天津农垦集团总公司

Tianjin Farms Agribusiness Group Corporation

总公司机关办公楼

Tianjin Farms Agribusiness Group Corporation is a key group supported by Tianjin Municipal Government. It is authorized to manage all the state-owned assets in the group.

In 2005, the total assets of Tianjin Farms Agribusiness Group Corporation reached 4.88 billion yuan. The corporation covers an area of 136,000 mu. There are 39 affiliates and 111 business units subordinate to the corporation. The total product of industry and agriculture in 2005 amounted to 2.358 billion yuan and the total profit aggregated 0.2 billion yuan. The main businesses of the corporation include: milk business (including milk cow breeding and Haihe milk product), wine business (including Dynasty, Welkin, Summer Palace), special agriculture (including terrestrial heat cultivate, lawn), real estate businesses and commercial services (including taxi services, gas station, office building services).

The key enterprise in the group is Sino-France Joint-venture Dynasty Winery Co., Ltd., which is a famous high-grade winery. In 2005, Dynasty Winery produced 46.71 million bottles wine of all kinds and reached a sale of 959 million yuan. Now Dynasty Winery is producing 90 varieties of wine in European style, which have won 14 international gold medals and was awarded by CMB international top-quality medal. Dynasty Winery Corporation is appraised as a leading industrialized enterprise, and Dynasty Wine is ranked by the Ministry of Agriculture as a polluteless, virusless and nourishing green-food. Dynasty Wine has been number 1 in high-grade wine market for consecutive seven years at home since 1998. Designated as state banquet wine, Dynasty Wine also provides for 231 Chinese consulates overseas and the products have businesses in dozens of foreign countries or regions, include America, Canada, England, France, Japan and Australia. Coming into the stock market in Jan. 2005, Dynasty Winery raised as much as 100 million dollars and the market value amounted to 3.75 billion yuan. The Dynasty's brand value reached 2.709 billion yuan in 2005, and that ranked first in domestic winery industry.

王朝公司全景

海河乳业厂景

2006 No. 22 总第22期

中英文对照

Chinese/English

天津统计年鉴

Tianjin Statistical Yearbook

天津市统计局 编

Compiled by Tianjin Municipal Bureau of Statistics

中国统计出版社

China Statistics Press

天津市生产总值(亿元)
Tianjin's GDP (100 million RMB)

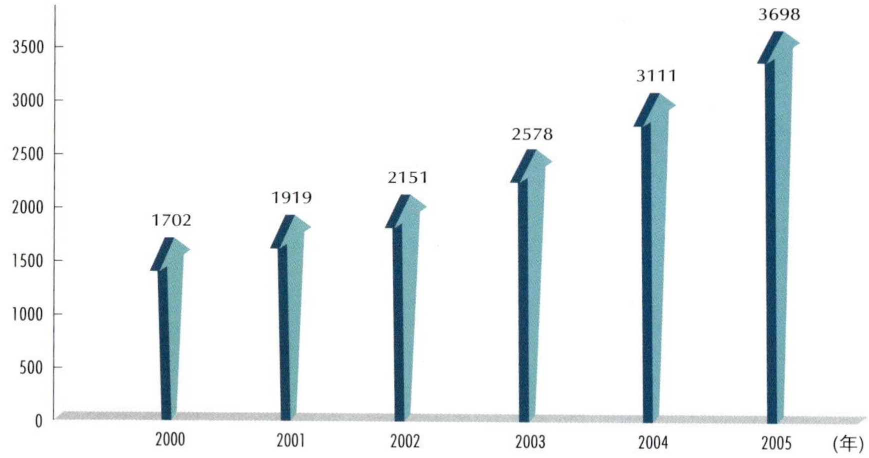

天津市人均生产总值(元)
Per Capita Gross Domestic Product of Tianjin (RMB)

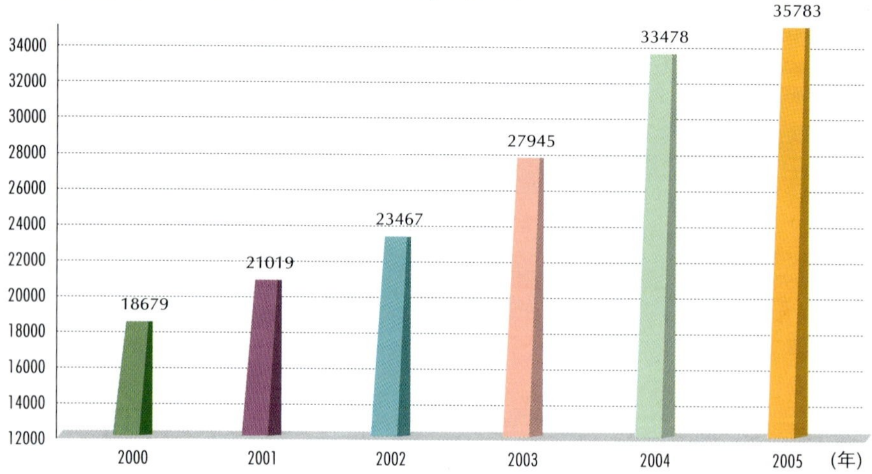

产业结构(%)
Industrial Structure (%)

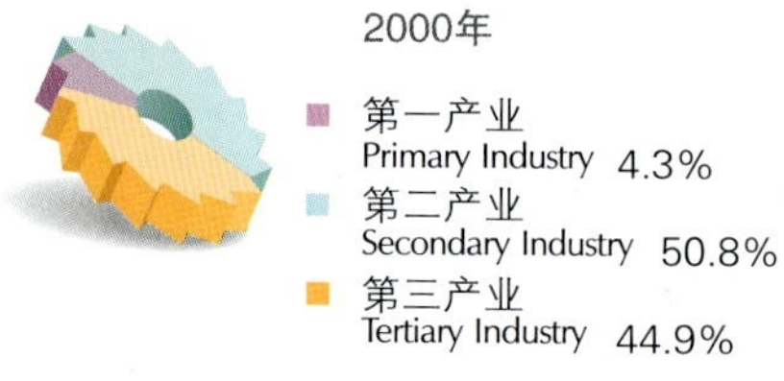

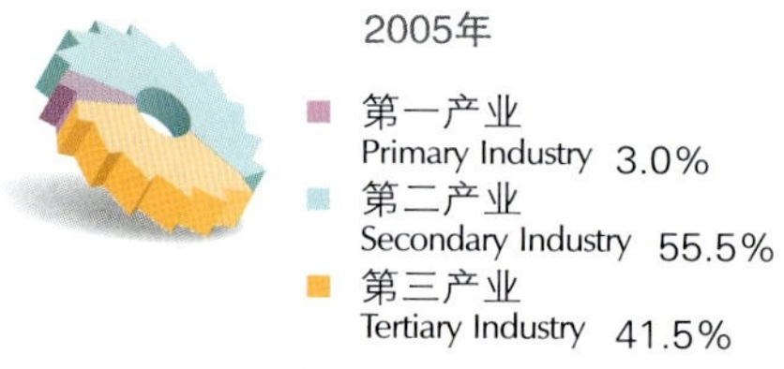

2001-2005 辉煌"十五" 和谐天津

Tianjin - a Harmonious City with Remarkable Achievements in the Tenth Five-year Plan Period

天津全市财政收入(亿元)
Tianjin Municipal Financial Revenue (100 million RMB)

2005年天津市平均每天主要经济社会活动情况
Average Daily Social and Economic Activities of Tianjin in 2005

- 地区生产总值10.13亿元 Gross Domestic Product (1013 million yuan)
- 工业增加值5.16亿元 Added Value of Industry (516 million yuan)
- 第三产业增加值4.20亿元 Added Value of Tertiary Industry (420 million yuan)
- 全市财政收入19885万元 Total Financial Revenue (198.85 million yuan)
- 原油产量4.88万吨 Output of Crude Oil (48,800 tons)
- 轿车产量892辆 Output of Cars (892)
- 移动电话机产量17.31万部 Output of Mobile Phones (173,100 pieces)
- 港口货物吞吐量65.94万吨 Freight Handled at Port (659,400 tons)
- 社会货物运输量110万吨 Freight Transportation (1100,000 tons)
- 邮电业务总量4831万元 Business Value of Post and Telecommunications (48.31 million yuan)
- 社会消费品零售总额3.26亿元 Total Retail Sales of Consumer Goods (326 million yuan)
- 外贸出口总值7510万美元 Total Value of Exports in Foreign Trade (75.10 million USD)
- 接待来津国际旅游者2028人次 Reception of International Tourists (2,028 man-times)
- 竣工房屋建筑面积5.54万平方米 Floor Space of Building Completed (55,400 m^2)
- 天然气和煤气售气量260.39万立方米 Sales of Natural Gas and Fuel Gas (2,603,900 m^3)
- 新增移动电话用户2192户 Increased Mobile Phone Users (2192)
- 生活用水量79.1万吨 Daily Consumption Water (791,000 tons)
- 报纸出版239.88万份 Newspapers Issued (2,398,800 copies)

全社会固定资产投资与城市基础设施投资(亿元)
Total Investment in Fixed Assets and Urban Infrastructure Investment (100 million RMB)

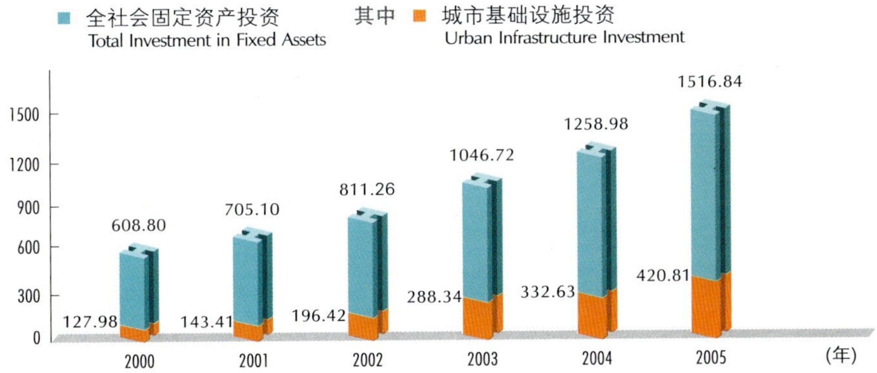

万元地区生产总值、万元工业增加值能耗(吨标准煤)
Energy Consumption of Every 10,000 Yuan Regional Gross Product and Value Added in Industry (tons of SCE)

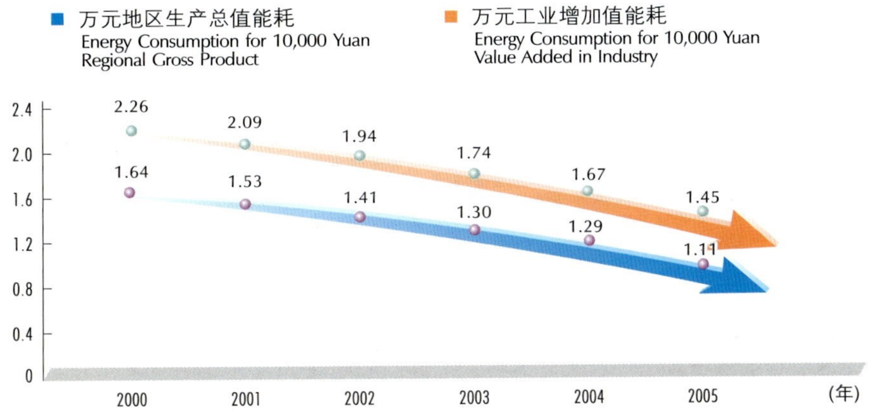

城市居民人均可支配收入(元)
Per Capita Annual Disposable Income of Urban Households (RMB)

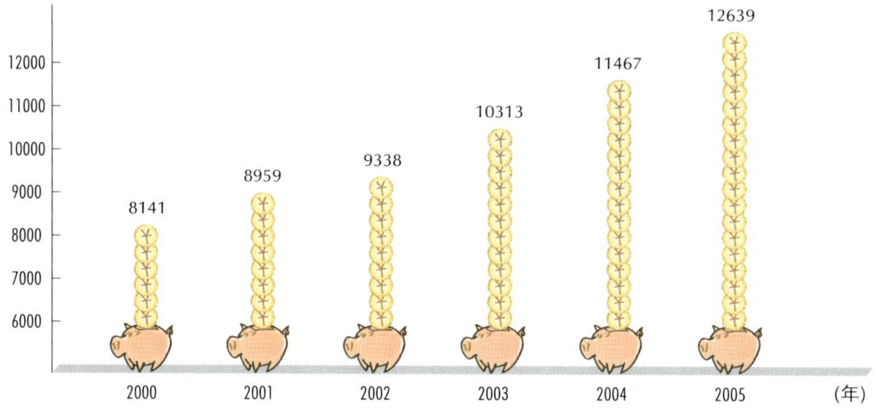

2005年城市居民人均消费性支出构成(%)
Composition of Per Capita Annual Expenditure for Consumption of Urban Households in 2005 (%)

- 食　品 Food 36.7%
- 衣　着 Clothing 7.2%
- 家庭设备、用品及服务 Household Equipment, Utensils and Services 5.5%
- 医疗保健 Medical Care 10.3%
- 交通与通讯 Traffic and Telecommunication 10.3%
- 娱乐、教育、文化服务 Entertainment, Education and Cultural Services 13.3%
- 居　住 Residence 13.4%
- 杂项商品与服务 Miscellaneous Products and Services 3.3%

城市居民人均住宅建筑面积(平方米)
Per-capita Floor Space of Urban Residential Buildings (m^2)

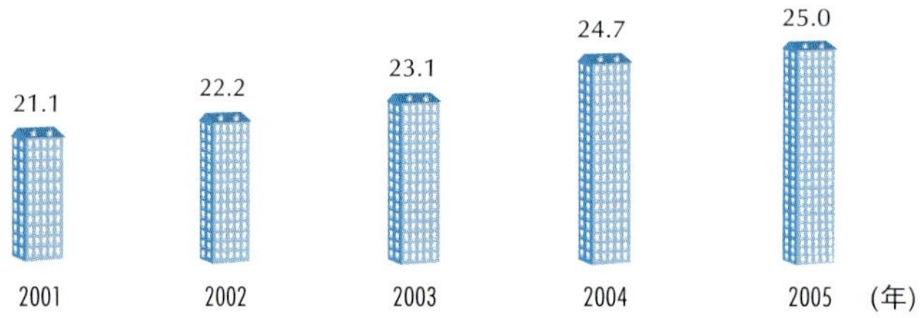

城市绿化覆盖率(%)
Coverage Rate of Afforestation in Urban Areas (%)

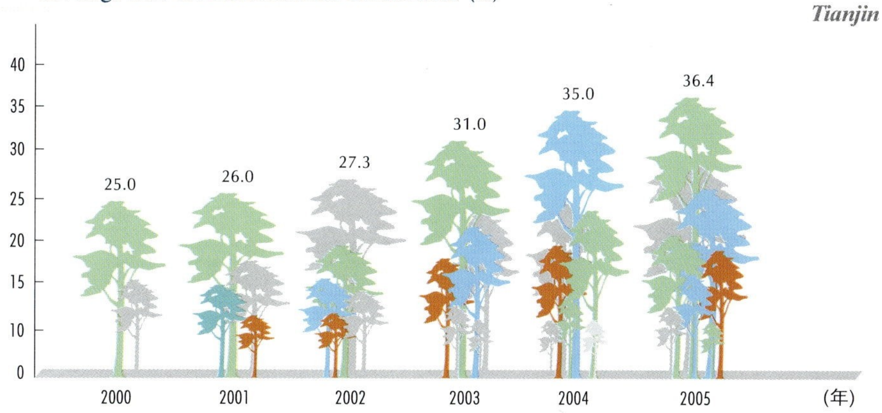

2005年六大优势产业产值构成(%)
Output Value of Six Advantageous Industries in 2005

产值总计 4851.35亿元
Total Output Value 485,135 million RMB

- 电子信息产品制造业 37.5%
  Electronic and Information Product Manufacturing Industry
- 冶金工业 25.9%
  Metallurgical Industry
- 石油及化学工业 24.2%
  Petroleum and Chemical Industry
- 汽车制造业 8.1%
  Automobile Manufacturing Industry
- 生物技术与现代医药制造业 3.4%
  Biotechnology and Modern Pharmaceutical Industry
- 新能源及环保业 0.9%
  New Energy Source and Environment Protection Industry

港口货物吞吐量(万吨)
Volume of Freight Handled in Tianjin Port (10,000 tons)

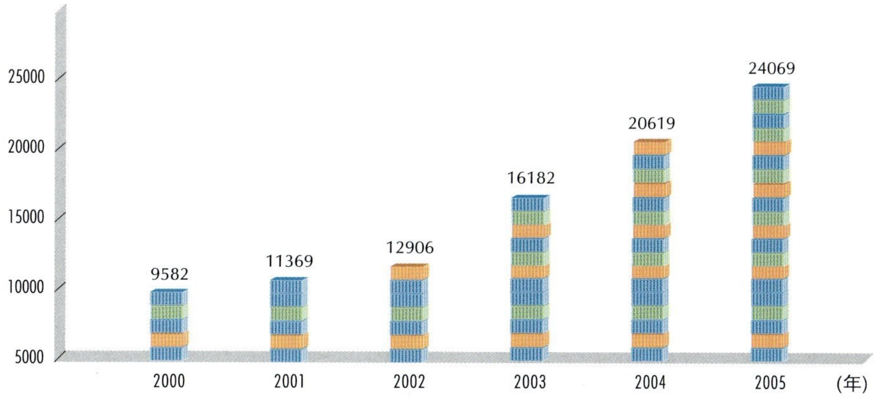

邮电业务总量(亿元)
Business Value of Post and Telecommunication Services (100 million RMB)

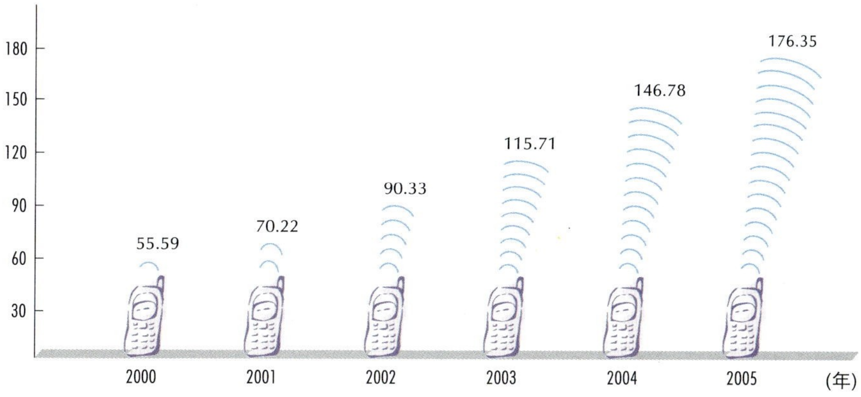

社会消费品零售总额(亿元)
Total Retail Sales of Consumer Goods (100 million RMB)

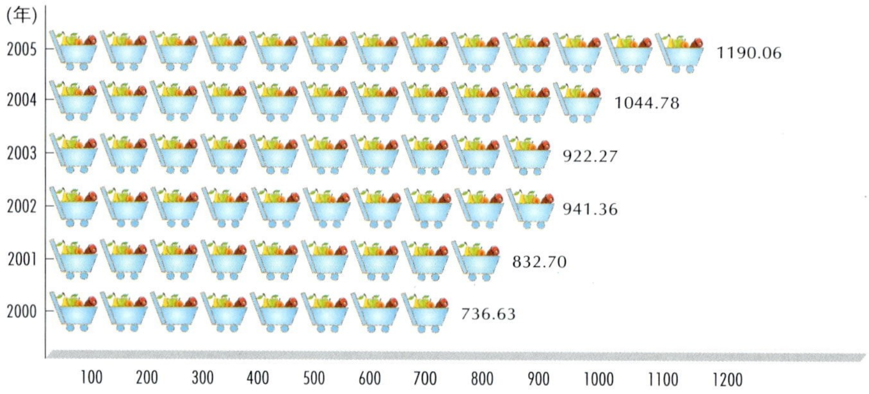

外贸进出口总值(亿美元)
Total Value of Import & Export in Foreign Trade (100 million USD)

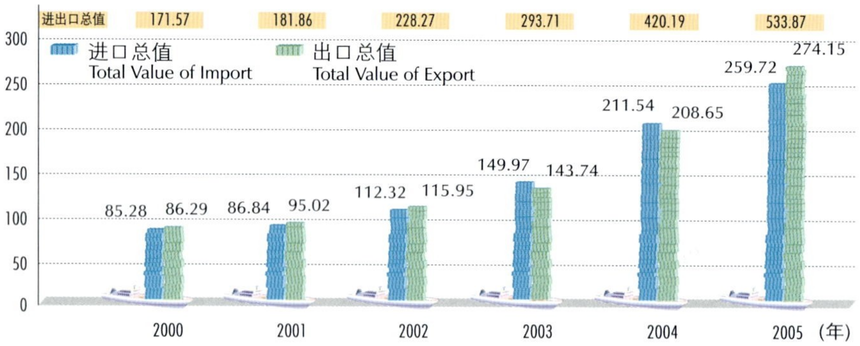

2005年实际直接利用外资额结构(%)
Composition of Actual Used Foreign Direct Investment (%)

按在天津投资的国家和地区分
By the countries or regions investing in Tianjin

- 中国香港 Hong Kong, China 20.7%
- 日 本 Japan 17.1%
- 英属维尔京群岛 Virgin Islands of the United Kingdom 15.7%
- 韩 国 Republic of Korea 13.1%
- 美 国 United States 5.6%
- 新加坡 Singapore 5.3%
- 其 他 Others 22.5%

年末金融机构(含外资)本外币存贷款余额(亿元)

Balance of Home and Foreign Currency Deposits and Loans in Financial(Including Foreign) Institutions at the End of 2005 (100 million RMB)

存款 Deposits　贷款 Loans

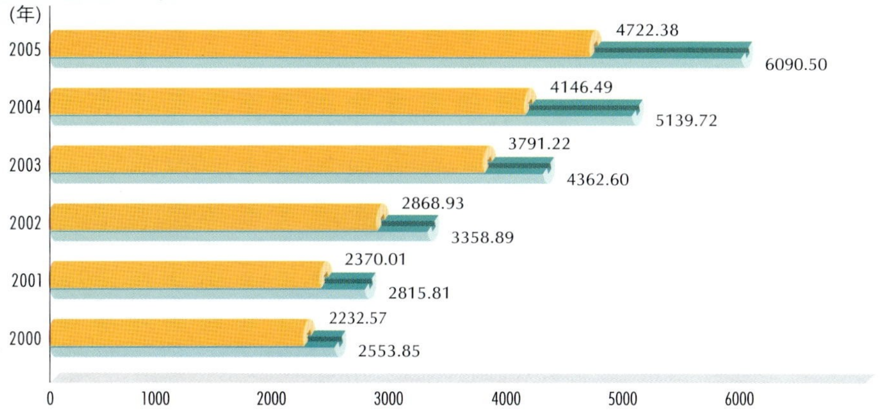

平均每万人口拥有大学生(人)

Number of University or College Students Per 10,000 Population (persons)

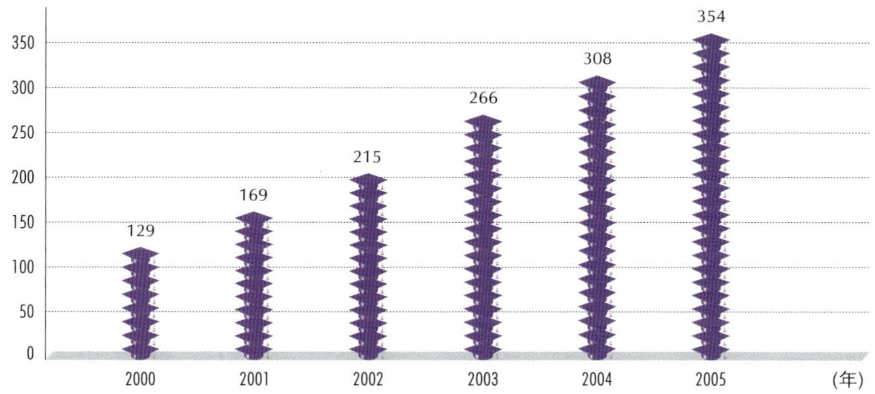

价格指数(上年=100)

Price Index (Preceding year=100)

城市居民消费价格指数 The Urban Residents' consumption Price Index

城市商品零售价格指数 The Retail Price Index of Commodities in the Urban Area

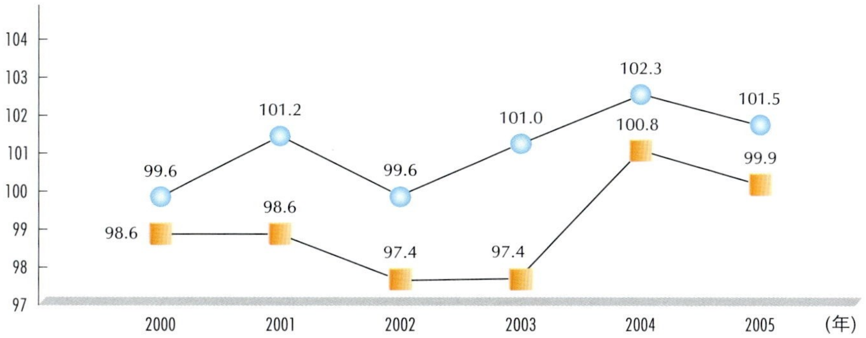

滨海新区生产总值(亿元)

Gross Domestic Product of Binhai New Area (100 million RMB)

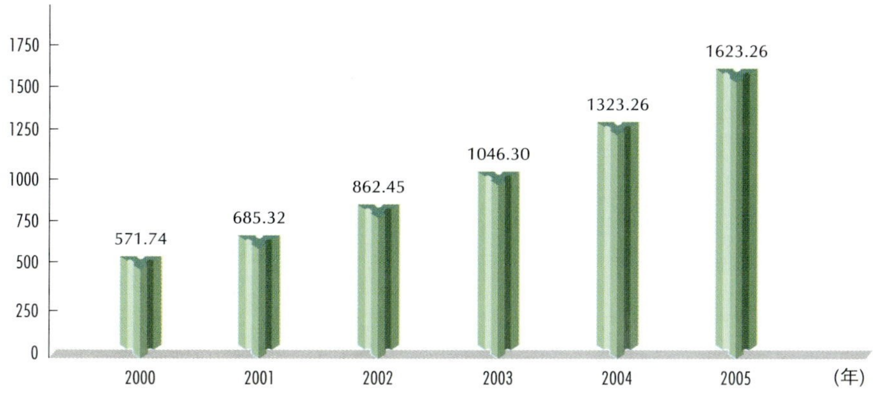

《天津统计年鉴—2006》编辑委员会

主 编：韩启祥

副主编：

杨福刚 董顺荣 吴振远 李文海
童月梅 武军定 张 强 杜 瑾
杨宝勤 李荣朴 温广玲 杨玉存

编 委（以姓氏笔画为序）：

牛文辉 王玉珠 王玉刚 刘金江
朱永强 许德发 宋卫东 李恭谦
杜 威 杜洪策 沈孝来 吴 浩
吴学平 郑渤玫 恽 菁 徐继良
高艾玲 高慧蓉 曹宗泉 褚丽萍
潘志德 魏云秀

责任编辑：李立新 戴 华

编辑人员（以姓氏笔画为序）：

刁志缨 马 兰 于海芳 王 稳
王福娣 王继英 王雪飞 冯 萍
卢智伟 孙 静 许士龙 朱永筠
陆 盈 宋笑丛 李 力 李 萍
张秀歧 张建强 何一磊 陈孔政
赵忆群 荣 斌 姜 岩 郭秀兰
陶玉华 梁 伟 曾祥菊 韩爱兵

区县篇资料整理人员

（以姓氏笔画为序）：

王 缜 王 静 王玉伟 冯 昕
杨淑东 张 娟 李兴萍 李赛南
陆诗凤 肖 宇 陈 乐 郑国义
赵守臣 赵文新 殷惠蔷 董树山
葛 铭 潘绍红

英文翻译：黄 瑛

排 版：张 柳 朱 云 纪艳娟

电子版制作：张鑫宇

彩页编辑：孙炳文

Editorial Board and Staff

Editor-in-chief:

Han Qixiang

Deputy Editor-in-chief:

Yang Fugang　Dong Shunrong　Wu Zhenyuan　Li Wenhai
Tong Yuemei　Wu Junding　Zhang Qiang　Du Jin
Yang Baoqin　Li Rongpu　Wen Guangling　Yang Yucun

Editorial Board: (in order of strokes of Chinese surname)

Niu Wenhui　Wang Yuzhu　Wang Yugang　Liu Jinjiang
Zhu Yongqiang　Xu Defa　Song Weidong　Li Gongqian
Du Wei　Du Hongce　Shen Xiaolai　Wu Hao
Wu Xueping　Zheng Bomei　Yun Jing　Xu Jiliang
Gao Ailing　Gao Huirong　Cao Zongquan　Chu Liping
Pan Zhide　Wei Yunxiu

Coordinators:

Li Lixin　Dai Hua

Editorial Staff: (in order of strokes of Chinese surname)

Diao Zhiying　Ma Lan　Yu Haifang　Wang Wen
Wang Fudi　Wang Jiying　Wang Xuefei　Feng Ping
Lu Zhiwei　Sun Jing　Xu Shilong　Zhu Yongjun
Lu Ying　Song Xiaocong　Li Li　Li Ping
Zhang Xiuqi　Zhang Jianqiang　He Yilei　Chen Kongzheng
Zhao Yiqun　Rong Bin　Jiang Yan　Guo Xiulan
Tao Yuhua　Liang Wei　Zeng Xiangju　Han Aibing

Data Provider on Districts and Counties Chapter:
(in order of strokes of Chinese surname)

Wang Zhen　Wang Jing　Wang Yuwei　Feng Xin
Yang Shudong　Zhang Juan　Li Xingping　Li Sainan
Lu Shifeng　Xiao Yu　Chen Yue　Zheng Guoyi
Zhao Shouchen　Zhao Wenxin　Yin Huiqiang　Dong Shushan
Ge Ming　Pan Shaohong

English Translator:

Huang Ying

Typeset:

Zhang Liu　Zhu Yun　Ji Yanjuan

Electric CD:

Zhang Xinyu

Color Inset Editor:

Sun Bingwen

编 者 说 明

一、《天津统计年鉴》是一部全面反映天津市国民经济和社会发展情况的大型资料工具书，创刊于1984年，逐年出版，形成系列。本书以其丰富翔实的统计资料而成为社会各界了解天津、认识天津最具权威性的工具资料书。

二、《天津统计年鉴－2006》全书中英文对照，同步配备电子版光盘。

三、书内文字资料载有："2005年天津市国民经济和社会发展统计公报"，"2005年天津市国民经济保持平稳快速运行"，辉煌"十五"、和谐天津等一系列反映"十五"时期天津市各行业发展的分析文章。为方便读者使用，书中在每篇后附有统计指标解释。索引中标明了全书结构。

四、本年鉴的统计数据大部分取自统计年报，少部分来自抽样调查和专业部门统计资料。

五、本年鉴所使用的度量衡单位均采用国际统一标准计量单位；行业分类标准均采用国家GB/T4754－2002标准；计算人均指标时，从2005年开始采用常住人口计算，2005年以前采用户籍人口计算。

六、本年鉴中部分数据的合计数和相对数由于四舍五入取舍不同而产生的计算误差，均未做机械调整。

七、本年鉴表中的符号使用说明："空格"表示该项统计指标无数据、数据不足本表最小单位或数据不详；"#"表示其中的主要项；由于版面原因，部分计量单位如：100 000 000用10^8表示，10 000用10^4表示。

八、由于同普查结果衔接、国家统计制度变化或主管部门提供的数据有调整等原因，年鉴中部分指标的历史年度数据有变动。读者在使用历史资料时，凡以前年度的年鉴与本年鉴数据有出入的，均以本年鉴为准。

九、《天津统计年鉴》公开出版以来，受到了国内外广大读者的关心和支持，对本年鉴的内容和编辑工作提出了许多宝贵意见，对此我们深表谢意。限于我们的水平，书中难免还有不足之处，敬请广大读者继续给予批评指正，帮助我们进一步改进年鉴编辑工作，更好地为广大读者服务。

Preface

Ⅰ. Tianjin Statistical Yearbook is a large – sized statistics publication to reflect various aspects of Tianjin's economic and social development, which was started in 1984 and published year after year, having become a series of yearbooks. Possessing plentiful and detailed statistical materials, the yearbook has become the most authoritative statistics publication for various circles to understand and know Tianjin.

Ⅱ. Tianjin Statistical Yearbook 2006 is written in Chinese & English, and is equipped with electric CD.

Ⅲ. Written materials in the book include:" Statistical Communique on the 2005 National Economic and Social Development of Tianjin"," Tianjin national economy has maintained steady and rapid operation in 2005", " Proud the 10th Five – Year plan Period and Harmonious Tianjin", a series of reports reflecting the development of Tianjin in the 10th Five – Year plan Period and so on. In order to help readers using these statistical materials better, Explanatory Notes On Main Statistical Indicators are attached after each chapter. Whose structure is marked in the index.

Ⅳ. The major data sources of this book are obtained from annual statistical report, a few from sample surveys and materials of departments statistics.

Ⅴ. The units of measurement used in this book are internationally standard measurement units, sector listed in this table is classified by the standard of GB/T4754 – 2002. When calculating per capit indicators, we use permanent pepulation since 2005 and use registered population before 2005.

Ⅵ. Statistical discrepancies due to rounding are not adjusted in this book.

Ⅶ. Notations used in this book: "(blank)" indicates the data not available or the figure is not large enough to be measured with the smallest unit in the table. " # " indicates the major items of the total. When the unit is 100,000,000, we shorten some of them as 10^8, 10,000 we shorten some of them as 10^4, so as to save the space for printing.

Ⅷ. As a result of joining with various census, change of statistics institution, data adjustment of special department and so on, some data in this yearbook are different from former yearbook. When using historical data, users should take the data of this book as standard.

Ⅸ. Since Tianjin Statistical Yearbook had been published openly, we have been concerned and supported by the readers at home and abroad. They advance much valuable suggestion on content and edition of the yearbook, we deeply thanks for this all. Based on our limited level, perhaps there are some mistakes in this book, we welcome all of the readers give us your criticism in order to help us further improving our edition level, and providing services for the readers better.

篇目索引

篇　目　　起始页码

SUBJECT INDEX

目　录

CONTENTS

二、人口和劳动就业

POPULATION,LABOR AND EMPLOYMENT

三、固定资产投资和房地产
INVESTMENT IN FIXED ASSETS AND REAL ESTATE

四、能源生产和消费

ENERGY PRODUCTION AND CONSUMPTION

五、财　政
GOVERNMENT FINANCE

六、价格指数
PRICE INDICES

七、人民生活
PEOPLE'S LIFE

八、城市建设和环境保护

URBAN CONSTRUCTION AND ENVIRONMENT PROTECTION

九、农村经济

RURAL ECONOMY

十、工　业
INDUSTRY

十一、建筑业
CONSTRUCTION

十二、交通运输和邮电
TRANSPORTATION,POST AND TELECOMMUNICATIONS

十三、国内贸易
DOMESTIC TRADE

十四、对外经济贸易和旅游
FOREIGN ECONOMY TRADE AND TOURISM

十五、金融业
FINANCIAL INTERMEDIATION

十六、教育和科技

EDUCATION AND SCIENCE & TECHNOLOGY

十七、文化和体育
CULTURE AND SPORTS

十八、卫生、社会保障和社会福利
PUBLIC HEALTH, SOCIAL SECURITY AND SOCIAL WELFARE

十九、公共管理和社会组织

PUBLIC MANAGEMENT AND SOCIAL ORGANIZATIONS

二十、企业改革与市场发展
REFORM OF ENTERPRISE AND DEVELOPMENT OF MARKET

二十一、滨海新区
BINHAI NEW AREA

二十二、区县基本情况

BASIC STATISTICS ON DISTRICTS AND COUNTIES

2005年天津市国民经济和社会发展统计公报

天津市统计局

2006年3月3日

2005年是实施"十五"计划的最后一年，全市各地区、各部门在市委、市政府的正确领导下，以邓小平理论和"三个代表"重要思想为指导，以科学发展观统领经济社会发展全局，齐心协力，团结奋斗，坚决落实国家宏观调控政策措施，积极推进结构调整、科技创新和对外开放，努力转变经济增长方式，全面加快"三步走"战略和五大战略举措的实施。全市经济保持平稳快速运行，各项社会事业协调发展，人民生活不断改善，圆满完成"十五"计划确定的主要任务。

一、经济发展

经济总量

全年实现全市生产总值(GDP)3663.86亿元，按可比价格计算比上年增长14.5%。全市人均生产总值达到35457元，约合4328美元，增长12.8%。能源利用效率不断提高。万元生产总值综合能耗为1.28吨标准煤，比2000年下降了0.36吨。

三次产业全面增长。第一产业完成增加值109.42亿元，增长4.3%。第二产业完成增加值2050.34亿元，增长17.5%。第三产业完成增加值1504.1亿元，增长11.4%。三次产业对经济增长的贡献率分别为1.0%、66.5%和32.5%。三次产业结构由2000年的4.3:50.8:44.9变化为2005年的3:56:41。

"十五"期间，全市地区生产总值年均增长13.9%，超出"十五"计划目标3.9个百分点，高于"九五"时期平均增速2.6个百分点。其中三次产业年均分别增长5.7%、16.5%和11.6%。

财政收入再上新台阶。全年全市财政收入突破700亿元，达到725.52亿元，按可比口径计算比上年增长26.8%。全年实现地方一般预算财政收入331.74亿元，增长28.2%。主要税种均保持了快速增长，其中增值税增长21.8%，企业所得税增长27.8%，营业税增长23.0%，个人所得税增长17.8%。全年财政支出520.28亿元，比上年增长20.6%。其中，基本建设支出73.23亿元，增长5.5%；企业挖潜改造资金支出29.12亿元，增长7.1%；支援农业支出12.85亿元，增长17.6%。

"十五"期间，全市财政收入年均增长24.3%，增幅比"九五"时期提高了8.4个百分点，累计实现财政收入2360亿元，是"九五"时期的2.5倍。财政收入占地区生产总值的比重逐年提高，2005年为19.8%，比2000年上升5.4个百分点。

劳动与就业

全年全市新增就业岗位安置就业26.21万人次，比上年增加4.76万人次，增长22.2%。实施积极的再就业政策，开发了公共卫生保洁、劳动保障协管、交通协管、旧楼区准物业管理等多渠道社会公益性岗位，全年下岗失业人员实现再就业14.22万人。2005年末，全市社会从业人员总量达到538万人，比2000年末增加51.11万人。其中，从事第二产业的226万人，比"九五"期末增加了3.8万人，从事第三产业的229.2万人，比"九五"期末增加了45.7万人，成为吸收劳动力的重要渠道。全年人才和劳务市场共接待331.83万人次进场择业洽谈，90.19万人次达成初步意向。

"十五"期间，我市实现新增就业岗位数量多于新增下岗失业人员数量，累计安置下岗失业人员57.2万人次。城镇登记失业率由2002年的3.91%下降到2005年的3.7%。

价　格

全年城市居民消费价格指数为101.5，涨幅比上年回落0.8个点。从八大类构成看，食品类价格上涨3.4%，涨幅比上年回落6.5个百分点；居住类价格上涨6.7%，比上年上升3.1个百分点；娱乐教育文化用品价格与上年持平；其他五类消费价格水平呈现不同程度的下跌。城市商品零售价格指数为99.9，由上年的上涨转为下降。工业品出厂价格指数为100.1，涨幅比上年回落 4 个点。其中生产资料出厂价格上涨1%，生活资料出厂价格下降2.7%。原材料燃料及动力购进价格指数为104.9，涨幅比上年回落10.5个点。房屋销售价格上涨6.0%，涨幅比上年回落7.5个百分点；其中商品房价格上涨6.3%，涨幅比上年回落5.4个百分点。

"十五"期间，我市价格总水平运行平稳。居民消费价格累计上涨5.7%，年均上涨1.1%，比"九五"时期的年均上涨率低0.9个百分点。商品零售价格总水平年平均下降1.2%，工业品出厂价格总水平年平均下降0.4%。

固定资产投资

全年全社会固定资产投资完成1516.84亿元，增长20.5%。其中城镇固定资产投资完成1385.56亿元，增长22.4%。第二产业投资快速增长，完成543.16亿元，增长25.2%，占全市城镇固定资产投资的比重为39.2%。其中制造业完成投资350.30亿元，增长39.3%。第三产业投资完成837.35亿元，增长20.4%，占全市的比重达到60.4%。其中交通运输仓储邮政业完成投资167.84亿元，增长87.8%；房地产业完成投资339.47亿元，增长23.2%。制造业、交通运输仓储邮政业和房地产业成为拉动全市投资增长的主要行业，这三个行业共完成投资857.61亿元。合计增长39.1%，占全市的比重达到61.9%，对全市投资增长的贡献率达到95.1%。重点建设项目完成情况较好。全市58个重点项目累计完成投资387.02亿元，其中，能源及交通项目完成投资128.37亿元，高科技项目完成投资20.12亿元。民间资本增速快、比重升，全年完成511.42亿元，增长32.4%，占全市的比重为33.7%，比上年提高 3 个百分点。外商及港澳台资本150.02亿元，下降19.0%，所占比重为9.9%。

"十五"期间，我市累计完成全社会固定资产投资5338.9亿元，年均完成投资在千亿元以上，比"九五"时期年均完成水平高出近 1 倍。投资年均递增速度19.4%，比"九五"期间提高8.8个百分点。

农　业

全年农业总产值完成238.34亿元，比上年增长4.8%。其中种植业产值97.49亿元，增长0.2%；畜牧业产值102.71亿元，增长7.5%；渔业产值36.25亿元，增长10.6%；林业产值1.89亿元，增长13.6%。养殖业占农业总产值的比重达到58.3%，比上年提高2.1个百分点。

主要农副产品产量增加。全年粮食种植面积431.49万亩，粮食总产量137.5万吨，比上年增产12.23万吨。棉花产量8.35万吨，比上年减少3.68万吨。肉类总产量57.78万吨，增长7.5%。牛奶产量63.41万吨，增长16.9%。水产品产量33.81万吨，增长9.1%。蔬菜产量542.74万吨，下降7.3%。禽蛋产量23.47万吨，下降3.7%。

农业园区化、设施化水平显著提高。建成了以津南国家级农业现代化示范园区和宁河国家级原种猪场为龙头的一批高水平种养业园区，重点畜禽和水产品生产基本实现了园区化。资产在1000万元以上的龙头企业达到130家，其中国家级龙头企业达到10家。进入产业化体系的农户占总农户比重达到70%，比"九五"末提高37个百分点。节水灌溉面积达到295万亩，比"九五"末增长46.8%。百亩耕地拥有机械动力达到98.4千瓦，比"九五"末提高20.7%。

农业科研取得新进展。"十五"期间，全市取得农业科技成果466项，其中137项成果获得国家级、市级科技奖励，在黄瓜育种、杂交粳稻育种、农产品保鲜、葡萄酒加工和动物胚胎克隆技术等方面处于全国领先水平。

工　业

全年全市工业完成增加值1884.8亿元，增长17.9%。其中，规模以上工业完成增加值1783.02亿元，增长

20.4%,完成工业总产值6774.10亿元,增长20.8%。

优势产业拉动作用明显。电子信息、汽车、石化、冶金、生物技术与现代医药、新能源及环保等六大优势产业完成工业总产值4851.35亿元,占全市的比重达到71.6%,对全市工业增长的贡献率达到78.6%。高新技术产业完成产值2141.37亿元,增长16.4%,占全市规模以上工业的比重为31.6%,其中电子信息业产值1682.37亿元,增长17.3%,占全市工业的24.8%。

产销衔接良好,出口增长较快。全年全市规模以上工业实现销售产值6816.56亿元,比上年增长21.4%,产销率达到100.6%。其中出口交货值实现1759.22亿元,增长24.3%,占销售产值的25.8%。

适应市场需求的工业产品产量快速增长。全年天然原油产量1782.88万吨,比上年增长23.6%;天然气8.79亿立方米,增长5.8%;发电量365.69亿千瓦时,增长8.7%;生铁660.24万吨,增长33.8%;钢材1664.04万吨,增长22.2%;无缝钢管174.59万吨,增长10.6%;水泥519.15万吨,增长4.2%;移动电话机6319.82万部,增长28.4%;轿车32.56万辆,增长48.1%;布2.58亿米,增长7.0%;服装17815.94万件,增长13.0%;精制食用植物油51.57万吨,增长22.3%;微波炉1431.15万台,增长5.1%;中成药6150.64吨,增长24.2%;大规模半导体集成电路51841万块,增长10.8%;干电池(折1号电池)37034万只,增长26.8%。

工业经济效益在上年大幅度增长的基础上继续保持了较高增幅。全市规模以上独立核算工业企业全年实现产品销售收入6865.24亿元,比上年增长22.9%。实现利税总额760.75亿元,增长27.2%。利润和税金保持同步增长,实现利润520.18亿元,增长27.2%,实现税金总额240.57亿元,增长27.1%。全市工业经济效益综合指数为214.85,比上年提高20.5个点。其中,总资产贡献率为14.34%,提高1.0个百分点;成本费用利润率为8.26%,提高0.3个百分点。

"十五"时期,全部工业总产值年均增长21.5%,比"九五"时期提高6.3个百分点。其中规模以上工业实现总产值连续突破4个千亿元,年均增长23.7%;工业增加值比2000年增长1.4倍,年均增长19.6%。

建筑业

全年建筑业完成增加值165.54亿元,增长13.5%;完成总产值725.26亿元,增长14.9%。全年房屋建筑施工面积3770.28万平方米,增长9.7%;房屋建筑竣工面积1317.95万平方米。全市有总承包和专业承包资格的建筑企业1180家,实现利润14.63亿元,增长27.7%,实现税金21.58亿元,增长17.3%。

"十五"期间,全市建筑业增加值年均增长10.7%,比"九五"时期提高4.2个百分点。建设工程质量稳步提高。有28项工程获国家级奖项,280项工程获市优工程奖。

交通运输邮电仓储业

全年交通运输邮电仓储业完成增加值308.38亿元,比上年增长7.8%。货运量继续增加。全年货运总量39748.7万吨,比上年增长4.8%。其中,公路运输19850万吨,增长1.0%;铁路运输6793.95万吨,增长11.2%;水路运输12367.77万吨,增长7.7%。公路、水路、铁路三种主要运输方式货运量比重分别为49.9%、31.1%和17.1%。港口货物吞吐量24068.8万吨,比上年增长16.7%,其中进港9369.3万吨,增长26.6%,出港14699.5万吨,增长11.2%。集装箱吞吐量480.1万国际标准箱,增长25.8%。机场货邮吞吐量8.02万吨,增长13.0%。

旅客运输增长迅速。全年旅客运输量4687.29万人,比上年增长14.2%。其中,铁路1558.43万人,增长4.6%;公路2961万人,增长20.5%。机场旅客吞吐量213.65万人,增长25.3%。

年末全市机动车保有量112.6万辆,其中轿车50.3万辆。私人机动车达到81.5万辆,其中轿车37.4万辆。

运能运力继续提高。"十五"期间,新建和改造港口泊位21个,五万吨级以上泊位由"九五"末期的3个增至15个,累计新增能力9362万吨,开辟内外贸集装箱航线44条,新建3个内陆"无水港",与世界上160多个国家和地区的300多个港口有贸易往来。天津机场航线达到65条,通航城市54个。

电信和邮政业务加快发展。全年邮电业务总量完成178亿元,比上年增长21.1%。其中电信业务总量166亿元,增长20.3%,邮政业务总量12亿元,增长33.3%。年末长途光缆线路总长度达到3376公里,局用电话交换机总容量433万门,公网固定电话用户达到439万户。全年公网电话本地通话量103亿次,长途电话通话量9.5亿次,其中国际及港澳台长途电话0.22亿次,增长37.5%。年末移动电话用户503万户,当年新增用户200万户,短信业务总量达到45亿条,增长55.2%。全年发送函件8754万件,其中特快专递332万件,增长13.3%。当年新增邮政局所54处,总数达到454处。

国内商业

全年批发零售贸易餐饮业完成增加值488.63亿元,比上年增长13.5%。全市规模以上商贸企业商品购进总额3620.5亿元,全部商贸企业及个体经营户商品销售总额达到4820.22亿元。

零售市场购销活跃。全年社会消费品零售总额完成1190.06亿元,增长13.9%。消费热点趋多,汽车类零售额增长1.2倍,石油及制品类、电子出版物及音像制品类、家俱类零售额增幅均超过40%。餐饮业零售额完成159.49亿元,增长20.9%。"十五"期间,全市社会消费品零售总额累计达到4931.17亿元,年均增长13.5%。

批发交易市场建设快速发展。2005年末,全市成交金额超亿元的大型批发市场达57个。会展经济蓬勃兴旺,津洽会、啤酒节、PECC博览会、手机配套会等成为天津的品牌展会。

商业设施建设快速推进。友谊新天地等一批大型商业设施建成开业。"十五"期间,全市累计竣工商业设施面积431万平方米,5000平方米以上大型商业设施增加123个。菜市场改造建设、社区商业等商业设施建设成效明显。

金融保险业

全市金融保险业实现增加值160.64亿元,比上年增长15.7%。引进了华夏银行和民生银行,渤海财产保险公司开业,天津农村合作银行正式成立,总部设在天津的渤海银行目前已正式开业,成为1996年以来获准成立的第一家全国性股份制银行。年末全市各类金融机构达2926家,从业人员4.62万人。

存贷款规模继续扩大。截止年末,全市金融机构(含外资)本外币各项存款余额6090.50亿元,比年初增加907.35亿元,比上年多增128.03亿元。其中,企事业单位存款余额2448.99亿元,增长19.0%;城乡居民储蓄存款余额2584.40亿元,增长14.3%。全市金融机构(含外资)本外币各项贷款余额4722.38亿元,比年初增加648.94亿元,比上年多增154.47亿元。其中,短期贷款余额2077.95亿元,增长11.1%;中长期贷款余额2255.23亿元,增长21.9%。住房按揭贷款余额375.2亿元,增长22.6%,汽车消费贷款余额14.56亿元,下降33.8%。年末全市银行类机构1548家。

金融要素市场平稳。2005年末全市共有境内上市股票24只。全年各类证券成交额1097.5亿元,其中股票成交额1018.53亿元,债券成交额44.67亿元,基金成交额34.3亿元。期货市场全年成交量258.86万手,成交金额1201.47亿元。年末共有证券营业部75家,期货经纪公司营业部12家,证券投资咨询机构2家。证券帐户开户数101.3万户。全年调剂外汇总额21.3亿美元,比上年增长34.1%,其中调入外汇12.46亿美元,增长60.2%,调出外汇8.83亿美元,增长9.0%。

保险业务快速发展。全年保费收入90.64亿元,比上年增长11.8%,其中财产险保费收入21.78亿元,人身险保费收入68.86亿元。各项赔款和给付17.46亿元,其中财产险赔付款10.74亿元,人身险赔付6.72亿元。至年末,全市共有保险类机构427家。

房地产业

全年房地产业实现增加值116.04亿元,增长6.7%。全年房地产开发投资327.54亿元,增长24.1%。其中住宅投资完成234.93亿元,增长34.1%,商业营业用房投资完成41.75亿元,增长47.8%。我市房地产市场在国家重点宏观调控下,保持了平稳有序的发展态势。全年商品房开发施工面积3470.57万平方米,增长21.1%,其中住宅2827.87万平方米,增长20.2%;商品房竣工面积1479.22万平方米,增长33.5%,其中住宅1270.96万平方米,增长25.3%。商品房现房销售面积938.02万平方米,增长10.7%;实现商品房现房销售收入367.56亿元,增长39.3%。全年存量房交易面积854.9万平方米,其中,私房799.1万平方米,公房置换55.8万平方米。存量房交易金额212.3亿元,其中,私房195.3亿元,公房置换17亿元。

二、改革开放

所有制结构

全市公有制经济完成增加值1758.65亿元,占全市生产总值的48%,非公有制经济完成增加值1905.21亿元,占全市的比重为52%。非公有制经济比重比上年提高 2 个百分点。

工业所有制结构继续呈现多元化。全市规模以上工业企业中,外商及港澳台商投资企业完成总产值3298.04亿元,增长19.0%,占48.7%;股份制企业完成总产值2525.72亿元,增长26.8%,占37.3%;私营企业完成总产值653.67亿元,增长22.7%,占9.6%。全市规模以上国有及国有控股工业企业共完成总产值2567.26亿元,比上年增长27.0%。

私营个体经济不断壮大。全市私营个体经济增加值达到886.65亿元,增长18.8%,占全市生产总值的比重为24.2%。年末私营个体经济注册资金1620.33亿元,比年初增加349.05亿元。私营和个体经营户达到25.43万户,其中私营企业7.73万户。从业人员114.16万人,比年初增加12.29万人,其中私营88.7万人。全年实现销售及营业收入1306.17亿元,增长36.2%,其中私营企业完成747.87亿元,增长38.2%,个体经济完成558.30亿元,增长33.5%。全年实现税收61.07亿元,增长21.4%,其中私营48.86亿元,增长27.9%。

国有资产管理与国有企业改革

全市国有及国有控股企业资产总额5701亿元,所有者权益1915亿元,国有资本分布在重要行业和关键领域的比重达到70%,17户国有企业入选中国企业500强。国有资本合理流动的力度加大,全年872宗国有产权进入产权交易市场公开挂牌交易,实现交易额218.68亿元。其中跨区域交易额30.31亿元,市内交易额188.37亿元。

国有企业改革和调整取得新进展。截止2005年末,全市有2637户市属国有企业实现多元化改制,改制面由上年的61.7%上升到76.6%。全市国有大中型骨干企业80%以上完成了公司制改革。工业战略东移加快推进,累计有210户企业迁入滨海新区。

社会保障

城镇职工养老、医疗、工伤、生育、失业保险体系和城乡最低生活保障制度进一步健全,覆盖面进一步扩大。全市养老保险参保职工200.62万人,医疗保险参保人员299.34万人,失业保险参保职工197.51万人,工伤保险参保职工162.91万人,生育保险覆盖157.42万人。进一步完善了对低收入者的救助制度,符合低保条件的困难群众实现应保尽保。连续 5 年调整全市企业职工最低工资标准,由2000年的350元增加到2005年的590元。

地区合作

全年吸引外地资金实际到位额339.93亿元,比上年增长42.4%。从资金来源看,来自京冀地区的投资到位额138亿元,“长三角”地区72亿元,“珠三角”地区51亿元,分别比上年增长92.9%、60.3%和69.7%。房地产业吸引内资实际到位额达到149亿元,占全市的43.8%。

天津对甘肃省、西藏昌都地区、重庆万州区和新疆喀什地区的对口支援和帮扶工作进一步加强,有力地促进了当地经济的发展。

对外贸易

全年全市外贸进出口总值533.87亿美元,增长27.1%。其中出口274.15亿美元,增长31.4%,进口

259.72亿美元，增长22.8%，实现贸易顺差14.43亿美元。对美国、欧盟、东盟、日本和韩国等主要贸易伙伴的出口占全市的比重达到79%。机电产品出口185亿美元，比上年增长26%，占全市的67.5%，比重比上年提高7.4个百分点。高新技术产品出口124.7亿美元，增长24.5%；占全市出口总额的45.5%。外商投资企业出口220.23亿美元，占全市出口总额的80.3%，增长29.1%，国有企业出口33.79亿美元，增长23.8%。

“十五”时期全市外贸进出口总额达到1658亿美元，比“九五”时期增长1.8倍，其中，出口838亿美元，进口820亿美元，均比“九五”时期增长1.8倍。

利用外资

全年全市新批外商投资企业1309家，增长18.8%；全市直接利用外资合同金额73.23亿美元，增长31.0%；实际到位33.29亿美元，增长34.6%。外商独资企业成为直接利用外资的主要形式，全年实际到位22.72亿美元，占全市的比重达到68.3%。服务业直接利用外资增长较快，全年到位7.9亿美元，占全市的比重为23.7%，增长19.7%。来自法国、德国、香港、新加坡和韩国的合同外资额分别增长3.2倍、1.7倍、1.1倍、95.2%和86.0%。

“十五”时期，全市实际直接利用外资累计达到103.35亿美元，年均递增32%。截止2005年末，在津投资的国家和地区达110个，世界500强企业已有114家在津落户。“十五”时期，制造业实际到位外资比“九五”时期增长1.3倍。

对外经济合作

2005年我市对外承包工程、劳务合作、设计咨询新签合同907个，合同额4.3亿美元，比上年增长30.4%，实现营业额3.2亿美元，增长18.7%，在外投资涉及化工、制药、建材、食品、服装等多领域。当年派出各类劳务人员4800多人次，期末在境外1.31万人。全年新批境外机构75个，新批境外投资生产企业54个，总投资5048.83万美元，其中中方投资4371.54万美元。截止年末，全市共有对外经济合作经营企业54家，对外承包工程和劳务合作涉及81个国家和地区。引进国外先进技术力度加大，全年签定技术引进合同580项，合同金额6.57亿美元。国际交流活动频繁，成功举办了亚欧财长会议、意大利天津周、新加坡天津周等活动，扩大了天津的影响。

旅　游

全年接待国际旅游者74.01万人次，比上年增长20.2%；旅游创汇5.09亿美元，增长23.4%。接待外省市游客人数和旅游收入均比上年增长12.8%。全市共有14.6万人次出国出境旅游，增长47.3%，旅游支出19.21亿元，增长47.4%。年末全市拥有星级宾馆、饭店111家；国际、国内旅行社达263家，其中，国际旅行社28家，国内旅行社235家。

滨海新区

全年滨海新区实现生产总值1608.63亿元，按可比价格计算，比上年增长19.8%；完成工业总产值3996.73亿元，增长30.7%；完成固定资产投资693.31亿元，增长22.6%；外贸出口184.69亿美元，占全市的比重为67.4%，增长34.8%；直接利用外资合同金额51亿美元，占全市的比重为69.6%，增长37.6%；直接利用外资到位额26.46亿美元，占全市的比重为79.5%，增长52.1%；实现社会消费品零售额206.52亿元，增长14.7%。

新一轮开发建设力度加大。对外现代交通体系的建设步伐加快，京津城际轨道客运专线、京津塘高速公路二线、天津滨海国际机场改造扩建、天津港扩建等重点工程项目的相继开工建设。天津碱厂搬迁改造项目启动，天津新港船厂搬迁项目签约，中国石化天津100万吨乙烯炼化一体化项目获得国务院批准，中国唯一民航科技产业化基地签约落户滨海新区，临港工业区完成围海造陆12.1平方公里。

对腹地的辐射和服务作用进一步增强。国际贸易与航运服务中心和电子口岸工程建成投入使用，进出口通关时间平均缩短了三分之一。全年天津口岸进出口总值达到819.29亿美元,增长20.9%。在天津口岸进出口额中,北京、河北、内蒙古、山西、河南、辽宁、山东等地区进出口额比重达到53.9%。天津保税区空港物流园区正式运行,全年保税区实现进出区货物总值187.6亿美元,比上年增长42.9%。

三、城市建设和管理

基础设施建设

城市基础设施建设取得快速进展。年末实有城市铺装道路长度5460公里,铺装道路面积6669万平方米,建成区人均道路面积10.41平方米。中心城区快速路实现通车120公里,地铁一号线建成试通车,京津城际快速铁路工程开工建设,蓟港铁路,黄万铁路正在建设中。"十五"期间,津滨轻轨投入运行,新增高速公路299公里,建成了津蓟、津晋、唐津等高速公路,高速公路总里程达到603公里。五年来,新建和改造京津、杨北、津港等55条干线公路,改造农村公路2804公里,新建和改造了紫金山路、咸阳路、水上北路等385条城市主次干道,新建大中型桥梁94座。

公用事业

2005 年,全市自来水综合生产能力为358.95万立方米/日,全年自来水售水量67501万立方米,其中生活用水28885万立方米。城市居民家庭燃气用户227.64万户,气化率为98.45%。地下管网服务能力增强。"十五"期间,全市新增供水管道1951公里,新增供气管道2609公里,新增排水管道3857公里。继续发展集中供热,当年新增供热面积2600万平方米,五年全市新增住宅集中供热面积4894万平方米,集中供热普及率达到83.2%,比"九五"末提高29.7个百分点。新建、扩建了纪庄子、咸阳路、北仓等 9 座污水处理厂,建成了双口、大韩庄、双港、蓟县 4 座垃圾处理场。全市污水和垃圾处理能力分别达到75%和81%,比"九五"末分别提高16和18个百分点。新建、改建了一批公交场所,公交运营车辆6794辆,年内更新691辆;完善了公交线网,年内新辟公交线路30条,市内公交线路达到428条。全年公共交通客运量89000万人次。运营出租车31939辆。

海河综合开发与市容整治

海河综合开发取得快速进展。经过三年建设,清淤工程基本完成,完成堤岸改造17公里,大沽桥通车,奉化桥、保定桥主体完工。新建和拓宽海河西路等28条临河道路,建成音乐公园等 6 处大型绿地,整修风貌建筑42栋,凤凰广场商贸区、运河商贸区、水上运动世界等商贸区相继开工建设,促进了现代服务业发展。

市容市貌变化显著。"十五"期间,新建绿地面积8576万平方米,建成区绿化覆盖率由"九五"末的25.1%提高到36.4%,城市人均公共绿地面积达到8.5平方米,比"九五"末增加3.1平方米。"十五"期间,全面完成海河干流综合治理,基本完成引滦水源保护工程;建成了翔宇公园、北辰公园、红桥公园等一批公园和大型绿地;完成了津河、卫津河、长泰河等10条、总长104公里市区二级河道改造,改善了河道两岸环境。

资源与环境保护

加强土地资源管理取得成效。在全市范围内推行国有土地有偿使用制度,经营性用地实现了"招、拍、挂",建立了新的城市基础设施建设投融资体制。严格控制建设用地规模,全年征地4212.7公顷,"十五"期间,连续五年实现耕地占补平衡。对各类开发区清理整顿取得明显成效。

创建国家环保模范城市取得成功,顺利通过了国家环保总局的检查评估。蓝天、碧水、污染防治、生态保护、创模细胞和安静六大环保工程的实施成效显著。全市二级以上良好天数占全年天数由2001年的47%上升到2005的81.6%。饮用水水质达标率和城市水功能区水质达标率均达到100%,保障了广大市民饮水安全;工业废水排放达标率95%以上。加强噪声污染控制,共建成安静居住小区97个,环境噪声达标区面积569.9平方公里,城市环境噪声达标区覆盖率达到80%。建成烟尘控制区48个,烟尘控制面积574.6平方公里。工业固体废物处置利用率达到99%。5 年来,全市共创建生态村113个,创建国家级优美乡镇 4 个。年末全市有环境监测站21个，国家级生态示范区2个，国家级生态示范区试点5个，自然保护区8个，自然保护区面积16.3万公顷。

信息化建设

“十五”以来，我市建设提升了电子政务平台、电子商务平台和公共信息服务平台；“南开之星”超级计算中心、互联网数据中心(IDC)、国家防病毒中心、今晚呼叫中心等一批信息化功能设施相继建成并投入使用。2005年末，全市铺设光纤达70万芯公里，通信能力城乡覆盖率达到100%。宽带城域网核心交换能力达到2000G，城市出口带宽121G，互联网拨号上网用户266万户，宽带用户65万户。启动数字电视试点工作，具备150套数字电视播出能力，试点用户1万户。

城市信息化建设步伐加快。市电子政务专网覆盖了全市副局级以上单位近200个，区县电子政务网络已延伸至区属委办局和乡镇街，市区两级政府全部建立了门户网站，初步实现了政务公开、网上办公、招商引资、便民服务等功能。经过连续四年政府网上办公“百项工程”的实施，市级政府机关累计实现网上办公项目1200余项，涉及79个委办局。开通8890为民服务呼叫中心成为群众与服务部门和服务企业联系的桥梁。金税、金盾、金审等一批重点信息系统工程相继启动。信息技术改造提升传统产业效果明显。全市年销售收入超过10亿元以上的大型商场都实现了商业信息化，90%的大型企业、50%中小企业开展了电子商务。全市1800所大中小学实现了“校校通”，其中800所实现了光纤接入。

质量监督

2005年，全市共有依法设置的质检机构19个，计量检定机构22个。通过国家审定的免检企业有11家，累计44家，通过国家审定的免检产品有11种，累计达到47种。2005年新创中国名牌产品6个，累计达到15个。新创天津名牌产品19个，累计达到209个。全年制定和修订企业产品标准3636种，企业标准总量达3.3万种。定期监督检验3636家企业的4493批次产品，批次合格率为88.5%。专项监督检验商业企业207家，检查商品352批次，批次合格率72%，完成计量仪器检定10.28万台(件)，其中强检计量器具占88.5%。取得食品生产许可证(QS产品)食品企业有243家。累计发放体系认证证书3033个。取得“3C”产品认证企业有609家，发证3244张。进出口商品检验检疫力度加大，全年共受理出入境报检15万多批，货值122亿美元，比上年增长21.8%。

四、社会事业

科　技

全年受理专利申请11657件，专利授权3045项。我市科研成果获2005年度国家科学技术奖14项。市级科技成果登记1508项，其中属于国际领先水平75项，达到国际先进水平321项。应用技术成果1232项，软科学成果86项，基础理论成果190项。全年技术合同交易额达到50.71亿元。当年执行科技发展计划项目2009项，其中科技攻关计划468项，成果推广及产业化计划404项，中小企业创新基金122项，火炬计划103项，星火计划105项。当年新增国家火炬计划项目20项，新增国家星火计划项目35项，新增国家重点新产品项目38项。全年研究与实验发展(R&D)经费支出占全市地区生产总值的比重达到2%，我市综合科技进步水平居全国第三位。

科技创新能力显著增强，取得了一批标志性的成果。抗艾滋病病毒药物“西夫韦肽”获得国家发明专利授权和美国专利授权，已完成一期临床试验。基因芯片研究已申请专利94项，体液重要致病菌检测基因芯片进入临床试验。药物研发取得进展，全年获新药证书51个，新药临床批文92个。利用胚胎克隆技术在国内首次克隆出波尔山羊。集成电路SOC芯片设计达到90纳米的国际先进水平。铜铟硒薄膜太阳能电池、纯电动汽车等研发居于国内领先水平。无缝钢管、皮质激素、复方丹参滴丸、力神锂离子电池、中空纤维膜材料和组件等一批自主创新新一代标志性产品已形成产业规模。年末全市共有国家级和市级企业技术中心150家，其中国家级企业技术中心13家。

积极引进海内外优秀人才，全年引进各类人才7900多人，新建博士后工作站10家，全市博士后流动站、工作站达到126个，在站博士后500余人。全市高级以上技术工人达到15.7万人，占技术工人队伍的22.4%，比“九五”末提高11.7个百分点。

新技术产业园区保持快速发展。全年园区实现技工贸总收入751.29亿元，比上年增长29.7%；技工贸总产值627.44亿元，增长28.6%；实现利润总额41.02亿元，增长76.9%；实现税金总额40亿元，增长14.0%；出口销售收入24.53亿美元，增长50.1%。华苑产业区显示了核心区的带动作用，全年完成工业总产值258亿元，比上年增长45.1%；外贸出口值7.36亿元，增长46.6%；财政收入14.3亿元，增长20%以上。

教　育

全年全市普通高校和高等职业技术学院共招生10.36万人，比上年增长7.7%，当年毕业6.92万人，年末共有在校学生33.16万人。全年招收研究生1.02万人，比上年增长9.7%，当年毕业0.6万人，年末在学研究生2.85万人。年内全市共有12576名贫困学生得到国家助学贷款，发放金额7946万元。高等教育毛入学率超过50%。高校毕业生就业率达91.4%。成人高等教育初步形成高标准职教体系，当年招生3.52万人，毕业2.88万人，年末在校学生8.44万人。

全市当年招收初中生9.98万人，当年毕业13.91万人，年末在校学生34.02万人。招收普通高中生7.44万人，当年毕业5.73万人，年末在校学生21.72万人。中等职业学校当年招生4.42万人，在校学生13.54万人。小学当年招生7.84万人，毕业11.48万人，在校学生55.19万人。幼儿园在园幼儿20.47万人，学龄儿童入学率99.97%，小学生升学率96.22%。已累计建成48所示范性高中，接受优质高中阶段教育的学生超过75%。

文　化

年末全市共有艺术表演团体16个，文化馆、科技馆19个，博物馆17个，公共图书馆32个。全市现有广播节目9套，综合人口覆盖率为100%；市级电视节目13套，综合人口覆盖率为99.83%，全市有线电视用户达到194万户。我市承办的第十五届全国书市取得巨大成功，包括港澳台在内的35个外地展团、500余家出版社，近10万书商来津参与订货，参加书市选购图书的总人数达到50万人次。成功举办了“2005相约环渤海中外交响乐经典作品演出季”、“华夏神韵——第二届中国民族戏曲优秀剧目大汇演”和天津市精品剧目国内巡回演出活动。精心组织了意大利天津周各项文化活动。举办了首届社区文化艺术节、第二届老年文化艺术节、第三届家庭文化艺术节和第五届滨海艺术节，群众文化活动丰富多彩。

卫　生

年末全市共有各类卫生机构2489个，其中医院272个，卫生防疫、防治机构41个，妇幼保健机构23个。卫生机构床位数4.3万张，其中医院、卫生院4.2万张。全市卫生技术人员6.1万人，其中执业医师及执业助理医师2.51万人，注册护士1.96万人。公共卫生体系建设取得新进展，疾病预防控制中心、120急救中心扩建工程竣工投入使用。社区卫生服务网络逐步完善，乡镇卫生院标准化建设启动。农村新型合作医疗扩展到8个区县，免费为320万农民进行健康体检。全年无偿献血9.1万人次。

体　育

在全国十运会上，参赛的天津体育健儿不畏强手，顽强拼搏，夺得了15.5枚金牌、13.5枚银牌和11枚铜牌，奖牌榜位次由上一届的第17位提高到第10位，创造了天津体育史上的最好成绩。“十五”期间，竞技体育有了长足进步，五年间，我市运动员在全国重大赛事中共夺得65枚金牌、56.5枚银牌、52枚铜牌，在国际重大赛事中夺得17枚金牌、9枚银牌、5枚铜牌。在2004年雅典奥运会上，夺得3枚金牌和1枚银牌。天津女排夺得国内赛事大满贯。群众体育工作始终保持全国领先，建成了一批规模大、档次高、功能全的健身公园和健身广场，群众体育活动场地和设施得到明显改善。全市已建立3000余个晨晚练辅导站，社会体育指导员达到

13000余名，全市经常参加体育活动的人数已达总人口的35%。

社会福利与救助

政府抚恤、补助各类优抚对象2.45万人，城乡低保对象18.27万人。各种福利院床位19748张，收养13471人。全市城乡老年福利机构258个。全市有救助站9个，全年救助13684人次。全市社区服务设施2139处，社区服务中心111个。全年销售社会福利彩票4.02亿元，筹集福利资金1.5亿元。全年接受社会捐赠1760.5万元。

残疾人事业

当年全市特殊教育招收新生200余人，在校生达到2600余人，残疾儿童少年义务教育入学率、保留率达到95%以上。年内新办福利企业5家。“十五”期间累计安排8.03万残疾人就业，其中城镇3.23万人，农村4.8万人。2005年，我市残疾人运动员在全国比赛中获得34枚金牌，28枚银牌和42枚铜牌；在世界大赛中获得8枚金牌，7枚银牌和5枚铜牌。在第六届全国残疾人艺术汇演中，我市残疾人演员获得2金1银3铜。举办了第二届残疾儿童艺术节和天津市残疾青年书画展。新建城市道路和建筑物普遍建设无障碍设施，并对原有道路和建筑物进行了大规模无障碍改造。

五、人口与人民生活

人　口

年末全市常住人口为1043万人，户籍人口939.31万人，其中，农业人口376.91万人，非农业人口562.40万人。2005年全市人口出生率为7.44‰，人口死亡率为6.01‰，人口自然增长率为1.43‰，我市人口进入低速增长期。

居民收入与消费

全年城镇单位从业人员人均劳动报酬23929元，增长13.2%。城市居民人均可支配收入12639元，增长10.2%；农村居民人均纯收入7202元，增长10.4%。居民生活水平继续提升。2005年城市居民人均消费性支出9653元，增长9.7%。其中衣着、医疗保健和交通通讯支出分别增长了11.9%、20.9%和26.7%。农村居民人均生活消费支出3590元，增长8.9%，其中衣着、交通通讯支出分别增长23.1%和12.0%。城乡居民生活质量继续提高，年末城市居民每百户家庭拥有移动电话122.1部、家用电脑51.1台、微波炉74.3台、热水器86.5台、轿车3辆。农村居民家庭每百户拥有洗衣机95台、电冰箱84台、抽油烟机18台、热水器32台、微波炉16台、移动电话89部、电脑10台。

“十五”时期，我市居民收入和消费水平有了显著提高。城市居民人均可支配收入和农村居民人均纯收入五年平均递增10.7%和10.5%，城市居民恩格尔系数达到36.7%，农村居民恩格尔系数达到38.3%，分别比“九五”末期降低3.4和4.3个百分点。

居　住

城乡居民居住条件和环境不断改善。城镇居民人均住房建筑面积25.8平方米，比“九五”末增加8.6平方米。农村居民人均住房面积26.1平方米，比“九五”末增加2.5平方米。全年拆迁房屋面积346.3万平方米，动迁居民6.2万户。累计有9400户中低收入群众住上经济适用房和廉租房。实施了旧楼区综合整治，累计完成了640片、1813万平方米旧楼区整修。据抽样调查显示，截至2005年末，居民家庭拥有自有产权住房的比率已达53.1%，比上年上升4.6个百分点，居住环境的改善和生活质量的提高使得居民家庭用于居住方面的支出稳步增长，城市和农村居民人均居住支出分别比上年增长5.0%和11.5%。

经济和社会发展中存在的主要问题是：加快结构调整、转变经济增长方式的任务还很重，经济总量还不够大，服务业发展相对滞后，个体私营经济比重偏低，就业压力比较大，社会保障体系还有待于进一步完善。

注：1. 2005年各项统计数据为快报数。

2. 按国家统计局要求，本公报中全市生产总值、社会消费品零售额历史数据根据经济普查结果作了相应调整。

3. 全市生产总值、各产业增加值绝对数按当年价格计算，增长速度按可比价格计算。

4. 规模以上工业企业包括全部国有和年销售收入在500万元及以上的非国有工业企业。

5. 高等教育毛入学率指在校大学生人数（不包括外地在津学生）与学龄组人口的比例，表明一个地区提供高等教育机会的综合水平。

6. 恩格尔系数是指食品支出占居民消费性支出的比重，恩格尔系数的降低标志着居民生活水平的提高。

STATISTICAL COMMUNIQUE ON THE 2005 NATIONAL ECONOMIC AND SOCIAL DEVELOPMENT OF THE CITY OF TIANJIN

Tianjin Municipal Bureau of Statistics

March 3. 2006

In 2005, under the correct leadership of Tianjin municipal Party committee of the Communist Party of China and Tianjin Municipal Government, the people of Tianjin followed the guidance of Deng Xiaoping Theory and the important principle of the "Three Represents", implemented the view of scientific development and macroeconomic control measures in an all - round way. Great efforts were made to carry out structural adjustment, technologic innovation, opening up to the outside world, changing the form of economic growth, quickening to implement the "three - step" development strategy and five strategic measures. The economic growth kept steady and rapid, social undertakings progressed in a comprehensive way, the peoples' living standard continued to improve. The targets defined in the Tenth - Five - Year Plan were fulfilled successfully.

Ⅰ. Economic Development

Economic Aggregate

The gross domestic product(GDP) of Tianjin was 366.386 billion yuan, up by 14.5% over the previous year at comparable prices. The per capita GDP in Tianjin was 35,457 yuan(4,328 USD), up 12.8%. The energy sources were used more efficiently than before. In 2005, for an output of 10,000 yuan, the comprehensive energy consumption is 1.28 tons of standard coal, 0.36 ton less than in 2000.

The year 2005 witnessed a balances development of the primary, secondary and tertiary industries in Tianjin. The added value of primary industry was 10.942 billion yuan, up by 4.3% over the previous year. The secondary industry accomplished added value 205.034 billion yuan, up by 17.5% over last year. The tertiary industry accomplished added value 150.41 billion yuan, up by 11.4%. To the economic growth in Tianjin, the three industries contributed 1.0%, 66.5% and 32.5% respectively. The ratio between the three industries changed from 4.3: 50.8: 44.9 in 2000 to 3:56:41 in 2005.

During the 10th Five - Year Plan Period, the GDP of Tianjin grew 13.9% each year on an average basis, 3.9 percentage points higher than the goal of the 10th Five - Year Plan, and 2.6 percentage points higher than the average annual growth rate during the 9th Five - Year Plan. Of which, the three industries grew 5.7%, 16.5% and 11.6% respectively each year on an average basis.

Financial revenue stepped onto a new stage. In 2005, the financial revenue exceeded 70 billion yuan and reached 72.552 billion yuan, calculated on comparable basis, the revenue is 26.8% more than in the previous year. The revenue within the general budget is 33.174 billion yuan, up 28.2%. The revenue from major taxes has also increased rapidly, the value - added tax has increased by 21.8%; business income tax, 27.8%; business tax, 23.0%; individual income tax, 17.8%. The financial expenditure in the year was 52.028 billion yuan, an increase of 20.6% over the previous year. Of the total, the expenditure on fundamental construction was 7.323 billion yuan, up 5.5%; the expenditure on enterprise improvement and upgrading was 2.912 billion yuan, up 7.1%; the expenditure on agriculture was 1.285 billion yuan, up 17.6%.

During the 10th Five-Year Plan, financial revenue grew 24.3% each year on an average basis, 8.4 percentage points higher than the average annual growth rate during the 9th Five-Year Plan. Financial revenue accumulated to 236 billion yuan, 2.5 times that in the 9th Five-Year Plan. Financial revenue accounted for 19.8% of Tianjin's GDP, 5.4 percentage points higher than that in 2000.

Labor and Employment

In 2005, the number of people employed in new job posts was 262,100, an increase of 47,600 people over the previous year, up 22.2%. Proactive reemployment policies were adopted and a wide variety of new job posts were offered in such fields as public place cleaning, labor security assistant management, traffic assistant management, and property management in old building blocks. A total of 142,200 laid-off workers were reemployed in the year 2005. At the end of the year 2005, the total number of employees in Tianjin was 5.38 million, an increase of 511,000 people over 2000. Of which, the number of employees in the secondary industry was 2.26 million, an increase of 38,000 people over 2000; the number of employees in the tertiary industry was 2.292 million, an increase of 457,000 people over 2000. In the human resources and labor market, 3,318,300 people were interviewed for jobs, and 901.900 people reached preliminary agreement with their potential employers.

During the 10th Five-Year Plan, the newly employed outnumbered the newly laid-off. A total of 572.000 laid-off workers were reemployed. The registered unemployment rate in the urban area dropped to 3.7% from 3.91% in 2002.

Price

The urban residents' consumption price index is 101.5, its rise being 0.8 percentage point lower that in the previous year. The price of food products rose by 3.4%, 6.5 percentage points lower that in the previous year. The price residence products rose by 6.7%, 3.1 percentage points higher than that in the previons year. The price of recreation, education and cultural products remained at the same level as in the last year. The price levels of the other five categories of products have dropped by different degrees. The retail price index of commodities in the urban area is 99.9, being decrease from increase in the previous year. In 2005, the ex-factory price index of industrial products was 100.1, the rise being 4 percentage points lower than in the previous year. Of which, the ex-factory price of productive materials rose by 1.0%, the ex-factory price of living materials dropped by 2.7%. The purchasing price index of raw materials, fuels and motive power was 104.9, the rise being 10.5 percentage points lower than in the previous year. The sales price of housing rose by 6.0%, the rise being 7.5 percentage points lower than in the previous year. The price of commercial residences rose by 6.3%, the rise being 5.4 percentage points lower than in the previous year.

During the tenth five-year plan period, the price level of Tianjin remained stable. The urban residents' consumption price accumulatively rose 5.7%, rose 1.1% each year on an average basis, 0.9 percentage points lower than the average growth rate during the 9th Five-Year Plan. The retail price of commodities dropped 1.2% each year on an average basis. The ex-factory price of industrial products dropped 0.4% each year on an average basis.

Investment In Fixed Assets

In 2005, the total fixed asset investment in Tianjin was 151.684 billion yuan, 20.5% more than in the previous year. Of the total, the fixed asset investment in the urban area was 138.556 billion yuan, up 22.4%. Of the total fixed asset investment in the urban area, 54.316 billion yuan went to the secondary industry, up 25.2%, accounting for 39.2% of the total investment in the urban area. Of which, 35.03 billion yuan went to manufacturing, up 39.3%. 83.735 billion yuan went to the tertiary industry, up 20.4%, accounting for 60.4% of the total investment in the urban area. Of which, investment of transportation and storage, post services was 16.784 billion, up 87.8%, investment of real estate was 33.947 billion yuan, up 23.2%. The major sectors that contribute to the growth of investment include: manufacturing, transportation and storage, post services, real estate industry, the total investment of the three industries was 85.761 billion yuan, up 39.1%, accounting for 61.9% of the total investment. To the growth of investment in Tianjin, the three industries contributed 95.1%. Construction of key projects ran smoothly. In 2005, a total of 38.702 billion yuan were invested in 58 key engineering projects in Tianjin, of which, energy and transport projects invested 12.837 billion yuan, high science & technology projects invested 2.012 billion yuan. The investment from private, individual was 51.142 billion yuan, up 32.4%, accounting for 33.7% of the total investment, 3 percentage points higher than the previous year. Foreign funded and Hangkong, Macao, Taiwan investment was 15.002 billion yuan, down by 19%, accounting for 9.9% of the total investment.

During the 10th Five-Year Plan, the completed investment in fixed assets of Tianjin accumulated to 533.89 billion yuan, 1 time as much as that in the 9th Five-Year Plan. During these five years, the investment grew 19.4% each year on an average basis, an increase of 8.8 percentage points over the 9th Five-Year Plan.

Agriculture

The total agricultural output value in 2005 is 23.834 billion yuan, up 4.8% over the previous year. The crop cultivation yielded 9.749 billion yuan, 0.2% more than in the last year; livestock husbandry yielded 10.271 billion yuan, a rise of 7.5%; the fishing industry yielded 3.625 billion yuan, up 10.6%; forestry industry increased 13.6% to 189 million yuan. Livestock husbandry accounted for 58.3% of the total output value in agriculture, 2.1 percentage points higher than in the last year.

The output of major agricultural and sideline products have increased. In 2005, the sown area of grain was 4,314,900 mu, the total output of grains is 1,375,000 tons, an increase of 122,300 tons over the previous year. The output of cotton is 83,500 tons, 36,800 tons less than in the previous year. The output of meat is 577,800 tons, up 7.5%; the output of milk is 634,100 tons, up 16.9%; the output of aquatic products is 338,100 tons, up 9.1%; the output of vegetable is 5,427,400 tons, a drop of 7.3%; the output of eggs is 234,700 tons, a drop of 3.7%.

Agricultural farms and agricultural facilities have been improved greatly. Several high-level plantations and breeding farms have been established, with Jinnan National Paradigmatic Farm of Modern Agriculture and Ninghe National Original-Breed Pig Farm as outstanding examples. Major animals and poultry and aquatic products are mainly produced on centralized farms. At the end of 2005, there were 130 leading enterprises with assets over 10 million yuan, including 10 national leading enterprises. 70% of the rural families have been involved in the system of agricultural industrialization, 37 percentage points higher than that in 2000. Water-saving irrigating area was 2.95 million mu, up 46.8% over 2000. Machinery power per 100 mu was 98.4 kw, up 20.7% over 2000.

New progress has been made in the development of agricultural science and technology. During the tenth five - year plan period, 466 items of scientific and technological achievements were made in agriculture in Tianjin. 137 items of the achievements have won scientific and technological awards at the municipal or state level. In such fields as cucumber breeding, rice hybridization and breeding, agricultural products preserving, wine processing, and animal embryo cloning, Tianjin enjoys a leading position in China.

Industry

In 2005, Tianjin industry realized an added value of 188.48 billion yuan, a rise of 17.9% over the previous year. The industrial enterprises above the designated size accomplished added value 178.302 billion yuan, up 20.4%. The output value of the industrial enterprises above the designated size is 677.41 billion yuan, a growth of 20.8%.

The advantageous industries play a significant role in pushing forward the development of economy. In 2005, six advantageous industries in Tianjin (electronic information, automobile, petrochemical industry, metallurgy, biotechnology and modern medicine, new energy sources and environment protection) accomplished a total industrial output of 485.135 billion yuan, accounting for 71.6% of the total in Tianjin, their contribution rate to industrial growth in Tianjin is 78.6%. In 2005, the new and high - tech industries accomplished an output value of 214.137 billion yuan, a growth of 16.4% over the previous year, accounting for 31.6% of the total output value of industries above the designated size, of which, the electronic information products manufacturing industry accomplished an output value of 168.237 billion yuan, up 17.3%, accounting for 24.8% of the total output value of industries.

The production and marketing situation were adapted to each other better, exports of industrial products increased quickly. The sales output value was 681.656 billion yuan, up 21.4%. The sales rate of industrial products in Tianjin was 100.6%. The value of exports of industrial products was 175.922 billion yuan, up 24.3%, accounting for 25.8% of the total sales output value.

The output of major industrial products increased quickly. In 2005, the output of crude oil was 17.8288 million tons, up 23.6%. The output of natural gas was 0.879 billion cu.m, up 5.8%. Electric power generation was 36.569 billion kwh, up 8.7%. The output of pig iron was 6.6024 million tons, up 33.8%. The output of steel was 16.6404 million tons, up 22.2%. The output of seamless steel pipe was 1.7459 million tons, up 10.6%. The output of cement was 5.1915 million tons, up 4.2%. The output of mobile phone was 63.1982 million, up 28.4%. The output of cars was 0.3256 million sets, up 48.1%. The output of cloth was 0.258 billion meters, up 7.0%. The output of garments was 178.1594 million pieces, up 13.0%. The output of vegetable oil was 0.5157 million tons, up 22.3%. The output of microwave oven was 14.3115 million sets, up 5.1%. The output of traditional Chinese medicine was 61.5064 million tons, up 24.2%. The output of semiconductor integrated circuit was 518.419 million pcs, up 10.8%. The output of dry battery was 370.34 million, up 26.8%.

The industrial economic benefit maintained its momentum of growth by leaps and bounds. In 2005, the independent industrial enterprises above the designated size in Tianjin earned an revenue of 686.524 billion yuan from their major business, up 22.9% over the previous year. Their profit payments and tax turnover were 76.075 billion yuan, up 27.2%. The profit has grown in pace with tax payment, yielding a profit of 52.018 billion yuan, up 27.2%, and a tax payment of 24.057 billion yuan, up 27.1%. Overall economic benefit index of industrial enterprises above designated size in Tianjin was 214.85, an increase of 20.5 percentage points over the previous year. Of which, the total asset contribution factor is 14.34%, 1.0 percentage points higher; the rate of profit based on the cost of production and expenses is 8.26%, 0.3 percentage point higher.

During the 10th Five - Year Plan, the gross output value of industrial sector of Tianjin grew 21.5% each year on an average basis, up by 6.3 percentage points over the 9th Five - Year Plan Period. The gross output value of industrial enterprises above designated size grew 23.7% each year on an average basis, the added value of industrial enterprises above designated size grew 19.6% each year on an average basis, 1.4 times than that in 2000.

Construction

The added value of construction was 16.554 billion yuan, up 13.5%, the output value of Tianjin totaled 72.526 billion yuan, up by 14.9%. Construction area of houses was 37.7028 million square meters, up 9.7%; area of houses completed was 13.1795 million square meters. There were 1,180 construction enterprises. The profit of these enterprises was 1.463 billion yuan, up 27.7%, the tax was 2.158 billion yuan, up 17.3%.

During the 10th Five - Year Plan, the added value of the construction sector in Tianjin grew 10.7% each year on an average basis, an increase of 4.2 percentage points over the 9th Five - Year Plan. The quality of construction projects improved stably. There were 28 projects awarded national grade awards, 280 projects awarded municipal grade awards.

Transportation, Posts & Telecommunications and Storage

In 2005, the transportation, posts & telecommunications and storage accomplished an added value of 30.838 billion yuan, up 7.8%. Cargo transport continued to develop. In 2005, total volume of cargo transport was 397.487 million tons, up by 4.8% over the previous year. Of this total, the cargo transportation by highways was 198.5 million tons, up 1.0%, by railways, 67.9395 million tons, up 11.2%; by water transport, 123.6777 million tons, up 7.7%. Share of transportation volume by three means of highway, waterway and railway was 49.9%, 31.1% and 17.1% respectively. The cargoes loaded and unloaded at Tianjin Port weighed 240.688 million tons, up 16.7% over previous year. Of which, the import transportation volume was 93.693 million tons, up 26.6%, the export transportation volume was 146.995 million tons, up 11.2%. The transportation volume of containers was 4.801 million international standard containers, up 25.8%. The freight turnover was 80,200 tons, up 13.0%.

Passenger transportation grew rapidly. In 2005, the volume of passenger transportation was 46.8729 million, up by 14.2%. Of the total, passenger carried by railways were 15.5843 million persons, up by 4.6%; by highways, 29.61 million persons, up by 20.5%. Annual passenger turnover was 2.1365 million persons, up 25.3%.

At the end of 2005, there were 1.126 million automobiles, of which, 0.503million were cars. There were 0.815 million private automobiles, of which, 0.374 million were cars.

The capacity of transportation increased. During the 10th Five - Year Plan, there were 21 newly constructed berths, 15 berths with 50,000 tons class. The accumulative newly capacity was 93.62 million tons. 44 lines have been opened for container ships. Tianjin newly opened 3 inland ports. Tianjin Port has established business relationships with more than 300 ports in 160 countries and areas in the world. The number of airlines was 65, and connected with 54 cities.

The business in post and telecommunication industry has developed rapidly. In 2005, the total business of post and telecommunication industry was 17.8 billion yuan, a growth of 21.1% over the previous year. Of the total, the telecommunication business was 16.6 billion yuan, up 20.3%, the post business was 1.2 billion yuan , up 33.3%. At the end of the year, the long-distance optic cable reached a length of 3,376 km; the total exchange capacity was 4.33 million telephones and the number of fixed telephone users hit 4.39 million. Local calls numbered 10.3 billion times, long-distance calls numbered 0.95 billion times, of which, international and Hongkong, Macao and Taiwan calls numbered 0.022 billion times, up 37.5%. The number of mobile phone users was 5.03 million, including 2 million new users. A total of 4.5 billion messages were sent through mobile phones, a growth of 55.2%. Throughout the year, 87.54 million mailing matters were posted, including 3.32 million EMS matters, up 13.3%. 54 new post offices were established, increasing the total number of post offices to 454.

Domestic Commerce

In 2005, the wholesale, retail trade and catering services accomplished an added value of 48.863 billion yuan, up 13.5% over the previous year. The commerce and trade enterprises above the designated size in Tianjin purchased goods worth 362.05 billion yuan. The total sales volume of all commerce and trade enterprises and individual business entities reached 482.022 billion yuan.

The retail market was also vibrant with purchase and sale. In 2005, the total retail volume of consumer goods was 119.006 billion yuan, a rise of 13.9% over the previous year. The consumption interest seems to be more and more diversified. The retail volume of automobiles grow by 1.2 times; the retail volume has grown by more than 40% for petroleum and its products, electronic publications and audio-visual products, and furniture. The retail volume of catering business increased by 20.9% to 15.949 billion yuan. During the 10th Five-Year Plan, the total retails sales of consumer goods accumulated to 493.117 billion, grew 13.5% each year on an average basis.

Rapid progress has also been made in the construction of wholesale markets. By the end of 2005, there were 57 large-scale wholesale markets with a transaction volume of over 100 million yuan each. Exhibition and fair-based economy has also thrived. Tianjin Business Negotiation Fair, Beer Festival, PECC Exposition, and Mobile Phone Equipment Fair have become well-known business events in Tianjin.

Rapid progress has been made in the construction of business facilities in Tianjin. Many large commercial establishments have been completed and opened to the public, such as Friendship - New Horizon Plaza. The commercial establishments completed during the tenth five-year plan period cover an area of 4.31 million m^2. And 123 more large commercial establishments covering more than 5000 m^2 were also built. Obvious effects have been achieved after the construction of such commercial establishments as vegetable markets and community business centers.

Finance and Insurance Industries

In 2005, the added value of finance and insurance industries was 16.064 billion yuan, up 15.7% over the previous year. Huaxia Bank and China Minsheng Banking Corp. Ltd. established offices in Tianjin. Bohai Property Insurance Corporation started business. Tianjin Rural Cooperation Bank established. China Bohai Bank, which central department locates in Tianjin, started business, becoming the first national share - holding bank approved after the year of 1996. By the end of 2005, there were 2,926 banking institutions in Tianjin, with a staff of 46,200 people.

The deposit and loan continued to increase. At the end of 2005, the total amount of home and foreign currency deposited in Chinese and foreign financial institutions in Tianjin was worth 609.05 billion yuan, an increase of 90.735 billion yuan compared to the beginning of the year, 12.803 billion yuan more than the increase in the same period of the previous year. Of this total, savings of enterprises reached 244.899 billion yuan, up by 19.0%; the savings by residents reached 258.44 billion yuan, up by 14.3%. The balance of loans in home and foreign currency reached 472.238 billion yuan, an increase of 64.894 billion yuan compared to the beginning of the year, 15.447 billion yuan more than the increase in the same period of the previous year. Of this total, short - term loans reached 207.795 billion yuan, up 11.1%; medium - term & long - term loans reached 225.523 billion yuan, up 21.9%. Housing loans reached 37.52 billion yuan, up 22.6%, automobiles consume loans reached 1.456 billion yuan, down by 33.8%. By the end of 2005, there were 1,548 banking institutions in Tianjin.

The securities business has developed steadily in general. At the end of 2005, there were 24 kinds of listed stocks in domestic stock market in Tianjin. The business volume of securities was 109.75 billion yuan. Of this total, the transaction volume of stocks was 101.853 billion yuan, that of treasure bonds, 4.467 billion yuan, that of funds, 3.43 billion yuan. In the futures market, 2,588,600 transactions were made, with a business volume of 120.147 billion yuan. By the end of 2005, there were 75 securities business departments, 12 futures departments, 2 securities investment consultation companies. Account - opening by investors in stock market reached 1,013,000 households. Over the year, the total volume of foreign exchange swap was 2.13 billion USD, up 34.1%. Of this total, foreign exchange swap to Tianjin was 1.246 billion USD, up 60.2%, foreign exchange swap from Tianjin was 0.883 billion USD, up 9.0%.

The insurance market has become more and more diversified, and the business volume has increased again. In 2005, the insurance premium brought an income of 9.064 billion yuan, a rise of 11.8% over the previous year. Of this total, the premium income from property insurance was 2.178 billion yuan, the personal insurance income was 6.886 billion yuan. The total expenditure on insurance payment was 1.746 billion yuan, the payment for property insurance was 1.074 billion yuan, the payment for personal insurance was 0.672 billion yuan. By the end of 2005, there were 427 insurance institutions in Tianjin.

Real Estate

The added value in the real estate industry was 11.604 billion yuan, up 6.7%; the investment in this industry was 32.754 billion yuan, up 24.1%, including the investment in residential houses 23.493 billion yuan, up 34.1%, and investment in houses for business operations 4.175 billion yuan, up 47.8%. As a result of the regulation and control of the national macro policies, the investment and development of real estate have maintained a momentum of steady, orderly development in 2005. The commercial housing under development covers an area of 34,705,700m^2, up 21.1%, including constructed residential houses 28,278,700m^2, up 20.2%. The commercial housing that has been completed covers 14,792,200 m^2, up 33.5%, including completed residential houses 12,709,600 m^2, up 25.3%. The floor space of completed commercial houses sold in the year was 9,380,200 m^2, up 10.7%; the sales revenue was 36.756 billion yuan, up 39.3%. In the year, the amount of stock housing transactions was 8,549,000 m^2, including 7,991,000 m^2 for private housings, 558,000 m^2 for public housings. The transaction volume of the stock housing was 21.23 billion yuan, including 19.53 billion yuan for private housing purchase and 1.7 billion yuan for public housing purchase or exchanges.

II Reform and Opening up to the Outside World

Ownership Structure

In 2005, the public - owned economy completed added value 175.865 billion yuan, accounting for 48 percent of the GDP in Tianjin; the non - public - owned economy completed added value 190.521 billion yuan, accounting for 52 percent of the GDP in Tianjin, 2 percentage points higher than in 2004.

The ownership structures of the industries are quite diversified. In 2005, of the total output value of industrial enterprises above the designated size in Tianjin, the enterprises with investment from abroad or Hong Kong, Macao or Taiwan accomplished an output value of 329.804 billion yuan, up 19.0%, accounting for 48.7% of the total output value; the stock ownership enterprises accomplished an output value of 252.572 billion yuan, up 26.8%, accounting for 37.3% of the total; the private enterprises accomplished 65.367 billion yuan, up 22.7%, accounting for 9.6% of the total. In Tianjin, the state - owned industrial enterprises and state - owned holding industrial enterprises above the designated size accomplished an output value of 256.726 billion yuan, an increase of 27.0% over the previous year.

The private and individual economy has undergone continuous development. The private and individual economy realized incremental value 88.665 billion yuan, up 18.8%, accounting for 24.2% of the total output value in Tianjin. At the end of 2005, the registered capital in private and individual economy was 162.033 billion yuan, 34.905 billion yuan higher than at the beginning of the year. The number of private and individual economic entities reached 254,300, of which, the number of private reached 77,300. The number of people working in this field was 1,141,600, an increase of 122,900 people over the beginning of the year, including 887,000 people working in private economy. The total sale and business income in the year was 130.617 billion yuan, up 36.2%. Of the total, that of private enterprises was 74.787 billion yuan, up 38.2%; that of individual was 55.83 billion yuan, up 33.5%. The total tax revenue in the year was 6.107 billion yuan, up 21.4%. Of which, that of private enterprises was 4.886 billion yuan, up 27.9%.

Management of State - owned Assets and Reform of State - owned Enterprises

The assets of state - owned and state - holding enterprises amounted to 570.1 billion yuan, the creditor's equity amounted to 191.5 billion yuan. State - owned capital accounting for 70 of major sectors and fields. The state - owned assets further circulated. At the Tianjin Property Right Exchange, 872 projects were registered. The transaction volume of state - owned assets was 21.868 billion yuan, of this total, the transaction volume among districts was 3.031 billion yuan, the transaction volume among Tianjin units was 18.837 billion yuan.

New progress was made in the reform and adjustment of state - owned enterprises. By the end of 2005, 2,637 enterprises carried out reform, accounting for 76.6% of all municipal state - owned enterprises. More than 80% large & medium - sized state - owned enterprises have completed reform of corporation system. The strategic eastward movement of Tianjin industry was further carried out. By the end of the year, there were 210 enterprises moved to new coastal area.

Social Security

The system of endowment, medical, employment injury, maternity and unemployment insurance for urban workers and subsistence allowance system in the rural and urban areas has been improved so that they have a wider coverage than before. In 2005, 2,006,200 workers were involved in endowment insurance, 2,993,400 workers were involved in medical insurance, 1,975,100 workers were involved in unemployment insurance, 1,629,100 workers were involved in employment injury insurance, and 1,574,200 people in maternity insurance. The relief system for those with low incomes has been improved, too. Great efforts have been made to make sure that subsistence allowance is provided to the needy. The minimum salary standard was adjusted in successive 5 years. In 2005, the minimum salary of enterprise workers in Tianjin was set at 590 yuan from 350 yuan in 2000.

Domestic Cooperation

In 2005, the actual investment in Tianjin was 33.993 billion yuan, up 42.4%. As for the sources of capital, the actual investment in Tianjin from Beijing and Hebei Province was 13.8 billion yuan, up 92.9%; that from the Yangtze Delta was 7.2 billion yuan, up 60.3%; that from the Pearl River Delta was 5.1 billion yuan, up 69.7%. As for the destinations of the capital, the real estate industry in Tianjin has attracted the most domestic capital, with an actual investment of 14.9 billion yuan, 43.8% of the total investment in Tianjin.

Assistance and support of Tianjin to GanShu, Changdu of Tibet, Wanzhou District of ChongQing and Kashi of Xinjiang was further enhanced and promoted the development of local economy.

Foreign Trade

In 2005 in Tianjin, the total import and export through foreign trade reached US $53.387 billion, up 27.1%, the export value is US $27.415 billion, up 31.4%; the import value is US $25.972 billion, up 22.8%. A favorable trade balance of US $1.443 billion has been achieved. The exports to US, EU, ASEAN, Janpan and Korea accounted for 79% of the total exports. In 2005, the export volume of electromechanical equipment in Tianjin (ranked the fourth in China) increased 26% to US $18.5 billion, accounting for 67.5% of the total export in Tianjin, 7.4 percentage points higher than the previous year. The export of high - tech products reached US $12.47 billion, up 24.5%, accounting for 45.5% of the total export in Tianjin. the foreign - funded enterprises exported goods worth US $22.023 billion, a growth of 29.1% over the previous year, accounting for 80.3% of the total export in Tianjin. The state - owned enterprises exported goods worth US $3.379 billion, up 23.8%.

During the 10th Five - Year Plan, the total value of exports and imports of Tianjin accumulated to US$ 165.8 billion, an increase of 1.8 times over the 9th Five - Year Plan. Of this total, the value of exports accumulated to US$ 83.8 billion, the value of imports was US$ 82 billion, increase of 1.8 times over the 9th Five - Year Plan respectively.

Foreign Investment

In 2005, 1,309 enterprises with foreign investment were approved in Tianjin, 18.8% more than in the previous year. The contracted value of foreign capital to be directly used was US $7.323 billion, up 31.0%; the foreign capital that was actually used was US $3.329 billion, up 34.6%. Establishing solely foreign - funded enterprises has become a major way to make use of foreign capital directly. In 2005, the actual investment was US $2.272 billion, accounting for 68.3% of the total in Tianjin. In the service sector in 2005, US $790 million foreign capital was actually used, accounting for 23.7% of the total foreign capital actually used in Tianjin, up 19.7%. The contracted value of foreign capital from France, German, Hongkong, Singapore and Korea increased by 3.2 times, 1.7 times, 1.1 times, 95.2% and 86.0% respectively.

During the 10th Five - Year Plan, foreign funds actually utilized accumulated to US $ 10.335 billion, grew 32% each year on an average basis. By the end of 2005, enterprises from 110 countries and areas have invested in Tianjin. Of the top 500 enterprises in the world, 114 have invested in Tianjin. During the 10th Five - Year Plan, foreign funds of manufacturing actually utilized increased by 1.3 times over the 9th Five - Year Plan.

Foreign Economic Cooperation

In 2005, Tianjin signed 907 contracts with foreign enterprises on projects undertaking, cooperation of labor service, design and consultation services, with a contract value of US $430 million, a rise of 30.4% over the previous year, yielding a business turnover of US $320 million, up 18.7%. The investment abroad covers many fields, such as chemical industry, medicine production, building materials, food, and clothing. In 2005, a total of 4,800 contract workers were sent abroad. By the end of the year, there were 13,100 Tianjin workers abroad. 75 overseas institutions and 54 overseas manufacturing enterprises were approved in 2005, with a total investment of US $50,488,300, including Chinese investment US $43,715,400. By the end of 2005, there were 54 enterprises of foreign economic cooperation in Tianjin, which undertook projects from and offered labor cooperation services to 81 countries and areas. Greater efforts were made in introducing advanced technology from abroad. In 2005, 580 contracts were signed on technology introduction, with a contract value of US $657 million. International activities increased, Tianjin successfully hosted many activities which enlarged the affection of Tianjin, including ASEM Finance Ministers' Meeting, Italy Tianjin Week, Singapore Tianjin Week.

Tourism

In 2005, 740,100 tourists from all over the world visited Tianjin, 20.2% more than in the previous year. Tourist industry earned foreign exchange US $509 million, a growth of 23.4%. The number of domestic tourists and the income from domestic tourism both increased by 12.8% over the previous year. In the year, 146,000 Tianjin citizens traveled abroad, up 47.3%, causing an expenditure of 1.921 billion yuan, up 47.4%. By the end of the year 2005, there are 111 hotels above star level in Tianjin, there were 263 travel agencies, including 28 international agencies and 235 domestic agencies.

New Coastal Area

In 2005, the total output value in the area is 160.863 billion yuan, a growth of 19.8%. The total industrial output value is 399.673 billion yuan, an increase of 30.7%; the investment of fixed assets is 69.331 billion yuan, up 22.6%. The export through foreign trade was US $18.469 billion, up 34.8%, accounting for 67.4% of the total export quantity in Tianjin. The contracted value of foreign capital was US $5.1 billion, up 37.6%, accounting for 69.6% of the total. The new area made direct use of foreign investment US $ 2.646 billion, up 52.1%, accounting for 79.5% of the total. The retail volume of consumer goods is 20.652 billion yuan, an increase of 14.7%.

The pace of construction modern transport system was quickened. Many key projects started to construct, including Beijing - Tianjin Express Way, Beijing - Tianjin - Tanggu Express Way Second Line, expansion of Tianjin Binhai Airport, widening construction of Tianjin Port. Reconstruction of Tianjin Soda Plant started. The project of moving Tainjin New Port Ship Plant signed. Ethane project with annual productive power over 1,000,000tons was approved by the State Council. The first national aviation industry base would build in new coastal area. Port industry park had completed producing land of 12.1 sq.km.

The function of servicing inland districts was improved. International trade & shipping service center and E - port project put into use. The time of entering and outing port shortened one third. In 2005, the total volume of import and export through Tianjin port is US $ 81.929 billion, up 20.9%. Of the total import and export volume through Tianjin port, the goods transported from Beijing, Inner Mongolia, Shanxi, Henan, Liaoning, Shandong accounting for 53.9% of the total. TPFTZ Logistics Park operated well. The total goods getting in or out of TPFTZ were worth US $ 18.76 billion, up 42.9%.

Ⅲ Urban Construction and Management

Construction of Infrastructure

The construction of infrastructure in Tianjin progressed quickly. By the end of 2005, length of paved roads was 5,460 km, area of paved roads was 66.69 million sq.m, Per capita area of roads was 10.41 sq.m. In the central urban area, the urban express way that has been put in operation is 120 km long. The end of the year saw the completion of the subway 1st line. The Beijing - Tianjin Express Railway Project started to construct. Jigang railway and Huangwan railway was constructing. During the 10th Five - Year Plan, the Jinbin light - rail express railway was put into operation. A total of 299 km expressway had been completed. The length of expressway reached 603 km. In the past five years, there were 55 highway had been constructed and reconstructed, including Bejing - Tianjin, Yangbei and Jingang highway. There were 2,804 km rural highway had been reconstructed. The city constructed and reconstructed 385 urban roads, including Zijinshan, Xianyang, Shuishangbei road. It also constructed 94 large - sized and medium - sized bridges.

Public Utilities

In 2005, the comprehensive production capacity of tap water in Tianjin was 3.5895 million m^3 per day. Throughout the year, 675.01 million m^3 tap water was sold, including 288.85 million m^3 water for daily use. In the urban area, 98.45% of the families, i.e. 2.2764 million families, use fuel gas. During the tenth five - year plan period, the length of new water supply pipelines was 1,951 km, the length of new gas supply pipelines was 2,609 km, the length of new water drainage pipelines was 3,857 km. In 2005, new central heating services were opened to an area of 26 million m^2, newly increased heating area reached 48.94 million m^2, and the rate of central heating availability reached 83.2%,29.7 percentage points higher than 2000.9 sewage processing factories were built or rebuilt, including Jizhuangzi sewage processing factory, Xianyanglu sewage processing factory, Beicang sewage processing factory. 4 rubbish processing stations were built, including Shuangkou rubbish processing station, Dahanzhuang rubbish processing station, Shuanggang rubbish processing station, Jixian rubbish processing station. The sewage and rubbish processing capacity reached 75% and 81% respectively, 16 and 18 percentage points higher than 2000 respectively. Several public transportation sites were built or rebuilt. By the end of 2005, there were 6,794 public transportation vehicles, with a net increase of 691. With the opening of 30 new public transportation routes, there are 428 public transport routes in Tianjin now. The public transportation system in Tianjin had a transportation volume of 890 million passengers in 2005. There are 31,939 taxis in Tianjin.

Comprehensive Development Along Haihe River and City Appearance Reorganizing

The steps were quickened to comprehensively develop the belt along Haihe River. After the construction of three years, the project of clearing silt completed. 17 km long dyke were rebuilt or constructed. In the year, Dagu Bridge put in use. Fenghua Bridge and Baoding Bridge completed main engineering. 28 roads(including Haihe west road) along the river were rebuilt. 6 greenland(including music park) were completed. 42 scenery buildings were reconstructed. Many trade projects started to construct, and accelerated the development of modern services, including Fenghuang Square Trade Zone, Cannel Trade Zone, Water Sport World.

The look of city changed obviously. During the 10th Five - Year Plan, the newly increased green land in Tianjin was 85.76 million sq.m, The green coverage rate in the built - up area reached 36.4% from 25.1% in 2000. The per capita area of public green land in the city was 8.5m^2, an increase of 3.1 m^2 than 2000. During the 10th Five - Year Plan, protecting Luanhe project completed. A lot of parks and green land were built, including Xiangyu Park, Beichen Park, Hongqiao Park. 10 rivers, including Jinhe, Weijin river, Changtai river, with 104 km were reconstructed and the river environment was improved.

Resource and Environment Protection

Tianjin implemented more rigid measures for land administration. The tender, auction, and listing systems for transfer of use right of operational land were implemented fully. New infrastructure financing system was founded. Land supply was controlled rigidly, 4212.7 hectares of land were supplied in 2005. During the 10th Five - Year Plan, the usage and supplement remained balance for 5 successive years. Achievement was made in reorganization of developed zones.

In 2005, Tianjin passed the evaluation of the State Environment Protection Administration and became a model city of environment protection in China. Obvious effects have been achieved in six environment protection projects: Blue Sky Project, Limpid Water Project, Pollution Prevention and Control Project, Ecological Protection Project, Model Cell Project, and Quietness Project. The rate of high - quality environment air was 81.6% in 2005 from 47% in 2001. The up - to - standard rate of drinking water and that of the water quality in the urban water function area are both 100%. The up - to - standard rate of discharged waste water is over 95%. Noise pollution has also been effectively controlled, and 97 quiet residential communities have been established. The area with up - to - standard urban environment noise level is 569.9 km^2, with a coverage percentage of 80%. 48 smoke control areas have been established, and the smoke control area is 574.6 km^2. The comprehensive utilization rate of industrial solid rubbish is 99%. In the past 5 years, 113 ecological villages were built, 4 national - grade beautiful towns were built. At the end of 2005, there were 21 environment monitoring stations, 2 national model ecological areas, 5 national experimental ecological areas, and 8 nature reserves (with an area of 163,000 ha.) in Tianjin.

Information Construction

During the 10th Five - Year Plan, the city constructed e - government network, e - business network and public information service network. A lot of information facilities put into use, including "Nankai Star" super computer center, IDC, State Anti - virus Center, Jinwan Calling center. By the end of 2005, there were 700,000 km of optic fiber had been laid, communication power had covered the whole city, the kernel capacity of the trunk board - band network reached 2,000 Gbps, the brand width at the exit of the city was 121 Gbps. Number of subscriber of Internet dialing number was 2.66 million, number of subscriber of wild - belt Internet was 0.65 million. Digit television started to installed with 150 channels, the users was 10,000 households.

The steps of information construction have been quickened in Tianjin. By the end of 2005, the municipal e - government network had been accessible to nearly 200 institutions above the sub - bureau level. The e - government network at the district or county level had been extended to the committees, offices, bureaus, towns, townships and streets in the district or county. Portal websites had been established for governments at the city and district level. With this development, the government affairs have become more transparent and open to the public. Apart from this, the networks also enabled on - line office, contributed to business invitation and investment attraction, and provided convenient services to the citizens. Through four years' effort to carry out "100 projects" on the web, the municipal government organs have finished over 1200 tasks of 79 bureaus(offices) online. The opening of the 8890 service hotline serves as a bridge connecting the citizens with service departments and enterprises. A series of key information system projects have been started, such as Gold Tax, Gold Shield, Gold Auditing, etc.. The improvement of information technology has boosted the development of conventional industries. In 2005, all the large - scale marketplaces with an annual sales revenue of more than 1 billion yuan adopted information technology in their commercial activities. 90% of the large - scale enterprises and 50% of the small and medium - sized enterprises in Tianjin were also involved in e - business. Through the network, 1800 schools in Tianjin have been effectively linked with each other. In 800 schools, network access is made possible through optic fibers.

Quality Supervision and Inspection

In 2005, there were 19 legal quality inspection institutions and 22 measurement verification institutions in Tianjin. 44 enterprises and 47 products had been approved to be exempted from inspection (including 11 enterprises and 11 products that won the approval within the year 2005). Six products became name - brand products in China, making the total 15; 19 products became name - brand products in Tianjin, making the total 209. 3,636 enterprise and product standards were established or amended, making the total number of enterprise standards 33,000. In 2005, 3,636 enterprises and 4,493 batches of their products were inspected. The up - to - standard rate of the production batches was 88.5%. 207 commercial enterprises and 352 of batches commodities were inspected. The up - to - standard rate of the batches was 72%. 102,800 sets (pieces) of measurement instrument were verified in 2005. In total, 243 enterprises had food production licenses. A total of 3,033 system authentification certificates had been issued. 609 enterprises had won China Compulsory Certification (3C) for their products, and a total of 3,244certificates had been issued. A sum of 150,000 batches goods were inspected by Tianjin Entry - exit Inspection and Quarantine Bureau, with the value of 12.2 billion USD, up 21.8% than the previous year.

Ⅳ Social Undertakings

Science and Technology

In 2005, the number of patent applications in Tianjin was 11,657, the number of patents granted was 3,045. 14 national awards have been won. In 2005, Tianjin won 1,508 municipal awards for its scientific achievements, 75 of which reached the leading level in the world and 321 of which came up to the advanced world standard. Of which, there were 1,232 applied achievements, 86 soft science achievements, 190 basic theory achievements. The transaction value of technology contracts was 5.071 billion yuan in 2005. In 2005, the city carried out 2,009 science & technology development projects, including 468 science & technology storming projects, 404 applied achievements, 122 innovation funds of medium & small - sized enterprises, 103 torch plan, 105 spark plan. There were 20 newly increased torch plan, 35 newly increased spark plan and 38 newly increased new products projects. R&D expenditure accounting for 2% of GDP in 2005. Tianjin secures the third position in China in terms of overall scientific and technological strength.

The improved innovation ability in science and technology has contributed to a series of significant achievements. Sifuvirtide, a new anti - HIV medicine, has won patents from China and US, and the first phase of clinical experiment has been completed. In the research of gene chips, applications have been made for 94 patents of special genes in major pathogens and probes both at home and abroad. The gene chips for the detection of major pathogens in body fluid are now under clinical experiments. Progress has also been made in the research and development of new medicines. In 2005, 51 new medicine certificates and 92 clinical medicine experiment approval documents were obtained. With embryo cloning technology, a Boer goat was cloned in China for the first time. In the design of SOC chips (system on chip), the international advanced level of 90 nanometer was achieved. Apart from this, Tianjin also enjoys a leading position in China in the development of CIS thin - film solar cells and exclusively electricity - powered automobiles. By the end of 2005, there were 150 enterprise technology centers above the municipal level in Tianjin, including 13 enterprise technology centers at the state level.

Proactive efforts have been made to attract excellent talents from home and abroad. In 2005, a total of over 7,900 talents were introduced to Tianjin. 10 post - doctoral work stations were established. Thus, there were in total 126 post - doctoral mobile stations and work stations in Tianjin, with over 500 post - doctors working there. There was a senior technical staff of 157,000 workers, accounting for 22.4% of total technical staff, 11.7 percentage points higher than that in 2000.

The New Technology Industrial Park has been developing at a high speed. In 2005, the park had a total income of 75.129 billion yuan through technology, industry and trade, a rise of 29.7% over the previous year. The total output value of technology, industry and technology was 62.744 billion yuan, up 28.6%; the total profit was 4.102 billion yuan, up 76.9%; the total tax payment was 4 billion yuan, up 14.0%; the total revenue from export and sales was US $2.453 billion, up 50.1%. Huayuan Industrial Park has played a leading role as a kernel park: it achieved a total industrial output value of 25.8 billion yuan, 45.1% more than in the previous year; its export volume through foreign trade was 736 million yuan, up 46.6%; its financial revenue was 1.43 billion yuan, a rise of more than 20%.

Education

In 2005, institutions of higher education and senior vocational schools enrolled 103,600 students, 7.7% more than in the previous year. 69,200 students graduated from these schools in 2005, and at the end of the year, there were 331,600 students studying in these schools. The year 2005 also saw the recruitment of 10,200 graduate students, up 9.7% over the previous year. 6,000 graduate students graduated in 2005, and at the end of the year, there were 28,500 graduate students. In 2005, a total of 12,576 students from poverty-stricken families got student loans totaling 79.46 million yuan. The gross rate of admission to higher education institutions was more than 50%, the employment rate of graduates from institutions of higher education was 91.4%. Adult education has formed high level teaching system. In 2005, the adult education institutions of higher learning in Tianjin enrolled 35,200 students, thus the total number of these students was 84,400, 28,800 students graduated from these schools.

In 2005, 99,800 students were admitted to junior high schools and 139,100 students graduated from these schools. At the end of the year, there were 340,200 students studying in these schools. 74,400 students were admitted to senior high schools, and 57,300 students graduated from the schools. At the end of the year, there were 217,200 students in senior high schools. There were 135,400 enrolled students in secondary vocational schools, with 44,200 new entrants. In primary schools, 78,400 children were enrolled, and 114,800 students graduated. The number of students studying the primary schools was 551,900. In kindergartens, there were 204,700 children. 99.97% of school-age children were enrolled to schools to receive education, and 96.22% of the primary school graduates were admitted to junior high schools. By the end of 2005, there were 48 model senior high schools in Tianjin. The percentage of students who receive high-quality senior school education was over 75%.

Culture

At the end of the year, there were 16 arts performing troupes, 19 cultural centers and science and technology centers, 17 museums, and 32 public libraries in Tianjin. In 2005, there are 9 radio channels (accessible to 100% of Tianjin citizens), and 13 TV channels (accessible to 99.83% of Tianjin citizens). In the whole city, 1,940,000 families have access to cable TV programs. The fifteenth national book fair was held in Tianjin. From areas outside Tianjin, including Hong Kong, Macao and Taiwan, 35 delegations, over 500 publishing units, and nearly 100,000 book sellers came to the fair. About 500,000 people went to the book fair to buy books. The performance market was also vibrant in Tianjin. Many performance activities were organized, such as "Meet at Bohai Bay - Chinese and Foreign Classic Symphonies Concert 2005", "Charm of China - the second joint performance of Chinese folk operas", and the around-China performance of excellent plays of Tianjin. In the "China Tianjin Week" in Italy, the culture and arts of Tianjin were shown. Tianjin citizens have a wide variety of cultural activities, including the first community culture and arts festival, the second elderly people's culture and arts festival, the third family culture and arts festival, the fifth Binhai arts festival.

Public Health

At the end of 2005, there were in Tianjin 2,489 public health organizations, including 272 hospitals and clinics, 41 disease control organizations, and 23 health centers for women and children. There were 43,000 beds in the public health organizations, including 42,000 beds in hospitals and clinics. In Tianjin, there were 61,000 health personnel, including 25,100 practicing physicians and practicing assistant physicians, and 19,600 registered nurses. New progress has been made in the improvement of public health system. The Disease Prevention and Control Center and 120 Emergency Center have been expanded and put in use. The community health service network has also been improved. The project to standardize clinics at the town or township level has also been launched. New - style cooperative medical services in the rural areas are available to 8 districts and counties. 3.2 million peasants have received free physical checkups. In the year, 91,000 people donated their blood for free.

Sports

At the tenth national sports meet in 2005, through severe competition, Tianjin athletes won 15.5 gold medals, 13.5 silver medals and 11 bronze medals and achieved the best record in the history of Tianjin sports, Tianjin listed 10th from 17th in the last national sports meet. During the 10th Five - Year Plan, giant strides have been taken and great achievements have been made in Tianjin sports. Tianjin athletes won 65 gold medals, 56.5 silver medals and 52 bronze medals in national games. Tianjin athletes won 17 gold medals, 9 silver medals and 5 bronze medals in international games. At the 28th Olympic Games, the athletes from Tianjin won 3 gold medals,1 silver medals. In 2005, Tianjin Women's Volleyball Team won all championship in the national women's volleyball tournament. Mass sports have also developed on a large scale in Tianjin. As a result, the citizens have become more conscious of the importance of body - building. By the end of 2005, over 3000 instruction stations had been established in Tianjin for morning and evening exercises. There were over 13,000 instructors of mass sports. 35% of the population have regular sports exercises.

Social Welfare and Relief

In 2005, 24,500 people were subject to special care given to servicemen and the family members of revolutionary martyrs and servicemen. 182,700 people from the urban or rural areas received subsistence allowances. The welfare institutions have 19,748 beds and 13,471 people are living there. There were 258 welfare institutions for the elderly. There are 9 rescue units in Tianjin, which offered help to 13,684 people in 2005. There are 2,139 community service facilities and 111 community service centers. With the sale of 402 million yuan social welfare lotteries, a total of 150 million yuan has been raised as welfare fund. Throughout the year, 17.605 million yuan was donated from all walks of life.

Disable Undertaking

The special education agencies enrolled 200 students in 2005. At the end of 2005, there were 2,600 students receiving special education. Enrollment rate of handicapped children compulsory education was over 95%. In 2005, 5 welfare factories were newly founded. During the 10th Five - Year Plan, a total of 80,300 disable people were employed, including 32,300 urban people and 48,000 rural people. In this year, the disable athletes from Tianjin won 34 gold medals, 28 silver medals and 42 bronze medals in national games, won 8 gold medals, 7 silver medals and 5 bronze medals in international games. In the sixth national arts report - back performance of disable people, disable people of

Tianjin won 2 gold medals, 1 silver medals and 3 bronze medals. The Second Children Art Festival and Tianjin Young Disable People Calligraphy & Picture Exhibition were organized. Newly built roads and buildings all constructed non - hinder facilities, a lot of public facilities were renovated for disable people.

Ⅴ Population and People's Life

Population

At the end of 2005, the total number of permanent residents in Tianjin was 10.43 million. The registered population was 9,393,100, of which, the agricultural population was 3,769,100, the non - agricultural population was 5,624,000. With a birth rate of 7.44‰, and a death rate of 6.01‰, the natural population change rate in Tianjin was 1.43‰ in 2005. The population of Tianjin increased with a low growth rate.

Income of Residents and Consumption

In 2005, the per capita remuneration payment for urban workers in Tianjin was 23,929 yuan, up 13.2% over 2004. The per capita disposable income in urban families was 12,639 yuan in 2005, up 10.2%. The per capita net income of peasants is 7,202 yuan, up 10.4% over the previous year. The consumption level of urban and rural residents in Tianjin has also improved. In 2005, the nonproductive expenditure in Tianjin urban families was 9,653 yuan, up 9.7% over the previous year. The expenditures on clothing, health care and transportation & telecommunications increased by 11.9%, 20.9% and 26.7% respectively. In the countryside, the per capita personal consumption is 3,590 yuan, up 8.9%. Of the total, expenditures on clothing and transportation & telecommunications increased by 23.1% and 12.0% respectively. The living level of rural and urban residents further improved. By the end of 2005, for every 100 urban households in Tianjin, there were 122.1 mobile phones, 51.1 computers, 74.3 microwave ovens, 86.5 hot - water shower baths, 3 cars. In the countryside, for every 100 rural households, there were 95 washing machines, 84 refrigerators, 18 smoke absorbers, 32 water heaters, 16 microwave ovens, 89 mobile phones, and 10 computers.

During the 10th Five - Year Plan, the level of income and expenditure were improved obviously. The per capita disposable income of urban residents grew 10.7% each year on an average basis, the per capita net income of rural residents grew 10.5% each year on an average basis. The Engel's coefficient of urban residents was 36.7%, a decline of 3.4 percentage points from the year 2000. The Engel's coefficient of rural residents was 38.3%, a decline of 4.3 percentage points from the year 2000.

Living Conditions

The housing conditions and living environment have been improved both in the urban and rural areas. In 2005, the per capita floor space of urban residents was 25.8 m^2, 8.6 m^2 more than in 2000. In the countryside, the per capita floor space was 26.10 m^2, an increase of 2.5 m^2 more than 2000. In 2005, 3,463,000m^2 of old buildings were demolished and 62,000 households moved to new houses. By the end of 2005, a total of 640 blocks of old buildings on an area of 18.13 million m^2 had been refitted. A total of 9,400 families with medium or low income had moved to economical houses or low - rent houses. According to sample survey statistics, by the end of 2005, the families living in houses with their own property rights accounted for 53.1% of the total, a rise of 4.6 percentage points over the previous year. The expenditures on housing of residents increased stably, per capita expenditure on housing of urban residents and rural residents increased by 5.0% and 11.5% respectively.

The main problems in national economy and social development were as follows: task of quickening structure adjustment and changing the form of economic growth is yet arduous; the aggregate economic value is yet not large; the development of the tertiary industry is yet to be quickened; the proportion of individual and private economy is yet to be improved. heavier pressure of employment, and social security system to be improved.

Note:

1. All figures in the communique are preliminary statistics.
2. As required by the National Bureau of Statistics, the historical data on regional GDP and total retail sales of consumer goods of Beijing were adjusted correspondingly in accordance with the result of the economic census.
3. Figures in value term on added value and output value of GDP and all industries are at current prices, where as growth rates are calculated at comparable prices.
4. Industrial enterprises above designated size refer to all state-owned enterprises and other enterprises with annual sales of over 5 million yuan.
5. The gross rate of admission to higher education institutions refer to the proportion of students of higher education institutions and population at school-age, it indicates the general level of providing chances of higher education.
6. The Engel Coefficient is the ratio of the expenditure on foodstuffs share in the average consuming expenditure, the decrease of the Engel Coefficient identify the improvement of living standards of the people.

辉煌“十五” 和谐天津

“十五”时期，是天津市历史上经济发展和综合经济实力提高最快的时期，以2002年提前一年全面实现“三五八十”四大奋斗目标和2003年实现“三步走”战略第一步目标为标志，天津经济和社会进入了追求高水平，实现新跨越，更加协调发展的新阶段。

一、经济发展步入新阶段，综合实力和运行质量双提升

综合实力显著增强。天津市生产总值由“九五”期末的1701.88亿元，增长到2005年的3697.62亿元，年均增长14.0%，比“十五”计划目标快4.0个百分点，高于“九五”时期年均增长幅度2.7个百分点，为建国以来天津市各个五年计划时期平均增速最快的五年。“十五”期间，天津市人均GDP在2003年突破3000美元，圆满完成“三步走”战略第一步目标；2005年按常住人口计算，人均GDP约合4368美元，五年年均增长13.1%。工业的快速增长使三次产业在国民经济中的比例结构发生了变化，2005年为3.0：55.5：41.5。与2000年相比，第一产业比重下降了1.3个百分点，第二产业比重上升了4.7个百分点，第三产业比重回落3.4个百分点。

财政收入五年间跃上5个百亿元台阶，由2000年的244.81亿元，增长到2005年的725.81亿元，平均增长24.3%，增幅比“九五”时期提高了8.4个百分点，累计实现收入2360亿元，是“九五”时期的2.5倍。财政收入占地区生产总值的比重延续了“九五”以来逐年提高的升势，2005年为19.6%，比2000年上升5.2个百分点。

经济发展进入新一轮增长周期。自2001年开始，天津市经济进入新一轮增长周期的上升期，2003－2005年成为高峰期。本轮经济增长以“三步走”战略第一、二步目标的实现为动力，伴随比较宽松的国际经济环境和后期“有保有压”的宏观调控，走出了一条既稳又快的增长轨迹，经济增长速度的高低差为3.7个百分点，与“九五”时期的5个百分点相比呈现缩小趋势，经济增长的稳定性不断增强。

经济运行质量明显提高。五年间全市规模以上独立核算工业企业累计实现利税总额达2477.51亿元，是“九五”时期的2.8倍。2005年全市工业产品销售收入达到7125.93亿元，比2000年增长1.7倍；实现利润总额达到551.6亿元，比2000年增长2.3倍。进入“十五”期间，随着经济增长，工业化和城市化进程加快，能源消费的弹性系数明显提高，2004年全市能源消费弹性系数高达0.95。同样电力消费弹性系数变动呈现相同的变动趋势，这一时期天津电力消费弹性系数变动在0.27和1.11之间，全国弹性系数的变动区间为0.36至1.78，天津市经济发展的稳定性高于全国，而且消费同样的能源创造的GDP的价值增长速度快于全国水平。能源利用效率不断提高。2005年天津市万元生产总值综合能耗为1.11吨标准煤，比2000年的1.64吨下降了0.53吨。

市场物价保持基本稳定。城市居民消费价格指数(CPI)涨幅适度，2001年为101.2，2002年为99.6，2003年为101.0，2004年为102.3，2005年价格指数有所回落，为101.5，五年平均涨幅为1.1%。商品零售价格呈下降趋势，五年平均降幅为1.2%。生产领域价格得到有效调控，涨幅趋于回落，上下游价格离差趋于缩小。工业品出厂价格五年年均下降0.4%。原材料、燃料及动力购进价格五年平均涨幅为4.5%，2004年最高达到15.4%，2005年回落到4.9%，工业品出厂价格与原材料、燃料及动力购进价格离差由2004年最大的11.3点，缩小到2005年的4.8点。房地产价格指数攀升势头得到有效控制，五年平均涨幅为5.2%，2004年最高为13.5%，2005年涨幅回落，为6.0%。

二、农业生产出现新变化，农民生产生活条件显著改善

落实中央一号文件精神，从2004年开始，免征农业税，对种粮农民实行直接补贴，发放良种补贴和农机具购置补贴，对农业的支持力度加大。农林牧渔业总产值和增加值2004年分别跨上200亿元和100亿元的台阶，2005年全市农林牧渔业总产值完成238.34亿元，比2002年增加82亿元，年均增长6.0%以上。农业产业内部结构调整力度不断加大，养殖业产值占农林牧渔业总产值的比重达58.3%，比2000年提高12.5个百分点。农业产业化经营取得新进展。2005年末，全市共有农业生产加工销售一体化的龙头企业400多个，资产在1000万元以上的龙头企业130个。全市进入农业产业化体系的农户占农户总数的70%。农业生产园区化、设施化水平显著提高。建成了以津南国家级农业现代化示范园区和宁河国家级原种猪场为龙头的一批高水平种养业园区。

粮食生产止跌回升，主要农副产品产量稳步增长。鼓励农民种粮的一系列补贴政策促进了粮食产量的增加。2004年和2005年粮食生产连续两年增收，扭转持续 4 年的滑跌态势。2005年粮食种植面积431.49万亩，比上年增长9.2%，粮食总产量达137.50万吨，比2000年增长10.8%。2003 年和2004年棉花种植面积连续两年达百万亩以上，分别为105.9万亩和130.35万亩，2005年略有减少但仍达到91.85万亩，比2000年增长3.1倍。肉蛋菜奶全面增长。蔬菜产量542.74万吨。肉类总产量57.78万吨，比2000年增长95.9%。水产品总产量33.81万吨，比2000年增长40%。牛奶产量63.41万吨，比2000年增长近 3 倍。

建设社会主义新农村，农村城市化取得新进展。2005年天津市城镇化率达到75%，高于2000年 3 个百分点。创新小城镇试点建设（宅基地换房），实现农民向城镇集中，工业向小区集中，耕地向种田大户集中。“十五”期间，先后实施了户厕改造和人畜饮水解困等惠农工程，农村居民生活环境得到了显著改善。扩大新型农村合作医疗试点，2004年底四个试点区县已有55%的农民参加了新型农村合作医疗，2005年扩大到八个区县。

三、工业经济实现新突破，六大产业形成集聚优势

实施新一轮嫁接改造调整，积极发展高新技术产业，做大做强优势产业，加快工业东移等发展战略的实施取得明显进展，初步形成以滨海新区现代制造业为主、中心城区都市型工业和郊县区域特色工业为补充的工业布局。工业经济的总量规模和发展速度实现新突破，成为全市经济的主要推动力量。2005年全部工业总产值突破7000亿元，比2000年增长1.6倍，“十五”时期年均增长21.5%，比“九五”时期提高6.3个百分点。其中规模以上工业实现总产值连续突破 4 个千亿元，由2000年的2606.38亿元增长到2005年6774.1亿元，年均增长23.7%；工业增加值1836.3亿元，比2000年增长1.4倍，年均增长19.6%。

优势产业迅速壮大，支撑作用明显。电子信息、汽车、石油化工、冶金、生物技术与现代医药、新能源及环保等六大优势产业产值占全市工业比重超过70%，对全市工业增长的贡献率达到78.6%，成为拉动工业增长的主要支撑力量。其中电子信息产业迅速崛起为第一支柱产业，涌现出一批技术含量高、市场竞争力强的产品，摩托罗拉手机、三星手机、力神电池等产品在全国有很高的市场占有率。

科技创新取得新进展，高技术、低能耗的增长方式更加明显。2005年高新技术产业完成工业总产值占全市工业总产值比重达到31.6%。工业国际化水平快速提升。2005年，全市工业实现出口交货值1759.22亿元，比2000年增长2.2倍，年均增长26.5%，出口占销售产值的比重为四分之一强，有力地拉动了全市工业的快速增长。其中外商及港澳台商投资企业、高新技术产业出口比重增长较快，成为了促进天津市工业出口加快增长的主导因素。

四、投资建设呈现新飞跃，年均超过千亿元

投资规模进一步扩张，对经济增长的拉动作用增强。“十五”期间全市全社会完成固定资产投资达到5338.9亿元，年均增长19.4%，比“九五”期间提高8.8个百分点，年均完成投资在千亿元以上，比“九五”时期年均完成水平高出近 1 倍。

投资结构不断改善，促进了产业结构的全面升级。第三产业投资比重不断攀升，“十五”期间累计达到3203.2亿元，超过同期第一、二产业投资的总和。第三产业投资整体呈现房地产业投资稳步增长、交通运输网络建设和改造快速推进、城市建设投资大幅度增加的态势。

投资效果显著，建成一批大项目。“十五”期间，列入本市重点建设的项目近200个，已有一汽丰田汽车、中新药业现代中药产业园、天钢东移改造、盘山电厂二期等140个项目建成投产或交付使用，累计完成投资约1384亿元，占同期全社会固定资产投资的四分之一。

基础设施投资创新高。“十五”期间，天津市累计完成城市基础设施投资1379.5亿元，比“九五”期间多出一倍。现代综合交通体系建设全面推进，京津城际轨道交通、京津塘高速公路二线、天津滨海国际机场扩建工程陆续展开，天津港15万吨深水航道建成，黄万铁路和多条疏港公路正在施工。唐津、津蓟、津晋等 5 条高速公路建成，高速公路通车里程达603公里，津滨轻轨投入运营，地铁一号线基本建成，市区快速路通车120公里。五年来，新建和改造京津、杨北、津港等 55 条干线公路，改造农村公路2804公里，新建和改造了紫金山路、咸阳路、水上北路等385条城市主次干道，新建大中型桥梁94座。年末全市实有城市铺装道路长度5460公里，铺装道路面积6669万平方米，建成区人均道路面积10.41平方米。

海河综合开发取得快速进展。经过三年建设，清淤工程基本完成，完成堤岸改造17公里，大沽桥通车，奉化桥、保定桥主体完工。新建和拓宽海河西路等28条临河道路，建成音乐公园等6处大型绿地，整修风貌建筑42栋，凤凰广场商贸区、运河商贸区、水上运动世界等商贸区相继开工建设，促进了现代服务业发展。

五、市场流通形成新格局，零售额保持稳步增长

商业流通规模不断扩大。2005年全市贸易企业商品销售总额4820.22亿元，比2000年增长2.37倍。2005年，全市社会消费品零售总额达1190.06亿元，年均增长13.5%。餐饮、旅游、汽车、通讯、住房和教育文化娱乐等新的消费热点不断涌现，成为活跃市场、拉动经济快速发展的重要因素。

商品交易市场发展壮大，辐射功能进一步增强。2005年末，全市各类市场总数达693个，其中商品批发交易市场150个，成交金额超亿元的大型批发市场达到57个。以大型批发市场为龙头，区域市场为骨干，初级市场为基础，多层次、多门类的市场体系在流通中发挥了重要作用，交易商品涉及上百个大类，辐射全国20多个省区。

商业设施建设继续保持快速发展。伊都锦、新澳购物中心、万达商业广场等大型零售商场相继建成开业。大超市、大卖场、专卖店、便利店、餐饮店星罗棋布，各社区配套齐全，消费购物环境进一步改善。

六、对外开放取得新成就，滨海新区龙头地位提升

对外开放已经成为全市经济发展的强大引擎。“十五”以来，抓住世界经济全球化、我国正式加入WTO及国际产业结构加快调整和转移机遇，天津市进一步发挥区位优势，对外开放进入全方位、多层次、宽领域的发展阶段。“十五”时期，对外贸易取得了令人瞩目的成绩，对外贸易总额位居全国第七。2005年外贸进出口总值达到533.87亿美元，其中出口达到274.15亿美元，年均增长26%。“十五”累计出口837.51亿元，相当于“九五”的2.8倍。外贸出口依存度由2000年的43.6%提高到2005年的60.7%。出口结构继续改善，由初级产品出口为主向机电产品出口为主快速转变，机电产品出口占全市出口总额的比重由2000年的48.8%提高到2005年的75%。

招商引资成效显著。随着天津市经济持续快速增长，外商投资环境的进一步改善，以及招商引资力度加大，促进了天津市利用外资的大发展。2005年全市实际直接利用外资额达到33.29亿美元，“十五”时期累计达到103.35亿美元，年均递增32%。世界500强企业已有114家在津落户。“十五”时期，来自亚洲、非洲、欧洲、北美洲、拉丁美洲和大洋洲的合同外资都有不同程度增长。制造业仍是外商投资的主要行业，高新技术产业外商投资增长较快。“十五”时期制造业实际外资比“九五”时期增长1.3倍，电子行业实际到位外资增长1.2倍。对内招商引资工作迈上了新台阶，五年实际利用内资额达到803.1亿元。

滨海新区不断发展壮大，成为全市最大的经济增长点，在全市经济发展中的战略地位不断提升。2005年滨海新区生产总值在2004年突破千亿元的基础上继续以19.8%的速度快速增长，总量达到1608.63亿元，五年年均增长19.6%，对全市经济增长的贡献突出。现代化工业向新区聚集，电子通讯、石油开采及石油化工、海洋化工、现代冶金、机械制造、生物医药和食品加工等产业群落不断壮大和巩固。港口服务和辐射功能明显加强。“十五”时期，天津口岸进出口规模持续扩大，“十五”期间连上4个百亿元台阶。2005年全市口岸进出口总值达到819.29亿美元，比2000年增长1.7倍，五年年均增长22.4%。“十五”时期累计达到2648亿美元，是“九五”的2.2倍。天津口岸与河北、山西、内蒙古、新疆等省区建立了跨口岸区域合作机制。2005年天津港完成港口货物吞吐量2.41亿吨，比2000年增长了1.5倍；完成集装箱吞吐量480.1万国际标准箱，比2000年增长了1.8倍。

七、各项改革积极推进，民营经济快速发展

“十五”时期，在经济社会各领域改革不断深化，一些重要领域和关键环节的改革取得重大进展，为发展注入了强大动力。建立了国有资产监督管理体制，市属国有企业产权制度改制面达到76.6%，新一轮嫁改调蓬勃展开，行政管理体制改革和财税、金融、投资体制改革和各项社会事业改革全面推进。

“十五”时期，全市非公有制经济得到长足发展。2005年非公经济增加值占全市生产总值的比重达到52%，比“九五”期末提高了16.9个百分点。2005年末私营个体从业人员114.17万人，比2000年末增加55.1万人。民间投资渐趋活跃。“十五”期间，天津市的民间投资总量为1655.6亿元，占全社会固定资产投资的比例达到31%。

八、经济社会协调发展，社会事业全面进步

科技综合实力加强，科技综合实力继续保持在全国前列。“十五”期间，天津市深入实施“科教兴市”战略，深化科技体制改革，加速科技创新。五年间，全市共获科技成果6339项，其中达到国际领先水平284项，达到国际先进水平1320项，获国家科学技术奖59项。天津成功入选了首批国家电子信息产业基地。科技创新在生物、集成电路、医学、能源等方面取得一系列重大突破，具备了国际一流水平。2005年研发经费占地区生产总值的比例上升到2%。“十五”时期天津市专利申请量比“九五”时期增长2.7倍，使天津市成为近年来全国专利申请量增长最快地区之一，自主知识产权也向高科技含量、高附加值发展。大中型工业企业自主创新的力度明显加大，至2005年年末，全市共有国家级和市级企业技术中心150家。

重视社会发展，教育、文化、体育、卫生等各项社会事业全面进步。整合教育资源，各级各类教育全面发展。接受高等教育的规模不断扩大。高等教育毛入学率超过50%，普通高校在校大学生超过33万人。建成48所示范性高中。全市新增劳动者平均受教育年限达到14年。文化事业更加繁荣。全市文艺创作精品迭出，文艺演出好戏连台，群众文化蓬勃发展，文化设施建设成就突出，新闻出版业繁荣兴旺，广播电视业欣欣向荣。先后建成了天津博物馆、泰达图书馆、华夏未来少儿艺术中心。天津广电集团、天津日报报业集团、今晚传媒集团等文化产业集团集团化规模效益明显。启动了卫生资源调整工程，重新整合了医院布局，全市各类卫生机构的总数达2489个，医院床位数达3.9万张。建设了市疾病控制中心、海河医院、120急救中心等，形成了指挥有力、反映灵敏、功能完善、运转协调的突发公共卫生事件应急体系。竞技体育实现新突破。第十届全国运动会上，天津体育健儿勇夺15.5枚金牌、13.5枚银牌和11枚铜牌，名列奖牌榜第十位，实现了天津竞技体育的重大突破，取得了天津体育史上的最好成绩。天津女排连夺全国冠军。群众体育深入广泛开展。社会治安秩序继续保持全国最好的地区之一，社会治安秩序保持了总体稳定。

九、人民生活明显改善，建设和谐社会迈出坚实步伐

“十五”期间，随着经济的快速增长，天津市城乡居民的收入水平逐年提高。2005年天津市城市居民人均可支配收入和农村居民人均纯收入分别为12639元和7202元，五年平均递增10.7%和10.5%，2005年储蓄存款年末余额2462.41亿元，是2000年的2.1倍。城乡收入差距在逐渐缩小，城乡收入比例由2000年的1.86:1下降到2005年的1.75:1。居民消费结构加快转型升级，家用轿车、信息通信产品、住房等消费热点持续升温，城市居民恩格尔系数由2000年的40.1%下降到2005年的36.7%，农村居民恩格尔系数由2000年的42.6%下降到2005年的38.3%。

就业总体形势好转。实施积极的就业政策，千方百计增加就业岗位，就业再就业工作成效显著。全市就业总量从2000年的486.89万人增加到2005年的542.52万人，五年间就业总量增加了55.63万人。城镇登记失业率得到有效控制，城镇登记失业率由2000年的3.91%下降到2005年的3.7%，下降了0.21个百分点。

社会保障体系不断健全完善。进一步扩大保险覆盖面，基本建立了城镇职工养老、医疗、工伤、生育、失业保险体系和城乡最低生活保障制度。天津市养老保险覆盖全市200.62万名职工，医疗保险覆盖299.34万人，失业保险覆盖197.51万人，工伤保险覆盖162.91万人，生育保险覆盖157.42万人。符合低保条件的困难群众实现应保尽保。完善对低收入者的救助制度，对失业职工、失地农民、拆迁居民和贫困家庭提供帮助。

城乡居民居住条件和环境不断改善。通过建立廉租房、经济租赁房、经济适用房三条住房保障线，使拆迁家庭享受社会保障住房政策，解决了住房问题，对解决中低收入群众的住房安置、提高人民生活质量，全面建设小康社会也起到了积极的作用。2005年城市居民人均住宅建筑面积25.0平方米，比“九五”末期增加7.8平方米。污水集中处理率和生活垃圾无害化处理率分别达到58%和80.5%，城市绿化覆盖率36.4%，人均绿地面积8.4平方米。实施了一批便民工程，完成近百万平方米的里巷道路改造，改造一批低洼片排水设施，连续三年对旧楼区进行了综合整修。众多功能齐备、配套完善、环境幽雅的住宅小区的建成，使居民居住环境得到了有效改善。

人口、资源、环境协调发展。人口进入低速增长期，2005年常住人口为1043万人，“十五”时期年均增长8.2‰。环保工作成效显著。蓝天、碧水、安静、细胞、生态环保和污染防治等六大环保工程的全面实施，使城市环境和市容市貌明显改观。2005年，天津市创建国家环境保护模范城市工作顺利通过了国家评估验收，成为全国首个创模达标的直辖市。城市交通更加发达。公交线路达到432条,公交线网在全市的覆盖率由55%上升到70%以上。公用事业不断发展。城市居民家庭燃气用户227.76万户,气化率为98.5%;全市的热化率达到83.2%,比“九五”末提高25.5个百分点。实施改造津河、卫津河、复兴河等市区二级河道10条。

“十五”辉煌成就为未来天津发展奠定了坚实基础,今后五年,天津市正在进入重大的历史发展机遇期,滨海新区被纳入国家发展战略的总体布局,经济发展具备许多有利条件,也还面临不少困难和激烈竞争。在新时期,全市上下要在市委、市政府的正确领导下,坚定信心,扎实工作,聚精会神搞建设,一心一意谋发展,不断推进改革开放,争取更快、更好的发展,实现新的辉煌。

(黄瑛 王雪飞)

滨海新区迅速崛起

“十五”时期,滨海新区经济持续快速、稳定增长,社会各项事业全面进步。为建成现代化制造、研发基地,北方国际航运中心和国际物流中心,成为宜居的滨海新城,打下了良好的物质、技术和精神基础。

一、经济持续快速发展,成为全市最大增长点

2005年,新区完成生产总值1608.63亿元,按可比价格计算,平均每年递增19.6%,占全市经济总量的比重达到43.9%。

二、现代化工业基地进一步壮大和巩固

“十五”以来,工业规模不断扩大,工业经济高速增长。2005年,新区工业总产值达到3996.73亿元,比2000年增长2.3倍,年均递增27.1%。

现代化工业继续向新区聚集,电子通讯、石油开采及石油化工、海洋化工、现代冶金、机械制造、生物医药和食品加工等产业群落进一步壮大和巩固。电子信息制造业保持强势发展。形成了以摩托罗拉、通用半导体、三星集团、松下电子、三井高科技、飞思卡尔半导体、中芯国际集成电路等为主的电子信息产业群。2005年,新区电子及通信设备制造业完成总产值1446.09亿元,比2000年增长1.8倍,年均递增22.9%,占新区工业总产值的36.2%,为第一大行业。

海洋工业稳步发展。进入“十五”以来,新区全面推动海洋经济发展,海洋工业是重头戏。一是以中海油天津分公司和中石油大港油田为主体的石油开采业,不断加大油气开采力度,渤南油气群、曹妃甸11-1/2、渤中25-1及旅大10-1等先后投产,油气产量大幅增长。二是以中石化天津分公司和中石油大港公司为主体的石化行业,保持较快增长。三是塘沽海洋高新区发展加快,2005年实现增加值48.0亿元,比2000年增长21.6倍。四是海水淡化产业取得重大进展,日产1000吨海水淡化示范工程已通过验收,日产1万吨海水淡化项目开工建设,日产3万吨中水回用项目已投入使用。

以汽车制造为主体的机械制工业发展势头强劲。2002年天津丰田的投产,使新区汽车整车制造实现突破,不仅填补了新区汽车制造的空白,更带动了机械工业迅速发展。2005年汽车产业实现新突破,新皇冠轿车3月份投产。船舶公司通过不断加大改革力度,船舶制造业开始走出低谷,步入发展阶段。

三、北方国际航运中心和国际物流中心功能彰显

港口生产保持快速增长态势,继2001年货物吞吐量突破亿吨之后,仅用3年又跨上了一个亿吨的台阶,实现了新的突破。2004年天津港货物吞吐量位居全国第三位,2005年达到2.41亿吨,比2000年增长1.5倍,年均递增20.2%;集装箱吞吐量480万标箱,增长1.8倍,年均递增22.9%。2003年开工建设的十五万吨级航道,目前已通过国家验收,促进了进港船舶的大型化。“南散北集”的港口布局结构调整已见成效。为扩大港口辐射范围,天津港在石家庄、西安、兰州、成都设立了货物运输服务中心,与北京、山西、河北等12省市签订了《跨区域口岸合作天津议定书》,与新疆、内蒙古签署了口岸合作备忘录。保税区投资建设了空港物流加工区,国际汽车城建成开业,全力构筑多层次、多元化的国际物流体系,为货物的大进大出提供便捷的交易平台,已逐步建成电子、钢材、工程机械、石油化工等多种产品的分拨中心。空港国际物流区公共保税库投入运营,区港联动获得国务院批准,保税物流园区建设已经启动,国际贸易、保税仓储和物流分拨三大功能进一步增强。2005年,完成进出区货物总值187.6亿美元,比2000年增长3倍,年均递增32.0%。分拨、销售的进口汽车5.1万辆,占全国的60.0%,保持了全国最大的整车进口集散地的地位。目前,新区初步形成了天津港集装箱物流中心,散货物流中心,保税区海空港物流区等六个物流基地;京津两地空港以及海空港实现直接通关,形成了海空港一体的国际物流体系。新区的服务和辐射功能显著增强。

四、对外对内开放迈上新的台阶

"十五"以来,新区抓住中国入世的机遇,克服全球经济低迷,国内外市场竞争日益激烈的不利因素,不断优化投资环境,不断创新招商模式,拓展招商渠道,招商引资取得丰硕成果。"十五"时期,新区累计合同外资金额146亿美元,实际利用外资金额76.54亿美元,年均递增30%。利用外资质量不断提高,2005年《财富》全球500强企业中,共有来自境外10个国家和地区的57个跨国公司在开发区投资,投资企业达123家。积极构建与世界交流平台,努力扩大出口,与主要贸易联系日益紧密,为推动新区经济健康发展创造市场条件。2005年,新区实现外贸出口184.69亿美元,比2000年增长3.1倍,年均递增近三分之一。开发区是新区出口的主体,2005年实现出口139.71亿美元,比2000年增长3.3倍,占新区出口总量的75.6%。

积极推进对内开放,促进横向联合。"十五"时期,新区累计签订在津投资协议2290个,协议金额259.3亿元,实际到位额193.18亿元。

五、生产建设日新月异,现代化港口城市标志区风貌初露端倪

改善投资环境,增强区域服务功能,建设现代化滨海新城,是新区发展的重要目标。"十五"时期,新区累计固定资产投资2247.2亿元,其中,第一产业投资7.79亿元;第二产业投资1242.21亿元;第三产业投资997.2亿元。不断加大基础设施投资力度,累计投资额为608.57亿元,占新区固定资产投资总量的27.1%。城市基础设施不断完善,城市载体功能进一步提升,现代化港口城市标志区风貌初露端倪。一是三港(海港、空港、信息港)建设取得成效。天津港以建设世界一流大港为目标,经过对航道、码头、仓储、运输等环节的大规模改造和提升,已步入了一个跨越式发展的新阶段。天津滨海国际机场功能进一步完善,机场海关大楼投入使用,空港国际物流区基础设施已经完成,海关监管库、公共保税库、企业服务中心已经投入使用。信息港建设全面铺开,一批信息化重点建设项目建成并投入使用,新区范围内宽带网络已经形成,华北地区最大的互联网数据中心 IDC,具有良好的网络环境和设备环境,可以提供国际一流水平的 IT 外包技术服务,全国领先的天津市电子政务专网四个核心节点之一——滨海新区核心节点,对于促进滨海新区的电子政务建设将发挥巨大作用。二是城市载体功能显著提高。津滨高速公路、滨海立交桥、亚洲规模最大的单塔斜拉桥——海河大桥、滨海通用直升机场、滨海大道高速段、津沽二线高速段、塘沽区河北路、汉沽区新开路、津滨轻轨一期工程竣工通车、滨海500KV 变电站、滨海天然气输气干线等一批重点工程相继竣工投入使用。三是城市服务功能提高。塘沽区解放路商业街开街、天津海关大楼竣工投入运营、基辅号航母落位汉沽八卦滩、海河外滩公园对外开放、泰达足球场投入使用、泰达国际心血管病医院建成开诊、泰达图书馆及档案馆建成开放、泰达会展中心和金融区投入使用、保税区国际商务交流中心投入使用等等,使新区的服务功能登上一个较高层次。四是城市环境面貌焕然一新,治黑、治白、植绿见到成效。清理整顿煤碳仓储库场工作顺利完成、困扰塘沽城区七十多年的三号路碱渣山得到彻底根治,建成了碱渣山公园、森林公园、"挖湖造山"等绿化工程。开发区被国家环保总局和联合国环境署列入第一批"中国工业园区环境管理"试点园区,大港区被命名为全国环保模范城区,大港和塘沽区被命名为全国卫生城区。

六、科技创新能力提高,社会事业全面发展

积极推进"科教兴区"战略,创造高新技术产业发展的良好环境和氛围和环境,促进高新技术产业发展的政策体系不断完善。先后成立了天津市新兴产业投资公司、天津创业投资有限公司、诚信(天津)创业投资有限公司等风险投资公司;建立了天大科技园、泰达华生生物园、泰达软件园、国家纳米产业化基地、开泰企业孵化器等高科技创业孵化基地;引进了中科院水声工程中心、天津大学国家工业结晶技术中心、中国医学科学院血液学研究所泰达生命科学研究中心、国家计算机病毒应急处理中心、天津中新药业中药现代化技术工程中心、中新药业研究中心、华立达企业技术中心和天津市光电子联合科学研究中心等工程技术研究中心。

教育体系日臻完善,教育教学整体水平提高。中小学布局得到调整,建成了开发区国际学校和一批示范中学、模范小学,居民和流动人口子女九年制义务教育入学率100%,基本普及高中教育。教育规模扩大,大港区大学城已有南开大学滨海学院、天津医科大学临床学院、天津外国语学院滨海校区、国家法官学院天津分院等7所院校入住,北大青鸟软件学院和天津生物工程职业技术学院正积极筹建。

卫生事业稳步发展,新区医疗卫生服务网络体系逐步形成。泰达国际心血管病医院运行顺利,泰达医院进行了扩建改造,天津市急救中心泰达分中心投入运行,建成新大港医院等。天津医科大学滨海中心医院正积极筹建。农村村级医疗点普及。

文化、体育事业迈上新水平。定期举办专业性、群众性的文体活动,区域文化生活日渐丰富,成功举办了世界杯足球赛亚洲区预选赛中国队对马来西亚队比赛;国际大学生龙舟赛、国际女排赛、全国足球超级联赛、乒乓球超级联赛、全国女排联赛和"星耀泰达"亚洲名人音乐会、中国国际男子篮球对抗赛、全国武术套路冠军赛等多场国际、国内赛事和大型文艺演出。各区开展了多项具有特色的群众喜闻乐见的文化体育活动,丰富了群众生活,扩大了新区的影响。

(胡全洋)

工业生产再创新高

"十五"期间,全市工业生产保持了持续快速健康发展的好势头,整体素质和竞争力明显增强。

一、工业生产快速发展,整体实力明显增强

"十五"期间,天津市工业生产在高平台上实现高增长,总体规模不断壮大。截止"十五"末期,工业企业达30381户,从业人员167.29万人,拥有资产6143.17亿元。2005年,全市全部工业总产值达到7169.62亿元,比2000年增长1.6倍,年均增长21.5%,其中规模以上工业总产值达到6774.10亿元,比2000年增长1.9倍,年均增长23.7%,工业增加值达到1836.30亿元,比2000年增长1.4倍,年均增长19.6%,在快车道上加速发展。

生产与效益的同步增长。2005年,全市规模以上独立核算工业企业实现产品销售收入7125.93亿元,比2000年增长1.7倍;实现利税总额815.63亿元,比2000年增长2.0倍,其中实现利润总额551.60亿元,比2000年增长2.3倍;经济效益综合指数达214.79,比2000年提高60多个点,达到有史以来的最高点,使工业整体经济效益上了一个新台阶。

二、结构调整效果明显,优势产业和高新技术产业较快发展

1.加大投资力度,为天津工业发展增强了后劲

工业投资本着择优扶强的原则,集中力量发展优势产业和高新技术产业,建设了一大批重点技术改造和基建项目。"十五"期间,本市共完成工业投资1755亿元,比"九五"时期增加677.82亿元,增长62.9%。随着投资力度的加大,中石化20万吨聚脂、飞思卡尔、中芯国际芯片、力神锂离子电池、天钢东移改造、钢管公司二套轧机改造、天汽夏利换型、一汽丰田轿车、纺织产业园棉纺和剑龙工业项目、中维制药、君安生物制药等一批大项目相继建成或交付使用,生产效益已逐步显现。

2.优势产业和高新技术产业得到长足发展

"十五"期间,本市工业围绕把天津建成面向世界的现代化工业基地的目标,实施了新一轮嫁改调,使行业结构进一步优化。在全市37个工业行业中,有14个行业产值总量超百亿元,22个行业产值超50亿元,分别比2000年增加6个和8个行业。轻重工业比重由2000年的34:66发展变化为2005年的20:80。

"十五"期间,天津市工业把发展重点放在提高优势产业集中度和抢占制高点上,成功策划了一批代表产业发展方向、技术含量高、对产业升级和结构调整有突破性带动作用的大项目,引进了一大批新技术、新产品,构建和培育了产业链和产业集群,使工业结构进一步优化,优势产业的规模进一步扩大。电子信息、汽车、石油化工、冶金、生物技术与现代医药、新能源及环保等六大优势产业实现了高增长。2005年,优势产业实现工业总产值4851.35亿元,占全市工业比重超过70%,对全市工业增长的贡献率接近80%,成为拉动工业增长的主要支撑力量,同时,优势产业的经济效益也保持良好的发展势态,2005年,产品销售收入、实现利税总额和利润总额分别占全市的72.1%、79.3%和84.4%,销售收入利润率达8.9%,比全市平均水平高1.2个百分点。

3.工业产品结构继续改善,新产品比重占近三成

从主要产品产量看,2005年,移动电话机达到6319.82万部,比2000年增长3.8倍;房间空调器434.43万台,增长3.2倍;微波炉1431.15万台,增长

8.1倍；轿车32.56万辆，增长3倍；天然原油1782.89万吨，增长1.3倍；生铁660.24万吨，增长1.9倍；粗钢955.28万吨，增长1.7倍；成品钢材1664.04万吨，增长4.4倍；无缝钢管174.59万吨，增长2.2倍。新产品产值完成1971.66亿元，比2000年增长2.8倍，占全市工业的29.1%，比2000年提高8.6个百分点。

4.出口成为拉动工业增长的重要一极

2005年，全市规模以上工业实现销售产值6816.56亿元，工业品产销率达100.6%。工业品出口呈现稳定增长态势，实现出口交货值1759亿元，比2000年增长2.2倍，年均增长26.5%，出口占销售产值的四分之一强，有利地拉动了全市工业的快速增长。

三、多种经济类型竞相发展，形成了多点支撑的良好格局

国有经济在改革调整中有进有退，2005年，国有工业企业完成总产值占全市的比重为7.9%，比2000年降低了10.2个百分点。

股份制企业、私营企业经济得到较快发展。2005年，股份制企业完成总产值2525.72亿元，比2000年增长2倍，年均增长24.8%；私营企业完成总产值638.31亿元，比2000年增长3.8倍，占全市工业比重由2000年的2.7%，提高到2005年的9.4%，私营经济已经成为全市工业发展中不可或缺的一支重要力量。

外商及港澳台商投资企业发展迅速。2005年，外商及港澳台商投资企业完成总产值3319.23亿元，比2000年增长2.2倍，年均增长26%，比全市平均增速高2.3个百分点。外商及港澳台商投资企业在全市工业经济中的份额稳步提高，2005年工业总产值占全市的49.0%，比2000年的45.9%提高3.1个百分点；完成工业增加值773.42亿元，占全市的42.1%，与2000年所占比重持平。外商及港澳台商投资工业已成为天津工业经济中举足轻重的力量。

“十五”以来，天津市工业生产形成多点支撑局面，大型企业快速发展，中小型企业也加快发展步伐。大型企业对全市工业增长的拉动作用明显增强，2005年末，全市大型工业企业以不足全市1%的企业数完成工业总产值2625.04亿元；完成工业增加值576.07亿元，分别占全市的38.8%和30.9%。“十五”期间，在国家及天津市有关政策的扶持下，中小企业企业加快了发展步伐，企业生产经营能够状况得到改善。2005年完成工业总产值4149.06亿元，比上年增长23.3%，完成增加值1269.23亿元，比上年增长22.2%，总产值和增加值增幅均高于全市平均水平。

四、企业改制成效显著

“十五”期间，天津市大力开展国有经济的战略调整，国有及国有控股企业步入良性循环发展轨道，生产焕发出勃勃生机。2005年，国有及国有控股工业企业完成总产值2628.84亿元，比2000年增长1.8倍，年均增长23.3%，占全市工业总产值的比重为38.8%，比2000年提高5.9个百分点；完成增加值864.79亿元，比2000年增长1.1倍，年均增长16.2%，占全市工业增加值的比重为47.1%，比2000年提高3.5个百分点。

“十五”期间，现代企业制度改革在全市工业企业中全面展开并取得了明显成效，现代企业制度的基本框架在天津市大多数企业中初步确立。企业改制面逐年扩大。截止2005年底，实施监测重点企业中改制面达87.7%，比2000年提高13.9个百分点，公司治理结构不断完善。企业内部改革进展顺畅，企业经营者在企业生产中所起的作用不断加强。实现了投资主体多元化，企业实力得到加强，综合经济效益有较大提高。

（寇枫）

农业经济实现新突破

“十五”期间，天津市进一步深化和优化农业生产结构，加快农业现代化建设步伐，着力提升农业综合生产能力，实现新的历史性突破。

一、农业经济实现历史性突破，综合生产能力显著增强

“十五”时期，以种植业为基础，养殖业为发展重点的都市型农业经济结构进一步得到优化，全市农业经济呈现出在高位基础上持续稳定健康发展的良好态势，农业综合生产能力显著增强。

1.农业经济总量实现新的历史性突破

“十五”期间，全市农业经济继续保持高位稳步发展。继2004年天津市农林牧渔业总产值和增加值分别跨上200亿元和100亿元台阶后，2005年再创新高。全市共完成农林牧渔业总产值238.34亿元，比2000年增长82亿元，按可比价格计算，比2000年增长近35%，年均增长6.0%以上；全市实现农林牧渔业增加值109.60亿元，比 2000 年增长 36.1亿元，按可比价格计算，比 2000 年增长 31%，年均递增近6.0 %。

2005 年，天津市平均每个农业从业人员创造农林牧渔业总产值2.96万元，比 2000 年增加 1.00 万元，增长 32.8 %；平均每个农业劳动力提供粮食1.71吨、蔬菜7.20吨、肉类 710公斤、牛奶 750公斤、水产品 420公斤，分别比2000 年增长9.6 %、8.1 %、91.9%、2.6倍和 40 .0%；全市农业劳动生产率达1.36万元，比 2000年增长11.3 %。

2.粮食生产实现恢复性增长，蔬菜种植向效益型转化，棉花作物大幅增加

2004 年以来，随着中央“一号文件”和市委、市政府粮食直补、良种补贴等支持粮食生产政策措施的实施，极大调动农民种粮积极性，天津市粮食生产在2004 和 2005 年连续实现增收，扭转了自 1999年以来粮食生产连年滑跌的态势。2005 年全市粮食总产量达 137.50万吨，比 2000年增长 10.8 %；粮食单位面积产量达 318.7公斤/亩，比2000 年增长33.3 %。粮食生产结构形成了以小麦、玉米、水稻、大豆四大品种为主体的高产、高效，比例合理的生产格局。2005年四大品种粮食种植面积占粮食总面积的比重达97.7 %，比 2000 年提高 4.7个百分点；四大品种粮食产量占粮食总产量的比重达 99.3 %，比 2000 年提高2.9个百分点。

“十五”时期，天津市蔬菜生产加快由产品型向效益型转型的步伐。大量引进更新品种，广泛采用先进科学技术，大力发展工厂化栽培，并按照国际通例制定严格检测标准，致力发展无公害蔬菜生产，有力促进了天津市蔬菜生产效益的提高。2005年全市蔬菜产量达 542.74万吨，比 2000 年增长2.3%；全市无公害蔬菜基地认定面积达 85万亩，占菜田面积的 80 %以上。

棉花生产呈现快速发展。全市棉花种植面积在2003年和 2004 年连续两年达百万亩以上，2005 年仍保持在 91.85万亩，成为天津市种植业生产稳定发展、经济效益明显提高的重要支柱。

3.畜牧水产养殖业生产发展继续保持快速发展

“十五”期间，天津市畜牧业保持快速发展。设施畜牧业示范小区建设步伐加快，综合生产能力显著增强，有效提升了畜禽产品的档次和经济效益。各农业区县中靠发展畜牧业生产致富的专业乡、专业村和专业户不断增加，畜牧业生产已成为天津市农村经济快速发展的重要支柱。

2005 年，全市肉类总产量达57.78万吨，比 2000年增95.9%，年均增长14.4 %，比“九五”期间年均增速提高 1.1 个百分点。全市生猪出栏 481.45万头，比 2000 年增长91 %；牛奶产量63.41万吨，比 2000年增长近 3 倍；牛、羊出栏 37.83万头和140.11万只，分别比 2000 年增长1.1倍和 47.4 %。家禽出栏9205.64万只，比 2000 年增长 1.1倍。

“十五”期间，天津市不断扩大以出口为主的水产养殖区域，积极引进培育优质高值品种，广泛推广海淡混养、鱼虾蟹混养等先进科技手段，大幅度提高渔业生产效益，促进了渔业生产的快速发展。2005 年，全市水产品总产量 33.81万吨，比 2000 年增长40%；其中淡水产品产量占水产品总产量的比重达到85.5%，比 2000 年提高约 2 个百分点。

二、优化农业生产结构，加快农业现代化进程

“十五”时期以来，天津市的农业经济内部结构不断优化，已基本形成“粮、经布局合理，种、养比例协调”的良好生产格局；农业生产基础设施、生产方式都发生了历史性的变化，农业现代化进程明显加快。

农业生产园区化、设施化水平显著提高。建成了以津南国家级农业现代化化示范园区和宁河国家级原种猪场为龙头的一批高水平种养业园区，种植业小区达到 341个，设施化面积 42万亩，养殖业园区达到1800个，重点畜禽和水产品生产基本实现了园区化。

农业产业化水平显著提高。资产在1000万元以上的龙头企业达到 130家，其中国家级龙头企业达到10家；进入产业化体系的农户占总农户比重达到70 %，比“九五”末提高37个百分点。

农业生产标准化水平显著提高。市级、区县和产区质量安全检测体系初步形成，主要农产品实现依标生产。无公害蔬菜面积达到 86万亩，占蔬菜总面积的 83 %；无公害奶牛存栏达到13万头，占奶牛存栏数的 76 %；无公害水产品养殖面积达到29.4万亩，占养殖面积的 50 %。

同时，农业基础设施和装备水平也明显提高。全市节水灌溉面积达到 290万亩，比“九五”末 201万亩提高 44 %；百亩耕地拥有机械动力达到 97.04千瓦，比“九五”末 81.5千瓦提高 19 %。

农业生产结构效益明显提升。养殖业比重由

2000 年的 45.8 %上升到 2005 年的 58.3 %，提高12.5个百分点；养殖业增加值占农林牧渔业增加值的比重达 55.2 %，比2000年提高 13.1个百分点。其中养殖效益高、市场需求大的畜牧业生产五年来持续保持快速发展。2005 年畜牧业产值达 102.71亿元，比 2000 年增长 74 %，年均递增16%，占农业总产值的比重也由“九五”末的 33.1 %上升到“十五”末的43.1 %，提高了10.0个百分点。

种植业生产结构在“十五”时期得到进一步优化，棉花、油料、蔬菜和水果等经济作物生产增速加快，比重上升。2005 年，全市经济作物播种面积占农作物总播种面积的比重达 56.2 %，比 2000 年提高9.6 个百分点。

三、农业科技进步贡献率显著提高

“十五”期间，全市取得农业科技成果 466项，有137项成果获得国家级、市级科技奖励；在黄瓜育种、杂交粳稻育种、农产品保鲜、葡萄酒加工和动物胚胎克隆技术等方面均处于全国领先水平。科技推广取得丰硕成果，实施重点技术推广项目 200多个，使20多万农民掌握先进的农业生产科学技术，创造社会经济效益 34亿元。实施了农村劳动力“351培训工程”。2005 年农业科技进步贡献率达到55 %，比“九五”末提高 2 个百分点。先进科学技术进一步拓展了农业功能，全市已形成黄瓜良种、原种猪等服务全国的良种产业基地，建设了一批以科普教育、自助采摘、旅游休闲为主的新型农业基地，有力提升了农业生产效益。

（韩爱兵）

零售市场繁荣兴旺

“十五”时期，随着国家扩大内需政策的实施和社会购买力的不断增加，天津市商业经济进入新的发展时期。全市贸易流通规模进一步扩大，社会消费品零售额保持了稳步增长，经济结构得到调整，商业经济的运行质量不断提高。

一、商品流通规模不断扩大，对天津经济的贡献加大

改革开放以来，特别是“十五”时期天津市流通业蓬勃发展。2005年全市批发零售贸易业销售总额达到4820.22亿元，其中批发3861.83亿元，零售958.39亿元，分别比2000年增长2.37倍、2.68倍和1.53倍，5年间年均分别增长27.5%、29.8%和20.4%。商业网点及从业人员成倍增长。商贸流通业在天津经济发展中继续发挥带动作用，有力地促进了第三产业的快速发展。

二、市场繁荣活跃，社会消费品零售总额保持较高增长

“十五”时期，天津市零售市场总体运行态势良好。商品货源充足，价格稳定，交易活跃，社会消费品零售总额连年保持两位数增长。2005年，全市社会消费品零售总额1190.06亿元，比上年增长13.9%，“十五”时期年均增长13.5%。其中吃、穿、用三种商品分别实现零售总额393.19亿元、235.32亿元和530.46亿元，分别比2000年增长30.6%、92.5%和73.1%，年均分别增长5.5%、14.0%和11.6%。

“十五”期间，随着居民收入的稳步增长，生活水平的不断提高，以食品为主体的消费结构也发生了变化。到2005年底，在社会消费品零售总额中，吃的商品所占零售额比重由2000年的40.9%下降到33.0%，而用品类商品零售额的比重则由2000年的41.6%上升到44.6%，成为拉动零售市场增长的主体。在食品消费上，主食消费减少，副食消费比重上升，绿色食品、营养保健品、奶制品、果汁饮品等消费需求上升；穿着方面更注重品牌的选择，突出个性化、多样化和时代感；在生活用品消费方面，大件耐用消费品如彩电、冰箱等升级换代逐步加快，规格、档次不断提高。特别是平板电视、数码产品、电脑和食品加工机等家电商品成为近年来的消费主流。

三、餐饮市场快速发展

餐饮市场持续升温，全市餐饮业零售额以平均每年15.1%的速度增长，2005年达到159.49亿元，比2000年增长1.02倍，增速居各行业之首。五年间天津市积极发展餐饮业，在整体推进的同时，突出重点，进行改组改造，鼓励、引导私营餐饮企业发展；在弘扬津菜的同时，不断引进西餐企业和全国各地风味、特色小吃，使餐饮市场呈现百花齐放的局面。一方面通过培育天津特色菜基地，新建规范化的小吃街等促进餐饮业发展；另一方面举办一系列影响大、参与程度高的技术竞赛活动发展餐饮市场。几年来，在天津市餐饮市场上涌现出一批具有现代经营理念的规模大、环境好、服务优、档次高的企业。一些大型餐饮企业如“鸿起顺”、“狗不理”、“桂发祥”、“红旗饭庄”等纷纷发展连锁、直营、特许等多种经营业态。“粤唯鲜”、“友鹏”等私营企业快速成长，特别是餐饮超市的经营方式，在天津市开创了餐饮企业经营的新模式。西餐业发展迅猛，各式西餐厅生意红火，2001年天津市举办了首届“西餐节”，进一步促进了西餐业的发展。随着生活节奏的加快及口味的变化，各类快餐业发展迅猛。到2005年，“麦当劳”、“肯德基”、“德克士”、“家必得”在天津市连锁分店已发展到80多家，不仅活跃和丰富了天津市餐饮市场，而且使天津市餐饮业总体规模不断扩大。餐饮业的快速发展也反映天津市居民消费水平的提高，为天津商务活动创造了良好条件。

四、商业结构调整步伐加快，促进了零售市场发展

“十五”时期，天津市商业结构调整步伐加快，力度加大。通过股份制改造，培育上市企业，利用资本市场融资，加快企业发展，推进国有资本从小企业退出，发展非公有制商业；通过走联合发展之路，与国外实力雄厚的商业跨国集团合资合作，以优势资源引进良性有效资产，进一步壮大实力，提高企业竞争力，如与中外跨国集团和知名企业签定合作项目，兴建综合购物中心、大型超市、配送中心，扩大加盟连锁经营等，使天津市零售市场形成了一个多元化、多层次和多业态的新格局。

经济结构向多元化发展。在所有制结构调整中，天津市通过引进外资，发展私营、个体经济，使三资企业和私营、个体经济得到迅猛发展。2005年，天津市“三资”经济实现零售额45.54亿元，比2000年增长49.3%，年均增长8.3%，占全市零售总额的比重为4.4%。个体、私营经济实现零售额728.3亿元，比2000年增长3.17倍，年均增长33.0%，占全市零售额的比重为69.7%，比2000年提高了46个百分点。公有制经济实现零售额284.44亿元，占全市零售额的比重为23.9%，比2000年降低了7.7个百分点。

新业态、新营销方式快速发展。“十五”时期，天津市以发展连锁企业，建立新业态零售业为重点，进一步推进行业结构调整。到2004年天津市各种超市、专业(专卖)店已达1907家，遍及全市各区县，方便了居民生活。家乐福、家乐、乐购、沃尔玛等现代大型综合超市成为天津市连锁企业发展的龙头。其中民营企业——家乐超市在天津市已有分店16家，分别坐落在8个区，年销售额超20亿元，成为天津市最大的连锁企业。一些传统零售企业在寻求向外发展的同时，也在进行内部变革，引进新的营销理念，将购物、餐饮、娱乐、休闲融为一体，形成“一站式”购物。

零售企业向大型化、集团化、专业化方向发展。“十五”时期，天津市按照“以市场为导向，以资产为纽带，以效益为目标，合理配置资源”的思路，加快推进企业组织结构的调整，通过重组、引进、转型等多种方式进行了卓有成效的改革，使企业找到了适合自身发展的道路，并在竞争中站稳了脚跟。2005年年销售额超亿元的零售企业达65家，与2000年相比成倍增长。2000年，国美电器进入天津市场，给家电市场带来不小冲击的同时，也带来一种全新的、规范化的经营管理模式，是天津市第一家专营家电商品的大型零售企业。

五、市场规模壮大，大型市场发展势头强劲，辐射功能进一步增强

随着天津市经济快速稳定发展，全市商品交易市场进一步发展壮大，形成了以大型批发市场为龙头，区域市场为骨干，初级市场为基础，多层次、多门类的市场体系。到2005年，全市各类市场总数达693个，其中商品批发交易市场150个。2004年全市各类市场实现成交额929.33亿元，占贸易业销售总额的近三分之一，其中75个亿元以上的骨干市场总成交额达到608.35亿元，占全市商品交易市场成交总额的65.5%，交易商品涉及上百个大类，辐射全国20多个省区。

六、商业设施和环境的改善加速了零售市场的发展

近几年，天津市加大了商业环境的建设力度，大卖场和便利店星罗棋布，到2004年末全市共有商业零售网点11044个，营业面积85万平方米。在市中心形成了以滨江道为中轴，和平路、南京路为纵深的商业区建设。改建后的和平路和滨江道，百年老店、大型商场、各品牌专卖店、专业店云集，成为天津商业的“金街”和“银街”，不仅实现了错位经营，增强了商圈的集聚效应，而且成为津门一景，给沿街商家带来了效益，为企业提供了良好的发展空间。各商业企业也适时进行内部的店堂改造，以舒适的环境、醒目的标识、优美的音乐给顾客营造更加轻松的购物环境。华联商厦运动休闲区塑胶跑道的铺设、麦当劳滨江道店的重新装修、伊势丹精品区的开辟等给顾客耳目一新的感觉。对繁荣天津市零售市场起到了积极的促进作用。各区县相继建立起各自的商业中心或商圈。同时，社区商业、便利店等多形式、多业态的商业设施见缝插针，形成了一个集中与分散、高档与普及相交叉的商业布局，大大方便了居民群众，初步建成了天津市零售市场多层次格局。

（张琦）

投资总量年均超过千亿

“十五”期间，全市投资结构不断改善，投融资体制改革不断突破，投资调控手段不断成熟，对优化经济结构、改善投资环境、促进企业技术进步、增强可持续发展能力和提高人民生活水平发挥了积极的作用。

一、投资规模进一步扩张，为国民经济实现平稳较快发展奠定了基础

1.年均完成投资超过千亿元，平均增长速度大大高于“九五”时期

“十五”期间，天津市累计完成全社会固定资产投资5338.9亿元，年均完成投资在千亿元以上，比“九五”时期年均完成水平高出近1倍。投资年均递增速度为19.4%，比“九五”期间提高8.8个百分点。

2.投资贡献率上升，对经济增长的带动作用增强

多年以来，天津市经济增长呈现明显的投资主导型特征。有关测算表明，天津市固定资产投资与GDP之间的相关系数高达0.997，显示出投资与GDP之间的紧密联系。“十五”期间，固定资产投资贡献率达到46.3%，投资已成为这一阶段拉动天津市经济增长的第一要素。

二、投资结构不断改善，促进了产业结构的全面升级

随着天津市投资规模的不断扩大，三次产业投资比重由“九五”期间的0.6:49.7:49.7调整为“十五”的0.8:39.2:60。

1.投资结构进一步调整优化

第二产业投资较快增长，巩固了天津市工业基地的地位。“十五”期间，天津市第二产业共完成投资2095.2亿元，年均增长12.7%，增速高于“九五”时期7.9个百分点。随着工业东移步伐的加快，工业投资规模不断扩大。全市工业累计完成投资1755亿元，年均增长速度达到13.4%，比“九五”时期提高了8.8个百分点。在工业投资快速增长的带动下，八年“嫁改调”引进的资金、技术、管理积聚潜能不断释放，天津市工业的整体素质和与国际接轨的能力得到显著提升，形成了一批优势企业和拳头产品，使本市老工业基地的地位和作用得到巩固，为天津工业发展增强了后劲。

第三产业投资增长迅猛，全面提升了城市形象和功能。“十五”期间，第三产业投资增长迅速，其总量远远超过了第一、二产业投资的总和，达到3203.2亿元；年均增长速度达到24.4%，远远高于“九五”期间17.5%的平均增长水平；所占比重也由“九五”期间的49.7%提高到60%。从投资方向上看，房地产投资稳步增长。全市房地产开发累计完成投资1140亿元，年均增长18.3%；累计竣工商品房面积4935.5万平方米，相当于“九五”时期的2.3倍。大交通体系网络建设和改造快速推进。“十五”期间，天津市相继建成了津滨高速、津沽二线、津蓟高速、丹拉公路和津滨轻轨一期工程，不仅使公路运输功能进一步增强，同时构筑起快速的交通体系；市内卡口道路改造以及地铁一号线工程基本完工，极大地提高了市民的出行能力；天津移动和联通扩容为电信行业的竞争提供了动力，满足了用户对电信服务业多元化和个性化的需求。文教卫体等社会事业及其他方面投入不断加大。先后建成了60所示范高中校，全市70%左右的学生可以进入优质高中学习；天津图书大厦、泰达图书馆、天津博物馆等一批文化工程进一步提升了天津的文化品位和人文内涵；卫生资源调整进展顺利，改造了海河医院和一中心医院，完成了传染病医院和人民医院工程的建设，新建了泰达国际心血管医院；加紧启动实施了一批高等院校布局调整以及奥林匹克体育中心；还建成了友谊路家世界购物广场、万达商业广场、滨江金耀广场等一批大型现代化商贸设施。

2.投资主体结构变化明显，民间投资登上舞台

进入“十五”以来，由于我国社会主义市场经济的不断发展以及投资环境的不断改善，天津市投资主体结构变化十分明显。从投资份额看，国有经济投资依旧占据主力地位，但相对份额减少；民间投资高于以往任何一个历史时期，份额呈明显的上升势头；外商投资份额呈波动变化且有下滑迹象。

民间投资三分天下有其一。“十五”期间，天津市民间投资已覆盖所有国民经济行业，其总量达到1655.6亿元，占全社会固定资产投资的比例为31%，

主要投向为房地产业和制造业；同时，民间投资以24.5%的增长速度位居三种所有制投资之首。

国有投资仍占主体。国有投资在基础产业部门中，继续发挥着人、财、物及管理体制上的优势，占据着主力位置。“十五”期间，国有投资累计完成2882.2亿元，占全社会固定资产投资的比重为54%，虽然占比依旧较高，但比“九五”时期已下降了近10个百分点。

3.资金来源多渠道趋势更加明显，投资自主增长能力不断增强

以贷款、自筹资金为主体的资金构架初步形成。靠扩大招商引资、资本运作、吸引民间资金等多种手段，“十五”期间建设资金到位率大幅度提高，并形成了以贷款、自筹资金为主体的建设资金构架。其中：国内贷款和自筹资金累计到位4013.6亿元，占全部到位资金的74%；国内贷款、自筹资金和其他资金在当年到位资金中所占比重分别比“九五”时期提高了4、4.8和3.5个百分点。这说明在影响投资增长的动力机制中，政策性因素在不断减弱，市场机制因素在不断提高，投资自主增长的能力在不断增强。

国家预算内资金和利用外资比重持续走低。“十五”期间，全市固定资产投资资金来源中国家预算内资金累计到位98.3亿元，仅占全部投资来源的1.8%，所占比重比“九五”时期低0.8个百分点；受外资大项目减少影响，“十五”期间累计利用外资432.7亿元，占全部投资来源的8%，所占比重比“九五”时期低10.2个百分点。

三、投资效果显著，增强了天津市的整体经济实力

“十五”期间，列入天津市重点建设的项目近200个，约有140个项目建成投产或交付使用，累计完成投资1384亿元，占同期全社会固定资产投资的四分之一。工业方面，投产的一批高新技术产业项目和传统技术改造项目，使工业利税大幅度提高；农业方面，农业产业化已形成一定规模，农业综合生产能力和农产品商品化程度明显提高；电力方面，全市电力改造项目基本完成，大大缓解了电力紧张的局面；城市基础设施投资的增长更是带动了城市生产、生活环境的改变，极大地消除了“瓶颈”制约。重点项目主要新增能力：原油开采853.7万吨/年，发电101万千瓦，汽车21万辆/年，港口吞吐能力8400万吨/年，高速公路216公里，市区道路面积461万平方米，新建桥梁46座，医院病床5255个，大中小学学生席位15.6万个等。总之，“十五”期间，天津市建成投产了一大批项目，为全市经济和社会发展奠定了坚实的物质技术基础。

四、投资管理水平不断提高，为全市固定资产投资健康发展提供了保障

1.按照国家宏观调控的要求，狠抓结构调整

为控制部分行业和地区盲目投资、低水平重复建设的苗头，国家自2003年下半年开始在审批、信贷、土地方面采取了一系列宏观调控措施，并于2004年上半年颁发了《国务院办公厅关于清理固定资产投资项目的通知》(国办发[2004]38号)。天津市认真贯彻落实国家有关调控措施，努力化解不利因素，同时加大投资结构调整力度。一是努力加快国家鼓励和不限制行业的投资项目建设，二是积极适应市场要求，调整了房地产投资结构，增加了中小户型商品房和经济适用房的建设。正是由于及时采取了有保有压的得力措施，天津市固定资产投资保持了平稳较快的增长速度，对国民经济的健康快速发展起到了重要的支撑作用。

2.突出抓好重点项目前期工作和重大项目储备库建设

“十五”期间，围绕“三步走”战略实施方案，积极筹划建设项目，充实项目库。共提出了350多个重大建设项目，投资总额近万亿元，每年从中筛选若干个项目作为重点前期项目，责成专人抓好落实。项目前期工作得到加强，一些重大项目取得了突破性进展，增强了天津市投资持续增长的后劲。

3.多渠道筹措建设资金，扩大了资金来源

一方面，政府加强了对土地市场的管理和宏观调控，规范了国有土地有偿使用办法，确保了土地出让收益；另一方面，一些单位按照市场化方式，公开招投标拍卖冠名权、广告发布权等也取得了一定的收益。充足的到位资金保证了建设项目的顺利实施。

4.体制改革取得突破，确立了企业的投资主体地位

2004年，根据《国务院关于投资体制改革的决定》精神，天津市对企业投资管理体制进行了重大改革，取消了传统审批制度下的相关程序，区别不同情况，分别实行核准制和备案制。改革后，企业投资决策自主权进一步得到落实，投资积极性进一步提高。

（毛涛）

对外贸易实现新跨越

“十五”期间，随着我国加入世贸组织以及天津市对外开放的扩大和外向型经济的加快发展，全市的对外贸易进入了一个崭新的发展阶段，进出口规模迅速扩大，经济外向度不断提高。对外贸易总额位居全国第七，出口增幅连续三年位居沿海省市第5位。

1.对外贸易快速增长，有力地带动了国民经济快速增长

“十五”时期，全市实现外贸出口总额838亿美元，比“九五”时期增长1.8倍；进口819.67亿美元，比“九五”时期增长1.8倍。进口和出口均实现快速增长，而且出口规模持续攀升，创历史最高水平。2005年当年新增出口额达到65.35亿美元，国民经济增长对外贸出口的依存度达到60.7%，比2000年提高17.1个百分点。

2.进出口商品结构进一步优化

“十五”时期以来，天津对进出口商品结构进行了较大的调整和优化，出口商品逐步朝精加工、深加工、高附加值的方向发展，质量稳步提高，品牌效应显现，形成了以机电、纺织、服装产品为主，具有较高附加值和比较优势的出口商品体系。

2005年，全市机电产品出口比重由2000年的48.8%上升到75%，成为天津出口第一大类商品。在进口方面，市内急需的原材料和机械设备进口增加，如钢材、纺织机械、轴承、电子设备等，弥补了市内资源的不足，增加了市场的有效供给，促进了国民经济的持续、健康发展。

3.外贸经营主体不断壮大

随着天津市外贸体制改革的不断深化，外贸经营主体不断壮大，并呈现多元化发展态势。到2005年底，全市有各类进出口企业4835家，比2000年底增加1836家，再加上已经开业投产的近6000家外商直接投资企业，基本形成一个国有企业、外商投资企业、集体私营企业共同开拓市际市场的多层次的外经贸队伍格局。

4.对传统市场出口保持较高增长，新兴市场得到迅速拓展

“十五”时期，天津积极实施“市场多元化”战略，2005年底，与世界上200多个国家和地区建立了贸易关系，比2000年底增加13个。在对欧盟、美国、日本等传统市场出口保持较高的增速的同时，非洲、拉丁美洲、中东、俄罗斯和东欧等新兴的市场也得到了迅速拓展。2005年对欧盟、日本、美国、香港四大传统市场出口比上年分别增长49.5%、19.5%、27.8%、22.4%，对非洲和拉丁美洲分别增长57.8%和23.4%，对俄罗斯增长5倍。

（程新娣）

直接利用外资增势强劲

“十五”期间，天津市对外开放进一步扩大，投资环境不断改善，利用外资增势强劲，质量明显提高。“十五”时期全市直接协议利用外资达到228.6亿美元，实际利用外资总额116.2亿美元。比“九五”时期分别增长1.6倍和1.3倍，其中直接协议利用外资平均每年增长28.7%；实际利用外资平均每年增长32%。

1.大项目增多，平均规模不断扩大

“十五”时期批准的外商直接投资单个项目平均合同外资金额达到422万美元，比“九五”时期单个项目平均合同外资金额210万美元增长1倍，直接利用外资项目平均每年增长15.9%，创历史新高。“十五”期间，全市引进超亿美元以上项目21个（含增资），特别是丰田整车、三星手机项目的引进巩固了天津市主导产业优势；中芯国际、飞思卡尔等项目引进弥补了天津市芯片产业不足；卡博特、LG化工等项目开拓了引资新空间。截止目前，已有114家世界500强公司在天津投资设立了311家外商投资企业，项目总投资120.58亿美元，500强企业在天津投资的项目平均规模为3877万美元，是天津市外商投资项目平均规模的10倍。提升了引进项目质量和支柱产业的优势聚集度。

2.投资方式发生明显变化

外商独资企业是利用外资增长最快的方式，成为天津市第一大投资方式。“十五”时期外商独资企业合同外资和实际外资分别达到148.97亿美元和68.21亿美元，分别占总数的74.4%和66%，分别比“九五”时期增长2.8倍和1.6倍，说明外商独资企业日益成为外商投资到天津的重要方式，外商已从过去试探性的合资、合作进入到对股权的控制和市场的深度开发上。

3.利用外资的地区结构逐步调整

亚洲国家和地区一直是天津市吸引外资的最主

要来源地。“十五”时期，来自亚洲国家和地区的合同外资累计达到111.33亿美元，占合同外资总额的55.6%，比“九五时期”提高11.6个百分点，其中来自香港的合同外资累计达到68.28亿美元，占合同外资总额的34.1%，来自台湾地区的合同外资累计达到7.61亿美元，占合同外资总额的3.8%。2005年来自非洲、欧洲、北美洲、拉丁美洲和大洋洲的合同外资都有不同程度增长。其中来自美国的合同外资五年累计达到30.43亿美元，占合同外资总额的15.2%。

4.制造业仍是外商投资的主要行业，高新技术产业和第三产业外商投资增长较快

“十五”时期制造业的合同外资和实际直接利用外资分别比“九五”时期增长1.9倍和1.3倍。高新技术和第三产业合同外资快速增长，2005年与2000年相比，电子行业合同和实际到位外资分别增长65%和1.2倍，第三产业分别增长2.5倍和48%，其中主要服务行业的合同外资涨幅较大。

5.滨海新区拉动作用明显

“十五”期间，滨海新区直接利用外资合同外资额和实际直接利用外资分别为145.99亿美元和69.56亿美元，比“九五”时期分别增长1.7倍和1.1倍；年均分别增长31.8%和26.4%。

6.外资企业的经营情况良好，经济效益显著

2005年全市三资企业实现进出口总额428.36亿美元，占全市对外贸易总额的80%，比2000年增长2.1倍。实现销售(营业)收入和利润总额均比上年增长20%以上。

（程新娣）

建筑业总产值年均增百亿

“十五”期间，天津市建筑业取得了长足的发展，对保持国民经济的快速平稳增长发挥了重要作用。同时在深化改革、完善机制、提高工程质量、增加经济效益方面也取得了很大的进展。

一、建筑业生产规模快速扩张

在海河综合开发改造和大规模城市建设的强力拉动下，天津市建筑业获得了难得的发展机遇。“十五”期间，天津市建筑业企业完成建筑业总产值达到2625.3亿元，比“九五”时期增长1.5倍，平均每年增加百亿元；累计建成各类房屋6852万平方米，比“九五”时期增长66.2%；房屋建筑施工面积由2000年的2254万平方米，扩大到2005年的3941万平方米，平均每年增长11.8%。

随着社会主义市场经济的发展，天津市建筑业通过行政、法律、经济等手段，不断推进企业资产重组及所有制结构调整，建筑市场由国有和集体企业一统天下逐步过渡到多种经济类型共同竞争的格局。从经济类型来看，国有和集体所有制建筑施工企业完成的建筑业总产值所占比重逐步回落，外商、港澳台商、私营以及以股份制企业为主导的其他经济类型企业逐步进入建筑市场，完成建筑业总产值比重逐年攀升。2000年，本市其他经济类型建筑企业完成建筑业总产值32.1亿元，而到2005年完成360.9亿元，总量增长了10倍，所占市场份额由2000年的13.5%发展到2005年的47.8%；而国有和集体企业完成建筑业总产值比重则分别由2000年的70.4%和15.2%回落为2005年的37.5%和5.4%，比重大幅下降。

二、建筑施工队伍有序发展

2001 年 7 月 1 日国家建设部颁布了新的《建筑企业资质管理规定》，天津市行业主管部门按照新的资质就位要求，引导全市建筑施工企业对内加大改革力度，深化体制改革、加强质量管理，对外进行企业间的收购兼并和资产重组，调整所有制结构，各种经济资源得到新的整合，建筑队伍的整体素质明显增强，企业在建筑市场的竞争力得到明显提高。目前，天津市建筑业企业已形成了以智力密集型的总承包企业(集团)为龙头，以高资质的技术密集型的独立承包施工企业为主体，以工程专业分包和劳务企业为依托的产业大军，建筑企业资质级别结构呈现金字塔型，企业结构得到优化。截止到2005年，天津市已拥有新资质等级建筑企业1108家，其中总承包序列245家，专业承包序列863家，总承包序列中获批特级资质等级的企业 4 家，一、二级资质等级的126家；专业承包企业中一、二级资质等级企业186家。随着建筑业企业的发展壮大，建筑业为全市提供了大量的就业岗位，已成为吸纳农村剩余劳动力，解决农民就业，增加农民收入的重要途径。到2005年，全社会建筑业从业人数达39.1万人，比2000年增加11.7万人，占社会劳动者人数的7.2%。

三、建筑企业实力明显增强

为了适应不断扩大的固定资产投资规模和高、

大、难工程的需要，天津市建筑企业不断加大对技术装备的投入，技术装备、机械化施工程度明显提高。到2005年底，全市建筑业企业共拥有资产739.4亿元，比2000年增长1.3倍，其中：固定资产净值127.4亿元，比2000年的54.3亿元增长了1.3倍；实收资本为148.8亿元，比2000年增长1.4倍；全市建筑业企业所拥有的机械设备10万台，企业自有机械设备净值达69.5亿元，企业自有机械设备总功率为246.3万千瓦，全市建筑企业技术装备率达到26064元/人，动力装备率9.24千瓦/人，与2000年相比都保持了大幅增长。特别是近年来，天津市建筑施工企业通过引进新技术，对企业的机械设备进行了有效的更新改造，使整个行业的技术装备得到了加强，广大建筑工人的施工条件进一步改善，劳动强度降低，工程质量、劳动效率和经济效益大大提高。

四、建筑企业效益显著提高

随着建筑业生产的快速发展，天津市建筑业企业继续加强经营管理，大力开展成本核算和控制，大幅降低管理费用，建筑业企业效益显著提高。2005年，全市建筑企业实现利润17亿元，比2000年增长5.3倍；产值利润率从2000年的1.1%提高到2005年的2.3%；实现利税39.8亿元，比2000年增长3.2倍；产值利税率和人均利税分别为5.3%和10178元/人，比2000年提高了1.3个百分点和6697元。建筑业企业在着力发展生产的基础上，不断优化劳动组合，开展技术革新，提高技术含量，使全员劳动生产率大幅提高。2005年全市建筑业企业按总产值计算的全员劳动生产率达19.3万元/人，比2000年增长1.2倍，其中国有经济为22.8万元/人，比2000年增长1.5倍。人均竣工产值、人均施工面积、人均竣工面积分别为11.76万元/人、100.78平方米/人、38平方米/人，与“十五”初期相比都有较大幅度增长。

五、建筑业发展贡献巨大

首先，建筑业作为重要的产业部门之一，为促进天津经济发展发挥了重要作用。2005年建筑业增加值达到165.54亿元，比2000年增长了1.3倍，“十五”期间累计向国家缴纳税金93.5亿元。其次大规模的城市建设使城市面貌发生了巨大的变化，一大批项目使城市功能进一步改善，投资环境进一步优化，为提高城市综合竞争力打下了坚实的基础。最后，住宅建设呈现跨跃式发展，市民居住水平得到了极大改善，而建筑企业在这一历史性进步中扮演了重要角色。2005年住宅施工面积已达到1941万平方米，竣工住宅面积729万平方米，城市居民人均住宅建筑面积达到24.97平方米。

（毛涛）

运输邮电业再上新台阶

“十五”期间，随着天津市国民经济的快速发展，交通运输、仓储及邮电业企业加大基础设施投资力度，努力寻求挖潜增盈的措施和途径，为整个国民经济的正常运行提供了坚实的保障。2005年，全行业增加值308.38亿元，比2000年增长72.4%，年均递增11.5%。经过“十五”期间的快速发展，天津市已基本形成较为发达的立体交通网络和快速、高效、大容量的信息网络系统，城市载体功能进一步增强。

基础设施建设投入不断加大，客货运输再上新水平。“十五”期间，天津市加大公路网建设投资，截止2005年底，天津市公路网总里程10836公里，其中，等级公路10791公里。高速公路已达593公里，与“九五”时期末的305公里相比增长94.4%，津蓟等多条高速公路在“十五”期间实现通车。“十五”期间，天津市民用车拥有辆突破百万辆，其中汽车拥有量已达70.7万辆。2005年，天津市各种运输工具运输旅客4679万人次，比2000年增长34.7%；旅客周转量142.1亿人公里，增长60.7%。运输货物4.0亿吨，增长50.9%；货物周转量12461亿吨公里，增长1.7倍。

发展城市公共交通，便利居民出行。为根本解决市区道路交通拥堵问题，“十五”期间天津市完善了城市道路层次化、网络化，建设完善快速路系统，建设主要路口的立交，提高道路通行能力，积极改变中心城区、海河两岸长期阻断不通历史，建设了一批主、次干道项目。截止2005年底，市区道路长度达1100多公里，道路面积2480多万平方米。市内道路网质量的进一步提高，也使得城市公共交通得到了充分发展。公交行业及时按照市民居住需求调整、改造、延伸公交线路，优先发展大容量快速公共交通，完善常规公共汽车线网和运营设施，加大车辆更新力度，提高车辆、设施水平，形成快速、便捷、发达的公共交通网络，使公交车辆万人拥有率达到11.23标台。公交车、出租车、轻轨、地铁为天津市居民出行提供了多种便利交通工具。2005年,城市公共交通客运量达9亿人次,比2000年5.4亿人次增长66.7%。

水上运输业创新高。天津市地处环渤海中部,经济辐射十多个省市,辐射总面积占全国面积近一半。西北、东北、华北中东部地区的煤炭、金属矿石、钢材等散货,通过天津市海港装船运往国内外各地区,为天津市大力发展海洋散货运输提供了得天独厚的发展空间。"九五"期间落户天津的中远散货运输有限公司也伴随着"十五"经济发展的快速步伐,壮大成为拥有百亿资产,年利润30多亿元的世界水上散货运输的领航企业。随着天津港基础设施的不断完善,已有多家私营航运企业在天津落户,使天津的航运市场更加繁荣、发达。2005年,水上运输企业完成货运量1.24亿吨,比2000年增长2倍,完成货物周转量12031亿吨公里,增长1.8倍。

民用航空振翅欲飞。"十五"期间,随着天津作为环渤海经济发展龙头作用的凸现,越来越多的航空公司看好并进入天津航空市场,目前在天津执行航线的国际国内航空公司已达20余家,其中,国内现有的11家航空公司全部在天津机场建立了基地或办事处,韩国大韩、韩亚、荷兰马丁、新加坡货航等多家国际知名航空公司陆续与天津机场建立合作关系,同时国际上还有6家航空公司在天津设立办事处,国内东方航空、深圳航空、厦门航空、上海航空等几大航空公司也继国航、海航之后与天津机场建立了密切合作伙伴关系。天津机场的航班执行航线已达到65条,其中国际航线17条,国内航线48条;执行班次为769班次/周,其中国际班次为91班次/周,国内班次为678班次/周;通航54个城市。奥凯、春秋两家国内民营航空公司开辟了天津航线,其中奥凯航空公司在天津机场设立了基地。随着航班航线密度不断加大,以往被首都机场分流的旅客逐渐回流,2005年天津机场旅客吞吐量达219.4万人次,首次突破200万人次大关,比2000年增长1.5倍,"十五"期间年平均旅客吞吐量141万人,比"九五"期间的84万人,增68%。机场货邮吞吐量达8万吨,比2000年增长53.8%。

港口发展实现新跨越。天津港与世界上160多个国家和地区的300多个港口保持贸易往来。开辟集装箱班轮航线70多条,每月集装箱航班近300班,目前天津港已与美国、韩国、日本、荷兰等12个港口建立了友好港。为更好地服务腹地经济发展,2005年,天津港为加强港口服务需求信息,谋划市场经营方向,针对航运市场发展和货物流通服务方式的新特点,提出"将码头建到西部去",在新疆、河北等地开辟"无水港",并针对重点货类开辟"绿色通道",对西部地区货物直接装船作出承诺,积极利用运输通道把西部大开发急需的设备及其他生产生活资料运往内地。在天津港的腹地中,有约占全国3/5的煤、1/4的盐、1/6的油和矿需要经海上运输并进行国内外贸易。现在,天津港70%以上的货物吞吐量和55%的口岸进出口货值来自天津市以外的其他省市。经过"十五"期间的快速发展,天津港于2004年率先成为环渤海地区货物吞吐量突破2亿吨的我国北方最大港口。2005年,全港完成货物吞吐量2.4亿吨,比2000年的0.96亿吨增长1.5倍;完成集装箱480万 TEU,比2000年的170万 TEU 增长了1.8倍。"十五"期间,天津港年均货物吞吐量1.7亿吨,比"九五"时期增长了1.3倍;集装箱吞吐量年均321万 TEU,比"九五"时期增长了1.8倍。天津港以年均22%的速度快速发展显示了建设中国北方国际航运中心和国际物流中心的巨大潜力。

电信、邮政业务快速增长。"十五"期间,随着天津市电信用户对电信业务个性化、多元化需求的不断提高,为电信行业的竞争提供了源源不断的动力,使通信业务迅猛发展。电信业务价值的创造已不仅是通过运营规模,更重要的是依靠拓展业务范围和提高服务质量来实现,电信以其便利性和个性化特点使其拥有量迅速上升。2005年,天津市邮政、电信行业完成邮电业务总量176.3亿元,"十五"时期平均增长26%,呈现良好的发展态势。

(卢智伟)

房地产业不断壮大

"十五"期间,在强劲市场需求的带动下,天津市房地产市场急剧升温,商品房销售火爆,房地产投资、施工、销售等各项指标呈全面增长态势,房地产业正在成为拉动天津经济增长的主要动力。

一、房地产开发企业发展状况

到2005年年底,天津市共有房地产开发企业974家,其中拥有一级资质的房地产企业17家,二级资质的73家，三级及三级以下资质的企业884家，涌现出顺驰地产、泰达建设集团、天房发展、万隆集团、津投金厦、住宅建设集团、万兆投资发展集团等一批实力雄厚、管理先进的典型企业。

2005年底天津市房地产开发企业拥有资本金373.5亿元，比2000年增长1.3倍；资产2021.4亿元，比2000年增长2.4倍；其中非国有资本占资产总量的80%，比2000年提高17.8个百分点；资产负债率72.8%，比2000年下降4.6个百分点。受国家宏观调控政策影响，房地产开发企业资产质量不断提高，企业实力明显增强。

二、商品房供给市场发展状况

1.房地产开发投资规模日益扩大

由于海河综合开发改造、地铁、轻轨等重大基础设施的建设，加上危旧房屋拆迁力度的加大，形成了对天津市房地产市场的刚性需求，同时也为天津房地产的发展注入新的活力，市场需求大幅度增长，房地产开发投资规模稳步扩大，已成为全社会固定资产投资的重要组成部分。“十五”期间全市完成房地产开发投资达到1140亿元，年均增长18.3%，比“九五”期间提高5.2个百分点；占全社会固定资产投资的比重为21.3%，比“九五”期间提高2.3个百分点。

在房地产开发投资快速增长的同时，商品房施工、竣工规模也快速扩张。全市房地产施、竣工房屋面积自2000年以来以年均14.2%和20.4%的速度快速递增。2005年房地产施、竣工房屋面积分别达到3470.6万平方米和1479.2万平方米，比2000年增长了94.6%和1.5倍。

2.商品住宅建设的主体地位得到加强

天津市“十五规划”明确提出要把房地产业培育成为天津市支柱产业之一，在这一产业政策引导下，天津市房地产开发企业抓住契机，调整结构，不断加大以普通住宅为主的住宅建设力度，房地产开发结构出现新变化，商品住宅建设主体地位继续得到加强。“十五”期间，商品住宅投资累计760.7亿元，商业营业用房投资为124.6亿元，办公楼投资为47.5亿元，占房地产开发投资的比重分别为66.7%、10.9%和4.2%；同期竣工商品住宅面积为4335.7万平方米，竣工商业营业用房面积为356万平方米，竣工办公楼面积为131.9万平方米，占全部竣工房屋面积的比重分别为87.8%、7.2%和2.7%，商品住宅的主体地位十分明显。

3.房地产开发建设资金到位情况理想

近几年，一方面由于房地产市场销售状况比较理想，房地产开发资金回笼较快；另一方面也因为房地产开发商自身实力增强，银行信贷对房地产开发的支持力度相应增大，天津市房地产开发资金到位情况一直比较理想。在各类资金中，自筹资金、定金及预付款、国内贷款之和已占据房地产开发资金总量的九成以上，居于房地产开发投资资金的绝对主导地位。“十五”以来，自筹资金年均增长32.8%，增速居各类资金之首；国内贷款年均增长27.9%，居第二位；定金及预付款年均增长23.7%，居第三位。从各类资金所占比重看，自筹资金、定金及预付款、国内贷款三者之间的比例由2000年的30.6:38.2:25.3演变为2005年的32.5:28.4:22.3，其中，自筹资金所占比重上升了1.9个百分点，定金及预付款所占比重下降9.8个百分点，国内贷款比重下降了3个百分点。

三、房地产消费市场状况

1.房地产市场销售看好

“十五”以来，全市商品房销售面积、销售额分别以年均19.1%和32.1%的速度快速增长，累计实现商品房现房销售3673万平方米，销售额达到1097.3亿元。特别是2003年以后，由于海河综合开发改造和大规模城市建设带来了拆迁的急剧放量，也带动了商品房销售量和销售价格的大幅度提升。2005年商品房现房销售面积938万平方米，销售额367.6亿元，分别为2000年的2.4倍和4倍。

2.商品房价格上涨

2005年商品房现房平均价格为3919元/平方米，比2000年每平方米价格提高了1591元，涨幅达68.3%。从各类房屋价格的变化情况看，以住宅平均价格涨幅最高，为69.9%；其次是其他用房，涨幅为34.9%；商业营业用房平均价格涨幅居第三位，为21.6%；办公楼涨幅为13.3%，居第四位。

（毛涛）

金融业蓬勃健康发展

“十五”期间，天津市国民经济保持了持续、快速、稳定运行的良好态势，综合经济实力不断增强，促进和推动了天津金融业的较快发展。

一、金融机构不断完善，组织体系更加健全

“十五”期间，天津金融业不断发展壮大，金融组织体系更加健全。目前，我市基本形成了国有商业银行、股份制银行、外资银行、政策性银行以及非银行金融机构等多层次、多种类金融机构竞相发展的金融组织体系。截至2005年底，全市共有各类金融机构2874家，比“九五”末期增长17.2%，金融机构从业人员达4.67万人，比“九五”末期增长11.5%。一批有影响、实力强的金融、保险、证券机构相继在津成立，为活跃天津经济、提供社会保险和融通资金发挥了重要作用。

银行类金融机构蓬勃发展。2001年深圳发展银行、上海浦东发展银行入驻天津，2002年美国花旗集团在津设立花旗银行天津分行，2004年中德住房储蓄银行在津开业，年底民生银行天津分行成立。2005年华夏银行天津分行开业，天津市农村信用合作社改革为农村合作银行。此外，总部设在天津滨海新区的渤海银行在津成立。

保险公司竞相落户津门。2001年，第一家总部设在天津的保险公司恒安人寿保险公司正式挂牌，新华人寿保险公司、华泰财产保险公司等也相继在天津设立分公司。2002年，光大永明人寿保险公司和天安保险股份有限公司在津成立。2003年，太平保险公司天津分公司开业。2004年，中国保险市场最大的中外合资保险公司恒安标准人寿保险公司又落户天津。2005年，第一家总部在天津的财产保险公司渤海财产保险股份有限公司正式在津成立。

证券公司平稳运行。2001年，资金规模位居全国前五位的综合性证券公司渤海证券公司在津挂牌开业。中新药业、天药股份、天房发展等公司成功上市，我市通过资本市场融资工作取得突破性进展。截至2005年底，我市共有各类证券经营公司 79 家。

二、银行业蓬勃发展

“十五”期间，我市金融机构本外币存贷款余额逐年稳步增长，2001 至 2005 年，存款余额年均增长21.3%，贷款余额年均增长18.8%。截止 2005 年末，全市中外金融机构本外币存款余额达到6090.50亿元，比上年末增长18.5%，净增额为950.78亿元。其中企事业单位存款余额2448.99亿元，比上年末增长18.9%，净增额为390.08亿元；城乡居民储蓄存款余额2584.40亿元，比上年末增长14.3%，净增额为322.91亿元。虽然居民储蓄存款总量不断增加，但占存款的比重持续降低，由2001年的51.2%降至2005年的42.4%，五年间下降了8.8个百分点，主要原因为企事业存款的比例加大（由2001年的36.7%上升至2005年的40.2%）及居民投资渠道的多元化。至2005年末，我市金融机构本外币贷款余额达到4722.38亿元，按可比口径计算比上年末增长13.9%，净增额为575.89亿元。其中，中长期贷款余额2255.23亿元，比上年末增长21.9%。

三、证券市场逐步规范，发展潜力较大

“十五”期间，我市证券市场发展迅速，市场规范化程度进一步提高，为金融市场改革发展和经济结构的调整做出了重要贡献。

2001 年是中国证券业的规范整顿之年，天津市在一级市场融资有了突破性进展，二级市场发展呈现稳中有进的局面。2001年全市上市公司新增融资额34亿元。2005年，证券市场运行较平稳，融资总额达170亿元，当年新增融资额10亿元，年末共有境内上市股票27只。

四、保险业稳步发展，保费收入逐年增加

“十五”期间，随着天津城乡居民收入水平的提高和居民保险意识的增强，我市保险业务一直保持平稳增长，保险市场体系不断完善，管理和服务水平逐步提高。

2002 年，我市保险公司抓住银行再次降息的机遇，及时推出了新型保险品种，促进了保费收入的快速增长。全年实现保费收入64.97亿元，同比增长55.8%，是历史上增长最快的一年。保险密度649.13元，同比增加233.75元，是全国平均水平的2.73倍；保险深度3.21%，同比增加0.93个百分点，高出全国平均水平0.21个百分点。近几年，天津保险市场在2002年高速发展的基础上继续保持平稳增长，截至2005年底，天津市共有各类保险机构达431家，全年实现保费收入90.64亿元，同比增长11.9%。其中财产险保费收入21.78亿元，增长16.1%（主要是我市机动车辆保险增长较快，成为拉动财产险增长的主要险种）。支付各项赔款给付17.46亿元，比上年增长0.2%，其中财产险赔付款10.74亿元，比上年增长11.5%。保险密度869.02元，保险深度2.47%。

五、金融业增加值总量不断加大，对全市经济的贡献显著提高

“十五”期间，我市金融保险业增加值年均可比增长17.2%，占全市GDP的比重稳中有升(由2001年的3.5%升至2005年的4.3%)。2003年，全市存贷款业务量大幅增加，使得银行利息收入持续快速增加，带动金融保险业经营效益明显提高。各商业银行纷纷加大处置不良贷款的力度，提高了贷款的收息率，有力地带动了增加值的快速增长，金融业增加值可比增速达25.5%，是“十五”期间增长最快的一年。2005年，金融保险业稳健运行。全市金融保险业实现增加值159.24亿元，可比增长15.6%。

综上所述，“十五”期间，天津市金融业总体运行状况良好，各类金融机构竞相发展，金融市场进一步活跃，金融增加值总量不断加大，对全市经济的发展做出了突出贡献。

(张颖)

旅游业充满活力

“十五”期间天津市旅游业迎来了快速发展的大好时机。旅游服务业各项经济指标再创历史最好水平。

一、发展速度明显加快，旅游经济增势强劲

“十五”末的2005年全市接待海外旅游者达74.01万人次，比“九五”末的2000年增长1.1倍，年平均增长15.7%；实现旅游外汇收入5.07亿美元，比2000年增长1.2倍，年平均增长17%。

二、全面深度开发旅游资源，景观建设实现新突破

“十五”以来，以“河、海、山、城”为载体，全面整合、深度开发旅游资源，旅游景区景点建设取得重大进展。以海河为轴线、以市区为中心、以滨海和蓟县为两翼的旅游开发格局进一步拓展。“一带五区”的开发建设实现重点突破，已形成了市区、滨海、蓟县、西青四大旅游集聚区。市区的河流景观、园林景观、街市景观、建筑景观、灯光景观不断涌现，新建和改造的金街、鼓楼步行街、古文化街、五大道风情区、天塔湖风景区、天津博物馆等一批新景点脱颖而出，已成为拉动天津旅游业发展的巨大引擎。滨海休闲度假旅游区发展势头强劲，基辅航母、海河外滩公园、“东方公主”号游轮、新洋市场、海洋观光、渔家风情和开发区新貌成为滨海旅游的新亮点。西青生态民俗旅游区新建或扩建的热带植物观光园、御河人家、明清街二期工程、石家大院、安家大院、年画馆等交相辉映，形成了多点支撑的整体气势。蓟县山野名胜旅游区基础设施进一步改善，新建了盘山观光索道和滑雪场，恢复了水胜景观、万松寺、乾隆御路、诗刻长廊，扩建了梨木台、奇石林、玉龙滑雪场等新景区，特别是农家乐旅游迅速扩张，农家旅店增至百村千户，旅游脱贫致富的道路越走越宽广。宝坻、静海、东丽、津南等区县也都开发建设了一批新景点。

三、旅游产业规模不断扩大，旅游生产力全面增长

“十五”以来，天津市旅游产业规模不断扩大，旅游产业水平逐步提高，旅游生产力全面增长，天津市旅游业已经发展成为具有一定产业规模和产业水平的现代服务业中的重点产业，对全市国民经济和社会发展贡献日趋显著。

到2005年底，全市拥有星级宾馆、饭店110家，比2000年增加62家，客房1.52万间，比2000年增长77.7%。国际、国内旅行社达265家，比2000年增加82家，其中，国际旅行社29家，增加10家；全市旅游景点60多处，其中，A级景区30处；全国工农业旅游示范点5个。

四、国内外旅游客源市场开发不断深化，区域合作加快，旅游产业对外开放力度进一步扩大

“十五”期间，天津市旅游业突出了“新世纪、新天津、新景观”的宣传主题，着力打造“近代缩影、渤海明珠”的旅游形象。策划推出了名馆博览游、名人故居游、名街休闲游、水路风光游、渔阳山野游、滨海风情游、西青民俗游、宗教文化游、工业观光游、农业观光游等系列精品线路。培育推出了海河旅游节、天津民俗文化旅游节、妈祖文化旅游节、五大道欧陆风情旅游节、渔阳金秋山野旅游节、黄崖关长城国际马拉松旅游活动等国内外知名品牌的大型旅游节会活动。做大做足三大黄金周，假日经济格外红火。天津旅游市场日趋繁荣，形成了津京对流、城乡对流、南北对流、出入境对流四大客源对流的良性循环，天津作为旅游目的地的形象和地位明显提升。

“十五”期间，环渤海区域旅游经济合作体系逐渐形成。京津冀与港澳台“3+3”迎奥运旅游市场互动交流活动的开展、2005年环渤海港口城市旅游合作组织成立大会暨邮轮经济发展研讨会在津召开，标志着区域旅游经济合作不断向深度和广度发展。

(张辉)

科技实力明显增强

"十五"以来,天津科技事业紧紧围绕全市科技发展目标,深入实施"科教兴市"战略,深化科技体制改革,加大研发创新力度,取得了丰硕的成果。

一、全市综合科技实力明显增强

"十五"期间,全市科技创新环境得到进一步改善,近两年,天津综合科技进步水平连续居全国省市第三位。

1. 科技投入持续增长

"十五"以来,全社会科技人员投入强度不断提高,天津每万名从业人员拥有科技人员由2000年的352人增加到2005年的474人,科技人员内部结构继续得到优化,高素质人员不断增加,2005年科学家和工程师为6.23万人,比2000年增加1.32万人,R&D人员折合全时人员3.40万人/年,比2000年增长46.55%。几年来,天津科技经费筹集与支出实现同步持续增长。2005年科技经费筹集额达到183.05亿元,比2000年增加128.70亿元,年均增长27.49%;科技经费支出额达166.94亿元,增加117.57亿元,年均增长27.59%;研发经费(R&D)投入从2000年的24.69亿元增加到2005年的72.92亿元,年均增长24.18%。R&D占GDP的比重由2000年的1.51%增长到2005年的1.97%。

2. 科技产出绩效斐然

随着科技投入力度的加大和科技环境的改善,天津科技成果层出不穷。2001-2005年,全市共获科技成果6339项,其中达到国际领先水平284项,达到国际先进水平1320项;获国家科学技术奖59项。获市科学技术奖1158项,其中获二等奖以上385项,占市科学技术获奖总数的33.25%。独立自然科学机构开展课题研究7726项,经费投入23.2亿元,仅2005年投入就达到6.33亿元,其中研发经费投入3.73亿元,比"九五"末分别增长126.88%和297.87%。理工农医类高等院校开展各类课题研究累计达到22989项,科技经费累计投入28.73亿元,比"九五"时期增长129.66%。其中国家级项目累计达到2972项,经费累计投入4.55亿元。国家级项目中国家自然科学基金项目累计达到2385项,经费累计投入2.05亿元。2005年国家级项目753项,比"九五"末增长61.94%。国家级项目中国家自然科学基金项目达到608项,增长69.36%。

专利申请量取得了突出成绩,增幅连续五年名列全国前茅。天津已成为近年来全国专利申请量增长最快地区之一,自主知识产权也向高科技含量、高附加值发展。2001-2005年天津专利申请量累计达到35313件,比"九五"时期增长268.96%。其中发明专利申请量大幅增长,五年累计达到14662件,比"九五"时期增长9倍。

二、科技创新体系日臻完善

"十五"以来,天津科技创新体系进一步完善,以科研机构和高等院校为知识创新主体、企业为技术创新主体、科技服务机构为桥梁的科技创新体系进一步完善。

1. 科研机构、高等院校知识创新主体作用进一步突出

近年来,天津科研机构和高等院校在科技创新、培养人才和发展经济等方面做出了积极的贡献。2004年天津101所高等院校、科研机构承担的科技项目(课题)达8687项,占全市的64.13%,比2000年增加2889项,年均增长10.64%。特别是高等院校除教学之外,还承担了全市57.49%的项目(课题)任务。此外,在研究与试验发展(R&D)活动中,科研院所和高等院校承担了90%以上的基础研究和应用研究项目(课题)任务。这些科技知识的生产活动为天津企业生产的技术创新提供了知识源泉和动力。

2. 企业技术创新主体作用逐渐显现

"十五"期间,工业企业逐渐成为天津开展技术创新活动的主体。近几年,天津工业企业坚持走科技路,吃科技饭,科技创新的动力增强,自主创新的投入力度明显加大。

首先,加强了各类研究中心、工程中心和企业技术开发中心的建设。自1996年首批企业技术中心被批准认定,到2005年底全市经批准认定的企业技术中心已达150家,其中国家级企业技术中心12家,比2000年增加5家,市级企业技术中心138家,增加75家。在一些大中型企业和企业集团中初步建立了以企业技术中心为主体的企业创新体系。

其次,大中型工业企业科技投入逐年加大,成为企业技术创新主体。2005年,全市企业从事科技活动人员为6.84万人,其中工业企业为5.37万人,占全市企业从事科技活动人员的比重为78.5%。在工业企业中,大中型工业企业从事科技活动人员为3.22万人,占工业企业从事科技活动人员的比重为59.96%,成为企业技术创新的主体。大中型工业企业研究与

实验发展(R&D)人员一直保持平稳增长态势,2005年为1.52万人,比2000年增加0.25万人。R&D人员占单位从业人员的比重为的2.50%,略高于2000年的2.11%。企业科技经费投入成倍增长。2005年大中型工业企业科技活动经费达93.68亿元,比2000年增加73.14亿元,增长3.56倍。R&D活动经费投入逐年递增,2005年大中型工业企业R&D经费支出为38.43亿元,比2000年增加26.81亿元,增长2.31倍,企业自主创新能力不断增强。

第三,企业运用知识产权制度的能力和水平提高。企业自主知识产权拥有量逐年增加,技术开发活动成果层出不穷。2004年工业企业专利申请数为3812项,比2000年增加3069项。其中,大中型工业企业为2977项,比2000年增加2724项。

3.技术市场成为研发成果转化的纽带和桥梁

经过多年努力,天津科技服务体系逐渐形成,并在实践中进一步完善,特别是技术市场现已成为科技与经济结合的纽带,成为技术成果进入生产领域的桥梁,成为科学技术由知识形态转化为物质形态、由潜在的生产能力转化为现实生产力的助推器。“十五”以来,技术市场交易更加活跃,累计签订技术合同40799项,技术合同成交额204.67亿元,比“九五”期间增长111.71%。2005年签订技术合同11295项,技术合同成交额50.71亿元,比“九五”末增长93.11%。

(郭秀兰)

社会事业全面发展

“十五”期间天津市社会综合发展水平始终位居全国前列,教育、卫生、文化、体育等各项社会事业全面发展,社会保障制度不断完善,基层社会管理体制改革取得新进展,社会治安继续保持全国最好地区之一,人民生活质量显著提高,经济与社会发展更加协调。

一、教育事业再上新水平

“十五”期间,天津市不断加大教育改革和创新力度,积极推进素质教育,努力改善办学条件,提高教育现代化、信息化水平,加快培养中小学学科带头人,积极实施高校高层次创新人才工程,教师队伍素质不断提高,学校布局调整成效显著,教育整体水平迈上新台阶,教育事业取得了重大进展。

1.教育投入明显增长

“十五”期间,天津市在确保教育经费“三个增长”的基础上,不断加大政府对教育的投入,财政性教育经费支出由“九五”末的30.87亿元增加到2005年的89.55亿元。同时逐步完善多渠道筹措教育经费的体制,鼓励和支持社会力量以各种形式捐资助学,全市教育经费总量逐年增加,为加快教育设施建设、顺利推进学校布局调整提供了有力保障,教职工待遇、办学经费和条件等也得到明显改善。

2.教育整体水平位居全国前列

基础教育不断加强。“十五”期间,天津市3至6岁儿童入园率达到91%,农村基本普及学前一年、二年教育。义务教育和特殊教育入学率继续保持在99%和95%以上,初中三年保留率超过96%。高中阶段教育进入全面普及阶段,全市高中阶段毛入学率超过90%,接受优质教育的高中生比例超过了75%。

高等教育开始进入普及化阶段。“十五”期间,天津市高等教育毛入学率按照新口径达到51%,普通高校在校生超过32万人,每十万人口在校大学生达到4000人,天津已经成为继上海、北京之后第三个率先进入高等教育普及化阶段的城市。

职业教育继续保持优势。“十五”期间,天津市大力整合职业教育资源,逐步建立起适应经济发展要求的高标准职业教育体系。目前全市拥有独立设置的高等职业技术学院23所,其中国家级示范性重点建设学院2所;拥有中等职业学校151所,其中国家级、省部级重点学校65所;拥有国家级中、高等职业教育师资培训基地4个。高等职业院校在校生规模超过12万人,相当于2000年的3.6倍。

二、卫生事业稳步发展

“十五”期间,天津市进一步推进医疗卫生体制改革,优化卫生资源配置,完善卫生服务、医疗保障、卫生监督体系,促进卫生事业得到良好的发展,人民群众的健康水平显著提高。

1.卫生资源的质量进一步优化

“十五”期间天津市启动了卫生资源调整工程,通过资源整合逐步优化医疗卫生布局,促进了卫生事业的发展。三个医学中心、五个区域性医疗中心和一批重点专科医院技术水平不断提高,重点学科中获得国家自然科学二等奖1项,国家科学技术二等奖6项。中医针灸、肝移植、血液病学、乳腺癌防治、中西医结合治疗胆胰病等学科保持全国领先地位。

2005年末全市各类卫生机构的总数达2489个，各类床位数达41556张，每千人口医院、卫生院床位4.48张。全市卫生系统职工人数为8.00万人，其中：卫生技术人员6.13万人，千人口拥有卫生技术人员6.5人。

2.服务网络进一步健全

"十五"期间天津市建成了由9个社区卫生服务指导中心、70个社区卫生服务中心、470个社区卫生服务站为主体的城市社区卫生服务网络。卫生服务站覆盖率达到93.4%，80%的家庭有了固定的社区医生，使广大群众享受到了方便、快捷、优质的基本医疗服务。

农村初级卫生保健取得显著成绩，以县医院、防病站、妇幼保健院为龙头，县、乡、村三级卫生机构组成的农村医疗预防保健网络逐步完善。

2005年全市各类医疗保健机构共完成诊疗3463.8万人次，比2002年增加了15.3%；收治入院病人67.0万人，比2002年增加了22.3%；二级以上医院病床使用率平均为72.5%，比2000年提高了16.4个百分点。

3.疾病控制和公共卫生水平显著提高

"十五"期间，通过广泛开展社区综合防治和健康教育，全市妇女、儿童保健基本知识和城乡居民主要慢性病防病知识知晓率显著提高。甲、乙类传染病发病率始终处于较低水平。2005年全市7种计划免疫疫苗全程接种率达97%以上，儿童保健系统管理覆盖率达90.08%，孕产妇系统管理覆盖率达96%，碘缺乏病等地方病的防治工作取得成就。

4.居民健康水平全面提高

随着天津市卫生事业的较快发展，天津市居民的健康水平得到全面提高。天津市人口平均期望寿命由2000年的75.14岁提高到2005年的77.33岁。

三、文化事业百花争艳、成绩斐然

"十五"期间，天津市积极推进文化体制改革，不断加大文化创新力度，实现了文化建设与经济社会协调发展。

1.文艺创作精品迭出，文艺演出好戏连台

全市文艺工作者辛勤耕耘，开拓创新，不断推出思想深刻、艺术精湛、独具天津特色的优秀文艺作品，在全国性文艺评奖中屡屡获奖。五年间，累计创作新剧(节)目39台，整理加工剧(节)目195台，获得各类奖项370个。京剧《华子良》入选国家舞台艺术十大精品剧目，获得文化部"文华大奖"，话剧《为你喝彩》等7个剧目获得中宣部"五个一工程"奖，儿童剧《尼玛·太阳》等12个剧目获得"文华新剧目奖"，杂技《单手倒立》荣获第十届法国未来杂技节金奖第一名暨法兰西共和国总统金奖。

对外文化交流更加活跃，五年间共引进和派出文化交流项目562个、13500人次，比利时中国天津文化节、天津民乐团赴维也纳"金色大厅"演出、华夏未来少儿艺术团"环球之旅"等节目的艺术水平、组织规模堪称一流，深受各国朋友的喜爱，进一步扩大了天津文化的影响。

2.群众文化蓬勃发展

"十五"期间，天津市切实加强群众文化的基本阵地、基本队伍、基本活动内容和基本活动方式的建设，积极推动音乐、舞蹈、美术、摄影、书法等业余文艺创作，在全国"群星奖"作品评选中获奖总数名列前茅。"和平杯"中国京剧票友邀请赛、农民艺术节、妈祖文化旅游节、"沽上春好"大型灯会等已经连续举办多届，成为天津市群众文化的代表作。

3.文化设施建设成就突出

"十五"以来，天津市不断加大对文化设施建设的投入，先后建成了天津博物馆、泰达图书馆、华夏未来少儿艺术中心，同时完成了6个区县图书馆、文化馆的新建和改扩建，天津图书馆开通了"天图网"，信息化工程取得新进展。

目前，全市共有电影放映场所(电影院、影剧院、俱乐部)45家，拥有座席30576个；艺术表演场所28个，座席数15529个；公共图书馆32个，总建筑面积16.87万平方米，藏书869万册；博物馆18个，文物藏品57万件，文物保护单位8个，藏品2995件。

4.新闻出版业繁荣兴旺

近年来天津市图书报刊出版行业始终保持旺盛的发展势头，2005年，出版各类图书4434种，总印数达5917万册，与2000年相比，分别增长72.6%和0.6%；出版报纸44种，比2000年增加了18种，总印数达到87557万份，比2000年增长46.2%。

5.广播电视业欣欣向荣

天津人民广播电台现有自办节目9套，平均每日播出时间190小时58分，与2000年110小时42分相比增加了80小时16分。全年制作广播节目55846小时，与2000年34006小时相比，增加了21840小时。

天津电视台现有自办节目13套，平均每周播出时间1171小时30分，与2000年560小时29分相比增加了

611小时1分。全年播出电视剧596部，共14758集。

全年制作电视节目8947小时，与2000年6873小时相比，增加了2074小时。

有线电视用户普及率大幅度提高，2005年达到194万户，入户率为61.47%。

四、体育事业实现跨越发展

"十五"期间，天津市体育事业蓬勃发展，成就令人瞩目。

竞技体育不断取得新突破。"十五"期间，天津市运动员在全国重大赛事中共夺得65枚金牌、56.5枚银牌、52枚铜牌，在国际重大赛事中夺得17枚金牌、9枚银牌、5枚铜牌。有1名运动员先后2次冲击世界记录，其中打破2项世界记录，平1项世界记录。

2002年天津市承办了首届世界大学生滑水锦标赛，这是继第43届世乒赛、第34届世体赛之后，天津承办的又一重大国际赛事，来自美国、澳大利亚、英国、瑞典等21个国家和地区的100余名运动员参加了比赛，盛况空前。

体育彩票市场保持持续、健康发展，销售额连续5年保持在5亿元之上，为天津市举办各项体育公益事业积累了雄厚的资金。

群众体育工作始终保持全国领先。"十五"期间，全市100%的街道建立了社区体协，3000余个晨晚练辅导站遍布大街小巷，13000余名社会体育指导员活跃其中，指导群众健身，形成独特的健身景观。群众健身意识不断增强，全市经常参加体育活动的人数已达总人口的47%。

五、社会保障体系建设全面提速

"十五"期间，天津市积极发展社会福利、社会救济、优抚安置和社会互助等社会保障事业，逐步建立并完善社会救助体系、社会互助体系和灾害救助体系，为困难群众和弱势群体撑起"保护伞"，切实维护广大人民群众的切身利益，保持社会稳定。

1.社会福利事业快速发展

随着社会经济整体水平的提高，不仅政府加大了对社会福利事业的投入力度，各种社会力量也纷纷兴办福利机构，共同推动天津市福利事业快速发展。2005年全市收养性福利单位共有267所，拥有床位总数16113张，年末在院收养人员达11176人。随着老龄人口的逐年增加以及生活方式的转变，社会兴办的老年福利机构发展较快，床位数由2000年的7998张增至2005年的13636张，增长70.5%，年末在院收养人数也由2000年的4900人增至2005年的8858人，增长了80.8%。

2.抚恤、救济事业费大幅度增加

"十五"期间，天津市继续加大抚恤和救济事业费的投入，提高优抚和救济对象的保障水平，2005年全市抚恤事业费达到12879万元，比2000年增长53.0%；社会救济费达到48720万元，相当于2000年的5.7倍，其中城镇低保救济费从2000年的3211万元增加到2005年的26680万元，五年时间增长了7.3倍。

六、新型社区建设步伐加快，社区功能日益完善

截至2005年底，全市城镇社区服务中心达111个，在社区救助和福利、再就业和社会保障社会化服务等方面发挥了较好的作用；城镇社区服务设施达2139个，为城镇居民提供了较好的活动场所和活动内容，参加社区活动人次由2000年的54.5万人次增加到2005年的56.9万人次，增长了4.45%。全市便民利民网点数发展到8907个，比2000年增长了12.3%，城镇居民的生活变得更加方便快捷。

"十五"期间，天津市在保持经济持续、快速、健康发展的同时，实现了社会事业的全面进步，促进了经济与社会的协调可持续发展。

（陶玉华）

天津市人口进入低速增长期

"十五"期间，天津市人口进入低速增长期，人口出生率持续下降，全市基本稳定在低生育水平，人口分布日趋合理，全体人口素质普遍提高。

一、人口自然增长趋缓，外来人口增多

2005年底，天津市常住人口为1043万人，比"九五"末期增加41.86万人，增长4.18%，年平均增长0.82%，比"九五"时期的增速降低0.41个百分点。进入新世纪以来，天津市外来人口大量涌入和自然增加人口规模持续缩小的特点愈发明显。具体表现为：

1.外来人口越来越成为天津人口总量增长的主要来源

新世纪以来，天津经济增长、城市建设和社会发展加快带动了人口的迁移流动。来津的常住外来人口由2000年87.34万人，2005年增加到114.35万人，增幅达30.93%。在全市新增人口中外来人口占新增人口总量的64.90%。外来人口已成为天津市人口总量的重要组成部分。

2.人口自然变动持续低水平,市中心区连续12年呈现负增长

2005年全市人口出生率为7.44‰,死亡率为6.01‰,自然增长率为1.43‰。人口自然增长率与2000年1.46‰的水平相比,略有下降。近年来,天津市人口自然增长率一直处于较低水平,并且呈现波动下降的态势,基本保持在1.1‰-1.6‰之间,平均自然增加人口在2万人以内。

二、人口空间分布日趋合理,城镇化进程不断推进

"十五"期间,随着城市布局的变化和滨海新区、城郊经济的发展,天津市人口的空间分布呈现新特点。市内六区和三县的人口比重表现为减少的态势;滨海三区和其他六区的人口表现为较强的增长势头,全市人口分布呈现出中心城区人口进一步向外扩散、人口向东南地区聚集的显著特征。五年来处于东南地区的河东、河西、东丽、塘沽、大港、津南6区新增人口25.39万人,增长了7.55%,占全市总人口的比重也增加了1.08个百分点。与此同时,随着武清高新产业园区、宝坻开发区、绿色种植基地示范区的建设,人口向北部聚集的态势也初见端倪,五年来两区共增人口6.45万人,增长了4.37%,占全市总人口的比重增长了0.02个百分点。

城镇化水平是反映一个地区现代化程度的重要标志。近年来天津市城镇规模不断扩大,城镇人口规模也有了较大增长,推进了天津市城镇化进程。天津市城镇化水平2005年末由"九五"末的71.99%上升到75.11%以上。

三、总体人口年龄结构继续老化

天津市是较早进入老龄化社会的城市,近年来,天津持续呈现低龄人口减少,老年人口增加的人口特点。2005年,全市常住人口中0-14岁人口占总人口的比重为12.60%;15-64岁人口占总人口的77.72%;65岁及以上人口占总人口的9.68%。与2000年相比,0-14岁人口的比重下降了4.13个百分点,65岁及以上人口的比重上升了1.30个百分点。65岁以上老年人口已达100.90万,比2000年增加17.06万人。少年人口比重的不断下降和老年人口比重的持续增长,使老少比由2000年的50.07%上升到2005年的76.81%。老化程度已显示出由早期向中期发展的态势。

四、人口的性别构成相对平稳

2005年,在全市常住人口中,男性人口有523.47万人,占总人口的50.21%,女性人口有519.06万人,占49.79%,性别比为100.85,即每100个女性人口,相对有100.85个男性。比2000年时的103.99相比,缩小了3.14个点。

五、人口文化素质进一步提高

近年来,天津市着力提高全民素质,加大教育投入,教育事业发展步伐不断加快,人口总体文化素质进一步提高。天津市2005年在全市6岁及以上人口中,接受过大学本科及以上文化教育的人口所占比例达6.8%,接受过大学专科文化教育的人口比例达7.22%,接受过高中、中专教育的比例为21.03%,接受过初中教育的比例为37.86%,接受过小学教育的比例为21.84%。与2000年相比,接受过大学本科及以上、大学专科和初中文化教育的人口比例上升,分别上升了2.77、1.80和1.56个百分点。

平均受教育年限是衡量人口文化素质的标志之一。五年来,天津市6岁及以上人口平均受教育年限由2000年的8.93年,提高到9.42年。

这些变化表明天津市人口的文化程度已由初低级向中高级转变,体现了天津市提高人口素质和培养大量合格人才,为早日跨入现代化城市的基础性战略部署已逐步取得成效。

(姜岩)

就业规模迅速扩大 就业结构显著改善

"十五"期间,天津市实施积极有效的劳动就业政策,不断创新工作思路,千方百计增加就业岗位,就业再就业工作收到明显效果,呈现就业总量增加,就业结构优化的良好势头。

一、就业总量迅速扩大

1.经济发展带动就业年均增加11.13万人

"十五"期间,天津市的经济和社会发展取得了令人瞩目的成就,为促进就业创造了有利条件,带动了就业总量的增长。2005年末,全市社会从业人员总量达到542.52万人,比2000年末增加55.63万人,平均每年增加11.13万人就业。特别是"十五"后三年,就业总量呈现迅速扩大的态势,三年中年均增加16.64万

人，使天津市的就业压力得到有效缓解。

五年中，新增就业岗位91.5万个，实现新增就业岗位数量多于新增下岗失业人员数量，分流安置下岗失业人员57.2万人。城镇登记失业率由2002年的3.91%下降到2005年的3.7%，下降了0.21个百分点，城镇登记失业人数由12.9万人下降到11.7万人，减少了1.2万人，使城镇登记失业人员和失业率保持在与天津市经济发展相适应的较低常量，有效地促进了经济建设和社会发展。

2.困难群体就业得到有效缓解

针对就业困难群体，通过政府出资购买、大力开发社会公益性岗位、发展公益性再就业公司等措施手段实施就业援助，建立了困难群体再就业帮扶机制，帮助和促进“4050”下岗失业人员再就业。先后开发了公共卫生保洁、劳动保障协管、交通协管、旧楼区准物业管理等多渠道社会公益性岗位，安排下岗失业人员4.3万人实现再就业，扩大了就业容量，缓解了下岗失业人员特别是“4050”人员的就业困难。

3.就业方式灵活多样

随着劳动力市场建设的日趋成熟，市场导向就业机制不断完善，“劳动者自主择业、市场调节就业和政府促进就业”的机制初步建立，劳动者就业观念发生了重大变化，企业用工机制改革不断深入，就业方式呈现多样化，各种灵活就业方式越来越被各类单位和个人所接受。2005年末，全市城镇单位中使用各类其他从业人员24.2万人，是“九五”期末时其他从业人员的2.9倍。

二、就业结构显著改善

五年来，全市呈现一、二产业从业人员比重下降，第三产业从业人员比重迅速提高的良好态势。“十五”期末，全市三次产业就业人员的比重为15.1:41.9:43.0，与“九五”期末的16.7:45.6:37.7相比，一、二产业从业人员比重分别下降1.6和3.7个百分点，第三产业从业人员比重上升5.3个百分点。

1.第三产业成为扩大就业的主导产业

到2005年末，全市第三产业就业总量达到233.35万人，比“九五”期末增加了49.9万人，增长27.2%，比重提高5.3个百分点。其中，城镇第三产业从业人员达到168.33万人，比“九五”期末增加30.01万人，比重提高7.2个百分点。第三产业已成为吸收劳动力的重要渠道，为拉动就业增长发挥了重要作用，其对全市就业增长的贡献率达到89.7%。

2.第二产业优化调整

随着第二产业资本技术构成的不断提高，在产品创新、机制转换的过程中，劳动力结构也在震荡调整，一方面大量淘汰低素质劳动力，另一方面对高素质、高技能人才呈现出旺盛的需求，表现为大量减员的同时又出现较大的人员需求，呈现总量稳定、结构优化的良好局面。到2005年末，第二产业社会从业人员227.38万人，比“九五”期末增加了5.23万人，就业比重降低了3.7个百分点。

三、非公经济成为重要的就业增长点

“十五”期间，天津市非公有制经济快速发展，成为全市经济的重要组成部分，在非公有制经济实体中就业的人员也显著增加，2005年末达到262.2万人，比2000年末增加147.8万人。非公有制经济从业人员占全部从业人员的比重由23.5%上升到48.3%，提高24.8个百分点。

1.私营个体经济成为重要的就业增长点

私营个体经济依靠灵活性优势迅速发展壮大，成为解决就业的重要渠道。2005年末，全市私营个体经济从业人员达到114.17万人，比“九五”期末增加了55.1万人，增长了近1倍，占全部从业人员比重达到21%，提高了8.9个百分点。其中私营经济从业人员由2000年末的37.95万人迅速增长到2005年末的88.71万人，增长了1.3倍，占全部从业人员比重达到16.4%，比2000年末提高了8.6个百分点。据市工商部门统计，个体经济从业人员2005年末达到25.46万人(市工商局按从事个体经济的登记注册人数)，占全部从业人员比重为4.7%。

2.三资企业从业人员迅速增长

各类合资、合作经营、外商独资经营企业迅速发展，从业人员队伍迅速壮大，为天津市经济增长、扩大社会就业发挥了重要作用。“十五”期间，天津市三资企业从业人员由36.6万人发展到51.1万人，增长了39.6%，占全市从业人员比重由7.5%提高到9.4%，提高了1.9个百分点。

(杨霞)

城市居民生活质量不断提升

“十五”期间在全市经济保持持续、快速增长的同时，城市居民家庭收入水平增长加快，生活质量不断改善，社会保障体系进一步完善。

一、居民家庭可支配收入增速加快

据市城调队1500户抽样调查资料显示，2005年天津市城市居民家庭人均可支配收入为12639元，比2000年增长66.2%，年平均增长速度为10.7%。

1.工资及补贴收入是推动居民家庭收入增长的最主要因素

“十五”期间，随着天津企业经济效益不断提高，单位从业人员劳动报酬稳步增加；在财政收入快速增长的基础上，机关事业单位职工工资有了较大幅度提高；全方位开放格局的形成，其他所有制单位吸收了大量就业人员，使家庭中工资及补贴收入保持平稳较快增长，成为“十五”期间城市居民家庭收入加快增长的最主要的因素。2005年天津市城市居民家庭来自工资及补贴方面的收入人均8016元，比2000年增长67.7%，年均增速达到10.9%。

2.个体经济健康发展，居民家庭投资领域拓宽，收入来源多元化

随着就业观念、就业形式、就业格局的变化，非工资性收入已成为家庭收入重要组成部分。“十五”期间天津市加大对个体私营经济的扶植力度，市政府《关于促进个体私营经济和中小企业发展有关问题的意见》政策的落实，为个体私营经济健康发展提供了有利保证。居民家庭来自个体经营净收益成倍增加，2005年家庭人均个体经营净收益666元，比2000年增长2.5倍。

居民投资意识的增强，市场投资渠道的拓宽，居民所得红利、利息和各类投资收益等财产性收入日益增多。2005年家庭人均财产性收入148元，比2000年增长32.2%。其中，随着收入水平的提高和住房条件的改善，购房投资的居民增多，出租房屋收入迅速增长，2005年家庭人均出租房屋收入比2002年增长5.6倍；住房市场的启动，带动了住房公积金的使用，2005年居民家庭人均提取住房公积金收入为218元。

3.社保体系更加完善，离退休人员和低收入群体得到实惠

“十五”期间，天津市连续多年提高离退休人员养老待遇标准，并补齐企业离退休人员统筹外退休金，实现了退休金足额发放，使居民家庭收入中来自养老金收入大幅增长。2005年城市居民家庭来自离退休人员养老金收入人均3377元，比2000年增长70.5%，年均递增11.3%。

在“十五”期间，天津市出台了多项保障措施，提高了最低工资标准、失业人员救济金标准以及最低生活保障标准，困难职工和困难家庭生活得到“应保尽保”。2005年10%最低收入家庭的人均可支配收入比2000年增长43.7%，年均递增7.5%。

二、消费热点纷呈，生活质量显著提高

“十五”期间，天津市城市居民家庭生活质量显著提高，消费观念和消费结构发生明显变化，居民家庭用于吃、穿、用的消费比重下降，用于医疗保健、交通和通讯、居住方面的消费比重上升。2005年，居民家庭用于食品支出占消费性支出的比重为36.7%，比2000年下降3.4个百分点；用于衣着支出的比重为7.2%，比2000年下降1.7个百分点；用于家庭设备用品及服务支出的比重为5.5%，比2000年下降6.3个百分点；用于杂项商品和服务支出的比重为3.3%，比2000年下降1.5个百分点，而居民家庭用于医疗保健、交通和通讯、居住方面支出所占比重分别为10.2%、10.3%和13.4%，分别比2000年上升了3.6个、4.6个和4.2个百分点。调查显示，2005年城市居民家庭消费性支出为9653元，比2000年增长57.7%，年平均增长速度为9.5%。

1.食品支出增加，在外用餐消费快速增长

“十五”期间，随着天津市居民家庭生活水平的不断提高，越来越多的居民家庭更加注重生活质量和生活品位，绿色食品、方便食品倍受青睐，家庭在外用餐支出明显增加。2005年城市居民家庭人均用于食品类支出为3543元，比2000年增长44.3%。其中，家庭人均在外用餐支出比2000年增长1.1倍，占食品总支出的比重达23.9%。

2.衣着消费档次提高

“十五”期间，居民的衣着消费稳步上升，成衣消费增加，且更加追求高档、时尚和个性化。在近年来市场上衣着总体价格水平下降的情况下，居民家庭购买服装和鞋类的混合平均单价却不断上升。2005年天津市城市居民家庭用于衣着类支出人均699元，比2000年增长28.4%。

3.新兴耐用消费品迅速普及

新兴家庭设备迅速普及，“十五”期间居民家庭以电动助力车、家用电脑、微波炉等为代表的新的家电产品消费增势强劲。到2005年末，城市居民家庭百户已拥有电动助力车11.1辆，家用电脑51.1台，微波炉74.3台，淋浴热水器86.5台，影碟机56.1台，摄像机

5.7台，消毒碗柜2.6台，饮水机40.1台，健身器材3.1套。

4.医疗保健消费增幅显著

天津市居民家庭自我保健意识进一步增强，“花钱买健康，健康是财富”已被广大居民家庭认同，“十五”期间，居民家庭用于医疗保健支出显著增长。2005年天津市城市居民家庭人均用于医疗保健支出996元，比2000年增长1.4倍。主要是滋补保健品、保健器具和药品费支出增加。

5.汽车消费成为最大亮点，移动电话拥有量超过固定电话

2005年天津市城市居民家庭人均用于交通和通讯方面的支出为998元，比2000年增长1.9倍。“十五”期间，随着天津市畅通工程和卡口路段拓宽改造工程的相继完工，市区道路交通状况和交通设施进一步改善；公交行业淘汰中小型客车、购进大批节能、环保大客车的投入运营，让天津市广大居民外出更加方便、舒适、快捷，居民家庭交通费支出较快增长。同时，由于2004年部分家用汽车价格下调及新款车的推出，造就了天津市车市火爆。调查数据显示，居民家庭购买的车型以经济型轿车为主，并开始由低档向中档车发展。在汽车销售价格不断下降的情况下，居民平均购车单价由每辆4－7万元向10万元左右车型发展，拥有私家车的居民家庭越来越多，截至2005年末，天津市城市居民家庭百户拥有家用汽车3辆，比2000年增加2.8辆，增长14倍。

信息产业长足发展，为居民信息消费增长提供了基础。截至2005年末，天津市城市居民家庭百户拥有移动电话已达122.1部，普通固定电话93.4部，移动电话的百户拥有量超过固定电话，居民家庭通信消费结构发生了根本性改变。同时，手机拥有量的增加带动了通信服务支出大幅增长，2005年比2000年增长1.1倍。

6.教育、旅游、健身、娱乐消费明显增长

“十五”期间，居民家庭更加重视并加大对教育的投入，精神文化生活需求也不断扩大，旅游、健身、娱乐已成为居民家庭业余生活的消费主流。2005年城市居民家庭人均用于教育文化娱乐和服务支出为1284元，比2000年增长56.2%。其中，用于各种教育的支出比2000年增长81.9%，用于参观游览、健身活动和团体旅游等文化娱乐服务支出比2000年增长1.1倍。另据专项调查资料显示，黄金周每人出游一次花费由2001年的211.80元，上升为2005年的301.57元，增长了42.4%，黄金周旅游“大餐”彰显黄金本色。

7.美容成为消费新热点

“十五”期间，随着人民生活水平的不断提高和天津市美容业的进一步规范，美容消费正呈现专业化、品牌化和高质化趋势。美容消费人群和消费产品迅速扩张。美容产业正在成为继房地产、汽车、通信和旅游之后的第五大消费热点。2005年城市居民家庭人均用于美容支出比2000年增长1倍；家庭人均用于美容化妆品支出比2000年增长71.5%。

8.购建房支出增势强劲，居住条件明显改善

“十五”期间，随着天津市城市规划建设项目的实施，海河开发建设的全面铺开，加之一大批适合中低收入家庭的经济适用房竣工并交付使用及二级房屋市场公产住房置换程序的进一步规范，使广大居民家庭在住房消费上有了更大的选择余地。2005年天津市城市居民家庭人均用于购建房支出达到2800元，比2000年增长1.1倍。截至2005年末，居民家庭拥有产权住房的比率已达53.1%，拥有两居室及以上住房的家庭占71.2%。

9.居民家庭社会保障意识进一步增强

“十五”期间天津市努力扩大社会保障覆盖面，加大单位征缴力度，广大居民家庭自我保障意识也进一步增强。2005年天津市城市居民家庭人均用于社会保障支出813元，比2002年增长81.3%。

10.服务性消费发展潜力巨大

“十五”期间，随着第三产业的发展和居民收入的不断增加，居民生活质量由生存型向享受型发展，城市居民对服务性消费需求不断上升。2005年居民家庭人均服务性消费支出为2798元，比2002年增长37.8%。

（吴向晨）

农村居民生活水平明显提高

“十五”期间，天津市积极贯彻落实中央“多予、少取、放活”的惠农方针，相继出台了一系列促进农村居民增收和改善农村居民生活的重要举措。农村居民收入水平快速提高，生活质量显著改善。

一、农村居民收入实现两位数增长

“十五”时期，在各项有利政策的带动下，加之近

两年来主要农产品价格回升，天津市农村居民人均纯收入连跨五千、六千、七千三个千元大台阶，从2000年的4370元增加到2005年7202元，增加2832元，年均增加额达566元以上，年均增速10.5%，继续保持两位数增长。

1.工资性收入仍是农村居民增收的主要渠道

“十五”期间，在多种政策的带动下，农村居民工资性收入较快增长。2005年人均达到3840元，比2000年增加1467元，年均增加293元，年均增速10.1%，占纯收入的比重为53.3%。“十五”期间，工资性收入对纯收入增长的贡献率达51.8%。

农村居民从本地企业劳动得到的收入快速增长。2005年，天津市农村居民从本地企业劳动得到收入达2512元，年均增长10.8%，其中从私营个体企业得到收入1478元，年均增长30.0%；从股份制和“三资”等企业得到收入281元，年均增长32.8%。

外出打工者增多，外出从业收入增加。“十五”期间，天津市农村劳动力转移步伐日益加快。据测算，2005年，天津市外出从业劳动力达到34万余人，比2000年增加14万人左右，年均增长11.2%。随着外出从业劳动力的增多，农村居民外出从业收入快速增长。2005年，天津市农村居民外出从业收入人均达251元，比2000年增加了108元，年均增加22元，年均增长11.9%。

政策增资带动乡、村等非企业组织工资性收入进一步增长。“十五”期间，天津市农村居民人均从非企业组织中得到的收入由585元增加到684元，年均增长3.2%，其中从行政事业单位得到收入204元，年均增长10.6%；从乡村集体得到的收入480元，年均增长0.8%。

2.惠农政策相继出台，拉动农业收入走出低谷

“十五”期间，天津市相继出台了加大农业结构调整力度，大力发展农业产业化，全面取消农业税，实行粮食直接补贴、良种补贴、购买大型农机具补贴等惠农增收政策，有效地降低了农业生产成本，极大地调动了广大农村居民的生产积极性，加之近两年来，粮食、生猪等主要农产品价格回升，天津市农村居民家庭经营农业收入逐渐走出低谷。2005年，天津市农村居民家庭经营农业纯收入人均达到1814元，比2000年增加了574元，年均增收达到115元，比“九五”期间多75元，年均增速达到7.9%，比“九五”期间提高了4.0个百分点，占纯收入的比重为25.2%，比2000年降低了3.2个百分点。“十五”期间，农业纯收入对纯收入增长的贡献率达15.1%，比“九五”期间提高了2.9个百分点。

从农业内部结构看，2005年种植业收入人均1399元，年均增加85元，年均增长7.5%；畜牧业收入人均191元，年均增加17元，年均增长12.7%；渔业收入人均208元，年均增加12元，年均增长6.8%。

3.家庭经营非农业发展壮大，非农业收入全面增长

“十五”期间，天津市农村小城镇建设速度的不断加快，为农村居民家庭经营建筑业、批发和零售业、居民服务和其他服务业提供了广阔的发展空间。各区县充分利用各自的资源优势，大力发展旅游业，农家旅店如雨后春笋应运而生，并不断发展壮大。2005年，天津市农村居民家庭经营非农业收入达1145元，比2000增加了624元，年均增加125元，比“九五”期间多49元，年均增速17.1%，占纯收入的比重为15.9%，比2000年提高了4.0个百分点。

4.农村经济持续快速发展，转移性、财产性收入显著增加

“十五”期间，小城镇建设步伐日益加快，经济开发区和各类工业园区不断增多，大量农村耕地被征用，外来打工人员逐年增加，城乡结合部、开发区和工业园区附近居民纷纷出租富余房屋，使天津市农村居民土地征用补偿收入、转让土地承包经营权收入租金收入等从无到有由少到多。从2004年开始，天津市对种粮农民实行了粮食直接补贴、良种补贴和购买大型农机具补贴等扶持政策，使农民每年得到的补贴收入近30元。在上述因素拉动下，2005年，天津市农村居民转移性、财产性收入人均达到403元，比2000年增加一倍多，年均增速15.7%，占纯收入的比重为5.6%。

二、生活水平大幅度提高，消费结构进一步优化

“十五”时期，随着收入的快速增长，天津市农村居民的生活水平节节升高”。2005年天津市农村居民人均生活消费支出达3590元，比2000年增加1197元，增长50.0%，年均增长8.5%，比“九五”时期提高了1.6个百分点。

1.恩格尔系数快速降低，居民饮食习惯明显转变

2005年，天津市农村居民人均食品消费支出1376元，比2000年增加356元，增长34.9%，年均增长6.2%，比“九五”时期快了5.4个百分点。食品消费占生活消费支出的比重，即恩格尔系数为38.3，比2000降低了4.3个百分点，农村居民生活大步向全面小康

迈进。

在食品支出增长的同时，天津市农村居民家庭饮食结构和饮食习惯也发生了明显转变。2005年天津市农村居民人均在外饮食消费支出155元，比2000年增加90元，年均增速达18.9%，拉动“十五”时期食品消费支出增幅提高了8.8个百分点，成为天津市农民饮食消费的新亮点。

2.居住支出大幅上升，居住环境显著改善

“十五”期间，天津市进一步加快农村城市化和小城镇建设步伐，农村房地产市场迅猛发展。2005年，天津市农村居民人均居住支出844元，比2000年增加392元，增长86.7%，年均增长13.3%。人均住房面积超过26.1平方米，比“九五”末期2000年的23.6平方米，增加了2.5平方米。

“十五”期间，天津市先后实施了户厕改造和人畜饮水解困等惠农工程，农村居民居住质量逐渐提高。调查显示，2005年末，天津市饮用自来水的农户比重达61.7%，使用水冲式厕所的农户比重达43.7%，比“九五”末期分别提高了22个和28.2个百分点；整治村容村貌，加强街道路面建设，使室外道路为硬质路面的农户比重提高了18.3个百分点，农村居民的生活条件得到显著改善。

3.电话、手机迅速普及，交通通讯支出成倍增长

“十五”时期，固定电话、移动电话和小汽车等交通通讯工具在天津市农村居民家庭中日渐普及。2005年，天津市农村居民人均交通通讯消费支出达270元，比2000年增加162元，增长1.5倍，年均增长20.1%。2005年天津市农村居民家庭每百户拥有普通电话近88部，比“九五”末期的51部增加了37部，增长72.5%；拥有移动电话89部，比“九五”末期的11部增加了78部，增长了7.1倍；拥有生活用汽车近6辆，比“九五”末期的2.2辆增加了3.8辆，增长了1.7倍。

4.时尚观念不断强化，衣着消费支出连年增加

时尚观念的不断强化，天津市农村居民在衣着方面的消费支出连年增加。2005年，天津市农村居民人均衣着消费支出362元，比2000年增加139元，增长62.3%，年均增长10.2%，比“九五”时期快了6.7个百分点。

5.现代家电走入农家，生活质量持续攀升

“十五”期间，耐用消费品开始进入更新换代时期，百户拥有量稳步增长。如洗衣机由2000年的85台增加到2005年的95台，电冰箱由65台增长到84台。电动自行车、微波炉等现代家电悄然兴起，快速步入农家，拉进了农村与城市间的距离。

6.医疗保健意识逐步增强，医疗保健支出明显提高

“十五”时期，在经历了“非典”、“禽流感”疫情后，广大农村居民保健意识日益增强，农村新型医疗制度逐步推广。截至“十五”末期，天津市累计参加人数已近120万人，占全部乡村人口的30%，较好地解决了农民因患大病造成的生活困难和致贫、返贫问题。2005年，天津市农村居民医疗保健支出人均268元，比2000年增加116元，增长76.3%，年均增长12.0%。

7.旅游、娱乐渐成时尚，文教娱乐用品及服务支出稳步增长

近年来，随着天津市广大农村居民生活条件的改善，大家在平时看看报、下下棋、养养花、溜溜鸟、扭扭秧歌，自娱自乐，其乐融融，越发懂得享受生活，享受清闲。每逢节假日，休闲娱乐，购物旅游，已不再是奢侈的行为。据调查，2005年三个黄金周期间，天津市农村居民累计外出人次数已达240万人次。

农村居民家庭更加注重教育投资。2005年，天津市农村居民人均教育服务支出为186元，比2000年增加了23元，年均增长2.7%。每百户拥有家用电脑10台，其中接入互联网的2台，农村居民信息化程度大幅提高。2005年，天津市农村居民文教娱乐用品及服务消费支出人均252元，比2000年增加47元，增长22.9%，年均增长4.2%。

8.消费结构优化，农村居民生活向享受型发展

农村居民生活向享受型发展的步伐日益加快，消费结构进一步优化。2005年，天津市农村居民服务性消费支出人均1049元，比2000年增加482元，增长85.0%，年均增长13.1%。从支出构成看，2005年食品、居住和衣着三项基本消费，占生活消费支出的比重仍然位居前三位，比重分别为38.3%、23.5%和10.1%；享受型消费支出占生活消费支出的比重为48.5%，比2000年的44%提高了4.5个百分点，消费结构进一步调整优化。

按照全国农村全面小康标准测算，2005年，天津市农村全面小康社会实现程度已接近70%，比“九五”末期提高了10余个百分点，平均每年前进2个百分点，这标志着天津市农村居民生活质量和生活水平在

“十五”期间实现了新的跨越，津郊农民生活越来越富足，越来越幸福。

（王福泉 张春华）

物价水平温和上涨

“十五”期间，整体价格总水平的变动幅度控制在合理的区间，既有利于促进国民经济持续、快速、健康发展，又能保障居民生活，保持社会稳定。

一、“十五”时期天津市物价运行的基本情况

“十五”时期，天津市积极应对“非典”和“禽流感”等突发事件，采取了有效措施，保持物价基本稳定，将物价涨幅控制在各方面都能承受的范围内，居民消费价格总水平保持了温和上涨。“十五”时期天津市居民消费价格累计上涨5.7%，年均递增1.1%，比“八五”时期的年均增长15.6%低14.5个百分点，比“九五”时期的年均增长2.0%低0.9个百分点。

在这一时期价格总水平变动经历了价格回暖、价格上升、涨幅回落三个阶段。第一阶段为“十五”前两年，即2001、2002年，在此期间上游产品价格仍处于下行通道，工业品出厂价格连续两年比上年同期下降4.1%。虽然市场自发力量开始复苏，但居民消费价格的上升依旧主要靠政策性调价拉动。由于积极的财政政策、稳健的货币政策和启动消费市场、扩大内需等政策的效果逐步显现，2001年居民消费价格总水平走出了长达3年的低谷，比上年同期上涨1.2%。但由于经济环境中的就业压力依然较大，有效需求仍显不足，市场物价下降局面尚未完全改变，2002年居民消费价格总水平再次出现回落，比上年同期下降0.4%。第二阶段为“十五”中期，即2003、2004年，由于我国主要农产品的种植面积和总产量连续几年减少，在产量下降和需求增长的双重压力下，农副产品类价格迅猛上涨；同时在经过连续几年的经济“加速增长”之后，经济运行中出现了“局部过热”现象，钢铁、有色金属、煤、电、油等一些主要生产资料供应出现了严重的“瓶颈”制约；加上随着世界经济复苏加快，尤其是制造业增长明显，国际市场上原材料价格出现了较明显的上涨，市场价格总水平出现回升。2003、2004年天津市工业品出厂价格分别比上年同期上涨了2.5%和4.1%，居民消费价格总水平也持续上涨，分别比上年同期上涨1.0%和2.3%。第三阶段为“十五”末期，即2005年，为了保持经济快速、平稳地运行，国家根据形势发展变化采取了“有保有压、区别对待”的宏观调控措施，进行适时适度微调，宏观经济的结构性过热等问题得到较明显的抑制，经济继续朝着健康协调的方向发展，各种产品价格涨幅回落。与上年同期相比，2005年天津市工业品出厂价格仅上涨0.1%；居民消费价格也呈温和上涨，比上年同期上涨1.5%，涨幅比上年回落0.8个百分点。

“十五”时期，天津市工业品出厂价格总水平年平均下降0.4%，居民消费价格总水平年平均上涨1.1%，商品零售价格总水平年平均下降1.2%。

二、“十五”时期天津市物价运行的特点

1.食品价格的高低对价格总水平的回升起着决定作用

食品类价格历来是牵动物价上涨的“龙头”，“十五”时期天津市食品类价格的变动对价格总水平的回升仍然起着举足轻重的作用。2001年由于严重的旱情造成粮食大量减产，致使粮价逐步回升，并带动其它农副产品的价格止跌回升。2002年随着农业种植结构的进一步调整和深化以及科学技术的普及和应用，经济作物的生产也发生了突飞猛进地发展。由于品种的丰富和货源的充足，主要农副产品价格稳中趋降。但受国际和国内市场供求关系的影响，2003年、2004年粮食价格的恢复性上升带动了相关食品价格的全面攀升。由于国家连续实施的一系列重视农业生产、促进农业增长的政策，使得全国粮食恢复性增产，粮食生产情况向好，粮食供给形势继续改善，从而粮食价格在高价位上平稳回落。粮油的稳定也使主要副食品价格上涨缺乏动力，涨幅回落。

“十五”期间天津市食品消费价格累计上升17.5%，年均增长3.3%，意味着到2005年天津市食品消费价格总体水平比“九五”末期2000年高17.5%。从构成食品类价格变动的十六类商品看，价格下降的只有两类。与居民生活息息相关的“菜篮子”、“米袋子”价格涨幅止跌回升，“十五”期间粮食价格年均递增6.3%，肉禽及其制品价格年均递增4.3%，蛋类价格年均递增6.4%，水产品价格年均递增8.4%，菜类价格年均递增3.5%，干鲜果类价格年均递增4.7%。

2.主要工业消费品价格继续走低

“十五”时期市场供过于求的总体格局依然没有

发生大的实质性变化，多数工业消费品仍处于供大于求的状态，多数日用工业消费品价格仍旧继续下降。“十五”时期，在工业出厂价格中，耐用消费品年平均下降5.3%。在居民消费价格中，衣着类年平均下降7.8%，降幅较“九五”时期扩大7.8个百分点；西药价格年平均下降8.1%，降幅较“九五”时期扩大6.4个百分点；通讯工具价格年平均下降24.4%，降幅较“九五”时期扩大16.8个百分点。

但自2003年上半年起工业消费品市场供过于求的局面开始出现转好的信号，部分商品价格止跌转升或降幅趋缓。据商务部对2005下半年600种主要商品供求情况的分析，供过于求的商品占71.3%，比供求矛盾最严重的2002年下半年缩小16.7个百分点。“十五”期间包括洗衣机、电冰箱、空调器等商品的家庭设备类价格年平均下降4.8%，降幅较“九五”时期缩小0.2个百分点；包括电视机、照相机、音响、摄像机等文娱用耐用消费品价格年平均下降8.3%，降幅较“九五”时期缩小5.8个百分点。

3.居住和服务项目价格保持合理上涨

为加快住房制度改革，“十五”期间天津市连续两次上调了公有住房租金，带动全市房租价格年均上涨8.0%。针对天津市水资源严重短缺的情况，又先后两次上调了居民生活用的水价格，带动水价年均上涨14.6%。同时为促进城市基础设施建设，又对民用电、管道燃气、煤制品、取暖费等价格也进行了调整，由于上述项目价格的调整，使“十五”期间居住类价格平均每年递增4.4%。为促进公用公益事业的发展，解决基础产品、基础设施、公用事业价格结构性矛盾，缓和行业亏损的状况以及减轻财政压力，“十五”期间天津市适时适度地对学杂费、托幼费、医疗保健服务价格、公交汽车票和出租汽车票等服务项目类价格进行了调整，并对公园门票价格实行淡旺季价格，放开了幼儿园收费。“十五”时期天津市服务项目类价格年均以4.8%的速度上涨，其中学杂托幼费价格累计上涨63.9%，年均递增10.4%；市区公共交通价格累计上涨41.3%，年均递增7.2%。

“十五”期间，天津市继续完善价格形成机制改革，坚持深化价格改革，整顿和规范市场价格秩序，不断理顺价格关系，充分发挥了价格的杠杆作用；注意把握好价格调控的方向、时机、节奏和力度，将价格总水平的变动幅度控制在合理的区间。在宏观经济形势复杂，全国价格总水平变化较大的情况下，天津市价格总水平始终能够保持相对平稳运行的态势。

（于海芳）

重点企业改制稳步推进

“十五”期间，现代企业制度框架已在天津大多数企业中建立起来，企业通过改制内部管理更加科学化，经济效益明显好转。

一、企业改制面逐年扩大，公司治理结构不断完善

截至2005年底，实施监测的179户重点企业中，有157户企业进行了改制，改制面达87.7%，比2000年73.8%的改制面提高了13.9个百分点；已改制的157户企业中，成立董事会的有156户，占99.4%；成立监事会的有114户，占72.6%，成立股东会的有81户，占改制企业的69.3%（改制为国有独资公司的41户企业不需要成立股东会）；公司法所赋予企业股东会、董事会和监事会的各项职权90%以上都能得到有效实施，在已改制的企业中全部明确了出资人，用法律来界定出资者和企业经营者之间的关系，明确各自的权利、义务和责任；企业所有权和经营权逐步得到分离，企业经营体制更趋向市场经济运行规则。

二、实现了投资主体多元化和企业内部管理科学化

通过建立现代企业制度的改革，重点监测企业的资本金结构发生较大变化。截至2005年底，国家资本金所占比重由2000年的63.5%下降到35.2%，减少了28.3个百分点；法人资本所占比重由2000年的24.7%上升到45.2%，增加了20.5个百分点；外商资本所占比重由2000年的6.3%上升到11.7%，增加了5.4个百分点，个人资本所占比重由2000年的4.2%上升到7.3%，增加了3.1个百分点，其他资本所占比重的增加，表明企业投资主体正在向多元化方向转变。

企业内部劳动、人事和分配制度改革进展顺利，各项管理制度发生了深刻变化。如用工上形成职工能进能出、管理人员能上能下，分配上形成员工收入能增能减的长效激励机制，截至2005年底，179户重点企业在劳动用工方面，有178户全面实现劳动合同制度，占总数的99.4%，150户已实行全员竞争上岗，占总数的83.8%;111户企业已不存在“干部”和“工人”的身份界限,占总数的62.0%;142户企业内部管理人员实行公开竞聘,占总数的79.3%;174户企业能够给职工足额缴纳社会保险金,占97.2%。

三、各主要经济指标保持稳步增长

资产与投资同步增长。从2000年起截至2005年底,重点监测企业户平均年末资产达到13.8亿元,平均每年增长11.5%;户平均累计对外投资为1.02亿元,平均每年增长18.1%;户平均股东权益为5.4亿元,平均每年增长12.5%。

主要经济指标增幅强劲,经济效益大幅提高。五年来,重点企业坚持科技创新,加大新产品开发和设备改造力度,在产品增值企业增效上下功夫,不断增强企业产品市场竞争力,产品销售收入大幅上升。2005年重点监测的179户重点企业,全年主营业务收入达到2062.9亿元,平均每户企业11.5亿元,年均增长24.8%;户平均利润总额达到6470.2万元,年均增长66.6%。

从业人员劳动报酬增加。2005年179户重点监测企业,从业人员的人均劳动报酬达到2.89万元,比2000年增加1.52万元。

四、整体综合经济效益指标提高

“十五”期间,由于重点企业经营机制转变加上产业结构调整,使企业整体素质和各项综合经济指标都有很大提高,资产的利用效率及回报收益也都得到相应的提高。截至2005年,劳动生产率由23.31万元/人上升到73.79万元/人,上升了3.2倍,总资产使用率由47.8%上升到83.7%,上升35.9个百分点,总资产报酬率由2.0%上升到5.5%,上升3.5个百分点。资产利税率由2.8%上升到8.1%,比2000年提高5.3个百分点;净资产收益率由1.0%上升到8.9%,比2000年提高7.9个百分点。表明“十五”期间天津重点企业改制进程和整体经营状况处于良好水平。

(许士龙)

企业集团进入快速发展阶段

“十五”期间,天津企业集团优化产业结构,加速资源整合,充分显示出集团化经营的优势,截止到2005年底,资产规模达亿元以上的企业集团170家,经营业务遍布三次产业的41个行业,并且培育出一批较强经济实力和经营能力的重点大型企业集团,成为天津经济发展中的龙头企业。

一、改制取得新进展

经过几年的努力,天津企业集团的体制改革取得了明显成效,截至2005年,170家资产规模达亿元以上的企业集团基本都按照现代企业制度的要求建立了母子公司体制,并且有95.3%的母公司和其所属的全部子公司已明确了出资人。随着集团母公司核心地位的加强,使其在对集团内各项事务的统一决策中发挥着更重要的作用。

在170家企业集团中,已有164家的集团母公司完成了企业改制,改制面高达96.5%。在已改制的集团母公司中,能够按照公司法的规定要求建立股东会、董事会和监事会的分别占已完成改制企业集团总数的57.9%、96.9%和75.0%。同时,在建有董事会的集团母公司中,有74.2%的董事会成员是由出资人委派;有24.0%的董事会设立了独立董事;有22.0%的董事会下设了专门委员会;总经理由董事会聘任的占55.3%。

二、内部管理进一步规范

从劳动人事制度上看:2005年,在170家企业集团中,多数企业集团实行了以劳动合同、公开竞聘和竞争上岗为主的多种形式的劳动人事管理制度。其中,全面实行劳动合同制度的占90.6%;实行全员竞争上岗制度的占80.6%;管理人员实行公开竞聘、择优录用制度的占78.8%。同时有占68.8%的企业集团已打破“工人”、“干部”界限。

在收入分配制度上,有87.1%的企业集团实行以岗位工资为主的工资制度,44.1%的企业集团实行企业经营者年薪制;44.7%和31.2%的企业集团实行科技人员工资分配激励机制和工资集体协商制;按照经营者和职工持股分配的企业集团均占14.7%左右。

在内部制度建设方面,有 89.4%的企业集团建立了重大事项决策程序制度;72.9%的企业集团建立了预算管理制度;48.2%的企业集团建有财务总监委派制度;建立奖惩制度且能够严格执行的企业集团占78.8%。

三、经济实力明显增强

“十五”期间,天津170家企业集团各项经济指标均保持快速平稳增长,比2000年有较大幅度提高,经济效益增长显著。

截至2005年底，天津170家企业集团资产总额已达4312.1亿元，“十五”期间年平均增长14.2％，其中超百亿元资产企业集团已达7家，资产总计占170家企业集团的42.0％。所有者权益由2000年的794.9亿元增加到1495.5亿元，年均增长13.5％。

2005年，170家企业集团完成营业收入2606.5亿元，五年间，年均增长18.5％。其中营业收入在50亿元以上的企业集团已达13家，超百亿元企业集团8家。出口销售总额折人民币151.5亿元，年平均增速为4.6％。2004年两家企业集团中首次出现对境外投资，投资额3054万元，2005年两集团对外投资再次增加2536万元，标志着天津企业集团开始“走出去”，向国际市场发展。

2005年，170家企业集团实现利润97.4亿元，年均增长53.8％，利润总额超亿元企业集团20家，充分显示出天津企业集团经营能力和经济效益的大幅提升。

从反映企业经营质量的综合效益指标看，劳动生产率55.2万元/人，比2000年增加了35.2万元/人，增长超过1.6倍；总资产使用率、净资产收益率、成本费用利润率、资金利润率、销售利润率、资产利税率和总资产报酬率均比2000年有不同程度的提高。综合效益指标的迅速提升说明天津企业集团经营质量与企业素质的全面提高。

四、发展潜力增大

截止到2005年底，170家企业集团研发人员8832人，五年间年均增长5.4％，研发人员的人均劳动报酬由2000年的人均1.3万元增长到2.6万元，年均增长14.9％。

从研发费用的投入看：170家企业集团全年支出研发费用总额为24.5亿元，年均增长55％。

从新产品销售看：170家企业集团全年的新产品销售收入总额达171.1亿元，年均增长9.4％。

五、第三产业发展形势喜人

“十五”期间，随着天津产业结构的调整，第三产业企业集团获得了较快地发展。截止到2005年底，第三产业集团的资产总额已达2023.7亿元，年均增长23.3％；所有者权益633.3亿元，年均增长21.7％；营业收入780.2亿元，年均增长17.6％；利润总额45.6亿元，年均增长47.2％。同时，第三产业集团的资产、所有者权益所占全部企业集团的比重分别比2000年提高14.9、11.8个百分点。

六、民营企业集团发展迅速

“十五”期间，天津民营企业集团获得了较快发展。截至2005年底，天津资产在亿元以上的民营企业集团已达99家，资产、收入、利润和从业人员分别占全市企业集团的21.7％、23.6％、38.7％和21.4％。并且涌现出一批如家世界集团、天士力集团、顺驰集团等在行业中起重要作用的大企业集团，引领着民营企业集团前进的方向。

七、在全市经济中的主导作用日益增强

170家企业集团中共包括成员企业1765家，占全市78749个经营性法人单位的2.2％。但从2005年主要经济指标来看，这些企业拥有的资产、营业收入和实现的利润已分别达到6123.1亿元、4532.6亿元和156.8亿元，从行业上看，170家企业集团在化学原料及化学品制造、医药制造业、黑色金属冶炼及压延加工业、房屋和土木工程建筑业、批发零售业和房地产业等行业上都具有一定或绝对优势。在天津重点支持的22家大企业集团、大公司中，基本涵盖了天津工业六大支柱行业和商业、建筑业，经济指标迅速增长，成为天津企业集团中的领头羊。

（杨波）

第1篇
CHAPTER 1

综 合
General Survey

自然状况(2005 年)

Natural Conditions,2005

地理位置:天津市位于北纬38度34分至40度15分,东经116度43分至118度 4 分之间,处于国际时区的东八区。地处华北平原的东北部,海河流域下游,东临渤海,北依燕山,西靠首都北京,距北京 120 公里。

Geographic Location :Located at latitude 38°34′N40°15′N and longitude 116°43′E118°04′E, Tianjin belongs to the 8th eastern international time zone. Tianjin lies on the northeast of North China Plain and the lower reaches of Haihe River Basin. On its east is Bohai Sea; north, Yanshan Mountain; and west, Beijing. In Tianjin, Only 120 kilometers away from Beijing.

地　势:天津市是"退海之地",绝大部分是由古黄河三次北徙冲积而成的平原,地势由西北山区向东南逐渐降低,呈簸箕形向渤海倾斜。有山地、丘陵和平原三种地形。平原面积占总面积的94%。一般海拔 2～5 米,最北部燕山南麓的低山丘陵区海拔在100～500米之间,最高处八仙山海拔1052米。

Topography: Most parts of Tianjin area are alluvial plain, created by ancient Yellow River's moving to north part three times. The topography is higher in the Northwest, lower in the Southeast, the whole topography inclines to Bohai Sea. There are three topography, including mountain, hill and plain. Plain occupies 94% of the total area. The general sea level elevation is 2～5 meters, that of North part hills is 100～500 meters, the highest site, Eight Immortals Desk Mountain 1,052 meters.

行政区域面积:天津市行政区域总面积11760平方公里。南北长189公里,东西宽117公里。其中市辖区面积7399平方公里,市辖县面积4361平方公里。疆域周长约1290.81公里,其中海岸线长153.33公里,陆界长约1137.48公里。

Area of the Administrative Region :The administrative region of Tianjin covers an area of 11,760 km^2, Tianjin is 189 km long from south to north and 117 km wide from east to west. Its urban districts cover an area of 7,399 km^2 and its rural counties cover 4,361 km^2. The circumference of the whole city is about 1290.814 km, including a coastline of 153.334 km and a land line of over 1137.48 km.

河　流:天津市地处海河流域下游,是海河五大支流南运河、子牙河、大清河、永定河、北运河的汇合处和入海口,素有"九河下梢"、"河海要冲"之称。

River:Tianjin locates at the lower reaches of Haihe River Basin, five major branches of Haihe River - South Canal, Ziya River, Daqing River, Yongding River, and North Canal - converge and flow into the sea. The city of Tianjin is well-known for its abundance in rivers and closeness to the sea.

气　候:天津属暖温带半湿润大陆季风型气候,夏季受海洋之惠、冬季受内陆补偿、四季分明,景象多姿。气候的主要特征是:季风显著、温差较大。

Climate:Located in the warm temperate zone, Tianjin has sub-humid continental monsoon climate. As it is influenced by the sea and ocean in Summer and by the continent in winter, the four seasons here are clearly cut, which results in a great variety of temperature throughout the year.

自然资源(2005 年)

天津自然资源丰富,这在国内外大城市中不多见。一是充足的油气资源。天津有渤海和大港两大油田,是国家重点开发的油气田,2005年产原油1783万吨、天然气8.8亿立方米。二是取之不尽的海盐资源。天津有153多公里的海岸线,中国最著名的海盐产区长芦盐场就位于这里,2005年产原盐230万吨,占全国海盐总产量的十分之一。三是丰富的金属和非金属矿产资源。金属矿产主要有锰硼石、锰、金、钨、钼、铜、锌、铁等10多种。非金属矿产主要有水泥石灰岩、重晶石、迭层石、大理石、天然石、紫砂陶土、麦饭石等,都具有较高的开采价值。四是蕴藏较为丰富的地下热水资源。水温多为30℃至90℃,具有埋藏浅、水质好的特点,已发现的10个具有勘探和开发利用价值的地热异常区,热水总储藏量达1103.6亿立方米,是中国迄今最大的中低温地热田。五是土地资源丰富。天津市土地总面积119.19万公顷。其中耕地面积44.55万公顷,占全市土地总面积的37.4.%;居民点及工矿用地26.25万公顷;未利用地面积13.82万公顷。全市的土地,除北部蓟县山区、丘陵外,其余地区大都是在深厚积沉物上发育的土壤。在海河下游的滨海地区有待开发的近1214平方公里的盐碱荒地,这些地区交通条件好,开发费用低,是国内其他大城市所不具备的。

Natural Resources, 2005

Tianjin enjoys a rich supply of natural resources, which is quite rare in large cities both at home and abroad. First of all, Tianjin has abundant oil and gas resources. Its Bohai and Dagang Oil Fields are key state oil and gas projects, In 2005, turning out 17,830,000 tons of crude oil and 880,000,000 m^3 of natural gas . Secondly, with its coastline stretching 153 km, Tianjin has inexhaustible sea salt resources. Changlu Salt Field, In 2005, with an annual output of 2,300,000 tons of salt (10% of the total sea salt output in China), is the most famous sea salt production base in China. Thirdly, Tianjin possesses rich mineral resources, metal and nonmetal. The major metal minerals include jimboite, manganese, gold, wolfram, molybdenum, copper, zinc, iron, etc.. The nonmetal minerals here - cement rock, barytes, stromatolith, marble, natural rock, purple sand porcelain clay, maifan stone, etc. - are of considerable mining values. Fourthly, plentiful underground warm water is available in Tianjin. The underground warm water temperature ranges from 30℃ to 90℃ and, in addition to its excellent quality, the warm water is deposited at a shallow position. In ten areas with geothermal resources worth further prospecting and tapping, the total hot water reserve amounts to 110.36 billion m3. This is the largest medium and low - temperature geothermal field in China. Fifthly, Tianjin has abundant land resources. The total area of land in Tianjin is 1,191,900 ha., including arable land 445,500 ha. (37.4% of the total land area of Tianjin), residential, industrial and mining land 262,500 ha., and unused land Area 138,200 ha.. Except for the mountainous and hilly areas in the north, the land in Tianjin abounds in fertile soil formed on a deep layer of accumulated matters. In the coastal area at the lower reaches of Haihe River, about 1214km^2 salt and alkaline wasteland and shallows have great potentials for development, and because of the convenient transportation in these areas, it is possible to develop the land at low cost. Such favorable conditions are not available in other large cities in China.

1-1　行政建制(2005 年底)

ADMINISTRATIVE DIVISIONS,(END OF 2005)

单位:个　　(unit)

项　目	Item	行政区域面积（平方公里）(sq. km)	街道办事处 Subdistrict Offices	居民委员会 Resident's Committees	镇政府 Town Governments	乡政府 Township Governments	村民委员会 Village Committees
全市总计	**Total**	**11 760**	**101**	**1 645**	**120**	**20**	**3 838**
市辖区	**Districts Under City Administration**	**7 399**	**100**	**1 564**	**73**	**9**	**2 226**
和平区	Heping District	10	6	89			
河东区	Hedong District	40	13	233			
河西区	Hexi District	38	12	251			
南开区	Nankai District	39	12	254			
河北区	Hebei District	30	10	98			
红桥区	Hongqiao District	21	10	171			
塘沽区	Tanggu District	782	11	83	1		34
汉沽区	Hangu District	409	4	45	4		58
大港区	Dagang District	1 041	5	79	3		74
东丽区	Dongli District	478	5	45	3	1	114
西青区	Xiqing District	566	2	57	7		149
津南区	Jinnan District	388		26	8		165
北辰区	Beichen District	473	4	80	9		126
武清区	Wuqing District	1 575	6	27	19	5	741
宝坻区	Baodi District	1 509		26	19	3	765
市辖县	**Counties Under City Administration**	**4 361**	**1**	**81**	**47**	**11**	**1 612**
宁河县	Ninghe County	1 296		26	11	3	283
静海县	Jinghai County	1 476		35	16	2	384
蓟　县	Jixian County	1 590	1	20	20	6	945

资料来源:天津市民政局。
Information Source:Tianjin Municipal Civil Affairs Bureau.

1-2　土地面积(2005 年)

AREA OF LAND,2005

分　组	Groups	面积（平方公里）Area (sq. km)	占全市土地总面积比重(%) Percentage to Total Area(%)
全市总计	**Total**	**11 919.70**	**100.0**
农用地	**Land for Agricultural Production**	**7 075.00**	**59.4**
耕　地	Cultivated Land	4 455.14	37.4
园　地	Garden Plot	371.01	3.1
林　地	Afforested Land	366.31	3.1
牧草地	Grassland	6.04	0.1
其他农用地	Others	1 876.50	15.7
建设用地	**Land for Construction**	**3 462.84**	**29.0**
居民点及工矿用地	Land for Residents and Industry	2 625.16	22.0
交通用地	Land for Transportation	183.95	1.5
水利设施用地	Land for Water Conservancy	653.73	5.5
未利用地面积	**Unused Area**	**1 381.86**	**11.6**
未利用土地	Unused Soil	406.92	3.4
其他土地	Other Land	974.94	8.2

资料来源:天津市国土资源和房屋管理局。
Information Source:Bureau of Land Resources and Housing Management of Tianjin.

1-3 各月份气象资料(2005年)

EACH MONTH OF METEOROLOGICAL DATA, 2005

月份 Month	平均气温 Average Temperature (℃)	最高气温 The Highest Temperature (℃)	最低气温 The Lowest Temperature (℃)	相对湿度 Average Relative Humidity (%)	日照时数(小时) Hours of Sunshine (hour)	降水量(毫米) Precipitation (mm)	一日最大降水量(毫米) Largest Precipita-tion in a Day (mm)	平均风速(米/秒) Average Wind Speed (m/sec)
一月 January	-3.9	5.6	-12.6	51	178.4	1.6	1.6	2.4
二月 February	-3.1	10.3	-14.2	53	132.3	6.0	5.5	2.8
三月 March	5.4	25.0	-7.5	39	244.3	0.0	0.0	3.4
四月 April	16.3	33.1	3.2	37	219.5	8.5	5.6	3.3
五月 May	19.8	33.8	8.7	50	237.8	37.4	23.2	3.1
六月 June	25.7	39.5	16.1	65	229.1	170.9	74.5	2.5
七月 July	27.8	37.5	19.7	72	183.4	154.2	72.1	2.1
八月 August	25.7	35.5	17.0	78	148.9	209.0	125.4	1.7
九月 September	21.7	31.8	11.7	68	199.3	29.2	12.1	1.8
十月 October	14.8	26.5	1.8	57	215.9	0.9	0.8	2.2
十一月 November	7.1	20.0	-2.2	60	174.4			1.9
十二月 December	-3.0	9.6	-10.1	50	184.9	0.8	0.3	3.3

1-4 各区县气象资料(2005年)

METEOROLOGICAL DATA OF DISTRICT AND COUNTY, 2005

地区 Region	最高气温 The Highest Temperature (℃)	最低气温 The Lowest Temperature (℃)	全年平均气温 Annual Average Temperature (℃)	平均相对湿度 Average Relative Humidity (%)	日照时数(小时) Hours of Sunshine (hour)	降水量(毫米) Precipitation (mm)	无霜期(天) Non-Frosting Period (day)	雾天数(天) Foggy Days (day)
市区 Urban District	38.6	-10.0	13.9	50	2 102.0	620.6	255	7
塘沽区 Tanggu District	36.6	-11.7	13.4	60	2 339.1	493.2	249	11
汉沽区 Hangu District	35.9	-13.9	12.3	58	2 622.7	450.7	206	18
大港区 Dagang District	38.5	-10.7	13.4	53	2 443.9	483.9	256	5
东丽区 Dongli District	36.8	-10.7	13.0	57	2 521.2	443.9	226	9
西青区 Xiqing District	39.5	-14.2	12.9	57	2 348.2	618.5	208	9
津南区 Jinnan District	38.0	-12.4	13.2	64	2 424.5	531.3	220	11
北辰区 Beichen District	39.6	-15.3	12.7	59	2 366.8	536.5	227	8
武清区 Wuqing District	38.9	-16.3	12.2	58	2 408.7	380.4	198	13
宝坻区 Baodi District	37.5	-14.8	11.9	57	2 336.7	467.1	200	19
宁河县 Ninghe County	35.9	-11.8	12.4	60	2 718.2	478.3	232	17
静海县 Jinghai County	39.3	-13.8	13.1	57	2 372.8	565.2	213	14
蓟县 Jixian County	37.5	-10.4	13.0	51	2 470.2	552.9	198	6

资料来源:天津气候服务中心。
Information Source: Tianjin Meteorological Service Center.

1-5 主要年份国民经济主要指标和增长速度

MAIN INDICATORS AND INCREASE RATE OF NATIONAL ECONOMY IN MAIN YEARS

年 份 Year	户籍人口数(万人) Registered Population (10 000 persons)	社会从业人员数(万人) Number of Persons Employed (10 000 persons)	#城镇单位从业人员 Persons Employed in Urban Units	地区生产总值(亿元) Gross Domestic Product (100 million yuan)	人均地区生产总值(元) Per Capital GDP (yuan)	社会劳动生产率(元/人) Society Labour Productivity (yuan/person)
1952	439.22	159.50	45.18	12.80	299	825
1957	529.65	186.50	86.24	24.11	468	1 311
1962	595.63	203.80	106.48	24.25	414	1 166
1965	637.80	227.50	120.30	35.96	571	1 602
1970	652.70	270.20	135.81	50.99	791	1 960
1975	702.86	328.60	181.46	69.73	1 011	2 232
1978	724.27	366.70	217.40	82.65	1 160	2 300
1980	748.91	394.79	242.69	103.53	1 392	2 670
1985	804.80	455.98	276.48	175.78	2 199	3 892
1990	866.25	470.07	284.31	310.95	3 621	6 617
1995	894.67	515.30	289.59	931.97	10 441	18 126
1996	898.45	512.00	283.98	1 121.93	12 513	21 842
1997	899.80	513.33	281.34	1 264.63	14 065	24 667
1998	905.09	508.10	218.56	1 374.60	15 232	26 944
1999	910.17	508.14	211.76	1 500.95	16 537	29 540
2000	912.00	486.89	201.75	1 701.88	18 679	34 208
2001	913.98	488.34	192.30	1 919.09	21 019	39 357
2002	919.05	492.61	185.50	2 150.76	23 467	43 851
2003	926.00	510.90	191.01	2 578.03	27 945	51 380
2004	932.55	527.78	193.91	3 110.97	33 478	59 903
2005	939.31	542.52	194.12	3 697.62	35 783	69 095
平均每年递增%						
Average Annual						
Increase Rate%						
1953-1957	3.8	3.2	13.8	12.8	8.8	9.0
1958-1962	2.4	1.8	4.3	-1.8	-4.3	-4.2
1963-1965	2.3	3.7	4.2	15.3	12.6	12.4
1966-1970	0.5	3.5	2.5	7.7	7.1	4.6
1971-1975	1.5	4.0	6.0	7.2	5.7	3.3
1976-1980	1.3	3.7	6.0	7.3	6.0	3.1
1981-1985	1.4	2.9	2.6	9.3	7.7	5.7
1986-1990	1.5	0.6	0.6	5.2	3.7	4.4
1991-1995	0.6	1.9	0.4	11.7	10.9	9.8
1996-2000	0.4	-1.1	-7.0	11.3	10.8	12.0
2001-2005	0.6	2.2	-0.8	14.0	13.1	12.3
1981-1990	1.5	1.8	1.6	7.3	5.7	5.0
1991-2000	0.5	0.4	-3.4	11.5	10.8	10.9
1953-2005	1.4	2.3	2.8	8.8	7.2	6.3
1979-2005	1.0	1.5	-0.4	10.3	9.1	8.6
1998-2005	0.5	0.7	-4.5	12.5	11.8	11.9
2005 比 2004	0.7	2.8	0.1	14.7	12.9	11.3

注:1.本表地区生产总值、人均地区生产总值按现价计算,速度按可比价计算。2.社会劳动生产率按现价地区生产总值计算,速度按可比价计算。

Note:a)Gross domestic product,per capita GDP are calculated at current prices,increase rate are based on comparable prices. b)Society labour productivity are calculated at current prices of GDP,increase rate are based on comparable prices.

1-5 续表 1　Continued

单位:亿元　(100 million yuan)

年份 Year	农业总产值 Gross Output Value of Agriculture	工业总产值 Gross Output Value of Industry	轻工业 Light Industry	重工业 Heavy Industry	中资金融机构人民币存款余额 RMB Deposits of Chinese Financial Institutions	#储蓄存款余额 Savings Deposit Balance
1952	2.73	19.71	16.36	3.35	2.66	0.50
1957	3.23	40.44	29.01	11.43	3.08	1.05
1962	2.78	45.39	29.12	16.27	10.33	0.93
1965	4.82	66.35	39.08	27.27	12.19	1.57
1970	5.20	102.77	54.83	47.94	14.54	1.59
1975	5.39	145.57	74.47	71.10	25.69	2.88
1978	6.72	157.90	81.47	76.43	33.24	4.02
1980	9.25	195.94	106.00	89.94	44.92	7.96
1985	20.44	319.47	164.22	155.25	114.25	29.38
1990	51.72	679.94	354.50	325.44	263.21	126.92
1995	125.44	1 879.65	752.03	1 127.62	1 079.97	549.97
1996	133.53	2 177.42	1 014.46	1 162.96	1 399.06	724.91
1997	140.47	2 450.21	1 130.04	1 320.17	1 634.95	863.36
1998	156.16	2 562.62	1 157.09	1 405.53	1 860.84	1 020.14
1999	150.11	2 751.37	1 128.47	1 622.90	2 060.02	1 130.19
2000	156.30	3 080.74	1 263.10	1 817.64	2 281.55	1 172.40
2001	169.51	3 366.53	1 153.73	2 212.80	2 562.55	1 284.95
2002	181.07	3 717.72	1 207.88	2 509.84	3 018.26	1 486.38
2003	193.44	4 370.76	1 254.68	3 116.08	4 033.51	1 825.32
2004	221.35	6 186.04	1 398.65	4 787.39	4 729.61	2 116.73
2005	238.34	7 169.62	1 569.06	5 600.56	5 684.40	2 462.41
平均每年递增% Average Annual Increase Rate%						
1953-1957	3.8	16.6	13.5	29.5	3.0	16.0
1958-1962	-2.6	0.4	-1.3	4.5	27.4	-2.3
1963-1965	18.8	15.5	12.8	20.6	5.7	19.0
1966-1970	1.1	10.3	7.5	14.5	3.6	0.3
1971-1975	1.1	8.5	6.7	10.6	12.1	12.6
1976-1980	3.5	6.0	7.7	4.1	11.8	22.5
1981-1985	9.7	9.7	10.1	9.1	20.5	29.8
1986-1990	8.6	10.6	10.2	11.2	18.2	34.0
1991-1995	7.0	20.7	16.3	24.9	32.6	34.1
1996-2000	6.2	15.2	15.8	14.8	16.1	16.3
2001-2005	6.1	21.5	10.4	27.4	20.0	16.0
1981-1990	9.2	10.2	10.1	10.1	19.6	31.9
1991-2000	6.6	17.9	16.0	19.7	24.1	24.9
1953-2005	5.2	12.0	9.8	15.1	15.6	17.4
1979-2005	7.9	15.1	12.7	16.4	21.0	26.8
1998-2005	5.8	18.2	10.9	22.2	16.9	14.0
2005 比 2004	4.8	19.5	9.3	22.8	20.2	16.3

注:1.农业总产值按现价计算,速度按可比价计算。2.工业总产值 1995 年以后为现价新规定,以前为原规定,速度按可比价计算,以下各表同。3.金融机构人民币存、贷款余额为当年年末数。

Note:a)Gross output value of agriculture are calculated at current prices,increase rate are based on comparable prices. b)Gross output value of industry are calculated at current prices of new stipulation after 1995,others are former stipulation. Increase rate are based on comparable prices,same to next tables. c)RMB deposits and loans of financial institutions are by the end of the year.

1-5 续表 2 Continued
单位:亿元 (100 million yuan)

年 份 Year	中资金融机构人民币贷款余额 RMB Loans of Chinese Financial Institutions	全市财政收入 Total Financial Revenue	全市财政支出 Total Financial Expenditures	全社会固定资产投资额 Total Investment in Fixed Assets	#地 方 Local	全社会新增固定资产 Total Newly Increased in Fixed Assets
1952	0.46	3.88	1.08	1.03	0.32	
1957	10.91	7.99	1.63	2.40	1.13	
1962	24.96	9.77	2.49	1.86	1.33	
1965	25.25	13.33	3.50	2.91	1.84	
1970	39.04	28.02	6.40	6.17	4.34	
1975	68.59	39.17	10.61	16.25	8.88	
1978	80.14	39.25	14.51	20.30	10.03	
1980	102.66	40.94	14.67	23.92	14.53	17.84
1985	191.04	48.21	26.97	65.90	50.80	42.62
1990	415.91	44.88	40.20	87.69	57.47	65.16
1995	1 113.95	117.34	90.37	393.18	309.75	300.86
1996	1 357.38	137.45	110.19	435.81	325.71	313.12
1997	1 502.91	169.12	140.08	498.66	376.69	320.46
1998	1 629.12	186.55	155.15	575.86	452.11	439.58
1999	1 825.26	206.89	177.62	567.36	405.31	459.54
2000	1 863.60	244.81	209.57	608.80	463.83	434.28
2001	2 159.86	304.52	259.78	705.10	567.40	476.92
2002	2 519.04	375.92	300.07	811.26	677.60	537.98
2003	3 426.02	451.74	350.63	1 046.72	893.73	656.99
2004	3 821.38	502.17	431.49	1 258.98	1 067.97	696.56
2005	4 417.45	725.81	520.28	1 516.84	1 288.85	847.79
平均每年递增% Average Annual Increase Rate%						
1953-1957	88.3	15.5	8.6	20.8	36.6	
1958-1962	18.0	4.1	8.8	24.4	45.7	
1963-1965	0.4	10.9	12.0	26.4	20.7	
1966-1970	9.1	16.0	12.8	6.7	4.1	
1971-1975	11.9	6.9	10.6	22.0	14.0	
1976-1980	8.4	0.9	6.7	6.5	7.7	
1981-1985	13.2	3.3	12.9	20.8	29.6	23.6
1986-1990	16.8	-1.4	8.3	6.7	2.3	13.4
1991-1995	21.8	21.2	17.6	36.8	43.3	35.1
1996-2000	10.8	15.9	18.3	10.6	9.1	9.1
2001-2005	18.8	24.3	19.9	19.4	22.9	13.4
1981-1990	15.1	0.9	10.6	16.8	19.6	17.9
1991-2000	16.2	18.5	18.0	26.3	28.9	25.9
1953-2005	18.9	10.4	12.4	14.4	16.7	
1979-2005	16.0	11.4	14.2	17.2	19.8	
1998-2005	14.4	20.0	17.8	12.7	14.5	12.7
2005 比 2004	17.2	26.8	20.6	20.5	20.7	21.7

注:1994 年以前全市财政收支为原地方预算内财政收支口径;1994 年以后为分税制后的全市财政收支数。
Note: Before 1994, total financial revenue and expenditure intra-budgetary refer to original local financial budgetary revenue and expenditure; but it has been total financial revenue and expenditure of the city since the reform of tax system was implemented in 1994.

1-5 续表 3　Continued

年　份 Year	房屋建筑竣工面积（万平方米）Floor Space of Buildings Completed (10 000 sq. m)	#住　宅 Residential Buildings	社会货运量（万吨）Freight Traffic (10 000 tons)	港口货物吞吐量（万吨）Freight Handled at Ports (10 000 tons)	邮电业务总量（万元）Total Business of Post and Telecommunications Service (10 000 yuan)	社会消费品零售总额（亿元）Total Retail Sales of Consumer Goods (100 million yuan)
1952			1 748	74	894	7.19
1957			2 984	284	935	10.55
1962			3 498	391	1 436	12.31
1965			3 450	549	1 621	12.32
1970			4 837	817	1 660	14.57
1975			6 766	826	2 385	21.18
1978			9 241	1 131	2 710	25.20
1980	395.3	239.0	13 949	1 192	3 163	34.64
1985	598.1	342.1	18 249	1 856	5 290	64.12
1990	363.3	189.5	15 929	2 063	32 735	139.88
1995	736.5	486.9	24 040	5 787	187 195	375.64
1996	725.1	494.7	24 133	6 188	256 978	470.04
1997	655.2	412.0	25 090	6 789	342 848	535.02
1998	790.4	516.5	24 505	6 818	474 067	587.12
1999	873.6	596.2	27 052	7 298	567 242	657.28
2000	968.0	673.3	26 400	9 582	753 669	736.63
2001	1 020.1	682.4	28 608	11 369	702 206	832.70
2002	1 181.2	759.3	31 016	12 906	903 296	941.36
2003	1 255.1	775.3	35 252	16 182	1 157 060	922.27
2004	1 518.1	1 052.2	37 934	20 619	1 467 836	1 044.78
2005	2 023.1	1 305.1	40 263	24 069	1 763 477	1 190.06
平均每年递增%						
Average Annual						
Increase Rate%						
1953-1957			11.3	30.9	0.9	5.5
1958-1962			3.2	6.6	9.0	0.8
1963-1965			-0.5	12.0	4.1	4.0
1966-1970			7.0	8.3	0.5	3.7
1971-1975			6.9	0.2	7.5	7.8
1976-1980			15.6	7.6	5.8	8.8
1981-1985	8.6	7.4	5.5	9.3	10.8	9.3
1986-1990	-9.5	-11.1	-2.7	2.1	24.9	6.5
1991-1995	15.2	20.8	8.6	22.9	41.7	9.2
1996-2000	5.6	6.7	2.0	10.6	32.1	14.8
2001-2005	15.9	14.2	8.8	20.2	26.0	11.4
1981-1990	-0.8	-2.3	1.3	5.6	17.7	7.8
1991-2000	10.3	13.5	5.2	16.6	36.8	12.0
1953-2005			6.1	11.5	14.5	7.5
1979-2005			5.6	12.0	25.2	10.4
1998-2005	15.1	15.5	6.1	17.1	27.5	12.4
2005 比 2004	33.3	24.0	6.1	16.7	20.1	14.0

注：2003 年起社会消费品零售总额为新口径。增长速度均为可比口径，并已扣除物价因素。
Note: Since 2003, retail sales of consumer goods has been calculated on new statistical coverage. The increase rate of retail on sales of consumer goods are calculated at comparable coverage and have deducted price sectors.

1－5 续表 4 Continued

年 份 Year	实际利用外资额（万美元） Foreign Capital Actually Used (USD 10 000)	#客商直投 Foreign Direct Investment	天津口岸进出口总值（亿美元） Total Value of Imports & Exports In Tianjin Port (USD 100 million)	#出 口 Exports	外贸进出口总值（亿美元） Total Value of Imports & Exports in Foreign Trade (USD 100 million)	#出 口 Exports
1952						1.90
1957					2.50	2.48
1962					2.40	2.34
1965					3.54	3.41
1970					3.58	3.19
1975					8.86	7.72
1978					9.88	8.65
1980	271	271			18.27	15.42
1985	7 558	4 409	96.18	20.07	14.86	11.53
1990	33 467	8 315	85.95	42.53	22.10	17.86
1995	211 010	152 064	217.46	127.81	65.46	29.98
1996	298 358	200 587	216.85	122.89	82.97	40.49
1997	342 301	251 135	215.62	131.24	100.23	50.18
1998	305 787	251 803	223.19	134.84	106.16	54.99
1999	274 535	253 203	248.29	139.18	126.05	63.32
2000	282 467	256 000	298.03	165.29	171.57	86.29
2001	329 688	322 000	323.71	178.13	181.86	95.02
2002	386 901	380 591	365.35	190.55	228.27	115.95
2003	170 550	163 325	461.67	259.57	293.71	143.74
2004	270 236	247 243	677.66	384.80	420.19	208.65
2005	364 573	332 885	819.29	446.83	533.87	274.15
平均每年递增%						
Average Annual						
Increase Rate%						
1953－1957						5.5
1958－1962					－0.8	－1.2
1963－1965					13.8	13.5
1966－1970					0.2	－1.4
1971－1975					19.9	19.4
1976－1980					15.6	14.8
1981－1985	94.6	74.7			－4.1	－5.7
1986－1990	34.7	13.5	－2.2	16.2	8.3	9.1
1991－1995	44.5	78.8	20.4	24.6	24.3	10.9
1996－2000	6.0	11.0	6.5	5.3	21.3	23.5
2001－2005	27.2	32.0	22.4	22.0	25.5	26.0
1981－1990	61.9	40.8			1.9	1.5
1991－2000	23.8	40.9	13.2	14.5	22.7	17.1
1953－2005						9.8
1979－2005					15.9	13.7
1998－2005	7.5	14.5	18.2	16.5	23.3	23.6
2005 比 2004	34.9	34.6	20.9	16.1	27.1	31.4

注：2003 年实际利用外资额采用商务部口径，速度按可比口径计算；以下相关表同。
Note：since 2003，foreign direct investment refer to new coverage of Ministry of Commerce，its increase rate is calculated on the basis of comparable coverage，same as following next.

1－5 续表 5　Continued

年　份 Year	城镇单位从业人员劳动报酬总额（亿元） Total Remuneration of Persons Employed in Urban Units (100 million yuan)	＃国有单位 State－owned Units	城镇单位从业人员人均劳动报酬（元） Per Capita Remuneration of Persons Employed in Urban Units(yuan)	＃国有单位 State－owned Units	城市居民人均可支配收入（元） Per Capita Annual Disposable Income of Urban Households (yuan)	城市居民人均消费性支出（元） Per Capita Annual Expenditure for Consumption of Urban Households (yuan)
1952	2.56	2.56		573	200	176
1957	5.05	5.05		749	240	216
1962	7.11	7.11		685	252	238
1965	8.48	7.29	714	745	261	234
1970	8.58	7.17	652	673	281	255
1975	10.66	8.61	618	663	324	295
1978	14.00	11.51	640	690	388	345
1980	19.32	15.77	820	865	527	475
1985	34.14	24.69	1 250	1 223	876	771
1990	69.38	55.50	2 438	2 611	1 639	1 440
1995	184.80	135.22	6 501	6 963	4 930	4 064
1996	212.05	154.34	7 643	8 072	5 968	4 680
1997	223.25	160.47	8 238	8 689	6 609	5 204
1998	225.39	151.80	9 895	10 169	7 111	5 471
1999	234.42	151.93	11 046	11 169	7 650	5 852
2000	253.53	161.86	12 414	12 690	8 141	6 121
2001	277.56	176.26	14 242	14 823	8 959	6 987
2002	304.23	182.27	16 223	16 632	9 338	7 192
2003	350.60	194.80	18 511	18 929	10 313	7 868
2004	407.99	222.60	21 146	22 031	11 467	8 802
2005	458.26	247.30	24 122	24 832	12 639	9 653
平均每年递增% **Average Annual Increase Rate%**						
1953－1957	12.1	12.1		3.3	1.5	2.0
1958－1962	4.7	4.7		－3.9	－1.3	－0.3
1963－1965	10.0	4.6		6.7	5.0	3.2
1966－1970	0.6	0.1	－1.4	－1.5	1.9	2.1
1971－1975	4.4	3.7	－1.1	－0.3	2.9	3.0
1976－1980	11.2	11.5	4.5	4.1	8.8	8.6
1981－1985	8.4	5.8	5.3	3.7	7.2	6.6
1986－1990	5.2	7.4	4.4	6.3	3.5	3.5
1991－1995	5.2	3.4	5.3	5.3	7.8	6.4
1996－2000	4.4	1.6	11.6	10.5	8.4	6.4
2001－2005	11.3	7.6	12.9	13.1	8.0	8.3
1981－1990	6.8	6.6	4.8	4.4	5.1	5.0
1991－2000	4.9	2.5	8.4	7.9	8.1	6.5
1953－2005	6.9	5.7		4.1	4.8	4.5
1979－2005	7.4	5.8	8.0	7.8	7.4	6.8
1998－2005	8.9	5.1	13.9	13.5	8.0	7.6
2005 比 2004	10.7	9.5	12.4	11.0	8.6	8.0

注：1.1998 年以前有关劳动报酬指标的绝对数为职工工资，计算增长速度时已扣除物价因素。2.计算城市居民人均收支增长速度按可比口径，并已扣除物价因素。

Note: a) Before 1998, total remuneration and per capita remuneration refer to wage of staff and workers, average annualincrease rate of these indicators have deducted price sectors. b) The increase rate of income and expenditure are calculated at comparable coverage and have deducted price sectors.

1-5 续表 6 Continued

年 份 Year	农村居民人均纯收入(元) Per Capita Annual Net Income of Rural Households (yuan)	农村居民人均生活消费支出(元) Per Capita Annual Expenditure for Consumption of Rural Households (yuan)	各类学校在校学生数(万人) Students Enrollment By Level of School (10 000 persons)	国有单位自然科学技术人员数(人) Natural Scientific & Technical Personnel of State-owned Units (person)	医院卫生院床位数(张) Hospital Beds (unit)	卫生技术人员数(人) Medical Technical Personnel (person)	#执业及助理医师 Certified And Assistant Doctors
1952	70		57.14		3 457	8 481	3 326
1957	92		83.92		6 156	15 124	5 522
1962	65		106.37		10 521	23 858	8 627
1965	92		148.10		11 266	26 393	10 585
1970	145		148.17		11 361	23 591	9 046
1975	147		169.71		15 961	33 734	12 326
1978	153	132	162.30	102 022	17 288	40 653	15 776
1980	278	208	139.06	127 803	18 753	50 662	20 474
1985	564	426	121.09	194 837	25 191	60 412	25 555
1990	1 069	733	134.97	271 761	33 382	67 485	32 034
1995	2 531	1 717	155.28	248 739	37 280	71 806	33 693
1996	3 142	2 101	161.40	265 924	38 284	71 014	32 975
1997	3 548	2 110	164.41	260 927	39 467	70 431	32 475
1998	3 890	2 260	164.11	259 374	39 134	68 070	31 482
1999	4 055	2 334	162.53	257 169	38 579	65 901	30 273
2000	4 370	2 393	162.22	249 934	38 842	65 145	30 031
2001	4 825	2 618	160.54	240 361	40 394	63 475	29 215
2002	5 315	2 778	161.69	226 639	38 837	56 705	23 888
2003	5 861	3 015	163.23	232 324	38 074	55 629	22 780
2004	6 525	3 297	161.67	212 049	38 876	60 722	25 299
2005	7 202	3 590	162.05	206 222	39 491	61 284	25 088
平均每年递增% Average Annual Increase Rate%							
1953-1957	5.6		8.0		12.2	12.3	10.7
1958-1962	-6.7		4.9		11.3	9.5	9.3
1963-1965	12.3		11.7		2.3	3.4	7.1
1966-1970	9.5				0.2	-2.2	-3.1
1971-1975	0.3		2.8		7.0	7.4	6.4
1976-1980	13.6		-3.9		3.3	8.5	10.7
1981-1985	15.2	15.4	-2.7	8.8	6.1	3.6	4.5
1986-1990	13.6	11.5	2.2	6.9	5.8	2.2	4.6
1991-1995	18.8	18.6	2.8	-1.8	2.2	1.2	1.2
1996-2000	11.5	6.7	0.9	0.1	0.8	-1.9	-2.3
2001-2005	10.5	8.5		-3.8	0.3	-1.2	-3.5
1981-1990	14.4	13.4	-0.3	7.8	5.9	2.9	4.6
1991-2000	15.1	12.6	1.9	-0.8	1.5	-0.4	-0.6
1953-2005	9.1		2.0		4.7	3.8	3.9
1979-2005	15.3	13.0		2.6	3.1	1.5	1.7
1998-2005	9.3	6.9	-0.2	-2.9		-1.7	-3.2
2005 比 2004	10.4	8.9	0.2	-2.7	1.6	0.9	-0.8

1－6 国民经济结构和社会发展结构指标(2001－2005年)
STRUCTURAL INDICATORS ON NATIONAL ECONOMY AND SOCIAL DEVELOPMENT, 2001－2005

单位：%　　(%)

指　标	Item	2001	2002	2003	2004	2005
人口与就业	**Population and Employment**					
人　口	**Population**					
农非结构	Grouped by Non－agricultural and Agricultural					
非农业	Non－agricultural	58.6	58.9	59.4	59.6	59.9
农　业	Agricultural	41.4	41.1	40.6	40.4	40.1
性别结构	Grouped by Sex					
男	Male	50.5	50.5	50.5	50.5	50.4
女	Female	49.5	49.5	49.5	49.5	49.6
就　业	**Employment**					
社会从业人员产业结构	Grouped by Industry					
第一产业	Primary Industry	16.9	16.7	16.3	15.7	15.1
第二产业	Secondary Industry	43.6	41.7	42.9	42.4	41.9
第三产业	Tertiary Industry	39.5	41.6	40.8	41.9	43.0
宏 观 经 济	**Macro Economy**					
国民经济核算	**National Accounting**					
地区生产总值产业结构	Grouped by Industry					
第一产业	Primary Industry	4.1	3.9	3.5	3.4	3.0
第二产业	Secondary Industry	50.0	49.7	51.9	54.2	55.5
第三产业	Tertiary Industry	45.9	46.4	44.6	42.4	41.5
投　资	**Investment**					
全社会固定资产投资结构	Structure of Total Investment in Fixed Assets					
建设工程	Construction	57.9	57.4	56.8	54.8	56.2
安装工程	Installation	4.4	5.3	5.8	4.9	5.0
设备、工具、器械购置	Purchase of Equipment and Instruments	22.2	23.1	18.9	22.5	20.8
其他费用	Others	15.5	14.2	18.5	17.8	18.0
资金来源结构	Structure of Sources of Funds					
国家预算内投资	State Budgetary Appropriation	2.3	2.6	1.4	1.5	1.8
国内贷款	Domestic Loans	21.9	22.8	30.2	28.1	24.7
利用外资	Foreign Investment	15.8	8.4	5.9	7.3	6.7
自筹和其他投资	Fundraising and Others Investment	60.0	66.2	62.5	63.1	66.8
财　政	**Government Finance**					
地方财政收入结构	Structure of Local Fiscal Revenue					
#增值税	Value－added Tax	18.4	18.6	18.4	11.6	15.6

1－6续表1 Continued
单位：% (%)

指 标	Item	2001	2002	2003	2004	2005
营业税	Operating Tax	22.8	24.8	26.2	25.9	23.4
企业所得税	Income Tax of Enterprises	20.9	12.6	9.7	10.6	10.0
个人所得税	Individual Income Tax	8.8	6.3	5.1	5.3	4.6
利用外资	**Utilization of Foreign Capital**					
实际利用外资结构	Structure of Foreign Capital Actually Utilized					
对外借款	Foreign Loans	2.3	1.6	4.2	8.5	8.7
客外商直接投资	Foreign Direct Investment	97.7	98.4	95.8	91.5	91.3
能 源	**Energy**					
能源使用结构	Structure of Energy Consumption					
#第一产业	Primary Industry	2.5	2.6	1.9	1.8	1.9
第二产业	Secondary Industry	62.2	65.3	64.0	65.2	65.7
第三产业	Tertiary Industry	22.3	19.4	21.1	20.9	20.3
产 业	**Industrial**					
农 业	**Agriculture**					
农林牧渔业产值结构	Structure of Gross Output Value					
农 业	Farming	51.2	47.5	45.6	43.1	40.9
林 业	Forestry	0.9	0.8	0.8	0.7	0.8
牧 业	Animal Husbandry	35.8	38.3	39.9	41.8	43.1
渔 业	Fishery	12.1	13.4	13.7	14.4	15.2
工 业	**Industry**					
全部工业总产值结构	Structure of Gross Output Value of Industry					
轻工业	Light Industry	34.3	32.5	28.7	22.6	21.9
重工业	Heavy Industry	65.7	67.5	71.3	77.4	78.1
建筑业	**Construction**					
建筑业总产值结构	Structure of Gross Output Value of Construction					
房屋和土木工程建筑业	Building and Civil Engineering	80.6	81.9	81.9	81.0	80.9
建筑安装业	Equipment Installation	17.6	13.9	13.8	12.2	13.9
建筑装饰业	Building Decoration	1.8	3.2	3.1	4.1	3.0
其他建筑业	Others		1.0	1.2	2.7	2.2
交通运输业	**Transportation**					
货运量结构	Structure of Freight Traffic					
铁 路(天津地区)	Railway(Tianjin Area)	13.0	14.6	16.1	16.1	18.0

1-6续表2　Continued

单位：%　　(%)

指　标	Item	2001	2002	2003	2004	2005
公　路	Highway	67.8	63.0	56.9	51.6	49.3
水运、民航	Waterway and Civil Aviation	17.6	20.8	25.4	30.6	30.7
管道运输	Pipelines	1.6	1.6	1.6	1.7	2.0
国内商业	**Domestic Trade**					
社会消费品零售总额构成	Composition of Retail Sales of Consumer Goods					
市	City		93.4	93.2	93.4	93.5
县	Country		3.5	3.8	3.7	3.6
县以下	Under Country Level		3.1	3.0	2.9	2.9
对外经济贸易	**Foreign Trade**					
进出口贸易总值结构	Structure of Imports and Exports					
出口总值	Exports	52.2	50.8	48.9	49.7	51.4
进口总值	Imports	47.8	49.2	51.1	50.3	48.6
国际旅游	**International Tourism**					
来津旅游人员结构	Structure of Tourists					
外国人、华侨	Foreigners and Overseas Chinese	81.1	81.3	83.7	85.6	86.1
港澳台同胞	Compatriots form Hongkong,Macao and Taiwan	18.9	18.7	16.3	14.4	13.9
金融业	**Financial Intermediation**					
中资金融机构人民币存款结构	Structure of RMB Deposits in Chinese Financial Institution					
#企业存款	Deposits of Enterprises	37.0	37.0	38.2	38.5	38.4
储蓄存款	Savings Deposits	50.1	49.2	45.3	44.8	43.3
中资金融机构人民币贷款结构	Structure of RMB Loans in Chinese Financial Institution					
#工业贷款	Industrial Loans	20.1	17.9	12.5	10.6	9.6
商业贷款	Commercial Loans	11.6	9.6	8.0	6.8	5.8
中长期贷款	Medium - term & Long - term Loans	29.5	33.6	42.9	46.8	49.9
教育、科技、文化、卫生	**Education,Science,Culture and Health Care**					
教　育	**Education**					
在校学生结构	Sturctureof Student Enronllment					
大学生	University and College Students	9.6	12.2	15.0	17.7	20.5
中学生	Secondary Students	49.0	49.0	49.1	48.0	46.6
小学生	Primary Students	41.4	38.8	35.9	34.3	32.9

1-6 续表 3 Continued
单位:% (%)

指 标	Item	2001	2002	2003	2004	2005
专任教师结构	Full-time Teachers by Type					
大 学	University and College	11.3	12.6	13.8	16.7	18.9
中 学	Secondary Schools	47.5	47.5	47.5	46.1	45.2
小 学	Primary Schools	41.2	39.9	38.7	37.2	35.9
科 技	**Science and Technolgy**					
科技经费筹集额结构	Structure of Funding for Scientific and Technological					
#政府资金	Government Fund	19.2	21.4	18.7	17.8	18.4
企业资金	Enterprises Fund	62.8	64.7	67.9	71.4	73.6
金融机构贷款	Loans from Banks	8.8	2.9	7.6	6.1	5.0
卫 生	**Health Care**					
卫生机构结构	Structure of Health Care Institution					
#医院、卫生院	Hospitals and Health Care Centers	18.6	18.4	18.2	18.4	18.5
卫生技术人员结构	Structure of Medical Professionals					
#执业及助理医师	Certified And Assistant Doctors	46.0	42.1	40.9	41.7	40.9
注册护士	Registered Nurses	33.6	34.0	34.5	32.3	32.0
生 活、环 境	**People's Livelihood and Environment**					
生 活	**People's Livelihood**					
城市居民消费结构	Consumption Structure of Urban Residents					
食品类	Food	37.0	36.2	37.7	37.2	36.7
衣着类	Clothing	7.6	8.1	7.4	7.1	7.2
用品及其他	Articlesfor Daily Use and Others	43.8	42.7	41.0	41.7	42.7
居 住	Residence	11.6	13.0	13.9	14.0	13.4
农村居民消费结构	Consumption Structure of Rural Residents					
食品类	Food	40.5	38.2	38.3	38.5	38.3
衣着类	Clothing	9.2	9.5	8.8	8.9	10.1
用品及其他	Articlesfor Daily Use and Others	30.5	31.5	29.9	29.6	28.1
居 住	Residence	19.8	20.8	23.0	23.0	23.5
环 境	**Environment**					
空气质量结构	Strcuture of Air Quality					
二级和好于二级的天数	Days of Grade II and Better than Grade II	46.8	75.1	72.3	81.7	81.6

1-7 国民经济和社会发展比例和效益指标(2001-2005年)

MAIN INDICATORS ON PROPORTION AND EFFICIENCY IN NATIONAL ECONOMY AND SOCIAL DEVELOPMENT,2001-2005

单位:%　　(%)

指　标	Item	2001	2002	2003	2004	2005
人口与就业	**Population and Employment**					
人　口	**Population**					
出生率(‰)	Birth Rate	7.6	7.5	7.1	7.3	7.4
死亡率(‰)	Death Rate	5.9	6.0	6.0	6.0	6.0
自然增长率(‰)	Natural Growth Rate	1.6	1.5	1.1	1.3	1.4
就　业	**Employment**					
城镇登记失业率	Unemployment Rate in Urban Areas	3.6	3.9	3.8	3.8	3.7
宏观经济	**Macro Economy**					
国民经济核算	**National Accounting**					
经济增长贡献率	Contribution to Gross Domestic Product					
第一产业	Primary Industry	2.3	2.0	1.6	1.2	0.9
第二产业	Secondary Industry	54.2	57.9	63.0	66.6	66.1
#工　业	Industy	48.8	53.4	59.2	66.1	62.4
第三产业	Tertiary Industry	43.5	40.1	35.4	32.2	33.0
固定资产投资	**Investment in Fixed Assets**					
全社会固定资产投资相当于地区生产总值比例	Proportion of Total Investment in Fixed Assets to GDP	36.7	37.7	40.6	40.5	41.0
新增固定资产交付使用率	Rate of Fixed Assets Transferred and in Use	67.6	66.3	62.8	55.3	55.9
财　政	**Government Finance**					
全市财政收入相当于地区生产总值比例	Proportion of Total Financial Revenue to GDP	15.9	17.5	17.5	16.1	19.6
全市财政支出相当于地区生产总值比例	Proportion of Total Financial Expenditures to GDP	13.5	14.0	13.6	13.9	14.1
预算外资金收入相当于全市财政收入比例	Proportion of Extra-budgetaty Receipt to Toatl Financial Revenue	16.1	13.6	13.2	9.5	8.3
利用外资	**Utillization of Foreign Capital**					
客商直接投资相当于签约额比例	Proportion of Foreign Direct Investment to Foreign Investment Contracted	69.5	65.5	46.5	44.2	45.5
能　源	**Energy**					
能源消费弹性系数	Elasticity Ratio of Energy Consumption	0.37	0.28	0.43	0.95	0.77
万元地区生产总值耗能(吨标准煤)	Energy Consumption per 10 000 yuan GDP(ton of SCE)	1.53	1.41	1.30	1.29	1.11

1－7 续表 1 Continued

单位：% (%)

指 标	Item	2001	2002	2003	2004	2005
产 业	**Industrial**					
农 业	**Agriculture**					
每公顷耕地农业机械总动力(千瓦)	Total Power of Agricultural Machinery per Hectare of Cultivated Land(kw)	14.23	14.49	14.38	14.64	14.76
每公顷播种面积农产品产量(吨)	Output of Crops per Hectare of Sown Area(ton)					
粮 食	Grain	4.36	4.43	4.62	4.75	4.78
棉 花	Cotton	1.41	1.39	1.34	1.38	1.37
油 料	Oil－bearing Crops	1.90	1.80	1.95	2.54	2.53
工 业	**Industry**					
总资产贡献率	Ratio of Total Assets to Industrial Output Value	9.3	8.7	9.9	12.8	14.5
成本费用利润率	Ratio of Profits to Industrial Cost	6.6	5.8	6.0	7.5	8.5
工业增加值率	Ratio of Value Added to Gross Indusrial Output Value	24.8	25.4	26.5	26.1	27.1
建筑业	**Construction**					
技术装备率(元/人)	Value of Machinery per Laborer(yuan/person)	12 881	19 423	24 203	27 354	26 064
产值利税率	Ratio of Per－tax Profits to Gross Output Value	4.2	4.7	4.8	4.9	5.3
全员劳动生产率(万元/人)	Overall Laborer Productivity(10^4 yuan/person)	11.12	11.75	14.65	17.12	19.21
邮电通信业	**Post and Communications**					
电话普及率(含移动电话)(部/百人)	Access to Telephones (include mobile phone)(set/100 person)	56.0	65.4	82.3	89.5	90.1
移动电话普及率(部/百人)	Access to Mobile Phones(set/100 person)	23.5	33.3	41.4	45.4	48.2
每一邮电局所服务面积(平方公里)	Average Service Area per Post and Telecommunications Office (sq.km)	21.95	19.93	19.26	17.03	14.41
对外经济贸易	**Foreign Economy Trade**					
进出口总值相当于地区生产总值比例	Proportion of Total Value of Imports & Exports in Foreign Trade to GDP	78.4	87.8	94.3	111.8	118.3
出口总值相当于地区生产总值比例	Proportion of Total Value of Exports to GDP	41.0	44.6	46.1	55.5	60.7
国际旅游	**International Tourism**					
每一来津游客花费(美元)	Expenditure Per International Tourist in Tianjin(USD)	665	677	674	670	688
金融业	**Financial Intermediation**					

1－7 续表 2　Continued
单位：%　　　　(%)

指　　标	Item	2001	2002	2003	2004	2005
中资金融机构人民币存款相当于地区生产总值比例	RMB Chinese Bank Deposits as Percentage of GDP	133.5	140.3	156.5	152.0	153.7
中资金融机构贷款相当于地区生产总值比例	RMB Chinese Bank Loans as Percentage of GDP	112.6	117.1	132.1	122.8	119.5
教育、科技、文化	**Education,Science and Culture**					
教　育	**Education**					
学龄儿童入学率	Percentage of School－age Children Enrolled	100.0	100.0	100.0	100.0	100.0
初中毕业升学率	Entering Junior Secondary Schools	91.0	92.0	93.1	94.0	94.5
学校教师负担系数	Student－teacher Ratio(in percentage)	14	15	14	14	14
科　技	**Science**					
研究与实验发展经费支出相当于地区生产总值比例	R&d Expenditures as Percentage of GDP			1.65	1.81	1.97
文　化	**Culture**					
每百万人有艺术表演团体(个)	Number of Troupes per Million Persons(unit)	1.64	1.63	1.62	1.71	1.53
每百万人有公共图书馆(个)	Number of Public Libraries per Persons(unit)	3.39	3.37	3.35	3.43	3.07
每百万人有博物馆(个)	Number of Museums per Million Persons (uint)	1.64	1.63	1.84	1.82	1.73
生活和环境	**People's Livelihood and Environment**					
婚　姻	**Marriages and Divorces**					
离婚率(‰)	Divorces Rate(‰)	2.0	2.1	2.4	3.2	3.3
生　活	**People's Livelihood**					
城市与农村居民收入增长率比例(以农村居民收入指数为100)	Proportion of Growth Rate of Annual Income of Urban Residents to the Growth Rate of Annual Net Income of Rural Residents	99.7	94.6	100.2	99.9	97.7
福　利	**Welfare**					
离退休退职费相当于劳动报酬比例	Pensions for Retired Veterans,Retired and Resigned Persons as Percentage of Total Wages	26.3	29.6	30.0	30.3	32.7
离退休退职人员相当于在职人员比例	Proportion of the Number of Workers Who Have Retired or Resigned to the Number of Employed Ones	53.9	62.1	63.6	68.7	77.2
环境保护	**Environmental Protection**					
城市环境噪声达标区覆盖率	Coverage Rate of Urban Enviromental Noise Reaching Standard Areas	77	78.1	83.5	82.4	77.7
污水处理率	Percentage of Sewage Disposed	61.2	43.2	43.9	53.7	58.0
工业固体废物综合利用率	Reat of Comprehensive Using Industrial Waste Residue	94.7	96	96.1	97.3	98.3

1-8 平均每天社会经济活动(2001-2005年)

AVERAGE DAILY SOCIAL AND ECONOMIC ACTIVITIES,2001-2005

指 标	Item	单 位	Unit	2001	2002	2003	2004	2005
全市每天创造的财富	**Daily Production**							
地区生产总值	Gross Domestic Product	万元	10^4 yuan	52 577	58 924	70 631	85 233	101 305
第一产业	Primary Industry	万元	10^4 yuan	2 157	2 307	2 463	2 884	3 079
第二产业	Secondary Industry	万元	10^4 yuan	26 275	29 290	36 639	46 191	56 197
工 业	Industry	万元	10^4 yuan	23 812	26 533	33 367	42 458	51 645
建筑业	Construction	万元	10^4 yuan	2 463	2 757	3 272	3 733	4 552
第三产业	Tertiary Industry	万元	10^4 yuan	24 145	27 327	31 529	36 158	42 029
全市财政收入	Total Financial Revenue	万元	10^4 yuan	8 342	10 299	12 376	13 758	19 885
主要工业产品产量	Output of Major Industrial Products							
钢	Steel	吨	ton	10 830	13 221	15 505	21 602	26 172
钢 材	Steel Products	吨	ton	12 191	22 086	28 259	47 127	45 590
水 泥	Cement	吨	ton	9 287	10 349	12 310	14 261	14 223
原 油	Crude Oil	吨	ton	26 583	33 313	36 063	39 622	48 846
原 盐	Salt	吨	ton	6 534	6 586	6 041	6 608	6 304
发电量	Electricity	万千瓦时	10^4 kwh	5 957	7 365	8 766	9 308	10 019
汽 车	Motor Vehicle	辆	unit	161	259	473	628	898
彩色电视机	Color Television	台	set	1 409	2 092	3 080	2 998	1 778
摩托车	Motorcycle	辆	unit	1 381	2 178	3 145	3 421	3 053
自行车	Bicycle	辆	unit	8 829	17 373	22 847	52 823	35 800
微波炉	Microwave Oven	台	set	8 768	12 313	26 572	37 720	39 210
移动电话	Mobile Phone	部	unit	41 028	78 100	86 020	134 989	173 146
布	Cloth	万米	10^4 m	71	74	69	84	71
纱	Yarn	吨	ton	223	252	205	206	201
农用化肥	Chemical Fertilizer	吨	ton	408	439	449	437	464
化学农药	Chemical Pesticide	吨	ton	19	90	58	12	35
硫 酸	Sulfuric Acid	吨	ton	309	333	300	274	327
烧 碱	Caustic Soda	吨	ton	1 353	1 744	2 189	2 223	2 204
合成洗涤剂	Synthetic Detergents	吨	ton	156	148	139	138	38
饮料酒	Alcoholic Beverages	吨	ton	567	565	677	648	570
主要农产品产量	Output of Major Farm Products							
粮 食	Grain	吨	ton	3 927	3 776	3 268	3 432	3 767
棉 花	Cotton	吨	ton	174	171	259	330	229
油 料	Oil bearing Crops	吨	ton	107	93	84	42	35
肉 类	Meat	吨	ton	997	1 230	1 436	1 472	1 583
蛋 类	Eggs	吨	ton	712	670	664	668	643
牛 奶	Milk	吨	ton	659	920	1 184	1 486	1 737
蔬 菜	Vegetables	吨	ton	15 466	16 008	16 515	16 039	14 870
水产品	Aquatic Products	吨	ton	725	782	817	849	926

1－8 续表 Continued

指　标	Item	单　位	Unit	2001	2002	2003	2004	2005
全市每天消费量	**Daily Consumption**							
最终消费	Final Consumption Expenditure	万元	10^4 yuan	25 984	28 506	32 686	36 812	41 285
居民消费	Resident Consumption	万元	10^4 yuan	18 290	19 360	21 403	24 031	26 850
城镇居民	Urban	万元	10^4 yuan	15 705	16 639	18 479	20 898	23 499
农村居民	Rural	万元	10^4 yuan	2 585	2 721	2 924	3 133	3 351
政府消费	Government Consumption Expenditure	万元	10^4 yuan	7 694	9 146	11 283	12 781	14 435
社会消费品零售总额	Total Retail Sales of Consumer Goods	万元	10^4 yuan	22 814	22 788	25 268	28 624	32 604
生活用煤、气、水、电	Coal, Gas, Water & Electricity For Living							
煤	Coal	万吨	10^4 tons	0.38	0.22	0.25	0.23	0.24
液化石油气	Liquid Petroleum Gas	吨	ton	295	263	293	245	195
天然气和煤气	Natural Gas And Coal Gas	万立方米	10^4 cu. m	160	105	82.5	78.9	105
水	Water	万吨	10^4 tons	89.2	81.9	81.7	78.9	79.1
电	Electricity	万千瓦时	10^4 kwh	716	804	869	916	1 040
每天其他经济活动	**Other Daily Economic Activities**							
社会货物运输量	Freight Traffic	万吨	10^4 tons	78.4	85.0	96.6	103.9	110.3
客运量	Passenger Traffic	万人次	10^4 persons times	9.0	9.5	9.6	11.2	12.8
港口货物吞吐量	Freight Handled at Ports	万吨	10^4 tons	31.1	35.4	44.3	56.5	65.9
邮电业务总量	Total Business of Post and Telecommunications Service	万元	10^4 yuan	1 924	2 475	3 170	4 021	4 831
出版图书	Books Published	万册	10^4 copies	17.1	19.0	18.6	22.7	16.2
出版报纸	Newspapers Published	万份	10^4 copies	197.5	221.3	225.7	237.5	239.9
出版杂志	Magazines Published	万册	10^4 copies	12.5	13.2	12.6	12.3	11.5
邮寄函件	Letters Delivered	万件	10^4 copies	46.8	55.2	60.4	29.0	23.0
外贸出口总值	Total Value of Exports in Foreign Trade	万美元	USD 10^4	2 603	3 177	3 938	5 716	7 511
实际利用外资额	Foreign Capital Actually Used	万美元	USD 10^4	903	1 060	467	740	999
竣工房屋建筑面积	Floor Space of Buildings Completed	万平方米	10^4 sq. m	2.67	3.24	3.44	4.16	5.54
接待来津国际旅游人数(过夜)	Accommodated International Tourists (Stay for Night)	人次	person－times	486	560	472	755	849
每天人口和婚姻动态	**Daily Population Changes And Marriages**							
出生人口	Births	人	person	208	206	197	204	211
死亡人口	Deaths	人	person	163	166	167	166	170
结婚对数	Marriages	对	couple	159	148	172	210	173
离婚对数	Divorces	对	couple	27	29	33	44	47

注:生活用水为城市数。
Note: Water for Living refer to urban area.

1－9 国民经济主要指标人均水平(2001－2005年)
PER CAPITA ANNUAL LEVEL OF MAIN INDICATORS ON NATIONAL ECONOMY,2001－2005

指 标	Item	单 位 Unit		2001	2002	2003	2004	2005
1.地区生产总值	Gross Domestic Product	元	yuan	21 019	23 467	27 945	33 478	35 783
2.全市财政收入	Total Financial Revenue	元	yuan	3 335	4 102	4 897	5 404	7 024
3.全市财政支出	Total Financial Expenditures	元	yuan	2 845	3 274	3 801	4 643	5 035
4.全社会固定资产投资	Total Investment in Fixed Assets	元	yuan	7 723	8 852	11 346	13 548	14 679
5.工业总产值	Gross Output Value of Industry	元	yuan	36 874	40 563	47 378	62 026	69 383
6.主要工业产品产量	Output of Major Industrial Products							
原 油	Crude Oil	吨	ton	1.06	1.33	1.43	1.55	1.73
天然气	Natural Gas	立方米	cu.m	98	97	92	93	85
发电量	Electricity	千瓦时	kwh	2 382	2 933	3 468	3 630	3 539
钢	Steel	吨	ton	0.43	0.53	0.61	0.84	0.92
钢 材	Steel Products	吨	ton		0.88	1.12	1.84	1.61
水 泥	Cement	吨	ton	0.37	0.41	0.49	0.56	0.50
布	Cloth	米	m	28	30	27	33	25
纱	Yarn	公斤	kg	8.9	10.0	8.1	8.0	7.1
7.农业总产值	Gross Output Value of Agriculture	元	yuan	1 857	1 976	2 097	2 382	2 307
8.主要农产品产量	Output of Major Farm Products							
粮 食	Grain	公斤	kg	157	150	129	135	133
棉 花	Cotton	公斤	kg	7.0	6.8	10.3	12.9	8.1
油 料	Oil－Bearing Crops	公斤	kg	4.3	3.7	3.3	1.7	1.2
蔬 菜	Vegetables	公斤	kg	618	638	653	630	525
肉 类	Meat	公斤	kg	40	49	57	58	56
蛋 类	Eggs	公斤	kg	28	27	26	26	23
奶 类	Milk	公斤	kg	26	37	47	58	61
水产品	Aquatic Products	公斤	kg	29.0	31.2	32.3	33.3	32.7
鲜 果	Fresh Fruits	公斤	kg	32.1	32.6	34.3	31.8	26.9
9.社会消费品零售额	Total Retail Sales of Consumer Goods	元	yuan	9 121	10 271	9 997	11 243	11 517
10.城市居民主要商品购买量	Perchase Volume of Major Products of Urban Households							
粮 食	Grain	公斤	kg	100.3	74.7	80.8	80.8	81.4
食用植物油	Edible Vegetable－oil	公斤	kg	7.9	7.9	9.3	9.7	8.7
猪牛羊肉	Pork,Beef and Mutton	公斤	kg	21.5	22.0	24.2	24.0	24.0
鸡 蛋	Eggs	公斤	kg	17.5	16.3	18.8	16.8	18.5
鲜 菜	Fresh Vegetables	公斤	kg	128.9	125.0	138.9	138.9	132.4
鱼	Fish	公斤	kg	9.5	9.2	9.5	9.3	9.6
鲜 奶	Milk	公斤	kg	16.2	16.9	23.1	23.1	23.6
鲜瓜果	Fresh Fruits	公斤	kg	79.2	68.4	80.4	71.1	73.4
服 装	Garments	件	piece	7.1	6.9	6.3	6.1	6.1
鞋 类	Shoes	双	pair	2.6	2.5	2.4	2.4	2.3
11.外贸出口总值	Total Value of Exports in Foreign Trade	美元	USD	1 041	1 265	1 558	2 245	2 653
12.社会货物运输量	Freight Traffic	吨	ton	31.3	33.8	38.2	40.8	39.0

1－10　地区生产总值(1978－2005年)
GROSS DOMESTIC PRODUCT, 1978－2005

单位:亿元　　(100 million yuan)

年　份 Year	地区生产总值 Gross Domestic Product	第一产业 Primary Industry	第二产业 Secondary Industry	工　业 Industry	建筑业 Construction	第三产业 Tertiary Industry	人均地区生产总值(元) Per Capita GDP (yuan)	社会劳动生产率(元/人) Society Labour Productivity (yuan/person)
1978	82.65	5.03	57.53	54.39	3.14	20.09	1 160	2 300
1979	93.01	6.54	64.82	61.01	3.81	21.65	1 272	2 489
1980	103.53	6.53	72.56	67.48	5.08	24.44	1 392	2 670
1981	107.96	5.18	76.97	71.06	5.91	25.81	1 433	2 672
1982	114.11	7.00	79.86	72.30	7.56	27.24	1 488	2 737
1983	123.42	7.60	84.47	76.69	7.78	31.35	1 583	2 883
1984	147.53	11.13	96.47	87.97	8.50	39.93	1 869	3 342
1985	175.78	12.95	114.92	104.80	10.12	47.91	2 199	3 892
1986	194.74	16.51	123.33	111.90	11.43	54.90	2 407	4 221
1987	220.12	19.63	138.02	125.05	12.97	62.47	2 683	4 695
1988	259.71	26.21	160.96	146.73	14.23	72.54	3 118	5 548
1989	283.49	26.85	177.54	160.73	16.81	79.10	3 355	6 064
1990	310.95	27.32	181.38	165.59	15.79	102.25	3 621	6 617
1991	342.65	29.26	196.60	179.75	16.85	116.79	3 942	7 216
1992	411.04	30.26	233.41	212.80	20.61	147.37	4 694	8 516
1993	538.94	35.40	308.40	280.73	27.67	195.14	6 107	10 900
1994	732.89	46.55	414.95	371.43	43.52	271.39	8 251	14 426
1995	931.97	60.80	518.55	467.93	50.62	352.62	10 441	18 126
1996	1 121.93	67.67	609.10	549.81	59.29	445.16	12 513	21 842
1997	1 264.63	69.52	676.01	609.65	66.36	519.10	14 065	24 667
1998	1 374.60	74.14	697.99	622.15	75.84	602.47	15 232	26 944
1999	1 500.95	71.14	758.51	682.52	75.99	671.30	16 537	29 540
2000	1 701.88	73.69	863.83	785.96	77.87	764.36	18 679	34 208
2001	1 919.09	78.73	959.06	869.15	89.91	881.30	21 019	39 357
2002	2 150.76	84.21	1 069.08	968.44	100.64	997.47	23 467	43 851
2003	2 578.03	89.91	1 337.31	1 217.88	119.43	1 150.82	27 945	51 380
2004	3 110.97	105.28	1 685.93	1 549.70	136.26	1 319.76	33 478	59 903
2005	3 697.62	112.38	2 051.17	1 885.04	166.13	1 534.07	35 783	69 095

注:本表数据已依据2004年第一次经济普查结果进行了修订,1－11表至1－15表同

Note: The historical data in this table were adjusted correspondingly in accordance with the result of the first economic census in 2004, same as table 1－11 to table 1－15.

1-11　地区生产总值增长速度（1978-2005 年）
INCREASE RATE OF GROSS DOMESTIC PRODUCT,1978-2005

单位：%　　　　(%)

年　份 Year	地区生产总值 Gross Domestic Product	第一产业 Primary Industry	第二产业 Secondary Industry	工　业 Industry	建筑业 Construction	第三产业 Tertiary Industry	人均地区生产总值 Per Capita GDP	社　会 劳动生产率 Society Labour Productivity
1978	20.9	15.6	23.3	21.1	67.9	16.0	19.6	17.1
1979	10.0	17.4	10.4	10.4	10.7	7.0	7.2	5.9
1980	10.0	-0.2	11.4	10.6	22.0	8.7	8.1	6.0
1981	4.8	-20.9	7.0	6.6	12.2	4.8	3.4	0.5
1982	4.3	12.9	3.5	2.4	17.5	5.3	2.5	1.1
1983	8.3	9.2	6.0	6.0	6.3	14.8	6.6	5.5
1984	19.3	22.8	16.6	17.5	6.2	25.9	17.7	15.6
1985	10.6	21.1	10.5	10.0	16.5	8.8	9.2	8.1
1986	5.8	8.0	5.5	5.0	11.8	6.0	4.5	3.6
1987	7.6	6.0	8.3	8.2	8.9	6.3	6.1	5.9
1988	5.8	7.7	7.7	8.3	1.2	0.4	4.1	6.0
1989	1.6	11.4	-1.9	-2.2	1.2	9.3	0.2	1.8
1990	5.4	4.6	1.1	2.0	-8.4	16.4	3.8	4.8
1991	6.0	3.4	5.5	5.8	2.1	7.5	4.7	4.9
1992	11.7	0.7	11.5	12.4	1.2	14.6	10.8	9.8
1993	12.1	7.4	12.9	13.6	3.6	11.7	11.2	9.4
1994	14.3	5.3	14.7	14.1	22.7	15.6	13.6	11.2
1995	14.9	6.3	14.1	14.5	9.9	17.9	14.3	13.5
1996	14.3	8.2	14.3	14.6	10.1	15.4	13.6	14.4
1997	12.1	7.7	11.7	11.8	10.1	13.4	12.0	12.3
1998	9.3	6.7	7.4	7.0	12.7	13.0	8.9	9.9
1999	10.0	0.1	11.7	12.6	-0.8	8.9	9.4	10.5
2000	10.8	3.7	11.5	12.2	0.9	10.5	10.3	13.1
2001	12.0	6.3	12.8	12.7	14.3	11.7	11.8	14.3
2002	12.7	6.1	14.3	14.6	12.2	11.4	12.1	11.9
2003	14.8	6.1	18.0	18.6	12.4	11.9	14.0	12.2
2004	15.8	5.1	19.8	21.5	1.7	11.9	14.9	11.8
2005	14.7	4.3	17.6	17.9	13.5	11.7	12.9	11.3

1-12 地区生产总值及构成
GROSS DOMESTIC PRODUCT AND COMPOSITION

项　目　Item	绝对数(亿元) Number (100 million yuan)		2005比2004年增长% Increase Rate in 2005 over 2004	构　成(%) Composition in Percentage(%)	
	2004	2005		2004	2005
地区生产总值 Gross Domestic Product	**3 110.97**	**3 697.62**	**14.7**	**100.0**	**100.0**
第一产业 Primary Industry	**105.28**	**112.38**	**4.3**	**3.4**	**3.0**
第二产业 Secondary Industry	**1 685.93**	**2 051.17**	**17.6**	**54.2**	**55.5**
工　业 Tertiary Industry	1 549.67	1 885.04	17.9	49.8	51.0
建筑业 Construction	136.26	166.13	13.5	4.4	4.5
第三产业 Tertiary Industry	**1 319.76**	**1 534.07**	**11.7**	**42.4**	**41.5**
交通运输、仓储和邮政业 Transport, Storage and Post Services	222.83	227.16	0.4	7.1	6.2
信息传输、计算机服务和软件业 Information Transmitting, Conputer Services and Software	65.14	77.13	16.2	2.1	2.1
批发和零售业 Wholesale and Retail Trade	372.32	436.14	15.3	12.0	11.8
住宿和餐饮业 Accommodation and Catering Services	56.45	70.15	16.7	1.8	1.9
金融业 Finance Intermediation	136.97	159.24	15.6	4.4	4.3
房地产业 Real Estate	106.14	128.77	12.6	3.4	3.5
租赁和商务服务业 Leasing and Business Services	26.92	45.60	17.5	0.9	1.2
科学研究、技术服务和地质勘查业 Scientific Research, Technical Service and Geological Prospecting	63.12	78.98	15.2	2.0	2.1
水利、环境和公共设施管理业 Management for Water Conservancy, Environment and Public Facilities	18.65	21.89	13.4	0.6	0.6
居民服务和其他服务业 Resident Services and Other Social Services	60.96	66.90	11.4	2.0	1.8
教　育 Education	77.01	93.25	14.4	2.5	2.5
卫生、社会保障和社会福利业 Health Care, Social Security and Social Welfare	39.05	40.35	4.9	1.2	1.1
文化、体育和娱乐业 Culture, Sports and Recreational Services	13.12	13.24	12.6	0.4	0.4
公共管理和社会组织 Public Management and Social Organizations	61.08	75.27	15.2	2.0	2.0

1－13　支出法地区生产总值(2001－2005年)
GROSS DOMESTIC PRODUCT BY EXPENDITURE APPROACH,2001－2005

单位:亿元　(100 million yuan)

年　份 Year	2001	2002	2003	2004	2005
地区生产总值 Gross Domestic Product	**1 919.09**	**2 150.76**	**2 578.03**	**3 110.97**	**3 697.62**
最终消费 Final Consumption Expenditure	948.42	1 040.49	1 193.05	1 343.65	1 506.91
居民消费 Household Consumption	667.57	706.66	781.22	877.16	980.05
农村居民 Rural Households	94.35	99.33	106.75	114.36	122.32
城镇居民 Urban Households	573.22	607.33	674.47	762.80	857.73
政府消费 Government Consumption	280.85	333.83	411.83	466.49	526.86
资本形成总额 Gross Capital Formation	927.90	1 048.50	1 313.06	1 661.24	1 968.45
固定资本形成总额 Gross Fixed Capital Formation	805.34	926.65	1 180.54	1 446.49	1 753.92
存货增加 Changes in Inventories	122.56	121.85	132.52	214.75	214.53
货物和服务净出口 Net Export of Goods and Services	42.77	61.77	71.92	106.08	222.26

1－14　居民消费水平(2001－2005年)
HOUSEHOLD CONSUMPTION ,2001－2005

单位:元/人　(yuan/person)

指　标　Item	2001	2002	2003	2004	2005
全市居民消费水平 All Households	**6 763**	**7 120**	**7 789**	**8 621**	**9 484**
农村居民 Agricultural	3 267	3 466	3 758	4 079	4 360
城镇居民 Non－Agricultural	8 231	8 604	9 377	10 348	11 394
农村居民与城镇居民对比(以农村居民为1) Ratio of Consumption of Agricultural to Non－Agricultural(Agricultural as 1)	**1:2.52**	**1:2.48**	**1:2.49**	**1:2.54**	**1:2.61**

1－15　主要社会经济效益指标(2001－2005年)
MAJOR ECONOMIC EFFICIENCY INDICATORS,2001－2005

项　目　Item	2001	2002	2003	2004	2005
社会劳动生产率(元/人) Overall Labor Productivity(yuan/person)	**39 357**	**43 851**	**51 380**	**59 903**	**69 095**
第一产业 Primary Industry	9 602	10 210	10 869	12 683	13 653
第二产业 Secondary Industry	44 115	51 148	62 959	76 061	90 907
第三产业 Tertiary Industry	46 823	50 125	55 696	61 479	67 519
资本形成率(投资率)(%) Rate of Capital Formation (Investment Rate)(%)	**48.4**	**48.8**	**50.9**	**53.4**	**53.2**
消费率(%) Consumption Rate(%)	**49.4**	**48.4**	**46.3**	**43.2**	**40.8**

1－16　最终消费及构成

FINAL CONSUMPTION EXPENDITURE AND COMPOSITION

项　　目　　Item	绝对数(亿元) Number (100 million yuan)		构　成(%) Composition in Percentage(%)	
	2004	2005	2004	2005
最终消费				
Final Consumption Expenditure	**1 343.65**	**1 506.91**	**100**	**100**
居民消费				
Household Consumption	**877.16**	**980.05**	**65.3**	**65.3**
			(100)	**(100)**
农村居民				
Rural Households	114.36	122.32	13.0	12.5
食品类支出				
Food	35.60	38.61	4.0	4.0
衣着类支出				
Clothing	8.24	10.16	0.9	1.0
居住类支出				
Residence	11.99	12.60	1.4	1.3
家庭设备、用品及服务类支出				
Household Facilities, Articles and Services	3.28	3.03	0.4	0.3
医疗保健类支出				
Medicine and Medical Services	7.29	7.52	0.8	0.8
公共医疗消费支出				
Commonality Medicine and Medical Services	0.00	0.01	0.0	0.0
交通和通信类支出				
Transport and Communication Services	6.76	7.58	0.8	0.8
文教娱乐用品及服务类支出				
Recreation, Education and Cultural Services	6.95	7.07	0.8	0.7
金融中介服务虚拟支出				
Invented Expenditure for Finance Agent Service	15.31	17.69	1.7	1.8
自有住房服务虚拟支出				
Invented Expenditure for Own Housing Service	15.86	14.96	1.8	1.5
其他商品和服务类支出				
Other Goods and Services	3.08	3.09	0.4	0.3
城镇居民				
Urban Households	762.80	857.73	87.0	87.5
食品类支出				
Food	241.65	266.70	27.6	27.2
衣着类支出				
Clothing	46.04	52.61	5.3	5.4
居住类支出				
Residence	90.68	97.23	10.3	9.9
家庭设备、用品及服务类支出				
Household Facilities, Articles and Services	36.67	39.46	4.2	4.0
医疗保健类支出				
Medicine and Medical Services	60.74	75.00	6.9	7.7
公共医疗消费支出				
Commonality Medicine and Medical Services	34.5	42.23	3.9	4.3
交通和通信类支出				
Transport and Communication Services	58.07	75.12	6.6	7.7
文教娱乐用品及服务类支出				
Recreation, Education and Cultural Services	90.85	96.63	10.4	9.9
金融中介服务虚拟支出				
Invented Expenditure for Finance Agent Service	43.92	47.47	5.0	4.8
自有住房服务虚拟支出				
Invented Expenditure for Own Housing Service	23.97	30.28	2.7	3.1
实物消费支出				
Practicality	11.54	11.09	1.3	1.1
其他商品和服务类支出				
Other Goods and Services	24.17	23.91	2.8	2.4
政府消费				
Government Consumption	**466.49**	**526.86**	**34.7**	**34.7**

1－17　天津在全国的地位

POSITION OF TIANJIN IN THE WHOLE NATION

指　标	Item	2000 天　津 Tianjin	2000 占全国比重 As Percentage To Nation (%)	2005 天　津 Tianjin	2005 占全国比重 As Percentage To Nation (%)
年末常住人口(万人)	**Permanent Population(year－end)(10 000 persons)**	**1 001.14**	**0.8**	**1 043.00**	**0.8**
社会从业人员(万人)	**Total Persons Employed(10 000 persons)**	**486.89**	**0.7**	**542.52**	**0.7**
地区生产总值(亿元)	**Gross Domestic Product(100 million yuan)**	**1 701.88**	**1.7**	**3 697.62**	**2.0**
第一产业	Primary Industry	73.69	0.5	109.4	0.5
第二产业	Secondary Industry	863.83	1.8	2 050.3	2.4
第三产业	Tertiary Industry	764.36	2.0	1 504.1	2.0
财政、金融(亿元)	**Governmet Finance and Banking(100 million)**				
地方一般预算财政收入	Local General Budgetary Financial Revenue	133.61	1.0	331.9	2.2
一般预算财政支出	General Budgetary Financial Expenditure	187.05	1.2	442.1	1.8
金融机构本外币存款余额	Balance of Home and Foreign Currency Deposits	2 553.85	1.8	6 090.50	2.0
金融机构本外币贷款余额	Balance of Home and Foreign Currency Loans	2 232.57	1.9	4 722.38	2.3
保费收入	Premium	31.47	2.0	90.64	1.8
规模以上工业增加值(亿元)	**Gross Output Value of Industry(Above Designated Size)(100 million yuan)**	**630.09**	**2.5**	**1 836.30**	**2.8**
轻工业	Light Industry	190.61	2.0	346.45	1.7
重工业	Heavy Industry	439.49	2.8	1 489.84	3.3
主要工业产品产量	**Output of Major Industrial Products**				
钢(万吨)	Steel(10 000 tons)	356.76	2.8	955.3	2.7
生　铁(万吨)	Pig Iron(10 000 tons)	227.99	1.7	660.2	2.0
水　泥(万吨)	Cement(10 000 tons)	267.81	0.4	519.2	0.5
发电量(亿千瓦时)	Electricity(100 million kwh)	211.49	1.6	365.7	1.5
原　油(万吨)	Crude Oil(10 000 tons)	763.99	4.7	1 782.9	9.9
原　盐(万吨)	Salt(10 000 tons)	241.5	7.7	230.1	5.2
天然气(亿立方米)	Natural Gas(100 million cu. m)	9.10	3.3	8.8	1.8
轿　车(万辆)	Motor Vehicles(10 000 units)	8.20	13.5	32.56	11.8
自行车(万辆)	Bicycles(10 000 units)	311.99	10.7	1 306.7	23.2
移动电话机(万部)	Mobile Phone(10 000 units)	1 316.37	25.1	6 319.82	20.8
化学纤维(万吨)	Chemical Fibers(10 000 tons)	11.19	1.6	20.54	1.3
纱(万吨)	Yarn(10 000 tons)	8.80	1.3	7.32	0.5
布(亿米)	Cloth(100 million m)	2.92	1.1	2.58	0.5
彩色电视机(万台)	Color Television Sets(10 000 sets)	72.28	1.8	64.9	0.8

1－17 续表 Continued

指 标	Item	2000 天 津 Tianjin	2000 占全国比重 As Percentage To Nation (%)	2005 天 津 Tianjin	2005 占全国比重 As Percentage To Nation (%)
空调器(万台)	Air Conditioners(10 000 sets)	104.15	5.7	434.43	6.4
主要农产品产量(万吨)	**Output of Major Farm Products(10 000 tons)**				
粮 食	Grain	124.05	0.3	137.5	0.3
肉 类	Meat	29.49	0.5	57.8	0.7
蛋 类	Eggs	25.6	1.1	23.47	0.8
水产品	Aquatic Products	24.22	0.1	33.81	0.7
全社会固定资产投资额(亿元)	**Total Investment in Fixed Assets(100 million yuan)**	**608.8**	**1.9**	**1 516.84**	**1.7**
#房地产开发投资额	Real Estate Development	133.93	2.7	327.5	2.1
运输、邮政、电信	**Transportation,Post & Telecommunications Service**				
港口货物吞吐量(万吨)	Freight Handled at Ports(10 000 tons)	9 582	7.6	24 069	8.2
社会货物运输量(万吨)	Freight Traffic(10 000 tons)	26 523	1.9	40 263	2.2
邮电业务总量(亿元)	Post & Telecommunications Services (100 million yuan)	75.37	1.6	176.35	1.4
商业、外贸、外经	**Commerce,Foreign Trade & Foreign Capital**				
社会消费品零售总额(亿元)	Total Retail Sales of Consumer Goods (100 million yuan)	736.63	2.2	1 190.1	1.8
外贸出口总额(亿美元)	Total Value of Exports in Foreign Trade(USD 100 million)	86.29	3.5	274.15	3.6
实际利用外资额(亿美元)	Foreign Capital Actually Used(USD 100 million)	28.25	4.8	36.46	5.7
教育、科技、卫生、文化	**Education,Science & Technology,Health Care,Culture**				
高等学校在校学生数(万人)	Number of Students at Colleges and Universities(10 000 persons)	11.77	2.1	33.16	2.1
技术市场成交额(亿元)	Transaction Volume in the Technology Market(100 million yuan)	26.26	4.0	50.71	3.3
专利申请授权量(项)	Patent Applications Granted(item)	1 611	1.5	3 045	1.4
医院、卫生院(个)	Number of Hospitals(unit)	488	0.7	461	0.8
医院、卫生院床位(万张)	Number of Hospital Beds(10 000 units)	3.88	1.3	3.95	1.3
图书出版数(万册)	Number of Books Published(10 000 copies)	5 881	0.9	5 917	0.9
杂志出版数(万册)	Number of Magazines Issued(10 000 copies)	5 291	1.8	4 192	1.5
报纸出版数(亿份)	Number of Newspapers Issued(100 million copies)	5.99	1.8	8.76	2.2

主要统计指标解释

生产总值(原国内生产总值) 指按市场价格计算的一个国家(或地区)所有常住单位在一定时期内生产活动的最终成果。

从价值形态看,它是所有常驻单位在一定时期内所生产的全部货物和服务价值超过同期投入的全部非固定资产货物和服务价值的差额,即所有常驻单位的增加值之和;从收入形态看,它是所有常驻单位在一定时期内所创造并分配给常驻单位和非常驻单位的初次分配收入之和;从产品形态看,它是最终使用的货物和服务减去进口货物和服务。在实际核算中,其三种表现形态体现为三种计算方法,即生产法、收入法和支出法。三种方法分别从不同的方面反映生产总值及其构成。根据国务院和国家统计局有关我国 GDP 核算和数据发布制度的规定,天津市国内生产总值自 2004 年起更名为“天津市生产总值”简称“天津市 GDP”。

绿色 GDP 人类的经济活动包括两方面的活动。一方面为社会创造着财富,即所谓“正面效应”,但另一方面又在以种种形式和手段对社会生产力的发展起着阻碍作用,即所谓“负面效应”。改革现行的国民经济核算体系,对环境资源进行核算,从现行 GDP 中扣除环境资源成本和对环境资源的保护服务费用,其计算结果可称之为“绿色 GDP”。绿色 GDP 指标,实质上代表了国民经济增长的净正效应。绿色 GDP 占 GDP 的比重越高,表明国民经济增长的正面效应越高,负面效应越低,反之亦然。

劳动者报酬 指劳动者因从事生产活动所获得的全部报酬。包括劳动者获得的各种形式的工资、奖金和津贴,既包括货币形式的,也包括实物形式的,还包括劳动者所享受的公费医疗和医药卫生费、上下班交通补贴和单位支付的社会保险费、住房公积金等。对于个体经济来说,其所有者所获得的劳动报酬和经营利润不易区分,这两部分统一作为劳动者报酬处理。

生产税净额 指生产税减生产补贴后的余额。生产税指政府对生产单位生产、销售和从事经营活动以及因从事生产活动使用某些生产要素(如固定资产、土地、劳动力)所征收的各种税、附加费和规费。生产补贴与生产税相反,指政府对生产单位的单方面转移支付,因此视为负生产税,包括政策亏损补贴、价格补贴等。

固定资产折旧 指一定时期内为弥补固定资产损耗按照核定的固定资产折旧率提取的固定资产折旧,或按国民经济核算统一规定的折旧率虚拟计算的固定资产折旧。它反映了固定资产在当期生产中的转移价值。各类企业和企业化管理的事业单位的固定资产折旧是指实际计提的折旧费;不计提折旧的政府机关、非企业化管理的事业单位和居民住房的固定资产折旧是按照统一规定的折旧率和固定资产原值计算的虚拟折旧。原则上,固定资产折旧应按固定资产的重置价值计算,但是目前我国尚不具备对全社会固定资产进行重估价的基础,所以暂时只能采用这种办法。

营业盈余 指常住单位创造的增加值扣除劳动者报酬、生产税净额和固定资产折旧后的余额。它相当于企业的营业利润加上生产补贴,但要扣除从利润中开支的工资和福利等。

最终消费 指常住单位在一定时期内对于货物和服务的全部最终消费支出,也就是常住单位为满足物质、文化和精神生活的需要,从本国经济领土和国外购买的货物和服务的支出。不包括非常住单位在本国经济领土内的消费支出。最终消费分为居民消费和政府消费。

居民消费 指常住住户对货物和服务的全部最终消费支出。它除了常住住户直接以货币形式购买货物和服务的消费之外,还包括以其他方式获得的货物和服务的消费,即单位以实物报酬及实物转移的形式提供给劳动者的货物和服务;住户生产并由住户自己消费的货物和服务,其中的服务仅指住户的自有住房服务和支付报酬的家庭服务;金融机构提供的金融媒介服务;保险公司提供的保险服务。

政府消费 指政府部门为全社会提供公共服务的消费支出和免费或以较低价格向住户提供的货物和服务的净支出。前者等于政府服务的产出价值减去政府单位所获得的经营收入后的价值,政府服务的产出价值等于它的经常性业务支出加上固定资产折旧;后者等于政府部门免费或以较低价格向住户提供的货物和服务的市场价值减去向住户收取的价值。

资本形成总额 指常住单位在一定时期内获得的减去处置的固定资产加存货的净变动额,包括固定资本形成总额和存货增加。

固定资本形成总额 指生产者在一定时期内获得的固定资产减处置的固定资产的价值总额,固定资产是通过生产活动生产出来的，其使用年限在一年以上，单位价值在规定标准以上的资产，不包括自然资产。固定资本形成总额可分为有形固定资本形成总额和无形固定资本形成总额。有形固定资本形成总额包括一定时期内完成的建筑工程、安装工程、设备工器具购置(减处置)价值以及土地改良、新增役、种、奶、毛、娱乐用牲畜和新增经济林木价值。无形固定资本形成总额包括矿藏的勘探、计算机软件等获得减处置。

存货增加 指常住单位在一定时期内存货实物量变动的市场价值，即期末价值减期初价值的差额，再扣除当期由于价格变动而产生的持有收益。存货增加可以是正值，也可以是负值；正值表示存货增加，负值表示存货减少。它包括生产单位购进的原材料、燃料和储备物资等存货，以及生产单位生产的产成品、在制品存货等。

货物和服务净出口 指货物和服务出口减货物和服务进口的差额。出口包括常住单位向非常住单位出售和无偿转让的各种货物和服务的价值；进口包括常住单位从非常住单位购买或无偿得到的各种货物和服务的价值。由于服务活动的提供与使用同时发生，因此服务的进出口业务并不发生出入境现象，一般把常住单位从国外得到的服务作为进口，常住单位向国外提供的服务作为出口。货物的出口和进口都按离岸价格计算。在计算地区货物和服务净出口时，还包括地区间货物和服务的流入流出。

用公式表示：

货物和服务净出口(净流出)＝货物和服务出口(流出)－进口(流入)

行业划分标准 本《年鉴》中各专业指标的行业分类标准均采用《国民经济行业分类》标准(GB/T 4754－2002)。

国民经济行业分类标准(GB/T 4754－2002)

门　类	大类	中类	小类
A 农、林、牧、渔业	5	18	38
B 采矿业	6	15	33
C 制造业	30	169	482
D 电力、燃气及水的生产和供应业	3	7	10
E 建筑业	4	7	11
F 交通运输、仓储和邮政业	9	24	37
G 信息传输、计算机服务和软件业	3	10	14
H 批发和零售业	2	18	93
I 住宿和餐饮业	2	7	7
J 金融业	4	16	16
K 房地产业	1	4	4
L 租赁和商务服务业	2	11	27
M 科学研究、技术服务和地质勘察业	4	19	23
N 水利、环境和公共设施管理业	3	8	18
O 居民服务和其他服务业	2	12	16
P 教　育	1	5	13
Q 卫生、社会保障和社会福利业	3	11	17
R 文化、体育和娱乐业	5	22	29
S 公共管理和社会组织	5	12	24
T 国际组织	1	1	1
(合计)　20	**95**	**396**	**913**

三次产业 根据《国民经济行业分类》标准(GB/T 4754－2002)规定，三次产业划分范围如下：

第一产业：包括农、林、牧、渔业。

第二产业：包括采矿业，制造业，电力、燃气及水的生产和供应业，建筑业。

第三产业：包括除第一、二产业以外的其他行业，具体包括 交通运输、仓储和邮政业，信息传输、计算机服务和软件业，批发和零售业，住宿和餐饮业，金融业，房地产业，租赁和商务服务业，科学研究、技术服务和地质勘查业，水利、环境和公共设施管理业，居民服务和其他服务业，教育，卫生、社会保障和社会福利业，文化、体育和娱乐业，公共管理和社会组织等。

现行价格(或称当年价格) 指报告期的实际价格，如工业品的出厂价格，农副产品的收购价格，商业的零售价格等。它反映当年的实际情况，使国民经济各项指标互相衔接，便于对生产、流通、分配、消费之间进行综合平衡。

可比价格 指计算各种总量指标所采用的扣除了价格变动因素的价格，可进行不同时期总量指标的对比。按可比价格计算总量指标有两种方法：一种是直接用产品产量乘某一年的不变价格计算；另一种是用价格指数进行缩减。

平均增长速度 我国计算平均增长速度有两种方法：一种是习惯上经常使用的“水平法”，又称几何平均法，是以间隔期最后一年的水平同基期水平对比来计算平均每年增长(或下降)速度；另一种是“累计法”，又称代数平均法或方程法，是以间隔期内各年水平的总和同基期水平对比来计算平均每年增长(或下降)速度。在一般正常情况下，两种方法计算的平均每年增长速度比较接近；但在经济发展不平衡、出现大起大落时，两种方法计算的结果差别较大。

本《年鉴》内所列的平均增长速度，除固定资产投资类指标用“累计法”计算外，其余均用“水平法”计算。从某年到某年平均增长速度的年份，均不包括基期年在内。

企业登记注册类型 以工商行政管理部门对企业登记注册的类型为依据，将企业登记注册类型划分为三大类：第一类是内资企业，包括国有企业、集体企业、股份合作企业、私营企业、股份有限公司、有限责任公司、联营企业和其他内资企业。第二类是港、澳、台商投资企业，包括合资经营企业、合作经营企业、港澳台商独资经营企业、港澳台商投资股份有限公司。第三类是外商投资企业，包括中外合资、中外合作、外资企业和外商投资股份有限公司。由于个体经营不属于企业，因此在《关于划分企业登记注册类型的规定》中，未将个体经营列入。但国家明确规定其仍属于国家统计范围，并在分类中单列。企业登记注册类型不同于经济类型，特别是其中的国有企业和集体企业不同于经济类型中的国有经济和集体经济。

内资企业 包括国有企业、集体企业、股份合作企业、私营企业、股份有限公司、有限责任公司、联营企业和其他内资企业。

国有企业 指企业全部资产归国家所有，并按《中华人民共和国企业法人登记管理条例》规定登记注册的非公司制的经济组织。不包括有限责任公司中的国有独资公司和联营企业中的国有与国有联营企业。

集体企业 指企业资产归集体所有，并按《中华人民共和国企业法人登记管理条例》规定登记注册的经济组织。不包括股份合作企业和联营企业中的集体与集体联营企业。

股份合作企业 指以合作制为基础，由企业职工共同出资入股，吸收一定比例的社会资产投资组建，实行自主经营，自负盈亏，共同劳动，民主管理，按劳分配与按股分红相结合的一种集体经济组织。

私营企业 指由自然人投资设立或由自然人控股，以雇佣劳动为基础的营利性经济组织。包括按照《公司法》、《合伙企业法》、《私营企业暂行条例》规定登记注册的私营有限责任公司、私营股份有限公司、私营合伙企业和私营独资企业。

股份有限公司 指根据《中华人民共和国公司登记管理条例》规定登记注册，其全部注册资本由等额股份构成并通过发行股票筹集资本，股东以其认购的股份对公司承担有限责任，公司以其全部资产对其债务承担责任的经济组织。

有限责任公司 指根据《中华人民共和国公司登记管理条例》规定登记注册，由两个以上，五十个以下的股东共同出资，每个股东以其所认缴的出资额对公司承担有限责任，公司以其全部资产对其债务承担责任的经济组织。有限责任公司包括国有独资公司以及其他有限责任公司。

国有独资公司 指国家授权的投资机构或者国家授权的部门单独投资设立的有限责任公司。

其他有限责任公司 指国有独资公司以外的其他有限责任公司。

联营企业 指两个及两个以上相同或不同所有制性质的企业法人或事业单位法人，按自愿、平等、互利的原则共同投资组成的经济组织。

其他内资企业 指上述内资企业之外的其他内资经济组织。

港澳台商投资企业 包括合资经营企业（港或澳、台资）、合作经营企业（港或澳、台资）、港澳台商独资经营企业和港澳台商投资股份有限公司。

港、澳、台商独资经营企业 指依照《中华人民共和国外资企业法》及有关法律的规定，在内地由港澳台地区投资者全额投资设立的企业。

港、澳、台商投资股份有限公司 指根据国家有关规定，经外经贸部（现为商务部）依法批准设立，其中港、澳、台商的股本占公司注册资本的比例达25%以上的股份有限公司。凡其中港、澳、台商的股本占公司注册资本的比例小于25%的，属于内资企业中的股份有限公司。

外商投资企业 包括中外合资经营企业、中外合作经营企业、外资（独资）企业和外商投资股份有限公司。

个体经营 指除农户外，生产资料归劳动者个人所有，以个体劳动为基础，劳动成果归劳动者个人占有和支配的一种经营单位。包括按照《民法通则》和《城乡个体经营户管理暂行条例》规定登记注册的个体工商户和个人合伙，以及没有领取营业执照，但从事个体经营活动的城镇、农村个体经营单位。

行政机关、事业单位和社会团体填写登记注册类型参照企业登记注册类型，主要按其经费来源和管理方式划分。具体规定如下：

(1)**行政机关**:包括国家机关和政党机关，原则上均列为“国有”。但有特殊规定的，如供销社等，则列为“集体”。

(2)**事业单位**:包括经国家机构编制部门和有关业务主管部门批准成立的各类事业单位，不包括实行企业化管理的事业单位。事业单位的划分办法如下：

① 由国家财政预算拨款或列入财政预算外资金管理以及经费主要来源于国有主管部门或国有上级单位的事业单位，列为“国有”。

②经费主要来源于集体单位的事业单位，列为“集体”。

③ 公民个人（或个人合伙）开办的事业单位，列为“私营”。

④ 上述以外的其他事业单位，如果其经费来源不明确，按管理方式进行归类。

(3)**社会团体**:包括经民政部门批准成立以及未纳入社会团体管理条例范围的工会、妇联等各类社会团体。社会团体的划分办法如下：

① 未纳入民政部社会团体管理条例范围的工会、妇联、共青团、青联、工商联、科协、侨联等社会团体，国家拨款设立的基金会或基金管理组织以及经费主要来源于国有业务主管部门或国有上级单位的社会团体，列为“国有”。

②经费主要来源于集体单位的社会团体，列为“集体”。

③ 公民个人（或个人合伙）开办的社会团体，划为“私营”。

④ 上述以外的其他社会团体，如果其经费来源不明确，改按管理方式进行归类。

经济类型 本《年鉴》中的经济类型分组，从1998年开始是在企业登记注册类型分组基础上的再加工，其中国有经济包括国有企业、国有独资和国有与国有联营企业；集体经济包括集体企业、股份合作企业和集体与集体联营企业。私有经济包括私营企业和个体经营。

Explanatory Notes on Main Statistical Indicators

Gross Domestic Product refers to the final products at market prices produced by all resident units in a country(or a region) during a certain period of time.

The form of value added refers to the total value of all products and services produced by all resident units during a certain period of time minus total value of inputs of non－fixed－assets products and services or the summation of the value added of all resident units; the form of prduct refers to all final goods and services minus improts of goods and services. In the practice of national accounting, it is calculated by three approaches, i. e. product approach, income approach and expenditure approach, respectively, to reflect Gross Product and its composition of different aspects. According to the regulations of GDP national accounting as Tianjin Gross Product Value, for short Tianjin GDP.

Green Economic GDP The human economic activities include two components. On one hand, creating wealth for social, namely so－called "positive effect", but on the other hand, obstructing the development of the social productivity with all kinds of measures, namely so－called "negative effect" Green Economic GDP, i.e. the current GDP minus the environment resources cost and the protection service charge of the environment resources through reforming the current national economy accounts system and accounting the environment resources. Green Economic GDP, represents the net positive effect of national economy growth. The higher the weight of the Green Economic GDP accounted for the GDP, the higher the positive effect of national economy is, the lower the negative effect is, contrarily, the lower the positive effect of national economy is, the higher the negative effect is.

Laborer Remuneration refers to the whole payment of various forms earned by the laborers from the productive activities they are engaged in. It includes wages, bonuses and allowances the laborers earned in monetary form and in kind. It also includes the free medical services provided to the laborers and the medicine expenses, traffic subsidies, social insurance fee and housing provident fund paid by the laborer's working units for them. As the individual economy is concerned, since the laborer's remuneration is not easily distinguished from the operating profit, both are treated as laborer's remuneration.

Net Taxes on Production refers to the residual of the taxes on production minus the subsidies on production. The taxes on production refers to the various taxes, extra charges and fees levied on the production units on their production, sale and business activities as well as on some sectors of production, such as fixed assets, land and labour force, used in the production activities they are engaged in. In contrast to the taxes on production, the subsidies on production refer to the unilateral transfer of part of the government's revenue to the production units and are therefore regarded as negative taxes on production. They include subsidies on the loss due to implementation of government policies, price subsidies, etc.

Depreciation of Fixed Assets refers to the depreciation of fixed assets of a given period, drawn in accordance with the stipulated depreciation rate for the purpose of compensating the wear loss of the fixed assets or the depreciation of fixed assets calculated in a fictitious way in accordance with the stipulated unified depreciation rate in the national economic accounting system. It reflects the value of transfer of the fixed assets in the production of the current period. The depreciation of fixed assets in various enterprises and institutions managed as enterprises refers to the depreciation expenses actually drawn. In government agencies and institutions not managed as enterprises which do not draw the depreciation expenses, as well as for the houses of residents, the depreciation of fixed assets is the imputed depreciation, which is calculated in accordance with the stipulated unified depreciation rate. In principle, the depreciation of fixed assets should be calculated on the basis of the re－purchased value of the fixed assets. However, there is no actual condition to re－evaluate all the fixed assets in China. Therefore, this method is temporarily adopted at present.

Operating Surplus refers to the balance of the value added created by the resident units deducting the laborer's remuneration, net taxes on production and the depreciation of fixed assets. It is equivalent to the business profit of the enterprises plus subsidies on production, but the wages and welfare expenses paid from the profits should be deducted.

Final Consumption refers to the total expenditure of resident units on final consumption of goods and services in a certain period, namely the expenditure of the resident units for purchases of goods and services from domestic economic territory and abroad to meet the requirements of material, cultural and spiritual life. It excludes the consumption expenditure of non-resident units on consumption in the economic territory of the country. The final consumption is classified into households consumption and government consumption.

Households Consumption refers to the total expenditure of resident households on the final consumption of goods and services. In addition to the consumption of goods and services bought by the households directly with money, the households consumption also includes expenditure on goods and services obtained by the households on other ways, i.e. the goods and services provided to the households by the units in the form of payment in kind and transfer in kind; the goods and services produced and consumed by the households themselves, in which the services refer only to the owner-occupied housing and domestic services provided by the paid household workers; financial intermediate services provided by financial institutions; insurance services provided by insurance companies.

Government Consumption refers to the expenditure on the consumption of the public services provided by the government to the whole society and the net expenditure on the goods and services provided by the government to the households at free charge or lower prices. The former equals to the output value of the government services minus the value of operating income obtained by the government departments, the output value of the government services equals to its current operating expenditure plus depreciation of fixed assets. The latter equals to the market value of the goods and services provided by the government free of charge or at low prices to the households minus the value received by the government from the households.

Total Capital Formation refers to the fixed assets acquired minus those disposed and the net value of inventory, including the total fixed assets formation and the increase in inventory.

Total Fixed Capital Formation refers to the value of fixed assets acquired minus those disposed of during a given period. Fixed assets are the assets produced through production activities with specified unit value which could be used for over one year, excluding natural assets. Total fixed capital formation can be categorized into total tangible assets formation and total intangible assets formation. The total tangible assets formation include the value of the construction projects, installation projects completed and the equipment, apparatus and instruments purchased as well as the value of land improved, the value of draught animals, breeding stock, animal for milk, wool and for recreational animals purpose and the newly increased forest with economic value during a given period. The total intangible assets formation includes the prospecting of minerals, the acquisition of computer software minus the disposal of them.

Increase in Inventory refers to the market value of the change in inventory of resident units during a given period, i.e. the difference of value between the beginning and the end of the period minus the current gains due to the change in prices. The increase in inventory can be positive or negative. A positive value indicates the increase in inventory while a negative value indicates the decrease in stock. The inventory includes the raw materials, fuel and reserve materials purchased by the production units as well as the inventory of finished products, semi-finished products, etc.

Net Export of Goods and Services refers to the difference of the exports of goods and services minus the imports of goods and services. The imports include the value of various goods and services sold or gratuitously transferred by the resident units to the non-resident units. The imports include the value of various goods and services purchased or gratuitously acquired by the resident units from the non-resident units. Because the provision of services and the use of them happen simultaneously, the import and export of services do not appear to have the phenomena of crossing the border of the country. The acquisition of services by the resident units from abroad is usually treated as import while the acquisition of services by non-resident units in this country is usually treated as export. The export and import of goods are calculated at FOB. The formula for calculating is as follows:

Net export of goods and services = value of export of goods and services － value of import of goods and services

Standard of Industry Categorized In this statistical yearbook, the industry category adopts the standard (GB/T 4754－2002).

National Economy Industry Category (GB/T 4754－2002)

Industry	Large	Middle	Small
A Farming, Forestry, Animal Husbandry and Fishery	5	18	38
B Minerals Mining	6	15	33
C Manufacturing	30	169	482
D Production & Supply of Power, Gas and Water	3	7	10
E Construction	4	7	11
F Transport, Storage, Post Services	9	24	37
G Information Transmitting, Computer Services and Software	3	10	14
H Wholesale and Retail Trade	2	18	93
I Accommodation and Catering Services	2	7	7
J Finance	4	16	16
K Real Estate	1	4	4
L Leasing and Business Services	2	11	27
M Scientific Research, Technical Services and Geological Prospecting	4	19	23
N Management for Water Conservancy, Environment and Public Facilities	3	8	18
O Resident Services and Other Social Services	2	12	16
P Education	1	5	13
Q Health Care, Social Security and Social Welfare	3	11	17
R Culture, Sports and Recreational Services	5	22	29
S Public Management and Social Organizations	5	12	24
T International Organizations	1	1	1
(Total) 20	**95**	**396**	**913**

Three Industries According to the standard of national economy industry category (GB/T 4754－2002), three industries are categorized as following.

Primary Industry include agriculture, forestry, animal husbandry and fishery.

Secondary Industry include minerals mining, manufacturing, production and supply of electricity, gas and water, construction.

Tertiary Industry include all other industries not included in primary or secondary industry, including transport, storage, post services; information transmitting, computer services and software; wholesale and retail trade; accommodation and catering services; finance; real estate; leasing and business services; scientific research, technical services and geological prospecting; management for water conservancy, environment and public facilities; resident services and other social services; education; health care, social security and social welfare; culture, sports and recreational services; public management and social organizations and so on.

Actual Price (current year price) include all other industries not included in primary or secondary industry, including transport, storage, post services; information transmitting, computer services and software; wholesale and retail trade; accommodation and catering services; finance; real estate; leasing and business services; scientific research, technical services and geological prospecting; management for water conservancy, environment and public facilities; resident services and other social services; education; health care, social security and social welfare; culture, sports and recreational services; public management and social organizations and so on.

Comparable Prices refer to prices that are used to remove the factors of price change in calculating economic aggregates, so as to facilitate comparison of aggregates over time. Two methods are used for calculating economic aggregates at comparable prices, a) Multiplying the output of products by their constant prices of certain year; b) Deflation of data at current prices by relevant price index.

Average Annual Growth Rate Two methods for calculating average annual growth rate are applied in China, one is often called "level approach", or the method of calculating geometric average, which is derived by comparing the level of the last year of the interval with that of the beginning year; the other is called "accumulative approach" or algebraic average or equation method, which is derived by the summation of the actual figure of each year in the interval divided by the figure in the base year. Usually the results calculated by the two methods are fairly close, but they differed sharply when uneven economic development occurred with striking fluctuations in growth.

The average annual growth rate listed in this statistical yearbook are calculated by "level approach" except for the growth rate of investment in fixed assets. The base years are not listed when the years are listed for average annual growth rates.

Registration Status of Enterprises Enterprises are classified into 3 categories, in the light of the registration status of an enterprise in industrial and commercial administration agencies. Domestic - funded enterprises include state - owned enterprises, collective - owned enterprises, cooperative enterprises, private enterprises, share - holding corporations Ltd., limited liability corporations, joint ownership enterprises and other domestic - funded enterprises. Hongkong, Macao and Taiwan funded enterprises include joint venture enterprises, cooperative enterprises, sole investment enterprises and share - holding corporations Ltd. Foreign funded enterprises include Chinese - foreign joint venture enterprises, Chinese - foreign cooperative enterprises, sole foreign funded enterprises and share - holding corporations Ltd. with foreign investment. Due to individuals don't belong to enterprises, individuals don't be listed according to the "Regulation of Registered Status of Enterprises". But individuals belong to statistical category. Registered status of enterprises is different to ownership, especially, state - owned and collective - owned enterprises are different to state - owned and collective - owned economy.

Domestic - funded Enterprises include state - owned enterprises, collective - owned enterprises, cooperative enterprises, private enterprises, share - holding corporations Ltd., limited liability corporations, joint ownership enterprises and others.

State - owned Enterprises refer to non - corporation economic units where the entire assets are owned by the state and which have registered in accordance with the Regulation of the People's Republic of China on the Management of Registration of Corporate Enterprises. Excluded from this category are sole state - funded corporations in the limited liability corporations. Excluded from this category are enterprises with exclusive investment from state - owned, state - owned cooperative enterprises in the join ownership enterprises.

Collective - owned Enterprises refer to economic units where the assets are owned collectively and which have registered in accordance with the Regulation of the People's Republic of China on the Management of Registration of Corporate Enterprises. Excluded from this category are collective - owned and collective - owned cooperative enterprises in joint ownership enterprises, excluded cooperative enterprises.

Cooperative Enterprises refer to a form of collective economic units (enterprises) where capitals come mainly from employees as their shares, with certain proportion of capital from the outside, where production is organized on the basis of independent operation, independent accounting for profits and losses, joint work, democratic management, and a distribution system that integrates remuneration according to work with divided according to capital share.

Private Enterprises refer to profit - making economic units invested and established by natural persons, or controlled by natural persons using employed labour. Included in this category are private limited liability corporations, private share - holding corporations Ltd., private partnership enterprises and private - funded enterprises registered in accordance with the Corporation Law, Partnership Enterprises Law and Interim Regulations on Private Enterprises.

Share - holding Corporations Ltd. refer to economic units registered in accordance with the Regulation of the People's Republic of China on the Management of Registration of Corporations, with total registered capitals divided into equal shares and raised through issuing stocks. Each investor bears limited liability to the corporation depending on the holding of shares,and the corporation bears liability to its debt to the maximum of its total assets.

Limited Liability Corporations refer to economic units established with investment from 2 – 50 investors and registered in accordance with the Regulation of the People's Republic of China on the Management of Registration of Corporations, each investor bearing limited liability to the corporation depending on its share of investment, and the corporation bearing liability to its debt to the maximum of its total assets. Limited liability corporations include exclusive state – funded limited liability corporations and other limited liability corporations.

Sole State – funded Corporations refer to limited liability corporations established with exclusive investment from investment institutions or departments authorized by the state.

Other Limited Liability Corporations refer to the limited liability corporations other than sole state – funded corporations.

Joint Ownership Enterprises refer to economic units established by two or more corporate enterprises or corporate institutions of the same or different ownership, through joint investment on the basis of equality, voluntary participation and mutual benefits. They include state joint ownership enterprises, collective joint ownership enterprises, joint state – collective enterprises, other joint ownership enterprises.

Other Domestic – funded Enterprises refer to domestic – funded economic units other than those mentioned above.

Enterprises with Investment from Hongkong, Macao and Taiwan include joint venture enterprises with funds from Hongkong, Macao and Taiwan, cooperative enterprises with funds from Hongkong, Macao and Taiwan, enterprises with exclusive investment from Hongkong, Macao and Taiwan, share – holding corporations Ltd. with investment from Hongkong, Macao and Taiwan.

Enterprises with Exclusive Investment from Hongkong, Macao and Taiwan refer to enterprises established in the mainland of China with exclusive investment from investors from Hongkong, Macao and Taiwan in accordance with the Law of the People's Republic of China on Foreign – Funded Enterprises and other relevant laws.

Share – holding Corporations Ltd. with Investment from Hongkong, Macao and Taiwan refer to share – holding corporations Ltd. established with the approval from the Ministry of Foreign Trade and Economic Relations (the Ministry of Commerce) in line with relevant state regulations, where the share of investment from Hongkong, Macao or Taiwan business men exceeds 25% of the total registered capital of the corporation. In case, the share of investment from Hongkong, Macao or Taiwan is less than 25% of the total registered capital, the enterprise is to be classified as domestic – funded share – holding corporation Ltd.

Foreign Funded Enterprises include joint venture enterprises with foreign investment, cooperation enterprises with foreign investment, enterprises with exclusive foreign investment, share – holding corporations Ltd. with foreign investment.

Individual refer to economic units which the production materials are owned by individual, where production is organized on the basis of individual operation, labors results are owned and used by laborer, including economic units where have registered in accordance with Civil Law General Rule and individual industrialists and businessmen or a group of citizens which have registered in urban and rural industrial and commercial administration agencies, urban and rural individual where have no business licenses but undertake individual operation.

Government Agencies, Institutions and Social Organization are classified into following categories by source of funds and way of management taking reference of the registration status of enterprises.

(1)**Government agencies** include state and party agencies, classified in principle as "state – owned". There are exceptions, such as supply and marketing cooperatives which are classified as "collective – owned".

(2)**Institutions** include institutions of various types established with the approval by organization and staffing department of the government, but exclude institutions where enterprise management system is introduced. Institutions are further classified as follows:

(a) Institutions whose main budget is listed in the government budget appropriations or extra - budget funds, or allocated from the budget of their competent government agencies. Such institutions are classified as "state - owned".

(b) Institutions whose budget mainly comes from collective units. Such institutions are classified as "collective - owned".

(c) Institutions established by individual(individual partnership), which are classified as "private".

(d) Institutions other than those mentioned above whose source of budget is not clear. Such institutions are classified by way of management.

(3) **Social organizations** include social organizations established with the approval from the Ministry of Civil Affairs, and organizations that are not covered by social organizations management regulations such as trade unions, women's federations etc.. Social organizations are further classified as follows:

(a) Social organizations that are not covered by social organizations management regulations of the Ministry of Civil Affairs, such as trade unions, women's federations, communist youth leagues, youth associations, industrial and commerce associations, scientists associations, overseas Chinese associations, etc., foundations and fund management organization established with funds from state, and social organizations whose funds mainly come from the budget of their competent government agencies. Such institutions are classified as "state - owned".

(b) Social organizations whose budget mainly comes from collective units. Such institutions are classified as "collective - owned".

(c) Social organizations established by individual(individual partnership), which are classified as "private".

(d) Social organizations other than those mentioned above whose source of budget is not clear. Such institutions are classified by way of management.

Type of Ownership refers to enterprises classified as various type of ownership in accordance with registered categories of enterprises after 1998. In which, state - owned economy refer to state - owned enterprises, sole state - funded enterprises, state joint ownership enterprises, collective - owned economy refer to collective - owned enterprises, cooperative enterprises, collective joint ownership enterprises; private economy refer to private enterprises and individual.

第2篇
CHAPTER 2

人口和劳动就业
Population, Labor and Employment

2-1 人口主要指标(1990-2005年)

MAJOR POPULATION STATISTICS,1990-2005

年 份 Year	常住人口(万人) Permanent Population (10 000 persons)	户籍人口(万人) Registered Population (10 000 persons)	户籍户数(万户) Registered Households (10 000 households)	人口密度(人/平方公里) Population Density (person/sq. km)	人口出生率 Birth Rate (‰)	人口死亡率 Death Rate (‰)	人口自然增长率 Natural Growth Rate (‰)
1990	884.03	866.25	258.31	764	15.62	5.79	9.83
1991	908.89	872.63	262.75	770	11.94	5.78	6.16
1992	920.41	878.97	266.77	776	12.50	6.00	6.50
1993	928.02	885.89	270.77	782	10.71	6.20	4.51
1994	935.28	890.55	273.87	745	10.98	6.19	4.79
1995	941.83	894.67	276.89	749	10.23	6.23	4.00
1996	948.19	898.45	279.62	752	10.09	6.53	3.56
1997	952.59	899.80	284.08	753	9.98	6.95	3.03
1998	956.64	905.09	288.20	757	9.89	6.49	3.40
1999	959.48	910.17	291.32	762	9.68	6.73	2.95
2000	1 001.14	912.00	293.04	763	7.72	6.17	1.55
2001	1 004.06	913.98	295.63	765	7.58	5.94	1.64
2002	1 007.18	919.05	299.67	769	7.49	6.04	1.45
2003	1 011.30	926.00	303.27	775	7.14	6.04	1.10
2004	1 023.67	932.55	316.62	780	7.31	5.97	1.34
2005	1 043.00	939.31	322.95	797	7.44	6.01	1.43

注:1.人口密度2005年按市民政局行政区划面积计算,2005年以前按市规划局土地面积计算。2.人口自然变动"三率"为历年人口调查数据。

Note:a)The population density in 2005 is calculated with administrative areas measured by Tianjin Civil Administration Bureau, and those before 2005 are calculated with areas measured by Tianjin Bureau of Planning . b)The three ratio of population changing are obtained from population survey.

2-2 户籍人口主要构成(1990-2005年)

COMPOSITION OF REGISTERED POPULATION,1990-2005

单位:% (%)

年 份 Year	按户口性质分 By Registered Character		按性别分 By Sex		
	非农业 Non-agricultural	农 业 Agricultural	男 性 Male	女 性 Female	性别比(女=100) Sex Ratio(Female=100)
1990	56.04	43.96	50.79	49.21	103.20
1991	56.19	43.81	50.76	49.24	103.07
1992	56.29	43.71	50.73	49.27	102.96
1993	56.44	43.56	50.71	49.29	102.87
1994	56.60	43.40	50.70	49.30	102.85
1995	56.77	43.23	50.66	49.34	102.67
1996	57.12	42.88	50.62	49.38	102.50
1997	57.27	42.73	50.58	49.42	102.33
1998	57.60	42.40	50.53	49.47	102.14
1999	58.09	41.91	50.51	49.49	102.06
2000	58.39	41.61	50.51	49.49	102.05
2001	58.56	41.44	50.48	49.52	101.92
2002	58.88	41.12	50.45	49.55	101.84
2003	59.37	40.63	50.47	49.53	101.89
2004	59.64	40.36	50.46	49.54	101.86
2005	59.87	40.13	50.44	49.56	101.77

2－3 按地区分的户数、人口数及人口密度

HOUSEHOLDS, POPULATION AND POPULATION DENSITY BY REGION

地区 Region		户数（万户）Households (10 000 households)		人口数（万人）Population (10 000 persons)		年平均人口（万人）Average Annual Population (10 000 persons)	人口密度（人/平方公里）Population Density (person/sq.km)
		2004	2005	2004	2005	(2005)	(2005)
全市常住人口	**Total Permanent Population**	**319.83**	**346.18**	**1 023.67**	**1 043.00**	**1 033.34**	**887**
全市户籍人口	**Total Registered Population**	**316.62**	**322.95**	**932.55**	**939.31**	**935.93**	**797**
市辖区	**Districts Under City Administration**	**265.43**	**270.08**	**764.37**	**769.60**	**766.99**	**1 037**
#市内六区	Six Urban Districts	133.90	135.24	383.64	384.57	384.11	21 718
滨海区	Coastal Districts	36.43	37.21	99.95	101.22	100.59	453
和平区	Heping District	13.47	13.01	47.07	43.84	45.45	43 845
河东区	Hedong District	24.66	25.35	67.75	69.23	68.49	17 469
河西区	Hexi District	25.68	26.01	73.00	73.96	73.48	19 457
南开区	Nankai District	27.61	27.79	79.08	79.73	79.41	20 683
河北区	Hebei District	22.38	22.85	61.77	62.65	62.21	21 151
红桥区	Hongqiao District	20.10	20.23	54.97	55.16	55.06	25 945
塘沽区	Tanggu District	17.18	17.62	48.17	48.85	48.51	624
#经济技术开发区	TEDA	0.72	0.82	2.18	2.65	2.42	
汉沽区	Hangu District	6.30	6.39	16.85	16.91	16.88	413
大港区	Dagang District	12.95	13.20	34.93	35.46	35.20	341
东丽区	Dongli District	12.17	12.45	31.32	31.82	31.57	665
西青区	Xiqing District	11.61	11.96	30.91	31.48	31.20	556
津南区	Jinnan District	13.46	13.78	37.54	38.07	37.81	982
北辰区	Beichen District	12.06	12.51	32.31	33.02	32.67	698
武清区	Wuqing District	25.01	25.60	81.10	81.72	81.41	519
宝坻区	Baodi District	19.86	20.37	65.22	65.28	65.25	433
天津铁厂	Tianjin Iron Works	0.93	0.96	2.38	2.42	2.40	
市辖县	**Counties Under City Administration**	**51.19**	**52.87**	**168.18**	**169.71**	**168.95**	**389**
宁河县	Ninghe County	11.03	11.28	36.28	36.74	36.51	283
静海县	Jinghai County	17.01	17.30	51.59	52.27	51.93	354
蓟　县	Jixian County	23.15	24.29	80.31	80.70	80.51	508

注：和平区人数、户数中含全市委培大学生数。
Note: Population and households of Heping District include the students commissioned in the universities.

2-4 按户口性质分的户籍户数
HOUSEHOLDS BY REGISTERED CHARACTER

单位:万户 (10 000 households)

地区	Region	非农业 Non-agricultural Households 2004	非农业 Non-agricultural Households 2005	农业 Agricultural Households 2004	农业 Agricultural Households 2005
全市总计	**Total**	**201.56**	**206.68**	**115.06**	**116.27**
市辖区	**Districts Under City Administration**	**189.87**	**193.56**	**75.56**	**76.52**
#市内六区	Six Urban Districts	133.06	134.41	0.84	0.83
滨海区	Coastal Districts	29.17	29.70	7.26	7.51
和平区	Heping District	13.47	13.01		
河东区	Hedong District	24.62	25.31	0.04	0.04
河西区	Hexi District	25.48	25.86	0.20	0.15
南开区	Nankai District	27.15	27.29	0.46	0.50
河北区	Hebei District	22.36	22.83	0.02	0.02
红桥区	Hongqiao District	19.98	20.11	0.12	0.12
塘沽区	Tanggu District	14.87	15.25	2.31	2.37
#经济技术开发区	TEDA	0.72	0.82		
汉沽区	Hangu District	4.78	4.83	1.52	1.56
大港区	Dagang District	9.52	9.62	3.43	3.58
东丽区	Dongli District	4.73	4.97	7.44	7.48
西青区	Xiqing District	3.40	3.50	8.21	8.46
津南区	Jinnan District	4.09	4.20	9.37	9.58
北辰区	Beichen District	5.06	5.39	7.00	7.12
武清区	Wuqing District	4.98	5.51	20.03	20.09
宝坻区	Baodi District	4.45	4.92	15.41	15.45
天津铁厂	Tianjin Iron Works	0.93	0.96		
市辖县	**Counties Under City Administration**	**11.69**	**13.12**	**39.50**	**39.75**
宁河县	Ninghe County	3.41	3.59	7.62	7.69
静海县	Jinghai County	3.86	4.07	13.15	13.23
蓟 县	Jixian County	4.42	5.46	18.73	18.83

2-5 按户口性质分的户籍人口数
REGISTERED POPULATION BY REGISTERED CHARACTER

单位:万人 (10 000 persons)

地 区 Region	非农业 Non-agricultural Population		农 业 Agricultural Population	
	2004	2005	2004	2005
全市总计 Total	**556.17**	**562.40**	**376.38**	**376.91**
市辖区 Districts Under City Administration	**527.27**	**532.42**	**237.10**	**237.18**
#市内六区 Six Urban D istricts	381.82	382.86	1.82	1.71
滨海区 Coastal Districts	79.09	80.23	20.86	20.99
和平区 Heping District	47.07	43.84		
河东区 Hedong District	67.68	69.17	0.07	0.06
河西区 Hexi District	72.61	73.66	0.39	0.30
南开区 Nankai District	78.00	78.65	1.08	1.08
河北区 Hebei District	61.75	62.63	0.02	0.02
红桥区 Hongqiao District	54.71	54.91	0.26	0.25
塘沽区 Tanggu District	42.15	42.81	6.02	6.04
#经济技术开发区 TEDA	2.18	2.65		
汉沽区 Hangu District	12.32	12.36	4.53	4.55
大港区 Dagang District	24.62	25.06	10.31	10.40
东丽区 Dongli District	11.40	12.06	19.92	19.76
西青区 Xiqing District	7.95	8.34	22.96	23.14
津南区 Jinnan District	10.06	10.38	27.48	27.69
北辰区 Beichen District	12.57	13.21	19.74	19.81
武清区 Wuqing District	11.91	12.48	69.19	69.24
宝坻区 Baodi District	10.09	10.44	55.13	54.84
天津铁厂 Tianjin Iron Works	2.38	2.42		
市辖县 Counties Under City Administration	**28.90**	**29.98**	**139.28**	**139.73**
宁河县 Ninghe County	8.52	8.77	27.76	27.97
静海县 Jinghai County	8.89	9.20	42.70	43.07
蓟 县 Jixian County	11.49	12.01	68.82	68.69

2-6 按性别分的户籍人口数
REGISTERED POPULATION BY SEX

单位:万人 (10 000 persons)

地 区 Region		男 性 Male		女 性 Female		性别比(女=100) Sex Ratio(Female=100)	
		2004	2005	2004	2005	2004	2005
全市总计	**Total**	**470.57**	**473.77**	**461.98**	**465.54**	**101.86**	**101.77**
市辖区	**Districts Under City Administration**	**385.00**	**387.38**	**379.37**	**382.22**	**101.49**	**101.35**
#市内六区	Six Urban Districts	192.50	192.79	191.14	191.78	100.71	100.53
滨海区	Coastal Districts	51.63	52.25	48.32	48.97	106.85	106.67
和平区	Heping District	23.09	21.43	23.98	22.41	96.30	95.65
河东区	Hedong District	34.14	34.89	33.61	34.34	101.59	101.58
河西区	Hexi District	36.21	36.62	36.79	37.34	98.40	98.10
南开区	Nankai District	40.09	40.36	38.99	39.37	102.82	102.50
河北区	Hebei District	31.19	31.61	30.58	31.04	101.99	101.82
红桥区	Hongqiao District	27.78	27.88	27.19	27.28	102.17	102.23
塘沽区	Tanggu District	24.84	25.19	23.33	23.66	106.49	106.44
#经济技术开发区	TEDA	1.10	1.35	1.08	1.30	102.03	103.45
汉沽区	Hangu District	8.55	8.57	8.30	8.34	102.95	102.69
大港区	Dagang District	18.24	18.49	16.69	16.97	109.29	108.94
东丽区	Dongli District	15.74	16.00	15.58	15.82	101.04	101.09
西青区	Xiqing District	15.35	15.61	15.56	15.87	98.65	98.36
津南区	Jinnan District	18.78	19.04	18.76	19.03	100.05	100.09
北辰区	Beichen District	16.19	16.53	16.12	16.49	100.48	100.30
武清区	Wuqing District	40.67	40.96	40.43	40.76	100.61	100.49
宝坻区	Baodi District	32.92	32.96	32.30	32.32	101.93	101.95
天津铁厂	Tianjin Iron Works	1.22	1.24	1.16	1.18	105.36	105.61
市辖县	**Counties Under City Administration**	**85.57**	**86.39**	**82.61**	**83.32**	**103.56**	**103.70**
宁河县	Ninghe County	18.41	18.65	17.87	18.09	102.99	103.16
静海县	Jinghai County	26.26	26.63	25.33	25.64	103.64	103.88
蓟 县	Jixian County	40.90	41.11	39.41	39.59	103.77	103.83

2-7 计划生育情况(2000-2005年)
FAMILY PLANNING, 2000-2005

指 标 Item	2000	2001	2002	2003	2004	2005
政策生育率(%) Family Planning Rate(%)	98.51	98.67	98.80	98.73	98.99	99.02
一孩率(%) One-child Rate(%)	76.55	76.54	70.30	76.36	78.25	73.62
二孩率(%) Two-child Rate(%)	22.27	22.58	29.19	22.59	20.55	24.91
多孩率(%) Multi-child Rate(%)	1.18	0.88	0.51	1.05	1.20	1.47
总和生育率 General Fertility Rate	0.88	1.05	1.02	1.03	1.00	1.00

资料来源:政策生育率为计生委年报数;其余指标为历年人口抽样调查数据.
Data Source: Family planning rate is obtained from annual reports of Tianjin Birth Control Committee; other data of this table are obtained from annual sample survey.

2-8 人口婚姻登记情况(2001-2005年)
MARRIAGE REGISTRATION, 2001-2005

指 标 Item	2001	2002	2003	2004	2005
结婚对数合计(对) Total Marriages (couple)	**57 922**	**54 180**	**62 973**	**76 950**	**63 600**
#恢复结婚对数 Remarriage with Former Spouse	697	716	515	1 446	1 303
涉外婚姻 Chinese-Foreigner Marriage	273	288	343	361	399
#女性(人) Female(person)	235	242	278	298	345
初婚人数(万人) First Marriages(10 000 persons)	10.0	9.3	10.9	13.2	10.3
再婚人数(万人) Remarriages(10 000 persons)	1.5	1.5	1.6	2.2	2.4
离婚对数(对) Divorces(couple)	**9 851**	**10 576**	**12 041**	**16 146**	**17 073**
法院判决离婚 Mediated by The Court	3 791	4 143	3 647	3 590	3 554
民政协议离婚 Approved by Civil Administration Agencies	6 060	6 433	8 394	12 556	13 519

资料来源:结婚对数是民政事业统计年报数,离婚对数是民政事业统计年报与法院统计年报数之和。
Data Source: The data of marriage couples are obtained from the annual reports of civil administration agencies, and the divorce couples are the sum of data obtained from annual reports of civil administration agencies and courts.

2-9 各种特征年龄组的户籍人口(2005年)
REGISTERED POPULATION BY AGE GROUPS,2005

单位:万人 (10 000 persons)

年龄组 Age Groups	合计 Total	#市内六区 Six Urban Districts	男性 Male	#市内六区 Six Urban Districts	女性 Female	#市内六区 Six Urban Districts
按学龄人口分组 Grouped by School Age						
0-2 岁 Age 0-2	17.11	4.00	9.12	2.07	7.99	1.93
3-5 岁 Age 3-5	20.50	4.80	10.87	2.47	9.63	2.33
6-14 岁 Age 6-14	75.45	19.08	39.65	9.74	35.80	9.34
15-17 岁 Age 15-17	43.79	14.19	22.55	7.15	21.24	7.04
18-21 岁 Age 18-21	63.07	29.54	32.28	15.13	30.79	14.41
按婚育人口分组 Grouped by Marriage Age and Child-bearing Age						
进入法定婚龄人口 Reaching Legal Marriage Age	16.20	8.74	8.82	5.03	7.38	3.71
育龄妇女人口 Women at Child-bearing Age						
(15-49 岁) (Between 15-49)	266.91	108.89			266.91	108.89
按劳龄人口分组 Grouped by Labor Age						
进入劳龄人口 Reaching Labor Age						
(国内标准) (Domestic Standard)	15.07	4.88	7.78	2.48	7.29	2.40
(国际标准) (International Standard)	13.54	3.89	6.98	1.95	6.56	1.94
劳动年龄内人口 Within Labor Age						
(国内标准) (Domestic Standard)	641.95	270.89	338.52	143.68	303.43	127.21
(国际标准) (International Standard)	723.10	303.64	364.84	154.04	358.26	149.60
退出劳龄人口 Over Labor Age						
(国内标准) (Domestic Standard)	11.25	4.94	4.76	2.03	6.49	2.91
(国际标准) (International Standard)	6.10	2.73	2.97	1.30	3.13	1.43
按老年人口分组 Grouped by Aged Population						
60 岁及以上人口 Age 60 and over	142.42	70.01	68.64	32.89	73.78	37.12
占总人口比重(%) Proportion in Total(%)	15.16	18.20	14.49	17.06	15.85	19.36
65 岁及以上人口 Age 65 and over	103.15	53.05	49.30	24.48	53.85	28.57
占总人口比重(%) Proportion in Total(%)	10.98	13.79	10.41	12.70	11.57	14.90
80 岁及以上人口 Age 80 and over	17.96	9.98	8.08	4.55	9.88	5.43
占总人口比重(%) Proportion in Total(%)	1.91	2.59	1.70	2.36	2.12	2.83

2-10 人口普查、人口抽样调查数据

BASIC STATISTICS ON POPULATION CENSUS AND SAMPLE SURVEY

指　标	Item	第四次人口普查(1990.7.1) the Fourth Population Census (1990.7.1)	第五次人口普查(2000.11.1) the Fifth Population Census (2000.11.1)	人口抽样调查(2005.11.1) Sample Survey on Population (2005.11.1)
常住人口(万人)	**Permanent Population(10 000 persons)**	**878.54**	**1 000.91**	**1 042.53**
1.按性别分	By Sex			
男性人口	Male	447.07	510.23	523.47
女性人口	Female	431.47	490.68	519.06
性别比(女=100)	Sex Ratio(Female=100)	103.62	103.99	100.85
2.按行政区划分	By Administrative Division			
市镇人口	Urban Population	611.11	720.56	783.06
乡村人口	Rural Population	267.43	280.35	259.47
3.按民族分	By Nationality			
汉族人口	Han Nationality	858.28	974.22	1 012.15
少数民族人口	Uinority Nationality	20.26	26.69	30.38
4.按受教育程度分	By Educational Level			
#大学及以上	University and above	18.25	38.46	72.06
大学专科	Junior College	22.78	51.69	67.86
高中(中专)	Senior(Specialized) Secondary School	139.95	208.75	209.86
初　中	Junior Secondary School	258.29	346.12	377.79
小　学	Primary School	260.33	250.81	217.94
5.按年龄组分	By Age			
0-14 岁	Age 0-14	199.48	167.46	131.36
15-64 岁	Age 15-64	622.27	749.61	810.27
65 岁及以上	Age 65 and above	56.79	83.84	100.90
6.人口负担系数(%)	Population Dependency Ratio(%)			
人口总负担系数	Total Dependency Ratio	41.18	33.52	28.66
负担少儿系数	Children Dependency Ratio	32.06	22.34	16.21
负担老年系数	The Aged Dependency Ratio	9.13	11.18	12.45
老少比	Ratio of Aged to Children	28.47	50.07	76.81
总户数(万户)	**Number of Households(10 000 households)**	**255.20**	**313.58**	**346.18**
#家庭户户数	Family Households	253.93	303.15	335.10
家庭平均户规模(人/户)	**Average Family Size(person/household)**	**3.44**	**3.09**	**2.95**

注:2005 年数据为快速汇总推算结果。
Noet: Data in 2005 were calculated by the quick sum method.

2-11 按地区分的6岁及以上各种受教育程度人口(2005年)

EDUCATION STATUS OF POPULATION AGED 6 AND ABOVE BY REGION,2005

单位:人 (person)

地区 Region	合计 Total	小学 Primary School	初中 Junior Middle School	高中 Senior Middle School	大学专科 Junior College	大学本科 University	研究生 Graduate Student
全市总计 Total	**462 414**	**106 586**	**184 762**	**102 634**	**35 243**	**30 853**	**2 336**
市辖区 Districts under City Administration	**388 017**	**78 538**	**149 563**	**93 993**	**33 456**	**30 141**	**2 326**
#市内六区 Six Urban Districts	180 211	20 039	52 219	58 901	23 976	22 999	2 077
滨海区 Coastal Districts	59 242	11 116	24 137	15 161	4 962	3 693	173
和平区 Heping District	13 893	1 634	4 134	4 516	1 969	1 546	94
河东区 Hedong District	34 717	3 728	10 081	11 634	4 592	4 387	295
河西区 Hexi District	35 876	3 879	9 659	10 631	4 901	6 322	484
南开区 Nankai District	41 483	4 028	10 472	13 163	6 360	6 495	965
河北区 Hebei District	29 822	3 553	9 477	10 348	3 651	2 628	165
红桥区 Hongqiao Distric	24 420	3 217	8 396	8 609	2 503	1 621	74
塘沽区 Tanggu District	32 389	4 396	13 437	8 992	2 928	2 510	127
汉沽区 Hangu District	7 714	2 228	3 128	1 745	461	149	3
大港区 Dagang District	19 138	4 492	7 572	4 424	1 573	1 034	43
东丽区 Dongli District	20 849	5 826	10 722	3 331	658	305	7
西青区 Xiqing District	20 276	6 010	9 228	2 981	931	1 115	11
津南区 Jinnan District	19 199	6 194	9 722	2 327	554	401	1
北辰区 Beichen District	20 683	5 247	9 659	3 722	899	1 108	48
武清区 Wuqing District	37 680	13 190	19 057	4 269	862	299	3
宝坻区 Baodi District	29 877	10 916	14 819	3 301	614	221	6
市辖县 Counties under City Administration	**74 397**	**28 048**	**35 199**	**8 641**	**1 787**	**712**	**10**
宁河县 Ninghe County	16 084	6 336	7 730	1 707	251	59	1
静海县 Jinghai County	23 598	9 664	10 831	2 381	485	234	3
蓟县 Jixian County	34 715	12 048	16 638	4 553	1 051	419	6

注:此表为2005年人口抽样调查数据,2-12至2-15表同。
Note:Sample Surrey on population in 2005,Same as following table 2-12 to 2-15.

2－12 按地区分的15岁及以上各种婚姻状况人口(2005年)
MARRIAGE STATUS OF POPULATION AGED 15 AND ABOVE BY REGION,2005

单位:人 (person)

地区	Region	合计 Total	未婚 Unmarried	初婚有配偶 First Marriages	再婚有配偶 Remarriages	离婚 Divorces	丧偶 Widowed
全市总计	**Total**	**444 364**	**93 055**	**317 617**	**8 110**	**4 988**	**20 594**
和平区	Heping District	13 483	3 009	9 012	235	263	964
河东区	Hedong District	33 941	7 251	24 043	470	501	1 676
河西区	Hexi District	34 873	9 308	22 618	495	578	1 874
南开区	Nankai District	40 367	10 594	26 816	492	510	1 955
河北区	Hebei District	29 233	6 347	20 491	377	386	1 632
红桥区	Hongqiao Distric	23 861	4 978	16 791	296	360	1 436
塘沽区	Tanggu District	31 332	10 468	19 113	500	383	868
汉沽区	Hangu District	7 665	1 024	5 811	221	180	429
大港区	Dagang District	17 935	2 552	14 268	376	228	511
东丽区	Dongli District	20 166	3 792	14 869	422	211	872
西青区	Xiqing District	19 559	4 552	13 756	334	174	743
津南区	Jinnan District	18 490	3 339	13 783	389	188	791
北辰区	Beichen District	19 964	4 371	14 117	312	221	943
武清区	Wuqing District	35 220	4 845	27 721	811	174	1 669
宝坻区	Baodi District	27 976	5 007	21 003	634	157	1 175
宁河县	Ninghe County	14 963	2 818	11 117	381	91	556
静海县	Jinghai County	22 395	2 847	17 827	478	181	1 062
蓟县	Jixian County	32 941	5 953	24 461	887	202	1 438
#女性	**Female**	**223 253**	**43 217**	**158 977**	**4 218**	**2 509**	**14 332**
和平区	Heping District	7 039	1 403	4 650	102	149	735
河东区	Hedong District	17 141	3 360	12 119	226	267	1 169
河西区	Hexi District	17 790	4 495	11 377	244	321	1 353
南开区	Nankai District	20 395	4 886	13 580	229	296	1 404
河北区	Hebei District	14 690	2 865	10 301	188	201	1 135
红桥区	Hongqiao Distric	12 105	2 286	8 450	138	196	1 035
塘沽区	Tanggu District	15 405	5 595	8 750	217	228	615
汉沽区	Hangu District	3 855	434	2 928	105	90	298
大港区	Dagang District	8 966	1 166	7 115	181	145	359
东丽区	Dongli District	10 205	1 880	7 428	217	94	586
西青区	Xiqing District	9 623	2 084	6 770	170	67	532
津南区	Jinnan District	9 236	1 509	6 920	196	91	520
北辰区	Beichen District	10 092	2 083	7 104	156	103	646
武清区	Wuqing District	17 599	1 965	13 947	473	64	1 150
宝坻区	Baodi District	14 002	2 234	10 590	353	44	781
宁河县	Ninghe County	7 452	1 262	5 589	197	32	372
静海县	Jinghai County	11 202	1 208	8 991	260	63	680
蓟县	Jixian County	16 456	2 502	12 368	566	58	962

2－13 按区域分的不同年龄组人口(2005 年)
POPULATION GROUPED BY AGE AND REGION, 2005

单位:人 (person)

地 区 Region	合 计 Total	0－14 岁 Age 0－14	15－59 岁 Age 15－59	60 岁及以上 Age 60 and Above	#65 岁及以上 Age 65 and Above
全 市 Total	**509 736**	**64 226**	**376 226**	**69 284**	**49 335**
市辖区 Districts under City Administration	**423 741**	**48 538**	**316 301**	**58 902**	**42 050**
#市内六区 Six Urban Districts	191 828	15 187	143 744	32 897	24 604
滨海区 Coastal Districts	64 965	7 893	50 418	6 654	4 499
市辖县 Counties under City Administration	**85 995**	**15 688**	**59 925**	**10 382**	**7 285**

2－14 按户口登记地分的外来常住人口构成(2005 年)
RESIDENCES CARD LOCATION OF NON－NATIVES, 2005

单位:% (%)

户口登记地 Residences Card Location	占外来常住人口的比重 Percentage in Total Non－natives	户口登记地 Residences Card Location	占外来常住人口的比重 Percentage in Total Non－natives
河 北 Hebei	22.89	北 京 Beijing	0.92
山 东 Shandong	19.80	湖 南 Hunan	0.90
黑龙江 Heilongjiang	11.62	重 庆 Chongqing	0.88
河 南 Henan	9.06	福 建 Fujian	0.87
安 徽 Anhui	5.65	江 西 Jiangxi	0.67
四 川 Sichuan	3.50	广 东 Guangdong	0.42
湖 北 Hubei	3.39	新 疆 Xinjiang	0.41
内蒙古 Inner Mongolia	3.22	贵 州 Guizhou	0.35
吉 林 Jilin	3.18	宁 夏 Ningxia	0.26
江 苏 Jiangsu	2.54	上 海 Shanghai	0.24
辽 宁 Liaoning	2.08	青 海 Qinghai	0.23
山 西 Shanxi	1.73	广 西 Guangxi	0.21
甘 肃 Gansu	1.63	海 南 Hainan	0.17
陕 西 Shanxi	1.52	云 南 Yunnan	0.15
浙 江 Zhejiang	1.51	西 藏 Tibet	

2-15 按地区分的15岁及以上人口的主要生活来源(2005年)
MAIN SOURCE OF SUPPORT OF POPULATION AGED 15 AND OVER BY REGION,2005

单位:人 (person)

地区	Region	劳动收入 Labour Income	离退休金、养老金 Pensions for Retirement	失业保险金 Unemployment Insurance	最低生活保障金 Subsistence Allowance
全市总计	**Total**	**263 533**	**62 914**	**678**	**2 206**
和平区	Heping District	6 177	4 225	31	94
河东区	Hedong District	16 655	8 730	75	266
河西区	Hexi District	16 815	9 179	107	196
南开区	Nankai District	19 236	10 390	90	166
河北区	Hebei District	14 543	7 696	84	233
红桥区	Hongqiao District	11 550	6 094	48	304
塘沽区	Tanggu District	21 747	3 451	56	167
汉沽区	Hangu District	4 004	1 385	25	92
大港区	Dagang District	12 098	1 668	10	70
东丽区	Dongli District	12 481	1 562	17	92
西青区	Xiqing District	12 117	1 229	15	83
津南区	Jinnan District	12 568	860	16	76
北辰区	Beichen District	11 168	2 099	24	115
武清区	Wuqing District	25 674	1 219	9	80
宝坻区	Baodi District	19 957	856	19	37
宁河县	Ninghe County	10 044	382	14	20
静海县	Jinghai County	14 522	727	20	39
蓟县	Jixian County	22 177	1 162	18	76

地区	Region	下岗生活费 Laid-off Living Income	内退生活费 Internal Retirement Living Income	财产性收入 Income from Properties	家庭其他成员供养 Supplied by Other Members of Family	其他 Others
全市总计	**Total**	**1 233**	**1 743**	**725**	**104 561**	**6 773**
和平区	Heping District	65	76	6	2 602	207
河东区	Hedong District	140	389	9	7 022	654
河西区	Hexi District	202	182	9	7 878	303
南开区	Nankai District	161	204	38	9 559	524
河北区	Hebei District	144	138	15	5 950	429
红桥区	Hongqiao District	68	106	16	5 162	512
塘沽区	Tanggu District	103	230	29	5 385	166
汉沽区	Hangu District	17	90	36	1 795	221
大港区	Dagang District	14	25	86	3 813	154
东丽区	Dongli District	46	41	46	5 196	684
西青区	Xiqing District	51	29	96	5 504	434
津南区	Jinnan District	24	68	40	4 498	340
北辰区	Beichen District	81	49	62	5 659	709
武清区	Wuqing District	21	35	56	7 805	322
宝坻区	Baodi District	28	8	44	6 767	257
宁河县	Ninghe County	11	11	6	4 222	254
静海县	Jinghai County	27	12	36	6 756	256
蓟县	Jixian County	30	50	95	8 988	347

2-16 社会从业人员(1990-2005年)
TOTAL PERSONS EMPLOYED,1990-2005

单位:万人 (10 000 persons)

年份 Year	劳动力资源总数 Number of Labour Force	社会从业人员合计 Number of Persons Employed	按城乡分组 Grouped by Urban and Rural Areas					
			城镇 Urban Areas	国有单位 State-owned Units	集体单位 Collective-owned Units	其他单位 Others	个体、私营单位 Private and Individual Units	乡村 Rural Areas
1990	558.93	470.07	290.01	217.26	62.55	4.50	5.70	180.06
1991	564.15	479.67	300.58	219.34	66.17	6.05	9.02	179.09
1992	569.70	485.70	303.70	212.73	72.39	8.85	9.73	182.00
1993	566.10	503.10	312.70	210.90	75.50	16.30	10.00	190.40
1994	694.30	513.00	318.60	206.50	71.40	24.40	16.30	194.40
1995	701.60	515.30	319.80	202.10	68.40	29.20	20.10	195.50
1996	708.80	512.00	317.10	199.10	62.80	31.00	24.20	194.90
1997	716.26	513.33	318.60	196.16	58.19	35.80	28.45	194.73
1998	728.68	508.10	312.65	183.49	53.00	41.58	34.58	195.45
1999	740.76	508.14	313.89	176.54	47.54	49.80	40.01	194.25
2000	753.27	486.89	296.61	163.84	40.58	55.37	36.82	190.28
2001	761.11	488.34	295.37	153.25	32.13	60.94	49.05	192.97
2002	771.69	492.61	295.71	137.81	26.60	82.54	48.76	196.90
2003	793.86	510.90	299.95	128.52	22.80	93.72	54.91	210.95
2004	798.43	527.78	302.47	126.36	20.21	103.59	52.31	225.31
2005	858.88	542.52	312.76	99.18	11.31	148.01	54.26	229.76

年份 Year	按三次产业分 Grouped by Three Industries					
	绝对数 Number			构成(%) Composition in Percentage(%)		
	第一产业 Primary Industry	第二产业 Secondary Industry	第三产业 Tertiary Industry	第一产业 Primary Industry	第二产业 Secondary Industry	第三产业 Tertiary Industry
1990	93.63	232.17	144.27	19.9	49.4	30.7
1991	94.27	237.24	148.16	19.7	49.5	30.8
1992	92.50	238.40	154.80	19.0	49.1	31.9
1993	89.00	245.20	168.90	17.7	48.7	33.6
1994	85.60	246.50	180.90	16.7	48.0	35.3
1995	82.90	247.10	185.30	16.1	47.9	36.0
1996	82.10	241.40	188.50	16.0	47.2	36.8
1997	81.26	235.69	196.38	15.8	45.9	38.3
1998	80.88	233.21	194.01	15.9	45.9	38.2
1999	79.57	230.33	198.24	15.7	45.3	39.0
2000	81.29	222.15	183.45	16.7	45.6	37.7
2001	82.70	212.65	192.99	16.9	43.6	39.5
2002	82.25	205.38	204.98	16.7	41.7	41.6
2003	83.19	219.44	208.27	16.3	42.9	40.8
2004	82.83	223.89	221.06	15.7	42.4	41.9
2005	81.79	227.38	233.35	15.1	41.9	43.0

注:1998-2004年城镇从业人员中包括由于各种原因已经离开本人的生产或工作岗位,但仍与本单位保留劳动关系的职工。
Note:From 1998 to 2004,the number of urban employment personnel include those staff and workers who still keep their relation with their units,but have left their working post at there.

2-17 城镇单位从业人员(1990-2005年)
PERSONS EMPLOYED IN URBAN UNITS, 1990-2005

单位:万人 (10 000 persons)

年份 Year	合计 Total	按三次产业分 Grouped by Three Industries			按登记注册类型分 Grouped by Registration Status		
		第一产业 Primary Industry	第二产业 Secondary Industry	第三产业 Tertiary Industry	国有单位 State-owned Units	集体单位 Collective-owned Units	其他单位 Others
总计 Total							
1990	284.31	4.10	167.68	112.53	217.26	62.55	4.50
1991	291.56	4.34	171.57	115.65	219.34	66.17	6.05
1992	293.97	4.10	171.41	118.46	212.73	72.39	8.85
1993	293.45	2.55	171.18	119.72	206.52	70.89	16.04
1994	291.94	2.30	168.72	120.92	201.75	66.21	23.98
1995	289.59	1.90	167.33	120.36	197.01	64.19	28.39
1996	283.98	1.73	163.07	119.18	194.32	59.62	30.04
1997	281.34	1.71	158.68	120.95	191.64	55.28	34.42
1998	218.56	1.43	113.47	103.66	144.18	36.26	38.12
1999	211.76	1.10	110.27	100.39	135.08	30.46	46.22
2000	201.75	1.11	105.63	95.01	125.00	25.82	50.93
2001	192.30	1.09	99.82	91.39	116.24	20.05	56.00
2002	185.50	1.09	92.68	91.73	107.79	16.47	61.24
2003	191.01	0.97	97.60	92.44	101.57	13.95	75.49
2004	193.91	0.87	96.82	96.22	102.09	12.46	79.36
2005	194.12	0.81	97.52	95.79	99.18	11.33	83.61
#女性 Female							
1990	120.90	1.25	71.76	47.89	84.44	34.39	2.07
1991	124.24	1.44	73.87	48.93	85.78	35.61	2.85
1992	124.05	1.23	73.38	49.44	83.89	35.89	4.27
1993	123.14	0.86	72.00	50.28	81.46	34.00	7.68
1994	123.73	0.81	72.00	50.92	80.64	31.79	11.30
1995	123.60	0.68	72.03	50.89	79.27	30.81	13.52
1996	120.23	0.57	69.84	49.82	77.39	28.59	14.25
1997	118.75	0.55	67.48	50.72	76.61	26.15	15.99
1998	89.89	0.46	46.11	43.32	56.17	15.93	17.79
1999	82.95	0.31	41.33	41.31	51.80	13.22	17.93
2000	77.28	0.33	38.85	38.10	47.26	10.76	19.26
2001	77.40	0.36	40.09	36.95	43.26	8.11	26.03
2002	73.59	0.33	36.00	37.26	39.60	6.52	27.47
2003	76.27	0.28	38.49	37.50	37.73	5.33	33.21
2004	73.66	0.26	35.30	38.10	37.56	4.39	31.71
2005	68.66	0.23	33.01	35.42	33.94	4.09	30.63

注:1998年以前为职工人数。
Note: The data Before 1998 of this table refer to staff and workers.

2-18 按国民经济行业分各类从业人员(2005年)

PERSONS EMPLOYED GROUPED BY SECTOR,2005

单位:万人 (10 000 persons)

项 目 Item	社会从业人员 Persons Employed	城镇单位从业人员 Persons Employed In Urban Units	在岗职工人数 On-post Staff and Workers	其他从业人员 Other Persons Employed
总 计 **Total**	**542.52**	**194.12**	**169.90**	**24.22**
按三次产业分 **Grouped by Three Industries**				
第一产业 Primary Industry	81.79	0.81	0.80	0.01
第二产业 Secondary Industry	227.38	97.52	89.28	8.24
第三产业 Tertiary Industry	233.35	95.79	79.82	15.97
按国民经济行业分 **Grouped by Sector**				
农、林、牧、渔业 Farming,Forestry,Animal Husbandry and Fishery	81.79	0.81	0.80	0.01
采矿业 Minerals Mining	6.22	7.31	6.42	0.89
制造业 Manufacturing	187.33	77.72	71.45	6.27
电力、燃气及水的生产和供应业 Production & Supply of Power,Gas and Water	4.40	3.36	3.09	0.27
建筑业 Construction	29.43	9.12	8.32	0.80
交通运输、仓储及邮政业 Transport,Storage,Post Services	33.86	11.77	10.45	1.32
信息传输、计算机服务和软件业 Information Transmitting,Computer Services and Software	3.73	2.43	2.18	0.25
批发和零售业 Wholesale and Retail Trade	67.09	11.74	8.81	2.93
住宿和餐饮业 Accommodation and Catering Services	11.27	3.00	2.19	0.81
金融业 Finance Intermediation	5.81	5.12	3.55	1.57
房地产业 Real Estate	5.83	2.32	1.70	0.62
租赁和商务服务业 Leasing and Business Services	12.45	6.59	4.49	2.10
科学研究、技术服务和地质勘察业 Scientific Research,Technical Services and Geological Prospecting	6.10	5.31	4.74	0.57
水利、环境和公共设施管理业 Management for Water Conservancy,Environment and Public Facilities	5.08	3.60	3.13	0.47
居民服务和其他服务业 Resident Services and Other Social Services	37.58	4.20	2.14	2.06
教 育 Education	16.63	16.97	16.20	0.77
卫生、社会保障和社会福利业 Health Care, Social Security and Social Welfare	9.29	7.71	6.77	0.94
文化、体育和娱乐业 Culture, Sports and Recreational Services	3.58	1.75	1.52	0.23
公共管理和社会组织 Public Management and Social Organizations	15.05	13.29	11.95	1.34

2-19 社会从业人员及构成
NUMBER AND COMPOSITION OF PERSONS EMPLOYED

项目	Item	绝对数(万人) Number (10 000 persons) 2004	2005	构成(%) Composition in Percentage(%) 2004	2005
总计	**Total**	**527.78**	**542.52**	**100.0**	**100.0**
按登记注册类型分	**Grouped by Registration Status**				
内资单位	Domestic Investment Economy				
国有单位	State-owned Units	126.36	99.18	24.0	18.3
集体单位	Collective-owned Units	195.95	181.18	37.1	33.4
联营单位	Joint-owned Units	4.47	1.35	0.8	0.2
股份有限公司	Share Holding Corporations Ltd.	13.29	10.20	2.5	1.9
有限责任公司	Limited-Liability Corporations	19.05	14.78	3.6	2.7
股份合作单位	Cooperative Units	4.14	1.08	0.8	0.2
私营单位	Private	76.66	88.71	14.5	16.4
个体	Individual	25.22	25.46	4.8	4.7
其他单位	Others	13.26	69.44	2.5	12.8
港澳台投资单位	Units with Funds from Hongkong, Macao and Taiwan	11.72	9.94	2.2	1.8
外商投资单位	Foreign Funded Units	37.66	41.20	7.2	7.6
按国民经济行业分	**Grouped by Sector**				
农、林、牧、渔业	Farming, Forestry, Animal Husbandry and Fishery	82.83	81.79	15.6	15.1
采矿业	Minerals Mining	8.91	6.22	1.7	1.2
制造业	Manufacturing	182.85	187.33	34.6	34.5
电力、燃气及水的生产和供应业	Production & Supply of Power, Gas and Water	3.63	4.40	0.7	0.8
建筑业	Construction	28.50	29.43	5.4	5.4
交通运输、仓储及邮政业	Transport, Storage, Post Services	32.65	33.86	6.2	6.2
信息传输、计算机服务和软件业	Information Transmitting, Computer Services and Software	3.05	3.73	0.6	0.7
批发和零售业	Wholesale and Retail Trade	64.49	67.09	12.2	12.4
住宿和餐饮业	Accommodation and Catering Services	10.41	11.27	2.0	2.1
金融业	Finance Intermediation	5.48	5.81	1.0	1.1
房地产业	Real Estate	5.08	5.83	1.0	1.1
租赁和商务服务业	Leasing and Business Services	11.21	12.45	2.1	2.3
科学研究、技术服务和地质勘察业	Scientific Research, Technical Services and Geological Prospecting	5.75	6.10	1.1	1.1
水利、环境和公共设施管理业	Management for Water Conservancy, Environment and Public Facilities	4.28	5.08	0.8	0.9
居民服务和其他服务业	Resident Services and Other Social Services	34.16	37.58	6.5	6.9
教育	Education	17.40	16.63	3.3	3.1
卫生、社会保障和社会福利业	Health Care, Social Security and Social Welfare	9.29	9.29	1.8	1.7
文化、体育和娱乐业	Culture, Sports and Recreational Services	3.61	3,58	0.7	0.6
公共管理和社会组织	Public Management and Social Organizations	14.20	15.05	2.7	2.8

2-20 城镇单位从业人员及构成

NUMBER AND COMPOSITION OF PERSONS EMPLOYED IN URBAN UNITS

项目	Item	绝对数(万人) Number (10 000 persons)		构成(%) Composition in Percentage(%)	
		2004	2005	2004	2005
总计	**Total**	**193.91**	**194.12**	**100.0**	**100.0**
按登记注册类型分	**Grouped by Registration Status**				
国有单位	State-owned Units	102.09	99.18	52.7	51.1
集体单位	Collective-owned Units	12.46	11.33	6.4	5.8
其他单位	Others	79.36	83.61	40.9	43.1
#外商及港澳台商投资单位	Units with Funds from Foreign Countries, HongKong,Macao & Taiwan	48.30	51.15	24.9	26.3
股份有限公司	Share Holding Corporations Ltd.	9.59	10.20	4.9	5.3
按国民经济行业分	**Grouped by Sector**				
农、林、牧、渔业	Farming,Forestry,Animal Husbandry and Fishery	0.87	0.81	0.4	0.4
采矿业	Minerals Mining	7.69	7.31	4.0	3.8
制造业	Manufacturing	76.79	77.72	39.6	40.1
电力、燃气及水的生产和供应业	Production & Supply of Power,Gas and Water	3.07	3.36	1.6	1.7
建筑业	Construction	9.27	9.12	4.8	4.7
交通运输、仓储及邮政业	Transport,Storage,Post Services	13.33	11.77	6.9	6.1
信息传输、计算机服务和软件业	Information transmitting,Computer Services and Software	1.91	2.43	1.0	1.2
批发和零售业	Wholesale and Retail Trade	11.69	11.74	6.0	6.0
住宿和餐饮业	Accommodation and Catering Services	3.33	3.00	1.7	1.6
金融业	Finance Intermediation	5.07	5.12	2.6	2.6
房地产业	Real Estate	2.59	2.32	1.3	1.2
租赁和商务服务业	Leasing and Business Services	5.05	6.59	2.6	3.4
科学研究、技术服务和地质勘察业	Scientific Research,Technical Services and Geological Prospecting	5.18	5.31	2.7	2.7
水利、环境和公共设施管理业	Management for Water Conservancy, Environment and Public Facilities	3.97	3.60	2.1	1.9
居民服务和其他服务业	Resident Services and Other Social Services	4.77	4.20	2.5	2.2
教育	Education	16.51	16.97	8.5	8.7
卫生、社会保障和社会福利业	Health Care,Social Security and Social Welfare	7.55	7.71	3.9	4.0
文化、体育和娱乐业	Culture,Sports and Recreational Services	2.00	1.75	1.0	0.9
公共管理和社会组织	Public Management and Social Organizations	13.27	13.29	6.8	6.8
按企业、事业、机关分	**Grouped By Enterprise,Institution and Agency**				
企业	Enterprises	148.10	147.93	76.4	76.2
中央	Central	26.41	26.27	13.6	13.5
地方	Local	121.69	121.66	62.8	62.7
#国有	State-owned	37.10	35.08	19.1	18.1
事业	Institutions	33.46	33.63	17.2	17.3
中央	Central	2.23	2.36	1.1	1.2
地方	Local	31.23	31.27	16.1	16.1
机关	Agencies	12.35	12.56	6.4	6.5
中央	Central	1.16	1.14	0.6	0.6
地方	Local	11.19	11.42	5.8	5.9

2-21 城镇单位在岗职工及构成

ON-POST STAFF AND WORKERS OF PERSONS EMPLOYED IN URBAN UNITS

项目	Item	绝对数(万人) Number (10 000 persons) 2004	2005	构成(%) Composition in Percentage(%) 2004	2005
总计	**Total**	**172.56**	**169.90**	**100.0**	**100.0**
按登记注册类型分	**Grouped by Registration Status**				
国有单位	State-owned Units	91.26	87.53	52.9	51.5
集体单位	Collective-owned Units	10.60	9.12	6.1	5.4
其他单位	Others	70.70	73.25	41.0	43.1
#外商及港澳台商投资单位	Units with Funds from Foreign Countries, HongKong, Macao & Taiwan	44.97	46.08	26.1	27.1
股份有限公司	Share Holding Corporations Ltd.	8.18	8.55	4.7	5.0
按国民经济行业分	**Grouped by Sector**				
农、林、牧、渔业	Farming, Forestry, Animal Husbandry and Fishery	0.86	0.80	0.5	0.5
采矿业	Minerals Mining	6.76	6.42	3.9	3.8
制造业	Manufacturing	72.24	71.45	41.9	42.1
电力、燃气及水的生产和供应业	Production & Supply of Power, Gas and Water	2.91	3.09	1.7	1.8
建筑业	Construction	8.63	8.32	5.0	4.9
交通运输、仓储及邮政业	Transport, Storage, Post Services	11.67	10.45	6.8	6.1
信息传输、计算机服务和软件业	Information transmitting, Computer Services and Software	1.84	2.18	1.1	1.3
批发和零售业	Wholesale and Retail Trade	9.36	8.81	5.4	5.2
住宿和餐饮业	Accommodation and Catering Services	2.58	2.19	1.5	1.3
金融业	Finance Intermediation	3.54	3.55	2.1	2.1
房地产业	Real Estate	1.62	1.70	0.9	1.0
租赁和商务服务业	Leasing and Business Services	3.83	4.49	2.2	2.6
科学研究、技术服务和地质勘察业	Scientific Research, Technical Services and Geological Prospecting	4.70	4.74	2.7	2.8
水利、环境和公共设施管理业	Management for Water Conservancy, Environment and Public Facilities	3.38	3.13	2.0	1.8
居民服务和其他服务业	Resident Services and Other Social Services	2.58	2.14	1.5	1.3
教育	Education	15.70	16.20	9.1	9.5
卫生、社会保障和社会福利业	Health Care, Social Security and Social Welfare	6.78	6.77	3.9	4.0
文化、体育和娱乐业	Culture, Sports and Recreational Services	1.78	1.52	1.0	0.9
社会管理和社会组织	Public Management and Social Organizations	11.80	11.95	6.8	7.0

2－22 城镇单位其他从业人员及构成

OTHER PERSONS EMPLOYED IN URBAN UNITS

项 目	Item	绝对数(万人) Number (10 000 persons)		构 成(%) Composition in Percentage(%)	
		2004	2005	2004	2005
总 计	**Total**	**21.36**	**24.22**	**100.0**	**100.0**
按登记注册类型分	**Grouped by Registration Status**				
国有单位	State－owned Units	10.84	11.65	50.8	48.1
集体单位	Collective－owned Units	1.86	2.21	8.7	9.1
其他单位	Others	8.66	10.36	40.5	42.8
#外商及港澳台商投资单位	Units with Funds from Foreign Countries, HongKong,Macao & Taiwan	3.33	5.07	15.6	20.9
股份有限公司	Share Holding Corporations Ltd.	1.41	1.65	6.6	6.8
按国民经济行业分	**Grouped by Sector**				
农、林、牧、渔业	Farming,Forestry,Animal Husbandry and Fishery	0.01	0.01	0.1	0.1
采矿业	Minerals Mining	0.93	0.89	4.3	3.7
制造业	Manufacturing	4.55	6.27	21.3	25.9
电力、燃气及水的生产和供应业	Production & Supply of Power,Gas and Water	0.16	0.27	0.7	1.1
建筑业	Construction	0.64	0.80	3.1	3.3
交通运输、仓储及邮政业	Transport,Storage,Post Services	1.66	1.32	7.8	5.5
信息传输、计算机服务和软件业	Information transmitting,Computer Services and Software	0.07	0.25	0.3	1.0
批发和零售业	Wholesale and Retail Trade	2.33	2.93	10.9	12.1
住宿和餐饮业	Accommodation and Catering Services	0.75	0.81	3.5	3.3
金融业	Finance Intermediation	1.53	1.57	7.2	6.5
房地产业	Real Estate	0.97	0.62	4.5	2.5
租赁和商务服务业	Leasing and Business Services	1.22	2.10	5.7	8.7
科学研究、技术服务和地质勘察业	Scientific Research,Technical Services and Geological Prospecting	0.49	0.57	2.3	2.3
水利、环境和公共设施管理业	Management for Water Conservancy, Environment and Public Facilities	0.59	0.47	2.8	1.9
居民服务和其他服务业	Resident Services and Other Social Services	2.20	2.06	10.3	8.5
教 育	Education	0.81	0.77	3.8	3.2
卫生、社会保障和社会福利业	Health Care,Social Security and Social Welfare	0.77	0.94	3.6	3.9
文化、体育和娱乐业	Culture,Sports and Recreational Services	0.22	0.23	1.0	0.9
公共管理和社会组织	Public Management and Social Organizations	1.46	1.34	6.8	5.6

2－23 城镇单位从业人员变动情况(2005年)
CHANGES OF PERSONS EMPLOYED IN URBAN UNITS,2005

单位:人 (person)

项 目 Item	合 计 Total	按登记注册类型分 Grouped by Registration Status			按企事业机关分 Grouped by Enterprise, Institution and Agency		
		国有单位 State－owned Units	集体单位 Collective－owned Units	其他单位 Others	企 业 Enterprise	事 业 Institu－tion	机 关 Agency
从业人员增加合计							
Number of Persons Employed Increased	**270 952**	**84 150**	**17 404**	**169 398**	**241 840**	**22 999**	**6 113**
1.从农村招收人员							
Recruited from Rural Area	62 419	13 086	1 529	47 804	61 709	660	50
2.从城镇招收失业人员							
Recruited from Urban Area	26 862	7 540	1 692	17 630	24 855	1 328	679
3.录用的退伍军人							
Employment of Demobilized Soldiers	2 320	1 605	82	633	1 672	199	449
4.录用及使用的大中专技校毕业生							
Employment of Graduate	48 028	18 514	1 315	28 199	38 211	7 875	1 942
5.调入人数							
Job Changes	60 504	23 686	5 008	31 810	49 575	8 856	2 073
#市外调入							
From Outside Tianjin	3 205	2 337	9	859	2 766	423	16
6.其 他							
Others	70 819	19 719	7 778	43 322	65 818	4 081	920
从业人员减少合计							
Number of Persons Employed Decreased	**270 274**	**102 583**	**21 080**	**146 611**	**243 087**	**22 061**	**5 126**
1.离退休退职人员							
Retire and Quit	35 225	21 245	2 779	11 201	25 465	8 153	1 607
2.开除、除名、辞退							
Discharge	18 852	5 584	1 058	12 210	18 238	517	97
3.终止、解除合同							
Contract Expiration	95 123	25 281	3 773	66 069	93 135	1 767	221
4.在岗人员转不在岗							
Not On－post from On－post	21 886	12 909	3 113	5 864	20 128	1 622	136
5.死 亡							
Death	1 511	1 075	91	345	1 023	361	127
6.调出人数							
Job Changes	52 774	26 396	5 192	21 186	43 693	7 229	1 852
#调至市外							
To Outside Tianjin	996	385	10	601	786	187	23
7.其 他							
Others	44 903	10 093	5 074	29 736	41 405	2 412	1 086

2－24 市属部分局(总公司)国有经济单位从业人员年末人数

YEAR－END NUMBER OF PERSONS EMPLOYED BY STATE－OWNED UNITS IN PART OF BUREAUS(CORPORATIONS)

单位:人 (person)

局(总公司)	Bureau(Corporation)	2004	2005
经委系统	**Tianjin Economical Committee System**		
机电工业控股集团公司	Tianjin Machinery & Electric Industry Holding Group Company	11 506	10 129
中环电子信息集团有限公司	Tianjin Zhonghuan Electronics & Information Group	13 894	12 991
冶金集团(控股)有限公司	Tianjin Metallurgical Group(Holding) Corporation	10 471	9 107
渤海化工集团公司	Tianjin Bohai Chemical Industry Group Corporation	31 621	29 597
纺织集团(控股)有限公司	Tianjin Textile Industrial General Corporation	25 253	24 343
一轻集团(控股)有限公司	Tianjin First Light Industry Group(Holding Share) Co.,Ltd	5 054	4 340
二轻集团(控股)有限公司	The Second Light Industry Group(Holding) Co.,Ltd	3 004	2 318
医药集团有限公司	Tianjin Pharmaceutical Holdings	3 946	2 340
汽车工业(集团)有限公司	Tianjin Automobile Industry Group Co.,Ltd	1 531	556
飞鸽集团有限公司	Tianjin Flying Pigeon Group Co.,Ltd	1 699	1 195
塑料集团	Tianjin Plastics Group	739	763
天铁冶金集团有限公司	Tianjin Tian Tie Metallurgical Group Co.,Ltd	19 509	19 267
建筑材料集团(控股)有限公司	Tianjin Building Materials Group(Holding) Co.,Ltd	3 790	3 187
农委系统	**Tianjin Agricultural Committee System**		
农业局	Tianjin Agriculture Bureau	425	435
畜牧局	Tianjin Animal Husbandry Bureau	311	323
农垦集团总公司	Tianjin State Farms Agribusiness Group Company	3 906	3 465
水产局	Tianjin Aquatic Products Bureau	1 075	847
建委系统	**Tianjin Construction Committee System**		
建工集团总公司	Tianjin Construction Engineering Group Corporation	6 758	3 707
市政工程局	Tianjin Municipal Engineering Bureau	14 044	13 985
房地产管理局	Tianjin Real Estate Administrative Bureau	8 621	9 164
住宅建设发展集团	Tianjin House Construction Development Group	1 909	1 285
公共交通集团公司	Tianjin Public Traffic Group Corporation	10 084	10 507
自来水集团	Tianjin Tap Water Group	3 567	3 737
燃气集团	Tianjin Gas Group	6 453	6 630
交委系统	**Tianjin Transportation Committee System**		
天津港(集团)有限公司	Tianjin Port Group Corporation Ltd.	11 497	11 143
天津交通运输总公司	Tianjin Communication Corporation	6 948	6 181
商委系统	**Tianjin Commercial Committee System**		
粮食粮油集团有限公司	Tianjin Grain & Oil Group Co.,Ltd	3 456	2 978
一商集团有限公司	Tianjin First Commercial Group Co.,Ltd	3 055	1 933
二商集团有限公司	Tianjin Second Commercial Group Co.,Ltd	4 920	3 332

2-25 市属部分局(总公司)国有经济单位从业人员年平均人数

AVERAGE NUMBER OF PERSONS EMPLOYED BY STATE-OWNED UNITS IN PART OF BUREAUS(CORPORATIONS)

单位:人 (person)

局(总公司)	Bureau(Corporation)	2004	2005
经委系统	**Tianjin Economical Committee System**		
机电工业控股集团公司	Tianjin Machinery & Electric Industry Holding Group Company	12 322	10 531
中环电子信息集团有限公司	Tianjin Zhonghuan Electronics & Information Group	14 807	13 136
冶金集团(控股)有限公司	Tianjin Metallurgical Group(Holding) Corporation	10 656	9 380
渤海化工集团公司	Tianjin Bohai Chemical Industry Group Corporation	33 284	30 791
纺织集团(控股)有限公司	Tianjin Textile Industrial General Corporation	26 226	24 637
一轻集团(控股)有限公司	Tianjin First Light Industry Group(Holding Share) Co.,Ltd	5 444	4 584
二轻集团(控股)有限公司	The Second Light Industry Group(Holding) Co.,Ltd	3 430	2 551
医药集团有限公司	Tianjin Pharmaceutical Holdings	4 133	2 496
汽车工业(集团)有限公司	Tianjin Automobile Industry Group Co.,Ltd	1 622	861
飞鸽集团有限公司	Tianjin Flying Pigeon Group Co.,Ltd	1 517	1 288
塑料集团	Tianjin Plastics Group	774	741
天铁冶金集团有限公司	Tianjin Tian Tie Metallurgical Group Co.,Ltd	19 487	18 927
建筑材料集团(控股)有限公司	Tianjin Building Materials Group(Holding)Co.,Ltd	4 587	3 574
农委系统	**Tianjin Agricultural Committee System**		
农业局	Tianjin Agriculture Bureau	422	430
畜牧局	Tianjin Animal Husbandry Bureau	302	317
农垦集团总公司	Tianjin State Farms Agribusiness Group Company	4 037	3 707
水产局	Tianjin Aquatic Products Bureau	1 180	971
建委系统	**Tianjin Construction Committee System**		
建工集团总公司	Tianjin Construction Engineering Group Corporation	7 211	4 082
市政工程局	Tianjin Municipal Engineering Bureau	14 033	14 027
房地产管理局	Tianjin Real Estate Administrative Bureau	9 051	9 096
住宅建设发展集团	Tianjin House Construction Development Group	1 962	1 461
公共交通集团公司	Tianjin Public Traffic Group Corporation	10 070	10 316
自来水集团	Tianjin Tap Water Group	3 542	3 710
燃气集团	Tianjin Gas Group	6 551	6 540
交委系统	**Tianjin Transportation Committee System**		
天津港(集团)有限公司	Tianjin Port Group Corporation Ltd.	11 353	11 446
天津交通运输总公司	Tianjin Communication Corporation	7 133	6 316
商委系统	**Tianjin Commercial Committee System**		
粮食粮油集团有限公司	Tianjin Grain & Oil Group Co.,Ltd	3 517	3 080
一商集团有限公司	Tianjin First Commercial Group Co.,Ltd	3 144	2 706
二商集团有限公司	Tianjin Second Commercial Group Co.,Ltd	5 154	3 991

2－26 城乡私营、个体从业人员(2005 年)
(按行业分)
PERSONS EMPLOYED OF PRIVATE AND INDIVIDUAL IN URBAN AND RURAL AREAS,2005
(GROUPED BY SECTOR)

单位:万人 (10 000 persons)

项目	Item	城乡 Urban and Rural Areas 合计 Total	私营 Private	个体 Individual
总计	**Total**	**114.17**	**88.71**	**25.46**
农、林、牧、渔业	Farming,Forestry,Animal Husbandry and Fishery	0.84	0.69	0.15
采矿业	Minerals Mining	0.10	0.03	0.07
制造业	Manufacturing	37.53	32.23	5.30
电力、燃气及水的生产和供应业	Production & Supply of Power,Gas and Water	0.07	0.06	0.01
建筑业	Construction	4.31	4.09	0.22
交通运输、仓储及邮政业	Transport,Storage,Post Services	4.52	3.49	1.03
信息传输、计算机服务和软件业	Information transmitting,Computer Services and Software	0.87	0.82	0.05
批发和零售业	Wholesale and Retail Trade	37.40	24.26	13.14
住宿和餐饮业	Accommodation and Catering Services	3.65	1.31	2.34
房地产业	Real Estate	2.25	2.23	0.02
租赁和商务服务业	Leasing and Business Services	5.74	5.36	0.38
居民服务和其他服务业	Resident Services and Other Social Services	4.40	1.92	2.48
卫生、社会保障和社会福利业	Health Care,Social Security and Social Welfare	0.20	0.15	0.05
文化、体育和娱乐业	Culture,Sports and Recreational Services	0.61	0.49	0.12
其他行业	Others	11.68	11.58	0.10

项目	Item	#城镇 Urban Areas 合计 Total	私营 Private	个体 Individual
总计	**Total**	**54.26**	**44.51**	**9.75**
农、林、牧、渔业	Farming, Forestry,Animal Husbandry and Fishery	0.16	0.14	0.02
采矿业	Minerals Mining	0.02	0.02	
制造业	Manufacturing	11.30	10.44	0.86
电力、燃气及水的生产和供应业	Production & Supply of Power,Gas and Water	0.03	0.03	
建筑业	Construction	2.25	2.16	0.09
交通运输、仓储及邮政业	Transport,Storage,Post Services	2.78	2.23	0.55
信息传输、计算机服务和软件业	Information transmitting,Computer Services and Software	0.59	0.56	0.03
批发和零售业	Wholesale and Retail Trade	20.08	14.31	5.77
住宿和餐饮业	Accommodation and Catering Services	1.72	0.79	0.93
房地产业	Real Estate	1.50	1.49	0.01
租赁和商务服务业	Leasing and Business Services	3.65	3.48	0.17
居民服务和其他服务业	Resident Services and Other Social Services	2.36	1.17	1.19
卫生、社会保障和社会福利业	Health Care,Social Security and Social Welfare	0.13	0.10	0.03
文化、体育和娱乐业	Culture,Sports and Recreational Services	0.33	0.27	0.06
其他行业	Others	7.36	7.32	0.04

资料来源:天津市工商局。
Data source:Tianjin Municipal Industry & Commerce Bureau.

2－27 离退休退职人员情况(2001－2005年)
BASIC STATISTICS ON RETIRED AND QUITED PERSONNEL, 2001－2005

指　　标　Item	2001	2002	2003	2004	2005
离退休、退职人数(万人) Number of Retired and Quited Personnel(10 000 persons)	**99.2**	**109.9**	**111.2**	**118.6**	**131.2**
劳动部门 Labour Department	98.6	109.3	110.6	118.0	130.6
国有单位 State－owned Units	72.0	76.8	76.6	83.0	94.6
集体单位 Collective－owned Units	16.8	18.0	18.6	19.1	20.9
其他单位 Others	9.8	14.5	15.4	15.9	15.1
民政部门 Civil Administration Department	0.6	0.6	0.6	0.6	0.6
离退休退职人员与在职职工之比(以在职职工为100) Ratio of Retired and Quited Personnel to On－post Staff and Workers(take on－post staff and workers as 100)	**53.9**	**62.1**	**63.6**	**68.7**	**77.2**

资料来源：天津市劳动和社会保障局、民政局。
Data Source: Tianjin Municipal Labour & Social Insurance Bureau and Tianjin Municipal Civil Administration Bureau.

2－28 城镇登记失业人员情况(2001－2005年)
BASIC STATISTICS ON REGISTERED PERSONS UNEMPLOYED IN URBAN AREA, 2001－2005

单位：万人　　(10 000 persons)

指　　标　Item	2001	2002	2003	2004	2005
新登记失业人数 Number of Newly Registered Unemployed Personnel	**9.99**	**11.02**	**7.61**	**6.61**	**6.03**
#女　性 Female	5.49	6.13	3.96	3.33	3.14
由就业转失业人数 Unemployment Turned from Employment	7.45	8.76	5.60	4.01	4.11
本期失业人员就业人数 Newly Employed Personnel Turning from Unemploymen	**9.09**	**9.51**	**8.48**	**6.87**	**6.09**
期末实有登记失业人数 Registered Unemployed Personnel Year－end	**11.40**	**12.90**	**12.03**	**11.77**	**11.72**
#女　性 Female	6.27	6.71	6.25	5.92	6.09
长期失业者 Permanent Unemployed Personnel	10.26	10.91	4.81	5.20	
登记失业率(%) Registered Unemployed Rate(%)	**3.60**	**3.91**	**3.80**	**3.76**	**3.70**

资料来源：天津市劳动和社会保障局。
Data Source: Tianjin Municipal Labour & Social Insurance Bureau.

2-29 全市职业技能培训(2001-2005年)
VOCATIONAL TECHNICAL TRAINING,2001-2005

项 目 Item	2001	2002	2003	2004	2005
参加职业技能鉴定人次(人次) Persons Attending Vocational Technical Appraisal(person/time)	**124 817**	**151 266**	**155 120**	**206 427**	**227 984**
初级工 Junior Worker	84 405	103 595	106 367	138 398	144 874
中级工 Middle Worker	32 261	37 961	39 554	49 393	59 594
高级工 Senior Worker	7 202	8 458	8 350	14 634	17 058
技 师 Technician	869	1 097	809	3 596	6 082
高级技师 Senior Technician	80	155	40	406	376
取得职业资格证书人数(人) Persons Gaining Vocational Certificate(person)	**115 179**	**140 943**	**145 246**	**193 218**	**215 217**
初级工 Junior Worker	78 109	97 065	99 820	131 097	137 961
中级工 Middle Worker	29 826	34 793	36 847	44 877	55 256
高级工 Senior Worker	6 319	7 862	7 761	13 565	16 102
技 师 Technician	849	1 072	784	3 292	5 549
高级技师 Senior Technician	76	151	34	387	349

2-30 全市就业和再就业情况(2003-2005年)
STATISTICS ON EMPLOYMENT AND RE-RMPLOYMENT,2003-2005

单位:万人 (10 000 persons)

项 目 Item	2003	2004	2005
新增就业岗位人数 Persons Employed on New Job Posts	**18.12**	**21.45**	**26.21**
下岗失业人员 Laid-off and Unemployed	12.08	13.70	14.22
下岗人员 Laid-off	6.10	6.83	7.16
失业人员 Unemployed	5.98	6.87	7.06
其他人员 Others	6.04	7.75	11.99
领取再就业优惠证人数 Persons Gaining Re-employment Favourable Prove	**12.09**	**11.10**	**6.14**
#4050人员 Persons at 40 and 50 Years Old	7.08	3.01	2.05

主要统计指标解释

常住人口 指实际经常居住在某地区一定时间(指半年以上)的人口。按人口普查和抽样调查规定,主要包括:1.除离开本地半年以上(不包括在国外工作或学习的人)的全部常住本地的户籍人口;2.户口在外地,但在本地居住半年以上者,或离开户口地半年以上而调查时在本地居住的人口;3.调查时居住在本地,但在任何地方都没有登记常住户口,如手持户口迁移证、出生证、退伍证、劳改劳教释放证等尚未办理常住户口的人,即所谓"口袋户口"的人。

户籍人口 指公民依照《中华人民共和国户口登记条例》,已在其经常居住地的公安户籍管理机关登记了常住户口的人。这类人口不管其是否外出,也不管外出时间长短,只要在某地注册有常住户口,则为该地区的户籍人口。

人口密度 指单位土地面积上的人口数。通常使用常住人口计算人口密度,用于说明人口的拥挤程度。通常以每平方公里的居民人数来表示。计算公式:

人口密度=(常住人口/总土地面积)

人口出生率 指一定时期内出生的人口数与该时期内平均人口数之比,通常以年为单位计算,用千分比来表示,表明某年1000人中活产的人数。计算公式:

人口出生率=(年内出生人数/年平均人口数)×1000‰

人口死亡率 指一定时期内死亡的人口数与该时期内平均人口数之比,通常以年为单位计算,用千分比来表示,表明某年1000人中死亡的人数。计算公式:

人口死亡率=(年内死亡人数/年平均人口数)×1000‰

人口自然增长率 指一定时期内人口自然增长数(出生人数减死亡人数)与该时期内平均人口数之比,通常以年为单位计算,用千分比来表示,计算公式:

人口自然增长率=〔(年内出生人数-年内死亡人数)/年平均人口数〕×1000‰

人口自然增长率=人口出生率-人口死亡率

政策生育率 表明的是平均100个出生人口中符合生育政策规定的存活活产数。计算公式:

政策生育率=(符合政策生育规定的出生人数/本期出生总数)×100%

总和生育率 总和生育率是将特定时点上全体妇女生育率综合起来,以一个数字来表示。实际上,它就是假设一个妇女在整个育龄期都按照某一年的年龄别生育率生育,她所生育孩子的总数,即平均每个妇女在育龄期生育的孩子数。

总负担系数 指14岁及以下少年儿童人口数和65岁及以上老年人口数与15-64岁劳动力年龄人口数的比例。表明的是每百名劳动年龄人口负担多少非劳动年龄人口。计算公式:

总负担系数=〔(14岁及以下人数+65岁及以上人数)/15-64岁人数〕×100%

劳动力资源 指在劳动年龄内,具有劳动能力,在正常情况下,可能或实际参加社会劳动的总人口数。具体的范围是:劳动年龄内(16周岁及以上),有劳动能力、实际参加社会劳动和未参加社会劳动的人员。

社会从业人员 是指在劳动年龄内,有劳动能力,参加社会劳动取得劳动报酬或经营收入的人员。具体指城镇单位从业人员,乡镇企业从业人员,乡村农林牧渔劳动者,私营、个体雇员,私营、个体雇主以及其他从业人员。从空间范围上讲社会从业人员既包括城镇中的从业人员,又包括乡村中的从业人员。

城镇单位从业人员 是指在各级国家机关、政党机关、社会团体、事业单位以及城镇范围内的各类企业中工作,并取得劳动报酬的全部人员。包括在岗职工和其他从业人员,但不包括不在岗职工。

城镇私营和个体从业人员 城镇私营从业人员指在工商管理部门注册登记,其经营地址设在县城关镇(含城关镇)以上的私营企业从业人员;包括私营企业投资者和雇工。城镇个体从业人员指在工商管理部门注册登记,并持有城镇户口或在城镇长期居住,经批准从事个体工商经营的从业人员;包括个体经营者和在个体工商户劳动的家庭帮工和雇工。

在岗职工 是指调查时期(时点)在单位工作并领取工资的职工。具体是指那些与本单位签有劳动合同或在本单位在册,并在本单位从事有报酬的劳动人员,在岗职工还包括单位派出学习、工作及病伤产假(六个月内)且仍在单位支付劳动报酬的人员。

单位其他从业人员 按劳动统计规定不作在岗职工统计,但实际参加各单位生产或工作并取得劳动报酬的人员。包括再就业的离退休人员、民办教师、在各单位工作的港、澳、台、外籍人员、聘用的外单位不在岗人员、聘用的失业人员、聘用和使用的外来人员、聘用的其他人员以及在本单位从事第二职业的外单位人员，但不包括在单位中工作并领取报酬的在校学生。

城镇登记失业人员 指有非农业户口，在一定的劳动年龄（16岁至退休年龄）内，有劳动能力，无业且要求就业，并在当地劳动保障机构进行求职登记的人员。

城镇登记失业率 报告期末城镇登记失业人数占期末从业人员总数与期末实有城镇登记失业人数之和的比重。计算公式：

城镇登记失业率＝〔期末实有城镇登记失业人数/（期末从业人员总数＋期末实有城镇登记失业人数）〕×100%

法定婚龄、劳龄人口 我国进入婚龄法定人口标准为男22岁、女20岁；进入劳龄人口、劳动年龄内人口、退出劳龄人口的国内标准分别是男16岁、16－59岁、60岁和女16岁、16－54岁、55岁；国际标准男女均为15岁、15－64岁、65岁。

2005年人口抽样调查资料说明 2005年人口抽样调查是继第五次人口普查后的一次简易普查，天津市调查的样本量为50万人，占全市总人口的5%.调查登记的标准时点为2005年11月1日零时；调查样本设计以全市为总体，以各区县为次总体，采取分层、多阶段、整群、概率比例的抽样方法，在全市18个区县中，抽取了240个街（乡、镇）级行政单位的944个居（村）委会和2054调查小区，实际调查登记了19.95万户、65.80万人。表2－11至2－15为这次调查加权汇总数据。

Explanatory Notes on Main Statistical Indicators

Permanent Resident Population refers to the total number of people alive at a given area within a period (over half a year). According to the regulation of population census and sample survey, permanent resident population include (a) registered population in this area except those who have left this area over half a year(exclude those going abroad to work or study). (b) population with residence registered in other area, but having actually resided in this area over half a year or having left place of residence registration over half a year and resided in this area during the period of population survey. (c) population with residence registration in this enumeration area not yet settled, i. e. residence card on hand, migration certificate, birth certificate, demobilized soldier card, release certificate, etc.

Registered Population refers to the population with registered in accordance with the regulation of the People's Republic of China on the Management of Registration Residence in public security organs in this area. No matter he is out or not, how long the time is, which is often expressed in.

Population Density refers to the total number of people within unit land area. Usually, population density is calculated using permanent resident population and indicates crowd degree of population. It is often expressed in the number of people per square kilometer. The following formula is used:

Population Density = (permanent resident population)/(Total Area of Land)

Birth Rate refers to the ratio of the number of births to the average population during a certain period of time, usually using a year as unit for calculation, which is often expressed in ‰ and indicates the alive births per 1000 persons. The following formula is used

Birth Rate = (Number of Births)/(Annual Average Number of Population) × 1000‰

Death Rate refers to the ratio of the number of deaths to the average population during a certain period of time, usually using a year as unit for calculation, which is often expressed in ‰ and indicates the deaths per 1000 persons. The following formula is used

Death Rate = (Number of Deaths)/(Annual Average Number of Population) × 1000‰

Natural Growth Rate of Population refers to the ratio of natural increase in population (number of births minus number of deaths) in a certain period of time to the average population of the same period, usually using a year as unit for calculation, which is often expressed in ‰. The following formula is used:

Natural Growth Rate of Population = (Number of Births − Number of Deaths)/(Annual Average Number of Population) × 1000‰

Natural Growth Rate of Population = Birth Rate − Death Rate

Birth Control Rate refers to the number of alive births matching the birth control policy per 100 births. The following formula is used :

Birth Control Rate = (the number of births matching the birth control policy)/(the Total Births of the Same Period) × 1000‰

Total of Birth Rate refers to the total of birth rate of women aged 15 − 49 during a certain period of time, which is expressed in a data. It actually refers to the number of children of average woman aged 15 − 49.

Gross Dependency Coefficient refers to the ratio of children aged 0 − 14 and elderly population aged 65 and over to the working − age population aged 15 − 64. It describes in general the number of non − working − age population that every 100 people at working ages will take care of. The following formula is used:

Gross Dependency Coefficient = [(population aged 0 − 14) + (population aged 65 and over)]/(population aged 15 − 64) × 100%

Labour Force Resources refer to the number of population at working ages (aged 16 and over) who have capacity for physical labour, have engaged in social labour or not.

Social Employment Personnel refer to the persons aged 16 and over who are engaged in social labour and receive remuneration payment or earn business income, including employment personnel worked in units in urban areas, employment personnel worked in township enterprises, rural labour engaged in farming, forestry, animal husbandry and fishery, employees in private enterprises and individual economy, employers of private enterprises and individual economy and other employment personnel. Social employment personnel not only include those in urban areas, also include those in rural areas.

Persons Employed in Urban Units refer to all the persons working in government agencies of various levels, political and party organizations, social organizations, enterprises and institutions, and receiving remuneration payment. They include on − post staff and workers and other employment personnel in various units, but exclude staff and workers who have left their working units.

Persons Employed in Private Enterprises and Individual Economy in Urban Areas Persons employed in private enterprises refer to the persons employed in the private enterprises which have been registered at the departments of industrial and commercial administration and are situated at a town (i. e. at own where the county government is located) for business operation or at urban areas with the level higher than a county town. The individual economy in urban areas refer to persons who hold the certificates of residence in urban areas or have resided in the urban areas for a long time and have been registered at the departments of industrial and commercial administration and approved to be engaged in individual industrial or commercial business, including self − employed persons as well as helpers and hired labourers who work in the individual households engaged in industrial or commercial business.

On − post Staff and Workers refer to staff and workers who work in and receive wages from their working units during a survey period. They include the persons who have signed working contracts with units or registered in units, also include those receive wages from units but are temporarily absent from work for reasons of study, work or on sick, injury or maternal leave no more than six months.

Other Persons Employed in Various Units refer to the numbers receiving wages or other forms of payment, include re − employed retirees, teachers in schools run by the local people, foreigners and Chinese compatriots from HongKong, Macao, and Taiwan working in various units, employees of other units working temporarily at current posts, unemployment personnel, non − locals, and employees holding the second job of other units, exclude students enrolled in universities and colleges who work at the units and receive wages.

Registered Urban Unemployed Persons refer to the persons who are registered as permanent residents in the urban areas engaged in non－agricultural activities, aged within the range of working age(16－retired age), capable to labour, unemployed but desirous to be employed and have been registered at the local employment service agencies to apply for a job.

Registered Urban Unemployment Rate refers to the ratio of the number of the registered unemployed persons to the sum of the number of employed persons and the registered unemployed persons. The formula is as follows：

Registered urban unemployment rate = number of urban registered unemployed persons/ (urban employed persons + number of registered urban unemployed persons) × 100%

Legal marriage age, labor age population：The standard of legal marriage age is 22 for male and 20 for female; the domestic standard of "reaching labor age", "within labor age" and "over labor age" are 16, 16 to 59, 60 for male respectively and 16, 16 to 54, 55 for female respectively; the international standard of these items are 15, 15－64 and 65 respectively for both male and female.

Brief introduction for sample survey on population in 2005: 2005 sample survey of population was a simple survey after the fifth population census. The survey sample volume is 500,000 people in Tianjin, the sampling fraction was 5%. The reference time of sample survey was zero o'clock of November 1, 2005, the survey took the whole city as total and districts as inferior total. The sample survey was conducted with a multi－stage systematic cluster sampling scheme. A total of 0.658 million people were selected as the sample from 0.1995 million households from 2,054 area in 944 resident's committees & village committees in 240 streets(towns) of 18 districts(counties). From Table 2－11 to Table 2－15, data were calculated by the weighted sum method.

第3篇
CHAPTER 3

固定资产投资和房地产
Investment in Fixed Assets and Real Estate

3-1 全社会固定资产投资(1990-2005年)
TOTAL INVESTMENT IN FIXED ASSETS,1990-2005

单位:亿元　　(100 million yuan)

年份 Year	全社会固定资产投资 Total Investment in Fixed Assets	国有经济 State-owned	集体经济 Collective-owned	#农村 Rural	个体经济 Individuals	#农村 Rural
总计 Total						
1990	87.69	72.18	10.56	9.48	4.95	4.36
1991-1995	1 234.54	1 024.85	166.69	145.27	43.00	36.99
1991	128.95	109.69	12.18	10.84	7.08	6.68
1992	169.88	137.81	25.21	23.59	6.86	6.08
1993	226.56	187.83	30.51	27.34	8.22	6.36
1994	315.97	265.32	40.14	36.98	10.51	8.51
1995	393.18	324.20	58.65	46.52	10.33	9.36
1996-2000	2 686.49	2 280.95	320.22	271.91	85.32	62.96
1996	435.81	351.59	66.67	57.35	17.55	15.28
1997	498.66	422.84	61.77	52.39	14.05	10.63
1998	575.86	491.87	68.39	56.70	15.60	12.45
1999	567.36	488.45	61.59	49.00	17.32	11.50
2000	608.80	526.20	61.80	56.47	20.80	13.10
2001-2005	5 338.90	4 706.89	483.10	426.14	148.91	115.76
2001	705.10	612.50	66.10	61.50	26.50	16.40
2002	811.26	695.75	85.90	74.00	29.61	20.01
2003	1 046.72	919.59	98.04	89.73	29.09	22.86
2004	1 258.98	1 114.98	109.72	99.06	34.28	27.20
2005	1 516.84	1 364.07	123.34	101.85	29.43	29.29
#地方 Local Investment						
1990	57.47	41.96	10.56	9.48	4.95	4.36
1991-1995	259.75	750.06	166.69	145.27	43.00	36.99
1991	93.13	73.87	12.18	10.84	7.08	6.68
1992	123.85	91.78	25.21	23.59	6.86	6.08
1993	176.14	137.41	30.51	27.34	8.22	6.36
1994	256.88	206.23	40.14	36.98	10.51	8.51
1995	309.75	240.77	58.65	46.52	10.33	9.36
1996-2000	2 023.65	1 618.11	320.22	271.91	85.32	62.96
1996	325.71	241.49	66.67	57.35	17.55	15.28
1997	376.69	300.87	61.77	52.39	14.05	10.63
1998	452.11	368.12	68.39	56.70	15.60	12.45
1999	405.31	326.40	61.59	49.00	17.32	11.50
2000	463.83	381.23	61.80	56.47	20.80	13.10
2001-2005	4 495.49	3 863.48	483.10	426.14	148.91	115.76
2001	567.40	474.80	66.10	61.50	26.50	16.40
2002	677.60	562.09	85.90	74.00	29.61	20.01
2003	893.73	766.60	98.04	89.73	29.09	22.86
2004	1 067.91	923.91	109.72	99.06	34.28	27.20
2005	1 288.85	1 136.08	123.34	101.85	29.43	29.29

注:本表国有经济中包括"三资"、股份制、联营、私营经济。以下各表同。
Note: State-owned units of this table included foreign funded economic units, share holding economic units, joint ownership economic units and private economy. The same as in the following tables.

3-2 全社会新增固定资产(1990-2005年)
TOTAL NEWLY INCREASED IN FIXED ASSETS,1990-2005

单位:亿元 (100 million yuan)

年份 Year	全社会新增固定资产 Total Newly Increased in Fixed Assets	国有经济 State-owned	集体经济 Collective-owned	#农村 Rural	个体经济 Individuals	#农村 Rural
总计 **Total**						
1990	65.16	49.66	10.55	9.55	4.95	4.36
1991-1995	878.36	698.11	137.24	128.77	43.01	36.99
1991	74.11	54.99	12.03	10.85	7.09	6.68
1992	102.27	73.24	22.17	21.26	6.86	6.08
1993	140.00	105.82	25.96	24.11	8.22	6.36
1994	261.12	216.98	33.63	32.36	10.51	8.51
1995	300.86	247.08	43.45	40.19	10.33	9.36
1996-2000	1 966.98	1 641.13	250.01	219.84	75.84	57.00
1996	313.12	246.63	48.94	41.61	17.55	15.28
1997	320.46	259.08	47.33	41.76	14.05	10.63
1998	439.58	379.21	44.77	42.54	15.60	12.45
1999	459.54	383.73	58.49	47.78	17.32	11.50
2000	434.28	372.48	50.48	46.15	11.32	7.14
2001-2005	3 216.24	2 627.54	449.52	407.78	139.18	113.28
2001	476.92	385.67	64.75	61.00	26.50	16.40
2002	537.98	427.98	80.39	71.14	29.61	20.01
2003	656.99	534.66	96.66	87.03	25.67	22.86
2004	696.56	567.65	98.46	92.64	30.45	27.20
2005	847.79	711.58	109.26	95.97	26.95	26.81
#地方 **Local Investment**						
1990	49.46	33.96	10.55	9.55	4.95	4.36
1991-1995	672.19	491.94	137.24	128.77	43.01	36.99
1991	47.38	28.26	12.03	10.85	7.09	6.68
1992	69.15	40.12	22.17	21.26	6.86	6.08
1993	93.59	59.41	25.96	24.11	8.22	6.36
1994	244.01	199.87	33.63	32.36	10.51	8.51
1995	218.06	164.28	43.45	40.19	10.33	9.36
1996-2000	1 540.88	1 215.03	250.01	219.84	75.84	57.00
1996	241.66	175.17	48.94	41.61	17.55	15.28
1997	243.63	182.25	47.33	41.76	14.05	10.63
1998	351.27	290.90	44.77	42.54	15.60	12.45
1999	353.35	277.54	58.49	47.78	17.32	11.50
2000	350.97	289.17	50.48	46.15	11.32	7.14
2001-2005	2 584.74	1 994.69	450.87	408.28	139.18	113.28
2001	356.46	263.86	66.10	61.50	26.50	16.40
2002	434.61	324.61	80.39	71.14	29.61	20.01
2003	543.59	421.26	96.66	87.03	25.67	22.86
2004	522.43	393.52	98.46	92.64	30.45	27.20
2005	727.65	591.44	109.26	95.97	26.95	26.81

3-3　全社会固定资产投资和房屋建筑面积

TOTAL INVESTMENT IN FIXED ASSETS AND FLOOR SPACE OF BUILDINGS

指　　标	Item	2003	2004	2005	2005 比 2004 年增长 % Increase Rate in 2005 over 2004
投资总额(亿元)	**Total Investment(100 million yuan)**	**1 046.72**	**1 258.98**	**1 516.84**	**20.5**
按经济类型分	**Grouped by Ownership**				
国有经济	State - owned	919.59	1 114.98	1 364.07	22.3
集体经济	Collective - owned	98.04	109.72	123.34	12.4
#农　村	Rural	89.73	99.06	101.85	2.8
个体经济	Individuals	29.09	34.28	29.43	-14.1
#农　村	Rural	22.86	27.20	29.29	7.7
按隶属关系分	**Grouped by Administrative Relationship**				
中　央	Central Government	152.99	191.07	227.99	19.3
地　方	Local Government	893.73	1 067.91	1 288.85	20.7
按城乡分	**By Urban and Rural**				
城镇投资	Urban Investment	933.86	1 132.33	1 385.56	22.4
#房地产开发	Real Estate Development	211.39	263.92	327.54	24.1
农村投资	Rural Investment	112.58	126.26	131.14	3.9
按构成分	**Grouped by Use of Funds**				
建筑工程	Construction	594.72	690.33	852.60	23.5
安装工程	Installation	61.06	61.76	75.59	22.4
设备工器具购置	Purchases of Equipment and Instrument	197.32	282.48	316.10	11.9
其他费用	Others	193.62	224.41	272.55	21.5
按三次产业分	**Grouped by Industries**				
第一产业	Primary Industry	9.38	11.55	13.71	18.7
第二产业	Secondary Industry	377.64	501.70	614.63	22.5
第三产业	Tertiary Industry	659.70	745.73	888.50	19.1
房屋建筑面积(万平方米)	**Floor Space of Buildings(10 000 sq.m)**				
施工面积	Floor Space Under Construction	4 377.95	5 242.05	6 295.19	20.1
竣工面积	Floor Space Completed	2 072.42	2 353.92	2 863.36	21.6
#住　宅	Residential Buildings	1 121.96	1 428.39	1 662.53	16.4

3-4 按行业分全社会固定资产投资
TOTAL INVESTMENT IN FIXED ASSETS GROUPED BY SECTOR

单位:万元 (10 000 yuan)

行　业　Sector	2004	2005	2005 比 2004 年 增长% Increase Rate in2005 over 2004
总　计			
Total	**12 589 831**	**15 168 404**	**20.5**
农、林、牧、渔业			
Farming, Forestry, Animal Husbandry and Fishery	115 587	137 077	18.6
采矿业			
Minerals Mining	1 185 043	1 243 053	4.9
制造业			
Manufacturing	3 078 502	4 178 023	35.7
电力、燃气及水的生产和供应业			
Production & Supply of Power, Gas and Water	484 630	577 491	19.2
建筑业			
Construction	268 872	147 804	-45
交通运输、仓储和邮政业			
Transport, Storage, Post Services	937 390	1 722 811	83.8
信息传输、计算机服务和软件业			
Information Transmitting, Computer Services and Software	282 423	265 065	-6.1
批发和零售业			
Wholesale and Retail Trade	242 471	274 144	13.1
住宿和餐饮业			
Accommodation and Catering Services	100 587	57 925	-42.4
金融业			
Finance Intermediation	9 502	5 841	-38.5
房地产业			
Real Estate	3 072 891	3 718 385	21
租赁和商务服务业			
Leasing and Business Services	41 778	59 873	43.3
科学研究、技术服务和地质勘查业			
Scientific Research, Technical Services and Geological Prospecting	22 732	46 199	103.2
水利、环境和公共设施管理业			
Management for Water Conservancy, Environment and Public Facilities	1 853 525	1 798 851	-2.9
居民服务和其他服务业			
Resident Services and Other Social Services	53 737	60 222	12.1
教　育			
Education	381 898	404 478	5.9
卫生、社会保障和社会福利业			
Health Care, Social Security and Social Welfare	106 671	95 672	-10.3
文化、体育和娱乐业			
Culture, Sports and Recreational Services	189 854	147 388	-22.4
公共管理和社会组织			
Public Management and Social Organizations	161 738	228 102	41

3-5 全市固定资产投资额及新增固定资产

INVESTMENT IN FIXED ASSETS AND NEWLY INCREASED FIXED ASSETS

单位：万元 (10 000 yuan)

项 目	Item	2004	2005	2005比2004年增长% Increase Rate in 2005 over 2004
固定资产投资额	**Total Investment in Fixed Assets**	**11 323 315**	**13 855 642**	**22.4**
按三次产业分	**Grouped by Industries**			
第一产业	Primary Industry	30 948	50 472	63.1
第二产业	Secondary Industry	4 338 860	5 429 365	25.1
#工 业	Industry	4 183 425	5 323 543	27.3
第三产业	Tertiary Industry	6 953 507	8 375 805	20.5
按隶属关系分	**Grouped by Administrative Relationship**			
中 央	Central Government	1 910 736	2 279 888	19.3
地 方	Local Government	9 412 579	11 575 754	23
按建设性质分	**Grouped by Type of Construction**			
#新 建	New Construction	4 683 185	5 906 967	26.1
改、扩建及其他	Expansion, Reconstruction and Others	4 000 965	4 673 272	16.8
按构成分	**Grouped by Use of Funds**			
建筑工程	Construction	6 270 195	7 876 445	25.6
安装工程	Installation	572 948	710 873	24.1
设备工器具购置	Purchases of Equipment and Instrument	2 351 885	2 660 897	13.1
其他费用	Others	2 128 287	2 607 427	22.5
按登记注册类型分	**Grouped by Registered Categories**			
内资企业	Domestic-funded Enterprises	9 475 186	11 723 920	23.7
国有企业	State-owned Enterprises	3 408 609	4 229 851	24.1
集体企业	Collective-owned Enterprises	106 598	190 026	78.3
股份合作企业	Cooperative Enterprises	50 145	130 828	160.9
私 营	Private Enterprises	719 685	1 383 094	92.2
股份有限公司	Share Holding Corporations Ltd.	1 504 883	1 666 833	10.8
有限责任公司	Limited Liability Corporations	3 458 617	3 802 831	10
#国有独资	Sole State-funded Corporations	1 387 978	1 940 401	39.8
联营企业	Joint Ownership Enterprises	112 965	122 206	8.2
#国有与国有联营企业	State Joint Ownership Enterprises	83 778	99 593	18.9
集体与集体联营企业	Collective Joint Ownership Enterprises	14 713	4 313	-70.7
其他内资企业	Other Domestic-funded Enterprises	113 684	198 251	74.4
港澳台商投资企业	Enterprises with Investment from Hongkong, Macao and Taiwan	499 510	496 515	-0.6
外商投资企业	Foreign Funded Enterprises	1 347 844	1 616 264	19.9
个体经济	Individuals	775	18 943	2 344.3
新增固定资产	**Newly Increased Fixed Assets**	**5 787 754**	**7 248 716**	**25.2**
第一产业	Primary Industry	21 133	41 660	97.1
第二产业	Secondary Industry	2 959 144	2 920 481	-1.3
#工 业	Industry	2 918 123	2 867 340	-1.7
第三产业	Tertiary Industry	2 807 477	4 286 575	52.7
固定资产交付使用率(%)	**Rate of Fixed Assets Put into Use(%)**	**51.1**	**52.3**	

注：表中按建设性质分组数据不含房地产开发投资。
Note: The data of this table grouped by type of construction exclude real estate development.

3－6　按行业分全市固定资产投资
INVESTMENT IN FIXED ASSETS BY SECTOR

单位:万元　　　　(10 000 yuan)

行　业　Sector	2004	2005	2005比2004年增长% Increase Rate in 2005 over 2004
总　计 **Total**	**11 323 315**	**13 855 642**	**22.4**
农、林、牧、渔业 Farming,Forestry,Animal Husbandry and Fishery	30 948	50 472	63.1
采矿业 Minerals Mining	1 185 043	1 243 053	4.9
制造业 Manufacturing	2 514 700	3 502 999	39.3
电力、燃气及水的生产和供应业 Production & Supply of Power,Gas and Water	483 682	577 491	19.4
建筑业 Construction	155 435	105 822	－31.9
交通运输、仓储和邮政业 Transport,Storage,Post Services	893 541	1 678 371	87.8
信息传输、计算机服务和软件业 Information Transmitting,Computer Services and Software	282 225	264 845	－6.2
批发和零售业 Wholesale and Retail Trade	202 395	233 653	15.4
住宿和餐饮业 Accommodation and Catering Services	91 214	48 426	－46.9
金融业 Finance Intermediation	9 502	5 841	－38.5
房地产业 Real Estate	2 754 372	3 394 727	23.2
租赁和商务服务业 Leasing and Business Services	31 566	48 753	54.4
科学研究、技术服务和地质勘查业 Scientific Research,Technical Services and Geological Prospecting	22 732	46 199	103.2
水利、环境和公共设施管理业 Management for Water Conservancy,Environment and Public Facilities	1 841 543	1 786 977	－3
居民服务和其他服务业 Resident Services and Other Social Services	9 975	18 385	84.3
教　育 Education	372 062	394 620	6.1
卫生、社会保障和社会福利业 Health Care,Social Security and Social Welfare	103 507	92 424	－10.7
文化、体育和娱乐业 Culture,Sports and Recreational Services	184 222	141 542	－23.2
公共管理和社会组织 Public Management and Social Organizations	154 651	221 042	42.9

3-7 按制造业主要行业分全市固定资产投资
INVESTMENT IN FIXED ASSETS OF MAIN MANUFACTURING

单位:万元 (10 000 yuan)

行业	Sector	2004	2005	2005比2004年增长% Increase Rate in2005 over 2004
总计	**Total**	**2 514 700**	**3 502 999**	**39.3**
农副食品加工业	Processing of Food from Agricultural Products	47 542	90 764	90.9
食品制造业	Manufacture of Foods	44 723	64 945	45.2
饮料制造业	Manufacture of Beverages	23 022	46 857	103.5
纺织业	Manufacture of Textile	52 275	163 631	213
纺织服装、鞋、帽制造业	Manufacture of Textile Wearing Apparel, Footware and Caps	20 551	41 363	101.3
皮革、皮毛、羽毛及其制品业	Manufacture of Leather,Fur,Feather and Related Products	4 509	7 729	71.4
木材加工及木、竹、藤、棕、草制品业	Processing of Timber,Manufacture of Wood,Bamboo,Rattan,Palm and Straw Products	4 764	4 028	-15.4
家具制造业	Manufacture of Furniture	13 454	25 843	92.1
造纸及纸制品业	Manufacture of Paper and Paper Products	11 192	14 741	31.7
印刷和记录媒介的复制	Printing,Reproduction of Recording Media	1 392	19 448	1 297.1
文教体育用品制造业	Manufacture of Articles for Culture,Education and Sport Activity	880	12 762	1 350.2
石油加工、炼焦及核燃料加工业	Processing of Petroleum,Coking,Processing of Nuclear Fuel	62 181	83 060	33.6
化学原料及化学制品制造业	Manufacture of Raw Chemical Materials and Chemical Products	167 794	256 040	52.6
医药制造业	Manufacture of Medicines	135 212	118 674	-12.2
化学纤维制造业	Manufacture of Chemical Fibers	17 634	7 240	-58.9
橡胶制品业	Manufacture of Rubber	5 094	68 075	1 236.4
塑料制品业	Manufacture of Plastics	107 677	113 249	5.2
非金属矿物制品业	Manufacture of Non-metallic Mineral Products	85 504	116 501	36.3
黑色金属冶炼及压延加工业	Smelting and Pressing of Ferrous Metals	441 781	826 155	87
有色金属冶炼及压延加工业	Smelting and Pressing of Non-ferrous Metals	19 597	21 628	10.4
金属制品业	Manufacture of Metal Products	77 236	132 857	72
通用设备制造业	Manufacture of General Purpose Machinery	54 285	155 789	187
交通运输设备制造业	Manufacture of Transport Equipment	329 513	397 093	20.5
电气机械及器材制造业	Manufacture of Electrical Machinery and Equipment	144 651	102 206	-29.3
通信设备、计算机及其他电子设备制造业	Manufacture of Communication Equipment,Computers and Other Electronic Equipment	513 229	450 622	-12.2
仪器仪表及文化、办公用机械制造业	Manufacture of Measuring Instruments and Machinery for Cultural Activity and Office Work	26 607	26 872	1

3-8 按行业分全市新增固定资产
NEWLY INCREASED FIXED ASSETS BY SECTOR

单位:万元 (10 000 yuan)

行　业　Sector	2004	2005	2005 比 2004 年增长% Increase Rate in 2005 over 2004
总　计 Total	**5 787 754**	**7 437 441**	**28.5**
农、林、牧、渔业 Farming, Forestry, Animal Husbandry and Fishery	21 133	41 660	97.1
采矿业 Minerals Mining	1 220 131	716 585	-41.3
制造业 Manufacturing	1 309 968	1 865 570	42.4
电力、燃气及水的生产和供应业 Production & Supply of Power, Gas and Water	388 024	285 185	-26.5
建筑业 Construction	41 021	53 141	29.5
交通运输、仓储和邮政业 Transport, Storage, Post Services	415 360	660 215	59
信息传输、计算机服务和软件业 Information Transmitting, Computer Services and Software	123 431	127 659	3.4
批发和零售业 Wholesale and Retail Trade	188 526	132 891	-29.5
住宿和餐饮业 Accommodation and Catering Services	84 244	13 092	-84.5
金融业 Finance Intermediation	6 246	5 841	-6.5
房地产业 Real Estate	1 016 185	2 909 258	186.3
租赁和商务服务业 Leasing and Business Services	11 279	6 634	-41.2
科学研究、技术服务和地质勘查业 Scientific Research, Technical Services and Geological Prospecting	22 098	14 929	-32.4
水利、环境和公共设施管理业 Management for Water Conservancy, Environment and Public Facilities	513 663	284 966	-44.5
居民服务和其他服务业 Resident Services and Other Social Services	6 700	4 800	-28.4
教　育 Education	169 677	152 792	-10
卫生、社会保障和社会福利业 Health Care, Social Security and Social Welfare	104 339	102 374	-1.9
文化、体育和娱乐业 Culture, Sports and Recreational Services	34 525	3 755	-89.1
公共管理和社会组织 Public Management and Social Organizations	111 204	56 094	-49.6

3-9 按制造业主要行业分全市新增固定资产
NEWLY INCREASED FIXED ASSETS OF MAIN MANUFACTURING

单位:万元 (10 000 yuan)

行业	Sector	2004	2005	2005比2004年增长% Increase Rate in2005 over 2004
总计	**Total**	**1 309 968**	**1 865 570**	**42.4**
农副食品加工业	Processing of Food from Agricultural Products	15 669	37 097	136.8
食品制造业	Manufacture of Foods	25 354	30 634	20.8
饮料制造业	Manufacture of Beverages	31 716	11 120	-64.9
纺织业	Manufacture of Textile	6 855	35 470	417.4
纺织服装、鞋、帽制造业	Manufacture of Textile Wearing Apparel, Footware and Caps	5 461	36 003	559.3
皮革、皮毛、羽毛及其制品业	Manufacture of Leather, Fur, Feather and Related Products	4 389	829	-81.1
木材加工及木、竹、藤、棕、草制品业	Processing of Timber, Manufacture of Wood, Bamboo, Rattan, Palm and Straw Products	5 364	9 639	79.7
家具制造业	Manufacture of Furniture	10 854	8 777	-19.1
造纸及纸制品业	Manufacture of Paper and Paper Products	7 875	7 280	-7.6
印刷和记录媒介的复制	Printing, Reproduction of Recording Media	1 392	11 518	727.4
文教体育用品制造业	Manufacture of Articles for Culture, Educationty and Sport Activity	580	4 500	675.9
石油加工、炼焦及核燃料加工业	Processing of Petroleum, Coking, Processing of Nuclear Fuel	57 188	48 662	-14.9
化学原料及化学制品制造业	Manufacture of Raw Chemical Materials and Chemical Products	84 627	97 191	14.8
医药制造业	Manufacture of Medicines	52 023	72 887	40.1
化学纤维制造业	Manufacture of Chemical Fibers	13 224	4 280	-67.6
橡胶制品业	Manufacture of Rubber	1 916	13 675	613.7
塑料制品业	Manufacture of Plastics	65 977	76 807	16.4
非金属矿物制品业	Manufacture of Non-metallic Mineral Products	87 614	71 742	-18.1
黑色金属冶炼及压延加工业	Smelting and Pressing of Ferrous Metals	128 484	619 942	382.5
有色金属冶炼及压延加工业	Smelting and Pressing of Non-ferrous Metals	305	10 535	3 354.1
金属制品业	Manufacture of Metal Products	46 644	62 437	33.9
通用设备制造业	Manufacture of General Purpose Machinery	43 171	81 257	88.2
交通运输设备制造业	Manufacture of Transport Equipment	270 942	182 401	-32.7
电气机械及器材制造业	Manufacture of Electrical Machinery and Equipment	39 758	56 903	43.1
通信设备、计算机及其他电子设备制造业	Manufacture of Communication Equipment, Computers and Other Electronic Equipment	230 498	202 825	-12.0
仪器仪表及文化、办公用机械制造业	Manufacture of Measuring Instruments and Machinery for Cultural Activity and Office Work	16 983	11 171	-34.2

3-10 全市固定资产投资资金来源
SOURCE OF FUNDS FOR INVESTMENT IN FIXED ASSETS

单位:万元 (10 000 yuan)

项 目	Item	2004	2005	2005比2004年增长% Increase Rate in 2005 over 2004
资金来源合计	**Total Funds**	**14 305 044**	**18 706 157**	**30.8**
上年末结余资金	Balance of Funds Brought Forward from The Previous Year	1 459 330	1 595 826	9.4
本年资金来源小计	Subtotal of The Sources of Funds in This Year	12 845 714	17 110 331	33.2
国家预算内资金	State Budgetary Appropriation	186 317	311 579	67.2
国内贷款	Domestic Loans	3 616 042	4 227 194	16.9
债 券	Bonds	3 183		
利用外资	Foreign Investment	938 721	1 137 705	21.2
#外商直接投资	Foreign Direct Investment	796 942	1 046 214	31.3
自筹资金	Fundraising	6 033 443	8 322 423	37.9
#企、事业单位自有资金	Fundraising of Enterprises and Institutions	4 711 134	6 333 895	34.4
其他资金来源	Others	2 068 008	3 111 430	50.5

3-11 全市施工和竣工房屋建筑面积
FLOOR SPACE OF BUILDINGS UNDER CONSTRUCTION AND COMPLETED

单位:万平方米 (10 000 sq. m)

项 目	Item	2004	2005	2005比2004年增长% Increase Rate in 2005 over 2004
全市房屋建筑施工面积	**Floor Space of Buildings under Construction**	**4 160.45**	**5 210.19**	**25.2**
#房地产开发企业	Real Estate Development	2 865.55	3 470.57	21.1
#住宅施工面积	Residential Buildings	2 441.49	2 896.83	18.7
#房地产开发企业	Real Estate Development	2 352.98	2 827.87	20.2
全市房屋建筑竣工面积	**Floor Space of Buildings Completed**	**1 518.13**	**2 023.09**	**33.3**
#房地产开发企业	Real Estate Development	1 108.13	1 479.22	33.5
#住宅竣工面积	Residential Buildings	1 052.19	1 305.08	24
#房地产开发企业	Real Estate Development	1 014.46	1 270.96	25.3

注:房屋竣工面积不含农村集体和个人建房数。
Note:Floor space of buildings completed exclude rural collective－owned and individual houses.

3－12 按行业分全市固定资
SOURCE OF FUNDS FOR INVESTM

行 业 Sector	资金来源合计 Total Funds	上年末结余资金 Balance of Funds Brought Forward from the Previous Year	本年资金来源小计 Subtotal of the Sources of Funds in this Year
总 计			
Total	**18 706 157**	**1 595 826**	**17 110 331**
农、林、牧、渔业			
Farming, Forestry, Animal Husbandry and Fishery	54 672	7 885	46 787
采矿业			
Minerals Mining	1 245 100		1 245 100
制造业			
Manufacturing	3 958 900	246 699	3 712 201
电力、燃气及水的生产和供应业			
Production & Supply of Power, Gas and Water	682 332	69 609	612 723
建筑业			
Construction	108 081	534	107 547
交通运输、仓储和邮政业			
Transport, Storage, Post Services	1 507 402	13 953	1 493 449
信息传输、计算机服务和软件业			
Information Transmitting, Computer Services and Software	266 053	1 935	264 118
批发和零售业			
Wholesale and Retail Trade	247 759	9 480	238 279
住宿和餐饮业			
Accommodation and Catering Services	62 505	300	62 205
金融业			
Finance Intermediation	5 841		5 841
房地产业			
Real Estate	7 419 640	1 061 855	6 357 785
租赁和商务服务业			
Leasing and Business Services	52 736	2 460	50 276
科学研究、技术服务和地质勘查业			
Scientific Research, Technical Services and Geological Prospecting	2 043 887	49 066	1 994 821
水利、环境和公共设施管理业			
Management for Water Conservancy, Environment and Public Facilities	1 995 999	48 107	1 947 892
居民服务和其他服务业			
Resident Services and Other Social Services	18 385	555	17 830
教 育			
Education	437 758	25 604	412 154
卫生、社会保障和社会福利业			
Health Care, Social Security and Social Welfare	182 025	80 427	101 598
文化、体育和娱乐业			
Culture, Sports and Recreational Services	144 168	5 207	138 961
公共管理和社会组织			
Public Management and Social Organizations	268 913	20 257	248 656

产投资资金来源（2005 年）

ENT IN FIXED ASSETS BY SECTOR,2005

国家预算内资金 State Budgetary Appropriatio	国内贷款 Domestic Loans	利用外资 Foreign Investment	#外 商直接投资 Foreign Direct Investment	自筹资金 Fundraising	#企事业单位自有资金 Fundraising of Enterprises Investment	其他资金 Others
311 579	**4 227 194**	**1 137 705**	**1 046 214**	**8 322 423**	**6 333 895**	**3 111 430**
2 430	2 570	300	300	35 987	27 198	5 500
		294 922	294 922	949 578	930 337	600
1 000	592 394	744 085	686 330	2 345 760	2 107 121	28 962
18 000	201 394	14 096		317 561	261 268	61 672
14 082	24 000			69 465	61 424	
158 666	535 874	23 291	18 291	764 168	698 124	11 450
	8 330			253 788	253 788	2 000
	2 960	12 977	12 977	215 154	215 154	7 188
	12 887	1 476	1 476	47 591	47 591	251
				5 841	5 841	
	2 789 834	34 895	27 229	2 101 470	1 286 524	2 815 103
240	2 000			47 336	23 885	700
133	1 235 978	10 474	3 500	669 510	15 928	33 478
45 248	1 209 562	6 974		652 630	118 320	33 478
		562	562	16 943	15 368	
16 487	82 178			234 802	165 160	78 687
27 100	14 900			48 646	33 477	10 952
9 567	59 412	627	627	46 574	24 051	22 781
18 626	46 000			152 249	43 336	31 781

3-13 按行业分全市固定资产投资施工项目个数
（不含农村集体及个人投资）
NUMBER OF PROJECTS UNDER CONSTRUCTION IN FIXED ASSETS
(EXCLUDE RURAL COLLECTIVE - OWNED UNITS AND INDIVIDUAL ECONOMY)

单位：个 (unit)

项目	Item	2004	2005	2005比2004年增长% Increase Rate in 2005 over 2004
总计	**Total**	**1 640**	**1 770**	**7.9**
农、林、牧、渔业	Farming, Forestry, Animal Husbandry and Fishery	35	58	65.7
采矿业	Minerals Mining	9	24	166.7
制造业	Manufacturing	602	753	25.1
电力、煤气及水的生产和供应业	Production & Supply of Power, Gas and Water	105	105	
建筑业	Construction	28	23	-17.9
交通运输、仓储和邮政业	Transport, Storage, Post Services	85	78	-8.2
信息传输、计算机服务和软件业	Information Transmitting, Computer Services and Software	51	44	-13.7
批发和零售业	Wholesale and Retail Trade	80	87	8.8
住宿和餐饮业	Accommodation and Catering Services	17	24	41.2
金融业	Finance Intermediation	3		
房地产业	Real Estate	27	24	-11.1
租赁和商务服务业	Leasing and Business Services	16	17	6.3
科学研究、技术服务和地质勘查业	Scientific Research, Technical Services and Geological Prospecting	25	16	-36
水利、环境和公共设施管理业	Management for Water Conservancy, Environment and Public Facilities	274	254	-7.3
居民服务和其他服务业	Resident Services and Other Social Services	6	8	33.3
教育	Education	135	124	-8.1
卫生、社会保障和社会福利业	Health Care, Social Security and Social Welfare	44	31	-29.5
文化、体育和娱乐业	Culture, Sports and Recreational Services	35	26	-25.7
公共管理和社会组织	Public Management and Social Organizations	63	74	17.5

3-14 按行业分全市固定资产投资建成投产项目个数

(不含农村集体及个人投资)

NUMBER OF PROJECTS IN FIXED ASSETS COMPLETED AND PUT INTO USE

(EXCLUDE RURAL COLLECTIVE-OWNED UNITS AND INDIVIDUAL ECONOMY)

单位:个(unit)

项目	Item	2004	2005	2005 比 2004 年增长% Increase Rate in 2005 over 2004
总计	**Total**	**864**	**826**	**-4.4**
农、林、牧、渔业	Farming,Forestry,Animal Husbandry and Fishery	17	36	111.8
采矿业	Minerals Mining	6	16	166.7
制造业	Manufacturing	282	335	18.8
电力、煤气及水的生产和供应业	Production & Supply of Power,Gas and Water	65	48	-26.2
建筑业	Construction	15	14	-6.7
交通运输、仓储和邮政业	Transport,Storage,Post Services	41	41	
信息传输、计算机服务和软件业	Information Transmitting,Computer Services and Software	5	7	40
批发和零售业	Wholesale and Retail Trade	57	55	-3.5
住宿和餐饮业	Accommodation and Catering Services	11	6	-45.5
金融业	Finance Intermediation			
房地产业	Real Estate	9	8	-11.1
租赁和商务服务业	Leasing and Business Services	8	3	-62.5
科学研究、技术服务和地质勘查业	Scientific Research,Technical Services and Geological Prospecting	16	6	-62.5
水利、环境和公共设施管理业	Management for Water Conservancy,Environment and Public Facilities	178	147	-17.4
居民服务和其他服务业	Resident Services and Other Social Services	4	1	-75
教育	Education	78	57	-26.9
卫生、社会保障和社会福利业	Health Care,Social Security and Social Welfare	26	16	-38.5
文化、体育和娱乐业	Culture,Sports and Recreational Services	14	3	-78.6
公共管理和社会组织	Public Management and Social Organizations	32	27	-15.6

3-15 全市能源工业固定资产投资额
INVESTMENT IN FIXED ASSETS OF ENERGY INDUSTRY

单位:万元 (10 000 yuan)

部门	Department	2004	2005	2005比2004年增长% Increas Rate in 2005 over 2004
总计	**Total**	**1 717 724**	**1 894 661**	**10.3**
石油和天然气开采业	Petroleum and Natural Gas Extraction	1 171 861	1 234 110	5.3
电力、热力的生产和供应业	Production and Supply of Electric Power and Heating Energy	348 477	412 464	18.4
水的生产和供应业	Production and Supply of Water	101 836	102 969	1.1
燃气生产和供应业	Production and Supply of Gas	33 369	62 058	86
石油加工、炼焦业及核燃料加工	Petroleum Processing,Coking and Nuclear Fuel Processing	62 181	83 060	33.6
能源投资占全市固定资产投资比重(%)	**As Percentage of Total Investment in Fixed Assets(%)**	**15.2**	**13.7**	

3-16 全市城市基础设施固定资产投资
URBAN INFRASTRUCTURE INVESTMENT IN FIXED ASSETS

单位:万元 (10 000 yuan)

部门	Department	2004	2005	2005比2004年增长% Increase Rate in 2005 over 2004
总计	**Total**	**3 326 252**	**4 208 066**	**26.5**
交通运输、仓储和邮政业	Transport,Storage,Post Services	893 541	1 678 371	87.8
电信和其他信息传输服务业	Telecommunication and Other Information Transmitting Services	282 225	263 845	-6.5
电力、热力的生产和供应业	Production and Supply of Electric Power and Heating Energy	348 477	412 464	18.4
燃气生产和供应业	Production and Supply of Gas	33 369	62 058	86
水的生产和供应业	Production and Supply of Water	101 836	102 969	1.1
公共设施管理	Management for Public Facilities	1 666 804	1 688 359	1.3
城市基础设施占全市固定资产投资比重(%)	**As Percentage of Total Investment in Fixed Assets(%)**	**29.4**	**30.4**	

3-17 地方固定资产投资额
LOCAL INVESTMENT IN FIXED ASSETS

单位:万元 (10 000 yuan)

项 目	Item	2004	2005	2005比2004年增长% Increase Rate in 2005 over 2004
总 计	**Total**	**9 412 579**	**11 575 754**	**23.0**
按构成分	**Grouped by Use of Funds**			
建筑工程	Construction	4 919 954	6 393 726	30.0
安装工程	Installation	404 742	531 180	31.2
设备工器具	Equipment and Instruments	2 025 038	2 336 711	15.4
其他费用	Others	2 062 845	2 314 137	12.2
按建设性质分	**Grouped by Type of Construction**			
新 建	New Construction	4 145 635	5 122 917	23.6
扩 建	Expansion	1 177 134	1 398 027	18.8
改 建	Reconstruction	660 371	981 039	48.6
其 他	Others	834 253	798 368	-4.3
按行业分	**Grouped by Sector**			
农、林、牧、渔业	Farming, Forestry, Animal Husbandry & Fishery	30 948	50 472	63.1
采矿业	Minerals Mining	13 182	8 943	-32.2
制造业	Manufacturing	2 425 085	3 391 942	39.9
电力、煤气及水的生产和供应业	Production & Supply of Power, Gas and Water	320 609	368 289	14.9
建筑业	Construction	125 866	102 040	-18.9
交通运输、仓储和邮政业	Transport, Storage, Post Services	873 869	1 309 803	49.9
信息传输、计算机服务和软件业	Information Transmitting, Computer Services and Software	196	10 387	5 199.5
批发和零售业	Wholesale and Retail Trade	185 395	217 709	17.4
住宿和餐饮业	Accommodation and Catering Services	91 214	48 426	-46.9
金融业	Finance Intermediation	2 465		
房地产业	Real Estate	2 710 393	3 394 727	25.2
租赁和商务服务业	Leasing and Business Services	31 566	48 753	54.4
科学研究、技术服务和地质勘查业	Scientific Research, Technical Services and Geological Prospecting	15 938	41 023	157.4
水利、环境和公共设施管理业	Management for Water Conservancy, Environment and Public Facilities	1 840 734	1 786 917	-2.9
居民服务和其他服务业	Resident Services and Other Social Services	9 975	18 385	84.3
教 育	Education	293 488	326 756	11.3
卫生、社会保障和社会福利业	Health Care, Social Security and Social Welfare	103 507	92 424	-10.7
文化、体育和娱乐业	Culture, Sports and Recreational Services	184 222	141 542	-23.2
公共管理和社会组织	Public Management and Social Organizations	153 927	217 216	41.1

注:表中按建设性质分组数据不包括房地产开发投资。
Note: Investment grouped by type of construction excludes real estate development.

3-18 全市房地产开发投资、建设情况(1990-2005年)

CONSTRUCTION OF REAL ESTATE DEVELOPMENT,1990-2005

单位:万元 (10 000 yuan)

年份 Year	本年完成投资额 Investment Completed in This Year	住宅 Residential Buildings	办公楼 Office Buildings	商业营业用 Commerce Buildings	其他 Others
1990	24 934	19 589			
1991	32 403	27 237			
1992	45 842	33 994			
1993	180 957	136 882			
1994	256 571	136 627			
1995	694 364	444 015	86 703	78 455	85 191
1996	715 103	428 672	66 798	124 930	94 703
1997	808 041	396 370	86 881	140 582	184 208
1998	1 067 035	630 053	65 161	111 459	260 362
1999	1 169 569	868 972	36 045	46 569	217 983
2000	1 339 294	900 198	31 251	71 834	336 011
2001	1 612 662	963 985	45 157	156 497	447 023
2002	1 758 446	1 031 788	75 122	147 244	504 292
2003	2 113 876	1 509 252	77 808	242 564	284 252
2004	2 639 165	1 752 377	157 504	282 388	446 896
2005	3 275 403	2 349 240	119 477	417 449	389 237

单位:万平方米 (10 000 sq. m)

年份 Year	施工面积 Floor Space of Building under Construction	#住宅 Residential Buildings	竣工面积 Floor Space of Building Completed	#住宅 Residential Buildings
1990	129.71	117.30	60.79	53.03
1991	117.70	104.50	50.90	46.37
1992	185.29	157.66	64.81	55.71
1993	377.66	296.42	89.03	80.13
1994	418.46	313.11	128.08	111.43
1995	1 016.95	788.22	394.75	344.58
1996	988.66	712.76	366.51	318.50
1997	1 116.23	773.92	299.63	254.39
1998	1 379.77	1 093.69	428.74	357.17
1999	1 596.67	1 274.32	454.81	431.12
2000	1 783.00	1 582.15	583.51	532.63
2001	1 863.48	1 590.62	690.48	626.63
2002	2 135.56	1 746.13	746.44	673.00
2003	2 314.43	1 953.50	911.27	750.67
2004	2 865.55	2 352.98	1 108.13	1 014.46
2005	3 470.57	2 827.87	1 479.22	1 270.96

3－19　全市房地产开发投资情况
INVESTMENT ON REAL ESTATE DEVELOPMENT

单位:万元　　(10 000 uan)

项　目	Item	2004	2005	2005 比 2004 年增长% Increase Rate in 2005 over 2004
本年完成投资额	**Investment Completed in This Year**	**2 639 165**	**3 275 403**	**24.1**
按隶属关系分	**Grouped by Administrative Relationship**			
中　央	Central Government	43 979		
地　方	Local Government	2 595 186	3 275 403	26.2
按登记注册类型分	**Grouped by Registered Categories**			
1.内资企业	Domestic－funded Enterprises	2 355 030	3 031 982	28.7
国有企业	State－owned Enterprises	537 313	527 458	－1.8
集体企业	Collective－owned Enterprises	54 608	54 111	－0.9
股份合作企业	Cooperative Enterprises	7 980	24 911	212.2
私　营	Private Enterprises	600 638	1 027 038	71
股份有限公司	Share Holding Corporations Ltd.	158 540	239 426	51
有限责任公司	Limited Liability Corporations	899 280	1 091 243	21.3
#国有独资	Sole State－funded Corporations	38 278	111 421	191.1
联营企业	Joint Ownership Enterprises	10 548	30 590	190
#国有联营	State Joint Ownership Enterprises	8 335	28 877	246.5
集体联营	Collective Joint Ownership Enterprises	713	713	
其他内资企业	Other Domestic－funded Enterprises	86 123	37 205	－56.8
2.港澳台商投资企业	Enterprises with Investment from Hongkong,Macao and Taiwan	150 293	124 790	－17
3.外商投资企业	Foreign Funded Enterprises	133 842	118 631	－11.4
按构成分	**Grouped by Use of Funds**			
建筑工程	Construction	1 511 837	1 773 711	17.3
安装工程	Installation	96 744	203 581	110.4
设备工器具	Equipment and Instruments	50 340	51 975	3.2
其他费用	Others	980 244	1 246 136	27.1
按工程用途分	**Grouped by Use of Projects**			
住　宅	Residential Buildings	1 752 377	2 349 240	34.1
#别墅、高档公寓	Top Grade Apartment	240 878	311 449	29.3
办公楼	Office Buildings	157 504	119 477	－24.1
商业营业用房	Commerce Buildings	282 388	417 449	47.8
其　他	Others	446 896	389 237	－12.9
本年新增固定资产	**Newly Increased Fixed Assets in This Year**	**947 872**	**2 659 678**	**180.6**

3-20 全市房地产开发建设情况

CONSTRUCTION OF REAL ESTATE DEVELOPMENT

项　目	Item	2004	2005	2005 比 2004 年增长% Increase Rate in 2005 over 2004
施工房屋面积(万平方米)	**Floor Space of Buildings Under Construction(10^4 sq.m)**	**2 865.55**	**3 470.57**	**21.1**
住　宅	Residential Buildings	2 352.98	2 827.87	20.2
办公楼	Office Buildings	134.19	159.19	18.6
商业营业用房	Houses for Business Use	302.65	368.41	21.7
其　他	Others	75.73	115.10	52
竣工房屋面积(万平方米)	**Floor Space of Buildings Completed(10^4 sq.m)**	**1 108.13**	**1 479.22**	**33.5**
住　宅	Residential Buildings	1 014.46	1 270.96	25.3
办公楼	Office Buildings	32.40	39.30	21.3
商业营业用房	Houses for Business Use	43.24	121.07	180
其　他	Others	18.03	47.89	165.6
竣工房屋价值(万元)	**Value of Buildings Completed(10^4 yuan)**	**2 492 781**	**2 787 124**	**11.8**
住　宅	Residential Buildings	2 191 809	2 174 910	-0.8
办公楼	Office Buildings	116 690	137 296	17.7
商业营业用房	Houses for Business Use	127 392	340 606	167.4
其　他	Others	56 890	134 312	136.1
资金来源合计(万元)	**Total Funds(10^4 yuan)**	**4 733 583**	**7 277 942**	**53.8**
上年末结余资金	Balance of Funds Brought Forward from The Previous Year	660 593	1 001 288	51.6
本年资金来源合计	Subtotal of The Sources of Funds in This Year	4 072 990	6 216 654	52.6
国家预算内资金	State Budgetary Appropriation			
国内贷款	Domestic Loans	835 002	1 383 517	65.7
债　券	Bonds			
利用外资	Foreign Investment	56 508	34 895	-38.2
#外商直接投资	Foreign Direct Investment	38 314	27 229	-28.9
自筹资金	Fundraising	1 246 887	2 017 535	61.8
#企、事业单位自有资金	Fundraising of Enterprises and Institutions	671 868	1 202 589	79
其他资金来源	Others	1 934 593	2 780 707	43.7

3－21 农村集体固定资产投资完成情况

INVESTMENT IN FIXED ASSETS OF RURAL COLLECTIVE UNITS

项 目	Item	2003	2004	2005
固定资产投资合计(万元)	**Total Investment in Fixed Asstes(10 000 yuan)**	**897 262**	**990 627**	**1 018 499**
#农、林、牧、渔业	Farming,Forestry,Animal Husbanday,Fishery	33 101	43 450	38 528
工 业	Industry	496 264	554 484	663 884
交通运输业	Transportation	12 643	6 590	6 006
建筑业	Construction	77 919	88 163	16 031
文教卫生社会福利业	Culture,Health Care,Social Welfare	3 149	3 901	4 071
新增固定资产(万元)	**Newly Increased Fixed Assets(10 000 yuan)**	**870 309**	**926 360**	**959 718**
房屋面积(万平方米)	**Floor Space of Buildings(10 000 sq.m)**			
施工面积	Under Construction	734.24	768.05	766.89
竣工面积	Completed	599.84	605.32	610.29

3－22 城镇和农村个人建房情况

BUILDING CONSTRUCTION BY INDIVIDUAL IN URBAN AND RURAL AREAS

项 目 Item	单 位 Unit	2003	2004	2005
城镇建房				
Building Construction in Urban				
户 数	户			
Number of Households	household	246	429	57
竣工房屋面积	平方米			
Floor Space of Buildings Completed	sq.m	33 789	63 119	2 259
#住 宅				
Residential Buildings		23 900	55 923	1 605
竣工房屋价值	万元			
Value of Buildings Completed	10 000 yuan	2 452	3 876	1 363
#住 宅				
Residential Buildings		1 722	3 364	593
农村建房				
Building Construction in Rural				
投资总额	万元			
Total Investment	10 000 yuan	228 571	272 013	292 900
竣工房屋面积	万平方米			
Floor Space of Buildings Completed	10 000 sq.m	214.11	224.16	229.75
#住 宅				
Residential Buildings		175.16	192.24	196.17
竣工住宅价值	万元			
Value of Residential Buildings Completed	10 000 yuan	114 950	130 186	142 302
竣工住宅造价	元/平方米			
Cost of Residential Buildings Completed	yuan/sq.m	656	677	725

3-23 重点建设项目一览表(2005 年)

BASIC STATISTICS ON KEY PROJECTS,2005

项 目 名 称 Name of project	开工时间 Starting Time	计划总投资 (万元) Total Planned Investment (10 000 yuan)	累计完成投资 (万元) Investment Accumulated (10 000 yuan)	本年完成投资 (万元) Investment in 2005 (10000 yuan)
总 计(58 项)		**18 341 679**	**7 130 856**	**3 870 236**
一、工业项目合计(10 项)		**5 193 159**	**1 394 891**	**733 403**
1.100 万吨/年乙烯及配套项目		2 008 700	19 500	19 500
2.蓝星集团化工新材料基地一期工程		492 132	2 000	2 000
3.LG 渤化 35 万吨/年氯乙烯项目	2 005.05	244 497	50 720	50 720
4.渤化集团 2.8 万吨环氧丙烷项目		45 510		
5.天津钢铁有限公司填平补齐项目	2 001.10	550 000	969 237	398 000
6.天津钢管有限公司冷轧不锈钢薄板项目	2 004.09	156 867	15 477	15 477
7.天铁集团板材基地	2 005.05	864 453	28 029	12 959
8.高新纺织工业基地	2 003.09	503 000	195 176	131 995
9.鼎盛公司工程机械(科技)产业基地项目	2 004.04	28 000	20 000	8 000
10.天津一汽丰田汽车有限公司新花冠项目	2 005.06	300 000	94 752	94 752
二、高科技项目(10 项)		**1 161 887**	**451 698**	**201 198**
11.中芯国际芯片扩能		672 300	330 336	103 626
12.中环半导体工业园	2 004.10	28 913	25 428	21 029
13.天津普林电器公司新工厂建设项目		32 000	5 000	5 000
14.摩托罗拉集成电子方案部(IESS)天津生产基地		49 800	22 819	22 819
15.泰达新水源公司万吨级海水淡化				
高技术产业化示范工程	2 004.01	16 000	11 632	4 201
16.金耀生物工程产业化基地项目	2 005.06	210 000	11 577	11 577
17.天士力集团公司中药产业园二期工程	2 005.05	105 000	16 032	7 128
18.中维药业公司 VBI 合成高校分子新工艺				
高技术产业化示范工程	2 004.07	18 000	16 391	13 335
19.君安生物制药公司新型抗肿瘤骨转移药物产业化		11 846	12 483	12 483
20.医药集团发酵类产品 VB2 新技术产业化建设项目		18 028		
三、能源及交通项目合计(13 项)		**5 470 019**	**1 840 895**	**1 283 714**
21.陈热二期扩建及配套工程	2 004.03	119 823	52 751	26 600
22.杨电扩建工程	1 997.04	291 970	57 464	39 423
23.盘山电厂配套等电网工程建设	2 003.01	119 730	88 403	55 721
24.京津高速公路复线	2 004.01	1 000 000	94 129	72 121
25.京沪高速公路天津段	2 003.12	820 000	318 291	189 207
26.威乌高速公路西段(津晋高速天津段)	2 001.03	145 600	252 826	54 248
27.津蓟高速二期(延长线)		130 000	1 000	1 000
28.津汕高速公路		400 000		

3-23 续表 Continued

项 目 名 称 Name of project	开工时间 Starting Time	计划总投资 (万元) Total Planned Investment (10 000 yuan)	累计完成投资 (万元) Investment Accumulated (10 000 yuan)	本年完成投资 (万元) Investment in 2005 (10 000 yuan)
29.京津公路拓宽改造工程	2 005.02	50 000	47 892	47 892
30.黄骅南至万家码头铁路工程	2 004.11	139 900	93 768	86 174
31.京津城际铁路客运专线项目	2 005.07	1 234 000	156 625	153 737
32.天津机场改扩建工程	2 005.08	186 000	62 550	62 550
33.天津港扩建	2 001.01	832 996	615 196	495 041
四、基础设施和环保项目(15 项)		**4 458 874**	**3 013 224**	**1 275 671**
34.海河开发基础设施	2 003.02	280 695	530 720	213 820
35.地铁一号线	2 000.10	786 800	725 627	256 797
36.城市快速路工程	2 003.07	1 428 733	1 174 042	436 449
37.市区道路改造	2 004.01	681 750	117 676	117 628
38.城市供水改造	2 001.05	230 472	54 588	21 938
39.污水处理项目	2 003.09	108 933	31 206	14 685
40.城市垃圾处理项目	2 004.03	58 000	6 941	3 641
41.河道治理工程	2 004.04	20 000	94 838	46 226
42.停车场(楼)工程	2 004.01	143 357	26 010	5 510
43.公交枢纽站工程	2 005.09	68 948	3 685	3 685
44.城市绿化工程		388 535	45 267	45 267
45.铁路沿线治理二期工程	2 004.03	7 268	87 398	46 198
46.临港工业区造陆工程	2 003.03	84 543	104 174	52 775
47.空港物流加工区基础设施		52 000	2 052	2 052
48.滨海新区交通环境治理项目		118 840	9 000	9 000
五、农林水利项目(1 项)		**239 940**	**22 000**	**22 000**
49.天津市引滦入津水源保护工程		239 940	22 000	22 000
六、社会事业项目(5 项)		**947 800**	**318 173**	**264 275**
50.高等教育布局调整项目		628 546	184 355	184 355
51.示范校建设	2 003.01	85 598	24 286	24 286
52.天津市兴华剧院	2 005.06	10 000	8 909	5 851
53.公共卫生结构调整及公共卫生体系项目	2 002.12	81 736	33 091	33 091
54.天津奥林匹克中心体育场	2 003.08	141 920	67 532	16 692
七、商贸旅游项目(4 项)		**870 000**	**89 975**	**89 975**
55.天津国际游乐港		600 000		
56.凤凰商贸广场		60 000	20 518	20 518
57.现代城大型商业设施	2 005.05	100 000	30 957	30 957
58.国际轻工商贸城		110 000	38 500	38 500

3-24 建设项目主要新增生产能力(2005年)

MAIN NEWLY INCREASED PRODUCTION CAPACITY OF CONSTRUCTION PROJECTS,2005

生产能力名称	Item	建设规模 Construction Size	累计新增生产能力 Accumulated Newly Increased
天然原油(万吨/年)	Natural Petroleum(10 000 tons/year)	271.83	261.83
生　铁(万吨/年)	Pig Iron(10 000 tons/year)	525	499
炼　钢(万吨/年)	Steel - making(10 000 tons/year)	720	50
钢　材(万吨/年)	Steel Products(10 000 tons/year)	1 108	85
热轧钢材(万吨/年)	Steel - Rolling(10 000 tons/year)	1 027	98
输电线路长度(公里)	Lenght of Transmit Electricity Line(km)	170	
变电设备能力(万千伏安)	Capacity of Transformer Equipments(10 000 kVA)	198.6	
乙　烯(吨/年)	Ethene(ton/year)	118	
轿车制造(辆/年)	Car(unit/year)	302 000	102 000
塑料树脂及其聚合物(吨/年)	Plastic Resin and Plastic Resin Polymer(ton/year)	550 000	
烧　碱(吨/年)	Caustic Soda(tòn/year)	30 000	
程控交换机(万线/年)	Telephone Exchanges(10 000 lines/year)	19.52	2.11
新建公路(公里)	Length of New Highways(km)	329.94	114.18
改建公路(公里)	Length of Reconstructed Highways(km)	152.62	152.62
高等院校:学生席位(个)	Universities and Colleges:Students Capacity(unit)	13 177	8 737
建筑面积(平方米)	Floor Space of Construction(sq.m)	201 054	126 047
中等学校:学生席位(个)	Secondary Schools:Students Capacity(unit)	8 085	8 085
建筑面积(平方米)	Floor Space of Construction(sq.m)	96 692	96 492
小学校:学生席位(个)	Primary School:Students Capacity(unit)	15 085	9 905
建筑面积(平方米)	Floor Space of Construction(sq.m)	98 893	63 177
医院病床(张)	Number of Hospital Beds(bed)	3 880	1 670
城市道路扩建长度(公里)	Length of Urban Roads Expanded(km)	240.70	
城市道路扩建面积(万平方米)	Areas of Urban Roads Expanded(10 000 sq.m)	250.46	28.41
城市排水管道铺设长度(公里)	Length of Urban Drain Pipes Paved(km)	133.82	32.74
城市永久性桥梁(座)	Urban Permanent Bridges(unit)	18	1
新(扩)建港口码头(年吞吐量)	Newly Built Ports(annual handling capacity,10 000 tons/year)	6 490	150
新(扩)建港口码头(泊位:个)	Newly Built Ports(number of berths:unit)	11	2

3－25 房地产开发企业投资额、销售额五十强(2005年)

TOP 50 REAL ESTATE ENTERPRISES ORDERED BY INVESTMENT AND SALES, 2005

投资额名次 Position of Investment	企业名称 Name of Enterprises	销售额名次 Position of Sales	企业名称 Name of Enterprises
1	天津市房地产发展(集团)股份有限公司	1	天津优联投资发展集团有限公司
2	天津市远驰房地产开发有限公司	2	天津万兆投资发展集团有限公司
3	天津融创置地有限公司	3	天津市融创奥城投资有限公司
4	天津市融创奥城投资有限公司	4	天津乐康置业有限公司
5	天津泰达建设集团有限公司	5	天津阳光壹佰房地产开发有限公司
6	天津优联投资发展集团有限公司	6	天津市津南区建设开发公司
7	天津海景实业有限公司	7	天津浩天房地产开发有限公司
8	天津万科房地产有限公司	8	天津市凯立房地产开发有限公司
9	天津富力城房地产开发有限公司	9	天津市津东房地产开发集团有限公司
10	天津市金厦中天房地产开发有限公司	10	天津市红勘房地产开发有限公司
11	天津阳光鑫地投资有限公司	11	天津市房地产发展(集团)股份有限公司
12	天津梅江建设发展有限公司	12	天津兴海房地产开发有限公司
13	天津市美震房地产开发有限公司	13	天津顺驰发展有限公司
14	天津塘沽贻成实业有限公司	14	天津开发区亚资置业有限公司
15	天津大天房地产发展有限公司	15	天津顺驰地产有限公司
16	天津市天创置业有限公司	16	天津开发区建隆置业有限公司
17	天津乐康置业有限公司	17	天津合生珠江房地产开发有限公司
18	天津市宁发发展有限公司	18	天津阳光鑫地投资有限公司
19	天津阳光壹佰房地产开发有限公司	19	天津市康因实业有限公司
20	天津津滨创辉发展有限公司	20	天津顺驰融业置地有限公司
21	天津万兆投资发展集团有限公司	21	天津市大通建设发展集团有限公司
22	天津经济技术开发区房地产开发公司	22	天津燕宇置业有限公司
23	天津市古文化街海河楼开发经营有限公司	23	天津市福通房地产开发有限公司
24	天津开发区永泰房地产开发有限公司	24	天津兴利房地产开发公司
25	天津浩天房地产开发有限公司	25	天津万邦房地产开发有限公司
26	天津合生珠江房地产开发有限公司	26	天津市美震房地产开发有限公司
27	天津市塞斯置业发展有限公司	27	天津龙都置业投资集团有限公司
28	天津广顺房地产开发有限责任公司	28	天津飞林房地产开发有限公司
29	天津中信置业有限公司	29	天津市祥建房地产开发有限公司
30	天津万通时尚置业有限责任公司	30	天津泰达建设集团有限公司
31	天津市安居建设发展总公司	31	天津市塘沽海洋高新技术开发总公司
32	天津都市阳光房地产开发有限公司	32	天津市东丽区房地产开发总公司
33	天津市顺潮房地产开发有限公司	33	天津塘沽贻成实业有限公司
34	天津市塘沽经济开发区鸿发房地产有限公司	34	天津广达房地产开发有限公司
35	天津海泰科技发展股份有限公司	35	天津世纪房地产开发有限公司
36	天津市津南区建设开发公司	36	天津万科房地产有限公司
37	天津宝利集团有限公司	37	天津市开发区正信房地产开发有限公司
38	天津隆侨房地产开发有限公司	38	天津市港容城市环境开发有限公司
39	天津市万豪大厦有限公司	39	天津开发区立泰置业有限公司
40	天津顺驰融信置地有限公司	40	天津海泰科技发展股份有限公司
41	天津市红碟房地产开发有限公司	41	天津市双盈房地产开发有限公司
42	天津市万顺置业有限公司	42	天津市佳特置业有限公司
43	天津天保控股有限公司	43	天津市万顺置地有限公司
44	天津麦迪逊投资发展有限公司	44	天津市君利房地产开发有限公司
45	金地(集团)天津房地产开发有限公司	45	天津天保控股有限公司
46	天津市河西区建设开发总公司	46	天津市耀居置业有限公司
47	天津顺驰发展有限公司	47	天津锦嵘置业有限公司
48	天津市现代投资有限公司	48	天津市利泰房地产开发经营公司
49	天津市海达房地产开发实业总公司	49	天津顺弛建设有限公司
50	天津亿城地产有限公司	50	天津龙都房地产开发有限公司

主要统计指标解释

固定资产投资额 是以货币表现的在一定时期内建造和购置固定资产的工作量以及与此有关的费用的总称。全社会固定资产投资的统计范围包括城镇固定资产投资、农村固定资产投资和城乡个人投资。全市固定资产投资的统计范围是全社会固定资产投资中扣除农村固定资产投资和城乡个人投资。

房地产开发投资 指房地产开发公司、商品房建设公司及其他房地产开发单位进行土地开发工程、商品房屋建设工程所完成的投资额。是以货币表现的房地产开发工作量。

固定资产投资按构成分组：

建筑工程 指各种房屋建筑物的建造工程，又称建筑工程量。这部分投资额必须兴工动料，通过施工才能实现。建筑工程包括各种房屋的建造，设备基础及各种窑炉的砌筑和金属结构工程，为施工而进行的建筑场地布置、地质勘探、平整场地、施工用水、电、气、路和清理绿化等。矿井的开凿、铁路、公路、桥梁、水利及防空、地下建筑等特殊工程。

安装工程 指各种设备、装置的安装工程，又称安装工作量。在安装工程投资额中，不包括被安装设备本身的价值。安装工程包括生产、动力、起重、运输、传动和医疗试验等各种需安装设备的装配与设备相连的工作台、梯子栏杆以及管线敷设、保温、油漆、防腐和单机试运系统联动无负簧试运(不包括投料试运)。

设备、工具、器具购置 指购置和自制达到固定资产标准的设备、工具、器具的价值。但新建单位、扩建单位的新建车间，按照设计和计划要求购置或自制的全部设备、工具、器具，不论是否达到固定资产标准均计入"设备、工具、器具购置"中。

其他费用 指除建筑安装、设备工具器具购置和商品房屋购置以外的构成固定资产投资完成额的各种费用。主要包括牲畜购置费、林木营建费、办公和生活家具、器具购置费、土地青苗补偿费和安置补助费、建设单位管理费、研究试验费、勘查设计费、联合试运转费、引进技术和进口设备项目的其他费用、生产职工培训费、施工机构迁移费、报废工程损失费和供电站费、矿山巷道维修费等。

固定资产投资按建设性质分组： 是反映固定资产投资使用方向，研究各类性质的比重和对比分析投资效果。具体包括：

新建 一般指从无到有"平地起家"新开始建设的企事业和行政单位及新建输电线路、输油管道、铁路、公路等独立工程。有的项目原有基础很小，经扩大建设后，其新增加的固定资产价值(原值)超过原有固定资产价值三倍以上的也应算为新建。

扩建 指为扩大原有产品生产能力或新的产品能力，在厂内或其他地点增建主要生产车间(或主要工程)，独立的生产线等。事业单位和行政单位在原单位增建业务用房，也作为扩建。

改建或更新改造 现有企事业单位为了技术进步对现有设施、工艺条件进行技术改造或更新(包括相应配套的辅助性生产、生活设施建设)。有的还充分发挥现有的生产能力，进行填平补齐而增建不直接增加本单位主要产品生产能力的车间等，也属于改建。

新增固定资产 指报告期内交付使用的固定资产价值，包括建成投入生产或交付使用的工程投资和达到固定资产标准的设备、工具器具的投资以及有关的摊入费用和属于增加固定资产价值的其他建设费用。

固定资产交付使用率 指报告期内新增固定资产与同期完成投资额的比率。它反映各个时期固定资产动用速度，衡量建设过程中投资效果的一个综合性指标。

施工房屋建筑面积 指报告期内施工的全部房屋建筑面积。包括本期新开工的面积和上期开工跨入本期继续施工的房屋面积，以及上期已停建在本期复工的房屋面积。

竣工房屋建筑面积 指在报告期内房屋建筑按设计要求已全部完工，达到住人和使用条件，经验收鉴定合格(或达到竣工验收标准)，可正式移交使用的各栋房屋建筑面积的总和。

Explanatory Notes on Main Statistical Indicators

Total Investment in Fixed Assets refers to the volume of activities in construction and purchases of fixed assets and related fees, expressed in monetary terms. Total investment in fixed assets in the whole country includes urban investment, rural investment and individual investment. Investment in fixed assets in Tianjin refers to total investment in fixed assets in the whole country deducting rural investment and individual investment.

Investment in Real Estate Development refers to the investment by the real estate development companies, commercial buildings construction companies and other real estate development units of various types of ownership in the construction of house buildings. It is finished work in monetary terms.

Commercial Houses refer to residential buildings and other commercial houses of commercial houses development companies that are qualified for sale, excluding non-commercial houses. (1) Investment commercial houses include: (a) making a requisition of land and pull down a houses in development area, (b) funds of residential buildings construction and installation, (c) municipal administration engineering system in red line of development area, (d) residential building complementary service facilities in development area. (2) Investment in construction of other commercial houses include funds of factory buildings, warehouses and other commercial houses.

Investment in Fixed Assets by Structure :

Construction Project refers to the construction of various houses and buildings, it also is called the work volume of construction, including construction of various houses, equipment foundations and industrial kilns and stoves, preparation works for project construction, and clearing up works post project construction, geological examination, land-leveling, water, electricity, gas road-cleaning, planting trees, drilling of mines, pavement of railways and roads, highway, bridge, construction of projects of water conservancy, construction of underground air-raid shelters and construction of other special projects.

Installation Project refers to the installation of various kinds of equipment and instruments (work volume of installation) . The value of equipment installed is excluded in the value of installation projects. Including various kinds of equipment, i. e. production, power-driven, lifting, transport, transmission, medical experiment etc. and working table, stepladder railing, putting up of pipes, keep warm, paint, rot-proofing, try operation (excluding put in material try operation).

Purchase of Equipment and Instruments refers to the total value of equipment, tools, and vessels purchased or self-produced which come up to standards for fixed assets. Equipment, tools and vessels purchased or self- produced for new workshops by newly established or expanded units are categorized as "purchase of equipment and instruments" no matter whether they come up to the standards for fixed assets or not.

Other Expenses refers to investment excluded in above items, which consist of construction and installation, purchase of equipment and instruments, purchase of commercial buildings, including purchase of animals by agricultural and forestry units, planting and operating of various economic forest, purchase of office and home furniture, purchase of instruments and vessels, compensation for the loss of land and young crops, subsidies for moving, administration expenses of construction units, and expenses on research and testing, geological prospecting and designing, joint trial running, and the other purchase introduction of technology and imports of equipment, expenses on training of staff and workers, transportation of construction machines, loss of discarded projects, powers upply station, mine harbor maintenance.

Investment in Fixed Assets by Type of Construction refers to reflect use direction of investment in fixed assets, researching various proportions and analyzing result of investment. It includes :

New Construction refers to newly constructed units. In the case, in which the value of the original fixed assets is quite small, and the value of newly added fixed assets exceeds the original ones by three times, the expansion construction is considered as new construction.

Expansion Construction refers to construction of new major production workshop or independent production line within a factory or in other locations, or construction of a branch factory so as to increase the production capacity of the original products. Newly constructed business houses in institutions and administrative organizations are also classified as expansion.

Reconstruction refers to technical innovation and transformation of the existing equipment and technical conditions undertaken by enterprises and institutions for the purposes of technological advancement, (including accessory facilities for production or for living and welfare purposes). The construction of new workshops for improving existing production capacity rather than increasing production capacity is also considered as reconstruction.

Newly Increased Fixed Assets refers to the newly increased value of fixed assets through investment, including the value of projects completed and put into production, the value of equipment, tools, and vessels considered as fixed assets, as well as the relevant expenses as investment in fixed assets and other construction expansion of increased the volume in fixed assets.

Rate of Projects of Fixed Assets Completed and Put into Operation refers to the ratio of the newly increased fixed assets to the total investment made in the same period. This is a comprehensive indicator, reflecting the speed of the employment of fixed assets and the investment efficiency.

Floor Space of Buildings under Construction refers to total floor space of all buildings under construction during the reference period, including floor space of newly started buildings during the reference period, floor space of construction extended from the previous year to the current period, and floor space of construction suspended during the previous period and resumed in the current period.

Floor Space of Buildings Completed refer to the floor space of all buildings completed in the reference period, which have been appraised and accepted(or come up to the designed standards) and have been transferred to the owners for use.

第4篇
CHAPTER 4

能源生产和消费
Energy Production and Consumption

4-1 能源生产总量及构成(1990-2005年)

TOTAL PRODUCTION OF ENERGY AND ITS COMPOSITION,1990-2005

年份 Year	能源生产总量 (万吨标准煤) Total Energy Production (10 000 tons of SCE)	占能源生产总量的比重% As Percentage of Total Energy Production	
		原油 Crude Oil	天然气 Natrual Gas
1990	719.41	93.23	6.77
1991	726.45	93.39	6.61
1992	757.45	92.75	7.25
1993	790.99	93.38	6.62
1994	936.65	89.84	10.16
1995	978.82	90.61	9.39
1996	1 036.17	89.15	10.85
1997	1 014.77	90.93	9.07
1998	1 079.73	91.46	8.54
1999	1 084.63	90.45	9.55
2000	1 201.94	90.81	9.19
2001	1 494.84	92.73	7.27
2002	1 844.92	94.16	5.84
2003	1 983.56	94.80	5.20
2004	2 171.95	95.12	4.88
2005	2 663.93	95.61	4.39

4-2 能源终端消费量(1990-2005年)

FINAL CONSUMPTION OF ENERGY,1990-2005

单位:万吨标准煤 (10 000 tons of SCE)

年份 Year	能源终端消费量 Final Consumption of Energy	第一产业 Primary Industry	第二产业 Secondary Industry	第三产业 Tertiary Industry	生活消费 Living Consumption
1990	1 961.58	64.12	1 320.02	365.11	212.33
1991	1 920.61	56.99	1 260.45	381.56	221.61
1992	2 062.35	65.24	1 383.16	394.86	219.09
1993	2 233.06	65.80	1 540.61	412.10	214.55
1994	2 250.85	55.70	1 583.40	424.92	186.83
1995	2 539.46	69.30	1 773.03	478.40	218.73
1996	2 374.07	70.72	1 735.50	311.33	256.52
1997	2 312.79	44.76	1 605.60	420.96	241.47
1998	2 353.71	44.00	1 588.62	437.27	283.82
1999	2 352.21	53.61	1 435.11	535.14	328.35
2000	2 553.60	58.17	1 570.08	635.23	290.12
2001	2 724.32	68.83	1 694.78	608.05	352.66
2002	2 966.56	76.64	1 935.92	575.96	378.04
2003	3 084.49	58.86	1 975.56	650.27	399.80
2004	3 522.15	62.00	2 296.39	737.35	426.41
2005	3 901.28	73.28	2 562.80	791.21	473.99

4-3 综合能源平衡表(标准量)
OVERALL ENERGY BALANCE SHEET(STANDARD EQUIVALENT)

单位:万吔标准煤 (10 000 tons of SCE)

项 目	Item	2004	2005
可供本地区消费的能源量	**Volume of Energy Available for Consumption in This Area**	**3 725.50**	**4 115.52**
年初库存量	Stock in The Beginning of The Year	309.99	323.55
一次能源生产量	Primary Energy Output	2 171.94	2 663.93
回收能	Recovery of Energy		27.71
外省(区、市)调入量	Inflow from Other Provinces(Regions,Cities)	4 788.39	6 790.41
进口量	Import	500.26	632.50
我轮、机在外国加油量	Our Steamship and Plane Oiled Abroad	114.08	93.86
本市调出量(-)	Outflow to Other Provinces(Regions,Cities)(-)	-3 502.82	-5 681.20
出口量(-)	Export(-)	-264.42	-302.68
外轮、机在本市加油量(-)	Foreign Steamship and Plane Oiled in Tianjin(-)	-43.89	-53.54
年末库存量	Stock in Year-end	-348.03	-379.02
加工转换投入(-)产出(+)量	**Input(-) or Output(+) of Processing and Transformation**	**-79.02**	**-108.19**
火力发电	Fuel Power Generation		
供 热	Heating		
洗选煤	Clean Coal		
炼 焦	Coke Making	-65.74	-9.00
炼 油	Oil Refining	-88.03	-99.18
制 气	Gas Making	74.76	
#焦碳再投入量(-)	Input of Coke(-)		
煤制品加工	Processing of Coal Products		
损失量	**Loss Volume**	**95.51**	**105.72**
终端消费量	**End-user Consumption**	**3 522.15**	**3 901.28**
第一产业	Primary Industry	62.00	73.28
第二产业	Secondary Industry	2 296.39	2 562.80
工 业	Industry	2 259.61	2 512.38
建筑业	Construction	36.78	50.42
第三产业	Tertiary Industry	737.35	791.21
交通运输、仓储及邮政业	Transportation,Storage and Post Services	333.04	336.94
批发和零售业、住宿和餐饮业	Wholesale and Retail Trade,Accommodation and Catering Services	249.54	287.70
其 他	Others	154.77	166.57
生活消费	Living Consumption	426.41	473.99
平衡差额	**Balance**	**28.82**	**0.33**
消费量合计	**Total of Consumption**	**3 696.68**	**4 115.19**

4-4 能源消耗基本情况(1990-2005年)

BASIC INDICATORS OF ENERGY CONSUMPTION,1990-2005

年 份 Year	能源消耗(万吨标准煤) Energy Consumption (10 000 tons of SCE)	#工 业 Industry	电力消耗(亿千瓦小时) Electricity Power Consumption (100 million kwh)	#工 业 Industry
1990	2 037.93	1 355.97	124.15	97.78
1991	1 989.63	1 294.48	130.11	102.72
1992	2 140.73	1 433.05	134.29	103.08
1993	2 292.67	1 565.67	151.55	117.36
1994	2 345.10	1 653.91	167.42	128.55
1995	2 568.79	1 714.57	178.99	122.14
1996	2 500.22	1 816.55	187.51	111.35
1997	2 452.34	1 698.19	194.09	142.45
1998	2 502.24	1 698.82	200.38	147.43
1999	2 553.07	1 608.66	211.19	151.09
2000	2 793.71	1 776.94	236.55	171.83
2001	2 918.04	1 855.60	250.47	181.89
2002	3 022.15	1 969.20	281.00	205.33
2003	3 214.97	2 087.57	313.00	230.16
2004	3 696.68	2 434.14	350.97	259.61
2005	4 115.19	2 726.29	396.33	292.49

年 份 Year	生产总值能耗(吨标准煤/万元) Energy Consumption of GDP (tons of SCE/10 000 yuan)	生产总值电耗(千瓦小时/万元) Electricity Power Consumption of GDP (kwh/10 000 yuan)	工业增加值能耗(吨标准煤/万元) Energy Consumption of Value Added in Industry (tons of SCE/10 000 yuan)	工业增加值电耗(千瓦小时/万元) Electricity Power Consumption of Value Added in Industry (kwh/10 000 yuan)
1990	3.56	2 169.35	5.27	3 800.23
1991	3.28	2 145.44	4.76	3 774.25
1992	3.16	1 983.31	4.68	3 368.99
1993	3.02	1 997.23	4.50	3 376.83
1994	2.70	1 930.33	4.17	3 242.53
1995	2.58	1 796.02	3.78	2 691.53
1996	2.19	1 646.08	3.49	2 141.55
1997	1.92	1 520.31	2.92	2 450.07
1998	1.79	1 434.95	2.73	2 369.84
1999	1.66	1 374.94	2.30	2 156.90
2000	1.64	1 389.94	2.26	2 186.25
2001	1.53	1 313.51	2.09	2 053.52
2002	1.41	1 308.20	1.94	2 023.65
2003	1.30	1 268.95	1.74	1 912.95
2004	1.29	1 228.33	1.67	1 776.40
2005	1.11	1 040.80	1.45	1 551.64

注:1.能源消耗指标采用等价值计量。2.生产总值、工业增加值的能耗和电耗2005年为2005年可比价,2005年以前年份为2000年可比价。
Note:a) Indicators of energy consumption are converted into same value. b) In 2005, energy or electricity power consumption of GDP, energy or electricity power consumption of value added in industry are calculated at 2005 comparable prices; data before 2005, they are calculated at 2000 comparable prices.

4-5　电力平衡表(2000—2005年)
ELECTRICITY BALANCE SHEET,2000—2005

单位:亿千瓦小时　　(100 million kwh)

项　目 Item	2000	2001	2002	2003	2004	2005
可 供 量						
Total Energy Available for Consumption	**236.55**	**250.48**	**281.00**	**313.00**	**350.97**	**396.33**
生产量						
Output	219.13	224.53	276.10	325.60	343.22	376.36
火　电						
Thermal Power	219.13	224.53	276.10	325.60	343.22	376.36
外省(区、市)调入量						
Inflow from Other Provinces(Regions,Cities)	17.65	26.19	5.18	4.10	8.08	20.38
本市调出量						
Outflow to Other Provinces	0.23	0.24	0.28	16.70	0.33	0.41
消 费 量						
Total Energy Consumption	**236.55**	**250.47**	**281.00**	**313.00**	**350.97**	**396.33**
在消费量中:						
Consumption by Sector:						
农、林、牧、渔业						
Farming,Forestry,Animal Husbandry and Fishery	8.35	8.12	10.54	9.49	8.93	9.73
工　业						
Industry	171.83	181.89	205.33	230.16	259.61	292.49
建筑业						
Construction	1.47	1.48	1.53	1.74	1.99	3.77
交通运输、仓储和邮政业						
Transport, Storage and Post Services	4.26	4.55	4.88	5.68	6.72	6.52
批发和零售业、住宿和餐饮业						
Wholesale and Retail Trade, Accommodation and Catering Services	12.63	11.03	12.82	15.28	17.59	16.55
其　他						
Others	13.31	17.26	16.56	18.92	22.68	29.31
生活消费						
Living Consumption	24.70	26.14	29.34	31.73	33.45	37.96
在消费量中:						
Consumption by Usage:						
终端消费						
Final Consumption	220.98	236.55	265.39	293.85	329.38	373.37
#工　业						
Industry	156.26	167.97	189.72	211.01	238.02	269.53
输配电损失量						
Losses in Transmission	15.57	13.92	15.61	19.15	21.59	22.96
平衡差额						
Balance		**0.01**				

4－6 能源消费弹性系数(1991－2005年)

ELASTICITY OF ENERGY CONSUMPION,1991－2005

年 份 Year	能源消费比上年增长(%) Growth Rate of Energy Consumption over Preceding year(%)	电力消费比上年增长(%) Growth Rate of Electricity Power Consumption over Preceding year(%)	生产总值比上年增长(%) Growth Rate of GDP over Prec－eding year (%)	能源消费弹性系数 Elasticity Ratio of Energy Consumption	电力消费弹性系数 Elasticity Ratio of Electric Power Consumption
1991	－2.4	4.8	6.0		0.80
1992	7.6	3.2	11.7	0.65	0.28
1993	7.1	12.9	12.1	0.59	1.07
1994	2.3	10.5	14.3	0.16	0.73
1995	9.5	6.9	14.9	0.64	0.46
1996	－2.7	4.8	14.3		0.33
1997	－1.9	3.5	12.1		0.29
1998	2.0	3.2	9.3	0.22	0.34
1999	2.0	5.4	10.0	0.20	0.54
2000	9.4	12.0	10.8	0.87	1.11
2001	4.5	5.9	12.0	0.37	0.49
2002	3.6	12.2	12.7	0.28	0.96
2003	6.4	11.4	14.8	0.43	0.77
2004	15.0	12.1	15.8	0.95	0.77
2005	11.3	12.9	14.7	0.77	0.88

4－7 平均每天能源消费量(2000—2005年)

AVERAGE DAILY ENERGY CONSUMPTION BY VARIETY,2000—2005

能源品种 Item	单 位 Unit	2000	2001	2002	2003	2004	2005
合 计	**万吨标准煤**						
Total	**10 000 tons of SCE**	**7.65**	**7.99**	**8.28**	**8.81**	**10.13**	**11.27**
煤 炭	万 吨						
Coal	10 000 tons	6.77	7.22	8.02	8.78	9.61	10.41
焦 炭	万 吨						
Coke	10 000 tons	0.39	0.35	0.41	0.39	0.90	0.90
原 油	万 吨						
Crude Oil	10 000 tons	1.94	2.05	1.85	2.06	2.15	2.36
燃料油	万 吨						
Fuel Oil	10 000 tons	0.22	0.24	0.24	0.31	0.31	0.31
汽 油	万 吨						
Gasoline	10 000 tons	0.31	0.32	0.26	0.29	0.33	0.33
煤 油	万 吨						
Kerosene	10 000 tons	0.05	0.03	0.04	0.05	0.04	0.04
柴 油	万 吨						
Diesel Oil	10 000 tons	0.54	0.50	0.50	0.53	0.62	0.67
天然气	亿立方米						
Natural Gas	100 million cu.m	0.01	0.02	0.02	0.02	0.02	0.02
电 力	亿千瓦小时						
Electricity	100 million kwh	0.65	0.69	0.77	0.86	0.96	1.09

4－8 生活能源消费量(2000—2005年)

ENERGY CONSUMPTION FOR NON－PRODUCTION PURPOSE,2000—2005

能源品种 Item	单 位 Unit	2000	2001	2002	2003	2004	2005
合 计	**万吨标准煤**						
Total	**10 000 tons of SCE**	**290.12**	**352.66**	**378.04**	**399.80**	**426.41**	**473.99**
煤 炭	万 吨						
Coal	10 000 tons	99.65	88.20	79.87	91.44	84.27	88.98
液化石油气	万 吨						
LPG	10 000 tons	11.76	10.77	9.59	10.70	8.93	7.13
天然气和煤气	亿立方米						
Natural Gas and Coal Gas	100 million cu. m	4.28	3.94	3.83	3.01	2.88	3.85
热 力	万百万千焦						
Heat	10 billion kilo－joule	3 182.29	3 302.62	3 803.57	3 983.72	4 340.00	4 482.00
电 力	亿千瓦小时						
Electricity	100 million kwh	24.70	26.14	29.34	31.73	33.45	37.96

4－9 人均生活能源消费量(1990—2005年)

ANNUAL PER CAPITA ENERGY CONSUMPTION FOR NON－PRODUCTION PURPOSE,1990—2005

年 份 Year	平均每人生活消费能源(千克标准煤) Annual Per Capita Consumption for Non－production Purpose (Kg of SCE)	煤 炭 (千克) Coal (kg)	电 力 (千瓦小时) Electricity (kwh)	液化石油气 (千克) LGP (kg)	天然气和煤气 (立方米) Natural Gas and Coal Gas (cu. m)
1990	247.1	247.1	93.4	3.2	20.6
1991	254.9	254.2	102.0	2.8	26.5
1992	250.2	223.7	116.2	3.2	24.5
1993	243.1	211.6	126.6	3.0	23.8
1994	210.3	168.2	151.3	3.5	31.2
1995	245.0	165.2	160.9	4.5	31.3
1996	286.1	213.6	188.9	6.4	21.0
1997	268.6	187.8	211.2	5.4	22.4
1998	314.5	141.2	227.3	5.4	21.6
1999	361.8	130.7	264.8	18.6	22.0
2000	318.4	109.4	271.1	12.9	47.0
2001	386.3	96.6	286.3	11.8	43.1
2002	412.5	87.1	320.1	10.5	41.8
2003	433.4	99.1	343.9	11.6	32.6
2004	458.9	90.7	360.0	9.6	31.0
2005	458.7	86.1	367.4	6.9	37.3

4-10 工业行业主要能源终端消费量(2005 年)

THE FINAL CONSUMPTION OF MAIN ENERGY BY INDUSTRIAL SECTOR, 2005

行业	Sector	煤炭(万吨) Coal (10 000 tons)	焦炭(万吨) Coke (10 000 tons)	原油(万吨) Crude Oil (10 000 tons)	汽油(万吨) Gasoline (10 000 tons)
总计	**Total**	**841.23**	**329.06**	**23.48**	**9.39**
煤炭开采和洗选业	Coal Mining and Dressing				0.01
石油和天然气开采业	Petroleum and Natural Gas Extraction	17.91		23.18	1.15
有色金属矿采选业	Nonferrous Metals Mining and Dressing	1.52			
非金属矿采选业	Nonmetal Minerals Mining and Dressing	2.90			0.08
农副食品加工业	Agricultural Products and Byproducts Processing	9.42			0.23
食品制造业	Food Manufacturing	11.99			0.16
饮料制造业	Beverage Manufacturing	41.73			0.09
烟草制品业	Tobacco Products	2.77			
纺织业	Textile Industry	30.63			0.25
纺织服装鞋帽制造业	Textile Garments, Shoes, Caps Manufacturing	10.10			0.40
皮革毛皮羽毛(绒)及其制品业	Leather, Furs, Feather and Related Products	1.99			0.09
木材加工及木、竹、藤、棕、草制品业	Timber Processing, Bamboo, Cane, Palm Fiber and Straw Products	4.74			0.08
家具制造业	Furniture Manufacturing	3.65	0.02		0.15
造纸及纸制品业	Papermaking and Paper Products	23.23	0.40		0.29
印刷业和记录媒介的复制	Printing and Record Medium Reproduction	2.30			0.14
文教体育用品制造业	Cultural, Educational and Sports Goods	1.79	0.08	0.09	0.05
石油加工炼焦及核燃料加工业	Petroleum Processing, Coking and Nuclear Fuel Processing	5.45	0.01		0.04
化学原料及化学制品制造业	Raw Chemical Materials and Chemical Products	121.42	1.04	0.01	0.85
医药制造业	Medical and Pharmaceutical Products	18.22			0.13
化学纤维制造业	Chemical Fiber	3.77			0.02
橡胶制品业	Rubber Products	20.28	0.12	0.02	0.23
塑料制品业	Plastic Products	7.26			0.27
非金属矿物制品业	Nonmetal Mineral Products	106.23	0.26	0.13	0.37
黑色金属冶炼及压延加工业	Smelting and Pressing of Ferrous Metals	263.51	320.71		0.37
有色金属冶炼及压延加工业	Smelting and Pressing of Nonferrous Metals	5.19	0.14		0.07
金属制品业	Metal Products	22.91	1.35		0.72
通用设备制造业	General Purpose Equipment Manufacturing	15.03	4.35		0.61
专用设备制造业	Special Purpose Equipment Manufacturing	3.00	0.23		0.30
交通运输设备制造业	Transport Equipment Manufacturing	21.91	0.25	0.04	1.07
电气机械及器材制造业	Electric Equipment and Machinery	11.42	0.10	0.01	0.39
通信设备计算机及其他电子设备制造业	Telecommunications Equipment, Computer and Other Electronic Equipment Manufacturing	4.94			0.24
仪器仪表及文化办公用机械制造业	Instruments, Meters, Cultural and Office Machinery	1.18			0.10
工艺品及其他制造业	Craftwork and Other Manufacturing	7.75			0.09
废弃资源和废旧材料回收加工业	Waste Resources and Materials Recovering and Processing	0.05			0.01
电力热力的生产和供应业	Production and Supply of Electric & Heat Energy	31.99			0.27
燃气生产和供应业	Production and Supply of Gas	2.29			0.05
水的生产和供应业	Production and Supply of Water	0.76			0.02

4-10 续表 1　Continued

行　业　　Sector		柴　油（万吨）Diesel Oil (10 000 tons)	燃料油（万吨）Fuel Oil (10 000 tons)	天然气（亿立方米）Natural Gas (100 million cu. m)
总　计	**Total**	**24.11**	**53.86**	**3.99**
煤炭开采和洗选业	Coal Mining and Dressing			
石油和天然气开采业	Petroleum and Natural Gas Extraction	10.96		1.16
有色金属矿采选业	Nonferrous Metals Mining and Dressing	0.01		
非金属矿采选业	Nonmetal Minerals Mining and Dressing	0.27		
农副食品加工业	Agricultural Products and Byproducts Processing	0.49	0.06	
食品制造业	Food Manufacturing	0.61		0.05
饮料制造业	Beverage Manufacturing	0.39		
烟草制品业	Tobacco Products			
纺织业	Textile Industry	0.15		0.03
纺织服装鞋帽制造业	Textile Garments,Shoes,Caps Manufacturing	0.11		0.01
皮革毛皮羽毛(绒)及其制品业	Leather,Furs,Feather and Related Products	0.01		
木材加工及木、竹、藤、棕、草制品业	Timber Processing,Bamboo,Cane, Palm Fiber and Straw Products	0.06		0.04
家具制造业	Furniture Manufacturing	0.07		0.02
造纸及纸制品业	Papermaking and Paper Products	0.29	0.06	
印刷业和记录媒介的复制	Printing and Record Medium Reproduction	0.03		
文教体育用品制造业	Cultural, Educational and Sports Goods	0.07		
石油加工炼焦及核燃料加工业	Petroleum Processing,Coking and Nuclear Fuel Processing	0.35	15.64	
化学原料及化学制品制造业	Raw Chemical Materials and Chemical Products	1.35	20.19	0.21
医药制造业	Medical and Pharmaceutical Products	0.57		0.03
化学纤维制造业	Chemical Fiber	0.02		
橡胶制品业	Rubber Products	0.14	0.73	
塑料制品业	Plastic Products	0.24	0.02	0.04
非金属矿物制品业	Nonmetal Mineral Products	1.81	5.20	0.12
黑色金属冶炼及压延加工业	Smelting and Pressing of Ferrous Metals	1.54	8.49	1.62
有色金属冶炼及压延加工业	Smelting and Pressing of Nonferrous Metals	0.24	0.36	0.03
金属制品业	Metal Products	0.73	0.98	0.08
通用设备制造业	General Purpose Equipment Manufacturing	0.42	0.02	0.08
专用设备制造业	Special Purpose Equipment Manufacturing	0.33	0.03	0.01
交通运输设备制造业	Transport Equipment Manufacturing	0.91		0.08
电气机械及器材制造业	Electric Equipment and Machinery	0.44	0.01	0.04
通信设备计算机及其他电子设备制造业	Telecommunications Equipment,Computer and Other Electronic Equipment Manufacturing	0.56	2.01	0.27
仪器仪表及文化办公用机械制造业	Instruments,Meters,Cultural and Office Machinery	0.03		0.01
工艺品及其他制造业	Craftwork and Other Manufacturing	0.03	0.04	
废弃资源和废旧材料回收加工业	Waste Resources and Materials Recovering and Processing	0.02		
电力热力的生产和供应业	Production and Supply of Electric & Heat Energy	0.82	0.02	
燃气生产和供应业	Production and Supply of Gas	0.04		0.06
水的生产和供应业	Production and Supply of Water			

4-10 续表 2　Continued

行　　业	Sector	热　力（万百万千焦）Heat (10 000 million kilo-joule)	电　力（亿千瓦时）Electricity (100 million kwh)	其他石油制品（万吨）Other Petroleum Product (10 000 tons)
总　　计	**Total**	**5 325.54**	**269.53**	**122.50**
煤炭开采和洗选业	Coal Mining and Dressing			
石油和天然气开采业	Petroleum and Natural Gas Extraction	2.25	12.86	
有色金属矿采选业	Nonferrous Metals Mining and Dressing		0.70	
非金属矿采选业	Nonmetal Minerals Mining and Dressing	157.24	1.34	
农副食品加工业	Agricultural Products and Byproducts Processing	39.08	2.17	
食品制造业	Food Manufacturing	90.20	2.62	
饮料制造业	Beverage Manufacturing	41.00	3.07	
烟草制品业	Tobacco Products		0.18	
纺织业	Textile Industry	114.80	8.47	
纺织服装鞋帽制造业	Textile Garments,Shoes,Caps Manufacturing	6.75	1.44	
皮革毛皮羽毛(绒)及其制品业	Leather,Furs,Feather and Related Products	0.06	0.65	
木材加工及木、竹、藤、棕、草制品业	Timber Processing,Bamboo,Cane, Palm Fiber and Straw Products		0.66	
家具制造业	Furniture Manufacturing	2.80	1.27	
造纸及纸制品业	Papermaking and Paper Products	63.96	3.49	
印刷业和记录媒介的复制	Printing and Record Medium Reproduction	1.78	0.80	
文教体育用品制造业	Cultural, Educational and Sports Goods	3.56	0.66	
石油加工炼焦及核燃料加工业	Petroleum Processing,Coking and Nuclear Fuel Processing	19.13	4.03	84.04
化学原料及化学制品制造业	Raw Chemical Materials and Chemical Products	4 391.72	55.34	36.90
医药制造业	Medical and Pharmaceutical Products	118.65	3.70	0.01
化学纤维制造业	Chemical Fiber		0.79	
橡胶制品业	Rubber Products	64.05	3.24	0.01
塑料制品业	Plastic Products	9.38	6.48	
非金属矿物制品业	Nonmetal Mineral Products	2.07	8.94	0.81
黑色金属冶炼及压延加工业	Smelting and Pressing of Ferrous Metals	46.67	59.50	0.03
有色金属冶炼及压延加工业	Smelting and Pressing of Nonferrous Metals	0.04	1.97	
金属制品业	Metal Products	5.21	8.64	0.01
通用设备制造业	General Purpose Equipment Manufacturing	24.27	6.30	0.09
专用设备制造业	Special Purpose Equipment Manufacturing	15.83	2.19	0.03
交通运输设备制造业	Transport Equipment Manufacturing	24.11	8.99	0.47
电气机械及器材制造业	Electric Equipment and Machinery	5.77	7.39	0.06
通信设备计算机及其他电子设备制造业	Telecommunications Equipment,Computer and Other Electronic Equipment Manufacturing	33.57	17.42	
仪器仪表及文化办公用机械制造业	Instruments,Meters,Cultural and Office Machinery	6.46	1.07	0.02
工艺品及其他制造业	Craftwork and Other Manufacturing	0.20	0.63	
废弃资源和废旧材料回收加工业	Waste Resources and Materials Recovering and Processing		0.03	
电力热力的生产和供应业	Production and Supply of Electric & Heat Energy	34.93	29.84	0.02
燃气生产和供应业	Production and Supply of Gas		0.67	
水的生产和供应业	Production and Supply of Water		1.99	

主要统计指标解释

能源生产总量 指一定时期内全国一次能源生产量的总和。该指标是观察全国能源生产水平、规模、构成和发展速度的总量指标。一次能源生产量包括原煤、原油、天然气、水电、核能及其他动力能(如风能、地热能等)发电量,不包括低热值燃料生产量、生物质能、太阳能等的利用和由一次能源加工转换而成的二次能源产量。

能源消费总量 指一定时期内全国物质生产部门、非物质生产部门和生活消费的各种能源的总和。该指标是观察能源消费水平、构成和增长速度的总量指标。能源消费总量包括原煤和原油及其制品、天然气、电力,不包括低热值燃料、生物质能和太阳能等的利用。能源消费总量分为终端能源消费量、能源加工转换损失量和能源损失量三部分。

(1)**终端能源消费量:** 指一定时期内全国生产和生活消费的各种能源在扣除了用于加工转换二次能源消费量和损失量以后的数量。

(2)**能源加工转换损失量:** 指一定时期内全国投入加工转换的各种能源数量之和与产出各种能源产品之和的差额。该指标是观察能源在加工转换过程中损失量变化的指标。

(3)**能源损失量:** 指一定时期内能源在输送、分配、储存过程中发生的损失和由客观原因造成的各种损失量,不包括各种气体能源放空、放散量。

能源消费弹性系数 反映能源消费增长速度与国民经济增长速度之间比例关系的指标。计算公式为:能源消费弹性系数=能源消费量年平均增长速度/国民经济年平均增长速度

电力消费弹性系数 反映电力消费增长速度与国民经济增长速度之间比例关系的指标。计算公式为:电力消费弹性系数=电力消费量年平均增长速度/国民经济年平均增长速度

Explanatory Notes on Main Statistical Indicators

Total Energy Production refers to the total production of primary energy by all energy producing enterprises in the country in a given period of time. It is a comprehensive indicator to show the capacity, scale, composition and development of energy production of the country. The production of primary energy includes that of coal, crude oil, natural gas, hydro-power and electricity generated by nuclear energy and other means such as wind power and geothermal power. However, it excludes the production of fuels of low calorific value, bio-energy, solar energy and the secondary energy converted from the primary energy.

Total Energy Consumption refers to the total consumption of energy of various kinds by material production sectors, non material production sectors and households in the country in a given period of time. It is a comprehensive indicator to show the scale, composition and development of energy consumption. The total energy consumption includes that of coal, crude oil and their products, natural gas and electricity; However, it excludes the consumption of fuel of low calorific value, bio-energy and solar energy. Total domestic energy consumption can be divided into three parts: final energy consumption, loss during the process of energy conversion, and energy loss.

(1)**Final Energy Consumption**: It refers to the total energy consumption by material production sectors, non material production sectors and households in the country (region) in a given period of time, but excludes the consumption in conversion of the primary energy into the secondary energy and the loss in the process of energy conversion.

(2)**Loss During the Process of Energy Conversion**: It refers to the total input of various kinds of energy for conversion, minus the total output of various kinds of energy in the country in a given period of time. It is an indicator to show the loss that occurs during the process of energy conversion.

(3)**Energy Loss**: It refers to the total of the loss of energy during the course of energy transport, distribution and storage and the loss caused by any objective reason in a given period of time. The loss of various kinds of gas due to gas discharges and stocktaking is excluded.

Elasticity Ratio of Energy Consumption is an indicator to show the relationship between the growth rate of energy consumption and the growth rate of the national economy. The formula is:

Elasticity Ratio of Energy Consumption = (Average Annual Growth Rate of Energy Consumption)/(Average Annual Growth Rate of National Economy)

Elasticity Ratio of Electricity Consumption is an indicator to show the relationship between the growth rate of electricity consumption and the growth rate of the national economy. The formula is:

Elasticity Ratio of Electricity Consumption = (Average Annual Growth Rate of Electricity)/(Average Annual Growth Rate of National Economy)

第5篇
CHAPTER 5

财 政
Government Finance

5-1 全市财政收支(1994-2005年)

TOTAL FINANCIAL REVENUE AND EXPENDITURE,1994-2005

年 份 Year	全市财政收入 Total Financial Revenue	一般预算收入 General Budgetary Financial Revenue	基金预算收入 Fund Revenue	全市财政支出 Total Financial Expenditure	一般预算支出 General Budgetary Financial Expenditure	基金预算支出 Fund Expenditure
绝对数(亿元)						
Value						
(100 million yuan)						
1994	95.99	95.99		69.00	69.00	
1995	117.34	117.34		90.37	90.37	
1996	137.45	137.45		110.19	110.19	
1997	169.12	151.42	17.70	140.08	122.78	17.30
1998	186.55	170.07	16.47	155.15	137.93	17.22
1999	206.89	187.14	19.75	177.62	157.41	20.21
2000	244.81	222.70	22.11	209.57	187.05	22.52
2001	304.52	279.41	25.12	259.78	234.67	25.11
2002	375.92	339.81	36.11	300.07	265.21	34.86
2003	451.74	410.95	40.79	350.63	312.08	38.56
2004	502.17	445.15	57.03	431.49	375.02	56.47
2005	725.81	645.09	80.71	520.28	442.12	78.16
比上年增长%						
Increase Rate over						
Preceding Year(%)						
1995	22.2	22.2		31.0	31.0	
1996	15.8	15.8		21.9	21.9	
1997	13.5	10.2		13.8	11.4	
1998	10.3	12.3	-6.9	8.0	6.9	16.8
1999	10.9	10.0	19.9	14.5	14.1	17.3
2000	18.3	19.0	11.9	16.4	17.1	11.2
2001	24.4	25.5	13.6	25.7	27.3	11.8
2002	18.4	14.7	43.8	15.5	13.0	39.6
2003	20.2	21.0	12.9	16.8	17.8	10.0
2004	26.7	25.4	39.8	23.3	20.2	48.8
2005	26.8	26.3	41.5	20.6	17.9	38.4

资料来源:天津市财政局
Information source:Tianjin Municipal Finance Bureau.
注:1.本表收支均未含以港养港收支。2.增长速度均按可比口径计算。3.5-2至5-7表同。
Note:a)Revenue and expenditure in this table exclude expenses charged and used for operation of Tianjin Port. b)Increase rate is calculated on the basis of comparable coverage . c)Same as following table 5-2 to 5-7.

5-2 地方一般预算财政收入(1994-2005年)

LOCAL GENERAL BUDGETARY FINANCIAL REVENUE,1994-2005

年份 Year	地方一般预算收入 Local General Budgetary Finan-cial Revenue	#增值税(25%) Value-added Tax(25%)	#营业税 Operating Tax	#企业所得税 Income Tax of Enterprises	#个人所得税 Individual Income Tax
绝对数(亿元)					
Value					
(100 million yuan)					
1994	46.83	14.26	15.17	11.21	2.41
1995	58.94	16.66	19.86	12.67	3.77
1996	76.02	17.25	24.67	19.06	5.30
1997	89.91	17.30	27.60	21.48	6.49
1998	101.40	18.99	30.71	20.34	7.91
1999	112.81	20.83	33.88	24.02	8.86
2000	133.61	26.12	38.16	29.25	11.34
2001	163.64	34.87	42.99	39.38	16.58
2002	171.83	38.73	51.65	26.24	13.20
2003	204.53	45.19	64.32	23.80	12.53
2004	246.18	35.17	78.39	32.12	15.98
2005	331.85	64.24	96.45	41.11	18.82
比上年增长%					
Increase Rate over					
Preceding Year(%)					
1995	16.0	28.8	42.6	13.0	56.5
1996	29.0	3.6	24.2	50.4	40.4
1997	18.3	0.3	11.9	12.7	22.5
1998	12.8	9.8	11.3	-5.3	21.9
1999	11.3	9.7	10.3	18.1	12.1
2000	18.4	25.4	12.6	21.8	27.9
2001	22.5	33.5	12.7	34.6	46.2
2002	16.9	11.1	20.1	9.6	23.1
2003	24.8	16.7	24.5	13.6	18.7
2004	28.9	16.7	21.9	34.8	27.5
2005	28.2	21.8	23.0	27.8	17.5

注:2002年开始中央与地方实施所得税收入分享改革,所得税中央与地方分享比例2002年为5:5,2003年以来为6:4。下同。

Note:Since 2002,the distribution of income tax is reformed,central government and local government go shares for income tax at equal share of 50% each in 2002,central government shares 60% and local government shares 40% since 2003. Same as following table next.

5-3 一般预算财政支出(1994-2005年)

GENERAL BUDGETARY FINANCIAL EXPENDITURE,1994-2005

年 份 Year	一般预算支出 General Budgetary Financial Expenditure	#基本建设 Capital Construction	#支援农业 Supporting Agriculture	#教育支出 Operating Expense of Education	#城市维护费 City Maintenance	#科技三项费用 Science and Technology Promotion
绝对数(亿元) Value (100 million yuan)						
1994	69.00	9.69	2.29	11.41	6.88	0.94
1995	90.37	17.95	2.81	13.41	7.82	0.99
1996	110.19	23.20	3.11	16.62	10.33	1.16
1997	122.78	22.69	3.72	19.07	12.30	1.43
1998	137.93	24.16	4.00	21.74	15.13	1.58
1999	157.41	22.87	4.38	25.33	14.89	2.32
2000	187.05	29.71	4.65	30.87	15.90	3.69
2001	234.67	37.43	5.74	36.26	16.09	6.06
2002	265.21	39.36	7.05	41.57	20.44	6.68
2003	312.08	52.43	8.04	47.58	27.61	7.80
2004	375.02	69.39	10.93	55.40	40.81	9.20
2005	442.12	73.23	12.85	67.20	52.02	10.86
比上年增长% Increase Rate over Preceding Year(%)						
1995	31.0	85.3	22.7	17.5	13.7	10.3
1996	21.9	29.3	10.6	23.9	32.1	17.4
1997	11.4	-2.2	19.6	14.7	19.1	22.8
1998	6.9	6.5	7.6	14.0	23.0	10.4
1999	14.1	-5.4	9.5	16.5	-1.6	47.0
2000	17.1	29.9	6.2	21.9	6.7	59.2
2001	27.3	26.0	23.4	17.4	1.2	64.0
2002	13.0	5.2	22.9	14.7	27.0	10.2
2003	17.8	33.2	14.3	14.4	35.1	16.8
2004	20.2	30.9	35.6	16.4	48.3	17.9
2005	17.9	5.5	17.6	21.3	27.5	18.0

5-4 财政收入
FINANCIAL REVENUE

单位:万元 (10 000 yuan)

项　目	Item	2004	2005	2005 比 2004 年 增长% Increase Rate in 2005 over 2004
合　计	**Total**	**5 021 743**	**7 258 066**	**26.8**
#一般预算收入	General Budgetary Financial Revenue	4 451 457	6 450 919	26.3
一、地方财政收入	**Local Financial Revenue**	**3 032 086**	**4 125 654**	**30.6**
1.一般预算收入	**General Budgetary Financial Revenue**	**2 461 800**	**3 318 507**	**28.2**
#税收收入	Revenue from Taxs	2 016 395	2 705 011	23.4
#增值税(25%)	Value-added Tax(25%)	351 718	642 377	21.8
营业税	Operating Tax	783 942	964 545	23.0
个人所得税	Individual Income Tax	159 822	188 224	17.5
企业所得税	Income Tax of Enterprises	321 246	411 131	27.8
国有企业计划亏损补贴	Planning Subsidies to Loss-suffering State-owned Enterprises	-25 000	-25 000	
罚没收入	Penalty and Confiscatory Income	65 998	67 835	2.8
行政性收费收入	Income from Administrative Fees	294 509	458 474	55.7
专项收入	Special Project Income	72 140	89 995	24.7
基金预算收入	**Budgetary Fund Revenue**	**570 286**	**807 147**	**41.5**
2.市级财政收入	**Financial Revenue at City Level**	**1 475 646**	**2 071 234**	**30.7**
一般预算收入	General Budgetary Financial Revenue	1 145 896	1 483 171	21.5
基金预算收入	Budgetary Fund Revenue	329 750	588 063	61.7
区县级财政收入	**Financial Revenue at District & County Level**	**1 556 440**	**2 054 420**	**30.1**
一般预算收入	General Budgetary Financial Revenue	1 315 904	1 835 336	29.2
基金预算收入	Budgetary Fund Revenue	240 536	219 084	37.7
二、上划中央收入小计	**Revenue Transferred to Central Government**	**1 989 657**	**3 132 412**	**24.4**

5-5 财政支出
FINANCIAL EXPENDITURE

单位:万元 (10 000 yuan)

项 目	Item	2004	2005	2005 比2004年 增长% Increase Rate in 2005 over 2004
合 计	**Total**	**4 314 902**	**5 202 795**	**20.6**
1.一般预算支出	**General Budgetary Financial Expenditure**	**3 750 212**	**4 421 207**	**17.9**
#基本建设支出	Capital Construction	693 881	732 323	5.5
企业挖潜改造资金	Innovation Funds of Enterprises	271 803	291 198	7.1
科技三项费用	Science and Technology Promotion	91 979	108 550	18.0
支援农村生产支出	Supporting Agricultural Production	109 317	128 503	17.6
工交流通等部门事业费	Operating Expenses of Industrial, Transportation and Commercial Departments	18 623	19 374	4.0
城市维护费	Expenditure for City Maintenance	408 127	520 168	27.5
文体广播事业费	Operating Expenses of Culture,Sports and Broadcasting	86 942	107 471	23.6
教育支出	Operating Expense of Education	553 991	672 034	21.3
科学支出	Operating Expense of Science	22 915	27 989	22.1
医疗卫生支出	Expenditure for Health Care	183 378	189 803	3.5
社会保障和优抚救济支出	Social Security and Pensions, Relief	398 033	459 111	15.4
政策性补贴支出	Expenditure for Price Subsidies	25 190	30 072	19.4
基金预算支出	**Budgetary Fund Expenditure**	**564 690**	**781 588**	**38.4**
2.市级财政支出	**Financial Expenditure at City Level**	**2 052 968**	**2 560 824**	**24.7**
一般预算支出	General Budgetary Financial Expenditure	1 717 388	2 000 867	16.5
基金预算支出	Budgetary Fund Expenditure	335 580	559 957	66.9
区县级财政支出	**Financial Expenditure at District & County Level**	**2 261 934**	**2 641 971**	**16.8**
一般预算支出	General Budgetary Financial Expenditure	2 032 824	2 420 340	19.1
基金预算支出	Budgetary Fund Expenditures	229 110	221 631	-3.5

5－6　区县级一般预算财政收入(2005 年)

GENERAL BUDGETARY FINANCIAL REVENUE AT DISTRICT & COUNTY LEVEL,2005

单位:万元　　(10 000 yuan)

地　区	Region	一般预算财政收入 General Budgetary Financial Revenue	增值税 Value－added Tax	营业税 Operating Tax	个人所得税 Individual Income Tax
总　计	**Total**	**1 835 336**	**413 346**	**437 987**	**77 114**
区级合计	**Total at District Level**	**1 719 016**	**389 126**	**422 356**	**74 444**
和平区	Heping District	102 253	8 016	33 973	4 898
河东区	Hedong District	77 253	9 602	25 725	2 786
河西区	Hexi District	113 046	11 478	33 959	4 748
南开区	Nankai District	102 657	11 289	28 904	3 778
河北区	Hebei District	49 676	7 222	14 892	1 866
红桥区	Hongqiao District	30 382	3 751	9 223	979
塘沽区	Tanggu District	108 465	14 615	35 998	3 009
汉沽区	Hangu District	17 930	5 059	2 948	408
大港区	Dagang District	50 838	10 143	10 791	1 765
东丽区	Dongli District	97 988	24 741	15 399	3 891
西青区	Xiqing District	112 110	26 243	19 577	3 489
津南区	Jinnan District	63 602	15 434	12 495	1 762
北辰区	Beichen District	92 430	31 013	12 711	2 761
武清区	Wuqing District	77 473	17 656	20 843	5 524
宝坻区	Baodi District	35 326	4 384	12 489	754
天津经济技术开发区	TEDA	456 985	159 642	95 278	21 402
天津保税区	TFTZ	72 907	11 870	23 997	5 334
天津新技术产业园区	THIP	57 695	16 968	13 154	5 290
县级合计	**Total at County Level**	**116 320**	**24 220**	**15 631**	**2 670**
宁河县	Ninghe County	32 144	3 278	3 973	681
静海县	Jinghai County	36 167	8 978	6 749	902
蓟　县	Jixian County	48 009	11 964	4 909	1 087

5-6 续表 Continued
单位:万元 (10 000 yuan)

地 区	Region	城市维护建设税 Tax on Urban Maintenance and Construction	企业所得税 Income Tax of Enterprises	其他各项收 入 Others
总 计	**Total**	**118 929**	**291 144**	**496 816**
区级合计	**Total at District Level**	**110 527**	**274 304**	**448 259**
和平区	Heping District	7 161	16 069	32 136
河东区	Hedong District	7 366	5 674	26 100
河西区	Hexi District	7 123	9 651	46 087
南开区	Nankai District	6 929	9 312	42 445
河北区	Hebei District	4 027	5 336	16 333
红桥区	Hongqiao District	2 668	2 573	11 188
塘沽区	Tanggu District	8 891	9 065	36 887
汉沽区	Hangu District	1 798	1 063	6 654
大港区	Dagang District	4 646	5 375	18 118
东丽区	Dongli District	13 683	10 518	29 756
西青区	Xiqing District	10 396	14 207	38 198
津南区	Jinnan District	5 542	12 502	15 867
北辰区	Beichen District	8 516	12 410	25 019
武清区	Wuqing District	5 392	9 430	18 628
宝坻区	Baodi District	2 754	2 455	12 490
天津经济技术开发区	TEDA	7 319	122 255	51 089
天津保税区	TFTZ	2 130	16 451	13 125
天津新技术产业园区	THIP	4 186	9 958	8 139
县级合计	**Total at County Level**	**8 402**	**16 840**	**48 557**
宁河县	Ninghe County	1 376	1 612	21 224
静海县	Jinghai County	2 571	3 160	13 807
蓟 县	Jixian County	4 455	12 068	13 526

5－7 区县级一般预算财政支出(2005 年)
GENERAL BUDGETARY FINANCIAL EXPENDITURE AT DISTRICT & COUNTY LEVEL,2005

单位:万元 (10 000 yuan)

地区	Region	一般预算财政支出 General Budgetary Financial Expenditure	#基本建设支出 Capital Construction	#支援农村生产支出 Supporting Agricultural Production	#教育支出 Operating Expense of Education
总计	**Total**	**2 420 340**	**583 116**	**56 753**	**445 832**
区级合计	**Total at District Level**	**2 210 806**	**581 396**	**40 942**	**382 769**
和平区	Heping District	110 159	20 675		27 717
河东区	Hedong District	89 493			28 300
河西区	Hexi District	98 196	1 037		30 344
南开区	Nankai District	103 337	950		27 807
河北区	Hebei District	80 487	530		26 395
红桥区	Hongqiao District	60 566			20 879
塘沽区	Tanggu District	147 046	23 117	2 533	30 934
汉沽区	Hangu District	37 350	260	1 504	10 008
大港区	Dagang District	96 104	12 048	2 884	34 422
东丽区	Dongli District	104 696	7 830	3 804	19 110
西青区	Xiqing District	154 484	65 614	3 315	16 015
津南区	Jinnan District	100 953	24 719	4 062	17 564
北辰区	Beichen District	113 068	26 869	3 454	20 578
武清区	Wuqing District	145 158	317	14 207	36 236
宝坻区	Baodi District	74 173		5 179	25 540
天津经济技术开发区	TEDA	537 149	304 670		8 804
天津保税区	TFTZ	109 067	70 073		
天津新技术产业园区	THIP	49 320	22 687		2 116
县级合计	**Total at County Level**	**209 534**	**1 720**	**15 811**	**63 063**
宁河县	Ninghe County	55 877	20	3 627	15 065
静海县	Jinghai County	70 653		7 739	22 037
蓟　县	Jixian County	83 004	1 700	4 445	25 961

5－7 续表 Continued
单位：万元 (10 000 yuan)

地　区	Region	#医疗卫生支出 Expenditure for Health Care	#社会保障补助支出 Subsidies for Social Security	#公检法司支出 Public Security Agency, Procura－torial Agency & Court of Justice
总　计	**Total**	**96 206**	**21 254**	**128 995**
区级合计	**Total at District Level**	**86 806**	**19 684**	**112 724**
和平区	Heping District	6 660	784	9 988
河东区	Hedong District	6 709	1 589	8 547
河西区	Hexi District	6 587	1 444	8 894
南开区	Nankai District	7 252	1 821	10 256
河北区	Hebei District	6 657	1 101	6 530
红桥区	Hongqiao District	5 803	1 402	5 941
塘沽区	Tanggu District	4 545	5 427	15 400
汉沽区	Hangu District	3 315	688	3 335
大港区	Dagang District	3 500	1 071	5 355
东丽区	Dongli District	5 290	334	6 405
西青区	Xiqing District	4 938	257	5 922
津南区	Jinnan District	4 774	560	4 521
北辰区	Beichen District	5 027	482	4 098
武清区	Wuqing District	7 958	124	7 241
宝坻区	Baodi District	3 013	1 213	4 000
天津经济技术开发区	TEDA	4 745	807	4 982
天津保税区	TFTZ		500	1 206
天津新技术产业园区	THIP	33	80	103
县级合计	**Total at County Level**	**9 400**	**1 570**	**16 271**
宁河县	Ninghe County	1 326	211	2 480
静海县	Jinghai County	4 286	221	5 843
蓟　县	Jixian County	3 788	1 138	7 948

5－8　天津市国家税务局各项税收情况(2001－2005年)

TAX REVENUE OF TIANJIN NATIONAL TAX BUREAU, 2001－2005

单位:万元　(10 000 yuan)

项　目	Item	2001	2002	2003	2004	2005
总　计	**Total**	**2 913 569**	**3 412 625**	**4 064 420**	**5 087 574**	**7 189 915**
税收合计	**Total Tax**	**2 895 242**	**3 876 635**	**4 693 511**	**6 306 091**	**8 377 271**
#增值税	Value－added Tax	2 057 409	2 952 659	3 595 089	4 631 805	5 836 010
消费税	Consumption Tax	147 029	200 445	289 421	352 408	447 750
营业税	Operating Tax	44 771	33 876	28 396	30 143	32 106
企业所得税	Income Tax of Enterprises	107 394	72 838	134 168	203 579	365 496
#国有企业	State－owned Enterprises	23 030	23 975	22 144	27 551	37 525
集体企业	Collective－owned Enterprises	1 340	4 558	4 933	10 022	8 410
股份合作企业	Cooperative Enterprises		87	711	706	1 462
联营企业	Joint Ownership Enterprises	745	613	322	1 028	2 704
股份有限公司	Share－holding Corporations Ltd.	82 261	38 156	82 605	92 248	291 765
私营企业	Private Enterprises		245	1 396	7 676	23 583
外商投资企业和外国企业所得税	Income Tax of Foreign and Foreign－founded Enterprises	463 259	531 775	553 412	982 337	1 470 901
个人所得税	Individual Income Tax	71 130	80 752	86 507	96 567	107 602
城市维护建设税	Tax on Urban Maintenance and Construction	2 167	2 104	3 223	5 042	7 036
房产税	Tax on Real Estates	502	526	574	626	681
印花税	Stamp Tax	1 403	1 473	2 562	3 440	4 970
城镇土地使用税	Tax on the Use of Town Land	153	153	129	124	136
车船使用税	Tax on the Use of Vehicle and Ship	25	34	30	20	24
出口退税合计	**Total Tax Returned from Export Enterprises**		**－495 912**	**－679 190**	**－1 266 686**	**－1 232 311**
其他收入合计	**Total Others**	**18 327**	**31 902**	**50 099**	**48 169**	**44 955**
#教育费附加收入	Revenue from Extra－Charges for Education	929	902	1 381	2 156	3 014

主要统计指标解释

财政收入 指国家可直接支配的财力，主要包括税收收入和其他收入两大类。1994 年我国统一实行分税制财政体制，按税种分为上划中央收入和地方财政收入。上划中央收入包括：增值税的 75% 和消费税的 100%等；地方财政收入包括：增值税的 25%、营业税（不含银行总行、铁道、保险总公司的营业税）、地方企业交纳的企业所得税、外商投资企业和外国企业所得税、个人所得税、土地使用税、固定资产投资方向调节税、城市维护建设税（不含银行总行、铁道、保险总公司集中交纳的部分）、资源税（不包括海洋石油资源税）、房产税、车船使用税、印花税、屠宰税、农牧业税、耕地占用税、契税、遗产和赠与税、土地增值税、国有土地有偿使用收入以及基金收入等。地方财政收入加上划中央收入为全市财政收入。需要指出的是，1994 年以后地方财政收入与以前实行的总额分成财政体制下的地方财政收入在内容和范围上有一定差别，从 2002 年 1 月 1 日起我国所得税收入分配方式又有重大改革，2002 年所得税收入中央分享 50%，地方分享 50%。因此，历年数据不完全可比。

一般预算财政收入 是通过一定的形式和程序，由各级财政部门组织并纳入预算管理的各项收入，也就是会计制度改革以前所称的“预算收入”。

基金预算收入 是按规定收取，转入或通过当年财政安排，由财政管理并具有指定用途的政府性基金预算收入等。

一般预算财政支出 是各级财政部门对集中的一般预算收入有计划地分配和使用而安排的支出。

基金预算支出 是各级财政部门用基金预算收入安排的支出。

Explanatory Notes on Main Statistical Indicators

Government Revenue refers to the revenue of the government directly disposable finance, including various tax revenue and other revenue. In accordance with the classification of the structure of the government finance in 1994 on the basis of the classification of channels for collection of tax revenue, the revenue of the central government and the revenue of the local governments have different coverage. Revenue of the central government includes 75% of the value added tax and 100% of the value consumption tax, etc, The revenue of the local governments includes 25% of the value added tax, business tax, (excluding business taxes of head offices of bank, profits of railways, head office of insurance company) , income tax of the local enterprises subordinated to the local government, income tax of foreign, Hongkong, Macao and Taiwan funded enterprises, personal income tax, tax on the use of urban land, tax on the adjustment of the investment in fixed assets, tax on town maintenance and construction, tax on resources (excluding tax on ocean petroleum resources), tax on real estates, tax on the use of vehicles and ships, stamp tax, slaughter tax, tax on agriculture and animal husbandry, tax on the occupancy of cultivated land, contract tax, inheritance tax, gift tax, land value added tax, income of non - gratuitous use on the state - owned land and income of funds. Total of government revenue included the revenue of the central government and the revenue of the local governments. Now the content and coverage of the local financial revenue is difference from that before 1994, please pay attention to distinguish when you use. From January 1,2002 , distribution of income tax changed, central government share in 50% and local government share in 50% , the figures in 2002 are not comparable with the previous years.

General Budgetary Financial Revenue refers to financial revenue with budgetary management through certain form and procedure by financial departments at each level, also called "budgetary revenue" before reformation of accounting system.

Fund Budgetary Revenue refers to government fund budgetary revenue with financial management and assigned uses gathered by rules or through financial arrangement.

General Budgetary Financial Expenditure refers to expenditure distributed and used from general budgetary financial revenue by financial departments at each level.

Fund Budgetary Expenditure refers to expenditure arranged from fund budgetary revenue by financial departments at each level.

第 6 篇
CHAPTER 6

价格指数
Price Indices

6-1 城市物价总指数(1978-2005 年)

URBAN GENERAL PRICE INDICES,1978-2005

年 份 Year	上年=100 Preceding Year=100		1978=100		1990=100	
	商品零售价格指数 Retail Price Index	居民消费价格指数 Consumer Price Index	商品零售价格指数 Retail Price Index	居民消费价格指数 Consumer Price Index	商品零售价格指数 Retail Price Index	居民消费价格指数 Consumer Price Index
1978	100.0	100.0	100.0	100.0		
1979	101.1	101.0	101.1	101.0		
1980	105.5	105.1	106.7	106.2		
1981	101.5	101.3	108.3	107.5		
1982	100.5	100.5	108.8	108.1		
1983	100.5	100.5	109.3	108.6		
1984	101.8	101.8	111.3	110.6		
1985	113.9	113.1	126.8	125.0		
1986	107.2	106.8	135.9	133.6		
1987	106.9	106.8	145.3	142.6		
1988	117.7	116.9	171.0	166.7		
1989	115.1	114.7	196.8	191.2		
1990	102.7	103.0	202.1	197.0	100.0	100.0
1991	108.0	110.2	218.3	217.1	108.0	110.2
1992	109.4	111.4	238.8	241.8	118.2	122.8
1993	114.3	117.6	273.0	284.4	135.0	144.4
1994	115.6	124.0	315.6	352.6	156.1	179.0
1995	110.6	115.3	349.0	406.6	172.7	206.4
1996	105.1	109.0	366.8	443.2	181.5	225.0
1997	100.7	103.1	369.4	456.9	182.7	232.0
1998	96.6	99.5	356.8	454.6	176.5	230.8
1999	97.5	98.9	347.9	449.6	172.1	228.3
2000	98.6	99.6	343.1	447.8	169.7	227.3
2001	98.6	101.2	338.2	453.2	167.3	230.1
2002	97.4	99.6	329.5	451.4	163.0	229.2
2003	97.4	101.0	320.9	455.9	158.7	231.4
2004	100.8	102.3	323.5	466.4	160.0	236.8
2005	99.9	101.5	323.1	473.4	159.8	240.3

6－2　城市居民消费价格分类指数

（上年＝100）

URBAN CONSUMER PRICE INDICES BY CATEGORY

(Preceding Year＝100)

项　目　Item	2003	2004	2005
居民消费价格总指数			
General Consumer Price Index	**101.0**	**102.3**	**101.5**
#服务项目价格指数			
Services	107.8	100.3	101.6
1.食　品			
Food	**103.3**	**109.9**	**103.4**
粮　食			
Grain	102.1	123.7	103.8
淀粉及薯类			
Starches and Tubers	94.6	102.3	109.3
干豆类及豆制品			
Bean and Related Products	105.5	119.9	100.8
油脂类			
Oil or Fat	111.5	120.1	94.7
肉禽及其制品			
Meat,Poultry and Related Products	102.2	113.9	104.5
蛋　类			
Eggs	102.0	123.8	103.5
水产品			
Aquatic Products	111.0	131.6	95.7
菜　类			
Vegetables	121.6	94.5	112.1
调味品			
Flavoring	104.2	104.3	101.7
糖			
Sugar	99.6	99.8	103.0
茶及饮料			
Tea and Drink	99.2	99.7	101.0
干鲜瓜果			
Dried and Fresh Melons and Fruits	99.8	109.2	109.6
糕点饼干面包			
Pasty,Biscuit and Bread	100.4	105.9	105.3
奶及奶制品			
Milk and Related Products	95.7	100.0	100.3
在外用膳食品			
Catering Trade	100.0	103.9	104.1
其他食品及食品加工服务			
Other Food and Cooking Services	97.3	101.9	101.4
2.烟酒及用品			
Tobacco,Liquor and Related Goods	**98.8**	**101.0**	**99.7**
烟　草			
Tobacco	98.4	101.5	101.2
酒			
Liquor	99.1	106.0	103.2
吸烟饮酒用品			
Related Goods	98.9	91.4	88.6
3.衣　着			
Clothing	**88.1**	**92.1**	**96.3**
服　装			
Garments	87.6	92.5	99.9

6-2 续表 Continued

项 目 Item	2003	2004	2005
衣着材料 Clothing Materials	100.2	100.6	100.0
鞋袜帽 Shoes,Socks and Hats	86.0	88.7	85.2
衣着加工服务 Processing Services	100.0	100.0	99.7
4.家庭设备用品及维修服务 **Household Appliances,Articles and Repair Services**	**96.5**	**98.3**	**99.1**
耐用消费品 Durable Consumer Goods	95.9	97.5	97.6
室内装饰品 Indoors Decorations	100.6	100.0	95.9
床上用品 Bed Articles	90.7	89.0	103.2
家庭日用杂品 Daily Use Household Articles	95.0	101.2	100.4
家庭服务及加工维修服务 Household Services and Repair Services	103.0	98.4	107.2
5.医疗保健和个人用品 **Medical,Health Care and Individual Goods**	**94.0**	**93.4**	**97.6**
医疗保健 Medicine and Medical Services	92.1	91.6	97.6
个人用品及服务 Individual Goods and Services	100.0	98.7	97.4
6.交通和通讯 **Transportation and Telecommunications**	**97.0**	**96.8**	**98.6**
交 通 Transportations	99.2	98.7	104.1
通 讯 Telecommunications	95.3	95.5	94.8
7.娱乐教育文化用品及服务 **Recreational,Educational & Cultural Artcles and Services**	**110.7**	**99.2**	**100.0**
文娱用耐用消费品及服务 Durable Consumer Goods & Services for Recreational Use	93.2	91.9	95.1
教 育 Education	118.5	101.5	100.5
文化娱乐用品 Recreation and Culture Articles	121.4	94.9	103.5
旅游及外出 Tourism	83.5	106.5	100.8
8.居 住 **Residence**	**101.7**	**103.6**	**106.7**
建房及装修材料 Building and Decoration Materials	98.8	100.7	102.1
租 房 Rent	104.6	100.3	102.1
自有住房 Individual Housing	99.0	100.4	103.6
水、电、燃料 Water,Electricity and Fuel	102.7	108.4	112.5

6-3 城市商品零售价格分类指数
(上年=100)
URBAN RETAIL PRICE INDICES BY CATEGORY
(Preceding Year=100)

项 目 Item	2003	2004	2005
商品零售价格总指数			
General Retail Price Index	**97.4**	**100.8**	**99.9**
1.食 品			
Food	**103.7**	**110.2**	**103.5**
粮 食			
Grain	102.1	123.7	103.8
淀粉及薯类			
Starches and Tubers	94.6	102.3	109.3
干豆类及豆制品			
Bean and Related Product	105.5	119.9	100.8
油脂类			
Oil or Fat	111.5	120.1	94.7
肉禽及其制品			
Meat,Poultry and Related Products	102.0	113.9	104.5
蛋 类			
Eggs	102.1	123.8	103.5
水产品			
Aquatic Products	111.0	131.6	95.7
菜 类			
Vegetables	123.7	94.5	112.1
调味品			
Flavoring	104.4	104.3	101.7
糖			
Sugar	99.5	99.8	103.0
干鲜瓜果			
Dried and Fresh Melons and Fruits	100.3	109.2	109.6
糕点饼干面包			
Pasty,Biscuit and Bread	100.4	105.9	105.3
奶及奶制品			
Milk and Related Products	95.7	100.0	100.3
在外用膳食品			
Catering Trade	100.0	103.9	104.1
其它食品			
Other Food	97.2	101.9	101.3
2.饮料烟酒			
Beverages,Tobacco and Liquor	**98.8**	**102.3**	**101.8**
茶及饮料			
Tea and Beverages	99.1	99.7	101.0
烟 草			
Tobacco	98.4	101.5	101.2
酒			
Liquor	99.1	106.0	103.2
3.服装鞋帽			
Garments,Shoes and Hats	**87.4**	**91.7**	**96.1**
服 装			
Garments	87.8	92.6	99.9
鞋袜帽			
Shoes,Socks and Hats	86.1	88.9	85.2
其 他			
Others	91.0	95.7	98.3

6-3 续表 1 Continued

项 目 Item	2003	2004	2005
4.纺织品			
Textiles	**95.3**	**94.5**	**102.2**
衣着材料			
Clothing Materials	100.2	100.6	100.0
床上用品			
Bed Articles	90.6	88.4	103.2
5.家用电器及音像器材			
Household Appliances and Stereo Sets & Camera Faciles	**90.9**	**93.5**	**96.3**
家庭设备			
Hosehold Facilities	94.3	96.1	98.3
文娱用耐用消费品			
Durable Consumer Goods for Recreational Use	84.2	87.3	92.7
音像器材类			
Stereo Sets & Camera Facilities	94.1	98.4	96.5
6.文化办公用品			
Culture and Office Articles	**98.1**	**96.2**	**98.8**
7.日用品			
Articles for Daily Use	**96.8**	**100.3**	**100.4**
日用百货			
General Merchandise for Daily Use	96.4	101.6	99.6
日用杂品			
Sundry Articles	99.3	98.1	100.4
洗涤用品			
Washing Articles	101.1	100.1	100.6
其他日用品			
Other Articles for Daily Use	94.2	99.5	101.4
8.体育娱乐用品			
Sport and Recreation Articles	**99.2**	**95.3**	**97.6**
体育用品			
Sport Article	98.5	98.7	100.6
娱乐用品			
Recreation Articles	99.6	93.1	95.8
9.交通、通讯用品			
Transportation and Telecommunications Articles	**90.0**	**87.8**	**88.6**
交通运输机械			
Transportation Machine	96.2	93.0	99.1
通讯器材类			
Telecommunications Facilities	65.3	72.2	70.5
10.家 具			
Furniture	**99.2**	**99.9**	**97.2**
11.化妆品			
Cosmetics	**99.2**	**100.9**	**98.2**
12.金银珠宝			
Gold and Silver Jewelry	**115.5**	**119.1**	**102.9**
13.中西药品及医疗保健用品			
Traditional Chinese & Western Medicine and Medical,Health Care Goods	**90.1**	**86.9**	**96.5**
医疗器具及用品			
Medical Facilities and Goods	103.1	100.0	98.4
中药材及中成药			
Traditional Chinese Medicine Material and Medicine	96.3	94.0	95.3

6-3 续表 2　Continued

项　　目　　Item	2003	2004	2005
西　药 Western Medicine	85.2	81.1	96.2
保健器具及用品 Health Care Facilities and Goods	94.7	93.4	98.6
14.书报杂志及电子出版物 Books, Newspapers and Magazines, Electronics Publications	**99.5**	**99.5**	**100.6**
教材及参考书 Teaching Materials and Reference Books	96.9	97.0	100.9
书报杂志 Books, Newspapers and Magazines	102.0	100.5	100.0
电子音像制品 Electronics Music and Picture Goods	99.9	104.3	101.8
15.燃　料 Fuels	**109.9**	**110.5**	**112.9**
煤炭及制品类 Coal and Related Products	97.1	124.3	121.9
石油及制品类 Petroleum and Related Products	110.7	109.7	112.4
16.建筑材料及五金电料 Construction Materials and Hardware Materials	**99.1**	**100.6**	**101.6**
建筑装璜材料 Construction and Decoration Materials	98.7	100.7	102.1
五金电料类 Hardware Materials	100.0	100.0	100.0

6-4　居民货币购买力指数(1991-2005年)

INDICES OF MONETARY PURCHASING POWER OF RESIDENTS, 1991-2005

年　份 Year	上年=100 Preceding Year=100	1990=100
1991	90.7	90.7
1992	89.8	81.4
1993	85.0	69.3
1994	80.6	55.9
1995	86.7	48.4
1996	91.7	44.4
1997	97.0	43.1
1998	100.5	43.3
1999	101.1	43.8
2000	100.4	44.0
2001	98.8	43.5
2002	100.4	43.6
2003	99.0	43.2
2004	97.8	42.2
2005	98.5	41.6

6-5 固定资产投资价格指数(2001-2005年)

(上年=100)

PRICE INDICES OF INVESTMENT IN FIXED ASSETS,2001-2005

(Preceding Year=100)

项 目 Item	2001	2002	2003	2004	2005
固定资产投资价格总指数 General Price Index of Investment In Fixed Assets	**99.7**	**99.5**	**102.6**	**107.3**	**101.2**
建筑安装、装饰工程 Building Installation	100.1	100.7	104.9	111.3	101.4
#材料费用 Expense of Materials	99.8	100.3	106.0	114.8	101.1
设备工器具购置 Purchase of Equipment,Tools and Instruments	98.5	94.9	97.8	100.5	99.1
其他费用 Others	100.1	100.2	100.4	101.0	102.6

6-6 工业品出厂价格指数(2001-2005年)

(上年=100)

EX-FACTORY PRICE INDICES OF INDUSTRIAL PRODUCTS,2001-2005

(Preceding Year=100)

项 目 Item	2001	2002	2003	2004	2005
工业品出厂价格总指数 General Industrial Producer Price Index	**95.9**	**95.9**	**102.5**	**104.1**	**100.1**
轻工业 Light Industry	97.8	97.9	99.6	101.2	98.2
以农产品为原料 Using Farm Products as Raw Materials	97.8	98.4	103.6	104.0	98.9
以非农产品为原料 Using Non-farm Products as Raw Materials	97.9	97.3	98.1	100.3	98.0
重工业 Heavy Industry	94.8	94.5	105.1	106.3	101.5
采掘业 Mining and Quarrying Industry	89.3	100.2	124.7	121.0	131.0
原料工业 Raw Materials Industry	99.7	98.7	113.5	118.4	108.1
加工工业 Processing Industry	93.1	90.7	97.5	97.2	92.9
生产资料 Production Goods	95.0	95.5	103.3	105.6	101.0
采掘业 Mining and Quarrying Industry	89.5	100.3	124.7	121.1	130.4
原料工业 Raw Materials Industry	99.5	98.5	113.0	117.7	107.4
加工工业 Processing Industry	93.3	92.8	98.2	99.7	95.4
生活资料 Consumer Goods	97.6	95.7	100.0	99.2	97.3
食 品 Food	96.6	100.2	103.1	103.5	98.3
衣 着 Clothing	100.1	99.2	101.2	100.9	98.0
一般日用品 Daily Use Articles	98.5	98.6	99.9	99.8	101.0
耐用消费品 Durable Consumer Goods	97.1	89.7	96.4	95.6	95.1

6-7 按行业分工业品出厂价格指数(2005年)

(上年=100)

EX-FACTORY PRICE INDICES OF INDUSTRIAL PRODUCTS BY SECTOR, 2005

(Preceding Year=100)

行业 Sector	2005	行业 Sector	2005
煤炭开采和洗选业 Coal Mining and Dressing	107.2	化学纤维制造业 Chemical Fiber	107.4
石油和天然气开采业 Petroleum and Natural Gas Extraction	132.7	橡胶制品业 Rubber Products	103.4
有色金属矿采选业 Nonferrous Metals Mining and Dressing	107.0	塑料制品业 Plastic Products	101.5
非金属矿采选业 Nonmetal Minerals Mining and Dressing	150.4	非金属矿物制品业 Nonmetal Mineral Products	101.3
农副食品加工业 Agricultural Products and Byproducts Processing	94.2	黑色金属冶炼及压延加工业 Smelting and Pressing of Ferrous Metals	102.2
食品制造业 Food Manufacturing	101.3	有色金属冶炼及压延加工业 Smelting and Pressing of Nonferrous Metals	114.6
饮料制造业 Beverage Manufacturing	102.1	金属制品业 Metal Products	102.4
烟草制品业 Tobacco Processing	100.0	通用设备制造业 General Purpose Equipment Manufacturing	100.8
纺织业 Textile Industry	100.3	专用设备制造业 Special Purpose Equipment Manufacturing	99.4
纺织服装、鞋、帽制造业 Textile Garments, Shoes, Caps Manufacturing	95.1	交通运输设备制造业 Transport Equipment Manufacturing	92.3
皮革、毛皮、羽毛(绒)及其制品业 Leather, Furs, Down and Related Products	102.8	电气机械及器材制造业 Electric Equipment and Machinery	100.6
木材加工及木、竹、藤、棕、草制品业 Timber Processing, Bamboo, Cane, Palm Fiber and Straw Products	103.9	通信设备、计算机及其他电子设备制造业 Telecommunications Equipment, Computer and Other Electronic Equipment Manufacturing	87.2
家具制造业 Furniture Manufacturing	99.6	仪器仪表及文化、办公用机械制造业 Instruments, Meters, Cultural and Office Machinery	94.6
造纸及纸制品业 Papermaking and Paper Products	99.8	工艺品及其他制造业 Handiwork and Other Manufacturing	98.4
印刷业和记录媒介的复制 Printing and Record Medium Reproduction	100.4	废弃资源和废旧材料回收加工业 Waste Resources and Materials Recovering and Processing	127.2
文教体育用品制造业 Cultural, Educational and Sports Goods	100.1	电力、热力的生产和供应业 Production and Supply of Electric Power and Heat Energy	109.0
石油加工、炼焦及核燃料加工业 Petroleum Processing, Coking and Nuclear Fuel Processing	118.7	煤气生产和供应业 Production and Supply of Gas	100.6
化学原料及化学制品制造业 Chemical Raw Materials and Chemical Products	102.1	水的生产和供应业 Production and Supply of Tap Water	102.4
医药制造业 Medical and Pharmaceutical Products	95.4		

6-8 工业主要原材料、燃料及动力购进价格指数(2001-2005年)

(上年=100)

MAIN RAW MATERIALS, FUELS AND MOTIVE POWER PURCHASING PRICE INDICES OF INDUSTRY, 2001-2005

(Preceding Year=100)

项 目 Item	2001	2002	2003	2004	2005
原材料燃料动力购进价格总指数 Raw Materials Fuel and Motive Power Purchasing Price Index	**98.8**	**95.9**	**108.7**	**115.4**	**104.9**
燃料、动力类 Fuels and Energy	98.4	102.0	113.1	118.3	122.9
黑色金属材料类 Ferrous Metals	100.8	98.4	119.6	134.3	103.3
有色金属材料及电线类 Non ferrous Metals	95.3	96.8	107.8	130.5	117.3
化工原料类 Chemical Raw Materials	98.9	94.5	111.3	114.4	111.7
木材及纸浆类 Wood and Paper Pulps	101.1	102.9	100.9	99.0	104.6
建筑材料及非金属矿类 Construction Materials	97.2	98.3	106.9	106.3	114.5
其他工业原材料及半成品类 Other Industrial Raw Materials and Semi-products	97.7	95.1	95.9	105.5	98.3
农副产品类 Farm and Sideline Products	100.5	92.7	122.5	115.6	91.9
纺织原料类 Textile Raw Materials	99.5	89.3	106.2	118.6	97.9

6-9 房地产价格指数(2001-2005年)

(上年=100)

PRICE INDICES OF REAL ESTATE, 2001-2005

(Preceding Year=100)

项 目 Item	2001	2002	2003	2004	2005
房屋销售价格指数 Price Index of Real Estate Sales	**101.2**	**101.6**	**104.1**	**113.5**	**106.0**
商品房 Commercial House	101.9	101.9	104.0	111.7	106.3
经济适用房 Low-cost and Policy-related House	103.9	103.9	106.6	111.2	104.7
普通住宅 Common Residence	101.7	101.1	103.2	111.7	107.1
高档住宅 High-grade Residence	98.3	100.9	100.6	110.3	107.2
二手房 Second-hand House	97.0	99.6	105.0	119.5	105.0
房屋租赁价格指数 Price Index of Real Estate Rent	**110.1**	**106.0**	**100.7**	**101.2**	**101.3**
住 宅 Residence	120.9	113.8	107.9	100.4	101.6
办公楼 Office	95.6	95.2	96.1	101.7	102.7
商业娱乐用房 Business and Entertainment Housing	100.6	102.9	99.9	103.1	100.4
工业仓储用房 Industry storehouses	100.1	96.1	90.3	101.4	100.4
土地交易价格指数 Price Index of Land Transaction	**101.6**	**102.8**	**103.0**	**116.3**	**103.9**

主要统计指标解释

城市商品零售价格指数 是工业、商业、餐饮业和其他零售企业向城市居民、机关团体出售生活消费品和办公用品的价格水平变动趋势和变动程度的相对数。其目的在于掌握零售商品价格的变动趋势，为国家宏观调控和国民经济核算提供参考依据。

商品零售价格的调查范围涉及到各种类型的工业、商业、餐饮业和其他行业的零售商品以及农民对非农业居民出售商品的价格。包括食品、饮料烟酒、服装鞋帽、纺织品、家用电器及音像器材、文化办公用品、日用品、体育娱乐用品、交通通信用品、家具、化妆品、金银珠宝、中西药品及医疗保健用品、书报杂志及电子出版物、燃料、建筑材料及五金电料等16个大类。

城市居民消费价格指数 是反映城市居民购买的消费品及服务价格水平的变动趋势和变动程度的相对数。它是宏观经济分析和决策、价格总水平监测和调控以及国民经济核算的重要指标。其按年度计算的变动率通常被用来作为反映通货膨胀(或紧缩)程度的指标。

城市居民消费价格的调查范围包括城市居民购买并用于日常生活消费的商品和服务项目价格。按用途划分为8个大类，包括食品、烟酒及用品、衣着、家庭设备用品及维修服务费、医疗保健及个人用品、交通和通信、娱乐教育文化用品及服务、居住等。

固定资产投资价格指数 是反映一定时期内固定资产投资额价格变动趋势和程度的相对数。固定资产投资额是由建筑安装工程投资完成额、设备、工器具购置投资完成额和其他费用投资完成额三部分组成的。编制固定资产投资价格指数首先分别编制上述三部分投资的价格指数，然后采用加权算术平均法求出固定资产投资价格总指数。该指数可以准确地反映固定资产投资中涉及的各类商品和取费项目价格变动趋势和变动幅度，消除按现价计算的固定资产投资指标中的价格变动因素，真实地反映固定资产投资的规模、速度、结构和效益，为国家科学地制定、检查固定资产投资计划并提高宏观调控水平，为完善国民经济核算体系提供科学的、可靠的依据。

工业品出厂价格指数 是反映一定时期内全部工业产品出厂价格总水平的变动趋势和程度的相对数，包括工业企业售给本企业以外所有单位的各种产品和直接售给居民用于生活消费的产品。通过工业品出厂价格指数能观察出厂价格变动对工业总产值的影响。

工业原材料、燃料及动力购进价格指数 是反映一定时期内全部工业企业作为生产投入，从物资交易市场和能源、原材料生产企业购买原材料、燃料和动力产品时，所支付的价格水平变动趋势和程度的相对数，是扣除工业企业物质消耗成本中的价格变动影响的重要依据。

房地产价格指数 是反映全部房地产价格总水平的变动趋势和程度的相对数。包括土地交易价格指数、房地产销售价格指数、房地产租赁价格指数。

土地交易价格指数 是反映一定时期内房地产开发商或其他建设单位在进行商品房、生产和商业用房及其他生产经营用地开发前为取得土地使用权而实际支付的价格的变动趋势和程度的相对数。

房屋销售价格指数 是反映一定时期内房屋销售价格总水平变动趋势和程度的相对数。

房屋租赁价格指数 是反映一定时期内房屋租赁价格总水平变动趋势和程度的相对数。

Explanatory Notes on Main Statistical Indicators

Urban Retail Price Index reflects the trend and degree of changes in retail prices of living consumer goods and office equipment which are sold to residents and organizations by retail enterprises. It can be used to know about the change tendency of the price of retailed goods, provides reliable data for government decision making and further improving the current national accounting system.

Its survey field covers the retail price of industry, commerce, catering trade and other sectors and prices of goods sold to non－agricultural population by farmers. Now it is classified into 16 categories by food, beverages, tobacco and liquor, garments, shoes and hats, textiles, household appliances, stereo sets & camera facilities, cultural and office goods, articles for daily use, sports and recreational goods, transport and communications goods, furniture, cosmetics, jewelry, traditional Chinese and western medicines, newspapers, magazines and electronics publications, fuels, building decoration materials, hardware materials.

Urban Consumer Price Index reflects the trend and degree of changes in prices of consumer goods and services purchased by urban households. It is a indicator used for government decision making, price monitoring & controlling and improving the current national accounting system. The annual price index is used to reflect the degree of inflation and deflation.

Its survey field covers the prices of goods and services purchased by urban households and used for living. It is classified into 8 categories by food, tobacco and use articles, clothing, household facilities and articles, repair services, medicine and medical articles, means of transportation and communication, recreation, education and culture articles, residence, services.

Price Index of Investment in Fixed Assets reflects the trend and degree of changes in prices of investment in fixed assets during a given period. The investment in fixed assets consists of three components, namely the investment in construction and installation, the investment in purchases of equipment and instrument, and the investment in other items. Price index of investment in fixed assets is calculated as the weighted arithmetic mean of the price indices of the three components of investment in fixed assets. Removing the factor of price change in the aggregates of investment at current prices, this indicator shows the changes in the prices of commodities and fees involved in the investment of fixed assets, and can be used to observe the actual size, growth, structure, and efficiency of investment in fixed assets and provides reliable and scientific data for government planning, management, decision making, and further improving the current national accounting system.

Ex－factory Price Index of Industrial Products reflects the trend and degree of changes in general ex－factory prices of all industrial products during a given period, including sales of industrial products by an industrial enterprise to all units outside the enterprise, as well as sales of consumer goods to residents. It can be used to analyze the impact of ex－factory prices on gross industrial output value.

Purchasing Price Index of Raw Material, Fuel and Power reflects the trend and degree of changes in purchasing price of raw material, fuel and power paid by industrial enterprises when they purchase production as input from the market or other energy and raw material producers during a given period, and provide basis for measuring the material consumption of industrial enterprises after removing influence of price from cost.

Price Index of Real Estate reflects the trend and degree changes in real estate price, including price index of land transaction, price index of real estate sales, price index of real estate leasing.

Price Index of Land Transaction reflects the trend and degree changes in land transaction price which paid actually by developing enterprises or construction units to get land use rights before development of commodity buildings during a given period.

Price Index of Housing Sales reflects the trend and degree changes in housing sales during a given period.

Price Index of Housing Leasing reflects the trend and degree changes in housing leasing during a given period.

第7篇
CHAPTER 7

人民生活
People's Life

7-1 城乡居民物质文化生活水平提高情况(2001-2005年)
IMPROVEMENT IN URBAN AND RURAL RESIDENTS' MATERIAL AND CULTURAL LIFE,2001-2005

指　　标	Item	2001	2002	2003	2004	2005
居民收入支出(元)	**Income and Expenditure of Urban and Rural Residents(yuan)**					
城镇单位从业人员人均劳动报酬	Per Capita Annual Remuneration of Persons Employed in Urban Units	14 242	16 223	18 511	21 146	24 122
城市居民人均可支配收入	Per Capita Annual Disposable Income	8 959	9 338	10 313	11 467	12 639
城市居民人均消费性支出	Per Capita Annual Expenditures for Consumption	6 987	7 192	7 868	8 802	9 653
农村居民人均纯收入	Per Capita Annual Net Income of Farmer	4 825	5 315	5 861	6 525	7 202
农村居民人均生活消费支出	Per Capita Annual Living Expenditures of Farmer	2 618	2 778	3 015	3 297	3 590
储　蓄(万元)	**Savings(10000 yuan)**					
人均年末储蓄存款余额	Per Capita Saving Deposit Balance	1.41	1.62	1.97	2.27	2.36
住　房(平方米)	**Floor Space of Residential Buildings(sq.m)**					
城市人均住宅建筑面积	Per Capita Floor Space of Urban Residential Buildings	21.1	22.2	23.1	24.7	25.0
农村人均住房面积	Per Capita Living Floor Space of Rural Residents	23.9	24.3	24.4	25.2	26.1
交通和通信	**Traffic and Telecommunications**					
城市每万人拥有公共交通车辆(标台)	Number of Public Transportations Vehicles Per 10 000 Persons in City(standard vehicles)	8.9	9.3	9.4	10.7	11.2
城市每万人拥有铺装道路长度(公里)	Length of Paved Roads Per 10 000 Persons in City(km)	6.40	6.57	6.55	6.71	8.52
每人每年函件交寄(件)	Per Capita Annual Letters Delivered(piece)	18.7	22.0	23.9	11.4	8.1
全市每百人拥有电话机(含移动)(部)	Telephones Owned Per 100 Persons (Include Mobile)(sets)	56.0	65.4	82.3	89.5	90.1
电、水、燃气、供热	**Electricity,Water,Gas and Heating**					
全市人均生活用电量(千瓦小时)	Per Capita Electric Consumption for Living of All Residents(kwh)	286	320	344	360	367
城市人均生活用水量(吨)	Per Capita Water Consumption for Living of Urban Households(ton)	53	48.5	47.8	45.6	45.1
城市用气普及率(%)	Popularization Rate of Urban Households in Gas Use(%)	94.8	95.1	97.1	98.5	98.5
城市住宅集中供热面积(万平方米)	Heating Area of Urbon Residential Buildings(10 000 sq.m)	6 591	7 381	8 118	8 970	10 967

7-1 续表 Continued

指 标	Item	2001	2002	2003	2004	2005
文 化	**Culture**					
每百户城市居民家庭拥有(台)	Number of Sets Per 100 Urban Households(set)					
彩色电视机	Color TV Sets	134	135	135	137	136
家用电脑	Micro - Computer	21	26	34	41	51
每百户农村居民家庭拥有(台)	Possession Per 100 Rural Households(set)					
彩色电视机	Color TV Sets	103	105	110	115	116
家用电脑	Micro - Computers	3	5	7	8	10
平均每人每年有图书(册)	Per Capita Number of Books Per Year(copy)	6.8	7.5	7.3	8.9	8.9
平均每百人每天有报纸(份)	Number of Newspapers Per 100 Persons Per Day(copy)	21.6	24.1	24.5	25.6	23.9
教 育	**Education**					
每万人口中有各级学校在校学生(人)	Number of Students Enrollment Per 10 000 Population(person)	1 759	1 764	1 769	1 740	1 731
#大学生	University Students	169	215	266	308	354
卫 生	**Public Health**					
每万人拥有医院、卫生院床位(张)	Number of Hospital Beds Per 10 000 Persons(bed)	44.2	42.4	41.3	41.8	37.9
每万人拥有医生(人)	Number of Doctors Per 10 000 Persons (person)	32.0	26.0	24.7	27.2	24.3
赡养人口(人)	**Persons Supported by Others(person)**					
城镇每一就业者赡养人口	Number of Persons Supported by Each Urban Employment	1.46	1.46	1.46	1.41	1.38
农村每一劳动力负担人口	Number of Persons Supported by Each Rural Labourer	1.50	1.48	1.48	1.48	1.42
城市绿化	**City Afforestation**					
建成区绿化覆盖率(%)	Coverage Rate of Afforestation in Developed Area(%)	26.0	27.3	31.0	35.0	36.4
城市人均公共绿地(平方米)	Per Capita Public Green Areas in Urban Areas(sq. m)	4.9	5.6	6.7	8.1	8.1
环境卫生与保护	**Environment Sanitation and Protection**					
年末拥有公共厕所(座)	Public Lavatories(unit)	2 740	2 723	2 430	2 731	2 075
城市环境噪声达标面积(平方公里)	Standardization Areas of City Environment Noise(sq. km)	375	477	539	560	570

7-2　城镇单位从业人员劳动报酬总额(1990-2005年)
TOTAL REMUNERATION OF PERSONS EMPLOYED IN URBAN UNITS,1990-2005

单位:万元　　(10 000 yuan)

年份 Year	合计 Total	按三次产业分 Grouped by Three Industries			按登记注册类型分 Grouped by Registration Status		
		第一产业 Primary Industry	第二产业 Secondary Industry	第三产业 Tertiary Industry	国有单位 State-owned Units	集体单位 Collective-owned Units	其他单位 Others
1990	693 799.9	7 922.4	384 745.7	301 131.8	555 045.8	126 263.4	12 490.7
1991	797 340.6	9 044.1	448 747.2	339 549.3	623 445.1	154 187.4	19 708.1
1992	915 613.9	10 256.6	540 256.4	365 100.9	719 664.3	165 127.4	30 822.2
1993	1 167 779.8	7 155.8	691 240.2	469 383.8	903 227.9	192 110.6	72 441.3
1994	1 540 420.1	7 987.2	869 252.5	663 180.4	1 160 716.0	216 900.1	162 804.0
1995	1 848 027.9	8 603.4	1 055 034.7	784 389.8	1 352 214.5	259 963.3	235 850.1
1996	2 120 491.6	9 611.0	1 163 182.5	947 698.1	1 543 422.3	271 357.8	305 711.5
1997	2 232 525.8	10 438.1	1 187 059.3	1 035 028.4	1 604 714.3	264 608.8	363 202.7
1998	2 253 865.6	10 749.2	1 185 574.2	1 057 542.2	1 517 991.3	239 448.3	496 426.0
1999	2 344 186.1	9 713.4	1 215 273.1	1 119 199.6	1 519 302.4	212 537.6	612 346.1
2000	2 535 342.8	10 707.3	1 311 485.3	1 213 150.2	1 618 601.9	198 578.4	718 162.5
2001	2 775 592.7	11 572.1	1 374 770.9	1 389 249.7	1 762 580.1	168 567.3	844 445.3
2002	3 042 326.7	13 831.2	1 457 423.5	1 571 072.0	1 822 701.1	154 713.5	1 064 912.1
2003	3 506 036.0	13 186.3	1 727 566.1	1 765 283.6	1 947 978.7	154 880.0	1 403 177.3
2004	4 079 878.3	13 776.8	1 991 231.4	2 074 870.1	2 225 960.7	162 127.1	1 691 790.5
2005	4 582 620.0	13 168.1	2 197 189.1	2 372 262.8	2 472 988.3	166 904.2	1 942 727.5

注:1.1998年以前为职工工资总额。2.1993年以前各项指标中均不包括交通费、洗理费。下同。
Note:a)Data before 1998 of this table refer to total wages of staff and workers. b)Each item before 1993,excludes expenses of transport and washing. Same as following next.

7-3　城镇单位从业人员人均劳动报酬(1990-2005年)
PER CAPITA REMUNERATION OF PERSONS EMPLOYED IN URBAN UNITS,1990-2005

单位:元　　(yuan)

年份 Year	合计 Total	按三次产业分 Grouped by Three Industries			按登记注册类型分 Grouped by Registration Status		
		第一产业 Primary Industry	第二产业 Secondary Industry	第三产业 Tertiary Industry	国有单位 State-owned Units	集体单位 Collective-owned Units	其他单位 Others
1990	2 438	1 932	2 270	2 715	2 611	1 866	2 946
1991	2 724	3 102	2 572	2 980	2 912	2 114	3 455
1992	3 118	2 430	3 088	3 188	3 383	2 285	3 553
1993	4 080	2 972	4 167	3 980	4 410	2 780	5 869
1994	5 364	2 610	5 116	5 297	5 806	3 370	7 100
1995	6 501	4 844	6 237	6 357	6 963	4 138	8 640
1996	7 643	5 710	7 131	7 787	8 072	4 745	10 522
1997	8 238	6 476	7 691	8 372	8 689	5 083	10 599
1998	9 895	7 541	9 778	10 062	10 169	6 020	12 818
1999	11 046	8 476	11 000	11 127	11 169	6 821	13 601
2000	12 414	9 414	12 259	12 622	12 690	7 485	14 317
2001	14 242	10 333	13 503	15 107	14 823	8 159	15 263
2002	16 223	12 492	15 432	17 081	16 632	9 152	17 449
2003	18 511	13 257	17 772	19 357	18 929	10 865	19 424
2004	21 146	15 450	20 398	21 972	22 031	12 545	21 421
2005	24 122	15 954	23 370	24 936	24 832	14 693	24 583

7－4　城镇单位从业人员劳动报酬总额

TOTAL REMUNERATION OF PERSONS EMPLOYED IN URBAN UNITS

单位:万元　　(10 000 yuan)

项　目	Item	2004	2005	2005比2004年增长% Increase Rate in 2005 over 2004
总　计	**Total**	**4 079 878.3**	**4 582 620.0**	**12.3**
按登记注册类型分	**Grouped by Registration Status**			
国有单位	State－owned Units	2 225 960.7	2 472 988.3	11.1
集体单位	Collective－owned Units	162 127.1	166 904.2	2.9
其他单位	Others	1 691 790.5	1 942 727.5	14.8
#外商及港澳台商投资单位	Units with Funds from Foreign Countries, HongKong,Macao & Taiwan	1 051 909.8	1 192 183.1	13.3
股份有限公司	Share Holding Corporations Ltd.	249 175.7	328 255.0	31.7
按国民经济行业分	**Grouped by Sector**			
农、林、牧、渔业	Farming,Forestry,Animal Husbandry and Fishery	13 776.8	13 168.1	－4.4
采矿业	Minerals Mining	200 493.6	201 973.4	0.7
制造业	Manufacturing	1 469 338.4	1 606 401.2	9.3
电力、燃气及水的生产和供应业	Production & Supply of Power,Gas and Water	114 232.9	155 120.0	35.8
建筑业	Construction	207 166.5	233 694.5	12.8
交通运输、仓储及邮政业	Transport,Storage,Post Services	342 927.5	352 055.3	2.7
信息传输、计算机服务和软件业	Information transmitting,Computer Services and Software	74 477.4	84 530.3	13.5
批发和零售业	Wholesale and Retail Trade	212 519.6	227 133.8	6.9
住宿和餐饮业	Accommodation and Catering Services	43 913.4	44 198.9	0.7
金融业	Finance Intermediation	139 640.7	203 182.3	45.5
房地产业	Real Estate	41 898.6	50 001.0	19.3
租赁和商务服务业	Leasing and Business Services	74 910.1	92 766.9	23.8
科学研究、技术服务和地质勘察业	Scientific Research,Technical Services and Geological Prospecting	160 326.2	188 409.0	17.5
水利、环境和公共设施管理业	Management for Water Conservancy, Environment and Public Facilities	68 738.0	74 351.8	8.2
居民服务和其他服务业	Resident Services and Other Social Services	47 980.2	54 087.5	12.7
教　育	Education	361 617.8	417 452.3	15.4
卫生、社会保障和社会福利业	Health Care,Social Security and Social Welfare	165 948.0	192 381.9	15.9
文化、体育和娱乐业	Culture,Sports and Recreational Services	45 108.1	44 785.9	－0.7
公共管理和社会组织	Public Management and Social Organizations	294 864.5	346 925.9	17.7
按企业、事业、机关分	**Grouped By Enterprise,Institution and Agency**			
企　业	Enterprises	3 075 190.6	3 430 435.7	11.6
中　央	Central	770 301.1	907 068.2	17.8
地　方	Local	2 304 889.5	2 523 367.5	9.5
#国　有	State－owned	639 807.3	686 183.5	7.2
事　业	Institutions	728 345.1	823 225.8	13.0
中　央	Central	59 566.7	69 603.2	16.8
地　方	Local	668 778.4	753 622.6	12.7
机　关	Agencies	276 342.6	328 958.5	19.0
中　央	Central	33 016.8	35 703.6	8.1
地　方	Local	243 325.8	293 254.9	20.5

7-5 城镇单位从业人员人均劳动报酬
PER CAPITA REMUNERATION OF PERSONS EMPLOYED IN URBAN UNITS

单位:元 (yuan)

项目	Item	2004	2005	2005比2004年增长% Increase Rate in 2005 over 2004
总计	**Total**	**21 146**	**24 122**	**14.1**
按登记注册类型分	**Grouped by Registration Status**			
国有单位	State-owned Units	22 031	24 832	12.7
集体单位	Collective-owned Units	12 545	14 693	17.1
其他单位	Others	21 421	24 583	14.8
#外商及港澳台商投资单位	Units with Funds from Foreign Countries, HongKong, Macao & Taiwan	22 042	25 705	16.6
股份有限公司	Share Holding Corporations Ltd.	26 038	31 846	22.3
按国民经济行业分	**Grouped by Sector**			
农、林、牧、渔业	Farming, Forestry, Animal Husbandry and Fishery	15 450	15 954	3.3
采矿业	Minerals Mining	27 005	28 248	4.6
制造业	Manufacturing	18 971	21 595	13.8
电力、燃气及水的生产和供应业	Production & Supply of Power, Gas and Water	36 305	46 625	28.4
建筑业	Construction	21 597	25 540	18.3
交通运输、仓储及邮政业	Transport, Storage, Post Services	25 723	30 117	17.1
信息传输、计算机服务和软件业	Information transmitting, Computer Services and Software	38 055	37 375	-1.8
批发和零售业	Wholesale and Retail Trade	17 766	19 116	7.6
住宿和餐饮业	Accommodation and Catering Services	13 246	14 458	9.1
金融业	Finance Intermediation	27 085	39 528	45.9
房地产业	Real Estate	18 313	22 462	22.7
租赁和商务服务业	Leasing and Business Services	15 900	15 081	-5.2
科学研究、技术服务和地质勘察业	Scientific Research, Technical Services and Geological Prospecting	31 472	36 398	15.7
水利、环境和公共设施管理业	Management for Water Conservancy, Environment and Public Facilities	17 441	19 247	10.4
居民服务和其他服务业	Resident Services and Other Social Services	13 101	13 119	0.1
教育	Education	22 013	24 608	11.8
卫生、社会保障和社会福利业	Health Care, Social Security and Social Welfare	22 607	25 109	11.1
文化、体育和娱乐业	Culture, Sports and Recreational Services	22 503	25 481	13.2
公共管理和社会组织	Public Management and Social Organizations	22 266	26 322	18.2
按企业、事业、机关分	**Grouped By Enterprise, Institution and Agency**			
企业	Enterprises	20 891	23 820	14.0
中央	Central	28 939	34 899	20.6
地方	Local	19 115	21 380	11.8
#国有	State-owned	17 744	19 165	8.0
事业	Institutions	21 818	24 579	12.7
中央	Central	26 593	29 866	12.3
地方	Local	21 475	24 183	12.6
机关	Agencies	22 359	26 391	18.0
中央	Central	28 414	30 966	9.0
地方	Local	21 731	25 925	19.3

7-6 在岗职工工资总额
TOTAL WAGES OF ON-POST STAFF AND WORKERS

单位:万元 (10 000 yuan)

项 目	Item	2004	2005	2005比2004年增长% Increase Rate in 2005 over 2004
总 计	**Total**	**3 777 433.4**	**4 198 023.7**	**11.1**
按登记注册类型分	**Grouped by Registration Status**			
国有单位	State-owned Units	2 145 955.0	2 354 416.8	9.7
集体单位	Collective-owned Units	143 664.3	143 864.6	0.1
其他单位	Others	1 487 814.1	1 699 742.3	14.2
#外商及港澳台商投资单位	Units with Funds from Foreign Countries, HongKong, Macao & Taiwan	923 607.8	1 031 654.6	11.7
股份有限公司	Share Holding Corporations Ltd.	222 990.3	292 090.9	31.0
按国民经济行业分	**Grouped by Sector**			
农、林、牧、渔业	Farming, Forestry, Animal Husbandry and Fishery	13 635.6	13 035.4	-4.4
采矿业	Minerals Mining	189 884.7	188 186.0	-0.9
制造业	Manufacturing	1 343 188.2	1 448 728.4	7.9
电力、燃气及水的生产和供应业	Production & Supply of Power, Gas and Water	108 469.4	149 981.4	38.3
建筑业	Construction	199 035.2	224 434.9	12.8
交通运输、仓储及邮政业	Transport, Storage, Post Services	322 174.5	330 296.5	2.5
信息传输、计算机服务和软件业	Information transmitting, Computer Services and Software	72 849.1	81 893.5	12.4
批发和零售业	Wholesale and Retail Trade	181 975.0	184 406.1	1.3
住宿和餐饮业	Accommodation and Catering Services	36 397.0	34 346.2	-5.6
金融业	Finance Intermediation	111 677.2	166 445.0	49.0
房地产业	Real Estate	35 268.8	42 506.8	20.5
租赁和商务服务业	Leasing and Business Services	62 105.4	72 594.6	16.9
科学研究、技术服务和地质勘察业	Scientific Research, Technical Services and Geological Prospecting	152 904.6	180 484.0	18.0
水利、环境和公共设施管理业	Management for Water Conservancy, Environment and Public Facilities	65 478.7	70 267.1	7.3
居民服务和其他服务业	Resident Services and Other Social Services	39 694.2	39 019.0	-1.7
教 育	Education	353 435.3	409 435.9	15.8
卫生、社会保障和社会福利业	Health Care, Social Security and Social Welfare	161 368.6	184 482.6	14.3
文化、体育和娱乐业	Culture, Sports and Recreational Services	41 505.0	39 655.8	-4.5
公共管理和社会组织	Public Management and Social Organizations	286 386.9	337 824.5	18.0

7-7 在岗职工平均工资报酬
AVERAGE WAGES OF ON-POST STAFF AND WORKERS

单位:元 (yuan)

项目	Item	2004	2005	2005比2004年增长% Increase Rate in 2005 over 2004
总计	**Total**	**21 754**	**25 271**	**16.2**
按登记注册类型分	**Grouped by Registration Status**			
国有单位	State-owned Units	23 221	26 759	15.2
集体单位	Collective-owned Units	13 157	15 713	19.4
其他单位	Others	21 160	24 642	16.5
#外商及港澳台商投资单位	Units with Funds from Foreign Countries, HongKong, Macao & Taiwan	20 745	24 683	19.0
股份有限公司	Share Holding Corporations Ltd.	27 589	33 770	22.4
按国民经济行业分	**Grouped by Sector**			
农、林、牧、渔业	Farming, Forestry, Animal Husbandry and Fishery	15 514	16 034	3.4
采矿业	Minerals Mining	28 193	29 571	4.9
制造业	Manufacturing	18 431	21 183	14.9
电力、燃气及水的生产和供应业	Production & Supply of Power, Gas and Water	36 691	48 417	32.0
建筑业	Construction	22 412	26 777	19.5
交通运输、仓储及邮政业	Transport, Storage, Post Services	27 305	31 836	16.6
信息传输、计算机服务和软件业	Information transmitting, Computer Services and Softwware	38 257	40 569	6.0
批发和零售业	Wholesale and Retail Trade	18 992	20 603	8.5
住宿和餐饮业	Accommodation and Catering Services	14 058	15 861	12.8
金融业	Finance Intermediation	31 454	46 874	49.0
房地产业	Real Estate	21 545	26 727	24.1
租赁和商务服务业	Leasing and Business Services	16 717	17 898	7.1
科学研究、技术服务和地质勘察业	Scientific Research, Technical Services and Geological Prospecting	33 134	38 973	17.6
水利、环境和公共设施管理业	Management for Water Conservancy, Environment and Public Facilities	19 173	21 113	10.1
居民服务和其他服务业	Resident Services and Other Social Services	15 467	18 895	22.2
教育	Education	22 582	25 268	11.9
卫生、社会保障和社会福利业	Health Care, Social Security and Social Welfare	23 958	27 435	14.5
文化、体育和娱乐业	Culture, Sports and Recreational Services	23 067	25 892	12.2
公共管理和社会组织	Public Management and Social Organizations	24 358	28 432	16.7

7-8 其他从业人员劳动报酬总额
TOTAL REMUNERATION OF OTHER PERSONS EMPLOYED

单位:万元 (10 000 yuan)

项目	Item	2004	2005	2005比2004年增长% Increase Rate in 2005 over 2004
总计	**Total**	**302 444.9**	**384 596.3**	**27.2**
按登记注册类型分	**Grouped by Registration Status**			
国有单位	State-owned Units	80 005.7	118 571.5	48.2
集体单位	Collective-owned Units	18 462.8	23 039.6	24.8
其他单位	Others	203 976.4	242 985.2	19.1
#外商及港澳台商投资单位	Units with Funds from Foreign Countries, HongKong,Macao & Taiwan	128 302.0	160 528.5	25.1
股份有限公司	Share Holding Corporations Ltd.	26 185.4	36 164.1	38.1
按国民经济行业分	**Grouped by Sector**			
农、林、牧、渔业	Farming,Forestry,Animal Husbandry and Fishery	141.2	132.7	-6.0
采矿业	Minerals Mining	10 608.9	13 787.4	30.0
制造业	Manufacturing	126 150.2	157 672.8	25.0
电力、燃气及水的生产和供应业	Production & Supply of Power,Gas and Water	5 763.5	5 138.6	-10.8
建筑业	Construction	8 131.3	9 259.6	13.9
交通运输、仓储及邮政业	Transport,Storage,Post Services	20 753.0	21 758.8	4.8
信息传输、计算机服务和软件业	Information transmitting,Computer Services and Software	1 628.3	2 636.8	61.9
批发和零售业	Wholesale and Retail Trade	30 544.6	42 727.7	39.9
住宿和餐饮业	Accommodation and Catering Services	7 516.4	9 852.7	31.1
金融业	Finance Intermediation	27 963.5	36 737.3	31.4
房地产业	Real Estate	6 629.8	7 494.2	13.0
租赁和商务服务业	Leasing and Business Services	12 804.7	20 172.3	57.5
科学研究、技术服务和地质勘察业	Scientific Research,Technical Services and Geological Prospecting	7 421.6	7 925.0	6.8
水利、环境和公共设施管理业	Management for Water Conservancy, Environment and Public Facilities	3 259.3	4 084.7	25.3
居民服务和其他服务业	Resident Services and Other Social Services	8 286.0	15 068.5	81.9
教育	Education	8 182.5	8 016.4	-2.0
卫生、社会保障和社会福利业	Health Care,Social Security and Social Welfare	4 579.4	7 899.3	72.5
文化、体育和娱乐业	Culture,Sports and Recreational Services	3 603.1	5 130.1	42.4
公共管理和社会组织	Public Management and Social Organizations	8 477.6	9 101.4	7.4

7－9　其他从业人员人均劳动报酬
PER CAPITA REMUNERATION OF OTHER PERSONS EMPLOYED

单位:元　　(yuan)

项　目	Item	2004	2005	2005比2004年增长% Increase Rate in 2005 over 2004
总　计	**Total**	**15 673**	**16 124**	**2.9**
按登记注册类型分	**Grouped by Registration Status**			
国有单位	State－owned Units	9 275	10 221	10.2
集体单位	Collective－owned Units	9 211	10 453	13.5
其他单位	Others	23 535	24 182	2.7
#外商及港澳台商投资单位	Units with Funds from Foreign Countries, HongKong,Macao & Taiwan	40 068	35 032	－12.6
股份有限公司	Share Holding Corporations Ltd.	17 607	21 808	23.9
按国民经济行业分	**Grouped by Sector**			
农、林、牧、渔业	Farming,Forestry,Animal Husbandry and Fishery	11 031	10 702	－3.0
采矿业	Minerals Mining	15 393	17 535	13.9
制造业	Manufacturing	27 565	26 295	－4.6
电力、燃气及水的生产和供应业	Production & Supply of Power,Gas and Water	30 302	22 410	－26.0
建筑业	Construction	11 424	12 050	5.5
交通运输、仓储及邮政业	Transport,Storage,Post Services	13 542	16 552	22.2
信息传输、计算机服务和软件业	Information transmitting,Computer Services and Software	30 781	10 847	－64.8
批发和零售业	Wholesale and Retail Trade	12 833	14 575	13.6
住宿和餐饮业	Accommodation and Catering Services	10 350	11 051	6.8
金融业	Finance Intermediation	17 421	23 115	32.7
房地产业	Real Estate	10 186	11 791	15.8
租赁和商务服务业	Leasing and Business Services	12 856	9 628	－25.1
科学研究、技术服务和地质勘察业	Scientific Research,Technical Services and Geological Prospecting	15 478	14 531	－6.1
水利、环境和公共设施管理业	Management for Water Conservancy, Environment and Public Facilities	6 195	7 636	23.3
居民服务和其他服务业	Resident Services and Other Social Services	7 561	7 323	－3.2
教　育	Education	10 547	10 547	0.0
卫生、社会保障和社会福利业	Health Care,Social Security and Social Welfare	7 571	8 427	11.3
文化、体育和娱乐业	Culture,Sports and Recreational Services	17 559	22 700	29.3
公共管理和社会组织	Public Management and Social Organizations	5 707	7 012	22.9

7-10 市属部分局(总公司)国有经济单位从业人员劳动报酬总额
TOTAL REMUNERATION OF PERSONS EMPLOYED BY STATE - OWNED UNITS IN PART OF BUREAUS(CORPORATIONS)

单位:万元 (10 000 yuan)

局(总公司)	Bureau(Corporation)	2004	2005
经委系统	**Tianjin Economical Committee System**		
机电工业控股集团公司	Tianjin Machinery & Electric Industry Holding Group Company	17 334.2	17 124.2
中环电子信息集团有限公司	Tianjin Zhonghuan Electronics & Information Group	23 936.3	24 271.5
冶金集团(控股)有限公司	Tianjin Metallurgical Group(Holding) Corporation	14 303.8	14 445.7
渤海化工集团公司	Tianjin Bohai Chemical Industry Group Corporation	66 927.2	71 409.2
纺织集团(控股)有限公司	Tianjin Textile Industrial General Corporation	31 312.0	32 746.7
一轻集团(控股)有限公司	Tianjin First Light Industry Group(Holding Share) Co.,Ltd	8 328.3	8 248.8
二轻集团(控股)有限公司	The Second Light Industry Group(Holding) Co.,Ltd	4 386.7	3 900.7
医药集团有限公司	Tianjin Pharmaceutical Holdings	7 937.9	5 302.2
汽车工业(集团)有限公司	Tianjin Automobile Industry Group Co.,Ltd	3 814.4	2 980.7
飞鸽集团有限公司	Tianjin Flying Pigeon Group Co.,Ltd	1 463.9	1 340.3
塑料集团	Tianjin Plastics Group	841.9	934.2
天铁冶金集团有限公司	Tianjin Tian Tie Metallurgical Group Co.,Ltd	39 982.4	41 434.5
建筑材料集团(控股)有限公司	Tianjin Building Materials Group(Holding)Co.,Ltd	5 777.5	5 648.8
农委系统	**Tianjin Agricultural Committee System**		
农业局	Tianjin Agriculture Bureau	771.2	971.7
畜牧局	Tianjin Animal Husbandry Bureau	608.4	686.2
农垦集团总公司	Tianjin State Farms Agribusiness Group Company	6 694.4	7 321.2
水产局	Tianjin Aquatic Products Bureau	2 910.6	2 386.7
建委系统	**Tianjin Construction Committee System**		
建工集团总公司	Tianjin Construction Engineering Group Corporation	10 284.0	7 425.6
市政工程局	Tianjin Municipal Engineering Bureau	29 373.2	32 913.3
房地产管理局	Tianjin Real Estate Administrative Bureau	17 970.8	22 903.5
住宅建设发展集团	Tianjin House Construction Development Group	3 475.9	3 017.6
公共交通集团公司	Tianjin Public Traffic Group Corporation	12 895.5	14 708.8
自来水集团	Tianjin Tap Water Group	9 787.2	10 348.8
燃气集团	Tianjin Gas Group	15 966.0	17 992.7
交委系统	**Tianjin Transportation Committee System**		
天津港(集团)有限公司	Tianjin Port Group Corporation Ltd.	59 157.4	68 353.4
天津交通运输总公司	Tianjin Communication Corporation	8 874.2	9 013.8
商委系统	**Tianjin Commercial Committee System**		
粮食粮油集团有限公司	Tianjin Grain & Oil Group Co.,Ltd	5 513.0	5 385.7
一商集团有限公司	Tianjin First Commercial Group Co.,Ltd	4 844.5	4 494.1
二商集团有限公司	Tianjin Second Commercial Group Co.,Ltd	6 790.0	6 167.5

7-11 市属部分局(总公司)国有经济单位从业人员人均劳动报酬

PER CAPITA REMUNERATION OF PERSONS EMPLOYED BY STATE - OWNED UNITS IN PART OF BUREAUS(CORPORATIONS)

单位:元 (yuan)

局(总公司)	Bureau(Corporation)	2004	2005
经委系统	**Tianjin Economical Committee System**		
机电工业控股集团公司	Tianjin Machinery & Electric Industry Holding Group Company	14 068	16 261
中环电子信息集团有限公司	Tianjin Zhonghuan Electronics & Information Group	16 166	18 477
冶金集团(控股)有限公司	Tianjin Metallurgical Group(Holding) Corporation	13 423	15 401
渤海化工集团公司	Tianjin Bohai Chemical Industry Group Corporation	20 108	23 192
纺织集团(控股)有限公司	Tianjin Textile Industrial General Corporation	11 939	13 292
一轻集团(控股)有限公司	Tianjin First Light Industry Group(Holding Share) Co.,Ltd	15 298	17 995
二轻集团(控股)有限公司	The Second Light Industry Group(Holding) Co.,Ltd	12 789	15 291
医药集团有限公司	Tianjin Pharmaceutical Holdings	19 206	21 243
汽车工业(集团)有限公司	Tianjin Automobile Industry Group Co.,Ltd	23 517	34 619
飞鸽集团有限公司	Tianjin Flying Pigeon Group Co.,Ltd	9 650	10 406
塑料集团	Tianjin Plastics Group	10 877	12 607
天铁冶金集团有限公司	Tianjin Tian Tie Metallurgical Group Co.,Ltd	20 517	21 892
建筑材料集团(控股)有限公司	Tianjin Building Materials Group(Holding)Co.,Ltd	12 595	15 805
农委系统	**Tianjin Agricultural Committee System**		
农业局	Tianjin Agriculture Bureau	18 275	22 598
畜牧局	Tianjin Animal Husbandry Bureau	20 146	21 647
农垦集团总公司	Tianjin State Farms Agribusiness Group Company	16 583	19 750
水产局	Tianjin Aquatic Products Bureau	24 666	24 580
建委系统	**Tianjin Construction Committee System**		
建工集团总公司	Tianjin Construction Engineering Group Corporation	14 262	18 191
市政工程局	Tianjin Municipal Engineering Bureau	20 932	23 464
房地产管理局	Tianjin Real Estate Administrative Bureau	19 855	25 180
住宅建设发展集团	Tianjin House Construction Development Group	17 716	20 654
公共交通集团公司	Tianjin Public Traffic Group Corporation	12 806	14 258
自来水集团	Tianjin Tap Water Group	27 632	27 894
燃气集团	Tianjin Gas Group	24 372	27 512
交委系统	**Tianjin Transportation Committee System**		
天津港(集团)有限公司	Tianjin Port Group Corporation Ltd.	52 107	59 718
天津交通运输总公司	Tianjin Communication Corporation	12 441	14 271
商委系统	**Tianjin Commercial Committee System**		
粮食粮油集团有限公司	Tianjin Grain & Oil Group Co.,Ltd	15 675	17 486
一商集团有限公司	Tianjin First Commercial Group Co.,Ltd	15 409	16 608
二商集团有限公司	Tianjin Second Commercial Group Co.,Ltd	13 174	15 454

7-12 职工劳保福利费发放情况(2001-2005年)
TOTAL INSURANCE WELFARE OF STAFF AND WORKERS,2001-2005

指标 Item	2001	2002	2003	2004	2005
在职职工保险福利费用总额(万元) Total Insurance Welfare of On-post Staff & Workers(10 000 yuan)	**264 423.4**	**221 265.1**	**265 528.4**	**323 589.0**	**227 405.7**
国有单位 State-owned Units	170 572.3	140 320.9	176 980.3	219 670.2	150 358.8
集体单位 Collective-owned Units	10 314.9	8 231.4	7 738.1	26 307.8	5 761.8
其他单位 Others	83 536.2	72 712.8	80 810.0	77 611.0	71 285.1
非在职职工保险福利费用总额(万元) Total Insurance Welfare of Staff & Workers not On-post(10 000 yuan)	**858 471.6**	**997 655.8**	**1 136 250.0**	**1 358 726.3**	**1 672 527.2**
#国有单位 State-owned Units	692 157.4	775 335.7	864 488.0	1 075 570.6	1 303 996.9
在职职工人均保险福利费(元) Per Capita Insurance Welfare of On-post Staff & Workers(yuan)	**1 218**	**1 039**	**1 246**	**1 539**	**1 369**
国有单位 State-owned Units	1 399	1 079	1 432	1 864	1 699
集体单位 Collective-owned Units	342	350	373	1 460	663
其他单位 Others	1 285	1 224	1 175	1 044	1 034
非在职职工人均保险福利费(元) Per Capita Insurance Welfare of Staff & Workers not On-post(yuan)	**8 705**	**9 127**	**10 270**	**11 513**	**12 809**
#国有单位 State-owned Units	9 612	10 094	11 281	12 954	13 791

注:1.本资料来源于市劳动和社会保障局、民政局。2.非在职职工保险福利费不含民政部门支付。
Note:a)Data are gotten from Tianjin Municipal Labour & Social Insurance Bureau and Tianjin Municipal Civil Administration Bureau. b)Insurance welfare of staff and workers not on the job exclude those paid by civil administration department.

7-13 职工保险福利费构成(2001-2005年)
COMPOSITION OF INSURANCE WELFARE OF STAFF AND WORKERS,2001-2005

单位:万元 (10 000 yuan)

指标 Item	2001	2002	2003	2004	2005
在职职工 On-post Staff & Workers	**264 423.4**	**221 265.1**	**265 528.4**	**323 589.0**	**2 274 057.7**
集体福利设施、事业补贴费 Collective Welfare Facilities,Insurance Subsidies	42 345.8	40 950.9	46 666.4	43 561.9	37 976.7
文体宣传费 Culture and Sport Expenses	9 229.8	9 088.6	9 300.5	8 833.1	9 287.7
医疗卫生费 Medical,Health Care Expenses	149 881.4	100 772.9	102 014.0	96 968.3	82 265.7
其他 Others	62 966.4	70 452.7	107 547.5	174 225.7	97 875.6
非在职职工 Staff and Workers not On-post	**858 471.6**	**997 655.8**	**1 136 250.0**	**1 358 726.3**	**1 672 527.2**
离休费 Retirement Pay	40 207.5	46 185.6	51 122.5	69 304.2	60 036.0
退休费 Pension Cost	683 579.8	847 180.6	978 888.5	1 158 782.4	1 440 551.5
退职生活费 Resignation Living Fee	4 921.7	7 379.7	7 165.5	7 019.0	
医疗卫生费 Medical,Health Care Expenses	93 045.0	60 589.4	64 498.4	70 006.1	90 251.9
其他 Others	36 717.6	36 320.5	34 575.1	53 614.6	81 687.8

7-14 城市居民家庭人均收支及增幅(1990-2005年)

PER CAPITA INCOME & EXPENDITURES AND INCREASE RATE OF URBAN HOUSEHOLDS,1990-2005

年份 Year	人均年可支配收入(元) Per Capita Annual Disposable Income (yuan)	人均年消费性支出(元) Per Capita Annual Expenditures for Consumption (yuan)	人均收入增幅(%) Increase Rate of Per Capita Disposable Income (%)	人均支出增幅(%) Increase Rate of Per Capita Expenditures for Consumption (%)	扣除物价人均收入增幅(%) Increase Rate of Per Capita Disposable Income After Deducting Price Factor (%)	扣除物价人均支出增幅(%) Increase Rate of Per Capita Expenditures for Consumption After Deducting Price Factor (%)
1990	1 638.92	1 440.47	10.9	11.6	7.7	8.3
1991	1 844.98	1 585.71	12.6	10.1	2.2	-0.1
1992	2 238.38	1 907.17	21.3	20.3	8.9	8.0
1993	2 769.26	2 322.19	23.7	21.8	5.2	3.6
1994	3 982.13	3 301.37	43.8	42.2	16.0	14.7
1995	4 929.53	4 064.10	23.8	23.1	7.4	6.8
1996	5 967.71	4 679.61	21.1	15.1	11.1	5.6
1997	6 608.56	5 204.29	10.7	11.2	7.4	7.9
1998	7 110.54	5 471.01	7.6	5.1	8.1	5.6
1999	7 649.83	5 851.53	7.6	7.0	8.8	8.1
2000	8 140.55	6 121.07	6.4	4.6	6.8	5.0
2001	8 958.70	6 987.22	10.1	14.2	8.7	12.8
2002	9 337.54	7 191.97	11.6	5.4	12.1	5.8
2003	10 312.91	7 867.53	10.4	9.4	9.4	8.3
2004	11 467.16	8 802.44	11.2	11.9	8.7	9.4
2005	12 638.55	9 653.26	10.2	9.7	8.6	8.0

7-15 城市居民家庭基本情况(2002-2005年)

BASIC INDICATORS OF URBAN HOUSEHOLDS,2002-2005

指标	Item	2002	2003	2004	2005
调查户数(户)	Number of Households Surveyed (household)	1 500	1 500	1 500	1 500
平均每户人口(人)	Average Persons Per Household (person)	3.02	2.99	2.96	2.92
平均每户就业人口(人)	Average Employees Per Household (person)	1.44	1.41	1.47	1.45
平均每户就业面(%)	Percentage of Employment Per Household (%)	47.7	47.2	49.7	49.7
平均每一就业者负担人口(人)	Persons Supported By Each Employee (person)	2.11	2.12	2.01	2.01
居民家庭人均收入(元)	**Per Capita Annual Disposable Income(yuan)**				
家庭总收入	Gross Income per Household	9 838.57	10 971.57	12 279.73	13 563.32
#可支配收入	Average per Capita Disposable Income	9 337.54	10 312.91	11 467.16	12 638.55
工薪收入	Salaries	6 050.77	6 663.54	7 508.72	8 174.64
经营净收入	Net Income from Household Business	463.56	468.96	600.40	665.53
财产性收入	Property Income	124.04	96.41	123.55	148.15
转移性收入	Transferred Income	3 200.19	3 742.66	4 047.06	4 574.99
#养老金或离退休金	Pensions and Retirement Pay	2 333.00	2 851.34	3 126.76	3 376.79
居民家庭人均支出(元)	**Per Capita Annual Expenditures(yuan)**				
家庭总支出	Gross Expenditures Per Household	9 689.20	11 087.99	13 322.83	14 450.32
#消费支出	Average Per Capita Consumption Expenditures	7 191.97	7 867.53	8 802.44	9 653.26
#服务性消费支出	Service Consumption Expenditure	2 031.26	2 125.33	2 502.25	2 798.38

7－16 城市不同收入水平居民家庭基本情况(2005年)

(按平均每人每年可支配收入分组)

BASIC INDICATORS OF URBAN HOUSEHOLDS WITH DIFFERENT INCOME LEVEL,2005

(GROUPED BY PER CAPITA DISPOSABLE INCOME PER YEAR)

项目	Item	调查户数(户) Number of Households Surveyed (household)	平均每户人口(人) Average Persons Per Household (person)	平均每户就业人口(人) Average Employees Per Household (person)	平均每一就业者负担人口(人) Persons Supported by Each Employee (person)
全市	**Total**	**1 500**	**2.92**	**1.45**	**2.01**
1.最低收入户	Lowest Income Households				
(5217.78元以下)	(Below 5217.78 yuan)	150	3.17	1.23	2.58
#更低收入户	Even More Lowest Income Households				
(4373.25元以下)	(Below 4373.25 yuan)	75	3.25	1.23	2.64
2.低收入户	Low Income Households				
(5234.44－6774.77元)	(5234.44－6774.77 yuan)	150	3.25	1.40	2.32
3.中等偏下收入户	Lower Middle Income Households				
(6776.66－9447.50元)	(6776.66－9447.50 yuan)	300	3.04	1.40	2.17
4.中等收入户	Middle Income Households				
(9468.56－12423.87元)	(9468.56－12423.87 yuan)	300	2.85	1.44	1.98
5.中等偏上收入户	Upper Middle Income Households				
(12451.25－17492.80元)	(12451.25－17492.80 yuan)	300	2.80	1.55	1.81
6.高收入户	High Income Households				
(17530.59－22184.00元)	(17530.59－22184.00 yuan)	150	2.77	1.60	1.73
7.最高收入户	Highest Income Households				
(22312.00元以上)	(Over 22312.00 yuan)	150	2.67	1.44	1.85

项目	Item	平均每人年总收入(元) Per Capita Annual Actual Income (yuan)	#平均每人年可支配收入(元) Per Capita Annual Disposable Income (yuan)	平均每人年消费性支出(元) Per Capita Annual Expenditures for Consumption (yuan)	#平均每人年服务性消费支出(元) Per Capita Annual Expenditures for Services (yuan)
全市	**Total**	**13 563.32**	**12 638.55**	**9 653.26**	**2 798.38**
1.最低收入户	Lowest Income Households				
(5217.78元以下)	(Below 5217.78 yuan)	4 457.22	4 161.26	5 061.74	1 455.41
#更低收入户	Even More Lowest Income Households				
(4373.25元以下)	(Below 4373.25 yuan)	3 998.54	3 564.32	4 914.46	1 508.22
2.低收入户	Low Income Households				
(5234.44－6774.77元)	(5234.44－6774.77 yuan)	6 414.50	6 014.21	6 043.08	1 864.48
3.中等偏下收入户	Lower Middle Income Households				
(6776.66－9447.50元)	(6776.66－9447.50 yuan)	8 666.71	8 111.95	7 357.52	1 997.52
4.中等收入户	Middle Income Households				
(9468.56－12423.87元)	(9468.56－12423.87 yuan)	11 651.58	10 889.99	9 127.68	2 526.96
5.中等偏上收入户	Upper Middle Income Households				
(12451.25－17492.80元)	(12451.25－17492.80 yuan)	16 017.04	14 900.52	10 917.44	3 115.45
6.高收入户	High Income Households				
(17530.59－22184.00元)	(17530.59－22184.00 yuan)	21 582.45	19 538.08	13 271.82	4 275.73
7.最高收入户	Highest Income Households				
(22312.00元以上)	(Over 22312.00 yuan)	34 921.05	33 003.13	19 467.67	5 736.42

7－17 城市居民家庭平均每人全年消费性支出分类(2005年)

THE CLASSIFICATION OF PER CAPITA ANNUAL EXPENDITURES FOR CONSUMPTION OF URBAN HOUSEHOLDS,2005

单位:元 (yuan)

项 目	Item	总平均 Average	最低收入 10% Lowest Income (10 percent)	低收入 10% Low Income (10 percent)	中等偏下收入 20% Lower Middle Income (20 percent)
消费性支出	**Total Expenditures for Consumption**	**9 653.26**	**5 061.74**	**6 043.08**	**7 357.52**
一、食 品	Food	3 542.90	2 483.47	2 697.62	3 121.69
(一)粮油类	Grain and Oil	415.01	392.17	375.65	408.73
1.粮 食	Grain	257.99	254.79	235.93	260.26
2.淀粉及薯类	Starches and Tubers	34.41	31.87	31.30	32.36
3.干豆类及豆制品	Beans and Bean Products	35.00	27.06	31.55	33.07
4.油脂类	Oil and Fats	87.60	78.45	76.87	83.03
(二)肉禽蛋水产品类	Meat,Poultry,Egg and Aquatic Products	949.68	762.12	785.70	894.96
1.肉 类	Meat	453.68	368.80	405.49	439.50
2.禽 类	Poultry	93.52	65.11	79.10	93.05
3.蛋 类	Eggs	115.45	138.75	99.23	111.88
4.水产品类	Aquatic Products	287.03	189.45	201.87	250.53
(三)蔬菜类	Vegetables	270.39	225.06	238.14	252.93
(四)调味品	Condiments	61.62	49.35	52.62	59.65
(五)糖烟酒饮料类	Sugar,Tobacco,Liquor and Beverages	378.89	195.67	249.66	316.47
1.糖 类	Sugar	29.98	17.64	21.46	25.92
2.烟草类	Tobacco	144.56	79.29	93.31	137.16
3.酒 类	Liquor	113.39	53.46	75.05	88.73
4.饮 料	Beverages	90.96	45.27	59.84	64.67
(六)干鲜瓜果类	Dry and Fresh Melons and Fruits	282.58	176.56	204.55	242.25
(七)糕点、奶及奶制品	Cake,Milk and Related Products	257.07	177.27	189.44	215.73
(八)其他食品	Other Food	80.06	56.63	51.09	61.79
(九)饮食服务	Dining	847.60	448.58	550.77	669.18
#在外饮食	Dining Out	847.23	448.41	550.37	668.74
二、衣 着	Clothing	698.91	235.79	318.08	452.29
#服 装	Garments	488.89	151.24	213.81	308.22
衣着材料	Clothing Materials	11.52	3.55	5.18	8.53
鞋 类	Shoes	160.05	65.28	76.93	107.68
衣着加工服务费	Tailoring and Laundering Service Fees	7.95	1.45	3.42	4.42
三、家庭设备、用品及服务	Household Facilities,Articles and Services	524.20	163.31	253.50	313.94
#耐用消费品	Durable Consumer Goods	294.67	72.69	103.07	153.46
室内装饰品	Room Decorations	25.89	1.30	6.90	10.83
家庭服务	Household Services	37.47	7.88	24.16	17.28
四、医疗保健	Medicine and Medical Services	996.35	412.78	514.77	801.24
五、交通与通讯	Transport and Communication Services	998.01	311.39	381.42	630.64
六、娱乐、教育、文化服务	Recreation,Education and Cultural Services	1 283.70	862.04	1 057.31	969.85
#文化娱乐用品	Cultural and Recreational Articles	382.50	122.54	170.04	260.76
七、居 住	Residence	1 291.60	513.91	665.56	889.53
#燃 料	Fuels	119.67	106.01	108.09	112.39
八、杂项商品与服务	Miscellaneous Commodities and Services	317.58	79.11	154.83	178.33

7－17 续表 Continued
单位:元 (yuan)

项目	Item	中等收入 20% Middle Income (20 percent)	中等偏上收入 20% Upper Middle Income (20 percent)	高收入 10% High Income (10 percent)	最高收入 10% Highest Income (10 percent)
消费性支出	**Total Expenditures for Consumption**	**9 127.68**	**10 917.44**	**13 271.82**	**19 467.67**
一、食　品	Food	3 520.33	4 019.36	4 284.15	5 047.29
(一)粮油类	Grain and Oil	421.42	438.47	427.57	427.76
1.粮　食	Grain	257.67	270.48	255.35	260.75
2.淀粉及薯类	Starches and Tubers	36.22	36.41	35.99	36.23
3.干豆类及豆制品	Beans and Bean Products	35.42	36.30	43.14	40.53
4.油脂类	Oil and Fats	92.11	95.29	93.09	90.25
(二)肉禽蛋水产品类	Meat,Poultry,Egg and Aquatic Products	989.96	1 050.47	1 025.93	1 114.69
1.肉　类	Meat	466.92	495.06	461.16	519.21
2.禽　类	Poultry	97.25	103.01	100.05	109.70
3.蛋　类	Eggs	115.05	116.76	113.28	118.48
4.水产品类	Aquatic Products	310.74	335.64	351.45	367.30
(三)蔬菜类	Vegetables	278.59	290.84	300.39	310.21
(四)调味品	Condiments	64.12	68.05	66.36	67.30
(五)糖烟酒饮料类	Sugar,Tobacco,Liquor and Beverages	379.15	433.58	467.11	687.53
1.糖　类	Sugar	29.36	35.12	38.14	45.97
2.烟草类	Tobacco	152.11	160.70	150.86	244.24
3.酒　类	Liquor	103.66	127.90	155.04	234.19
4.饮　料	Beverages	94.02	109.86	123.07	163.12
(六)鲜瓜果类	Dry and Fresh Melons and Fruits	292.04	330.43	371.59	378.45
(七)糕点、奶及奶制品	Cake,Milk and Related Products	270.60	287.31	346.88	340.75
(八)其他食品	Other Food	74.02	94.76	108.97	137.17
(九)饮食服务	Dining	750.44	1 025.45	1 169.35	1 583.43
#在外饮食	Dining Out	750.19	1 024.92	1 168.88	1 583.26
二、衣　着	Clothing	624.17	890.78	1 266.99	1 431.35
#服　装	Garments	429.23	626.51	897.79	1 043.55
衣着材料	Clothing Materials	9.98	15.17	16.59	25.71
鞋　类	Shoes	150.50	201.92	284.97	293.55
衣着加工服务费	Tailoring and Laundering Service Fees	6.85	11.48	12.11	19.76
三、家庭设备、用品及服务	Household Facilities,Articles and Services	447.28	508.31	980.13	1 492.99
#耐用消费品	Durable Consumer Goods	254.85	251.87	570.74	1 011.93
室内装饰品	Room Decorations	17.10	33.94	49.56	90.13
家庭服务	Household Services	23.40	36.97	109.17	90.33
四、医疗保健	Medicine and Medical Services	1 048.24	1 258.90	1 426.63	1 593.41
五、交通与通讯	Transport and Communication Services	835.38	1 171.71	1 160.26	3 250.03
六、娱乐、教育、文化服务	Recreation,Education and Cultural Services	1 093.45	1 402.59	2 000.05	2 180.32
#文化娱乐用品	Cultural and Recreational Articles	340.08	451.68	610.37	936.49
七、居　住	Residence	1 239.20	1 343.53	1 603.57	3 607.53
#燃　料	Fuels	129.77	116.80	111.04	161.34
八、杂项商品与服务	Miscellaneous Commodities and Services	319.64	322.26	550.05	864.75

7-18 城市居民家庭平均每人主要消费品全年购买量(2005年)

PER CAPITA ANNUAL PURCHASES OF MAJOR CONSUMER GOODS OF URBAN HOUSEHOLDS,2005

商品名称	Item	单位	Unit	总平均 Average	最低收入 10% Lowest Income (10 percent)	低收入 10% Low Income (10 percent)	中等偏下收入 20% Lower Middle Income (20 percent)
粮食	Grain	公斤	kg	81.41	83.72	74.65	85.13
淀粉及薯类	Starches and Tubers	公斤	kg	16.52	16.13	15.61	16.12
油脂类	Oil and Fats	公斤	kg	8.74	8.70	8.35	8.76
#食用植物油	Edible Vegetable Oil	公斤	kg	8.72	8.67	8.31	8.73
肉类	Meat	公斤	kg	28.12	23.45	25.67	27.92
#猪肉	Pork	公斤	kg	17.28	14.66	16.51	17.49
牛肉	Beef	公斤	kg	3.37	3.22	2.64	3.17
羊肉	Mutton	公斤	kg	3.37	2.70	2.99	3.47
禽类	Poultry	公斤	kg	6.00	4.45	5.45	6.12
#鸡	Chicken	公斤	kg	3.46	2.99	3.45	3.59
蛋类	Eggs	公斤	kg	19.77	24.21	17.14	19.30
#鲜蛋	Fresh Eggs	公斤	kg	18.48	23.14	16.08	17.97
鱼	Fish	公斤	kg	9.59	7.51	7.89	9.44
虾	Shrimp	公斤	kg	4.28	2.82	3.18	3.85
鲜菜	Fresh Vegetables	公斤	kg	132.39	118.49	124.59	131.25
干菜	Dry Vegetables	公斤	kg	0.45	0.24	0.42	0.36
酒类	Liquor	公斤	kg	11.90	6.51	10.10	12.28
#白酒	Wine	公斤	kg	2.45	2.08	2.29	2.62
啤酒	Beer	公斤	kg	9.22	4.31	7.68	9.49
碳酸饮料	Beverages	公斤	kg	4.38	2.32	3.89	3.65
茶叶	Tea	公斤	kg	0.28	0.22	0.24	0.27
鲜果	Fresh Fruits	公斤	kg	46.37	33.42	35.84	40.80
鲜瓜	Fresh Melons	公斤	kg	27.07	18.16	20.74	24.69
糕点	Cake	公斤	kg	6.93	4.86	5.74	6.04
鲜奶	Milk	公斤	kg	23.57	16.34	17.15	19.61
服装	Garments	件	piece	6.08	3.30	3.88	5.06
#男士服装	Men's Clothing	件	piece	2.53	1.44	1.67	2.17
女士服装	Women's Clothing	件	piece	3.08	1.66	1.89	2.59
童装	Children's Clothing	件	piece	0.47	0.20	0.32	0.29
鞋类	Shoes	双	pair	2.29	1.51	1.74	2.08

7-18 续表　Continued

商品名称	Item	单位	Unit	中等收入 20% Middle Income (20 percent)	中等偏上收入 20% Upper Middle Income (20 percent)	高收入 10% High Income (10 percent)	最高收入 10% Highest Income (10 percent)
粮　食	Grain	公斤	kg	82.15	83.82	77.40	76.07
淀粉及薯类	Starches and Tubers	公斤	kg	17.07	17.15	16.23	16.86
油脂类	Oil and Fats	公斤	kg	9.24	9.08	8.34	7.88
#食用植物油	Edible Vegetable Oil	公斤	kg	9.21	9.06	8.32	7.88
肉　类	Meat	公斤	kg	28.79	30.15	27.70	31.71
#猪　肉	Pork	公斤	kg	17.41	18.13	16.23	19.70
牛　肉	Beef	公斤	kg	3.71	3.59	3.88	3.15
羊　肉	Mutton	公斤	kg	3.49	3.78	3.16	3.43
禽　类	Poultry	公斤	kg	6.21	6.52	6.01	6.56
#鸡	Chicken	公斤	kg	3.54	3.50	3.18	3.68
蛋　类	Eggs	公斤	kg	19.60	19.99	19.07	19.83
#鲜　蛋	Fresh Eggs	公斤	kg	18.28	18.69	17.71	18.28
鱼	Fish	公斤	kg	10.23	10.16	9.95	11.45
虾	Shrimp	公斤	kg	4.53	4.96	5.09	5.42
鲜　菜	Fresh Vegetables	公斤	kg	134.79	136.82	137.00	141.17
干　菜	Dry Vegetables	公斤	kg	0.45	0.51	0.81	0.43
酒　类	Liquor	公斤	kg	11.26	12.35	13.40	18.28
#白　酒	Wine	公斤	kg	2.37	2.54	1.99	3.09
啤　酒	Beer	公斤	kg	8.68	9.52	11.00	14.78
碳酸饮料	Beverages	公斤	kg	4.33	4.67	4.53	8.37
茶　叶	Tea	公斤	kg	0.32	0.31	0.28	0.29
鲜　果	Fresh Fruits	公斤	kg	48.94	51.98	57.27	58.26
鲜　瓜	Fresh Melons	公斤	kg	27.14	29.84	35.52	35.69
糕　点	Cake	公斤	kg	7.09	7.49	8.66	9.45
鲜　奶	Milk	公斤	kg	26.90	25.97	30.97	28.97
服　装	Garments	件	piece	5.99	7.56	8.68	8.68
#男士服装	Men's Clothing	件	piece	2.41	3.19	3.67	3.32
女士服装	Women's Clothing	件	piece	3.17	3.72	4.32	4.51
童　装	Children's Clothing	件	piece	0.41	0.65	0.69	0.85
鞋　类	Shoes	双	pair	2.24	2.80	2.74	2.87

7-19 城市居民家庭平均每百户主要消费品全年购买量(2001-2005年)

PER 100 URBAN HOUSEHOLDS ANNUAL PURCHASES OF MAJOR CONSUMER GOODS,2001-2005

商品名称	Item	2001	2002	2003	2004	2005
摩托车(辆)	Motorcycle(unit)	0.2	0.3	0.2	0.2	0.1
自行车(辆)	Bicycle(unit)	13.8	18.9	19.7	18.8	21.1
助力车(辆)	Helping Hand Car(unit)		0.9	2.9	4.1	4.7
家用汽车(辆)	Automobile (unit)	0.2	0.3	0.5	0.5	1.0
电风扇(台)	Electric Fan(unit)	4.4	5.3	6.4	3.7	6.6
洗衣机(台)	Washing Machine(unit)	5.6	4.8	6.8	6.1	5.8
电冰箱(台)	Refrigerator(unit)	6.4	5.7	4.9	5.2	5.2
冰　柜(台)	Freezer(unit)	0.6	0.9	0.5	0.2	0.5
彩色电视机(台)	Color TV Set(unit)	9.0	9.9	6.8	8.6	7.0
影碟机(台)	Video Disc Player(unit)	3.6	4.7	4.4	5.3	4.7
录放像机(台)	Videorecorder(unit)		0.1	0.2	0.2	0.2
摄像机(台)	Pickup Camera (unit)		0.1	0.1	0.5	0.6
组合音响(台)	Hi-Fi Stereo Component System(unit)	1.2	1.5	1.1	0.7	0.8
收录机(台)	Recorder(unit)	3.6	6.9	6.4	5.4	3.4
家用电脑(台)	Micro-Computer(unit)	5.2	5.7	5.6	5.3	5.9
照像机(架)	Camera(set)	1.6	1.1	1.1	2.3	1.7
微波炉(台)	Microwave Oven(unit)	11.2	6.3	7.0	4.6	3.7
空调器(台)	Air-conditioner(unit)	7.6	6.7	6.7	5.9	7.1
电炊具(台)	Electric Cooking Appliance(unit)	9.4	8.7	9.5	7.4	7.2
淋浴热水器(台)	Shower (unit)	6.8	6.9	6.2	6.8	6.6
排油烟机(台)	Smoke Absorber(unit)	4.8	5.1	6.2	5.0	4.9
吸尘器(台)	Dust Catcher(unit)	1.2	1.5	1.9	1.0	0.7
移动电话(部)	Mobile Telephone(unit)		11.9	22.0	22.3	18.8

7－20 城市居民家庭平均每百户耐用消费品年末拥有量(2001－2005年)
PER 100 URBAN HOUSEHOLDS YEAR－END POSSESSIONS OF MAJOR DURABLE CONSUMER GOODS,2001－2005

商品名称	Item	2001	2002	2003	2004	2005
成套家具(套)	Composite Furniture(set)	75.0	85.0	91.9	98.5	95.7
摩托车(辆)	Motorcycle (unit)	9.6	8.5	8.9	8.5	8.1
自行车(辆)	Bicycle (unit)	239.0	226.1	228.5	222.4	202.4
助力车(辆)	Helping Hand Car(unit)		2.1	4.4	7.4	11.1
家用汽车(辆)	Automobile (unit)	0.2	1.2	2.2	2.3	3.0
电风扇(台)	Electric Fan(unit)	132.6	118.7	119.9	114.6	95.8
洗衣机(台)	Washing Machine(unit)	95.6	96.0	96.3	95.9	109.1
电冰箱(台)	Refrigerator(unit)	102.6	102.1	98.5	98.9	97.8
冰　柜(台)	Freezer(unit)	19.2	18.0	16.7	16.8	14.5
彩色电视机(台)	Color TV Set(unit)	134.0	135.0	134.5	136.5	136.3
影碟机(台)	Video Disc Player(unit)	41.0	45.1	49.6	55.3	56.1
录放像机(台)	Video－recorder(unit)	31.8	30.4	30.3	28.0	24.2
摄像机(台)	Pickup Camera (unit)	2.0	2.7	3.4	3.9	5.7
组合音响(台)	Hi－Fi Stereo Component System(unit)	21.4	25.1	26.8	28.9	28.8
收录机(台)	Tape Recorder(unit)	68.4	55.7	56.8	54.7	46.2
家用电脑(台)	Micro－Computer(unit)	21.2	26.3	34.1	41.2	51.1
照像机(架)	Camera(unit)	59.6	60.0	56.3	54.3	52.5
钢　琴(架)	Piano(unit)	0.6	1.5	1.4	1.1	1.3
微波炉(台)	Microwave Oven(unit)	43.0	51.1	61.4	68.9	74.3
空调器(台)	Air－conditioner(unit)	73.8	80.9	90.9	95.3	102.1
电炊具(台)	Electric Cooking Appliance(unit)	95.4	91.9	101.1	103.0	97.3
淋浴热水器(台)	Shower(unit)	78.6	79.0	82.7	85.8	86.5
排油烟机(台)	Smoke Absorber(unit)	74.8	75.9	82.4	87.1	85.1
吸尘器(台)	Dust Catcher(unit)	22.0	21.1	24.3	26.7	24.7
移动电话(部)	Mobile Telephone(unit)	21.2	45.2	77.8	107.1	122.1

7－21　农村居民家庭基本情况(2002－2005年)
BASIC INDICATORS OF RURAL HOUSEHOLDS,2002－2005

项　目	Item	单　位	Unit	2002	2003	2004	2005
户均常住人口	Average Permanent Residents Per Household	人	person	3.64	3.60	3.56	3.55
#劳动力	Labors Per Household	人	person	2.46	2.44	2.41	2.49
平均每个劳动力负担人口	Dependents Per Labor	人	person	1.48	1.48	1.48	1.42
年末户均生产性固定资产原值	Year－end Productive Original Value of Fixed Assets Per Household	元	yuan	7 728	7 051	8 311	10 150
#役畜、产品畜	Draught Animals and Commodity Animals	元	yuan	779	729	469	515
大中型铁木农具	Large and Medium Wood and Iron Farm Tools	元	yuan	335	263	363	162
农林牧渔业机械	Machinery for Farming,Forestry,Animal Husbandry and Fishery	元	yuan	1 375	1 300	1 480	1 910
户均经营耕地面积	Cultivated Land Areas Per Household	公顷	hectare	0.34	0.31	0.32	0.32
年内人均新建住房面积	New Living Space Per Capita in Current Year	平方米	sq.m	0.42	0.29	0.31	0.73
年末人均住房面积	Year－end Living Space Per Capita	平方米	sq.m	24.33	24.44	25.22	26.06
全年人均纯收入	Annual Net Income Per Capita	元	yuan	5 315	5 861	6 525	7 202
全年人均生活消费支出	Per Capita Living Expenditures	元	yuan	2 778	3 015	3 297	3 590
年末百户生产性固定资产拥有量	Year－end Productive Original Value of Fixe Assets Per Household						
汽　车	Motor Vehicles	辆	set	6.50	5.83	5.50	6.67
大中型拖拉机	Large and Medium Tractors	台	set	1.67	1.67	2.50	1.67
小型和手扶拖拉机	Mini－tractors	台	set	25.67	22.33	21.67	18.00
水　泵	Pumps	台	set	20.88	18.67	19.25	19.00

7－22　农村居民家庭劳动力文化程度(2002－2005年)
EDUCATION LEVEL OF LABORS IN RURAL HOUSEHOLDS,2002－2005

单位:人　　(person)

项　目	Item	2002	2003	2004	2005
每百个劳动力中:	In Per 100 Labors:				
不识字或识字很少	Illiterate or Semi－illiterate	1.69	1.65	1.64	1.64
小　学	Primary School	28.01	25.37	24.65	18.08
初　中	Junior Middle School	54.94	55.84	53.13	59.68
高　中	Senior Middle School	10.49	11.13	14.78	13.90
中　专	Specialized Secondary School	3.65	4.64	4.35	4.89
大专及以上	Junior College	1.22	1.37	1.45	1.81

7-23 农村居民人均纯收入
PER CAPITA NET INCOME OF FARMER

单位:元 (yuan)

项 目	Item	2003	2004	2005	2005比2004年增长% Increase Rate in 2005 over 2004
人均纯收入	**Per Capita Annual Net Income**	**5 861**	**6 525**	**7 202**	**10.4**
1.工资性收入	Rewards of Labours	3 248	3 579	3 840	7.3
#在非企业组织中劳动得到	From Collective Organization	676	710	684	-3.7
在本地企业中劳动得到	From Labour In Local Enterprises	2 143	2 366	2 512	6.2
#从乡镇集体企业中劳动得到	From Collective Enterprises	937	882	654	-25.9
2.家庭经营纯收入	Income from Family Busines	2 349	2 604	2 959	13.6
#农 业	Planting	1 178	1 316	1 399	6.3
畜牧业	Animal Husbandry	166	192	191	-0.5
采矿业和制造业	Minerals Mining and Manufacturing	26	29	38	31.0
建筑业	Construction	165	147	182	23.8
交通运输、仓储和邮政业	Transportation,Post and Telecommunications	231	277	371	33.9
批发和零售业	Wholesale,Retail & Catering Trade	106	121	165	36.4
住宿和餐饮业	Accommodation Catering Service	55	62	82	32.3
3.转移性、财产性纯收入	Transfer and Property Income	264	342	403	17.8

7-24 农村居民人均纯收入构成
COMPOSITION OF PER CAPITA NET INCOME OF FARMER

单位:% (%)

项 目	Item	2003	2004	2005
人均纯收入	**Per Capita Annual Net Income**	**100**	**100**	**100**
1.工资性收入	Rewards of Labours	55.4	54.9	53.3
#在非企业组织中劳动得到	From Collective Organization	11.5	10.9	9.5
在本地企业中劳动得到	From Labour In Local Enterprises	36.6	36.3	34.9
#从乡镇集体企业中劳动得到	From Collective Enterprises	16.0	13.5	9.1
2.家庭经营纯收入	Income from Family Busines	40.1	39.9	41.1
#农 业	Planting	20.1	20.2	19.4
畜牧业	Animal Husbandry	2.8	2.9	2.7
采矿业和制造业	Minerals Mining and Manufacturing	0.4	0.4	0.5
建筑业	Construction	2.8	2.3	2.5
交通运输、仓储和邮政业	Transportation,Post and Telecommunications	3.9	4.2	5.2
批发和零售业	Wholesale,Retail & Catering Trade	1.8	1.9	2.3
住宿和餐饮业	Accommodation Catering Service	0.9	1.0	1.1
3.转移性、财产性纯收入	Transfer and Property Income	4.5	5.2	5.6

7-25 农村居民人均生活消费支出
PER CAPITA ANNUAL LIVING EXPENDITURES OF FARMER

单位:元 (yuan)

项目	Item	2003	2004	2005	2005比2004年增长% Increase Rate in 2005 over 2004
人均生活消费支出	**Per Capita Annual Living Expenditures**	**3 015**	**3 297**	**3 590**	**8.9**
食品	Food	1 156	1 270	1 376	8.3
衣着	Clothing	266	294	362	23.1
居住	Residence	694	757	844	11.5
家庭设备、用品及服务	Household Facilities, Articles and Services	105	117	108	-7.7
医疗保健	Medicine and Medical Services	230	260	268	3.1
交通通讯	Transportation and Communications	216	241	270	12.0
文教娱乐用品及服务	Culture, Education and Recreation Articles and Services	246	248	252	1.6
其他商品和服务	Other Commodities and Services	102	110	110	

7-26 农村居民人均生活消费支出构成
COMPOSITION OF PER CAPITA LIVING EXPENDITURES OF FARMER

单位:% (%)

项目	Item	2003	2004	2005
人均生活消费支出	**Per Capita Annual Living Expenditure**	**100**	**100**	**100**
食品	Food	38.3	38.5	38.3
衣着	Clothing	8.8	8.9	10.1
居住	Residence	23.0	23.0	23.5
家庭设备、用品及服务	Household Facilities, Articles & Services	3.5	3.6	3.0
医疗保健	Medicine and Medical Services	7.6	7.9	7.5
交通通讯	Transportation and Communications	7.2	7.3	7.5
文教娱乐用品及服务	Culture, Education and Recreation Articles and Services	8.2	7.5	7.0
其他商品和服务	Other Commodities and Services	3.4	3.3	3.1

7－27　农村居民家庭每百户耐用消费品年末拥有量(2001－2005年)
PER 100 RURAL HOUSEHOLDS YEAR－END POSSESSIONS OF DURABLE CONSUMER GOODS,2001－2005

商品名称	Item	2001	2002	2003	2004	2005
自行车(辆)	Bicycle(unit)	200	204	198	191	183
电动自行车(辆)	Bicycle(unit)		2	3	4	8
摩托车(辆)	Motorcycle(unit)	40	41	45	49	50
生活用汽车(辆)	Car(unit)	2	3	3	4	6
电风扇(台)	Electric Fan(set)	182	180	171	158	137
空调器(台)	Air－Conditioner(set)	20	26	32	36	42
洗衣机(台)	Washing Machine(set)	90	86	90	92	95
电冰箱(台)	Refrigerator(set)	66	72	75	78	84
微波炉(台)	Oven(unit)	4	7	10	12	16
吸尘器(台)	Dust Catcher(unit)	5	5	6	6	6
热水器(台)	Shower(set)			15	21	32
抽油烟机(台)	Smoke Absorbet(set)			12	14	18
移动电话(部)	Mobile Telephone(unit)	19	36	54	65	89
家用电脑(台)	Micro－Computers(unit)	3	5	7	8	10
彩色电视机(台)	Color TV Set(set)	103	105	110	115	116
照相机(架)	Camera(set)	19	20	20	20	20
影碟机(台)	Video Disc Player(set)	24	27	31	33	40
收录机(台)	Tape Recorders(set)	21	19	19	18	19
摄像机(台)	Vidicon(set)			1	1	1

7－28　农村居民人均食品消费量(2001－2005年)
PER CAPITA ANNUAL CONSUMPTION ON FOOD OF RURAL HOUSEHOLDS,2001－2005

单位:千克　　(kg)

商品名称	Item	2001	2002	2003	2004	2005
粮　食	Grain	207.4	199.0	195.0	182.3	173.5
蔬菜及其制品	Vegetables and Related Products	117.5	132.4	134.3	136.4	124.7
食用植物油	Vegetable Oil	9.2	10.8	9.3	9.4	9.4
食用动物油	Animal Oil	1.0	0.9	0.7	0.5	0.3
猪　肉	Pork	8.9	8.9	9.4	9.3	9.8
牛　肉	Beef	0.9	0.6	0.7	0.9	1.0
羊　肉	Mutton	1.0	1.1	1.0	1.1	1.2
家　禽	Poultry	0.9	1.1	1.1	0.9	0.7
肉禽制品	Meat,Poultry and Related Products	0.6	0.9	1.2	1.1	1.1
蛋类及其制品	Eggs and Related Products	12.0	14.4	16.6	18.0	17.4
奶及其制品	Milk and Related Products	1.0	1.3	1.9	2.4	3.4
水产品	Aquatic Products	7.3	8.7	9.4	10.2	12.8
水果及其制品	Fruits and Related Products	28.6	30.2	30.1	31.4	28.8
食　糖	Sugar	1.2	2.0	1.1	0.7	0.6
白　酒	wine	3.2	3.3	3.2	3.1	3.5
啤　酒	Beer	8.1	7.3	7.0	7.3	7.3

主要统计指标解释

城镇单位从业人员劳动报酬　是指各单位在一定时期内直接支付给本单位全部从业人员的劳动报酬总额。包括在岗职工工资总额和本单位其他从业人员劳动报酬两部分。

在岗职工工资总额　指各单位在一定时期内直接支付给本单位在岗职工的全部劳动报酬总额。在岗职工工资总额构成包括:计时工资(含计时标准工资)、计件工资、奖金、计件超额工资、津贴和补贴、加班加点工资、特殊情况下支付的工资等。

其他从业人员劳动报酬　指各单位在一定时期内直接支付给本单位其他从业人员的全部劳动报酬。包括支付给再就业的离退休人员的劳动报酬和民办教师、港澳台和外籍人员的劳动报酬总额。还包括支付给聘用的外单位不在岗人员、聘用的失业人员、聘用和使用的外来人员、聘用的在本单位从事第二职业人员的劳动报酬。

职工保险福利费总额　指各单位在工资以外实际支付给职工个人和用于集体的劳动保险福利费用总额。

城市居民家庭就业人口　指从事社会劳动并取得报酬或经营收入的人口,不论在全民、集体和其他所有制单位工作或从事个体劳动,不论有固定性职业或临时性职业都是就业人口。

城市居民家庭总收入　指城市居民家庭中生活在一起的所有家庭成员在调查期得到的工薪收入、经营净收入、财产性收入、转移性收入的总和,不包括出售财物收入和借贷收入。收入的统计标准以实际发生的数额为准,无论收入是补发还是预发,只要是调查期得到的都应如实计算,不作分摊。

城市居民家庭可支配收入　指城市居民家庭可用于最终消费支出和其他非义务性支出以及储蓄的总和,即居民家庭可以用来自由支配的收入。它是家庭总收入扣除交纳的所得税、个人交纳的社会保障费以及调查户的记帐收入补贴后的收入。计算公式为:

可支配收入＝家庭总收入－交纳所得税－个人交纳的社会保障支出－记帐补贴

城市居民家庭消费支出　指城市居民家庭用于本家庭日常生活消费需要的全部支出,包括食品、衣着、家庭设备用品及服务、医疗保健、交通和通讯、娱乐教育文化服务、居住、杂项商品和服务等八大类。

城市居民家庭服务性消费支出　指城市居民家庭用于本家庭支付社会提供的各种文化和生活方面的非商品性服务费用。不包括为别人付款的服务费用。

农村居民常住人口　指全年经常在家或在家居住六个月以上,而且经济和生活与本户连成一体的人口。外出从业人员在外居住时间虽然在六个月以上,但收入主要带回家中,经济与本户连成一体,仍视为家庭常住人口;在家居住、生活和本户连成一体的国家职工、退休人员也视为家庭常住人口。但是现役军人、中专及以上(走读生除外)的在校学生、以及常年在外(不包括探亲、看病等)且已有稳定的职业与居住场所的外出从业人员,不应当作为家庭常住人口。

农村居民纯收入　指农村住户当年从各个来源得到的总收入相应地扣除所发生的费用后的收入总和。纯收入主要用于再生产投入和当年生活消费支出,也可用于储蓄和各种非义务性支出。计算公式为:

农村居民纯收入＝总收入－家庭经营费用支出－税费支出—生产性固定资产折旧－农村亲友赠送

农村居民工资性收入　指农村住户成员受雇于单位或个人,靠出卖劳动而获得的收入。包括:

(1)在非企业组织中劳动得到的收入:指农村住户成员在不具备企业性质的行政事业单位和各种组织中劳动得到的收入。包括村干部和民办教师的工资(奖金、补贴),乡及以上行政、事业单位工作人员的工资(奖金、补贴)等。

(2)在本地劳动得到的收入:指农村住户成员在所属乡(镇)地域范围内受雇于单位或个人,靠出卖劳动而获得的收入。

(3)常住人口外出从业得到的收入:指农村住户成员到住户所属乡镇地域范围以外从业得到的收入。

农村居民家庭经营收入　指农村住户以家庭为生产经营单位进行生产筹划和管理而获得的收入。家庭经营活动按行业划分为农业、林业、畜牧业、渔业、工业、建筑业、交通运输和邮电业、批发和零售贸易餐饮业、社会服务业、文教卫生业和其他家庭经营。

农村居民财产性收入　指金融资产或有形非生产性资产的所有者向其他机构单位提供资金或将有形非生产性资产供其支配,作为回报而从中获得的收入。包括利息收入、股息收入、租金收入、土地征用补偿收入等。

农村居民转移性收入　指农村住户和住户成员无须付出任何对应物而获得的货物、服务、资金或资产所有权等，不包括无偿提供的用于固定资本形成的资金。一般情况下，指农村住户在二次分配中的所有收入。包括家庭非常住人口寄回或带回、城市亲友赠送、农村亲友赠送等。

农村居民生活消费支出 指农村住户用于物质生活和精神生活方面的支出。包括食品，衣着，居住，家庭设备、用品及服务，医疗保健，交通和通讯，文化教育娱乐用品及服务，其他商品和服务等消费支出。

Explanatory Notes on Main Statistical Indicators

Reward of Employment Personnel Worked in Urban Units refer to total reward payment of employment personnel worked in units during a certain period. It includes total wages of working staff and workers and reward of other employment personnel.

Total Wages of Working Staff and Workers refer to the total reward payment to working staff and workers in their units during a certain period of time. It includes time wage, piece wage, cash awards, exceed wage, subsidy, working overtime wage and other special wage.

Total Reward Payment to Other Employment Personnel refers to the total reward payment to other persons employed in their units during a certain period of time. It includes reward payment to re－employed retirees, teachers in schools run by the local people, foreigners and Chinese compatriots from HongKong, Macao, and Taiwan working in various units, employees of other units working temporarily at current posts, unemployment personnel, non－locals, and employees holding the second job of other unit.

Total Insurance Welfare Funds of Staff and Workers refer to the total labour insurance welfare funds payment to every staff and worker in various units and collective of the units.

Employment Personnel of Urban Households refer to the persons who are engaged in social labor and receive payment or earn business income, including the staff and workers in the state－owned, the staff and workers in collective－owned, other employed, employed persons individual business, etc. No matter he is permanent or temporary.

Total Income of Urban Households refers to the total income of the sample households, including wage, income from business, income from property, transfer income, excluding proceeds from sales of belongings and credit income. It is calculated on real income, no matter the income is supplied again or beforehand.

Disposable Income of Urban Households refers to the disposable income of the sample households, including those which can be used for final expenditure and other non－obligation expenditure and savings. It refers to the difference of total income minus income tax, expenditure for social security and subsidies of account. The following formula is used

Disposable Income of Urban Households = Total Income－Income Tax－Expenditure for Social Security －Survey Subsidies

Expenditure for Consumption of Urban Households refers to total expenditure of the sample households for consumption in daily life. It is classified into 8 categories food, clothing, household facilities and articles service, medicine and medical service, transportation and communication, recreation, education and culture service, residence, miscellaneous commodities services.

Service Expenditure for Consumption of Urban Households refers to total non－commodity expenditure of the sample households for consumption in culture and life. It excludes service expenditure paid for other persons.

Rural Permanent Resident Population refers to population staying at home permanently or for over 6 months during a year and sharing life economically with the household. Members of the household staying away from the household for over 6 months but keeping a close economic life with the household by sending the majority of income to the household are regarded as resident population of the household. Government staff and workers or retirees living as close members of the household are also considered as resident population. However, servicemen, students of secondary technical schools or schools of higher education and persons with stable jobs and residence outside the household (excluding those visiting relatives or seeking medical service) are not included as resident population of the household.

Net Income of Rural Households refers to the total income of the rural households after the deduction of the expenses for the various cost, which can then be spent for investment in reproduction, expenditure for living consumption, saving, non – productive construction. The formula for calculating is as follows:

Net Income of Rural Households = Total Income – Expenses for Productive Operation – Taxes – Depreciation of Fixed Assets for Production – Gifts to Relatives

Income from Wages and Salaries of Rural Households refers to income from labour earned by members of rural households employed by other units or individuals. It includes:

(a) Income by members of rural households employed by administration business units and social organizations, including wages (Cash awards and subsidy) of village staff and teachers in schools run by the local people, wages (Cash awards and subsidy) of staff employed by administration business units at township and higher level.

(b) Income earned at local region income from labour earned by members of rural households employed by other units or individuals at local township.

(c) Income of permanent residence outside the household income from labour earned by members of rural households employed by other units or individuals at outside local region.

Income of Productive Operation of Rural Households refers to income obtained from family productive operation. Family productive operation cover farming, forestry, animal husbandry, fishery, industry, construction, transport, post, telecommunication, wholesale and retail trade, catering, social services, culture, education, health care and other household operation.

Property Income of Rural Households refers to the income received as returns by owners of financial assets or tangible non – productive assets by providing capital or tangible non – productive assets to other institutional units. It includes interest income, bonus stock income, rent income, compensatory income of collected land.

Transfer Income of Rural Households refers to the receipt by rural households and their members of goods, services, capitals or rights of assets without giving or repaying accordingly, excluding capitals provided to them for the formation of fixed assets. In general, it refers to all income received by rural household through redistribution. It includes income receipt by non – permanent residents, gifts of urban & rural relatives.

Total Income of Rural Households refers to the sum of income earned from various sources by the rural households and their members during the referance period, and is classified as income from wages and salaries, income from household operations, property income and transfer income.

Expenditure on Rural Household Operations refers to expenditure by rural households on goods and services consumed (including own – produced goods) in household – based production or operations. Consumption of own – produced goods which are not included as household income is not considered as expenditure. Chemical fertilizers and pesticides in stock are not included as expenditure of the current period.

Expenditure on Consumption of Rural Households That Expenditure was use on matter life and energy life by rural households, including food expenditure, clothing expenditure, residence, household facilities, articles and services, medicines and medical services, transportation and communications, cultural, education and recreation articles and services, other commodity and services.

第8篇
CHAPTER 8

城市建设和环境保护
Urban Construction and Environment Protection

8-1 城市建设用地
CITY CONSTRUCTION LAND-USED

单位：平方公里 (sq. km)

指　　标	Item	2003	2004	2005
建成区面积	**Developed Area**	**487.47**	**500.14**	**530.00**
市中心区	Central Districts	253.63	257.18	269.05
滨海新区	Binhai New Area	166.24	175.15	188.65
塘沽地区小计	Tanggu District	108.69	117.04	127.26
塘沽城区和天津港	Central District of Tanggu and Tianjin Port	80.69	87.44	93.11
经济技术开发区	TEDA	23.00	24.60	28.86
天津港保税区	TPFTZ	5.00	5.00	5.29
汉沽区	Hangu District	15.60	16.16	16.16
大港区	Dagang District	41.95	41.95	45.23
西青区	Xiqing District	15.40	15.49	15.49
津南区	Jinnan District	6.92	6.94	6.95
武清区	Wuqing District	31.04	31.14	34.95
宝坻区	Baodi District	14.24	14.24	14.91
城市建设用地	**City Construction Land-used**	**487.47**	**500.14**	**530.00**
居住用地	Dwelling	119.81	159.49	167.56
公共设施用地	Public Facilities	51.02	60.08	65.42
工业用地	Industry	116.87	114.90	119.63
仓储用地	Warehouse	34.67	30.34	27.02
对外交通用地	Traffic	20.36	16.96	18.31
道路广场用地	Road and Square	44.16	41.60	43.00
市政公用设施用地	Public Facilities of Municipal Administration	14.07	16.04	19.13
绿　地	Green Land	45.19	48.71	58.25
特殊用地	Special Land	41.32	12.01	11.67

资料来源：天津市建委。
Information Source: Tianjin Municipal Urban & Rural Construction Commission.

8－2 市政公用设施水平
LEVEL OF MUNICIPAL PUBLIC FACILITIES

指标	Item	单位	Unit	2003	2004	2005
城市人口密度	Population Density of Urban Districts	人/平方公里	person/sq.km	841	852	857
人均城市建设维护基金	Per Capita Fund on Urban Construction and Maintenance	元/人	yuan/person	2 219	2 744	2 898
人均住宅建筑面积	Per Capita Floor Space of Residential Buildings	平方米	sq.m	23.10	24.65	24.97
人均日生活用水量	Per Capita Daily Consumption of Tap Water for Residential Use	公斤	kg	131.0	124.9	123.6
用水普及率	Percentage of Population with Access to Tap Water	%	%	100	100	100
每万人拥有公共交通车辆	Number of Public Transportation Vehicles per 10 000 Persons	标台	unit	9.4	10.7	11.2
用气普及率	Percentage of Population with Access to Gas	%	%	97.1	98.5	98.5
人均拥有道路面积	Per Capita Area of Paved Roads	平方米	sq.m	8.8	9.3	10.4
排水管道密度	Density of Drainpipes	公里/平方公里	km/sq.km	18.7	18.7	20.6
污水处理率	Percentage of Sewage Disposed	%	%	43.9	53.7	58.0
人均公共绿地面积	Per Capita Public Green Areas	平方米	sq.m	6.7	8.1	8.4
建成区绿化覆盖率	Coverage Rate of Afforestation in Developed Area	%	%	31.0	35.0	36.4
垃圾粪便无害化处理率	Innocuous Disposal Rate of Garbage, Excrement and Urine	%	%	60.6	61.0	80.5

8－3 城市房屋建筑面积
FLOOR SPACE OF BUILDINGS IN CITY

单位：万平方米 (10 000 sq.m)

项目	Item	2003	2004	2005	2005比2004年增长% Increase Rate in 2005 over 2004
年末实有房屋建筑面积	**Total Floor Space of Buildings (year－end)**	**19 324.10**	**20 902.87**	**22 578.12**	**8.0**
#房管部门直管产	Under House Management Department	3 052.42	2 945.73	2 949.64	0.1
私　产	Private Property	8 564.05	10 178.76	11 089.90	9.0
#物业管理房	Under Products Management	7 300.00	9 628.91	11 505.96	19.5
年末实有住宅建筑面积	**Residential Buildings (year－end)**	**12 575.38**	**13 465.32**	**14 043.16**	**4.3**
#房管部门直管产	Under House Management Department	1 780.52	1 713.28	1 678.62	－2.0
私　产	Private Property	8 093.38	9 050.02	10 120.23	11.8
#物业管理房	Under Products Management	5 957.00	8 256.94	9 938.63	20.4
人均住宅建筑面积(平方米/人)	**Per Capita Floor Space of Residential Buildings (sg.m/person)**	**23.1**	**24.7**	**25.0**	**1.2**

8-4 城市市政设施情况
MUNICIPAL FACILITIES IN CITY

指标	Item	单位	Unit	2003	2004	2005	2005比2004年增长% Increase Rate in 2005 over 2004
年末实有道路	**Road(year-end)**						
铺装道路长度	Length of Paved Roads	公里	km	4 084	4 240	5 460	29.3
铺装道路面积	Area of Paved Roads	万平方米	10^4 sq.m	5 489	5 897	6 669	13.1
#人行道面积	Area of Footway	万平方米	10^4 sq.m	969	1 030	1 070	3.9
年末实有桥梁	**Bridges(year-end)**						
桥梁座数	Number of Bridges	座	unit	490	511	563	10.2
#立交桥	Flyover	座	unit	51	50	66	32.0
年末实有路灯盏数	**Number of Road Lamps(year-end)**	**盏**	**unit**	**178 826**	**181 072**	**175 696**	**-3.0**
排泄污水能力	**Capacity of Sewage Drainage**						
污水年排放量	Annual Volume of Sewage Drainage	万吨	10^4 tons	53 730	55 223	59 484	7.7
排水管道长度	Length of Drainpipes	公里	km	9 124	9 332	10 889	16.7
污水处理厂	Sewage Treatment Works	座	set	3	12	9	-25.0
污水处理厂能力	Disposal Capacity of Sewage Treatment Works	万吨/日	10^4 tons/day	76.0	93.2	157.8	69.3

注:铺装道路含市区公路。
Note:Paved roads include highway of urban areas.

8-5 城市自来水
URBAN TAP WATER

指标	Item	单位	Unit	2003	2004	2005	2005比2004年增长% Increase Rate in 2005 over 2004
综合生产能力	Production Capacity	万吨/日	10^4 tons/day	343.1	338.3	359.0	6.1
供水管道	Length of Water Supply Pipelines	公里	km	6 822	6 781	7 093	4.6
供水总量	Total Annual Volume of Water Supply	万吨	10^4 tons	64 537	64 490	68 236	5.8
售水总量	Total Annual Volume of Water Sold	万吨	10^4 tons	54 758	53 805	60 173	11.8
#生活用水	For Residential Use	万吨	10^4 tons	29 829	28 807	28 885	0.5
生产用水	For Productive Use	万吨	10^4 tons	24 889	24 997	31 430	25.7
用水人口	Number of Residents With Access to Tap Water	万人	10^4 persons	623.9	632.0	640.5	1.3

8－6　城市燃气设备能力、销售量和用气户数
GAS EQUIPMENT, GAS SOLD AND GAS USERS CAPACITY IN CITY

项　目	Item	2003	2004	2005	2005 比2004年增长% Increase Rate in 2005 over 2004
液化石油气	**Liquefied Petroleum Gas**				
储气能力(吨)	Storage Capacity(ton)	14 881	21 524	15 829	－26.5
销售量(吨)	Volume of Gas Sold(ton)	79 736	69 779	61 503	－11.9
工业用	For Industrial Use	36 942	42 347	37 704	－11.0
民　用	For Residential Use	42 794	27 432	23 799	－13.2
用气户数(户)	Gas Users(household)	419 502	422 416	449 511	6.4
工业用	For Industrial Use	11 880	5 323	5 838	9.7
民　用	For Residential Use	407 622	417 093	443 673	6.4
天　然　气	**Natural　Gas**				
储气能力(万立方米)	Storage Capacity(10 000 cu.m)	126.0	120.6	120.4	－0.1
管道长度(公里)	Length of Pipelines(km)	5 380	5 715	6 751	18.1
销售量(万立方米)	Volume of Gas Sold(10 000 cu.m)	41 567	52 710	68 966	30.8
工业用	For Industrial Use	15 630	25 147	26 190	4.1
福利用	For Welfare Use	11 190	11 839	14 568	23.1
民　用	For Residential Use	14 180	15 145	15 465	2.1
用气户数(户)	Gas Users (household)	1 361 443	1 422 495	1 493 271	5.0
工业用	For Industrial Use	148	242	270	11.6
福利用	For Welfare Use	6 678	7 468	7 347	－1.6
民　用	For Residential Use	1 354 617	1 414 785	1 485 654	5.0
煤　制　气	**Coal　Gas**				
储气能力(万立方米)	Storage Capacity(10 000 cu.m)	60.0	60.0	60.0	
管道长度(公里)	Length of Pipelines(km)	1 423	1 432	1 461	2.0
销售量(万立方米)	Volume of Gas Sold(10 000 cu.m)	24 172	23 683	26 078	10.1
#工业用	For Industrial Use	14 820	13 978	16 246	16.2
福利用	For Welfare Use	1 413	1 782	2 052	15.2
民　用	For Residential Use	7 938	7 594	7 421	－2.3
用气户数(户)	Gas Users(household)	334 505	345 450	349 590	1.2
#工业用	For Industrial Use	12	13	12	－7.7
福利用	For Welfare Use	1 135	1 162	1 278	10.0
民　用	For Residential Use	333 358	344 275	348 300	1.2

注：工业用液化石油气数据含福利、商业和其他用。
Note: Volume of liquefied petroleum gas sold for industrial use include those of welfare, commerce and other use.

8-7 城市园林绿化情况
PARKS,GARDENS AND GREEN AREAS IN CITY

指 标	Item	2003	2004	2005	2005比2004年增长% Increase Rate in 2005 over 2004
公 园(含动物园)(个)	Parks (Including Zoo)(unit)	196	186	183	2.0
花 圃(个)	Gardens(unit)	23	13	15	15.4
园林绿地总面积(公顷)	Total Area of Parks,Gardens and Green Areas(hectare)	13 238.8	14 238.1	15 740.7	10.6
#公共绿地	Public Green Area	4 161.3	5 094.4	5 368.6	5.4
#公园面积	Area of Parks	2 829.4	2 424.0	2 325.3	-4.1
花圃面积	Area of Gardens	71.4	63.8	65.8	3.1
专用绿地	Special-purpose Green Area	2 338.4	2 326.0	2 685.0	29.0
年末实有树木(万株)	Trees(year-end)(10 000 trees)	2 386.9	2 714.2	3 106.4	14.4
#行道树	Roadside Trees	171.6	137.2	148.3	8.1
全年植树(万株)	Trees Planted(10 000 trees)	213.0	262.1	122.8	-53.4

8-8 公园分布
DISTRIBUTION OF PARKS

地 区	Region	公园个数(个) Number of Parks(unit)			公园面积(公顷) Area of Parks(hectare)		
		2003	2004	2005	2003	2004	2005
合 计	**Total**	**196**	**186**	**183**	**2 829.4**	**2 424.0**	**2 325.3**
和平区	Heping District	14	14	11	30.9	35.5	12.8
河东区	Hedong District	16	14	14	52.8	45.3	47.9
河西区	Hexi District	28	28	28	136.9	136.9	145.0
南开区	Nankai District	16	14	14	262.2	291.2	294.1
河北区	Hebei District	20	19	19	75.6	73.0	73.0
红桥区	Hongqiao District	25	25	25	51.2	54.4	54.4
塘沽区	Tanggu District	9	9	9	368.6	448.6	475.7
开发区	TEDA District	16	16	16	147.3	144.0	146.4
汉沽区	Hangu District	6	6	6	58.1	56.5	56.5
大港区	Dagang District	6	6	6	757.5	801.6	628.5
东丽区	Dongli District	10	8	8	398.5	22.2	24.0
西青区	Xiqing District	4	1	1	208.5		0.2
津南区	Jinnan District	9	6	6	124.4	143.2	191.8
北辰区	Beichen District	5	7	7	11.5	15.9	15.9
武清区	Wuqing District	10	10	10	117.7	122.5	122.5
宝坻区	Baodi District	2	3	3	27.7	33.2	33.2

8－9 城市集中供热
HEATING IN CITY

项 目	Item	单 位	Unit	2003	2004	2005	2005 比2004年增长% Increase Rate in 2005 over 2004
供热能力	Heating Capacity						
蒸 汽	Steam	吨/小时	ton/hour	3 234	3 407	3 294	－3.3
热 水	Hot Water	兆瓦/小时	1 million kw/hour	9 390	10 111	10 563	4.5
供热总量	Volume Supplied						
蒸 汽	Steam	万吉焦/年	10^4 billion joule/year	1 486	1 764	1 966	11.5
热 水	Hot Water	万吉焦/年	10^4 billion joule/year	6 191	6 530	7 572	16.0
管道长度	Length of Pipelines	公里	km	7 387	8 038	8 705	8.3
供热面积	Heating Area	万平方米	10^4 sq.m	10 787	11 441	14 041	22.7
#住 宅	Residential Buildings	万平方米	10^4 sq.m	8 118	8 970	10 967	22.3

8－10 城市公共交通
PUBLIC TRAFFIC IN CITY

指 标	Item	单 位	Unit	2003	2004	2005	2005 比2004年增长% Increase Rate in 2005 over 2004
公共汽车	**Public Transportation Vehicles**						
营运车辆	Operation Vehicles	辆	unit	6 066	6 331	6 768	6.9
线路条数	Number of Routes	条	route	347	402	432	7.5
线路长度	Length of Routes	公里	km	8 206	8 114	9 354	15.3
乘客人数	Passengers	万人次	10^4 person－time	62 048	78 502	89 529	14.0
日均乘客人数	Average Daily Passengers	万人次	10^4 person－time	172	218	249	14.2
营运出租汽车	**Operating Taxis**	**辆**	**unit**	**31 939**	**31 939**	**31 939**	

8－11 城市环境卫生事业发展情况
DEVELOPMENT OF URBAN ENVIRONMENT SANITATION

指 标	Item	单 位	Unit	2003	2004	2005	2005 比2004年增长% Increase Rate in 2005 over 2004
清运垃圾粪便工作量	**Volume of Garbage, Excrement and Urine Disposal**						
清扫街道面积	Area Cleaned	万平方米	10^4 sq.m	6 408	6 090	7 357	20.8
清运垃圾	Volume of Garbage Disposal	万吨	10^4 ton	172	204	167	－18.1
清运粪便	Volume of Excrement and Urine Disposal	万吨	10^4 ton	25.2	26.4	27.3	3.4
垃圾无害化处理量	Volume of Garbage Innocuous Disposal	万吨	10^4 ton	104.1	110.7	119.0	7.5
环境卫生设施	**Environmental Sanitation Facilities**						
公共厕所	Lavatories	座	unit	2 430	2 731	2 778	1.7
垃圾无害化处理厂	Garbage Innocuous Disposal Plant	座	unit	3	6	6	
无害化处理厂能力	Capacity of Innocuous Disposal Plant	吨/日	ton/day	3 800	5 690	6 800	19.5
环卫职工人数	**Number of Environment Sanitation Staff & Workers**	**人**	**person**	**16 857**	**18 477**	**19 087**	**3.3**

8-12 水资源情况(2000-2005年)

WATER RESOURCES, 2000-2005

年份 Year	水资源总量(亿立方米) Total Amount of Water Resources (100 million cu. m)	地表水资源量 Surface Water	地下水资源量 Under-ground Water	地表水与地下水资源重复量 Duplicated Measurement Between Surface	人均水资源量(立方米/人) Per Capita Water Resources (cu. m/person)
2000	3.15	0.62	2.75	0.22	31.46
2001	5.66	3.53	2.41	0.28	56.37
2002	3.67	1.85	2.09	0.27	36.44
2003	10.60	6.15	4.82	0.37	104.82
2004	14.31	9.79	5.16	0.64	139.79
2005	10.63	7.13	4.44	0.94	101.92

8-13 供水用水情况(2000-2005年)

WATER SUPPLY AND WATER USE, 2000-2005

单位:万立方米 (10 000 cu. m)

年份 地区	Year Region	供用水总量 Water Supply & Use	地表水 Surface Water	地下水 Under-ground Water	#农业用水 Agricu-lture Use
2000		226 345	144 164	82 181	119 469
2001		188 141	111 738	76 403	99 056
2002		199 610	117 421	82 189	106 244
2003		205 118	133 713	71 405	114 072
2004		219 623	148 932	70 691	121 529
2005 合计	**Total**	**225 193**	**160 224**	**64 969**	**135 267**
市内六区	Six Urban Districts	53 905	53 905		
塘沽区	Tanggu District	7 393	5 775	1 618	344
汉沽区	Hangu District	4 532	720	3 812	1 878
大港区	Dagang District	3 938	170	3 768	254
东丽区	Dongli District	2 001	98	1 903	409
西青区	Xiqing District	13 990	11 190	2 800	12 016
津南区	Jinnan District	6 327	3 200	3 127	3 860
北辰区	Beichen District	4 925	2 665	2 260	3 595
武清区	Wuqing District	28 639	18 702	9 937	24 570
宝坻区	Baodi District	65 806	55 114	10 692	62 411
宁河县	Ninghe County	14 531	8 300	6 231	12 725
静海县	Jinghai County	4 824		4 824	3 137
蓟县	Jixian County	14 382	385	13 997	10 068

资料来源:天津市水利局。
Information Source: Tianjin Municipal Water Conservancy Bureau.

8－14 工业废水、废气、固体废物排放及处理情况(2002－2005年)

EMISSION AND TREATMENT OF INDUSTRIAL WASTE WATER, WASTE GAS, WASTE RESIDUE AND DUST, 2002－2005

指 标 Item	2002	2003	2004	2005
工业废水				
Industrial Waste Water				
工业废水排放量(万吨)				
Volume of Waste Water Discharged(10 000 tons)	21 959	21 605	22 628	30 081
工业废水排放达标率(%)				
Rate of Reaching the Standard of Industrial Waste Water(%)	100	100	99	99.6
工业废气				
Industrial Waste Gas				
工业废气排放总量(亿标立方米)				
Total Volume of Industrial Waste Gas Emission(100 million cu. m)	3 678	4 360	3 058	4 602
生产工艺过程中废气排放量				
Volume of Waste Gas from the Process of Production	956	893	835	1 222
燃料燃烧过程中废气排放量				
Volume of Waste Gas from the Burning Process of Fuel	2 722	3 467	2 223	3 380
废气中二氧化硫排放量(万吨)				
Sulphur Dioxide in Waste Gas(10 000 tons)	20	26	20	24
工业粉尘产生量(万吨)				
Amount of Industrial Dust Producted(10 000 tons)	24	21	26	28
工业粉尘排放量				
Volume of Industrial Dust Emission	3	2	2	2
工业粉尘去除量				
Volume of Industrial Dust Removed	21	19	24	26
工业粉尘去除率(%)				
Rate of Industrial Dust Removed(%)	89	90	93	93
工业固体废物				
Industrial Waste Residue				
工业固体废物产生量(万吨)				
Amount of Industrial Waste Residue Produced(10 000 tons)	643	644	753	1 123
#已处理量				
Volume of Treatment	26	57	21	20
已综合利用量				
Volume of Comprehensive Utilization	643	619	782	1 153
工业固体废物处理率(%)				
Disposal Rate of Industrial Waste Residue(%)	4	8	3	1
工业固体废物综合利用率(%)				
Rate of Comprehensive Using Industrial Waste Residue(%)	96	96	97	98

8-15 城市空气质量状况、环境噪声情况(2002-2005年)

URBAN AIR QUALITY CONDITIONS AND ENVIRONMENTAL NOISE SITUATION,2002-2005

指 标 Item	2002	2003	2004	2005
空气质量状况				
Air Quality Conditions				
可吸入颗粒物(毫克/立方米)				
(PM10)Paticulate Matters (milligram/cu. m)	0.138	0.133	0.111	0.106
二氧化硫(毫克/立方米)				
(SO2)Sulphur Dioxide (milligram/cu. m)	0.069	0.073	0.073	0.077
二氧化氮(毫克/立方米)				
(NO2)Nitrogen Dioxide (milligram/cu. m)	0.046	0.051	0.052	0.047
空气质量达到及好于二级的天数(天)				
Days of Air Quality Equal to or Above Grade II (days)	274	264	299	298
环境空气质量优良率(%)				
Ambient Air Quality Fine Rate	75.0	72.3	81.7	81.6
环境噪声情况				
Environmental noise Situation				
城市交通噪声等效声级(分贝)				
Equivalent Sound Level of City Traffic Noise(decibel)	68	68	68	68
城市环境噪声达标面积(平方公里)				
Standardization Areas of City Environment Noise(sq. km)	477	539	560	570
城市环境噪声达标区覆盖率(%)				
Coverage Rate of City Environment Noise Reaching Standard Areas(%)	78.1	83.5	82.4	77.7

8-16 环境保护系统人员构成(2002-2005年)

COMPOSITION OF ENVIRONMENT PROTECTION PERSONNEL,2002-2005

指 标	Item	2002	2003	2004	2005
年末实有人数(人)	**Persons(year-end)(person)**	**1 679**	**1 703**	**1 781**	**1 853**
科技人员	Science and Technology Personnel	737	724	728	839
#科研人员	Scientific Research Personnel	175	176	176	176
监测人员	Monitoring Personnel	391	402	421	688
行政干部	Administrative Personnel	418	438	457	522
科技业务人员占全部人员比重(%)	**Percentage of Science and Technology Personnel in Total(%)**	**44**	**43**	**41**	**45**

8-17 环境管理"三同时"制度执行情况(2002-2005年)

IMPLEMENTATION OF "THREE MEANTIME" SYSTEM OF ENVIRONMENTAL MANAGEMENT,2002-2005

指 标	Item	2002	2003	2004	2005
当年建成投产项目数(个)	Projects Putting into Use(unit)	4 464	1 439	1 121	1 181
应执行"三同时"项目数(个)	Number of Project Executing "Three Meantime"(unit)	4 464	1 439	1 121	1 181
实际执行"三同时"项目(个)	Number of Actual Executing Project(unit)	4 464	1 439	1 121	1 181
项目实际投资额(亿元)	Actual Investment of Project(100 million yuan)	82	93	113	253
#环保工程实际投资额	Actual Investment of Protecting Environment	2	3	4	24
"三同时"执行率(%)	Rate of Executing "Three Meantime"(%)	100	100	100	100
"三同时"合格率(%)	Qualified Rate of Executing "Three Meantime"(%)	100	100	100	100

注:"三同时"指同时设计、同时施工、同时使用。
Note:"Three Meantime" refers to design,construction,and use at the same time.

8－18 排污费征收、工业污染治理情况(2002－2005年)

COLLECTION OF DISCHARGE FEE AND INDUSTRIAL POLLUTION HARNESSING PROJECTS,2002－2005

指 标 Item	2002	2003	2004	2005
排污费收支情况				
Revenue And Expenditure of Discharge Fee				
排污费交纳单位(个)				
Unit of Paying Discharge Fee(unit)	12 527	6 766	6 508	5 875
排污费征收额(万元)				
Collection of Discharge Fee(10 000 yuan)	11 157	14 219	14 675	20 177
工业污染治理情况				
Industrial Pollution Harnessing Projects				
本年完成投资(万元)				
Investment Completed This Year(10 000 yuan)	99 227	87 152	72 546	186 316
治理废水				
Treating Waste Water	23 152	28 612	20 352	28 530
治理废气				
Treating Waste Gas	44 391	45 627	42 940	101 091
治理固体废物				
Treating Waste Residue	18 487	6 587	1 560	4 328
治理噪声				
Treating Noise Pollution	1 128	719	711	1 707
其 他				
Others	12 069	5 608	6 984	50 660
本年安排治理项目(个)				
Number of Project of Treated This Year(unit)	445	319	262	235
本年竣工项目(个)				
Number of Project Completed This Year(unit)	295	182	194	178
治理废水				
Treating Waste Water	79	58	73	60
治理废气				
Treating Waste Gas	150	79	72	70
治理固体废物				
Treating Waste Residue	9	10	10	20
治理噪声				
Treating Noise Pollution	19	3	9	4
其 他				
Others	38	32	30	24

主要统计指标解释

建成区面积 指城市行政区内实际已成片开发建设、市政公用设施和公共设施基本具备的区域。对核心城市，它包括集中连片的部分以及分散的若干个已经成片建设起来的市政公用设施和公共设施基本具备的地区；对一城多镇来说，它包括由几个连片开发建设起来的市政公用设施和公共设施基本具备的地区组成。因此建成区范围，一般是指建成区外轮廓线所能包括的地区，也就是这个城市实际建设用地所达到的范围。

城市园林绿地面积 指报告期末用作园林和绿化的各种绿地面积。包括公共绿地、居住区绿地、单位附属绿地、防护绿地、生产绿地、道路绿地和风景林地面积。

建成区绿化覆盖率 指报告期末建成区内绿化覆盖面积与建成区面积之比。用百分数表示。计算公式：

建成区绿化覆盖率 =（建成区内绿化覆盖面积/建成区面积）×100%

公共绿地 指向公众开放的市级、区级、居住区级各类公园、街旁游园，包括其范围内的水域。其中居住区级公园应不小于1万平方米，街旁游园的宽度不小于8米，面积不小于400平方米。

人均公共绿地面积 指报告期末区域内城市人口平均每人拥有的公共绿地面积。计算公式：人均公共绿地面积 = 区域内公共绿地面积/区域内城市人口数

房屋建筑面积 指从房屋外墙线算起的各层平面面积的总和，包括可供使用的有效面积和房屋结构（如柱、墙）占用的面积。多层建筑按各层（包括地下室）面积总和计算。

住宅建筑面积 指施工和竣工房屋建筑面积中供居住用的施工和竣工房屋建筑面积。

噪声等效声级(简称 LEQ) 指在规定的时间内，某一连续稳态声的 A〔计权〕声压，具有与时变的噪声相同的均方 A〔计权〕声压，则这一连续稳态声的声级，就是此时变噪声的等效声级。噪声等效声级（分贝）数值越小越好。

Explanatory Notes on Main Statistical Indicators

Developed Areas refer to the land in administrative areas having been developed concentratedly with municipal public facilities. For core city, developed areas include concentrated areas and decentralized areas, having basic perfect municipal public facilities; for the city with several towns, developed areas are composed of several concentrated areas with municipal public facilities. Therefore, the scope of developed areas refers to actual construction land of a city.

Area of Urban Gardens and Green Areas refers to the total area used for gardens and green by the report period, including public green land, residential zone green land, units green land, protection green land, production green land, roadside green land and suburban scenic spots.

The Rate of Green Coverage of the Developed Zones is the ratio of gardens and green areas to the developed zones areas, which is often expressed in %. The following formula is used

The Rate of Green Coverage of the Developed Zones = (gardens and green areas) / (the developed zones areas) × 100%

Public Green Area refers to green area of various parks and roadside gardens opened to the public, including waters within the above region. Of which, residential zone gardens should not less than 10,000 square meters, roadside gardens should not less than 8 meters wide and 400 square meters.

Per Capita Public Green Area refers to public green owned by each urban population. The following formula is used

Per Capita Public Green Area = public green area/number of urban population

Floor Space of Buildings under Construction refers to total floor space of the horizontal section of outer walls above the plinth of the buildings, including the effective area and the area occupied by the structure.

Floor Space of Residential Buildings refers to the floor space of residential buildings among the total space of buildings under construction or completed.

Level of Equivalent Noise (LEQ) In the specified time interval, it refer to the A sound pressure of a continuous steady state sound, with the same mean square A sound pressure as the time variant noise. This sound level of a continuous steady state sound is the equivalent sound level of the time variant noise. The smaller of the value of noise equivalent sound level (dB), the better.

第9篇
CHAPTER 9

农村经济
Rural Economy

9-1 农村社会经济主要指标
MAJOR INDICATORS OF AGRICULTURAL SOCIETY AND ECONOMY

项　目	Item	2003	2004	2005	2005 比2004年增长% Increase Rate in 2005 over 2004
基本情况	**Basic Statistics**				
乡镇政府(个)	Township and Town Governments (unit)	140	140	140	
乡村总户数(万户)	Number of Rural Households(10 000 households)	115.27	117.88	119.76	1.6
乡村总人口(万人)	Rural Population(10 000 persons)	391.28	395.18	397.51	0.6
农业现代化	**Agricultural Modernization**				
农机总动力(万千瓦)	Total Power of Agricultural Machinery(10 000 kw)	601.66	608.13	611.94	0.6
大中型拖拉机(台)	Large and Medium-sized Tractors(set)	9 290	9 400	10 260	9.1
小型拖拉机(万台)	Mini-tractors(10 000 sets)	3.58	3.64	3.54	-2.7
年末实有机电井(眼)	Motor-pumped Well(year-end)	25 509	25 855	26 648	3.1
有效灌溉面积(万公顷)	Effective Irrigated Areas(10 000 hectares)	35.41	35.34	35.52	0.5
节水灌溉面积(万公顷)	Water-saving Irrigated Areas(10 000 hectares)	17.47	18.57	19.67	5.9
农村用电量(万千瓦时)	Rural Electricity Consumption(10 000 kwh)	423 157	484 221	522 492	7.9
化肥施用量(折纯)(万吨)	Consumption of Chemical Fertilizers(pureness)(10 000 tons)	17.80	22.85	23.29	1.9
农药使用量(吨)	Consumption of Farm Pesticides(ton)	2 547	3 057	3 349	9.6
农作物总播种面积(万公顷)	**Total Sown Areas of Farm Crops (10 000 hectares)**	**50.15**	**50.43**	**49.94**	**-1**
#粮　食	Grain	25.81	26.35	28.77	9.2
蔬　菜	Vegetables	13.46	13.19	12.97	-1.7
总产量(万吨)	**Yield of Farm Crops(10 000 tons)**				
#粮　食	Grain	119.29	125.27	137.50	9.8
蔬　菜	Vegetables	602.78	585.43	542.74	-7.3
水果产量(万吨)	**Yield of Fruits(10 000 tons)**	**84.33**	**69.05**	**68.24**	**-1.2**
#果用瓜	Melon-Fruits	52.69	39.47	40.45	2.5
年末实有林地面积(万公顷)	**Forest Area(year-end)(10 000 hectares)**	**18.21**	**18.75**	**19.05**	**1.6**
#当年造林面积	Afforested Area in Current Year	0.69	0.53	0.36	-32.1

9-1续表 Continued

项 目	Item	2003	2004	2005	2005比2004年增长% Increase Rate in 2005 over 2004
畜牧业生产	**Production of Animal Husbandry**				
生猪年末存栏(万头)	Pigs in Hand(year-end)(10 000 heads)	245.09	252.42	255.45	1.2
生猪当年出栏(万头)	Number of Slaughtered Pigs(10 000 heads)	412.94	446.61	481.45	7.8
牛年末存栏(万头)	Cattle in Hand(year-end)(10 000heads)	42.91	43.42	44.40	2.3
#乳 牛	Cows	13.30	16.14	17.61	9.1
牛当年出栏(万头)	Number of Slaughtered Cattle(10 000 heads)	32.82	33.84	37.83	11.8
羊年末存栏(万只)	Sheep&Goats in Hand(year-end)(10 000heads)	106.49	93.61	84.69	-9.5
羊当年出栏(万只)	Number of Slaughtered Sheep and Goats (10 000 heads)	142.45	143.97	140.11	-2.7
家禽年末存栏(万只)	Poultry in Hand(year-end)(10 000heads)	3 488.75	3 218.25	2 894.32	-10.1
#产蛋鸡	Hens	1 741.08	1 620.43	1 701.35	5.0
家禽当年出栏(万只)	Number of Slaughtered Poultry(10 000 heads)	9 441.88	8 500.13	9 205.64	8.3
畜禽产品产量(万吨)	**Output of Animal and Poultry(10 000 tons)**				
肉类总产量	Output of Meat	52.41	53.73	57.78	7.5
#猪 肉	Pork	30.56	33.05	35.63	7.8
牛羊肉	Beef and Mutton	8.53	8.73	9.28	6.3
禽 肉	Poultry	12.81	11.53	12.49	8.3
禽蛋产量	Output of Poultry Eggs	24.25	24.38	23.47	-3.7
奶类产量	Output of Milk	43.23	54.24	63.41	16.9
渔业生产	**Production of Fishery**				
水产养殖面积(万公顷)	Cultured Areas of Aquatic Products (10 000 hectares)	3.83	4.04	4.17	3.2
#淡 水	Fresh Water	3.33	3.50	3.69	5.4
水产品产量(万吨)	Output of Aquatic Products(10 000 tons)	29.83	31.00	33.81	9.1
#淡 水	Fresh Water	24.74	26.14	28.92	10.6
农林牧渔业总产值(亿元)	**Gross Output Value of Farming,Forestry,Animal Husbandry and Fishery(100 million yuan)**	**193.44**	**221.35**	**238.34**	**4.8**
农 业	Farming	88.20	95.29	97.49	0.2
林 业	Forestry	1.61	1.66	1.89	13.6
牧 业	Animal Husbandry	77.22	92.55	102.71	7.5
渔 业	Fishery	26.41	31.85	36.25	10.6

注:农林牧渔业总产值按当年价格计算,增长速度按可比价格计算(下同)。
Note:Gross output value of farming,forestry,animal husbandry and fishery are calculated at current prices,increase rate are based on comparable prices(same as following next).

9－2 农村基层组织情况(2005 年)

BASIC CONDITION OF RURAL GRASSROOTS UNITS,2005

地 区	Region	乡镇政府(个) Township and Town Governments (unit)	# 镇政府 Town Governments	乡村户数(户) Number of Rural Households (household)	乡村人口(人) Rural Population (person)	乡村从业人员(人) Number of Rural Persons Employed (person)
总 计	**Total**	**140**	**120**	**1 197 576**	**3 975 117**	**1 784 996**
塘沽区	Tanggu District	1	1	28 529	76 089	26 823
汉沽区	Hangu District	4	4	18 551	56 188	26 415
大港区	Dagang District	3	3	33 984	103 662	40 012
东丽区	Dongli District	4	3	88 015	245 276	99 550
西青区	Xiqing District	7	7	84 748	241 832	114 812
津南区	Jinnan District	8	8	92 497	283 201	134 006
北辰区	Beichen District	9	9	85 855	269 479	114 967
武清区	Wuqing District	24	19	200 853	692 363	372 947
宝坻区	Baodi District	22	19	163 524	576 965	256 726
宁河县	Ninghe County	14	11	79 829	289 061	113 942
静海县	Jinghai County	18	16	133 098	438 635	161 554
蓟 县	Jixian County	26	20	188 093	702 366	323 242

9－3 按国民经济行业分各类乡村从业人员

NUMBER OF RURAL PERSONS EMPLOYED GROUPED BY SECTOR

单位:人 (person)

行 业	Sector	2004	2005	2005 比 2004 年增长% Increase Rate in 2005 over 2004
总 计	**Total**	**1 757 417**	**1 784 996**	**1.6**
农、林、牧、渔业	Farming,Forestry,Animal Husbandry and Fishery	805 407	795 452	－1.2
采矿业	Minerals Mining	3 575	4 235	18.5
制造业	Manufacturing	467 736	484 935	3.7
电力、燃气及水的生产和供应业	Production & Supply of Power,Gas and Water	2 953	3 221	9.1
建筑业	Construction	125 905	129 448	2.8
交通运输、仓储及邮政业	Transport,Storage,Post Services	116 760	121 346	3.9
信息传输、计算机服务和软件业	Information Transmitting, Computer Services & Software	1 123	970	－13.6
批发和零售业	Wholesale and Retail Trade	113 079	118 026	4.4
住宿和餐饮业	Accommodation and Catering Services	29 637	32 203	8.7
金融业	Finance Intermediation	1 614	1 446	－10.4
房地产业	Real Estate	1 047	821	－21.6
租赁和商务服务业	Leasing and Business Services	8 796	8 542	－2.9
科学研究、技术服务和地质勘察业	Scientific Research,Technical Services & Geological Prospecting	299	124	－58.5
水利、环境和公共设施管理业	Management for Water Conservancy, Environment & Public Facilities	1 206	1 307	8.4
居民服务和其他服务业	Resident Services and Other Social Services	59 164	62 893	6.3
教 育	Education	4 442	4 787	7.8
卫生、社会保障和社会福利业	Health Care, Social Security and Social Welfare	6 117	6 129	0.2
文化、体育和娱乐业	Culture, Sports and Recreational Services	1 333	1 410	5.8
公共管理和社会组织	Public Management and Social Organizations	7 224	7 701	6.6

9-4 农业生产条件情况(1990-2005年)

CONDITIONS OF AGRICULTURAL PRODUCTION, 1990-2005

年 份 Year	年末实有常用耕地面积(万公顷) Cultivated Area (year-end) (10 000 hectares)	年末实有林地面积(万公顷) Forest Area (year-end) (10 000 hectares)	#当年造林面积 Afforested Area in The Year	水产养殖面积(万公顷) Cultured Area of Aquatic Products (10 000 hectares)	有效灌溉面积(万公顷) Effective Irrigated Area (10 000 hectares)
1990	43.15	4.47	0.73	2.68	32.69
1991	43.16	6.40	0.55	2.65	32.88
1992	42.95	7.12	0.72	2.70	32.75
1993	42.87	7.37	0.77	2.73	32.85
1994	42.74	8.32	0.78	2.90	32.96
1995	42.61	8.70	0.48	3.12	33.24
1996	42.58	9.26	0.62	3.41	33.26
1997	42.52	9.85	0.90	3.81	33.28
1998	42.49	11.14	0.91	3.71	33.29
1999	42.46	12.74	0.94	3.76	34.39
2000	42.43	13.69	0.93	3.64	35.32
2001	42.39	14.19	0.50	3.67	35.43
2002	42.28	17.53	0.85	3.82	35.44
2003	41.85	18.21	0.69	3.83	35.41
2004	41.53	18.75	0.53	4.04	35.34
2005	41.45	19.05	0.36	4.17	35.52

年 份 Year	农用机械总动力(万千瓦) Total Power of Agricultural Machinery (10 000 kw)	机耕面积(万公顷) Cultivated Area Using Machinery (10 000 hectares)	机播面积(万公顷) Sown Area Using Machinery (10 000 hectares)	化肥施用量(折纯)(万吨) Consumption of Chemical Fertilizers (Pureness) (10 000 tons)	农村用电量(万千瓦小时) Rural Electricity Consumption (10 000 kwh)
1990	311.27	39.90	13.21	40.99	165 331
1991	303.76	40.17	14.53	42.53	180 834
1992	308.63	40.65	17.13	41.19	218 273
1993	302.22	38.47	15.00	40.13	231 072
1994	335.72	39.93	17.22	41.06	250 611
1995	364.08	38.08	19.50	45.29	325 482
1996	384.22	39.85	22.28	48.82	358 184
1997	417.37	39.66	25.00	49.15	330 249
1998	440.57	40.13	24.99	51.48	337 565
1999	481.54	39.62	24.93	47.24	343 667
2000	593.40	39.62	25.73	16.64	354 946
2001	603.32	37.26	24.11	17.31	377 823
2002	612.72	38.17	23.95	17.59	402 785
2003	601.66	37.05	23.57	17.80	423 157
2004	608.13	37.35	27.66	22.85	484 221
2005	611.94	37.62	28.94	23.29	522 492

注:化肥施用量2000年以前为实物量。
Note: Consumption of chemical fertilizers refered to full-scale quantity before 2000.

9-5 农林牧渔业总产值及增长速度(1990-2005年)
GROSS OUTPUT VALUE AND INCREASE RATE OF FARMING, FORESTRY, ANIMAL HUSBANDRY AND FISHERY, 1990-2005

年份 Year	合计 Total	农业 Farming	林业 Forestry	牧业 Animal Husbandry	渔业 Fishery
总产值(亿元) Gross Output Value (100 million yuan)					
1990	51.72	34.71	0.45	11.54	5.02
1991	54.55	36.68	0.34	12.88	4.65
1992	58.50	39.24	0.45	13.44	5.37
1993	66.32	44.28	0.44	15.82	5.78
1994	88.74	57.71	0.60	22.91	7.52
1995	125.44	85.25	0.85	28.76	10.58
1996	133.53	90.17	0.96	30.27	12.13
1997	140.47	89.77	1.00	33.99	15.71
1998	156.16	98.83	1.19	38.09	18.05
1999	150.11	91.58	1.42	38.95	18.16
2000	156.30	83.42	1.37	51.75	19.76
2001	169.51	86.73	1.46	60.76	20.56
2002	181.07	86.06	1.52	69.21	24.28
2003	193.44	88.20	1.61	77.22	26.41
2004	221.35	95.29	1.66	92.55	31.85
2005	238.34	97.49	1.89	102.71	36.25
增长速度(比上年)(%) Increase Rate over Preceding Year(%)					
1990	6.7	6.6	17.4	7.4	5.0
1991	6.7	7.0	-16.3	10.2	-0.2
1992	4.1	4.5	21.5	3.0	3.4
1993	4.3	5.6	-12.3	7.8	-9.6
1994	7.3	4.3	4.1	14.3	8.4
1995	13.0	13.5	-1.0	5.1	33.4
1996	7.5	8.5	10.3	3.5	10.6
1997	7.6	5.1	2.6	10.5	15.7
1998	11.8	8.2	39.7	15.4	21.2
1999	0.4	-6.3	15.1	13.7	3.1
2000	4.2	-4.4	-5.7	19.6	6.1
2001	8.0	4.1	7.2	15.9	3.0
2002	6.0	-8.9	13.7	14.9	36.2
2003	6.6	0.02	3.8	13.6	6.7
2004	5.2	3.1	2.6	5.8	10.5
2005	4.8	0.2	13.6	7.5	10.6

9-6 农林牧渔业总产值结构(1990-2005年)
STRUCTURE OF GROSS OUTPUT VALUE OF FARMING,FORESTRY,
ANIMAL HUSBANDRY AND FISHERY,1990-2005

单位:% (%)

年份 Year	合计 Total	农业 Farming	林业 Forestry	牧业 Animal Husbandry	渔业 Fishery
1990	100.0	67.1	0.9	22.3	9.7
1991	100.0	67.2	0.6	23.6	8.6
1992	100.0	67.1	0.8	23.0	9.1
1993	100.0	66.8	0.7	23.9	8.6
1994	100.0	65.0	0.7	25.8	8.5
1995	100.0	68.0	0.7	22.9	8.4
1996	100.0	67.5	0.7	22.7	9.1
1997	100.0	63.9	0.7	24.2	11.2
1998	100.0	63.3	0.8	24.4	11.5
1999	100.0	61.0	0.9	25.9	12.2
2000	100.0	53.4	0.9	33.1	12.6
2001	100.0	51.2	0.9	35.8	12.1
2002	100.0	47.5	0.8	38.3	13.4
2003	100.0	45.6	0.8	39.9	13.7
2004	100.0	43.1	0.7	41.8	14.4
2005	100.0	40.9	0.8	43.1	15.2

9-7 农作物播种面积(1990-2005年)
SOWN AREAS OF FARM CROPS,1990-2005

单位:万公顷 (10 000 hectares)

年份 Year	合计 Total	粮食 Grain	棉花 Cotton	油料 Oil-bearing Crops	蔬菜 Vegetables	其他农作物 Others
1990	54.95	45.23	1.04	2.21	5.08	1.39
1991	55.30	45.19	1.74	1.93	5.24	1.20
1992	54.56	44.03	1.67	1.85	5.71	1.30
1993	54.61	44.64	0.57	1.83	6.12	1.45
1994	53.00	41.74	1.33	1.72	7.02	1.19
1995	54.91	43.78	1.00	1.69	7.50	0.94
1996	56.44	45.57	0.38	1.37	8.08	1.04
1997	55.73	43.99	0.28	1.61	8.82	1.03
1998	56.32	44.45	0.35	1.69	8.64	1.19
1999	56.29	43.10	0.60	1.62	9.86	1.11
2000	53.31	34.59	1.51	2.63	12.83	1.75
2001	54.45	32.85	4.50	2.05	12.95	2.10
2002	52.28	31.13	4.48	1.89	12.84	1.94
2003	50.15	25.81	7.06	1.58	13.46	2.24
2004	50.43	26.35	8.69	0.61	13.19	1.59
2005	49.94	28.77	6.12	0.51	12.97	1.57

9-8 主要农产品产量情况(1990-2005年)
YIELD OF MAJOR FARM CROPS,1990-2005

单位:万吨 (10 000 tons)

年份 Year	粮食 Grain	#小麦 Wheat	#玉米 Corn	棉花 Cotton	油料 Oil-bearing Crops	蔬菜 Vegetables
1990	188.75	64.74	74.00	1.53	4.68	268.14
1991	198.50	62.00	79.90	2.55	4.50	282.56
1992	198.74	62.00	76.04	1.63	3.96	310.41
1993	199.82	59.07	80.80	0.76	4.45	354.34
1994	190.33	50.76	77.65	0.93	4.03	407.86
1995	207.46	65.40	80.50	1.12	4.01	434.17
1996	207.00	67.35	75.41	0.51	3.13	452.71
1997	206.16	77.41	65.45	0.39	3.01	486.23
1998	210.12	76.06	75.51	0.63	3.76	505.35
1999	174.85	71.60	56.30	0.57	2.34	486.07
2000	124.05	59.91	40.95	1.75	3.31	530.60
2001	143.33	45.09	75.19	6.36	3.90	564.50
2002	137.82	44.11	71.05	6.24	3.40	584.31
2003	119.29	35.91	64.81	9.47	3.08	602.78
2004	125.27	37.81	70.71	12.03	1.55	585.43
2005	137.50	47.42	73.16	8.36	1.29	542.74

年份 Year	肉类 Meats	#猪肉 Pork	#牛羊肉 Beef and Mutton	禽蛋 Poultry Eggs	奶类 Milk	水产品 Aquatic Products
1990	9.13	7.07	0.84	13.01	7.40	10.83
1991	9.89	7.19	1.05	15.01	8.41	10.81
1992	11.31	7.43	1.24	14.95	9.10	11.10
1993	11.47	7.26	1.61	15.08	9.14	11.39
1994	13.69	8.32	2.37	17.48	9.43	12.83
1995	15.86	9.59	3.09	16.94	10.47	15.35
1996	16.94	10.50	3.30	16.65	10.69	16.99
1997	18.70	11.77	3.44	17.71	12.13	18.98
1998	21.74	13.88	3.74	22.68	11.69	21.38
1999	23.53	14.59	4.24	23.56	12.94	23.03
2000	29.49	17.96	4.76	25.60	16.52	24.22
2001	36.40	21.92	5.97	26.00	24.06	26.46
2002	44.88	26.09	7.39	24.47	33.59	28.56
2003	52.41	30.56	8.53	24.25	43.23	29.83
2004	53.73	33.05	8.73	24.38	54.24	31.00
2005	57.78	35.63	9.28	23.47	63.41	33.81

9-9 农村居民家庭户均生产性固定资产原值(2001-2005年)
ORIGINAL VALUE OF PRODUCTIVE FIXED ASSETS PER RURAL HOUSEHOLD,2001-2005

单位:元 (yuan)

项目	Item	2001	2002	2003	2004	2005
年末户均生产性固定资产原值	**Original Value of Productive Fixed Assets(year-end)**	**6 624**	**7 228**	**7 051**	**8 311**	**10 150**
1.农、林、牧、渔业	Farming,Forestry,Animal Husbandry and Fishery	4 039	4 161	4 232	4 781	5 006
#役畜、产品畜	Draught Animals and Commodity Animals	513	779	729	469	515
大中型铁木农具	Large and Medium Wood & Iron Farm Tools	424	335	263	363	162
农林牧渔业机械	Machinery for Farming,Forestry,Animal Husbandry and Fishery	1 484	1 375	1 300	1 480	1 910
2.制造业	Manufacturing	148	288	230	286	1 151
3.批发和零售业	Wholesale and Retail Trade	233	208	289	247	448
4.住宿和餐饮业	Accommodation and Catering Services	185	165	201	348	33
5.文化、体育和娱乐业	Culture,Sports and Recreational Services	21	25	30	25	
6.其他	Others	1 998	2 381	2 069	2 624	3 512

注:本表数据为农村住户抽样调查数。
Note:The data of this table are collected from sample survey on rural households.

9-10 农村居民家庭每百户生产性固定资产拥有量(2001-2005年)
NUMBER OF PRODUCTIVE FIXED ASSETS PER 100 RURAL HOUSEHOLDS,2001-2005

项目	Item	2001	2002	2003	2004	2005
汽车(辆)	Motor Vehicles(set)	5.17	6.50	5.83	5.50	6.67
大中型拖拉机(台)	Large and Medium Tractors(set)	3.17	1.67	1.83	2.50	1.67
小型和手扶拖拉机(台)	Mini-tractors(set)	23.33	25.67	22.33	21.67	18.00
机动脱粒机(台)	Motorized Threshing Machines(set)	2.27	3.18	2.69	1.67	0.67
胶轮大车(辆)	Carts with Rubber Tires(set)	12.67	9.83	7.17	3.83	4.67
水泵(台)	Pumps(set)	20.80	20.88	18.67	19.25	19.00
役畜(头)	Draught Animals(head)	17.25	17.67	17.08	10.50	5.50
产品畜(头)	Commodity Animals(head)	24.00	36.33	35.17	22.50	25.00

注:本表数据为农村住户抽样调查数。
Note:The data of this table are collected from sample survey on rural households.

9-11 各区县耕地面积(2005年)
AREAS UNDER CULTIVATION BY DISTRICT AND COUNTY,2005

单位:公顷 (hectare)

地 区 Region	年末实有耕地 Cultivated Areas (year-end)	水田 Paddy Fields	旱地 Dry Fields	粮食占耕地 Areas for Grain	蔬菜占耕地 Areas for Vegetables
塘沽区 Tanggu District	5 161	566	4 595	1 449	815
汉沽区 Hangu District	4 216	138	4 078	536	227
大港区 Dagang District	13 419		13 419	12 972	440
东丽区 Dongli District	12 955	1 599	11 356	2 201	1 958
西青区 Xiqing District	15 279	1 319	13 960	7 575	3 895
津南区 Jinnan District	14 553	329	14 224	5 148	1 553
北辰区 Beiche District	18 459	28	18 431	9 101	2 849
武清区 Wuqing District	89 851	64	89 787	54 020	15 895
宝坻区 Baodi District	76 114	5 624	70 490	46 675	14 336
宁河县 Ninghe County	38 666	4 547	34 119	12 168	6 527
静海县 Jingha County	69 178		69 178	47 660	2 969
蓟 县 Jixian County	53 989	164	53 825	35 348	6 042

9-12 各区县农业现代化情况(2005年)
AGRICULTURAL MODERNIZATION BY DISTRICT AND COUNTY,2005

地 区 Region	农业机械总动力(万千瓦) Total Power of Agricultural Machinery (10 000 kw)	农村用电量(万千瓦时) Rural Electricity Consumption (10 000 kwh)	有效灌溉面积(万公顷) Effective Irrigated Areas (10 000 hectares)	化肥施用量(折纯)(吨) Consumption of Chemical Fertilizers (Pureness) (ton)	农用薄膜使用量(吨) Consumption of Agricul-tural Membrane (ton)	农药使用量(吨) Consumption of Farm Pesticides (ton)
塘沽区 Tanggu District	27.89	4 851	0.52	1 072	247	55
汉沽区 Hangu District	15.71	12 713	0.45	3 136	139	377
大港区 Dagang District	27.34	17 858	1.09	3 057	29	68
东丽区 Dongli District	44.43	24 515	1.30	3 148	694	127
西青区 Xiqing District	44.48	49 178	1.53	9 012	1 314	99
津南区 Jinnan District	47.44	41 947	1.38	1 127	386	79
北辰区 Beichen District	41.57	42 151	1.45	5 660	1 406	219
武清区 Wuqing District	98.79	143 164	7.41	52 712	2 721	380
宝坻区 Baodi District	71.35	24 521	6.56	65 466	2 698	400
宁河县 Ninghe County	52.43	18 944	3.59	17 938	1 319	285
静海县 Jinghai County	68.87	117 896	5.55	33 375	1 534	544
蓟 县 Jixian County	70.55	32 046	4.22	36 519	914	699

9-13 各区县农林牧渔业总产值和增加值(2005年)
GROSS OUTPUT VALUE AND VALUE-ADDED OF FARMING, FORESTRY, ANIMAL HUSBANDRY AND FISHERY BY DISTRICT AND COUNTY, 2005

单位:万元 (10 000 yuan)

地区 Region	合计 Total	农业 Farming	林业 Forestry	牧业 Animal Husbandry	渔业 Fishery
总产值 Gross Output Value					
塘沽区 Tanggu District	48 369	11 334	90	11 189	25 756
汉沽区 Hangu District	80 803	22 952	16	12 290	45 545
大港区 Dagang District	40 657	13 170	162	19 276	8 049
东丽区 Dongli District	86 202	39 639	1 311	27 549	17 703
西青区 Xiqing District	133 256	61 070	466	31 695	40 025
津南区 Jinnan District	58 445	22 604	232	19 927	15 682
北辰区 Beichen District	128 135	47 936	369	65 970	13 860
武清区 Wuqing District	504 587	250 807	4 448	208 509	40 823
宝坻区 Baodi District	318 680	143 278	944	149 480	24 978
宁河县 Ninghe County	260 128	116 343	933	119 861	22 991
静海县 Jinghai County	259 824	126 692	3 566	110 889	18 677
蓟县 Jixian County	445 053	154 073	4 236	266 543	20 201
增加值 Value-added					
塘沽区 Tanggu District	17 742	4 245	41	3 668	9 788
汉沽区 Hangu District	33 147	12 509	10	2 865	17 763
大港区 Dagang District	16 673	4 068	102	9 069	3 434
东丽区 Dongli District	38 179	18 670	577	10 524	8 408
西青区 Xiqing District	64 265	30 350	281	14 453	19 181
津南区 Jinnan District	28 285	10 581	95	9 347	8 262
北辰区 Beichen District	61 916	28 635	185	27 191	5 905
武清区 Wuqing District	216 537	125 064	2 669	72 897	15 907
宝坻区 Baodi District	134 664	55 979	530	68 163	9 992
宁河县 Ninghe County	120 948	54 520	431	55 096	10 901
静海县 Jinghai County	127 874	72 835	2 122	46 606	6 311
蓟县 Jixian County	191 058	81 123	2 772	97 948	9 215

9－14 各区县主要农作物播种面积(2005 年)

SOWN AREAS OF MAJOR FARM CROPS BY DISTRICT AND COUNTY,2005

单位:公顷 (hectare)

地区	Region	粮食作物 Grain Crops	#小麦 Wheat	#稻谷 Rice	#玉米 Corn
塘沽区	Tanggu District	1 019	10	7	560
汉沽区	Hangu District	536		138	276
大港区	Dagang District	16 004	4 486		6 447
东丽区	Dongli District	2 627		326	1 589
西青区	Xiqing District	8 702	2 588	1 333	3 906
津南区	Jinnan District	4 333		318	2 988
北辰区	Beichen District	10 554	1 416	13	7 600
武清区	Wuqing District	93 643	38 361	64	53 712
宝坻区	Baodi District	71 296	28 653	5 624	33 566
宁河县	Ninghe County	12 474	463	4 550	5 635
静海县	Jinghai County	61 809	15 019		33 724
蓟　县	Jixian County	66 810	24 880	583	39 810

地区	Region	油料作物 Oil－bearing Crops	#花生 Peanuts	棉花 Cotton	蔬菜 Vegetable
塘沽区	Tanggu District			2 014	1 592
汉沽区	Hangu District			837	381
大港区	Dagang District	75		471	811
东丽区	Dongli District			5 784	5 026
西青区	Xiqing District	23	5	2 804	9 185
津南区	Jinnan District			3 887	3 318
北辰区	Beichen District	663	343	2 915	6 549
武清区	Wuqing District	1 317	408	10 103	33 072
宝坻区	Baodi District	380	200	9 974	14 828
宁河县	Ninghe County	155	47	19 528	9 807
静海县	Jinghai County	1 259	108	13 067	6 664
蓟　县	Jixian County	1 077	1 077	1 048	14 493

9－15 各区县主要农作物产量(2005年)

YIELD OF MAJOR FARM CROPS BY DISTRICT AND COUNTY,2005

地 区 Region		粮食作物 Grain Crops	#小 麦 Wheat	#稻 谷 Rice	#玉 米 Corn
产 量(吨) Total Yield (ton)					
塘沽区	Tanggu District	4 107	37	33	2 797
汉沽区	Hangu District	4 084		1 057	2 151
大港区	Dagang District	43 137	3 815		29 523
东丽区	Dongli District	12 015		2 311	7 467
西青区	Xiqing District	45 686	11 906	8 532	22 849
津南区	Jinnan District	23 360		2 456	17 499
北辰区	Beichen District	53 179	6 811	100	42 007
武清区	Wuqing District	595 700	223 465	554	367 072
宝坻区	Baodi District	405 227	149 621	46 794	194 397
宁河县	Ninghe County	88 259	2 151	39 097	41 040
静海县	Jinghai County	299 366	56 047		211 585
蓟 县	Jixian County	412 222	149 904	4 089	252 777
单 产 Unit Yield					
(公斤/公顷)(kg/hectare)					
塘沽区	Tanggu District	4 030	3 700	4 714	4 995
汉沽区	Hangu District	7 619		7 659	7 793
大港区	Dagang District	2 695	850		4 579
东丽区	Dongli District	4 574		7 089	4 699
西青区	Xiqing District	5 250	4 600	6 401	5 850
津南区	Jinnan District	5 391		7 723	5 856
北辰区	Beichen District	5 039	4 810	7 692	5 527
武清区	Wuqing District	6 361	5 825	8 656	6 834
宝坻区	Baodi District	5 684	5 222	8 320	5 791
宁河县	Ninghe County	7 075	4 646	8 593	7 283
静海县	Jinghai County	4 843	3 732		6 274
蓟 县	Jixian County	6 170	6 025	7 014	6 350

9-15 续表 Continued

地　区 Region	油料作物 Oil-bearing Crops	#花　生 Peanuts	棉　花 Cotton	蔬　菜 Vegetables
产　量(吨) Total Yield (ton)				
塘沽区 Tanggu District			1 727	59 506
汉沽区 Hangu District			957	33 307
大港区 Dagang District	102		1 151	32 118
东丽区 Dongli District			5 417	218 279
西青区 Xiqing District	51	27	8 374	365 699
津南区 Jinnan District			4 125	126 341
北辰区 Beichen District	1 479	951	2 663	320 297
武清区 Wuqing District	3 104	1 299	11 635	1 423 740
宝坻区 Baodi District	832	474	16 784	608 541
宁河县 Ninghe County	346	135	22 715	402 820
静海县 Jinghai County	2 605	361	15 111	416 387
蓟　县 Jixian County	4 231	4 231	1 817	1 013 045
单　产 Unit Yield				
(公斤/公顷)(kg/hectare)				
塘沽区 Tanggu District			857	37 378
汉沽区 Hangu District			1 143	87 420
大港区 Dagang District	1 360		2 444	39 603
东丽区 Dongli District			937	43 430
西青区 Xiqing District	2 217	5 400	2 986	39 815
津南区 Jinnan District			1 061	38 077
北辰区 Beichen District	2 231	2 773	914	48 908
武清区 Wuqing District	2 357	3 184	1 152	43 050
宝坻区 Baodi District	2 189	2 370	1 683	41 040
宁河县 Ninghe County	2 232	2 872	1 163	41 075
静海县 Jinghai County	2 069	3 343	1 156	62 483
蓟　县 Jixian County	3 929	3 929	1 734	69 899

9－16　各区县畜牧业生产情况（2005 年）

PRODUCTION OF ANIMAL HUSBANDRY BY DISTRICT AND COUNTY, 2005

地　区 Region		猪出栏（万头）Slaughtered Pigs (10 000 heads)	牛出栏（万头）Slaughtered Cattle (10 000 heads)	羊出栏（万只）Slaughtered Sheep and Goats (10 000 heads)	家禽出栏（万只）Slaughtered Poultry (10 000 heads)	#鸡 Cocks and Hens	产蛋鸡存栏（万只）Hens in Hand (10 000 heads)	乳牛存栏（头）Cows in Hand (head)
塘沽区	Tanggu District	10.34	0.17	1.15	44.40	44.10	4.87	723
汉沽区	Hangu District	7.88	0.14	0.74	123.76	123.76	8.10	990
大港区	Dagang District	5.72	0.38	4.69	308.20	308.20	39.90	740
东丽区	Dongli District	14.28	0.54	3.76	395.69	394.98	13.32	1 391
西青区	Xiqing District	13.36	0.18	1.86	874.61	744.83	42.07	4 161
津南区	Jinnan District	8.37	0.29	1.42	1 201.20	1 200.00	33.00	545
北辰区	Beichen District	18.85	0.83	11.18	647.16	588.99	113.27	25 041
武清区	Wuqing District	70.11	6.35	36.75	3 169.03	2 984.67	220.00	62 596
宝坻区	Baodi District	101.23	7.40	17.60	464.26	316.35	238.19	4 732
宁河县	Ninghe County	90.58	0.92	7.38	911.71	911.71	112.57	30 001
静海县	Jinghai County	46.73	1.83	28.82	1 527.69	1 523.75	93.14	20 856
蓟　县	Jixian County	164.14	17.64	24.72	1 386.97	1 010.22	609.69	2 886

地　区 Region		肉类总产量（吨）Output of Meat (ton)	#猪　肉 Pork	#牛羊肉 Beef & Mutton	#禽　肉 Meat of Poultry	禽蛋产量（吨）Output of Poultry Eggs (ton)	#鸡　蛋 Eggs	牛奶产量（吨）Output of Milk (ton)
塘沽区	Tanggu District	9 003	7 238	893	872	595	564	1 455
汉沽区	Hangu District	9 002	5 912	322	2 449	1 432	1 423	2 945
大港区	Dagang District	10 069	4 000	1 446	4 623	3 950	3 950	2 937
东丽区	Dongli District	20 836	10 644	2 343	7 828	1 773	1 773	6 532
西青区	Xiqing District	24 482	10 336	763	13 383	5 617	4 070	12 645
津南区	Jinnan District	15 992	6 410	1 039	8 543	3 005	3 000	3 481
北辰区	Beichen District	27 520	13 917	4 911	9 395	22 382	21 919	102 078
武清区	Wuqing District	114 404	49 080	23 001	41 920	32 733	29 260	238 278
宝坻区	Baodi District	110 482	75 921	19 305	11 500	44 568	44 568	18 022
宁河县	Ninghe County	84 783	63 407	3 173	17 984	16 200	15 700	70 901
静海县	Jinghai County	75 467	35 983	12 700	26 784	16 420	16 420	105 950
蓟　县	Jixian County	163 500	114 800	26 500	22 100	79 444	73 500	13 533

9－17 林业生产、果园面积及产量
FORESTRY PRODUCTION,ORCHARD AREAS AND OUTPUT

项 目	Item	2003	2004	2005
年末实有林地面积(万公顷)	**Forestry Areas(year－end)(10 000 hectares)**	**18.21**	**18.75**	**19.05**
#当年造林面积	Afforested Areas in Current Year	0.69	0.53	0.36
封山育林面积(万公顷)	**Afforested Areas on Sealed Moutain(10 000 hectares)**	**1.27**	**2.21**	**2.20**
育苗面积	Areas Used for Cultivating Sapling	0.79	0.89	0.52
年末实有果园面积(万公顷)	**Areas of Orchards(year－end)(10 000 hectares)**	**4.11**	**3.64**	**3.71**
干果产量(吨)	**Output of Dry Fruits(ton)**	**666**	**697**	**754**
#核 桃	Walnuts	384	412	442
栗 子	Chestnut	239	285	312
园林水果产量(吨)	**Output of Fruits in Orchards(ton)**	**316 429**	**295 819**	**277 877**
#苹 果	Apples	68 069	64 721	66 039
梨	Pears	25 851	25 182	22 553
桃	Peaches	49 071	49 006	48 997
鲜 枣	Fresh Jujubes	15 678	13 560	24 691
葡 萄	Grapes	140 060	132 084	93 229
柿 子	Persimmons	10 036	6 301	11 402

9－18 各区县渔业生产情况(2005年)
FISHERY PRODUCTION BY DISTRICT AND COUNTY,2005

地 区 Region	水产品总产量(吨) Total Aquatic Products (ton)	海水产品 Seawater Aquatic Products	淡水产品 Freshwater Aquatic Products	水产养殖面积(公顷) Cultured Areas of Aquatic Products (hectare)	海水养殖 Seawater Cultured	淡水养殖 Freshwater Cultured
塘沽区 Tanggu District	25 970	20 656	5 314	4 226	1 741	2 485
汉沽区 Hangu District	26 449	14 552	11 897	1 395	674	721
大港区 Dagang District	7 585	2 155	5 430	5 464	2 258	3 206
东丽区 Dongli District	21 291		21 291	2 784		2 784
西青区 Xiqing District	50 645		50 645	5 149		5 149
津南区 Jinnan District	14 348		14 348	2 663		2 663
北辰区 Beichen District	13 512		13 512	2 132		2 132
武清区 Wuqing District	54 456		54 456	6 378		6 378
宝坻区 Baodi District	35 280		35 280	3 492		3 492
宁河县 Ninghe County	16 475	125	16 350	3 000	133	2 867
静海县 Jinghai County	26 293		26 293	2 602		2 602
蓟 县 Jixian County	27 421		27 421	1 800		1 800

9－19 农垦集团总公司主要指标(2002－2005年)

MAJOR INDICATORS OF STATE FARMS OF AGRIBUSINESS GROUP CORPORATION,2002－2005

项 目	Item	2002	2003	2004	2005
直属企事业单位(个)	**Number of Units(unit)**	**36**	**40**	**40**	**40**
#农场个数	Farms	15	15	15	14
工业企业个数	Industrial Enterprises	12	12	14	12
商业企业个数	Commercial Enterprises	3	2	2	2
土地面积(公顷)	**Land Areas (hectare)**	**10 992**	**9 025**	**9 269**	**9 077**
#耕地面积	Cultivated Areas	3 965	3 051	3 168	3 039
工农业总产值(万元)	**Gross Output Value of Agriculture and Industry (10 000 yuan)**	**160 151**	**173 676**	**183 295**	**236 404**
#农业总产值	Gross Agricultural Output Value	25 430	27 154	28 353	32 638
增加值(万元)	**Value－added(10 000 yuan)**	**61 993**	**66 910**	**76 605**	**73 001**
第一产业	Primary Industry	6 721	7 380	5 859	5 825
第二产业	Secondary Industry	47 713	50 767	59 727	56 103
第三产业	Tertiary Industry	7 559	8 763	11 019	11 073
种植业生产情况	**Production of Planting**				
农作物播种面积(公顷)	Sown Areas of Farm Crops(hectare)	3 453	2 513	2 911	2 997
#粮食作物	Grain	1 934	1 077	1 323	1 414
商品蔬菜	Vegetables for Sale	63	72	6	56
农作物总产量(吨)	Total Yield of Farm Crops(ton)				
#粮　食	Grain	9 069	5 782	8 237	7 942
商品蔬菜	Vegetables for Sale	2 115	3 620	255	2 712
水果生产情况	**Production of Fruits**				
果园面积(公顷)	Areas of Orchards(hectare)	259	184	213	181
水果总产量(吨)	Total Yield of Fruits(ton)	1 193	1 268	1 886	853
畜牧水产生产情况	**Production of Animal Husbandry and Fishery**				
奶牛年末存栏(头)	Cows in Hand(year－end)(head)	19 059	19 979	21 157	21 469
#成母牛	Female Cows	10 666	11 966	12 499	11 040
牛奶总产量(吨)	Output of Milk(ton)	74 281	79 455	81 741	79 585

9－19 续表 Continued

项 目	Item	2002	2003	2004	2005
鸡年末存栏(万只)	Cocks and Hens in Hand(year－end)(10 000 heads)	37.30	22.69	22.74	22.59
#产蛋鸡	Hens	35.30	22.29	22.74	22.59
鸡蛋总产量(吨)	Total Output of Eggs(ton)	3 369	4 516	4 842	3 905
肉类总产量(吨)	Total Output of Meat(ton)	549	833	673	1 054
养殖水面(公顷)	Cultured Water Areas(hectare)	834	516	422	646
水产品产量(吨)	Total Aquatic Products(ton)	5 579	4 077	3 754	6 877
农业机械总动力(万千瓦)	**Total Power of Agricultural Machinery(10 000 kw)**	**1.39**	**1.05**	**1.16**	**1.09**
#大中型拖拉机(台)	Large and Medium－sized Tractors(set)	50	38	28	31
小型拖拉机(台)	Mini－tractors(set)	12	8	7	4
汽 车(辆)	Number of Motor Vehicles(set)	317	296	276	321
#载重汽车(辆)	Trucks(set)	87	62	57	62
用电量(万千瓦小时)	**Electricity Consumption(10 000 kwh)**	**4 635**	**4 328**	**7 123**	**5 295**
化肥施用量(折纯)(吨)	**Consumption of Chemical Fertilizers (pureness)(ton)**	**616**	**758**	**648**	**686**
主要工业产品产量	**Output of Major Industrial Products**				
葡萄酒(吨)	Wine(ton)	29 690	27 150	36 650	38 151
淀 粉(吨)	Starch(ton)	60	22		
奶 粉(吨)	Milk Powder(ton)	2 277	2 200	3 007	2 028
消毒牛奶(吨)	Sterilized Milk(ton)	52 233	65 157	70 011	66 125
饲料添加剂(吨)	Added Preparation for Forage(ton)	404	151	307	288
固定资产投资总额(万元)	**Total Investment in Fixed Assets(10 000 yuan)**	**13 302**	**16 744**	**27 860**	**10 000**
新增固定资产	Newly Increased Fixed Assets	12 702	7 697	20 705	10 000
外贸出口总值(万元)	**Total Value of Exports(10 000 yuan)**	**13 708**	**14 010**	**10 332**	**6 897**
利润总额(万元)	**Total Profits(10 000 yuan)**	**6 712**	**7 808**	**22 757**	**20 038**
年末职工人数(人)	**Number of Staff and Workers(year－end)(person)**	**9 349**	**7 958**	**7 122**	**6 489**
工资总额(万元)	**Total Wages(10 000 yuan)**	**9 857**	**10 392**	**11 838**	**12 934**
职工年平均工资(元)	Annual Average Wage(yuan)	9 706	11 829	15 954	18 739
年末固定资产原值(万元)	**Original Value of Fixed Assets(year－end) (10 000 yuan)**	**107 317**	**111 067**	**121 421**	**148 534**
年末固定资产净值(万元)	Net Value of Fixed Assets(year－end)(10 000 yuan)	74 772	76 113	84 774	107 894

9－20 大型水库基本情况(2005 年)

LARGE RESERVOIRS OF TIANJIN,2005

项目	Item	于桥水库 Yuqiao Reservoir	北大港水库 Beidagang Reservoir	团泊洼水库 Tuanbowa Reservoir
建设地点	Construction Site	蓟县 Jixian	大港区 Dagang	静海县 Jinghai
所属河系	Location River	蓟运河 Jiyun River	大清河 Daqing River	独流碱河 Duliujian River
总库容(万立方米)	Total Capacity of Reservoir(10 000 cu. m)	155 900	50 000	18 000
设计灌溉面积(万公顷)	Designed Irrigated Areas(10 000 hectares)	4.20	1.38	3.00
有效灌溉面积(万公顷)	Effective Irrigated Areas(10 000 hectares)	3.00	0.66	2.60

9－21 中型水库基本情况(2005 年)

MEDIUM RESERVOIRS OF TIANJIN,2005

水库名称 Name of Reservoir	座落地点 Site	所在河系 Location River	总库容(万立方米) Total Capacity of Reservoir (10 000 cu. m)	灌溉面积(万公顷) Irrigated Areas (10 000 hectares)		年设计灌溉用水(万立方米) Annual Irrigated Water (10 000 cu. m)
				设计 Designed Areas	有效 Effective Areas	
七里海水库 Qilihai Reservoir	宁河县 Ninghe	潮白新河 Chaobaixin River	2 400	1.00	0.40	1 800
新地河水库 Xindihe Reservoir	东丽区 Dongli	金钟河 Jinzhong River	2 200	0.27	0.27	1 000
鸭淀水库 Yadian Reservoir	西青区 Xiqing	津港运河 Jingang Canal	3 150	0.47	0.47	1 997
黄港一库 Huanggang Ⅰ Reservoir	塘沽区 Tanggu	黑猪河 Heizhu River	1 295	0.09	0.06	800
黄港二库 Huanggang Ⅱ Reservoir	塘沽区 Tanggu	黑猪河 Heizhu River	4 615	0.21	0.18	400
北塘水库 Beitang Reservoir	塘沽区 Tanggu	永定新河 Yongdingxin River	1 580			
营城水库 Yingcheng Reservoir	汉沽区 Hangu	蓟运河 Jixian Canal	3 000	0.04	0.04	400
钱圈水库 Qianquan Reservoir	大港区 Dagang	马厂减河 Machangjian River	2 650	0.20	0.10	
沙井子水库 Shajingzi Reservoir	大港区 Dagang	青县、静海县、黄骅县 Qingxian,Jinghai & Huanghua County	2 000	0.07	0.07	300
上马台水库 Shangmatai Reservoir	武清区 Wuqing	北运河 North Canal	2 680	0.86	0.86	1 900
津南水库 Jinnan Reservoir	津南区 Jinnan	海河 Haihe River	2 966	0.15	0.15	600
尔王庄水库 Erwangzhuang Reservoir	宝坻区 Baodi	潮白新河 Chaobaixin River	4 530			

主要统计指标解释

乡村总人口 指乡村户数中的常住人口。包括常住人口中外出的民工、合同工及户口在家的在外学生。但不包括户口在家领取工资的国家正式职工。

乡村从业人员 指乡村人口中16岁以上实际参加生产经营活动并取得实物或货币收入的人员，即包括劳动年龄内经常参加劳动的人员，也包括超过劳动年龄但经常参加劳动的人员，但不包括户口在家的在外学生、现役军人和丧失能力的人，也不包括待业人员和家务劳动者。从业人员年龄为16岁以上。从业人员按从事主业时间最长（时间相同按收入算），分为农业从业人员、工业从业人员、建筑业从业人员、交运仓储及邮电通讯业从业人员、批发零售及餐饮业从业人员、其它从业人员。

农林牧渔业总产值 指以货币表现的农林牧渔业全部产品总量。它用价值量形式综合说明了一定时期（通常指一年）农林牧渔业生产的总成果和总规模，是观察农林牧渔业生产水平和发展速度；研究农林牧渔业内部比例关系和农林牧渔业在国民经济中的产业布局的一个重要指标，同时，也是计算农林牧渔业劳动生产率和农林牧渔业增加值的基础资料。

农林牧渔业增加值 指各种经济类型的农业生产单位和农户从事农业生产经营活动所提供的社会最终产品的货币表现。其计算方法有两种，一是生产法：农牧渔业增加值＝农林牧渔业总产值－农林牧渔业中间消耗；二是分配法：农林牧渔业增加值＝固定资产折旧＋劳动者报酬＋生产税净额（生产税－生产补贴）＋营业盈余。

农业机械总动力 指主要用于农、林、牧、渔业的各种动力机械的动力总和。包括耕作机械、收获机械、农产品加工机械、运输机械、植保机械、牧业机械、林业机械、渔业机械和其它农业机械的动力。

农村用电量 指在本年度内，农村生产上和生活上的全年用电总度数（全年累计数）。但不包括农村中的全民所有制工业、交通、基建单位的用电量，也不包括县办工业和城镇生活用电量。

有效灌溉面积 指灌溉工程或设备已基本配套，有一定水源，土地比较平整，在一般年景可以进行正常灌溉的耕地面积。在一般情况下，有效灌溉面积应等于灌溉工程或设备已经配套，能够进行灌溉的水田和水浇地面积之和。

造林面积 指报告期内在荒地、荒山、沙丘等一切可造林的土地上，采用人工播种、植苗、飞机播种等方法种植成片的乔木林和灌木林，经过检查验收符合技术规程要求，并按《中华人民共和国森林法实施细则》规定，成活率达85％以上的造林面积。包括四旁植树如一侧在四行以上，连续面积0.066公顷以上的面积，造林面积不包括补植面积和治沙及沿河种草面积。

当年出栏头数 指农林牧渔企业生产单位饲养的，供屠宰并已出栏的全部牲畜头数。包括交售给国家，集市上出售的部分。

肉类总产量 指当年出栏并已屠宰的猪、牛、羊、马、骡、驴、家禽、兔等肉产量。即屠宰后除去头、蹄、下水后带骨肉的重量，也叫胴体重。

水产品产量 指本年度内捕捞的水产品（包括人工养殖并捕捞的水产品和捕捞天然生长的水产品）产量。不论自食或出售的，都应计算在内。用作继续扩大再生产的水产品（如鱼苗、鱼种、鱼饵及转塘鱼、存塘鱼等）不作水产品产量统计。在淡水生长的各种水生植物，如莲藕、菱角等，因属农作物范畴，均不包括在水产品产量之内。

Explanatory Notes on Main Statistical Indicators

Total Population of Rural refer to the permanent residents in rural, including those work in other places, contract workers, students having left place of residence registration in other places of which permanent population, excluding the staff and worker of receiving wages from state－owned units and having resided in this enumeration area.

Employment Personnel in Rural Areas refers to the total number of people aged over 16 who are engaged in production and business activities that generate incomes in cash or in kind. It includes all the working laborers, no matter whether they are within the working age or not. But students studying outside with their registered residence at home, active army, people who lost their ability to work, unemployed people and those engaged in housework are not included. The age of employment personnel are 16 and over. Employment personnel in rural areas are divided into agricultural personnel, industrial personnel, construction personnel, personnel engaged in transportation, storage, post and telecommunications, personnel engaged in wholesale, retail and catering business, other employment personnel according to the working time of main working.

Gross Output Value of Farming, Forestry, Animal Husbandry and Fishery refers to the total volume of products of farming, forestry, animal husbandry and fishery in value terms, which reflects the total scale and total result of agricultural production during a given period of time, which observe development level and speed of farming, forestry, animal husbandry and fishery, study proportional relations of farming, forestry, animal husbandry and fishery and proportional relations in national economic, which is also calculated labor productivity of farming, forestry, animal husbandry and fishery and value - added of farming, forestry, animal husbandry and fishery.

Value - added of Farming, Forestry, Animal Husbandry and Fishery refers to the final results of various agricultural production and trade units in money terms. It is calculated with two approaches. First, production approach, value - added of farming, forestry, animal husbandry and fishery = gross output value of farming, forestry, animal husbandry and fishery - intermediate input of farming, forestry, animal husbandry and fishery. Second, distribution approach, value - added of farming, forestry, animal husbandry and fishery = depreciation of fixed assets + laborers remuneration + net taxes on production (taxes on production subsidies production) + operating surplus.

Total Power of Farm Machinery refers to total mechanical power of machinery used in farming, forestry, animal husbandry, and fishery, including cultivating, harvesting, farming products process, transport, plant protection, stock breeding, forestry and fishery and other power of farm machinery.

Rural Electricity Consumption refers to the value of consumption electricity of rural in a year on production and life, but excluding value of consumption electricity by state - owned industry, transport, basic construction units and county - run industry, urban household consumption of electricity.

Effective Irrigated Area refers to areas that are effectively irrigated, i. e. level land which has water source and complete sets of irrigation facilities to lift and move adequate water for irrigation purpose under normal conditions. In general, irrigated area equal sum area of paddy fields and irrigated land for irrigated engineering or complete sets.

Afforested Area refers to the area of forest land where tree and bush by artificially seed, young plant, plane seed on the waste land, barren mountain, dune. during the reference period. Live rate of forest area coverage above 85% in accordance with the Regulation of the People's Republic of China on the Management of Forest Law, including the area of forest land inside farm land and the area of tree planted by the side of farm houses and along the roads, continuing area coverage above 0.066 hectare, excluding the area of sand and planted grass lands along the river.

Number of Livestock Slaughtered refers to the total number of animals for butchering by farming, forestry, animal husbandry and fishery, including parts of selling to country and markets.

Output of Meat refers to output of having butchered of pork, beef, mutton, horse, mule, donkey, fowls, rabbit in the current year, namely the heaviness minus head, hoof, offal.

Total Output of Aquatic Products Amount of fishing (including artificially cultured, naturally grown) ,in respective consumption by peasants themselves or sold. It excludes aquatic (i. e. fish fry, fish grows, fish bait and transferred fish from piscina, leave fish) for continuing expanded reproduction aquatic. Various fresh water plants (i. e. lotus roots, water chestnut) are not included.

第10篇 CHAPTER 10

工业 Industry

10－1 工业总产值及增长速度(1990－2005年)

GROSS OUTPUT VALUE AND INCREASE RATE OF INDUSTRY,1990－2005

年 份 Year	全部工业总产值 Total	按轻重分 Grouped by Light & Heavy Industry		按经济类型分 Grouped by Ownership		
		轻工业 Light Industry	重工业 Heavy Industry	国有经济 State－owned	集体经济 Collective－owned	其他经济 Others
绝对数(亿元) Gross Output Value (100million yuan)						
1990	679.94	354.50	325.44	404.28	243.44	36.73
1991	786.60	392.29	394.31	436.43	295.72	54.45
1992	997.91	465.48	532.43	492.15	402.42	103.34
1993	1 401.84	530.05	871.79	628.76	573.51	199.57
1994	1 754.30	760.80	993.50	648.10	675.59	430.61
1995	1 879.65	752.03	1 127.62	582.51	704.36	592.78
1996	2 177.42	1 014.46	1 162.96	587.86	798.77	790.79
1997	2 450.21	1 130.04	1 320.17	636.94	963.77	849.50
1998	2 562.62	1 157.09	1 405.53	572.64	731.59	1 258.39
1999	2 751.37	1 128.47	1 622.90	572.33	704.71	1 474.33
2000	3 080.74	1 263.10	1 817.64	558.50	815.26	1 706.98
2001	3 366.53	1 153.73	2 212.80	546.00	643.48	2 177.05
2002	3 717.72	1 207.88	2 509.84	519.19	660.91	2 537.62
2003	4 370.76	1 254.68	3 116.08	599.97	542.67	3 228.12
2004	6 186.04	1 398.65	4 787.39	716.56	327.25	5 142.24
2005	7 169.62	1 569.06	5 600.56	738.92	389.16	6 041.54
比上年增长% Increase Rate over Preceding Year(%)						
1990	7.8	5.3	11.2	－0.1	16.0	38.6
1991	12.2	7.1	17.8	2.4	24.5	42.2
1992	24.2	22.5	26.3	7.3	37.2	90.0
1993	25.1	8.9	40.5	－1.6	37.5	95.7
1994	19.1	33.8	8.2	－6.6	29.0	99.1
1995	23.5	11.2	34.8	－3.3	－22.6	110
1996	24.7	31.8	19.5	4.9	45.8	18.7
1997	12.9	13.6	12.2	7.8	－8.8	48.2
1998	8.5	9.9	7.2	－2.1	－1.3	19.9
1999	13.0	5.9	19.4	－0.2	3.2	22.2
2000	17.5	19.7	16.0	13.9	6.1	20.8
2001	14.0	－6.6	28.4	2.0	－17.7	33.0
2002	19.6	13.3	23.7	16.8	9.58	22.7
2003	24.1	18.5	27.0	12.2	8.3	28.7
2004	31.0	19.4	35.5	31.1	6.3	34.4
2005	19.5	9.3	22.8	19.5	－3.9	21.5

注:工业总产值绝对数按当年价格计算,增长速度按可比价格计算(下同)。

Note:Gross output value of industry are at current prices,increase rate are based on comparable prices(same as following next).

10－2　工业企业单位数

（全部国有及规模以上工业）

NUMBER OF INDUSTRIAL ENTERPRISES(ALL STATE－OWNED AND ABOVE DESIGNATED SIZE)

单位：个　　(unit)

项　目	Item	2004	2005
全市总计	**Total**	**6 460**	**6 144**
#国有及国有控股企业	State－owned and State－holding Enterprises	1 896	1 497
按登记注册类型分	**Grouped by Status of Registration**		
内资企业	Domestic－funded Enterprises	4 803	4 517
国有企业	State－owned Enterprises	1 263	937
集体企业	Collective－owned Enterprises	584	604
股份合作企业	Cooperative Enterprises	144	145
私营企业	Private Enterprises	1 796	1 765
股份有限公司	Share－holding Corporations Ltd.	120	88
有限责任公司	Limited Liability Corporations	793	904
#国有独资	Sole State－funded Corporations	72	52
联营企业	Joint Ownership Enterprises	64	44
#国有与国有联营企业	State Joint Ownership Enterprises	28	14
集体与集体联营企业	Collective Joint Ownership Enterprises	12	7
其他内资企业	Other Domestic－funded Enterprises	39	30
港澳台商投资企业	Enterprises with Investment from Hongkong, Macao and Taiwan	372	353
外商投资企业	Foreign Funded Enterprises	1 285	1 274
按经济类型分	**Grouped by Ownership**		
国有经济	State－owned	1 363	1 003
集体经济	Collective－owned	740	756
私有经济	Private and Individual	1 796	1 765
港澳台商投资经济	Hongkong,Macao and Taiwan Funded	372	353
外商投资经济	Foreign Funded	1 285	1 274
其　他	Others	904	993
按隶属关系分	**Grouped by Administrative Relationship**		
中央工业	Central Industry	161	110
地方工业	Local Industry	6 299	6 034
#市管工业	City Industry	2 863	2 748
#工业系统	Industry System	1 214	1 233
区县管工业	District & County Industry	565	454
街管工业	Neighbour Industry	30	31
乡镇管工业	Town and Country Industry	2 561	2 446
按轻重分	**Grouped by Light & Heavy Industry**		
轻工业	Light Industry	2 551	2 495
重工业	Heavy Industry	3 909	3 649

10－2 续表 Continued

项 目	Item	2004	2005
按规模分组:	**Grouped by Size of Enterprises**		
大 型	Large－sized	42	45
中 型	Medium－sized	472	504
小 型	Small－sized	5 946	5 595
按行业分组:	**Grouped by Sector**		
煤炭开采和洗选业	Coal Mining and Dressing	5	3
石油和天然气开采业	Petroleum and Natural Gas Extraction	5	5
有色金属矿采选业	Nonferrous Metals Mining and Dressing	1	1
非金属矿采选业	Nonmetal Minerals Mining and Dressing	7	20
农副食品加工业	Agricultural Products and Byproducts Processing	186	179
食品制造业	Food Manufacturing	149	138
饮料制造业	Beverage Manufacturing	53	50
烟草制品业	Tobacco Products	1	1
纺织业	Textile Industry	329	314
纺织服装鞋帽制造业	Textile Garments,Shoes,Caps Manufacturing	251	295
皮革毛皮羽毛(绒)及其制品业	Leather,Furs,Feather and Related Products	79	77
木材加工及木、竹、藤、棕、草制品业	Timber Processing,Bamboo,Cane, Palm Fiber and Straw Products	76	66
家具制造业	Furniture Manufacturing	73	89
造纸及纸制品业	Papermaking and Paper Products	169	184
印刷业和记录媒介的复制	Printing and Record Medium Reproduction	140	118
文教体育用品制造业	Cultural,Educational and Sports Goods	60	63
石油加工炼焦及核燃料加工业	Petroleum Processing,Coking and Nuclear Fuel Processing	46	39
化学原料及化学制品制造业	Raw Chemical Materials and Chemical Products	635	573
医药制造业	Medical and Pharmaceutical Products	112	112
化学纤维制造业	Chemical Fiber	18	21
橡胶制品业	Rubber Products	112	108
塑料制品业	Plastic Products	287	271
非金属矿物制品业	Nonmetal Mineral Products	237	245
黑色金属冶炼及压延加工业	Smelting and Pressing of Ferrous Metals	334	269
有色金属冶炼及压延加工业	Smelting and Pressing of Nonferrous Metals	124	94
金属制品业	Metal Products	520	523
通用设备制造业	General Purpose Equipment Manufacturing	513	464
专用设备制造业	Special Purpose Equipment Manufacturing	307	289
交通运输设备制造业	Transport Equipment Manufacturing	461	436
电气机械及器材制造业	Electric Equipment and Machinery	395	369
通信设备计算机及其他电子设备制造业	Telecommunications Equipment,Computer and Other Electronic Equipment Manufacturing	333	339
仪器仪表及文化办公用机械制造业	Instruments,Meters,Cultural and Office Machinery	153	142
工艺品及其他制造业	Craftwork and Other Manufacturing	172	128
废弃资源和废旧材料回收加工业	Waste Resources and Materials Recovering and Processing	13	25
电力热力的生产和供应业	Production and Supply of Electric & Heat Energy	70	62
燃气生产和供应业	Production and Supply of Gas	13	14
水的生产和供应业	Production and Supply of Water	21	18

10－3 地方工业企业单位数
(全部国有及规模以上工业)

NUMBER OF LOCAL INDUSTRIAL ENTERPRISES(ALL STATE－OWNED AND ABOVE DESIGNATED SIZE)

单位:个 (unit)

项 目	Item	2004	2005
全 市 总 计	**Total**	**6 299**	**6 034**
按登记注册类型分	**Grouped by Status of Registration**		
内资企业	Domestic－funded Enterprises	4 650	4 415
国有企业	State－owned Enterprises	1 158	873
集体企业	Collective－owned Enterprises	581	601
股份合作企业	Cooperative Enterprises	143	144
私营企业	Private Enterprises	1 796	1 765
股份有限公司	Share－holding Corporations Ltd.	113	81
有限责任公司	Limited Liability Corporations	763	880
#国有独资	Sole State－funded Corporations	67	50
联营企业	Joint Ownership Enterprises	57	41
#国有与国有联营企业	State Joint Ownership Enterprises	22	11
集体与集体联营企业	Collective Joint Ownership Enterprises	12	7
其他内资企业	Other Domestic－funded Enterprises	39	30
港澳台商投资企业	Enterprises with Investment from Hongkong,Macao and Taiwan	369	351
外商投资企业	Foreign Funded Enterprises	1 280	1 268
按经济类型分	**Grouped by Ownership**		
国有经济	State－owned	1 247	934
集体经济	Collective－owned	736	752
私有经济	Private and Individual	1 796	1 765
港澳台商投资经济	Hongkong,Macao and Taiwan Funded	369	351
外商投资经济	Foreign Funded	1 280	1 268
其 他	Others	871	964
按隶属关系分	**Grouped by Administrative Relationship**		
#市管工业	City Industry	2 863	2 748
#工业系统	Industry System	1 212	1 231
区县管工业	District & County Industry	565	454
街管工业	Neighbour Industry	30	31
乡镇管工业	Town and Country Industry	2 561	2 446
按轻重分	**Grouped by Light & Heavy Industry**		
轻工业	Light Industry	2 520	2 469
重工业	Heavy Industry	3 779	3 565

10－3 续表　Continued

单位：个　(unit)

项　目	Item	2004	2005
按规模分	**Grouped by Size of Enterprises**		
大　型	Large－sized	34	38
中　型	Medium－sized	444	481
小　型	Small－sized	5 821	5 515
按行业分	**Grouped by Sector**		
煤炭开采和洗选业	Coal Mining and Dressing	5	3
有色金属矿采选业	Nonferrous Metals Mining and Dressing	1	1
非金属矿采选业	Nonmetal Minerals Mining and Dressing	7	20
农副食品加工业	Agricultural Products and Byproducts Processing	185	179
食品制造业	Food Manufacturing	147	136
饮料制造业	Beverage Manufacturing	53	50
纺织业	Textile Industry	327	312
纺织服装鞋帽制造业	Textile Garments, Shoes, Caps Manufacturing	251	295
皮革毛皮羽毛(绒)及其制品业	Leather, Furs, Feather and Related Products	78	77
木材加工及木、竹、藤、棕、草制品业	Timber Processing, Bamboo, Cane, Palm Fiber and Straw Products	74	64
家具制造业	Furniture Manufacturing	73	89
造纸及纸制品业	Papermaking and Paper Products	169	184
印刷业和记录媒介的复制	Printing and Record Medium Reproduction	130	112
文教体育用品制造业	Cultural, Educational and Sports Goods	60	63
石油加工炼焦及核燃料加工业	Petroleum Processing, Coking and Nuclear Fuel Processing	41	34
化学原料及化学制品制造业	Raw Chemical Materials and Chemical Products	614	558
医药制造业	Medical and Pharmaceutical Products	111	108
化学纤维制造业	Chemical Fiber	18	21
橡胶制品业	Rubber Products	112	108
塑料制品业	Plastic Products	286	270
非金属矿物制品业	Nonmetal Mineral Products	228	243
黑色金属冶炼及压延加工业	Smelting and Pressing of Ferrous Metals	334	269
有色金属冶炼及压延加工业	Smelting and Pressing of Nonferrous Metals	124	94
金属制品业	Metal Products	513	518
通用设备制造业	General Purpose Equipment Manufacturing	509	461
专用设备制造业	Special Purpose Equipment Manufacturing	291	281
交通运输设备制造业	Transport Equipment Manufacturing	432	423
电气机械及器材制造业	Electric Equipment and Machinery	379	358
通信设备计算机及其他电子设备制造业	Telecommunications Equipment, Computer and Other Electronic Equipment Manufacturing	328	333
仪器仪表及文化办公用机械制造业	Instruments, Meters, Cultural and Office Machinery	146	136
工艺品及其他制造业	Craftwork and Other Manufacturing	171	128
废弃资源和废旧材料回收加工业	Waste Resources and Materials Recovering and Processing	13	25
电力热力的生产和供应业	Production and Supply of Electric & Heat Energy	54	49
燃气生产和供应业	Production and Supply of Gas	13	14
水的生产和供应业	Production and Supply of Water	21	18

10-4 工业总产值
（全部国有及规模以上工业）
GROSS OUTPUT VALUE OF INDUSTRY(ALL STATE-OWNED AND ABOVE DESIGNATED SIZE)

单位:亿元 (100 million yuan)

项　目	Item	2004	2005	2005 比2004年增长% Increase Rate in 2005 over 2004
全市总计	**Total**	**5 853.72**	**6 774.10**	**20.8**
#国有及国有控股企业	State-owned and State-holding Enterprises	2 046.36	2 628.84	27.0
按登记注册类型分	**Grouped by Status of Registration**			
内资企业	Domestic-funded Enterprises	3 007.55	3 454.87	22.5
国有企业	State-owned Enterprises	551.50	532.12	25.4
集体企业	Collective-owned Enterprises	195.06	194.41	1.6
股份合作企业	Cooperative Enterprises	79.34	65.25	-8.5
私营企业	Private Enterprises	678.41	638.31	-6.0
股份有限公司	Share-holding Corporations Ltd.	700.88	979.39	29.1
有限责任公司	Limited Liability Corporations	765.03	1 020.20	24.5
#国有独资	Sole State-funded Corporations	162.92	205.09	33.4
联营企业	Joint Ownership Enterprises	28.08	17.42	-24.8
#国有与国有联营企业	State Joint Ownership Enterprises	2.14	1.73	-5.1
集体与集体联营企业	Collective Joint Ownership Enterprises	3.88	1.51	-20.5
其他内资企业	Other Domestic-funded Enterprises	9.26	7.78	-9.1
港澳台商投资企业	Enterprises with Investment from Hongkong, Macao and Taiwan	262.89	314.85	26.8
外商投资企业	Foreign Funded Enterprises	2 583.28	3 004.38	18.2
按经济类型分	**Grouped by Ownership**			
国有经济	State-owned	716.56	738.93	27.3
集体经济	Collective-owned	278.28	261.17	-1.5
私有经济	Private and Individual	678.41	638.31	-6.0
港澳台商投资经济	Hongkong, Macao and Taiwan Funded	262.89	314.85	26.8
外商投资经济	Foreign Funded	2 583.28	3 004.38	18.2
其　他	Others	1 334.31	1 816.46	25.1

10－4 续表 1　Continued

单位:亿元　　(100 million yuan)

项　　目	Item	2004	2005	2005 比 2004 年增长% Increase Rate in 2005 over 2004
按隶属关系分	**Grouped by Administrative Relationship**			
中央工业	Central Industry	898.31	1 091.57	29.2
地方工业	Local Industry	4 955.41	5 682.53	19.2
#市管工业	City Industry	3 496.34	4 012.37	19.0
#工业系统	Industry System	1 851.24	2 250.36	22.4
区县管工业	District & County Industry	178.22	285.67	23.5
街管工业	Neighbour Industry	10.52	5.69	－46.0
乡镇管工业	Town and Country Industry	1 109.78	1 226.84	22.8
按轻重分	**Grouped by Light & Heavy Industry**			
轻工业	Light Industry	1 265.73	1 372.88	9.6
重工业	Heavy Industry	4 587.98	5 401.23	24.0
按规模分	**Grouped by Size of Enterprises**			
大　型	Large－sized	2 263.68	2 625.04	16.9
中　型	Medium－sized	1 837.13	2 366.05	27.3
小　型	Small－sized	1 752.91	1 783.01	1.6
按行业分	**Grouped by Sector**			
煤炭开采和洗选业	Coal Mining and Dressing	24.38	16.07	－33.7
石油和天然气开采业	Petroleum and Natural Gas Extraction	314.65	474.76	59.2
有色金属矿采选业	Nonferrous Metals Mining and Dressing	35.08	39.63	17.5
非金属矿采选业	Nonmetal Minerals Mining and Dressing	5.54	10.42	45.3
农副食品加工业	Agricultural Products and Byproducts Processing	130.36	130.01	7.0
食品制造业	Food Manufacturing	65.26	85.17	6.1
饮料制造业	Beverage Manufacturing	53.93	65.35	20.7
烟草制品业	Tobacco Products	9.28	7.11	－23.5
纺织业	Textile Industry	73.20	82.08	13.3
纺织服装鞋帽制造业	Textile Garments,Shoes,Caps Manufacturing	61.03	89.18	7.1
皮革毛皮羽毛(绒)及其制品业	Leather,Furs,Feather and Related Products	32.35	32.61	0.2
木材加工及木、竹、藤、棕、草制品业	Timber Processing,Bamboo,Cane,Palm Fiber and Straw Products	17.75	21.28	19.9

10-4 续表 2 Continued

单位:亿元 (100 million yuan)

项 目	Item	2004	2005	2005 比 2004 年 增长% Increase Rate in 2005 over 2004
家具制造业	Furniture Manufacturing	36.48	41.41	13.1
造纸及纸制品业	Papermaking and Paper Products	46.28	50.15	11.4
印刷业和记录媒介的复制	Printing and Record Medium Reproduction	20.08	17.06	2.1
文教体育用品制造业	Cultural,Educational and Sports Goods	27.42	28.85	12.6
石油加工炼焦及核燃料加工业	Petroleum Processing,Coking and Nuclear Fuel Processing	257.95	373.94	11.1
化学原料及化学制品制造业	Raw Chemical Materials and Chemical Products	402.62	340.23	-15.6
医药制造业	Medical and Pharmaceutical Products	117.84	139.70	10.8
化学纤维制造业	Chemical Fiber	5.24	6.67	27.2
橡胶制品业	Rubber Products	53.85	48.74	5.7
塑料制品业	Plastic Products	105.53	110.56	15.9
非金属矿物制品业	Nonmetal Mineral Products	77.73	95.47	17.0
黑色金属冶炼及压延加工业	Smelting and Pressing of Ferrous Metals	769.44	838.93	29.7
有色金属冶炼及压延加工业	Smelting and Pressing of Nonferrous Metals	101.50	96.23	-1.6
金属制品业	Metal Products	204.50	241.46	7.6
通用设备制造业	General Purpose Equipment Manufacturing	214.06	232.62	23.1
专用设备制造业	Special Purpose Equipment Manufacturing	102.77	121.36	16.3
交通运输设备制造业	Transport Equipment Manufacturing	436.55	585.79	36.8
电气机械及器材制造业	Electric Equipment and Machinery	312.64	333.88	19.6
通信设备计算机及其他电子设备制造业	Telecommunications Equipment,Computer and Other Electronic Equipment Manufacturing	1 368.10	1 616.84	18.6
仪器仪表及文化办公用机械制造业	Instruments,Meters,Cultural and Office Machinery	55.33	51.05	-7.8
工艺品及其他制造业	Craftwork and Other Manufacturing	36.35	28.09	-4.0
废弃资源和废旧材料回收加工业	Waste Resources and Materials Recovering and Processing	7.76	7.50	-20.6
电力热力的生产和供应业	Production and Supply of Electric & Heat Energy	239.13	288.58	32.9
燃气生产和供应业	Production and Supply of Gas	12.64	14.06	8.1
水的生产和供应业	Production and Supply of Water	19.10	11.28	-41.0

10－5 地方工业总产值
（全部国有及规模以上工业）
GROSS OUTPUT VALUE OF LOCAL INDUSTRY(ALL STATE－OWNED AND ABOVE DESIGNATED SIZE)

单位：亿元 (100 million yuan)

项 目	Item	2004	2005	2005比2004年增长% Increase Rate in 2005 over 2004
全 市 总 计	**Total**	**4 955.41**	**5 682.53**	**19.2**
按登记注册类型分	**Grouped by Status of Registration**			
内资企业	Domestic－funded Enterprises	2 133.54	2 385.56	19.1
国有企业	State－owned Enterprises	261.98	319.16	24.4
集体企业	Collective－owned Enterprises	194.16	193.74	1.8
股份合作企业	Cooperative Enterprises	79.18	65.12	－8.5
私营企业	Private Enterprises	678.41	638.31	－6.0
股份有限公司	Share－holding Corporations Ltd.	238.89	241.47	14.5
有限责任公司	Limited Liability Corporations	645.73	903.00	26.5
#国有独资	Sole State－funded Corporations	113.06	167.24	38.9
联营企业	Joint Ownership Enterprises	25.94	16.98	－25.9
#国有与国有联营企业	State Joint Ownership Enterprises	1.62	1.29	－15.9
集体与集体联营企业	Collective Joint Ownership Enterprises	3.88	1.51	－20.5
其他内资企业	Other Domestic－funded Enterprises	9.26	7.78	－9.1
港澳台商投资企业	Enterprises with Investment from Hongkong,Macao and Taiwan	262.22	314.22	26.9
外商投资企业	Foreign Funded Enterprises	2 559.65	2 982.75	18.6
按经济类型分	**Grouped by Ownership**			
国有经济	State－owned	376.66	487.69	28.7
集体经济	Collective－owned	277.21	260.38	－1.4
私有经济	Private and Individual	678.41	638.31	－6.0
港澳台商投资经济	Hongkong,Macao and Taiwan Funded	262.22	314.22	26.9
外商投资经济	Foreign Funded	2 559.65	2 982.75	18.6
其 他	Others	801.26	999.18	19.2

10－5 续表 1　Continued
单位:亿元　(100 million yuan)

项　目	Item	2004	2005	2005 比 2004 年增长% Increase Rate in 2005 over 2004
按隶属关系分	**Grouped by Administrative Relationship**			
#市管工业	City Industry	3 496.34	4 012.37	19.0
#工业系统	Industry System	1 851.18	2 250.23	22.4
区县管工业	District & County Industry	178.22	285.67	23.5
街管工业	Neighbour Industry	10.52	5.69	－46.0
乡镇管工业	Town and Country Industry	1 109.78	1 226.84	22.8
按轻重分	**Grouped by Light & Heavy Industry**			
轻工业	Light Industry	1 249.40	1 357.18	9.5
重工业	Heavy Industry	3 706.01	4 325.36	22.6
按规模分	**Grouped by Size of Enterprises**			
大　型	Large－sized	1 708.04	1 990.57	16.0
中　型	Medium－sized	1 552.79	1 970.42	23.1
小　型	Small－sized	1 694.58	1 721.54	1.5
按行业分	**Grouped by Sector**			
煤炭开采和洗选业	Coal Mining and Dressing	24.38	16.07	－33.7
有色金属矿采选业	Nonferrous Metals Mining and Dressing	35.08	39.63	17.5
非金属矿采选业	Nonmetal Minerals Mining and Dressing	5.54	10.42	45.3
农副食品加工业	Agricultural Products and Byproducts Processing	130.36	130.01	7.0
食品制造业	Food Manufacturing	65.02	84.73	5.9
饮料制造业	Beverage Manufacturing	53.93	65.35	20.7
纺织业	Textile Industry	72.81	81.70	13.4
纺织服装鞋帽制造业	Textile Garments,Shoes,Caps Manufacturing	61.03	89.18	7.1
皮革毛皮羽毛(绒)及其制品业	Leather,Furs,Feather and Related Products	32.33	32.61	0.2
木材加工及木、竹、藤、棕、草制品业	Timber Processing,Bamboo,Cane,Palm Fiber and Straw Products	17.42	21.09	21.1

10－5 续表 2 Continued
单位:亿元 (100 million yuan)

项 目	Item	2004	2005	2005 比 2004 年 增长% Increase Rate in 2005 over 2004
家具制造业	Furniture Manufacturing	36.48	41.41	13.1
造纸及纸制品业	Papermaking and Paper Products	46.28	50.15	11.4
印刷业和记录媒介的复制	Printing and Record Medium Reproduction	19.20	16.32	1.9
文教体育用品制造业	Cultural,Educational and Sports Goods	27.42	28.85	12.6
石油加工炼焦及核燃料加工业	Petroleum Processing,Coking and Nuclear Fuel Processing	42.05	63.26	21.5
化学原料及化学制品制造业	Raw Chemical Materials and Chemical Products	311.19	322.67	10.4
医药制造业	Medical and Pharmaceutical Products	115.23	136.59	10.8
化学纤维制造业	Chemical Fiber	5.24	6.67	27.2
橡胶制品业	Rubber Products	53.85	48.74	5.7
塑料制品业	Plastic Products	105.40	109.81	16.0
非金属矿物制品业	Nonmetal Mineral Products	75.65	93.59	16.7
黑色金属冶炼及压延加工业	Smelting and Pressing of Ferrous Metals	769.44	838.93	29.7
有色金属冶炼及压延加工业	Smelting and Pressing of Nonferrous Metals	101.50	96.23	－1.6
金属制品业	Metal Products	179.51	220.62	10.2
通用设备制造业	General Purpose Equipment Manufacturing	213.96	232.29	23.1
专用设备制造业	Special Purpose Equipment Manufacturing	95.11	118.33	19.5
交通运输设备制造业	Transport Equipment Manufacturing	419.62	568.27	37.6
电气机械及器材制造业	Electric Equipment and Machinery	307.14	329.72	21.0
通信设备计算机及其他电子设备制造业	Telecommunications Equipment,Computer and Other Electronic Equipment Manufacturing	1 361.40	1 614.07	19.1
仪器仪表及文化办公用机械制造业	Instruments,Meters,Cultural and Office Machinery	53.75	50.48	－6.2
工艺品及其他制造业	Craftwork and Other Manufacturing	36.35	28.09	－4.0
废弃资源和废旧材料回收加工业	Waste Resources and Materials Recovering and Processing	7.76	7.50	－20.6
电力热力的生产和供应业	Production and Supply of Electric & Heat Energy	42.12	63.81	66.0
燃气生产和供应业	Production and Supply of Gas	12.64	14.06	8.1
水的生产和供应业	Production and Supply of Water	19.10	11.28	－41.0

10－6　主要工业产品产量(1990－2005年)

OUTPUT OF MAJOR INDUSTRIAL PRODUCTS,1990－2005

年　份 Year	布（万米）Cloth (10 000 m)	纱（万吨）Yarn (10 000 tons)	机制纸及纸板（万吨）Machine-made Paper and Paperboards (10 000 tons)	合成洗涤剂（万吨）Synthetic Detergent (10 000 tons)	饮料酒（万吨）Alcoholic Beverages (10 000 tons)	家用电冰箱（万台）Household Refrige-rators (10 000 units)	电视机（万台）Television Sets (10 000 units)	#彩色电视机 Color Television Sets
1990	49 194	11.69	26.75	8.54	9.28	23.34	143.93	62.46
1991	46 790	11.23	27.18	9.34	10.75	6.71	140.27	72.63
1992	43 031	10.86	33.32	10.56	10.88	9.27	140.99	68.29
1993	39 259	11.59	36.84	10.00	11.40	2.71	134.88	73.30
1994	41 437	13.19	31.01	9.68	11.09	3.95	124.00	80.37
1995	49 803	12.35	41.42	11.95	12.34	3.70	160.82	109.54
1996	39 662	10.51	45.89	12.07	10.72	0.29	157.34	117.80
1997	49 845	13.61	40.56	10.28	13.73	0.69	84.36	59.16
1998	33 326	8.37	33.64	9.65	15.25	2.29	82.94	47.87
1999	27 308	8.45	25.50	8.75	14.21	9.93	84.67	50.34
2000	29 217	8.80	25.18	7.19	15.75	8.42	94.27	72.28
2001	25 861	8.13	20.63	5.68	20.71	3.85	66.24	51.42
2002	27 082	9.18	27.98	5.41	20.64	19.14	87.06	76.35
2003	25 114	7.47	17.76	5.09	24.72	29.17	121.09	112.41
2004	30 805	7.51	36.03	5.04	23.65	28.25	110.99	109.42
2005	25 850	7.32	18.89	1.40	20.81	19.30	66.01	64.90

年　份 Year	原油（万吨）Crude Oil (10 000 tons)	发电量（亿千瓦小时）Electricity (100 million kwh)	钢（万吨）Steel (10 000 tons)	水泥（万吨）Cement (10 000 tons)	硫酸（万吨）Sulfuric Acid (10 000 tons)	烧碱（万吨）Caustic Soda (10 000 tons)	农用化肥（万吨）Chemical Fertilizer (10 000 tons)	化学农药（万吨）Chemical Pesticide (10 000 tons)
1990	469.50	94.85	166.74	122.14	7.70	25.23	7.21	1.97
1991	474.90	90.27	175.43	137.24	8.31	27.25	7.85	2.12
1992	491.76	98.62	183.45	144.58	8.15	27.99	7.84	2.01
1993	517.00	126.65	221.98	152.39	7.36	28.27	10.61	2.37
1994	589.00	122.47	188.55	177.00	7.79	29.28	15.75	2.81
1995	620.82	133.65	171.57	200.62	5.58	32.57	9.74	1.69
1996	646.60	146.04	200.99	207.88	8.11	50.75	11.31	2.95
1997	645.90	166.53	236.79	209.00	11.33	44.15	10.91	3.27
1998	691.28	172.51	255.27	250.00	10.36	39.90	10.26	3.38
1999	686.72	182.56	317.69	240.51	11.47	47.04	26.82	3.68
2000	763.99	211.49	356.76	267.81	11.17	49.28	17.04	2.79
2001	970.29	217.43	395.30	338.99	11.27	49.39	14.91	0.71
2002	1 215.94	268.83	482.58	377.75	12.15	63.65	16.03	3.30
2003	1 316.30	319.95	565.95	449.31	10.96	79.89	16.40	2.10
2004	1 446.21	339.76	788.48	520.52	9.99	81.14	15.96	0.44
2005	1 782.89	365.70	955.28	519.15	11.95	80.45	16.94	1.26

10－7　主要工业产品产量
OUTPUT OF MAJOR INDUSTRIAL PRODUCTS

产品名称	Item	单　位	Unit	2004	2005
原　油	Crude Oil	万吨	10 000 tons	1 446.21	1 782.89
原油加工量	Crude Oil Processed	万吨	10 000 tons	742.61	467.02
发电量	Electricity	亿千瓦小时	100 million kwh	339.76	365.70
供热量	Heating Supply	万百万千焦	10 000 billion joule	6 868.85	5 651.98
天然气	Natural Gas	亿立方米	100 million cu.m	8.72	8.80
液化气	Liquefied Petroleum Gas	万吨	10 000 tons	47.69	44.78
原　盐	Salt	万吨	10 000 tons	241.20	230.10
食用植物油	Edible Vegetable Oil	万吨	10 000 tons	52.61	51.57
饮料酒	Alcoholic Beverages	万吨	10 000 tons	23.65	20.81
#啤　酒	Beer	万吨	10 000 tons	17.12	14.49
方便主食品	Staple Foods	万吨	10 000 tons	15.05	10.88
软饮料	Soft Drinking	万吨	10 000 tons	93.90	81.40
卷　烟	Cigarettes	万箱	10 000 cases	22.00	26.50
家　具	Furniture	万件	10 000 pcs	323.90	403.97
地　毯	Carpet	万元	10 000 yuan	115 869	120 186
化学纤维	Chemical Fiber	万吨	10 000 tons	28.04	20.54
纱(混合)	Yarn	万吨	10 000 tons	7.51	7.32
布(混合)	Cloth	万米	10 000 m	30 804.85	25 849.89
毛　线	Knitting Wool	吨	ton	2 747.62	2 845.31
呢　绒	Woolen Piece Goods	万米	10 000 m	799.70	770.10
服　装	Garments	万件	10 000 pieces	23 727.48	17 815.94
人造板	Artificial Board	万立方米	10 000 cu.m	11.64	16.16
机制纸及纸板	Machine－made Paper & Paperboard	万吨	10 000 tons	36.03	18.89
电子琴	Electronic Organ	万架	10 000 units	124.84	130.64
硫　酸	Sulfuric Acid	万吨	10 000 tons	9.99	11.95
纯　碱	Soda Ash	万吨	10 000 tons	87.09	86.87
烧　碱	Caustic Soda	万吨	10 000 tons	81.14	80.45
电　石	Calcium Carbide	万吨	10 000 tons	1.09	
合成氨	Synthetic Ammonia	万吨	10 000 tons	18.28	22.58
农用化肥	Chemical Fertilizer	万吨	10 000 tons	15.96	16.94
化学农药	Chemical Pesticide	吨	ton	4 446.25	12 606.71
乙　烯	Ethene	万吨	10 000 tons	22.79	20.71

10－7 续表 Continued

产品名称	Item	单 位	Unit	2004	2005
油 漆	Paint	吨	ton	90 657.65	66 229.00
染 料	Dyestuff	吨	ton	106 946.73	62 617.00
轮胎外胎	Tires	万条	10 000 units	4 398.08	676.01
农用塑料薄膜	Plastic Film for Farm Use	吨	ton	13 181.31	16 603.87
合成洗涤剂	Synthetic Detergents	万吨	10 000 tons	5.04	1.40
化学原料药	Chemical Raw Medicine	吨	ton	25 475.90	11 240.93
中成药	Traditional Chinese Patent Medicine	吨	ton	6 500	6 200
水 泥	Cement	万吨	10 000 tons	520.52	519.15
平板玻璃	Plate Glass	万重量箱	10 000 weight cases	433.71	379.75
生 铁	Pig Iron	万吨	10 000 tons	524.18	660.24
钢	Steel	万吨	10 000 tons	788.48	955.28
钢 材	Steel Products	万吨	10 000 tons	1 720.14	1 664.04
黄 金	Gold	千克	kg	33 980	41 755.00
焦 炭	Coke	万吨	10 000 tons	376.65	360.24
电焊条	Welding Rod	万吨	10 000 tons	106.57	129.10
内燃机	Internal Combustion Engine	万千瓦	10 000 kw	1 671.79	1 839.81
金属切削机床	Metal－cutting Machine	台	unit	595	524
升降移动机械	Lift	台	unit	16 008	17 173
汽 车	Motor Vehicle	辆	unit	229 167	327 756
#轿 车	Car	辆	unit	222 065	325 594
摩托车	Motorcycle	万辆	10 000 units	124.87	111.42
自行车	Bicycle	万辆	10 000 units	1 928.03	1 306.70
家用电冰箱	Household Refrigerator	万台	10 000 units	28.25	19.30
房间空气调节器	Air Conditioner	万台	10 000 units	384.12	434.43
微波炉	Microwave Oven	万台	10 000 units	1 376.78	1 431.15
移动电话	Mobile Phone	万部	10 000 units	4 927.09	6 319.82
微型计算机	Micro－computer	万部	10 000 units	2.37	2.14
半导体集成电路	Semiconductor Integrated Circuit	亿块	100 million pcs	4.80	5.20
电视机	Television Sets	万台	10 000 units	110.99	66.01
#彩色电视机	Color Television Sets	万台	10 000 units	109.42	64.90
录像机	Videocorder	万台	10 000 units	210.38	152.28
吸尘器	Vacuum Cleaners	万台	10 000 units	359.06	322.16

10－8 主要产品销售量和产销率

SALES VOLUME AND SALES RATIO OF MAJOR INDUSTRIAL PRODUCTS

产品名称	Item	单位	Unit	2004		2005	
				销售量 Sales Volume	产销率(%) Sales Ratio(%)	销售量 Sales Volume	产销率(%) Sales Ratio(%)
生　铁	Pig Iron	万吨	10 000 tons	132.08	25.2	128.79	19.5
钢　材	Steel Products	万吨	10 000 tons	1 677.47	97.5	1 706.16	100.4
无缝钢管	Seamless Steel Pipe	万吨	10 000 tons	144.04	98.3	174.99	100.2
硫　酸	Sulfuric Acid	万吨	10 000 tons	10.07	100.8	11.68	97.7
烧　碱	Caustic Soda	万吨	10 000 tons	80.40	99.1	81.31	96.7
纯　碱	Soda Ash	万吨	10 000 tons	84.81	97.4	83.59	96.2
轮胎外胎	Tires	万条	10 000 units	4 412.82	100.3	676.21	100.0
水　泥	Cement	万吨	10 000 tons	508.64	97.7	512.39	98.7
平板玻璃	Plate Glass	万重量箱	10 000 weight cases	407.85	94.7	370.82	97.6
焦　碳	Coke	万吨	10 000 tons	250.81	66.6	237.57	66.4
原　油	Crude Oil	万吨	10 000 tons	1 411.54	97.6	1 770.74	99.3
汽　车	Motor Vehicle	万辆	10 000 units	21.62	94.4	32.65	99.6
电视机	Television Sets	万台	10 000 units	112.81	101.6	66.82	101.2
#彩色电视机	Color Television Sets	万台	10 000 units	110.58	101.1	65.41	100.8
家用电冰箱(柜)	Household Refrigerator	万台	10 000 units	27.50	97.3	18.97	98.3
吸尘器	Vacuum Cleaners	万台	10 000 units	361.23	100.6	321.76	99.9
房间空气调节器	Air Conditioner	万台	10 000 units	449.49	91.0	434.78	100.1
微波炉	Microwave Ovens	万台	10 000 units	1 397.95	101.5	1 429.29	99.9
移动电话机	Mobile Phone	万部	10 000 units	4 938.42	100.2	6 311.18	99.9
纱(混合)	Yarn	万吨	10 000 tons	5.17	68.9	4.85	66.3
布(混合)	Cloth	万米	10 000 m	30 365.33	98.6	26 022.32	100.7
毛　线	Knitting Wool	吨	ton	2 789.63	101.5	3 202.31	112.5
呢　绒	Woolen Piece Goods	万米	10 000 m	763.25	95.4	773.03	100.4
合成洗涤剂	Synthetic Detergents	万吨	10 000 tons	5.01	99.4	1.94	102.7
录像机	Videocorder	万部	10 000 units	211.39	100.5	154.76	101.6
照相机	Cameras	万台	10 000 units	120.77	105.3	75.49	101.5
服　装	Garments	万件	10 000 pieces	23 597.80	99.8	17 959.02	99.4
自行车	Bicycle	万辆	10 000 units	1 888.02	97.9	1 286.87	99.4
微型计算机	Micro－computer	万部	10 000 units	2.40	99.5	2.07	96.8
人造板	Artificial Board	万立方米	10 000 cu. m	11.94	102.6	15.98	98.9
摩托车	Motorcycles	万辆	10 000 units	119.74	95.9	113.47	101.1

10－9 工业企业主要财务指标(1990－2005年)

MAIN FINANCIAL INDICATORS OF INDUSTRIAL ENTERPRISES,1990－2005

单位:亿元 (100 million yuan)

年 份 Year	固定资产原价 Original Value of Fixed Assets	固定资产净值年平均余额 Annual Average Balance of Net Value of Fixed Assets	流动资产年平均余额 Annual Average Balance of Circulating Funds	主营业务收入 Business Revenue	利税总额 Total Pre－tax Profits	从业人员年平均人数(万人) Annual Average Persons Employed (10 000 persons)
全 市 Total						
1990	329.93	217.17	148.83	465.55	48.36	159.31
1991	379.97	252.86	173.89	538.50	52.61	155.64
1992	458.50	276.80	207.99	646.92	59.40	160.30
1993	611.67	312.14	559.47	1 040.49	83.94	178.08
1994	852.75	429.40	756.09	1 101.71	109.86	177.93
1995	1 273.46	628.11	888.92	1 376.70	133.51	173.58
1996	1 338.28	892.14	1 044.83	1 498.67	139.73	165.56
1997	1 590.96	1 092.54	1 232.07	1 668.15	139.96	158.52
1998	1 899.35	1 289.83	1 386.17	1 943.89	148.69	142.99
1999	2 157.03	1 446.46	1 490.98	2 182.17	175.66	128.75
2000	2 488.60	1 561.39	1 488.27	2 656.98	274.27	120.19
2001	2 763.94	1 657.85	1 772.75	2 983.26	326.55	122.15
2002	2 940.21	1 729.50	1 874.76	3 437.46	325.07	120.95
2003	3 036.78	1 793.13	1 991.12	4 202.02	401.35	115.28
2004	3 415.23	2 076.99	2 682.47	5 861.43	608.91	122.85
2005	3 845.17	2 155.41	3 058.69	7 125.93	815.63	122.21
#国有经济 State－owned						
1990	273.52	176.86	112.41	356.60	37.35	97.07
1991	314.71	207.30	129.89	407.79	39.01	96.74
1992	376.34	245.69	255.46	459.59	37.32	96.08
1993	467.63	292.18	345.77	663.86	37.91	117.79
1994	612.46	363.96	444.30	584.78	44.50	93.50
1995	942.91	644.15	474.69	625.98	44.91	90.70
1996	910.56	647.65	518.45	594.08	37.06	83.05
1997	1 031.89	732.58	577.59	625.22	39.26	78.99
1998	1 130.86	773.73	601.69	587.69	29.63	69.34
1999	1 261.91	817.29	631.78	594.55	26.88	56.84
2000	1 193.87	836.48	648.06	667.84	18.70	48.12
2001	1 151.07	699.45	615.11	649.26	17.08	42.99
2002	1 087.90	693.21	605.08	629.86	22.63	36.42
2003	1 066.98	704.47	576.42	817.42	52.83	30.71
2004	882.16	585.60	575.46	738.40	40.14	23.52
2005	898.32	549.77	627.10	841.32	50.27	20.61

注:1.本表数据范围1998年以前为街乡及以上工业,以后为规模以上工业。2.从业人员年平均人数1998年以前为职工平均人数。

Note:a)Figures Before 1998 of this table refer to industrial enterprises at township and higher level. Since 1998,figures refer to enterprises above designated size. b)Annual average employment personnel before 1998 refer to staff and workers.

10-10 工业企业主
MAIN FINANCIAL INDICATORS OF

项 目	Item	从业人员年平均人数（人） Annual Average Persons Employed (person)	工业增加值（万元） Value Added of Industry (10 000 yuan)	实收资本（万元） Total Capital Hold (10 000 yuan)
全 市 总 计	**Total**	**1 222 079**	**18 362 950**	**19 546 303**
#国有及国有控股企业	State－owned and State－holding Enterprises	406 521	8 647 939	9 557 752
按登记注册类型分	**Grouped by Status of Registration**			
内资企业	Domestic－funded Enterprises	793 692	10 628 785	11 239 511
国有企业	State－owned Enterprises	132 258	1 208 174	1 958 060
集体企业	Collective－owned Enterprise	78 368	517 957	247 764
股份合作企业	Cooperative Enterprises	17 613	113 366	109 982
私营企业	Private Enterprises	214 175	1 320 414	1 560 676
股份有限公司	Share－holding Corporations Ltd.	74 096	4 834 265	2 600 910
有限责任公司	Limited Liability Corporations	267 810	2 570 515	4 696 611
#国有独资	Sole State－funded Corporations	72 591	437 609	2 282 337
联营企业	Joint Ownership Enterprises	6 457	34 240	58 541
#国有与国有联营企业	State Joint Ownership Enterprises	1 264	4 305	20 736
集体与集体联营企业	Collective Joint Ownership Enterprises	1 457	6 178	8 973
其他内资企业	Other Domestic－funded Enterprises	2 915	29 855	6 967
港澳台商投资企业	Enterprises with Investment from Hongkong, Macao and Taiwan	82 183	968 161	1 123 644
外商投资企业	Foreign Funded Enterprises	346 204	6 766 004	7 183 148
按经济类型分	**Grouped by Ownership**			
国有经济	State－owned	206 113	1 650 087	4 261 133
集体经济	Collective－owned	97 438	637 501	366 719
私有经济	Private and Individual	214 175	1 320 414	1 560 676
港澳台商投资经济	Hongkong, Macao and Taiwan Funded	82 183	968 161	1 123 644
外商投资经济	Foreign Funded	346 204	6 766 004	7 183 148
其 他	Others	275 966	7 020 783	5 050 983
按隶属关系分	**Grouped by Administrative Relationship**			
中央工业	Central Industry	103 883	5 363 706	3 798 917
地方工业	Local Industry	1 118 196	12 999 244	15 747 386
#市管工业	City Industry	596 434	8 835 638	12 320 596
#工业系统	Industry System	348 694	4 228 213	6 261 851
区县管工业	District & County Industry	54 765	637 807	590 716
街管工业	Neighbour Industry	3 127	20 370	12 028
乡镇管工业	Town and Country Industry	414 224	3 049 198	2 552 195
按轻重分	**Grouped by Light & Heavy Industry**			
轻工业	Light Industry	475 854	3 464 522	5 082 091
重工业	Heavy Industry	746 225	14 898 428	14 464 212
按规模分	**Grouped by Size of Enterprises**			
大 型	Large－sized	261 351	5 670 654	4 417 153
中 型	Medium－sized	384 435	8 052 239	8 431 816
小 型	Small－sized	576 293	4 640 057	6 697 334

要财务指标(2005 年)
INDUSTRIAL ENTERPRISES,2005

资产总计(万元) Total Assets (10 000 yuan)	流动资产年平均余额(万元) Annual Average Balance of Circulating Funds (10 000 yuan)	固定资产原价(万元) Original Value of Fixed Assets (10 000 yuan)	固定资产净值年平均余额(万元) Annual Average Balance of Net Value of Fixed Assets (10 000 yuan)	主营业务收入(万元) Business Revenue (10 000 yuan)	利税总额(万元) Total Pre-tax Profits (10 000 yuan)	#利润总额 Total Profits
63 479 196	**30 586 887**	**38 451 665**	**21 554 108**	**71 259 252**	**8 156 311**	**5 515 983**
32 671 390	12 426 089	25 131 980	13 506 598	27 385 763	4 258 560	2 626 588
39 656 208	16 398 138	27 386 989	15 071 758	36 407 188	4 897 462	3 091 869
9 670 630	4 014 579	5 432 647	3 437 106	5 492 148	256 937	4 436
1 135 194	722 217	489 038	289 818	2 037 889	173 485	100 313
523 616	331 585	125 546	80 471	640 122	45 876	25 214
4 525 419	2 472 187	1 663 814	1 144 806	7 095 929	590 148	349 608
8 416 817	2 420 216	11 043 391	4 967 710	9 449 508	2 749 758	1 999 892
15 123 181	6 300 253	8 513 426	5 074 095	11 370 746	1 060 970	599 498
6 182 941	2 240 747	3 518 742	2 034 643	2 903 415	245 215	120 580
214 624	109 465	100 424	66 862	248 117	13 834	8 317
46 249	15 681	31 773	25 912	17 614	528	-1 149
17 886	9 732	13 552	6 893	15 879	2 254	1 480
46 728	27 637	18 704	10 891	72 729	6 453	4 591
3 225 872	1 713 511	1 739 777	1 071 168	3 415 231	332 273	245 069
20 597 116	12 475 237	9 324 899	5 411 181	31 436 834	2 926 576	2 179 045
15 899 819	6 271 007	8 983 163	5 497 661	8 413 177	502 680	123 867
1 676 695	1 063 534	628 135	377 182	2 693 890	221 615	127 006
4 525 419	2 472 187	1 663 814	1 144 806	7 095 929	590 148	349 608
3 225 872	1 713 511	1 739 777	1 071 168	3 415 231	332 273	245 069
20 597 116	12 475 237	9 324 899	5 411 181	31 436 834	2 926 576	2 179 045
17 554 275	6 591 411	16 111 878	8 052 109	18 204 192	3 583 018	2 491 387
10 875 849	2 830 410	14 905 665	7 338 147	10 742 368	2 991 511	2 074 046
52 603 347	27 756 476	23 546 001	14 215 961	60 516 884	5 164 800	3 441 937
39 859 304	20 916 938	18 349 262	10 866 069	43 118 519	3 673 884	2 485 777
23 474 723	11 330 045	10 781 708	6 164 037	23 875 424	1 861 271	1 020 394
2 394 035	1 317 566	967 810	634 575	2 755 504	150 230	79 581
59 292	33 095	22 795	11 361	54 485	4 852	3 013
9 401 419	4 890 137	3 793 629	2 450 081	13 025 472	1 200 915	786 219
16 019 202	7 794 914	7 497 351	4 708 996	14 618 457	1 282 493	744 306
47 459 994	22 791 973	30 954 314	16 845 111	56 640 796	6 873 819	4 771 677
22 737 973	10 768 641	14 129 392	7 555 101	28 434 755	3 082 138	2 023 620
20 870 065	9 564 549	15 411 399	8 233 244	23 895 282	3 592 679	2 608 831
19 871 158	10 253 696	8 910 875	5 765 763	18 929 215	1 481 495	883 532

10－11 地方工业企业

MAIN FINANCIAL INDICATORS OF LO

项 目	Item	从业人员年平均人数（人）Annual Average Persons Employed (person)	工业增加值（万元）Value Added of Industry (10 000 yuan)	实收资本（万元）Total Capital Hold (10 000 yuan)
全 市 总 计	**Total**	**1 118 196**	**12 999 244**	**15 747 386**
按登记注册类型分	**Grouped by Status of Registration**			
内资企业	Domestic－funded Enterprises	692 239	5 317 951	7 489 148
国有企业	State－owned Enterprises	94 577	640 920	1 153 421
集体企业	Collective－owned Enterprise	78 008	518 683	247 114
股份合作企业	Cooperative Enterprises	17 601	113 443	109 831
私营企业	Private Enterprises	214 175	1 320 414	1 560 676
股份有限公司	Share－holding Corporations Ltd.	47 591	534 371	753 358
有限责任公司	Limited Liability Corporations	231 043	2 126 473	3 603 944
#国有独资	Sole State－funded Corporations	40 656	426 585	1 596 793
联营企业	Joint Ownership Enterprises	6 329	33 793	53 836
#国有与国有联营企业	State Joint Ownership Enterprises	1 136	3 858	16 031
集体与集体联营企业	Collective Joint Ownership Enterprises	1 457	6 178	8 973
其他内资企业	Other Domestic－funded Enterprises	2 915	29 855	6 967
港澳台商投资企业	Enterprises with Investment from Hongkong,Macao and Taiwan	81 881	965 526	1 104 458
外商投资企业	Foreign Funded Enterprises	344 076	6 715 767	7 153 780
按经济类型分	**Grouped by Ownership**			
国有经济	State－owned	136 369	1 071 363	2 766 245
集体经济	Collective－owned	97 066	638 304	365 918
私有经济	Private and Individual	214 175	1 320 414	1 560 676
港澳台商投资经济	Hongkong,Macao and Taiwan Funded	81 881	965 526	1 104 458
外商投资经济	Foreign Funded	344 076	6 715 767	7 153 780
其 他	Others	244 629	2 287 871	2 796 308
按隶属关系分	**Grouped by Administrative Relationship**			
#市管工业	City Industry	596 434	8 835 638	12 320 596
#工业系统	Industry System	348 667	4 228 034	6 260 841
区县管工业	District & County Industry	54 765	637 807	590 716
街管工业	Neighbour Industry	3 127	20 370	12 028
乡镇管工业	Town and Country Industry	414 224	3 049 198	2 552 195
按轻重分	**Grouped by Light & Heavy Industry**			
轻工业	Light Industry	471 355	3 392 610	5 015 512
重工业	Heavy Industry	646 841	9 606 634	10 731 874
按规模分	**Grouped by Size of Enterprises**			
大 型	Large	189 915	3 654 731	3 215 080
中 型	Medium－sized	360 076	4 947 240	6 122 976
小 型	Small－sized	568 205	4 397 273	6 409 330

主要财务指标(2005 年)

CAL INDUSTRIAL ENTERPRISES, 2005

资产总计(万元) Total Assets (10 000 yuan)	流动资产年平均余额(万元) Annual Average Balance of Circulating Funds (10 000 yuan)	固定资产原价(万元) Original Value of Fixed Assets (10 000 yuan)	固定资产净值年平均余额(万元) Annual Average Balance of Net Value of Fixed Assets (10 000 yuan)	主营业务收入(万元) Business Revenue (10 000 yuan)	利税总额(万元) Total Pre-tax Profits (10 000 yuan)	#利润总额 Total Profits
52 603 347	**27 756 476**	**23 546 001**	**14 215 961**	**60 516 884**	**5 164 800**	**3 441 937**
28 945 859	13 696 375	12 530 729	7 766 313	25 899 392	1 945 090	1 055 926
6 558 834	2 951 707	2 450 711	1 676 379	3 245 954	94 188	9 928
1 124 876	714 067	486 015	288 265	2 023 425	172 378	99 499
521 817	329 942	125 267	80 315	638 849	45 835	25 198
4 525 419	2 472 187	1 663 814	1 144 806	7 095 929	590 148	349 608
3 297 866	1 572 152	1 656 622	831 488	2 662 423	265 486	137 614
12 662 652	5 522 403	6 033 593	3 670 494	9 916 627	757 113	421 345
5 075 862	1 682 326	2 853 721	1 685 380	2 252 748	202 548	115 008
207 667	106 281	96 004	63 676	243 456	13 488	8 143
39 291	12 497	27 354	22 727	12 953	182	-1 323
17 886	9 732	13 552	6 893	15 879	2 254	1 480
46 728	27 637	18 704	10 891	72 729	6 453	4 591
3 183 845	1 681 283	1 732 935	1 067 506	3 410 922	325 845	238 874
20 473 644	12 378 818	9 282 337	5 382 141	31 206 571	2 893 866	2 147 137
11 673 988	4 646 530	5 331 786	3 384 485	5 511 655	296 918	123 613
1 664 579	1 053 742	624 834	375 472	2 678 153	220 466	126 176
4 525 419	2 472 187	1 663 814	1 144 806	7 095 929	590 148	349 608
3 183 845	1 681 283	1 732 935	1 067 506	3 410 922	325 845	238 874
20 473 644	12 378 818	9 282 337	5 382 141	31 206 571	2 893 866	2 147 137
11 081 873	5 523 917	4 910 296	2 861 550	10 613 654	837 557	456 529
39 859 304	20 916 938	18 349 262	10 866 069	43 118 519	3 673 884	2 485 777
23 473 517	11 329 700	10 780 612	6 163 064	23 873 861	1 861 220	1 020 399
2 394 035	1 317 566	967 810	634 575	2 755 504	150 230	79 581
59 292	33 095	22 795	11 361	54 485	4 852	3 013
9 401 419	4 890 137	3 793 629	2 450 081	13 025 472	1 200 915	786 219
15 772 490	7 665 506	7 375 874	4 636 406	14 424 550	1 218 025	737 672
36 830 857	20 090 970	16 170 127	9 579 555	46 092 335	3 946 775	2 704 265
16 331 839	8 914 856	6 584 287	3 586 052	21 904 143	2 252 496	1 604 060
17 355 323	8 889 336	9 052 773	5 401 299	20 293 845	1 574 086	1 043 039
18 916 185	9 952 284	7 908 942	5 228 609	18 318 897	1 338 218	794 838

10－12 分行业工业企业

MAIN FINANCIAL INDICATORS OF INDUSTRIAL

行 业	Sector	从业人员年平均人数(人) Annual Average Persons Employed (person)	工业增加值(万元) Value Added of Industry (10 000 yuan)	实收资本(万元) Total Capital Hold (10 000 yuan)
总 计	**Total**	**1 222 079**	**18 362 950**	**19 546 303**
煤炭开采和洗选业	Coal Mining and Dressing	104	9 793	20 334
石油和天然气开采业	Petroleum and Natural Gas Extraction	53 107	4 137 081	2 297 694
有色金属矿采选业	Nonferrous Metals Mining and Dressing	2 850	13 182	28 000
非金属矿采选业	Nonmetal Minerals Mining and Dressing	12 895	71 561	51 665
农副食品加工业	Agricultural Products and Byproducts Processing	25 226	254 311	267 941
食品制造业	Food Manufacturing	24 742	245 698	341 023
饮料制造业	Beverage Manufacturing	12 801	247 141	298 564
烟草制品业	Tobacco Products	1 004	50 600	0
纺织业	Textile Industry	62 316	214 467	476 955
纺织服装鞋帽制造业	Textile Garments, Shoes, Caps Manufacturing	87 181	264 922	178 751
皮革毛皮羽毛(绒)及其制品业	Leather, Furs, Feather and Related Products	18 774	56 206	61 472
木材加工及木、竹、藤、棕、草制品业	Timber Processing, Bamboo, Cane, Palm Fiber and Straw Products	7 339	42 853	45 492
家具制造业	Furniture Manufacturing	21 371	94 151	186 307
造纸及纸制品业	Papermaking and Paper Products	19 403	147 334	226 269
印刷业和记录媒介的复制	Printing and Record Medium Reproduction	9 813	51 477	126 511
文教体育用品制造业	Cultural, Educational and Sports Goods	14 568	68 506	93 812
石油加工炼焦及核燃料加工业	Petroleum Processing, Coking and Nuclear Fuel Processing	16 171	343 847	418 232
化学原料及化学制品制造业	Raw Chemical Materials and Chemical Products	71 041	938 897	1 251 757
医药制造业	Medical and Pharmaceutical Products	39 939	472 818	1 026 183
化学纤维制造业	Chemical Fiber	2 758	9 995	18 679
橡胶制品业	Rubber Products	22 535	113 917	187 159
塑料制品业	Plastic Products	43 452	321 816	377 656
非金属矿物制品业	Nonmetal Mineral Products	29 863	306 009	489 717
黑色金属冶炼及压延加工业	Smelting and Pressing of Ferrous Metals	89 932	1 724 509	1 505 185
有色金属冶炼及压延加工业	Smelting and Pressing of Nonferrous Metals	8 777	183 690	131 484
金属制品业	Metal Products	68 139	474 838	450 881
通用设备制造业	General Purpose Equipment Manufacturing	63 303	618 641	721 199
专用设备制造业	Special Purpose Equipment Manufacturing	41 009	386 817	397 851
交通运输设备制造业	Transport Equipment Manufacturing	98 556	1 387 529	1 916 753
电气机械及器材制造业	Electric Equipment and Machinery	54 655	582 019	1 184 512
通信设备计算机及其他电子设备制造业	Telecommunications Equipment, Computer and Other Electronic Equipment Manufacturing	121 221	3 320 336	2 806 388
仪器仪表及文化办公用机械制造业	Instruments, Meters, Cultural and Office Machinery	16 090	134 600	503 327
工艺品及其他制造业	Craftwork and Other Manufacturing	24 049	57 749	75 040
废弃资源和废旧材料回收加工业	Waste Resources and Materials Recovering and Processing	1 619	17 483	21 699
电力热力的生产和供应业	Production and Supply of Electric & Heat Energy	24 842	901 656	897 191
燃气生产和供应业	Production and Supply of Gas	6 818	45 266	240 303
水的生产和供应业	Production and Supply of Water	3 816	51 237	224 317

主要财务指标(2005 年)

ENTERPRISES BY INDUSTRIAL SECTOR,2005

资产总计 (万元) Total Assets (10 000 yuan)	流动资产年平均余额 (万元) Annual Average Balance of Circulating Funds (10 000 yuan)	固定资产原价 (万元) Original Value of Fixed Assets (10 000 yuan)	固定资产净值年平均余额 (万元) Annuale Average Balance of Net Value of Fixed Assets (10 000 yuan)	主营业务收入 (万元) Business Revenue (10 000 yuan)	利税总额 (万元) Total Pre-tax Profits (10 000 yuan)	#利润总额 Total Profits
63 479 196	**30 586 887**	**38 451 665**	**21 554 108**	**71 259 252**	**8 156 311**	**5 515 983**
297 503	252 490	11 736	8 767	351 150	3 142	1 647
4 809 939	1 084 532	7 993 394	3 505 725	4 421 976	2 580 844	2 054 574
129 781	64 676	39 720	20 374	394 032	11 186	9 460
302 810	139 227	140 062	87 732	104 495	16 731	4 356
839 290	483 927	398 965	263 304	1 529 633	46 501	30 746
823 876	391 863	573 603	346 059	773 032	76 483	39 047
786 491	343 677	465 026	305 719	678 943	118 827	52 291
98 105	62 591	60 703	36 903	105 325	56 055	1 893
1 682 485	871 613	904 988	572 588	854 367	56 726	25 638
516 741	310 453	258 395	158 846	940 733	78 694	45 053
248 190	154 811	107 984	69 344	317 532	15 778	12 325
146 869	88 712	54 629	33 670	203 143	12 673	8 726
468 430	204 560	175 562	118 118	431 744	30 774	23 756
596 758	250 604	362 594	301 879	520 733	27 728	9 921
765 569	420 291	191 306	109 726	178 018	19 845	10 870
238 085	132 245	154 845	81 610	280 614	16 196	13 439
2 082 467	746 303	2 464 771	1 355 537	3 829 282	-30 529	-182 504
3 403 113	1 530 444	2 071 959	1 220 647	3 477 280	296 434	162 021
3 379 199	1 349 704	1 057 523	630 023	1 908 316	311 854	204 403
50 457	24 391	40 062	40 259	78 954	-1 394	-3 745
606 896	317 586	348 942	207 483	582 626	50 550	24 046
1 225 216	560 282	674 767	424 591	1 070 649	76 785	48 816
1 402 589	672 657	764 289	529 822	989 825	69 253	32 556
8 338 527	3 985 806	3 362 265	2 090 719	9 180 689	716 688	432 261
824 935	437 884	166 368	110 260	1 017 949	41 534	16 681
1 681 872	1 084 499	615 070	391 650	2 707 128	172 633	126 827
2 321 211	1 310 648	972 633	590 109	2 550 478	292 432	217 303
1 490 270	976 416	543 637	319 153	1 307 761	174 302	131 755
4 979 805	2 382 678	2 563 078	1 378 385	6 031 282	668 845	277 623
3 497 014	1 836 763	1 270 585	774 128	3 561 963	240 840	176 213
9 086 626	6 531 840	3 534 049	1 951 201	16 770 528	1 471 176	1 313 751
534 803	347 970	198 499	120 047	583 825	47 169	26 935
242 516	131 004	98 057	66 314	286 528	18 433	13 045
55 241	32 109	15 253	11 494	100 256	1 892	978
4 334 414	821 382	4 929 666	2 777 028	2 750 148	365 645	165 427
538 417	153 702	339 527	207 249	263 902	-2 113	-11 133
652 690	96 550	527 155	337 648	124 415	5 702	-1 016

10－13 分行业国有大中型工

MAIN FINANCIAL INDICATORS OF LARGE AND MEDIUM－SIZED

行 业	Sector	企业单位数（个）Number of Enter－prises (unit)	从业人员年平均人数（人）Annual Average Persons Employed (persons)	工业总产值（万元）Gross Industrial Output Value (10 000 yuan)
总 计	**Total**	**73**	**140 762**	**6 466 056**
#石油和天然气开采业	Petroleum and Natural Gas Extraction	3	38 974	446 625
非金属矿采选业	Nonmetal Minerals Mining and Dressing	2	10 761	70 730
农副食品加工业	Agricultural Products and Byproducts Processing	4	2 206	75 859
食品制造业	Food Manufacturing	1	507	8 946
饮料制造业	Beverage Manufacturing	3	2 155	104 928
烟草制品业	Tobacco Products	1	1 004	71 105
纺织业	Textile Industry	1	4 077	20 323
纺织服装鞋帽制造业	Textile Garments，Shoes，Caps Manufacturing	1	489	4 981
石油加工炼焦及核燃料加工业	Petroleum Processing，Coking and Nuclear Fuel Processing	3	2 055	190 551
化学原料及化学制品制造业	Raw Chemical Materials and Chemical Products	6	7 828	343 456
医药制造业	Medical and Pharmaceutical Products	3	5 278	120 254
塑料制品业	Plastic Products	1	1 082	35 472
非金属矿物制品业	Nonmetal Mineral Products	2	1 252	12 961
黑色金属冶炼及压延加工业	Smelting and Pressing of Ferrous Metals	7	21 715	2 622 174
金属制品业	Metal Products	6	3 543	153 401
通用设备制造业	General Purpose Equipment Manufacturing	2	1 876	28 891
专用设备制造业	Special Purpose Equipment Manufacturing	4	2 729	34 685
交通运输设备制造业	Transport Equipment Manufacturing	6	8 213	181 149
电气机械及器材制造业	Electric Equipment and Machinery	1	1 469	17 652
通信设备计算机及其他电子设备制造业	Telecommunications Equipment，Computer and Other Electronic Equipment Manufacturing	1	354	4 773
电力热力的生产和供应业	Production and Supply of Electric & Heat Energy	10	14 857	1 763 257
燃气生产和供应业	Production and Supply of Gas	3	5 907	97 950
水的生产和供应业	Production and Supply of Water	1	1 830	54 524

业企业主要财务指标(2005)

STATE - OWNED ENTERPRISES BY INDUSTRIAL SECTOR,2005

工业增加值(万元) Value Added of Industry (10 000 yuan)	实收资本(万元) Total Capital Hold (10 000 yuan)	资产总计(万元) Total Assets (10 000 yuan)	流动资产年平均余额(万元) Annual Average Balance of Circulating Funds (10 000 yuan)	固定资产原价(万元) Original Value of Fixed Assets (10 000 yuan)	固定资产净值年平均余额(万元) Annual Average Balance of Net Value of Fixed Assets (10 000 yuan)	主营业务收入(万元) Business Revenue (10 000 yuan)	利税总额(万元) Total Pre - tax Profits (10 000 yuan)	#利润总额 Total Profits
1 452 717	**3 148 357**	**11 311 872**	**4 183 426**	**6 934 127**	**4 136 634**	**7 429 281**	**516 094**	**171 754**
63 147	733 088	1 328 115	731 714	828 168	594 968	752 341	23 500	- 16 608
54 874	39 506	268 618	131 119	105 367	62 160	65 073	11 977	779
11 739	22 109	95 114	50 617	38 165	25 800	116 770	310	- 177
3 200	4 322	10 704	4 922	4 366	2 399	8 330	521	33
26 392	16 483	71 011	29 921	39 006	17 086	100 171	10 539	848
50 600	0	98 105	62 591	60 703	36 903	105 325	56 055	1 893
9 149	9 089	36 598	16 946	40 063	23 651	22 466	- 588	- 1 244
1 289	1 832	4 222	2 275	2 046	1 088	5 900	230	- 3
15 473	52 260	172 641	86 275	111 319	59 994	205 694	4 709	51
84 313	439 361	527 111	239 338	356 917	206 601	396 655	11 423	1 476
9 220	356 570	1 126 378	385 954	216 300	107 191	459 697	54 746	43 666
3 140	30 140	62 357	17 332	33 029	20 748	36 468	- 1 317	- 1 516
3 961	9 039	26 195	6 606	20 653	19 092	13 669	451	78
650 004	652 786	3 725 120	1 413 143	1 759 943	1 053 078	2 723 884	230 650	152 494
14 437	38 449	161 567	107 385	47 206	31 075	217 182	1 748	- 95
7 853	7 073	42 158	21 577	30 695	15 335	27 239	1 746	179
6 628	38 199	61 273	44 969	44 362	21 035	46 194	2 519	- 309
46 855	41 137	324 269	197 157	126 598	53 856	184 462	11 709	8 162
6 409	8 126	27 048	10 873	20 574	5 981	17 127	1 708	801
2 654	10 193	25 930	6 533	19 099	12 800	5 623	729	240
312 286	327 030	2 252 253	460 063	2 374 023	1 362 707	1 657 589	106 319	5 387
34 860	185 378	414 799	103 679	267 248	161 580	179 672	- 8 139	- 15 463
34 236	119 951	420 133	31 238	377 628	234 261	57 365	- 6 955	- 10 117

10－14 分地区工业企业主要财务指标（2005 年）
MAIN FINANCIAL INDICATORS OF INDUSTRIAL ENTERPRISES BY REGION，2005

单位：亿元 (100 million yuan)

地 区	Region	企业单位数（个）Number of Enter－prises (unit)	资产总计 Total Assets	固定资产原 价 Original Value of Fixed Assets	固定资产净值年平均余额 Annual Average Balance of Net Value of Fixed Assets	流动资产年平均余额 Annual Average Balance of Circulating Funds
全 市 总 计	**Total**	**6 144**	**6 347.92**	**3 845.17**	**2 155.41**	**3 058.69**
和平区	Heping District	88	286.48	154.03	91.28	131.83
河东区	Hedong District	193	457.62	129.01	75.30	188.97
河西区	Hexi District	263	277.83	110.38	67.94	142.98
南开区	Nankai District	552	335.79	119.35	72.62	173.86
河北区	Hebei District	240	300.25	224.28	140.09	102.30
红桥区	Hongqiao District	126	46.69	17.76	10.29	25.66
塘沽区	Tanggu District	517	1 411.71	946.37	471.30	826.12
汉沽区	Hangu District	134	70.69	45.75	26.47	31.21
大港区	Dagang District	221	538.89	665.98	327.42	189.23
东丽区	Dongli District	430	478.08	291.80	159.73	190.29
西青区	Xiqing District	641	794.47	454.33	271.71	389.15
津南区	Jinnan District	487	203.48	85.24	58.24	100.42
北辰区	Beichen District	676	513.65	196.23	127.32	276.55
武清区	Wuqing District	443	217.79	147.88	84.75	107.54
宝坻区	Baodi District	360	51.26	29.93	21.54	26.00
宁河县	Ninghe County	174	62.55	28.57	18.65	30.59
静海县	Jinghai County	327	187.23	65.45	44.44	101.28
蓟 县	Jixian County	272	113.47	132.83	86.33	24.71

地 区	Region	主营业务收 入 Business Revenue	主营业务税金及附加 Sales Tax and Extra Charge	利税总额 Total Pre－tax Profit	利润总额 Total Profit	工业总产值 Gross Industrial Output Value	工业增加值 Value Added of Industry
全 市 总 计	**Total**	**7 125.93**	**77.74**	**815.63**	**551.60**	**6 774.10**	**1 836.30**
和平区	Heping District	230.47	0.70	13.13	5.96	197.58	36.35
河东区	Hedong District	250.35	0.66	19.39	12.53	202.42	46.88
河西区	Hexi District	207.93	0.51	12.99	9.08	181.46	39.57
南开区	Nankai District	264.75	0.72	24.31	14.93	224.18	58.51
河北区	Hebei District	210.90	0.90	11.95	2.13	202.95	41.07
红桥区	Hongqiao District	30.24	0.36	2.83	1.42	24.93	5.52
塘沽区	Tanggu District	1 962.36	20.85	350.83	289.87	1 910.79	603.70
汉沽区	Hangu District	82.02	0.49	8.12	2.42	81.98	30.20
大港区	Dagang District	636.04	12.49	80.82	43.75	614.42	192.88
东丽区	Dongli District	434.31	5.18	41.77	23.29	406.95	137.97
西青区	Xiqing District	1 203.75	17.88	86.86	43.10	1 181.01	252.30
津南区	Jinnan District	227.08	0.56	19.27	13.08	222.28	43.43
北辰区	Beichen District	547.01	2.80	50.63	32.34	512.61	147.58
武清区	Wuqing District	235.57	0.31	23.21	17.03	241.10	59.77
宝坻区	Baodi District	94.61	0.15	8.23	5.71	80.89	9.10
宁河县	Ninghe County	77.67	1.17	5.24	2.82	81.58	12.53
静海县	Jinghai County	288.17	9.89	29.02	15.79	272.17	74.38
蓟 县	Jixian County	142.71	2.11	27.03	16.34	134.80	44.55

10－15 工业企业主要经济效益指标(1990－2005年)

MAIN INDICATORS ON ECONOMIC BENEFIT OF INDUSTRIAL ENTERPRISES,1990－2005

年 份 Year	产销率(%) Sales Ratio (%)	资 金利税率(%) Ratio of Pre-tax Profits to Total Assets (%)	总资产贡献率(%) Ratio of Total Assets to Industrial Output Value (%)	成本费用利润率(%) Ratio of Profits to Industrial Cost (%)	万元产值耗能源(现价、吨标准煤) Energy Consumption per 10 000 yuan Output Value (tons of SCE)	工 业增加值率(%) Ratio of Value Added to Gross Industrial Output Value (%)	全员劳动生产率(元/人) Overall Labor Productivity (yuan/person)
全 市 合 计							
Total							
1990	88.8	10.7			1.99		
1991	93.1	9.6			1.65	22.5	8 574
1992	92.7	9.2			1.44	22.7	9 864
1993	97.6	9.6	9.1	3.5	1.12	20.8	11 814
1994	85.2	9.3			0.94	20.9	15 214
1995	86.4	8.8	9.6	4.5	0.91	21.9	20 084
1996	91.6	7.2	8.3	5.0	0.83	21.3	20 993
1997	96.4	6.0	7.1	3.7	0.69	20.4	23 073
1998	97.9	5.6	6.6	2.9	0.66	20.1	29 055
1999	98.6	6.0	6.5	3.6	0.58	20.7	35 730
2000	98.4	9.0	8.9	6.5	0.58	24.2	52 425
2001	96.7	9.5	9.3	6.6	0.55	24.8	59 605
2002	99.1	9.0	8.7	5.8	0.53	25.4	69 728
2003	98.9	10.6	9.9	6.0	0.48	26.5	93 235
2004	99.0	12.8	12.8	7.5	0.39	26.1	124 367
2005	100.6	15.6	14.5	8.5	0.38	27.1	150 260
#国有经济							
State－owned							
1990	92.1	10.7					
1991	97.6	7.3				22.9	10 126
1992	98.2	7.9				23.2	11 371
1993	100.8	6.7	7.0	0.7		20.3	10 813
1994	97.9	6.3				23.0	15 910
1995	107.5	5.6	6.5	0.5		27.3	20 536
1996	98.2	3.3	5.0	0.3		27.3	18 365
1997	95.8	3.2	4.7			25.0	19 587
1998	99.2	2.2	4.1			25.8	21 340
1999	101.0	1.9	3.2			28.4	26 743
2000	100.0	1.3	1.3			28.0	32 545
2001	99.0	1.3	2.4			23.2	29 470
2002	100.5	1.7	2.4			22.5	32 058
2003	100.2	4.1	4.2	1.6		28.9	56 402
2004	101.0	3.5	3.3	0.4		28.0	85 329
2005	102.0	4.3	3.7	1.5		22.3	80 057

10－16　工业企业主要经济效益指标(2005年)

MAIN INDICATORS ON ECONOMIC BENEFIT OF INDUSTRIAL ENTERPRISES, 2005

项　目	Item	单　位	Unit	全　市 Total	#地　方 Local
全　市	**Total**				
总资产贡献率	Ratio of Total Assets to Industrial Output Value		%	14.5	11.2
增加值率	Ratio of Value Added to Gross Industrial Output Value		%	27.1	22.9
全员劳动生产率	Overall Labor Productivity	元/人	yuan/person	150 260	116 252
流动资产周转次数	Number of Times of Turnover of Circulating Funds	次	times	2.3	2.2
亏损企业个数	Number of Loss - suffering Enterprises	个	unit	1 599	1 567
亏损企业亏损额	Total Loss of Loss - suffering Enterprises	亿元	100 million yuan	74.49	48.49
国有及国有控股经济	**State - owned and State - holding**				
总资产贡献率	Ratio of Total Assets to Industrial Output Value		%	14.5	6.9
增加值率	Ratio of Value Added to Gross Industrial Output Value		%	32.9	21.4
全员劳动生产率	Overall Labor Productivity	元/人	yuan/person	212 730	109 459
流动资产周转次数	Number of Times of Turnover of Circulating Funds	次	times	2.2	1.7
亏损企业个数	Number of Loss - suffering Enterprises	个	unit	752	722
亏损企业亏损额	Total Loss of Loss - suffering Enterprises	亿元	100 million yuan	42.55	16.54
国有经济	**State - owned**				
总资产贡献率	Ratio of Total Assets to Industrial Output Value		%	3.7	3.1
增加值率	Ratio of Value Added to Gross Industrial Output Value		%	22.3	22.0
全员劳动生产率	Overall Labor Productivity	元/人	yuan/person	80 057	78 563
流动资产周转次数	Number of Times of Turnover of Circulating Funds	次	times	1.3	1.2
亏损企业个数	Number of Loss - suffering Enterprises	个	unit	625	601
亏损企业亏损额	Total Loss of Loss - suffering Enterprises	亿元	100 million yuan	14.39	10.61
集体经济	**Collective - owned**				
总资产贡献率	Ratio of Total Assets to Industrial Output Value		%	12.6	12.7
增加值率	Ratio of Value Added to Gross Industrial Output Value		%	24.4	24.5
全员劳动生产率	Overall Labor Productivity	元/人	yuan/person	65 426	65 760
流动资产周转次数	Number of Times of Turnover of Circulating Funds	次	times	2.5	2.5
亏损企业个数	Number of Loss - suffering Enterprises	个	unit	118	118
亏损企业亏损额	Total Loss of Loss - suffering Enterprises	亿元	100 million yuan	1.36	1.36
"三资"经济	**Foreign, Hongkong, Macao and Taiwan Funded**				
总资产贡献率	Ratio of Total Assets to Industrial Output Value		%	15.5	15.4
增加值率	Ratio of Value Added to Gross Industrial Output Value		%	23.3	23.3
全员劳动生产率	Overall Labor Productivity	元/人	yuan/person	180 542	180 330
流动资产周转次数	Number of Times of Turnover of Circulating Funds	次	times	2.5	2.5
亏损企业个数	Number of Loss - suffering Enterprises	个	unit	462	462
亏损企业亏损额	Total Loss of Loss - suffering Enterprises	亿元	100 million yuan	29.46	29.46
股份制经济	**Share - holding**				
总资产贡献率	Ratio of Total Assets to Industrial Output Value		%	23.9	9.4
增加值率	Ratio of Value Added to Gross Industrial Output Value		%	38.8	22.9
全员劳动生产率	Overall Labor Productivity	元/人	yuan/person	258 700	93 885
流动资产周转次数	Number of Times of Turnover of Circulating Funds	次	times	2.8	1.9
亏损企业个数	Number of Loss - suffering Enterprises	个	unit	197	189
亏损企业亏损额	Total Loss of Loss - suffering Enterprises	亿元	100 million yuan	27.54	5.32

10－17 国有及国有控股大中型工业企业主要经济指标
MAIN ECONOMIC INDICATORS OF LARGE & MEDIUM－SIZED STATE－OWNED AND STATE－HOLDING ENTERPRISES

单位:亿元 (100 million yuan)

指标	Item	全市工业 Total	国有及国有控股大中型 Large & Medium－sized State－owned and State－holding 绝对数 Absolute Number	占全市比重％ As Percentage of Whole Industry(％)
2004 年				
企业单位数(个)	Number of Enterprises(unit)	6 460	188	2.9
从业人员年平均人数(万人)	Annual Average Employment Personnel (10 000 persons)	122.85	30.13	24.5
工业总产值	Gross Industrial Output Value	5 853.72	1 742.62	29.8
工业增加值	Value Added of Industry	1 527.84	576.52	37.7
资产总计	Total Assets	5 612.47	2 104.15	37.5
#流动资产年平均余额	Annual Average Balance of Circulating Funds	2 682.47	738.48	27.5
固定资产净值年平均余额	Annual Average Balance of Net Value of Fixed Assets	2 076.99	978.29	47.1
主营业务收入	Business Revenue	5 861.43	1 831.45	31.2
#主营业务成本	Cost of Sales	4 978.28	1 494.15	30.0
主营业务税金及附加	Sales Tax and Extra Charges	53.51	39.40	73.6
利税总额	Total Pre－tax Profits	608.91	254.06	41.7
总资产贡献率(％)	Ratio of Total Assets to Industrial Output Value(％)	12.8	13.5	
全员劳动生产率(元/人)	Overall Labor Productivity(yuan/person)	124 367	191 334	
亏损企业个数(个)	Number of Loss－suffering Enterprises(unit)	1 943	45	2.3
亏损企业亏损额	Total Loss of Loss－suffering Enterprises	60.87	15.52	25.5
2005 年				
企业单位数(个)	Number of Enterprises(unit)	6 144	174	2.8
从业人员年平均人数(万人)	Annual Average Employment Personnel (10 000 persons)	122.21	29.49	24.1
工业总产值	Gross Industrial Output Value	6 774.10	2 312.13	34.1
工业增加值	Value Added of Industry	1 836.30	780.37	42.5
资产总计	Total Assets	6 347.92	2 539.74	40.0
#流动资产年平均余额	Annual Average Balance of Circulating Funds	3 058.69	911.52	29.8
固定资产净值年平均余额	Annual Average Balance of Net Value of Fixed Assets	2 155.41	1 104.77	51.3
主营业务收入	Business Revenue	7 125.93	2 401.95	33.7
#主营业务成本	Cost of Sales	6 039.33	1 959.80	32.5
主营业务税金及附加	Sales Tax and Extra Charges	77.74	55.50	71.4
利税总额	Total Pre－tax Profits	815.63	403.74	49.5
总资产贡献率(％)	Ratio of Total Assets to Industrial Output Value(％)	14.5	18.5	
全员劳动生产率(元/人)	Overall Labor Productivity(yuan/person)	150 260	264 587	
亏损企业个数(个)	Number of Loss－suffering Enterprises(unit)	1 599	39	2.4
亏损企业亏损额	Total Loss of Loss－suffering Enterprises	74.49	30.86	41.4

10－18 大中型工业企业主要经济指标
MAIN ECONOMIC INDICATORS OF LARGE & MEDIUM－SIZED INDUSTRIAL ENTERPRISES

单位:亿元 (100 million yuan)

指标	Item	大中型 Large & Medium－sized 绝对数 Absolute Number	大中型 占全市比重% As Percentage of Whole Industry(%)	#国有大中型 State－owned 绝对数 Absolute Number	#国有大中型 占全市比重% As Percentage of Whole Industry(%)
2004 年					
企业单位数(个)	Number of Enterprises(unit)	514	8.0	80	1.2
从业人员年平均人数(万人)	Annual Average Employment Personnel (10 000 persons)	61.73	50.2	14.88	12.1
工业总产值	Gross Industrial Output Value	4 100.81	70.1	613.41	10.5
工业增加值	Value Added of Industry	1 116.32	73.1	161.08	10.5
资产总计	Total Assets	3 562.52	63.5	902.88	16.1
#流动资产年平均余额	Annual Average Balance of Circulating Funds	1 672.49	62.3	313.50	11.7
固定资产净值年平均余额	Annual Average Balance of Net Value of Fixed Assets	1 469.48	70.8	429.69	20.7
主营业务收入	Business Revenue	4 164.67	71.1	652.63	11.1
#主营业务成本	Cost of Sales	3 477.31	69.8	583.40	11.7
主营业务税金及附加	Sales Tax and Extra Charges	47.18	88.2	7.89	14.8
利税总额	Total Pre－tax Profits	494.71	81.2	42.59	7.0
总资产贡献率(%)	Ratio of Total Assets to Industrial Output Value(%)	15.7		5.2	
全员劳动生产率(元/人)	Overall Labor Productivity(yuan/person)	180 837		108 282	
亏损企业个数(个)	Number of Loss－suffering Enterprises(unit)	106	5.5	29	1.5
亏损企业亏损额	Total Loss of Loss－suffering Enterprises	30.62	50.3	8.83	14.5
2005 年					
企业单位数(个)	Number of Enterprises(unit)	549	8.9	73	1.2
从业人员年平均人数(万人)	Annual Average Employment Personnel (10 000 persons)	64.58	52.8	14.08	11.5
工业总产值	Gross Industrial Output Value	4 991.10	73.7	646.61	9.5
工业增加值	Value Added of Industry	1 372.29	74.7	145.27	7.9
资产总计	Total Assets	4 360.80	68.7	1 131.19	17.8
#流动资产年平均余额	Annual Average Balance of Circulating Funds	2 033.32	66.5	418.34	13.7
固定资产净值年平均余额	Annual Average Balance of Net Value of Fixed Assets	1 578.83	73.2	413.66	19.2
主营业务收入	Business Revenue	5 233.00	73.4	742.93	10.4
#主营业务成本	Cost of Sales	4 384.02	72.6	676.81	11.2
主营业务税金及附加	Sales Tax and Extra Charges	64.83	83.4	8.35	10.7
利税总额	Total Pre－tax Profits	667.48	81.8	51.61	6.3
总资产贡献率(%)	Ratio of Total Assets to Industrial Output Value(%)	17.8		5.8	
全员劳动生产率(元/人)	Overall Labor Productivity(yuan/person)	212 499		103 204	
亏损企业个数(个)	Number of Loss－suffering Enterprises(unit)	94	5.9	25	1.6
亏损企业亏损额	Total Loss of Loss－suffering Enterprises	45.79	61.5	6.50	8.7

10－19 工业系统分主管部门工业企业主要财务指标(2005 年)

MAIN FINANCIAL INDICATORS OF INDUSTRIAL ENTERPRISES BY ADMINISTRATIVE DEPARTMENT,2005

单位:万元 (10 000 yuan)

主管系统 Administrative Department	企业单位数(个) Number of Enterprises (unit)	资产总计 Total Assets	固定资产原价 Original Value of Fixed Assets	固定资产净值年平均余额 Annual Average Balance of Net Value of Fixed Assets	流动资产年平均余额 Annual Average Balance of Circu－lating Funds	主营业务收入 Business Revenue
冶金集团(控股)有限公司						
Tianjin Metallurgical Group(Holding) Corporation	44	1 746 827	274 045	203 180	1 133 376	1 841 190
渤海化工集团公司						
Tianjin Bohai Chemical Industry Group Corporation	219	2 229 221	1 549 105	863 003	861 133	1 811 808
机电工业控股集团公司						
Tianjin Machinery & Electric Industry Holding Group Company	188	1 837 886	692 220	403 117	982 030	1 746 529
中环电子信息集团有限公司						
Tianjin Zhonghuan Electronics & Information Group	163	2 795 563	1 306 306	592 094	1 889 301	6 149 545
纺织集团(控股)有限公司						
Tianjin Textile Industrial General Corporation	353	1 457 190	713 216	469 710	577 202	432 956
一轻集团(控股)有限公司						
Tianjin First Light Industry Group(Holding Share) Co.,Ltd	213	1 152 204	473 601	282 491	576 933	1 007 169
二轻集团(控股)有限公司						
The Second Light Industry Group(Holding) Co.,Ltd	75	974 710	401 591	257 755	477 530	1 231 499
医药集团有限公司						
Tianjin Pharmaceutical Holdings	48	1 089 903	351 441	208 225	399 194	697 416
建筑材料集团(控股)有限公司						
Tianjin Building Materials Group(Holding)Co.,Ltd	51	506 017	344 681	230 807	218 605	180 247
汽车工业(集团)有限公司						
Tianjin Automobile Industry Group Co.,Ltd	38	2 511 952	1 388 848	668 248	1 152 637	3 565 611
飞鸽集团有限公司						
Tianjin Flying Pigeon Group Co.,Ltd	34	105 292	37 794	23 763	67 165	43 597
钢管有限责任公司						
Tianjin Pipe Group Co.,Ltd	25	1 835 920	1 501 861	938 089	561 753	1 658 269
有色金属集团有限公司						
Tianjin Non－ferrous Metals Group Co.,Ltd	21	178 977	42 547	28 838	118 588	287 836
天铁冶金集团有限公司						
Tianjin Tian Tie Metallurgical Group Co.,Ltd	1	1 486 646	784 035	451 031	804 494	1 965 822
摩托集团						
Tianjin Motors Group	1	276 023	163 762	80 476	127 546	375 509
塑料集团						
Tianjin Plastics Group	16	109 367	67 134	44 323	36 712	71 144

10－19 续表 Continued
单位:万元 (10 000 yuan)

主管系统 Administrative Department	主营业务税金及附加 Sales Tax and Extra Charges	利税总额 Total Pre－tax Profits	利润总额 Total Profits	工业总产值 Gross Industrial Output Value	工业总产值比上年增长% Increase Rate of Gross Industrial Output Value Preceding Year	工业增加值 Value Added of Industry
冶金集团(控股)有限公司 Tianjin Metallurgical Group(Holding) Corporation	902	31 044	17 519	1 275 820	25.0	117 418
渤海化工集团公司 Tianjin Bohai Chemical Industry Group Corporation	14 777	98 672	21 644	1 811 735	14.7	383 330
机电工业控股集团公司 Tianjin Machinery & Electric Industry Holding Group Company	2 974	123 357	80 134	1 577 521	23.2	294 986
中环电子信息集团有限公司 Tianjin Zhonghuan Electronics & Information Group	1 778	374 185	298 598	6 170 391	23.0	638 015
纺织集团(控股)有限公司 Tianjin Textile Industrial General Corporation	1 199	13 256	－264	407 939	11.6	99 801
一轻集团(控股)有限公司 Tianjin First Light Industry Group(Holding Share) Co.,Ltd	8 065	73 432	36 257	806 507	26.0	187 121
二轻集团(控股)有限公司 The Second Light Industry Group(Holding) Co.,Ltd	107	18 694	11 554	1 194 151	4.3	74 767
医药集团有限公司 Tianjin Pharmaceutical Holdings	2 492	127 754	70 031	504 864	14.3	242 503
建筑材料集团(控股)有限公司 Tianjin Building Materials Group(Holding)Co.,Ltd	928	5 474	－5 004	202 112	13.3	56 734
汽车工业(集团)有限公司 Tianjin Automobile Industry Group Co.,Ltd	158 784	479 498	169 688	3 541 194	43.0	634 623
飞鸽集团有限公司 Tianjin Flying Pigeon Group Co.,Ltd	38	685	105	58 457	30.1	6 016
钢管有限责任公司 Tianjin Pipe Group Co.,Ltd	5 337	173 213	113 773	1 512 246	50.7	316 100
有色金属集团有限公司 Tianjin Non－ferrous Metals Group Co.,Ltd	76	1 583	－927	254 786	0.2	15 473
天铁冶金集团有限公司 Tianjin Tian Tie Metallurgical Group Co.,Ltd	4 949	120 962	58 123	1 761 168	17.0	256 284
摩托集团 Tianjin Motors Group	23 757	31 523	61	373 539	－6.1	76 720
塑料集团 Tianjin Plastics Group	121	－82	－1 334	72 190	17.5	8 833

10－20 高新技术产业主要经济指标
MAIN INDICATORS OF HIGH & NEW TECHNOLOGY INDUSTRY

单位:亿元 (100 million yuan)

项 目 Item	工业总产值 Gross Industrial Output Value		主营业务收入 Business Revenue		利税总额 Total Pre－tax Profits	
	2004	2005	2004	2005	2004	2005
全 市 总 计						
Total	**1 731.02**	**2 141.37**	**1 728.01**	**2 238.35**	**202.40**	**214.30**
按规模分						
Grouped by Size of Enterprises						
大型企业						
Large－sized	1 014.04	943.19	1 034.06	1 045.52	142.00	124.05
中型企业						
Medium－sized	510.09	917.35	491.40	885.18	42.13	67.05
小型企业						
Small－sized	206.89	280.83	202.55	307.65	18.27	23.20
按经济类型分						
Grouped by Ownership						
国有经济						
State－owned	23.85	21.64	21.79	39.59	0.91	3.43
集体经济						
Collective－owned	52.26	14.06	43.07	34.25	3.99	3.03
私有经济						
Private and Individual	11.00	10.53	11.57	26.64	1.30	3.74
外商投资经济						
Foreign Funded	1 477.66	1 707.09	1 443.74	1 859.39	169.94	168.62
港澳台商投资经济						
Hongkong,Macao and Taiwan Funded	46.08	143.11	40.69	75.79	5.80	11.63
其他经济						
Others	120.17	244.94	167.15	202.69	20.46	23.85
按技术领域分						
Grouped by Technical Field						
电子信息						
Electronics and Information	1 351.73	1 682.37	1 311.22	1 728.45	154.39	157.13
航空航天						
Aviation and Spaceflight	0.59	2.20	0.56	2.30	0.31	0.51
光机电一体化						
Photoeletric Mechanical Electron Incorporated	161.19	172.86	164.03	177.85	13.69	16.77
生物技术和医药						
Biology Technology and Pharmaceutical	134.64	163.85	175.65	207.25	27.07	33.52
新材料						
New Materials	55.25	61.44	50.32	64.74	5.31	2.35
新能源和节能材料						
New Energy and Energy Saving Materials	26.51	58.41	25.20	57.54	1.54	4.00
环境保护						
Environmental Protection	1.11	0.24	1.03	0.22	0.09	0.02

10-21 电子信息产品制造业主要经济指标(2005年)
MAIN INDICATORS OF ELECTRONIC AND INFORMATION PRODUCTS MANUFACTURING,2005

单位:亿元 (100 million yuan)

项 目 Item	工业总产值 Gross Industrial Output Value	主营业务收入 Business Revenue	利税总额 Total Pre-tax Profits
全 市 总 计			
Total	**1 783.30**	**1 834.20**	**162.58**
按规模分			
Grouped by Size of Enterprises			
大型企业			
Large-sized	865.38	925.35	112.10
中型企业			
Medium-sized	740.97	725.54	39.90
小型企业			
Small-sized	176.95	183.31	10.58
按经济类型分			
Grouped by Ownership			
国有经济			
State-owned	4.66	5.21	-0.58
集体经济			
Collective-owned	15.73	16.36	1.39
私有经济			
Private and Individual	23.04	23.54	3.02
外商及港澳台商投资经济			
Foreign,Hongkong,Macao and Taiwan Funded	1 658.96	1 710.57	152.23
其他经济			
Others	80.91	78.52	6.52
按行业分			
Grouped by Sector			
雷达业			
Radar	0.08	0.07	0.01
通信设备业			
Telecommunications Equipment	969.06	1 034.04	120.69
广播电视设备业			
Equipment of Radio and Television	1.21	1.23	0.04
电子计算机业			
Electronic Computer	132.33	152.80	0.25
家电业			
Home Appliances	92.70	91.82	10.67
电子测量仪器业			
Instruments of Electronic Survey	2.64	2.59	0.50
电子工业专用设备业			
Industrial Electronic Equipment for Special Use	19.80	23.49	3.17
电子元件业			
Electronic Element	275.19	262.99	11.42
电子器件业			
Electronic Implements	168.34	143.62	7.43
电子信息机电产品业			
Machinery & Electric Products	119.61	119.36	8.03
电子信息专用材料业			
Electronic and Information Materials for Special Use	2.34	2.19	0.37

10－22 主营业务收入百强工业企业(2005年)

TOP 100 INDUSTRIAL ENTERPRISES ON BUSINESS REVENUE,2005

名 次 Position	企业名称 Name of Enterprises	名 次 Position	企业名称 Name of Enterprises
1	摩托罗拉(中国)电子有限公司	51	俊安(天津)实业有限公司
2	中海石油(中国)有限公司天津分公司	52	天津阿尔卑斯电子有限公司
3	天津三星通信技术有限公司	53	天津通广集团数字通信有限公司
4	天津一汽丰田汽车有限公司	54	天津渤海化工有限责任公司天津碱厂
5	天津天铁冶金集团有限公司	55	天津市轧一制钢有限公司
6	中国石油化工股份有限公司天津分公司	56	现代电子(天津)多媒体有限公司
7	天津市电力公司	57	天津嘉里粮油工业有限公司
8	中国石油天然气股份有限公司大港油田公司	58	天津大通铜业有限公司
9	天津天钢集团有限公司	59	天津军粮城发电有限公司
10	中国石油天然气股份有限公司大港石化分公司	60	罗姆半导体(中国)有限公司
11	乐金电子(天津)电器有限公司	61	天津天士力集团有限公司
12	天津钢管集团有限公司	62	天津大桥焊材集团有限公司
13	天津三星电子显示器有限公司	63	天津市东益钢铁有限公司
14	天津津亚电子有限公司	64	富士能(天津)光学有限公司
15	天津一汽夏利汽车股份有限公司	65	天津胜达轧钢有限公司
16	飞思卡尔半导体(中国)有限公司	66	日新(天津)塑胶有限公司
17	大港油田集团有限责任公司	67	SEW传动设备(天津)有限公司
18	奥的斯电梯(中国)投资有限公司	68	天津新港船厂
19	天津三星电子有限公司	69	三星高新电机(天津)有限公司
20	天津友发钢管集团有限公司	70	天津顶津食品有限公司
21	天津金耀集团有限公司	71	天津市福坤工贸有限公司
22	天津大沽化工股份有限公司	72	康地万达(天津)有限公司
23	中金黄金股份有限公司	73	中盛粮油工业(天津)有限公司
24	新大洲本田摩托有限公司	74	中美天津史克制药有限公司
25	天津市荣程联合钢铁集团有限公司	75	大宇微波炉(天津)有限公司
26	天津中新药业集团股份有限公司	76	天津华能杨柳青热电有限责任公司
27	天津新利钢铁有限公司	77	诺和诺德(中国)制药有限公司
28	天津通广三星电子有限公司	78	天津大桥大寺电焊条有限公司
29	天津三星视界有限公司	79	天津市万达轮胎集团有限公司
30	鹏思特(天津)实业有限公司	80	蓝星石化有限公司天津石油化工厂
31	天津渤天化工有限责任公司	81	天津市兆博实业有限公司
32	天津市金桥焊材集团有限公司	82	天津力神电池股份有限公司
33	天津三星光电子有限公司	83	西门子电气传动有限公司
34	天津大无缝铜材有限公司	84	天津市星宇达钢管有限公司
35	北海粮油工业(天津)有限公司	85	天津市景田集团公司
36	天津大唐盘山发电有限公司	86	赫比(天津)电子有限公司
37	天津丰田汽车发动机有限公司	87	天津富士达自行车有限公司
38	天津三美电机有限公司	88	上海烟草(集团)公司天津卷烟厂
39	天津富士通天电子有限公司	89	天津浩安矿产有限公司
40	天津国华盘山发电有限责任公司	90	天津可口可乐饮料有限公司
41	天津钢管还原铁厂	91	亚光耐普罗精密注塑(天津)有限公司
42	天津三星视界移动有限公司	92	普利司通(天津)轮胎有限公司
43	天津中集北洋集装箱有限公司	93	天津英泰汽车饰件有限公司
44	天津乐金大沽化学有限公司	94	中法合营王朝葡萄酿酒有限公司
45	天津三星电机有限公司	95	斯必克制冷技术(天津)有限公司
46	中国石化集团天津石油化工公司	96	天津爱普生有限公司
47	天津市冷轧薄板厂	97	天津市瑞丰带钢有限公司
48	天津市飞龙制管有限公司	98	天津俊安煤焦化工有限公司
49	天津顶益国际食品有限公司	99	天津市达亿钢铁有限公司
50	天津市轧三金属材料科技有限公司	100	天津荣程祥矿产有限公司

10－23 实现利税百强工业企业(2005年)

TOP 100 INDUSTRIAL ENTERPRISES ON TOTAL PRE－TAX PROFITS,2005

名 次 Position	企业名称 Name of Enterprises	名 次 Position	企业名称 Name of Enterprises
1	中海石油(中国)有限公司天津分公司	51	斯必克制冷技术(天津)有限公司
2	摩托罗拉(中国)电子有限公司	52	飞思卡尔半导体(中国)有限公司
3	中国石油天然气股份有限公司大港油田公司	53	赫比(天津)电子有限公司
4	天津一汽丰田汽车有限公司	54	西门子电气传动有限公司
5	天津钢管集团有限公司	55	天津大港华实发电有限责任公司
6	天津三星通信技术有限公司	56	天津市大邱庄薄板有限公司
7	天津天铁冶金集团有限公司	57	PPG涂料(天津)有限公司
8	奥的斯电梯(中国)投资有限公司	58	天津市福坤工贸有限公司
9	天津市电力公司	59	日新(天津)塑胶有限公司
10	天津国华盘山发电有限责任公司	60	天津华丰汽车装饰有限公司
11	天津一汽夏利汽车股份有限公司	61	天津英泰汽车饰件有限公司
12	天津大唐盘山发电有限公司	62	天津市景田集团公司
13	天津天钢集团有限公司	63	世讯工业(天津)有限公司
14	天津三星电子有限公司	64	鹏思特(天津)实业有限公司
15	上海烟草(集团)公司天津卷烟厂	65	天津力生制药股份有限公司
16	中美天津史克制药有限公司	66	天津可口可乐饮料有限公司
17	天津金耀集团有限公司	67	普利司通(天津)轮胎有限公司
18	天津华能杨柳青热电有限责任公司	68	壳牌(天津)石油化工有限公司
19	天津三星电子显示器有限公司	69	爱信(天津)车身零部件有限公司
20	中法合营王朝葡萄酿酒有限公司	70	天津市金桥焊材集团有限公司
21	天津天士力集团有限公司	71	天津市兆博实业有限公司
22	天津友发钢管集团有限公司	72	中金黄金股份有限公司
23	大港油田集团有限责任公司	73	亚光耐普罗精密注塑(天津)有限公司
24	天津大沽化工股份有限公司	74	天津电装电子有限公司
25	天津通广三星电子有限公司	75	申克(天津)矿业设备有限公司
26	天津天狮生物发展有限公司	76	天津三星光电子有限公司
27	天津丰田汽车发动机有限公司	77	天津丰津汽车传动部件有限公司
28	新大洲本田摩托有限公司	78	天津广宇发展股份有限公司
29	天津市瑞通钢铁有限公司	79	天津赛象电气自动化技术有限公司
30	天津三星视界有限公司	80	约翰·迪尔天拖有限公司
31	天津津亚电子有限公司	81	阿克苏诺贝尔涂料(天津)有限公司
32	SEW传动设备(天津)有限公司	82	诺和诺德(中国)制药有限公司
33	天津中新药业集团股份有限公司	83	新大洲本田摩托有限公司天津分公司
34	天津新利钢铁有限公司	84	中国大冢制药有限公司
35	天津荣程祥矿产有限公司	85	天津宝洁工业有限公司
36	施耐德电气低压(天津)有限公司	86	天马缝纫机制造有限公司
37	天津中集北洋集装箱有限公司	87	德芬工业减速机(天津)有限公司
38	天津市荣程联合钢铁集团有限公司	88	天津中天仕名科技集团有限公司
39	诺维信(中国)生物技术有限公司	89	威娜化妆品(中国)有限公司
40	天津胜达轧钢有限公司	90	天津新伟祥工业有限公司
41	天津力神电池股份有限公司	91	天津市云峰钢铁有限公司
42	天津渤天化工有限责任公司	92	天津正大饲料科技有限公司
43	天津悦泰石化科技有限公司	93	西湖(天津)橡塑制品有限公司
44	天津顶津食品有限公司	94	天津东洋油墨有限公司
45	天津顶益国际食品有限公司	95	丹佛斯(天津)有限公司
46	天津军粮城发电有限公司	96	天津南辰钢铁有限公司
47	罗姆半导体(中国)有限公司	97	天津天管特钻具有限公司
48	天津塑力线缆集团有限公司	98	万新塑胶制品(天津)有限公司
49	天津大港广安津能发电有限责任公司	99	天津南侨油脂有限公司
50	乐金电子(天津)电器有限公司	100	天津丰田合成有限公司

主要统计指标解释

工业总产值　是以货币表现的工业企业在报告期内生产的工业产品总量。它是反映一定时间内工业生产总规模和总水平的重要指标。工业总产值采用“工厂法”计算。1995 年全国第三次工业普查对工业总产值的范围和计算方法作出新规定。工业总产值包括本年生产成品价值，对外加工费收入，自制半成品、在产品期末期初差额价值。新规定与原规定的变化：一是对工业产值中凡自备原材料，不论其加工繁简程度如何，一律按全价计算产值。凡来料加工，一律按加工费计算总产值；二是自制半成品、在产品期末期初差额价值的计算改变了生产周期六个月以上的原则，而以当期会计是否将其计入成本核算作为是否计入产值的依据；三是现价产值按不含增值税的价格计算。1995 年以后各年工业总产值均是按新规定计算的。

规模以上工业企业　包括全部国有(含国有联营、国有独资公司)和年销售收入在 500 万元及以上的非国有工业企业。

工业行业类别　根据新颁布的行业分类标准《国民经济行业分类》(GB/T 4754－2002) “工业”包括“采矿业”、“制造业”和“电力、燃气及水的生产和供应业”三个门类。

轻工业　一般指提供生活消费品和制作手工工具的工业。

重工业　一般指生产生产资料为国民经济各部门提供物质技术基础的工业。

大、中、小型企业　根据 2003 年国家统计局制定的《统计上大中小型企业划分办法(暂行)》，以从业人员数、销售额和资产总额三项指标为依据，将工业企业划分为大、中、小型，而不再按照企业产品的年生产能力和生产用固定资产原值划分。划分标准如下：

指标名称	单　位	大　型	中　型	小　型
从业人员数	人	2 000 及以上	300－2 000 以下	300 以下
销售额	万元	30 000 及以上	3 000－30 000 以下	3 000 以下
资产总额	万元	40 000 及以上	4 000－40 000 以下	4 000 以下

实收资本(股本)　指投资人作为资本投入到企业中的各种资产的价值。企业实收资本按照投资主体一般分为六种：

①**国家资本：**　指有权代表国家投资的政府部门或机构以国有资产投入企业形成的资本。不论企业的资本是哪个政府部门或机构投入的，只要是以国家资本形式投资的，均作为国家资本计算。

②**集体资本：**　指由本企业劳动群众集体所有和集体企业联合经济组织范围内的劳动群众集体所有的资产投入形成的资本金，以及企业在实行新制度以前国家减免税款形成的资本金。

③**法人资本：**　指其他法人单位投入本企业的资本。

④**个人资本：**　指社会个人或者本企业内部职工以个人合法财产投入企业形成的资本。

⑤**港澳台资本：**　指我国香港、澳门和台湾地区的投资者投入企业的资本。

⑥**外商资本：**　指外国投资者投入企业的资本。

产品销售收入　指企业销售产品的销售收入和提供劳务等主要经营业务取得的收入总额。现行的会计制度要求企业采用“权责发生制”原则计算产品销售收入，即以销售实现为依据。

产品销售成本　指企业销售产品和提供劳务等主要经营业务的实际成本。该指标不包括期间费用，即不包括管理费用、销售费用和财务费用。企业应当按照权责发生制原则确认当期费用，即对应属于本期的各项费用，不论其是否实际支付，均应确认为本期的费用；对于不属于本期的费用，即使款项已经在本期付出，也不应确认为本期费用。

产品销售费用　指企业在销售产品、自制半成品和提供劳务等主要经营业务过程中所发生的各项费用以及专设销售机构的各项费用。包括运输费、装卸费、包装费、保险费、展览费、广告费、租赁费(不包括融资租赁费)，以及为销售本企业产品而专设的销售机构的职工工资、福利费、业务费、折旧费等其他费用。

产品销售税金及附加　指企业销售产品和提供劳务等主要经营业务应负担的城市维护建设税、消费税、资源税和教育费附加。

产品销售利润　指企业销售产品和提供劳务等主要经营业务收入扣除其成本、费用、税金后的利润。该指标计算公式为：

产品销售利润＝产品销售收入－产品销售成本－产品销售费用－产品销售税金

营业利润　指企业生产经营活动所取得的利润，包括主营业务利润和其他业务利润。其计算公式为：

营业利润 = 产品销售利润 + 其他业务利润 - 管理费用 - 财务费用

利润总额 指企业在一定时期的最终经营成果。企业在生产经营过程中，通过销售过程将产品卖给购买方，实现收入，收入扣除当初的投入成本以及其他一系列费用，再加减非经营性质的收支及投资收益，即为企业的利润总额或亏损总额。亏损以"-"号表示，计算公式为：

利润总额 = 营业利润 + 投资收益 + 补贴收入 + 营业外收入 - 营业外支出 + 以前年度损益调整

利税总额 指利润总额、产品销售税金及附加和本期应交增值税之和。

Explanatory Notes on Main Statistical Indicators

Gross Industrial Output Value is the total volume of industrial products sold or available for sale in value terms which reflect the total achievements and overall scale of industrial production during a given period. The gross industrial output value is calculated with "factory method" . Data of the gross industrial output value were adjusted in accordance with the 1995 industrial census. It includes the value of the finished products, the value of industrial services rendered to other units, and the changes in the value of the semi-finished products and products in process between the beginning and end of the period. The changes between the new regulation and the old regulation: the first, calculating output value as whole price for ready source materials by themselves, calculating output value as cost for processed with imported materials; the second, the changes producing circulation above six months for the value of the semi-finished products and products in process between the beginning and end of the period, calculating output value in accordance with financial accounting in current period; the third, output value of current price excluded value added tax. It is not comparable with the data before 1995.

Industrial Enterprises above Designated Size refer to all state-owned(including sole state-funded enterprises, state-owned joint ownership enterprises), and other non-state-owned industrial enterprises with annual sales of over 5 million yuan.

Industrial Sector Classification State draws up the new industrial classification of China Industrial Classification by Sector of the National Economy (GB/T4754-2002) in 2003. Industry is classified into three categories, minerals mining, manufacturing, production & supply of power, gas & water.

Light Industry refers to the industry that produces consumer goods and hand tools.

Heavy Industry refers to the industry which produces capital goods, and provides various sectors of the national economy with necessary material and technical basis.

Large, Medium, Small-sized Enterprises Industrial enterprises are classified into large, medium, small-sized enterprises according to employment personnel, sales revenue and total assets in accordance with the regulation of Classification (temporary) of Large, Medium, Small-sized Enterprises on Statistics, are not classified according to production capacity and original value of fixed assets. The standard of classification as following

Indicator	Unit	Large-sized	Medium-sized	Small-sized
Employment personnel	person	2 000 and over	300-2 000 below	below 300
Sales Revenue	10 000 yuan	30 000 and over	30 00-30 000 below	below 3 000
Total assets	10 000 yuan	40 000 and over	4 000-40 000 below	below 4 000

Capital Obtained refers to the sum of capital received by the enterprise from investors. It can be classified into 6 kinds according to investors.

(a) **State capital** refers to capital which is formed through state-owned investment into the enterprises by government agencies or institutions that could represent the state in the investment.

(b) **Collective capital** refers to capital which is formed through state-owned investment into the enerprises by collective institutions or units that could represent the state in the investment, also include the capital which is formed through decrease tax before the enterprise implement new regulation.

(c)**Corporate capital** refers to capital which is formed through investment by other corporate units.

(d) **Individual capital** refers to capital which is formed through investment by individuals outside the enterprise or employees of the enterprise using their personal legal properties.

(e) **Capital from Hongkong, Macao and Taiwan** refers to capital which is formed through investment by investors from Hongkong,Macao and Taiwan of China using their assets of various forms.

(f)**Foreign capital** refers to capital which is formed through investment by foreign investors.

Sales Revenue of Products refers to the revenue from the sales of products by industrial enterprises and the revenue from services provided, etc. According to the requirement of current accountancy regulation,enterprise calculate sales revenue of products using the principle of power occurrence system,i. e. it is calculated on the basis of sales.

Sales Cost of Products refers to the actual cost of products of industrial enterprises and industrial services provided, etc. It excludes period cost,i. e. management cost,sales cost and finance cost. Enterprise should calculate sales cost according to the principle of power occurrence system,i. e. cost of current period should be calculated no matter whether it has be paid or not; cost of non - current period should not be calculated even it has been paid at current period.

Sales Expenses of Products refers to the expenses of selling products, semi - processed goods of industrial enterprises and industrial services provided, expenses of sales department, which is included the expenses on transportation, load and unload, package, insurance, exhibition,advertisement and wage of staff and workers of sales department, welfare, business and depreciation.

Tax and Extra Charges on Sales of Products refer to the tax on city maintenance and construction, consumption tax,resources tax and extra charges for education, which should be borne by the enterprises in selling products and providing industrial services during the reference period.

Sales Profit of Products refers to the profit gained by the enterprises by deducting cost, charges and taxes from the business income of the enterprises obtained in selling products and providing industrial services. The following formula is used

Sales Profit of Products = Sales Revenue - Sales Cost of Products - Sales Expenses of Products - Sales Tax of Products

Business Profits refers to the profits on producing and operating by the enterprises, including main operating profits and other profits. The following formula is used

Business Profits = Sales Profits + Other Profits - overhead costs - financial expenses

Total Profits refer to the final achievements of production and operation of the enterprises, represented by the total profits or losses (loss is expressed by the negative figure) , i. e. sales revenue deduce devotion cost, expenses, expenditure of activities other than operation, add income of activities other than operation and investment earnings. The following formula is used

Total Profits = Profits from Operation + Investment Earnings + Income from Subsidies + Income of Activities other than Operation - Expenditure of Activities other than Operation + Adjustment of Profits and Losses of Previous Years

Total Value of Profit and Tax (Pre - tax) refers to the sum of the total net profits, products sales tax & surcharges and the value added tax payable of industrial enterprises, namely pre - tax profits.

第11篇
CHAPTER 11

建筑业
Construction

11－1 建筑企业基本情况(1990－2005年)

BASIC STATISTICS ON CONSTRUCTION ENTERPRISES,1990－2005

年 份 Year	企业个数(个) Number of Enterprises (unit)	从业人员平均人数(万人) Annual Average Employed Personnel (10 000 persons)	建筑业总产值(万元) Gross Output Value of Construction (10 000 yuan)	房屋建筑施工面积(万平方米) Floor Space of Building Under Construction (10 000 sq.m)	房屋建筑竣工面积(万平方米) Floor Space of Building Completed (10 000 sq.m)	#住 宅 Residential Buildings
1990	82	18.71	317 009	675.46	333.60	
1991	83	18.95	361 739	582.73	295.41	
1992	96	18.76	484 293	721.50	344.70	158.50
1993	237	25.87	826 585	1 210.94	505.02	270.70
1994	482	36.28	1 305 160	1 359.96	600.15	376.97
1995	693	31.53	1 656 748	1 604.10	640.25	328.40
1996	461	29.06	1 735 679	1 579.53	567.98	285.82
1997	477	29.26	1 909 999	1 752.13	727.61	398.82
1998	500	29.34	2 111 208	2 059.23	868.00	527.98
1999	491	28.71	2 227 406	2 087.01	901.88	637.85
2000	456	27.44	2 380 991	2 253.99	1 056.40	658.85
2001	420	25.96	2 886 808	2 140.04	924.92	562.40
2002	925	34.56	4 061 628	2 817.84	1 332.10	726.87
2003	900	35.55	5 208 402	3 395.94	1 465.75	797.72
2004	1 155	38.27	6 551 996	3 547.76	1 644.90	758.00
2005	1 108	39.10	7 543 702	3 940.56	1 484.38	728.58

11－2 建筑企业主要经济效益指标和工程质量(1990－2005年)

MAIN INDICATORS OF ECONOMIC EFFICIENCY AND ENGINEERING QUALITY OF CONSTRUCTION ENTERPRISES,1990－2005

年 份 Year	全员劳动生产率(元/人) Overall Labor Productivity (yuan/person)	平均每一从业人员竣工面积(平方米) Per Capita Floor Space of Building Completed (sq.m)	产值利润率(%) Ratio of Profit to Gross Output Value (%)	产值利税率(%) Ratio of Pre－tax Profit to Gross Output Value (%)	按面积计算竣工率(%) Percentage of Building Completed in terms of Floor Space (%)
1990	15 874	16.7	－0.3	2.7	49.4
1991	17 952	14.7	0.8	3.4	50.7
1992	23 578	16.8	1.0	3.5	38.2
1993	33 126	18.6	2.9	5.5	38.7
1994	36 762	16.0	0.5	3.2	42.3
1995	52 545	19.6	0.6	3.4	37.2
1996	59 724	19.5	1.0	3.6	36.0
1997	65 274	24.9	1.1	3.7	41.5
1998	71 958	29.6	1.4	3.9	42.2
1999	77 583	31.4	1.0	3.6	43.2
2000	86 771	38.5	1.1	4.0	46.9
2001	111 194	35.6	1.3	4.2	43.2
2002	117 536	38.5	1.8	4.7	47.3
2003	146 499	41.2	1.9	4.8	43.2
2004	171 190	43.0	1.9	4.9	46.4
2005	192 931	38.0	2.3	5.3	37.7

11－3　建筑企业基本情况(2005 年)
(按登记注册类型和经济类型分)
BASIC STATISTICS ON CONSTRUCTION ENTERPRISES,2005
(GROUPED BY STATUS OF REGISTRATION AND OWNERSHIP)

项　目　Item	企业个数(个) Number of Enterprises (unit)		从业人员平均人数(万人) Average Employed Personnel (10 000 persons)		从业人员劳动报酬(万元) Earnings of Employed Personnel (10 000 yuan)		建筑业总产值(万元) Gross Output Value of Construction (10 000 yuan)	
	2004	2005	2004	2005	2004	2005	2004	2005
总　计 Total	**1 155**	**1 108**	**38.27**	**39.10**	**471 038**	**561 648**	**6 551 996**	**7 543 702**
按登记注册类型分 Grouped by Status of Registration								
内资企业 Domestic－funded Enterprises	1 119	1 070	37.79	38.55	463 076	552 390	6 421 746	7 397 444
国有企业 State－owned Enterprises	146	131	9.27	10.22	182 412	206 102	2 231 714	2 462 821
集体企业 Collective－owned Enterprises	133	105	4.27	3.09	42 979	36 881	431 881	331 891
股份合作企业 Cooperative Enterprises	36	27	0.48	0.56	7 374	11 032	61 945	73 496
私营企业 Private Enterprises	445	444	4.08	4.37	32 098	41 279	425 278	550 388
股份有限公司 Share－holding Corporations Ltd.	36	34	1.17	1.21	22 077	26 252	363 778	426 483
有限责任公司 Limited Liability Corporations	294	300	17.99	18.52	170 072	222 799	2 836 983	3 469 667
#国有独资 Sole State－funded Corporations	11	8	2.14	2.16	14 987	22 147	327 584	364 435
联营企业 Joint Ownership Enterprises	10	8	0.19	0.13	2 770	2 615	21 101	12 534
#国有与国有联营企业 State Joint Ownership Enterprises	3	1	0.02	0.01	259	96	3 077	474
集体与集体联营企业 Collective Joint Ownership Enterprises	3	4	0.06	0.07	701	895	3 839	4 920
其他内资企业 Other Domestic－funded Enterprises	19	21	0.34	0.45	3 294	5 430	49 066	70 164
港澳台商投资企业 Enterprises with Investment from Hongkong,Macao and Taiwan	19	20	0.26	0.24	4 980	6 312	76 386	79 607
外商投资企业 Foreign Funded Enterprises	17	18	0.22	0.31	2 982	2 946	53 864	66 651
按经济类型分 Grouped by Ownership								
国有经济 State－owned	160	140	11.43	12.38	197 658	228 345	2 562 375	2 827 729
集体经济 Collective－owned	172	136	4.82	3.72	51 054	48 807	497 665	410 307
私有经济 Private and Individual	445	444	4.08	4.37	32 098	41 279	425 278	550 388
港澳台商投资经济 Hongkong,Macao and Taiwan Funded	19	20	0.26	0.24	4 980	6 312	76 386	79 607
外商投资经济 Foreign Funded	17	18	0.22	0.31	2 982	2 947	53 864	66 651
其　他 Other	342	350	17.46	18.08	182 266	233 958	2 936 428	3 609 020

11－3 续表　Continued

项　目　Item	竣工产值（万元）Gross Output Value Completed (10 000 yuan)		房屋建筑施工面积（万平方米）Floor Space of Building Under Construction (10 000 sq. m)		房屋建筑竣工面积（万平方米）Floor Space of Building Completed (10 000 sq. m)		#住　宅 Residential Buildings	
	2004	2005	2004	2005	2004	2005	2004	2005
总　计 **Total**	**3 972 010**	**4 596 374**	**3 547.76**	**3 940.56**	**1 644.90**	**1 484.38**	**758.00**	**728.58**
按登记注册类型分 **Grouped by Status of Registration**								
内资企业 Domestic－funded Enterprises	3 927 521	4 549 337	3 486.30	3 872.55	1 624.69	1 464.78	758.00	728.58
国有企业 State－owned Enterprises	1 344 861	1 616 346	1 021.81	1 080.09	401.34	296.78	169.84	135.45
集体企业 Collective－owned Enterprises	345 855	289 006	470.43	313.15	284.18	208.81	164.46	101.52
股份合作企业 Cooperative Enterprises	52 584	62 454	18.68	7.08	13.19	2.10	8.19	0.26
私营企业 Private Enterprises	315 355	400 499	262.89	245.30	145.86	138.33	53.03	51.79
股份有限公司 Share－holding Corporations Ltd.	127 830	160 619	66.72	126.60	34.34	45.48	14.76	21.03
有限责任公司 Limited Liability Corporations	1 685 572	1 951 460	1 631.16	2 084.57	735.07	762.33	341.21	412.39
#国有独资 Sole State－funded Corporations	327 584	220 172	205.26	216.29	75.93	69.19	53.17	50.66
联营企业 Joint Ownership Enterprises	15 341	10 808	7.55	4.32	7.38	3.87	4.65	0.56
#国有与国有联营企业 State Joint Ownership Enterprises	3 077							
集体与集体联营企业 Collective Joint Ownership Enterprises	3 839	4 920	3.38	3.75	3.21	3.75	0.82	0.56
其他内资企业 Other Domestic－funded Enterprises	40 123	58 145	7.06	11.44	3.33	7.08	1.86	5.58
港澳台商投资企业 Enterprises with Investment from Hongkong, Macao and Taiwan	19 649	22 313	6.16					
外商投资企业 Foreign Funded Enterprises	24 840	24 724	55.30	68.01	20.21	19.60		
按经济类型分 **Grouped by Ownership**								
国有经济 State－owned	1 558 876	1 836 518	1 227.07	1 296.39	477.27	365.97	223.01	186.11
集体经济 Collective－owned	402 196	356 380	492.48	323.97	300.57	214.66	173.46	102.34
私有经济 Private and Individual	315 355	400 499	262.89	245.30	145.86	138.33	53.03	51.79
港澳台商投资经济 Hongkong, Macao and Taiwan Funded	19 649	22 313	6.16					
外商投资经济 Foreign Funded	24 840	24 724	55.30	68.01	20.21	19.60		
其　他 Other	1 651 094	1 955 940	1 503.86	2 006.89	700.99	745.82	308.50	388.34

11－4　建筑企业基本情况(2005 年)

(按行业和资质等级分)

BASIC STATISTICS ON CONSTRUCTION ENTERPRISES,2005

(GROUPED BY SECTOR AND QUALIFICATION GRADE)

指　标 Item	企业个数(个) Number of Enterprises (unit)		从业人员平均人数(万人) Average Employed Personnel (10 000 persons)		从业人员劳动报酬(万元) Earnings of Employed Personnel (10 000 yuan)		建筑业总产值(万元) Gross Output Value of Construction (10 000 yuan)	
	2004	2005	2004	2005	2004	2005	2004	2005
按行业类别分								
Grouped by Sector								
房屋工程建筑业								
Building Engineering	173	167	16.56	17.03	127 830	142 014	2 292 932	2 614 781
土木工程建筑业								
Civil Engineering	164	159	12.41	12.70	214 305	270 762	3 016 527	3 485 805
建筑安装业								
Building Installation	354	363	6.05	6.51	96 821	122 029	796 736	1 046 200
建筑装饰业								
Building Decoration	290	278	1.87	1.63	18 494	14 468	269 624	229 701
其他建筑业								
Others	174	141	1.38	1.23	13 588	12 375	176 177	167 215
按资质等级分								
Grouped by Quali-fication Grade								
施工总承包								
General Contractor	**259**	**245**	**28.28**	**28.44**	**331 396**	**402 607**	**4 886 950**	**5 606 342**
特　级								
Super Grade	3	4	5.26	4.55	40 292	71 782	923 931	1 151 948
一　级								
First Grade	47	49	13.53	15.16	194 444	238 421	2 872 284	3 355 988
二　级								
Second Grade	87	77	5.95	6.18	63 775	64 786	778 555	776 658
三　级								
Third Grade	122	115	3.54	2.55	32 885	27 618	312 180	321 748
专业承包								
Specialized Contractor	**896**	**863**	**9.99**	**10.66**	**139 642**	**159 041**	**1 665 046**	**1 937 360**
一　级								
First Grade	57	51	3.05	2.93	53 971	51 738	910 438	976 958
二　级								
Second Grade	147	135	2.25	3.07	28 901	43 256	269 240	361 103
三　级								
Third Grade	680	662	4.65	4.60	56 396	63 494	479 514	586 351
不分等级								
No Grade	12	15	0.04	0.06	374	553	5 854	12 948

11－4 续表　Continued

指　　标 Item	竣工产值 （万元） Gross Output Value Completed (10 000 yuan)		房屋建筑施工面积 （万平方米） Floor Space of Building Under Construction (10 000 sq. m)		房屋建筑竣工面积 （万平方米） Floor Space of Building Completed (10000 sq. m)		#住　宅 Residential Buildings	
	2004	2005	2004	2005	2004	2005	2004	2005
按行业类别分								
Grouped by Sector								
房屋工程建筑业								
Building Engineering	1 690 385	1 754 038	3 217.27	3 587.42	1 498.12	1 361.34	720.44	694.50
土木工程建筑业								
Civil Engineering	1 469 117	1 883 397	168.02	235.62	74.94	75.12	18.18	28.17
建筑安装业								
Building Installation	515 516	662 644	151.52	105.10	69.87	45.78	19.38	5.91
建筑装饰业								
Building Decoration	160 453	187 503						
其他建筑业								
Others	136 539	108 792	10.95	12.42	1.97	2.14		
按资质等级分								
Grouped by Quali－fication Grade								
施工总承包								
General Contractor	**2 991 292**	**3 343 088**	**3 335.29**	**3 750.23**	**1 559.15**	**1 387.07**	**752.89**	**715.34**
特　级								
Super Grade	412 662	368 203	276.85	325.79	105.25	80.86	42.83	34.03
一　级								
First Grade	1 749 775	2 171 502	1 908.93	2 367.24	800.02	760.55	329.34	375.78
二　级								
Second Grade	563 773	530 416	779.36	780.79	404.88	343.57	245.47	192.70
三　级								
Third Grade	265 082	272 967	370.15	276.41	249.00	202.09	135.25	112.83
专业承包								
Specialized Contractor	**980 718**	**1 253 286**	**212.47**	**190.33**	**85.75**	**97.31**	**5.11**	**13.24**
一　级								
First Grade	390 870	494 146	99.52	98.98	46.80	51.57	3.29	
二　级								
Second Grade	219 892	300 193	45.28	52.79	22.66	28.64		8.12
三　级								
Third Grade	365 475	454 586	67.67	38.56	16.29	17.10	1.82	5.12
不分等级								
No Grade	4 481	4 361						

11－5 建筑企业主要财务指标(2005年)
MAIN FINANCIAL INDICATORS OF CONSTRUCTION ENTERPRISES,2005

单位:万元 (10 000 yuan)

指标	Item	全市总计 Total	#国有经济 State－owned	#地方 Local
资本金	**Capital**			
资本金合计	Total Capital	1 487 546	510 687	275 845
年末资产负债	**Assets and Liabilities at Year－end**			
流动资产合计	Total Circulating Funds	5 429 042	2 087 763	969 445
固定资产合计	Total Fixed Assets	1 428 900	485 703	204 686
固定资产原价	Original Value of Fixed Assets	2 024 888	782 007	256 982
#生产经营用	Used in Production and Management	1 606 378	633 002	157 218
累计折旧	Accumulative Depreciation	750 917	331 560	75 904
资产总计	Total Assets	7 393 700	2 855 637	1 321 483
损益及分配	**Profit,Loss and Distribution**			
工程结算收入	Revenue of Project Settle Accounts	7 888 702	2 838 716	865 070
工程结算成本	Costs of Project Settle Accounts	7 088 871	2 580 905	777 474
工程结算税金及附加	Taxes & Extra Charges of Project Settle Accounts	219 852	82 714	24 546
工程结算利润	Profits of Project Settle Accounts	560 011	173 984	62 254
其他业务收入	Other Revenue from Business	190 254	71 972	40 538
其他业务利润	Other Profits from Business	10 817	4 754	3 526
管理费用	Management Expenses	378 910	129 691	49 848
#税　金	Taxes	8 168	3 980	2 469
利润总额	Total Profits	169 948	37 299	10 763
应交所得税	Income Taxes Payable	44 928	11 548	4 675
应付利润	Profits Payable	53 537	16 575	3 932
利税总额	Total Pre－tax Profits	397 968	123 993	37 778
工资、福利费	**Wage and Welfare Expenses**			
应付工资总额	Total Wage Payable	507 298	206 389	49 124
应付福利费总额	Total Welfare Expenses Payable	54 350	21 956	5 996

注:本表按原经济类型分组,下同。
Note: Data is grouped by original ownership in this table,same as following tables.

11－5 续表　Continued
单位:万元　　(10 000 yuan)

指　标	Item	#集体经济 Collective －owned	#私有经济 Private	#港澳台投资经济 Hongkong,Macao andTaiwan Funded	#外商投资经济 Foreign Funded
资本金	**Capital**				
资本金合计	Total Capital	101 776	254 829	21 195	26 879
年末资产负债	**Assets and Liabilities at Year－end**				
流动资产合计	Total Circulating Funds	346 988	433 078	73 666	83 568
固定资产合计	Total Fixed Assets	58 627	148 177	12 190	5 819
固定资产原价	Original Value of Fixed Assets	78 584	169 578	16 169	8 935
#生产经营用	Used in Production and Management	56 339	128 861	7 005	3 229
累计折旧	Accumulative Depreciation	25 809	41 218	5 831	4 266
资产总计	Total Assets	427 673	606 396	92 034	93 242
损益及分配	**Profit,Loss and Distribution**				
工程结算收入	Revenue of Project Settle Accounts	411 632	543 463	84 894	53 061
工程结算成本	Costs of Project Settle Accounts	357 063	465 815	63 654	47 456
工程结算税金及附加	Taxes and Extra Charges of Project Settle Accounts	14 200	17 889	1 375	819
工程结算利润	Profits of Project Settle Accounts	39 045	52 620	13 274	4 532
其他业务收入	Other Revenue from Business	3 732	16 605	23 404	1 563
其他业务利润	Other Profits from Business	1 477	1 496	－769	178
管理费用	Management Expenses	28 408	41 566	16 687	3 898
#税　金	Taxes	663	757	28	31
利润总额	Total Profits	11 301	9 223	－4 486	273
应交所得税	Income Taxes Payable	4 235	3 465	153	312
应付利润	Profits Payable	5 046	7 106	148	624
利税总额	Total Pre－tax Profits	26 164	27 869	－3 083	1 123
工资、福利费	**Wage and Welfare Expenses**				
应付工资总额	Total Wage Payable	44 584	37 259	6 180	2 694
应付福利费总额	Total Welfare Expenses Payable	4 223	4 020	132	252

11－6 建筑企业年末自有机械设备总功率和净值(1990－2005年)
TOTAL POWER AND NET VALUE OF MACHINERY AND EQUIPMENT OWNED BY CONSTRUCTION ENTERPRISES(YEAR－END),1990－2005

年 份 Year	年末自有机械设备总功率(万千瓦) Total Power of Machinery and Equipment Owned (year－end) (10 000 kw)	#国有经济 State－owned	#地 方 Local	年末自有机械设备净值(万元) Net Value of Machinery and Equipment Owned (year－end) (10 000 yuan)	#国有经济 State－owned	#地 方 Local
1990	91.7	86.7	41.4	79 168	77 633	28 493
1991	89.74	85.46	42.95	76 234	74 526	27 722
1992	94.60	89.90	42.60	76 234	74 252	29 646
1993	98.92	89.57	41.20	116 608	108 817	55 009
1994	116.58	103.91	37.47	172 348	153 207	47 757
1995	138.36	110.17	43.77	179 888	164 162	60 526
1996	137.98	109.22	40.47	384 677	178 790	47 006
1997	151.18	119.22	43.87	207 571	173 245	54 521
1998	173.03	111.19	39.28	206 033	163 854	49 153
1999	185.54	146.77	38.00	214 052	174 687	67 470
2000	157.27	102.26	36.14	217 748	122 519	45 433
2001	168.83	87.31	32.16	231 546	126 407	51 157
2002	221.56	85.37	33.03	529 838	166 556	83 098
2003	227.81	86.32	34.65	582 022	208 634	79 305
2004	258.80	96.86	42.66	622 763	223 307	63 141
2005	246.33	93.87	29.07	694 990	230 140	53 538

11－7 建筑企业技术装备率和动力装备率(1990－2005年)
VALUE AND POWER OF MACHINES PER LABORER OF CONSTRUCTION ENTERPRISES,1990－2005

年 份 Year	全部职工技术装备率(元/人) Value of Machines per Laborer (yuan/person)	#国有经济 State－owned	#地 方 Local	全部职工动力装备率(千瓦/人) Power of Machines Per Laborer (kw/person)	#国有经济 State－owned	#地 方 Local
1990	4 231	4 480	2 893	4.9	5.0	4.2
1991	4 023	4 259	2 697	4.7	4.9	4.1
1992	4 063	4 279	2 878	5.00	5.20	4.10
1993	4 507	5 490	4 461	3.80	4.50	3.30
1994	5 114	5 075	2 350	3.46	3.44	1.84
1995	6 281	6 622	4 299	4.83	4.44	3.11
1996	13 237	7 677	3 647	4.75	4.69	3.14
1997	7 094	7 680	4 300	5.17	5.28	3.46
1998	7 022	7 908	4 134	5.90	5.37	3.30
1999	8 774	11 542	10 233	7.61	9.70	5.76
2000	10 714	9 483	9 008	7.74	7.92	7.17
2001	12 881	14 697	11 768	9.39	10.15	7.40
2002	19 423	18 366	16 571	8.12	9.41	6.59
2003	24 203	27 824	24 187	9.47	11.51	10.57
2004	27 354	33 064	25 506	11.37	14.34	17.23
2005	26 064	26 376	16 793	9.24	10.76	9.12

11-8 建筑企业机械设备情况及经济效益指标
MACHINERY & EQUIPMENT AND ECONOMIC
EFFICIENCY INDICATORS OF CONSTRUCTION ENTERPRISES

指　　标　　Item	全　市 Total	#国有经济 State - owned	#地　方 Local
2004 年			
建筑业机械设备情况			
Machinery and Equipment of Construction Enterprises			
自有机械设备总台数(台)			
Number of Machinery and Equipment Owned(set)	99 495	29 482	15 497
自有机械设备总功率(万千瓦)			
Power of Machinery and Equipment Owned(10 000 kw)	258.80	96.86	42.66
自有机械设备净值(万元)			
Net Value of Machinerand Equipment Owned(10 000 yuan)	622 763	223 307	63 141
技术装备率(元/人)			
Value of Machines Per Laborer(yuan/person)	27 354	33 064	25 506
动力装备率(千瓦/人)			
Power of Machines Per Laborer(kw/person)	11.37	14.34	17.23
建筑业经济效益指标			
Economic Efficiency Indicators of Construction Enterprises			
全员劳动生产率(元/人)			
Overall Labor Productivity(yuan/person)	171 190	224 168	160 810
房屋竣工率(%)			
Percentage of Buildings Completed(%)	46.4	38.9	38.4
平均每一从业人员竣工面积(平方米/人)			
Per Capita Floor Space of Buildings Completed(sq. m/person)	43.0	41.8	34.5
每百元产值实现利税(元)			
Ratio of Pre - tax Profit to Gross Output Value(yuan)	4.9	3.6	3.3
百元产值占用流动资产(元)			
Ratio of Circulating Funds to Gross Output Value(yuan)	73.3	73.4	106.9
全员资金占有率(元/人)			
Per Capita Owned Capital(yuan/person)	160 429	205 314	209 159
2005 年			
建筑业机械设备情况			
Machinery and Equipment of Construction Enterprises			
自有机械设备总台数(台)			
Number of Machinery and Equipment Owned(set)	100 040	28 704	13 146
自有机械设备总功率(万千瓦)			
Power of Machinery and Equipment Owned(10 000 kw)	246.33	93.87	29.07
自有机械设备净值(万元)			
Net Value of Machinerand Equipment Owned(10 000 yuan)	694 990	230 140	53 538
技术装备率(元/人)			
Value of Machines Per Laborer(yuan/person)	26 064	26 376	16 793
动力装备率(千瓦/人)			
Power of Machines Per Laborer(kw/person)	9.24	10.76	9.12
建筑业经济效益指标			
Economic Efficiency Indicators of Construction Enterprises			
全员劳动生产率(元/人)			
Overall Labor Productivity(yuan/person)	192 931	228 354	172 133
房屋竣工率(%)			
Percentage of Buildings Completed(%)	37.7	28.2	40.0
平均每一从业人员竣工面积(平方米/人)			
Per Capita Floor Space of Buildings Completed(sq. m/person)	38.0	29.6	30.7
每百元产值实现利税(元)			
Ratio of Pre - tax Profit to Gross Output Value(yuan)	5.3	4.4	4.4
百元产值占用流动资产(元)			
Ratio of Circulating Funds to Gross Output Value(yuan)	72.0	73.8	106.5
全员资金占有率(元/人)			
Per Capita Owned Capital(yuan/person)	175 392	207 821	222 012

11－9　全市建筑企业建筑业总产值、利税总额五十强(2005 年)

TOP 50 CONSTRUCTION ENTERPRISES BY GROSS OUTPUT VALUE AND TOTAL PRE－TAX PROFITS OF CONSTRUCTION,2005

总产值名次 Position of Output Value	单位名称 Name of Enterprise	利税总额名次 Position of Total Pre－tax Profits	单位名称 Name of Enterprise
1	中铁十八局集团有限公司	1	海洋石油工程股份有限公司
2	海洋石油工程股份有限公司	2	中铁十八局集团有限公司
3	天津电力建设公司	3	天津航道局
4	中港第一航务工程局第一工程公司	4	中港第一航务工程局第一工程公司
5	天津市建工工程总承包有限公司	5	天津二十冶金建设有限公司
6	中国建筑第六工程局	6	天津电力建设公司
7	天津二十冶金建设有限公司	7	中港第一航务工程局第四工程公司
8	中国建筑第六工程局土木工程公司	8	天津城建集团有限公司
9	中港第一航务工程局第四工程公司	9	中港第一航务工程局
10	天津城建集团有限公司	10	路桥集团第一公路工程局天津工程处
11	天津三建建筑工程有限公司	11	天津市宝泉路桥有限公司
12	天津航道局	12	中国建筑第六工程局土木工程公司
13	天津第五市政公路工程有限公司	13	中国建筑第六工程局
14	天津二建建筑工程有限公司	14	天津市建工工程总承包有限公司
15	天津六建建筑工程有限公司	15	天津市西青区光源电力工程安装有限公司
16	中港第一航务工程局	16	渤海石油航务建筑工程公司
17	天津第一市政公路工程有限公司	17	天津第五市政公路工程有限公司
18	中国石化集团第四建设公司	18	天津三建建筑工程有限公司
19	天津一建建筑工程有限公司	19	中国石化集团第四建设公司
20	路桥集团第一公路工程局天津工程处	20	天津二建建筑工程有限公司
21	天津第三市政公路工程有限公司	21	中国水利水电基础工程局
22	中国建筑第六工程局第四建筑工程公司	22	天津市建设发展总公司
23	中国建筑第六工程局第二建筑工程公司	23	天津第一市政公路工程有限公司
24	中铁建工集团北方工程有限公司	24	中国建筑第六工程局第三建筑工程公司
25	天津路桥建设工程有限公司	25	天津六建建筑工程有限公司
26	天津四建建筑工程有限公司	26	中国建筑第六工程局第四建筑工程公司
27	天津送变电工程公司	27	天津市大港水利工程公司
28	渤海石油航务建筑工程公司	28	天津市建城地基基础工程有限公司
29	天津第六市政公路工程有限公司	29	天津武清建筑建材集团
30	中铁六局集团天津铁路建设有限公司	30	中国建筑第六工程局第二建筑工程公司
31	中国水利水电基础工程局	31	天津蓝巢电力检修有限公司
32	天津市雍阳公路工程有限公司	32	天津市光达电力有限责任公司
33	西门子楼宇科技(天津)有限公司	33	中铁建工集团北方工程有限公司
34	中国建筑第六工程局第三建筑工程公司	34	天津市青龙建筑安装工程公司
35	中国建筑第六工程局第五建筑工程公司	35	天津第三市政公路工程有限公司
36	天津第四市政建筑工程有限公司	36	天津送变电工程公司
37	天津电信建设工程有限公司	37	天津开发区市政工程修建服务公司
38	天津市龙祥建材建设工程有限公司	38	中铁六局集团天津铁路建设有限公司
39	天津市管道工程集团有限公司	39	天津新宇建筑工程有限公司
40	天津市水利工程有限公司	40	天津一建建筑工程有限公司
41	天津市青龙建筑安装工程公司	41	天津第六市政公路工程有限公司
42	天津富凯建设集团有限公司	42	天津市水利工程有限公司
43	天津市公路工程总公司	43	天津蓝巢特种吊装工程有限公司
44	天津市机电设备安装公司	44	天津市龙祥建材建设工程有限公司
45	静海公路工程有限公司	45	中国建筑第六工程局第五建筑工程公司
46	天津市地方铁路工程公司	46	天津市雍阳公路工程集团有限公司
47	天津振津工程集团有限公司	47	天津滨电电力工程公司
48	天津市建城地基基础工程有限公司	48	天津渔阳建工集团有限公司
49	天津和平建工集团有限公司	49	天津路桥建设工程有限公司
50	天津渔阳建工集团有限公司	50	天津和平建工集团有限公司

主要统计指标解释

建筑业总产值 是以货币表现的建筑安装企业在一定时期内生产的建筑业产品的总和。建筑业总产值包括三部分内容：

(1)建筑工程产值 指列入建筑工程预算内的各种工程价值，主要包括：各种用途的房屋、构筑物的建筑工程和暖气、卫生、通风、照明、煤气等设备安装价值；设备基础、支柱、操作台、梯子、烟囱、凉水塔的砌筑工程；各种锅炉炉体砌筑和金属结构安装工程；施工现场布置、场地平整、施工临时用水、电、道路的铺筑与架设；矿井的开凿、井巷掘进延伸、露天矿的剥离、石油、天然气钻井工程；铁路、公路、港口、桥梁的建筑工程；水利工程；防空、地下建筑等特殊工程。和对建筑物内部或外部进行装饰、装修的价值。

(2)设备安装工程产值 指设备安装工程价值，主要包括生产、动力、起重、运输、传动、医疗、实验、电讯、光纤、电话、计算机和电子设备等各种需要安装设备的装配与安装，与设备相联接的工作台、梯子、栏杆等装设工程；附属于被安装设备的管线敷设工程；被安装设备的绝缘、防腐保温、油漆等工作；为测定安装工作质量，对单个设备、系统设备进行单机试车和系统联动无负荷试运转工作，但产值中不包括被安装设备的价值。

(3)其他产值 建筑业总产值中除建筑工程、安装工程以外的产值。包括房屋、构筑物修理产值、非标准设备制造产值、总包企业向分包企业收取的管理费以及不能明确划分的施工活动所完成的产值。

①房屋、构筑物修理产值 指房屋和构筑物修理所完成的产值，但不包括被修理房屋、构筑物本身产值和生产设备的修理产值。

②非标准设备制造产值 指加工制造没有定型的非标准生产设备的加工费和原材料价值。

Explanatory Notes on Main Statistical Indicators

Gross Output Value of Construction refers to the total of construction products, expressed in money terms, completed by construction and installation enterprises during a given period of time. It includes three parts :

(a) **Output Value of Construction Projects** is the value of projects covered by the project budgets, including the value of various buildings and structures, the value of the installation projects of central heating, public health, ventilation, lighting, gas, etc., the building of the base of equipment, pillar, operation desk, ladder, funnel, water tower, the building boiler room and installation of metals construction, arrange construction site, level the land, temporary expenses of water, electrical, pave the way, cutting mine, well drilling construction of oil, gas, the building engineering of railways, highways, port and bridges, water engineering, output value of building decoration, air defense, underground.

(b) **Output Value of Installation Projects** is the value of the installation of equipment, (excluding the value of the equipment to be installed), mainly including production, power, lifting, transportation, medical treatment, experimentation, telecommunications, fiber optics, telephone, computer, electronic equipment, working desk, ladder, banisters, insulation, heat preservation, paint, etc.

(c) **Other Output Value** refers to output value outside of output value of construction projects and installation projects. It includes output value of repair of buildings and structures, output value of manufactured non－standard equipment, management fee of chief contractor received from subcontractor, other output value of construction.

a. Output value of repair of buildings and structures refer to the value created through the repairs of buildings or structures, but does not include the value of buildings or structures being repaired and the value of the repair of production equipment.

b. Output value of manufactured non－standard equipment refer to the value of non－standard production equipment (including raw materials and manufacturing cost) made for the construction projects.

第12篇
CHAPTER 12

交通运输和邮电
Transportation, Post and Telecommunications

12－1　社会客、货运输量和周转量（1990－2005年）

PASSENGER & FREIGHT TRAFFIC AND THE TURNOVER VOLUME OF PASSENGER & FREIGHT TRAFFIC,1990－2005

年　份 Year	客运量（万人） Passenger Traffic (10 000 persons)	#铁　路 Railways	#公　路 Highways	#水　运 Waterways	旅客周转量（百万人公里） Turnover Volume of Passenger Traffic (million passenger－km)	#铁　路 Railways	#公　路 Highways	#水　运 Waterways
1990	2 175	1 722	447			5 409	307	
1991	2 922	1 718	1 196			4 974	941	
1992	2 662	1 731	897			6 242	819	
1993	3 225	1 812	1 380	4	8 825	6 584	1 463	92
1994	3 373	1 863	1 463	6	8 299	5 778	1 639	49
1995	3 308	1 802	1 464	5	7 927	5 437	1 680	41
1996	3 125	1 580	1 496	5	7 599	4 917	1 772	43
1997	3 136	1 449	1 640	5	7 921	5 050	2 017	41
1998	3 207	1 511	1 651	4	7 950	5 280	1 914	33
1999	3 259	1 546	1 671	3	8 277	5 780	1 782	25
2000	3 474	1 594	1 820	2	8 845	6 022	1 864	26
2001	3 302	1 456	1 780	6	9 197	5 996	2 205	34
2002	3 457	1 498	1 870	5	9 255	5 782	2 272	33
2003	3 507	1 281	2 109	2	9 274	5 526	2 158	23
2004	4 103	1 491	2 457	2.5	11 713	7 112	2 404	30
2005	4 679	1 550	2 961	3.2	14 210	9 070	2 646	36

年　份 Year	货运量（万吨） Freight Traffic (10 000 tons)	#铁　路 Railways	#公　路 Highways	#水　运 Waterways	货物周转量（亿吨公里） Turnover Volume of Freight Traffic (100 million ton－km)	#铁　路 Railways	#公　路 Highways	#水　运 Waterways
1990	15 929	2 228	12 329	1 046	1 139	234	52	852
1991	18 308	2 290	14 537	1 163	1 216	204	37	973
1992	17 522	2 392	13 562	1 248	1 321	217	37	1 067
1993	21 640	2 618	17 244	1 347	1 341	264	46	1 030
1994	23 783	2 634	19 270	1 421	1 325	225	46	1 053
1995	24 040	2 722	19 323	1 517	1 412	230	41	1 139
1996	24 133	2 668	19 491	1 489	1 052	224	41	784
1997	25 090	2 548	20 515	1 390	1 031	219	44	765
1998	24 505	2 467	18 584	2 867	3 710	198	60	3 449
1999	27 052	2 380	20 049	3 884	4 759	200	60	4 497
2000	26 400	3 079	18 764	4 165	4 674	275	63	4 334
2001	28 608	3 727	19 382	5 037	5 166	230	65	4 870
2002	31 016	4 519	19 554	6 452	6 484	228	66	6 188
2003	35 252	5 662	20 072	8 944	8 169	259	68	7 840
2004	37 934	6 108	19 560	11 613	11 473	286	72	11 112
2005	40 263	7 241	19 850	12 375	12 461	353	74	12 031

注：铁路数据为天津地区辖区数，下同。
Note: The data of railways cover the regions under Tianjin administration, same as following next.

12－2　社会客、货运输量和周转量
PASSENGER & FREIGHT TRAFFIC AND THE TURNOVER VOLUME OF PASSENGER& FREIGHT TRAFFIC

指　　标	Item	2003	2004	2005	2005 比2004年 增长% Increase Rate in 2005 over 2004
客运量(万人)	**Passenger Traffic (10 000 persons)**	**3 507**	**4 103**	**4 679**	**14.0**
铁　路	Railways	1 281	1 491	1 550	4.0
公　路	Highways	2 109	2 457	2 961	20.5
水　运	Waterways	2	2.5	3.2	28.0
民　航	Civil Aviation	115	153	165	7.8
旅客周转量 (百万人公里)	**Turnover Volume of Passenger Traffic (million passenger－km)**	**9 274**	**11 713**	**14 210**	**21.3**
铁　路	Railways	5 526	7 112	9 070	27.5
公　路	Highways	2 158	2 404	2 646	10.1
水　运	Waterways	23	30	36	20.0
民　航	Civil Aviation	1 567	2 166	2 458	13.5
货运量(万吨)	**Freight Traffic (10 000 tons)**	**35 252**	**37 934**	**40 263**	**6.1**
铁　路	Railways	5 662	6 108	7 241	18.5
公　路	Highways	20 072	19 560	19 850	1.5
水　运	Waterways	8 944	11 613	12 375	6.6
民　航	Civil Aviation	1	1.7	1.9	11.8
管道输油气量	Traffic of Petroleum & Gas Pipelines	573	651	795	22.0
货物周转量 (亿吨公里)	**Turnover Volume of Freight Traffic (100 million ton－km)**	**8 169**	**11 473**	**12 461**	**8.6**
铁　路	Railways	259	286	353	23.4
公　路	Highways	68	72	74	2.8
水　运	Waterways	7 840	11 112	12 031	8.3
民　航	Civil Aviation	0.2	0.26	0.3	15.4
管道输油气量	Traffic of Petroleum & Gas Pipelines	1.9	2.6	3.1	19.2

12－3　运输线路长度
LENGTH OF TRANSPORT ROUTES

单位:公里　　(km)

指　　标	Item	2003	2004	2005	2005 比2004年 增长% Increase Rate in 2005 over 2004
公　路	**Highways**				
通车里程	Length of Highways Having Transport Service	10 168	10 514	10 836	3.1
等级公路	Expressway and Class I to IV Highway	9 901	10 420	10 791	3.6
#高速公路	Expressway	517	517	593	14.7
等外公路	Highway Below Class IV	267	94	44	－53.2
内河航道	**Navigable Inland Waterways**				
航道里程	Length of Navigable Inland Waterways	412	412	412	
民　航	**Civil Aviation**				
民用航空航线里程	Length of Civil Aviation	18 519	22 802	19 504	－14.5
管　道	**Pipelines**				
输油气管道里程	Length of Petroleum & Gas Pipelines	495	613	503	－17.9

注:内河航道里程为内河清淤里程。民用航空航线里程为国航天津分公司在天津机场起降飞机的里程。
Note: Length of navigable inland waterways refer to length of cleaning up the silt inland waterways. Length of civil aviation refer to the length of Air China Tianjin Company flights at Tianjin Airport.

12－4　港口客、货吞吐量（1990－2005 年）

VOLUME OF PASSENGER & FREIGHT HANDLED IN PORTS，1990－2005

年　份 Year	港口旅客吞吐量 （万人次） Volume of Passenger Handled in Ports (10 000 person－times)	港口货物吞吐量 （万吨） Volume of Freight Handled in Ports (10 000 tons)	出　港 Out－port	比　重(%) Proportion (%)	进　港 In－port	比　重(%) Proportion (%)	集装箱吞吐量 （万国际标准箱） Handled Containers (10 000 TEU)
1990	37.0	2 063	1 195	57.9	868	42.1	29
1991	47.7	2 378	1 488	62.6	890	37.4	34
1992	61.2	2 929	1 915	65.4	1 014	34.6	39
1993	57.6	3 719	2 527	68.0	1 192	32.0	48
1994	51.9	4 652	3 507	75.4	1 145	24.6	63
1995	50.4	5 787	4 551	78.6	1 236	21.4	70
1996	58.7	6 188	4 839	78.2	1 349	21.8	82
1997	52.7	6 789	5 198	76.6	1 591	23.4	94
1998	45.3	6 818	5 124	75.2	1 694	24.8	102
1999	48.7	7 298	5 280	72.4	2 018	27.6	130
2000	40.2	9 582	6 936	72.4	2 646	27.6	171
2001	37.1	11 369	8 086	71.1	3 283	28.9	201
2002	33.0	12 906	8 802	68.2	4 104	31.8	241
2003	22.7	16 182	10 912	67.4	5 270	32.6	302
2004	32.5	20 619	13 217	64.1	7 402	35.9	382
2005	31.6	24 069	14 700	61.1	9 369	38.9	480

注：货物吞吐量是全港数据，即包括货主码头数据。
Note：Volume of freight handled in ports refer to the figure of ports，including those of docks.

12－5　港口设施

PORTS FACILITIES

指　标	Item	2003	2004	2005	2005 比 2004 年增长% Increase Rate in 2005 over 2004
码头长度（米）	Length of Quay Line(m)	14 443	20 324	20 906	2.9
港口泊位（个）	Number of Berths(unit)	108	114	116	1.8
天津港（集团）有限公司	Tianjin Port Group Corporation Ltd.	76	74	76	2.7
货主码头	Docks	32	40	40	
#万吨级泊位	10,000 Ton Class	54	53	55	5.8
#天津港（集团）有限公司	Tianjin Port Group Corporation Ltd.	52	52	54	3.8
铁路专用线长度（米）	Length of Railways(m)	75 650	100 037	120 665	20.6
仓库总面积（平方米）	Areas of Store Houses(sq. m)	200 445	273 777	282 868	3.3
堆场总面积（平方米）	Areas of Goods Pile(sq. m)	3 295 601	3 743 714	4 636 202	23.8
集装箱堆场堆存能力（TEU）	Capacity of Piling Containers(TEU)	98 129	143 809	140 644	－2.2
装卸机械台数（台）	Number of Loading & Unloading Machines(unit)	1 102	1 422	1 932	35.9

注：本表除港口泊位含货主码头数据外，其余设施均为天津港（集团）有限公司数据。
Note：Number of berths include docks，other ports facilities refer to those owned by Tianjin Port Group Corporation Ltd.

12-6 港口分货类吞吐量
VOLUME OF FREIGHT HANDLED IN PORTS BY CATEGORY

单位:万吨 (10 000 tons)

指标 Item	合计 Total		出港量 Out-port		进港量 In-port	
	2004	2005	2004	2005	2004	2005
港口货物吞吐量 Volume of Freight Handled in Ports	**20 619**	**24 069**	**13 217**	**14 700**	**7 402**	**9 369**
国外 Abroad	10 792	12 310	5 610	5 591	5 182	6 719
国内 Domestic	9 827	11 759	7 607	9 109	2 220	2 650
分品种货物吞吐量 Volume of Freight Handled by Category						
煤炭及制品 Coal and Related Products	7 720	7 990	7 648	7 948	72	42
石油、天然气及制品 Petroleum,Natural Gas and Related Products	2 105	2 614	985	1 336	1 120	1 278
金属矿石 Metal Ores	2 864	4 072	46	54	2 818	4 018
钢铁 Steel and Iron	1 660	2 030	1 454	1 790	206	240
矿建材料 Mineral Building Materials	992	1 244	108	149	884	1 095
水泥 Cement	4	5	4	5	0	0
木材 Timber	38	34	22	20	16	14
非金属矿石 Nonmetal Ores	259	263	235	225	24	37
化学肥料及农药 Chemical Fertilizers and Pesticides	77	77	5	3	72	74
盐 Salt	16	39	16	4	0	35
粮食 Grain	271	251	71	41	200	210
机械、电器、设备 Machine, Electric Machine,Equipment	1 058	1 441	544	795	514	646
化工原料及制品 Chemical Materials and Related Products	812	931	546	603	266	328
有色金属 Nonferrous Metals	150	168	88	87	62	81
轻工、医药产品 Light Industry,Medical and Pharmaceutical Products	945	1 130	728	849	217	281
农林牧渔产品 Agricultural Products	437	416	195	184	242	232
其他 Others	1 211	1 365	522	607	689	758
集装箱吞吐量(万国际标准箱) Handled Containers (10 000 TEU)	**382**	**480**	**199**	**245**	**183**	**235**

12-7 公路及民航运输主要技术经济指标
MAIN TECHNICAL AND ECONOMIC INDICATORS OF HIGHWAY AND CIVIL AVIATION TRANSPORT

指标	Item	2003	2004	2005
公路	**Highways**			
载货汽车里程利用率(%)	Utilization Rate of Length of Trucks in Operation(%)	59.6	52.7	53.8
载客汽车里程利用率(%)	Utilization Rate of Length of Passenger Vehicles in Operation(%)	70.4	99.6	95.6
载货汽车每百吨公里耗汽油(升)	Gasoline Consumption of Trucks(L/100 ton-km)	7.9	7.4	6.7
载客汽车每百吨公里耗汽油(升)	Gasoline Consumption of Passenger Vehicles(L/100 ton-km)	15.1	23.1	25.1
载货汽车每百吨公里耗柴油(升)	Diesel Oil Consumption of Trucks(L/100 ton-km)	4.2	4.7	4.5
载客汽车每百吨公里耗柴油(升)	Diesel Oil Consumption of Passenger Vehicles(L/100 ton-km)	21.4	29.4	28.6
载货汽车实载率(%)	Utilization Rate of Capacity of Freight Trucks(%)	70.5	60.9	63.4
载客汽车实载率(%)	Utilization Rate of Capcity of Passenger Vehicles(%)	79.2	34.9	47.2
民航	**Civil Aviation**			
飞行小时(小时)	Flying Time(hour)	28 901	39 398	43 939
平均每可用机飞行小时(小时)	Flying Time Per Avaliable Aircraft(hour)	2 627	3 796	3 881
正班飞行距离(万公里)	Distance under Normal Conditions(10 000 km)	1 793.1	2 272.6	2 530.2
平均每可用机日生产飞行小时(小时)	Average Daily Flying Time Per Avaliable Aircraft (hour)	7.2	10.3	10.6
正班平均载运率(%)	Average Utilization Rate of Capacity under Normal Conditions(%)	66.0	71.8	72.4

注:本表公路数据为交通运输总公司数据,民航数据为国航天津分公司数据。
Note: In this table, the data of highway is provided by Tianjin Communication Corporation, and the data of civil aviation is provided by Air China Tianjin Company.

12-8 民用航空机场主要指标
MAIN INDICATORS OF CIVIL AVIATION AIRPORT

指标	Item	2004	2005	2005比2004年增长% Increase Rate in 2005 over 2004
机场旅客吞吐量(万人)	**Civil Aviation Passenger Traffic Handled at Airport (10 000 persons)**	**170.5**	**219.4**	**28.7**
国内旅客	Domestic Passenger Traffic		172.2	
国际旅客	International Passenger Traffic		41	
港、澳、台地区旅客	Hongkong, Macao & Taiwan Passenger Traffic		6.2	
机场货邮吞吐量(万吨)	**Civil Aviation Freight Traffic(10 000 tons)**	**7.1**	**8**	**13.0**
国内货邮	Domestic Routes		2.4	
国际货邮	International Routes		5.5	
港、澳、台地区货邮	Hongkong, Macao & Taiwan Regional Routes		0.1	
机场全年起、降架次(万架次)	**Times of Ascend and Descend of Civil Aircrafts in TBIA (10 000 times)**	**2.8**	**4.8**	**69.7**

12-9 民用车辆拥有量(2005年)
NUMBER OF CIVIL MOTOR VEHICLES OWNED,2005

单位:辆 (unit)

指标	Item	合计 Total	#个人 Private-owned	#当年新注册 Registered in 2005
总计	**Total**	**1 126 494**	**879 227**	**126 959**
民用汽车	Civil Motor Vehicles	706 690	479 495	121 398
1.载客汽车	Passenger Vehicles	542 657	386 240	109 269
#轿车	Cars	342 547	246 649	89 295
大型	Large-sized	14 064	1 046	1 900
中型	Medium-sized	25 839	11 190	1 171
小型	Small-sized	398 169	280 704	105 227
微型	Minisize	104 585	93 300	971
2.载货汽车	Trucks	119 550	61 772	10 334
#普通载货	Ordinary Trucks	90 758	49 065	7 079
重型	Heavy Trucks	18 906	5 872	470
中型	Medium-sized Trucks	17 061	7 228	1 004
轻型	Light Trucks	75 708	42 023	8 743
微型	Minisize Trucks	7 875	6 649	117
3.其他汽车	Other Civil Motor Vehicles	44 483	31 483	1 795
摩托车	Motorcycles	342 234	331 254	4 851
拖拉机	Tractor	64 330	64 330	
挂车	Trailer	11 664	3 892	654
其他类型车	Other Vehicles	1 576	256	56

12-10 邮电业基本情况(1990-2005年)
BASIC STATISTICS ON POST AND TELECOMMUNICATIONS,1990-2005

年份 Year	邮电业务总量(万元) Business Value of Post and Telecommunications (10 000 yuan)	邮电局所数(处) Number of Post and Telecommunications Offices(unit)	局用电话交换机容量(门) Capacity of Office Telephone Exchanges (line)	电话机(含移动、小灵通)(万部) Telephone (Include Mobile) (10 000)	平均每百人拥有电话机数(含移动)(部/百人) Popularization Rate of Telephone (Include Mobile) (unit/100 persons)
1990	32 735	281	230 586	31.78	3.7
1991	44 527	280	271 356	34.28	3.9
1992	61 063	273	359 932	42.27	4.8
1993	97 062	277	532 118	63.91	7.2
1994	132 464	297	1 137 748	96.03	10.8
1995	187 195	300	1 522 493	135.61	15.2
1996	256 978	314	1 694 092	174.65	19.4
1997	342 848	328	1 945 020	207.82	23.1
1998	474 067	399	2 447 630	259.58	28.7
1999	567 242	470	2 761 633	329.30	36.2
2000	753 669	563	3 182 465	431.28	46.6
2001	702 206	543	3 645 600	511.57	56.0
2002	903 296	597	3 865 700	601.45	65.4
2003	1 157 060	619	4 024 500	761.91	82.3
2004	1 467 836	700	4 237 700	835.01	89.5
2005	1 763 477	827	6 288 300	939.82	90.1

注:邮电业务总量1990年至2000年为1990年不变价,2001年开始为2000年不变价(下同)。
Note: The business value of post and telecommunications is calculated at 1980 constant prices before 1990, it is calculated at 1990 constant prices in 1990-2000, it has been calculated at 2000 constant prices since 2001(same as following next).

12－11 邮电业务基本情况
BASIC STATISTICS ON POST AND TELECOMMUNICATIONS SERVICES

指 标 Item	单位 Unit	2003	2004	2005	2005 比 2004 年增长% Increase Rate in 2005 over 2004
邮电业务总量 Business Value of Post and Telecommunications Services	万元 10^4 yuan	1 157 060	1 467 836	1 763 477	20.1
函 件 Letters	万件 10^4 pcs	22 033.93	10 591.27	8 384.81	－20.8
特快专递 Pieces of Express Mail Services	万件 10^4 pcs	321.50	372.67	410.24	10.1
订销报刊期发数 Number of Newspapers and Magazines Subscibed	万份 10^4 pcs	314.07	374.21	353	－5.7
集邮业务 Philately	万枚 10^4 pcs	6 793.54	5 352.98	5 000.22	－6.6
短信业务发送量 Number of Messages Send Out	万条 10^4 pcs			450 791.82	
长途电话 Long Distance Calls	万次 10^4 times	48 978.07	88 049.05	86 002.92	－2.3
国内长途电话 Domestic	万次 10^4 times	48 367.01	86 403.18	83 792.83	－3.0
国际电话及港澳台电话 International and Hongkong,Macao & Taiwan	万次 10^4 times	611.06	1 645.87	2 210.09	34.3
移动电话年末用户 Number of Mobile Telephone Subscribers at Year－end	万户 10^4 subscribers	383.31	423	502.90	18.9
本地电话年末用户 Number of Local Telephone Subscribers at Year－end	万户 10^4 subscribers	354.54	413.30	436.92	5.7
住宅电话年末用户 Number of Residential Telephone Subscribers at Year－end	万户 10^4 subscribers	238.36	241.17	351.59	45.8
公用电话 Number of Public Telephone Sets	万部 10^4 sets	22.69	33.64	34.01	1.1
数字数据用户 Digital and Data Users	户 Subscriber	7 690	6 600	6 054	－8.3
国际互联网络用户 Number of Subscriber of Internet Services	万户 10^4 subscriber	204.57	267.49	207.36	－22.5
邮电局所数 Number of Post & Telecommunications Offices	处 unit	619	700	827	18.1
#邮政局所数 Number of Post Offices	处 unit	364	460	454	－10.3
信筒信箱 Number of Post Boxes	处 unit	1 649	1 656	1 728	4.3
邮路总长度 Length of Postal Routes	公里 km	19 986	21 705	21 996	1.3
汽车邮路长度 Length of Postal Routes by Highway	公里 km	9 395	11 114	10 671	－4.0
铁路邮路长度 Length of Postal Routes by Railway	公里 km	5 071	5 071	5 754	13.5
邮政汽车 Automobile for Post Bussiness	辆 unit	744	812	1 104	36.0
农村投递线路 Rural Delivery Routes	公里 km	16 438	16 172	16 144	－0.2

12－12 电信主要通信能力
MAIN COMMUNICATION CAPACITY OF TELECOMMUNICATIONS

指　　标　　　　Item	2003	2004	2005
长途电话业务电路(2M) Number of Long－distance Telephones(line)	1 839	2 544	2 638
数据通信网长途电路(2M) Digital Long－distance Communication(line)	12 795	12 795	73 489
长途电话交换机容量(路端) Capacity of Long－Distance Telephone Exchanges(circuit)	265 427	270 160	267 869
局用电话交换机容量(万门) Capacity of Office Telephone Exchanges(10 000 lines)	402.5	423.8	628.8
移动电话交换机容量(万门) Capacity of Mobile Telephone Exchanges(10 000 subscribers)	515	559	619
电话机(含移动)(万部) Telephone(Include Mobile telephone)(10 000 subscribers)	761.9	835	939.8
长途光缆线路长度(公里) Length of Optical Cable Line(km)	2 386.6	1 873	3 013

12－13 邮政电信服务水平
LEVEL OF POST AND TELECOMMUNICATION SERVICES

指　　标　　　　Item	2003	2004	2005
平均每一邮电局所服务面积(平方公里) Average Area Served by Every Post Telecommunications Office(sq.km)	19.26	17.03	14.41
＃平均每一邮政局所服务面积 Average Area Served by Every Post Office	32.75	29.36	26.25
平均每一邮电局所服务人口(万人) Average People Served by Every Post office Telecommunications(10 000 persons)	1.50	1.33	1.26
＃平均每一邮政局所服务人口 Average People Served by Every Post office	2.54	2.30	2.30
平均每人每年发函件数(件) Annual Average Number of Letters Mailed per Capita(piece)	23.9	11.4	8.11
平均每百人每年订报刊数(件) Annual Average Number of Newspaper and Magazine Subscribed per 100 Persons(piece)	34.0	40.3	34.2
平均每百人拥有电话机(含移动)(部) Popularization Rate of Telephone (include mobil telephone)(sets)	82.3	89.5	90.1
平均每百人拥有移动电话(部) Popularization Rate of Mobile Telephone(sets)	41.4	45.4	48.2
平均每千人拥有公用电话(部) Per 1 000 Person Public Telephone (Sets)	24.6	36.2	32.9

12-14 邮政、电信局(所、厅)数

NUMBER OF POST AND TELECOMMUNICATIONS OFFICES BY REGION

单位:处 (unit)

地 区	Region	2003	2004	2005
全 市	**Total**	**619**	**700**	**827**
#邮政局(所)	Post Offices	364	406	454
市辖区	**Districts Under City Administration**	**483**	**556**	**679**
#市内六区	Six Urban Districts	199	241	320
滨海三区	Three Coastal Districts	107	122	141
和平区	Heping District	34	37	53
河东区	Hedong District	40	47	59
河西区	Hexi District	36	46	55
南开区	Nankai District	43	49	62
河北区	Hebei District	30	38	52
红桥区	Hongqiao District	16	24	39
塘沽区	Tanggu District	50	53	64
汉沽区	Hangu District	19	23	26
大港区	Dagang District	38	46	51
东丽区	Dongli District	18	22	26
西青区	Xiqing District	22	26	33
津南区	Jinnan District	22	23	23
北辰区	Beichen District	20	20	27
武清区	Wuqing District	54	57	58
宝坻区	Baodi District	41	45	51
市辖县	**Counties Under City Administration**	**136**	**144**	**148**
宁河县	Ninghe County	42	46	49
静海县	Jinghai County	51	56	59
蓟 县	Jixian County	43	42	40

主要统计指标解释

货运量 指在一定时期内,以重量单位(吨)计算的由各种运输工具实际完成运送过程的货物数量。

货物周转量 指在一定时期内,由各种运输工具实际完成运送过程的以综合货物运量和运送距离的乘积之和。

客运量 指在一定时期内,各运输部门实际运送的旅客人数,计算单位为人。

旅客周转量 指在一定时期内,实际运送的旅客人数与其相应的旅客运输距离乘积之和。

港口货物吞吐量 又称港口吞吐量,指经由水路运进、出港区范围,并经过装卸的货物数量。按货物流向分为进港吞吐量和出港吞吐量;按货物的贸易性质分为内贸和外贸吞吐量;按货物的类别分,可根据现行的交通行业标准《运输货物分类和代码》分类。

邮电业务总量 指以价值量形式表现的邮电通信企业为社会提供各类邮电通信服务的总数量。邮电业务量按专业分类包括函件、包件、汇票、报刊发行、邮政快件、特快专递、邮政储蓄、集邮、公众电报、用户电报、传真、长途电话、出租电路、无线寻呼、移动电话、分组交换数据通信、出租代维等。计算方法为各类产品乘以相应的平均单价(不变价)之和,再加上出租电路和设备、代用户维护电话交换机和线路等的服务收入。该指标综合反映了一定时期邮电业务发展的总成果,是研究邮电业务量构成和发展趋势的重要指标。计算公式为:

邮电业务总量 = ∑(各类邮电业务量 × 不变单价) + 出租代维及其他业务收入

= 邮政业务总量 + 电信业务总量

民用汽车拥有量 指报告期末,在公安交通管理部门按照《机动车注册登记工作规范》,已注册登记领有民用车辆牌照的全部汽车数量。汽车拥有量统计的主要分类:根据汽车结构分为载客汽车、载货汽车及其他汽车;根据汽车所有者不同分为个人(私人)汽车、单位汽车;根据汽车的使用性质分为营运汽车、非营运汽车和特种汽车;根据汽车大小规格不同载客汽车分为大型、中型、小型和微型,载货汽车分为重型、中型、轻型和微型。

长途电话交换机容量 指用于接入长途电话网的电话交换机设备的额定容量,包括国际电话交换机容量。

局用交换机容量 指安装在电信运营企业内用于接续本地固定电话的电话交换机容量,包括现用和备用的人工或自动交换机的全部容量。不包括用户交换机容量。

移动电话交换机容量 指移动电话交换机根据一定话务模型和交换机处理能力计算出来的最大同时服务用户的数量。

Explanatory Notes on Main Statistical Indicators

Freight Traffic refers to the volume (tons) of freight transported with various traffic facilities in a given period.

Turnover Volume of Freight Traffic refers to the sum of the volume of transported cargo multiplying by the transport distance in a given period.

Passengers Traffic refers to the sum of the passengers transported in some time in a given period.

Turnover Volume of Passengers Traffic refers to the sum of the volume of transported passengers multiplied by the transport distance in a given period.

Ports Cargo Handled Capacity refers to the volume of cargo passing in and out the harbor area and having been loaded and unloaded. The volume of freight handled may be classified as in - port & out - port.

It can also be classified as national trade and international trade by the attribute of trade or be classified by the classification of cargo according to the standard of traffic in use "The Classification and Code of Transported Cargo".

Business Volume of Post and Telecommunications refers to the total amount of post and telecommunication services, expressed in value terms, provided by the post and telecommunications departments for the society. Post and telecommunication services can be classified as letters, parcels, remittance, issue of newspapers and magazines, fast mail service, express mail service, savings deposits, stamps for collection, public and individual telegraph service, facsimiles, long-distance telephone service, leasing of telephone lines, urban paging service, mobile telephone service, data transfer and transmission, etc. The accounting approach is to multiply the service products of all types with their average unit price (constant price) to get sum of business value, plus income from other services such as leasing of telephone lines and equipment, maintenance of telephone switchboards and lines on behalf of customers. This indicator reflects the overall results of post and telecommunications service during a given period, and is important to study the composition of business service and the development of post and telecommunications service.

The formula is as follows:

Business volume of post and telecommunications = $\sum$(Transaction of post and telecommunication service x constant price) + Income from leasing, maintenance and other services = Business volume of post + Business volume of tele-communication

Possession of Civil Motor Vehicles refers to the total number of vehicles that are registered and received vehicles license tags according to the Work Standard for Motor Vehicles Registration formulated by transport management office under department of public security at the end of reference period. They are divided into following categories according to the structure of motor vehicles: passenger vehicles, trucks and others; and private vehicles and vehicles for units use according to ownerships; working vehicles, non-working vehicles and special motor vehicles according to kind of usage; large passenger vehicles, medium passenger vehicles, small passenger vehicles and mini passenger vehicle, heavy trucks, light-heavy trucks, light trucks and mini trucks according to sizes of vehicles.

Capacity of Long Distance Telephone Exchanges refers to the rated capacity of telephone exchanges to connect long distance telephone network, including capacity of international telephone exchanges.

Capacity of Office Telephone Exchanges refers to the capacity (measured in gate) of telephone exchanges installed in the offices of telecommunication service providers for communication between fixed telephones. It includes the capacity of both manual and automatic exchanges in use and for stand-by purpose, excluding the capacity of subscribers exchanges.

Capacity of Mobile Telephone Exchanges refers to the capacity of the maximum services provided to subscribers at one time basing on a certain model and transacting capacity of the mobile telephone exchanges.

第13篇 CHAPTER 13

国内贸易

Domestic Trade

13-1　社会消费品零售总额
TOTAL RETAIL SALES OF CONSUMER GOODS

单位:万元　(10 000 yuan)

指　　标　　Item	2003	2004	2005	2005比2004年增长% Increase Rate in 2005 over 2004
社会消费品零售总额 Total Retail Sales of Consumer Goods	**9 222 673**	**10 447 761**	**11 900 636**	**13.9**
按销售地区分 Grouped by Region				
市 City	8 591 908	9 754 723	11 129 495	14.1
县 County	352 577	390 492	421 948	8.1
县以下 Under County Level	278 188	302 546	349 193	15.4
按行业分 Grouped by Sector				
批发和零售业 Wholesale and Retail Trade	7 271 020	8 256 377	9 583 918	16.1
餐饮业 Catering Trade	1 099 120	1 318 682	1 594 866	20.9
其他行业 Others	852 533	872 702	721 852	-17.3

13-2　批发和零售业商品销售总额(2005年)
TOTAL SALES OF WHOLESALE AND RETAIL TRADE,2005

单位:万元　(10 000 yuan)

项　　目	Item	商品销售总额 Total Sales	#批　发 Wholesale
总　　计	**Total**	**53 838 826**	**43 497 267**
批发业	**Wholesale Trade**	**43 724 420**	**42 261 765**
农畜产品批发	Farm & Livestock Products	547 646	536 416
食品、饮料及烟草制品批发	Food,Beverage and Tobacco	1 407 252	1 317 674
纺织、服装及日用品批发	Textile,Garments and Daily Articles	1 546 039	1 528 170
文化、体育用品及器材批发	Cultural and Sports Goods & Equipment	307 712	290 147
医药及医疗器械批发	Medicine and Medical Appliance	1 614 067	1 380 387
矿产品、建材及化工产品批发	Mineral Products,Building Material and Chemical Products	30 802 273	30 166 883
机械设备、五金交电及电子产品批发	Machinery Equipment,Hardware,Transport,Electric and Electronic Products	5 954 293	5 551 955
贸易经纪与代理	Trade Agent	448 739	448 744
其他批发	Others	1 096 399	1 041 389
零售业	**Retail Trade**	**10 114 406**	**1 235 502**
综合零售	Comprehensive Retail	2 170 334	294 260
食品、饮料及烟草制品专门零售	Special Retail of Food,Beverage and Tobacco	369 219	22 691
纺织、服装及日用品专门零售	Special Retail of Textile,Garments and Daily Articles	469 567	63 210
文化、体育用品及器材专门零售	Special Retail of Cultural and Sports Goods & Equipment	395 736	28 509
医药及医疗器械专门零售	Special Retail of Medicine and Medical Appliance	410 794	72 208
汽车、摩托车、燃料及零配件专门零售	Special Retail of Motor Vehicles,Motorcycles,Parts and Fuel	2 237 940	380 019
家用电器及电子产品专门零售	Special Retail of Household Appliances and Electronic Products	1 526 143	135 350
五金、家具及室内装修材料专门零售	Special Retail of Hardware,Furniture and Decorati on Materials for Indoors	1 179 970	91 539
无店铺及其他零售	Non-shop and Other Retail	1 354 701	147 716

13－3 限额以上批发和零售业商品购进总额

TOTAL PURCHASES OF WHOLESALE AND RETAIL TRADE ABOVE DESIGNATED SIZE

单位：万元 (10 000 yuan)

项目 Item	商品购进总额 Total Goods Purchases		#进口 Imports	
	2004	2005	2004	2005
总计 Total	**35 788 881**	**41 923 855**	**2 388 884**	**1 974 435**
#国有及国有控股企业 State-owned and State-holding Enterprises	20 800 632	27 652 039	966 269	839 668
按登记注册类型分 Grouped by Registered Type				
内资企业 Domestic-funded Enterprises	33 328 032	39 848 073	1 525 787	1 260 697
国有企业 State-owned Enterprises	11 956 909	15 937 343	339 261	222 305
集体企业 Collective-owned Enterprises	981 333	736 553	4 528	23 607
股份合作企业 Cooperative Enterprises	141 823	130 483	62	
私营企业 Private Economy	7 666 514	7 452 351	566 326	429 419
股份有限公司 Share-holding Corporations Ltd.	2 661 422	4 769 702	127 818	84 630
有限责任公司 Limited Liability Corporations	9 428 290	10 350 407	466 800	490 877
#国有独资 Sole State-funded Corporations	1 468 290	2 062 914	189 501	222 300
联营企业 Joint Ownership Enterprises	229 915	293 572	6 047	995
#国有与国有联营企业 State Joint Ownership Enterprises	124 822	115 437		
集体与集体联营企业 Collective Joint Ownership Enterprises	2 640	9 824		
其他内资企业 Other Domestic-funded Enterprises	261 826	177 663	14 945	8 866
港澳台商投资企业 Enterprises with Investment from Hongkong, Macao and Taiwan	566 275	492 790	237 057	234 267
外商投资企业 Foreign Funded Enterprises	1 894 574	1 582 993	626 039	479 471
按经济类型分 Grouped by Ownership				
国有经济 State-owned	13 550 021	18 115 694	528 761	444 605
集体经济 Collective-owned	1 125 796	876 859	4 590	23 607
股份制经济 Share-holding	10 621 422	13 057 195	405 118	353 206
私营经济 Private and individual	7 666 514	7 452 351	566 326	429 419
"三资"经济 Hongkong, Macao, Taiwan and Foreign Funded	2 460 849	2 075 782	863 096	713 738
其他 Others	364 279	345 974	20 992	9 860

13－3 续表　Continued

项　　目　　Item	商品购进总额 Total Goods Purchases		#进　口 Imports	
	2004	2005	2004	2005
按国民经济行业分				
Grouped by Sector				
批发业				
Wholesale Trade	**32 394 907**	**38 288 382**	**2 314 309**	**1 954 908**
农畜产品批发				
Farm & Livestock Products	501 937	505 316	74 078	36 787
食品、饮料及烟草制品批发				
Food, Beverage and Tobacco	931 257	927 238	63 759	64 706
纺织、服装及日用品批发				
Textile, Garments and Daily Articles	915 125	1 069 760	97 306	133 528
文化、体育用品及器材批发				
Cultural and Sports Goods & Equipment	159 427	176 509	1 435	10 048
医药及医疗器械批发				
Medicine and Medical Appliance	956 347	1 428 967	16 188	78 755
矿产品、建材及化工产品批发				
Mineral Products, Building Material and Chemical Products	22 649 921	28 522 177	718 383	576 532
机械设备、五金交电及电子产品批发				
Machinery Equipment, Hardware, Transport, Electric and Electronic Product	5 293 931	4 540 129	1 216 904	886 501
贸易经纪与代理				
Trade Agent	124 472	381 679	14 155	122 414
其他批发				
Others	862 490	736 607	112 101	45 638
零售业				
Retail Trade	**3 393 974**	**3 635 473**	**74 574**	**19 527**
综合零售				
Comprehensive Retail	1 297 553	1 500 896		
食品、饮料及烟草制品专门零售				
Special Retail of Food, Beverage and Tobacco	55 292	57 613	1 027	2 723
纺织、服装及日用品专门零售				
Special Retail of Textile, Garments and Daily Articles	128 887	107 301		
文化、体育用品及器材专门零售				
Special Retail of Cultural and Sports Goods & Equipment	73 124	75 756		
医药及医疗器械专门零售				
Special Retail of Medicine and Medical Appliance	50 223	48 889	509	
汽车、摩托车、燃料及零配件专门零售				
Special Retail of Motor Vehicles, Motorcycles, Parts and Fuel	1 035 878	1 214 679	67 223	16 804
家用电器及电子产品专门零售				
Special Retail of Household Appliances and Electronic Products	385 897	465 557	3 706	
五金、家具及室内装修材料专门零售				
Special Retail of Hardware, Furniture and Decoration Materials for Indoors	180 966	85 027	1 037	
无店铺及其他零售				
Non－shop Stores and Other Retail	186 154	79 755	1 072	

13－4　限额以上批发和零售业商品销售和库存总额
TOTAL SALES AND INVENTORY OF WHOLESALE AND RETAIL TRADE ABOVE DESIGNATED SIZE

单位:万元　　(10 000 yuan)

项　目　Item	商品销售总额 Total Sales		#批　发 Wholesale		年末库存总额 Inventory(year－end)	
	2004	2005	2004	2005	2004	2005
总　计 **Total**	**36 362 168**	**43 160 074**	**31 993 312**	**38 977 967**	**2 216 822**	**2 045 196**
#国有及国有控股企业 State－owned and State－holding Enterprises	21 542 349	27 652 039	20 168 345	26 812 853	1 151 900	1 117 987
按登记注册类型分 **Grouped by Registered Type**						
内资企业 Domestic－funded Enterprises	33 783 858	40 834 674	29 860 980	36 971 279	1 809 706	1 834 703
国有企业 State－owned Enterprises	12 152 258	16 287 685	11 661 855	15 735 382	519 294	415 084
集体企业 Collective－owned Enterprises	996 078	753 898	787 679	643 765	64 362	46 988
股份合作企业 Cooperative Enterprises	150 974	134 528	114 354	109 399	15 690	13 093
私营企业 Private Economy	8 020 398	7 707 232	6 765 180	6 448 187	429 703	439 239
股份有限公司 Share－holding Corporations Ltd.	2 876 774	5 073 521	2 579 928	4 461 573	132 859	172 835
有限责任公司 Limited Liability Corporations	9 043 252	10 392 851	7 589 570	9 209 300	584 464	713 920
#国有独资 Sole State－funded Corporations	1 494 572	1 966 664	1 492 354	1 963 887	202 746	232 201
联营企业 Joint Ownership Enterprises	270 856	308 520	211 061	225 045	7 752	6 170
#国有与国有联营企业 State Joint Ownership Enterprises	125 338	117 007	96 582	86 088	2 034	3 387
集体与集体联营企业 Collective Joint Ownership Enterprises	2 681	9 870		9 870	136	304
其他内资企业 Other Domestic－funded Enterprises	273 268	176 440	151 353	138 628	55 582	27 375
港澳台商投资企业 Enterprises with Investment from Hongkong,Macao and Taiwan	608 689	505 481	464 804	431 653	150 009	65 620
外商投资企业 Foreign Funded Enterprises	1 969 621	1 819 919	1 667 528	1 575 034	257 107	144 873
按经济类型分 **Grouped by Ownership**						
国有经济 State－owned	13 772 168	18 371 355	13 250 791	17 785 357	724 074	650 671
集体经济 Collective－owned	1 149 733	898 296	902 033	763 034	80 188	60 385
股份制经济 Share－holding	10 425 454	13 499 708	8 677 144	11 706 987	514 577	654 554
私营经济 Private and individual	8 020 398	7 707 232	6 765 180	6 448 187	429 703	439 239
"三资"经济 Hongkong,Macao,Taiwan and Foreign Funded	2 578 310	2 325 400	2 132 332	2 006 687	407 116	210 493
其　他 Others	416 105	358 084	265 832	267 715	61 164	29 854

13－4 续表 Continued

项 目 Item	商品销售总额 Total Sales		#批 发 Wholes ale		年末库存总额 Inventory(year－end)	
	2004	2005	2004	2005	2004	2005
按国民经济行业分 Grouped by Sector						
批发业 Wholesale Trade	**32 705 486**	**39 313 949**	**31 349 636**	**38 265 676**	**1 794 860**	**1 758 245**
农畜产品批发 Farm & Livestock Products	435 871	440 823	408 507	440 752	179 914	194 292
食品、饮料及烟草制品批发 Food,Beverage and Tobacco	1 004 517	977 114	990 524	960 417	75 070	62 779
纺织、服装及日用品批发 Textile,Garments and Daily Articles	1 032 207	1 227 178	1 011 730	1 221 894	54 382	58 031
文化、体育用品及器材批发 Cultural and Sports Goods & Equipment	171 116	190 335	151 661	180 247	22 238	21 029
医药及医疗器械批发 Medicine and Medical Appliance	1 068 762	1 516 993	932 309	1 293 161	77 046	123 704
矿产品、建材及化工产品批发 Mineral Products,Building Material and Chemical Products	22 657 043	29 015 012	22 095 102	28 557 469	731 557	827 593
机械设备、五金交电及电子产品批发 Machinery Equipment,Hardware,Transport,Electric and Electronic Products	5 198 304	4 809 084	4 641 569	4 505 294	609 511	417 363
贸易经济与代理 Trade Agent	257 544	391 042	257 538	391 042	11 696	19 070
其他批发 Others	880 122	746 369	860 696	715 401	33 446	34 385
零售业 Retail Trade	**3 656 682**	**3 846 125**	**643 676**	**712 290**	**421 962**	**286 951**
综合零售 Comprehensive Retail	1 575 464	1 705 054	266 338	232 145	138 787	87 189
食品、饮料及烟草制品专门零售 Special Retail of Food,Beverage and Tobacco	69 079	66 557	4 544	5 551	6 621	6 579
纺织、服装及日用品专门零售 Special Retail of Textile,Garments and Daily Articles	206 733	131 524	63 932	32 603	112 020	33 013
文化、体育用品及器材专门零售 Special Retail of Cultural and Sports Goods & Equipment	79 449	80 113	5 325	9 670	17 613	16 994
医药及医疗器械专门零售 Special Retail of Medicine and Medical Appliance	54 638	49 591	8 623	12 902	8 442	3 689
汽车、摩托车、燃料及零配件专门零售 Special Retail of Motor Vehicles,Motorcycles,Parts and Fuel	914 022	1 195 336	119 025	331 084	85 781	74 666
家用电器及电子产品专门零售 Special Retail of Household Appliances and Electronic Products	366 395	440 964	58 329	38 691	29 843	42 134
五金、家具及室内装修材料专门零售 Special Retail of Hardware,Furniture and Decoration Materials for Indoors	198 252	89 454	45 659	12 092	12 003	11 431
无店铺及其他零售 Non－shop Stores and Other Retail	192 650	87 534	71 901	37 553	10 852	11 254

13－5 限额以上国有及国有控股批发和零售业主要指标(2005 年)

MAIN INDICATORS OF STATE－OWNED & STATE－HOLDING WHOLESALE AND RETAIL TRADE ABOVE DESIGNATED SIZE,2005

项 目 Item	机 构（个）Organization (unit)	商品购进总额（万元）Total Purchases (10 000 yuan)	商品销售总额（万元）Total Sales (10 000 yuan)
总 计 Total	**358**	**27 652 039**	**28 485 801**
批发业 Wholesale Trade	**270**	**26 182 984**	**26 834 425**
农畜产品批发 Farm & Livestock Products	12	353 634	350 534
食品、饮料及烟草制品批发 Food,Beverage and Tobacco	21	635 727	617 539
纺织、服装及日用品批发 Textile,Garments and Daily Articles	20	578 596	651 955
文化、体育用品及器材批发 Cultural and Sports Goods & Equipment	8	104 369	117 153
医药及医疗器械批发 Medicine and Medical Appliance	22	1 201 492	1 261 732
矿产品、建材及化工产品批发 Mineral Products,Building Material and Chemical Products	129	21 554 843	21 851 298
机械设备、五金交电及电子产品批发 Machinery Equipment,Hardware,Transport,Electric and Electronic Products	43	1 491 492	1 706 404
贸易与经济代理 Trade Agent	7	165 425	178 908
其他批发 Others	8	97 406	98 902
零售业 Retail Trade	**88**	**1 469 055**	**1 651 375**
综合零售 Comprehensive Retail	21	884 172	1 021 495
食品、饮料及烟草制品专门零售 Special Retail of Food,Beverage and Tobacco	16	22 618	28 008
纺织、服装及日用品专门零售 Special Retail of Textile,Garments and Daily Articles	3	3 031	4 103
文化、体育用品及器材专门零售 Special Retail of Cultural and Sports Goods & Equipment	24	50 565	56 974
医药及医疗器械专门零售 Special Retail of Medicine and Medical Appliance	2	3 840	4 503
汽车、摩托车、燃料及零配件专门零售 Special Retail of Motor Vehicles,Motorcycles,Parts and Fuel	16	496 518	526 004
家用电器及电子产品专门零售 Special Retail of Household Appliances and Electronic Products	1	1 056	1 123
五金、家具及室内装修材料专门零售 Special Retail of Hardware,Furniture and Decoration Materials for Indoors			
无店铺及其他零售 Non－shop Stores and Other Retail	5	7 255	9 166

13-6 星级住宿业企业基本情况(2005年)

BASIC STATISTICS ON ACCOMMODATION SERVICES OF STAR LEVEL ENTERPRISES,2005

项目	Item	门店总数(个) Number of Stores (unit)	从业人员(人) Employed Persons (person)	餐饮营业面积(平方米) Operational Area of Catering Services(sq.m)	床位数(个) Number of Beds (unit)
总计	**Total**	**99**	**17 647**	**200 496**	**20 316**
#国有及国有控股企业	State-owned and State-holding Enterprises	57	11 773	116 538	12 786
按登记注册类型分	**Grouped by Status of Registration**				
内资企业	Domestic-funded Enterprises	79	12 730	174 158	15 460
国有企业	State-owned Enterprises	40	6 988	98 885	9 108
集体企业	Collective-owned Enterprises	9	700	6 594	1 313
联营企业	Joint Ownership Enterprises	1	89	246	184
有限责任公司	Limited Liability Corporations	13	2 746	44 451	2 976
股份有限公司	Share-holding Corporations Ltd.	2	439	1 502	300
私营企业	Private Enterprises	14	1 768	22 480	1 579
#私营独资	Private-funded Enterprises	2	80	600	240
私营有限责任公司	Private Limited Liability Corporations	10	1 481	21 388	1 293
私营股份有限公司	Private Share-holding Corporations Ltd.	2	207	492	46
港澳台商投资企业	Enterprises with Funds from Hong Kong, Macao and Taiwan	6	2 396	15 707	1 567
#港澳台商合资经营	Joint-venture Enterprises	5	2 334	15 507	1 402
港澳台商合作经营	Cooperative Enterprises	1	62	200	165
外商投资企业	Foreign Funded Enterprises	14	2 521	10 631	3 289
#中外合资经营	Joint-venture Enterprises	6	1 722	6 828	1 848
中外合作经营	Cooperative Enterprises	7	760	3 403	1 418
外资企业	Enterprises with Sole Foreign Investment	1	39	400	23
按行业分	**Grouped by Sector**				
旅游饭店	Tourism Restaurant	79	15 657	181 585	17 237
一般旅馆	Hotel	17	1 779	17 721	2 818
其他住宿服务	Other Accommodation Services	3	211	1 190	261

13－6 续表 Continued
单位:万元 (10 000 yuan)

项　　目	Item	资产总计 Total Assets	负债合计 Total Liabilities	营业收入 Revenue of Sale	主营业务成本 Main Business Cost
总　　计	**Total**	**664 172**	**502 423**	**172 075**	**40 768**
#国有及国有控股企业	State－owned and State－holding Enterprises	505 623	409 611	115 283	26 496
按登记注册类型分	**Grouped by Status of Registration**				
内资企业	Domestic－funded Enterprises	425 148	281 351	106 107	25 379
国有企业	State－owned Enterprises	205 095	140 438	51 590	12 889
集体企业	Collective－owned Enterprises	13 934	4 293	4 630	1 638
联营企业	Joint Ownership Enterprises	2 923	1 281	434	2
有限责任公司	Limited Liability Corporations	104 358	81 077	29 130	6 366
股份有限公司	Share－holding Corporations Ltd.	30 455	18 056	3 447	189
私营企业	Private Enterprises	68 383	36 207	16 877	4 296
#私营独资	Private－funded Enterprises	2 456	2 106	968	641
私营有限责任公司	Private Limited Liability Corporations	32 505	19 210	13 589	2 469
私营股份有限公司	Private Share－holding Corporations Ltd.	33 423	14 891	2 321	1 186
港澳台商投资企业	Enterprises with Funds from Hong Kong, Macao and Taiwan	155 352	136 474	26 901	5 053
#港澳台商合资经营	Joint－venture Enterprises	154 484	136 372	26 109	4 997
港澳台商合作经营	Cooperative Enterprises	868	102	792	56
外商投资企业	Foreign Funded Enterprises	83 673	84 598	39 066	10 336
#中外合资经营	Joint－venture Enterprises	60 129	67 470	30 984	8 837
中外合作经营	Cooperative Enterprises	23 544	17 128	8 082	1 499
外资企业	Enterprises with Sole Foreign Investment				
按行业分	**Grouped by Sector**				
旅游饭店	Tourism Restaurant	640 611	487 671	159 687	37 893
一般旅馆	Hotel	18 308	13 178	10 973	2 826
其他住宿服务	Other Accommodation Services	5 253	1 574	1 414	49

13-7 天津市三星级以上饭店一览表(2005年)

LIST OF THREE,FOUR,FIVE-STAR HOTELS,2005

宾馆名称 Name of Hotel	星级 Star Level	客房数 Number of Guest Rooms	床位数 Number of Beds	地址 Address
喜来登大酒店	五星			河西区紫金山路
SHERATON TIANJIN HOTEL	★★★★★	300	380	Zijinshan Road,Hexi Dist.
泰达国际酒店暨会馆	五星			天津经济技术开发区第二大街
TEDA INTERNATIONAL HOTEL	★★★★★	236	331	Second Avenue of TEDA
天津泰达国际会馆	五星			南开区复康路7号增2号
TEDA INTERNATIONAL CLUB TIANJIN	★★★★★	114	220	No.7-2,Fukang Road,Nankai Dist.
天津天保国际酒店	五星			天津港保税区京门大道368号
TIANJIN TIANBAO INTERNATIONAL HOTEL	★★★★★	145	232	No.368,Jingmen Avenue,TPFTZ
天津金皇大酒店	五星			河西区南京路18号
TIANJIN GOLDEN CROWN HOTEL	★★★★★	259	353	No.18,Nanjing Road,Hexi Dist.
天津万丽泰达酒店及会议中心	五星			天津经济技术开发区第二大街29号
RENAISSANCE TIANJIN TEDA HOTEL & CONVENTION CENTRE	★★★★★	543		No.29,Second Avenue of TEDA
凯悦饭店	四星			和平区解放北路219号
HYATT TIANJIN	★★★★	428	632	No.219,North Jiefang Road,Heping Dist.
水晶宫饭店	四星			河西区友谊路28号
THE CRYSTAL PALACE HOTEL	★★★★	277	399	No.28,Youyi Road,Hexi Dist.
利顺德大饭店	四星			和平区台儿庄路33号
ASTOR HOTEL	★★★★	213	308	No.33,Tai'erzhuang Road,Heping Dist.
津利华大酒店	四星			河西区友谊路32号
GENEVA HOTEL	★★★★	260	359	No.32,Youyi Road,Hexi Dist.
天宇大酒店	四星			和平区电台道19号
TIANJIN TIAN YU HOTEL	★★★★	133	251	No.19,Diantai Road,Heping Dist.
天津假日饭店	四星			河北区中山路288号
HOLIDAY INN TIANJIN	★★★★	256	345	No.288,Zhongshan Road,Hebei Dist.
美都大酒店	四星			河西区围堤道117号
MEIDU HOTEL	★★★★	158	250	No.117,Weidi Road,Hexi Dist.
泰达中心酒店	四星			天津经济技术开发区第三大街16号
TEDA CENTRAL HOTEL	★★★★	187	276	No.16,Third Avenue of TEDA
君悦酒店	四星			和平区贵州路16号
JUNYUE HOTEL	★★★★	176	225	No.16,Guizhou Road,Heping Dist.
天鹅湖温泉度假村	四星			武清开发区福源道20号
SWAN LAKE SPRING VACATION VILLAGE	★★★★	197	394	No.20,Fuyuan Road,Wuqing Development Area
天津利顺德大厦	四星			和平区台儿庄路32号
ASTOR PLAZA	★★★★	83	120	No.32,Tai'erzhuang Road,Heping Dist.
舒泊花园大酒店	四星			和平区荣业大街2号
SUPER GARDEN HOTEL TIANJIN	★★★★	101	223	No.2,Rongye Avenue,Heping Dist.
胜利宾馆	四星			塘沽区津塘公路11号
VICTORY HOTEL TIANJIN CHINA	★★★★	326	590	No.11,Jintang Highway,Tanggu Dist.
凯德大酒店	四星			河北区自由道15号
KIND HOTEL	★★★★	148	278	No.15,Ziyou Road,Hebei Dist.
天津世纪酒店	四星			河西区黑牛城道179号
CENTURY HOTEL TIANJIN	★★★★	115	146	No.179,Heiniucheng Road,Hexi Dist.
天津惠中酒店	四星			天津经济技术开发区第三大街芳林泰达园A座
TIANJIN ELEGANCE HOTEL	★★★★	151		Building A,TEDA Fanglin Garden,Third Avenue of TEDA
北方宾馆	三星			塘沽区东沽闸北路1号
TIAN JIN VIEW HOTEL	★★★	176	352	No.1,Zhabei Road of Donggu,Tanggu Dist.
友谊宾馆	三星			和平区南京路94号
TIANJIN FRIENDSHIP HOTEL	★★★	298	576	No.94,Nanjing Road,Heping Dist.
凯撒皇宫大酒店	三星			河西区气象台路46号
CAESAR PALACE HOTEL	★★★	90	152	No.46,Qixiangtai Road,Hexi Dist.

13－7 续表 1　Continued

宾馆名称 Name of Hotel	星级 Star Level	客房数 Number of Guest Rooms	床位数 Number of Beds	地址 Address
天津市皇宫饭店	三　星			和平区解放北路 177 号
TIANJIN IMPERIAC HOTEL	★★★	53	90	No. 177, North Jiefang Road, Heping Dist.
东亚大酒店	三　星			和平区昆明路 86 号
EAST ASIA HOTEL CO. LTD	★★★	109	222	No. 86, Kunming Road, Heping Dist.
龙凤酒店	三　星			河东区光华路甲 1 号
LONGFENG HOTEL	★★★	150	320	No. 1, Guanghua Road, Hedong Dist.
华富宫大饭店	三　星			和平区南市旅馆街
GHAFU PALACE GRAND HOTEL	★★★	475	940	Nanshi Hotel Mall, Heping Dist.
金禧国际大酒店	三　星			南开区南开三马路 2 号
CAIRNHILL INTERNATIONAL HOTEL	★★★	320	438	No. 2, Sanmalu, Nankai Dist.
双鹿大厦	三　星			南开区南开三马路 165 号
SHUANGLU HOTEL	★★★	109	220	No. 165, Sanmalu, Nankai Dist.
金帆酒店	三　星			天津经济技术开发区第一大街 49 号
GOLDEN SAIL HOTEL	★★★	98	172	NO. 49, First Avenue of TEDA
夏日酒店	三　星			塘沽区滨海游乐城内
SUMMER HOTEL	★★★	76	140	Binhai Entertainment City, Tanggu Dist.
天大天财酒店	三　星			华苑新技术产业园区榕苑路 1 号
TIANCAI HOTEL	★★★	150	286	No. 1, Rongyuan Road, THIP, Huayuan
柳林宾馆	三　星			河西区柳林东
LIULIN HOTEL	★★★	100	194	East of Liulin, Hexi Dist.
津华饭店(天津第一饭店)	三　星			和平区解放北路 158 号
TIANJIN JINHUA HOTEL	★★★	99	128	No. 158, North Jiefang Road, Heping Dist.
月坛酒店	三　星			津南区咸水沽为民路 4 号
MOON HOTEL	★★★	113	212	No. 4, Weimin Road, Xianshuigu Town, Jinnan Dist.
新业国际饭店	三　星			塘沽区新港路 129 号
XINYE INTERNATIONAL HOTEL	★★★	46	90	No. 129, Xingang Road, Tanggu Dist.
银河大酒店	三　星			东丽区津塘公路十号桥
YINHE HOTEL	★★★	83	142	No. 10 Bridge, Jintang Highway, Dongli Dist.
升云大酒店	三　星			大港区上古林东环海鲜街 88 号
SHENGYUN HOTEL	★★★	47	103	No. 88, Haixian Street, Shanggulin, Dagang Dist.
正达酒店	三　星			河北区万柳村大街 6 号
ZHENGDA HOTEL	★★★	84	140	No. 6, Wanliucun Street, Hebei Dist.
贵达酒店	三　星			宁河县苗庄镇刘庄村
GUIDA HOTEL	★★★	39	80	Liu zhuang Village, Miaozhuang Town, Ninghe County
津海大酒店	三　星			静海县大邱庄镇黄山路 8 号
JINHAI RESTAURANT	★★★	130	285	No. 8, Huangshan Road, Daqiuzhuang Town, Jinghai County
尧舜大酒店	三　星			静海县大邱庄镇尧舜街
TIANJIN YAOSHUN HOTEL	★★★	78	120	Raoshun Street, Daqiuzhuang Town, Jinghai County
石化天华宾馆	三　星			大港区北围堤路(西)68 号
TIANHUA HOTEL	★★★	106	189	No. 68, North Weidi Road, Dagang Dist.
和平宾馆	三　星			和平区大理道 66 号
PEACE HOTEL	★★★	102		No. 66, Dali Road, Heping Dist.
天津金世界酒店	三　星			塘沽区新港二号路 2169 号
TIANJIN JINSHIJIE HOTEL	★★★	85	136	No. 2169, Xingang No. 2 Road, Tanggu Dist.
天津市中泰大酒店	三　星			塘沽区和平路 588 号
TIANJIN ZHONGTAI HOTEL	★★★	170		No. 588, Heping Road, Tanggu Dist.
大通会馆酒店	三　星			河东区中环线红星路东
TIANJIN DATONG CLUB	★★★	84		East of Hongxing Road, Middle of Ring Road, Hedong Dist.
华海大酒店	三　星			天津经济技术开发区第三大街 9 号
HUAHAI HOTEL	★★★	117	189	No. 9, Third Avenue of TEDA

13－7 续表 2 Continued

宾馆名称 Name of Hotel	星 级 Star Level	客房数 Number of Guest Rooms	床位数 Number of Beds	地 址 Address
天波大酒店 TIANBO HOTEL	三 星 ★★★	170	300	河东区六经路 11 号 No. 11, Liujing Road, Hedong Dist.
建设大厦 JIANSHE BUILDING TIANJIN	三 星 ★★★	52	104	蓟县中昌北路 North Zhongchang Road, Jixian County
水上会宾园饭店 HUIBINYUAN HOTEL	三 星 ★★★	168	321	南开区水上公园路 46 号 No. 46, Water Park Road, Nankai Dist.
体育宾馆 SPORTS HOTEL	三 星 ★★★	96	176	南开区宾水道延长线 Continuation of Binshui Road, Nankai Dist.
红楼大酒店 RED BUILDING HOTEL	三 星 ★★★	85	172	南开区卫津南路 38 号 No. 38, South Weijin Road, Nankai Dist.
长青温泉宾馆 HOT SPRING HOTEL TIANJIN	三 星 ★★★	259	500	河西区小围堤道 Xiaoweidi Road, Hexi Dist.
渤海度假村 BOHAI HOLIDAY RESORT TIANJIN	三 星 ★★★	345	820	塘沽区新北公路 21 号 No. 21, Xinbei Highway, Tanggu Dist.
天津远洋宾馆 OCEAN HOTEL TIANJIN	三 星 ★★★	122	301	河北区远洋广场 5 号 No. 5, Ocean Square, Hebei Dist.
渔阳宾馆 YUYANG HOTEL	三 星 ★★★	201	442	蓟县城内迎宾路 12 号 No. 12, Yingbin Road of County, Jixian County
大港油田宾馆 DAGANG OIL FIELD HOTEL	三 星 ★★★	195	367	大港油田三号院团结西路 No. 3 yard, Tuanjie West Road, Dagang Oil Field
东丽湖度假村 DONGLI LAKE HOLIDAY VILLAGE	三 星 ★★★	110	227	东丽区东丽湖北侧 North of Dongli Lake, Dongli Dist.
宝坻宾馆 BAODI HOTEL	三 星 ★★★	208	451	宝坻区城关镇广川路 23 号 No. 23, Guangchuan Road, Chengguan Town, Baodi County
雍阳宾馆 YONGYANG HOTEL	三 星 ★★★	130	300	武清区杨村镇雍阳东道 16 号 No. 16, East Yongyang Road, Yangcun Town, Wuqing Dist.
枫林宾馆 FENGLIN HOTEL	三 星 ★★★	84	89	南开区宾水西道 2 号 No. 2, West Binshui Road, Nankai Dist.
鸿发大厦 HONGFA BUILDING	三 星 ★★★	80	95	天津经济技术开发区洞庭路 41 号 No. 41, Dongting Road, TEDA
富蓝特大酒店 TIANJIN FRIEND HOTEL	三 星 ★★★	81	148	和平区新华路 231 号 No. 231, Xinhua Road, Heping Dist.
憩园山庄 QIYUAN HOTEL	三 星 ★★★	80	160	蓟县官庄镇营房村北 Guanzhuang Town, Jixian County
建行蓟县干训所 CHINA CONSTRUCTION BANK JIXIAN SANATORIUM	三 星 ★★★	40	90	蓟县兴华大街 20 号 No. 20, Xinghua Street, Jixian County
天津科技大厦 INTER TECH HOTEL	三 星 ★★★	113	195	河西区友谊路 25 号 No. 25, Youxi Road, Hexi Dist.
天水大酒店 NARCISSUS HOTEL	三 星 ★★★	38	38	河西区平山道 25 号 No. 25, Pingshan Road, Hexi Dist.
麓琳宾馆 LULIN HOTEL	三 星 ★★★	102	151	东丽区卫国道 216 号(余门) No. 216, Weiguo Road, Dongli Dist.
太阳雨大酒店 SUNNYRAIN HOTEL	三 星 ★★★	152		天津经济技术开发区第一大街明园路渤化小区 Bohua Area, Mingyuan Road, First Avenue of TEDA
天城度假村 TIANCHENG VACATION VILLAGE	三 星 ★★★	90	170	蓟县逯庄子乡东大屯北 North of Dongdatun, Daizhuangzi Township, Jixian County
海得润滋酒店 HYDRUS HOTEL	三 星 ★★★	158		大港区津岐公路千米桥北侧 North of Qianmi Bridge, Jinqi Road, Dagang Dist.
天津市华城宾馆 TIANJIN HUACHENG HOTEL	三 星 ★★★	97		南开区红旗路 253 号 No. 253, Hongqi Road, Nankai Dist.

13－8　限额以上餐饮业基本情况(2005 年)

BASIC STATISTICS ON CATERING SERVICES ENTERPRISES ABOVE DESIGNATED SIZE,2005

项　　目	Item	门店总数(个) Number of Stores(unit)	从业人员(人) Employed Per－sons (person)	营业面积(平方米) Operational Area(sq. m)	餐位数(位) Number of Beds(unit)
总　计	**Total**	**178**	**24 956**	**477 976**	**104 585**
#国有及国有控股企业	State－owned and State－holding Enterprises	16	2 477	38 770	6 521
按登记注册类型分	**Grouped by Status of Registration**				
内资企业	Domestic－funded Enterprises	158	16 638	390 621	76 883
国有企业	State－owned Enterprises	8	1 098	24 450	3 673
集体企业	Collective－owned Enterprises	12	1 166	28 019	7 939
股份合作企业	Cooperative Enterprises	1	86	2 500	800
有限责任公司	Limited Liability Corporations	34	5 595	107 032	17 602
股份有限公司	Share－holding Corporations Ltd.	5	434	5 740	3 670
私营企业	Private Enterprises	89	7 630	204 136	40 138
私营独资	Private－funded Enterprises	25	1 486	30 605	8 598
私营合伙	Private Limited Liability Corporations	3	220	4 060	890
私营有限责任公司	Private Share－holding Corporations Ltd.	61	5 924	169 471	30 650
其他内资	Other Enterprises	9	629	18 744	3 061
港澳台商投资企业	Enterprises with Funds from Hong Kong, Macao and Taiwan	6	428	7 931	5 030
外商投资企业	Foreign Funded Enterprises	14	7 890	79 424	22 672
#中外合资经营	Joint－venture Enterprises	5	411	2 738	1 538
中外合作经营	Cooperative Enterprises	1	42	260	20
外资企业	Enterprises with Sole Foreign Investment	8	7 437	76 426	21 114
按行业分组	**Grouped by Sector**				
正餐服务业	Restaurant	151	14 844	368 660	72 302
快餐服务业	Snack Counter	17	8 938	95 636	29 567
饮料及冷饮服务业	Cafe	1	125	200	60
其他餐饮服务业	Others	9	1 049	13 480	2 656

13－8 续表 Continued
单位:万元 (10 000 yuan)

项　　目	Item	资产总计 Total Assets	负债合计 Total Liabilities	营业收入 Revenue of Sales	主营业务成本 Main Business Cost
总　　计	**Total**	**302 789**	**197 607**	**295 264**	**146 051**
#国有及国有控股企业	State－owned and State－holding Enterprises	42 992	22 127	29 601	16 826
按登记注册类型分	**Grouped by Status of Registration**				
内资企业	Domestic－funded Enterprises	232 359	156 480	172 592	99 635
国有企业	State－owned Enterprises	26 537	14 736	11 188	6 771
集体企业	Collective－owned Enterprises	5 944	4 724	4 495	2 520
股份合作企业	Cooperative Enterprises	318	268	857	484
有限责任公司	Limited Liability Corporations	99 935	71 078	66 887	37 522
股份有限公司	Share－holding Corporations Ltd.	2 237	1 695	6 044	3 451
私营企业	Private Enterprises	90 611	60 747	75 579	43 625
私营独资	Private－funded Enterprises	5 790	3 956	11 817	7 027
私营合伙	Private Limited Liability Corporations	561	495	1 857	782
私营有限责任公司	Private Share－holding Corporations Ltd.	84 260	56 296	61 905	35 816
其他内资	Other Enterprises	6 777	3 232	7 542	5 262
港澳台商投资企业	Enterprises with Funds from Hong Kong, Macao and Taiwan	4 953	1 796	6 262	3 049
外商投资企业	Foreign Funded Enterprises	65 477	39 331	116 410	43 368
#中外合资经营	Joint－venture Enterprises	1 774	1 855	2 710	1 038
中外合作经营	Cooperative Enterprises				
外资企业	Enterprises with Sole Foreign Investment	63 703	37 476	113 700	42 330
按行业分	**Grouped by Sector**				
正餐服务业	Restaurant	198 441	137 860	143 958	80 732
快餐服务业	Snack Counter	73 070	42 616	122 694	46 715
饮料及冷饮服务业	Cafe	1 066	308	1 838	1 146
其他餐饮服务业	Others	30 213	16 824	26 774	17 459

13－9 限额以上批发和零售业财务状况(2005 年)
FINANCLAL STATUS OF WHOLESALE AND RETAIL TRADE ABOVE DESIGNATED SIZE,2005

单位:万元 (10 000 yuan)

项 目	Item	合 计 Total	#国有经济 State－owned	#集体经济 Collective－owned
资产负债	**Total Assets and Liabilities**			
资产合计	Total Assets	12 855 020	4 246 595	300 680
#流动资产年末合计	Total Circulating Assets(year－end)	10 163 866	3 135 941	228 960
#存 货	Inventory	2 031 879	701 169	53 187
负债合计	Total Liabilities	9 638 951	3 287 697	222 262
所有者权益合计	Owner's Equity	3 216 069	958 898	78 418
#实收资本	Paid－in Capital	2 618 696	894 350	69 131
#国家资本	State－owned	717 310	552 592	3 731
集体资本	Collective－owned	69 892	71	38 021
法人资本	Legal Units	1 113 754	304 219	18 265
个人资本	Private	540 140	36 501	9 114
港澳台商资本	Hongkong,Macao and Taiwan	60 895		
外商资本	Foreign	116 706	968	
损益及分配	**Profit,Loss and Distribution**			
营业收入	Sales Revenue	39 455 043	16 757 928	870 063
#主营业务收入	Sales Revenue of Major Business	38 803 540	16 743 673	859 712
主营业务成本	Cost of Major Business	36 776 733	16 169 602	821 499
主营业务税金及附加	Tax and Extra Charges on Major Business	40 072	9 244	1 862
主营业务利润	Profits of Major Business	1 450 726	478 203	24 506
其他业务利润	Profits of Other Business	138 309	27 657	3 954
营业费用	Operating Expenses	949 732	253 117	20 550
管理费用	Administrative Expenses	466 694	150 755	17 908
财务费用	Financial Expenses	114 830	50 152	2 634
营业利润	Operating Profits	336 995	111 754	－1 344
利润总额	Total Profits	390 775	143 358	1 511

13－10 限额以上批发业财务状况(2005 年)

FINANCIAL STATUS OF WHOLESALE ABOVE DESIGNATED SIZE,2005

单位:万元 (10 000 yuan)

指标	Item	合计 Total	#国有经济 State－owned	#集体经济 Collective－owned
资产负债	**Total Assets and Liabilities**			
资产合计	Total Assets	10 886 421	3 766 354	239 847
#流动资产年末合计	Total Circulating Assets(year－end)	8 970 539	2 882 435	182 240
#存货	Inventory	1 765 952	674 508	46 640
负债合计	Total Liabilities	8 210 138	2 911 109	177 099
所有者权益合计	Owner's Equity	2 676 283	855 245	62 749
#实收资本	Paid－in of Capital	2 199 521	820 888	50 938
#国家资本	State－owned	658 617	521 478	3 501
集体资本	Collective－owned	50 071		32 340
法人资本	Legal Units	955 265	264 143	8 687
个人资本	Private	421 626	35 267	6 410
港澳台商资本	Hongkong,Macao and Taiwan	50 202		
外商资本	Foreign	63 739		
损益及分配	**Profit,Loss and Distribution**			
营业收入	Sales Revenue	36 033 136	16 272 560	721 434
#主营业务收入	Sales Revenue of Major Business	35 411 838	16 258 979	711 294
主营业务成本	Cost of Major Business	33 762 834	15 741 145	686 753
主营业务税金及附加	Tax and Extra Charges on Major Business	33 152	7 849	1 471
主营业务利润	Profits of Major Business	1 203 453	436 516	15 369
其他业务利润	Profits of Other Business	62 577	19 949	3 352
营业费用	Operating Expenses	707 161	233 173	14 037
管理费用	Administrative Expenses	342 408	113 755	12 587
财务费用	Financial Expenses	93 739	43 944	2 199
营业利润	Operating Profits	346 912	113 496	－2 391
利润总额	Total Profits	406 518	152 793	3 036

13-11 限额以上零售业财务状况(2005年)
FINANCIAL STATUS OF RETAIL TRADE ABOVE DESIGNATED SIZE,2005

单位:万元 (10 000 yuan)

指 标	Item	合 计 Total	#国有经济 State-owned	#集体经济 Collective-owned
资产负债	**Total Assets and Liabilities**			
资产合计	Total Assets	1 968 599	480 241	60 832
#流动资产	Total Circulating Assets(year-end)	1 193 327	253 506	46 719
#存 货	Inventory	265 927	26 661	6 547
负债合计	Total Liabilities	1 428 813	376 588	45 163
所有者权益合计	Owner's Equity	539 786	103 653	15 669
#实收资本	Paid-in of Capital	419 176	73 462	18 193
#国家资本	State-owned	58 693	31 114	230
集体资本	Collective-owned	19 822	71	5 682
法人资本	Legal Units	158 489	40 076	9 578
个人资本	Private	118 514	1 234	2 703
港澳台商资本	Hongkong,Macao and Taiwan	10 693		
外商资本	Foreign	52 967	968	
损益及分配	**Profit,Loss and Distribution**			
营业收入	Sales Revenue	3 421 908	485 368	148 629
#主营业务收入	Sales Revenue of Major Business	3 391 703	484 695	148 418
主营业务成本	Cost of Major Business	3 013 899	428 457	134 746
主营业务税金及附加	Tax and Extra Charges on Major Business	6 921	1 396	391
主营业务利润	Profits of Major Business	247 273	41 686	9 136
其他业务利润	Profits of Other Business	75 732	7 708	602
营业费用	Operating Expenses	242 571	19 944	6 513
管理费用	Administrative Expenses	124 286	37 000	5 321
财务费用	Financial Expenses	21 091	6 207	435
营业利润	Operating Profits	-9 917	-1 741	1 047
利润总额	Total Profits	-15 743	-9 435	-1 525

13－12 限额以上零售业业态情况(2005 年)

BUSINESS STATUS OF RETAIL TRADE ABOVE DESIGNATED SIZE,2005

单位:万元 (10 000 yuan)

指　　标	Item	百货商店 Department Store	超级市场 Supermarket	专业(专卖)店 Monopolization Shop	其　他 Others
企业数(个)	Number of Units	42	41	144	178
从业人员平均人数(人)	Average Employed Persons (person)	13 694	19 360	15 894	9 924
资产合计	Total Assets	642 976	321 095	437 762	566 765
流动资产	Total Circulating Assets	279 164	216 974	269 132	428 057
存　货	Inventory	25 779	75 691	86 068	78 389
负债合计	Total Liabilities	423 081	278 597	300 618	426 517
营业收入	Sales Revenue	696 455	675 291	1 085 402	964 760
#主营业务收入	Sales Revenue of Major Business	695 557	657 420	1 083 434	955 291
主营业务成本	Cost of Major Business	626 266	524 915	993 773	868 944
税金及附加	Tax and Extra Charges	2 105	886	2 413	1 516
主营业务利润	Profits of Major Business	51 045	61 618	73 583	61 027
其他业务利润	Profits of Other Business	12 495	43 889	5 258	14 090
营业费用	Operating Expenses	37 447	107 001	51 878	46 246
管理费用	Administrative Expenses	42 175	18 961	29 100	34 051
财务费用	Financial Expenses	7 408	2 475	4 962	6 247
营业利润	Operating Profits	－13 479	－8 877	4 487	7 953
利润总额	Total Profits	－22 269	－7 875	3 707	10 694

13－13 营业收入五十强餐饮业企业(2005 年)

TOP 50 CATERING TRADE ENTERPRISES BY BUSINESS REVENUE,2005

名　次 Position	单位名称 Name of Enterprise	名　次 Position	单位名称 Name of Enterprise
1	天津肯德基有限公司	26	天津市康乐饮料有限公司
2	天津麦当劳食品有限公司	27	天津市康德劳动服务有限公司
3	天津市桂发祥十八街麻花总店有限公司	28	北京快客利食品工业有限公司天津分公司
4	天津市瀚金佰餐饮有限公司	29	天津市粤唯鲜娱乐苑集团有限公司
5	天津市鹏天阁时代酒楼有限公司	30	天津白金宫大酒楼有限公司
6	天津开发区海港世家餐饮有限公司	31	天津市鸿起顺餐饮有限责任公司
7	天津市桂发祥麻花饮食集团有限公司	32	天津市双街新家园海鲜餐饮有限公司
8	天津泰达标准食品有限公司	33	天津市峰光大酒楼有限公司
9	天津市翠亨邨餐饮娱乐有限公司	34	天津市月坛酒店有限公司
10	天津梅江南大岛酒楼有限公司	35	天津绿色时代餐饮有限公司
11	天津德克士食品开发有限公司	36	天津市楚云天餐饮有限责任公司
12	天津市森永泰餐饮有限公司	37	天津市集贤大酒家有限公司
13	泰达津菜城美食有限公司	38	天津市宴宾美食娱乐有限公司
14	天津市狗不理大酒店	39	天津市凯德龙园美食有限公司
15	天津市森泰餐饮有限公司	40	北京大食代餐饮有限公司天津分公司
16	天津海都世纪酒楼有限公司	41	天津市中山美食林快餐有限责任公司
17	天津市津南宝德福酒家	42	天津市起士林大饭店
18	天津天麟娱乐有限公司	43	天津市中天运河渔村餐饮发展有限公司
19	天津市丁香餐饮发展有限公司	44	天津市河东区鸿起顺饭庄有限公司
20	天津市食为天粮油便民连锁公司	45	天津津卫一九二八餐饮有限公司
21	天津市集贤佰悦海鲜酒楼有限公司	46	天津市河西区富祥酒楼
22	天津市天府饮食文化有限公司	47	天津市耳朵眼炸糕餐饮有限责任公司
23	天津市皇冠明珠餐饮娱乐发展有限公司	48	天津市麒麟轩餐饮有限公司
24	天津狗不理餐饮有限公司	49	天津市津轩阁餐饮有限公司
25	天津市大圆碗食品有限公司	50	天津有乐和食食品有限公司

13－14　销售总额百强批发贸易企业(2005年)

TOP 100 WHOLESALE TRADE ENTERPRISES BY TOTAL SALES,2005

名　次 Position	单位名称 Name of Enterprise	名　次 Position	单位名称 Name of Enterprise
1	中国石化销售有限公司华北分公司	51	天津钢管工程设备材料公司
2	天津宝钢北方贸易有限公司	52	天津市辰晔煤业有限责任公司
3	中国石油化工股份有限公司天津石油分公司	53	天津本钢钢铁贸易有限公司
4	中国石油天燃气股份有限公司华北销售大港分公司	54	天津中邮普泰移动通信设备有限责任公司
5	天津一汽夏利汽车股份有限公司销售分公司	55	天津市京津工贸开发公司
6	天津市亚益成工贸有限公司	56	天津市化工轻工材料总公司
7	中国铁路物资天津公司	57	天津开发区福源商贸有限公司
8	天津国能投资有限公司	58	天津市机电进出口有限公司
9	天津天铁冶金集团商贸有限公司	59	天津地天泰实业发展有限公司
10	天津钢管国际经济贸易有限公司	60	天津市大港区蓝盾商贸有限公司
11	天津市浩通物产有限公司	61	北方国际集团天津市新的纺织品进出口有限公司
12	天津市丽兴京津钢铁贸易有限公司	62	天津市福浩木业有限公司
13	国药控股天津有限公司	63	天津市正泰实业总公司
14	天津太平(集团)有限公司	64	天津汽车工业华北销售有限公司
15	天津中新药业集团股份有限公司	65	天津机械进出口有限公司
16	天津中联进出口贸易有限公司	66	天津中色东方商厦有限公司
17	中国烟草总公司天津市公司	67	渤海石油物资供应公司
18	天津港保税区瀚通国际贸易有限公司	68	天津市中油禄祺石油销售有限公司
19	天津市咸通生产资料有限责任公司	69	永立建机(天津)国际贸易有限公司
20	天津市化轻贸易有限公司	70	天津市物资实业发展中心
21	天津市盈通物资有限公司	71	天津市机电设备总公司
22	丰田通商(天津)有限公司	72	中国有色金属进出口天津公司
23	天津市金属材料总公司	73	天津市隆威物资有限公司
24	天津轧三物流有限公司	74	天津市北辰区北方实业发展有限公司
25	天津市顺鑫进出口贸易有限公司	75	众奥(天津)国际汽车物贸有限公司
26	天津大桥集团电焊条供销有限公司	76	天津市电力燃料公司
27	天津纺织集团进出口股份有限公司	77	天津海尔工贸有限公司
28	天津市基建物资总公司	78	天津市博通华信科技发展有限公司
29	天津服装进出口股份有限公司	79	天津市盈博商贸有限公司
30	天津天资棉纺织品物流有限公司	80	天津市外资企业物资供应服务公司
31	天津市燃料油公司	81	天津顶盛国际贸易有限公司
32	天津天士力医药有限公司	82	上海大众汽车有限公司天津分公司
33	天津里碑冷轧板材有限公司	83	天津港保税区捷丰国际贸易有限公司
34	中化物产股份有限公司天津分公司	84	天津开发区天恒工贸有限公司
35	北星(天津)汽车有限公司	85	天津市瑞通矿业贸易有限公司
36	中国中煤能源集团公司天津分公司	86	天津威斯特机械设备有限公司
37	中化天津进出口公司	87	天津市润德中天机电设备有限公司
38	三星爱商(天津)国际物流有限公司	88	天津裕华经济贸易总公司
39	天津市方正延中信息系统有限公司	89	仙妮蕾德(天津)企业有限公司
40	天津大沽贸易有限公司	90	天津广茂物流有限公司
41	松下电器机电(天津)有限公司	91	天津市闽东贸易有限公司
42	天津住友商事有限公司	92	天津开发区金泽石油化工有限公司
43	五矿钢铁天津有限公司	93	天津港保税区四辟国际贸易有限公司
44	天津太钢销售有限公司	94	天津市世茂国际贸易有限公司
45	天津晟达石化有限公司	95	天津经济技术开发区进出口公司
46	天津市浩物机电汽车贸易有限公司	96	天津市宏桥汇鑫商贸中心
47	天津开发区嘉诚钢材贸易有限公司	97	天津市金昌物资贸易公司
48	天津市润飞贸易有限公司	98	双日(天津)有限公司
49	天津立业钢铁贸易有限公司	99	天津市德利得物流有限公司
50	京瓷(天津)商贸有限公司	100	天津开发区泰盈商贸有限公司

13－15 销售总额百强零售贸易企业(2005年)

TOP 100 RETAIL TRADE ENTERPRISES BY TOTAL SALES,2005

名 次 Position	单位名称 Name of Enterprise	名 次 Position	单位名称 Name of Enterprise
1	中国石油天然气股份有限公司天津销售公司	51	天津市鑫亿海汽车贸易有限公司
2	天津家世界连锁超市有限公司	52	天津老百姓大药房连锁有限公司
3	天津国美电器有限公司	53	天津开发鑫兴物资贸易有限公司
4	天津劝业场(集团)股份有限公司	54	天津劝宝超市有限责任公司
5	中原百货集团股份有限公司	55	上海汽车工业天津销售有限公司
6	绫志时装有限公司	56	天津一商世纪联华商贸有限公司
7	天津一商发展有限公司	57	天津市合力叉车有限公司
8	天津百货大楼集团有限公司	58	天津市恩诚工贸有限公司
9	天津滨江商厦有限公司	59	天津市班尼路服饰有限公司
10	天津开发区世盛物业有限公司	60	米盖尔(天津)发展有限公司
11	天津壳牌机动车加油服务有限公司	61	天津月坛商厦集团股份有限公司
12	天津金元宝商厦集团有限公司	62	天津开发区合诚汽车销售有限公司
13	天津苏宁电器连锁加盟有限公司	63	天津市文物公司
14	天津家世界家居建材超市有限公司	64	天津一商世纪联华购物广场有限公司
15	天津市津工超市有限责任公司	65	天津市中乒北众汽车销售服务有限公司
16	天津劝业家乐福超市有限公司	66	天津市大港区迎宾超市
17	天津市大中电器有限公司	67	天津市贸顺汽车销售有限公司
18	天津福业商业有限公司	68	天津鸿达汽车销售有限公司
19	天津伊势丹有限公司	69	天津市好利来食品有限公司
20	天津滨江购物中心	70	天津市中乒北骏汽车销售有限公司
21	天津市中乒汽车服务有限公司	71	天津金文图书城股份有限公司
22	沃尔玛深国投百货有限公司天津和平路分店	72	天津市冀东汽车贸易有限公司
23	天津市风神汽车销售有限公司	73	天津中原百货滨海有限公司
24	天津物美未来商贸发展有限公司	74	天津路金汽车销售有限公司
25	天津时尚新世界购物广场有限公司	75	天津市天丰汽车销售服务有限责任公司
26	天津华润超级市场有限公司	76	天津市鹏峰汽车贸易有限公司
27	天津滨江服饰商厦	77	天津石油集团红桥石油有限公司
28	天津塘沽乐购生活购物有限公司	78	天津市亨得利钟表眼镜有限公司
29	天津市人人乐商业有限公司	79	天津市武清区海龙商贸有限公司
30	天津柳林丰田汽车销售服务有限公司	80	天津市蓟县家乐商贸有限公司
31	天津汽车工业交通出租车销售有限公司	81	天津凯旋门百货有限公司
32	天津开发区晟陆汽车销售服务有限公司	82	宁河家乐超市有限责任公司
33	天津凯通汽车服务发展有限公司	83	天津商场
34	天津开发区兴象科技有限公司	84	天津市鑫舜商贸有限公司
35	天津华苑丰田汽车销售服务有限公司	85	天津水牛城商业有限公司
36	天津市大唐通信有限公司	86	天津市米兰商业有限公司
37	天津开发区四联汽车贸易有限公司	87	天津津泰石油有限公司
38	天津中联百盛商业广场有限公司	88	天津市健龙商贸有限公司
39	锦江麦德龙现购自运有限公司天津红桥商场	89	天津市西青区百顺商贸有限公司
40	天津捷通汽车销售有限公司	90	天津恒裕隆汽车销售服务有限公司
41	天津开发区乐购生活购物有限公司	91	天津金马工贸中心
42	天津港保税区捷拓国际贸易有限公司	92	天津市大港区油田炼达超市有限公司
43	天津开发区柯兰德汽车贸易有限公司	93	天津市新航线贸易有限公司
44	天津金钟乐购生活购物有限公司	94	屈臣氏大药房有限公司
45	天津市中乒丰田汽车销售服务有限公司	95	天津东风汽车华北销售服务有限公司
46	天津市新中国现代文化用品有限责任公司	96	天津市新城市汽车销售服务有限公司
47	天津市大港滨城商贸有限责任公司	97	天津市美自达汽车销售有服务有限公司
48	天津新濠汽车贸易有限公司	98	天津市银诺威臣汽车销售服务有限公司
49	天津世宏远东国际贸易有限公司	99	天津华星捷盛汽车贸易有限公司
50	天津市大港区滨城购物有限公司	100	天津新世界百货有限公司

13－16　实际利用内资额(2002－2005年)
DOMESTIC CAPITAL ACTUALLY USED,2002－2005

单位:万元 (10 000 yuan)

单　位	Unit	2002	2003	2004	2005
总　计	**Total**	**610 903**	**1 122 103**	**2 387 495**	**3 399 285**
各区县	**Districts and Counties**	**323 095**	**603 411**	**1 796 824**	**3 042 565**
和平区	Heping District	31 800	92 099	195 000	311 013
河东区	Hedong District	22 204	28 180	72 374	117 794
河西区	Hexi District	22 000	32 650	92 800	158 764
南开区	Nankai District	25 500	24 690	114 500	293 522
河北区	Hebei District	20 800	32 400	82 000	126 100
红桥区	Hongqiao District	29 000	35 000	120 660	180 990
塘沽区	Tanggu District	68 110	82 862	181 897	290 000
汉沽区	Hangu District	7 395	10 900	26 100	36 800
大港区	Dagang District	7 360	22 365	55 000	182 850
东丽区	Dongli District	12 528	42 176	96 370	183 686
西青区	Xiqing District	8 356	38 863	110 000	154 049
津南区	Jinnan District	11 134	21 210	91 569	155 822
北辰区	Beichen District	14 864	35 101	74 601	104 441
武清区	Wuqing District	7 864	19 121	120 273	183 810
宝坻区	Baodi District	10 330	18 390	183 860	307 651
宁河县	Ninghe County	3 900	6 650	42 300	62 735
静海县	Jinghai County	6 938	39 229	67 520	94 528
蓟　县	Jixian County	13 012	21 525	70 000	98 010
“三区”	**"Three Districts"**	**97 908**	**167 230**	**271 081**	**356 720**
天津经济技术开发区	TEDA	32 944	43 568	90 567	117 738
天津保税区	TFTZ	23 054	56 151	93 000	124 600
天津新技术产业园区	THIP	41 910	67 511	87 514	114 382

13－17　外省市在津投资情况(2005 年)

DOMESTIC CAPITAL FROM OTHER PROVINCES AND MUNICIPALITIES, 2005

单　位	Unit	新签协议合同数(个) Number of Newly Signed Contracts (unit)	协　议合同额(万元) Total Amount of Capital Projects in Signed (10 000 yuan)	实际利用内资额(万元) Total Amount of Domestic Capital Actually Used (10 000 yuan)
总　计	**Total**	**2 343**	**5 203 059**	**3 399 285**
北京市	Beijing	459	1 671 108	1 331 377
河北省	Hebei	493	448 124	403 296
山西省	Shanxi	90	53 151	42 618
内蒙古自治区	Inner Mongolia	64	37 692	29 191
辽宁省	Liaoning	78	104 247	61 426
吉林省	Jilin	90	36 821	25 859
黑龙江省	Heilongjiang	127	74 345	45 353
上海市	Shanghai	72	640 542	357 274
江苏省	Jiangsu	76	195 121	100 485
浙江省	Zhejiang	118	492 392	262 336
安徽省	Anhui	31	20 365	11 150
福建省	Fujian	71	68 163	68 163
江西省	Jiangxi	22	20 421	18 771
山东省	Shandong	151	37 222	34 508
河南省	Henan	87	19 578	18 120
湖北省	Hubei	40	6 527	6 487
湖南省	Hunan	15	2 030	2 030
广东省	Guangdong	120	1 200 526	510 021
广西壮族自治区	Guangxi	4	100	100
海南省	Hainan	4	10 964	10 804
重庆市	Chongqing	10	1 895	1 695
四川省	Sichuan	41	35 879	34 202
贵州省	Guizhou	1	100	100
云南省	Yunnan	3	130	130
陕西省	Shanxi	25	11 372	11 337
甘肃省	Gansu	18	1 563	1 563
青海省	Qinghai	7	4 380	3 440
宁夏回族自治区	Ningxia	8	1 120	465
新疆维吾尔自治区	Xinjiang	18	7 181	6 984

主要统计指标解释

批发和零售业 根据新颁布的行业分类标准《国民经济行业分类》(GB/T4754－2002),将原批发零售贸易、餐饮业门类中的餐饮业调出,且不含原"金属和非金属废料和碎屑的加工处理"部分。

社会消费品零售总额 各种经济类型的批发和零售业、餐饮业和其他行业对城乡居民和社会集团的消费品零售额总和。

商品购进总额 指从本企业以外的单位和个人购进(包括从国外直接进口)作为转卖或加工后转卖的商品金额。包括从工农业生产者购进额,从批发和零售业购进额,进口额和其他购进组成。这个指标反映批发和零售企业从国内外市场上购进商品的总量。

商品销售总额 指售予本企业以外的单位和个人的商品金额(含增值税)。销售总额包括零售额和批发额两部分,其中零售额包括:售予居民和社会集团商品的金额;批发额包括:售予生产经营单位商品的金额和商品的金额。这个指标反映批发零售业在国内市场上销售商品以及出口商品的总量。

营业收入 指企业(单位)在生产经营活动中通过销售商品或提供劳务等取得的收入。营业收入包括主营业务收入和其他业务收入。主营业务收入是指企业在销售商品、提供劳务等主要业务活动所产生的收入总额。其他业务收入是指各类企业主营业务以外其他业务或不独立核算的附营业务所发生的收入。

商品销售税金及附加 批发和零售企业销售商品应负担的税金和餐饮企业应由各项经营业务负担的税金及附加。包括营业税、城市维护建设税、出口关税和教育费附加等。

限额以上批发和零售业、餐饮业企业划分标准 批发业是指年销售额2000万元及以上,年末从业人员20人及以上;零售业是指年销售额500万元及以上,年末从业人员60人及以上;餐饮业是指年销售额200万元及以上,年末从业人员40人及以上。

Explanatory Notes on Main Statistical Indicators

Wholesale and Retail Trade refers to original wholesale, retail trade and catering deducting catering according to the new classification of "national economic classification and code" (GB T4754－2002), excluding original "metal and non－metal waste materials processing".

Total Retail Sales of Consumer Goods refers to the sum of retail sales of consumer goods to urban and rural residents and social groups by the establishments in wholesale, retail, catering and other industries of various ownerships.

Total Purchases of Commodities refers to the total value of purchases of commodities by the establishments from other establishments or individuals (including direct import from abroad) for the purpose of reselling, either with or without further processing of the commodities purchased. The total purchases include agricultural and industrial products purchased from producers, commodities purchased from wholesale and retail trades, commodities directly imported from abroad, commodities purchased from other units. This indicator issued to show the total value of purchases of commodities by wholesale and retail establishments from domestic and overseas markets.

Total Sales of Commodities refers to value of commodities sold by the establishments to other establishments and individuals (including added－value tax). Total sales of commodities include retail sales and wholesale sales. Retail sales include value sold to individuals and social groups. Wholesale sales include value sold to productive units and exports value. The indicator reflects the sum of commodities sold in domestic markets and export commodities by retail and wholesale track.

Business Income refers to income of enterprises through selling commodities or providing services. It includes income of main business and other business income. Income of main business refers to income of main business activities. Other business income refers to income of other business or attached business not including main business.

Tax and Extra Charges on Sales of Commodity refers to tax of sold goods supported by wholesale and retail enterprises, tax and extra charges supported by catering enterprises, including business tax, tax on city maintenance, export tax and extra charges for education.

Classified Standard of Wholesale, Retail Trade and Catering Enterprises above Designated Size Wholesale enterprises refer to enterprises with sales over 20 million yuan, with laborers over 20 persons. Retail enterprises refer to enterprises with sales over 5 million yuan, with laborers over 60 persons. Catering enterprises refer to enterprises with sales over 2 million yuan, with laborers over 40 persons.

第14篇
CHAPTER 14

对外经济贸易和旅游

Foreign Economy Trade and Tourism

14－1 对外贸易进出口商品总值(1990－2005年)
TOTAL VALUE OF IMPORTS AND EXPORTS,1990－2005

年 份 Year	绝对数(万美元) Absolute Value(USD 10 000)			增长速度(%)(比上年) Increase Rate(%)(Over Preceding Year)		
	进出口总值 Imports & Exports	出口总值 Exports	进口总值 Imports	进出口总值 Imports & Exports	出口总值 Exports	进口总值 Imports
1990	220 979	178 555	42 424	－0.2	5.9	－19.7
1991	202 013	160 636	41 377	－8.6	－10.0	－2.5
1992	237 577	175 234	62 343	17.6	9.1	50.7
1993	277 666	194 234	83 432	16.9	10.8	33.8
1994	331 232	239 978	91 254	19.3	23.6	9.4
1995	654 556	299 841	354 715	97.6	24.9	288.7
1996	829 743	404 913	424 830	26.8	35.0	19.8
1997	1 002 286	501 818	500 468	20.8	23.9	17.8
1998	1 061 595	549 856	511 739	5.9	9.6	2.3
1999	1 260 465	633 199	627 265	18.7	15.2	22.6
2000	1 715 741	862 906	852 835	36.1	36.3	36.0
2001	1 818 636	950 177	868 459	6.0	10.1	1.8
2002	2 282 658	1 159 490	1 123 168	25.5	22.0	29.3
2003	2 937 141	1 437 396	1 499 745	28.7	24.0	33.5
2004	4 201 948	2 086 544	2 115 404	43.2	45.4	41.4
2005	5 338 661	2 741 476	2 597 186	27.1	31.4	22.8

注：自1998年始，用海关数据。
Note:Since 1998,the data of this table are gotten from Tianjin Custom.

14－2 天津口岸进出口贸易总值(1990－2005年)
TOTAL VALUE OF IMPORTS AND EXPORTS IN TIANJIN PORT,1990－2005

年 份 Year	按美元计算(亿美元) Calculated by USD(USD 100 million)			按人民币计算(亿元) Calculated by RMB(100 million yuan)		
	进出口总值 Imports & Exports	出口总值 Exports	进口总值 Imports	进出口总值 Imports & Exports	出口总值 Exports	进口总值 Imports
1990	85.95	42.53	43.42	410.84	203.29	207.55
1991	91.37	46.48	44.89	486.98	239.59	247.39
1992	104.61	54.60	50.01	572.23	298.68	273.55
1993	125.04	66.03	59.01	726.48	383.63	342.85
1994	161.67	86.81	74.86	1 397.96	750.65	647.31
1995	217.46	127.81	89.65	1 821.23	1 070.41	750.82
1996	216.85	122.89	93.96	1 804.19	1 022.44	781.75
1997	215.62	131.24	84.38	1 787.55	1 088.02	699.53
1998	223.19	134.84	88.35	1 852.48	1 119.17	733.31
1999	248.29	139.18	109.11	2 055.34	1 152.13	903.21
2000	298.03	165.29	132.74	2 479.60	1 375.20	1 104.40
2001	323.71	178.13	145.58	2 679.30	1 474.40	1 204.90
2002	365.35	190.55	174.80	3 025.46	1 577.94	1 447.52
2003	461.67	259.57	202.10	3 831.86	2 154.43	1 677.43
2004	677.66	384.80	292.86	5 608.66	3 184.80	2 423.86
2005	819.29	446.83	372.46	6 711.38	3 660.30	3 051.08

14－3 利用外资情况(1990－2005年)

UTILIZATION OF FOREIGN CAPITAL,1990－2005

年份 Year	绝对数(万美元) Absolute Value (USD 10 000)		增长速度(%)(比上年) Increase Rate(%) (Over Preceding Year)	
	直接利用外资 Foreign Direct Investment	借用国外资金 Foreign Loans	直接利用外资 Foreign Direct Investment	借用国外资金 Foreign Loans
合同额 Foreign Investment Contracted				
1990	16 367	2 000	93.6	－87.3
1991	19 656	4 100	20.1	87.0
1992	121 927	12 100	520.3	195.1
1993	225 567	9 154	85.0	－24.3
1994	350 234	52 000	55.3	468.1
1995	385 053	35 600	9.9	－31.5
1996	392 431	120 400	1.9	238.2
1997	385 066	202 100	－1.9	67.9
1998	363 729	132 989	－5.5	－34.2
1999	362 034	102 545	－0.5	－22.9
2000	460 000		27.1	
2001	463 000		0.7	
2002	581 220		25.5	
2003	351 297		74.3	
2004	558 855		59.1	
2005	732 281		31.0	
实际利用外资 Foreign Capital Actually Used				
1990	8 315	25 122	2.7	－28.6
1991	9 388	38 711	12.9	54.1
1992	23 138	59 922	146.5	54.8
1993	54 120	39 112	133.9	－34.7
1994	101 499	75 985	87.5	94.3
1995	152 064	58 924	49.8	－22.5
1996	200 587	97 771	31.9	65.9
1997	251 135	91 166	25.2	－6.8
1998	251 803	53 984	0.3	－40.8
1999	253 203	21 332	0.6	－60.5
2000	256 000	26 467	1.1	24.1
2001	322 000	7 688	25.8	－71.0
2002	380 591	6 310	18.2	－17.9
2003	163 325	7 225	62.9	14.5
2004	247 243	22 993	51.4	218.2
2005	332 885	31 688	34.6	37.8

注:自2003年开始,直接利用外资额采用商务部新口径,速度为可比口径;14－8、14－9、14－11表同。

Note: Foreign direct investment since 2003 refers to new coverage of Ministry of Commerce, and its increase rate is calculated on the basis of comparable coverage; same as following table 14－8, 14－9 and 14－11.

14-4 对外贸易进出口商品总值
TOTAL VALUE OF IMPORTS AND EXPORTS IN FOREIGN TRADE

单位:万美元 (USD 10 000)

项目	Item	2004 进出口总值 Imports & Exports	2004 出口总值 Exports	2004 进口总值 Imports
合计	**Total**	**4 201 948**	**2 086 544**	**2 115 404**
按口岸分	**By Port**			
本口岸	Local Port	3 023 364	1 362 977	1 660 387
外口岸	Outside Port	1 178 584	723 567	455 017
按经营单位分	**By Managing Unit**			
#国有企业	State-owned Enterprises	558 626	272 847	285 779
中外合资企业	Joint Venture Enterprises	1 249 724	552 966	696 758
中外合作企业	Cooperative Operation Enterprises	50 165	24 064	26 101
外商独资企业	Foreign-funded Sole Enterprises	2 106 856	1 128 520	978 336
按贸易性质分	**By Trade Kind**			
#一般贸易	General Trade	1 363 637	641 071	722 566
进料加工	Processing Using Import Material	2 047 260	1 315 981	731 279
外商投资企业进口设备	Equipments of Foreign-funded Enterprises Import	121 807		121 807
来料加工	Processing Using Provided Material	154 466	85 360	69 106
易货贸易	Dicker Trade			
捐赠	Donation	34		34
保税区仓储进出境货物	Goods Passed in and out TPFTZ	18 903	3 851	15 052
保税区仓储转口货物	Goods Transited in TPFTZ	490 046	39 033	451 013
按商品类别分	**By Category of Commodities**			
#食品及活动物	Food and Live Animals	46 306	33 129	13 177
饮料及烟类	Beverages and Tobacco	1 374	976	398
非食用原料(燃料油除外)	Non-edible Raw Materials(exclude Fuel Oil)	154 750	19 874	134 876
矿物燃料、润滑油及有关原料	Mineral Fuels, Lubricants and Related Materials	151 073	129 144	21 929
动植物油、脂及蜡	Animal and Vegetable Oils, Fats and Wax	63 675	353	63 322
化学成品及有关产品	Chemicals and Related Products	271 227	89 769	181 458
按原料分类的制成品	Related Products By Raw Materials	398 506	207 744	190 762
机械及运输设备	Machinery and Transport Equipment	2 732 338	1 357 589	1 374 749
杂项制品	Miscellaneous Products	1 766	535	1 231

14－4 续表 Continued
单位:万美元 (USD 10 000)

项 目	Item	2005 进出口总值 Imports & Exports	2005 出口总值 Exports	2005 进口总值 Imports
合 计	**Total**	**5 338 661**	**2 741 476**	**2 597 185**
按口岸分	**By Port**			
本口岸	Local Port	3 780 836	1 721 371	2 059 465
外口岸	Outside Port	1 557 825	1 020 105	537 720
按经营单位分	**By Managing Unit**			
#国有企业	State－owned Enterprises	662 241	337 853	324 388
中外合资企业	Joint Venture Enterprises	1 525 943	730 873	795 070
中外合作企业	Cooperative Operation Enterprises	54 359	27 372	26 987
外商独资企业	Foreign－funded Sole Enterprises	2 703 286	1 443 991	1 259 295
按贸易性质分	**By Trade Kind**			
#一般贸易	General Trade	1 796 779	908 314	888 465
进料加工	Processing Using Import Material	2 511 631	1 675 438	836 193
外商投资企业进口设备	Equipments of Foreign－funded Enterprises Import	105 352		105 352
来料加工	Processing Using Provided Material	180 376	100 172	80 204
易货贸易	Dicker Trade	18	18	
捐 赠	Donation	592	365	227
保税区仓储进出境货物	Goods Passed in and out TPFTZ	22 901	3 149	19 752
保税区仓储转口货物	Goods Transited in TPFTZ	703 944	45 542	658 402
按商品类别分	**By Category of Commodities**			
#食品及活动物	Food and Live Animals	54 284	38 897	15 387
饮料及烟类	Beverages and Tobacco	1 511	1 032	479
非食用原料(燃料油除外)	Non－edible Raw Materials(exclude Fuel Oil)	265 480	22 450	243 030
矿物燃料、润滑油及有关原料	Mineral Fuels, Lubricants and Related Materials	295 333	263 597	31 736
动植物油、脂及蜡	Animal and Vegetable Oils, Fats and Wax	59 278	953	58 325
化学成品及有关产品	Chemicals and Related Products	325 950	110 372	215 578
按原料分类的制成品	Related Products By Raw Materials	490 693	270 179	220 514
机械及运输设备	Machinery and Transport Equipment	3 355 482	1 713 725	1 641 757
杂项制品	Miscellaneous Products	479 360	315 398	163 962

14－5　对外贸易分国别、地区进出口总值

TOTAL VALUE OF IMPORTS AND EXPORTS IN FOREIGN TRADE BY COUNTRY AND REGION

单位:万美元　　(USD 10 000)

国　别、地　区	Country, Region	2004			2005		
		进出口总值 Imports & Exports	出口总值 Exports	进口总值 Imports	进出口总值 Imports & Exports	出口总值 Exports	进口总值 Imports
合　计	**Total**	**4 201 948**	**2 086 544**	**2 115 404**	**5 338 661**	**2 741 476**	**2 597 185**
亚　洲	**Asia**	**2 492 065**	**950 276**	**1 541 789**	**3 102 793**	**1 160 556**	**1 942 237**
#中国香港	Hongkong, China	203 195	121 492	81 703	252 677	148 670	104 007
中国澳门	Macao, China	338	292	46	649	467	182
朝　鲜	Democratic People's Republic of Korea	440	289	151	534	448	86
韩　国	Republic of Korea	698 417	178 388	520 029	867 484	234 554	632 930
日　本	Japan	747 865	238 457	509 408	815 729	284 909	530 820
菲律宾	Philippines	27 232	10 605	16 627	32 741	11 043	21 698
缅　甸	Burma	1 565	1 491	74	5 180	5 083	97
泰　国	Thailand	36 870	17 683	19 187	54 098	31 514	22 584
马来西亚	Malaysia	98 366	42 617	55 749	119 000	52 470	66 530
新加坡	Singapore	246 074	157 303	88 771	312 068	156 245	155 823
巴基斯坦	Pakistan	5 207	4 832	375	9 609	8 992	617
伊　朗	Iran	7 711	7 356	355	11 275	7 861	3 414
叙利亚	Syria	1 508	1 508		1 208	1 208	
中国台湾	Taiwan, China	163 456	27 270	136 186	153 385	29 894	123 491
黎巴嫩	Lebanon	1 144	498	646	685	627	58
约　旦	Jordan	1 034	954	80	1 615	1 599	16
也　门	Yeman	1 497	1 439	58	932	918	14
沙　特	Saudi Arabia	5 705	3 439	2 266	11 435	7 600	3 835
科威特	Koweit	1 082	414	668	1 300	1 042	258
巴　林	Bahrein	186	186		308	308	
非　洲	**Africa**	**30 704**	**23 024**	**7 680**	**46 877**	**36 342**	**10 535**
#埃　及	Egypt	3 619	2 679	940	4 199	3 229	970
苏　丹	Sudan	1 122	866	256	6 194	6 064	130
利比亚	Libya	443	443		672	672	
肯尼亚	Kenya	1 112	939	173	1 893	1 797	96
坦桑尼亚	Tanzania	810	727	83	1 258	998	260
欧　洲	**Europe**	**666 098**	**384 188**	**281 910**	**914 403**	**614 182**	**300 221**
#波　兰	Poland	2 890	2 282	608	3 910	3 014	896
俄罗斯	Russia	28 076	9 086	18 990	79 104	54 737	24 367
爱沙尼亚	Esthonia	343	229	114	438	320	118
拉托维亚	Latvia	310	218	92	541	509	32
立陶宛	Lithuania	276	192	84	907	792	115
斯洛文尼亚	Slovenia	266	236	30	679	624	55
斯洛伐克	Slovakia	644	204	440	3 771	1 182	2 589

14－5 续表　Continued
单位:万美元 (USD 10 000)

国 别、地 区	Country, Region	2004 进出口总值 Imports & Exports	2004 出口总值 Exports	2004 进口总值 Imports	2005 进出口总值 Imports & Exports	2005 出口总值 Exports	2005 进口总值 Imports
匈牙利	Hungary	7 820	6 912	908	13 434	12 789	645
捷　克	Czech	3 087	1 805	1 282	4 475	2 501	1 974
保加利亚	Bulgaria	424	395	29	1 569	931	638
阿尔巴尼亚	Albania	137	137		80	80	
罗马尼亚	Roumania	2 685	1 777	908	3 425	2 055	1 370
德　国	Germany	293 824	161 415	132 409	375 027	263 558	111 469
法　国	France	46 764	24 592	22 172	69 542	33 534	36 008
意大利	Italy	35 301	18 839	16 462	41 075	22 129	18 946
荷　兰	Netherlands	50 444	40 523	9 921	61 364	52 007	9 357
比利时	Belgium	16 950	10 573	6 377	21 033	10 812	10 221
英　国	United Kingdom	62 044	39 142	22 902	86 633	57 328	29 305
爱尔兰	Ireland	3 035	1 352	1 683	4 497	2 417	2 080
丹　麦	Danmark	18 359	5 831	12 528	23 307	9 838	13 469
芬　兰	Finland	32 119	27 218	4 902	37 520	31 865	5 655
瑞　典	Sweden	11 274	4 254	7 020	12 284	7 481	4 803
挪　威	Norway	8 434	3 691	4 743	6 542	1 966	4 576
瑞　士	Switzerland	6 929	368	6 561	11 775	5 632	6 143
奥地利	Austria	6 928	368	6 560	7 177	915	6 262
西班牙	Spain	13 415	9 256	4 159	24 597	17 769	6 828
希　腊	Greece	1 645	1 155	490	2 256	2 127	129
葡萄牙	Portugal	2 012	1 594	418	2 610	2 440	170
塞普路斯	Cyprus	239	209	30	307	271	36
马耳他	Malta	130	45	85	290	49	241
拉丁美洲及北美洲	**Latin and North America**	**954 274**	**696 028**	**258 246**	**164 053**	**92 685**	**71 368**
#墨西哥	Mexico	43 609	33 471	10 138	43 018	32 791	10 227
古　巴	Cuba	902	400	502	17 146	4 871	12 275
智　利	Chile	6 807	3 864	2 943	1 161	848	313
加拿大	Canada	41 806	24 933	16 873	53 849	35 479	18 370
美　国	United States	768 540	595 972	172 568	974 340	761 476	212 864
大洋洲及太平洋地区	**Oceania and Pacific Region**	**58 807**	**33 028**	**25 779**	**82 248**	**41 498**	**40 750**
#澳大利亚	Australia	51 759	30 071	21 688	71 773	36 844	34 929
新西兰	New Zealand	6 540	2 509	4 031	9 779	3 229	6 550

14-6 天津口岸进出口商品检验情况(2001-2005年)
INSPECTION OF IMPORTS AND EXPORTS COMMODITIES IN TIANJIN PORT,2001-2005

单位:批、万美元 (batch)(USD 10 000)

项目	Item	2001	2002	2003	2004	2005
进口商品检验	**Imports Inspection**					
批数	Batches	57 285	76 426	105 340	133 767	153 949
#经检验发现不合格商品	Disqualification	292	505	602	1 420	2 330
金额	Value	539 748	651 968	1 035 630	1 481 248	1 713 168
#经检验发现不合格商品	Disqualification	13 620	20 431	24 721	125 877	220 364
出口商品检验	**Exports Inspection**					
批数	Batches	125 642	147 379	171 394	166 023	185 513
#经检验发现不合格商品	Disqualification	129	140	163	675	766
金额	Value	636 064	774 081	1 030 159	1 624 435	1 848 814
#经检验发现不合格商品	Disqualification	192	288	355	16 106	16 123

14-7 设立境外企业和机构情况
OVERSEAS ENTERPRISES AND AGENCIES

项目	Item	2004	2005	至2005年底累计 Accumulated at the end of 2005
企业和机构总计(个)	Total (Unit)	58	75	617
企业	Enterprises	50	54	479
机构	Agencies	8	21	138
投资总额(万美元)	Total Investment(USD 10000)	6 205.59	5 048.83	49 688.11
#中方投资额	Chinese Investment	4 796.96	4 371.54	36 050.55
中方投资占比重(%)	Proportion of Chinese Investment(%)	77.3	86.6	72.6
投资国家和地区(个)	Number of Countries Regions(Unit)	21	31	88

14－8 直接利用外资签约情况
UTILIZATION OF FOREIGN DIRECT INVESTMENT

单位:个、万美元 (batch)(USD 10 000)

项目	Item	2003	2004	2005	2005 比2004年增长% Increased Rate in 2005 over 2004
合同数	**Number of Contracts**	**941**	**1 102**	**1 309**	**18.8**
合资企业	Joint Venture Enterprises	218	328	357	8.8
合作企业	Cooperative Operation Enterprises	23	30	16	－46.7
独资企业	Foreign－funded Sole Enterprises	700	744	936	25.8
合同投资总额	**Total Investment Contracted**	**591 200**	**959 300**	**1 297 272**	**35.2**
合资企业	Joint Venture Enterprises	156 229	261 910	461 763	76.3
合作企业	Cooperative Operation Enterprises	20 385	34 529	51 663	49.6
独资企业	Foreign－funded Sole Enterprises	414 586	662 861	783 846	18.3
合同外资金额	**Foreign Investment Contracted**	**351 297**	**558 855**	**732 281**	**31.0**
合资企业	Joint Venture Enterprises	62 060	92 537	170 925	84.7
合作企业	Cooperative Operation Enterprises	14 471	20 916	21 408	2.4
独资企业	Foreign－funded Sole Enterprises	274 766	445 402	539 948	21.2

14－9 实际利用外资情况
FOREIGN CAPITAL ACTUALLY USED

单位:万美元 (USD 10 000)

项目	Item	2003	2004	2005	2005 比2004年增长% Increased Rate in 2005 over 2004
总计	**Total**	**170 550**	**270 236**	**364 573**	**34.9**
借用国外资金	**Foreign Loans**	**7 225**	**22 993**	**31 688**	**37.8**
外国政府贷款	Foreign Government Loans		2 835	1 925	－32.1
国际金融组织贷款	Loans from International Financial Organizations		7 130	15 000	110.4
出口信贷	Export Loans	247			
外国银行商业贷款	Commercial Loans from Foreign Banks	6 978	13 028	14 763	13.3
对外发行债券、股票	External Bonds,Stocks				
直接利用外资	**Foreign Direct Investment**	**163 325**	**247 243**	**332 885**	**34.6**
合资企业	Joint Venture Enterprises	49 201	83 566	91 370	9.3
合作企业	Cooperative Operation Enterprises	2 967	10 002	14 303	43.0
独资企业	Foreign－funded Sole Enterprises	111 157	153 676	227 213	47.9

14－10 借用国外资金情况
BORROWING FOREIGN CAPITAL

单位:万美元 (USD 10 000)

项 目 Item	上年结转资金 Capital Carried From Last Year		当年新增借款 New Increased Loans		偿还本金 Repaid Principal	
	2004	2005	2004	2005	2004	2005
国外贷款合计						
Total Loans	**105 750**	**98 367**	**22 993**	**31 688**	**30 472**	**34 531**
按债务期限分						
By Period of Debt						
中长期						
Long－term & Medium－term	99 552	93 421	9 965	16 929	16 189	24 871
短　期						
Short－term	6 198	4 946	13 028	14 763	14 283	9 660
按借款方式分						
By Mode of Borrowing						
外国政府贷款						
Government Loans	43 044	42 891	2 835	1 925	2 403	6 919
国际金融组织贷款						
Loans from International Financial Organization	18 921	19 637	7 130	15 000	6 414	1 221
出口信贷						
Export Loans	22 035	17 250			5 454	3 089
外国银行商业贷款						
Commercial Loans of Foreign Banks	21 750	18 589	13 028	14 763	16 201	9 660

项 目 Item	外汇汇率差额 Margin of Foreign Exchange Rate		期末借款余额 Loaned Balance Year－end		偿还利息 Repaid Interest	
	2004	2005	2004	2005	2004	2005
国外贷款合计						
Total Loans	**156**	**－2 828**	**98 427**	**92 756**	**2 083**	**1 741**
按债务期限分						
By Period of Debt						
中长期						
Long－term & Medium－term	153	－2 828	93 481	82 707	2 078	1 740
短　期						
Short－term	3		4 946	10 049	5	1
按借款方式分						
By Mode of Borrowing						
外国政府贷款						
Government Loans	－585	－178	42 891	37 719	439	530
国际金融组织贷款						
Loans from International Financial Organization	60	－1 448	19 697	32 028	43	175
出口信贷						
Export Loans	669	－1 202	17 250	12 950	1 136	809
外国银行商业贷款						
Commercial Loans of Foreign Banks	12		18 589	10 050	465	227

14-11 外商及港澳台商投资企业投资情况(2005年)

INVESTMENT OF FOREIGN-FUNDED AND HONGKONG,MACAO AND TAIWAN FUNDED ENTERPRISES,2005

项目	Item	直接利用外资合同数(个) Contractual Projects of Foreign Direct Investment (unit)		直接利用外资合同投资总额(万美元) Total Volume of Foreign Direct Investment Contracted (USD 10 000)	
		2005	至2005年底累计 Accumulated at the end of 2005	2005	至2005年底累计 Accumulated at the end of 2005
总　计	**Total**	**1 309**	**18 401**	**1 297 272**	**7 906 260**
按投资方式分	**By Mode of Investment**				
合资企业	Joint Venture Enterprises	357	6 633	461 763	3 144 451
合作企业	Cooperative Operation Enterprises	16	604	51 663	640 237
独资企业	Foreign-funded Sole Enterprises	936	11 164	783 846	4 121 572
按行业分	**By Sector**				
农　业	Agriculture	13	135	5 665	51 882
制造业	Manufacturing	707	10 319	745 948	4 609 801
建筑业	Construction	20	350	29 086	130 856
交通运输及仓储业	Transportation and Storage	10	170	71 074	298 088
批发零售贸易及餐饮业	Wholesale,Retail Trade and Catering	275	5 323	109 966	945 572
房地产业	Real Estate	75	702	199 372	1 308 258
社会服务业	Social Services	209	1 363	136 161	258 458
其他行业	Others		465		303 347
按国别(地区)分	**By Country(Region)**				
#中国香港	Hongkong,China	291	5 758	381 161	2 656 398
中国台湾	Taiwan,China	80	1 738	39 133	287 905
韩　国	Republic of Korea	299	2 335	132 280	699 877
日　本	Japan	97	1 742	114 929	693 588
美　国	United States	156	2 871	133 146	1 163 571
新加坡	Singapore	47	557	61 357	274 056
英　国	United Kingdom	23	192	8 386	1 176 618
德　国	Germany	27	239	39 114	145 115
法　国	France	21	149	18 762	70 763
意大利	Italy	10	90	8 542	49 408
英属维尔京群岛	Virgin Islands	77	371	154 840	698 357

14－11 续表　Continued

项　　目	Item	#直接利用外资合同额（万美元）Foreign Capital of Foreign Direct Investment Contracted (USD 10 000)		实际直接利用外资（万美元）Foreign Capital Actually Used (USD 10 000)	
		2005	至2005年底累计 Accumulated at the end of 2005	2005	至2005年底累计 Accumulated at the end of 2005
总　　计	**Total**	**732 281**	**5 821 281**	**332 885**	**3 034 131**
按投资方式分	**By Mode of Investment**				
合资企业	Joint Venture Enterprises	170 925	1 800 238	91 370	1 216 048
合作企业	Cooperative Operation Enterprises	21 408	511 511	14 303	19 512
独资企业	Foreign－funded Sole Enterprises	539 948	3 509 532	227 213	1 622 963
按行业分	**By Sector**				
农　业	Agriculture	4 411	29 124	2 292	7 559
制造业	Manufacturing	404 086	3 362 623	242 750	1 934 635
建筑业	Construction	21 154	95 158	8 892	51 680
交通运输及仓储业	Transportation and Storage	24 393	202 150	9 352	117 176
批发零售贸易及餐饮业	Wholesale,Retail Trade and Catering	60 644	746 027	33 343	480 143
房地产业	Real Estate	120 340	1 011 145	23 834	198 955
社会服务业	Social Services	97 253	226 580	12 422	90 110
其他行业	Others		148 474		153 873
按国别(地区)分	**By Country(Region)**				
#中国香港	Hongkong,China	217 681	1 986 202	68 947	1 000 183
中国台湾	Taiwan,China	23 090	208 770	7 225	99 094
韩　国	Republic of Korea	76 291	403 334	43 664	246 163
日　本	Japan	55 889	441 243	57 012	374 091
美　国	United States	86 005	939 804	18 619	391 799
新加坡	Singapore	33 131	130 510	17 667	102 594
英　国	United Kingdom	6 583	59 789	8 730	48 583
德　国	Germany	27 434	101 541	9 244	61 465
法　国	France	14 687	51 111	2 588	22 189
意大利	Italy	6 632	37 822	1 580	13 608
英属维尔京群岛	Virgin Islands	64 644	423 666	52 153	228 422

14-12 外商及港澳台商投资企业生产经营情况(2005年)
PRODUCTION AND OPERATION OF FOREIGN-FUNDED AND HONGKONG,MACAO AND TAIWAN FUNDED ENTERPRISES,2005

单位:万元 (10 000 yuan)

项 目 Item	企业个数(个) Number of Enterprises (unit)	全部从业人员数(人) Number of Persons Employed (person)	全部从业人员劳动报酬 Total Remuneration of Persons Employed	销售(营业)收入 Sales (Business) Revenue	利润总额 Total Profits
合　计　Total	**5 590**	**532 463**	**1 291 465**	**39 472 910**	**2 577 550**
按投资方式分　By Mode of Investment					
港澳台合资 Hongkong,Macao and Taiwan Joint Venture	826	71 559	147 912	3 593 419	197 859
港澳台合作 Hongkong,Macao and Taiwan Cooperative Operation	63	4 149	8 933	144 609	15 010
港澳台独资 Hongkong,Macao and Taiwan Funded	1 073	71 981	156 113	2 922 573	164 655
中外合资 Joint Venture	1 106	154 365	379 162	15 497 423	672 677
中外合作 Cooperative Operation	118	10 576	25 859	370 232	73 111
外商独资 Foreign-funded Sole	2 404	219 833	573 486	16 944 653	1 454 238
按国民经济行业分　By Sector					
农、林、牧、渔业 Farming,Forestry,Animal Husbandry and Fishery	20	695	1 193	32 458	-226
采矿业 Minerals Mining	12	412	953	264 148	1 718
制造业 Manufacturing	3 432	461 781	1 072 267	34 296 665	2 200 094
#食品制造业 Food Manufacturing	129	12 720	27 199	467 130	32 548
饮料制造业 Beverage Manufacturing	58	7 237	24 155	475 429	42 445
纺织业 Textile Industry	104	9 860	15 351	202 074	7 073
纺织服装、鞋、帽制造业 Textile Industry	218	29 207	39 379	336 139	5 005
家具制造业 Furniture Manufacturing	64	11 180	15 211	224 158	4 393
化学原料及化学制品制造业 Chemical Raw Materials and Chemical Products	196	11 237	44 074	974 599	54 260
医药制造业 Medical and Pharmaceutical Products	74	11 011	47 651	602 193	77 385
塑料制品业 Plastic Products	396	37 639	73 594	1 192 151	55 276
非金属矿物制品业 Nonmetal Mineral Products	112	6 823	17 046	367 126	10 446
黑色金属冶炼及压延加工业 Smelting and Pressing of Ferrous Metals	29	4 909	7 899	226 253	2 806
通用设备制造业 General Purpose Equipment Manufacturing	165	23 901	86 216	1 729 354	142 278
专用设备制造业 Special Purposes Equipment Manufacturing	213	17 916	38 941	722 250	100 054
交通运输设备制造业 Transport Equipment Manufacturing	215	46 863	87 915	4 061 682	154 768

14－12 续表 1 Continued

单位：万元 (10 000 yuan)

项　目　Item	企业个数（个）Number of Enterprises (unit)	全部从业人员数（人）Number of Persons Employed (person)	全部从业人员劳动报酬 Total Remuneration of Persons Employed	销售（营业）收入 Sales (Business) Revenue	利润总额 Total Profits
电气机械及器材制造业 Electric Equipment and Machinery	121	15 767	29 460	669 708	39 597
通信设备、计算机及其他电子设备制造业 Telecommunications Equipment, Computer and Other Electronic Equipment Manufacturing	399	121 084	336 667	17 445 468	1 324 786
电力、燃气及水的生产和供应业 Production & Supply of Power, Gas and Water	13	2 605	11 519	205 591	23 581
建筑业 Construction	123	2 024	4 222	138 772	－5 312
交通运输、仓储及邮政业 Transport, Storage, Post Services	210	11 118	48 389	662 340	100 319
信息传输、计算机服务和软件业 Information Transmitting, Computer Services and Software	68	2 630	12 904	55 350	10 813
批发和零售业 Wholesale and Retail Trade	1 151	19 094	60 238	3 031 430	127 954
住宿和餐饮业 Accommodation and Catering Services	76	12 438	18 977	183 398	6 905
金融业 Finance Intermediation	18	371	4 617	90 705	19 001
房地产业 Real Estate	177	3 752	12 346	276 171	17 067
租赁和商务服务业 Leasing and Business Services	122	1 615	9 120	36 168	38 774
科学研究、技术服务和地质勘察业 Scientific Research, Technical Services and Geological Prospecting	96	3 437	21 884	154 297	38 360
水利、环境和公共设施管理业 Management for Water Conservancy, Environment and Public Facilities	9	101	254	1 687	－53
居民服务和社会服务业 Resident Services and Other Social Services	38	8 986	9 323	29 016	1 235
文化、体育和娱乐业 Culture, Sports and Recreational Services	15	966	1 579	5 951	－3 160
其　他 Others	10	438	1 682	8 764	480
按坐落地点分 By Site of Location					
和平区 Heping District	446	11 178	34 659	1 126 933	59 984
河东区 Hedong District	192	11 515	24 988	790 854	18 128
河西区 Hexi District	571	43 577	120 312	3 024 692	85 734
南开区 Nankai District	525	32 015	97 944	1 462 137	100 114
河北区 Hebei District	149	8 782	17 625	261 091	23 967
红桥区 Hongqiao District	55	2 053	3 752	74 444	7 303
塘沽区 Tanggu District	1 531	133 061	442 175	16 083 251	1 558 370
汉沽区 Hangu District	44	3 399	5 422	125 103	3 776
大港区 Dagang District	58	7 430	15 262	371 288	5 348
东丽区 Dongli District	403	42 536	82 088	1 777 140	111 742
西青区 Xiqing District	463	89 750	185 804	8 680 965	289 039
津南区 Jinnan District	319	36 041	60 042	797 237	55 934
北辰区 Beichen District	363	30 726	71 026	2 420 628	66 923
武清区 Wuqing District	202	44 698	82 578	1 600 071	134 291
宝坻区 Baodi District	64	13 574	16 208	166 891	5 147
宁河县 Ninghe County	53	2 885	4 340	70 442	3 955
静海县 Jinghai County	115	15 168	20 248	406 228	23 873
蓟　县 Jixian County	37	4 075	6 993	233 515	23 925

14－12 续表 2　Continued
单位:万元　(10 000 yuan)

项　　目	Item	企业个数(个) Number of Enterprises (unit)	全部从业人员数(人) Number of Persons Employed (person)	全部从业人员劳动报酬 Total Remuneration of Persons Employed	销售(营业)收入 Sales (Business) Revenue	利润总额 Total Profits
按国别(地区)分	**by Country(Region)**					
亚　洲	**Asia**	**3 871**	**386 456**	**807 415**	**24 108 843**	**1 040 305**
#孟加拉国	Bangladesh	8	231	237	10 399	－801
中国香港	Hongkong, China	1 514	104 180	229 710	4 978 622	303 282
印度尼西亚	Indonesia	7	124	347	28 143	181
日　本	Japan	783	105 967	241 193	8 506 354	332 554
中国澳门	Macao, China	28	1 986	4 307	182 871	5 093
马来西亚	Malaysia	32	3 844	5 196	57 736	－6 878
新加坡	Singapore	173	16 597	29 356	492 560	53 239
韩　国	Republic of Korea	818	106 564	205 160	8 086 616	285 182
泰　国	Thailand	17	1 645	4 237	169 709	－1 603
中国台湾	Taiwan, China	420	41 523	78 942	1 499 109	69 149
亚洲其他国家(地区)	Others	2	53	111	2 348	－896
非　洲	**Africa**	**33**	**1 086**	**3 497**	**106 031**	**11 971**
欧　洲	**Europe**	**427**	**31 486**	**131 488**	**2 728 671**	**295 791**
#比利时	Belgium	7	107	487	7 435	635
丹　麦	Danmark	14	2 334	18 090	294 425	35 006
英　国	United Kingdom	86	7 265	21 931	413 514	54 087
德　国	Germany	94	6 290	24 998	812 139	89 039
法　国	France	53	5 838	29 968	509 944	69 064
意大利	Italy	29	2 135	5 854	127 890	－7 553
荷　兰	Netherlands	31	1 478	10 216	220 872	15 095
西班牙	Spain	16	1 335	2 905	49 971	89
芬　兰	Finland	9	252	1 500	32 716	4 509
匈牙利	Hungary	6	52	79	379	43
挪　威	Norway	2	144	628	3 868	552
罗马尼亚	Roumania	6	92	147	1 812	－12
瑞　典	Sweden	22	1 071	2 582	83 148	16 799
瑞　士	Switzerland	23	2 501	10 387	155 054	18 149
俄罗斯	Russia	7	121	291	5 669	146
拉丁美洲	**Latin**	**149**	**26 207**	**59 530**	**1 266 872**	**－31 814**
#巴　西	Brazil	40	2 960	6 785	62 547	3 348
凯曼群岛	Cayman	12	3 836	10 543	141 756	－76 236
巴拿马	Panama	8	106	305	788	－50
英属维尔京群岛	Virgin Islands	72	18 123	39 137	1 035 781	40 725
北美洲	**North America**	**988**	**77 959**	**275 824**	**10 720 417**	**1 250 865**
#加拿大	Canada	111	5 085	9 358	155 908	5 129
美　国	United States	870	72 076	265 197	10 549 536	1 246 337
大洋洲	**Oceania**	**103**	**8 421**	**12 541**	**524 042**	**10 479**
#澳大利亚	Australia	70	5 266	7 817	336 397	10 621

14－13 新批准外商及港澳台商投资企业投资情况(2005年)
STATISTICS ON INVESTMENT OF NEW APPROVED FOREIGN－FUNDED AND HONGKONG, MACAO AND TAIWAN FUNDED ENTERPRISES, 2005

企业名称 Name of Enterprise	投资国别(地区) Investment Country(Region)	合同投资总额(万美元) Value of Investment Contracted(USD 10 000)	#合同外资额 Foreign Capital Contracted
天津乐金渤海化学有限公司 Tianjing LG Bohai Chemical Company Limited	韩　国 Korea	30 000	10 000
锦湖轮胎(天津)有限公司 Kumho Tire Tianjin Co.,Ltd.	中国香港 Hongkong,China	24 600	8 200
天津威斯特地产置业有限公司 Tianjin West Real Estate Co.,Ltd.	中国香港 Hongkong,China	9 998	5 000
天津鸿坤生物工程技术有限公司 Tianjin Hong Kun Biological Technological Co.,Ltd.	英属维尔京群岛 Virgin Islands	9 998	9 998
天津金润发置业发展有限公司 Tianjin Jinrunfa Development Co.,Ltd.	中国香港 Hongkong,China	9 988	9 988
天津市雅禄线缆有限公司 Tianjing Yalu Wire Co.,Ltd.	中国香港 Hongkong,China	9 907	3 625
天津市琦特电力开发有限公司 Tianjin Qite Electric Power Development Co.,Ltd.	英属维尔京群岛 Virgin Islands	9 907	3 480
天津市齐天源线缆有限公司 Tianjin Qitianyuan Wire And Cable Co.,Ltd.	中国香港 Hongkong,China	9 800	5 000
天津欧洲工业园有限公司 Tianjin Euro－Industrial Park Co.,Ltd.	法　国 France	9 800	8 000
天津港远航散货码头有限公司 Tianjin Port Yuanhang Bulk Cargo Terminal Co.,Ltd.	中国香港 Hongkong,China	9 800	3 840
B&F(天津)环球实业发展有限公司 B&F Best International Founding Group Co.,Ltd.	澳大利亚 Australia	9 800	9 800
天津港联盟国际集装箱码头有限公司 Tianjin Port Alliance International Container Termin Co.,Ltd.	中国香港 Hongkong,China	9 775	4 000
勤威(天津)工业有限公司 CMW (Tianjin) Industry Co.,Ltd.	开曼群岛 Cayman Islands	9 600	3 200
天津天狮生命源有限公司 Tianjin Tiens Life－Resources Co.,Ltd	英属维尔京群岛 Virgin Islands	9 000	3 000
顺吉(天津)国际贸易有限公司 Suen Jih (Tianjin) Marketing & Distribution Inc.	中国台湾 Taiwan,China	9 000	3 000
汉拿(天津)房地产开发有限公司 Halla (Tianjin) Real Estate Development Co.,Ltd.	韩　国 Korea	9 000	3 000
君盛意(天津)实业有限公司 JunShengYi (Tianjin) Industrial Co.,Ltd.	泰　国 Thailand	8 970	2 990
天韵(天津)生物医药咨询有限公司 Tianyun (Tianjin) Bio－Pharmaceutiacl Consultation Co.,Ltd.	中国香港 Hongkong,China	8 000	3 000
电装(天津)空调部件有限公司 Denso (Tianjin) Thermal Products Co.,Ltd.	日　本 Japan	7 600	4 200
天津市新创置业有限公司 Tianjin New Century Real Estate Development Ltd.	新加坡 Singapore	7 500	2 500
天津华联冶金装备有限公司 Tianjin Hhalian Metalurgy Equipment Co.,Ltd.	中国香港 Hongkong,China	7 400	3 000
华研国际(天津)发展有限公司 Cric of Tianjin	加拿大 Canada	7 398	2 466
和记黄埔地产(天津)有限公司 Hutchison Whampoa Properties (Tianjin) Limited	英属维尔京群岛 Virgin Islands	7 283	4 750
天津塑力集团超高压电缆有限公司 Tianjin Suli Group Extra High Voltage Cable Co.,Ltd.	中国香港 Hongkong,China	6 609	4 500
远洋地产(天津)有限公司 Sino－Ocean Real Estate (Tianjin) Co.,Ltd.	中国香港 Hongkong,China	6 288	2 096
澳盛国际(天津)发展有限公司 Osh International (Tianjin) Development Co.,Ltd.	中国香港 Hongkong,China	6 028	6 028
天津天狮生命科学有限公司 Tianjin Tiens Life－Sciences Co.,Ltd	英属维尔京群岛 Virgin Islands	6 000	2 000
天津超能之光环保科技有限公司 Tianjin Chaoneng Environmental Production Technological Co.,Ltd.	中国香港 Hongkong,China	6 000	2 000

注:本表企业为合同投资总额在2500美元以上的企业。
Note: This table is new appoved foreign－funded and Hongkong, Macao and Taiwan funded enterprises with contracted investment of over 25 million USD.

14－13 续表 1　Continued

企 业 名 称 Name of Enterprise	投资国别(地区) Investment Country(Region)	合同投资总额(万美元) Value of Investment Contracted(USD 10 000)	#合同外资额 Foreign Capital Contracted
麦克罗通信工程(天津)有限公司 Mai Ke Luo Communication Engineering (Tianjin) Co.,Ltd.	美　国 United States	6 000	3 000
第一澳元(天津)柔性电路有限公司 Great Pacific (Tianjin) Flex Circuit Co.,Ltd.	中国香港 Hongkong,China	6 000	2 990
富士康(天津)精密工业有限公司 Foxconn (Tianjin) Precision Industry Co.,Ltd.	开曼群岛 Cayman Islands	5 800	1 980
现阳汽配(天津)有限公司 Hyun Yang Automotive Parts (Tianjin) Co.,Ltd.	韩　国 Korea	5 000	3 000
天津优耐房地产开发有限公司 Tianjin Unid&C Real Estate Development Co.,Ltd.	韩　国 Korea	5 000	3 000
天津荣胜荣置业有限公司 Tianjin Rong Sheng Rong Real Estate Co.,Ltd.	塞浦路斯 Cyprus	5 000	5 000
嘉誉(天津)实业有限公司 Fortune (Tianjin) Co.,Ltd.	英属维尔京群岛 Virgin Islands	5 000	5 000
SEW－精密机械(天津)有限公司 Sew－Precision Gears (Tianjin) Co.,Ltd.	德　国 Germany	5 000	2 000
HYDE(天津)投资咨询有限公司 Hyde Investment Consultancy (Tianjin) Co.,Ltd.	加拿大 Canada	5 000	5 000
赛富成长基金(天津)创业投资企业 SAIF(Tianjin) Growth Fund	毛里求斯 Mauritius	5 000	2 000
天津晟实国际贸易有限责任公司 Tianjin Sheng Shi International Trade Company	英属维尔京群岛 Virgin Islands	4 932	2 466
天津中集集装箱有限公司 Tianjin Cimc Container Co.,Ltd.	中国香港 Hongkong,China	4 900	2 300
派克特精液压(天津)有限公司 Parker Tejing Hydraulics(Tianjin)Co.,Ltd.	美　国 United States	4 900	2 000
金威啤酒(天津)有限公司 Kingway Brewery (Tianjin) Co.,Ltd.	中国香港 Hongkong,China	4 838	1 620
沃尔福(天津)科技发展有限公司 Wolfgang (Tianjin) Technology Development Co.,Ltd.	德　国 Germany	4 800	4 800
天津金汇联成项目开发建设有限公司 Tianjin Jinhui Unite Success Item · Development Construction Co.,Ltd.	澳大利亚 Australia	4 800	2 400
天津丰爱汽车座椅部件有限公司 Tianjin Feng'ai Automotive Seat Parts Co., Ltd.	日　本 Japan	4 750	1 650
中菲(天津)纺织有限公司 Phil China (Tianjin) Textile Co.,Ltd.	菲律宾 Philippines	4 500	1 500
天津市西君房地产开发建设有限公司 Tianjin Xijun Real Estate Development & Construction Co.,Ltd.	萨摩亚 Samoa	4 500	3 500
普洛斯(天津)置业发展有限公司 ProLogis Park Tianjin Development Co.,Ltd.	巴巴多斯 Barbados	4 500	1 500
天津万科新锐房地产有限公司 Tianjin Vanke Fresh Drive Real Estate Co.,Ltd.	中国香港 Hongkong,China	4 439	1 480
天津塑力线缆集团有限公司 Tianjin Suli Cable Group Co.,Ltd.	英属维尔京群岛 Virgin Islands	4 377	4 377
约翰迪尔(天津)有限公司 John Deere (Tianjin) Company, Limited.	美　国 United States	4 000	1 400
依德尔(天津)房地产开发有限公司 Edle(Tianjin) Real Estate Development Co.,Ltd.	德　国 Germany	4 000	2 000
亨特尔(天津)科技开发有限公司 Huntere (Tianjin) Technology Development Co.,Ltd.	日　本 Japan	4 000	1 500
天津嘉禾韦仑木业有限公司 Tianjin Mellow Flooring Co.,Ltd.	中国香港 Hongkong,China	3 600	3 600
歌美飒风电(天津)有限公司 Gamesa Wind (Tianjin) Co.,Ltd.	西班牙 Spain	3 600	1 200
天津加蕾房地产开发有限公司 Tianjin Jia Lei Real Estate Development Corp.ltd.	新加坡 Singapore	3 500	1 200

14－13 续表 2　Continued

企　业　名　称 Name of Enterprise	投资国别(地区) Investment Country(Region)	合同投资总额 (万美元) Value of Investment Contracted(USD 10 000)	#合同外资额 Foreign Capital Contracted
博大印刷(天津)有限公司 Boda Printing (Tianjin) Co.,Ltd.	中国香港 Hongkong,China	3 500	3 500
天津博纳正信实业有限公司 TianJin Bona Fides Industry Co.,Ltd.	中国香港 Hongkong,China	3 300	2 650
肯纳金属(中国)有限公司 Kennametal (China) Co.,Ltd.	美　国 United States	3 100	1 200
奥联(天津)玻璃有限公司 O－I Tianjin Glass Co.,Ltd	中国香港 Hongkong,China	3 100	1 050
中体产业集团股份有限公司 China Sports Industry Group Co.,Ltd.	中国香港 Hongkong,China	3 065	3 065
维斯塔斯风力发电设备(中国)有限公司 Vestas Wind Turbine Equipment (China) Co.,Ltd.	丹　麦 Denmark	3 000	1 200
天津禹甸国际贸易有限公司 Tianjin Yudian International Trade Co.,Ltd.	中国台湾 Taiwan,China	3 000	1 000
天津唐财港口发展有限公司 Tianjin Tang Choy Port Development Co.,Ltd.	中国香港 Hongkong,China	3 000	2 000
天津隆德汽车电子有限公司 Tiajin Longde Auto－electronic Co.,Ltd.	韩　国 Korea	3 000	2 800
福满多投资有限公司 Fumanduo Investment Co.,Ltd.	英属维尔京群岛 Virgin Islands	3 000	3 000
超汇桂盟传动(天津)有限公司 Kmc Transmission (Tianjin) Co.,Ltd.	中国香港 Hongkong,China	3 000	1 200
天津众茂科技产业有限公司 Tianjin H G Co.,Ltd.	美　国 United States	2 998	1 500
天津市胜名置业有限公司 Tian Jin Shi Sheng Ming Real Estate Co.,Ltd.	意大利 Italy	2 998	2 998
天津珅利投资担保有限公司 Tianjin Shenli Invertment & Guarantee Co.,Ltd.	中国香港 Hongkong,China	2 998	2 998
天津仁和焕置业有限公司 Tianjin Humality Realstate Co.,Ltd.	韩　国 Korea	2 998	2 998
天津和信昌工业有限公司 Landmark International Industry Co.,Ltd.	萨摩亚 Samoa	2 998	1 200
天津宝龙置业发展有限公司 Tianjin Powerlong Real Estate Development Co.,Ltd	中国澳门 Macao,China	2 998	1 200
铭涛(天津)国际物流有限公司 Mantis (Tianjin) International Logistics Co.,Ltd.	加拿大 Canada	2 998	2 998
京薇国际投资顾问(天津)有限公司 Jingwei International Investment(Tianjin) Co.,Ltd.	大洋洲其他国家(地区) Oceanic Region	2 998	2 998
天津华曦科技有限公司 Tianjin Huaxi Science and Technology Co.,Ltd.	中国香港 Hongkong,China	2 990	1 200
龙泰普罗威瓦(天津)生物科技有限公司 Longtai Provivo (Tianjin) Biotechnology Co.,Ltd.	中国香港 Hongkong,China	2 990	2 990
龙泰普罗必(天津)保健食品有限公司 Longtai Probiotic (Tianjin) Health Food Co.,Ltd.	中国香港 Hongkong,China	2 990	2 990
鑫立鹏(天津)房地产开发有限公司 Xin Li Peng (Tianjin) Real Estate EMPOLDER Co.,Ltd.	中国香港 Hongkong,China	2 980	1 200
卡博特高性能材料(天津)有限公司 Cabot Performance Products (Tianjin) Co.,Ltd.	美　国 United States	2 980	1 200
嘉鹏(天津)实业发展有限公司 Jiapeng (Tianjin) Industrial Development Co.,Ltd.	美　国 United States	2 980	2 980
中盛国威(天津)置业有限公司 Zhongsheng Gouwei (Tianjin) Rael Estate Co., Ltd.	中国香港 Hongkong,China	2 960	2 960
中企伟达(天津)基础设施建设有限公司 Zhongqi Weida (Tianjin) Basic Facilities Construction Co.,Ltd.	中国香港 Hongkong,China	2 960	2 960

14－13续表3 Continued

企业名称 Name of Enterprise	投资国别(地区) Investment Country(Region)	合同投资总额(万美元) Value of Investment Contracted(USD 10 000)	#合同外资额 Foreign Capital Contracted
广厦建筑材料(天津)有限公司 Guangsha Building Materials(Tianjin) Co.,Ltd.	韩　国 Korea	2 960	2 960
东方天宏(天津)实业有限公司 Dong Fang Tian Hong (Tianjin) Industrial Co.,Ltd.	加拿大 Canada	2 950	1 500
天津市基辅航母金星大酒店有限公司 Tianjin Kiew Airfraft Carrier Golden－Star Hotel Co.,Ltd.	德　国 Germany	2 900	1 180
天津北方五金机电城有限公司 Tianjin Northern Hardware & Machinery Market Co., Ltd.	中国香港 Hongkong,China	2 900	1 160
隆达利(天津)纳米材料有限公司 Longdali(Tianjin) Nanomaterial Co.,Ltd.	中国香港 Hongkong,China	2 900	1 900
歌赛尔科技发展(天津)有限公司 GESL Tech Development(Tianjin) Co.,Ltd.	德　国 Germany	2 890	1 445
天津平和特殊玻璃有限公司 Tianjin Pinghe Special Glass Co.,Ltd.	中国香港 Hongkong,China	2 880	2 880
天津酮云电力设备制造有限公司 Tianjin Tongyun Electric Power Equipmenr Manufacture Co., Ltd.	英属维尔京群岛 Virgin Islands	2 839	2 839
藤田科技发展(天津)有限公司 Tengtian Science & Technulogy Development(Tianjin) Co., Ltd.	日　本 Japan	2 800	2 000
天津美特五金冲压制品有限公司 Tianjin Meite Mental Products Co.,Ltd.	美　国 United States	2 700	1 700
天津睿亨国际贸易有限公司 Tianjin Veeken International Trading Co.,Ltd.	中国香港 Hongkong,China	2 600	2 600
天津丽兴渤宇金属制品有限公司 Tianjin Licingboyu Metal Products Co.,Ltd.	英属维尔京群岛 Virgin Islands	2 600	1 050
天津津易达国际贸易有限公司 Tianjin Billionway International Trading Co.,Ltd.	英属维尔京群岛 Virgin Islands	2 600	1 400
浩渤(天津)不锈钢设备制造有限公司 Haobo (Tianjin) Stainless Steel Equipment Fabrication Co., Ltd.	加拿大 Canada	2 600	1 050
甘地特(天津)糖果有限公司 Candy Tech (Tianjin) Factory Co.,ltd.	毛里求斯 Mauritius	2 550	1 020
液化空气天津滨海有限公司 Air Liquide Tianjin Binhai Co.,Ltd.	法　国 France	2 500	1 000
天津智元生物技术有限公司 Sinocro Biosciences Limited	英属维尔京群岛 Virgin Islands	2 500	2 000
天津远东投资管理有限公司 Tianjin Fareast Investment Management,Inc.	美　国 United States	2 500	1 000
天津永裕房地产开发有限公司 Tianjin Yongyu Rael Estate Co.,Ltd.	中国香港 Hongkong,China	2 500	2 500
天津唐财大明文化教育发展有限公司 Tianjin Tangchoy Daming Cultural & Educational Development Co., Ltd.	中国香港 Hongkong,China	2 500	1 500
天津市盛元科技发展有限公司 Tianjin Shenyuan Science Technology Development Co., Ltd.	英属维尔京群岛 Virgin Islands	2 500	2 500
天津赛诺精细化工有限公司 Tianjin Sano Fine Chemicals Co.Ltd.	美　国 United States	2 500	2 250
天津瑞金房地产开发有限公司 Tianjin Ruijin Rael Estate Development Co.,Ltd.	荷　兰 Netherlands	2 500	1 200
天津津港物流发展有限公司 Tianjin Jingang Logistics Development Co.,Ltd.	英属维尔京群岛 Virgin Islands	2 500	1 000
天津港保税区斯维尔顿国际贸易有限公司 Tianjin Port Free Trade Zone Swrd International Trad Co., Ltd.	美　国 United States	2 500	2 500
天津奥纪托投资管理咨询有限公司 Tianjin Aojituo Investment Management Consulting Co.,Ltd.	中国香港 Hongkong,China	2 500	2 500
斯特福(天津)科技发展有限公司 Xitafu (Tianjin) Technology Development Co.,Ltd.	美　国 United States	2 500	2 500
雷玛(天津)汽车过滤制品有限公司 Kamas(Tianjin)Auto－Filters'Manufacturing Co.,Ltd.	美　国 United States	2 500	2 500
古河(天津)精密铝业有限公司 Furukawa－Sky Aluminum (Tianjin) Corporation Co.,Ltd.	日　本 Japan	2 500	1 000

14－14 接待入境旅游人数和居住天数(2001－2005年)
NUMBER OF INTERNATIONAL TOURISTS AND DWELLING DAYS,2001－2005

单位:人次、天 (person－times)(day)

项目	Item	2001	2002	2003	2004	2005
接待人数总计(含不过夜)	**Total Tourists(include not stay for night)**	**421 422**	**506 038**	**489 017**	**615 900**	**740 071**
接待人数(过夜)	Accommodated Tourists(stay for night)	177 330	204 559	172 104	275 753	309 789
外国人	Foreigners	143 735	166 205	144 087	236 004	266 672
#日本	Japan	47 418	52 748	45 268	80 015	89 648
菲律宾	Philippines	566	553	438	1 029	1 356
新加坡	Singapore	4 449	5 251	4 198	7 194	9 004
泰国	Thailand	530	622	425	958	853
印尼	Indonesia	689	562	510	832	1 166
美国	United States	12 279	16 197	10 705	19 271	21 427
加拿大	Canada	2 031	2 055	1 651	2 981	3 624
英国	United Kingdom	3 050	3 199	2 754	5 897	6 571
法国	France	2 389	2 079	2 030	4 421	4 970
德国	Germany	2 896	3 381	3 409	6 198	8 112
意大利	Italy	1 155	1 330	1 277	2 093	3 547
俄罗斯	Russia	6 654	4 352	3 337	3 846	2 782
澳大利亚	Australia	2 394	2 828	1 875	3 556	4 447
港澳台同胞	Hongkong,Macao & Taiwan Compatriots	33 595	38 354	28 017	39 749	43 117
平均每人居住天数	**Per Capita Staying Days in Tianjin**	**8.4**	**8.9**	**9.6**	**8.3**	**8.9**

14－15 接待入境旅游外汇收入(2001－2005年)
FOREIGN EXCHANGE EARNING FROM INTERNATIONAL TOURISTS,2001－2005

单位:万美元 (USD 10 000)

项目	Item	2001	2002	2003	2004	2005
总计	**Total**	**28 017**	**34 238**	**32 947**	**41 253**	**50 930**
长途交通	Long－distance Transportation Expense	12 385	12 905	12 403	12 012	21 526
飞机	Civil Aviation	10 039	10 460	10 047	10 030	13 636
火车	Railway	446	1 391	1 326	1 174	1 147
汽车	Motor Vehicles	1 394	443	447	324	1 043
海运	Sea Transportation	507	611	583	484	5 700
游览	Tour	1 388	2 004	1 916	2 179	1 435
住宿	Accommodation	3 424	4 496	4 333	4 841	5 166
餐饮	Catering Service	2 202	2 479	2 394	2 172	4 428
娱乐	Entertainment	1 362	2 528	2 427	2 077	2 090
购物	Shopping	4 747	5 451	5 266	11 714	10 046
邮电通讯	Posts and Telecommunications	781	1 231	1 177	1 655	933
市内交通	Local Transportation Expense	581	1 151	1 117	1 102	1 160
其他	Others	1 147	1 993	1 913	3 501	4 146

14-16 天津与国外结成友好城市一览表
LIST OF FOREIGN SISTER CITIES WITH TIANJIN

友好城市 Sister City	国别 Country of Origin	缔结时间 Time of Conclusion	友好城市 Sister City	国别 Country of Origin	缔结时间 Time of Conclusion
神户市	日本	1973年6月24日	乌兰巴托市	蒙古	1992年9月27日
Kobe	Japan	June 24,1973	Ulan Bator	Mongolia	Sept. 27,1992
费城	美国	1980年2月10日	哈尔科夫市	乌克兰	1993年6月14日
Philadephia	U.S.A	Feb. 10,1980	Kharkov	Ukraine	June 14,1993
墨尔本市	澳大利亚	1980年5月5日	延雪坪市	瑞典	1993年9月23日
Melbourne	Australia	May 5,1980	Jon Koping	Sweden	Sept. 23,1993
四日市	日本	1980年10月28日	仁川市	韩国	1993年12月7日
Yokkaichi	Japan	Oct. 28,1980	Inchon	Republic of Korea	Dec. 7,1993
萨拉热窝市	波黑共和国	1980年5月28日	萨尔州	德国	1994年9月27日
Sarajevo	Bosnia Herzegovina	Oct. 10,1984	State of Saarland	Germany	Sept. 27,1994
北加莱海峡大区	法国	1984年10月10日	罗兹市	波兰	1994年10月11日
Region Nord Pas de Clais	France	Oct. 10,1984	Lodz	Poland	Oct. 11,1994
伦巴第大区	意大利	1985年5月9日	里约热内卢市	巴西	1995年4月18日
Lombardia Region	Italy	May 9,1985	Rio de Janeiro	Brazil	Apr. 18,1995
格罗宁根市	荷兰	1985年9月12日	橘郡	美国	1997年8月1日
Groningen	Holand	Sept. 12,1985	Orange County	U.S.A	Aug. 1,1997
千叶市	日本	1989年5月7日	亚马逊洲	巴西	1997年10月21日
Chiba	Japan	May 7,1989	State of Amazon	Brazil	Oct. 21,1997
普罗夫迪夫大区	保加利亚	1989年10月15日	海防市	越南	1999年1月8日
Plovdiv	Bulgaria	Oct. 15,1989	Haiphong City	Vietnam	Jan. 8,1999
伊兹密尔市	土耳其	1991年9月25日	南浦市	朝鲜	2002年8月11日
Izmir	Turkey	Sept. 25,1991	Nampo City	DPRK	Aug. 11,2002
阿比让市	科特迪瓦	1992年9月26日			
La Ville D'abidjan	Cote Divoire	Sept. 26,1992			

14-17 对外承包工程和劳务合作(2001-2005年)
CONTRACTED FOREIGN PROJECTS AND LABOR COOPERATION,2001-2005

项目	Item	2001	2002	2003	2004	2005
签订合同份数(个)	Number of Contracts(unit)	811	501	1 107	777	907
# 对外承包工程	Contracted Foreign Projects	15	89	633	159	68
劳务合作	Labor Cooperation	496	405	461	598	828
签订合同金额(万美元)	Contracted Value(USD 10 000)	30 829	28 532	40 419	54 709	43 230
# 对外承包工程	Contracted Foreign Projects	10 712	17 373	31 227	44 087	32 563
劳务合作	Labor Cooperation	9 458	10 736	8 746	9 125	10 003
实际营业额(万美元)	Fulfilling Value(USD 10 000)	30 499	26 834	40 515	52 688	32 017
# 对外承包工程	Contracted Foreign Projects	6 084	16 443	28 863	40 597	18 013
劳务合作	Labor Cooperation	9 691	10 139	11 161	11 581	13 630
年末在外劳动人数(人)	Number of Outside Laborers Year-end(person)	15 069	11 876	11 320	12 485	13 140
# 对外承包工程	Contracted Foreign Projects	789	415	768	1 241	1 091
劳务合作	Labor Cooperation	14 265	11 421	10 544	11 190	11 990

14－18　按国别(地区)分对外承包工程、劳务合作(2005 年)

CONTRACTED FOREIGN PROJECTS AND LABOR COOPERATION BY COUNTRY(REGION), 2005

国别、地区	Country, Region	对外承包工程 Contracted Foreign Projects		劳务合作 Labor Cooperation	
		合同个数(个) Number of Projects(unit)	合同金额(万美元) Contracted Value(USD 10 000)	合同个数(个) Number of Projects(unit)	合同金额(万美元) Contracted Value(USD 10 000)
合　计	**Total**	**68**	**32 563**	**828**	**10 003**
亚　洲	**Asia**	**15**	**21 365**	**317**	**8 365**
孟加拉	Bangladesh	1	1 123		
缅　甸	Myanmar	1	23		
柬埔寨	Cambodia	1	10	29	174
印度尼西亚	Indonesia	3	10 000		
约　旦	Jordan			1	180
韩　国	Republic of Korea	1	6	13	2 338
新加坡	Singapore			76	665
沙特阿拉伯	Saudi Arabia			1	3
巴基斯坦	Pakistan	1	258		
蒙　古	Mongolia	1	42		
中国台湾	Taiwan, China			38	904
阿拉伯联合酋长国	United Arab Emirates	2	2 170	41	54
泰　国	Thailand	1			
日　本	Japan			64	2 394
伊　朗	Iran	2	1 905		
印　度	India	1	5 828		
中国香港	Hongkong, China			54	1 653
非　洲	**Africa**	**49**	**7 266**	**13**	**208**
安哥拉	Angola	2	164		
加　蓬	Gabon	3	599		
几内亚比绍	Guinea Bissau	1	10		
马达加斯加	Madagascar	1	1 155		
阿尔及利亚	Algeria			1	16
毛里求斯	Mauritius			2	150
尼日尔	Niger	1	2		
尼日利亚	Nigeria	2	2 726		
苏　丹	Sudan	33	2 580		
莱索托	Lesotho			10	42
厄立特里亚	Eritrea	1	30		
欧　洲	**Europe**	**4**	**3 932**		
哈萨克斯坦	Kazakhstan	1	670		
白俄罗斯	Belorussia	2	3 124		
挪　威	Norway	1	138		
拉丁美洲	**Latin America**			**9**	**243**
巴拿马	Panama			4	129
尼加拉瓜	Nicaragua			5	114
北美洲	**North America**			**25**	**781**
美　国	United States			25	781
国　内	**Domestic**			**464**	**406**

14－19 外商及港澳台商投资企业利润总额百强企业(2005年)

TOP 100 FOREIGN－FUNDED AND HONGKONG,MACAO AND TAIWAN FUNDED ENTERPRISES BY PROFITS,2005

名　次 Position	企业名称 Name of Enterprise	名　次 Position	企业名称 Name of Enterprise
1	摩托罗拉(中国)电子有限公司	51	天津电装电子有限公司
2	天津三星通信技术有限公司	52	壳牌润滑油有限公司
3	天津丰田汽车有限公司	53	天津天马缝纫机制造有限公司
4	天津三星电子有限公司	54	丹佛斯(天津)有限公司
5	绫致时装(天津)有限公司	55	天津天永高速公路有限公司
6	天津三星电子显示器有限公司	56	阿克苏诺贝尔涂料(天津)有限公司
7	中美天津史克制药有限公司	57	掌中万维(中国)信息科技有限公司
8	天津通广三星电子有限公司	58	亚光耐普罗精密注塑天津有限公司
9	奥的斯电梯(中国)投资有限公司	59	西湖(天津)橡塑制品有限公司
10	天津天狮生物发展有限公司	60	天津英泰汽车饰件有限公司
11	中国天津奥的斯电梯有限公司	61	万新塑胶制品(天津)有限公司
12	SEW传动设备(天津)有限公司	62	丰田通商(天津)有限公司
13	天津中集北洋集装箱有限公司	63	天津天管特钻具有限公司
14	天津丰田汽车发动机有限公司	64	天津雅马哈电子乐器有限公司
15	中法合营王朝葡萄酿酒有限公司	65	天津三星视界移动有限公司
16	天津津亚电子有限公司	66	天津东海理化汽车部件有限公司
17	天津三星视界有限公司	67	天津市海运股份有限公司
18	诺维信(中国)生物技术有限公司	68	天津可口可乐饮料有限公司
19	施耐德电气低压(天津)有限公司	69	天津太平货柜有限公司
20	华利行(天津)国际贸易有限公司	70	天津惠海船务企业有限公司
21	罗姆集成电路设计(天津)有限公司	72	中国大冢制药有限公司
22	飞思卡尔半导体(中国)有限公司	73	天津东洋油墨有限公司
23	天津港集装箱码头有限公司	74	可立新电子(天津)有限公司
24	天津喜来健医疗器械有限公司	75	天津津政交通发展有限公司
25	赫比(天津)电子有限公司	76	天津丰田合成有限公司
26	天津天惠船务企业有限公司	77	天津天利航空机电有限公司
27	乐金电子(天津)电器有限公司	78	天津富士通天电子有限公司
28	天津顶津食品有限公司	79	天津南侨油脂有限公司
29	天津天昂高速公路有限公司	80	美卓矿机(天津)有限公司
30	世讯工业(天津)有限公司	81	劲量(中国)有限公司
31	斯必克冷却技术(天津)有限公司	82	麦格昆磁(天津)有限公司
32	西门子电气传动有限公司	83	美孚石油(天津)有限公司
33	天津新展高速公路有限公司	84	飞马(天津)缝纫机有限公司
34	天津顶益国际食品有限公司	85	亚实履带(天津)有限公司
35	天津港远航矿石码头有限公司	86	富港电子(天津)有限公司
36	天津住友商事有限公司	87	北星(天津)汽车有限公司
37	爱信(天津)车身零部件有限公司	88	天津双协机械工业有限公司
38	PPG涂料(天津)有限公司	89	通用半导体(中国)有限公司
39	天津彼恩特通信有限公司	90	天津泰康实业有限公司
40	天津华丰汽车装饰有限公司	91	永立建机(天津)国际贸易有限公司
41	天津泰达津联电力有限公司	92	天津泰丰工业园投资(集团)有限公司
42	申克(天津)矿业设备有限公司	92	博爱(中国)膨化芯材有限公司
43	天津肯德基有限公司	93	天津群泰房地产开发有限公司
44	日新(天津)塑胶有限公司	94	因塔思(天津)电子有限公司
45	天津赛象电气自动化技术有限公司	95	飞比达电子元器件(天津)有限公司
46	天津丰津汽车传动部件有限公司	96	天津三电汽车空调有限公司
47	德芬工业减速机(天津)有限公司	97	威娜化妆品(中国)有限公司
48	天津东方海陆集装箱码头有限公司	98	天津南玻工程玻璃有限公司
49	天津正大饲料科技有限公司	99	天津泰达阿尔卑斯物流有限公司
50	约翰·迪尔天拖有限公司	100	天津津住汽车线束有限公司

14－20　外商及港澳台商投资企业出口创汇百强企业(2005年)

TOP 100 FOREIGN－FUNDED AND HONGKONG,MACAO AND TAIWAN FUNDED ENTERPRISES BY EXPORTS,2005

名　次 Position	企业名称 Name of Enterprise	名　次 Position	企业名称 Name of Enterprise
1	摩托罗拉(中国)电子有限公司	51	安施电子(天津)有限公司
2	天津三星通信技术有限公司	52	天津三和电机有限公司
3	乐金电子(天津)电器有限公司	53	天津国际联合轮胎橡胶有限公司
4	新科(天津)建设工程有限公司	54	功学社
5	飞思卡尔半导体(中国)有限公司	55	英保达资讯(天津)有限公司
6	天津三星电子显示器有限公司	56	天津鑫山家具有限公司
7	天津三星电子有限公司	57	天津三王风展轮胎有限公司
8	天津津亚电子有限公司	58	天津新午星机电有限公司
9	天津通广三星电子有限公司	59	天津新伟祥工业有限公司
10	天津三美电机有限公司	60	九维机电(天津)有限公司
11	天津中集北洋集装箱有限公司	61	天津韩飞鞋业有限公司
12	天津富士通天电子有限公司	62	天津中远关西涂料化工有限公司
13	天津三星电机有限公司	63	天津天狮生物发展有限公司
14	天津阿尔卑斯电子有限公司	64	雅士佳(天津)汽车零件有限公司
15	扎努西电气机械天津压缩机有限公司	65	天津彼恩特通信有限公司
16	罗姆集成电路设计(天津)有限公司	66	天津星湖实业有限公司
17	天津富士光机有限公司	67	诺曼地橡胶有限公司
18	现代电子(天津)多媒体有限公司	68	万新塑胶制品(天津)有限公司
19	天津三星视界移动有限公司	69	天津新韩精机有限公司
20	大宇微波炉(天津)有限公司	70	天津安费诺凯翼电子科技有限公司
21	三星高新电机(天津)有限公司	71	天津华住金属制品有限公司
22	天津大星电子有限公司	72	天津劳尔工业有限公司
23	中国天津奥的斯电梯有限公司	73	科莱恩颜料(天津)有限公司
24	天津三星光电子有限公司	74	劲量(中国)有限公司
25	天津富士达自行车有限公司	75	麦格昆磁(天津)有限公司
26	天津三星视界有限公司	76	天津南华制鞋有限公司
27	天津爱普生有限公司	77	天津天石休闲用品有限公司
28	美克国际家私(天津)制造有限公司	78	天津勤美达工业有限公司
29	天津雅马哈电子乐器有限公司	79	天津科林自行车有限公司
30	通用半导体(中国)有限公司	80	亚光耐普罗精密注塑天津有限公司
31	天津太平货柜有限公司	81	天津长威科技有限公司
32	天津三洋通信设备有限公司	82	天津成湖实业有限公司
33	中芯国际集成电路制造(天津)有限公司	83	罗姆(天津)电子有限公司
34	鹏思特(天津)实业有限公司	84	赫比(天津)电子有限公司
35	大真空有限公司	85	博爱(中国)膨化芯材有限公司
36	可立新电子(天津)有限公司	86	天津中辰番茄制品有限公司
37	世讯工业(天津)有限公司	87	天津中央电子有限公司
38	三洋能源(天津)有限公司	88	天津磁化电子有限公司
39	日新(天津)塑胶有限公司	89	天星科生皮革制品有限公司
40	丹佛斯(天津)有限公司	90	昌进特(天津)电子有限公司
41	京瓷太阳能有限公司	91	天津柯雅美术材料有限公司
42	天津富川电机有限公司	92	天禧(天津)餐具有限公司
43	大宇空调(天津)有限公司	93	天津沃茨阀门有限公司
44	天津津住汽车线束有限公司	94	天津斯坦雷电气有限公司
45	天津松下电子部品有限公司	95	阿克苏诺贝尔涂料(天津)有限公司
46	西迪斯(天津)电子有限公司	96	天津大像电子有限公司
47	亚实履带(天津)有限公司	97	天津燕桥焊接材料有限公司
48	天津汇宇实业有限公司	98	天津津英纺纱有限公司
49	诺维信(中国)生物技术有限公司	99	天津惠中化学有限公司
50	天津矢崎汽车配件有限公司	100	天津珍熙美容实业有限公司

14-21 外商及港澳台商投资企业实缴税金总额百强企业(2005年)

TOP 100 FOREIGN-FUNDED AND HONGKONG,MACAO AND TAIWAN FUNDED ENTERPRISES BY PAID-UP TAXES,2005

名 次 Position	企业名称 Name of Enterprise	名 次 Position	企业名称 Name of Enterprise
1	摩托罗拉(中国)电子有限公司	51	仙妮蕾德(天津)企业有限公司
2	天津丰田汽车有限公司	52	加德士润滑油有限公司
3	天津欧尚超市有限公司	53	美孚石油(天津)有限公司
4	新大洲本田摩托有限公司	54	天津华丰汽车装饰有限公司
5	天津三星通信技术有限公司	55	伍德沃德(天津)控制器有限公司
6	丰田通商(天津)有限公司	56	天津矢崎汽车配件有限公司
7	中国天津奥的斯电梯有限公司	57	天津日石润滑油脂有限公司
8	绫致时装(天津)有限公司	58	天津阿尔斯通水电设备有限公司
9	中法合营王朝葡萄酿酒有限公司	59	天津罗升企业有限公司
10	中美天津史克制药有限公司	60	中国大冢制药有限公司
11	天津珍熙美容实业有限公司	61	欧姆龙贸易(天津)有限公司
12	天津三星视界有限公司	62	天津电装空调有限公司
13	乐金电子(天津)电器有限公司	63	卡夫天美食品(天津)有限公司
14	天津津亚电子有限公司	64	天津中集北洋集装箱有限公司
15	天津通广三星电子有限公司	65	诺维信(中国)生物技术有限公司
16	天津顶益国际食品有限公司	66	天津天狮生物发展有限公司
17	天津丰田汽车发动机有限公司	67	天津南侨油脂有限公司
18	鹏思特(天津)实业有限公司	68	天津雀巢有限公司
19	壳牌润滑油有限公司	69	北星(天津)汽车有限公司
20	PPG涂料(天津)有限公司	70	博福-益普生(天津)制药有限公司
21	SEW传动设备(天津)有限公司	72	天津天马缝纫机制造有限公司
22	普利司通(天津)轮胎有限公司	73	北方浩伟(天津)国际贸易有限公司
23	天津嘉里粮油工业有限公司	74	天津港集装箱码头有限公司
24	施耐德电气低压(天津)有限公司	75	天津乐金大沽化学有限公司
25	天津艾达自动变速器有限公司	76	现代电子(天津)有限公司
26	西门子电气传动有限公司	77	天津津住汽车线束有限公司
27	天津三星电子有限公司	78	天津泰瑞房地产开发有限公司
28	诺和诺德(中国)制药有限公司	79	施维雅(天津)制药有限公司
29	天津三星光电子有限公司	80	天津丰田合成有限公司
30	顶盛(天津)国际贸易有限公司	81	天津东洋油墨有限公司
31	永立建机(天津)国际贸易有限公司	82	天津松下电子部品有限公司
32	天津英泰汽车饰件有限公司	83	爱信(天津)车身零部件有限公司
33	天津三星电子显示器有限公司	84	天津泰达津联电力有限公司
34	亚光耐普罗精密注塑天津有限公司	85	世讯工业(天津)有限公司
35	日新(天津)塑胶有限公司	86	天津棉花交易市场有限公司
36	天津钜祥精密模具有限公司	87	天津顶园食品有限公司
37	斯必克冷却技术(天津)有限公司	88	中盛粮油工业(天津)有限公司
38	天津宝洁工业有限公司	89	德芬工业减速机(天津)有限公司
39	天津富奥电装空调有限公司	90	丹佛斯(天津)有限公司
40	威娜化妆品(中国)有限公司	91	天津太平货柜有限公司
41	北海粮油工业(天津)有限公司	92	天津大邱庄薄板有限公司
42	天津可口可乐饮料有限公司	92	天津三电汽车空调有限公司
43	天津顶津食品有限公司	93	弗兰德机电传动(天津)有限公司
44	天津住友商事有限公司	94	天津丰田钢材加工有限公司
45	天津三五汽车部件有限公司	95	必迪艾(天津)轴承有限公司
46	天津电装电子有限公司	96	天津统一工业有限公司
47	天津肯德基有限公司	97	天津高乐高食品有限公司
48	天津合生珠江房地产开发有限公司	98	天津喜来健医疗器械有限公司
49	天津华润啤酒有限公司	99	天津雅马哈电子乐器有限公司
50	天津东海理化汽车部件有限公司	100	爱斯华(天津)华工有限公司

主要统计指标解释

利用外资 包括三部分，一是借用国外资金；二是直接利用投资；三是其他利用投资。外资包括现金、实物、工业产权或专有技术等。凡是本年内实际投资(不论是执行本年签订的协议或是执行过去几年签订的协议)均应计算在内。

借用国外资金 指由我国政府、部门、企业或其他经济组织从境外借入的资金或在境外发行的外币债券。按借款类别不同划分为：外国政府贷款、国际金融组织贷款、外国银行商业贷款、出口信贷和其他：包括对外发行债券、股票等。本年鉴公布的我市的对外借款统计数据中，不含外国及港、澳、台在津投资企业的对外借款。

直接利用投资 指国外及港澳台地区的法人和自然人按照我国有关政策、法规在中国大陆地区以现金、实物、无形资产等各种方式投资于非上市公司中的全部投资及在单个外国投资者所占股权比例不低于10%的上市公司中的投资。

其他利用投资 凡是国外及港澳台地区的法人和自然人按照我国有关政策、法规在中国大陆地区以现金、实物、无形资产等各种方式进行的投资中不属于客商直接投资的部分，均列入本类。

直接利用外资合同外资额 是根据外商投资企业合同(章程)规定，外方投资者应缴付的注册资本。包括外方从企业获得的利润对企业的再投资以及批准的企业投资总额内的外方股东贷款(2002 年以前还包括以企业名义从境内外借入的其他外资)。

实际利用外资 包括借用国外资金、直接利用投资和其他利用投资三部分实际到位的外资。借用国外资金按实际提取或拨交的使用数、直接利用投资按外方实际到位资金统计(以会计师事务所出具的验资报告为准)、其他利用投资按到位数计算。

口岸进出口总值 指天津口岸实际进出的货物总金额。包括天津经营单位和其他省市经营单位经天津口岸实现的进出口货物总额。按海关监管的贸易方式分为：一般贸易实际进出口货物，来料加工装配进出口货物，国家间、联合国及国际组织无偿援助物资和赠送品，华侨、港澳台同胞和外籍华人捐赠品，租赁期满归承租人所有的租赁货物，进料加工进出口货物，边境地方贸易及边境地区小额贸易进出口货物(边民互市贸易除外)，中外合资企业、中外合作经营企业、外商独资经营企业进出口货物和公用物品，到、离岸价格在规定限额以上的进出口货样和广告品(无商业价值、无使用价值和免费提供出口的除外)，从保税仓库提取在中国境内销售的进口货物，以及其他进出口货物。进出口总额用以观察一个国家在对外贸易方面的总规模。我国规定出口货物按离岸价格统计，进口货物按到岸价格统计。

外贸进出口总值 指所有天津进出口经营单位经天津口岸和其他省市口岸进出口货物的总金额。自1999 年 1 月开始使用海关统计数据。

Explanatory Notes on Main Statistical Indicators

Utilization of Foreign Capital includes foreign borrowing, foreign direct investment, and other foreign investment. Foreign capital includes cash, foods, industrial property right, special technique, etc. It includes actual investment in current year or signed in previous years.

Foreign Borrowing refer to funds borrowed from abroad by the Chinese government, departments, enterprises and other economic units, foreign currency bond issued abroad. Grouped by the category of borrowing, it includes (a) loans of foreign governments, (b) loans of international financial institutions, (c) commercial loans of foreign banks, (d) export credit of foreign banks, (e) bonds, shares issued abroad, etc. The data in this yearbook excludes foreign borrowing of foreign funded and Hongkong, Macao and Taiwan funded enterprises.

Foreign Direct Investment refers to the investment inside China by foreign funded and Hongkong, Macao and Taiwan funded enterprises, economic organizations or individuals, following the relevant policies and laws of China and using cash, practicalities technology, for the investment of corporations that are not listed in stock market, share ownership of single foreign investor is not lower than 10%.

Other Investment by Foreign Enterprises refers to the investment except foreign direct investment inside China by foreign funded and Hongkong, Macao and Taiwan funded enterprises, economic organizations or individuals, following the relevant policies and laws of China and using cash, practicalities technology.

Foreign Direct Investment Contracted refer to the total registered capital that according to the contract, foreign investor should provide. It includes re – investment of foreign investor using the profits obtained from enterprise, loans of foreigns shareholder among the total investment (also includes other investment of enterprise borrowed from China and abroad before 2002).

Foreign Capital Actually Used refers to the actual investment of foreign borrowing, foreign direct investment and other investment by foreign enterprises. It includes actual withdraw of foreign borrowing, actual capital of foreign direct investment (in accordance with the capital report of Accountant Services) , actual capital of other investment by foreign enterprises.

Total Imports and Exports at Customs refer to the value of commodities imported into and exported from Tianjin Custom. It includes the value of commodities imported into and exported from Tianjin Custom of Tianjin business units and business units of other provinces(municipalities). Imports and exports trade are the base on customs supervision, being divided into the actual imports and exports from common trade, imported and exported goods under the processing and assembling trades and materials, supplies and gifts as aid given gratis between governments and by the United Nations and other international organizations, and contributions donated by overseas Chinese, compatriots in HongKong and Macao and Chinese with foreign citizenship, leasing commodities owned by tenant at the expiration of leasing period, imported and exported commodities processed with imported materials, commodities trading in border areas (excluding mutual exchange goods) , the imported and exported commodities and articles for public use of the Sino – foreign joint ventures, cooperative enterprises and ventures exclusively with foreign own investment. Also included are import and export of samples and advertising goods for whose CIF or FOB value are beyond the permitted ceiling (excluding goods of no trading or use value and free commodities for export), imported goods sold in China from bonded warehouses and other imported or exported goods. The indicator of the total imports and exports at customs can be used to observe the total size of external trade in a country. In accordance with the stipulation of the Chinese government, imports are calculated at CIF, while exports are calculated at FOB.

Foreign Trade Imports & Exports include imports and exports of business units of Tianjin at Tianjin customs and other customs. The data of customs statistics has been used since January, 1999.

第15篇 CHAPTER 15

金融业

Financial Intermediation

15－1 各类金融机构和人员(2002－2005年)

FINANCIAL INSTITUTIONS AND PERSONNEL,2002－2005

项 目	Item	机 构(个) Institutions(unit)			
		2002	2003	2004	2005
各类金融机构	**Financial Institutions**	**2 850**	**2 837**	**2 833**	**2 874**
银行类机构	**Banking Institutions**	**1 653**	**1 594**	**1 564**	**1 552**
中央银行	Central Banks	2	2	2	2
政策性银行	Policy Banks	10	10	10	10
商业银行	Commercial Banks	1 627	1 567	1 537	1 526
国有独资商业银行	State－owned Sole Commercial Banks	1 361	1 279	1 238	1 215
股份制商业银行	Share－holding Commercial Banks	104	108	119	128
天津城市商业银行	Tianjin City Commercial Banks	160	180	180	180
渤海银行	China Bohai Bank				1
中德住房储蓄银行	Sino－German Bausparkasse				1
农村合作银行	Tianjin Rural Cooperative Bank				1
外资银行	Foreign Funded Banks	14	15	15	14
非银行类机构	**Non－banking Institutions**	**1 197**	**1 243**	**1 269**	**1 322**
保险公司	Insurance Companies	311	369	386	371
信托投资公司	Trust Investment Companies	3	2	2	2
证券经营公司	Securities Business Companies	85	78	79	79
农村信用社	Rural Credit Cooperatives	507	503	511	516
财务公司	Financial Affairs Companies	1	1	1	1
邮局储蓄所	Savings Deposit Offices of Postal Offices	286	286	286	349
金融资产管理公司	Finance Assets Supervision Corporation	4	4	4	4

项 目	Item	人 员(人) Personnel(person)			
		2002	2003	2004	2005
各类金融机构	**Financial Institutions**	**41 765**	**46 436**	**43 625**	**46 721**
银行类机构	**Banking Institutions**	**29 293**	**32 777**	**30 991**	**31 411**
中央银行	Central Banks	678	575	558	571
政策性银行	Policy Banks	288	292	364	359
商业银行	Commercial Banks	28 059	31 630	29 778	30 104
国有独资商业银行	State－owned Sole Commercial Banks	22 658	25 563	23 810	23 382
股份制商业银行	Share－holding Commercial Banks	1 934	2 362	2 563	3 061
天津城市商业银行	Tianjin City Commercial Banks	4 032	3 705	3 405	3 353
渤海银行	China Bohai Bank				105
中德住房储蓄银行	Sino－German Bausparkasse				36
农村合作银行	Tianjin Rural Cooperative Bank				167
外资银行	Foreign Funded Banks	268	280	291	377
非银行类机构	**Non－banking Institutions**	**12 472**	**13 659**	**12 634**	**15 310**
保险公司	Insurance Companies	3 246	5 000	3 753	4 735
信托投资公司	Trust Investment Companies	376	277	239	269
证券经营公司	Securities Business Companies	3 000	3 000	2 000	2 100
农村信用社	Rural Credit Cooperatives	4 701	4 701	4 857	5 333
财务公司	Financial Affairs Companies	16	16	16	16
邮局储蓄所	Savings Deposit Offices of Postal Offices	800	435	1 550	2 634
金融资产管理公司	Finance Assets Supervision Corporation	333	230	219	223

15－2 中资金融机构人民币各项存贷款余额(1990－2005年)

RMB SAVING DEPOSITS AND LOANS OF CHINESE FINANCIAL INSTITUTIONS, 1990－2005

单位:亿元 (100 million yuan)

年份 Year	存款合计 Total Deposits	企业存款 Deposits of Enterprises	财政性存款 Treasury Deposits	储蓄存款 Savings Deposits	农业存款 Agricultural Deposits	信托及其他类存款 Trust Deposits and Others	贷款合计 Total Loans	#工业贷款 Industrial Loans
1990	263.21	86.66	19.15	126.92	9.42	21.07	415.91	136.49
1991	336.56	106.84	24.73	163.18	13.15	28.67	487.43	158.14
1992	467.81	157.39	23.50	202.66	18.51	65.75	624.82	182.23
1993	586.12	193.71	23.78	269.70	21.75	77.19	768.57	223.91
1994	800.56	301.12	24.26	394.50	18.26	62.43	927.05	248.74
1995	1 079.97	385.21	37.59	549.97	22.87	84.33	1 113.95	289.50
1996	1 399.06	527.68	28.54	724.91	25.82	98.64	1 357.38	340.91
1997	1 634.95	638.88	26.22	863.36	28.76	77.73	1 502.91	379.86
1998	1 860.84	655.38	12.53	1 020.14	34.28	138.50	1 629.12	407.52
1999	2 060.02	736.03	45.78	1 130.19	37.94	110.08	1 825.26	429.22
2000	2 281.55	871.31	53.97	1 172.40	44.10	139.76	1 863.60	369.25
2001	2 562.55	946.89	63.82	1 284.95	56.32	210.56	2 159.86	433.16
2002	3 018.26	1 115.35	102.30	1 486.38	73.86	240.37	2 519.04	450.32
2003	4 033.51	1 542.75	136.89	1 825.32	164.72	363.83	3 426.02	429.13
2004	4 729.61	1 823.00	182.03	2 116.73	157.14	450.71	3 821.38	405.46
2005	5 684.40	2 185.23	234.75	2 462.41	163.66	638.35	4 417.45	425.74

年份 Year	#商业贷款 Commercial Loans	#建筑业贷款 Construction Loans	#私营及个体贷款 Loans to Private and Individuals	#乡镇企业贷款 Loans to Township Enterprises	#农业贷款 Agricultural Loans	#中长期贷款 Medium－term & Long－term Loans	#信托类贷款及其他 Trust Loans and Others
1990	162.49	8.23	0.09	10.75	27.29	50.00	20.57
1991	173.04	8.86	0.11	12.20	36.26	73.88	24.95
1992	196.20	9.75	0.14	13.50	49.78	105.67	67.56
1993	223.91	10.76	0.80	16.18	65.83	143.93	83.25
1994	219.58	13.06	1.44	67.29	16.58	210.87	71.98
1995	242.71	16.18	3.47	85.70	22.46	262.01	85.70
1996	278.76	31.82	11.48	106.12	29.66	305.50	116.22
1997	297.74	36.28	8.63	125.32	41.46	298.81	67.61
1998	295.91	37.38	10.11	147.17	50.65	302.69	94.42
1999	292.08	36.00	10.15	163.59	51.33	405.04	113.77
2000	235.64	44.85	15.64	163.14	42.65	431.27	113.89
2001	249.95	60.84	38.96	174.28	47.55	637.76	137.91
2002	240.68	77.45	34.76	192.22	74.99	846.93	179.49
2003	275.22	95.23	31.50	239.98	132.30	1 468.35	283.53
2004	261.13	80.47	26.89	278.72	175.25	1 789.78	278.48
2005	255.02	80.85	36.15	311.35	172.37	2 203.93	302.80

注:1.中长期贷款1994年以前为固定资产贷款,1998年起中长期贷款中含中期流动资金贷款。2.农业存款1996年以前为农村存款。3.信托类贷款及其他含票据融资款及垫款。4.15－3表同。

Note: a). Before 1994, medium－term & long－term loans refered to fixed assets loans, they had included medium－term circulating capital loans since 1998. b). Agricultural deposits refered to rural deposits before 1996. c). Trust loans and others include bill financing and all advanced money. d). Same as following table 15－3.

15-3 银行机构人民币存贷款余额(1990-2005年)

RMB SAVING DEPOSITS AND LOANS OF BANKING INSTITUTIONS,1990-2005

单位:亿元 (100 million yuan)

年份 Year	存款合计 Total Deposits	企业存款 Deposits of Enterprises	财政性存款 Treasury Deposits	储蓄存款 Savings Deposits	农业存款 Agricultural Deposits	信托及其他类存款 Trust Deposits and Others	贷款合计 Total Loans	#工业贷款 Industrial Loans
1990	236.31	83.78	19.15	101.88	18.58	12.92	387.72	134.42
1991	297.65	103.33	24.73	130.31	22.86	16.43	449.95	155.69
1992	376.19	141.99	23.50	160.47	24.27	25.96	539.53	178.32
1993	461.52	158.42	23.77	215.28	28.74	35.29	655.99	218.90
1994	596.96	250.75	24.26	317.46	2.31	2.18	788.51	243.47
1995	812.45	321.99	37.59	445.14	2.89	4.83	898.43	283.26
1996	1 071.75	443.35	28.54	593.35	2.59	3.93	1 147.90	332.65
1997	1 415.43	630.45	26.22	741.43	2.70	14.62	1 334.79	379.27
1998	1 605.63	648.00	12.53	880.82	2.78	61.50	1 427.53	406.79
1999	1 801.79	728.74	45.69	975.06	2.89	49.41	1 606.22	428.54
2000	2 000.58	861.62	53.88	1 011.47	2.54	71.07	1 635.99	368.86
2001	2 255.95	934.36	63.67	1 117.34	3.76	136.83	1 918.86	432.23
2002	2 672.47	1 090.57	102.16	1 308.25	3.69	167.80	2 233.48	448.66
2003	3 482.63	1 466.20	136.63	1 593.74	4.33	281.73	2 973.90	427.43
2004	4 096.92	1 763.90	175.18	1 815.25	7.60	334.99	3 301.60	403.82
2005	5 006.21	2 118.82	234.58	2 117.56	5.06	530.19	3 887.17	423.95

年份 Year	#商业贷款 Commercial Loans	#建筑业贷款 Construction Loans	#私营及个体贷款 Loans to Private and Individuals	#乡镇企业贷款 Loans to Township Enterprises	#农业贷款 Agricultural Loans	#中长期贷款 Medium-term & Long-term Loans	#信托类贷款及其他 Trust Loans and Others
1990	160.99	8.23	0.04	10.75	7.86	50.00	15.43
1991	171.22	8.86	0.03	12.20	9.74	73.88	18.34
1992	190.01	9.75	0.03	13.50	11.16	105.67	31.09
1993	210.73	10.76	0.05	16.18	14.20	143.93	41.23
1994	214.48	13.06	0.14	21.00	12.31	203.97	18.82
1995	237.52	16.18	0.10	25.42	16.37	257.00	21.28
1996	271.66	31.82	0.29	35.78	22.66	303.03	37.28
1997	297.74	36.28	8.63	41.29	30.43	297.02	12.53
1998	295.91	37.38	10.11	51.22	35.08	301.56	19.02
1999	292.08	35.99	10.15	57.22	31.64	404.36	34.23
2000	235.64	44.85	15.64	47.34	21.57	430.05	36.89
2001	249.93	60.81	38.96	49.35	19.92	634.26	66.47
2002	240.66	77.45	34.76	53.41	20.35	841.14	109.68
2003	275.20	95.23	31.50	59.10	16.52	1 460.80	167.50
2004	261.11	80.47	22.29	67.62	15.53	1 782.72	167.16
2005	255.02	80.85	32.21	66.89	14.62	2 198.34	211.45

注:自2001年起,银行机构没有信托类存贷款。
Note: Since 2001, banking institutions have no trust loans or deposits.

15－4 中资金融机构现金投放与回笼(1990－2005年)
CASH STATISTICS OF CHINESE FINANCIAL INSTITUTIONS,1990－2005

单位:亿元 (100 million yuan)

年 份 Year	现金收入 Cash Income	现金支出 Cash Expenditures	投 放 Currency Issuance
1990	239.92	242.00	2.08
1991	287.09	295.37	8.28
1992	407.75	418.72	10.97
1993	646.66	656.34	9.68
1994	892.28	893.48	1.20
1995	1 285.46	1 275.46	－10.00
1996	1 696.42	1 704.67	8.25
1997	2 637.49	2 636.20	－1.29
1998	3 209.96	3 218.63	8.67
1999	3 673.32	3 689.52	16.20
2000	4 277.52	4 268.38	－9.14
2001	4 782.14	4 793.23	11.09
2002	5 081.47	5 126.79	45.32
2003	6 561.94	6 651.99	90.05
2004	8 689.80	8 779.70	89.90
2005	9 675.45	9 779.48	104.03

15－5 中外资金融机构存贷款余额(2002—2005年)
SAVING DEPOSITS AND LOANS BALANCE OF CHINESE & FOREIGN FINANCIAL INSTITUTIONS,2002—2005

单位:亿元、亿美元 (100 million yuan、USD 100 million)

项 目	Item	2002	2003	2004	2005
存 款 余 额(折人民币)	**Saving Deposits Balance (as RMB)**	**3 358.89**	**4 362.60**	**5 139.72**	**6 090.50**
中资金融机构	Chinese Financial Institutions	3 297.79	4 317.98	5 044.07	5 990.37
人民币	RMB	3 018.26	4 033.51	4 729.61	5 684.40
外 汇	Foreign Exchange	33.77	34.37	37.99	37.91
外资金融机构	Foreign－funded Financial Institutions	61.08	44.63	95.65	100.13
外 汇	Foreign Exchange	7.23	4.26	9.06	8.48
人民币	RMB	1.24	9.37	20.67	31.69
贷 款 余 额(折人民币)	**Loans Balance (as RMB)**	**2 868.93**	**3 791.22**	**4 146.49**	**4 722.38**
中资金融机构	Chinese Financial Institutions	2 765.09	3 679.61	4 010.17	4 571.40
人民币	RMB	2 519.04	3 426.02	3 821.38	4 417.45
外 汇	Foreign Exchange	29.72	30.64	22.81	19.08
外资金融机构	Foreign－funded Financial Institutions	103.84	112.76	136.32	150.98
外 汇	Foreign Exchange	12.06	12.77	14.39	13.73
人民币	RMB	4.02	7.06	17.21	40.18

注:2002年汇率为1美元 ＝ 8.2773元人民币;2003年汇率为1美元 ＝ 8.2772元人民币;2004年汇率为1美元 ＝ 8.2765元人民币;2005年汇率为1美元 ＝ 8.0702元人民币。

Note: 1 US$ ＝ 8.2773 Yuan RMB in 2002; 1 US$ ＝ 8.2772 Yuan RMB in 2003; 1 US$ ＝ 8.2765 Yuan RMB in 2004; 1 US$ ＝ 8.0702 Yuan RMB in 2005.

15－6 中外资金融机构本外币信贷资金平衡表
RMB & FOREIGN CURRENCY CREDIT FUNDS BALANCE SHEET OF CHINESE & FOREIGN FINANCIAL INSTITUTIONS

单位：亿元 (100 million yuan)

项 目	Item	2004	2005	2005比2004年增长% Increase Rate in 2005 over 2004
资金来源合计	**All Sources**	**4 488.80**	**5 993.72**	**33.5**
各项存款余额总计	Total Deposits Balance	5 139.72	6 090.50	18.5
企事业存款	Deposits of Enterprises and Institutions	2 058.91	2 448.99	19.0
活期存款	Current Deposits	1 503.70	1 721.98	14.5
定期存款	Fixed Deposits	555.21	727.01	30.9
储蓄存款	Savings Deposits	2 261.49	2 584.40	14.3
活期存款	Current Deposits	667.57	791.54	18.6
定期存款	Fixed Deposits	1 593.92	1 792.86	12.5
信托存款	Trust Deposits	1.40	0.16	-88.6
委托存款	Entrust Deposits	115.52	105.70	-8.5
其他存款	Other Deposits	702.40	951.25	35.4
境外联行存放	External Inter-bank Deposits		44.17	
所有者权益	Owner's Equity	119.38	189.52	53.5
其 他	Others	-770.30	-330.47	
资金运用合计	**All Uses**	**4 488.80**	**5 993.72**	**33.5**
各项贷款余额总计	Total Loans Balance	4 146.49	4 722.38	15.3
短期贷款	Short-term Loans	1 923.29	2 077.95	11.1
中长期贷款	Medium-term and Long-term Loans	1 849.97	2 255.23	21.9
信托贷款	Trust Loans	8.77	6.72	-21.2
委托贷款	Entrust Loans	100.43	82.94	-17.4
其他贷款	Other Loans	74.15	71.52	-3.5
票据融资	Bill Financing	184.79	225.02	21.8
各项垫款	Money Advanced for sb. to be Paid Back Later	5.09	3.00	11.6
存放境内联行	Internal Inter-bank Deposits		979.44	
有价证券及投资	Securities & Investment	342.31	291.90	-14.7

注：表中增长速度按可比口径计算。15－7、15－8、15－9、15－14表同。
Note: The increase rates are calculated at comparable coverage. Same as following table 15－7, 15－8, 15－9, 15－14.

15－7 中资金融机构人民币存贷款情况(年末余额)
RMB SAVING DEPOSITS AND LOANS BALANCE OF CHINESE FINANCIAL INSTITUTIONS (YEAR－END)

单位:亿元 (100 million yuan)

项　目	Item	2003	2004	2005	2005比2004年增长% Increase Rate in 2005 over 2004
各项存款总计	**Total Deposits**	**4 033.51**	**4 729.61**	**5 684.40**	**20.2**
企业存款	Deposits of Enterprises	1 542.75	1 823.00	2 185.23	19.9
财政性存款	Treasury Deposits	136.89	182.03	234.75	29.0
储蓄存款	Savings Deposits	1 825.32	2 116.73	2 462.41	16.3
#定期储蓄	Fixed Deposits	1 294.04	1 475.47	1 697.42	15.0
农业存款	Agricultural Deposits	164.72	157.14	163.66	4.2
信托类存款	Trust Deposits	81.92	118.20	106.45	－9.9
其他类存款	Other Deposits	281.91	332.51	531.90	37.5
各项贷款总计	**Total Loans**	**3 426.02**	**3 821.38**	**4 417.45**	**17.2**
短期贷款	Short－term Loans	1 674.14	1 753.12	1 910.72	12.2
工业贷款	Industrial Loans	429.13	405.46	425.74	12.6
商业贷款	Commercial Loans	275.22	261.13	255.02	4.9
建筑业贷款	Construction Loans	95.23	80.47	80.85	4.6
私营及个体贷款	Loans to Private and Individuals	31.50	26.89	36.15	34.4
乡镇企业贷款	Loans to Township Enterprises	239.98	278.72	311.35	11.6
农业贷款	Agricultural Loans	132.30	175.25	172.37	－1.4
三资企业贷款	Loans to Hongkong, Macao, Taiwan and Foreign－funded Enterprises	83.41	63.24	38.86	－23.3
其他短期贷款	Other Short－term Loans	387.37	461.96	590.38	27.9
中期流动资金贷款	Medium－term Circulating Capital Loans	158.43	143.53		
中长期贷款	Medium－term and Long－term Loans	1 309.92	1 646.25	2 203.93	23.4
#技术改造贷款	Loans to Technical Innovation	26.71	18.54	15.27	－13.2
基本建设贷款	Loans to Capital Construction	806.36	946.21	1 229.95	30.5
信托类贷款	Trust Loans	87.90	108.82	90.61	－16.7
票据融资	Bill Financing	187.55	164.62	209.54	27.3
各项垫款	Money Advanced for sb. to be Paid Back Late	8.08	5.04	2.65	16.8

注:自2005年起,中期流动资金贷款并入中长期贷款。15－8表同。
Note: Since 2005, medium－term circulating capital loans have been merged into medium－term and long－term loans. Same as following table 15－8.

15-8 银行机构人民币存贷款情况(年末余额)

RMB SAVING DEPOSITS AND LOANS BALANCE OF BANKING INSTITUTIONS(YEAR-END)

单位:亿元 (100 million yuan)

项目	Item	2003	2004	2005	2005比2004年增长% Increase Rate in 2005 over 2004
各项存款总计	**Total Deposits**	**3 482.63**	**4 096.92**	**5 006.21**	**22.2**
企业存款	Deposits of Enterprises	1 466.20	1 763.90	2 118.82	20.1
财政性存款	Treasury Deposits	136.63	175.18	234.58	33.9
储蓄存款	Savings Deposits	1 593.74	1 815.25	2 117.56	16.7
#定期储蓄	Fixed Deposits	1 132.10	1 267.62	1 463.19	15.4
农业存款	Agricultural Deposits	4.33	7.60	5.06	-33.4
其他类存款	Other Deposits	281.73	334.99	530.19	61.4
各项贷款总计	**Total Loans**	**2 973.90**	**3 301.60**	**3 887.17**	**17.7**
短期贷款	Short-term Loans	1 345.60	1 354.72	1 477.38	9.1
工业贷款	Industrial Loans	427.43	403.82	423.95	5.0
商业贷款	Commercial Loans	275.20	261.11	255.02	-2.3
建筑业贷款	Construction Loans	95.23	80.47	80.85	0.5
私营及个体贷款	Loans to Private and Individuals	31.50	22.29	32.21	37.8
乡镇企业贷款	Loans to Township Enterprises	59.10	67.62	66.89	-1.1
农业贷款	Agricultural Loans	16.52	15.53	14.62	-5.9
三资企业贷款	Loans to Hongkong, Macao, Taiwan and Foreign-funded Enterprises	83.41	63.24	38.83	-38.6
其他短期贷款	Other Short-term Loans	357.21	440.64	565.01	28.5
中期流动资金贷款	Medium-term Circulating Capital Loans	158.43	143.53		
中长期贷款	Medium-term and Long-term Loans	1 302.37	1 636.19	2 198.34	23.5
#技术改造贷款	Loans to Technical Innovation	26.71	18.54	15.27	-17.6
基本建设贷款	Loans to Capital Construction	806.36	946.21	1 229.95	30.0
票据融资	Bill Financing	159.42	162.12	208.80	28.8
各项垫款	Money Advanced for sb. to be Paid Back Later	8.08	5.04	2.65	-47.4

15－9 中资金融机构现金收入和支出
CASH INCOME AND EXPENDITURES OF CHINESE FINANCIAL INSTITUTIONS

单位:亿元 (100 million yuan)

项　目	Item	2003	2004	2005	2005 比2004年增长% Increase Rate in 2005 over 2004
现金收入总计	**Total Cash Income**	**6 561.94**	**8 689.80**	**9 675.45**	**11.3**
商品销售收入	Income from Commodity Sales	1 122.42	1 302.97	1 464.86	12.4
服务事业收入	Income from Service Trade	281.56	334.30	379.40	13.5
税款收入	Income from Taxes	30.66	34.56	53.74	55.5
城乡个体经营收入	Income from Urban and Rural Individual Business	295.27	371.88	433.90	16.7
储蓄存款收入	Income from Savings Deposits	4 233.60	5 779.66	6 640.71	14.9
其他金融机构收入	Income from Other Financial Institutions	104.87	146.99	93.09	－36.7
居民归还贷款收入	Income from Repayment of Loans by Residents	91.78	148.93	192.10	29.0
汇兑收入	Income from Remittances	36.07	44.11	42.02	－4.7
有价证券收入	Income from Securities	28.04	18.77	11.35	－39.5
其他收入	Others	337.67	507.63	364.28	－28.2
现金支出总计	**Total Cash Expenditures**	**6 651.99**	**8 779.70**	**9 779.48**	**11.4**
工资性支出	Wages	582.02	647.14	676.52	4.5
#国家职工工资奖金	Wages and Bonuses to the Staff and Workers from Government	269.13	298.07	300.72	0.9
国家对个人其他支出	Other Payments to Individuals from Government	128.81	115.78	114.27	－1.3
其他单位工资性支出	Wages from Other Units	171.73	215.43	243.73	13.0
农副产品采购支出	Purchases of Agricultural and Sideline Products	112.90	142.28	157.82	10.9
工矿及其他产品采购支出	Expenditure for Purchases of Industrial and Mineral Products	88.07	131.43	167.37	27.4
行政企事业管理费支出	Government and Enterprises Overhead	351.52	406.13	451.35	11.1
城乡个体经营支出	Expenditure for Individual Business	569.39	615.41	688.30	11.8
储蓄存款支出	Expenditure for Savings Deposits	4 303.18	5 942.67	6 981.65	17.5
其他金融机构支出	Expenditure for Other Financial Institutions	96.22	96.73	71.04	－26.6
居民提取贷款支出	Expenditure for Loans by Residents	119.38	171.49	163.15	－4.9
汇兑支出	Expenditure for Remittances	16.36	18.02	22.51	24.9
有价证券支出	Expenditure for Securities	22.90	30.18	20.78	－31.2
其他支出	Others	390.05	578.22	378.99	－34.5
货币投放(＋)或回笼(－)	**Currency Issuance(＋) and Cash Withdrawal(－)**	**＋90.05**	**＋89.90**	**＋104.03**	**15.7**

15－10 金融机构法定存款利率表(1998－2005年)

NOMINAL INTEREST RATES ON DEPOSITS OF FINANCIAL INSTITUTIONS,1998－2005

单位:年利率% (annual interest rate %)

项目	Item	1998年3月25日 Mar. 25,1998	1998年7月1日 Jul. 1,1998	1998年12月7日 Dec. 7,1998
个人人民币储蓄存款	**RMB Household Deposits**			
活期	**Current Deposits**	**1.71**	**1.44**	**1.44**
定期	**Fixed Deposits**			
三个月	3 Months	2.88	2.79	2.79
半年	6 Months	4.14	3.96	3.33
一年	1 Year	5.22	4.77	3.78
二年	2 Years	5.58	4.86	3.96
三年	3 Years	6.21	4.95	4.14
五年	5 Years	6.66	5.22	4.50
存本取息、零存整取、整存零取	**Three Conveniens & Flexible Ways of Savings Deposits**			
一年	1 Year	4.14	3.96	3.33
三年	3 Years	5.22	4.77	3.78
五年	5 Years	6.21	4.95	4.14
企业单位存款	**Enterprises Deposits**			
活期	**Current Deposits**	**1.71**	**1.44**	**1.44**
定期	**Fixed Deposits**			
三个月	3 Months	2.88	2.79	2.79
半年	6 Months	4.14	3.96	3.33
一年	1 Year	5.22	4.77	3.78
二年	2 Years	5.58	4.86	3.96
三年	3 Years	6.21	4.95	4.14
五年	5 Years	6.66	5.22	4.50

项目	Item	1999年6月10日 June 10,1999	2002年2月21日 Feb. 21,2002	2004年10月29日 Oct. 29,2004
个人人民币储蓄存款	**RMB Household Deposits**			
活期	**Current Deposits**	**0.99**	**0.72**	**0.72**
定期	**Fixed Deposits**			
三个月	3 Months	1.98	1.71	1.71
半年	6 Months	2.16	1.89	2.07
一年	1 Year	2.25	1.98	2.25
二年	2 Years	2.43	2.25	2.70
三年	3 Years	2.70	2.52	3.24
五年	5 Years	2.88	2.79	3.60
存本取息、零存整取、整存零取	**Three Conveniens & Flexible Ways of Savings Deposits**			
一年	1 Year	1.98	1.71	1.71
三年	3 Years	2.16	1.89	2.07
五年	5 Years	2.25	1.98	2.25
企业单位存款	**Enterprises Deposits**			
活期	**Current Deposits**	**0.99**	**0.72**	**0.72**
定期	**Fixed Deposits**			
三个月	3 Months	1.98	1.71	1.71
半年	6 Months	2.16	1.89	2.07
一年	1 Year	2.25	1.98	2.25
二年	2 Years	2.43	2.25	2.70
三年	3 Years	2.70	2.52	3.24
五年	5 Years	2.88	2.79	3.60

15-11 金融机构法定贷款利率表(1998-2005年)

NOMINAL INTEREST RATES ON LOANS OF FINANCIAL INSTITUTIONS,1998-2005

单位:年利率% (annual interest rate %)

项目	Item	1998年3月25日 Mar. 25,1998	1998年7月1日 Jul. 1,1998	1998年12月7日 Dec.7,1998
流动资金贷款	**Loans for Circulating Funds**			
一般流动资金	General Circulating Funds			
半年	6 Months	7.02	6.57	6.12
一年	1 Year	7.92	6.93	6.39
个体工商户贷款	Loans to Individuals Engaged in Industrial and Business	在7.92%基础上上浮10% 10% Floating Over 7.92%	在6.93%基础上上浮10% 10% Floating Over 6.93%	
长期贷款	**Long-term Loans**			
基本建设贷款	Loans to Capital Construction			
一年以上至三年	1-3 Years	9.00	7.11	6.66
三年以上至五年	3-5 Years	9.72	7.65	7.20
五年以上至十年	5-10 Years	10.35	8.01	7.56

项目	Item	1999年6月10日 June 10,1999	2002年2月21日 Feb.21,2002	2004年10月29日 Otc.29,2004	2005年3月17日 Mar.17,2005
短期贷款	**Short-term Loans**				
一般流动资金	General Circulating Funds				
半年以内	Less than 6 Months	5.58	5.04	5.22	5.22
一年(六个月至一年)	1 Year(6 months to 1 year)	5.85	5.31	5.58	5.58
长期贷款	**Long-term Loans**				
基本建设贷款	Loans to Capital Construction				
一年以上至三年	1-3 Years	5.94	5.49	5.76	5.76
三年以上至五年	3-5 Years	6.03	5.58	5.85	5.85
五年以上至十年	5-10 Years	6.21	5.76	6.12	6.12
住房贷款	**Housing Loans**				
个人住房公积金贷款	Accumulation Fund Loans				
五年以内	Less than 5 Years	4.14	3.60	3.78	3.96
五年以上	More than 5 Years	4.59	4.05	4.23	4.41
商业银行自营性住房贷款	Self-supported by Commercial Banks				
半年以内	Less than 6 Months				4.698
一年(六个月至一年)	1 Year(6 months to 1 year)				5.022
一年以上至三年	1-3 Years				5.184
五年以内	Less than 5 Years	5.31	4.77	4.95	5.265
五年以上	More than 5 Years	5.58	5.04	5.31	5.508

注:1、从1998年11月起,金融机构对小企业贷款利率可在法定贷款利率基础上上浮20%。大中企业上浮10%。农村信用社贷款利率最高可上浮50%;金融机构贷款最低下浮10%。2、从1999年9月起,金融机构对中小企业贷款利率可在法定贷款利率基础上上浮30%,对大型企业贷款最高上浮10%;金融机构贷款贷款最低下浮10%。3、从2005年3月17日起,自营性个人住房贷款利率改按商业性贷款利率执行,上限放开,实行下限管理,下限利率水平为相应期限档次贷款基准利率的0.9倍。

Note:a)As of November 1998,the lending rate for small-sized enterprises could be 20% higher than nominal interest rates, and the lending rate for medium-and large-sized enterprises could be 10% higher than nominal interest rates. For all financial institutions,the lending rate could be 10% lower than nominal interest rates,while,for rural credit cooperatives,the lending rate could be 50% higher than nominal interest rates. b)As of September 1999,the lending rate for medium-and small-sized enterprises could be 30% higher than nominal interest rates;for large-sized enterprises ,the lending rate could be as much as 10% higher than nominal interest rates. For all financial institutions,the lending rate could be 10% lower than nominal interest rates. c)As of March 17 2005,the loan interest rate of self-supported by Commercial Banks is running as commercial loan interest rates,the upper limit loan interest rate is opened,the lower limit loan interest rate is managed, the lower limit loan interest rate is 0.9 times to the nominal interest rates at the same time grouping.

15－12 保险机构和人员(2005年)
INSURANCE INSTITUTIONS AND PERSONNEL,2005

项目	Item	机构(个) Institutions(unit)	人员(人) Personnel(person)
保险机构	**Insurance Institutions**	**431**	**26 288**
保险公司机构	**Insurance Company**	**371**	**25 691**
#总公司	Parent Company	3	3 347
# 中外合资、外资公司	Insurance Company Branches of Joint－venture with Foreign Investment and Sole Foreign Investment	2	3 263
分公司	Divisions	17	5 575
支公司	Sub－divisions	99	7 748
营销服务部	Operation & Service Offices	233	9 021
专业保险中介机构	**Professional Insurance Intermediary Institutions**	**56**	**576**
保险代理公司	Insurance Agent Companies	43	458
保险公估公司	Insurance Assessment Companies	4	42
保险经纪公司	Insurance Broker Companies	9	76
外资保险公司代表处	**Agencies of Foreign－founded Insurance Companies**	**4**	**21**

注:1、本表中支公司包含中心支公司。2 本表中保险机构从业人员含营销人员。
Note:a) In this table, sub－divisions insurance companies include center sub－divisions insurance companies. b) Personnel employed in insurance institutions in this table include operation and selling personnel.

15－13 保险业务主要指标(1990－2005年)
MAIN INDICATORS OF INSURANCE BUSINESS,1990－2005

年份 Year	保险金额(亿元) Amount Insured (100 million yuan)	保费(万元) Premium (10 000 yuan)	#人寿险 Life Insurance	#财产险 Property Insurance	赔款及给付(万元) Claim and Payment (10 000 yuan)	#人寿险 Life Insurance	#财产险 Property Insurance
1990	918.00	34 327	4 384	17 896	9 827	334	5 237
1991	1 009.18	39 474	5 832	20 222	14 715	894	8 651
1992	1 136.06	49 624	10 185	23 639	22 843	1 637	12 963
1993	1 514.16	67 412	14 492	32 496	34 689	4 866	17 885
1994	2 434.06	100 561	24 628	47 147	47 434	6 642	27 405
1995	2 274.74	123 655	31 588	61 338	52 985	6 545	30 973
1996	2 488.21	171 768	63 373	74 399	62 613	10 186	33 257
1997	3 306.04	243 377	125 327	112 401	83 528	18 334	61 900
1998	3 949.15	271 654	161 097	110 557	70 075	14 206	55 869
1999	4 848.10	291 382	175 804	115 578	69 163	14 703	54 460
2000	3 696.19	314 663	191 786	122 877	71 950	7 714	64 236
2001	5 176.91	417 049	276 050	140 999	119 062	56 364	62 698
2002	5 632.35	649 698	505 966	143 732	114 818	46 513	68 305
2003	6 497.87	753 098	597 450	155 648	173 608	72 493	101 115
2004	9 852.79	809 874	622 284	187 590	174 178	77 905	96 273
2005	12 141.02	906 391	585 605	217 762	174 637	37 163	107 353

15－14 保险业务情况

BASIC INDICATORS OF INSURANCE BUSINESS

项　目	Item	2004	2005	2005 比2004年 增长% Increase Rate in 2005 over 2004
保险金额(亿元)	**Amount Insured (100 million yuan)**	**9 852.79**	**12 141.02**	**59.6**
财产保险	Property Insurance	6 094.51	8 078.20	32.6
人寿保险	Life Insurance	3 758.28	4 062.82	14.6
保　费(万元)	**Premium (10 000 yuan)**	**811 117.06**	**906 390.56**	**11.8**
财产保险	Property Insurance	187 577.13	217 762.09	16.1
#机动车辆保险	Motor Vehicle Insurance	117 584.89	128 986.50	9.7
人寿保险	Life Insurance	538 836.20	585 604.88	8.7
人身意外伤害保险	Unforeseen Human Injury Insurance	14 044.99	17 864.63	27.2
健康保险	Health Insurance	70 658.74	85 158.95	20.5
赔款及给付额(万元)	**Claim and Payment (10 000 yuan)**	**174 177.81**	**174 637.17**	**0.3**
财产保险	Property Insurance	96 273.78	107 353.40	11.5
#机动车辆保险	Motor Vehicle Insurance	71 345.24	80 132.57	12.3
人寿保险	Life Insurance	44 711.25	37 163.21	－16.9
人身意外伤害保险	Unforeseen Human Injury Insurance	5 298.99	4 935.27	－6.9
健康保险	Health Insurance	27 893.79	25 185.29	－9.7
保险密度(元)	**Insurance Density(yuan)**	**809.17**	**869.02**	**7.4**
财产保险	Property Insurance	187.43	209.20	11.6
人寿保险	Life Insurance	621.74	654.54	5.3
保险深度(%)	**Insurance Depth(%)**	**2.76**	**2.47**	**－10.5**
财产保险	Property Insurance	0.64	0.61	－4.7
人寿保险	Life Insurance	2.12	1.86	－12.3
赔付率(%)	**Claim and Payment Rate(%)**	**21.51**	**19.27**	**－10.4**
财产保险	Property Insurance	51.32	48.88	－4.8
人寿保险	Life Insurance	12.52	9.58	－23.5

注：人寿保险金额为期末有效保险金额。
Note: Amount insured of life insurance is the efficiency amount insured at the end of term.

15－15　外资(合资)银行、保险公司在津分行、代表处一览(2005年)

BRANCHES OR OFFICES OF FOREIGN INVESTMENT(JOINT VENTURE) BANKS AND INSURANCE COMPANIES IN TIANJIN,2005

名　称 Name	行长、首席代表 Director	办公地址 Address
英国渣打银行有限责任公司天津分行	石新宇	天津津汇广场20层
Standard Chartered Bank Tianjin Branch	Edward	20 Floor Exchange Office Tower of Tianjin
法国巴黎银行有限公司天津分行	宋宝成	天津国际大厦16层
BNP Paribas Tianjin Branch	Victor Song	16 Floor International Building of Tianjin
香港上海汇丰银行有限公司天津分行	何伟民	天津远洋广场1层
The Hongkong Shanghai Banking Corporation Limited Tianjin Branch	Ho Wai Man	1 Floor Ocean Shipping Plaza of Tianjin
法国东方汇理银行股份有限公司天津分行	张家麟	天津国际大厦710室
Credit Agricole Indosurz Tianjin Branch	Charles Chang	Rm. 710 International Building of Tianjin
法国兴业银行有限公司天津分行	汪雁龄	天津河川大厦22层
Societe Generale Tianjin Branch	Denny Wong	22 Floor Innotec Tower of Tianjin
新加坡华侨银行有限公司天津分行	陈殿升	天津国际大厦511室
Oversea－Chinese Banking Corporation Ltd. Tianjin Branch	Tan Tian Seng	Rm. 511 International Building of Tianjin
美国摩根大通银行有限公司天津分行	佟静星	天津国际大厦14层
J.P.Morgan Chase Bank N.A,Tianjin Branch	Charles Tong	14 Floor International Building of Tianjin
韩国外换银行股份有限公司天津分行	李光铉	天津利顺德饭店1层
Korea Exchange Bank Tianjin Branch	Lee Kwang Hyun	1 Floor Astor Hotel of Tianjin
韩国朝兴银行股份有限公司天津分行	朴成根	天津国际大厦1901室
Cho Hung Bank Tianjin Branch	Park Sung Geun	Rm. 1901 International Building of Tianjin
日本三井住友银行股份有限公司天津分行	长冈令文	天津国际大厦1210室
Sumitomo Mitsui Banking Corporation Tianjin Branch	Nagaoka Norifumi	Rm. 1210 International Building of Tianjin
日本日联银行股份有限公司天津分行	山内一英	天津国际大厦811室
UFJ Bank Limited Tianjin Branch	Yamauchi Kazuhide	Rm. 811 International Building of Tianjin
韩国中小企业银行有限公司天津分行	金龙满	天津国际大厦911室
Industrial Bank of Korea Tianjin Branch	Kim Yong Man	Rm.911 International Building of Tianjin

15－15 续表 Continued

名　称 Name	行长、首席代表 Director	办公地址 Address
日本东京三菱银行股份有限公司天津分行	平山亮	天津国际大厦 21 层
The Bank of Tokyo－Mitsubishi Ltd.,Tianjin Branch	Ryo Hirayama	21 Floor International Building of Tianjin
美国花旗银行有限公司天津分行	沈筑非	天津津汇广场 1801 室
Citibank,N.A. Tianjin Branch	Fred Shen	Rm. 1801 Exchange Office Tower of Tianjin
中德住房储蓄银行	岳慕礼	天津河西区南京路 19 号增 1 号
Sino－German Bausparkasse	Joachim Dumitsch	19－1 Nanjing Road Hexi District Tianjin
星展银行(香港)有限公司天津代表处	李　虹	天津津汇广场 1902 室
DBS Bank (Hongkong) Limited,Tianjin Representative Office	Lillian H li	Rm. 1902 Exchange Tower of Tianjin
日本瑞穗实业银行股份有限公司天津代表处	孙国贤	天津国际大厦 2202 室
Mizuho Corporate Bank Ltd.,Tianjin Representative Office	Guo Xian Sun	Rm. 2202 International Building of Tianjin
荷兰银行有限公司天津代表处	许　燕	天津国际大厦 718 室
ABN AMRO Bank N.V.,Tianjin Rep. Office	Jennifer Xu	Rm. 718 International Building of Tianjin
东亚银行有限公司天津代表处	栗艳冰	天津国际大厦 907 室
The Bank of East Asia Limited,Tianjin Representative Office	Judy	Rm. 907 International Building of Tianjin
日本三井住友海上火灾保险公司天津代表处	山本猛志	天津国际大厦 2408 室
Mitsui Sumitomo Insurance Co.,Ltd. Tianjin Representative Office	Yama Moto Takeshi	Rm. 2408 International Building of Tianjin
日本东京海上日动火灾保险公司天津代表处	瓜生护	天津国际大厦 2201 室
The Tokio Marine and Nichido Fire Insurance Co.,Ltd. Tianjin Representative Office	Uriu Mamoru	Rm. 2201 International Building of Tianjin
爱和谊保险公司天津代表处	村中弘幸	天津国际大厦 1609 室
Aioi Insurance Co.,Ltd. Tianjin Representative Office	Hiroyuki Muranaka	Rm. 1609 International Building of Tianjin
裕利安宜信用保险股份公司天津代表处	王　洁	天津津汇广场 905 室
Euler Hermes Kreditversicherungs－AG Tianjin Representative Office	John Wang	Rm. 905 Exchange Office Tower of Tianjin

主要统计指标解释

保险密度　为按常住人口计算的人均保费收入。

保险深度　指保费收入相当于国内生产总值的比例。

存款　指企业、机关、团体或居民根据资金必须收回的原则，把货币资金存入金融机构保管并取得一定利息的一种信用活动形式。根据存款对象的不同可划分为企业存款、财政性存款、城乡储蓄存款、农村存款、信托及其他存款等，它是银行信贷资金的主要来源。

贷款　指金融机构根据资金必须归还的原则，按一定利率，为企业、个人等提供资金的一种信用活动形式。我国银行贷款分为工业贷款、农业贷款、商业贷款、建筑业贷款、私营和个体贷款、乡镇企业贷款、中长期贷款、信托及其他贷款等。

保险金额　指保险人承担赔偿或者给付保险金责任的最高限额。

保费　指投保人为取得保险人在约定范围内所承担赔偿责任而支付给保险人的费用。

赔款　指保险人根据保险合同的规定，向被保险人支付的赔偿保险责任损失的金额。

给付　包括死伤医疗给付和满期给付。死伤医疗给付是指保险人根据人寿保险及长期健康保险合同的规定，因被保险人在保险期内发生保险责任范围内的保险事故支付给被保险人（或受益人）的金额。满期给付是指被保险人生存期满，保险人按人寿保险合同规定支付给被保险人的满期保险金额。

Explanatory Notes on Main Statistical Indicators

Insurance Density refers to per capita premiums which is based on permanent resident population.

Insurance Depth refers to the proportion of premiums to gross domestic product.

Deposit is a form of credit by which enterprises, institutions, organizations or households can put money into banks and other credit institutions for safekeeping and interest earning under the principle of free withdrawal. According to different depositors, deposits are divided into enterprise deposits, treasury deposits, urban and rural savings deposits, rural deposits, entrust and other deposits. Deposits are major sources of credit funds of banks.

Loan is a form of credit by which banks and other credit institutions provide funds at certain interest rate to enterprises and individuals in the light of the principle of unconditional repayment. Loans from Chinese banks include industry loans, agriculture loans, commerce loans, construction loans, loans to private and individuals, township enterprises loans, medium & long term loans, entrust and other loans.

Amount Insured refers to the maximum that the insurant will get for the claim of the case insured.

Premium is the fee paid by the insurant to the insurer to obtain the obligation of compensation from the insurance within the agreed terms.

Settled Claim is the compensation paid by the insurer to insurant in accordance with the insurance contract.

Payment includes payment for death, injury or medical treatment and mature payment. Payment for death, injury or medical treatment refers to the money paid to insurant (or the beneficiary) in accordance with the life or health insurance contract when the insurant encounters accidents within the insured period covered in the contract. Mature payment refers to the mature payment to the insurant in accordance with the life insurance contract at the end of the insured period.

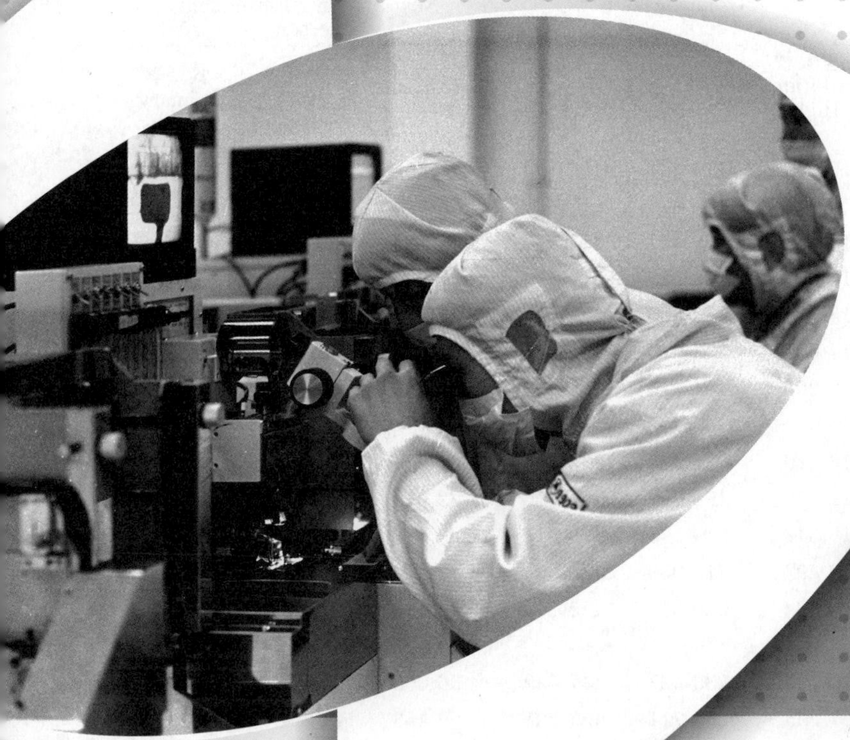

第16篇
CHAPTER 16

教育和科技
Education and Science & Technology

16－1 各级学校数、学生数和教职工数(1990－2005年)

SCHOOLS,STUDENTS AND TEACHERS BY LEVEL OF SCHOOL,1990－2005

年份 Year	学校数(所) Number of Schools (unit)			毕业生数(人) Graduates (person)			招生数(人) New Students Enrollment (person)		
	高等学校 Institutions of Higher Education	中等学校 Secondary Schools	小学 Primary Schools	高等学校 Institutions of Higher Education	中等学校 Secondary Schools	小学 Primary Schools	高等学校 Institutions of Higher Education	中等学校 Secondary Schools	小学 Primary Schools
1990	28	1 013	3 259	15 200	119 401	101 398	13 856	151 254	147 349
1991	27	1 003	3 232	15 059	129 497	117 856	14 523	171 048	132 025
1992	26	981	3 238	14 857	130 538	119 529	17 320	173 291	132 209
1993	26	975	3 243	13 494	132 538	121 237	21 678	180 770	143 268
1994	26	991	3 219	14 661	143 373	138 344	21 422	203 277	152 941
1995	25	1 059	3 216	20 203	151 024	156 641	22 055	229 589	148 922
1996	20	1 098	3 185	18 429	156 924	145 705	22 664	227 918	144 438
1997	20	1 108	3 030	19 535	191 798	133 616	22 016	230 692	133 012
1998	20	1 091	2 841	18 342	219 593	166 618	23 678	273 472	115 988
1999	21	1 041	2 642	19 292	216 950	156 584	31 670	254 033	104 452
2000	21	1 006	2 323	19 022	220 099	155 253	45 468	251 777	100 453
2001	33	1 012	1 307	19 103	233 427	147 639	56 066	249 761	95 492
2002	37	978	1 208	27 295	234 711	133 301	69 453	244 181	92 955
2003	37	897	1 136	40 221	244 398	132 022	86 115	259 174	84 963
2004	40	848	1 099	51 666	252 596	114 771	96 182	250 591	81 603
2005	42	803	1 062	69 211	243 305	106 447	103 616	234 837	78 373

年份 Year	在校学生数(人) Students Enrollment (10 000 persons)			教职工数(人) Teachers,Staff and Workers (person)			#专任教师数(人) Full－time Teachers (person)		
	高等学校 Institutions of Higher Education	中等学校 Secondary Schools	小学 Primary Schools	高等学校 Institutions of Higher Education	中等学校 Secondary Schools	小学 Primary Schools	高等学校 Institutions of Higher Education	中等学校 Secondary Schools	小学 Primary Schools
1990	51 039	443 400	855 319	28 821	73 855	56 773	11 121	47 056	47 110
1991	49 900	464 700	865 500	28 686	73 052	58 307	10 704	46 460	47 762
1992	52 127	483 238	872 412	22 338	73 563	59 781	10 391	46 935	49 030
1993	60 247	504 963	887 412	21 907	73 092	61 377	10 160	46 688	50 448
1994	66 672	533 908	896 174				10 170	46 591	51 616
1995	68 080	600 243	884 476	27 421	74 887	62 499	10 490	47 196	51 401
1996	71 354	662 873	879 772	26 203	76 640	62 207	9 811	48 771	51 202
1997	73 630	692 918	877 554	20 775	77 045	62 054	9 589	51 309	51 048
1998	78 651	735 764	826 732	20 349	77 569	60 500	9 496	51 643	49 420
1999	90 450	761 741	773 064	21 001	79 345	59 002	9 647	53 012	48 293
2000	117 690	712 762	717 146	25 952	80 321	56 948	10 137	53 844	46 697
2001	153 998	785 891	665 495	29 953	77 277	55 311	12 552	52 732	45 651
2002	196 892	792 772	627 242	32 019	76 590	54 237	14 175	53 386	44 922
2003	245 213	801 680	585 446	33 371	75 531	52 603	15 553	53 706	43 829
2004	286 145	775 673	554 844	36 400	73 720	50 989	18 973	52 270	42 122
2005	331 553	755 915	533 003	39 434	72 009	49 629	21 670	51 835	41 076

16－2　各级各类学校数、学生数和教职工数

SCHOOLS,STUDENTS AND TEACHERS BY LEVEL AND TYPE OF SCHOOL

学校类别	Item	学校数(所) Number of Schools (unit)		毕业生数(人) Graduates (person)		招生数(人) New Students Enrollment (person)	
		2004	2005	2004	2005	2004	2005
合　计	**Total**	**1 987**	**1 907**	**419 033**	**418 963**	**428 376**	**416 826**
高等学校	Institutions of Higher Education	40	42	51 666	69 211	96 182	103 616
中等专业学校	Specialized Secondary Schools	45	40	26 249	17 250	24 637	25 526
技工学校	Secondary Technical Schools	70	57	13 293	13 550	19 913	17 228
农业、职业中学	Rural,Vocational Secondary Schools	89	66	21 346	18 430	21 246	17 854
普通中学	Regular Secondary Schools	644	640	191 708	194 075	184 795	174 229
高　中	Senior Secondary Schools	230	232	52 635	57 263	72 335	74 449
初　中	Junior Secondary Schools	414	408	139 073	136 812	112 460	99 780
小　学	Primary Schools	1 099	1 062	114 771	106 447	81 603	78 373

学校类别	Item	在校学生数(人) Students Enrollment (person)		教职工数(人) Teachers, Staff and Workers(person)		#专任教师 Full－time Teachers	
		2004	2005	2004	2005	2004	2005
合　计	**Total**	**1 616 662**	**1 620 471**	**161 109**	**161 072**	**113 365**	**114 581**
高等学校	Institutions of Higher Education	286 145	331 553	36 400	39 434	18 973	21 670
中等专业学校	Specialized Secondary Schools	69 542	76 994	6 076	5 707	3 308	3 369
技工学校	Secondary Technical Schools	46 706	47 104	5 814	5 420	3 451	3 278
农业、职业中学	Rural,Vocational Secondary Schools	60 320	55 527	6 607	5 560	4 114	3 651
普通中学	Regular Secondary Schools	599 105	576 290	55 223	55 322	41 397	41 537
高　中	Senior Secondary Schools	198 537	217 180			13 105	14 207
初　中	Junior Secondary Schools	400 568	359 110			28 292	27 330
小　学	Primary Schools	554 844	533 003	50 989	49 629	42 122	41 076

16-3 平均每万人口拥有学生数(2002—2005 年)
NUMBER OF STUDENT ENROLLMENT PER 10 000 POPULATION,2002—2005

单位:人 (person)

项 目	Item	2002	2003	2004	2005
合 计	**Total**	**1 764**	**1 769**	**1 740**	**1 731**
高等学校	Institutions of Higher Education	215	266	308	354
中等学校	Secondary Schools	865	842	835	808
中等专业学校	Specialized Secondary Schools	81	79	75	82
技工学校	Secondary Technical Schools	52	56	51	50
农业、职业中学	Rural,Vocational Schools	72	67	65	59
普通中学	Regular Secondary Schools	660	667	645	616
高 中	Senior Secondary Schools	172	198	214	232
初 中	Junior Secondary Schools	488	469	431	384
小 学	Primary Schools	684	635	597	569

16-4 平均每一教师负担学生数(2002—2005 年)
STUDENT - TEACHER RATIO,2002—2005

单位:人 (person)

项 目	Item	2002	2003	2004	2005
合 计	**Total**	**15**	**14**	**14**	**14**
高等学校	Institutions of Higher Education	14	16	15	15
中等学校	Secondary Schools	16	15	15	14
中等专业学校	Specialized Secondary Schools	17	20	21	20
技工学校	Secondary Technical Schools	12	13	14	14
农业、职业中学	Rural,Vocational Schools	15	13	15	10
普通中学	Regular Secondary Schools	15	15	15	14
高 中	Senior Secondary Schools	15	15	15	15
初 中	Junior Secondary Schools	15	15	14	13
小 学	Primary Schools	14	13	13	13

16-5 各级学校学生升入学率(2002—2005 年)
PERCENTAGE OF GRADUATE STUDENTS AND ENROLLMENT IN ALL SCHOOLS BY LEVEL,2002—2005

单位:% (%)

指 标 Item	2002	2003	2004	2005
初中毕业生升学率 Percentage of Graduates in Junior Secondary Schools Entering Senior Secondary School	92.02	93.10	94.0	94.5
初中入学率 Percentage of Graduates in Primary Schools Entering Junior Secondary Schools	99.21	98.97	99.89	99.83
学龄儿童入学率 Percentage of School - age Children Enrolled	100.00	99.97	99.97	99.97

16－6　研究生在校、毕业、招生及指导教师人数(2002—2005年)
ENROLLED,GRADUATED AND RECRUITED STUDENTS FOR MASTER & DOCTOR DEGREE AND THEIR TEACHERS,2002—2005

单位:人　(person)

指　标　Item	2002	2003	2004	2005
总　计　Total				
在校生数　Students Enrollment	15 922	20 657	24 543	28 470
毕业生数　Graduates	2 790	3 252	4 995	6 142
招生人数　New Students Enrollment	6 574	8 506	9 259	10 169
指导教师　Teachers	3 056	3 273	3 699	4 271
攻读博士学位 Postgraduate for Doctor Degree				
在校生数　Students Enrollment	3 500	4 304	4 940	5 766
毕业生数　Graduates	642	585	982	944
招生人数　New Students Enrollment	1 387	1 680	1 717	1 787
攻读硕士学位 Postgraduate for Master Degree				
在校生数　Students Enrollment	12 422	16 353	19 603	22 704
毕业生数　Graduates	2 148	2 667	4 013	5 198
招生人数　New Students Enrollment	5 187	6 826	7 542	8 382

16－7　分学科在校研究生人数
NUMBER OF ENROLLED STUDENTS FOR MASTER & DOCTOR DEGREF BY SUBJECT

单位:人　(person)

学　科　Item	博士生 Doctor			硕士生 Master		
	2003	2004	2005	2003	2004	2005
总　计　Total	**4 304**	**4 940**	**5 766**	**16 353**	**19 603**	**22 704**
哲　学　Philosophy	73	84	98	175	196	217
经济学　Economics	1 358	1 441	616	4 188	4 859	2 161
法　学　Law	143	189	232	703	852	1 016
教育学　Education	18	21	24	846	802	792
文　学　Literature	132	172	209	1 002	1 353	1 770
历史学　History	213	245	270	251	316	371
理　学　Science	545	627	769	1 583	1 900	2 149
工　学　Engineering	1 478	1 752	2 153	6 425	7 695	8 663
医　学　Medicine	320	387	454	1 160	1 606	2 138
农　学　Agriculture	24	22	25	20	24	22
管理学　Management		877	916		2 859	3 405

16－8 各类高等学校基本情况

BASIC STATISTICS ON INSTITUTIONS OF HIGHER EDUCATION

项 目 Item		学校数(所) Number of Schools (unit)		在校学生数(人) Students Enrollment (person)		毕业生数(人) Graduates (person)	
		2004	2005	2004	2005	2004	2005
总 计	**Total**	**40**	**42**	**286 145**	**331 553**	**51 666**	**69 211**
综合大学	Comprehensive Universities	11	11	63 300	74 615	9 008	16 416
理工院校	Science and Engineering	13	14	114 131	135 758	23 161	30 104
农林院校	Agriculture and Forestry	1	1	8 286	10 005	1 036	1 600
医药院校	Medicine	3	3	16 094	18 841	2 457	3 001
师范院校	Teacher Training	2	2	26 010	29 551	5 358	5 166
语文院校	Linguistics and Literary	2	2	9 908	12 047	1 604	2 162
财经院校	Economics and Finance	3	3	34 328	36 207	6 441	7 888
政法院校	Political Science And law	1	1	2 419	2 174	662	1 025
体育院校	Physical Culture	1	1	5 545	5 145	1 171	922
艺术院校	Art Institutes	3	4	6 124	7 210	768	927

项 目 Item		招生数(人) New Students Enrollment (person)		教职工数(人) Teachers, Staff and Workers (person)		#专任教师 Full－time	
		2004	2005	2004	2005	2004	2005
总 计	**Total**	**96 182**	**103 616**	**36 400**	**39 434**	**18 973**	**21 670**
综合大学	Comprehensive Universities	23 667	27 672	8 271	9 308	3 999	4 857
理工院校	Science and Engineering	36 098	41 120	15 171	16 391	7 677	8 826
农林院校	Agriculture and Forestry	2 799	2 918	777	877	405	472
医药院校	Medicine	5 907	6 055	2 892	3 085	1 577	1 846
师范院校	Teacher Training	8 201	8 245	3 051	3 273	1 601	1 761
语文院校	Linguistics and Literary	3 559	3 995	968	995	624	701
政法院校	Political Science And law	623	9 427	270	3 254	153	149
财经院校	Economics and Finance	11 769	740	3 026	271	1 763	1 908
体育院校	Physical Culture	1 446	1 419	718	655	470	406
艺术院校	Art Institutes	2 113	2 025	1 256	1 325	704	744

16－9 高等学校分科学生数

NUMBER OF STUDENTS ENROLLMENT IN INSTITUTIONS OF HIGHER EDUCATION BY SUBJECT

单位：人 (person)

学科 Item		毕业生数 Graduates					
		合计 Total		本科 Regular College Course		专科 Specialized Subject	
		2004	2005	2004	2005	2004	2005
总计	**Total**	**51 666**	**69 211**	**29 208**	**33 759**	**22 458**	**35 452**
哲学	Philosophy	48	54	48	54		
经济学	Economics	3 210	5 532	2 033	2 617	1 177	2 915
法学	Law	2 210	3 129	1 015	1 205	1 195	1 924
教育学	Education	3 033	1 892	1 678	1 753	1 355	139
文学	Literature	6 566	9 400	3 502	4 736	3 064	4 664
历史学	History	175	112	175	112		
理学	Science	3 129	2 685	2 164	2 685	965	
工学	Engineering	20 964	28 827	11 938	12 615	9 026	16 212
农学	Agriculture	488	650	307	363	181	287
医学	Medicine	2 453	3 050	1 397	1 450	1 056	1 600
管理学	Management	9 390	13 880	4 951	6 169	4 439	7 711
总计中：师范	In total: Teacher Training	3 441	2 900	2 917	2 761	524	139

学科 Item		招生数 New Students Enrollment					
		合计 Total		本科 Regular College Course		专科 Specialized Subject	
		2004	2005	2004	2005	2004	2005
总计	**Total**	**96 182**	**103 616**	**51 191**	**53 013**	**44 991**	**50 603**
哲学	Philosophy	61	35	61	35		
经济学	Economics	7 655	6 325	3 729	3 538	3 926	2 787
法学	Law	3 081	3 963	1 808	2 028	1 273	1 935
教育学	Education	4 213	2 705	2 077	2 326	2 136	379
文学	Literature	13 587	14 976	8 531	10 177	5 056	4 799
历史学	History	199	205	163	205	36	
理学	Science	6 409	4 760	4 608	4 760	1 801	
工学	Engineering	34 517	41 872	16 753	16 932	17 764	24 940
农学	Agriculture	858	1 132	696	757	162	375
医学	Medicine	5 656	5 765	2 930	3 156	2 726	2 609
管理学	Management	19 946	21 878	9 835	9 099	10 111	12 779
总计中：师范	In total: Teacher Training	3 799	3 486	2 868	3 143	931	343

学科 Item		在校学生数 Students Enrollment					
		合计 Total		本科 Regular College Course		专科 Specialized Subject	
		2004	2005	2004	2005	2004	2005
总计	**Total**	**286 145**	**331 553**	**166 913**	**190 629**	**119 232**	**140 924**
哲学	Philosophy	236	208	236	208		
经济学	Economics	24 143	22 596	11 676	13 432	12 467	9 164
法学	Law	10 196	12 551	5 965	7 104	4 231	5 447
教育学	Education	13 379	9 849	8 011	9 056	5 368	793
文学	Literature	40 950	48 002	26 270	32 221	14 680	15 781
历史学	History	611	605	523	605	88	
理学	Science	20 878	16 849	14 785	16 849	6 093	
工学	Engineering	102 404	129 126	57 449	62 554	44 955	66 572
农学	Agriculture	2 868	3 606	2 209	2 658	659	948
医学	Medicine	15 690	18 217	9 521	11 344	6 169	6 873
管理学	Management	54 790	69 944	30 268	34 598	24 522	35 346
总计中：师范	In total: Teacher Training	13 242	13 354	11 552	12 675	1 690	679

16－10 高等学校分科专任教师数
（按职称分）
NUMBER OF FULL－TIME TEACHERS IN INSTITUTIONS OF HIGHER EDUCATION
（BY SUBJECT）

单位：人 (person)

学科	Item	合计 Total 2004	合计 Total 2005	正高级 Senior Title 2004	正高级 Senior Title 2005	副高级 Asso. Senior Title 2004	副高级 Asso. Senior Title 2005
总计	**Total**	**18 973**	**21 670**	**2 429**	**2 827**	**6 354**	**7 148**
哲学	Philosophy	476	599	66	80	203	240
经济学	Economics	1 253	1 443	169	197	393	429
法学	Law	534	678	59	83	175	203
教育学	Education	1 422	1 643	104	116	448	523
文学	Literature	3 737	4 283	348	414	1 064	1 229
历史学	History	238	264	63	68	90	95
理学	Science	2 359	2 649	468	539	877	934
工学	Engineering	6 093	6 882	703	816	2 194	2 397
农学	Agriculture	177	203	24	34	67	71
医学	Medicine	1 345	1 517	273	325	454	567
管理学	Management	1 339	1 509	152	155	389	460

学科	Item	中级 Middle Title 2004	中级 Middle Title 2005	初级 Junior Title 2004	初级 Junior Title 2005	无职称 No Title 2004	无职称 No Title 2005
总计	**Total**	**5 718**	**6 481**	**3 418**	**4 187**	**1 054**	**1 027**
哲学	Philosophy	152	214	45	62	10	3
经济学	Economics	384	480	222	266	85	71
法学	Law	146	202	115	150	39	40
教育学	Education	439	530	291	387	140	87
文学	Literature	1 227	1 346	849	1 076	249	218
历史学	History	61	67	14	24	10	10
理学	Science	636	741	288	360	90	75
工学	Engineering	1 763	1 966	1 124	1 326	309	377
农学	Agriculture	53	46	31	52	2	
医学	Medicine	400	427	186	179	32	19
管理学	Management	457	462	253	305	88	127

16-11 中等专业学校分科学生数及专业课教师数

NUMBER OF STUDENTS AND SPECIAL COURSE TEACHERS IN SPECIALIZED SECONDARY SCHOOLS BY SUBJECT

单位:人 (person)

学科	Item	在校学生数 Students Enrollment		毕业生数 Graduates	
		2004	2005	2004	2005
总计	**Total**	**69 542**	**76 994**	**26 249**	**17 250**
农林类	Agriculture and Forestry	1 204	1 093	987	274
资源与环境类	Resources and Environment	794	674	433	294
能源类	Energy	217	100	145	45
土木水利工程类	Civil and Hydraulic Engineering	6 268	5 090	2 084	1 512
加工制造类	Processing and Manufacturing	14 297	18 550	3 613	2 949
交通运输类	Communication and Transportation	1 902	3 026	477	656
信息技术类	Information Technology	20 768	22 769	8 472	4 911
医药卫生类	Medicine and Health	3 034	3 890	1 299	723
商贸与旅游类	Trade and Tourism	12 131	11 997	4 931	3 638
财经类	Finance and Economics	1 651	2 196	1 290	377
文化艺术与体育类	Culture, Arts and Physical Education	2 013	1 996	933	445
社会公共事业类	Public Affairs	2 570	2 982	1 413	1 063
师范类	Teacher Training	646	1 006	100	173
其他	Others	2 047	1 625	72	190

学科	Item	招生数 New students Enrollment		专业课教师数 Special Course Teachers	
		2004	2005	2004	2005
总计	**Total**	**24 637**	**25 526**	**1 683**	**1 641**
农林类	Agriculture and Forestry	654	541	58	56
资源与环境类	Resource and Environment	114	254	34	20
能源类	Energy	23	27	20	25
土木水利工程类	Civil and Hydraulic Engineering	1 876	1 450	162	142
加工制造类	Processing and Manufacturing	5 965	6 484	246	232
交通运输类	Communication and Transportation	643	798	59	40
信息技术类	Information Technology	7 197	7 147	385	334
医药卫生类	Medicine and Health	1 292	1 223	74	82
商贸与旅游类	Trade and Tourism	3 606	3 914	112	81
财经类	Finance and Economics	577	874	191	186
文化艺术与体育类	Culture, Arts and Physical Education	762	815	173	201
社会公共事业类	Public Affairs	435	1 347	16	79
师范类	Teacher Training	279	232	49	52
其他	Others	1 214	420	104	111

16-12 天津市重点中学一览表(2005年)
LIST OF KEY MIDDLE SCHOOLS,2005

学校名称 Name of School		班级(个) Classes (unit)		在校学生数(人) Students Enrollment (person)		教职工数(人) Teachers,Staff and Workers (person)	
		合计 Total	#高中 Senior Middle Schools	合计 Total	#高中 Senior Middle Schools	合计 Total	#高中 Senior Middle Schools
南开中学	Nankai Middle School	38	38	1 789	1 789	292	145
一中	No.1 Middle School	41	41	1 810	1 810	381	176
耀华中学	Yaohua Middle School	59	55	2 434	2 272	309	144
新华中学	Xinhua Middle School	38	38	1 705	1 705	307	146
实验中学	Shiyan Middle School	33	33	1 254	1 254	371	144
天津中学	Tianjin Middle School	34	28	1 537	1 376	195	90
二十中学	No.20 Middle School	24	24	1 011	1 011	215	108
二南开	No.2 Nankai Middle School	36	36	1 626	1 626	371	175
二十一中	No.21 Middle School	37	24	1 727	1 099	271	120
五十五中	No.55 Middle School	42	24	1 923	1 108	310	116
七中	No.7 Middle School	30	30	1 551	1 551	243	114
四十五中	No.45 Middle School	29	29	1 542	1 542	273	143
津华中学	Jinhua Middle School	30	30	1 511	1 511	240	89
海河中学	Haihe Middle School	29	29	1 489	1 489	401	107
四十二中	No.42 Middle School	33	33	1 512	1 512	334	124
四十一中	NO.41 Middle School	29	26	1 272	1 153	272	70
四中	No.4 Middle School	34	34	1 588	1 588	295	100
三十一中	No.31 Middle School	23	23	1 054	1 054	251	96
一0九中	No.109 Middle School	20	20	984	984	186	67
天大附中	Tianda Middle School	23	17	790	610	108	38
南大附中	Nanda Middle School	36	16	966	599	105	41
四十三中	No.43 Middle School	44	44	1 921	1 921	359	138
二十五中	No.25 Middle School	24	24	957	957	268	87
二中	No.2 Middle School	37	37	1 704	1 704	344	111
十四中	No.14 Middle School	27	27	1 073	1 073	220	76
五十七中	No.57 Middle School	25	25	1 174	1 174	236	91
外语附中	Foreign Language School	19	11	1 173	852	236	84
红光中学	Hongguang Middle School	33	12	786	398	194	43
铁一中	No.1 Railway Middle School	40	17	2 268	834	171	71
三中	No.3 Middle School	36	36	1 665	1 665	288	105
五中	No.5 Middle School	28	28	1 469	1 469	336	139
民族中学	Nationality Middle School	27	27	1 175	1 175	348	114
五十一中	No.51 Middle School	19	16	753		271	97

16－12 续表　Continued

学校名称 Name of School		班　级(个) Classes (unit)		在校学生数(人) Students Enrollment (person)		教职工数(人) Teachers, Staff and Workers(person)	
		合　计 Total	#高　中 Senior Middle Schools	合　计 Total	#高　中 Senior Middle Schools	合　计 Total	#高　中 Senior Middle Schools
英才中学	Yingcai Middle School	10	10	606	606	0	0
塘沽一中	Tanggu No.1 Middle School	36	36	1 644	1 644	389	277
塘沽二中	Tanggu No.2 Middle School	49	38	2 730	1 822	321	97
渤海石油一中	Bohai No.1 Middle School	24	14	744	391	114	50
汉沽一中	Hangu No.1 Middle School	44	44	2 222	2 222	198	172
大港一中	Dagang No.1 Middle School	30	30	1 432	1 432	114	70
油田实验中学	Oilfield Shiyan Middle School	24	24	1 034	1 034	125	90
第一百中学	No.100 Middle School	45	45	2 284	2 284	209	134
杨柳青一中	Yangliuqing No.1 Middle School	30	30	1 759	1 759	166	116
咸水沽一中	Xianshuigu No.1 Middle School	35	35	1 583	1 583	233	143
四十七中	No.47 Middle School	41	41	1 668	1 668	216	138
杨村一中	Yangcun No.1 Middle School	42	42	2 140	2 140	238	147
宝坻一中	Baodi No.1 Middle School	42	42	2 455	2 455	199	147
芦台一中	Lutai No.1 Middle School	24	24	2 092	2 092	195	122
静海一中	Jinghai No.1 Middle School	25	25	1 300	1 300	286	206
蓟县一中	Jixian No.1 Middle School	63	53	2 730	2 730	222	138

16－13　按部门分普通中小学生基本情况

BASIC STATISTICS ON SECONDARY SCHOOLS AND PRIMARY SCHOOLS BY DEPARTMENT

单位:人　(person)

项　目	Item	教育部门 Education Department		其他部门 Other Departments		民　办 Private Units	
		2004	2005	2004	2005	2004	2005
普通中学	**Middle Schools**						
在校学生数	Students Enrollment	556 158	500 392	13 549	19 038	29 398	56 860
毕业生数	Graduates	177 888	169 296	4 696	7 827	9 124	16 952
招生数	New Students Enrollment	170 731	149 701	4 032	5 865	10 032	18 663
小　学	**Primary Schools**						
在校学生数	Students Enrollment	536 665	507 248	14 047	13 204	4 132	12 551
毕业生数	Graduates	111 358	102 208	2 779	2 527	634	1 712
招生数	New Students Enrollment	78 507	74 048	2 503	2 099	593	2 226

注:本表不含民办公助和公办民助学校。
Note: This table exclude private units supported by state and state－owned units supported by private units.

16－14 普通中小学分布情况(2005年)

DISTRIBUTION OF REGULAR SECONDARY SCHOOLS AND PRIMARY SCHOOLS,2005

地区	Region	学校数(所) Number of Schools(Unit)		在校学生数(人) Students Enrollment(person)		专任教师数(人) Full－time Teachers(person)	
		普通中学 Regular Mid－dle Schools	小学 Primary Schools	普通中学 Regular Midd－le Schools	小学 Primary Schools	普通中学 Regular Mid－dle Schools	小学 Primary Schools
全市	**Total**	**640**	**1 062**	**576 290**	**533 003**	**41 537**	**41 076**
市辖区	**Districts Under City Administration**	**494**	**773**	**433 796**	**407 973**	**31 693**	**32 663**
和平区	Heping District	30	33	34 508	28 352	2 411	2 198
河东区	Hedong District	29	27	27 535	20 594	1 988	2 074
河西区	Hexi District	44	47	39 186	30 661	2 518	2 125
南开区	Nankai District	42	38	34 011	26 949	2 643	2 332
河北区	Hebei District	40	36	33 418	24 711	1 982	1 689
红桥区	Hongqiao District	31	33	26 393	16 834	1 821	2 065
塘沽区	Tanggu District	40	59	28 345	335 179	2 175	2 568
汉沽区	Hangu District	15	23	10 647	10 361	884	1 037
大港区	Dagang District	39	32	28 633	24 660	2 417	1 914
东丽区	Dongli District	27	42	16 893	25 397	1 324	1 822
西青区	Xiqing District	15	38	16 456	17 402	1 248	1 974
津南区	Jinnan District	20	43	19 281	25 814	1 179	1 555
北辰区	Beichen District	20	44	15 657	17 467	1 316	1 648
武清区	Wuqing District	51	139	47 022	51 856	3 610	3 674
宝坻区	Baodi District	49	134	54 269	50 189	4 028	3 790
天津铁厂	Tianjin Iron Works	2	5	1 542	1 547	149	198
市辖县	**Counties Under City Administration**	**146**	**289**	**142 494**	**125 030**	**9 844**	**8 413**
宁河县	Ninghe County	30	62	31 013	26 921	2 222	1 876
静海县	Jinghai County	52	97	41 391	40 445	2 784	2 767
蓟县	Jixian County	64	130	70 090	57 664	4 838	3 770

注:专任教师数中不包括民办教师数。
Note:Number of full－time teachers exclude civilian teachers.

16－15 普通中学、小学及幼儿园校舍情况(2005 年)
STATISTICS FOR SCHOOLHOUSES OF REGULAR SECONDARY SCHOOLS, PRIMARY SCHOOLS AND KINDERGARTENS, 2005

单位:平方米 (sq. m)

地区	Region	占地面积 Areas	校舍建筑面积 Floor Space of Schoolhouses			学生人均建筑面积 Average Floor Space of Students		
			普通中学 Regular Secondary Schools	小学 Primary Schools	幼儿园 Kinder－gartens	普通中学 Regular Secondary Schools	小学 Primary Schools	幼儿园 Kinder－gartens
全市	**Total**	**31 847 457**	**5 416 956**	**3 506 373**	**860 207**	**9.40**	**6.58**	**4.72**
市辖区	**Districts Under City Administration**	**22 980 867**	**4 359 783**	**2 723 961**	**696 867**	**9.40**	**6.10**	**8.21**
和平区	Heping District	537 142	324 232	148 047	46 490	9.40	5.22	9.24
河东区	Hedong District	831 494	251 458	141 854	54 778	9.13	6.89	8.22
河西区	Hexi District	1 025 025	436 594	172 026	72 163	11.14	5.61	7.78
南开区	Nankai District	1 093 901	426 534	165 745	74 512	12.54	6.15	8.10
河北区	Hebei District	934 498	308 075	146 306	50 344	9.22	5.92	8.25
红桥区	Hongqiao District	598 031	215 471	129 961	34 520	8.16	7.72	8.03
塘沽区	Tanggu District	1 713 362	369 944	342 012	58 031	9.20	6.73	7.82
汉沽区	Hangu District	512 670	76 163	58 676	9 204	7.15	5.66	4.50
大港区	Dagang District	2 677 481	368 995	168 041	74 352	12.89	6.81	8.36
东丽区	Dongli District	1 596 813	240 155	177 911	30 044	14.22	7.01	4.00
西青区	Xiqing District	1 179 280	160 245	167 229	24 787	9.74	9.61	2.85
津南区	Jinnan District	1 240 929	191 189	155 723	21 561	9.92	6.03	2.40
北辰区	Beichen District	1 298 806	188 769	162 630	40 040	12.06	9.31	4.06
武清区	Wuqing District	4 352 980	1 428 025	352 492	66 416	9.10	6.80	2.76
宝坻区	Baodi District	3 319 182	355 599	223 149	31 970	6.55	4.45	3.88
天津铁厂	Tianjin Iron Works	69 273	18 335	12 159	7 655	11.89	7.86	12.87
市辖县	**Counties Under City Administration**	**8 866 590**	**1 057 173**	**782 412**	**163 340**	**7.55**	**5.98**	**2.96**
宁河县	Ninghe County	1 554 919	190 915	163 156	9 424	6.16	6.06	1.74
静海县	Jinghai County	3 399 600	331 013	276 348	61 948	8.00	6.83	3.06
蓟县	Jixian County	3 912 071	535 245	342 908	91 968	7.64	5.95	3.03

注:占地面积包括中等师范学校、幼儿园教师进修学校、特殊教育学校及其他。
Note: Areas of schools include middle teacher training, kindergarten teacher training, special education and other schools.

16－16　其他教育基本情况(2002—2005年)
BASIC STATISTICS ON OTHER EDUCATION,2002—2005

单位:所、人 (unit)(person)

指　　标	Item	2002	2003	2004	2005
成 人 教 育	**Adult Education**				
成人高等学校	**Adult Higher Education Schools**				
学校数	Number of Schools	22	22	20	20
在校学生数	Students Enrollment	104 270	115 770	78 486	84 420
成人中等学校	**Secondary Schools for Adults**				
学校数	Number of Schools	74	29	25	15
在校学生数	Students Enrollment	20 505	7 619	5 367	2 905
特 殊 教 育	**Specific Education**				
盲聋哑学校	**Blind and Deaf－Mute Schools**				
学校数	Number of Schools	7	8	8	8
在校学生数	Students Enrollment	651	751	694	651
初　中	Junior Middle Schools	247	249	220	180
小　学	Primary Schools	404	502	474	471
教职工人数	Teachers,Staff and Workers	408	402	399	407
#专任教师数	Full－time Teachers	257	254	256	269
弱智学校	**Schools for Low Intelligence Student**				
学校数	Number of Schools	14	13	13	14
在校学生数	Students Enrollment	945	2 416	1 937	1 957
初　中	Junior Middle Schools	348	451	414	394
小　学	Primary Schools	597	1 965	1 523	1 563
教职工人数	Teachers,Staff and Workers	304	304	286	293
#专任教师数	Full－time teachers	220	200	200	215
工读学校	**Schools for Mistaken Students**				
学校数	Number of Schools	3	3	3	3
在校学生数	Students Enrollment	152	82	62	41
教职工人数	Teachers,Staff and Workers	117	113	107	88
#专任教师数	Full－time Eeachers	35	28	27	25

16－17　幼儿园基本情况(2002—2005年)
BASIC STATISTICS ON KINDERGARTENS,2002—2005

指　　标	Item	2002	2003	2004	2005
幼儿园所数(所)	Number of Kindergartens	1 166	1 778	1 636	1 657
入园儿童数(人)	Children Enrollment(person)	203 627	199 551	198 558	204 722
三岁及以上儿童	Children over Three Age	195 695	192 552	191 828	198 461
三岁及以下儿童	Children under Three Age	7 932	6 999	6 730	6 261
教职工数(人)	Teachers,Staff and Workers(person)	16 356	15 309	15 378	15 686
#教养员	Teachers and Health Workers	10 436	10 046	10 040	10 020

16－18 专业技术人员
SPECIAL TECHNICAL PERSONNEL

单位：人 (person)

项 目 Item	全 市 Total 2003	2004	2005	平均每万人口有科技人员 Scientific and Technological Personnel Per 10 000 Persons (2005)	平均每万名城镇单位从业人员有科技人员 Scientific and Technological Personnel Per 10 000 Persons Employed In Urban Units(2005)
合 计 Total	**465 039**	**439 578**	**424 845**	**407**	**2 189**
自然科学专业技术人员 Natural Science	**232 324**	**212 049**	**206 222**	**198**	**1 062**
# 工程技术人员 Engineering	134 556	114 331	107 745	103	555
农业技术人员 Agriculture	3 197	2 973	2 951	3	15
科学研究人员 Scientific Research	3 671	3 693	3 887	4	20
卫生技术人员 Health Care	60 517	59 920	59 604	57	307
教学人员 Teaching	30 383	31 132	32 035	31	165
社会科学专业技术人员 Social Science	**232 715**	**227 529**	**218 623**	**210**	**1 126**
# 科学研究人员 Scientific Research	1 040	878	1 002	1	5
教学人员 Teaching	97 685	99 838	99 029	95	510
经济人员 Economy	48 594	46 409	43 682	42	225
财会人员 Accountant	39 977	37 418	34 913	33	180
统计人员 Statistician	4 776	4 126	3 787	4	20
翻译人员 Translator	823	675	606	1	3
图书、档案、资料人员 Librarian and Archivist	5 828	5 605	5 461	5	28
编辑、记者、播音员 Editor, Reporter and Broadcasting	2 760	2 800	2 656	3	14
体育教练人员 Coach	548	529	546	1	3
工艺美术人员 Arts and Craft	437	330	295		2
文艺人员 Literature and Art	2 170	2 205	2 184	2	11

注：专业技术人员统计范围为公有制企事业单位。
Note: Special technical personnel refer to public－owned units.

16－19　专业技术人员构成(2005 年)
COMPOSITION OF SPECIAL TECHNICAL PERSONNEL,2005

单位:人　　　　(person)

项　目　Item	按性别分 By Sex	按受教育程度分 By Education Status		按职称分 By Title	
	#女专业技术人员数 Female	#受过高等专业教育人数 Having Higher Special Education Background	#受过中等专业教育人数 Having Special Secondary School Background	#高级职称人数 Senior Professional Certification	#中级职称人数 Medium Professional Certification
合　计 Total	**211 026**	**291 987**	**97 756**	**58 002**	**147 671**
自然科学专业技术人员 Natural Science	**92 240**	**143 385**	**51 616**	**32 642**	**65 795**
#工程技术人员 Engineering	30 492	77 207	23 001	16 493	32 481
农业技术人员 Agriculture	971	1 692	1 031	413	831
科学研究人员 Scientific Research	1 527	3 807	65	1 646	1 272
卫生技术人员 Health Care	41 236	32 427	24 210	5 626	18 190
教学人员 Teaching	18 014	28 252	3 309	8 465	13 021
社会科学专业技术人员 Social Science	**118 786**	**148 602**	**46 140**	**25 360**	**81 876**
#科学研究人员 Scientific Research	450	948	29	323	430
教学人员 Teaching	63 382	76 845	19 167	14 902	50 378
经济人员 Economy	15 238	23 611	10 039	1 864	7 844
财会人员 Accountant	22 318	19 887	10 389	800	6 370
统计人员 Statistician	2 690	1 893	1 003	205	882
翻译人员 Translator	322	589	17	190	216
图书、档案、资料人员 Librarian and Archivist	3 914	4 114	786	804	2 382
编辑、记者、播音员 Editor,Reporter and Broadcasting	1 184	2 467	92	892	888
体育教练人员 Coach	145	481	42	168	168
工艺美术人员 Arts and Craft	76	165	87	48	102
文艺人员 Literature and Art	796	726	1 043	737	973

16－20　自然科学专业技术人员构成(2005年)

(按国民经济行业分)

COMPOSITION OF SPECIAL TECHNICAL PERSONNEL OF NATURAL SCIENCE,2005

(GROUPED BY SECTOR)

单位:人　(person)

行　业　Sector	合　计 Total	#工程技术人员 Engineering	#卫生技术人员 Health Care	#教学人员 Teaching
总　计 Total	**206 222**	**107 745**	**59 604**	**32 035**
农、林、牧、渔业 Farming,Forestry,Animal Husbandry and Fishery	3 831	1 252	63	
采矿业 Minerals Mining	5 944	5 901	43	
制造业 Manufacturing	34 365	32 208	2 142	
电力、燃气及水的生产和供应业 Production & Supply of Power,Gas and Water	3 039	2 975	64	
建筑业 Construction	19 468	18 953	515	
交通运输、仓储及邮政业 Transport,Storage,Post Services	8 330	8 088	242	
信息传输、计算机服务和软件业 Information Transmitting,Computer Services and Software	2 724	2 718	6	
批发和零售业 Wholesale and Retail Trade	2 639	1 534	1 084	
住宿和餐饮业 Accommodation and Catering Services	105	91	14	
金融业 Finance Intermediation	998	998		
房地产业 Real Estate	2 463	2 405	35	
租赁和商务服务业 Leasing and Business Services	982	813	19	
科学研究、技术服务和地质勘察业 Scientific Research,Technical Services and Geological Prospecting	19 139	16 821	378	
水利、环境和公共设施管理业 Management for Water Conservancy, Environment and Public Facilities	5 356	5 220	89	
居民服务和其他服务业 Resident Services and Other Social Services	708	670	20	
教　育 Education	39 894	5 311	982	31 853
卫生、社会保障和社会福利业 Health Care,Social Security and Social Welfare	55 247	923	53 863	154
文化、体育和娱乐业 Culture, Sports and Recreational Services	755	655	43	27
公共管理和社会组织 Public Management and Social Organizations	235	209	2	1

16－21 社会科学专业技术人员构成(2005年)
(按国民经济行业分)
COMPOSITION OF SPECIAL TECHNICAL PERSONNEL OF SOCIAL SCIENCE,2005
(GROUPED BY SECTOR)

单位:人 (person)

行业 Sector	合计 Total	#教学人员 Teaching	#经济人员 Economy	#财会人员 Accountant	#图书、档案、资料人员 Librarian and Archivist
总计 Total	**218 623**	**99 029**	**43 682**	**34 913**	**5 461**
农、林、牧、渔业 Farming,Forestry,Animal Husbandry and Fishery	1 415	121	334	584	16
采矿业 Minerals Mining	2 990	398	874	700	112
制造业 Manufacturing	26 381	1 423	10 089	6 264	473
电力、燃气及水的生产和供应业 Production & Supply of Power,Gas and Water	2 119	35	619	576	61
建筑业 Construction	8 230	193	2 279	3 026	119
交通运输、仓储及邮政业 Transport,Storage,Post Services	9 235	158	4 873	1 877	75
信息传输、计算机服务和软件业 Information Transmitting,Computer Services and Software	881		368	225	23
批发和零售业 Wholesale and Retail Trade	9 761		5 188	2 722	77
住宿和餐饮业 Accommodation and Catering Services	511		136	225	6
金融业 Finance Intermediation	23 699		14 309	8 325	46
房地产业 Real Estate	2 792	269	849	844	49
租赁和商务服务业 Leasing and Business Services	2 180	81	756	694	79
科学研究、技术服务和地质勘察业 Scientific Research,Technical Services and Geological Prospecting	3 568	132	564	1 123	307
水利、环境和公共设施管理业 Management for Water Conservancy, Environment and Public Facilities	2 048	6	261	900	56
居民服务和其他服务业 Resident Services and Other Social Services	1 170	59	426	385	17
教育 Education	106 727	95 830	334	2 818	1 629
卫生、社会保障和社会福利业 Health Care,Social Security and Social Welfare	5 958	262	806	2 877	290
文化、体育和娱乐业 Culture, Sports and Recreational Services	8 149	61	109	642	1 990
公共管理和社会组织 Public Management and Social Organizations	809	1	508	106	36

16－22 独立科学研究和技术开发机构情况

BASIC INDICATORS OF INDEPENDENT INSTITUTIONS
OF SCIENTIFIC RESEARCH AND TECHNOLOGICAL DEVELOPMENT

指 标 Indicator	自然科学研究与技术开发机构 Institutions of Natural Scien－tific Research and Technical Development		社会、人文科研与开发机构 Institutions of Social Science and Humanities of Research and Development		科学技术情报和文献机构 Institutions of Scientific and Technological Information and Documents	
	2004	2005	2004	2005	2004	2005
机构数(个) Number of Institutions(unit)	**129**	**128**	**3**	**3**	**11**	**11**
科技活动人员(人) Number of Persons Engaged in Scientific and Technological Activities(person)	**9 857**	**10 309**	**288**	**299**	**602**	**612**
高级职称 Senior Professional Certification	3 320	3 421	135	140	222	220
中级职称 Medium Professional Certification	3 022	3 038	85	87	227	221
初级职称 Junior Professional Certification	2 395	2 504	50	51	119	125
其 他 Others	1 120	1 346	18	21	34	46
经费支出总额(万元) Total Expenditures of Operating Expense (10 000 yuan)	**143 416**	**150 918**	**2 112**	**2 301**	**6 940**	**8 280**

16－23 独立自然科学研究机构课题开展和投入

(按课题类型分)

PROJECTS AND INPUT OF INDEPENDENT
INSTITUTIONS OF NATURAL SCIENCE RESEARCH (GROUPED BY TYPE OF PROJECTS)

项 目 Item	课题数(项) Number of Projects (item)		投入人力(人年) Labor Force Input (person－year)		投入经费(万元) Funds Input (10 000 yuan)	
	2004	2005	2004	2005	2004	2005
合 计 Total	**1 555**	**1 552**	**4 998**	**4 796**	**58 094**	**63 290**
基础研究 Basic Research	36	49	84	135	613	946
应用研究 Application Research	153	152	529	467	3 095	3 884
试验发展 Experiment Development	466	545	2 052	2 147	27 895	32 449
R&D 成果应用 R&D Achievements Used	486	390	1 317	1 040	17 821	18 292
科技服务 Services of Science and Technology	390	386	969	913	8 187	6 536
生产性活动 Activities of Production	24	30	47	94	483	1 183

16－24 专利申请受理量和授权量
PATENT APPLICATIONS EXAMINED AND GRANTED

单位:项 (item)

项目 Item	申请受理量 Patent Applications Examined			申请授权量 Patent Applications Granted		
	2003	2004	2005	2003	2004	2005
合计 Total	**6 812**	**8 406**	**11 657**	**2 505**	**2 578**	**3 045**
按种类分 Grouped by Type						
发明 Inventions	3 328	4 013	4 470	241	432	763
实用新型 Utility Models	2 713	3 142	4 690	1 547	1 587	1 543
外观设计 Designs	771	1 251	2 497	717	559	739
按对象分 Grouped by Applicator						
职务发明 Service Inventions	**3 454**	**4 703**	**6 956**	**969**	**1 213**	**1 675**
#工矿企业 Industrial and Mineral Enterprises	2 791	3 812	5 600	675	810	1 240
大专院校 Universities and Colleges	436	674	1 008	175	267	317
科研单位 Scientific Research Institutions	193	183	303	97	105	103
机关团体 Government Agencies and Organizations	34	34	45	22	31	15
非职务发明 Non－service Inventions	**3 358**	**3 703**	**4 701**	**1 536**	**1 365**	**1 370**

16－25 科学技术成果(2002—2005 年)
ACHIEVEMENTS IN SCIENCE AND TECHNOLOGY,2002—2005

单位:项 (item)

项目 Item	2002	2003	2004	2005
市级科学技术成果登记数 Number of City Level Major Achievements in Science and Technology	**1 020**	**1 203**	**1 408**	**1 508**
国际领先 Leading Level in the World	32	59	75	75
国际先进 Advanced World Standard	197	311	282	321
国内领先 Leading Level in China	413	559	697	732
国内先进 Advanced National Standard	182	236	306	321
其他 Others	196	38	48	59
获天津市科学技术奖 Number of Tianjin Scientific and Technological Prizes Awarded	**246**	**218**	**215**	**210**
#自然科学奖 Awards for Natural Science	16	17	15	14
技术发明奖 Invention Prizes Awarded	5	5	10	17
科技进步奖 Scientific and Technological Progress Prize	223	195	190	179
获国家科学技术奖 Number of National Scientific and Technological Prizes Awarded	**13**	**14**	**9**	**14**
#自然科学奖 Awards for Natural Science		3	1	2
技术发明奖 Invention Prizes Awarded	1		2	1
科技进步奖 Scientific and Technological Progress Prize	11	11	6	11

16－26　天津市获国家科学技术奖科技成果一览(2005年)

LIST OF NATIONAL SCIENTIFIC AND TECHNOLOGICAL PRIZES AWARDED IN TIANJIN,2005

获奖项目和等级 Project and Grade Awarded	完成单位和个人 Name of Unit and Individual
自然科学二等奖(2项) **Second Class of National Awards for Natural Science (two items)**	
1. Atiyah－Singer 指标理论的若干研究 Selected Results in Atiyah－Singer Index Theory	张伟平 Zhang Weiping
2. 光折变新效应、机理与器件的研究 Study of New Photorefractive Phenomena, Mechanisms and Devicesx	许京军、张光寅、刘思敏、张国权、孔勇发 Xu Jingjun, Zhang Guangyin, Liu Simin, Zhang Guoquan, Kong Yongfa
技术发明二等奖(1项) **Second Class of National Invention Prizes Awarded (one item)**	
螺旋式浮环密封装置 Helical Grooved Floating Bushing Seal	王玉明 Wang Yuming
科技进步二等奖(11项) **Second Class of National Scientific and Technological Progress Award (eleven items)**	
1. 高效规整填料精馏塔技术及应用 High Efficiency Structured Packed Distillation Column Technology and Applications	余国琮、张鹏飞、许春建、朱慧铭、李凭力、田华明、周明、袁希钢、杨志才、冯惠生 天津大学 Yu Guocong, Zhang Pengfei, Xu Chunjian, Zhu Huiming, Li Pingli, Tian Huaming, Zhou Ming, Yuan Xigang, Yang Zhicai, Feng Huisheng Tianjin University
2. 大型旋转机械和振动机械重大振动故障治理与非线性动力学设计技术 Nonlinear Dynamical Design of Large－scale Rotating Machinery and Vibration Machinery, Fault Diagnosis Technique and Its Engineering Application	陈予恕、黄文虎、闻邦椿、朱均、武际可、薛禹胜、张文、曹树谦、吕和祥、丁千 天津大学 Chen Yushu, Huang Wenhu, Wen Bangchun, Zhu Jun, Wu Jike, Xue Yusheng, Zhang Weng, Cao Shuqian, Lv Hexiang, Ding Qian Tianjin University
3. 大型水利水电工程可视化仿真技术及其工程应用 Visual Simulation Technique and Its Application to Large－scal Hydraulic and Hydropower Engineering	钟登华、张社荣、刘东海、肖白云、何有忠、黄河、郑家祥、王忠耀、崔广涛、张宗亮 天津大学 Zhong Denghua, Zhang Sherong, Liu Donghai, Xiao Baiyu, He Youzhong, Huang He, Zheng Jiaxiang, Wang Zhongyao, Cui Guangtao, Zhang Zongliang Tianjin University
4. 井下工具检测技术及试验平台的研究与开发 Research and Development of Measuring Technology and Testing Platform for Downhole Tools	胡小唐、刘合、刘喜林、王凤山、杨乃群、徐世民、傅星、胡晓东、裴晓含、王金友 天津大学 Hu Xiaotang, Liu He, Liu Xilin, Wang Fengshan, Yang Naiqun, Xu Shimin, Fu Xing, Hu Xiaodong, Pei Xiaohan, Wang Jinyou Tianjin University
5. 天津港深水航道、港池、泊位适航水深应用与水深动态维护研究 Study on Applieation of Navigable Depthe and Dynamic Maintenance of Depth－Channel, Harbour Basine and Wharfin in Tianjin Port	黄力军、丁乃庆、刘富强、胡宁、张建国、钱平生、孙建鹏、王承刚、李进军、刘树东 天津港(集团)有限公司 Huang Lijun, Ding Naiqing, Liu Fuqiang, Hu Ning, Zhang Jianguo, Qian Pingsheng, Sun Jianpeng, Wang Chenggang, Li Jinjun, Liu Shudong Tianjin Port (Group) Co.,Ltd.
6. 新型高抗挤套管与复合管柱技术 New Casing With Super Collapse Resistence and Design Technology for Complex Casing String	高德利、严泽生、刘一江、张传友、徐志谦、王京、李铁成、付继成、李飞、张建设 天津钢管集团有限公司 Gao Deli, Yan Zesheng, Liu Yijiang, Zhang Chuanyou, Xu Zhiqian, Wang Jing, Li Tiecheng, Fu Jicheng, Li Fei, Zhang Jianshe Tianjin Steel Pipe Group Co., Ltd.
7. 长大隧道全断面岩石掘进机掘进技术研究与应用 Full Face Rock Tunnel Boring Machine Construction Technology and Applications	杜彦良、刘春、彭道富、崔原、杜立杰、沙明元、徐明新、孙谋、万治昌、房炳杰 中铁十八局集团有限公司 Du Yanliang, Liu Chun, Peng Daofu, Cui Yuan, Du Lijie, Sha Mingyuan, Xu Mingxin, Sun Mou, Wan Zhichang, Fang Bingjie China Railways 18th Bureau(Group) Co., Ltd.
8. 牵引供电自动化系统成套技术及应用 Complete Technology and Application of Railway Traction Power Supply Automation System	陈小川、高仕斌、王韧、徐志根、蒋先国、蒋勇、熊列彬、郭勤俭、陈德明、李岗 铁道第三勘察设计院 Chen Xiaochuan, Gao Shibin, Wang Ren, Xu Zhigen, Jiang Xianguo, Jiang Yong, Xiong Liebin, Guo Qinjian, Chen Deming, Li Gang The 3rd Survey & Design Institute of Ministry of Railways, China
9. 镍氢电池、电池组及相关材料产业化关键技术的研究与系统集成 Research and System Integration of Key Technology for Industrialization of MH/Ni Batteries, Battery Packs and Related Materials	吴锋、单忠强、方世璧、陈实、石力开、高学平、毛立彩、曲金秋、王国庆、宋德瑛 南开大学 Wu Feng, Shan Zhongqiang, Fang Shibi, Chen Shi, Shi Likai, Gao Xueping, Mao Licai, Qu Jinqiu, Wang Guoqing, Song Deying Nankai University
10. 中国海岸带环境遥感监测与信息系统技术集成及其应用 Integration of Environmental Remote Sensing and Geographical Information System Technologies with Its Applications in Coast Zone of China	周成虎、蒋兴伟、侯一筠、王钦敏、陈述彭、陈介中、王宏、恽才兴、杨晓梅、苏奋振 国家海洋信息中心 Zhou Chenghu, Jiang Xingwei, Hou Yiyun, Wang Qinmin, Chen Shupeng, Chen Jizhong, Wang Hong, Yun Caixing, Yang Xiaomei, Su Fenzhen NMDIS
11. 大型精对苯二甲酸生产过程智能建模、控制与优化技术 Intelligence Modeling, Control and Optimization Technology for Large－scale Purified Terephthalic Acid Plants	钱锋、钱积新、邢建良、郑国栋、冷家厂、颜学峰、赵均、王振新、杜文莉、王行愚 中国石化集团天津石油化工公司 Qian Feng, Qian Jixin, Xing Jianliang, Zheng Guodong, Ling Jiachang, Yan Xuefeng, Zhao Jun, Wang Zhenxin, Du Wenli, Wang Xingyu Tianjin Petrochemical Co., Sinopec Group

16－27　高等学校科研课题开展与投入(2005 年)
(理、工、农、医类)
PROJECTS OF DEVELOPMENT AND INPUT OF SCIENTIFIC RESEARCH IN UNIVERSITIES AND COLLEGES,2005
(SCIENCE,ENGINEERING,AGRICULTURE AND MEDICINE)

项　目	Item	课题数(项) Number of Projects (item)	投入人力(人年) Labor Force Input (person)	#科学家和工程师 Scientist and Engineer	投入经费(万元) Funds Input (10 000 yuan)
总　计	**Total**	**5 502**	**5 065**	**4 901**	**76 979**
按课题活动类型分	**Grouped by Type of Projects**				
基础研究	Basic Research	1 452	1 335	1 316	13 793
应用研究	Application Research	2 887	2 661	2 593	33 142
试验发展	Experiment Development	593	692	645	22 513
R&D 成果应用	R&D Achievement Used	329	215	202	4 731
科技服务	Service of Science and Technology	241	162	145	2 800
按(课题)项目类别分	**Grouped by Project**				
国家"973"项目	State "973" Project	42	46	44	1 663
国家科技攻关项目	State S&T Strategical Project	31	49	45	2 694
国家"863"项目	State "863" Project	72	78	77	4 300
国家自然科学基金项目	State Natural Scientific Fund Project	608	556	545	6 685
主管部门科技项目	S&T Project from Administrative Department	711	771	764	4 848
国家部委其他科技项目	S&T Project from Ministry	251	262	259	4 123
省、市、自治区科技项目	S&T Project from Province,Municipality,Autonomous Region	1 025	1 051	1 030	10 901
企事业单位委托科技项目	S&T Project from Enterprise,Institution	1 774	1 510	1 415	37 903
国际合作项目	International Cooperate Project	49	40	37	1 357
自选项目	Self－choosing Project	899	664	647	2 464
其他项目	Other Project	40	38	38	41

16－28　高等学校科技专著和论文(2002—2005 年)
(理、工、农、医类)
S&T WORKS AND PAPERS IN UNIVERSITIES AND COLLEGES,2002—2005
(SCIENCE,ENGINEERING,AGRICULTURE AND MEDICINE)

项　目	Item	单　位　Unit	2002	2003	2004	2005
科技专著	**Scientific and Technological Work**	**部 copy**	**143**	**135**	**60**	**88**
		万字 10 000 words	**4 209**	**4 056**	**1 524**	**1 635**
#自然科学	Natural Science	部 copy	25	26	7	10
		万字 10 000 words	503	910	200	272
工程科学	Engineering	部 copy	68	65	23	23
		万字 10 000 words	2 116	1 957	630	556
医学科学	Medicine	部 copy	48	43	30	45
		万字 10 000 words	1 571	1 186	695	709
农业科学	Agriculture	部 copy	2	1		10
		万字 10 000 words	19	3		98
科学论文	**Scientific Papers**	**篇 piece**	**8 624**	**9 540**	**11 460**	**13 077**
#国外发表	Published Abroad	篇 piece	1 201	1 312	1 968	2 293

16－29 新技术产业园区基本情况(1992—2005 年)

BASIC STATISTICS ON TIANJIN HIGH－TECH INDUSTRY PARK,1992－2005

单位:亿元 (100 million yuan)

年份 Year	技工贸总产值 Gross Output Value of Technology, Industry and Trade	技工贸总收入 Total Income from Technology, Industry and Trade	#技术收入 Income from Technology	利润总额 Profit	出口创汇总额(亿美元) Exports (USD 100 million)	交纳税金总额 Taxes
1992	7.62	9.02		0.86		0.43
1993	22.38	24.68	2.07	2.98		0.94
1994	39.79	41.57	2.47	3.61		2.06
1995	61.36	67.05	3.39	4.75		2.26
1996	86.17	96.96	6.41	6.99		3.76
1997	122.77	130.21	7.05	7.45		4.78
1998	152.40	172.46	8.95	6.76		8.74
1999	195.61	231.28	10.96	8.88		9.68
2000	274.61	296.99	13.88	16.31	9.13	14.73
2001	322.72	383.28	17.72	17.68	7.98	19.70
2002	416.60	498.40	20.90	23.70	12.90	20.40
2003	561.96	668.94	12.79	25.73	13.63	28.84
2004	595.79	659.43		23.19	16.34	35.08
2005	627.44	751.29	58.04	41.02	24.53	40.00

16－30 计量仪器检定情况(2002—2005 年)

STATISTICS FOR MEASURING IMPLEMENTS TEST,2002—2005

单位:台、件 (set)(piece)

类别	Sort	2002	2003	2004	2005
总计	**Total**	**1 309 119**	**1 325 488**	**1 481 652**	**1 027 813**
长度	Length	34 040	30 525	59 322	40 536
温度	Temperature	50 037	41 102	39 325	63 081
力学	Mechanics	431 922	447 634	767 458	347 050
#衡器	Weighing Apparatus	83 406	87 179	77 320	69 384
电学	Electrology	102 870	105 670	590 594	541 682
光学	Optics	260	254	1 596	426
声学	Acoustics	219	385	455	576
化学	Chemistry	2 751	3 018	2 351	2 126
电离辐射	Ionization Radiation	267	460	349	390
无线电	Radio	587 952	598 194	491	455
时间频率	Time Frequency	1 708	1 341	1 070	1 265
其他	Others	97 093	96 905	18 641	30 226

资料来源:天津市质量技术监督局,下表同。
Information Source: Tianjin Municipal Quality & Technology Supervision Bureau, same to next.

16－31 定期监督检验情况(2005年)

RESULTS OF FIXED－PERIOD CHECK ON THE QUALITY OF PRODUCTS UNDER STATE SUPERVISION,2005

项　　目	Item	检查企业(个) Number of Enterprises Checked (unit)	检查批次(批次) Checked－times (batch/times)	合格批次(批次) Batch－times with Qualified Quality (batch/times)	合格率(%) Rate of Qualified (%)
合　　计	**Total**	**3 636**	**4 493**	**3 883**	**86.42**
农副食品加工业	Agricultural Products and Byproducts Processing	445	485	378	77.94
食品制造业	Food Manufacturing	721	896	714	79.69
饮料制造业	Beverage Manufacturing	286	364	293	80.49
纺织业	Textile Industry	30	37	33	89.19
纺织服装鞋帽制造业	Textile Garments,Shoes,Caps Manufacturing	51	68	66	97.06
皮革毛皮羽毛(绒)及其制品业	Leather,Furs,Feather and Related Products	2	6	6	100.00
木材加工及木、竹、藤、草制品业	Timber Processing,Bamboo,Cane,Palm Fiber and Straw Products	1	1	1	100.00
家具制造业	Furniture Manufacturing	88	88	83	94.32
造纸及纸制品业	Papermaking and Paper Products	80	109	107	98.17
印刷业和记录媒介的复制	Printing and Record Medium Reproduction	15	15	15	100.00
文教体育用品制造业	Cultural,Educational and Sports Goods	1	2	2	100.00
石油加工炼焦及核燃料加工业	Petroleum Processing,Coking and Nuclear Fuel Processing	30	47	36	76.60
化学原料及化学制品制造业	Raw Chemical Materials and Chemical Products	217	372	350	94.09
橡胶制品业	Rubber Products	99	111	107	96.40
塑料制品业	Plastic Products	25	27	22	81.48
非金属矿物制品业	Nonmetal Mineral Products	247	300	286	95.33
黑色金属冶炼及压延加工业	Smelting and Pressing of Ferrous Metals	1	1	1	100.00
有色金属冶炼及压延加工业	Smelting and Pressing of Nonferrous Metals	4	5	3	60.00
金属制品业	Metal Products	165	176	167	94.89
通用设备制造业	General Purpose Equipment Manufacturing	98	137	133	97.08
专用设备制造业	Special Purpose Equipment Manufacturing	25	30	30	100.00
交通运输设备制造业	Transport Equipment Manufacturing	487	547	479	87.57
电气机械及器材制造业	Electric Equipment and Machinery	149	195	170	87.18
通信设备计算机及其他电子设备制造业	Telecommunications Equipment,Computer and Other Electronic Equipment Manufacturing	15	15	15	100.00
仪器仪表及文化办公用机械制造业	Instruments,Meters,Cultural and Office Machinery	5	5	4	80.00
工艺品及其他制造业	Craftwork and Other Manufacturing	349	454	382	84.14

16-32 产品质量专项监督检验情况(2005年)

RESULTS OF SPECIALIZED CHECK ON THE QUALITY OF PRODUCTS UNDER STATE SUPERVISION,2005

项目	Item	检查商业企业数(个) Number of Commercial Enterprises Checked (unit)	检查商品批次(批次) Batch-times Checked (batch/time)	合格批次(批次) Batch-times with Qualified Quality (batch/times)	批次合格率(%) Rate of Batch-times Qualified (%)
合计	**Total**	**207**	**352**	**254**	**72.16**
#农用产品	Agricultural Products	17	30	20	66.67
加工食品和饮料	Food and Beverage	78	115	57	49.57
纺织、鞋类产品	Textile and Shoes	16	30	30	100.00
化工产品	Chemical Products	40	75	65	86.67
建材产品	Building Raw Materials	34	60	47	78.33
机电产品	Mechanical and Electrical Products	22	42	35	83.33

16-33 技术监督机构人员、行政执法及科技成果情况

PERSONNEL,EXECUTING LAW OF ADMINISTRATION AND ACHIEVEMENT OF SCIENCE & TECHNOLOGY OF PRODUCT QUALITY & TECHNIQUE SUPERVISION AGENCIES

项目	Item	2004年 全市 Total (2004)	#市级单位 City Level	2005年 全市 Total (2005)	#市级单位 City Level
机构人员情况	**Agencies and Personnel**				
机构数(个)	Number of Agencies(unit)	80	14	79	12
职工人数(人)	Number of Employees(person)	2 039	802	2 007	797
行政机构人员	Administrative Agencies	660	110	640	105
事业机构人员	Institutions	1 379	692	1 367	692
#执法人员(人)	Staff of Executing Law(person)	889	223	853	223
行政执法情况	**Administrative Cases**				
受理案件数(件)	Number of Accepted and Heared Cases(case)	3 818	115	5 811	305
万元以上案件(件)	Cases over 10,000 yuan(case)	2 105	350	378	111
12365接待投诉、咨询(件)	"12365" Accepting Lawsuit and Consulting(case)	5 669	399	27 570	
罚没金额(万元)	Total Value of Punishment(10 000 yuan)	2 599	706	2 868	
科技项目情况	**Items of Science and Technology**				
项目总数(项)	Number of Items(item)	20	15		
经费金额(万元)	Outlay(10 000 yuan)	989	870		
科技成果获奖情况	**Prizes Awarded of Science and Technology Achievement**				
获奖项目数(项)	Number of Prizes Awarded(item)	2	2	8	7
省部级三等奖	Third Class Provincial and Ministerial Awards	2	2	1	1
地方局二等奖	Second Class Municipal Awards			4	4
地方局三等奖	Third Class Municipal Awards			3	2

16－34　天津市科学技术协会和所属学会科技活动(2005 年)
SCIENTIFIC AND TECHNOLOGICAL ACTIVITIES OF TIANJIN SCIENCE AND TECHNOLOGY ASSOCIATIONS AND AFFILIATED LEARNED SOCIETIES,2005

项　目	Item	合　计 Total	市及区、县科协 Science Association of City,District and County	市级学会 Institution of City Level
机构与人员	**Institutions and Personnel**			
机　构(个)	Institutions(unit)	490	19	471
人　员(人)	Personnel(person)	129 869	207	129 662
学术交流情况	**Academic Activities of Exchange**			
学术会议(次)	Academic Meetings(time)	559	11	548
国　内	Domestic	538	11	527
国　际	International	21		21
参加人数(人次)	Number of Participants(person－time)	74 678	1 074	73 604
国　内	Domestic	70 876	1 074	69 802
国　际	International	3 802		3 802
交流论文(篇)	Number of Papers Presented(piece)	13 159	25	13 134
国　内	Domestic	12 402	25	12 377
国　际	International	757		757
科技交流(个)	Exchange of Science and Technological(unit)	103	10	93
接　待	Received	63	4	59
外　派	Sent Abroad	40	6	34
交流人数(人次)	Number of Exchange(person－time)	521	77	444
接　待	Received	264	12	252
外　派	Sent Abroad	257	65	192
科学普及	**Activities for Popular Science**			
科普讲座(次)	Lectures of Popular Science(time)	3 151	2 402	749
参加人数(万人次)	Number of Participants(10 000 person－times)	82	67	15
科普展览(次)	Exhibitions of Popular Science(time)	1 431	1 272	159
参加人数(万人次)	Number of Participants(10 000 person－times)	101	85	16
科技培训	**Science and Technological Training**			
培训班数(个(期))	Number of Training Classes(unit(period))	459	146	313
培训人数(人次)	Number of Persons in Training Classes (person－time)	59 542	32 095	27 447
科技咨询服务(项)	**Service of Consultative Activities(item)**			
无偿咨询项目	Gratis Consultative Projects	893	110	783
完成技术合同数	Number of Consultative Contracts Completed	1 229	614	615
青少年科技活动	**Scientific and Technological Activities of Teenage**			
科技夏(冬)令营(次)	Scientific and Technological Summer(Winter)Camp(time)	108	101	7
参加人数(人次)	Number of Participants(person－time)	30 258	29 527	731
青少年科技竞赛(次)	Number of Teenagers Participating in Science and Technology Competition(time)	298	276	22
科技出版物	**Science and Technology Publication**			
出版科技期刊(种)	Science and Technology Magazine(kind)	54	2	52
年发行总数(万册)	Number of Issue(10 000 volumes)	172	100	72
年发表学术论文(篇)	Number of Papers Presented(piece)	7 178		7 178

16－35　大中型工业企业科技活动基本情况(2005 年)
(按企业类型和经济类型分)
S&T ACTIVITIES IN LARGE AND MEDIUM－SIZED ENTERPRISES,2005
(GROUPED BY TYPE AND OWNERSHIP)

项　目　Item	合　计 Total	按企业类型分 Grouped by Type of Enterprises	
		大　型 Large	中　型 Medium
1.有科技活动企业数(个)			
Number of Enterprises with Scientific and Technological Activities(unit)	209	25	184
2.从事科技活动人员(人)			
Employees Engaged in Scientific and Technological Activities(person)	32 184	14 873	17 311
#科学家和工程师			
Scientists and Engineers	20 042	9 113	10 929
研究与试验发展人员			
Personnel of R&D	15 195	6 357	8 838
3.科技活动经费筹集(万元)			
Funding for Scientific and Technological Activities(10 000 yuan)	1 026 670	449 179	577 491
4.科技活动经费支出(万元)			
Expenditures of Scientific and Technological Activities(10 000 yuan)	936 778	452 494	484 284
#研究与试验发展经费支出			
Expenditures of R&D	384 268	244 435	139 833
新产品开发经费支出			
Expenditures of New Product Development	400 514	223 824	176 690
5.科技活动项目数(项)			
Number of Scientific and Technological Activities(item)	1 679	757	922
#研究与试验发展项目数			
Number of R&D	1 080	416	664
6.科技机构数(个)			
Number of Scientific and Technological Institutions(unit)	195	48	147
科技机构人员数(人)			
Persons in Scientific and Technological Institutions(person)	13 272	5 922	7 350
科技机构经费支出(万元)			
Expenditures of Scientific and Technological Institutions(10 000 yuan)	434 190	299 987	134 203
#仪器设备经费支出			
Expenditures of Instrument and Equipment	357 238	183 626	173 612
7.新产品产值(万元)			
Output Value of New Products(10 000 yuan)	15 516 388	9 120 002	6 396 386
新产品销售收入(万元)			
Sales Revenue of New Products(10 000 yuan)	15 456 202	9 121 023	6 335 179
#出口销售收入(万元)			
Sales Revenue of Exports (10 000 yuan)	3 606 938	1 082 775	2 524 163
8.专利申请数(件)			
Number of Patent Applications(piece)	2 958	2 256	702
拥有发明专利数(件)			
Number of Patent Granted(piece)	2 099	1 940	159
9.技术改造经费支出(万元)			
Expenditures of Technical Innovation(10 000 yuan)	402 716	262 967	139 749
10.技术引进经费支出(万元)			
Expenditures of Technical Introduction(10 000 yuan)	313 480	59 386	254 094

16－35 续表　Continued

项　目　Item	按经济类型分　Grouped by Ownership			
	国有经济 State－owned	集体经济 Collective－owned	“三资”经济 Hongkong,Macao, Taiwan and Foreign Funded	其他经济 Others
1.有科技活动企业数(个)				
Number of Enterprises with Scientific and Technological Activities(unit)	43	9	62	95
2.从事科技活动人员(人)				
Employees Engaged in Scientific and Technological Activities(person)	10 950	848	6 641	13 745
#科学家和工程师				
Scientists and Engineers	7 238	502	4 957	7 345
研究与发展人员				
Personnel of R&D	3 864	662	4 449	6 220
3.企业科技活动经费筹集(万元)				
Funding for Scientific and Technological Activities(10 000 yuan)	291 424	6 008	478 239	250 999
4.企业科技活动经费支出(万元)				
Expenditures of Scientific and Technological Activities(10 000 yuan)	303 477	17 940	359 871	255 490
#研究与试验发展经费支出				
Expenditures of R&D	133 216	12 615	146 487	91 950
新产品开发经费支出				
Expenditures of New Product Development	98 627	3 864	141 986	156 037
5.企业科技活动项目数(项)				
Number of Scientific and Technological Activities(item)	660	44	254	721
#研究与试验发展项目数				
Number of R&D	272	31	218	559
6.科技机构数(个)				
Scientific and Technological Institutions(unit)	61	10	38	86
科技机构人员数(人)				
Persons in Scientific and Technological Institutions(person)	4 719	297	2 482	5 774
科技机构经费支出(万元)				
Expenditures of Scientific and Technological Institutions(10 000 yuan)	208 735	3 703	93 679	128 073
#仪器设备经费支出				
Expenditures of Instrument and Equipment	141 435	5 850	111 533	98 420
7.新产品产值(万元)				
Output Value of New Products(10 000 yuan)	1 847 813	46 857	11 751 657	1 870 061
新产品销售收入(万元)				
Sales Revenue of New Products(10 000 yuan)	1 888 483	41 367	11 814 000	1 712 352
#出口销售收入				
Sales Revenue of Exports(10 000 yuan)	69 932	7 200	3 408 876	120 930
8.专利申请数(件)				
Number of Patent Applications(piece)	170	41	1 992	755
拥有发明专利数(件)				
Number of Patent Granted(piece)	41	16	1 699	343
9.技术改造经费支出(万元)				
Expenditures of Technical Innovation(10 000 yuan)	187 007	12 334	115 265	88 110
10.技术引进经费支出(万元)				
Expenditures of Technical Introduction(10 000 yuan)	19 408		289 449	4 623

16－36 大中型工业企业科技活动基本情况(2005 年)
(按国民经济行业分)
S&T ACTIVITIES IN LARGE AND MEDIUM－SIZED ENTERPRISES,2005
(GROUPED BY SECTOR)

项目	Item	有科技活动企业数(个) Number of Enterprises with Scientific Technological Activities (unit)	从事科技活动人员(人) Employees Engaged in Scientific and Technological Activities (person)	#科学家和工程师 Scientists and Engineers	#研究与试验发展人员 Personnel of R&D (person)
总计	**Total**	**209**	**32 184**	**20 042**	**15 195**
#石油和天然气开采业	Petroleum and Natural Gas Extraction	4	2 594	1 837	1 505
非金属矿采选业	Nonmetal Minerals Mining and Dressing	2	528	372	438
农副食品加工业	Agricultural Products and Byproducts Processing	1	5	5	5
食品制造业	Food Manufacturing	1	171	130	57
饮料制造业	Beverage Manufacturing	4	245	245	152
烟草制品业	Tobacco Processing	1	149	115	117
纺织业	Textile Industry	8	2 799	293	315
纺织服装、鞋、帽制造业	Textile Garments,Shoes,Caps Manufacturing	2	165	62	65
皮革、毛皮、羽毛(绒)及其制品业	Leather,Furs,Feather and Related Products	1	30		
木材加工及木、竹、藤、棕、草制品业	Timber Processing,Bamboo,Cane,Palm Fiber and Straw Products				
家具制造业	Furniture Manufacturing				
造纸及纸制品业	Papermaking and Paper Products	2	75	51	40
印刷业和记录媒介的复制	Printing and Record Medium Reproduction	1	120	118	98
文教体育用品制造业	Cultural,Educational and Sports Goods	2	55	35	17
石油加工、炼焦及核燃料加工业	Petroleum Processing,Coking and Nuclear Fuel Processing	1	83	65	45
化学原料及化学制品制造业	Chemical Raw Materials and Chemical Products	17	1 750	1 142	1 076
医药制造业	Medical and Pharmaceutical Products	22	2 016	1 473	1 014
化学纤维制造业	Chemical Fiber				
橡胶制品业	Rubber Products	9	438	288	229
塑料制品业	Plastic Products	2	110	57	60
非金属矿物制品业	Nonmetal Mineral Products	5	121	111	10
黑色金属冶炼及压延加工业	Smelting and Pressing of Ferrous Metals	11	5 046	3 122	862
有色金属冶炼及压延加工业	Smelting and Pressing of Nonferrous Metals	1	12	6	12
金属制品业	Metal Products	8	644	362	250
通用设备制造业	General Purpose Equipment Manufacturing	17	2 371	1 390	1 542
专用设备制造业	Special Purpose Equipment Manufacturing	13	1 495	885	796
交通运输设备制造业	Transport Equipment Manufacturing	22	2 777	2 041	1 505
电气机械及器材制造业	Electric Equipment and Machinery	16	2 554	1 782	1 815
通信设备、计算机及其他电子设备制造业	Telecommunications Equipment,Computer and Other Electronic Equipment Manufacturing	24	4 375	2 970	2 620
仪器仪表及文化、办公用机械制造业	Instruments,Meters,Cultural and Office Machinery	3	228	165	191
电力、热力的生产和供应业	Production and Supply of Electric Power and Heat Energy	6	836	657	87
煤气生产和供应业	Production and Supply of Gas	1	26	14	20
水的生产和供应业	Production and Supply of Tap Water	1	216	216	216

16－36 续表 1　Continued

项　　目	Item	企业科技活动经费支出总额（万元）Expenditures of Scientific and Technological Activities of Enterprises (10 000 yuan)	#研究与试验发展经费支出 Expenditures of R&D	企业科技活动项目数（项）Number of Scientific and Activities (item)	新产品销售收入（万元）Sales Revenue of New Products (10 000 yuan)
总　　计	**Total**	**936 778**	**384 268**	**1 679**	**15 456 202**
#石油和天然气开采业	Petroleum and Natural Gas Extraction	90 779	17 195	197	417 857
非金属矿采选业	Nonmetal Minerals Mining and Dressing	3 397	2 199	27	11 350
农副食品加工业	Agricultural Products and Byproducts Processing	3	3		
食品制造业	Food Manufacturing	700	346	2	26 067
饮料制造业	Beverage Manufacturing	10 888	5 743	14	48 465
烟草制品业	Tobacco Processing	1 910	1 140	12	4 200
纺织业	Textile Industry	6 753	1 268	28	29 331
纺织服装、鞋、帽制造业	Textile Garments, Shoes, Caps Manufacturing	622	387	8	5 039
皮革、毛皮、羽毛(绒)及其制品业	Leather, Furs, Feather and Related Products	73			340
造纸及纸制品业	Papermaking and Paper Products	2 205	1 880	4	98
印刷业和记录媒介的复制	Printing and Record Medium Reproduction	813	463	7	5 002
文教体育用品制造业	Cultural, Educational and Sports Goods	233	73	4	28 363
石油加工、炼焦及核燃料加工业	Petroleum Processing, Coking and Nuclear Fuel Processing	452	168	17	1 888
化学原料及化学制品制造业	Chemical Raw Materials and Chemical Products	59 448	36 018	128	252 036
医药制造业	Medical and Pharmaceutical Products	77 591	36 318	224	175 073
化学纤维制造业	Chemical Fiber				
橡胶制品业	Rubber Products	6 799	2 797	31	146 496
塑料制品业	Plastic Products	1 028	1 023	7	12 595
非金属矿物制品业	Nonmetal Mineral Products	587	30	11	52 830
黑色金属冶炼及压延加工业	Smelting and Pressing of Ferrous Metals	228 903	90 275	279	1 783 448
有色金属冶炼及压延加工业	Smelting and Pressing of Nonferrous Metals	166	68	2	2 846
金属制品业	Metal Products	8 676	5 568	41	33 001
通用设备制造业	General Purpose Equipment Manufacturing	29 156	23 605	178	394 397
专用设备制造业	Equipment Manufacturing for Special Purpose	18 834	12 602	69	108 381
交通运输设备制造业	Transport Equipment Manufacturing	64 506	13 635	90	1 794 032
电气机械及器材制造业	Electric Equipment and Machinery	81 712	72 549	87	1 251 538
通信设备、计算机及其他电子设备制造业	Telecommunications Equipment, Computer and Other Electronic Equipment Manufacturing	222 559	52 911	110	8 770 690
仪器仪表及文化、办公用机械制造业	Instruments, Meters, Cultural and Office Machinery	3 402	2 338	12	97 844
电力、热力的生产和供应业	Production and Supply of Electric Power and Heat Ener	4 909	412	83	
煤气生产和供应业	Production and Supply of Gas	81	81	2	
水的生产和供应业	Production and Supply of Tap Water	8 941	3 021	3	

16－36 续表 2　Continued

项　目	Item	科技机构数（个）Number of Scientific and Technological Research Institutions (unit)	科技机构经费支出（万元）Expenditures of Scientific and Technological Research Institutions (10 000 yuan)	专利申请数（件）Number of Patent Applications (piece)	拥有发明专利数（件）Number of Invent Patent Owned (piece)
总　计	**Total**	**195**	**434 190**	**2 958**	**2 099**
#石油和天然气开采业	Petroleum and Natural Gas Extraction	23	45 003	70	15
非金属矿采选业	Nonmetal Minerals Mining and Dressing	2	1 339	4	
农副食品加工业	Agricultural Products and Byproducts Processing	1	3		
食品制造业	Food Manufacturing				
饮料制造业	Beverage Manufacturing	4	6 111	13	
烟草制品业	Tobacco Processing	1	601	4	1
纺织业	Textile Industry	7	1 337	5	
纺织服装、鞋、帽制造业	Textile Garments, Shoes, Caps Manufacturing	2	353	42	
皮革、毛皮、羽毛(绒)及其制品业	Leather, Furs, Feather and Related Products				
造纸及纸制品业	Papermaking and Paper Products	1	1 880	5	3
印刷业和记录媒介的复制	Printing and Record Medium Reproduction	1	813	5	
文教体育用品制造业	Cultural, Educational and Sports Goods	1	185		
石油加工、炼焦及核燃料加工业	Petroleum Processing, Coking and Nuclear Fuel Processing	1	452		
化学原料及化学制品制造业	Chemical Raw Materials and Chemical Products	21	47 812	161	31
医药制造业	Medical and Pharmaceutical Products	23	32 618	300	250
化学纤维制造业	Chemical Fiber				
橡胶制品业	Rubber Products	5	407	14	5
塑料制品业	Plastic Products	1	953	2	2
非金属矿物制品业	Nonmetal Mineral Products	2	24		
黑色金属冶炼及压延加工业	Smelting and Pressing of Ferrous Metals	15	166 767	35	11
有色金属冶炼及压延加工业	Smelting and Pressing of Nonferrous Metals			2	2
金属制品业	Metal Products	6	4 837	34	21
通用设备制造业	General Purpose Equipment Manufacturing	15	5 705	127	25
专用设备制造业	Equipment Manufacturing for Special Purpose	10	8 290	61	6
交通运输设备制造业	Transport Equipment Manufacturing	13	15 889	30	6
电气机械及器材制造业	Electric Equipment and Machinery	17	70 346	1 892	1 682
通信设备、计算机及其他电子设备制造业	Telecommunications Equipment, Computer and Other Electronic Equipment Manufacturing	17	17 642	93	21
仪器仪表及文化、办公用机械制造业	Instruments, Meters, Cultural and Office Machinery	1	435	35	4
电力、热力的生产和供应业	Production and Supply of Electric Power and Heat Energy	1	1 278	6	1
煤气生产和供应业	Production and Supply of Gas				
水的生产和供应业	Production and Supply of Tap Water	3	2 968	16	12

主要统计指标解释

学校(机构) 是按国家规定的设置标准和审批程序批准设立的,招收适龄人口实施各级各类教育活动的教育机构。

普通高等学校 是按国家规定的设置标准和审批程序批准举办的,通过全国普通高等教育统一招生考试,招收高中毕业生为主要培养对象,实施高等学历教育的全日制大学、独立设置的学院和高等专科学校、高等职业学校和其他机构。大学、独立设置的学院主要实施本科及本科层次以上的教育。高等专科学校、高等职业学校实施专科层次教育。

成人高等学校 是按国家规定的设置标准和审批程序批准举办的,通过全国成人高等教育统一招生考试,招收高中毕业或同等学历的人员为主要培养对象,利用函授、业余、脱产的多种形式对其实施高等学历教育的学校。包括:职工高等学校、农民高等学校、管理干部学院、教育学院、独立函授学院、广播电视大学、其他机构。

中等职业学校 是按国家规定的设置标准和审批程序批准成立的实施中等职业教育的学校(机构)。调整后的中等职业学校是指将普通中等专业学校(中等技术学校、中等师范学校)、成人中等专业学校、职业高中学校等各种实施中等职业教育的办学类型,通过合并、共建、联办、划转等形式调整为统一的办学类型,即中等职业学校。

职业中学(职业高中、职业初中) 职业中学是指经县或县以上教育行政部门批准设立,招收小学或初中毕业生实施中等职业技术教育的教学机构。职业中学按学校性质类别可分为:独立设置的职业中学(包括:职业初中、职业高中、职业初高中合设学校);附设有普通中学班的职业中学。

普通中等学校(普通高中、普通初中) 普通中等学校通常称普通中学,分为普通高级中学和普通初级中学两个阶段。普通初级中学是指独立设置的招收小学毕业的适龄人口进行初级中等基础教育的机构;普通高级中学是指独立设置的招收初中毕业的适龄人口进行高级中等基础教育的机构;完全中学是指普通初、高中合设的教育机构;一贯制学校是指在一所学校连续实施中小学教育的机构。其中包括实施九年义务教育的九年一贯制学校和实施高中教育的十二年一贯制学校。(说明:一贯制学校的办学条件如能划分为小学、初中、高中,则分开填报;如不能划分清楚,可按就高不就低的方法填入初中、高中报表中,不能重复填写。)

初等教育(普通小学) 普通小学是指由县或县以上教育行政部门批准,招收学龄儿童实施初等教育的教学机构。

学前教育(幼儿园) 幼儿园是指招收三周岁以上(含三周岁)学龄前幼儿,对其进行保育和教育的单位,包括全市各幼儿教学点;幼儿园以游戏为基本活动形式,寓教于乐、寓教于动。

工读学校 指由教育和公安部门联合举办的,对有轻微违法行为的中学生进行挽救教育的教学机构。

特殊教育学校 指某地独立设置的招收盲聋哑和智残儿童,以及其他特殊需要的儿童、青少年进行普通或职业初、中等教育的教学机构。

毕业生数 指上学年,具有学籍的学生学完教学计划规定的全部课程,考试及格,取得毕业证书,实际毕业的学生数。

招生数 指通过国家统一招生考试,按照国家招生计划实际招收入学的新生数。(高等教育包括春秋两季招收的学生。)

在校生数 指本学年初,具有学籍的注册学生总数。

教职工数 指在学校(机构)工作并由学校(机构)支付劳动报酬的教职工,人员包括在编人员,即根据原人事管理制度,人事关系和档案均在学校的人员;聘任制人员,即人事制度改革后,高校(机构)招聘录用的长期、全时工作人员。聘任制人员的人事关系在学校但档案不在学校。教职工数包括校本部教职工、科研机构人员、校办企业职工、其他附设机构人员。

专任教师 指具有教师资格,专门从事教学工作的人员。

科技活动 指在自然科学、农业科学、医药科学、工程与技术科学、人文与社会科学领域(简称科学技术领域)中与科技知识的产生、发展、传播和应用密切相关的有组织的活动。为核算科技投入的需要,科技活动可分为科学研究与试验发展(R&D)、科学研究与试验发展成果应用及相关的科技服务三类活动。

科学研究与试验发展 指在科学技术领域,为增加知识总量、以及运用这些知识去创造新的应用进行的系统的创造性的活动,包括基础研究、应用研究、试验发展三类活动。在工业企业开展的科学研究与试验发展(R&D)活动中,较为普遍的和大量的活动属于试验发展活动。

基础研究 指为了获得关于现象和可观察事实的基本原理的新知识(揭示客观事物的本质、运动规律,获得新发现、新学说)而进行的实验性或理论性研究,它不以任何专门或特定的应用或使用为目的。其成果以科学论文和科学著作为主要形式。

应用研究 指为获得新知识而进行的创造性研究,主要针对某一特定的目的或目标。应用研究是为了确定基础研究成果可能的用途,或是为达到预定的目标探索应采取的新方法(原理性)或新途径。其成果形式以科学论文、专著、原理性模型或发明专利为主。

试验发展 指利用从基础研究、应用研究和实际经验所获得的现有知识,为产生新的产品、材料和装置,建立新的工艺、系统和服务,以及对已生产和建立的上述各项作实质性的改进而进行的系统性工作。其成果形式主要是专利、专有技术、新产品原型或样机样件等。

研究与试验发展成果应用 指为使试验发展阶段产生的新产品、材料和装置,建立的新工艺、系统和服务以及作实质性改进后的上述各项能够投入生产或实际应用,解决所存在的技术问题而进行的系统性的工作。这类活动的成果形式大多是可供生产和实际操作的带有技术和工艺参数的图纸、技术标准和操作规范。

科技服务 与科学研究与试验发展有关并有助于科学技术知识的产生、传播和应用的活动,包括为扩大科技成果的使用范围而进行的示范性推广工作;为用户提供科技信息和文献服务的系统性工作;为用户提供可行性报告、技术方案、建议及进行技术论证等技术咨询工作;自然、生物现象的日常观测、监测,资源的考察和勘探;有关社会、人文、经济现象的通用资料的收集,如统计、市场调查等,以及这些资料的常规分析与整理;为社会和公众提供的测试、标准化、计量、计算、质量控制和专利服务,不包括工商企业为进行正常生产而开展的上述活动。

Explanatory Notes on Main Statistical Indicators

School (Institution) refer to educational establishments at different levels set up according to the government evaluation and approval procedures, enrolling school - age population.

Regular Institutions of Higher Learning refer to educational establishments set up according to the government evaluation and approval procedures, enrolling graduates from senior secondary schools and providing higher education courses and training for senior professionals. They include full - time universities, colleges, high professional schools, high professional vocational schools and others. Universities and colleges are mainly providing undergraduate courses; those high professional schools and high professional vocational schools are mainly providing professional trainings.

Institutions of Higher Learning for Adults refer to educational establishments, set up in line with relevant rules approved by the government, enrolling staff and workers with senior secondary school or equivalent education, and providing higher education courses in many forms of correspondence, spare time, or full time for adults. Professionals thus trained receive a qualification equivalent to graduates studying regular courses at regular universities, colleges and professional colleges. Institutions of higher learning for adults include schools of high education for staff and workers, schools of high education for peasants, colleges for management cadres, pedagogical colleges, independent correspondence colleges, Radio and TV universities and other educational establishments.

Secondary Professional Schools refer to educational establishments, set up in line with relevant rules approved by the government, implementing secondary professional education. Secondary professional schools are original specialized secondary schools (secondary technical schools, secondary teacher training schools), specialized secondary schools for adults, vocational secondary schools, which are named secondary professional schools after they are merged, constructed together and adjusted to be a kind of education type.

Vocational Secondary Schools (vocational senior secondary schools, vocational junior secondary schools) refer to educational establishments approved by county or above education administrative department, enrolling graduates from primary schools and junior secondary schools and providing vocational secondary education courses. They include vocational secondary schools (including vocational senior secondary schools, vocational junior secondary schools, vocational junior & senior secondary schools), vocational secondary schools with regular secondary school classes.

Regular Secondary Schools (regular senior secondary schools, regular junior secondary schools) are divided into regular senior secondary schools and regular junior secondary schools. Regular junior secondary schools refer to educational establishments enrolling graduates from primary schools and providing junior secondary education courses. Regular senior secondary schools refer to educational establishments enrolling graduates from junior secondary schools and providing senior secondary education courses. Whole seconary schools refer to educational establishments including senior secondary school and junior secondary school. Successive schools refer to educational establishments providing successive primary and secondary education courses, include nine - year successive schools and twelve - year successive schools. (Note: If successive schools can be divided into primary school, junior secondary school and senior secondary school, should fill in respectively, otherwise, should fill in junior secondary school or senior secondary school and have no repetition.)

Primary Education (Regular Primary Schools) refer to educational establishments approved by county or above education administrative department, enrolling school - age children and providing primary education courses.

Baby Education (Kindergartens) Kindergartens refer to educational units enrolling children aged 3 - 6, include all baby education units. Kindergartens take games as basic activities.

Schools for Juvenile Delinquents refer to educational establishments founded by education deparment and public security department, enrolling students of secondary schools with slight illegal behavior.

Special Education Schools refer to educational establishments, enrolling blind, deaf, dumb children, weak - minded children and providing regular or vocational primary and seconary education courses.

Graduates refer to the number of students who have student status, learn over all education courses, pass the examination and receive diploma.

New Students Enrollment refer to number of new students who have passed enrollment examination (Higher Learning include students enrolled in spring and autumn).

Students Enrollment refer to number of students with student status at the beginning of the school year.

Number of Teachers, Officers and Workers refer to work at schools (institutions) and receive wages from schools (institutions). They include personnel whose personal connections and files put in schools, engaged personnel, i.e. full - time personnel engaged by higher learning(institutions). The personal connections of engaged personnel are put in schools but files are not put in schools. Number of teachers, officers and workers include staff, personnel of science rearch institutions, staff and workers of enterprises founded by schools and personnel of other subordinated institutions.

Full - time Teachers refer to personnel who have qualifications of teacher and undertake educational working.

Science and Technology Activity refer to organizational activity aimed at developing, spreading and applying the scientific technology about natural science, agriculture science, medicine science, engineering and technology science, human and social science. In order to calculate the input of science and technology, science and technology activities are divided into R&D, Achievements Applying on Researches & Experiments Developing and Science and Technique Services.

Research and Experimental Development(R&D) refers to systematic and creative endeavor aimed at expanding the overall volume of knowledge and applying the knowledge in inventing new uses. It includes basic studies, application research and experimental development. For industrial enterprises, their R&D mainly belongs to experimental development activities.

Basic Research refers to empirical or theoretical research aiming at obtaining new knowledge on the fundamental principles of phenomena of observable facts to reveal the nature and law of movement of objects and to acquire new discoveries or new theories. Basic research takes no specific or designated application as the aim of the research. Results of basic research are mainly released or disseminated in the form of scientific papers or monographs.

Applied Research refers to creative research aiming at obtaining new knowledge on a specific objective or target. Purpose of the applied research is to identify the possible use of results from basic research, or to explore new (fundamental) methods or new approaches. Results of applied research are expressed in the form of scientific papers, monographs, fundamental models or invention patents.

Experiments and Development refer to systematic activities aiming at using the knowledge from basic and applied researches or from practical experience to develop new products, materials and equipment, to establish new production process, system and service, or to make substantial improvement on the existing products, process and services. Results of experiment and development activities are embodied in patents, exclusive technology, monotype of new products or equipment.

Achievements Applying on Researches & Experiments Developing It is meant that a lot of work is systematically taken to find solutions applicable both/either to technological problems in products, materials and devices put into production and in skills, systems and services into practical use. This kind of achievements include blueprint, technical standard and operating rules with technology and technological parameter for the purpose of production and practical operation.

Science and Technique Services A forward movement in research of the science and development of experiment is a help in creation, spread and application of scientific and technological knowledge, including seven principal matters : (a) extending application, on scope, of an achievement in science and technique by setting an example related there to in popularization, (b) furnishing users with the systematic information on sciences and value - lasting documents as a study, (c) making technique - inquiring business available to users for requirement of technologies either by way of a suggestion or of a scheme, either analysis or feasibility report, (d) people observing day by day and/or listening and reporting on or testing, by apparatus, things appearing in or changes brought about by the nature and living beings, (e) inspecting and/or searching for resources, (f) collecting, analyzing routinely and sorting out the general - purpose information on societies, humanities and economics, e.g. statistics and on - the - spot investigationon markets, (g) providing a test, standardization, measure, calculation, quality control and patent - related services to the society and the public, not to industrial enterprises and/or firms engaged in the above items - developing dealings made available to their normal production and/or operation.

第 17 篇
CHAPTER 17

文化和体育
Culture and Sports

17－1　文化事业机构和人员情况（2000－2005年）

BASIC STATISTICS OF CULTURAL INSTITUTIONS AND PERSONNEL，2000－2005

年　份 Year	电影事业 Film	艺术事业 Art	公共图书馆 Public Library	文物事业 Culturd Relic	群众文化事业 Mass Culture
机构数（个） Institutions（unit）					
2000	236	49	31	23	19
2001	236	49	31	23	19
2002	236	49	31	24	19
2003	236	49	31	26	19
2004	239	70	32	26	19
2005	190	61	32	27	19
人员数（人） Personnel（person）					
2000	1 930	2 468	1 111	887	798
2001	1 930	2 562	1 014	887	752
2002	1 930	2 483	974	918	755
2003	1 930	2 322	1 095	862	750
2004	1 959	2 937	1 082	875	706
2005	1 118	2 663	1 057	911	710

17－2　图书报纸杂志出版情况

BOOKS，NEWSPAPERS AND MAGAZINES PUBLICATION

项　目	Item	种类（种） Number of Publications（kind）			总印数（万册） Total Copies （10 000 volumes）		
		2003	2004	2005	2003	2004	2005
图书出版总计	**Books Publication Total**	**3 798**	**4 356**	**4 434**	**6 772**	**8 299**	**5 917**
#本　版	Local Publications	3 615	4 028	4 213	5 440	8 263	4 574
书　籍	Books	2 918	3 403	3 600	4 364	4 897	3 713
课　本	Textbook	815	898	794	2 332	3 366	2 133
图　片	Picture	65	55	40	76	36	71
报纸出版总计	**Newspapers Publication Total**	**45**	**41**	**44**	**82 387**	**86 687**	**87 557**
综合报	Comprehensive Newspapers	20	28	26	76 327	81 064	76 539
专业报	Professional Newspapers	25	13	14	6 060	5 623	11 018
省、直辖市级报纸合计	Newspapers at Provincial or Municipal Level	24	25	28	80 746	86 556	87 409
综合报	Comprehensive Newspapers	14	14	14	74 923	80 946	81 744
专业报	Professional Newspapers	10	11	14	5 823	5 610	5 665
区（市）级报纸合计	Newspapers at District （City）Level	21	16	16	1 641	131	148
综合报	Comprehensive Newspapers	6	14	16	1 404	117	148
专业报	Professional Newspapers	15	2		237	14	
杂志出版总计	**Magazines Publication Total**	**245**	**244**	**243**	**4 610**	**4 493**	**4 192**
综　合	Comprehensive	9	21	28	338	654	584
哲学、社会科学	Philosophy and Social Sciences	41	40	34	803	819	730
自然科学、技术	Natural Sciences and Technology	146	136	133	1 063	825	852
文化、教育	Culture and Education	33	29	28	1 569	1 304	964
文学、艺术	Literature and Art	14	16	16	802	861	832
#少年儿童读物	Juvenile and Children's Book	4	1	3	462	49	229
画　刊	Pictorial	2	2	1	34	30	1

17-3 书籍和课本分类出版情况

PUBLICATION OF BOOKS AND TEXTBOOKS BY CATEGORY

类 别 Item	种 类(种) Number of Publication(kind)			总印数(万册) Total Copies(10 000 volumes)		
	2003	2004	2005	2003	2004	2005
总 计 Total	**3 733**	**4 301**	**4 394**	**6 696**	**8 263**	**5 842**
马列主义、毛泽东思想 Marxism-Leninism, Mao Zedong Thought	6	4	13	11	10	8
哲 学 Philosophy	39	79	72	29	55	33
社会科学总论 General Social Sciences	14	42	59	6	33	46
政治、法律 Politics and Law	52	57	69	18	44	34
军 事 Military Affairs	1		3	1		1
经 济 Economics	255	231	270	125	118	131
文化、科学、教育、体育 Culture, Science, Education and Sports	1 579	1 507	1 521	5 349	5 267	3 902
语言、文字 Languages	286	339	317	166	234	195
文 学 Literature	277	401	465	205	348	379
艺 术 Art	611	809	680	506	1 774	721
历史、地理 History and Geography	42	84	121	21	47	57
自然科学总论 General Natural Sciences	29	8	6	13	8	5
数理科学、化学 Mathematics and Chemistry	87	113	106	39	75	65
天文学、地球科学 Astronomy and Geology	2	3	8	1	1	3
生物科学 Biology	5	9	11	1	5	7
医药、卫生 Medicine and Health Care	194	214	238	75	68	63
农业科学 Agricultural Science	15	39	36	3	9	8
工业技术 Industrial Technology	222	348	376	116	162	175
交通运输 Transportation	4	6	8	2	3	2
环境科学 Environmental Science	5	3	11	1	1	3
综合性图书 Comprehensive Books	8	5	4	10	1	4

17-4 录像和录音制品出版情况

PUBLICATION OF VIDEO PRODUCTS

项 目 Item	种 数(种) Kind		数 量(万盒、万张) Volume (10 000 cassettes, pieces)	
	2004	2005	2004	2005
数码激光视盘 VCD	132	50	91.48	140
高密度激光视盘 DVD	12	19	18.70	41
录 音 带 Audio-tapes	89	95	155.38	83.7
激光唱盘 CD	59	48	68.90	39.3

17－5 广播和电视节目制作情况(2005 年)
PRODUCTION OF BROADCASTING AND TELEVISION,2005

单位:小时 (hour)

项　　目 Item	全年制作节目时间 Annual Production of Programs	新闻资讯类 News	专题服务类 Special Topic Service	综艺益智类 Integrative Art and Improve Wise	广播/影视剧类 Broadcasting Film and Teleplay	广告类 Advertisement	其他类 Others
广播电台 Broadcasting Stations	**55 846**	**12 227**	**10 597**	**18 939**	**1 461**	**9 156**	**3 466**
电 视 台 Television Stations	**15 668**	**2 486**	**6 898**	**4 676**	**128**	**1 185**	**295**
天津电视台 Tianjin	8 947	1 402	6 025	1 193	128	199	
塘沽区电视台 Tanggu District	566	108	102	298		58	
汉沽区电视台 Hangu District	1 460	91	5	1 008		356	
大港区电视台 Dagang District	697	303	100	210		84	
武清区电视台 Wuqing District	779	164	272	212		105	26
宝坻区电视台 Baodi District	328	136	79	52		61	
宁河县电视台 Ninghe County	285	85	105			95	
静海县电视台 Jinghai County	1 590	87	98	1 308		79	18
蓟县电视台 Jixian County	1 016	110	112	395		148	251

17－6 广播和电视节目播出情况(2005 年)
PROGRAMS OF BROADCASTING AND TELEVISION,2005

单位:小时:分 (hour:minute)

项　　目 Item	全年播出节目时间 Annual Programs Hours	新闻资讯类 News	专题服务类 Special Topic Service	综艺益智类 Integrative Art and Improve Wise	广播/影视剧类 Broadcasting Film and Teleplay	广告类 Advertisement	其他类 Others
广播电台 Broadcasting Stations	**69 701:00**	**18 189:10**	**11 643:30**	**24 872:55**	**2 372:30**	**9 155:25**	**3 467:30**
电 视 台 Television Stations	**99 376:43**	**7 762:00**	**35 832:54**	**10 794:16**	**33 460:39**	**10 261:39**	**1 265:15**
天津电视台 Tianjin	60 919:03	3 798:10	31 713:24	3 683:51	14 193:04	7 530:34	
塘沽区电视台 Tanggu District	8 515:15	1 790:15	530:00	1 535:00	2 958:00	1 690:00	12:00
汉沽区电视台 Hangu District	6 510:10	130:00	305:55	1 728:15	4 018:20	327:40	
大港区电视台 Dagang District	5 916:50	697:00	1 394:00	1 277:00	2 464:15	84:35	
武清区电视台 Wuqing District	4 820:00	289:00	1 240:00	620:00	1 897:00	154:00	620:00
宝坻区电视台 Baodi District	2 612:00	273:00	237:00	156:00	1 460:00	122:00	364:00
宁河县电视台 Ninghe County	706:45	210:00	135:00		236:00	125:45	
静海县电视台 Jinghai County	5 096:40	464:35	165:35	1 399:10	2 970:00	79:05	18:15
蓟县电视台 Jixian County	4 280:00	110:00	112:00	395:00	3 264:00	148:00	251:00

17-7 广播电台和电视台情况(2002—2005年)
STATISTICS OF BROADCASTING AND TELEVISION STATIONS,2002—2005

单位:套、时:分、%　　(set)(hour:minute)(%)

项　目	Item	2002	2003	2004	2005
广播电台	**Broadcasting Stations**				
节目套数	Number of Programs	7	7	7	9
平均每日播音时间	Broadcasting Hours Per Day	130:07	148:32	158:15	190:58
广播覆盖率	Listener Rating	100	100	100	100
电 视 台	**Television Stations**				
节目套数	Number of Programs	15	16	17	18
平均每周播出时间	Program Hours Per Week	1 278:42	1 509:51	1 545:38	1 911:05
电视覆盖率	Viewer Rating	99	99	99	99.83

17-8 电影放映单位基本情况(2002—2005年)
FILM PROJECTING UNITS,2002—2005

单位:个　　(unit)

指　标	Item	2002	2003	2004	2005
电影院	Cinema	16	12	13	11
影剧院	Theater	13	11	12	12
开放礼堂俱乐部	Opening Auditorium	14	8	8	7
电影放映队	Projecting Team	139	139	139	139
对内俱乐部	Internal Club	15	15	15	15
电影放映单位拥有座席数	Seats	44 282	31 718	34 469	30 576
放映场次(场次)	Projecting Performances(times)	55 290	41 970	51 515	34 751
观众人次(万人次)	Audience (10 000 person - times)	180	103	117	65

17-9 艺术事业基本情况(2002—2005年)
BASIC STATISTICS ON ART,2002—2005

指　标	Item	2002	2003	2004	2005
艺术表演团体	**Art Performance Troupes**				
机构数(个)	Institutions(unit)	15	15	16	16
话剧团、儿童剧团	Drama and Children Troupes	2	2	2	3
歌舞剧团	Song and Dance Troupes	1	1	1	1
文工团、文宣队	Culturaland Performance Troupe	1	1	2	1
戏曲剧团	Local Opera Troupes	7	7	7	7
#京 剧	Local Beijing Opera Troupes	2	2	2	2
曲剧团、杂技团、木偶团	Recitation and Ballad Troupes,Acrobatic and Circus Troupes, Puppet Show Troup	3	3	3	3
乐团、合唱团	Philharmonic Troupes and Chorus	1	1	1	1
工作人员数(人)	Employment(person)	1 781	1 769	1 831	1 803
艺术表演场所	**Art Performance Places**				
机构数(个)	Institutions(unit)	32	32	29	28
剧场、音乐厅	Theatre and Concert Hall	31	31	28	27
书场、曲艺厅	Storytelling Places,Rectation and Balled Places	1	1	1	1
座席数(个)	Seats(unit)	17 858	15 792	17 233	15 529
工作人员数(人)	Employment(person)	650	537	500	395

17－10　艺术表演活动情况(2002—2005年)

ART PERFORMANCE,2002—2005

单位:场、万人次　　(times)(10 000 person－times)

指　标　Item	2002	2003	2004	2005
艺术表演团体　Art Performance Troupes				
演出场次　Number of Performances	2 242	2 191	2 500	2 332
#到农村演出　Shows In Rural Areas	452	433	400	444
观众人次　Number of Spectators	272	260	212	159
艺术表演场所　Art Performance Places				
演出场次　Number of Performances	39 000	30 336	28 600	20 025
观众人次　Number of Spectator	113	73	76	64

17－11　公共图书馆情况(2002—2005年)

PUBLIC LIBRARIES,2002—2005

项　目　Item	2002	2003	2004	2005
工作人员(人)　Employment (person)	974	1 095	1 082	1 057
藏　书(万册)　Collections (10^4 volumes)	822	840	827	869
借阅人次(万人次) Person－times of Borrowing (10^4 person－times)	232	187	170	212
借阅册次(万册次) Number of Books Borrowed (10^4 volume－times)	413	339	263	380
建筑面积(平方米) Floor Space of Buildings (sq.m)	103 000	100 444	170 000	168 685
阅览室座席(个)　Seating Capacity of Reading room (unit)	8 000	7 467	7 959	9 747

17－12　档案事业基本情况(2002—2005年)

BASIC STATISTICS ON ARCHIVES,2002—2005

项　目　Item	2002	2003	2004	2005
机构数(个)　Number of Institutions(unit)	**508**	**497**	**481**	**410**
档案馆　Archives	32	32	35	34
机关事业单位档案室　Archives in Government and Institutions	176	186	158	153
大型工业企业档案馆　Archives in Large Industrial Enterprises	300	279	288	223
专职工作人员(人)　Full－time Personnel(person)	**1 046**	**999**	**1 144**	**913**
档案馆　Archives	388	410	425	434
机关事业单位档案室　Archives in Government and Institutions	220	218	200	176
大型工业企业档案馆　Archives in Large Industrial Enterprises	438	371	519	303
兼职工作人员(人)　Part－time Personnel(person)	**2 690**	**2 466**	**3 746**	**2 000**
机关事业单位档案室　Archives in Government and Institutions	1 037	1 003	1 017	856
大型工业企业档案馆　Archives in Large Industrial Enterprises	1 653	1 463	2 729	1 144

17－13　档案馆档案资料馆藏与开发利用情况(2002—2005 年)

COLLECTION, DEVELOPMENT AND UTILIZATION OF MATERIALS IN ARCHIVES, 2002—2005

项　　目	Item	2002	2003	2004	2005
馆藏档案	**Collection of Archives**				
全　宗(个)	Full－Records(unit)	2 607	2 713	2 851	2 799
案　卷(万卷)	Files(10 000 volumes)	386	393	419	434
录音、录像、影片(盘)	Sounds and Movies Files(cassette)	5 500	6 900	7 300	30 000
照　片(张)	Photo Files(picture)	263 200	253 600	315 900	304 200
保存资料	**Collection of Materials**				
资料数量(万册)	Materials(10 000 volumes)	29	26	30	27
利用档案资料	**Utilization**				
利用人次(万人次)	Users(10 000 person－times)	4	3	3	4
利用档案(万卷次)	Access to Files(10 000 volume－times)	20	11	13	13
利用资料(册次)	Materials(volume－times)	10 500	6 700	13 700	8 000
利用档案资料(万页)	Copy Materials(10 000 pages)	8	8	8	10
编研档案资料	**Editing Materials**				
公开出版(种)	Public Publication(kind)	3	2	9	14
(万字)	(10 000 words)	270	11	330	208
内部参考(种)	Internal Reference(kind)	87	55	79	85
(万字)	(10 000 words)	1 764	278	819	456

17－14　机关事业单位档案资料保存与开发利用情况(2002—2005 年)

KEEPING, DEVELOPMENT AND UTILIZATION OF MATERIALS IN ARCHIVES, 2002—2005

项　　目	Item	2002	2003	2004	2005
保存档案	**Keeping Archives**				
全　宗(个)	Full－Records(unit)	254	263	232	191
案　卷(万卷)	Files(10 000 volumes)	91	125	96	82
底　图(万张)	Chart(10 000 pictures)	131	83	140	132
微缩胶片(万张)	Compressed Film(10 000 pictures)	9			
保存资料	**Keeping Materials**				
保存数量(万册)	Number of Materials(10 000 volumes)	5	5	5	5
借阅利用档案资料	**Lending**				
利用人次(万人次)	Users(10 000 person－times)	5	5	6	5
利用档案资料数量(万卷册数)	Access to Files(10 000 volumes)	11	12	10	9
编研档案资料	**Editing Materials and Archives**				
公开出版(种)	Public Publication(kind)	24	28	30	27
(万字)	(10 000 words)	302	1 247	394	1 400
内部参考(种)	Internal Reference(kind)	119	139	108	91
(万字)	(10 000 words)	1 165	1 335	5 499	1 207

17－15 大型工业企业档案资料保存与开发利用情况(2002—2005年)
KEEPING,DEVELOPMENT AND UTILIZATION OF ARCHIVES MATERIALS IN LARGE－SIZED INDUSTRIAL ENTERPRISES,2002—2005

项 目	Item	2002	2003	2004	2005
保存档案	**Keeping Archives**				
全 宗(个)	Full－Records(unit)	477	444	673	429
案 卷(万卷)	Files(10 000 volumes)	193	167	311	201
底 图(万张)	Chart(10 000 pictures)	345	333	339	114
缩微胶片(万张)	Compressed Film(10 000 pictures)	1	8		
保存资料	**Keeping Materials**				
保存数量(万册)	Number of Materials(10 000 volumes)	15	13	10	3
借阅利用档案资料	**Lending**				
利用人次(万人次)	Users(10 000 person－times)	9	8	11	6
利用档案资料数量(万卷册数)	Access to Files(10 000 volumes)	20	19	23	11
编研档案资料	**Editing Materials and Archives**				
公开出版(种)	Public Publication(kind)	4		1	1
(万字)	(10 000 words)	4		50	40
内部参考(种)	Internal Reference(kind)	262	266	468	739
(万字)	(10 000 words)	898	725	9 093	1 462

17－16 博物馆和文物保护单位基本情况(2002—2005年)
BASIC STATISTICS ON MUSEUMS AND CULTURAL RELIC PROTECTION UNITS,2002—2005

指 标	Item	单 位	Unit	2002	2003	2004	2005
博物馆	**Museums**						
单位数	Number of Units	个	unit	15	17	17	18
工作人员数	Employment	人	person	689	629	658	679
文物藏品	Number of Collection	万件	10^4 pieces	54	55	57	57
举办陈列	Number of Displays	个	unit	26	11		
举办展览	Number of Exhibitions	个	unit	53	46	31	68
参观人次	Numbers of Visitors	万人次	10^4 person－times	97	58	88	102
文物保护单位	**Cultural Relic Protection Units**						
单位数	Number of Units	个	unit	8	8	8	8
工作人员数	Employment	人	person	127	131	117	133
藏 品	Number of Collection	件	piece	3 073	2 975	2 239	2 995

17－17 群众文化事业基本情况(2002—2005年)
BASIC STATISTICS ON MASS ART,2002—2005

指 标	Item	单 位	Unit	2002	2003	2004	2005
单位数	Number of Units	个	unit	19	19	19	19
群众艺术馆	Mass Art Centers	个	unit	1	1	1	1
文化馆	Cultural Centers	个	unit	18	18	18	18
工作人员数	Employment	人	person	755	750	706	710
文化活动情况	Cultural Activity						
举办展览	Number of Exhibitions	次	time	238	144	220	177
组织文艺活动次数	Art Performances	次	time	1 422	1 097	1 143	1 345
举办训练班	Training Courses						
班 次	Number of Classes	班	class	431	595	603	660
结业人数	Number of Persons Completing Course	人	person	9 000	10 000	10 491	9 699

17－18　天津市举办运动竞赛情况(2002—2005 年)
(县及县以上)
SPORTS MEETINGS HELD IN TIANJIN, 2002—2005
(COUNTY－RUN AND OVER)

单位:次、万人　(times)(10 000 persons)

指　　标　Item	2002	2003	2004	2005
举办运动会次数 Sports Meetings	348	367	386	378
参加运动会人数 Athletes Attending Sports Meetings	21	25	28	33
体委系统　Physical Culture and Sports Commissions				
运动会次数　Times	87	82	96	108
参加人数　Person	8	12	14	18
其他系统　Other Departments				
运动会次数　Times	261	285	290	270
参加人数　Person	13	13	14	15

17－19　体委系统体育工作者(2002—2005 年)
PERSONNEL IN SPORTS COMMISSIONS SYSTEM, 2002—2005

单位:人　(person)

指　　标　Item	2002	2003	2004	2005
体育工作者人数 Personnel of Sports	3 602	4 100	4 080	3 920
专职教练员 Full－time Coaches	504	512	524	531
国家级教练员 National Coaches	6	6	5	8
每十万人口中有体育工作者 Number of Physical Personnel in Per 10^5 Persons	39	41	46	46

17－20　等级裁判员和运动员人数
NUMBER OF ATHLETES AND REFEREES IN GRADES

单位:人　(person)

指　　标　Item	裁判员　Referees			运动员　Athletes		
	2003	2004	2005	2003	2004	2005
总人数　Total	**404**	**424**	**436**	**1 283**	**1 250**	**1 132**
一　级　First Grade	68	82	88	72	86	62
二　级　Second Grade	336	342	348	1 211	1 164	1 070
#女　性　Female	**136**	**178**	**184**	**538**	**533**	**490**
一　级　First Grade	22	47	50	36	37	30
二　级　Second Grade	114	131	134	502	496	460

主要统计指标解释

电视人口覆盖率　指用普通的电视接收机，室外天线在离地面4米高处能在晚上正常收看电视节目的人数与全市总人口数之比。

广播人口覆盖率　指用普通的收音机在中午能正常收听广播节目的人数与全市总人口数之比。

文化事业机构　指从事专业文化工作和为专业文化工作服务的单独核算、独立建制的单位，不包括文化主管部门直属单位举办的其他行业和各部门的业余文化组织。

艺术表演团体　指从事戏曲、音乐、舞蹈、杂技等专业艺术表演有独立帐户、实行单独核算的团体。

电影放映单位　指具有放映机器设备，固定或不固定的放映场所与专职或兼职的放映技术人员，经文化部门登记批准，经常为一定的观众对象映出电影的机构。包括经批准对外开放进行营业、并与电影发行放映管理机构分帐的专用放映单位或军委系统租片在内。

等级运动员人数　指经考核正式批准授予等级运动员称号的人数。分为国际级运动健将、运动健将、一、二、三级运动员和少年级运动员。

等级裁判员人数　指经考核正式批准授予等级裁判员称号的人数。分为国际裁判、国家级裁判、一、二、三级裁判。

Explanatory Notes on Main Statistical Indicators

Viewer Rate refers to the ratio of the number of watching TV to the total population using normal television sets with outdoor antenna four meters apart from ground in the evening.

Listener Rate refers to the ratio of the number of listening radio to the total population using normal radiogram at noon.

Cultural Institutions refer to units which have their own organizational system and independent accounting system and specialize in or serve cutural development. They exclude other establishments run by these cultural institutions and amateur cultural groups established by various departments.

Art Troupe refers to the troupe which is engaged in drama, opera, music, dance, acrobatics or other art performance, opens independent accounts with banks and has self - supporting accounting system.

Film Projection Units refer to these units with film projection equipment, full or part - time projectionists, permanent or non - permanent places, approved by related administrative departments to show films regularly for certain groups of audience, including those film projection units which have been approved to give commercial shows and run business with independent accounting system as well as those film - renting units of the military system.

Number of Athletes in Grades refers to the number of athletes who have been given titles through examination. The titles of athletes include international masters of sports, masters of sports, first - grade, second - grade and third - grade sportsmen and young athletes.

Number of Referees in Grades refers to the number of referees who have been given titles after examination. They are classified as international referees, national referees and referees of the first, second and third grades.

第18篇 CHAPTER 18

卫生、社会保障和社会福利

Public Health, Social Security and Social Welfare

18－1　卫生事业基本情况(1990－2005年)

STATISTICS ON PUBLIC HEALTH ,1990－2005

年　份 Year	卫生事业机构(个) Number of Health Care Institutions (unit)	#医院、卫生院 Hospitals and Health Care Centers	卫生机构床位数(张) Beds (unit)	#医院、卫生院 Hospitals and Health Care Centers	卫生技术人员数(人) Medical Technical Personnel (person)	#执业及助理医师 Certified And Assistant Doctors	#注册护士 Registered Nurses
1990	3 392	293	35 581	33 382	67 485	32 034	21 228
1991	3 397	300	37 504	35 124	68 887	32 385	22 086
1992	3 287	301	38 137	36 035	69 815	32 320	22 804
1993	3 182	304	39 023	36 724	70 920	33 026	22 884
1994	3 182	419	38 986	37 157	71 217	33 373	22 936
1995	3 182	416	39 092	37 280	71 806	33 693	23 177
1996	4 171	476	39 612	38 284	71 014	32 975	23 156
1997	3 571	483	40 758	39 467	70 431	32 475	23 045
1998	3 190	482	40 471	39 134	68 070	31 482	22 209
1999	2 969	487	39 779	38 579	65 901	30 273	21 977
2000	2 983	488	40 039	38 842	65 145	30 031	21 667
2001	2 665	495	41 637	40 394	63 475	29 215	21 298
2002	2 636	486	40 090	38 837	56 705	23 888	19 257
2003	2 671	485	40 194	38 074	55 629	22 780	19 173
2004	2 577	474	40 994	38 876	60 722	25 299	19 602
2005	2 489	461	41 556	39 491	61 284	25 088	19 624

18－2　卫生事业机构数(2002－2005年)

NUMBER OF HEALTH CARE INSTITUTIONS,2002－2005

单位:个　　(unit)

名　称	Item	2002	2003	2004	2005
总　计	**Total**	**2 636**	**2 671**	**2 577**	**2 489**
医院、卫生院	Hospitals and Health Care Centers	486	485	474	461
疗养院	Sanatoriums	3	3	3	3
门诊部	Clinics	2 040	2 051	1 965	1 892
专科疾病防治院(所、站)	Specialized Prevention Stations	17	17	18	17
卫生防疫站	Sanitation and Antiepidemic Stations	25	25	24	24
妇幼保健院(所、站)	Maternity and Child Care Centers	21	22	23	23
卫生监督所	Health Office		3	3	3
医学科学研究机构	Research Institutes of Medical Science	9	8	8	8
高等医学教育机构	Education Institutions of High Medicine	3	3	3	3
其他卫生事业机构	Other Health Care Institutions	32	54	56	55
平均每个医院负担人口(人)	Average Burden Population of Each Hospital(person)	18 858	19 021	19 605	22 615

18－3 卫生事业基本情况(2005年)

(按市县、经济类型、管理部门分)

STATISTICS ON PUBLIC HEALTH, 2005

(GROUPED BY CITY & COUNTY, OWNERSHIP AND MANAGEMENT)

部门	Department	卫生机构(个) Health Care Institutions (unit)	卫生机构床位(张) Number of Institutions Beds (unit)	卫生技术人员(人) Medical Technical Personnel(person)	
				合计 Total	#执业及助理医师 Certified And Assistant Doctors
总计	**Total**	**2 489**	**41 556**	**61 284**	**25 088**
按市县分	**Grouped by City & County**				
市	City	2 046	38 352	54 302	21 832
县	County	443	3 204	6 982	3 256
按经济类型分	**Grouped by Ownership**				
国有经济	State－owned	1 263	37 754	54 143	21 678
集体经济	Collective－owned	239	1 978	2 986	1 692
联营、私营经济	Joint Ownership Enterprises and Private	868	1 170	3 115	1 177
其他	Others	119	654	1 040	541
按设置主办单位分	**Grouped by Management**				
政府办	Run by Government	505	32 570	48 004	18 806
#卫生部门	Health sector	480	32 552	47 935	18 759
企业办	Run by Enterprises	566	3 215	5 466	2 782
其他	Others	1 418	5 771	7 814	3 500

部门	Department	卫生技术人员(人) Medical Technical Personnel(person)			
		注册护士 Registered Nurses	药剂人员 Pharmacist	检验人员 Laboratory Technicians	其他人员 Others
总计	**Total**	**19 624**	**4 620**	**3 165**	**8 787**
按市县分	**Grouped by City & County**				
市	City	18 372	4 206	2 902	6 990
县	County	1 252	414	263	1 797
按经济类型分	**Grouped by Ownership**				
国有经济	State－owned	18 674	4 035	2 955	6 801
集体经济	Collective－owned	490	298	115	391
联营、私营经济	Joint Ownership Enterprises and Private	283	190	59	1 406
其他	Others	177	97	36	189
按设置主办单位分	**Grouped by Management**				
政府办	Run by Government	16 721	3 621	2 710	6 146
#卫生部门	Health sector	16 709	3 618	2 706	6 143
企业办	Run by Enterprises	1 651	429	215	389
其他	Others	1 252	570	240	2 252

18－4 卫生技术人员数(2005 年)
NUMBER OF MEDICAL TECHNICAL PERSONNEL,2005

单位:人 (person)

项 目	Item	总 计 Total	#执业及助理医师 Certified And Assistant Doctors	#注册护士 Registered Nurses	#药剂人员 Pharmacist	#检验人员 Laboratory Technicians
总 计	**Total**	**61 284**	**25 088**	**19 624**	**4 620**	**3 165**
医 院	Hospitals	45 718	16 883	17 512	3 653	2 291
#综合医院	Comprehensive Hospitals	29 550	10 985	11 443	2 322	1 554
专科医院	Special Hospitals	9 696	3 098	4 049	581	459
#口腔医院	Stomatitis Hospitals	597	278	165	17	7
眼科医院	Eye Hospitals	307	123	125	23	14
耳鼻喉科医院	E. N. T. Hospitals	47	9	10	2	2
肿瘤医院	Tumour Hospitals	1 107	344	458	59	32
胸科医院	Chest Hospitals	721	250	339	4	25
血液病医院	Blood Disease Hospitals	509	140	169	24	58
妇产科医院	Gynecology Hospitals	1 069	314	529	66	74
儿童医院	Children Hospitals	1 051	323	483	79	45
精神病医院	Mental Disease Hospitals	1 251	287	548	69	36
传染病医院	Infectious Disease Hospitals	446	109	199	45	31
皮肤病医院	Skin Disease Hospitals	17	11	3	2	1
骨科医院	Orthopaedics Hospitals	1 119	374	475	82	50
疗养院	Sanatoriums	203	54	95	10	3
社区卫生服务中心	Community Health Care Centers	70	45	22		
卫生院	Hospitals in Township	4 536	2 543	627	440	210
门诊部	Clinics	1 193	659	153	114	47
急救中心(站)	First－aid Centers	49	30	14	1	
采供血机构	Blood Collection and Supplying Institutions	149	27	43	1	
妇幼保健院(所、站)	Maternity and Child Care Centers	1 536	712	468	89	105
专科疾病防治院(所、站)	Specialized Prevention Stations	551	232	159	40	40
疾病预防控制中心(防疫站)	Disease Prevention and Control Centers	1 796	1 037	87	13	325
卫生监督所	Sanitation Supervision Institutions	161	100	5	1	9
其他卫生机构	Other Health Care Institutions	5 322	2 766	439	258	135

18－5　卫生机构的床位数(2002－2005 年)
NUMBER OF BEDS IN HEALTH CARE INSTITUTIONS, 2002－2005

单位:张　　(unit)

名　称	Item	2002	2003	2004	2005
总　计	**Total**	**40 090**	**40 194**	**40 994**	**41 556**
医　院	Hospitals	35 908	35 896	36 645	37 255
疗养院	Sanatoriums	633	633	643	643
卫生院	Hospitals in Township	2 296	2 178	2 231	2 236
门诊部	Clinics	59	114	111	201
妇幼保健院(所、站)	Maternity and Child Care Centers	779	837	839	818
专科疾病防治院(所、站)	Specialized Prevention Stations	380	499	500	360
其他卫生机构	Other Health Care Institutions	35	37	25	43
平均每千人口有医院床位	Hospital Beds per 1000 Population	3.80	3.77	3.82	3.79

18－6　医疗机构诊疗和病床使用情况(2002－2005 年)
DIAGNOSIS, TREATMENT AND BEDS USED OF MEDICAL INSTITUTIONS, 2002－2005

项　目　Item	2002	2003	2004	2005
诊疗情况(万人次)				
Diagnosis and Treatment(10^4 person－times)				
诊疗人数				
Patients Treated	2 277	2 226	2 455	2 704
#门　诊				
Out－patients	1 930	1 910	2 176	2 411
入院人数				
In－patients	46	45	52	57
平均每月诊疗人数(万人次)				
Number of Patients Treated Per Month(10^4 person－times)				
门诊诊疗人数				
Number of Out－patients	161	159	205	225
入院诊疗人数				
In－patients	4	4	4	5
病床使用情况				
Sickbeds Used				
病人治愈率(%)				
Recovering Rate(%)	40	37	37	36
病床周转次数(次)				
Turnover Beds(times)	13	13	14	16
病床使用率(%)				
Utilization Rate(%)	60	62	65	68
病床工作日(日)				
Working Days of Beds(day)	217	227	238	247
出院者平均住院日数(日)				
Average Hospitalization Period(day)	16	16	15	16

18－7 医院、卫生院、门诊部运营情况(2005年)
OPERATION OF HOSPITALS, HEALTH CLINICS AND OUT－PATIENT, 2005

指标	Item	医院 Hospitals	卫生院 Hospitals in Township	门诊部 Clinics
机构数(个)	Number of Institutions(unit)	266	191	117
总诊疗人次数(万人次)	Patients Treated(10^4 person－times)	2 703.72	515.21	119.99
#门诊人次数	Out－patients	2 411.29	491.56	115.19
急诊人次数	Emergency	223.36	7.38	0.69
观察室收容人数(人)	Observation Room(person)	1 018 887	22 482	5 221
健康检查人数(人)	Health Check(person)	948 514	59 042	22 154
入院人数(人)	In－patients(person)	571 114	69 061	57
出院人数(人)	Leaving Hospital(person)	571 211	68 997	57
住院病人手术人次(人次)	In－patients Surgery Trips(person－times)	187 379	15 766	15
治愈率(%)	Rate of Fully Recovery(%)	35.94	85.12	57.89
好转率(%)	Rate of Taking a Turn for the Better(%)	52.1	8.43	42.11

18－8 社区卫生服务站基本情况(2002－2005年)
BASIC INFORMATION OF HEALTH SERVICE STATIONS, 2002－2005

项目	Item	2002	2003	2004	2005
机构总数(个)	Number of Institutions(unit)	157	151	151	143
总人员数(人)	Total Personnel(person)	720	685	685	1 023
执业医师	Certified Doctors	1	1	1	2
执业助理医师	Certified Assistant Doctors	1	4	5	11
药剂人员	Pharmacists	60	49	62	28
检验人员	Laboratory Technicians	1	1	9	10
其他	Others	657	630	608	972
诊疗人次数(人次)	Number of Hospital Patients(person－times)	833 900	700 392	895 324	784 029
#出诊人次数	Home Visits	231 800	111 890	208 171	189 618

18－9 村卫生室基本情况(2002－2005年)
BASIC INFORMATION OF VILLAGE HEALTH ROOM, 2002－2005

项目	Item	2002	2003	2004	2005
机构总数(个)	Number of Institutions(unit)	2 373	2 266	2 252	2 322
执业助理医师(人)	Certified Assistant Doctors(person)	41	196	331	253
乡村医生和卫生员(人)	Village Health Room & Hygienists(person)	4 573	4 037	3 859	4 932
乡村医生	Village Health Room	4 446	3 978	3 805	4 862
卫生员	Hygienists	127	59	54	70
诊疗人次数(万人次)	Number of Hospital Patients(10^4 person－times)		642.23	697.02	722.94
#孕产妇检查人次数	Number of Checked Pregnant Women		1.41	0.67	0.28
儿童疫苗接种人次数	Number of Vaccinated Children		29.31	20.96	12.69

18－10 妇女儿童卫生保健状况（2002－2005 年）

BASIC STATISTICS OF MATERNITY AND CHILD CARE, 2002－2005

指 标	Item	2002	2003	2004	2005
妇幼保健经费（万元）	Expenses for maternity and child care（10^4 yuan）	997.0	1 156.0	1 858.0	1 718.0
计划生育事业费（万元）	Operating Expenses for Children Planning（10^3 yuan）	5 104.0	5 802.0	7 676.0	9 974.0
户籍人口（万人）	Registered Population（10^4 persons）	919.0	926.0	932.6	939.3
#女 性	Female	455.0	458.7	462.0	465.5
0－4 岁人口	Age 0－4	30.0	28.9	29.7	30.80
#女 性	Female	13.8	13.5	13.9	14.40
0－17 岁人口	Age 0－17	178.0	171.2	165.0	156.90
#女 性	Female	85.0	81.8	78.7	74.70
育龄妇女人口（15－49 岁）	Women of Child－bea ring Age(Age 15－49)	267.0	268.3	268.1	266.90
婴儿死亡率（‰）	Death Rate of Infant(‰)	8.1	8.5	7.3	6.2
5 岁以下儿童死亡率(‰)	Death Rate of Children at Age 5 and below(‰)	9.3	9.9	8.3	7.1
孕产妇死亡率(1/10 万)	Death Rate of Pregnant and Lying－in Woman(1/10^4)	11.5	11.3	12.2	14.7
卡介苗接种率(％)	BCG Vaccination Rate(％)	98.6	97.9	99.8	99.4
脊灰疫苗接种率(％)	Poliovirus Vaccination Rate(％)	97.4	98.3	100.0	99.4
白百破三联制剂接种率(％)	Pertussis, Diphtheria & Tetanus Vaccination Rate(％)	98.1	98.4	99.1	99.4
麻疹疫苗接种率(％)	Measles Virus Vaccination Rate(％)	99.9	98.1	99.3	97.7
乙肝疫苗接种率(％)	Hepatitis B Vaccination Rate(％)	99.8	96.9	99.8	99.8
5 岁以下儿童中、重度营养不良患病率(％)	Incidence Disease Rate from Medium and Serious Malnutrition of Children at Age 5 and below(％)	0.3	0.3	0.3	0.16
7 岁以下儿童保健管理率(％)	Management Rate of Children Health Care System at Age 7 and below(％)	90.1	87.9	86.3	83.4

18－11 全市居民前十位死亡原因、死亡专率

CAUSE OF DEATH AND DEATH RATE OF 10 MAJOR DISEASES

序位及死因	Position and Cause of Death	死亡专率 Death Rate (1/100 000)		占全部死亡人数的％ Proportion(％)	
		2004	2005	2004	2005
1.心脏病	Heart Trouble	157.59	164.72	24.79	27.01
2.脑血管病	Cerebrovascular Disease	149.00	147.78	23.44	24.23
3.恶性肿瘤	Malignant Tumour	131.82	125.86	20.74	20.64
4.呼吸系统疾病	Respiratory Disease	81.72	67.56	12.86	11.08
5.损伤和中毒外部原因	Trauma and Toxicosis	31.27	29.56	4.92	4.85
6.内分泌、营养和代谢的其他疾病	Internal System, Nutrition, Metabolive and Immunity Disease	19.62	18.69	3.09	3.06
7.消化系统疾病	Digestive Disease	16.92	12.57	2.66	2.06
8.泌尿生殖系统病	Urinary Disease	11.28	8.74	1.77	1.43
9.神经系统疾病	Neuropathy	8.10	8.27	1.27	1.36
10.先天畸形、变性和染色体异常	Inborn Abnormaliy, Chromosome Abnormality	2.48	2.59	0.39	0.46

18-12 社会保障事业发展情况(2002-2005年)

BASIC STATISTICS ON SOCIAL SECURITY,2002-2005

指标 Item	计量单位 Unit	2002	2003	2004	2005
医疗保险参保人员情况					
Medical Insurance					
参加基本医疗保险人数 Personnnel Participated in Medical Insurance	万人 10 000 persons	208.50	242.92	263.03	299.10
职工人数 Staff and Workers	万人 10 000 persons	139.20	165.17	158.24	180.80
退休人数 Retired Personnel	万人 10 000 persons	69.30	77.75	104.79	118.30
基本医疗保险基金收入 Revenue of Basic Medical Insurance Funds	亿元 100 million yuan	17.21	19.53	25.03	38.80
基本医疗保险基金支出 Expenditure of Basic Medical Insurance Funds	亿元 100 million yuan	15.07	20.40	27.17	35.90
基本医疗保险基金累计结余 Balance of Basic Medical Insurance Funds	亿元 100 million yuan	2.26	1.39	3.72	10.00
失业保险参保人员情况					
Unemployment Insurance					
参加失业保险职工人数 Personnnel Participated in Unemployment Insurance	万人 10 000 persons	189.55	193.45	195.06	197.50
领取失业保险金人数 Drawing Unemployment Insurance Funds	万人 10 000 persons	12.44	9.50	5.13	3.80
#本年新增 New Increased This Year	万人 10 000 persons	7.42	3.40	3.23	2.30
失业保险基金收入 Revenue of Unemployment Insurance Funds	亿元 100 million yuan	5.35	5.66	6.45	8.20
失业保险基金支出 Expenditure of Unemployment Insurance Funds	亿元 100 million yuan	5.58	4.43	3.06	2.30
失业保险基金累计结余 Balance of Unemployment Insurance Funds	亿元 100 million yuan	2.11	3.34	6.73	13.00
基本养老保险参保人员情况					
Pension Insurance					
参加基本养老保险职工人数 Personnnel Participated in Pension Insurance	万人 10 000 persons	204.61	185.67	194.20	200.60
基本养老保险实际缴费人数 Paying Expense for Pension Insurance	万人 10 000 persons	174.82	175.80	185.80	198.60
基本养老保险基金收入 Revenue of Pension Insurance Funds	亿元 100 million yuan	74.66	85.33	104.27	126.80
基本养老保险基金支出 Expenditure of Pension Insurance Funds	亿元 100 million yuan	67.03	81.78	94.20	102.20
基本养老保险基金累计结余 Balance of Pension Insurance	亿元 100 million yuan	18.55	22.10	32.18	60.00
社会保障标准					
Cocial Security Standaed					
职工工资最低标准 Minimum Standard of Wages of Staff and Workers	元 yuan	450	480	530	590
城镇居民生活保障最低标准 Minimum Standard of Living Security	元 yuan	241	241	241	265

18－13 社会福利事业、企业单位和工作人员数

NUMBER OF SOCIAL WELFARE INSTITUTIONS, ENTERPRISES, PERSONS ENGAGED

部门	Department	机构(个) Institutions or Enterprises(unit) 2004	2005	职工人数(人) Staff and Workers (person) 2004	2005
福利事业单位	Social Welfare Institutions	279	310	3 705	4 325
民政部门办	Run by Civil Adminstration Organs	25	29	1 474	1 563
社会办	Run by Society	254	281	2 231	2 762
福利企业单位	Social Welfare Enterprises	810	781	36 382	17 572
民政部门办	Run by Civil Adminstration Organs	86	75	4 950	5 017
社会办	Run by Society	724	706	31 432	12 555
优抚事业单位	Administration Agencies for Martyrs	9	9	398	398
烈士纪念建筑物管理单位	Martyr Memorial Building Management Units	10	10	168	176
救助管理单位	Collecting and Repatriation Units	8	9	186	183
殡仪服务单位	Funeral and Interment Units	25	25	967	1 003
彩票、募捐单位	Lottery & Collecting Purse Units		10		64
福利彩票发行单位	Welfare Lottery Issuing Units	5	6	41	42
城镇社区服务中心	Urban Community Service Institutions	108	111	821	920

18－14 收养性社会福利事业单位基本情况(2005年)

BASIC STATISTICS ON SOCIAL WELFARE INSTITUTIONS, 2005

指标	Item	单位数(个) Institutions (unit)	床位数(张) Number of Beds (unit)	职工人数(人) Staff and Workers (person)	年末在院收养人员(人) Adopted Personnel at the Year-end (person)	#女性 Female
总计	**Total**	**267**	**16 113**	**3 493**	**11 176**	**4 953**
民政部门办	**Run by Civil Administration Organ**	**9**	**2 477**	**794**	**2 318**	**1 044**
社会福利院	Social Welfare Homes	6	1 065	355	957	424
#市养老院	City Nursing Homes	1	505	185	505	300
儿童福利院	Welfare Homes for Children	2	818	154	767	432
#SOS儿童村	SOS Children's Village	1	200	27	158	61
精神病人福利院	Psychopath Welfare Homes	1	594	285	594	188
社会办	**Run by Society**	**258**	**13 636**	**2 699**	**8 858**	**3 909**
城镇老年福利机构	Run by Urban	127	9 963	2 133	6 628	3 386
农村老年福利机构	Run by Rural	131	3 673	566	2 230	523

18－15 社会福利企业情况(2002－2005年)
BASIC STATISTICS ON SOCIAL WELFARE ENTERPRISES, 2002－2005

指标	Item	2002	2003	2004	2005
民政部门办	**By Civil Administration Organ**				
工业	**Industry**				
单位数(个)	Number of Units(unit)	87	80	83	69
#国有经济	Stated－owned	33	36	32	29
职工人数(人)	Staff and Workers(person)	6 003	5 193	4 890	4 346
#盲聋哑残人数	Blind, Deaf, Mute, Disabled	2 352	2 058	2 008	1 823
销售收入(万元)	Sales Revenue(10 000 yuan)	46 577	51 331	60 466	57 294
#国有经济	Stated－owned	33 717	35 158	35 862	31 002
盈利金额(万元)	Profit(10 000 yuan)	2 685	3 140	4 931	1 656
亏损金额(万元)	Losses(10 000 yuan)	1 377	1 772	931	1 739
商业服务业	**Commerce and Service**				
单位数(个)	Number of Units(unit)	5	4	3	3
职工人数(人)	Staff and Workers(person)	91	76	60	48
销售收入(万元)	Sales Revenue(10 000 yuan)	615	851	625	112
盈利金额(万元)	Profit(10 000 yuan)	15	2	9	15
亏损金额(万元)	Losses(10 000 yuan)	174	252	8	6
社会办	**By Society**				
单位数(个)	Number of Units(unit)	802	759	724	697
职工人数(人)	Staff and Workers(person)	35 078	31 680	31 432	26 651
#盲聋哑残人数	Blind, Deaf, Mute, Disabled	16 204	14 668	14 185	12 422
销售收入(万元)	Sales Revenue(10 000 yuan)	389 057	495 872	529 044	770 751

18－16 抚恤事业单位情况(2002－2005年)
SITUATION OF ADMINISTRATION AGENCIES FOR MARTYRS, 2002－2005

指标	Item	2002	2003	2004	2005
优抚对象(人)	**Martyrs and Disabled Veterans(person)**	**26 344**	**25 413**	**24 582**	**24 521**
定期抚恤小计	Total of Regular Pensions	1 391	1 336	1 274	1 249
烈属	Members of Revolutionary Martyr's Family	954	882	830	799
牺牲病故军人家属	Families of Soldiers Sacrificed or Died of Illness	437	454	444	450
定期补助小计	Total of Periodic Grants	24 953	24 077	23 308	23 272
#现役军人家属	Servicemen's Families	4 659	4 373	3 833	3 890
革命伤残人员	Revolutionary Disabled	7 103	7 106	7 094	7 251
在乡复员军人	Demobilized Soldiers in Hometown	8 659	7 927	7 621	7 436
在乡退伍老红军战士	Demobilized Old Red Army Men in Hometown	3	2	2	2
优抚对象补助金额(万元)	**Funds for Family Members of Martyrs and Disabled Veterans(10 000 yuan)**	**3 123**	**5 715**	**5 757**	**5 878**
国家支出	Government Funds	3 944	3 809	4 014	4 232
集体供给	Collective Funds	2 179	1 906	1 743	1 646
抚恤事业费(万元)	**Pensions(10 000 yuan)**	**8 159**	**8 472**	**9 068**	**12 879**

18－17 城乡社会救济情况(2002－2005年)

BASIC STATISTICS OF URBAN & RURAL SOCIAL RELIEF, 2002－2005

指标 Item	2002	2003	2004	2005
城乡社会救济总人数(人)				
Number of Persons Receiving Relief Funds(person)	**332 470**	**273 627**	**239 834**	**182 696**
#城市居民最低生活保障人数				
Number of Persons Receiving Lowest Cost－of－living in Urban Areas	301 393	241 308	205 118	150 821
#下岗人员				
Laid－off Staff and Workers	74 345	37 381	18 618	63 612
农村居民最低生活保障人数				
Number of Persons Receiving Lowest Cost－of－living in Rural Areas	22 560	26 140	28 954	11 442
城乡临时救济人次数(人次)				
Number of Poor Persons Receiving Temporary Almsgiving(person－times)	**85 972**	**118 987**	**84 624**	**88 700**
城市临时救济人次数				
Number of Poor persons Receiving Temporary Almsgiving in Urban Area	56 587	76 577	38 667	44 244
农村临时救济人次数				
Number of Poor persons Receiving Temporary Almsgiving in Rural Area	29 385	42 410	45 957	44 456
社会救济费(万元)				
Relief Funds(10 000 yuan)	**29 772**	**33 499**	**36 128**	**48 720**
#农村社会救济费				
Rural Relief Funds	689	1 036	1 310	2 094
城镇低保救济费				
Urban Relief Funds	20 153	22 187	24 743	26 680
精简退职老职工救济费				
Relief for Old Staff and Workers Reduced and Discharged	712	487	505	696
自然灾害救济费(万元)				
Relief for Natural Disaster (10 000 yuan)	**804**	**1 745**	**1 721**	**1 170**

18－18 城镇社区服务情况(2002－2005年)

BASIC STATISTICS ON URBAN COMMUNITY SERVICE, 2002－2005

指标	Item	2002	2003	2004	2005
城镇社区服务设施数(个)	Number of Urban Welfare Facilities(unit)	2 425	1 913	1 976	2 139
社区从业人员(万人)	Persons Employed in Community	2	2	10	10
#安置下岗人员	Placement of Laid－off Staff and Workers	1	1	1	2
社区服务志愿者人数(万人)	Number of Service Volunteers in Community	32	30	33	36
便民利民服务网点(个)	Urban Service Points for Civilian(unit)	8 923	8 373	9 476	8 907
城镇社区服务中心	Urban Community Service Center				
单位数(个)	Number of Units(unit)	98	105	108	111
年末职工人数(人)	Number of Staff and Workers Year－end (person)	794	792	821	920
活动项目数(个)	Number of Project Activities (unit)	602	797	867	918
活动人次(人次)	Number of Persons Coming to Center(person－times)	554 855	594 781	673 304	568 796

主要统计指标解释

卫生技术人员 指卫生事业机构支付工资的全部固定职工和合同制职工中现任职务为卫生技术工作的人员。包括中医师、西医师、中西医结合高级医师、护师、中药师、西药师、检验师、其他技师、中医士、西医士、护士、助产士、中药剂士、西药剂士、检验士、其他技士、其他中医、护理员、中药剂员、西药剂员、检验员和其他初级卫生技术人员。不包括从事管理工作的卫生技术人员。

执业(助理)医师 指持有执业(助理)医师证书,并从事医疗卫生工作的人员。

妇幼保健经费 包括妇幼保健机构经费、业务费、妇幼医疗减免费等。

计划生育事业费 包括九个部分,即计划生育手术减免经费、避孕药具经费、基层计划生育专职干部经费、独生子女保健费、宣传经费、服务站经费、流动人口计划生育管理费、干部培训费、其他计划生育事业费。

婴儿死亡率 指一年内未满周岁死亡的婴儿数与当年活产数之比。计算公式为:

婴儿死亡率=(一年内未满周岁的婴儿死亡数/当年活产数)×1000‰

5岁以下儿童死亡率 指一年内未满5岁儿童死亡人数与当年活产数之比。计算公式为:

5岁以下儿童死亡率=(一年内未满5岁儿童死亡数/当年活产数)×1000‰

孕产妇死亡率 指年内孕产妇死亡人数与活产数之比。孕产妇死亡一般指从妊娠开始至产后42天内死亡者,包括外科原因、计划生育手术、宫外孕、葡萄胎死亡者,但不包括意外原因死亡者。

卡介苗、脊灰疫苗、百白破三联制剂、麻疹疫苗接种率 指按照儿童免疫程度进行合格接种的人数占全部应接种人数的百分比。应接种人数包括禁忌症人数和外地寄居3个月及以上的适龄人数,不包括外出3个月及以上的适龄人数。计算公式为:

单项疫苗接种率=(合格接种该疫苗人数/应接种人数)×100%

分子:按"合格接种判断"标准,判定当年实际完成合格接种的儿童数。

分母:按免疫程序规定当年应在12月龄内完成该项疫苗接种的儿童数。

5岁以下儿童中、重度营养不良患病率 指年内5岁以下儿童中,患中度和重度营养不良的儿童数与全部5岁以下儿童数之比。

7岁以下儿童保健管理率 指年内7岁以下儿童中当年实际接受1次及以上儿童保健服务的人数与当地7岁以下儿童数之比。

Explanatory Notes on Main Statistical Indicators

Medical Technical Personnel refer to all medical staff and workers employed by medical institutions, including doctors of Chinese and Western medicine, senior doctors who integrate traditional Chinese therapeutics with Western therapeutics in practice, senior nurses, pharmacists of Chinese and Western medicine, laboratory specialists, other specialists, paramedics of Chinese and Western medicine, nurses, midwives, druggists in Chinese and Western medicine, laboratory technicians, other technicians, other practitioners of Chinese medicine, nursing attendants, pharmacological workers of Chinese and Western medicine, laboratory workers, and other primary medical personnel, excluding management personnel.

Certified Physician(certified assistant physician) refer to personnel with certifications working in health care institutions.

Expenses for Maternity and Child Care include expenses for maternity and child care institutions, business cost, relief or free medicine for maternity and child, etc.

Operating Expenses for Family Planning include nine components, namely, expenses for relief or free family planning operation, expenses for birth control medicine & tools, expenses for family planning employee, health care expenses for only son and daughter, expenses for publicity, expenses for service station, expenses for family planning management of fluid population, expenses for personnel training, other operation expenses for family planning.

The Death Rate of Infant refers to the ratio of the number of dead infant below 1 year to the number of living in one year. The following formula is used:

The death rate of infant = (number of dead infant/number of living) × 1000‰

The Death Rate of Baby Below 5 **year - old** refers to the ratio of the number of dead baby below 5 to the living number. The following formula is used:

The death rate of baby below 5 year - old = (number of dead baby bellow 5 /number of living) × 1000‰

The Death Rate of Pregnant Woman refers to the ratio of the number of dead pregnant woman to the living number. The death of pregnant woman usually refers from gestation to die after give birth to child in 42 days, including surgery reason, family planning operation, pregnancy outside the womb, grape embryo dead women, excluding die due to accident trouble.

The Rate of Vaccine Inoculation of Bcg Vaccine, Poliomyelitis, Pertussis and Measles refers to the ratio of the number of children inoculating vaccine to the children on the age to inoculate vaccine. The children on the age to inoculate vaccine include the children avoiding to inoculate vaccine and living in some other place for 3 and more than 3 months, but exclude the children on age going out for 3 months. The following formula is used:

The rate of vaccine inoculation = (the number of children inoculating vaccine / the children on the age to inoculate vaccine) × 100%

The molecule: the actual number of children inoculating vaccine according to the standard of vaccine inoculation.

The denominator: the number of children according to the process of immunity should inoculate the vaccine in 12 months.

The Ratio of Innutritious Child below 5 **year - old** refers to the ratio of the number of children below five - year old have modest and heavy innutrition to the total number of children below 5.

The Ratio of Health Care and Management of Child below 7 **year - old** refers to the ratio of the number of children below 7 year - old who take child health care serves more than 1 time to the total number of local children below 7 year - old.

第 19 篇
CHAPTER 19

公共管理和社会组织
Public Management and Social Organizations

19-1 检察机关立案侦察经济案件情况(2005年)
ECONOMIC CASES UNDER INVESTIGATION BY PROCURATORIAL OFFICES,2005

项目 Item	侦查经济案件 Economic Cases Investigated	#贪污 Corrup-tion	#挪用公款 Misapprop-riate Public Funds	#贿赂案 Bribery	#受贿 Accepting Bribe
立案(件) Cases Registered(case)	**460**	**216**	**117**	**123**	**106**
#5万元至10万元 50000-100000 Yuan	211	132	4	75	73
10万元至50万元 100000-500000 Yuan	132	49	63	19	11
50万元至100万元 500000-1000000 Yuan	30	7	17	6	5
100万元以上 Over 1000000 Yuan	41	4	31	3	1
犯罪嫌疑人(人) Criminal in Cases Registered(person)	**473**	**225**	**120**	**124**	**107**
机关工作人员 Civil Servant	86	22	18	45	43
国有公司企业工作人员 Personnel of State-owned Enterprises	281	147	79	52	48
国有事业单位工作人员 Personnel of State-owned Institutions	38	21	9	8	8
委派到非国有单位从事公务人员 Functionary Appointed to Non-state Units	5	3	1	1	1
人民团体从事公务人员 Functionary Appointed to Mass Organizations	1		1		
其他依法从事公务人员 Other Personnel Line of Duty	45	29	10	6	6
其他 Others	17	3	2	12	1
结案 Cases Settled					
件数(件) Number of Cases(case)	380	186	86	108	97
人数(人) Number of Persons(person)	390	194	87	109	98
#移送起诉 Hand over to Suit					
件数(件) Number of Cases(case)	366	182	81	103	94
人数(人) Number of Persons(person)	376	190	82	104	95
撤销案件 Cases Withdrawed					
件数(件) Number of Cases(case)	6	2	4		
人数(人) Number of Persons(person)	6	2	4		
侦结认定金额(万元) Value Approved by Procuratorial Organs in Cases Settled(10 000 yuan)	**31 581.4**	**2 425.07**	**27 499.29**	**1 657.04**	**1 425.06**
挽回经济损失(万元) Retrieve Pecuniary Losses(10 000 yuan)	**3 301.41**	**606.7**	**2 219.2**	**475.51**	**338.33**

19-2 法院民事案件收案和结案情况(2005年)
CIVIL CASES ACCEPTED & SETTLED BY COURTS,2005

单位:件 (case)

项目	Item	收案 Cases Accepted	结案 Cases Settled	#调解 Mediation	#判决 Judgement
合同纠纷案件	**Contracts Disputes**	**48 750**	**47 789**	**8 973**	**23 409**
#买卖合同纠纷	Buying and Selling Contracts	8 879	8 694	2 291	4 047
房地产合同纠纷	Real Estate Contracts	884	910	106	543
借款合同纠纷	Debts Contracts	7 990	7 713	1 732	4 384
建设工程合同纠纷	Construction Project Contracts	1 275	1 259	295	624
运输合同纠纷	Transportation Contracts	396	380	84	189
婚姻家庭案件	**Marriages and Family Affair**	**12 324**	**12 188**	**4 756**	**4 538**
#离婚	Divorce	9 881	9 751	3 914	3 554
抚育	Foster	742	735	260	319
赡养	Support	649	646	157	286
继承纠纷案件	**Inheritance Disputes**	**329**	**306**	**97**	**138**
#继承	Inheritance	177	158	45	73
遗嘱	Testaments	6	6	3	2
继承权	Inheritance Right	10	9	1	5
抚养	Bring-up	6	5	2	3
其他	Others	129	127	46	54

19-3 法院行政案件收案和结案情况(2005年)
ADMINISTRATIVE CASES ACCEPTED AND SETTLED BY COURTS,2005

单位:件 (case)

项目	Item	收案 Cases Accepted	结案 Cases Settled	#维持 Affirmation of Original Judgement	#撤消 Cancel Settled	#撤诉 Withdraw	未结 Cases Unsettled
合计	**Total**	**738**	**689**	**241**	**38**	**148**	**142**
公安	Publi Security	95	90	39	9	21	15
资源	Resources	83	74	14	10	16	16
城建	City Construction	295	268	125	7	39	63
工商	Industry and Commerce	27	23	3		7	6
技术监督	Technology Supervision	3	5	2		1	
计划生育	Family Planning	5	5				
卫生	Health Care	16	12	3		3	5
物价	Price		1				
环保	Environment Protection	5	5	2			
交通	Transportation	32	31	10		13	3
税务	Tax	4	4	1		3	
海关(含商检)	Customs(Including Inspection & Quarantine)	1	1	1			
劳动和社会保险	Labour & Social Security	39	42	14	4	10	5
烟草专卖	Tobacco						
司法行政	Judicature	5	5	3		2	2
民政	Civil Affairs	8	8	2	1	3	1
教育	Education	12	13		1	3	
乡政府	Township Government	2	2			1	
其他	Others	106	100	22	6	26	26

19－4　调解工作基本情况(2002－2005 年)

BASIC STATISTICS ON MEDIATION,2002－2005

项　目　Item	单　位　Unit	2002	2003	2004	2005
司法助理员 Judicial Assistants	人 person	426	585	645	589
人民调解委员会 People's Mediation Committees	个 unit	6 095	6 136	133 510	5 984
调解民间纠纷 Civil Disputes	件 case	28 277	25 377	29 785	30 647
调解成功 Success	件 case	27 343	24 583	28 814	29 699
防止民事案件转化为刑事案件	件 case	94	57	84	127
Prevent Intensification of Civil Disputes	人 person	238	243	316	787
防止非正常死亡案件	件 case	48	27	45	34
Avoid Injuries and Deaths	人 person	80	34	55	42

19－5　律师工作基本情况(2002－2005 年)

BASIC STATISTICS ON LAWYERS,2002－2005

项　目　Item	单　位　Unit	2002	2003	2004	2005
律师事务所 Law Offices	所 unit	199	210	223	239
职业律师 Lawyers	人 person	2 177	1 729	2 445	2 518
#专职律师 Full－time Lawyers	人 person	1 398	1 618	1 705	1 722
兼职律师 Part－time Lawyers	人 person	304	111	111	134
聘请常年法律顾问的单位 Units with Permanent Legal Advisers	家 unit	3 093	6 026	4 582	4 657
民事代理 Civil Case	件 case	9 782	10 632	12 011	13 156
经济代理 Economic Case	件 case	6 486	6 084	5 454	5 641
刑事辩护 Criminal Defense	件 case	4 130	3 619	3 380	4 040
行政诉讼代理 Agent of Administrative Action	件 case	528	372	634	539
非诉讼事务 Off－court Case	件 case	8 135	17 621	24 396	20 277
解答法律咨询 Legal Advisory Services	人次 person－times	60 741	23 774	27 900	22 718
代写法律文书 Legal Document Written on Behalf of Clients	件 case	10 427	7 966	8 144	8 463

19－6　主要年份公证工作基本情况
BASIC STATISTICS ON NOTARIZATION IN MAIN YERS

单位:件　　(case)

项　目	Item	1995	2000	2004	2005
公证机构(个)	**Notary Offices(unit)**	**20**	**20**	**21**	**21**
公证员(人)	**Notarial Personnel(person)**	**286**	**278**	**267**	**267**
办理公证(件)	**Notarized Documents(case)**	**111 811**	**175 486**	**180 783**	**149 483**
国内公证总计	**Domestic Affairs Total**	**82 316**	**107 198**	**120 244**	**91 454**
民事公证	**Civil Legal Relations Notarized**	**35 055**	**37 249**	**52 082**	**46 455**
#收　养	Child Adoption	398	172	140	57
解除收养	Adoption Renouncements	44	3	3	1
继承权	Rights of Inheritance	2 378	3 526	6 392	6 228
遗　嘱	Testaments	804	1 606	802	906
亲属关系	Kinship Confirmation	252	429	230	812
房屋买卖	Purchases and Sales of House	660	2 926	3 721	3 420
房屋租赁	House Leases	198	12	269	428
委托书	Certificate of Entrustment	874	1 463	13 680	16 534
赠予书	Presentation Documents	3 334	2 453	1 341	1 072
声明书	Declarations	642	2 390	3 992	2 440
经济公证	**Business Notarized**	**47 261**	**69 949**	**68 162**	**44 999**
#购　销	Purchases and Sales of Contracts	485	38	65	74
联　营	Joint Business Contracts	42	3		450
贷　款	Loans Contracts	16 572	44 570	36 250	15 564
招标投标	Bidding	227	385	1 052	915
劳务合同	Labour Contracts	1 660	426	23	
建筑工程承包	Construction Project Contracts	521	178	505	475
农林牧副渔业承包	Farming,Forestry,Animal Husbandry,Sideline	492	783	317	60
财产租赁	Property Leases	2 831	620	1 730	2 056
法人资格	Legal Person Identification	782	153	45	19
法人委托书	Legal Person Certificate of Entrustment	303	401	4 082	3 094
涉外公证总计	**Foreign Affairs Total**	**29 495**	**67 803**	**60 539**	**58 029**
#出　生	Births	4 254	11 308	7 226	7 703
学　历	Schooling	5 632	11 919	7 010	6 393
经　历	Personal Histories	1 845	2 517	887	660
生存、居住	Survial and Residence		89	39	41
死　亡	Deaths		120	107	112
亲属关系	Kinship	2 011	5 313	5 157	5 023
婚姻状况	Marriages	3 056	5 067	2 998	2 360
继承权	Rights of Inheritance		3	9	
委托书	Trust Deeds		244	550	539
声明书	Declarations		450	1 087	980
受、未受刑事处分	Criminal Reeords & Undcriminal Records	3 444	9 131	6 773	7 014
文本相符	Confirmation of Copies and Photo－Offset Copies to Originals	581	7 445	4 587	3 971
其　他	Others	2 241	3 411	11 851	10 734

19－7 基层工会组织情况(2002－2005年)

STATISTICS ON GRASSROOTS UNIONS,2002－2005

项 目	Item	2002	2003	2004	2005
机构数(个)	**Institutions(unit)**	**13 947**	**12 440**	**15 980**	**16 199**
#国有企业	State－owned Enterprises	2 538	2 278	2 377	2 112
集体企业	Collective－owned Enterprises	1 850	1 862	1 933	1 722
私营企业	Private Enterprises	1 780	1 726	4 456	4 542
港澳台商投资企业	Enterprises with Investment from Hongkong,Macao and Taiwan	212	162	236	219
外商投资企业	Foreign Funded Enterprises	1 527	1 215	528	555
事 业	Institutions	2 615	2 979	3 353	3 505
机 关	Agencies	744	902	909	1 055
#建立职工代表大会制度的单位	Unit of Founding Employee Congress System	6 659	5 415	5 682	5 216
职工人数(人)	**Staff and Workers(person)**	**2 759 122**	**1 984 048**	**2 612 680**	**2 766 620**
#国有企业	State－owned Enterprises	1 045 361	805 061	857 775	869 485
集体企业	Collective－owned Enterprises	288 713	251 563	306 914	236 108
私营企业	Private Enterprises	108 924	125 662	311 062	366 225
港澳台商投资企业	Enterprises with Investment from Hongkong,Macao and Taiwan	33 680	16 026	41 656	41 802
外商投资企业	Foreign Funded Enterprises	178 955	119 011	142 305	163 375
事 业	Institutions	548 533	321 334	364 608	394 196
机 关	Agencies	84 984	85 860	94 330	98 276
#女职工	Female	894 837	798 939	905 524	921 897
#工会专职干部	Full－time Personnel	959	970	930	915

注:2003年职工人数不包括离退休及不在岗职工。
Note:In 2003,staff and workers exclude retired veterans,retired persons and those who are not on the job.

19－8 妇联组织情况(2002－2005年)

STATISTICS FOR WOMEN'S FEDERATION ORGANIZATIONS,2002－2005

项 目	Item	2002	2003	2004	2005
妇联组织机构(个)	**Woman Organizations(unit)**	**290**	**253**	**248**	**246**
区妇联	District Woman Organizations	15	15	15	15
县妇联	County Woman Organizations	3	3	3	3
乡妇联	Township Woman Organizations	177	140	141	140
街妇联	Street Woman Organizations	95	95	89	88
妇联干部总数(人)	**Cadres in Woman Organizations(person)**	**570**	**484**	**544**	**510**
市妇联	Municipal Woman Organizations	74	66	64	60
区妇联	District Woman Organizations	101	119	115	110
县妇联	County Woman Organizations	55	22	23	20
乡镇、街道妇联	Township and Street Woman Organizations	340	277	342	320

19-9 妇联工作情况(2002-2005年)

WOMEN'S FEDERATION WORKS, 2002-2005

项 目 Item	单 位 Unit	2002	2003	2004	2005
双学双比活动					
Double Study And Double Compare Activity					
实用技术培训情况					
Training of Practical Technology					
接受技术培训的妇女数					
Women Received Technology Training	人 person	163 239	152 426	136 421	210 049
女农民技术员					
Female Peasant Technician	人 person	8 035	3 010	3 307	21 195
获绿色证书人数					
Persons Obtaining Green Certificate	人 person	10 200	4 166	3 669	18 958
扶贫情况					
Poverty Helping					
"三八"绿色基地个数					
Number of "3.8" Green Base	个 unit	92	88	43	17
脱贫户数					
Number of Female of Escaping from Poverty	人 person	3 952	3 086	3 180	1 144
巾帼建功活动					
Activity of Women Making Contribution					
岗位建功成材					
Making Professional Contribution					
评选巾帼文明示范岗数					
Number of Civilization Post Chosen	个 unit	188	132	91	144
表彰标兵数					
Number of Prised Pacesetter	人 person	2 343	2 325	2 345	225
下岗女工再就业情况					
Reemployment of Laid-off Female Workers					
培训下岗女工人数					
Laid-off Trained	人 person	17 826	19 431	25 707	21 734
介绍下岗女工就业人数					
Laid-off Introduced to Employ	人 person	17 781	5 835	21 944	19 750
"三八"红旗手					
"3.8" Advanced Individual	人 person	1 969	554	1 314	624
"三八"红旗集体					
"3.8" Advanced Collectivity	个 unit	414	140	284	212
五好文明家庭					
"Five Good" Families	户 household	38 329	41 256	38 167	41 858
家庭教育场所					
Families Educational Places					
家长学校					
Householder School	个 unit	1 577	2 034	2 187	2 513
广播电视父母学校					
Broadcasting Parents School	个 unit	513	162	98	188
实施春蕾计划					
Actualizing Spring Bud Project					
资助女童入学或返校数					
Supporting Female Child Entering School	人 person	1 213	1 278	1 367	1 925
社会捐资总额					
Total of Social Donation	万元 10 000 yuan	99	80	226	143

19-10 受理消费者投诉情况(2005年)

BASIC STATISTICS ON ACCEPTED CASES OF CONSUMER INSTITUTION,2005

项目	Item	总计 Total	质量 Quality	安全 Safety	价格 Price	计量 Measur
受理投诉件数总计(件)	**Total Number of Accepted Cases(item)**	**4 237**	**3 248**	**108**	**219**	**39**
家用电子电器类	Household Electric Appliance	1 313	1 125	3	16	1
电视机	Television Set	144	129			
家庭影院	Household Cinema	7	7			
空调器类产品	Air-conditioner	145	111		1	
洗衣机类产品	Washing Machine	58	54			
电冰箱(冰柜)	Refrigerator(Freezer)	72	70			
厨房电器及相关产品	Kitchen Electric Appliances and Relative Product	79	66	2		
照摄像产品	Camera and DV	18	15		1	
通讯类产品	Telecommunications Product	638	563	1	10	
计算机类产品	Computer Series	52	42		3	
#计算机	Computer	49	39		3	
其　他	Others	100	68		1	1
家用机械类	Household Machinery	347	299	6	2	
汽　车	Car	63	50		2	
摩托车	Motorcycle	53	51			
热水器	Water Heater	127	109	5		
其　他	Others	104	89	1		
百货类	Daily Using Commodities	1 202	979	33	46	11
#化妆用品	Cosmetic	43	29	7	3	
保健用品	Health Care Goods	42	32	2		
家俱类产品	Furniture	201	158	3	14	
服装鞋帽	Garments,Shoes & hat	424	384	1	11	1
保健食品	Health Care Foodstuff	24	15		1	1
药　品	Medicine	15	5	4	1	
医疗辅助用品	Medical Treatment Articles	8	7			
房屋及装修建材	House and Decoration Materials	308	234	3	10	7
#房　屋	House	106	65	3	4	7
装饰材料	Decoration Materials	168	140		6	
农用生产资料类	Agricultural Production Materials	200	196			
#种子苗木、化肥	Seed,Young Plant,Chemical Fertilizer	182	180			
服务类	Service	783	366	58	141	18
#美容、美发、洗浴	Hairdressing and Wash	99	61	17	4	
电　信	Telecommunications	150	37	1	72	7
邮　政	Posts	6	2	1		
洗衣业	Laundry	86	73	7	4	
旅　游	Tourism	20	9	2		
房屋装修与物业管理	Building Decoration and Property Management	89	58	5	10	1
咨询中介	Consulting Agent	91	32		13	
其他商品类	Other Commodities	84	49	5	4	2
解决件数总计(件)	**Total Cases Solved(item)**	**4 237**				
为消费者挽回损失(万元)	**Exempting Expense for Consumers(10 000 yuan)**	**404.07**				

注:本资料为天津市消费者协会系统的统计数据,不含各监测站的统计资料。
Note: The data of this table are provided by Tianjin Municipal Consumer Institution,exclude those data calculated by each monitor station.

19－10 续表 Continued

项 目	Item	广 告 Adverti－sement	假 冒 Counter－feit	营销合同 Business Contract	其 他 Others
受理投诉件数总计(件)	**Total Number of Accepted Cases(item)**	**58**	**37**	**252**	**276**
家用电子电器类	Household Electric Appliance	16	12	64	76
电视机	Television Set	3			12
家庭影院	Household Cinema				
空调器类产品	Air－conditioner	4		22	7
洗衣机类产品	Washing Machine				4
电冰箱(冰柜)	Refrigerator(Freezer)			1	1
厨房电器及相关产品	Kitchen Electric Appliances and Relative Product			4	7
照摄像产品	Camera and DV				2
通讯类产品	Telecommunications Product	5	12	33	14
计算机类产品	Computer Series	3		2	2
#计算机	Computer	3		2	2
其 他	Others	1		2	27
家用机械类	Household Machinery	1	1	11	27
汽 车	Car	1		5	5
摩托车	Motorcycle				2
热水器	Water Heater		1	5	7
其 他	Others			1	13
百货类	Daily Using Commodities	16	14	31	72
#化妆用品	Cosmetic	1			3
保健用品	Health Care Goods	3	2		3
家俱类产品	Furniture	1	3	19	3
服装鞋帽	Garments, Shoes & hat	3	3	1	20
保健食品	Health Care Foodstuff	1	1	1	4
药 品	Medicine	1	1		3
医疗辅助用品	Medical Treatment Articles	1			
房屋及装修建材	House and Decoration Materials	3	6	35	10
#房 屋	House			24	3
装饰材料	Decoration Materials	3	6	8	5
农用生产资料类	Agricultural Production Materials			1	3
#种子苗木、化肥	Seed, Young Plant, Chemical Fertilizer			1	1
服务类	Service	20	1	104	75
#美容、美发、洗浴	Hairdressing and Wash	5		10	2
电 信	Telecommunications		1	10	22
邮 政	Posts			3	
洗衣业	Laundry				2
旅 游	Tourism			3	6
房屋装修与物业管理	Building Decoration and Property Management			15	
咨询中介	Consulting Agent	7		32	7
其他商品类	Other Commodities	2	3	6	13
解决件数总计(件)	**Total Cases Solved(item)**				
为消费者挽回损失(万元)	**Exempting Expense for Consumers(10 000 yuan)**				

主要统计指标解释

律师 指依法取得律师执业证书，担任法律顾问，民事(刑事、行政)案件代理人、刑事案件辩护人、办理非诉讼业务，解答法律询问，代写法律事务文书等，为社会提供法律服务的人员。

公证人员 指在公证处工作的人员总称，包括公证处主任、副主任、公证员、公证员助理(助理公证员)和其他从事辅助性工作的人员。

办理公证文书 指公证处根据当事人申请，依照事实和法律，按照法定程序制作的，具有法律效力的司法证明文书。根据公证书用途和使用地，公证书分为国内公证书、国内经济公证书、涉外民事公证书、涉外经济公证书四类。

调解人员 指在人民调解委员会担负调解民间纠纷工作的人员，包括调解委员会的委员和调解小组的调解员。

调解民间纠纷 指调解委员会按照法律规定，根据自愿原则，用说服教育的方法调解民间发生的有关民事权利和义务争执的件数，包括调解成功数和调解未成功数。

Explanatory Notes on Main Statistical Indicators

Lawyers are certified legal workers according to law, and who are employed by legal counseling firms to act as legal advisers, agents in criminal or civil lawsuits, or defenders in criminal lawsuits, or to handle non-litigious legal affairs, to advise on matters of law or to write legal papers for others, and provide service to the public.

Notary Personnel refers to people working for notary offices including: directors, deputy director, notaries, assistant notaries, and other people providing assistance.

Notary Documents refer to the judicatory notary documents drawn up by the request of the party and are in accordance with facts and laws and following certain legal proceedings. According to usage and locality, the notary documents are divided into following 4 types: domestic notary documents, domestic economic notary documents, foreign-related civil notary documents and foreign-related economic notary documents.

Mediators refer to workers on people mediation committees responsible for mediating in civil disputes and cases of slight infraction of the law. They include members of the mediation committees and mediators of mediation groups.

Mediation of Civil Disputes refers to number of cases made by mediation committees in mediating in civil disputes concerning civil rights and duties through persuasion and education in accordance with the provisions of law on a voluntary basis, so as to solve disputes by helping the parties involved come to an agreement and understanding, including those unsuccessful ones.

第 20 篇
CHAPTER 20

企业改革与市场发展

Reform of Enterprise and Development of Market

20－1 企业集团主要财务指标(2005年)

MAIN FINANCIAL INDICATORS OF ENTERPRISE GROUPS,2005

项目	Item	企业数(个) Number of Enterprises (unit)	从业人员(人) Employment Personnel (person)	从业人员劳动报酬总额(亿元) Total Reward of Employment Personnel (100 million yuan)
总计	**Total**	**170**	**472 438**	**109.00**
按审批部门分	**Grouped by Examining Department**			
国务院	The State Council	1	49 794	10.85
国务院主管部门	Governing Departments of the State Council	3	51 512	14.60
市政府	City Government	111	293 952	63.63
其他	Others	55	77 180	19.92
按国民经济行业分	**Grouped by Sector**			
农、林、牧、渔业	Agriculture	2	5 195	1.17
工业	Industry	77	293 831	69.97
#制造业	Manufacturing	74	248 133	57.33
建筑业	Construction	10	49 685	10.47
交通运输、仓储和邮政业	Transport,Storage and Post	8	22 928	5.57
批发和零售业	Wholesale and Retail Trade	26	68 547	9.82
住宿和餐饮业	Accommodation and Catering Services	3	3 220	0.59
房地产业	Real Estate	38	13 865	2.82
其他	Others	6	15 167	8.59
按登记注册类型分	**Grouped by Registered Categories**			
国有企业	State－owned Enterprises	4	3 938	0.66
国有独资公司	Sole State－funded Corporation	52	302 497	73.83
其他有限责任公司	Other Limited Liability Corporations	101	152 773	30.67
股份有限公司	Share－holding Corporations Ltd.	11	11 634	3.65
其他	Others	2	1 596	0.19
按控股情况分	**Grouped by Controlling Shares**			
国有绝对控股	State－owned Absolute Holding	67	367 934	92.18
国有相对控股	State－owned Relative Holding	4	3 327	0.68
集体绝对控股	Collective－owned Absolute Holding	29	25 512	3.14
集体相对控股	Collective－owned Relative Holding	3	1 994	0.21
其他	Others	67	73 671	12.79
按企业规模分	**Grouped by Size of Enterprises**			
大型	Large－sized	32	261 802	62.10
中型	Medium－sized	36	55 032	10.55
小型	Small－sized	34	48 663	8.85
其他	Others	68	106 941	27.50

注:本表统计范围为资产总计亿元以上企业集团。
Note:The data of this table refer to those enterprise groups with total assets of over 100 million yuan.

20－1 续表 1　Continued
单位:亿元　(100 million yuan)

项　目	Item	资　产 总　计 Total Assets	固定资产 净　值 Net Value of Fixed Assets	流动资产年平均余额 Annual Average Balance of Circulating Funds
总　计	**Total**	**4 312.14**	**970.51**	**1 972.86**
按审批部门分	**Grouped by Examining Department**			
国务院	The State Council	326.17	130.38	133.93
国务院主管部门	Governing Departments of the State Council	235.13	86.91	117.62
市政府	City Government	2 391.91	433.57	1 213.64
其　他	Others	1 358.93	319.65	507.67
按国民经济行业分	**Grouped by Sector**			
农、林、牧、渔业	Agriculture	50.85	11.21	29.48
工　业	Industry	2 001.37	522.94	892.96
#制造业	Manufacturing	1 784.35	439.34	809.14
建筑业	Construction	237.15	36.11	175.71
交通运输、仓储和邮政业	Transport,Storage and Post	121.61	56.22	24.16
批发和零售业	Wholesale and Retail Trade	376.44	99.35	192.54
住宿和餐饮业	Accommodation and Catering Services	14.62	3.59	6.08
房地产业	Real Estate	632.23	29.06	350.22
其　他	Others	877.87	212.03	301.71
按登记注册类型分	**Grouped by Registered Categories**			
国有企业	State－owned Enterprises	38.10	4.45	18.17
国有独资公司	Sole State－funded Corporation	2 958.10	690.48	1 331.45
其他有限责任公司	Other Limited Liability Corporations	1 191.86	225.62	579.19
股份有限公司	Share－holding Corporations Ltd.	115.04	48.31	40.90
其　他	Others	9.04	1.65	3.15
按控股情况分	**Grouped by Controlling Shares**			
国有绝对控股	State－owned Absolute Holding	3 354.48	813.64	1 534.58
国有相对控股	State－owned Relative Holding	22.96	2.19	18.27
集体绝对控股	Collective－owned Absolute Holding	124.98	20.95	64.64
集体相对控股	Collective－owned Relative Holding	6.79	2.10	1.56
其　他	Others	802.93	131.63	353.81
按企业规模分	**Grouped by Size of Enterprises**			
大　型	Large－sized	1 565.58	376.44	756.59
中　型	Medium－sized	474.16	122.06	221.61
小　型	Small－sized	199.46	49.55	107.01
其　他	Others	2 072.94	422.46	887.65

20－1 续表 2 Continued
单位:亿元 (100 million yuan)

项 目	Item	主营业务收入 Revenue of Main Business	利税总额 Total Pre－tax Profits	#利润总额 Total Profits
总 计	**Total**	**2 535.97**	**168.79**	**97.39**
按审批部门分	**Grouped by Examining Department**			
国务院	The State Council	213.67	9.72	2.27
国务院主管部门	Governing Departments of the State Council	178.65	19.66	12.17
市政府	City Government	1 427.40	82.83	42.78
其 他	Others	716.25	56.58	40.17
按国民经济行业分	**Grouped by Sector**			
农、林、牧、渔业	Agriculture	21.78	3.98	1.99
工 业	Industry	1 501.56	97.40	48.02
#制造业	Manufacturing	1 400.75	94.67	50.44
建筑业	Construction	244.77	8.96	1.80
交通运输、仓储和邮政业	Transport, Storage and Post	49.25	13.93	12.34
批发和零售业	Wholesale and Retail Trade	382.22	1.81	－0.64
住宿和餐饮业	Accommodation and Catering Services	7.15	0.57	0.25
房地产业	Real Estate	132.84	25.13	19.32
其 他	Others	196.40	17.01	14.31
按登记注册类型分	**Grouped by Registered Categories**			
国有企业	State－owned Enterprises	11.18	1.46	1.04
国有独资公司	Sole State－funded Corporation	1 542.44	78.51	38.45
其他有限责任公司	Other Limited Liability Corporations	933.25	74.91	45.74
股份有限公司	Share－holding Corporations Ltd.	47.08	13.88	12.16
其 他	Others	2.02	0.03	
按控股情况分	**Grouped by Controlling Shares**			
国有绝对控股	State－owned Absolute Holding	1 919.28	112.07	58.95
国有相对控股	State－owned Relative Holding	12.95	1.31	0.69
集体绝对控股	Collective－owned Absolute Holding	86.96	4.87	3.03
集体相对控股	Collective－owned Relative Holding	4.13	0.36	0.28
其 他	Others	512.65	50.18	34.44
按企业规模分	**Grouped by Size of Enterprises**			
大 型	Large－sized	1 433.32	90.23	51.26
中 型	Medium－sized	328.61	11.63	3.80
小 型	Small－sized	141.64	8.42	3.48
其 他	Others	632.40	58.51	38.85

20－2　企业集团主要经济效益指标(2005 年)

MAIN INDICATORS ON ECONOMIC EFFICIENCY OF ENTERPRISE GROUPS,2005

单位:%　　(%)

项　目	Item	资产负债率 Assets－Liability Ratio	净资产收益率 Earning Rate of Net Assets	资本保值增值率 Ratio of Maintenance or Addition of the Value of Assets
总　计	**Total**	**65.32**	**4.82**	**110.82**
按审批部门分	**Grouped by Examining Department**			
国务院	The State Council	61.63	1.07	101.03
国务院主管部门	Governing Departments of the State Council	51.45	7.46	121.41
市政府	City Government	63.26	3.77	109.10
其　他	Others	72.23	7.73	115.72
按国民经济行业分	**Grouped by Sector**			
农、林、牧、渔业	Agriculture	46.12	4.96	125.56
工　业	Industry	60.70	4.82	110.46
#制造业	Manufacturing	61.81	5.98	110.67
建筑业	Construction	79.71	2.16	100.19
交通运输、仓储和邮政业	Transport,Storage and Post	37.02	11.52	116.64
批发和零售业	Wholesale and Retail Trade	74.82	－1.49	95.28
住宿和餐饮业	Accommodation and Catering Services	79.97	5.25	117.84
房地产业	Real Estate	67.16	7.17	123.14
其　他	Others	71.36	3.72	108.71
按登记注册类型分	**Grouped by Registered Categories**			
国有企业	State－owned Enterprises	72.89	8.33	131.49
国有独资公司	Sole State－funded Corporation	67.01	2.77	109.21
其他有限责任公司	Other Limited Liability Corporations	63.68	8.22	113.32
股份有限公司	Share－holding Corporations Ltd.	38.92	12.43	112.70
其　他	Others	33.81	－1.05	167.58
按控股情况分	**Grouped by Controlling Shares**			
国有绝对控股	State－owned Absolute Holding	65.95	3.71	109.34
国有相对控股	State－owned Relative Holding	64.81	5.84	105.06
集体绝对控股	Collective－owned Absolute Holding	59.99	4.33	103.38
集体相对控股	Collective－owned Relative Holding	37.88	4.91	105.90
其　他	Others	63.77	9.24	118.87
按企业规模分	**Grouped by Size of Enterprises**			
大　型	Large－sized	63.87	7.06	114.23
中　型	Medium－sized	66.34	1.27	96.38
小　型	Small－sized	56.52	2.87	108.80
其　他	Others	67.03	4.05	112.23

20－2 续表 1　Continued

单位：%　(%)

项　目	Item	总资产报酬率 Rate of Return on Total Assets	资　产利税率 Ratio of Pre－tax Profits to Assets	资　金利润率 Fund－Profit Ratio
总　计	**Total**	**3.17**	**3.91**	**3.31**
按审批部门分	**Grouped by Examining Department**			
国务院	The State Council	1.40	2.98	0.86
国务院主管部门	Governing Departments of the State Council	5.86	8.36	5.59
市政府	City Government	2.34	3.46	2.60
其　他	Others	4.59	4.16	4.86
按国民经济行业分	**Grouped by Sector**			
农、林、牧、渔业	Agriculture	4.28	7.83	4.90
工　业	Industry	2.99	4.87	3.39
#制造业	Manufacturing	3.47	5.31	4.04
建筑业	Construction	1.43	3.78	0.85
交通运输、仓储和邮政业	Transport, Storage and Post	11.44	11.45	15.35
批发和零售业	Wholesale and Retail Trade	0.64	0.48	－0.22
住宿和餐饮业	Accommodation and Catering Services	2.45	3.87	2.59
房地产业	Real Estate	3.70	3.97	5.09
其　他	Others	3.55	1.94	2.79
按登记注册类型分	**Grouped by Registered Categories**			
国有企业	State－owned Enterprises	3.56	3.84	4.58
国有独资公司	Sole State－funded Corporation	2.20	2.65	1.90
其他有限责任公司	Other Limited Liability Corporations	4.74	6.29	5.68
股份有限公司	Share－holding Corporations Ltd.	11.85	12.07	13.64
其　他	Others	0.35	0.22	0.04
按控股情况分	**Grouped by Controlling Shares**			
国有绝对控股	State－owned Absolute Holding	2.69	3.34	2.51
国有相对控股	State－owned Relative Holding	4.30	5.67	3.35
集体绝对控股	Collective－owned Absolute Holding	3.17	3.90	3.55
集体相对控股	Collective－owned Relative Holding	4.06	5.34	7.54
其　他	Others	5.11	6.25	7.10
按企业规模分	**Grouped by Size of Enterprises**			
大　型	Large－sized	3.94	5.76	4.52
中　型	Medium－sized	1.29	2.45	1.11
小　型	Small－sized	2.24	4.22	2.22
其　他	Others	3.10	2.82	2.97

20－2 续表 2　Continued

项　目　Item		销　售利润率（%）Sales Profit Rate(%)	成本费用利润率（%）Ratio of Profits to Cost(%)	劳动生产率（万元/人）Labour Productivity (10 000yuan/person)
总　计	**Total**	**3.74**	**3.97**	**55.17**
按审批部门分	**Grouped by Examining Department**			
国务院	The State Council	0.97	1.07	46.73
国务院主管部门	Governing Departments of the State Council	6.71	7.18	35.24
市政府	City Government	2.92	3.86	49.84
其　他	Others	5.53	5.69	94.21
按国民经济行业分	**Grouped by Sector**			
农、林、牧、渔业	Agriculture	9.03	10.33	42.46
工　业	Industry	3.08	3.34	52.98
#制造业	Manufacturing	3.47	3.78	58.60
建筑业	Construction	0.73	0.76	49.80
交通运输、仓储和邮政业	Transport, Storage and Post	24.76	29.01	21.72
批发和零售业	Wholesale and Retail Trade	－0.16	－0.17	57.28
住宿和餐饮业	Accommodation and Catering Services	3.50	3.67	22.22
房地产业	Real Estate	14.50	17.34	96.76
其　他	Others	7.29	16.56	129.54
按登记注册类型分	**Grouped by Registered Categories**			
国有企业	State－owned Enterprises	8.94	9.51	29.44
国有独资公司	Sole State－funded Corporation	2.42	2.52	52.59
其他有限责任公司	Other Limited Liability Corporations	4.79	3.00	62.48
股份有限公司	Share－holding Corporations Ltd.	25.70	30.77	40.70
其　他	Others	0.08	0.08	13.21
按控股情况分	**Grouped by Controlling Shares**			
国有绝对控股	State－owned Absolute Holding	2.98	3.13	53.75
国有相对控股	State－owned Relative Holding	5.27	5.82	39.14
集体绝对控股	Collective－owned Absolute Holding	3.46	3.64	34.34
集体相对控股	Collective－owned Relative Holding	6.68	7.07	20.71
其　他	Others	6.57	7.26	71.14
按企业规模分	**Grouped by Size of Enterprises**			
大　型	Large－sized	3.49	3.70	56.17
中　型	Medium－sized	1.13	1.26	60.95
小　型	Small－sized	2.39	2.49	29.95
其　他	Others	5.93	6.15	61.23

20-3 重点企业主要财务指标(2005 年)
MAIN FINANCIAL INDICATORS OF KEY ENTERPRISES,2005

项 目	Item	企业数(个) Number of Enterprises (unit)	从业人员(人) Employment Personnel (person)	资本金合计(亿元) Total Capital (100 million yuan)
总 计	**Total**	**179**	**290 857**	**585.75**
按国民经济行业分	**Grouped by Sector**			
农、林、牧、渔业	Agriculture	1	893	0.96
工 业	Industry	116	224 134	439.43
#制造业	Manufacturing	107	173 358	349.84
建筑业	Construction	18	28 464	21.60
交通运输、仓储和邮政业	Transport,Storage and Post	6	22 071	70.01
批发和零售业	Wholesale and Retail Trade	28	12 162	21.94
住宿和餐饮业	Accommodation and Catering Services	1	249	0.06
房地产业	Real Estate	6	1 363	19.91
租赁和商务服务业	Leasing and Business Services	2	1 511	10.84
居民服务和其他服务业	Resident Services and Other Social Services	1	10	1.00
按登记注册类型分	**Grouped by Registered Categories**			
国有企业	State - owned Enterprises	21	23 153	21.19
国有独资公司	Sole State - funded Corporation	41	134 702	211.97
其他有限责任公司	Other Limited Liability Corporations	62	68 997	123.12
股份有限公司	Share - holding Corporations Ltd.	33	36 164	111.66
中外合资企业	Joint Ventures Enterprises with Foreign	16	22 631	105.84
港澳台合资企业	Joint Ventures Enterprises with Hongkong,Macao & Taiwan	5	4 903	11.88
其 他	Others	1	307	0.09
按控股情况分	**Grouped by Controlling Shares**			
国有绝对控股	State - owned Absolute Holding	123	236 596	443.29
国有相对控股	State - owned Relative Holding	21	12 538	52.84
集体绝对控股	Collective - owned Absolute Holding	5	5 106	2.97
集体相对控股	Collective - owned Relative Holding	2	586	1.15
其 他	Others	28	36 031	85.50
按企业规模分	**Grouped by Size of Enterprises**			
大 型	Large - sized	37	179 264	323.07
中 型	Medium - sized	112	100 679	221.28
小 型	Small - sized	20	7 137	8.69
其 他	Others	10	3 777	32.71

注:本表重点企业指本市跟踪监测建立现代化企业制度的企业。
Note:The key enterprises of this table refer to the enterprises which were followed and monitored the situation of establishing modern corporate system.

20－3 续表 1　Continued
单位:亿元　(100 million yuan)

项　目	Item	资　产 总　计 Total Assets	固定资产 净　值 Net Value of Fixed Assets	流动资产年 平均余额 Annual Average Balance of Circulating Funds
总　计	**Total**	**2 464.77**	**757.23**	**1 084.80**
按国民经济行业分	**Grouped by Sector**			
农、林、牧、渔业	Agriculture	1.69	0.68	0.63
工　业	Industry	1 697.17	591.94	711.56
#制造业	Manufacturing	1 402.81	467.28	614.54
建筑业	Construction	141.19	21.64	100.96
交通运输、仓储和邮政业	Transport, Storage and Post	302.13	105.52	77.42
批发和零售业	Wholesale and Retail Trade	140.19	28.16	84.42
住宿和餐饮业	Accommodation and Catering Services	0.26	0.07	0.17
房地产业	Real Estate	128.36	4.93	90.79
租赁和商务服务业	Leasing and Business Services	46.52	4.15	15.35
居民服务和其他服务业	Resident Services and Other Social Services	7.26	0.14	3.50
按登记注册类型分	**Grouped by Registered Categories**			
国有企业	State－owned Enterprises	113.42	27.62	59.82
国有独资公司	Sole State－funded Corporation	1 012.44	214.73	421.14
其他有限责任公司	Other Limited Liability Corporations	589.64	223.81	283.92
股份有限公司	Share－holding Corporations Ltd.	488.46	210.82	215.64
中外合资企业	Joint Ventures Enterprises with Foreign	216.02	69.71	81.00
港澳台合资企业	Joint Ventures Enterprises with Hongkong, Macao & Taiwan	44.12	10.40	22.85
其　他	Others	0.67	0.14	0.43
按控股情况分	**Grouped by Controlling Shares**			
国有绝对控股	State－owned Absolute Holding	1 972.87	647.34	839.05
国有相对控股	State－owned Relative Holding	188.10	24.16	115.99
集体绝对控股	Collective－owned Absolute Holding	21.62	3.88	14.42
集体相对控股	Collective－owned Relative Holding	8.67	0.85	7.19
其　他	Others	273.51	81.00	108.15
按企业规模分	**Grouped by Size of Enterprises**			
大　型	Large－sized	1 512.42	439.44	589.36
中　型	Medium－sized	726.85	299.06	361.35
小　型	Small－sized	41.67	8.83	23.82
其　他	Others	183.83	9.90	110.27

20－3 续表 2　Continued

单位：亿元　(100 million yuan)

项　目　Item		主营业务收入 Revenue of Main Business	利税总额 Total Pre－tax Profits	#利润总额 Total Profits
总　计	**Total**	**2 062.86**	**198.84**	**115.82**
按国民经济行业分	**Grouped by Sector**			
农、林、牧、渔业	Agriculture	0.49	－0.26	－0.26
工　业	Industry	1 479.20	138.44	63.43
#制造业	Manufacturing	1 367.76	128.73	60.05
建筑业	Construction	133.87	4.80	1.33
交通运输、仓储和邮政业	Transport, Storage and Post	251.26	50.94	48.70
批发和零售业	Wholesale and Retail Trade	167.86	0.23	－0.66
住宿和餐饮业	Accommodation and Catering Services	0.18	0.01	
房地产业	Real Estate	22.94	3.08	1.86
租赁和商务服务业	Leasing and Business Services	7.06	1.66	1.48
居民服务和其他服务业	Resident Services and Other Social Services		－0.06	－0.06
登记注册类型分	**Grouped by Registered Categories**			
国有企业	State－owned Enterprises	87.15	5.96	－0.81
国有独资公司	Sole State－funded Corporation	556.29	40.43	19.14
其他有限责任公司	Other Limited Liability Corporations	702.27	66.94	52.85
股份有限公司	Share－holding Corporations Ltd.	282.39	36.67	24.86
中外合资企业	Joint Ventures Enterprises with Foreign	392.82	40.67	15.21
港澳台合资企业	Joint Ventures Enterprises with Hongkong, Macao & Taiwan	41.50	8.08	4.53
其　他	Others	0.44	0.09	0.04
按控股情况分	**Grouped by Controlling Shares**			
国有绝对控股	State－owned Absolute Holding	1 450.65	140.52	90.07
国有相对控股	State－owned Relative Holding	115.96	9.02	6.27
集体绝对控股	Collective－owned Absolute Holding	24.31	0.85	0.59
集体相对控股	Collective－owned Relative Holding	6.39	0.83	0.66
其　他	Others	465.55	47.62	18.23
按企业规模分	**Grouped by Size of Enterprises**			
大　型	Large－sized	1 498.90	152.77	92.58
中　型	Medium－sized	490.06	42.70	21.80
小　型	Small－sized	43.41	－1.05	－1.58
其　他	Others	30.49	4.42	3.02

20－4 重点企业主要经济效益指标(2005 年)

MAIN INDICATORS ON ECONOMIC EFFICIENCY OF KEY ENTERPRISES, 2005

项 目	Item	劳动生产率(万元/人) Labour Productivity (10 000yuan/person)	资产负债率(%) Assets－Liability Ratio (%)	资产保值增值率(%) Ratio of Maintenance or Addition of the Value of Assets(%)
总 计	**Total**	**73.79**	**61.05**	**115.80**
按国民经济行业分	**Grouped by Sector**			
农、林、牧、渔业	Agriculture	5.92	114.05	142.90
工 业	Industry	68.21	60.20	118.04
#制造业	Manufacturing	81.63	61.78	120.09
建筑业	Construction	47.14	79.17	95.60
交通运输、仓储和邮政业	Transport, Storage and Post	128.22	45.08	124.46
批发和零售业	Wholesale and Retail Trade	139.34	81.13	92.96
住宿和餐饮业	Accommodation and Catering Services	7.23	68.94	93.04
房地产业	Real Estate	168.86	65.42	98.18
租赁和商务服务业	Leasing and Business Services	46.74	59.91	103.36
居民服务和其他服务业	Resident Services and Other Social Services		101.55	－10.28
按登记注册类型分	**Grouped by Registered Categories**			
国有企业	State－owned Enterprises	39.22	80.48	87.53
国有独资公司	Sole State－funded Corporation	45.40	61.60	117.41
其他有限责任公司	Other Limited Liability Corporations	103.27	67.02	118.67
股份有限公司	Share－holding Corporations Ltd.	81.12	52.57	112.24
中外合资企业	Joint Ventures Enterprises with Foreign	174.75	52.27	119.64
港澳台合资企业	Joint Ventures Enterprises with Hongkong, Macao & Taiwan	85.89	56.00	123.39
其 他	Others	14.91	39.48	104.77
按控股情况分	**Grouped by Controlling Shares**			
国有绝对控股	State－owned Absolute Holding	64.42	62.04	116.18
国有相对控股	State－owned Relative Holding	95.80	53.20	110.32
集体绝对控股	Collective－owned Absolute Holding	47.68	71.09	89.00
集体相对控股	Collective－owned Relative Holding	110.99	72.29	106.79
其 他	Others	130.79	58.19	120.02
按企业规模分	**Grouped by Size of Enterprises**			
大 型	Large－sized	87.54	59.94	122.47
中 型	Medium－sized	49.91	61.10	108.34
小 型	Small－sized	61.57	79.14	94.80
其 他	Others	81.04	65.90	97.67

20－4 续表1　Continued

单位：%　　（%）

项　目	Item	总资产报酬率 Rate of Return on Total Assets	净资产收益率 Earning Rate of Net Assets	销　售 利润率 Sales Profit Rate
总　计	**Total**	**5.51**	**8.93**	**5.40**
按国民经济行业分	**Grouped by Sector**			
农、林、牧、渔业	Agriculture	－15.54	110.95	－49.82
工　业	Industry	4.61	7.46	4.15
#制造业	Manufacturing	5.20	9.00	4.24
建筑业	Construction	1.54	1.37	0.99
交通运输、仓储和邮政业	Transport, Storage and Post	16.95	20.16	17.21
批发和零售业	Wholesale and Retail Trade	0.24	－3.06	－0.39
住宿和餐饮业	Accommodation and Catering Services	－0.46	－3.80	－0.67
房地产业	Real Estate	2.06	3.36	8.10
租赁和商务服务业	Leasing and Business Services	3.25	6.23	20.92
居民服务和其他服务业	Resident Services and Other Social Services	－0.36	57.30	
按登记注册类型分	**Grouped by Registered Categories**			
国有企业	State－owned Enterprises	0.25	－4.91	－0.89
国有独资公司	Sole State－funded Corporation	2.38	3.96	3.13
其他有限责任公司	Other Limited Liability Corporations	9.95	18.43	7.42
股份有限公司	Share－holding Corporations Ltd.	6.32	8.32	8.47
中外合资企业	Joint Ventures Enterprises with Foreign	7.79	12.36	3.85
港澳台合资企业	Joint Ventures Enterprises with Hongkong, Macao & Taiwan	11.46	18.22	10.75
其　他	Others	6.22	5.68	8.65
按控股情况分	**Grouped by Controlling Shares**			
国有绝对控股	State－owned Absolute Holding	5.38	8.61	5.91
国有相对控股	State－owned Relative Holding	4.17	6.48	5.22
集体绝对控股	Collective－owned Absolute Holding	3.18	8.07	2.39
集体相对控股	Collective－owned Relative Holding	9.28	18.41	10.20
其　他	Others	7.45	12.75	3.84
按企业规模分	**Grouped by Size of Enterprises**			
大　型	Large－sized	6.92	11.24	5.90
中　型	Medium－sized	3.94	6.00	4.34
小　型	Small－sized	－3.06	－18.76	－3.59
其　他	Others	2.10	3.71	9.85

20－4 续表 2　Continued
单位：%　　(%)

项　目　Item		资　金利润率 Fund－Profit Ratio	资产利税率 Ratio of Pre－tax Profits to Assets	成本费用利润率 Ratio of Profits to Cost
总　计	**Total**	**6.29**	**8.07**	**5.98**
按国民经济行业分	**Grouped by Sector**			
农、林、牧、渔业	Agriculture	－20.14	－15.54	－33.55
工　业	Industry	4.87	8.16	4.54
#制造业	Manufacturing	5.55	9.18	4.67
建筑业	Construction	1.09	3.40	1.02
交通运输、仓储和邮政业	Transport,Storage and Post	26.62	16.86	22.74
批发和零售业	Wholesale and Retail Trade	－0.59	0.17	－0.39
住宿和餐饮业	Accommodation and Catering Services	－0.50	2.85	－0.69
房地产业	Real Estate	1.95	2.40	9.39
租赁和商务服务业	Leasing and Business Services	7.58	3.58	24.74
居民服务和其他服务业	Resident Services and Other Social Services	－1.77	－0.89	－111.42
按登记注册类型分	**Grouped by Registered Categories**			
国有企业	State－owned Enterprises	－0.92	5.26	－0.95
国有独资公司	Sole State－funded Corporation	3.01	3.99	3.59
其他有限责任公司	Other Limited Liability Corporations	10.41	11.35	8.13
股份有限公司	Share－holding Corporations Ltd.	5.83	7.51	9.37
中外合资企业	Joint Ventures Enterprises with Foreign	10.09	18.83	4.15
港澳台合资企业	Joint Ventures Enterprises with Hongkong,Macao & Taiwan	13.61	18.32	12.60
其　他	Others	6.92	11.71	9.60
按控股情况分	**Grouped by Controlling Shares**			
国有绝对控股	State－owned Absolute Holding	6.06	7.12	6.63
国有相对控股	State－owned Relative Holding	4.48	4.79	5.60
集体绝对控股	Collective－owned Absolute Holding	3.18	3.92	2.44
集体相对控股	Collective－owned Relative Holding	8.24	9.53	11.38
其　他	Others	9.64	17.41	4.17
按企业规模分	**Grouped by Size of Enterprises**			
大　型	Large－sized	9.00	10.10	6.63
中　型	Medium－sized	3.30	5.87	4.63
小　型	Small－sized	－4.83	－2.52	－3.59
其　他	Others	2.51	2.40	11.30

20－5　企业家信心指数(2005 年)

CONFIDENCE INDEX OF ENTREPRENEUR,2005

指　标	Item	一季度 First Quarter	二季度 Second Quarter	三季度 Third Quarter	四季度 Fourth Quarter
总体状况	**Overall Confidence Index**	**137.05**	**129.92**	**129.02**	**131.50**
按行业门类分	**Grouped by Sector**				
工　业	Industry	137.66	126.37	125.02	126.65
采矿业	Minerals Mining	158.50	159.05	169.28	169.28
制造业	Manufacturing	137.86	125.28	123.21	122.09
电力、燃气及水的生产和供应业	Production & Supply of Electric Power,Gas & Water	108.95	104.40	101.68	148.96
建筑业	Construction	124.45	121.80	123.41	122.79
#房屋和土木工程建筑业	House & Civil Engineering	114.00	114.37	114.51	117.13
建筑安装业	Construction Installation	144.44	122.22	133.33	156.50
交通运输、仓储和邮政业	Transport,Storage and Post Services	136.61	126.72	127.49	124.84
#铁路运输业	Railway Transport	200.00	100.00	100.00	100.00
公路运输业	Highway Transport	109.52	114.29	114.29	109.52
水上运输业	Waterway Transport	171.63	129.29	128.07	116.04
航空运输业	Civil Aviation Transport	100.00	100.00	200.00	200.00
邮政业	Post Services	200.00	100.00	100.00	200.00
批发和零售业	Wholesale and Retail Trade	118.28	131.63	134.91	150.26
批发业	Wholesale Trade	114.58	127.31	131.85	149.56
零售业	Retail Trade	112.38	123.66	127.89	127.20
房地产业	Real Estate Trade	164.12	147.09	148.02	156.13
社会服务业	Social Services	144.12	141.18	129.41	137.78
租赁业	Leasing	175.00	175.00	175.00	175.00
商务服务业	Business Services	150.00	150.00	133.33	136.63
居民服务业	Resident Services	112.50	87.50	87.50	87.50
其他服务业	Other Social Services	100.00	100.00	100.00	100.00
信息传输和计算机服务及软件业	Information Transmitting,Computer Services and Software	138.40	155.67	155.67	155.52
信息传输业	Information Transmitting	138.06	200.00	200.00	183.33

20－5 续表 Continued

指 标	Item	一季度 First Quarter	二季度 Second Quarter	三季度 Third Quarter	四季度 Fourth Quarter
计算机服务业	Computer Services	137.50	137.50	137.50	137.50
软件业	Software	145.45	136.36	136.36	136.36
住宿和餐饮业	Accommodation and Catering Services	128.25	127.60	132.64	130.68
住宿业	Accommodation	126.04	128.57	131.10	126.16
餐饮业	Catering Services	133.33	125.00	133.33	141.67
按企业登记注册类型分	**Grouped By Status of Registration**				
国有企业	State－owned Enterprises	133.14	123.95	124.92	130.97
集体企业	Collective－owned Enterprises	110.03	115.73	114.29	111.90
股份合作企业	Cooperative Enterprises	132.42	96.71	119.53	128.59
联营企业	Joint Ownership Enterprises	116.67	116.67	116.67	116.67
有限责任公司	Limited Liability Corporations	126.05	129.48	130.24	126.81
股份有限公司	Share－holding Corporations Ltd.	170.18	139.79	116.35	109.79
私营企业	Private Enterprises	133.33	115.00	114.29	141.38
外商及港澳台商投资企业	Enterprises with Investment from Foreign, Hongkong, Macao and Taiwan	149.80	146.24	148.48	153.48
按企业规模分	**Grouped By Size of Enterprises**				
大型及特大型	Large and Super－sized	155.34	147.11	144.83	145.03
#特大型	Super－sized	177.24	161.94	149.62	146.38
大 型	Large－sized	144.57	139.68	142.51	130.29
中小型	Medium and Small－sized	126.94	123.84	124.04	118.78
#中 型	Medium－sized	129.73	129.07	129.69	118.65
小 型	Small－sized	124.86	119.94	119.83	119.64
其他分组	**Other**				
国家重点联系企业	State Key Enterprises	161.51	161.51	165.03	141.64
国家试点企业集团成员	State Experimental Enterprises Groups	159.14	113.51	149.30	146.60
乡镇企业	Township Enterprises	134.46	133.33	135.89	119.88
上市公司	Corporations Listed in the Stock Market	161.77	172.20	167.20	166.59

20－6 企业景气指数(2005年)

CLIMATE INDEX OF ENTERPRISES,2005

指 标 Item		一季度 First Quarter	二季度 Second Quarter	三季度 Third Quarter	四季度 Fourth Quarter
总体状况	**Overall Climate Index**	**131.09**	**126.29**	**128.84**	**128.98**
按行业门类分	**Grouped By Sector**				
工 业	Industry	135.50	126.51	131.74	130.62
采矿业	Minerals Mining	180.39	168.60	179.71	169.28
制造业	Manufacturing	135.54	126.16	131.05	129.07
电力、燃气及水的生产和供应业	Production & Supply of Electric Power,Gas & Water	89.85	74.77	88.36	103.46
建筑业	Construction	119.65	118.63	121.67	127.33
#房屋和土木工程建筑业	House & Civil Engineering	115.10	111.42	116.03	124.34
建筑安装业	Construction Installation	111.11	111.11	122.22	127.37
交通运输、仓储和邮政业	Transportation,Storage and Post Services	122.29	126.68	126.35	122.08
#铁路运输业	Railway Transport	200.00	100.00	100.00	100.00
公路运输业	Highway Transport	85.71	80.95	80.95	76.19
水上运输业	Waterway Transport	145.42	155.77	154.55	159.95
航空运输业	Civil Aviation Transport	100.00	200.00	200.00	200.00
邮政业	Post Services	200.00	100.00	100.00	200.00
批发和零售业	Wholesale,Retail	129.59	118.24	123.54	136.23
批发业	Wholesale Trade	125.15	115.57	117.78	132.44
零售业	Retail Trade	117.20	124.59	124.81	133.40
房地产业	Real Estate Trade	138.96	131.98	127.50	133.42
社会服务业	Social Services	112.17	117.09	99.20	98.94
租赁业	Leasing	125.00	125.00	100.00	125.00
商务服务业	Business Services	111.11	116.67	111.11	103.93
居民服务业	Resident Services	87.50	87.50	62.50	62.50
其他服务业	Other Social Services	100.00	100.00	100.00	100.00
信息传输和计算机服务及软件业	Information Transmitting,Computer Services and Software	137.75	159.67	167.35	159.34
信息传输业	Information Transmitting	136.91	200.00	198.85	182.39

20－6续表　Continued

指　　标	Item	一季度 First Quarter	二季度 Second Quarter	三季度 Third Quarter	四季度 Fourth Quarter
计算机服务业	Computer Services	125.00	125.00	150.00	150.00
软件业	Software	145.45	154.55	154.55	145.45
住宿和餐饮业	Accommodation and Catering Services	109.57	116.16	117.26	112.71
住宿业	Accommodation	107.05	114.64	114.64	114.77
餐饮业	Catering Services	116.67	116.67	125.00	109.18
按企业登记注册类型分	**Grouped By Status of Registration**				
国有企业	State－owned Enterprises	117.32	118.08	117.27	121.65
集体企业	Collective－owned Enterprises	84.19	105.14	102.38	101.71
股份合作企业	Cooperative Enterprises	111.00	103.85	142.61	120.90
联营企业	Joint Ownership Enterprises	116.67	116.67	116.67	116.67
有限责任公司	Limited Liability Corporations	137.47	126.86	134.16	134.48
股份有限公司	Share－holding Corporations Ltd.	160.79	107.51	108.53	110.72
私营企业	Private Enterprises	114.29	120.00	128.57	142.45
外商及港澳台商投资企业	Enterprises with Investment from Foreign, Hongkong, Macao and Taiwan	144.69	144.33	147.76	150.63
按企业规模分	**Grouped By Size of Enterprises**				
大型及特大型	Large and Super－sized	164.59	144.74	155.21	154.17
#特大型	Super－sized	184.74	162.12	154.14	156.82
大　型	Large－sized	154.67	136.02	155.73	125.13
中小型	Medium and Small－sized	114.88	115.4	115.86	104.69
#中　型	Medium－sized	119.69	121.71	122.66	105.14
小　型	Small－sized	111.27	110.69	110.79	101.79
其他分组	**Others**				
国家重点联系企业	State Key Enterprises	161.07	195.00	164.59	198.52
国家试点企业集团成员	State Experimental Enterprises Groups	149.70	106.19	144.88	138.00
乡镇企业	Township Enterprises	155.56	137.07	154.43	170.18
上市公司	Corporations Listed in the Stock Market	148.99	164.81	162.20	163.44

20－7 工业行业企业家信心指数(2005年)

CONFIDENCE INDEX OF INDUSTRIAL ENTREPRENEUR,2005

指　标	Item	一季度 First Quarter	二季度 Second Quarter	三季度 Third Quarter	四季度 Fourth Quarter
工业行业整体状况	**Overall Industrial Confidence Index**	**137.66**	**126.37**	**125.02**	**126.65**
按企业登记注册类型分	**Grouped By Status of Registration**				
国有企业	State－owned Enterprises	107.71	100.17	107.02	135.49
集体企业	Collective－owned Enterprises	100.00	100.00	103.85	100.00
有限责任公司	Limited Liability Corporations	123.85	111.34	111.96	98.04
股份有限公司	Share－holding Corporations Ltd.	177.79	134.21	103.54	100.50
私营企业	Private Enterprises	175.00	166.67	125.00	148.93
外商及港澳台商投资企业	Enterprises with Investment from Foreign,Hongkong,Macao and Taiwan	151.07	147.58	149.51	154.09
按行业门类分	**Grouped By Sector**				
采矿业	Minerals Mining	158.50	159.05	169.28	169.28
#石油和天然气开采业	Petroleum and Natural Gas Extraction	172.77	172.77	187.64	187.64
制造业	Manufacturing	137.86	125.28	123.21	122.09
#饮料制造业	Beverage Manufacturing	153.79	182.73	147.78	157.51
纺织业	Textile Industry	136.84	110.11	104.85	114.69
纺织服装鞋帽制造业	Textile Garments,Shoes,Caps Manufacturing	123.08	115.38	107.69	97.49
造纸及纸制品业	Papermaking and Paper Products	120.00	139.44	139.44	129.59
化学原料及化学制品制造业	Chemical Raw Materials and Products	119.38	82.62	128.17	109.49
医药制造业	Medical and Pharmaceutical Products	117.82	109.21	102.66	144.14
化学纤维制造业	Chemical Fiber	66.67	33.33	50.00	100.00
塑料制品业	Plastic Products	121.46	103.06	106.91	106.25
黑色金属冶炼及压延加工业	Smelting and Pressing of Ferrous Metals	138.73	109.75	126.77	82.21
交通运输设备制造业	Transport Equipment Manufacturing	128.17	134.95	125.62	124.21
电气机械及器材制造业	Electric Equipment and Machinery	171.48	151.41	158.08	109.76
通信设备、计算机及其他电子设备制造业	Telecommunications Equipment,Computer and Other Electronic Equipment Manufacturing	172.04	171.51	168.89	182.18
电力、燃气及水的生产供应业	Production & Supply of Electric Power,Gas & Water	108.95	104.40	101.68	148.96
按企业规模分	**Grouped By Size of Enterprises**				
大型及特大型	Large and Super－size	161.27	141.71	140.34	139.68
中小型	Medium and Small－sized	120.59	115.25	113.42	105.81
#中　型	Medium－sized	123.93	123.28	121.93	105.74
小　型	Small－sized	117.36	107.50	105.13	106.06
其他分组	**Others**				
国家重点联系企业	State Key Enterprises	162.11	162.11	162.11	136.76
国家试点企业集团成员	State Experimental Enterprises Groups	156.41	107.75	146.13	143.26
乡镇企业	Township Enterprises	118.36	116.67	120.50	129.82
上市公司	Corporations Listed in the Stock Market	164.49	165.36	155.36	162.78

20－8 工业企业景气指数(2005年)
CLIMATE INDEX OF INDUSTRIAL ENTERPRISES, 2005

指 标	Item	一季度 First Quarter	二季度 Second Quarter	三季度 Third Quarter	四季度 Fourth Quarter
工业行业整体状况	**Overall Industrial Climate Index**	**135.50**	**126.51**	**131.74**	**130.62**
按企业登记注册类型分	**Grouped By Status of Registration**				
国有企业	State－owned Enterprises	101.87	99.20	104.70	103.46
集体企业	Collective－owned Enterprises	89.29	92.59	88.46	88.46
有限责任公司	Limited Liability Corporations	131.75	131.54	131.35	125.85
股份有限公司	Share－holding Corporations Ltd.	170.11	99.06	101.98	102.99
私营企业	Private Enterprises	125.00	133.33	175.00	175.00
外商及港澳台商投资企业	Enterprises with Investment from Foreign, Hongkong, Macao and Taiwan	148.95	145.60	151.97	154.45
按行业门类分	**Grouped By Sector**				
采矿业	Minerals Mining	180.39	168.60	179.71	169.28
制造业	Manufacturing	135.54	126.16	131.05	129.07
电力、燃气及水的生产供应业	Production & Supply of Electric Power, Gas & Water	89.85	74.77	88.36	103.46
按企业规模分	**Grouped By Size of Enterprises**				
大型及特大型	Large and Super－size	166.03	149.06	153.06	150.97
中小型	Medium and Small－sized	113.45	110.17	115.58	98.06
#中 型	Medium－sized	115.38	112.93	116.67	99.18
小 型	Small－sized	111.57	107.50	114.53	93.94
不同观察指标景气指数	**Climate Index on Different Indicators**				
生产成本	Cost	64.33	79.45	82.10	85.19
生产总量	Gross Output	91.92	125.35	136.42	112.00
产品订货情况	Order for Product	115.18	121.05	123.82	119.94
产品销售量	Total Volume of Sales	91.15	109.92	125.99	116.02
产品销售价格	Price of Sales	103.77	95.42	108.45	84.64
产成品库存	Inventory of Product	124.01	127.08	125.76	122.03
税后利润	Profits after Tax	103.54	102.11	114.88	95.13
劳动力需求	Labour Demand	101.87	110.18	111.28	114.68
固定资产投资情况	Investment in Fixed Assets	115.97	104.37	111.15	114.67
科技开发情况	Science and Technology Development	116.24	107.87	106.06	106.12
其他分组	**Others**				
国家重点联系企业	State Key Enterprises	161.63	198.39	161.63	198.39
国家试点企业集团成员	State Experimental Enterprises Groups	146.35	99.94	141.44	134.13
乡镇企业	Township Enterprises	150.00	122.28	148.31	171.93
上市公司	Corporations Listed in the Stock Market	158.17	161.06	161.06	160.62

20-9 房地产销售、中介服务和物业管理情况
BASIC STATISTICS ON REAL ESTATE SALES,AGENCY SERVICES AND PROPERTY MANAGEMENT

指 标	Item	2003	2004	2005
商品房销售情况	**Statistics on Commercial Houses Sales**			
商品房销售面积(万平方米)	Floor Space of Commercial Houses Sold(10 000 sq.m)	786.50	847.03	938.01
住 宅	Residential Buildings	720.64	796.09	849.48
办公楼	Office Buildings	15.72	16.88	26.40
商业营业用房	Houses for Business Use	28.89	32.71	45.54
其 他	Others	21.25	1.35	16.59
商品房销售额(万元)	Total Sales of Commercial Houses(10 000 yuan)	1 980 448	2 638 180	3 675 570
住 宅	Residential Buildings	1 724 256	2 348 737	3 270 731
办公楼	Office Buildings	98 804	93 726	131 093
商业营业用房	Houses for Business Use	119 637	189 548	218 985
其 他	Others	37 751	6 169	54 761
房地产中介服务情况	**Statistics on Real Estate Agency Services**			
房屋代理总面积(万平方米)	Total Floor Space(10 000 sq.m)	254.35	235.85	232.32
房屋代理成交面积(万平方米)	Transaction Floor Space by Agency(10 000 sq.m)	254.35	235.85	222.32
房屋代理成交合同金额(万元)	Transaction Value by Agency(10 000 yuan)	970 338	577 071	1 054 655
房地产物业管理情况	**Statistics on Real Estate Property Management**			
企业总数(个)	Number of Enterprises(unit)	673	714	764
物业管理项目个数(个)	Number of Projects Managed(unit)	1 490	1 778	1 976
房屋建筑面积(万平方米)	Floor Space of Buildings(10 000 sq.m)	7 300	9 628.90	11 505.96
住 宅	Residential Buildings	5 957	8 256.94	9 938.63
办公用房	Office Buildings	622.50	513.55	787.55
商业营业用房	Houses for Business Use	244.80	280.44	279.30
工业仓储用房	Houses for Industry and Storage	382.70	337.31	285.55
其 他	Others	93.00	240.66	214.93
从业人员(人)	Personnel(person)	51 768	62 768	100 786
#管理人员	Administrative Personnel	7 877	6 938	16 898
年经营收入(万元)	Annual Income(10 000 yuan)	100 863	115 541	104 350
从业人员报酬(万元)	Remuneration of Employment Personnel(10 000 yuan)	31 620	31 904	36 695

注:商品房销售为现房销售。
Note: The sales of commercial houses are completed flats sales.

20-10 人才和劳务市场情况(1994-2005年)
STATISTICS ON TALENT AND LABOUR FORCE MARKET,1994-2005

单位:个、万人次 (unit)(10 000 person times)

年 份 Year	劳务市场 Labour Force Market			人才市场 Talent Market		
	进场单位数 Number of Units Entering	进场人次 Number of Persons Entering	达成意向人次 Number of Persons Reached Initial Intent	进场单位数 Number of Units Entering	进场人次 Number of Persons Entering	达成意向人次 Number of Persons Reached Initial Intent
1994	8 561	71.63	22.41	2 886	18.01	4.50
1995	13 737	136.60	30.84	4 002	23.54	7.07
1996	13 961	149.80	35.90	6 327	29.22	8.52
1997	15 769	161.54	33.73		29.89	9.74
1998	20 152	247.17	49.70	11 122	50.08	15.16
1999	27 226	276.68	50.27	12 285	42.26	12.26
2000	28 724	275.00	51.23	12 979	31.10	11.05
2001	28 855	269.85	50.56	15 455	34.89	11.17
2002	30 941	293.10	53.61	19 903	52.61	16.42
2003	32 939	249.00	45.50	19 142	43.26	15.72
2004		271.00	69.00	36 490	58.57	21.43
2005		275.80	70.10	34 628	56.03	20.09

20－11　技术市场基本情况

BASIC STATISTICS ON TECHNICAL MARKET

项　　目	Item	签订合同数(项) Number of Contracts Signed (item)		合同金额(万元) Value of Contracts Signed (10 000 yuan)	
		2004	2005	2004	2005
合　　计	**Total**	**8 002**	**11 295**	**450 276**	**507 093**
按技术合同类别分	**Grouped by the Type of Technical Contract**				
技术开发合同	Technology Development Contracts	2 746	2 942	298 501	269 098
技术转让合同	Technology Transfer Contracts	353	213	20 516	29 957
技术咨询合同	Technology Inquiry Contracts	1 658	2 100	28 167	55 816
技术服务合同	Technology Services Contracts	3 245	6 040	103 092	152 222
按合同卖方类别分	**Grouped by the Type of Sellers**				
科技机构	Technical Institution	2 093	1 887	104 947	128 903
高等院校	University	1 551	3 653	54 571	75 043
工业企业	Industrial Enterprises	970	1 725	196 013	134 960
技术贸易机构	Technology Trade Organization	2 476	2 780	43 484	56 228
个人及个人合伙	Private	29	22	3 541	7 133
其　他	Others	883	1 228	47 720	104 826
按合同买方类别分	**Grouped by the Type of Buyers**				
工业企业	Industrial Enterprises	5 533	7 530	195 263	329 265
科研机构	Technology Research Institution	467	1 268	15 435	27 029
各级管理部门	Various Management Sections	1 112	1 350	186 710	57 945
技术贸易机构	Technology Trade Organization	32	10	3 192	84
个人及个人合伙	Private	2	9	4	1 941
其　他	Others	856	1 128	49 672	90 829
按社会经济目标分	**Grouedbythe Social and Economic Activitie**				
农业、林业与渔业的发展	DevelopmentofFarming,ForestryandFishery	62	123	29 261	3 004
促进工业的发展	Promoting the Development of Industry	4 053	6 567	163 982	277 945
能源生产储存和分配	Production,Store and Distribution of Energ	392	439	34 836	18 535
交通、通讯事业的发展	Development of Transportation and Telecommunications	821	1 100	44 132	67 937
教育、卫生事业发展	Development of Education & Health Care	409	817	56 358	29 113
社会发展和社会经济服务	SocialDevelopmentandSocialEconomicServic	554	472	24 356	10 026
环境保护	Environmental Protecting	591	799	12 643	10 299
其　他	Others	1 120	978	84 708	90 234
按技术流向分类	**Grouped by the Buyer's Region**				
天　津	Tianjin	5 054	6 973	316 244	269 207
外　地	Others	2 948	4 322	134 032	237 886

20－12 天津市主要亿元

COMMODITY EXCHANGE MARKETS WITH TRANSACTION

市场名称	Name of Market	交易场所面积（平方米）Area of the Transaction Place (sq.m)	交易额（万元）Transaction Value (10 000 yuan)
天津储宝钢材现货交易市场	Tianjin Chubao Steel Spot Exchange Market	15 124	1 145 126
大胡同集团百货批发市场	Dahutong Small Goods Wholesale Market	78 300	454 239
天津万隆大胡同制业有限公司	Tianjin Wanlong Dahutong Development Co.,Ltd.	80 482	381 003
环渤海建筑材料中心批发市场有限公司	Huanbohai Wholesale Market of Building Materials	175 000	353 746
天津市宝钢储菱钢材交易市场	Tianjin Baogang Chuling Steel Exchange Market	1 000	325 918
天津石化交易中心市场	Tianjin Petroleum Chemical Products Exchange Market	1 786	207 933
五矿钢铁工贸天津公司	Minmetals Steel Industry & Trade Tianjin Company	34 000	205 960
红旗农贸批发市场	Hongqi Wholesale Market	180 000	198 942
北方日用工业品中心批发市场	North(Tianjin)Daily－use Industrial Products Wholesale Market	80 000	197 950
天津不锈钢材市场	Tianjin Stainless Steel Market	7 000	144 880
天津都行商城	Tianjin Duhang Trade Market	58 000	127 959
天津钢铁炉料交易市场	Tianjin Steel & Iron Materials Exchange Market	450	124 684
南马路五金城	Nanma Road Hardware Market	39 675	119 030
天津市冷冻食品批发市场	Tianjin Freezing Food Wholesale Market	1 200	117 000
何庄子蔬菜批发市场	Hezhuangzi Vegetables Wholesale Market	100 000	116 273
天津登发装饰基地	Tianjin Dengfa Decoration Base	180 000	100 820
天津轻纺商城	Tianjin Light and Textile Goods Market	16 000	98 630
中国(天津)粮油批发交易市场	China(Tianjin) Grain & Oil Wholesale Market	1 000	95 189
天津滨海国际汽车城	Tianjin Coastal International Auto City	2 800	89 330
旧机动车交易中心	Second Hand Motor Vehicle Exchange Market	2 000	76 150
兴业鞋帽批发市场	Xingye Shoes and Hats Market	7 650	72 090
金钟蔬菜批发市场	Jinzhong Vegetable Wholesale Market	6 600	69 830
信托贸易公司南开车辆商场	Trust Trade Corporation Nankai Vehicle Market	10 000	65 032
天津市兆鑫食品批销市场	Zhaoxin Eatable Wholesale & Sale Co.,Ltd.	2 240	63 000
天津市兴耀消费品综合批发市场	Xingyao Comprehensive Wholesale Market	2 660	61 051
一商旺地购物城有限公司	Tianjin First Trade Shopping City Co.,Ltd.	30 000	55 945
天昊集团铁东路摩托市场	Tianhao Group Tiedong Motorcycle Market	10 000	55 167
体北食品批发市场	Tibei Foodstuff Wholesale Market	18 000	53 477
津南区葛沽集贸综合市场	Jinnan Gegu Comprehensive Trade Market	51 294	51 103
静海县津海商城	Jinghai County Jinhai Market	40 000	50 492
蓟县城关市场	Chengguan Town Jixian County Bazaar Market	60 000	46 497
东丽商贸城	Dongli Trade Market	30 000	44 314
天津果品中心批发市场	Tianjin Fruit Center Wholesale Market	3 150	42 430
河北区幸福道农贸市场	Xingfu Road Farm Products Market	3 000	39 000
天津北方花卉有限公司	Tianjin North Flower Co.,Ltd.	30 000	36 000
红桥区彰武路市场	Zhangwu Road Farm Products Market	1 782	29 330
蝶桥旧机动车交易市场	Dieqiao Second Hand Motor Vehicle Exchange Market	150 000	27 956
天津市王顶堤集团汽车产品交易中心	Tianjin Wangdingdi Group Motor Vehicle Exchange Center	20 000	24 471
蓟县邦军农贸市场	Jixian Bangjun Farm Products Market	50 000	21 506
天津百货大楼家具城	Tianjin Department Store Furniture Center	15 000	19 992
天津华北建材陶瓷批发市场	Huabei Building Material,Ceramic Wholesale Market	11 800	18 991
武清泉州路市场	Wuqing Quanzhou Road Market	20 000	16 875
零号路农贸市场	Linghao Road Farm Products Market	3 314	16 549
天津百货大楼家居购物中心	Tianjin Department Store Living Purchasing Center	24 000	12 024
天津市温州城	Tianjin Wenzhou Market	7 000	10 820

商品交易市场情况(2005年)
VALUE OF OVER 100 MILLION IN TIANJIN,2005

市场类别	Market Type	交易地址	Transaction Place
金属材料	Metal Materials	北辰区顺义道	Shunyi Road,Beichen District
服装、小百货、鞋帽	Garments,Daily Consumer Goods,Shoes & Hats	红桥区南运河南路9号	No.9 Nanyunhe'nanlu Road,Hongqiao District
服　装	Garments	红桥区南运河南路	Nanyunhe'nanlu Road,Hongqiao District
建筑及装潢材料	Building and Decoration Materials	河西区解放南路473号	No.473 Jiefangnan Road,Hexi District
金属材料	Metal Materials	天津市北辰区顺义道	Shunyi Road,Beichen District
化工材料及制品	Chemical Materials and Related Products	河西区珠江道58号	No.58 Zhujiang Road,Hexi Distric
金属材料	Metal Materials	东丽区新兴村	North of Wangdingdi Crossbridge,Nankai District
蔬菜、水果、水产品	Vegetables,Fruits and Aquatic Products	南开区王顶堤复康路立交桥北	No.160 Zhuangguizhuang Road,Hedong District
灯具、花卉及其它	Lamp,Flower and Other Products	河东区张贵庄路160号	No.481 Huanghe Road,Nankai District
不锈钢材	Stainless Steel	南开区黄河道481号	No.481 Huanghe Road,Nankai District
服装、小百货、鞋帽	Garments,Daily Consumer Goods,Shoes & Hats	红桥区南运河南路	Nanyunhe'nanlu Road,Hongqiao District
金属材料	Metal Materials	河西区马场道103号	No.103 Machang Road,Hexi District
五　金	Hardware	天津市南开区南马路	Nanma Road Nankai District
食　品	Food	南开区天拖南保山道18号	No.18 Baoshan Road, Tiantuonan, Nankai District
蔬　菜	Vegetables	津南区双港镇何庄子南	South of Hezhuangzi,Shuanggang Town,Jinnan District
建筑及装潢材料	Building and Decoration Materials	大沽路与解放南路交口	Cross of Dagu Road and Jiefangnan Road
纺织品	Textiles	和平区张自忠路227号	No.227 Zhangzizhong Road, Heping District
粮　油	Grain and Oil	河西区台儿庄路39号	No.58 Zhujiang Road,Hexi Distric
机动车	Motor Vehicle	天津保税区天保大道86号	No.86 Tianbao Street TPFTZ
机动车	Motor Vehicle	河北区真理道54号	No.54 Zhenli Road,Hebei District
鞋	Shoes	南开区西湖道78号	No.78 Xihu Road,Nankai District
蔬　菜	Vegetables	东丽区大毕庄赵沽里	Zhaoguli Dabizhuang,Dongli District
机动车	Motor Vehicle	西青区王兰庄	Wanglanzhuang,Xiqing District
食　品	Food	东丽区张贵庄街跃进路	Yuejin Road Zhangguizhuang Street,Dongli District
农产品综合	Farm Products	河北区建昌道与外环线交口	Cross of Jianchang Road and Waihuan,Hebei District
装饰、家俱	Decoration, Furniture	河西区珠江道	Jiefangnan Road,Hexi District
摩托车	Motorcycle	北辰区铁东路普济河道立交桥北1公里	North of Pujihe Crossbridge,Tiedong Road,Beichen District
食品、饮料、烟酒	Food,Beverages,Tobacco and Liquo	河西区体北道一号	No.1 Tibei Road,Hexi District
食品、饮料、烟酒	Food,Beverages,Tobacco and Liquo	津南区葛沽镇葛沽二村	Gegu Second Village,Gegu Town,Jinnan District
工业品综合	Industrial Products	静海县东方红路15号	NO.15 Dofanghong Road,Jinghai County
农产品综合	Farm Products	蓟县兴华大街23号	No.23 Xinghua Street,Jixian County
农产品综合	Farm Products	东丽区福山路28号	No.28 Fushan Road,Dongli District
干鲜果品	Dry and Fresh Fruits	河西区珠江道55号增1号	Added No.1,No.55 Zhujiang Road,Hexi District
农产品综合	Farm Products	河北区幸福道1号路	No.1 Road,Xingfu Street,Hebei District
花　卉	Flower	西青区中北镇外环线七号桥北	North of No.7 Bridge Outer Circle Zhongbei Town, Xiqing District
农产品综合	Farm Products	红桥区红桥三号路咸阳北	North of Hongqiao Third Road,Hongqiao District
机动车	Motor Vehicle	河东区卫国道万东马路交口	Cross of Wandong Road and Weiguo Road,Hedong District
农产品综合	Farm Products	天津市西青区西营门王顶堤村	Wangdingdi Village,Xiyingmen,Xiqing District
家　俱	Furniture	蓟县京哈公路	Jingha Highroad,Jixian Country
建筑及装潢材料	Building and Decoration Materials	和平区和平路172号	No.172 Heping Road,Heping District
农产品综合	Farm Products	塘沽区津塘公路7－189号	No.7－189 Jintang Highway,Tanggu District
农产品综合	Farm Products	武清区泉州路南23号	No.23 Quanzhou Road, Wuqing District
农产品综合	Farm Products	天津市红桥区南运河南路9号	No.9 Nanyunhe'nanlu Road,Hongqiao District
建筑及装潢材料、家俱	Building and Decoration Materials,Furniture	天津市和平区和平路172号	No.172 Heping Road,Heping District
服装、鞋帽、针纺织品	Garments,Shoes and Hats,Textiles	东丽区大毕庄常青村	Changqing Village,Dabizhuang,Dongli District

主要统计指标解释

企业家信心指数　是根据企业家对企业外部市场经济环境与宏观政策的认识、看法、判断与预期而编制的指数，用以综合反映企业家对宏观经济环境的感受与信心。分行业企业家信心指数为各行业企业家对本行业企业外部市场经济环境与宏观政策的认识、看法、判断与预期。其表现形式为纯正数，以 100 作为景气指数的临界值，其数值范围在 0－200 之间。

企业景气指数　是根据企业家对本企业综合生产经营情况的判断和预期而编制的指数，用以综合反映企业的生产经营状况。分行业企业景气指数用以反映各行业企业的生产经营状况。其表现形式为纯正数，以 100 作为景气指数的临界值，其数值范围在 0－200 之间。

劳务人才市场交易情况　劳务人才市场是指劳动力供求双方实现劳务交换和劳动力流动的场所。主要反映进场单位数、进场人次、达成意向人次等情况。

技术市场　从狭义看，是指在一定时间、地点进行技术转让和技术商品交易的场所。目前统计反映的是企业购买技术开发、技术转让、技术咨询、技术服务项目的合同数和成交额。

Explanatory Notes on Main Statistical Indicators

Entrepreneur Confidence Index is an index made according to the entrepreneur´s understanding, view, judgment and forecast of the market economic environment out of the enterprise and macroscopic policy. It reflects the entrepreneur´s feeling and confidence in macroeconomic environment comprehensively. The enterprise confidence index by sectors is a reflection of the entrepreneur´s understanding, view, judgment and forecast of the market economic environment out of his own sector. It is expressed by a pure positive number between 0 and 200 with 100 as the boundary value of climate index.

Climate Index of Enterprise is an index made according to the entrepreneur´s judgment and forecast of the comprehensive production and management. The climate index by sectors reflects the production and management of each sector comprehensively. It is expressed by a pure positive number between 0 and 200 with 100 as the boundary value.

Employees Supply and Demand Dealings Market It is often known as an office to which employees made an application for having been either supplied or demanded daily. The principal datum there of are including numbers of the market entrance－making sectors or enterprises, of employees suppliers and demanders registered together with their agreements to have been reached between them.

Technique Market It can be regarded narrowly as technical－dealings office where technique transfer is made or technology－related good straded at certain time. As shown in statistical datum presently, turnovers are resulting either from purchase or from transfer of techniques, together with numbers related to the inquiry or services involved in technologies.

第21篇
CHAPTER 21

滨海新区
Binhai New Area

21-1 滨海新区行政建制(2005年)
ADMINISTRATIVE DIVISIONS OF BINHAI NEW AREA

单位:个 (Unit)

项　目 Item	行政区域面积(平方公里)(sq.km)	街道办事处 Subdistrict Offices	居民委员会 Resident's Committees	镇政府 Town Governments	村民委员会 Village Committees
合　计 Total	**2595.88**	**21**	**218**	**9**	**206**
塘沽区 Tanggu District	782.40	11	83	1	34
汉沽区 Hangu District	409.20	4	45	4	58
大港区 Dagang District	1 041	5	79	3	74
东丽区无瑕街 Wuxia Subdistrict, Dongli District	19.8	1	5		15
津南区葛沽镇 Gegu Town, Jinnan District	43.48		6	1	25

21-2 滨海新区建成区面积(2005年)
DEVELOPED AREA OF BINHAI NEW AREA

单位:平方公里 (sq.km)

项　目 Item	2003	2004	2005
合　计 Total	**166.24**	**175.15**	**188.65**
塘沽地区小计 Subtotal inTanggu District	108.69	117.04	127.26
塘沽城区和天津港 Central District of Tanggu and Tianjin Port	80.69	87.44	93.11
经济技术开发区 TEDA	23.00	24.60	28.86
天津港保税区 TPFTZ	5.00	5.00	5.29
汉沽区 Hangu District	15.60	16.16	16.16
大港区 Dagang District	41.95	41.95	45.23

21-3 滨海新区主要年份户籍人口主要指标
MAJOR REGISTERED POPULATION STATISTICS OF BINHAI NEW AREA IN MAIN YEARS

指　标 Item	单　位 Unit		1993	1995	2000	2005
户籍人口 Registered Population	万人	10^4 persons	99.18	100.70	104.58	109.39
人口密度 Population Density	人/平方公里	person/sq.km	437	444	462	483.33
户籍户数 Registered Households	万户	10^4 households	31.55	32.32	35.8	40.13
户规模 Family Size	人/户	person/household	3.14	3.12	2.91	2.73
按户口性质分 By Registered Charcter						
非农业 Non-agricultural	万人	10^4 persons	68.55	70.74	78.03	83.38
农　业 Agricultural	万人	10^4 persons	30.63	29.96	26.55	26.01
按性别分 By Sex						
男　性 Male	万人	10^4 persons	51.89	52.56	54.25	56.37
女　性 Female	万人	10^4 persons	47.29	48.14	50.34	53.02
性别比 Sex Ration	女=100	female=100	109.74	109.17	107.78	106.31

21－4 滨海新区主要经济指标

MAIN STATISTICS ON BINHAI NEW AREA

项 目	Item	2003	2004	2005	2005 比 2004 年增长% Increase Rate in 2005 over 2004
户籍人口(万人)	Registered Population(10 000 persons)	107.05	108.13	109.39	1.2
#非农业人口	Non－agricultural Population	81.05	82.03	83.38	0.4
单位从业人员期末人数(万人)	Number of Persons Employed Year－end (10 000 persons)	58.93	64.78	67.62	4.4
单位从业人员劳动报酬(亿元)	Total Remuneration of Persons Employed (100 million yuan)	116.68	151.45	177.36	17.1
单位从业人员人均劳动报酬(元)	Per Capita Remuneration of Persons Employed(yuan)	20 468	24 116	27 209	12.8
地区生产总值(亿元)	Gross Domestic Product(100 million yuan)	1 046.30	1 323.26	1 623.26	19.8
第一产业	Primary Industry	7.30	7.91	7.28	－4.8
第二产业	Secondary Industry	697.66	878.85	1 098.86	22.0
第三产业	Tertiary Industry	341.34	436.50	517.12	15.7
农业总产值(亿元)	Gross Output Value of Agriculture (100 million yuan)	15.81	16.86	18.02	7.0
工业总产值(亿元)	Gross Output Value of Industry (100 million yuan)	2 133.21	3 030.75	3 996.73	30.7
全社会固定资产投资(亿元)	Total Investment In Fixed Assets (100 million yuan)	464.08	565.47	693.31	22.6
#基础设施	Infrastructure	122.57	157.17	175.01	11.4
市重点项目	Key Projects	105.64	120.33	99.75	－17.1
财政收入(亿元)	General Budgetary Financial Revenue (100 million yuan)		206.03	317.16	53.9
财政支出(亿元)	General Budgetary Financial Expenditures (100 million yuan)		100.02	100.92	0.9
社会消费品零售总额(亿元)	Total Retail Sales of Consumer Goods (100 million yuan)	156.11	180.03	206.52	14.7
外贸出口总额(亿美元)	Exports(USD 100 million)	89.38	136.99	184.69	34.8
直接利用外资合同数(个)	Number of Foreign Investment Enterprises Newly Signed(unit)	458	477	625	31.0
直接利用外资合同金额(亿美元)	Contract Foreign Capital of Foreign Investment Enterprises Newly Signed(USD 100 million)	24.52	37.62	49.86	32.5
实际直接利用外资金额(亿美元)	Actual Direct Utilization of Foreign Capital (USD 100 million)	12.15	17.44	25.31	45.2
内联协议合同数(个)	Number of Projects Signed Contracts(unit)	503	719	797	10.8
外地在津投资协议额(亿元)	Total Domestic Investment Signed in Tianjin (100 million)	36.12	76.60	109.47	42.9
外地在津投资实际到位额(亿元)	Total Domestic Investment Actually Used in Tianjin(100 million)	25.41	52.71	89.83	70.4

21－5 滨海新区生产总值
GROSS DOMESTIC PRODUCT OF BINHAI NEW AREA

项　目	Item	2004	2005	2005 比 2004 年增长％(百分点) Increase Rate in 2005 over 2004(percent)
绝对数(亿元)	**Value(100 million yuan)**			
地区生产总值	Gross Domestic Product	1 323.26	1 623.26	19.8
第一产业	Primary Industry	7.91	7.28	－4.8
第二产业	Secondary Industry	878.85	1 098.86	22.0
#工　业	Industry	833.86	1 045.44	22.5
第三产业	Tertiary Industry	436.50	517.12	15.7
#交通运输、仓储和邮政业	Transport, Storage, Post Services	117.05	125.16	5.8
批发和零售业	Wholesale and Retail Trade	174.05	210.11	20.7
住宿和餐饮业	Accommodation and Catering Services	14.02	16.88	20.4
金融业	Finance Intermediation	7.33	11.00	13.7
房地产业	Real Estate	26.90	29.80	10.8
三次产业构成(％)	**Composition of Three Industries as Percentage(％)**			
地区生产总值	Gross Domestic Product	100	100	
第一产业	Primary Industry	0.60	0.45	－0.15
第二产业	Secondary Industry	66.42	68.89	2.47
#工　业	Industry	63.02	66.02	3.00
第三产业	Tertiary Industry	32.98	30.66	－2.32
#交通运输、仓储和邮政业	Transport, Storage, Post Services	8.85	8.60	－0.25
批发和零售业	Wholesale and Retail Trade	13.16	12.01	－1.15
住宿和餐饮业	Accommodation and Catering Services	1.06	0.93	－0.13
金融业	Finance Intermediation	0.55	0.54	－0.01
房地产业	Real Estate	2.03	1.74	－0.29
占全市比重(％)	**Percentage of The City's GDP(％)**			
地区生产总值	Gross Domestic Product	42.54	43.90	1.36
第一产业	Primary Industry	7.71	6.48	－1.23
第二产业	Secondary Industry	52.13	53.57	1.44
#工　业	Industry	53.81	55.46	1.65
第三产业	Tertiary Industry	33.01	33.71	0.70
#交通运输、仓储和邮政业	Transport, Storage, Post Services	41.39	55.10	13.71
批发和零售业	Wholesale and Retail Trade	46.75	48.18	1.43
住宿和餐饮业	Accommodation and Catering Services	24.84	24.07	0.77
金融业	Finance Intermediation	5.35	6.91	1.56
房地产业	Real Estate	25.36	23.14	－2.22

21-6 滨海新区固定资产投资
INVESTMENT IN FIXED ASSETS OF BINHAI NEW AREA

单位:万元 (10 000 yuan)

项 目	Item	2004	2005	2005比2004年增长% Increase Rate in 2005 over 2004
总 计		**4 366 445**	**5 349 906**	**22.5**
按三次产业分	**Grouped by Industries**			
第一产业	Primary Industry	13 057	9 490	-27.3
第二产业	Secondary Industry	2 481 757	3 042 056	22.6
第三产业	Tertiary Industry	1 871 631	2 298 360	22.8
按隶属关系分	**Grouped by Administrative Relationship**			
中 央	Central Government	1 335 808	1 417 176	6.1
地 方	Local Government	3 030 637	3 932 730	29.8
按建设性质分	**Grouped by Type of Construction**			
新 建	New Construction	1 706 936	2 057 382	20.5
改、扩建及其他	Expansion,Reconstruction and Others	2 659 509	3 292 524	23.8
按构成分	**Grouped by Use of Funds**			
建筑工程	Construction	2 781 180	3 493 970	25.6
安装工程	Installation	156 118	222 938	42.8
设备工器具购置	Purchases of Equipment and Instrument	1 083 898	1 111 086	2.5
其他费用	Others	345 249	521 912	51.2
按登记注册类型分	**Grouped by Registered Categories**			
内资企业	Domestic - funded Enterprises	3 629 600	4 369 293	20.4
国有企业	State - owned Enterprises	1 148 198	1 272 933	10.9
集体企业	Collective - owned Enterprises	28 995	12 098	-58.3
股份合作企业	Cooperative Enterprises	25 359	108 153	326.5
私营企业	Private Enterprises	253 971	386 186	52.1
股份有限公司	Share Holding Corporations Ltd.	1 087 892	1 236 971	13.7
有限责任公司	Limited Liability Corporations	1 071 001	1 324 007	23.6
#国有独资	Sole State - funded Corporations	290 855	962 079	230.8
联营企业	Joint Ownership Enterprises	6 920	3 913	-43.5
#国有与国有联营企业	State Joint Ownership Enterprises	78	900	1 053.8
集体与集体联营企业	Collective Joint Ownership Enterpri	713	3 013	322.6
其他内资企业	Other Domestic - funded Enterprises	7 264	25 032	244.6
港澳台商投资企业	Enterprises with Investment from Hongkong Macao and Taiwan	198 346	156 100	-21.3
外商投资企业	Foreign Funded Enterprises	538 499	824 513	53.1

注:本表数据不含农村集体和个人投资。
Note: The data in this table exclude rural collective - owned and individual investment.

21-6 续表
单位:万元 (10 000 yuan)

项 目 Item	2004	2005	2005比2004年增长% Increase Rate in 2005 over 2004
按行业分			
Grouped by Sectors			
农、林、牧、渔业			
Farming, Forestry, Animal Husbandry and Fishery	13 057	9 490	-27.3
采矿业			
Minerals Mining	1 184 567	1 240 463	4.7
制造业			
Manufacturing	1 035 852	1 655 401	59.8
电力、燃气及水的生产和供应业			
Production & Supply of Power, Gas and Water	146 983	109 673	-25.4
建筑业			
Construction	114 355	36 519	-68.1
交通运输、仓储和邮政业			
Transport, Storage, Post Services	519 741	716 861	37.9
批发和零售业			
Wholesale and Retail Trade	34 460	31 252	-9.3
住宿和餐饮业			
Accommodation and Catering Services	79 384	17 444	-78.3
金融业			
Finance Intermediation	2 782		
房地产业			
Real Estate	757 030	794 846	5.0
租赁和商务服务业			
Leasing and Business Services	18 334	14 595	-20.4
科学研究、技术服务和地质勘查业			
Scientific Research, Technical Services and Geological Prospecting	7 281	8 477	16.4
水利、环境和公共设施管理业			
Management for Water Conservancy, Environment and Public Facilities	259 014	486 503	87.8
居民服务和其他服务业			
Resident Services and Other Social Services	2 000	2 335	16.8
教 育			
Education	62 731	53 426	-14.8
卫生、社会保障和社会福利业			
Health Care, Social Security and Social Welfare	18 984	12 033	-36.6
文化、体育和娱乐业			
Culture, Sports and Recreational Services	73 244	60 774	-17.0
公共管理和社会组织			
Public Management and Social Organizations	36 646	99 814	172.4

21－7 滨海新区直接利用外资情况(2005年)

DIRECT UTILIZATION OF FOREIGN CAPITAL OF BINHAI NEW AREA,2005

项　目	Item	直接利用外资合同数(个) Number of Contracts (unit)	直接利用外资合同金额(万美元) Foreign Invest－ment Contracted (USD 10 000)	实际直接利用外资金额(万美元) Actual Direct Utilizati of Foreign Capital (USD 10 000)
合　计	**Total**	**625**	**498 589**	**253 139**
按投资方式分	**By Mode of Investment**			
合资企业	Joint Venture Enterprises	145	123 016	91 806
合作企业	Cooperative Operation Enterprises	5	11 066	6 791
独资企业	Foreign－funded Sole Enterprises	475	364 507	154 542
按行业分	**By Sector**			
#农、林、牧、渔业	Farming, Forestry, Animal Husbandry and Fishery	3	3 746	1 163
采矿业	Minerals Mining		726	36 837
制造业	Manufacturing	215	228 985	154 371
电力、燃气及水的生产和供应业	Production and Supply of Electric Power, Gas and Water	4	2 459	1 329
建筑业	Construction	8	11 368	4 346
交通运输、仓储和邮政业	Transport,Storage,Post Services	8	24 220	9 140
信息传输、计算机服务和软件业	Information Transmitting,Computer Services and Software	11	7 247	1 076
批发和零售业	Wholesale and Retail Trade	256	57 379	30 858
住宿和餐饮业	Accommodation and Catering Services	2	1 010	89
房地产业	Real Estate	35	83 891	7 952
租赁和商务服务业	Leasing and Business Services	70	59 249	2 221
科学研究、技术服务与地质勘查业	Scientific Research,Technical Services and Geological Prospecting	8	11 131	1 287
水利、环境和公共设施管理业	Management for Water Conservancy, Environment and Public Facilities	1	60	311
居民服务和其他服务业	Resident Services and Other Social Services	3	4 471	1 627
文化、体育与娱乐业	Culture,Sports and Recreational Services	1	2 647	438
按国别、地区分	**By Country(Region)**			
#中国香港	Hongkong,China	174	165 887	53 391
中国台湾	Taiwan,China	26	8 706	4 293
韩　国	Republic of Korea	89	43 434	27 354
日　本	Japan	41	30 047	34 056
美　国	United States	86	59 925	46 058
新加坡	Singapore	33	25 992	9 935
英　国	United Kingdom	11	5 352	7 266
德　国	Germany	17	17 136	3 008
法　国	France	11	11 548	2 045
意大利	Italy	6	6 225	1 348
英属维尔京群岛	Virgin Islands of United Kingdom	33	27 309	34 831

21-8 滨海新区限额以上工业

MAIN FINANCIAL INDICATORS OF

项 目	Item	从业人员年平均人数（人）Annual Average Persons Employed (person)	工业增加值（万元）Value Added of Industry (10 000 yuan)	实收资本（万元）Total Capital Hold (10 000 yuan)
总 计	**Total**	**381 476**	**11 063 495**	**10 038 557**
按登记注册类型分	**Grouped by Status of Registration**			
内资企业	Domestic - funded Enterprises	175 110	5 867 667	4 728 734
国有企业	State - owned Enterprises	23 620	221 803	733 146
集体企业	Collective - owned Enterprise	12 742	153 848	36 198
股份合作企业	Cooperative Enterprises	3 327	21 846	19 271
私营企业	Private Enterprises	18 305	243 006	145 502
股份有限公司	Share - holding Corporations Ltd.	34 766	4 446 306	2 010 023
有限责任公司	Limited Liability Corporations	83 080	791 232	1 854 413
#国有独资	Sole State - funded Corporations	52 728	376 705	1 428 063
联营企业	Joint Ownership Enterprises	585	4 941	9 210
#国有与国有联营企业	State Joint Ownership Enterprises	30	83	90
集体与集体联营企业	Collective Joint Ownership Enterprises			
其他内资企业	Other Domestic - funded Enterprises	87	4 426	800
港澳台商投资企业	Enterprises with Investment from Hongkong, Macao and Taiwan	38 112	453 762	712 562
外商投资企业	Foreign Funded Enterprises	166 852	4 722 327	4 517 433
按经济类型分	**Grouped by Ownership**			
国有经济	State - owned	76 378	598 591	2 161 299
集体经济	Collective - owned	16 069	175 694	55 469
私有经济	Private and Individual	18 305	243 006	145 502
港澳台商投资经济	Hongkong, Macao and Taiwan Funded	38 112	453 762	712 562
外商投资经济	Foreign Funded	166 852	4 722 327	4 517 433
其 他	Others	65 760	4 870 116	2 446 293
按隶属关系分	**Grouped by Administrative Relationship**			
中央工业	Central Industry	74 317	4 558 215	3 099 908
地方工业	Local Industry	307 159	6 505 280	6 938 649
#市管工业	City Industry	116 763	2 087 770	2 771 531
#工业系统	Industry System	20 486	296 153	258 563
区县管工业	District & County Industry			
街管工业	Neighbour Industry	12 870	178 109	45 950
乡镇管工业	Town and Country Industry	157 040	3 943 248	3 862 606
按轻重分	**Grouped by Light & Heavy Industry**			
轻工业	Light Industry	95 105	1 225 956	1 874 024
重工业	Heavy Industry	286 371	9 837 539	8 164 533
按规模分	**Grouped by Size of Enterprises**			
大 型	Large - sized	166 881	4 503 881	2 942 444
中 型	Medium - sized	112 581	5 120 461	4 724 241
小 型	Small - sized	102 014	1 439 153	2 371 873

企业主要财务指标(2005年)

INDUSTRIAL ENTERPRISES OF BINHAI NEW AREA,2005

资产总计(万元) Total Assets (10 000 yuan)	流动资产年平均余额(万元) Annual Average Balance of Circulating Funds (10 000 yuan)	固定资产原价(万元) Original Value of Fixed Assets (10 000 yuan)	固定资产净值年平均余额(万元) Annual Average Balance of Net Value of Fixed Assets (10 000 yuan)	主营业务收入(万元) Business Revenue (10 000 yuan)	利税总额(万元) Total Pre-tax Profits (10 000 yuan)	#利润总额 Total Profits
30 658 435	**15 141 948**	**21 668 526**	**11 377 348**	**40 393 777**	**5 471 135**	**3 968 918**
14 626 034	4 974 101	14 442 183	7 273 107	14 455 689	2 993 564	2 081 872
2 665 371	1 220 896	847 288	596 483	1 213 129	17 189	-8 976
230 638	172 626	75 938	44 228	431 154	23 669	6 348
82 610	48 499	34 196	20 904	93 317	7 020	3 667
984 651	506 156	318 320	230 239	1 250 777	77 868	40 102
5 787 066	1 082 684	9 854 929	4 384 614	7 685 859	2 551 364	1 901 684
5 035 086	1 998 939	3 442 981	1 982 513	3 745 555	313 667	137 398
3 499 405	1 325 661	2 426 118	1 378 221	2 108 718	194 187	95 716
26 370	10 105	15 102	12 202	29 480	2 665	1 615
315	229	150	66	150	-92	-92
5 858	3 724	2 295				
2 192 472	1 123 382	1 187 639	735 782	2 110 138	136 416	121 959
13 648 313	8 974 938	5 889 837	3 368 460	23 827 950	2 314 156	1 765 088
6 165 091	2 546 786	3 273 556	1 974 769	3 321 997	211 284	86 648
313 248	221 124	110 134	65 132	524 471	30 689	10 015
984 651	506 156	318 320	230 239	1 250 777	77 868	40 102
2 192 472	1 123 382	1 187 639	735 782	2 110 138	163 416	121 959
13 648 313	8 974 938	5 889 837	3 368 460	23 827 950	2 314 156	1 765 088
7 354 660	1 769 562	10 889 040	5 002 966	9 358 444	2 673 722	1 945 107
7 238 515	2 035 244	10 969 776	5 044 850	8 297 600	2 582 929	1 894 341
23 419 920	13 106 704	10 698 750	6 332 498	32 096 177	2 888 206	2 074 577
9 593 134	4 310 078	4 986 494	2 789 366	12 676 966	1 041 909	549 811
1 250 039	728 693	428 262	278 717	1 743 408	59 400	36 219
244 550	184 221	81 154	45 567	498 925	38 386	11 026
12 332 197	7 883 712	5 202 840	3 218 848	17 176 878	1 748 511	1 477 522
4 637 918	2 506 621	2 476 114	1 450 654	5 250 722	382 811	226 772
26 020 517	12 635 327	19 192 412	9 926 694	35 143 055	5 088 325	3 742 147
15 305 084	7 760 199	9 876 077	5 464 697	20 898 820	2 584 236	1 781 605
9 080 967	4 046 833	8 733 246	4 413 315	13 476 219	2 508 745	1 967 178
6 272 383	3 334 916	3 059 203	1 799 336	6 018 739	378 155	220 136

21－9 滨海新区财政收支(2005年)

FINANCIAL REVENUE AND EXPENDITURE OF BINHAI NEW AREA,2005

项目	Item	合计 Total	#塘沽区 Tanggu District	#汉沽区 Hangu District	#大港区 Dagang District	#经济技术开发区 TEDA	#天津保税区 TFTZ
财政收入合计	**Total Financial Revenue**	**317.16**	**24.94**	**4.91**	**13.19**	**141.25**	**22.73**
一般预算收入	**General Budgetary Financial Revenue**	**308.74**	**24.45**	**4.82**	**12.77**	**135.52**	**21.22**
#增值税	Value－added Tax	136.49	7.79	2.70	5.41	70.79	4.75
营业税	Operation Tax	31.81	7.20	0.59	2.16	9.65	4.95
企业所得税	Income Tax of Enterprises	79.76	3.02	0.35	1.80	31.13	7.98
个人所得税	Private Income Tax	15.19	1.53	0.24	0.92	5.39	1.75
其他收入	Other Income	45.49	4.91	0.94	2.48	18.56	1.79
基金预算收入	**Budgetary Fund Revenue**	**8.43**	**0.49**	**0.09**	**0.42**	**5.73**	**1.51**
财政支出合计	**Total Financial Expenditure**	**100.92**	**15.13**	**3.75**	**10.07**	**59.44**	**11.43**
一般预算支出	**General Budgetary Financial Expenditure**	**93.77**	**14.70**	**3.74**	**9.61**	**53.71**	**10.91**
#基本建设支出	Capital Construction	41.32	2.31	0.03	1.20	30.47	7.01
城市维护费	Expenditure for City Maintenance	4.13	1.13	0.62	0.55	1.43	0.40
企业挖潜改造资金	Innovation Funds of Enterprises	13.31	0.72	0.04		10.60	1.95
行政管理费	Administrative Expenses	6.68	2.03	0.52	1.04	2.26	0.69
公检法司支出	Expenditure for Public Security Agency, Procuratorial Agency and Court of Justice	3.03	1.54	0.33	0.54	0.50	0.12
教育支出	Operating Expense of Education	8.69	3.09	1.00	3.44	0.88	
医疗卫生支出	Expenditure for Health Care	1.62	0.45	0.33	0.35	0.47	
科学和科技支出	Operating Expense of Science	3.49	0.18	0.05	0.02	3.24	
文体广播事业费	Operating Expenses of Culture,Sports and Broadcasting	1.62	0.24	0.13	0.20	1.06	
社会保障和救济支出	Social Security and Pensions, Relief	1.54	0.90	0.23	0.24	0.12	0.05
农林水利气象支出	Expenditure for Operating Expenses of Agriculture,Forestry, Water Conservancy and Meteorology	0.71	0.25	0.15	0.29		
其他各项支出	Other Expensdiure	7.63	1.86	0.30	1.74	2.69	0.69
基金预算支出	**Budgetary Fund Expenditure**	**7.15**	**0.43**	**0.01**	**0.46**	**5.73**	**0.52**

注:此表财政收入是滨海新区地域内的三级财政收入(不含海关关税等中央级固定收入),包括塘沽区、汉沽区、大港区、经济技术开发区、天津保税区的区县三级财政收入和东丽区无瑕街、津南区葛沽镇的街镇财政收入,以及滨海新区范围内市级财政固定收入企业上缴的各项税收;财政支出是滨海新区内各区级财政实际支出,包括塘沽区、汉沽区、大港区、经济技术开发区、天津保税区的区级财政支出及东丽区无瑕街、津南区葛沽镇的街镇财政支出。

Note: Financial revenue refer to the three grades financial revenue from Binhai new area (excluded the fixed revenue of central government such as custom tariffs etc), including the three grades financial revenue of districts and counties from Tanggu District, Hangu District, Dagang District, TEDA and TFTZ, the financial revenue of sub－districts and towns from Wuxia Sub－district of Dongli District and Gegu Town of Jinnan District, and the taxes from the municipal enterprises in new coastal area with fixed financial revenue;Financial expenditure refer to real financial expenditure of districts in new coastal area, including the expenditure of districts from Tanggu District, Hangu District, Dagang District, TEDA and TFTZ, and the expenditure of sub－districts and towns from Wuxia Sub－district of Dongli District and Gegu Town of Jinnan District this table.

21－10 滨海新区金融机构现金收入和支出
CASH INCOME AND EXPENDITURES OF FINANCIAL INSTITUTIONS OF BINHAI NEW AREA

单位:万元 (10 000 yuan)

项 目	Item	2004	2005	2005 比 2004 年增长% Increase Rate in 2005 over 2004
现金收入总计	**Total Cash Income**	**11 302 770**	**15 450 691**	**36.7**
商品销售收入	Income from Commodity Sales	1 706 548	2 273 818	33.2
服务事业收入	Income from Service Trade	483 753	595 938	21.1
税款收入	Income from Taxes	104 952	141 564	34.9
城乡个体经营收	Income from Urban and Rural Individual Business	420 344	649 560	54.5
储蓄存款收入	Income from Savings Deposits	7 411 415	10 677 980	44.1
其他金融机构收入	Income from Other Financial Institutions	149 606	84 867	－43.3
居民归还贷款收入	Income from Repayment of Loans by Residents	141 649	303 539	114.3
汇兑收入	Income from Remittances	106 687	87 992	－17.5
有价证券收入	Income from Securities	32 109	28 826	－10.2
其他收入	Other Income	745 707	616 607	－17.3
现金支出合计	**Total Cash Expenditures**	**11 993 398**	**16 339 477**	**36.2**
工资性支出	Wages	722 567	1 012 231	40.1
#国家职工工资奖金	Wages and Bonuses to the Staff and Workers from Government	355 177	372 074	4.8
国家对个人其他支出	Other Payments to Individuals from Government	105 634	116 355	10.1
其他单位工资性支出	Wages from Other Units	251 928	513 174	103.7
农副产品采购支出	Purchases of Agricultural and Sideline Products	197 074	275 088	39.6
工矿及其他产品采购支出	Expenditure for Purchases of Industrial and Mineral Products	385 572	453 651	17.7
行政企事业管理费支出	Government and Enterprises Overhead	822 342	992 362	20.7
城乡个体经营支出	Expenditure for Individual Business	1 004 101	1 168 534	16.4
储蓄存款支出	Expenditure for Savings Deposits	7 899 376	11 583 636	46.6
其他金融机构支出	Expenditure for Other Financial Institutions	157 429	76 654	－51.3
居民提取贷款支出	Expenditure for Loans by Residents	119 165	256 350	115.1
汇兑支出	Expenditure for Remittances	32 601	24 482	－24.9
有价证券支出	Expenditure for Securities	21 311	19 346	－9.2
其他支出	Others	631 860	477 142	－24.5
货币投放(＋)或回笼(－)	**Currency Issuance(＋) and Cash Withdrawal(－)**	**690 628**	**888 787**	**28.7**

资料来源:中国银行业监督管理委员会天津滨海监管分局。21－11 表同。
Information Source:China Banking Regulatory Commission Tianjin Binhai Field Office. Same as the table 21－11.

21－11　滨海新区金融机构人民币信贷收支情况

RMB CREDIT INCOME & EXPENDITURES OF BANKING INSTITUTIONS OF BINHAI NEW AREA

单位:万元 (10 000 yuan)

项　目	Item	2004	2005	2005比2004年增长% Increase Rate in 2005 over 2004
各项存款总计	**Total Deposits**	**8 307 005**	**10 260 836**	**23.5**
企业存款	Deposits of Enterprises	4 092 403	5 306 792	29.7
财政性存款	Treasury Deposits	23 261	59 878	157.4
储蓄存款	Savings Deposits	3 240 842	3 810 519	17.6
#定期储蓄	Fixed Deposits	2 221 801	2 522 297	13.5
农业存款	Agricultural Deposits	270 264	221 765	－17.9
其他类存款	Other Deposits	680 235	861 882	26.7
各项贷款总计	**Total Loans**	**7 484 351**	**8 696 799**	**16.2**
短期贷款	Short－term Loans	3 569 482	4 484 335	25.6
#工业贷款	Industrial Loans	1 116 855	1 160 433	3.9
商业贷款	Commercial Loans	226 890	239 084	5.4
建筑业贷款	Construction Loans	101 124	110 442	9.2
私营及个体贷款	Loans to Private and Individuals	74 182	146 480	97.5
乡镇企业贷款	Loans to Township Enterprises	88 038	105 711	20.1
农业贷款	Agricultural Loans	455 097	504 050	10.8
三资企业贷款	Loans to Hongkong,Macao,Taiwan and Foreign Funded Enterprises	224 247	179 809	－19.8
其他短期贷款	Other Short－term Loans	1 283 049	2 038 326	58.9
中长期贷款	Medium－term and Long－term Loans	3 625 490	4 019 109	10.9
#技术改造贷款	Loans to Technical Innovation	50 618	41 936	－17.2
基本建设贷款	Loans to Capital Construction	1 983 030	2 443 073	23.2
票据融资	Bill Financing	289 379	190 855	－34.0
各项垫款	Money Advanced for sb. to be Paid Back Late		2 500	

21－12　滨海新区工业废水、废气、固体废物排放及处理情况(2002－2005年)
EMISSION AND TREATMENT OF INDUSTRIAL WASTE WATER, WASTE GAS, WASTE RESIDUE AND DUST OF BINHAI NEW AREA, 2002－2005

指　标　Item	2002	2003	2004	2005
工业废水				
Industrial Waste Water				
工业废水排放量(万吨)				
Volume of Waste Water Discharged(10 000 tons)	6 979.57	6 768.00	8 310.27	16 027.10
工业废水排放达标率(%)				
Rate of Reaching the Standard of Industrial Waste Water(%)	99.13	99.59	98.97	99.74
工业废气				
Industrial Waste Gas				
工业废气排放总量(亿标立方米)				
Total Volume of Industrial Waste Gas Emission(100 million cu.m	691.76	1 688.80	872.97	1 414.02
生产工艺过程中废气排放量				
Volume of Waste Gas from the Process of Production	166.86	160.11	681.82	380.27
燃料燃烧过程中废气排放量				
Volume of Waste Gas from the Burning Process of Fuel	524.90	1 528.69	191.15	1 033.75
工业粉尘产生量(万吨)				
Amount of Industrial Dust Producted(10 000 tons)	1.07	1.04	1.21	3.83
工业粉尘排放量				
Volume of Industrial Dust Emission	0.13	0.15	0.12	0.35
工业粉尘去除量				
Volume of Industrial Dust Removed	0.94	0.89	1.09	3.48
工业粉尘去除率(%)				
Rate of Industrial Dust Removed(%)	87.99	86.02	90.06	90.91
工业固体废物				
Industrial Waste Residue				
工业固体废物产生量(万吨)				
Amount of Industrial Waste Residue Produced(10 000 tons)	230.09	236.09	261.11	447.41
#已处理量				
Volume of Treatment	21.19	56.84	20.14	19.08
已综合利用量				
Volume of Comprehensive Utilization	209.31	211.63	291.76	480.06
工业固体废物综合利用率(%)				
Rate of Comprehensive Using Industrial Waste Residue(%)	89.74	89.64	93.50	96.30

21－13　滨海新区基础设施投资和城市市政设施(2002－2005年)
INFRASTRUCTURE INVESTMENT AND MUNICIPAL INFRASTRUCTURE OF BINHAI NEW AREA, 2002－2005

项　目	Item	2002	2003	2004	2005
基础设施投资(万元)	**Infrastructure Investment(10 000 yuan)**	**856 168**	**1 225 676**	**1 571 691**	**1 750 143**
铁路和轨道交通	Railway and Track Transportation	182 427	247 176	165 780	143 812
道路桥梁	Road and Bridge	219 427	230 354	190 142	152 897
港　口	Port	164 214	146 713	292 177	459 018
排　水	Drainage	13 339	25 622	7 375	2 175
供　水	Water Supply	10 243	2 333	11 128	6 006
供电供热	Power and Heat Supply	31 134	25 255	40 166	86 723
通　讯	Communication	14 493	1 500	15 733	56 304
绿化和环境工程	Afforest & Environment Engineering	73 585	110 983	146 290	64 269
其　他	Others	147 306	435 740	702 900	778 939
市政设施	**Municipal Infrastructire**				
铺装道路长度(公里)	Length of Paved Roads(km)	1 096.82	1 135.56	1 183.45	1 231.35
铺装道路面积(万平方米)	Area of Paved Roads(10 000 sq.m)	1 191.60	1 333.49	1 415.85	1 508.31
桥梁座数(座)	Number of Bridges(unit)	154	153	157	139
#立交桥(座)	Flyover(unit)	20	23	21	25
排水水泵站(座)	Pumping Station(unit)	116	136	136	136
排水管道长度(公里)	Length of Drainpipes(km)	1 549.55	1 684.14	1 738.67	1 885.47

21－14 经济技术开发区主要年份国民经济主要指标

MAIN STATISTICS ON ECONOMIC－TECHNOLOGICAL DEVELOPMENT AREA IN MAIN YEARS

年 份 Year	地区生产总值（万元） Gross Domestic Product (10 000 yuan)	工业总产值（万元） Gross Output Value of Industry (10 000 yuan)	#外商及港澳台商投资企业 Foreign Funded Enterprises	工业产品销售收入（万元） Sales Revenue of Industrial Product (10 000 yuan)	#外商及港澳台商投资企业 Foreign Funded Enterprises
1985					
1990	25 011	78 060	68 859	73 767	60 546
1995	801 102	2 664 551	2 621 361	2 526 011	2 483 428
1996	1 310 135	3 701 106	3 646 558	3 617 960	3 563 872
1997	1 536 270	4 702 422	4 590 240	4 630 014	4 519 091
1998	1 729 445	5 402 180	5 203 573	5 337 354	5 141 130
1999	2 019 633	6 085 483	5 863 637	6 018 543	5 802 137
2000	2 507 109	7 318 248	7 089 316	7 274 338	7 049 651
2001	3 081 804	8 651 050	8 394 351	8 633 748	8 378 463
2002	3 785 283	10 312 373	10 016 307	10 291 748	9 996 025
2003	4 475 502	12 513 994	12 158 648	12 494 722	12 143 923
2004	5 372 001	18 221 439	17 749 893	18 476 539	17 998 392
2005	6 420 489	23 051 921	22 471 809	23 521 464	22 908 165

年 份 Year	直接利用外资合同数（个） Number of Foreign Funded Enterprises Newly Signed(unit)	直接利用外资项目合同投资总额（万美元） Contract Investment of Foreign Funded Enterprises Newly Signed(USD 10 000)	出口总额（万美元） Exports (USD 10 000)	从业人员（人） Persons Employed (person)	#外商及港澳台商投资企业 Forign Funded Enterprises
1985	14	3 192		823	137
1990	54	12 237	6 370	14 462	8 115
1995	361	181 129	90 103	112 874	79 682
1996	187	191 604	145 020	140 150	99 853
1997	172	149 576	200 415	157 934	113 473
1998	194	148 207	208 135	171 604	121 093
1999	106	142 884	255 380	180 466	127 156
2000	99	277 902	326 691	191 058	134 496
2001	94	248 779	403 531	195 012	137 702
2002	111	260 676	570 563	205 884	146 808
2003	167	233 952	688 617	231 957	159 666
2004	164	321 112	1 117 503	258 064	179 747
2005	225	436 305	1 397 066	288 264	201 334

21－15 经济技术开发区国民经济主要指标
MAIN STATISTICS ON ECONOMIC－TECHNOLOGICAL DEVELOPMENT AREA

项目	Item	2004	2005	2005 比 2004 年增长% Increase Rate in 2005 over 2004
地区生产总值(万元)	Gross Domestic Product(10 000 yuan)	5 372 001	6 420 489	25.2
第二产业	Secondary Industry	4 402 936	5 394 349	29.0
#工　业	Industry	4 377 498	5 345 029	28.7
第三产业	Tertiary Industry	969 065	1 026 140	5.5
#交通运输、仓储和邮政业	Transport,Storage,Post Services	39 612	44 898	9.3
批发和零售业	Wholesale and Retail Trade	658 212	686 988	4.7
住宿和餐饮业	Accommodation and Catering Services	23 676	47 848	102.8
金融业	Finance Intermediation			
房地产业	Real Estate	131 562	167 835	22.9
工业产品销售收入(万元)	Sales Revenue of Industrial Products (10 000 yuan)	18 476 539	23 521 464	27.3
#外商及港澳台商投资企业	Foreign Funded Enterprises	17 998 392	22 908 165	27.3
工业总产值(万元)	Gross Output Value of Industry (10 000 yuan)	18 221 439	23 051 921	26.5
#外商及港澳台商投资企业	Foreign Funded Enterprises	17 749 893	22 471 809	26.6
出口总额(万美元)	Exports(USD 10 000)	1 117 503	1 397 066	25.0
直接利用外资合同数(个)	Number of Foreign Funded Enterprises Newly Signed(unit)	164	225	37.2
直接利用外资合同额(万美元)	Foreign Capital Contracted(USD 10 000)	192 235	259 510	35.0
实际直接利用外资金额(万美元)	Actual Direct Utilization of Foreign Capital(USD 10 000)	94 923	128 510	35.4
单位从业人员期末人数(人)	Number of Persons Employed Year－end (person)	258 064	288 264	11.7
外商及港澳台商投资企业	Foreign Funded Enterprises	179 747	201 334	12.0
内资企业	Domestic Funded Enterprises	78 317	86 930	11.0
按产业分组	Grouped by Industry			
第二产业	Secondary Industry	189 625	208 530	10.0
第三产业	Tertiary Industry	68 439	79 734	16.5
单位从业人员人均劳动报酬(元)	Per Capita Remuneration of Persons Employed(yuan)	21 744	24 624	13.2

21－16 经济技术开发区小区主要经济指标(2005 年)
MAIN STATISTICS ON SUBSIDIARIES AREAS OF TEDA,2005

项目	Item	西区 West Area	微电子工业区 MIP	逸仙科学工业区 YSP	化学工业区 CIP
工业总产值(万元)	Gross Output Value of Industry(10 000 yuan)	67 627	4 280 109	622 274	26 318
外贸出口总额(万美元)	Exports (USD 10 000)	32	282 781	14 655	1 052
固定资产投资(万元)	Total Investment In Fixed Assets(10 000 yuan)	195 421	140 520	33 942	129 561
#基础设施	Infrastructure	98 394	7 337	3 784	34 213
单位从业人员期末人数(人)	Number of Persons Employed Year－end (person)	688	18 856	6 473	1 559
直接利用外资项目数(个)	Number of Foreign Funded Enterprises Newly Signed(unit)	18	56	29	28
直接利用外资合同金额(万美元)	Foreign Capital Contracted (USD 10 000)	17 478	31 022	29 162	14 128

注:微电子工业区坐落于西青区、逸仙科学工业区坐落于武清区、化学工业区坐落于汉沽区。
Note: MIP is located at Xiqing district. YSP is located at Wuqing district. CIP is located at Han'gu district.

21－17　经济技术开发区城市建设情况
（截止2005年底）
URBAN CONSTRUCTION OF THE ECONOMIC－TECHNOLOGICAL DEVELOPMENT AREA
(By the End of 2005)

项　目	Item	单　位	unit	数　量 Amount
累计房屋开工面积	Total Floor Space Under Construction	万平方米	10 000 sq.m	1 506.2
#2005年	in 2005			280.6
累计房屋竣工面积	Total Floor Space Completed	万平方米	10 000 sq.m	927.0
#2005年	in 2005			110.8
已开发土地面积	Developed Area	平方公里	sq.km	40
桥　梁	Bridge	座	unit	9
路　灯	Street Lamp	盏	unit	12 180
污水处理量	Volume of Sewage Treatment	万立方米	10 000 cu.m	1 924.48
绿化面积	Area of Green Land	万平方米	10 000 sq.m	814.66
绿化覆盖率	Coverage Rate of Urban Green Areas	%	%	31.55
出租车辆	Number of Taxis	辆	unit	848
客运总量	Passenger Traffic	万人次	10 000 person－times	3 135.49
#轻　轨	Light Railway	万人次	10 000 person－times	676.58

21－18　经济技术开发区利用外资情况（1985－2005年）
FOREIGN INVESTMENT OF ECONOMIC－TECHNOLOGICAL DEVELOPMENT AREA, 1985－2005

年　份 Year	直接利用外资合同数（个） Number of Foreign Funded Enterprises Approved(unit)	直接利用外资合同金　额（万美元） Contract Investment (USD 10 000)	实际直接利用外资金　额（万美元） Contract Foreign Capital (USD 10 000)
1985－2005年累计 Total of 1985－2005	**4 076**	**2 137 019**	**1 181 100**
1985	14	1 436	568
1986	27	1 693	1 231
1987	34	844	1 099
1988	48	4 835	1 298
1989	40	6 764	4 071
1990	54	10 034	3 950
1991	121	12 653	11 006
1992	462	50 685	24 243
1993	909	75 853	34 460
1994	487	119 908	65 546
1995	361	158 959	72 216
1996	187	158 846	75 706
1997	172	130 815	75 558
1998	194	122 845	101 318
1999	106	127 987	100 071
2000	99	264 034	101 003
2001	94	220 008	180 072
2002	111	89 324	41 000
2003	167	127 751	63 251
2004	164	192 235	94 923
2005	225	259 510	128 510

注：表中数字以核发批准证书为准。
Note: The figures of this table are calculated according to the certificate of agreement.

21－19 经济技术开发区外商及港澳台商投资企业按投资方式及国别(地区)分类
(截至 2005 年底)

TEDA'S FOREIGN FUNDED ENTERPRISES BY INVESTING WAY AND COUNTRY(REGION)
(By the End of 2005)

国 别(地 区)	Country(Region)	企业个数(个) Number of Enterprises(unit)	直接利用外资项目合同投资总额(万美元) Total Volume of Contract (USD 10 000)	#直接利用外资合同金额(万美元) Foreign Capital (USD 10 000)
合 计	**Total**	**2 010**	**2 118 870**	**915 930**
按投资方式分	**Grouped by Investing Way**			
合资企业	Joint Ventures	815	824 570	320 332
合作企业	Cooperative Enterprises	57	85 457	27 934
独资企业	Sole－foreign Enterprises	1 138	1 208 843	567 663
按国别、地区分	**Grouped by Country, Region**			
美 国	United State	347	515 463	159 089
中国香港	Hongkong, China	596	390 500	177 207
韩 国	Republic of Korea	140	162 964	69 771
英属维尔京	Virgin Islands of United Kingdom	93	206 211	104 561
日 本	Japan	251	255 621	110 847
英 国	United Kingdom	41	43 506	17 423
新加坡	Singapore	89	43 530	20 175
中国台湾	Taiwan, China	130	28 533	13 683
开曼群岛	Qaman Islands	22	181 265	102 332
丹 麦	Denmark	6	36 913	15 728
德 国	Germany	37	35 200	17 908
荷 兰	Netherlands	15	31 344	16 756
瑞 士	Swiss	11	26 807	11 815
加拿大	Canada	52	38 291	19 977
中国澳门	Macao, China	20	17 863	7 598
法 国	France	20	18 739	7 256
西萨摩亚	Samoa Western	11	15 470	5 287
泰 国	Thailand	10	5 516	2 715
澳大利亚	Australia	21	9 929	5 890
马来西亚	Malaysia	9	4 720	2 876
芬 兰	Finland	5	1 788	1 055
比利时	Belgium	6	2 380	1 357
印度尼西亚	Indonesia	3	365	221
巴哈马	Bahama	1	600	300
以色列	Israel	1	556	186

注：表中数字以核发营业执照的企业为准，21－20 表同。
Note: The figures of this table refer to enterprises which have gotten business license, same as following table 21－20.

21-19 续表 Continued

国 别(地 区)	Country(Region)	企业个数(个) Number of Enterprises(unit)	直接利用外资项目合同投资总额(万美元) Total Volume of Contract (USD 10 000)	#直接利用外资合同金 额(万美元) Foreign Capital (USD 10 000)
新西兰	New Zealand	6	3 546	1 583
意大利	Italy	3	185	93
毛里求斯	Mauritius	9	14 029	8 484
菲律宾	Philippines	2	1 500	750
匈牙利	Hungary	6	1 203	1 145
罗马尼亚	Romania	1	50	50
巴拿马	Panama	3	208	73
捷 克	Czech	2	104	153
波 兰	Poland	1	150	105
蒙 古	Mongolia	2	1 014	810
西班牙	Spain	4	97	45
俄罗斯	Russia	2	83	42
挪 威	Norway	1	50	35
塞浦路斯	Cyprus	2	605	594
乌拉圭	Uruguay	1	68	24
约 旦	Jordan	1	42	10
奥地利	Austria	1	20	20
巴基斯坦	Pakistan	3	48	21
拉脱维亚	Latvia	1	30	30
秘 鲁	Peru	1	30	21
乌兹别克斯坦	Uzbekstan	1	950	870
柬埔寨	Cambodia	1	958	940
百慕大群岛	Bermuda	3	3 582	1 852
巴巴多斯	Barbados	2	10 200	3 300
卢森堡	Luxembourg	1	1 137	337
哥斯达黎加	Costa Rica	1	200	180
美属萨摩亚	American Samoa	3	739	728
也 门	Yemen	1	28	20
乌克兰	Ukraine	1	1 809	338
冈比亚	Gambia	1	321	218
爱尔兰	Ireland	1	20	20
英属印度洋群岛	British Indian Ocean Territory	1	20	20

21-20 经济技术开发区外商及港澳台商投资企业按行业分类

（截至2005年底）

TEDA'S FOREIGN FUNDED ENTERPRISES BY SECTOR

(By the End of 2005)

行业	Sector	企业个数（个）Number of Enterprises (unit)	直接利用外资项目合同投资总额（万美元）Total Volume of Contract (USD 10 000)	#直接利用外资合同金额（万美元）Foreign Capital (USD 10 000)
合计	**Total**	**2 010**	**2 118 870**	**915 930**
农业	Agriculture	2	2 220	2 005
渔业	Fishery	1	20	20
农、林、牧、渔服务业	FFAF Services	1	149	132
煤炭开采和洗选业	Coal Extraction and Washing	3	4 259	2 287
有色金属矿采选业	Non-ferrous Minerals Mining and Processing	1	77	60
其他矿采选业	Other Minerals Mining and Processing	1	70	70
农副食品加工业	Agriculture and Sideline Food Processing	66	61 263	33 571
食品制造业	Food Products	58	74 433	34 252
饮料制造业	Beverage Products	28	33 899	13 665
纺织业	Textile	36	21 053	7 742
纺织服装、鞋、帽制造业	Textile Garments, Shoes, Caps Manufacturing	76	15 285	10 293
皮革、毛皮、羽毛(绒)及其制品业	Leather, Fur, Down and Related Products	24	10 147	6 027
木材加工及木竹藤棕草制品业	Timber Processing and Timber, Bamboo, Cane, Palm Fiber and Straw Products	18	3 180	2 726
家具制造业	Furniture Products	26	20 925	9 868
造纸及纸制品业	Paper Marking and Paper Products	16	9 318	3 380
印刷业和记录媒介的复制	Printing and Record Medium Reproduction	28	10 877	7 538
文教体育用品制造业	Cultural, Educational and Sports Goods	21	8 172	2 575
石油加工、炼焦及核燃料加工业	Petroleum Processing and Coking and Nuclear Fuel Processing	10	4 980	2 623
化学原料及化学制品制造业	Raw Chemical Material and Chemical Product	111	144 125	60 353
医药制造业	Medical and Pharmaceutical Products	40	68 319	30 494
化学纤维制造业	Chemical Fiber Manufacturing	5	4 589	2 207
橡胶制品业	Rubber Products	20	39 016	16 053
塑料制品业	Plastic Products	64	36 326	14 985
非金属矿物制品业	Nonmetal Mineral Products	72	70 425	21 002
黑色金属冶炼及压延加工业	Smelting and Pressing of Ferrous Metals	11	18 098	6 934
有色金属冶炼及压延加工业	Smelting and Pressing of Non-ferrous Metals	8	11 265	3 714
金属制品业	Metal Products	43	14 391	6 244
通用设备制造业	General Equipment	69	48 521	25 093
专用设备制造业	Equipment for Special Purposes	111	57 616	22 854
交通运输设备制造业	Transportation Equipment	80	127 523	54 785
电气机械及器材制造业	Electric Equipment and Machinery	77	66 821	35 082
通信设备、计算机及其他电子设备制造业	Telecommunication Equipment, Computer and Other Electronic Equipment	183	724 474	284 809

21－19 续表 Continued

行 业	Sector	企业个数（个）Number of Enterprises (unit)	直接利用外资项目合同投资总额（万美元）Total Volume of Contract (USD 10 000)	#直接利用外资合同金额（万美元）Foreign Capital (USD 10 000)
仪器仪表及文化办公用机械制造业	Instruments, Meters, Cultural and Office Machinery	60	13 838	7 179
工艺品及其他制造业	Handicraft and Related Products	32	7 448	6 353
废弃资源和废旧材料回收加工业	Waste Resources and Materials Recovering and Processing	4	844	193
电力、热力的生产和供应业	Production and Supply of Power and Heating Energy	4	12 532	6 871
燃气生产和供应业	Gas Production and Supply	2	1 689	698
水的生产和供应业	Production and Supply of Water	1	3 928	1 803
房屋和土木工程建筑业	Buildingsand Civil Engineering Construction	20	37 611	11 108
建筑安装业	Equipment Installation	5	149	77
建筑装饰业	Building Decoration	50	10 874	9 025
其他建筑业	Other Construction	4	202	119
铁路运输业	Railroad Transportation	1	169	101
道路运输业	Road Transportation	6	4 339	2 400
城市公共交通业	Urban Public Transportation	2	68	35
水上运输业	Water Transportation	9	2 277	1 793
装卸搬运和其他运输服务业	Loading, Transportation and Other Transportation Services	22	5 940	1 991
仓储业	Storage	20	17 955	6 768
电信和其他信息传输服务业	Telecommunication and Other Information Transmitting Services	19	5 620	3 972
计算机服务业	Computer Services	1	28	10
软件业	Software	46	5 791	4 951
批发业	Wholesale	8	4 319	2 250
零售业	Retail	3	3 694	1 947
餐饮业	Catering	12	659	534
其他金融活动	Other Finance	1	121	121
房地产业	Real Estate	135	89 777	35 696
租赁业	Leasing Serving	2	1 670	700
商务服务业	Commercial Services	108	64 226	37 006
研究与试验发展	R&D	7	5 407	2 362
专业技术服务业	Professional Technology Services	36	12 587	7 903
科技交流和推广服务业	Scientific and Technological Exchange and Promotion Services	44	22 988	11 973
水利管理业	Water Conservancy	2	183	83
环境管理业	Management for Environment	5	3 571	2 463
公共设施管理业	Public Facilities Services	9	46 477	14 321
居民服务业	Resident Services	3	491	452
其他服务业	Other Services	3	58	20
教 育	Education	1	500	250
体 育	Sports	3	125	101
娱乐业	Entertainment	10	18 880	8 859

21－21 建区以来天津保税区国民经济主要指标(1992－2005年)
MAIN STATISTICS ON TIANJIN FREE TRADE ZONE SINCE ITS ESTABLISHMENT, 1992－2005

年份 Year	地区生产总值(万元) Gross Domestic Product (10 000 yuan)	工业总产值(万元) Gross Output Value of Industry (10 000 yuan)	固定资产投资(亿元) Investment in Fixed Assets (100 million yuan)	进出区货物总值(亿美元) Total Value of Goods from and to The Zone (USD 100 million)
1992	300		2.56	1.60
1993	6 500	800	15.09	8.60
1994	16 940	15 000	7.18	6.77
1995	33 930	46 800	2.51	12.78
1996	77 498	70 010	1.56	27.01
1997	121 687	69 706	2.32	40.97
1998	231 839	48 479	10.61	46.97
1999	284 363	41 436	14.66	46.48
2000	346 214	112 921	12.22	47.00
2001	443 845	169 446	12.57	50.01
2002	615 109	225 396	15.50	65.00
2003	830 186	418 136	31.20	92.31
2004	1 151 502	910 035	52.82	131.25
2005	1 535 838	1 622 752	72.17	187.61

年份 Year	直接利用外资合同数(个) Number of Foreign Funded Enterprises Newly Signed(unit)	直接利用外资合同金额(万美元) Contract Investment (USD 10 000)	实际直接利用外资金额(万美元) Foreign Direct Investment Actually Used (USD 10 000)	企业进出口总额(万美元) Foreign Trade of Enterprises (USD 10 000)	#进口 Import
1992	508	35 253	6 500		
1993	1 169	53 208	15 330	6 587	3 507
1994	390	22 179	11 011	7 413	3 985
1995	336	27 362	18 027	31 263	20 473
1996	370	35 906	20 310	39 281	23 962
1997	413	70 375	30 044	60 744	38 970
1998	427	50 213	30 511	71 190	45 438
1999	212	55 149	35 331	74 271	55 450
2000	168	33 779	35 497	99 284	76 873
2001	134	47 539	55 084	121 482	92 580
2002	188	52 549	23 500	212 003	173 978
2003	218	96 662	40 177	361 912	311 927
2004	257	152 384	56 361	543 963	473 052
2005	338	206 978	76 663	814 751	702 335

21－22 天津保税区主要经济指标
MAIN STATISTICS ON TIANJIN FREE TRADE ZONE

单位：万元 (10 000 yuan)

项目	Item	2003	2004	2005	2005比2004年增长% Increase Rate in 2005 over 2004
地区生产总值	Gross Domestic Product	830 186	1 151 502	1 535 838	37.1
第二产业	Secondary Industry	91 997	111 449	156 276	41.3
第三产业	Tertiary Industry	738 189	1 040 053	1 379 562	36.7
工业总产值	Gross Output Value of Industry	418 136	910 035	1 622 750	78.3
进出区货物总值（亿美元）	Total Value of Goods from and to The Zone(USD 100 million)	92.31	131.25	187.61	42.9
企业进出口额（亿美元）	Foreign Trade of The Enterprises (USD 100 million)	36.19	54.40	81.48	49.8
#进口	Imports	31.19	47.31	70.23	48.5
各项税收总额	Various Taxes	1 207	1 293 016	1 175 749	-9.1
#工商税及所得税	Industrial,Commercial and Income Tax	131 813	162 245	208 377	28.4
海关关税	Tariffs	542 691	535 393	408 772	-23.6
海关代征税	Tax Levied by The Customs as An Agent	532 557	595 378	558 600	-6.2
企业销售(营业)收入	Sales (Operating) Revenue of Enterprises	361.62	646.98	1 060.02	63.8
固定资产投资总额	Investment in Fixed Assets	233 066	429 251	620 573	44.6
#基础设施投资	Infrastructure Investment	144 962	151 590	91 713	-39.5

21－23 天津保税区基础设施形成能力
（截止2005年底）
CAPACITY OF INFRASTRUCTURE ON TIANJIN FREE TRADE ZONE
(By the End of 2005)

项目	Item	单位	unit	天津港保税区 Tianjin Port Tree Trade Zone	天津空港加工区 Tianjin AirPort Industrial Park
建成道路长度	Length of Completed Roads	公里	km	33.12	78.72
建成道路面积	Area of Completed Roads	万平方米	10 000 sq.m	39.69	104.10
绿地面积	Area of Green Areas	万平方米	10 000 sq.m	94.39	259.80
供水能力	Capacity of Water Supply	万立方米/日	10 000 cu.m/day	2.50	5.30
排水管道长度	Length of Drainpipes	公里	km	70.05	228.98
#污水管道		公里	km	18.45	93.40
供电能力	Capacity of Electricity Supply	千伏安	KVA	127 500	54 860
供气能力	Capacity of Gas Supply	万立方米/日	10 000 cu.m/day	1.40	1.00
供热能力	Heating Supply	吨/小时	ton/hour	250.00	93.00
局用电话交换机容量	Capacity of Office Telephone Exchanges	万门	10 000 lines	5.50	7.20

第22篇
CHAPTER 22

区县基本情况

Basic Statistics on Districts and Counties

22-1 和平区基本情况

BASIC STATISTICS OF HEPING DISTRICT

指标名称	Item	2004	2005
*户籍户数(万户)	Registered Households(10 000 househols)	13.40	12.95
*户籍人口(万人)	Registered Population(10 000 persons)	39.95	38.41
男	Male	19.29	18.56
女	Female	20.66	19.85
*人口出生率(‰)	Birth Rate of Population(‰)	4.09	4.00
*人口自然增长率(‰)	Natural Growth Rate of Population(‰)	-2.01	-1.51
城镇单位从业人员(万人)	Employment Personnel Worked in Urban Units(10 000 persons)	2.85	3.13
#在岗职工	Working Staff and Workers	2.34	2.74
地区生产总值(亿元)	Gross Domestic Product(10 000 yuan)	48.36	59.35
第二产业	Secondary Industry	2.26	4.36
#工　业	Industry	1.04	1.04
第三产业	Tertiary Industry	46.10	54.99
地区生产总值增速(%)	Increase Rate of Gross Domestic Product(%)	25.8	20.6
一般预算区级财政收入(万元)	General Budgetary Financial Revenue at District Level(10 000 yuan)	73 298	102 253
一般预算区级财政支出(万元)	General Budgetary Financial Expenditure at District Level(10 000 yuan)	89 414	110 159
#教育经费支出	Operating Expenses for Education	23 637	27 717
*固定资产投资(万元)	Investment in Fixed Assets(10 000 yuan)	1 759 518	1 782 316
规模以上工业企业	Industrial Enterprises above Designated Size		
单位数(个)	Number of Units(unit)	21	22
从业人员(万人)	Employment(10 000 persons)	0.13	0.11
总产值(万元)	Gross Output Value(10 000 yuan)	9 671	16 755
产品销售收入(万元)	Sales Revenue(10 000 yuan)	16 809	18 460
利税总额(万元)	Total Pre-tax Profits(10 000 yuan)	1 140	1 924
固定资产原值(万元)	Original Value of Fixed Assets(10 000 yuan)	3 595	2 868
流动资产合计(万元)	Total Circulating Funds(10 000 yuan)	23 024	13 665

注:1."*"为全区(县)数据,其余为区(县)属数。2.2004地区生产总值为第一次经济普查最终核实结果。3.固定资产投资不含农村集体和个人投资。4.22-2至22-18表同。

Note:a) The data with "*" of this table refer to the whole district(county)data,others refer to that of units under the leadership of this district (county). b) GDP is gained from the first economic census in 2004. c)The investment in fixed assets exclude rural collective and individual. d)Same as following table 22-2 to 22-18.

22－1 续表 Continued

指标名称	Item	2004	2005
社会消费品零售总额(万元)	Retail Sales of Consumer Goods(10 000 yuan)	925 524	1 127 010
* 私营工商企业	Private Industrial and Commercial Enterprises		
户　数(户)	Number of Enterprises(unit)	4 504	4 887
雇工人数(人)	Employees(person)	20 938	20 295
注册资本(万元)	Registered Capital(10 000 yuan)	453 695	487 802
总产值(万元)	Gross Output Value(10 000 yuan)		
营业收入(万元)	Business Revenue(10 000 yuan)	1 891 500	1 022 393
* 个体工商业	Individual Industrial and Commercial Enterprises		
户　数(户)	Number of Enterprises(unit)	6 652	4 390
从业人员(人)	Employment(person)	4 956	1 768
资　金(万元)	Fund(10 000 yuan)	28 983	13 436
营业额(万元)	Turnover(10 000 yuan)	299 106	171 761
实际直接利用外资(万美元)	Foreign Direct Investment (USD 10 000)	3 230	9 003
吸引内资到位额(万元)	Actual Domestic Investment(10 000 yuan)	195 000	311 013
工业企业出口交货值(万元)	Delivery Value of Industrial Enterprises(10 000 yuan)	8 682	11 490
* 小学校数(所)	Number of Primary Schools(unit)	32	31
* 小学在校学生数(人)	Students Enrollment of Primary Schools(person)	28 628	27 758
* 普通中学校数(所)	Number of Regular Secondary Schools(unit)	29	30
* 普通中学在校学生数(人)	Students Enrollment of Regular Secondary Schools(person)	35 901	34 508
幼儿园数(所)	Number of Kindergartens(unit)	32	28
卫生机构数(个)	Health Care Institutions(unit)	22	22
#医院、卫生院	Hospital and Health Center	11	10
卫生机构床位数(张)	Beds(unit)	663	663
#医院、卫生院	Hospital and Health Center	643	643
新增再就业人员(人)	Newly Re－employment Person(person)	2 950	3 100
* 人均公共绿地面积(平方米)	Per Capita Public Green Areas(sq. m)	2.16	1.84

22－2 河东区基本情况

BASIC STATISTICS OF HEDONG DISTRICT

指标名称	Item	2004	2005
* 户籍户数(万户)	Registered Households(10 000 househols)	24.66	25.35
* 户籍人口(万人)	Registered Population(10 000 persons)	67.75	69.23
男	Male	34.14	34.89
女	Female	33.61	34.34
* 人口出生率(‰)	Birth Rate of Population(‰)	3.76	4.33
* 人口自然增长率(‰)	Natural Growth Rate of Population(‰)	－2.37	－1.2
城镇单位从业人员(万人)	Employment Personnel Worked in Urban Units(10 000 persons)	2.09	2.30
#在岗职工	Working Staff and Workers	1.62	1.79
地区生产总值(亿元)	Gross Domestic Product(10 000 yuan)	42.52	50.74
第二产业	Secondary Industry	13.38	11.51
#工　业	Industry	5.64	8.96
第三产业	Tertiary Industry	29.14	39.23
地区生产总值增速(%)	Increase Rate of Gross Domestic Product(%)	22.6	19.5
一般预算区级财政收入(万元)	General Budgetary Financial Revenue at District Level(10 000 yuan)	62 057	77 253
一般预算区级财政支出(万元)	General Budgetary Financial Expenditure at District Level(10 000 yuan)	72 145	89 493
#教育经费支出	Operating Expenses for Education	22 864	28 300
* 固定资产投资(万元)	Investment in Fixed Assets(10 000 yuan)	282 298	487 782
规模以上工业企业	Industrial Enterprises above Designated Size		
单位数(个)	Number of Units(unit)	25	56
从业人员(万人)	Employment(10 000 persons)	0.13	0.38
总产值(万元)	Gross Output Value(10 000 yuan)	29 865	157 743
产品销售收入(万元)	Sales Revenue(10 000 yuan)	28 844	163 391
利税总额(万元)	Total Pre－tax Profits(10 000 yuan)	1 735	7 125
固定资产原值(万元)	Original Value of Fixed Assets(10 000 yuan)	22 016	27 276
流动资产合计(万元)	Total Circulating Funds(10 000 yuan)	58 671	68 573

22-2续表 Continued

指标名称	Item	2004	2005
社会消费品零售总额(万元)	Retail Sales of Consumer Goods(10 000 yuan)	520 664	626 136
* 私营工商企业	Private Industrial and Commercial Enterprises		
户　数(户)	Number of Enterprises(unit)	3 311	3 815
雇工人数(人)	Employees(person)	24 294	28 895
注册资本(万元)	Registered Capital(10 000 yuan)	312 749	414 335
总产值(万元)	Gross Output Value(10 000 yuan)	197 819	202 270
营业收入(万元)	Business Revenue(10 000 yuan)	414 275	683 269
* 个体工商业	Individual Industrial and Commercial Enterprises		
户　数(户)	Number of Enterprises(unit)	12 178	11 572
从业人员(人)	Employment(person)	12 178	11 572
资　金(万元)	Fund(10 000 yuan)	53 107	43 927
营业额(万元)	Turnover(10 000 yuan)	254 389	275 005
实际直接利用外资(万美元)	Foreign Direct Investment (USD 10 000)	1 557	879
吸引内资到位额(万元)	Actual Domestic Investment(10 000 yuan)	72 374	117 799
工业企业出口交货值(万元)	Delivery Value of Industrial Enterprises(10 000 yuan)	11 422	14 155
* 小学校数(所)	Number of Primary Schools(unit)	30	27
* 小学在校学生数(人)	Students Enrollment of Primary Schools(person)	22 661	20 594
* 普通中学校数(所)	Number of Regular Secondary Schools(unit)	33	30
* 普通中学在校学生数(人)	Students Enrollment of Regular Secondary Schools(person)	28 915	27 535
幼儿园数(所)	Number of Kindergartens(unit)	54	52
卫生机构数(个)	Health Care Institutions(unit)	18	18
#医院、卫生院	Hospital and Health Center	15	15
卫生机构床位数(张)	Beds(unit)	1 294	1 288
#医院、卫生院	Hospital and Health Center	980	1 028
新增再就业人员(人)	Newly Re-employment Person(person)	16 546	19 526
* 人均公共绿地面积(平方米)	Per Capita Public Green Areas(sq. m)	6.29	6.74

22-3 河西区基本情况

BASIC STATISTICS OF HEXI DISTRICT

指标名称	Item	2004	2005
*户籍户数(万户)	Registered Households(10 000 househols)	25.68	26.02
*户籍人口(万人)	Registered Population(10 000 persons)	73.00	73.96
男	Male	36.21	36.62
女	Female	36.79	37.34
*人口出生率(‰)	Birth Rate of Population(‰)	3.52	4.08
*人口自然增长率(‰)	Natural Growth Rate of Population(‰)	-2.93	-0.76
城镇单位从业人员(万人)	Employment Personnel Worked in Urban Units(10 000 persons)	3.04	3.47
#在岗职工	Working Staff and Workers	2.45	2.99
地区生产总值(亿元)	Gross Domestic Product(10 000 yuan)	52.57	60.99
第二产业	Secondary Industry	6.27	6.95
#工 业	Industry	4.31	4.97
第三产业	Tertiary Industry	46.30	54.04
地区生产总值增速(%)	Increase Rate of Gross Domestic Product(%)	23.1	18.2
一般预算区级财政收入(万元)	General Budgetary Financial Revenue at District Level(10 000 yuan)	84 005	113 046
一般预算区级财政支出(万元)	General Budgetary Financial Expenditure at District Level(10 000 yuan)	81 502	98 196
#教育经费支出	Operating Expenses for Education	25 936	30 344
*固定资产投资(万元)	Investment in Fixed Assets(10 000 yuan)	498 250	445 645
规模以上工业企业	Industrial Enterprises above Designated Size		
单位数(个)	Number of Units(unit)	60	75
从业人员(万人)	Employment(10 000 persons)	0.37	0.41
总产值(万元)	Gross Output Value(10 000 yuan)	51 521	70 926
产品销售收入(万元)	Sales Revenue(10 000 yuan)	54 724	80 133
利税总额(万元)	Total Pre-tax Profits(10 000 yuan)	4 918	4 208
固定资产原值(万元)	Original Value of Fixed Assets(10 000 yuan)	49 561	46 457
流动资产合计(万元)	Total Circulating Funds(10 000 yuan)	49 978	59 890

22－3 续表 Continued

指标名称	Item	2004	2005
社会消费品零售总额(万元)	Retail Sales of Consumer Goods(10 000 yuan)	975 965	1 161 949
* 私营工商企业	Private Industrial and Commercial Enterprises		
户　数(户)	Number of Enterprises(unit)	5 773	6 589
雇工人数(人)	Employees(person)	46 695	52 671
注册资本(万元)	Registered Capital(10 000 yuan)	486 566	611 032
总产值(万元)	Gross Output Value(10 000 yuan)	66 980	71 550
营业收入(万元)	Business Revenue(10 000 yuan)	239 110	262 900
* 个体工商业	Individual Industrial and Commercial Enterprises		
户　数(户)	Number of Enterprises(unit)	14 017	16 480
从业人员(人)	Employment(person)	16 457	20 984
资　金(万元)	Fund(10 000 yuan)	37 668	45 130
营业额(万元)	Turnover(10 000 yuan)	557 135	591 500
实际直接利用外资(万美元)	Foreign Direct Investment (USD 10 000)	2 630	3 597
吸引内资到位额(万元)	Actual Domestic Investment(10 000 yuan)	92 800	158 764
工业企业出口交货值(万元)	Delivery Value of Industrial Enterprises(10 000 yuan)	16 553	16 020
* 小学校数(所)	Number of Primary Schools(unit)	53	47
* 小学在校学生数(人)	Students Enrollment of Primary Schools(person)	31 125	30 661
* 普通中学校数(所)	Number of Regular Secondary Schools(unit)	46	44
* 普通中学在校学生数(人)	Students Enrollment of Regular Secondary Schools(person)	41 667	39 186
幼儿园数(所)	Number of Kindergartens(unit)	41	41
卫生机构数(个)	Health Care Institutions(unit)	24	24
# 医院、卫生院	Hospital and Health Center	18	18
卫生机构床位数(张)	Beds(unit)	916	1 285
# 医院、卫生院	Hospital and Health Center	916	1 285
新增再就业人员(人)	Newly Re－employment Person(person)	16 800	17 803
* 人均公共绿地面积(平方米)	Per Capita Public Green Areas(sq. m)	5.75	5.78

22-4 南开区基本情况
BASIC STATISTICS OF NANKAI DISTRICT

指标名称	Item	2004	2005
* 户籍户数(万户)	Registered Households(10 000 househols)	27.61	27.79
* 户籍人口(万人)	Registered Population(10 000 persons)	79.08	79.73
男	Male	40.09	40.36
女	Female	38.99	39.37
* 人口出生率(‰)	Birth Rate of Population(‰)	3.41	3.85
* 人口自然增长率(‰)	Natural Growth Rate of Population(‰)	-2.05	-0.63
城镇单位从业人员(万人)	Employment Personnel Worked in Urban Units(10 000 persons)	3.81	3.60
#在岗职工	Working Staff and Workers	2.82	2.59
地区生产总值(亿元)	Gross Domestic Product(10 000 yuan)	57.08	62.04
第二产业	Secondary Industry	12.11	13.70
#工　业	Industry	10.19	12.43
第三产业	Tertiary Industry	44.97	48.35
地区生产总值增速(%)	Increase Rate of Gross Domestic Product(%)	24.8	18.0
一般预算区级财政收入(万元)	General Budgetary Financial Revenue at District Level(10 000 yuan)	79 548	102 657
一般预算区级财政支出(万元)	General Budgetary Financial Expenditure at District Level(10 000 yuan)	80 964	103 337
#教育经费支出	Operating Expenses for Education	24 302	27 807
* 固定资产投资(万元)	Investment in Fixed Assets(10 000 yuan)	679 978	1 061 892
规模以上工业企业	Industrial Enterprises above Designated Size		
单位数(个)	Number of Units(unit)	97	128
从业人员(万人)	Employment(10 000 persons)	0.69	0.83
总产值(万元)	Gross Output Value(10 000 yuan)	121 734	221 953
产品销售收入(万元)	Sales Revenue(10 000 yuan)	117 204	229 041
利税总额(万元)	Total Pre-tax Profits(10 000 yuan)	11 849	21 967
固定资产原值(万元)	Original Value of Fixed Assets(10 000 yuan)	37 522	63 371
流动资产合计(万元)	Total Circulating Funds(10 000 yuan)	77 067	143 842

22-4 续表 Continued

指标名称	Item	2004	2005
社会消费品零售总额(万元)	Retail Sales of Consumer Goods(10 000 yuan)	921 212	1 113 669
* 私营工商企业	Private Industrial and Commercial Enterprises		
户　数(户)	Number of Enterprises(unit)	7 252	8 219
雇工人数(人)	Employees(person)	51 821	62 873
注册资本(万元)	Registered Capital(10 000 yuan)	557 126	677 666
总产值(万元)	Gross Output Value(10 000 yuan)	224 523	197 482
营业收入(万元)	Business Revenue(10 000 yuan)	551 789	679 627
* 个体工商业	Individual Industrial and Commercial Enterprises		
户　数(户)	Number of Enterprises(unit)	10 050	9 177
从业人员(人)	Employment(person)	10 969	10 667
资　金(万元)	Fund(10 000 yuan)	24 406	51 472
营业额(万元)	Turnover(10 000 yuan)	569 997	378 848
实际直接利用外资(万美元)	Foreign Direct Investment (USD 10 000)	5 697	4 628
吸引内资到位额(万元)	Actual Domestic Investment(10 000 yuan)	114 500	293 522
工业企业出口交货值(万元)	Delivery Value of Industrial Enterprises(10 000 yuan)	37 378	170 977
* 小学校数(所)	Number of Primary Schools(unit)	41	38
* 小学在校学生数(人)	Students Enrollment of Primary Schools(person)	28 289	26 949
* 普通中学校数(所)	Number of Regular Secondary Schools(unit)	43	42
* 普通中学在校学生数(人)	Students Enrollment of Regular Secondary Schools(person)	34 230	34 011
幼儿园数(所)	Number of Kindergartens(unit)	46	47
卫生机构数(个)	Health Care Institutions(unit)	26	27
# 医院、卫生院	Hospital and Health Center	17	19
卫生机构床位数(张)	Beds(unit)	1 423	1 423
# 医院、卫生院	Hospital and Health Center	1 423	1 423
新增再就业人员(人)	Newly Re-employment Person(person)	15 308	24 694
* 人均公共绿地面积(平方米)	Per Capita Public Green Areas(sq. m)	8.0	8.6

22－5　河北区基本情况
BASIC STATISTICS OF HEBEI DISTRICT

指标名称	Item	2004	2005
*户籍户数(万户)	Registered Households(10 000 househols)	22.38	22.85
*户籍人口(万人)	Registered Population(10 000 persons)	61.77	62.65
男	Male	31.19	31.61
女	Female	30.58	31.04
*人口出生率(‰)	Birth Rate of Population(‰)	3.51	4.30
*人口自然增长率(‰)	Natural Growth Rate of Population(‰)	－3.08	－2.06
城镇单位从业人员(万人)	Employment Personnel Worked in Urban Units(10 000 persons)	2.4	2.5
#在岗职工	Working Staff and Workers	1.9	2.0
地区生产总值(亿元)	Gross Domestic Product(10 000 yuan)	32.64	41.30
第二产业	Secondary Industry	9.23	9.12
#工　业	Industry	7.92	8.33
第三产业	Tertiary Industry	23.41	32.18
地区生产总值增速(％)	Increase Rate of Gross Domestic Product(％)	20.3	21.0
一般预算区级财政收入(万元)	General Budgetary Financial Revenue at District Level(10 000 yuan)	42 676	49 676
一般预算区级财政支出(万元)	General Budgetary Financial Expenditure at District Level(10 000 yuan)	47 986	80 487
#教育经费支出	Operating Expenses for Education	19 721	26 395
*固定资产投资(万元)	Investment in Fixed Assets(10 000 yuan)	277 770	389 750
规模以上工业企业	Industrial Enterprises above Designated Size		
单位数(个)	Number of Units(unit)	23	58
从业人员(万人)	Employment(10 000 persons)	0.30	0.36
总产值(万元)	Gross Output Value(10 000 yuan)	35 471	68 702
产品销售收入(万元)	Sales Revenue(10 000 yuan)	34 268	67 684
利税总额(万元)	Total Pre－tax Profits(10 000 yuan)	2 883	3 373
固定资产原值(万元)	Original Value of Fixed Assets(10 000 yuan)	22 805	36 943
流动资产合计(万元)	Total Circulating Funds(10 000 yuan)	31 074	46 803

22－5续表 Continued

指标名称	Item	2004	2005
社会消费品零售总额(万元)	Retail Sales of Consumer Goods(10 000 yuan)	798 600	970 580
* 私营工商企业	Private Industrial and Commercial Enterprises		
户　数(户)	Number of Enterprises(unit)	2 742	3 190
雇工人数(人)	Employees(person)	31 012	35 352
注册资本(万元)	Registered Capital(10 000 yuan)	264 925	299 452
总产值(万元)	Gross Output Value(10 000 yuan)	109 223	162 348
营业收入(万元)	Business Revenue(10 000 yuan)	358 966	480 813
* 个体工商业	Individual Industrial and Commercial Enterprises		
户　数(户)	Number of Enterprises(unit)	6 030	6 236
从业人员(人)	Employment(person)	6 625	6 851
资　金(万元)	Fund(10 000 yuan)	19 069	21 626
营业额(万元)	Turnover(10 000 yuan)	201 052	262 620
实际直接利用外资(万美元)	Foreign Direct Investment (USD 10 000)	1 049	2 789
吸引内资到位额(万元)	Actual Domestic Investment(10 000 yuan)	82 000	126 100
工业企业出口交货值(万元)	Delivery Value of Industrial Enterprises(10 000 yuan)	13 113	11 812
* 小学校数(所)	Number of Primary Schools(unit)	40	36
* 小学在校学生数(人)	Students Enrollment of Primary Schools(person)	26 039	24 711
* 普通中学校数(所)	Number of Regular Secondary Schools(unit)	38	40
* 普通中学在校学生数(人)	Students Enrollment of Regular Secondary Schools(person)	35 215	33 418
幼儿园数(所)	Number of Kindergartens(unit)	49	37
卫生机构数(个)	Health Care Institutions(unit)	22	22
# 医院、卫生院	Hospital and Health Center	18	18
卫生机构床位数(张)	Beds(unit)	1 615	1 535
# 医院、卫生院	Hospital and Health Center	1 615	1 535
新增再就业人员(人)	Newly Re－employment Person(person)	21 134	23 328
* 人均公共绿地面积(平方米)	Per Capita Public Green Areas(sq. m)	7.1	7.5

22－6　红桥区基本情况
BASIC STATISTICS OF HONGQIAO DISTRICT

指标名称	Item	2004	2005
* 户籍户数(万户)	Registered Households(10 000 househols)	20.10	20.23
* 户籍人口(万人)	Registered Population(10 000 persons)	54.96	55.16
男	Male	27.77	27.88
女	Female	27.19	27.28
* 人口出生率(‰)	Birth Rate of Population(‰)	4.3	4.4
* 人口自然增长率(‰)	Natural Growth Rate of Population(‰)	－2.2	－1.5
城镇单位从业人员(万人)	Employment Personnel Worked in Urban Units(10 000 persons)	2.49	2.36
# 在岗职工	Working Staff and Workers	2.00	1.82
地区生产总值(亿元)	Gross Domestic Product(10 000 yuan)	32.01	39.11
第二产业	Secondary Industry	8.32	3.61
# 工　业	Industry	7.57	2.65
第三产业	Tertiary Industry	23.70	35.50
地区生产总值增速(%)	Increase Rate of Gross Domestic Product(%)	19.3	20.2
一般预算区级财政收入(万元)	General Budgetary Financial Revenue at District Level(10 000 yuan)	24 809	30 382
一般预算区级财政支出(万元)	General Budgetary Financial Expenditure at District Level(10 000 yuan)	52 093	60 566
# 教育经费支出	Operating Expenses for Education	19 208	20 879
* 固定资产投资(万元)	Investment in Fixed Assets (10 000 yuan)	326 863	160 039
规模以上工业企业	Industrial Enterprises above Designated Size		
单位数(个)	Number of Units(unit)	55	42
从业人员(万人)	Employment(10 000 persons)	0.36	0.27
总产值(万元)	Gross Output Value(10 000 yuan)	76 755	65 301
产品销售收入(万元)	Sales Revenue(10 000 yuan)	66 266	63 051
利税总额(万元)	Total Pre－tax Profits(10 000 yuan)	3 079	3 466
固定资产原值(万元)	Original Value of Fixed Assets(10 000 yuan)	29 664	24 872
流动资产合计(万元)	Total Circulating Funds(10 000 yuan)	36 952	29 641

22－6续表 Continued

指标名称	Item	2004	2005
社会消费品零售总额(万元)	Retail Sales of Consumer Goods(10 000 yuan)	525 884	633 068
* 私营工商企业	Private Industrial and Commercial Enterprises		
户　数(户)	Number of Enterprises(unit)	1 618	1 842
雇工人数(人)	Employees(person)	13 788	15 472
注册资本(万元)	Registered Capital(10 000 yuan)	138 623	153 086
总产值(万元)	Gross Output Value(10 000 yuan)	36 007	34 033
营业收入(万元)	Business Revenue(10 000 yuan)	99 094	70 516
* 个体工商业	Individual Industrial and Commercial Enterprises		
户　数(户)	Number of Enterprises(unit)	7 903	9 120
从业人员(人)	Employment(person)	8 366	9 215
资　金(万元)	Fund(10 000 yuan)	19 217	22 581
营业额(万元)	Turnover(10 000 yuan)	989 447	1 147 992
实际直接利用外资(万美元)	Foreign Direct Investment (USD 10 000)	860	1 100
吸引内资到位额(万元)	Actual Domestic Investment(10 000 yuan)	120 660	180 990
工业企业出口交货值(万元)	Delivery Value of Industrial Enterprises(10 000 yuan)	24 830	14 745
* 小学校数(所)	Number of Primary Schools(unit)	33	30
* 小学在校学生数(人)	Students Enrollment of Primary Schools(person)	18 617	16 834
* 普通中学校数(所)	Number of Regular Secondary Schools(unit)	31	29
* 普通中学在校学生数(人)	Students Enrollment of Regular Secondary Schools(person)	28 707	26 393
幼儿园数(所)	Number of Kindergartens(unit)	18	16
卫生机构数(个)	Health Care Institutions(unit)	114	89
#医院、卫生院	Hospital and Health Center	15	14
卫生机构床位数(张)	Beds(unit)	1 023	1 044
#医院、卫生院	Hospital and Health Center	874	1 044
新增再就业人员(人)	Newly Re－employment Person(person)	14 188	17 592
* 人均公共绿地面积(平方米)	Per Capita Public Green Areas(sq. m)	3.03	3.24

22-7 塘沽区基本情况
BASIC STATISTICS OF TANGGU DISTRICT

指标名称	Item	2004	2005
*户籍户数(万户)	Registered Households(10 000 households)	17.18	17.62
#农业户	Agricultural Households	2.30	2.37
*户籍人口(万人)	Registered Population(10 000 persons)	48.17	48.85
1.农业人口	Agricultural Population	6.02	6.03
非农业人口	Non-agricultural Population	42.14	42.81
2.男	Male	24.84	25.18
女	Female	23.33	23.66
*人口出生率(‰)	Birth Rate of Population(‰)	6.5	7.5
*人口自然增长率(‰)	Natural Growth Rate of Population(‰)	1.3	3.0
城镇单位从业人员(万人)	Employment Personnel Worked in Urban Units(10 000 persons)	3.69	3.56
#在岗职工	Working Staff and Workers	3.28	3.27
*乡村从业人员(万人)	Rural Employment Personnel(10 000 persons)	2.29	2.68
#农林牧渔业劳动者人数	Farming,Forestry,Animal Husbandry and Fishery	0.63	0.68
地区生产总值(亿元)	Gross Domestic Product(10 000 yuan)	77.18	89.79
第一产业	Primary Industry	1.91	1.77
第二产业	Secondary Industry	27.59	25.31
#工　业	Industry	12.78	12.80
第三产业	Tertiary Industry	47.69	62.71
地区生产总值增速(%)	Increase Rate of Gross Domestic Product(%)	23.5	20.7
一般预算区级财政收入(万元)	General Budgetary Financial Revenue at District Level(10 000 yuan)	71 852	108 465
一般预算区级财政支出(万元)	General Budgetary Financial Expenditure at District Level(10 000 yuan)	100 957	147 046
#教育经费支出	Operating Expenses for Education	24 892	30 934
*固定资产投资(万元)	Investment in Fixed Assets(10 000 yuan)	1 749 836	3 475 198
年末实有耕地面积(万公顷)	Cultivated Land(year-end)(10 000 hectare)	0.52	0.48
农业机械总动力(万千瓦)	Total Power of Agricultural Machinery(10 000 kw)	26.71	27.89
化肥折纯量(吨)	Consumption of Chemical Fertilizers(Pureness)(ton)	1 048	1 072
农村用电量(万千瓦小时)	Rural Electricity Consumption(10 000 kwh)	3 459	4 851
农林牧渔业总产值(万元)	Gross Output Value of Farming,Forestry,Animal Husbandry and Fishery (10 000 yuan)	44 192	48 369
农林牧渔业总产值增速(%)	Increase Rate of Gross Output Value of Farming, Forestry,Animal Husbandry and Fishery(%)	12.2	7.7
粮食产量(万吨)	Total Yield of Grain(10 000 tons)	0.27	0.41
水产品产量(吨)	Total Yield of Aquatic Products(ton)	21 463	25 970
蔬菜总产量(吨)	Total Yield of Vegetable(ton)	58 740	59 506
*农村居民人均年纯收入(元)	Per Capita Annual Net Income of Rural Households(yuan)	7 223	7 932
*农村居民人均生活消费支出(元)	Per Capita Annual Expenditure for Consumption of Rural Households (yuan)	4 310	4 618

22－7 续表　Continued

指标名称	Item	2004	2005
乡镇企业单位数(个)	Number of Township Enterprises(unit)	65	52
乡镇企业人数(万人)	Employment of Township Enterprises(10 000 persons)	0.45	0.29
乡镇企业主营业务收入(万元)	Major Business Revenue of Township Enterprises(10 000 yuan)	121 817	72 142
规模以上工业企业	Industrial Enterprises above Designated Size		
单位数(个)	Number of Units(unit)	146	151
从业人员(万人)	Employment Personnel(10 000 persons)	1.33	1.39
总产值(万元)	Gross Output Value(10 000 yuan)	482 720	624 808
产品销售收入(万元)	Sales Revenue(10 000 yuan)	458 037	588 796
利税总额(万元)	Total Pre－tax Profits(10 000 yuan)	37 270	38 177
固定资产原值(万元)	Original Value of Fixed Assets(10 000 yuan)	349 396	394 782
流动资产合计(万元)	Total Circulating Funds(10 000 yuan)	332 519	387 265
社会消费品零售总额(万元)	Total Retail Sales of Consumer Goods(10 000 yuan)	713 187	856 228
* 私营工商企业	Private Industrial and Commercial Enterprises		
户　数(户)	Number of Enterprises(unit)	3 135	4 020
雇工人数(人)	Employees(person)	23 018	28 871
注册资本(万元)	Registered Capital(10 000 yuan)	523 295	650 247
总产值(万元)	Gross Output Value(10 000 yuan)	120 692	137 004
营业收入(万元)	Business Revenue(10 000 yuan)	235 266	251 465
* 个体工商业	Individual Industrial and Commercial Enterprises		
户　数(户)	Number of Enterprises(unit)	13 452	15 424
从业人员(人)	Employment(person)	16 212	19 681
资　金(万元)	Fund(10 000 yuan)	67 691	73 084
营业额(万元)	Turnover(10 000 yuan)	245 672	285 910
实际直接利用外资(万美元)	Foreign Direct Investment (USD 10 000)	6 001	8 707
吸引内资到位额(万元)	Actual Domestic Investment(10 000 yuan)	181 897	290 000
工业企业出口交货值(万元)	Delivery Value of Industrial Enterprises(10 000 yuan)	198 653	258 039
* 小学校数(所)	Number of Primary Schools(unit)	58	57
* 小学在校学生数(人)	Students Enrollment of Primary Schools(person)	32 649	33 033
* 普通中学校数(所)	Number of Regular Secondary Schools(unit)	36	36
* 普通中学在校学生数(人)	Students Enrollment of Regular Secondary Schools(person)	25 951	25 312
幼儿园数(所)	Number of Kindergartens(unit)	88	88
卫生机构数(个)	Health Care Institutions(unit)	177	174
# 医院、卫生院	Hospital and Health Center	28	28
卫生机构床位数(张)	Beds(unit)	2 231	2 219
# 医院、卫生院	Hospital and Health Center	1 987	2 017
新增再就业人员(人)	Newly Re－employment Person(person)	10 830	13 302

22-8 汉沽区基本情况
BASIC STATISTICS OF HANGU DISTRICT

指标名称	Item	2004	2005
* 户籍户数(万户)	Registered Households(10 000 househols)	6.30	6.39
# 农业户	Agricultural Households	1.53	1.56
* 户籍人口(万人)	Registered Population(10 000 persons)	16.85	16.91
1.农业人口	Agricultural Population	4.53	4.55
非农业人口	Non-agricultural Population	12.32	12.36
2.男	Male	8.55	8.57
女	Female	8.30	8.34
* 人口出生率(‰)	Birth Rate of Population(‰)	9.4	7.2
* 人口自然增长率(‰)	Natural Growth Rate of Population(‰)	1.3	1.5
城镇单位从业人员(万人)	Employment Personnel Worked in Urban Units(10 000 persons)	1.26	1.23
# 在岗职工	Working Staff and Workers	1.21	1.18
* 乡村从业人员(万人)	Rural Employment Personnel(10 000 persons)	2.55	2.64
# 农林牧渔业劳动者人数	Farming, Forestry, Animal Husbandry and Fishery	1.60	1.57
地区生产总值(亿元)	Gross Domestic Product(10 000 yuan)	19.79	24.08
第一产业	Primary Industry	3.15	3.31
第二产业	Secondary Industry	6.72	8.73
# 工　业	Industry	5.50	7.46
第三产业	Tertiary Industry	9.92	12.03
地区生产总值增速(%)	Increase Rate of Gross Domestic Product(%)	13.2	19.2
一般预算区级财政收入(万元)	General Budgetary Financial Revenue at District Level(10 000 yuan)	14 721	17 930
一般预算区级财政支出(万元)	General Budgetary Financial Expenditure at District Level(10 000 yuan)	29 526	37 350
# 教育经费支出	Operating Expenses for Education	8 359	10 008
* 固定资产投资(万元)	Investment in Fixed Assets(10 000 yuan)	107 012	221 041
年末实有耕地面积(万公顷)	Cultivated Land(year-end)(10 000 hectare)	0.42	0.42
农业机械总动力(万千瓦)	Total Power of Agricultural Machinery(10 000 kw)	14.81	15.71
化肥折纯量(吨)	Consumption of Chemical Fertilizers(Pureness)(ton)	3 171	3 136
农村用电量(万千瓦小时)	Rural Electricity Consumption(10 000 kwh)	13 036	12 713
农林牧渔业总产值(万元)	Gross Output Value of Farming, Forestry, Animal Husbandry and Fishery(10 000 yuan)	76 771	80 803
农林牧渔业总产值增速(%)	Increase Rate of Gross Output Value of Farming, Forestry, Animal Husbandry and Fishery(%)	9.2	5.3
粮食产量(万吨)	Total Yield of Grain(10 000 tons)	0.27	0.41
水产品产量(吨)	Total Yield of Aquatic Products(ton)	23 602	26 449
蔬菜总产量(吨)	Total Yield of Vegetable(ton)	31 936	33 307
* 农村居民人均年纯收入(元)	Per Capita Annual Net Income of Rural Households(yuan)	6 874	7 535
* 农村居民人均生活消费支出(元)	Per Capita Annual Expenditure for Consumption of Rural Households(yuan)	3 760	4 424

22－8 续表　Continued

指标名称	Item	2004	2005
乡镇企业单位数(个)	Number of Township Enterprises(unit)	130	139
乡镇企业人数(万人)	Employment of Township Enterprises(10 000 persons)	1.32	1.07
乡镇企业主营业务收入(万元)	Major Business Revenue of Township Enterprises(10 000 yuan)	270 394	321 627
规模以上工业企业	Industrial Enterprises above Designated Size		
单位数(个)	Number of Units(unit)	57	57
从业人员(万人)	Employment Personnel(10 000 persons)	1.42	1.27
总产值(万元)	Gross Output Value(10 000 yuan)	300 186	379 716
产品销售收入(万元)	Sales Revenue(10 000 yuan)	322 715	367 112
利税总额(万元)	Total Pre－tax Profits(10 000 yuan)	29 494	41 591
固定资产原值(万元)	Original Value of Fixed Assets(10 000 yuan)		71 383
流动资产合计(万元)	Total Circulating Funds(10 000 yuan)	108 177	112 714
社会消费品零售总额(万元)	Total Retail Sales of Consumer Goods(10 000 yuan)	165 077	197 735
* 私营工商企业	Private Industrial and Commercial Enterprises		
户　数(户)	Number of Enterprises(unit)	1 104	1 104
雇工人数(人)	Employees(person)	14 260	14 908
注册资本(万元)	Registered Capital(10 000 yuan)	69 939	99 031
总产值(万元)	Gross Output Value(10 000 yuan)	56 642	80 415
营业收入(万元)	Business Revenue(10 000 yuan)	66 139	79 639
* 个体工商业	Individual Industrial and Commercial Enterprises		
户　数(户)	Number of Enterprises(unit)	7 209	6 260
从业人员(人)	Employment(person)	7 239	5 428
资　金(万元)	Fund(10 000 yuan)	8 730	7 046
营业额(万元)	Turnover(10 000 yuan)	74 026	107 090
实际直接利用外资(万美元)	Foreign Direct Investment (USD 10 000)	2 818	3 389
吸引内资到位额(万元)	Actual Domestic Investment(10 000 yuan)	26 100	36 800
工业企业出口交货值(万元)	Delivery Value of Industrial Enterprises(10 000 yuan)	64 874	49 358
* 小学校数(所)	Number of Primary Schools(unit)	27	23
* 小学在校学生数(人)	Students Enrollment of Primary Schools(person)	10 890	10 361
* 普通中学校数(所)	Number of Regular Secondary Schools(unit)	15	15
* 普通中学在校学生数(人)	Students Enrollment of Regular Secondary Schools(person)	10 803	10 647
幼儿园数(所)	Number of Kindergartens(unit)	21	19
卫生机构数(个)	Health Care Institutions(unit)	16	15
# 医院、卫生院	Hospital and Health Center	8	8
卫生机构床位数(张)	Beds(unit)	992	992
# 医院、卫生院	Hospital and Health Center	972	972
新增再就业人员(人)	Newly Re－employment Person(person)	4 300	5 000

22－9 大港区基本情况

BASIC STATISTICS OF DAGANG DISTRICT

指标名称	Item	2004	2005
*户籍户数(万户)	Registered Households(10 000 househols)	12.95	13.20
#农业户	Agricultural Households	3.42	3.58
*户籍人口(万人)	Registered Population(10 000 persons)	34.92	35.46
1.农业人口	Agricultural Population	10.32	10.40
非农业人口	Non－agricultural Population	24.62	25.06
2.男	Male	18.24	18.49
女	Female	16.69	16.97
*人口出生率(‰)	Birth Rate of Population(‰)	11.8	11.8
*人口自然增长率(‰)	Natural Growth Rate of Population(‰)	8.1	8.2
城镇单位从业人员(万人)	Employment Personnel Worked in Urban Units(10 000 persons)	1.73	2.01
#在岗职工	Working Staff and Workers	1.71	1.98
*乡村从业人员(万人)	Rural Employment Personnel(10 000 persons)	3.80	4.00
#农林牧渔业劳动者人数	Farming,Forestry,Animal Husbandry and Fishery	1.60	1.60
地区生产总值(亿元)	Gross Domestic Product(10 000 yuan)	57.66	70.18
第一产业	Primary Industry	2.01	1.74
第二产业	Secondary Industry	34.34	42.16
#工　业	Industry	22.96	28.34
第三产业	Tertiary Industry	21.31	26.28
地区生产总值增速(%)	Increase Rate of Gross Domestic Product(%)	15.8	16.3
一般预算区级财政收入(万元)	General Budgetary Financial Revenue at District Level(10 000 yuan)	37 215	50 838
一般预算区级财政支出(万元)	General Budgetary Financial Expenditure at District Level(10 000 yuan)	59 100	96 104
#教育经费支出	Operating Expenses for Education	14 028	34 422
*固定资产投资(万元)	Investment in Fixed Assets(10 000 yuan)	578 430	564 834
年末实有耕地面积(万公顷)	Cultivated Land(year－end)(10 000 hectare)	1.34	1.34
农业机械总动力(万千瓦)	Total Power of Agricultural Machinery(10 000 kw)	26.76	27.34
化肥折纯量(吨)	Consumption of Chemical Fertilizers(Pureness)(ton)	2 818	3 057
农村用电量(万千瓦小时)	Rural Electricity Consumption(10 000 kwh)	15 378	17 858
农林牧渔业总产值(万元)	Gross Output Value of Farming,Forestry,Animal Husbandry and Fishery(10 000 yuan)	37 475	40 657
农林牧渔业总产值增速(%)	Increase Rate of Gross Output Value of Farming, Forestry,Animal Husbandry and Fishery(%)	27.1	8.5
粮食产量(万吨)	Total Yield of Grain(10 000 tons)	3.78	4.31
水产品产量(吨)	Total Yield of Aquatic Products(ton)	6 080	7 600
蔬菜总产量(吨)	Total Yield of Vegetable(ton)	50 521	32 118
*农村居民人均年纯收入(元)	Per Capita Annual Net Income of Rural Households(yuan)	6 903	7 577
*农村居民人均生活消费支出(元)	Per Capita Annual Expenditure for Consumption of Rural Households(yuan)	4 787	5 242

22-9续表 Continued

指标名称	Item	2004	2005
乡镇企业单位数(个)	Number of Township Enterprises(unit)	5 464	5 344
乡镇企业人数(万人)	Employment of Township Enterprises(10 000 persons)	5.80	6.90
乡镇企业主营业务收入(万元)	Major Business Revenue of Township Enterprises(10 000 yuan)	1 250 774	1 548 726
规模以上工业企业	Industrial Enterprises above Designated Size		
单位数(个)	Number of Units(unit)	263	200
从业人员(万人)	Employment Personnel(10 000 persons)	2.82	2.5
总产值(万元)	Gross Output Value(10 000 yuan)	951 367	1 160 650
产品销售收入(万元)	Sales Revenue(10 000 yuan)	929 253	1 252 019
利税总额(万元)	Total Pre-tax Profits(10 000 yuan)	51 339	70 786
固定资产原值(万元)	Original Value of Fixed Assets(10 000 yuan)	290 020	838 070
流动资产合计(万元)	Total Circulating Funds(10 000 yuan)	424 944	514 763
社会消费品零售总额(万元)	Total Retail Sales of Consumer Goods(10 000 yuan)	297 705	341 179
*私营工商企业	Private Industrial and Commercial Enterprises		
户　数(户)	Number of Enterprises(unit)	1 687	1 948
雇工人数(人)	Employees(person)	18 996	16 713
注册资本(万元)	Registered Capital(10 000 yuan)	179 021	247 244
总产值(万元)	Gross Output Value(10 000 yuan)	58 818	93 685
营业收入(万元)	Business Revenue(10 000 yuan)	108 161	107 409
*个体工商业	Individual Industrial and Commercial Enterprises		
户　数(户)	Number of Enterprises(unit)	7 492	4 952
从业人员(人)	Employment(person)	16 683	10 900
资　金(万元)	Fund(10 000 yuan)	30 019	22 106
营业额(万元)	Turnover(10 000 yuan)	95 720	108 440
实际直接利用外资(万美元)	Foreign Direct Investment (USD 10 000)	3 552	5 399
吸引内资到位额(万元)	Actual Domestic Investment(10 000 yuan)	55 000	182 850
工业企业出口交货值(万元)	Delivery Value of Industrial Enterprises(10 000 yuan)	221 074	317 723
*小学校数(所)	Number of Primary Schools(unit)	30	32
*小学在校学生数(人)	Students Enrollment of Primary Schools(person)	23 461	24 660
*普通中学校数(所)	Number of Regular Secondary Schools(unit)	38	39
*普通中学在校学生数(人)	Students Enrollment of Regular Secondary Schools(person)	26 732	28 633
幼儿园数(所)	Number of Kindergartens(unit)	75	61
卫生机构数(个)	Health Care Institutions(unit)	13	14
#医院、卫生院	Hospital and Health Center	13	14
卫生机构床位数(张)	Beds(unit)	600	950
#医院、卫生院	Hospital and Health Center	600	950
新增再就业人员(人)	Newly Re-employment Person(person)	7 595	12 568

22－10 东丽区基本情况

BASIC STATISTICS OF DONGLI DISTRICT

指标名称	Item	2004	2005
*户籍户数(万户)	Registered Households(10 000 househols)	12.17	12.45
#农业户	Agricultural Households	7.44	7.48
*户籍人口(万人)	Registered Population(10 000 persons)	31.32	31.82
1.农业人口	Agricultural Population	19.92	19.76
非农业人口	Non－agricultural Population	11.39	12.06
2.男	Male	15.74	16.00
女	Female	15.58	15.82
*人口出生率(‰)	Birth Rate of Population(‰)	9.3	7.9
*人口自然增长率(‰)	Natural Growth Rate of Population(‰)	3.9	4.3
城镇单位从业人员(万人)	Employment Personnel Worked in Urban Units(10 000 persons)	3.89	3.83
#在岗职工	Working Staff and Workers	3.73	3.57
*乡村从业人员(万人)	Rural Employment Personnel(10 000 persons)	9.66	9.96
#农林牧渔业劳动者人数	Farming,Forestry,Animal Husbandry and Fishery	1.92	1.80
地区生产总值(亿元)	Gross Domestic Product(10 000 yuan)	86.70	102.21
第一产业	Primary Industry	3.42	3.73
第二产业	Secondary Industry	45.70	52.87
#工　业	Industry	38.68	45.03
第三产业	Tertiary Industry	37.58	45.61
地区生产总值增速(%)	Increase Rate of Gross Domestic Product(%)	16.5	14.6
一般预算区级财政收入(万元)	General Budgetary Financial Revenue at District Level(10 000 yuan)	67 635	97 988
一般预算区级财政支出(万元)	General Budgetary Financial Expenditure at District Level(10 000 yuan)	76 139	104 696
#教育经费支出	Operating Expenses for Education	17 236	19 110
*固定资产投资(万元)	Investment in Fixed Assets(10 000 yuan)	888 940	1 325 078
年末实有耕地面积(万公顷)	Cultivated Land(year－end)(10 000 hectare)	1.31	1.30
农业机械总动力(万千瓦)	Total Power of Agricultural Machinery(10 000 kw)	44.92	44.43
化肥折纯量(吨)	Consumption of Chemical Fertilizers(Pureness)(ton)	3 311	3 148
农村用电量(万千瓦小时)	Rural Electricity Consumption(10 000 kwh)	24 834	24 515
农林牧渔业总产值(万元)	Gross Output Value of Farming,Forestry,Animal Husbandry and Fishery(10 000 yuan)	74 745	86 202
农林牧渔业总产值增速(%)	Increase Rate of Gross Output Value of Farming, Forestry,Animal Husbandry and Fishery(%)	－4.0	11.9
粮食产量(万吨)	Total Yield of Grain(10 000 tons)	1.32	1.20
水产品产量(吨)	Total Yield of Aquatic Products(ton)	21 987	21 291
蔬菜总产量(吨)	Total Yield of Vegetable(ton)	234 699	218 279
*农村居民人均年纯收入(元)	Per Capita Annual Net Income of Rural Households(yuan)	7 877	8 634
*农村居民人均生活消费支出(元)	Per Capita Annual Expenditure for Consumption of Rural Households(yuan)	5 268	5 433

22－10 续表 Continued

指标名称	Item	2004	2005
乡镇企业单位数(个)	Number of Township Enterprises(unit)	2 335	2 552
乡镇企业人数(万人)	Employment of Township Enterprises(10 000 persons)	10.6	10.8
乡镇企业主营业务收入(万元)	Major Business Revenue of Township Enterprises(10 000 yuan)	2 206 843	2 830 690
规模以上工业企业	Industrial Enterprises above Designated Size		
单位数(个)	Number of Units(unit)	264	247
从业人员(万人)	Employment Personnel(10 000 persons)	4.61	4.55
总产值(万元)	Gross Output Value(10 000 yuan)	1 510 421	1 904 805
产品销售收入(万元)	Sales Revenue(10 000 yuan)	1 282 516	1 886 821
利税总额(万元)	Total Pre－tax Profits(10 000 yuan)	75 962	172 488
固定资产原值(万元)	Original Value of Fixed Assets(10 000 yuan)	469 409	598 641
流动资产合计(万元)	Total Circulating Funds(10 000 yuan)	706 438	853 062
社会消费品零售总额(万元)	Total Retail Sales of Consumer Goods(10 000 yuan)	348 520	404 461
*私营工商企业	Private Industrial and Commercial Enterprises		
户　数(户)	Number of Enterprises(unit)	4 077	4 554
雇工人数(人)	Employees(person)	34 848	38 155
注册资本(万元)	Registered Capital(10 000 yuan)	533 521	627 268
总产值(万元)	Gross Output Value(10 000 yuan)	735 224	741 081
营业收入(万元)	Business Revenue(10 000 yuan)	613 912	622 440
*个体工商业	Individual Industrial and Commercial Enterprises		
户　数(户)	Number of Enterprises(unit)	8 260	7 779
从业人员(人)	Employment(person)	14 081	14 407
资　金(万元)	Fund(10 000 yuan)	27 644	28 305
营业额(万元)	Turnover(10 000 yuan)	211 010	174 530
实际直接利用外资(万美元)	Foreign Direct Investment (USD 10 000)	10 615	8 348
吸引内资到位额(万元)	Actual Domestic Investment(10 000 yuan)	96 370	183 686
工业企业出口交货值(万元)	Delivery Value of Industrial Enterprises(10 000 yuan)	557 769	651 002
*小学校数(所)	Number of Primary Schools(unit)	43	42
*小学在校学生数(人)	Students Enrollment of Primary Schools(person)	25 471	25 397
*普通中学校数(所)	Number of Regular Secondary Schools(unit)	25	27
*普通中学在校学生数(人)	Students Enrollment of Regular Secondary Schools(person)	16 885	16 893
幼儿园数(所)	Number of Kindergartens(unit)	60	61
卫生机构数(个)	Health Care Institutions(unit)	18	18
#医院、卫生院	Hospital and Health Center	12	12
卫生机构床位数(张)	Beds(unit)	722	722
#医院、卫生院	Hospital and Health Center	700	700
新增再就业人员(人)	Newly Re－employment Person(person)	2 936	2 230

22-11 西青区基本情况
BASIC STATISTICS OF XIQING DISTRICT

指标名称	Item	2004	2005
*户籍户数(万户)	Registered Households(10 000 househols)	11.61	11.96
#农业户	Agricultural Households	8.21	8.46
*户籍人口(万人)	Registered Population(10 000 persons)	30.91	31.48
1.农业人口	Agricultural Population	22.95	23.14
非农业人口	Non-agricultural Population	7.95	8.34
2.男	Male	15.34	15.61
女	Female	15.56	15.87
*人口出生率(‰)	Birth Rate of Population(‰)	9.7	10.7
*人口自然增长率(‰)	Natural Growth Rate of Population(‰)	1.2	5.1
城镇单位从业人员(万人)	Employment Personnel Worked in Urban Units(10 000 persons)	4.43	4.33
#在岗职工	Working Staff and Workers	4.28	3.39
*乡村从业人员(万人)	Rural Employment Personnel(10 000 persons)	11.81	11.48
#农林牧渔业劳动者人数	Farming,Forestry,Animal Husbandry and Fishery	3.88	3.74
地区生产总值(亿元)	Gross Domestic Product(10 000 yuan)	99.41	123.68
第一产业	Primary Industry	6.83	6.43
第二产业	Secondary Industry	57.36	73.81
#工　业	Industry	54.50	71.38
第三产业	Tertiary Industry	35.22	43.44
地区生产总值增速(%)	Increase Rate of Gross Domestic Product(%)	14.5	18.8
一般预算区级财政收入(万元)	General Budgetary Financial Revenue at District Level(10 000 yuan)	109 457	112 110
一般预算区级财政支出(万元)	General Budgetary Financial Expenditure at District Level(10 000 yuan)	104 511	154 484
#教育经费支出	Operating Expenses for Education	14 268	16 015
*固定资产投资(万元)	Investment in Fixed Assets(10 000 yuan)	836 516	1 088 194
年末实有耕地面积(万公顷)	Cultivated Land(year-end)(10 000 hectare)	1.53	1.53
农业机械总动力(万千瓦)	Total Power of Agricultural Machinery(10 000 kw)	45.64	44.48
化肥折纯量(吨)	Consumption of Chemical Fertilizers(Pureness)(ton)	10 890	9 012
农村用电量(万千瓦小时)	Rural Electricity Consumption(10 000 kwh)	49 820	49 178
农林牧渔业总产值(万元)	Gross Output Value of Farming,Forestry,Animal Husbandry and Fishery(10 000 yuan)	130 677	133 256
农林牧渔业总产值增速(%)	Increase Rate of Gross Output Value of Farming, Forestry,Animal Husbandry and Fishery(%)	6.3	-1.5
粮食产量(万吨)	Total Yield of Grain(10 000 tons)	4.49	4.57
水产品产量(吨)	Total Yield of Aquatic Products(ton)	46 144	50 645
蔬菜总产量(吨)	Total Yield of Vegetable(ton)	380 529	365 699
*农村居民人均年纯收入(元)	Per Capita Annual Net Income of Rural Households(yuan)	8 046	8 810
*农村居民人均生活消费支出(元)	Per Capita Annual Expenditure for Consumption of Rural Households(yuan)	3 767	4 099

22－11 续表　Continued

指标名称	Item	2004	2005
乡镇企业单位数(个)	Number of Township Enterprises(unit)	621	498
乡镇企业人数(万人)	Employment of Township Enterprises(10 000 persons)	7.42	8.19
乡镇企业主营业务收入(万元)	Major Business Revenue of Township Enterprises(10 000 yuan)	1 832 778	2 105 649
规模以上工业企业	Industrial Enterprises above Designated Size		
单位数(个)	Number of Units(unit)	382	478
从业人员(万人)	Employment Personnel(10 000 persons)	8.70	10.82
总产值(万元)	Gross Output Value(10 000 yuan)	2 585 677	3 376 196
产品销售收入(万元)	Sales Revenue(10 000 yuan)	2 536 683	3 371 601
利税总额(万元)	Total Pre－tax Profits(10 000 yuan)	285 187	247 480
固定资产原值(万元)	Original Value of Fixed Assets(10 000 yuan)	1 392 625	1 558 792
流动资产合计(万元)	Total Circulating Funds(10 000 yuan)	1 244 846	1 682 329
社会消费品零售总额(万元)	Total Retail Sales of Consumer Goods(10 000 yuan)	140 846	181 532
*私营工商企业	Private Industrial and Commercial Enterprises		
户　数(户)	Number of Enterprises(unit)	3 317	3 882
雇工人数(人)	Employees(person)	23 502	70 420
注册资本(万元)	Registered Capital(10 000 yuan)	456 932	584 825
总产值(万元)	Gross Output Value(10 000 yuan)	450 198	463 532
营业收入(万元)	Business Revenue(10 000 yuan)	442 211	479 106
*个体工商业	Individual Industrial and Commercial Enterprises		
户　数(户)	Number of Enterprises(unit)	7 355	5 820
从业人员(人)	Employment(person)	9 840	10 298
资　金(万元)	Fund(10 000 yuan)	26 710	28 629
营业额(万元)	Turnover(10 000 yuan)	327 420	277 126
实际直接利用外资(万美元)	Foreign Direct Investment (USD 10 000)	13 811	19 010
工业企业出口交货值(万元)	Delivery Value of Industrial Enterprises(10 000 yuan)	110 000	154 049
外贸出口交货值(万元)	Delivery Value of Exports Trade(10 000 yuan)	492 464	729 061
*小学校数(所)	Number of Primary Schools(unit)	40	38
*小学在校学生数(人)	Students Enrollment of Primary Schools(person)	18 684	17 402
*普通中学校数(所)	Number of Regular Secondary Schools(unit)	15	15
*普通中学在校学生数(人)	Students Enrollment of Regular Secondary Schools(person)	16 538	16 456
幼儿园数(所)	Number of Kindergartens(unit)	70	64
卫生机构数(个)	Health Care Institutions(unit)	15	15
#医院、卫生院	Hospital and Health Center	11	11
卫生机构床位数(张)	Beds(unit)	700	700
#医院、卫生院	Hospital and Health Center	700	700
新增再就业人员(人)	Newly Re－employment Person(person)	2 843	4 194

22－12 津南区基本情况
BASIC STATISTICS OF JINNAN DISTRICT

指标名称	Item	2004	2005
＊户籍户数(万户)	Registered Households(10 000 househols)	13.46	13.78
#农业户	Agricultural Households	9.37	9.58
＊户籍人口(万人)	Registered Population(10 000 persons)	37.54	38.07
1.农业人口	Agricultural Population	27.48	27.69
非农业人口	Non－agricultural Population	10.06	10.38
2.男	Male	18.78	19.05
女	Female	18.77	19.03
＊人口出生率(‰)	Birth Rate of Population(‰)	8.0	8.5
＊人口自然增长率(‰)	Natural Growth Rate of Population(‰)	3.3	5.5
城镇单位从业人员(万人)	Employment Personnel Worked in Urban Units(10 000 persons)	3.51	3.75
#在岗职工	Working Staff and Workers	3.35	3.62
＊乡村从业人员(万人)	Rural Employment Personnel(10 000 persons)	13.20	13.40
#农林牧渔业劳动者人数	Farming,Forestry,Animal Husbandry and Fishery	3.36	3.37
地区生产总值(亿元)	Gross Domestic Product(10 000 yuan)	72.33	85.70
第一产业	Primary Industry	2.94	2.83
第二产业	Secondary Industry	41.56	50.38
#工　业	Industry	35.90	43.91
第三产业	Tertiary Industry	27.83	32.49
地区生产总值增速(%)	Increase Rate of Gross Domestic Product(%)	15.0	15.3
一般预算区级财政收入(万元)	General Budgetary Financial Revenue at District Level(10 000 yuan)	40 683	63 602
一般预算区级财政支出(万元)	General Budgetary Financial Expenditure at District Level(10 000 yuan)	66 301	100 953
#教育经费支出	Operating Expenses for Education	14 206	17 564
＊固定资产投资(万元)	Investment in Fixed Assets(10 000 yuan)	217 870	336 448
年末实有耕地面积(万公顷)	Cultivated Land(year－end)(10 000 hectare)	1.46	1.46
农业机械总动力(万千瓦)	Total Power of Agricultural Machinery(10 000 kw)	47.44	47.44
化肥折纯量(吨)	Consumption of Chemical Fertilizers(Pureness)(ton)	1 694	1 127
农村用电量(万千瓦小时)	Rural Electricity Consumption(10 000 kwh)	35 872	41 947
农林牧渔业总产值(万元)	Gross Output Value of Farming,Forestry,Animal Husbandry and Fishery(10 000 yuan)	45 632	58 445
农林牧渔业总产值增速(%)	Increase Rate of Gross Output Value of Farming,Forestry,Animal Husbandry and Fishery(%)	1.5	3.3
粮食产量(万吨)	Total Yield of Grain(10 000 tons)	2.01	2.34
水产品产量(吨)	Total Yield of Aquatic Products(ton)	13 798	14 348
蔬菜总产量(吨)	Total Yield of Vegetable(ton)	176 724	126 341
＊农村居民人均年纯收入(元)	Per Capita Annual Net Income of Rural Households(yuan)	7 179	7 884
＊农村居民人均生活消费支出(元)	Per Capita Annual Expenditure for Consumption of Rural Households(yuan)	4 035	4 709

22-12 续表 Continued

指标名称	Item	2004	2005
乡镇企业单位数(个)	Number of Township Enterprises(unit)	7 655	7 908
乡镇企业人数(万人)	Employment of Township Enterprises(10 000 persons)	16.76	17.59
乡镇企业主营业务收入(万元)	Major Business Revenue of Township Enterprises(10 000 yuan)	2 197 559	2 487 591
规模以上工业企业	Industrial Enterprises above Designated Size		
单位数(个)	Number of Units(unit)	361	445
从业人员(万人)	Employment Personnel(10 000 persons)	6.51	7.43
总产值(万元)	Gross Output Value(10 000 yuan)	1 365 169	2 203 477
产品销售收入(万元)	Sales Revenue(10 000 yuan)	1 343 739	2 133 141
利税总额(万元)	Total Pre-tax Profits(10 000 yuan)	107 839	175 884
固定资产原值(万元)	Original Value of Fixed Assets(10 000 yuan)	488 999	683 949
流动资产合计(万元)	Total Circulating Funds(10 000 yuan)	641 152	929 943
社会消费品零售总额(万元)	Total Retail Sales of Consumer Goods(10 000 yuan)	162 817	194 473
* 私营工商企业	Private Industrial and Commercial Enterprises		
户　数(户)	Number of Enterprises(unit)	3 137	3 378
雇工人数(人)	Employees(person)	37 072	41 688
注册资本(万元)	Registered Capital(10 000 yuan)	382 394	488 123
总产值(万元)	Gross Output Value(10 000 yuan)	695 100	1 355 067
营业收入(万元)	Business Revenue(10 000 yuan)	707 900	1 064 709
* 个体工商业	Individual Industrial and Commercial Enterprises		
户　数(户)	Number of Enterprises(unit)	8 280	8 254
从业人员(人)	Employment(person)	15 487	16 069
资　金(万元)	Fund(10 000 yuan)	23 647	25 545
营业额(万元)	Turnover(10 000 yuan)	618 200	646 517
实际直接利用外资(万美元)	Foreign Direct Investment (USD 10 000)	9 135	12 232
吸引内资到位额(万元)	Actual Domestic Investment(10 000 yuan)	91 569	155 822
工业企业出口交货值(万元)	Delivery Value of Industrial Enterprises(10 000 yuan)	364 175	465 026
* 小学校数(所)	Number of Primary Schools(unit)	44	43
* 小学在校学生数(人)	Students Enrollment of Primary Schools(person)	27 568	25 814
* 普通中学校数(所)	Number of Regular Secondary Schools(unit)	26	20
* 普通中学在校学生数(人)	Students Enrollment of Regular Secondary Schools(person)	19 027	19 281
幼儿园数(所)	Number of Kindergartens(unit)	84	41
卫生机构数(个)	Health Care Institutions(unit)	16	16
# 医院、卫生院	Hospital and Health Center	12	12
卫生机构床位数(张)	Beds(unit)	553	553
# 医院、卫生院	Hospital and Health Center	529	529
新增再就业人员(人)	Newly Re-employment Person(person)	3 633	3 107

22－13　北辰区基本情况
BASIC STATISTICS OF BEICHEN DISTRICT

指标名称	Item	2004	2005
*户籍户数(万户)	Registered Households(10 000 househols)	12.06	12.51
#农业户	Agricultural Households	7.00	7.12
*户籍人口(万人)	Registered Population(10 000 persons)	32.31	33.02
1.农业人口	Agricultural Population	19.74	19.81
非农业人口	Non－agricultural Population	12.57	13.21
2.男	Male	16.19	16.53
女	Female	16.12	16.48
*人口出生率(‰)	Birth Rate of Population(‰)	7.9	8.9
*人口自然增长率(‰)	Natural Growth Rate of Population(‰)	1.3	4.4
城镇单位从业人员(万人)	Employment Personnel Worked in Urban Units(10 000 persons)	3.49	3.57
#在岗职工	Working Staff and Workers	3.22	3.31
*乡村从业人员(万人)	Rural Employment Personnel(10 000 persons)	11.43	11.49
#农林牧渔业劳动者人数	Farming,Forestry,Animal Husbandry and Fishery	3.12	2.94
地区生产总值(亿元)	Gross Domestic Product(10 000 yuan)	113.69	135.18
第一产业	Primary Industry	6.18	6.19
第二产业	Secondary Industry	78.31	94.62
#工　业	Industry	77.09	92.84
第三产业	Tertiary Industry	29.2	34.37
地区生产总值增速(%)	Increase Rate of Gross Domestic Product(%)	15.3	16.3
一般预算区级财政收入(万元)	General Budgetary Financial Revenue at District Level(10 000 yuan)	60 767	92 430
一般预算区级财政支出(万元)	General Budgetary Financial Expenditure at District Level(10 000 yuan)	68 189	113 068
#教育经费支出	Operating Expenses for Education	16 011	20 578
*固定资产投资(万元)	Investment in Fixed Assets(10 000 yuan)	383 590	428 433
年末实有耕地面积(万公顷)	Cultivated Land(year－end)(10 000 hectare)	1.85	1.85
农业机械总动力(万千瓦)	Total Power of Agricultural Machinery(10 000 kw)	45.37	41.57
化肥折纯量(吨)	Consumption of Chemical Fertilizers(Pureness)(ton)	6 086	5 660
农村用电量(万千瓦小时)	Rural Electricity Consumption(10 000 kwh)	35 857	42 151
农林牧渔业总产值(万元)	Gross Output Value of Farming,Forestry,Animal Husbandry and Fishery(10 000 yuan)	118 940	128 135
农林牧渔业总产值增速(%)	Increase Rate of Gross Output Value of Farming,Forestry,Animal Husbandry and Fishery(%)	8.1	4.6
粮食产量(万吨)	Total Yield of Grain(10 000 tons)	4.54	5.32
水产品产量(吨)	Total Yield of Aquatic Products(ton)	11 968	13 512
蔬菜总产量(吨)	Total Yield of Vegetable(ton)	366 554	320 297
*农村居民人均年纯收入(元)	Per Capita Annual Net Income of Rural Households(yuan)	7 997	8 776
*农村居民人均生活消费支出(元)	Per Capita Annual Expenditure for Consumption of Rural Households(yuan)	3 945	4 910

22－13 续表 Continued

指标名称	Item	2004	2005
乡镇企业单位数(个)	Number of Township Enterprises(unit)	744	831
乡镇企业人数(万人)	Employment of Township Enterprises(10 000 persons)	8.07	9.82
乡镇企业主营业务收入(万元)	Major Business Revenue of Township Enterprises(10 000 yuan)	3 071 244	4 786 172
规模以上工业企业	Industrial Enterprises above Designated Size		
单位数(个)	Number of Units(unit)	540	559
从业人员(万人)	Employment Personnel(10 000 persons)	8.63	8.95
总产值(万元)	Gross Output Value(10 000 yuan)	3 491 999	4 630 026
产品销售收入(万元)	Sales Revenue(10 000 yuan)	3 444 121	4 624 924
利税总额(万元)	Total Pre－tax Profits(10 000 yuan)	420 630	489 268
固定资产原值(万元)	Original Value of Fixed Assets(10 000 yuan)	1 118 389	1 384 473
流动资产合计(万元)	Total Circulating Funds(10 000 yuan)	1 783 538	2 488 647
社会消费品零售总额(万元)	Total Retail Sales of Consumer Goods(10 000 yuan)	270 266	249 712
* 私营工商企业	Private Industrial and Commercial Enterprises		
户　数(户)	Number of Enterprises(unit)	4 714	4 998
雇工人数(人)	Employees(person)	48 750	53 553
注册资本(万元)	Registered Capital(10 000 yuan)	715 980	749 868
总产值(万元)	Gross Output Value(10 000 yuan)	216 108	241 853
营业收入(万元)	Business Revenue(10 000 yuan)	538 141	578 394
* 个体工商业	Individual Industrial and Commercial Enterprises		
户　数(户)	Number of Enterprises(unit)	7 597	6 610
从业人员(人)	Employment(person)	15 592	11 827
资　金(万元)	Fund(10 000 yuan)	29 832	26 751
营业额(万元)	Turnover(10 000 yuan)	435 073	471 744
实际直接利用外资(万美元)	Foreign Direct Investment (USD 10 000)	12 310	17 766
吸引内资到位额(万元)	Actual Domestic Investment(10 000 yuan)	74 601	104 441
工业企业出口交货值(万元)	Delivery Value of Industrial Enterprises(10 000 yuan)	1 000 000	1 200 000
* 小学校数(所)	Number of Primary Schools(unit)	46	44
* 小学在校学生数(人)	Students Enrollment of Primary Schools(person)	18 395	17 467
* 普通中学校数(所)	Number of Regular Secondary Schools(unit)	20	20
* 普通中学在校学生数(人)	Students Enrollment of Regular Secondary Schools(person)	15 661	15 657
幼儿园数(所)	Number of Kindergartens(unit)	108	109
卫生机构数(个)	Health Care Institutions(unit)	20	17
# 医院、卫生院	Hospital and Health Center	16	13
卫生机构床位数(张)	Beds(unit)	634	667
# 医院、卫生院	Hospital and Health Center	634	667
新增再就业人员(人)	Newly Re－employment Person(person)	4 508	4 013

22－14 武清区基本情况

BASIC STATISTICS OF WUQING DISTRICT

指标名称	Item	2004	2005
*户籍户数(万户)	Registered Households(10 000 househols)	25.01	25.60
#农业户	Agricultural Households	20.03	20.09
*户籍人口(万人)	Registered Population(10 000 persons)	81.10	81.72
1.农业人口	Agricultural Population	69.19	69.24
非农业人口	Non－agricultural Population	11.90	12.48
2.男	Male	40.67	40.96
女	Female	40.43	40.76
*人口出生率(‰)	Birth Rate of Population(‰)	8.9	9.7
*人口自然增长率(‰)	Natural Growth Rate of Population(‰)	3.9	3.3
城镇单位从业人员(万人)	Employment Personnel Worked in Urban Units(10 000 persons)	6.58	6.36
#在岗职工	Working Staff and Workers	6.47	6.35
*乡村从业人员(万人)	Rural Employment Personnel(10 000 persons)	36.86	37.29
#农林牧渔业劳动者人数	Farming,Forestry,Animal Husbandry and Fishery	20.05	19.85
地区生产总值(亿元)	Gross Domestic Product(10 000 yuan)	100.28	114.54
第一产业	Primary Industry	21.17	21.65
第二产业	Secondary Industry	44.96	49.38
#工　业	Industry	40.89	45.17
第三产业	Tertiary Industry	34.15	43.51
地区生产总值增速(%)	Increase Rate of Gross Domestic Product(%)	15.0	15.1
一般预算区级财政收入(万元)	General Budgetary Financial Revenue at District Level(10 000 yuan)	64 698	77 473
一般预算区级财政支出(万元)	General Budgetary Financial Expenditure at District Level(10 000 yuan)	127 036	145 158
#教育经费支出	Operating Expenses for Education	30 416	36 236
*固定资产投资(万元)	Investment in Fixed Assets(10 000 yuan)	235 010	507 834
年末实有耕地面积(万公顷)	Cultivated Land(year－end)(10 000 hectare)	8.99	8.99
农业机械总动力(万千瓦)	Total Power of Agricultural Machinery(10 000 kw)	97.51	98.79
化肥折纯量(吨)	Consumption of Chemical Fertilizers(Pureness)(ton)	50 849	52 712
农村用电量(万千瓦小时)	Rural Electricity Consumption(10 000 kwh)	128 762	143 164
农林牧渔业总产值(万元)	Gross Output Value of Farming,Forestry,Animal Husbandry and Fishery(10 000 yuan)	464 030	504 587
农林牧渔业总产值增速(%)	Increase Rate of Gross Output Value of Farming,Forestry,Animal Husbandry and Fishery(%)	21.1	6.2
粮食产量(万吨)	Total Yield of Grain(10 000 tons)	53.28	59.57
水产品产量(吨)	Total Yield of Aquatic Products(ton)	44 350	54 456
蔬菜总产量(吨)	Total Yield of Vegetable(ton)	1 709 974	1 423 740
*农村居民人均年纯收入(元)	Per Capita Annual Net Income of Rural Households(yuan)	6 380	7 045
*农村居民人均生活消费支出(元)	Per Capita Annual Expenditure for Consumption of Rural Households(yuan)	2 617	3 031

22－14 续表 Continued

指标名称	Item	2004	2005
乡镇企业单位数(个)	Number of Township Enterprises(unit)	4 960	5 161
乡镇企业人数(万人)	Employment of Township Enterprises(10 000 persons)	11.56	9.28
乡镇企业主营业务收入(万元)	Major Business Revenue of Township Enterprises(10 000 yuan)	1 231 116	1 285 522
规模以上工业企业	Industrial Enterprises above Designated Size		
单位数(个)	Number of Units(unit)	427	439
从业人员(万人)	Employment Personnel(10 000 persons)	8.79	8.45
总产值(万元)	Gross Output Value(10 000 yuan)	1 740 111	1 859 243
产品销售收入(万元)	Sales Revenue(10 000 yuan)	1 716 734	1 755 968
利税总额(万元)	Total Pre－tax Profits(10 000 yuan)	168 636	194 595
固定资产原值(万元)	Original Value of Fixed Assets(10 000 yuan)	901 497	1 031 213
流动资产合计(万元)	Total Circulating Funds(10 000 yuan)	809 244	916 858
社会消费品零售总额(万元)	Total Retail Sales of Consumer Goods(10 000 yuan)	330 200	401 545
* 私营工商企业	Private Industrial and Commercial Enterprises		
户　数(户)	Number of Enterprises(unit)	3 547	2 647
雇工人数(人)	Employees(person)	26 227	27 500
注册资本(万元)	Registered Capital(10 000 yuan)	485 252	622 500
总产值(万元)	Gross Output Value(10 000 yuan)	233 587	270 900
营业收入(万元)	Business Revenue(10 000 yuan)	311 942	364 500
* 个体工商业	Individual Industrial and Commercial Enterprises		
户　数(户)	Number of Enterprises(unit)	18 153	19 479
从业人员(人)	Employment(person)	24 674	25 400
资　金(万元)	Fund(10 000 yuan)	39 752	55 800
营业额(万元)	Turnover(10 000 yuan)	154 520	154 350
实际直接利用外资(万美元)	Foreign Direct Investment (USD 10 000)	10 038	13 529
吸引内资到位额(万元)	Actual Domestic Investment(10 000 yuan)	120 273	183 810
工业企业出口交货值(万元)	Delivery Value of Industrial Enterprises(10 000 yuan)	630 000	725 000
* 小学校数(所)	Number of Primary Schools(unit)	192	182
* 小学在校学生数(人)	Students Enrollment of Primary Schools(person)	52 911	51 856
* 普通中学校数(所)	Number of Regular Secondary Schools(unit)	51	51
* 普通中学在校学生数(人)	Students Enrollment of Regular Secondary Schools(person)	48 436	47 105
幼儿园数(所)	Number of Kindergartens(unit)	258	239
卫生机构数(个)	Health Care Institutions(unit)	42	43
# 医院、卫生院	Hospital and Health Center	36	36
卫生机构床位数(张)	Beds(unit)	1 181	1 340
# 医院、卫生院	Hospital and Health Center	1 071	1 221
新增再就业人员(人)	Newly Re－employment Person(person)	15 215	16 300

22－15　宝坻区基本情况
BASIC STATISTICS OF BAODI DISTRICT

指标名称	Item	2004	2005
* 户籍户数(万户)	Registered Households(10 000 househols)	19.86	20.37
#农业户	Agricultural Households	15.41	15.45
* 户籍人口(万人)	Registered Population(10 000 persons)	65.22	65.28
1.农业人口	Agricultural Population	55.13	54.84
非农业人口	Non－agricultural Population	10.10	10.44
2.男	Male	32.92	32.96
女	Female	32.30	32.33
* 人口出生率(‰)	Birth Rate of Population(‰)	8.9	9.8
* 人口自然增长率(‰)	Natural Growth Rate of Population(‰)	2.7	－1.1
城镇单位从业人员(万人)	Employment Personnel Worked in Urban Units(10 000 persons)	3.00	2.99
#在岗职工	Working Staff and Workers	3.00	2.99
* 乡村从业人员(万人)	Rural Employment Personnel(10 000 persons)	25.39	25.67
#农林牧渔业劳动者人数	Farming,Forestry,Animal Husbandry and Fishery	13.58	13.58
地区生产总值(亿元)	Gross Domestic Product(10 000 yuan)	60.60	74.26
第一产业	Primary Industry	13.42	13.47
第二产业	Secondary Industry	19.54	33.56
#工　业	Industry	16.93	31.04
第三产业	Tertiary Industry	27.64	27.23
地区生产总值增速(%)	Increase Rate of Gross Domestic Product(%)	5.9	16.7
一般预算区级财政收入(万元)	General Budgetary Financial Revenue at District Level(10 000 yuan)	24 577	35 326
一般预算区级财政支出(万元)	General Budgetary Financial Expenditure at District Level(10 000 yuan)	56 831	74 173
#教育经费支出	Operating Expenses for Education	21 717	25 540
* 固定资产投资(万元)	Investment in Fixed Assets(10 000 yuan)	262 226	320 166
年末实有耕地面积(万公顷)	Cultivated Land(year－end)(10 000 hectare)	7.56	7.61
农业机械总动力(万千瓦)	Total Power of Agricultural Machinery(10 000 kw)	68.75	71.35
化肥折纯量(吨)	Consumption of Chemical Fertilizers(Pureness)(ton)	39 002	65 466
农村用电量(万千瓦小时)	Rural Electricity Consumption(10 000 kwh)	45 005	54 020
农林牧渔业总产值(万元)	Gross Output Value of Farming,Forestry,Animal Husbandry and Fishery(10 000 yuan)	298 819	318 680
农林牧渔业总产值增速(%)	Increase Rate of Gross Output Value of Farming,Forestry,Animal Husbandry and Fishery(%)	8.8	6.7
粮食产量(万吨)	Total Yield of Grain(10 000 tons)	36.31	40.52
水产品产量(吨)	Total Yield of Aquatic Products(ton)	33 878	35 280
蔬菜总产量(吨)	Total Yield of Vegetable(ton)	631 554	608 541
* 农村居民人均年纯收入(元)	Per Capita Annual Net Income of Rural Households(yuan)	6 054	6 692
* 农村居民人均生活消费支出(元)	Per Capita Annual Expenditure for Consumption of Rural Households(yuan)	2 805	3 191

22-15 续表 Continued

指标名称	Item	2004	2005
乡镇企业单位数(个)	Number of Township Enterprises(unit)	310	306
乡镇企业人数(万人)	Employment of Township Enterprises(10 000 persons)	6.5	6.1
乡镇企业主营业务收入(万元)	Major Business Revenue of Township Enterprises(10 000 yuan)	673 297	663 921
规模以上工业企业	Industrial Enterprises above Designated Size		
单位数(个)	Number of Units(unit)	353	359
从业人员(万人)	Employment Personnel(10 000 persons)	7.02	7.13
总产值(万元)	Gross Output Value(10 000 yuan)	799 917	605 162
产品销售收入(万元)	Sales Revenue(10 000 yuan)	624 297	634 187
利税总额(万元)	Total Pre-tax Profits(10 000 yuan)	70 028	71 289
固定资产原值(万元)	Original Value of Fixed Assets(10 000 yuan)	218 052	219 001
流动资产合计(万元)	Total Circulating Funds(10 000 yuan)	192 278	193 299
社会消费品零售总额(万元)	Total Retail Sales of Consumer Goods(10 000 yuan)	246 835	297 792
*私营工商企业	Private Industrial and Commercial Enterprises		
户　数(户)	Number of Enterprises(unit)	1 555	1 568
雇工人数(人)	Employees(person)	68 000	69 200
注册资本(万元)	Registered Capital(10 000 yuan)	238 423	259 329
总产值(万元)	Gross Output Value(10 000 yuan)	255 348	268 392
营业收入(万元)	Business Revenue(10 000 yuan)	51 866	52 098
*个体工商业	Individual Industrial and Commercial Enterprises		
户　数(户)	Number of Enterprises(unit)	14 047	14 396
从业人员(人)	Employment(person)	59 600	31 579
资　金(万元)	Fund(10 000 yuan)	48 466	76 502
营业额(万元)	Turnover(10 000 yuan)	90 944	278 744
实际直接利用外资(万美元)	Foreign Direct Investment (USD 10 000)	2 318	3 342
吸引内资到位额(万元)	Actual Domestic Investment(10 000 yuan)	183 860	307 651
工业企业出口交货值(万元)	Delivery Value of Industrial Enterprises(10 000 yuan)	325 142	375 214
*小学校数(所)	Number of Primary Schools(unit)	158	134
*小学在校学生数(人)	Students Enrollment of Primary Schools(person)	55 451	50 189
*普通中学校数(所)	Number of Regular Secondary Schools(unit)	49	49
*普通中学在校学生数(人)	Students Enrollment of Regular Secondary Schools(person)	53 876	54 269
幼儿园数(所)	Number of Kindergartens(unit)	162	153
卫生机构数(个)	Health Care Institutions(unit)	46	46
#医院、卫生院	Hospital and Health Center	41	41
卫生机构床位数(张)	Beds(unit)	1 000	1 155
#医院、卫生院	Hospital and Health Center	1 000	1 155
新增再就业人员(人)	Newly Re-employment Person(person)	2 400	3 000

22-16 宁河县基本情况
BASIC STATISTICS OF NINGHE COUNTY

指标名称	Item	2004	2005
*户籍户数(万户)	Registered Households(10 000 househols)	11.03	11.28
#农业户	Agricultural Households	7.61	7.70
*户籍人口(万人)	Registered Population(10 000 persons)	36.28	36.74
1.农业人口	Agricultural Population	27.76	27.97
非农业人口	Non-agricultural Population	8.52	8.77
2.男	Male	18.41	18.65
女	Female	17.87	18.08
*人口出生率(‰)	Birth Rate of Population(‰)	9.5	9.5
*人口自然增长率(‰)	Natural Growth Rate of Population(‰)	3.3	4.1
城镇单位从业人员(万人)	Employment Personnel Worked in Urban Units(10 000 persons)	2.49	1.77
#在岗职工	Working Staff and Workers	2.18	1.76
*乡村从业人员(万人)	Rural Employment Personnel(10 000 persons)	11.14	11.39
#农林牧渔业劳动者人数	Farming,Forestry,Animal Husbandry and Fishery	6.42	6.50
地区生产总值(亿元)	Gross Domestic Product(10 000 yuan)	47.68	54.86
第一产业	Primary Industry	11.93	12.09
第二产业	Secondary Industry	22.95	27.71
#工　业	Industry	21.02	25.39
第三产业	Tertiary Industry	12.80	15.06
地区生产总值增速(%)	Increase Rate of Gross Domestic Product(%)	12.8	15.0
一般预算区级财政收入(万元)	General Budgetary Financial Revenue at District Level(10 000 yuan)	15 566	32 144
一般预算区级财政支出(万元)	General Budgetary Financial Expenditure at District Level(10 000 yuan)	37 006	55 877
#教育经费支出	Operating Expenses for Education	12 583	15 065
*固定资产投资(万元)	Investment in Fixed Assets(10 000 yuan)	98 101	150 000
年末实有耕地面积(万公顷)	Cultivated Land(year-end)(10 000 hectare)	3.87	3.87
农业机械总动力(万千瓦)	Total Power of Agricultural Machinery(10 000 kw)	52.16	52.43
化肥折纯量(吨)	Consumption of Chemical Fertilizers(Pureness)(ton)	17 769	17 938
农村用电量(万千瓦小时)	Rural Electricity Consumption(10 000 kwh)	32 794	27 716
农林牧渔业总产值(万元)	Gross Output Value of Farming,Forestry,Animal Husbandry and Fishery(10 000 yuan)	231 532	260 128
农林牧渔业总产值增速(%)	Increase Rate of Gross Output Value of Farming, Forestry,Animal Husbandry and Fishery(%)	9.7	13.3
粮食产量(万吨)	Total Yield of Grain(10 000 tons)	4.24	8.83
水产品产量(吨)	Total Yield of Aquatic Products (ton)	16 150	16 475
蔬菜总产量(吨)	Total Yield of Vegetable(ton)	277 182	402 820
*农村居民人均年纯收入(元)	Per Capita Annual Net Income of Rural Households(yuan)	6 257	6 911
*农村居民人均生活消费支出(元)	Per Capita Annual Expenditure for Consumption of Rural Households(yuan)	2 395	2 860

22-16 续表 Continued

指标名称	Item	2004	2005
乡镇企业单位数(个)	Number of Township Enterprises(unit)	120	102
乡镇企业人数(万人)	Employment of Township Enterprises(10 000 persons)	1.17	1.00
乡镇企业主营业务收入(万元)	Major Business Revenue of Township Enterprises(10 000 yuan)	238 200	343 751
规模以上工业企业	Industrial Enterprises above Designated Size		
单位数(个)	Number of Units(unit)	190	196
从业人员(万人)	Employment Personnel(10 000 persons)	2.70	2.70
总产值(万元)	Gross Output Value(10 000 yuan)	749 869	808 078
产品销售收入(万元)	Sales Revenue(10 000 yuan)	677 986	759 999
利税总额(万元)	Total Pre-tax Profits(10 000 yuan)	51 421	58 945
固定资产原值(万元)	Original Value of Fixed Assets(10 000 yuan)	163 495	168 727
流动资产合计(万元)	Total Circulating Funds(10 000 yuan)	232 574	278 854
社会消费品零售总额(万元)	Total Retail Sales of Consumer Goods(10 000 yuan)	177 600	216 601
* 私营工商企业	Private Industrial and Commercial Enterprises		
户　数(户)	Number of Enterprises (unit)	1 399	1 565
雇工人数(人)	Employees(person)	14 896	14 131
注册资本(万元)	Registered Capital(10 000 yuan)	317 567	362 228
总产值(万元)	Gross Output Value(10 000 yuan)	126 982	109 715
营业收入(万元)	Business Revenue(10 000 yuan)	10 776	38 789
* 个体工商业	Individual Industrial and Commercial Enterprises		
户　数(户)	Number of Enterprises (unit)	6 789	7 220
从业人员(人)	Employment(person)	9 037	9 601
资　金(万元)	Fund(10 000 yuan)	14 581	17 256
营业额(万元)	Turnover(10 000 yuan)	116 084	186 050
实际直接利用外资(万美元)	Foreign Direct Investment (USD 10 000)	1 923	2 552
吸引内资到位额(万元)	Actual Domestic Investment(10 000 yuan)	42 300	62 735
工业企业出口交货值(万元)	Delivery Value of Industrial Enterprises(10 000 yuan)	330 000	350 000
* 小学校数(所)	Number of Primary Schools(unit)	63	63
* 小学在校学生数(人)	Students Enrollment of Primary Schools(person)	24 211	26 921
* 普通中学校数(所)	Number of Regular Secondary Schools(unit)	29	30
* 普通中学在校学生数(人)	Students Enrollment of Regular Secondary Schools(person)	36 350	31 013
幼儿园数(所)	Number of Kindergartens(unit)	140	140
卫生机构数(个)	Health Care Institutions(unit)	71	88
# 医院、卫生院	Hospital and Health Center	8	8
卫生机构床位数(张)	Beds(unit)	569	550
# 医院、卫生院	Hospital and Health Center	569	550
新增再就业人员(人)	Newly Re-employment Person(person)	3 200	4 100

22－17 静海县基本情况
BASIC STATISTICS OF JINGHAI COUNTY

指标名称	Item	2004	2005
* 户籍户数(万户)	Registered Households(10 000 households)	17.01	17.30
#农业户	Agricultural Households	13.15	13.23
* 户籍人口(万人)	Registered Population(10 000 persons)	51.59	52.27
1.农业人口	Agricultural Population	42.70	43.07
非农业人口	Non－agricultural Population	8.89	9.20
2.男	Male	26.26	26.63
女	Female	25.33	25.64
* 人口出生率(‰)	Birth Rate of Population(‰)	9.3	9.8
* 人口自然增长率(‰)	Natural Growth Rate of Population(‰)	3.6	4.1
城镇单位从业人员(万人)	Employment Personnel Worked in Urban Units(10 000 persons)	2.95	2.89
#在岗职工	Working Staff and Workers	2.86	2.83
* 乡村从业人员(万人)	Rural Employment Personnel(10 000 persons)	15.84	16.16
#农林牧渔业劳动者人数	Farming,Forestry,Animal Husbandry and Fishery	7.64	7.50
地区生产总值(亿元)	Gross Domestic Product(10 000 yuan)	71.09	85.18
第一产业	Primary Industry	12.72	12.79
第二产业	Secondary Industry	36.01	47.74
#工　业	Industry	33.19	44.66
第三产业	Tertiary Industry	22.36	24.65
地区生产总值增速(%)	Increase Rate of Gross Domestic Product(%)	14.1	14.5
一般预算区级财政收入(万元)	General Budgetary Financial Revenue at District Level(10 000 yuan)	28 089	36 167
一般预算区级财政支出(万元)	General Budgetary Financial Expenditure at District Level(10 000 yuan)	56 704	70 653
#教育经费支出	Operating Expenses for Education	19 495	22 037
* 固定资产投资(万元)	Investment in Fixed Assets(10 000 yuan)	170 969	240 556
年末实有耕地面积(万公顷)	Cultivated Land(year－end)(10 000 hectare)	6.92	6.92
农业机械总动力(万千瓦)	Total Power of Agricultural Machinery(10 000 kw)	68.00	68.87
化肥折纯量(吨)	Consumption of Chemical Fertilizers(Pureness)(ton)	31 424	33 376
农村用电量(万千瓦小时)	Rural Electricity Consumption(10 000 kwh)	108 140	117 896
农林牧渔业总产值(万元)	Gross Output Value of Farming,Forestry,Animal Husbandry and Fishery(10 000 yuan)	237 393	259 824
农林牧渔业总产值增速(%)	Increase Rate of Gross Output Value of Farming, Forestry,Animal Husbandry and Fishery(%)	11.4	10.2
粮食产量(万吨)	Total Yield of Grain(10 000 tons)	23.39	29.94
水产品产量(吨)	Total Yield of Aquatic Products(ton)	25 421	26 293
蔬菜总产量(吨)	Total Yield of Vegetable(ton)	423 204	416 387
* 农村居民人均年纯收入(元)	Per Capita Annual Net Income of Rural Households(yuan)	6 054	6 692
* 农村居民人均生活消费支出(元)	Per Capita Annual Expenditure for Consumption of Rural Households(yuan)	3 101	3 301

22－17 续表　Continued

指标名称	Item	2004	2005
乡镇企业单位数(个)	Number of Township Enterprises(unit)	319	442
乡镇企业人数(万人)	Employment of Township Enterprises(10 000 persons)	2.55	3.86
乡镇企业主营业务收入(万元)	Major Business Revenue of Township Enterprises(10 000 yuan)	863 000	1 002 520
规模以上工业企业	Industrial Enterprises above Designated Size		
单位数(个)	Number of Units(unit)	230	301
从业人员(万人)	Employment Personnel(10 000 persons)	3.94	5.38
总产值(万元)	Gross Output Value(10 000 yuan)	2 117 458	3 117 986
产品销售收入(万元)	Sales Revenue(10 000 yuan)	2 060 831	2 429 013
利税总额(万元)	Total Pre－tax Profits(10 000 yuan)	139 331	158 141
固定资产原值(万元)	Original Value of Fixed Assets(10 000 yuan)	430 286	618 007
流动资产合计(万元)	Total Circulating Funds(10 000 yuan)	831 921	1 206 518
社会消费品零售总额(万元)	Total Retail Sales of Consumer Goods(10 000 yuan)	140 891	175 483
*私营工商企业	Private Industrial and Commercial Enterprises		
户　数(户)	Number of Enterprises(unit)	2 560	3 087
雇工人数(人)	Employees(person)	22 548	26 487
注册资本(万元)	Registered Capital(10 000 yuan)	520 565	705 086
总产值(万元)	Gross Output Value(10 000 yuan)	39 960	494 006
营业收入(万元)	Business Revenue(10 000 yuan)	28 320	353 330
*个体工商业	Individual Industrial and Commercial Enterprises		
户　数(户)	Number of Enterprises(unit)	9 474	10 331
从业人员(人)	Employment(person)	23 472	23 698
资　金(万元)	Fund(10 000 yuan)	33 344	60 973
营业额(万元)	Turnover(10 000 yuan)	157 968	168 600
实际直接利用外资(万美元)	Foreign Direct Investment (USD 10 000)	2 568	4 488
吸引内资到位额(万元)	Actual Domestic Investment(10 000 yuan)	67 520	94 528
工业企业出口交货值(万元)	Delivery Value of Industrial Enterprises(10 000 yuan)	165 400	196 601
*小学校数(所)	Number of Primary Schools(unit)	99	97
*小学在校学生数(人)	Students Enrollment of Primary Schools(person)	42 144	40 445
*普通中学校数(所)	Number of Regular Secondary Schools(unit)	47	52
*普通中学在校学生数(人)	Students Enrollment of Regular Secondary Schools(person)	39 873	41 391
幼儿园数(所)	Number of Kindergartens(unit)	245	257
卫生机构数(个)	Health Care Institutions(unit)	100	109
#医院、卫生院	Hospital and Health Center	24	24
卫生机构床位数(张)	Beds(unit)	1 199	1 267
#医院、卫生院	Hospital and Health Center	1 133	1 218
新增再就业人员(人)	Newly Re－employment Person(person)	3 071	3 091

22－18　蓟县基本情况
BASIC STATISTICS OF JIXIAN COUNTY

指标名称	Item	2004	2005
* 户籍户数(万户)	Registered Households(10 000 households)	23.15	24.29
#农业户	Agricultural Households	18.74	18.83
* 户籍人口(万人)	Registered Population(10 000 persons)	80.31	80.70
1.农业人口	Agricultural Population	68.82	68.69
非农业人口	Non－agricultural Population	11.49	12.01
2.男	Male	40.90	41.11
女	Female	39.41	39.59
* 人口出生率(‰)	Birth Rate of Population(‰)	6.1	6.7
* 人口自然增长率(‰)	Natural Growth Rate of Population(‰)	1.8	－0.5
城镇单位从业人员(万人)	Employment Personnel Worked in Urban Units(10 000 persons)	4.78	4.59
#在岗职工	Working Staff and Workers	4.11	4.16
* 乡村从业人员(万人)	Rural Employment Personnel(10 000 persons)	32.09	32.32
#农林牧渔业劳动者人数	Farming,Forestry,Animal Husbandry and Fishery	16.69	16.31
地区生产总值(亿元)	Gross Domestic Product(10 000 yuan)	71.48	83.53
第一产业	Primary Industry	19.33	19.11
第二产业	Secondary Industry	19.25	24.23
#工　业	Industry	14.34	21.88
第三产业	Tertiary Industry	32.90	40.19
地区生产总值增速(%)	Increase Rate of Gross Domestic Product(%)	7.4	14.2
一般预算区级财政收入(万元)	General Budgetary Financial Revenue at District Level(10 000 yuan)	42 163	48 009
一般预算区级财政支出(万元)	General Budgetary Financial Expenditure at District Level(10 000 yuan)	70 276	83 004
#教育经费支出	Operating Expenses for Education	21 219	25 961
* 固定资产投资(万元)	Investment in Fixed Assets(10 000 yuan)	149 920	190 759
年末实有耕地面积(万公顷)	Cultivated Land(year－end)(10 000 hectare)	5.40	5.40
农业机械总动力(万千瓦)	Total Power of Agricultural Machinery(10 000 kw)	68.89	70.55
化肥折纯量(吨)	Consumption of Chemical Fertilizers(Pureness)(ton)	34 988	36 519
农村用电量(万千瓦小时)	Rural Electricity Consumption(10 000 kwh)	30 202	32 046
农林牧渔业总产值(万元)	Gross Output Value of Farming,Forestry,Animal Husbandry and Fishery(10 000 yuan)	425 855	445 053
农林牧渔业总产值增速(%)	Increase Rate of Gross Output Value of Farming, Forestry,Animal Husbandry and Fishery(%)	18.3	4.5
粮食产量(万吨)	Total Yield of Grain(10 000 tons)	37.51	41.22
水产品产量(吨)	Total Yield of Aquatic Products(ton)	26 362	27 421
蔬菜总产量(吨)	Total Yield of Vegetable(ton)	1 165 704	1 013 045
* 农村居民人均年纯收入(元)	Per Capita Annual Net Income of Rural Households(yuan)	6 056	6 693
* 农村居民人均生活消费支出(元)	Per Capita Annual Expenditure for Consumption of Rural Households(yuan)	2 649	2 754

22-18 续表 Continued

指标名称	Item	2004	2005
乡镇企业单位数(个)	Number of Township Enterprises(unit)	378	275
乡镇企业人数(万人)	Employment of Township Enterprises(10 000 persons)	4.70	3.40
乡镇企业主营业务收入(万元)	Major Business Revenue of Township Enterprises(10 000 yuan)	622 962	519 696
规模以上工业企业	Industrial Enterprises above Designated Size		
单位数(个)	Number of Units(unit)	272	136
从业人员(万人)	Employment Personnel(10 000 persons)	5.83	5.48
总产值(万元)	Gross Output Value(10 000 yuan)	994 612	672 280
产品销售收入(万元)	Sales Revenue(10 000 yuan)	891 531	626 705
利税总额(万元)	Total Pre-tax Profits(10 000 yuan)	95 576	58 165
固定资产原值(万元)	Original Value of Fixed Assets(10 000 yuan)	304 768	314 429
流动资产合计(万元)	Total Circulating Funds(10 000 yuan)	215 655	183 507
社会消费品零售总额(万元)	Total Retail Sales of Consumer Goods(10 000 yuan)	189 200	227 262
* 私营工商企业	Private Industrial and Commercial Enterprises		
户　数(户)	Number of Enterprises(unit)	797	1 091
雇工人数(人)	Employees(person)	12 696	17 200
注册资本(万元)	Registered Capital(10 000 yuan)	84 205	97 000
总产值(万元)	Gross Output Value(10 000 yuan)	80 765	83 800
营业收入(万元)	Business Revenue(10 000 yuan)	33 042	50 400
* 个体工商业	Individual Industrial and Commercial Enterprises		
户　数(户)	Number of Enterprises(unit)	13 900	14 659
从业人员(人)	Employment(person)	23 423	23 000
资　金(万元)	Fund(10 000 yuan)	30 894	301 000
营业额(万元)	Turnover(10 000 yuan)	71 860	116 000
实际直接利用外资(万美元)	Foreign Direct Investment (USD 10 000)	2 018	2 737
吸引内资到位额(万元)	Actual Domestic Investment(10 000 yuan)	70 000	98 010
工业企业出口交货值(万元)	Delivery Value of Industrial Enterprises(10 000 yuan)	365 000	500 100
* 小学校数(所)	Number of Primary Schools(unit)	196	130
* 小学在校学生数(人)	Students Enrollment of Primary Schools(person)	72 489	61 833
* 普通中学校数(所)	Number of Regular Secondary Schools(unit)	68	70
* 普通中学在校学生数(人)	Students Enrollment of Regular Secondary Schools(person)	75 539	65 973
幼儿园数(所)	Number of Kindergartens(unit)	191	205
卫生机构数(个)	Health Care Institutions(unit)	319	449
# 医院、卫生院	Hospital and Health Center	32	32
卫生机构床位数(张)	Beds(unit)	1 368	1 368
# 医院、卫生院	Hospital and Health Center	1 368	1 368
新增再就业人员(人)	Newly Re-employment Person(person)	2 976	2 070

附一
APPENDIX 1

天津市第一次经济普查资料

Tianjin Statistics of the First Economic Census

按行业划分的单位数及从业人数

NUMBER OF UNITS AND PERSONS EMPLOYED BY SECTOR

行业	Sector	法人单位 Institutional Units		产业活动单位 Unit with Industrial Undertakings	
		单位数（个） Number Units of	年末从业人数（人） Number of Persons Employed(person)	单位数（个） Number Units of	年末从业人数（人） Number of Persons Employed(person)
总计	**Total**	**93 228**	**3 365 282**	**109 419**	**3 489 469**
农、林、牧、渔业	**Farming, Forestry, Animal Husbandry and Fishery**			**90**	**354**
农业	Farming			3	6
畜牧业	Animal Husbandry			3	29
渔业	Fishery			1	16
农、林、牧、渔服务业	FFAF Services			83	303
采矿业	**Minerals Mining**	**112**	**73 866**	**124**	**43 948**
煤炭开采和洗选业	Coal Mining and Dressing	12	153	13	156
石油和天然气开采业	Petroleum and Natural Gas Extraction	26	59 981	35	31 646
黑色金属矿采选业	Mining and Processing of Ferrous Metal Ores	7	45	7	45
有色金属矿采选业	Mining and Processing of Non-ferrous Metal Ores	8	2 689	9	1 509
非金属矿采选业	Mining and Processing of Nonmetal Ores	57	10 966	57	10 494
其他采矿业	Mining of Other Ores	2	32	3	98
制造业	**Manufacturing**	**30 064**	**1 525 212**	**30 740**	**1 528 738**
农副食品加工业	Processing of Food from Agricultural Products	802	27 833	818	27 737
食品制造业	Food Manufacturing	845	31 244	880	30 633
饮料制造业	Beverage Manufacturing	291	15 875	306	14 840
烟草制品业	Tobacco Manufacturing	4	1 680	4	1 652
纺织业	Textile Industry	1 289	84 292	1 306	84 424
纺织服装鞋帽制造业	Textile Garments, Shoes, Caps Manufacturing	1 321	108 779	1 353	109 576
皮革毛皮羽毛(绒)及其制品业	Leather, Fur, Feather and Related Products	313	24 926	320	25 519
木材加工及木、竹、藤、棕、草制品业	Timber Processing, Manufacture of Wood, Bamboo, Rattan, Palm and Straw Products	425	10 455	435	10 693
家具制造业	Furniture Manufacturing	444	27 044	457	27 110
造纸及纸制品业	Papermaking and Paper Products	991	33 262	1 001	33 453
印刷业和记录媒介的复制	Printing and Reproduction of Recording Media	829	20 709	847	21 152
文教体育用品制造业	Manufacture of Articles for Culture, Education and Sport	357	19 819	369	19 835
石油加工、炼焦及核燃料加工业	Processing of Petroleum, Coking and Processing of Nuclear Fuel	156	14 531	162	14 618
化学原料及其品制造业	Raw Chemical Materials and Chemical Products	2 514	103 217	2 568	102 180

注：本表的农、林、牧、渔业为第二、三产业法人兼营的第一产业活动单位。
Note: Farming, Forestry, Animal Husbandry and Fishery in this table refer to the sideline of institutional units of Secondary Industry and Tertiary Industry.

续表 1 Continued

行　业	Sector	法人单位 Institutional Units		产业活动单位 Unit with Industrial Undertakings	
		单位数（个）Number Units of	年末从业人数（人）Number of Persons Employed(person)	单位数（个）Number Units of	年末从业人数（人）Number of Persons Employed(person)
医药制造业	Medical and Pharmaceutical Products	331	40 875	344	38 847
化学纤维制造业	Chemical Fiber	56	2 836	56	2 830
橡胶制品业	Rubber Products	530	32 260	540	32 396
塑料制品业	Plastic Products	1 566	66 410	1 589	67 098
非金属矿物制品业	Nonmetal Mineral Products	1 328	53 155	1 361	53 777
黑色金属冶炼及压延加工业	Smelting and Pressing of Ferrous Metals	863	95 944	881	96 263
有色金属冶炼及压延加工业	Smelting and Pressing of Nonferrous Metals	439	14 938	446	16 196
金属制品业	Metal Products	3 374	108 871	3 434	110 282
通用设备制造业	General Purpose Machinery Manufacturing	3 132	109 499	3 182	109 050
专用设备制造业	Special Purpose Machinery Manufacturing	1 568	61 511	1 616	64 286
交通运输设备制造业	Transport Equipment Manufacturing	2 213	123 712	2 256	124 305
电气机械及器材制造业	Electrical Equipment and Machinery	1 571	82 808	1 620	84 323
通信设备、计算机及其他电子设备制造业	Communications Equipment,Computer and Other Electronic Equipment Manufacturing	882	133 634	912	129 650
仪器仪表及文化、办公用机械制造业	Measuring Instruments and Machinery for Cultural Activity and Office Work	699	27 195	714	27 515
工艺品及其他制造业	Artwork and Other Manufacturing	877	47 087	908	47 684
废弃资源和废旧材料回收加工业	Recycling and Disposal of Waste	54	811	55	814
电力、燃气及水的生产和供应业	**Production and Supply of Electric Power, Gas and Water**	**205**	**34 642**	**421**	**42 101**
电力、热力的生产和供应业	Production and Supply of Power and Heat Power	115	22 934	286	28 330
燃气生产和供应业	Production and Supply of Gas	30	6 948	60	8 217
水的生产和供应业	Production and Supply of Water	60	4 760	75	5 554
建筑业	**Construction**	**3 210**	**295 407**	**4 024**	**316 989**
房屋和土木工程建筑业	Building and Civil Engineering	854	184 560	1 319	197 308
建筑安装业	Building Installation	959	68 859	1 087	73 341
建筑装饰业	Building Decoration	936	21 964	1 081	24 438
其他建筑业	Others	461	20 024	537	21 902
交通运输、仓储和邮政业	**Transport,Storage,Post Services**	**3 854**	**194 653**	**4 674**	**196 696**
铁路运输业	Railway Transport	53	61 211	111	58 766
道路运输业	Highway Transport	995	32 697	1 121	34 069

续表 2 Continued

行业	Sector	法人单位 Institutional Units		产业活动单位 Unit with Industrial Undertakings	
		单位数（个）Number Units of	年末从业人数（人）Number of Persons Employed(person)	单位数（个）Number Units of	年末从业人数（人）Number of Persons Employed(person)
城市公共交通业	City Public Traffic	123	20 685	156	20 605
水上运输业	Waterway Transport	105	24 571	134	21 106
航空运输业	Air Transport	7	2 559	28	3 009
管道运输业	Pipeline Transport	4	211	6	286
装卸搬运和其他运输服务业	Load & Unload and Others	1 882	24 881	2 108	27 890
仓储业	Storage Services	651	19 714	734	22 670
邮政业	Post Services	34	8 124	276	8 295
信息传输、计算机服务和软件业	**Information Transmitting, Computer Services and Software**	**1 230**	**28 071**	**1 469**	**30 246**
电信和其他信息传输服务业	Telecommunication and Other Information Transmitting Services	156	12 731	342	14 174
计算机服务业	Computer Services	699	9 332	734	9 794
软件业	Software	375	6 008	393	6 278
批发和零售业	**Wholesale and Retail Trade**	**23 727**	**293 370**	**28 407**	**325 353**
批发业	Wholesale	15 000	174 636	16 567	190 623
零售业	Retail Trade	8 727	118 734	11 840	134 730
住宿和餐饮业	**Accommodation and Catering Services**	**1 758**	**73 266**	**2 361**	**83 473**
住宿业	Accommodation	530	28 235	634	29 782
餐饮业	Catering Service	1 228	45 031	1 727	53 691
金融业	**Finance Intermediation**	**366**	**50 363**	**2 338**	**53 566**
银行业	Banking	236	35 541	2 071	38 600
证券业	Securities	61	2 154	99	2 271
保险业	Insurance	47	12 405	143	12 405
其他金融活动	Others	22	263	25	290
房地产业	**Real Estate**	**2 196**	**68 885**	**3 037**	**76 394**
租赁和商务服务业	**Leasing and Business Services**	**5 390**	**94 227**	**6 273**	**117 809**
租赁业	Leasing Serving	249	2 816	307	4 041
商务服务业	Business Serving	5 141	91 411	5 966	113 768
科学研究、技术服务和地质勘查	**Scientific Research, Technical Services and Geological Prospecting**	**3 379**	**90 517**	**3 667**	**95 860**
研究与试验发展	R&D	272	14 767	286	14 860

续表 3 Continued

行 业	Sector	法人单位 Institutional Units 单位数(个) Number Units of	法人单位 Institutional Units 年末从业人数(人) Number of Persons Employed(person)	产业活动单位 Unit with Industrial Undertakings 单位数(个) Number Units of	产业活动单位 Unit with Industrial Undertakings 年末从业人数(人) Number of Persons Employed(person)
专业技术服务业	Special Technical Services	1 904	57 033	2 096	62 354
科技交流和推广服务业	Science Exchanges and Technology Expansion	1 176	17 186	1 254	17 513
地质勘查业	Geological Prospecting	27	1 531	31	1 133
水利、环境和公共设施管理业	**Management for Water Conservancy, Environment and Public Facilities**	**759**	**35 183**	**918**	**37 125**
水利管理业	Management for Water Conservancy	268	8 007	287	8 491
环境管理业	Management for Environment	204	10 346	278	11 078
公共设施管理业	Management for Public Facilities	287	16 830	353	17 556
居民服务和其他服务业	**Resident Services and Other Social Services**	**4 419**	**71 412**	**5 129**	**78 449**
居民服务业	Resident Services	1 891	26 815	2 300	28 488
其他服务业	Other Social Services	2 528	44 597	2 829	49 961
教 育	**Education**	**2 522**	**178 193**	**3 556**	**195 834**
卫生、社会保障和社会福利	**Health Care,Social Security and Social Welfare**	**1 006**	**76 421**	**1 942**	**82 155**
卫 生	Health Care	752	70 985	1 653	76 481
社会保障业	Social Security	117	2 333	130	2 540
社会福利业	Social Welfare	137	3 103	159	3 134
文化、体育和娱乐业	**Culture, Sports and Recreational Services**	**808**	**22 207**	**913**	**22 991**
新闻出版业	News Publication	105	3 864	126	3 701
广播、电视、电影和音像	Broadcast,TV,Movies Record and Video Industry	117	4 174	130	4 259
文化艺术业	Culture and Art	231	6 642	249	6 791
体 育	Sports	110	3 112	122	3 161
娱乐业	Recreational Services	245	4 415	286	5 079
公共管理和社会组织	**Public Management and Social Organizations**	**8 223**	**159 387**	**9 336**	**161 388**
中国共产党机关	Chinese Communist Party Organizations	185	3 432	185	3 373
国家机构	Government Organizations	1 593	110 364	2 624	111 815
人民政协和民主党派	The People's Political Consultative Conferance Committees and Democracy Party Groupings	62	798	62	798
群众团体、社会团体和宗教组织	Mass Organizations,Social Organizations and Religious Groups	1 082	6 698	1 152	7 088
基层群众自治组织	Grass - roots Mass Autonomy Organizations	5 301	38 095	5 313	38 314

按隶属关系、地区划分的单位数及从业人数

NUMBER OF UNITS AND PERSONS EMPLOYED BY ADMINISTRATIVE RELATIONSHIP AND REGION

项目	Item	法人单位 Institutional Units		产业活动单位 Unit with Industrial Undertakings	
		单位数（个） Number of Units	年末从业人数（人） Number of Persons Employed(person)	单位数（个） Number of Units	年末从业人数（人） Number of Persons Employed(person)
总　　计	**Total**	**93 228**	**3 365 282**	**109 419**	**3 489 469**
按隶属关系分	**Grouped by Administrative Relationship**				
中　央	Central	1 493	384 324	2 374	363 733
市　属	Municipal	10 081	819 657	13 595	829 620
区　县	District and Country	12 665	475 743	16 084	496 419
街乡镇及以下	Steet,Town and Township below	10 526	250 291	11 433	255 412
其　他	Others	58 463	1 435 267	65 933	1 544 285
按地区分	**Grouped by Region**				
和平区	Heping District	5 543	245 496	6 797	226 178
河东区	Hedong District	5 190	184 897	6 584	216 020
河西区	Hexi District	8 140	269 767	9 956	282 017
南开区	Nankai District	8 791	257 198	10 335	270 064
河北区	Hebei District	4 441	215 699	5 834	190 688
红桥区	Hongqiao District	3 019	80 324	3 802	87 560
塘沽区	Tanggu District	5 886	198 923	6 975	216 528
汉沽区	Hangu District	1 449	55 656	1 709	57 899
大港区	Dagang District	2 792	156 270	3 322	159 448
东丽区	Dongli District	4 959	186 388	5 358	190 903
西青区	Xiqing District	5 193	233 722	5 575	239 028
津南区	Jinnan District	4 067	166 917	4 973	171 537
北辰区	Beichen District	5 918	214 692	6 579	226 588
武清区	Wuqing District	5 446	211 612	6 063	216 285
宝坻区	Baodi District	3 323	124 171	3 907	128 602
宁河县	Ninghe County	2 629	76 646	2 959	77 486
静海县	Jinghai County	4 545	135 337	5 095	139 709
蓟　县	Jixian County	2 980	98 605	4 225	104 642
经济技术开发区	TEDA	5 450	191 239	5 589	186 143
天津保税区	TFTZ	1 560	17 943	1 575	18 123
高新技术产业园区	THIP	1 907	43 780	1 917	42 989
外省市	Other Provinces(municipality)			290	41 032

按单位类别、登记注册类型划分的单位数及从业人数

NUMBER OF UNITS AND PERSONS EMPLOYED BY UNITS AND REGISTERED TYPE

项目	Item	法人单位 Institutional Units		产业活动单位 Unit with Industrial Undertakings	
		单位数(个) Number Units of	年末从业人数(人) Number of Persons Employed(person)	单位数(个) Number Units of	年末从业人数(人) Number of Persons Employed(person)
总　计	**Total**	**93 228**	**3 365 282**	**109 419**	**3 489 469**
按单位类型分	**Grouped by Type of Units**				
企　业	Enterprises	78 680	2 853 626	91 044	2 944 993
事业单位	Institutions Units	5 270	338 776	7 644	358 542
机　关	Agency	1 595	105 792	2 508	103 174
社会团体	Social Organizations	1 044	6 515	1 092	6 732
民办非企业	Non－enterprises Run by the Local People	818	14 205	818	13 859
其他组织机构	Other Organization	5 821	46 368	6 313	62 169
按登记注册类型分	**Grouped by Registered Type**				
内　资	Domestic－funded	87 347	2 818 790	102 394	2 924 251
国　有	State－owned	11 913	906 146	17 484	977 900
集　体	Collective－owned	11 074	315 480	13 505	335 794
股份合作	Cooperative	1 195	48 355	1 366	50 261
联营企业	Joint Ownership Enterprises	423	17 520	499	18 032
国有联营	State Joint Ownership	95	3 843	116	4 055
集体联营	Collective Joint Ownership	136	4 037	174	4 241
国有与集体联	State－owned and Collective Joint Ownership	106	7 205	114	7 247
其他联营	Other Joint Ownership	86	2 435	95	2 489
有限责任公司	Limited Liability Corporations	8 447	517 167	10 079	490 038
国有独资公司	Sole State－owned Corporations	325	87 965	404	51 011
其他有限责任	Other Limited Liability Corporations	8 122	429 202	9 675	439 027
股份有限公司	Share Holding Corporations Ltd.	1 747	146 975	2 713	153 272
私营企业	Private Enterprises	41 636	760 619	43 891	779 863
私营独资	Sole Private Enterprises	9 324	130 898	9 709	134 037
私营合伙	Join Hands with Private	2 769	45 558	2 861	46 494
私营有限责任公司	Private Limited Liability Corporations	27 947	547 650	29 618	560 902
私营股份有限公司	Private Share Holding Corporations Ltd.	1 596	36 513	1 703	38 430
其　他	Other	10 912	106 528	12 857	119 091
港、澳、台商投资企业	Enterprises with Investment from Hongkong, Macao and Taiwan	1 656	115 538	1 951	119 333
与港澳台商合资经营	Hongkong,Macao and Taiwan Joint Venture	684	60 085	813	62 518
与港澳台商合作经营	Hongkong,Macao and Taiwan Cooperative Operation	64	2 708	78	2 973
港澳台商独资	Hongkong,Macao and Taiwan Funded	888	51 120	1 039	52 209
港澳台商投资股份有限公司	Hongkong,Macao and Taiwan Share Holding Corporations Ltd.	20	1 625	21	1 633
外商投资企业	Foreign Funded Enterprises	4 225	430 954	5 074	445 885
中外合资经营	Chinese－foreign Joint Venture	1 331	173 865	1 601	180 548
中外合作经营	Chinese－foreign Cooperative Operation	147	12 881	173	14 289
外资企业	Foreign Investment Enterprise	2 705	238 148	3 213	243 740
外商投资股份有限公司	Foreign－funded Share Holding Corporations Ltd.	42	6 060	87	7 308

按行业、经济类型划分的法人数
NUMBER OF IMPERSONAL ENTITY BY SECTOR AND OWNERSHIP

单位：个 (unit)

行业 Sector	国有 State-owned	集体 Collective-owned	股份制 Joint-stock	私营 Private	其他内资 Other Domestic-funded	港澳台商投资 HongKong, Macao, Taiwan Funded	外商投资 Foreign Funded
总计 Total	**12 333**	**12 405**	**9 869**	**41 636**	**11 104**	**1 656**	**4 225**
采矿业 Minerals Mining	6	25	16	45	5	7	8
制造业 Manufacturing	1 353	5 356	2 519	15 809	1 517	854	2 656
电力、燃气及水的生产和供应业 Production and Supply of Electric Power, Gas and Water	66	20	49	46	1	7	16
建筑业 Construction	283	456	651	1 571	113	61	75
交通运输、仓储和邮政业 Transport, Storage, Post Services	441	640	481	1 785	221	143	143
信息传输、计算机服务和软件业 Information Transmitting, Computer Services and Software	86	32	158	839	59	10	46
批发和零售业 Wholesale and Retail Trade	1 622	3 322	2 817	13 746	1 067	354	799
住宿和餐饮业 Accommodation and Catering Services	236	356	170	734	168	24	70
金融业 Finance Intermediation	111	16	203	8	9	2	17
房地产业 Real Estate	250	151	645	896	91	80	83
租赁和商务服务业 Leasing and Business Services	801	659	775	2 513	428	52	162
科学研究、技术服务和地质勘查业 Scientific Research, Technical Services and Geological Prospecting	985	294	465	1 365	169	26	75
水利、环境和公共设施管理业 Management for Water Conservancy, Environment and Public Facilities	543	38	43	80	47	1	7
居民服务和其他服务业 Resident Services and Other Social Services	484	692	797	1 882	492	27	45
教育 Education	1 760	131	19	87	518	1	6
卫生、社会保障和社会福利业 Health Care, Social Security and Social Welfare	650	126	9	71	146	1	3
文化、体育和娱乐业 Culture, Sports and Recreational Services	456	58	42	156	78	6	12
公共管理和社会组织 Public Management and Social Organizations	2 200	33	10	3	5 975	0	2

全部企业主要经济指标
MAJOR INDICATORS OF ALL ENTERPRISES

单位:万元 (10000 yuan)

项　　目	Item	实收资本 Proceeds of Capital	主营业务收入 Revenue of Major Business
总　　计	**Total**	**47 573 355**	**121 479 680**
按注册登记类型分	**Grouped by Registered Type**		
国有企业	State - owned Enterprises	16 767 659	28 378 157
集体企业	Collective - owned Enterprises	1 804 370	5 874 734
股份制企业	Joint - stock Enterprises	10 696 097	31 835 389
私营企业	Private Enterprises	6 269 354	20 622 548
其他内资企业	Other Domestic - funded Enterprises	362 319	992 237
港澳台商投资企业	Enterprises with Investment from Hongkong, Macao and Taiwan	2 314 478	4 243 014
外商投资企业	Foreign Funded Enterprises	9 359 077	29 533 601
按行业分	**Grouped by Sector**		
采矿业	Minerals Mining	2 060 938	3 783 128
制造业	Manufacturing	16 840 689	54 453 598
电力、燃气及水的生产和供应业	Production and Supply of Electric Power, Gas and Water	1 468 776	2 888 171
建筑业	Construction	1 975 684	7 170 131
交通运输、仓储和邮政业	Transport, Storage, Post Services	4 882 172	5 055 005
信息传输、计算机服务和软件业	Information Transmitting, Computer Services and Software	555 369	1 015 678
批发和零售业	Wholesale and Retail Trade	4 642 652	36 364 942
住宿和餐饮业	Accommodation and Catering Services	442 780	553 975
金融业	Finance Intermediation	1 372 351	3 819 038
房地产业	Real Estate	3 620 929	3 789 733
租赁和商务服务业	Leasing and Business Services	6 902 709	793 646
科学研究、技术服务和地质勘查业	Scientific Research, Technical Services and Geological Prospecting	940 011	1 141 737
水利、环境和公共设施管理业	Management for Water Conservancy, Environment and Public Facilities	661 668	69 470
居民服务和其他服务业	Resident Services and Other Social Services	1 011 205	376 017
教　育	Education	13 368	17 977
卫生、社会保障和社会福利业	Health Care, Social Security and Social Welfare	15 664	6 437
文化、体育和娱乐业	Culture, Sports and Recreational Services	166 274	179 890
公共管理和社会组织	Public Management and Social Organizations	116	1 107

续表 Continued

单位:万元 (10 000 yuan)

项　　目	Item	利润总额 Total Profits	从业人员平均数(人) Average Persons Employed (persons)
总　　计	**Total**	**6 042 075**	**3 040 443**
按注册登记类型分	**Grouped by Registered Type**		
国有企业	State - owned Enterprises	603 489	624 682
集体企业	Collective - owned Enterprises	248 753	374 541
股份制企业	Joint - stock Enterprises	1 932 081	667 225
私营企业	Private Enterprises	585 940	762 035
其他内资企业	Other Domestic - funded Enterprises	23 688	57 612
港澳台商投资企业	Enterprises with Investment from Hongkong,Macao and Taiwan	267 649	115 169
外商投资企业	Foreign Funded Enterprises	2 380 476	439 179
按行业分	**Grouped by Sector**		
采矿业	Minerals Mining	988 767	68 822
制造业	Manufacturing	2 928 106	1 567 147
电力、燃气及水的生产和供应业	Production and Supply of Electric Power,Gas and Water	167 751	36 908
建筑业	Construction	142 395	453 991
交通运输、仓储和邮政业	Transport,Storage,Post Services	472 766	196 233
信息传输、计算机服务和软件业	Information Transmitting, Computer Services and Software	229 669	28 020
批发和零售业	Wholesale and Retail Trade	431 720	280 423
住宿和餐饮业	Accommodation and Catering Services	142	72 164
金融业	Finance Intermediation	208 229	39 566
房地产业	Real Estate	232 443	68 930
租赁和商务服务业	Leasing and Business Services	65 816	74 743
科学研究、技术服务和地质勘查业	Scientific Research,Technical Services and Geological Prospecting	135 408	70 338
水利、环境和公共设施管理业	Management for Water Conservancy, Environment and Public Facilities	8 897	6 986
居民服务和其他服务业	Resident Services and Other Social Services	27 484	60 844
教　育	Education	171	3 794
卫生、社会保障和社会福利业	Health Care,Social Security and Social Welfare	- 965	1 677
文化、体育和娱乐业	Culture, Sports and Recreational Services	3 134	9 798
公共管理和社会组织	Public Management and Social Organizations	142	59

企业采风

Brief Introduction of Enterprises

封二、封三 天津农垦集团总公司
TIANJIN FARMS AGRIBUSINESS GROUP INCORPORATION

1、天津港(集团)有限公司天津分公司
TIANJIN PORT(GROUP) CO.,LTD.

2、天津邮政
TIANJIN POST

3、中国网通(集团)有限公司天津市分公司
CNC TIANJIN COMPANY

4、中国联通天津分公司
CHINA UNICOM TIANJIN BRANCH

5、中国工商银行天津市分行
INDUSTRIAL & COMMERCIAL BANK OF CHINA TIANJIN MUNICIPAL BRANCH

6、中国建设银行天津市分行
CHINA CONSTRUCTION BANK TIANJIN MUNICIPAL BRANCH

7、中国人保财险天津市分公司
PICC PROPERTY AND CASUALTY COMPANY LIMITED TIANJIN BRANCH

8－9 天津钢管集团有限公司
TIANJIN PIPE GROUP CORPORATION LTD.

10、天津钢铁有限公司
TIANJIN IRON & STEEL CO.,LTD.

11、中国石化集团天津石油化工公司
SINOPEC GROUP TIANJIN PETROCHEMICAL CORPORATION

12、中国石油大港油田公司
PETROCHINA DAGANG OIL FIELD COMPANY

13、中国石油大港石化公司
PETROCHINA DAGANG PETROCHEMICAL CORPORATION

14、大港油田集团石油化工公司煅烧焦厂
DAGANG OILFIELD GROUP PETROCHEMICAL CORPORATION CALCINED PETROLEUM FACTORY

15、天津市建筑设计院
TIANJIN ARCHITECTURE DESIGN INSTITUTE

16、天津大学建筑学院
TIANJIN UNIVERSITY SCHOOL OF ARCHITECTURE

17、天津大学建筑设计规划研究总院
TIANJIN UNIVERSITY ACADEMY OF ARCHITECTURE DEVISE AND LAYOUT RESEARCH

18、天津大学管理学院
THE SCHOOL OF MANAGEMENT OF TIANJIN UNIVERSITY

19、天津科技大学
TIANJIN UNIVERSITY OF SCINENCE TECHNOLOGY

20、天津市四中心医院
TIANJIN FOURTH HOSPITAL

21、天津天士力制药股份有限公司
TASLY GROUP

22、津港评估
JINGANG PROPERTY CONSULTING AND APPRAISAL

23、天津泰达建设集团有限公司
TIANJIN TEDA CONSTRUCTION GROUP CO.,LTD.

24－25、天津城投集团
TIANJIN INFRASTRUCTURE INVESTMENT GROUP

26、天津住宅建设发展集团
TIANJIN RESIDENTIAL BUILDINGS CONSTRUCTION DEVELOPMENT GROUP

27、天津城建集团
TIANJIN URBAN CONSTRUCTION GROUP

28、天津第一市政公路工程有限公司
TIANJIN NO.1 MUNICIPAL HIGHWAY ENGINEERING CO., LTD.

29、天津第二市政公路工程有限公司
TIANJIN NO.2 MUNICIPAL HIGHWAY ENGINEERING CO., LTD.

30、天津第三市政公路工程有限公司
TIANJIN NO.3 MUNICIPAL HIGHWAY ENGINEERING CO., LTD.

31、天津第六市政建筑工程有限公司
TIANJIN NO.6 MUNICIPAL CONSTRUCTION CO., LTD.

32、天津市路桥建设工程有限公司
TIANJIN HIGHWAY & BRIDGE CONSTRUCTION ENGINEERING COMPANY LTD.

33、天津市津东房地产开发集团有限公司
TIANJIN JINDONG REAL ESTATE DEVELOPMENT GROUP CO., LTD.

34、天津市东达房地产开发有限公司
TIANJIN DONGDA REAL ESTATE DEVELOPMENT CO.,LTD.

35、天津市热力公司
TIANJIN HEAT—POWER COMPANY

36、天津送变电工程公司
TIANJIN POWER TRANSMISSION ENGINEERING CORPORATION

37、中航油津京管道运输中心
CHINA AVIATION OIL SUPPLY TSN—PEK PIPELINE TRANSPORTATION CENTER

38、天津一汽丰田发动机有限公司
TIANJIN FAW TOYOTA ENGINE CO., LTD.

39、津英纺纱有限公司
JINYING SPINNING CO.,LTD.

40、天津万华股份有限公司
TIANJIN WANHUA CO.,LTD.

41、天津市经纬电材有限公司
TIANJIN JINGWEI ELECTRIC WIRE CO.,LTD.

42、天津兴业置业集团
TIANJIN XINGYE PROPERTY GROUP

43、天津市王顶堤集团公司
TIANJIN WANGDINGDI GROUP CO.,LTD.

44－45、刘房子经济发展总公司
LIUFANGZI ECONOMY DEVELOPMENT GENERAL COMPANY

46、天津市西青区大寺镇人民政府
TIANJIN MUNICIPAL XIQING DISTRICT DASI TOWN PEOPLE'S GOVERNMENT

47、河兴庄农工商联合公司
HEXINGZHUANG AGRICULTURE INDUSTRY & COMMERCE GENERAL COMPANY

48、天津市侯台商贸集团有限公司
TIANJIN HOUTAI TRADE GROUP CO.,LTD.

中国统计出版社最新资料书简目

（仅供参考，以最后出书为准）

中国统计年鉴—2006
中国统计摘要—2006
2006 中国发展报告
中国城市统计年鉴—2005
中国劳动统计年鉴—2006
中国人口统计年鉴—2006
中国工业经济统计年鉴—2006
中国市场统计年鉴—2006
2005 中国经济景气年鉴
中国建筑业统计年鉴—2005
中国城市调查年鉴—2006
中国商品交易市场统计年鉴—2006
中国连锁餐饮企业统计年鉴—2005、2006
中国连锁零售业统计年鉴—2005、2006
中国能源统计年鉴—2004、2005
全国农产品成本收益资料汇编—2005
国际统计年鉴—2006
中国对外经济贸易统计年鉴—2005
中国基本单位统计年鉴—2005
中国民政统计年鉴—2006
中国高技术产业统计年鉴—2006
中国房地产行业名录
中国农村统计年鉴—2006
中国农村住户调查年鉴—2006(中文)
中国农村住户调查年鉴—2006(英文)
中国乡镇统计资料—2006
中国县(市)社会经济调查年鉴—2006
中国西部农村统计资料—2006
中国建制镇统计资料—2006
中国农产品价格调查年鉴—2006
中国国民经济核算年鉴—2006
中国经济普查年鉴—2004
中国棉花年鉴—2004、2005
中国百强县(市)发展年鉴—2006
中国教育经费统计年鉴—2005

北京统计年鉴—2006
天津统计年鉴—2006
河北经济年鉴—2006
山西统计年鉴—2006
内蒙古统计年鉴—2006
辽宁统计年鉴—2006
吉林统计年鉴—2006
黑龙江统计年鉴—2006
上海统计年鉴—2006
江苏统计年鉴—2006
浙江统计年鉴—2006
安徽统计年鉴—2006
福建统计年鉴—2006
江西统计年鉴—2006
山东统计年鉴—2006
河南统计年鉴—2006
湖北统计年鉴—2006
湖南统计年鉴—2006
广东统计年鉴—2006
广西统计年鉴—2006
海南统计年鉴—2006
重庆统计年鉴—2006
四川统计年鉴—2006
贵州统计年鉴—2006
云南统计年鉴—2006
西藏统计年鉴—2006
陕西统计年鉴—2006
甘肃年鉴—2006
青海统计年鉴—2006
宁夏统计年鉴—2006
新疆统计年鉴—2006
新疆生产建设兵团统计年鉴—2006
石家庄统计年鉴—2006
唐山统计年鉴—2006
邯郸统计年鉴—2006
张家口统计年鉴—2006
朔洲统计年鉴—2006
呼和浩特经济统计年鉴—2006
鄂尔多斯市统计年鉴—2006
包头统计年鉴—2006
沈阳年鉴—2006
大连统计年鉴—2006
鞍山统计年鉴—2006
长春统计年鉴—2006
吉林市社会经济统计年鉴—2006
四平统计年鉴—2006
延吉统计年鉴—2006
哈尔滨统计年鉴—2006
齐齐哈尔经济统计年鉴—2006
黑龙江垦区统计年鉴—2006
上海浦东新区统计年鉴—2006
南京统计年鉴—2006
苏州统计年鉴—2006
无锡统计年鉴—2006
常州统计年鉴—2006
徐州统计年鉴—2006
南通统计年鉴—2006
盐城统计年鉴—2006
镇江统计年鉴—2006
江阴统计年鉴—2006
杭州统计年鉴—2006
宁波统计年鉴—2006
绍兴统计年鉴—2006
台州统计年鉴—2006
舟山统计年鉴—2006
温州统计年鉴—2006
金华统计年鉴—2006
嘉兴统计年鉴—2006
湖洲统计年鉴—2006
安庆经济统计年鉴—2006
福州统计年鉴—2006
福州年鉴—2006
厦门经济特区年鉴—2006
福州经济技术开发区年鉴—2006
南昌经济社会统计年鉴—2006
上饶经济社会统计年鉴—2006
九江经济统计年鉴—2006
济南统计年鉴—2006
青岛统计年鉴—2006
潍坊统计年鉴—2006
淄博统计年鉴—2006
郑州统计年鉴—2006
洛阳统计年鉴—2006
三门峡统计年鉴—2006
南阳经济统计年鉴—2006
武汉统计年鉴—2006
宜昌统计年鉴—2006
十堰统计年鉴—2006
荆州统计年鉴—2006
长沙统计年鉴—2006
广州统计年鉴—2006
东莞统计年鉴—2006
惠州统计年鉴—2006
深圳统计年鉴—2006
南宁统计年鉴—2006
桂林经济社会统计年鉴—2006
柳州经济统计年鉴—2006
来宾统计年鉴—2006
河池地区经济社会统计年鉴—2006
海口统计年鉴—2006
成都统计年鉴—2006
贵阳统计年鉴—2006
昆明统计年鉴—2006
西安统计年鉴—2006
兰州年鉴—2006
西宁统计年鉴—2006
银川统计年鉴—2006
乌鲁木齐统计年鉴—2006
吐鲁番统计年鉴—2006

欲购以上图书请与中国统计出版社发行部联系。
编辑部电话：(010)63376907，63376908　同榻行书店电话：68783171，68783172
通讯地址：北京西城区三里河月坛南街75号　邮政编码：100826

(京)新登字 041 号

图书在版编目(CIP)数据

天津统计年鉴. 2006/天津市统计局编.
—北京: 中国统计出版社,2006.6
ISBN 7-5037-4877-X

Ⅰ.天…
Ⅱ.天…
Ⅲ.统计资料-天津市-2006-年鉴
Ⅳ.C832.21-54

中国版本图书馆 CIP 数据核字(2006)第 026088 号

天津统计年鉴—2006

作　　者/天津市统计局
责任编辑/蔡启新　叶礼奇
E-mail/yearbook@stats.gov.cn
责任校对/李立新　戴　华
封面设计/天津市河图广告传播有限公司
出版发行/中国统计出版社
通信地址/北京市西城区三里河月坛南街 75 号　中国统计出版社
邮　　编/100826
电　　话/(010)63376907
印　　刷/国家海洋信息中心印刷厂
经　　销/新华书店
开　　本/890×1240 毫米　1/16
字　　数/110 万字
印　　张/40.125 印张
印　　数/1-5000 册
版　　别/2006 年 8 月第 1 版
版　　次/2006 年 8 月第 1 次印刷
书　　号/ISBN 7-5037-4877-X/F·2224
定　　价/280.00 元(含光盘)

中国统计版图书,版权所有,侵权必究。
中国统计版图书,如有印装错误,本社发行部负责调换。
本书附同版本 CD-ROM 一张,光盘内容以书面文字为准。

天津港(集团)有限公司

Tianjin Port (Group) Co., Ltd.

董事长：王恩德

总裁：于汝民

天津港的历史可追溯到汉代，自唐代以来形成海港，1860年正式对外开埠。塘沽新港始建于1939年，建国后经过3年恢复性建设，于1952年10月17日重新开港。

天津港是中国最大的人工港。港区现有水陆域面积近200平方公里，陆域面积37平方公里，规划陆域面积80平方公里。天津港主航道35公里，航道底宽260米，水深15米，10万吨级船舶可全天候进出港，15万吨级船舶可乘潮进出港。天津港共拥有各类泊位140余个，其中万吨级以上泊位55个；天津港集团拥有各类泊位74个，万吨级以上泊位52个，泊位岸线总长1.5万米，泊位年设计通过能力1.5亿吨，其中集装箱设计通过能力355万TEU。

到2010年，港口货物吞吐量达到3亿吨，集装箱吞吐量达到1000万TEU，港口等级达到25万吨级。努力把天津港建设成为面向东北亚、辐射中西亚的集装箱枢纽港、中国北方最大的散货主干港、环渤海地区规模最大的综合性港口，力争成为世界一流大港。

The history of Tianjin Port can be traced back to Han Dynasty. Since Tang Dynasty, a harbor has been established here. In 1860, the port was open to other places formally. The construction of Tanggu new port started in 1939. Through 3 year resumptive construction after the founding of the People's Republic of China, the port was put into operation again on October 17, 1952.

Tianjin Port is the biggest artificial port in China. Within the port region, the water area and land area is nearly 200 square kilometers in total, of which land area is 37 square kilometers, layout area of the port region is 80 square kilometers. The main navigation channel of Tianjin Port is 35 kilometers in length, 260 meters in width of navigation channel bottom, 15 meters in water depth. 100,000-tonnage vessel can enter and exit the port at any time and 150,000-tonnage vessel can do it when there is tide. There are various berths totaling more than 140, including 74 berths of its own port, 55 berths with every throughput over 10,000 tons, including 52 berths of its ownport. The total length of the berth shoreline is 15,000 meters. The berth capacity is 150 million tons, of which the container capacity is 3.55 million TEU.

In 2010, the cargo throughput of Tianjin Port will be 300 million tons, container throughout will account for 10 million TEU and port level will reach 250,000-tonnage. Efforts will be made to become a container pivotal port facing Northeast Asia and radiating Middle West Asia, the biggest key port of bulk cargo in North China, the greatest comprehensive port in Bohai Sea region as well as the first-rate major port in the world.

地址：天津塘沽新港二号路35号 Add: No. 35, No. 2 Road Xin'gang, Tanggu District, Tianjin
邮政编码 Postal Code: 300456 电话 Tel: +86 22 25707550 25792985 传真 Fax: +86 22 25702080 http://www.portoftianjin.com

天津邮政
TIANJIN POST

特快专递

次晨达业务

邮政EMS在环渤海区域、长江三角洲、珠江三角洲共27个城市间开办的限时专递业务。贵公司在当日交寄的EMS邮件（长江三角洲，珠江三角洲上午11:00前，环渤海当日营业截止时间前），我们保证在次日上午10:00前（珠江三角洲11:00前）投交收件人。

EMS代收货款业务

一项邮政速递延伸服务，作为集运递、投送、收款及结算为一体的综合服务平台，非常适用于电子类、医药类等行业客户。

邮政金融

值得信赖的零售金融专家——邮政金融，天津市邮政储汇局负责全市邮政储蓄，国际、国内汇款及代理保险、国债和基金等各类中间业务的经营和管理工作。

邮政绿卡（储蓄卡）

邮政部门提供的一项多功能电子理财工具，适用于贵公司向员工发放薪酬。既可在本市和全国其他城市的银联ATM上取款，具有缴话费等多种功能，又可以在包括港澳地区在内的全国各地银联商户刷卡消费，并且即将在韩国、新加坡和泰国任一贴有“银联”标志的ATM上取款和刷卡消费。

目前，仅天津的银联特约商户已达7000余家。

西联汇款

中国邮政与美国西方联合金融服务有限公司合作开办的一项国际个人汇款业务，通达近200个国家和地区。

西联汇款短短几分钟便可到达。收款人凭密码取款，无需另开帐户，全球通取。

邮政11185客户服务中心

天津邮政11185客户服务中心是多功能的计算机电话集成语音信息服务平台。该平台连接邮政综合计算机网、金融网、实物网以及铁路、民航、商旅、社区等信息系统，向社会提供24小时全天候服务。

足不出户，尽享邮政服务

地址：天津市和平区花园路4号
Add: No. 4 Huayuan Road, Heping District, Tianjin
邮政编码 Postal Code: 300041
电话 Tel: +86 22 27121000
传真 Fax: +86 22 27121020

北京2008年奥运会合作伙伴
OFFICIAL PARTNER OF THE BEIJING 2008 OLYMPIC GAMES

中国网通（集团）有限公司 天津市分公司

CNC Tianjin Company

张立昌、戴相龙等市领导在天津网通霍海峰总经理的陪同下，参观天津网通设在PTC博览会上的展台

2004年，天津网通作为惟一一家通信企业率先入围全国质量管理奖入强行列

天津网通网管中心机房

在2004年PTC博览会上，天津网通向客户演示多媒体公话业务

中国网通（集团）有限公司天津市分公司（以下简称“天津网通”）是中国网通旗下分公司，是北京2008年奥运会固定通信服务合作伙伴，是天津地区规模占主导地位的电信运营商。

天津网通为客户提供固定电话、小灵通、宽带业务，近期还包装推出了IDC、小灵通机卡分离、固网预付费、“Q-BOX”、“宽带商务”等业务。目前，天津网通拥有500万客户。

天津网通将向广大客户提供更为标准化、亲情化、差异化的服务，为提高天津的信息化水平做出贡献，引领全市人民早日进入数字新时代、畅享数字新生活。

CNC Tianjin Company is subordinated to China Network Communications Corporation. It is a predominate telecommunications operator in Tianjin and the fixed telecommunications service partner for the 2008 Olympic Games.

Our businesses include fixed telecommunications, PHS and broadband network services. Currently, CNC has developed services such as IDC, Q-BOX, fixed network advance and broadband-business. At present, the number of our telephone users hit the mark of 5 million.

Striving to contribute to the information level in Tianjin, CNC is dedicated to more and more standardized, considerate services for our clients, so as to lead the whole municipalities into the great new era of digit.

天津网通网管中心大厦

地址：天津市和平区新兴路27号
Add: No. 27 Xinxing Road, Heping District, Tianjin
邮政编码 Postal Code: 300052
业务咨询电话 Tel-service: 10060
对外电话 Tel: +86 22 27830083
传真 Fax: +86 22 27839927
http://www.tjnetcom.com
http://www.online.tj.cn http://www.cncmax.tj.cn

China unicom 中国联通

CDMA无线上网卡

无线上网如宽带

无限速度 无线自由

随时随地高速上网 本地价格全国畅游

CDMA无线上网卡资费套餐

上网卡基础套餐	月基本费（元）	赠送时长（小时）可用于本地及国内漫游上网	超出套餐所含上网时长部分(元/分钟)
上网卡50	50	20 小时	0.10
上网卡100	100	60 小时	
上网卡200	200	200小时	
上网卡300	300	不限时	
CDMA无线上网卡具备通话功能，如果您使用CDMA无线上网卡打电话，本地通话：双向0.10元/分钟，漫游：0.60元/分钟。			

提示：以上套餐中只包含CDMA无线上网卡的上网费，不包含短信、用户订制等其他费用。

世界风 如意通 新势力

客户服务热线10010 话费查询专线10011
WWW.tj10010.com 中国联通天津分公司

中国工商银行 天津市分行

INDUSTRIAL AND COMMERCIAL BANK OF CHINA TIANJIN MUNICIPAL BRANCH

让财富与您更近
让服务与您更近

工商银行天津市分行作为中国资产规模最大的商业银行——工商银行在天津的一级分支机构，通过多年的不懈努力，积淀了良好的品牌形象，赢得了广大客户的普遍认可。截至2005年末，工商银行天津市分行总资产1211亿元，员工8000余人，开办有资产业务27个品种，负债业务24个品种，中间业务品种多达 227 项。并拥有丰富的客户资源、遍布全市的营业网点、先进的电子网络设备、完备的清算系统和畅通的汇路，在天津金融同业中占据着举足轻重的地位。

随着工商银行股份制改革的顺利推进，工商银行天津市分行将继续秉承崇尚信誉、追求卓越的经营理念，努力建设成资产质量好、服务水平高、具有较高公司市值的国际一流商业银行分行，更好地为广大客户提供全方位的金融服务！

工商银行天津市分行在本市同业首家实现各项存款突破1000亿元

ICBC Tianjin Municipal Branch is subordinated to Industrial and Commercial Bank of China (ICBC) which ranks first in the industry at home for many indexes such as total assets, total capital. After years of development, ICBC Tianjin Municipal Branch has established good reputation and widely wined trusts from our clients. At the end of 2005, the general assets reached 121.1 billion yuan, the staff amounted to 8,000, and the bank operated 27 capital businesses, 24 debt businesses and 227 intermediary businesses. With abundant resources of clients, advanced equipments of electronic network and a complete system of liquidation, ICBC Tianjin Municipal Branch holds an influential status in Tianjin finance.

As the program for stock system reform of ICBC progresses smoothly, ICBC Tianjin Municipal Branch will adhere to the faith of credit and excellence, dedicate ourselves to constructing a top-ranking international commercial bank with high-quality capitals, high-level services and high market value, and a bank which sincerely offers our clients with comprehensive and considerate services.

工商银行天津市分行与国内首家获政府批准的非银行性质的外资专业保理商——天津瀛寰东润国际保理有限公司签署合作协议

地址：天津市河西区围堤道123号
Add: No. 123 Weidi Road, Hexi District, Tianjin
邮政编码 Postal Code: 300074
电话 Tel: 95588
http://www.icbc.com.cn

中国建设银行 天津市分行
China Construction Bank Tianjin Municipal Branch

建设银行大楼

办公楼正门

营业厅

地址：天津市河西区南京路19号增1号
Add: Added No.1, No.19 Nanjing Road, Hexi District, Tianjin
邮政编码 Postal Code: 300203
电话 Tel: +86 22 23401616
传真 Fax: +86 22 23400520
http://www.ccb-tj.com

中国建设银行是一家具有五十多年历史的，以中长期信用为主要特色、资金实力雄厚、服务功能齐全的现代化商业银行。在英国《银行家》杂志“2005年全球最佳银行”评选中，中国建设银行荣获2005年“中国最佳银行”称号，是本年度中国银行业中惟一获此殊荣的银行。2005年10月27日，中国建设银行股份有限公司在香港联合交易所成功挂牌上市，建设银行成为中国四大国有商业银行中首家在海外公开上市的银行，实现了国有独资商业银行改革新的突破，并在国际化的道路上迈出了重要的一步。

中国建设银行天津市分行成立于1954年10月1日，是建设银行所属一级分行。50多年来，在积极服务天津市地方经济建设的同时，业务规模和经营效益成倍增长，并形成了独具特色的企业文化、品牌形象，积累了丰富的管理经验，培育了超前的服务理念，造就了专业的人才队伍，在中长期信贷、住房金融、审价咨询等业务领域具有市场领先地位。

随着中国建设银行成功实现股改上市，天津市分行正在按照股份制商业银行的全新要求，以富于创新的思路、百折不挠的勇气和奋力开拓的锐气，向着“专注为客户提供最佳服务，为股东创造最大价值，为员工提供最好发展机会的国际一流商业银行”的目标奋进！

China Construction Bank (CCB), which has a history of more than fifty years and fea-tures medium-term and long-term lending, is a modern commercial bank with a solid capital and complete service function. The magazine, *Banker* in Britain ranked China Construction Bank as "Best Bank in China" in "World Top Banks 2005" selection activity. In 27th Oct. 2005, China Construction Bank Corporation successfully came into the stock market in Hong Kong Stock Exchange. CBC became the first bank of China's four state-owned commercial banks that came into the market overseas. This marked a great breakthrough in the reform of state-owned commercial banks, and also a significant step that CBC went towards internationalization.

Found in 1st Oct. 1954, CBC Tianjin Branch is a branch bank directly under CBC. During the past 50 years, CBC Tianjin Branch actively serves for economic construction of Tianjin. Along with its business scale and benefits greatly increasing, CBC Tianjin Branch has accumulated abundant manage experiences and formed a unique enterprise culture and an eminent brand. With an advanced service notion and professional personnel, CBC Tianjin Branch dominates in a lot of businesses in the market, such as mediumterm and long-term credits, housing finance and price consultation.

As CBC has successfully come into the stock market, Tianjin Branch is making great effort to acclimatize itself to bran-new request of the stock commercial bank. We will work innovatively, unremittingly, and courageously to construct an international top-ranking commercial bank which is dedicated to providing the best service to clients, to creating maximal dividend for shareholders, and to offering the most advantageous developing opportunities for CBC personnel.

中国人保财险天津市分公司

PICC Property and Casualty Company Limited Tianjin Branch

崔津渡副市长来公司视察工作并听取马炳超总经理的工作汇报

中国人保财险天津市分公司是中国人民财产保险股份有限公司下属机构，在天津下设20个支公司，拥有员工八百多人，代理网点覆盖全市，占天津财险市场的主导地位。目前天津市及滨海新区许多国家重点工程、重大项目、大中型企业，以及世界500强在津投资的100多家企业中的大部分选择了在我公司投保，这些充分显示了人保财险公司的雄厚实力。

2003年7月，人保天津市分公司重组改制为人保财险天津市分公司，继续坚持“求实、诚信、拼搏、创新”的人保精神，“以市场为导向、以客户为中心”的经营理念，积极营造“和谐有序，团结进取”的企业文化氛围，坚持科学发展观，励精图治，开拓创新，团结奋进，铸就辉煌。“十一五”期间公司将向国内领先、国际一流的知识型、现代化非寿险公众公司的战略目标迈进。

地址：天津市河东区十一经路61号

Add: No. 61 Shiyijing Road, Hedong District, Tianjin

邮政编码 Postal Code: 300171

电话 Tel: +86 22 24148888

传真 Fax: +86 22 24311360

人保财险励精图治，再创辉煌誓师大会

PICC Property and Casualty Company Limited Tianjin Branch is a subordinated to PICC Property and Casualty Company Limited. It has 20 local subsidiaries, more than 800 staff and a lot of agent outlets in Tianjin. It is the leading insurer in Tianjin property and casualty insurance market. In present, many key projects, large-sized and middle-sized enterprises, more than 100 enterprises in Tianjin whose investors are the top 500 enterprises in the world choose PICC P&C, these show its strong strengths.

PICC Tianjin Branch was renewed and re-registered as Property and Casualty Company Limited Tianjin Branch on July 2003. It adheres to the enterprise spirit of “Pragmatism, Integrity, Devotion and Innovation”, conforms to the market-oriented and customer-centered approach in its operations, actively builds the enterprise culture of “harmonious operation, working in order, unity and make progress”. The company implements the view of scientific development and has made great achievement. During the “11th five-year plan”, it will continue on the path of becoming a domestic leader, first class international knowledge-based, modernized non-life insurance public company.

矗立在本市河东区十一经路与八纬路交口处的人保大厦

党委书记、董事长：孙宁豫

十六大代表、总经理：刘云生

天津钢管集团有限公司是中国目前最大的石油套管生产基地，拥有世界先进的生产技术和装备。公司已通过了美国API石油学会认证、ISO9001质量体系标准认证、ISO14001环境管理体系认证、OHSAS18001职业安全健康管理体系认证，同时还先后通过了17个国家和壳牌、美孚等48家国际大石油公司的认证。目前，石油管材国内市场占有率达到50%，产品出口到70多个国家和地区。

集团公司建有国家级技术中心和先进的钢管实验生产线，研制生产了抗腐蚀、热采井、高抗挤毁、特殊扣等一批高技术含量、高附加值新品，形成了具有自主知识产权的TP产品系列，其中50余项科研成果填补了国内空白。石油套管成为“中国名牌产品”，无缝钢管成为“中国名牌出口商品”。公司除生产无缝钢管以外，还生产石油钻杆、彩涂钢板、不锈钢薄板、铜线材、不锈钢管以及高压气瓶产品。公司还拥有华北地区最大的大型冶金机电设备制造企业，可以设计、制造各种大型工业炉、各类水电、风电、发电和港口机械等设备。

天津钢管集团有限公司先后获得了“国家质量管理卓越企业”、“第九届国家级企业管理现代化创新成果一等奖”、全国“五一”劳动奖状等荣誉，企业跻身中国企业500强、中国制造业500强和进出口企业500强。

地址: 天津市东丽区津塘公路396号
Add: No. 396 Jintang Highway, Dongli District, Tianjin
邮政编码 Postal Code: 300301
电话 Tel: +86 22 24802625
传真 Fax: +86 22 24360649
http://www.tpco.com.cn

石油套管

168厂生产线

套管生产线

天津钢管集团有限公司

Tianjin Pipe Group Corporation Ltd.

Tianjin Pipe (Group) Corporation (TPCO) is the largest OCTG production base in China and possesses international advanced production technology and equipment. It has passed the certification of API Petroleum Institute, the certification of ISO9001, ISO14001 environmental management system and the certification of OHSAS18001 profession safety management system. It also has passed the certification of 17 countries and 48 international petroleum corporations. In present, petroleum pipe occupies 50 percent of domestic market, its products exports to more than 70 countries and regions.

TPCO has built technology center of national level and advanced production line of steel pipe. It can produce a series of hi-tech new products, has formed the TP series products with autonomic intellectual property, of which, more than 50 scientific research results fill in the gaps of domestic related fields. Petroleum pipe become china famous product and seamless steel pipe become china famous export commodity. The corporation also produces steel plate, copper cash, high-pressure gas bottle and so on. It also has the largest metallurgical machinery & electric equipment enterprise in North China, which can produce large-sized equipment.

TPCO was awarded "national excellent enterprise on quality management", first class national innovation award of 9th enterprise management modernization, and the national labor prize. It listed top 500 national enterprises, top 500 national manufacturers and top 500 imp. & exp. enterprises.

天津钢铁有限公司
Tianjin Iron & Steel Co., Ltd.

天钢是集烧结、炼铁、炼钢、连铸、轧钢生产工艺为一体的国有大型钢铁企业。列2005年中国企业500强第251名，2005年中国制造业企业500强第127名。

2005年实现销售收入118.79亿元，同比增长15.35%，其中主业销售收入116.98亿元，同比增长15.68%。目前，天津市投资规模最大的工业项目，被市确定为工业战略东移新一轮嫁改调标志性重大项目——天钢东移工程已全面建成投产，天钢已形成了年产铁400万吨，钢400万吨，材600万吨的生产能力。主要产品：连铸方坯、连铸圆管坯、连铸板坯、无扭控冷热轧盘条、中厚板、棒材、热轧带钢、炼钢和铸造用生铁。其中，34Mn5、37Mn5石油套管用钢质量达到国际先进水平。低碳钢热轧圆盘条、钢筋混凝土热轧带肋钢筋、碳素结构钢和低合金结构钢热轧厚钢板及钢带荣获全国冶金产品实物质量金杯奖，造船板获劳埃德船级社认证。

Tianjin Iron & Steel Co., Ltd. is a large-sized united enterprise in iron refining, steel refining, steel rolling and so on. It listed No. 251 of top 500 national enterprises and No. 127 of national manufacturers in 2005.

In 2005, the sales income totaled 11.879 billion yuan, up 15.35%, of which, the sales income of main business totaled 11.698 billion yuan, up 15.68%. Being the largest industrial project, the eastward moving of Tianjin Iron & Steel Co., Ltd. has put into use. Its production capacities include: 4 million tons/year of iron, 4 million tons/year of steel, 6 million tons/year of materials. The product include: semifinished products, steel plate, belt steel, pig iron and so on. In which, 34 Mn5 and 37 Mn5 steel for oil pipe reach international advanced level. Some products were awarded golden cup prize. Shipbuilding steel plate passed the certificate of Lloyds.

地址：天津市东丽区津塘公路398号
Add: No. 398 Jintang Highway, Dongli District, Tianjin
邮政编码 Postal Code: 300301
电话 Tel: +86 22 84366800
传真 Fax: +86 22 84366820

双高炉外景

3座120T转炉

中厚板生产线

棒材生产线

高速线材

中国石化集团天津石油化工公司

SINOPEC Group Tianjin Petrochemical Corporation

中国石化股份有限公司天津分公司和中国石化集团天津石油化工公司（合称天津石化）是隶属于中国石化的国家特大型炼油、乙烯、化工、化纤联合企业，成立于1983年12月28日，位于天津市大港区北围堤路（西）160号，东临渤海油田，南靠大港油田，占地面积13.24平方公里，与天津市区和塘沽新港有铁路、公路相通，与大港油田和天津港南疆石化码头有输油管线相连，地理位置优越，海陆运输方便。天津石化总资产为135.08亿元，拥有炼油装置13套，化工装置11套，化纤装置5套；原油加工能力500万吨/年，生产能力为乙烯20万吨/年、对二甲苯 38万吨/年、PTA 30万吨/年、聚酯27万吨/年、涤纶短纤维16万吨/年、涤纶长丝9万吨/年、聚醚7万吨/年；原油储存能力64万立方米，在天津港石化码头建有原油、成品油库区和接卸设施。

天津石化各级领导班子率全体员工始终将企业的安全环境与健康工作当作头等大事来抓，坚定不移地贯彻执行“安全第一、预防为主”的安全生产方针，积极推行HSE管理体系，四年以来，始终保持“四个重大事故”为零的好成绩。同时，在公司科技人员的努力下，不断有炼油、化纤的新品和专利问世。天津石化将继续以优质的产品、先进的技术、严细的管理和良好的服务为中国石化事业的发展和全球经济的繁荣做出应有的贡献。

China Petrochemical Co., Ltd. Tianjin filiale and Sinopec Group Tianjin Petrochemical Corporation, all subordinated to Sinopec Corporation and together called as Tianjin Petrochemical, is a national super-sized united enterprise in oil refining, ethane, chemical industry, and chemical fiber. Established in 28th Dec. 1983, Tianjin Petrochemical is located at No. 160 North Weidi Road in Dagang District. With Bohai Oil Field to its east and Dagang Oil Field to its south, the enterprise covers an area of 13.24 sq. km. There are convenient traffic lines including railways and highways linking the corporation with Tianjin downtown and Tanggu New Port; and there are also oil pipes linking it with Dagang Oil Field and Nanjiang Petrochemical Dock of Tianjin Port. With 13 sets of oil refining equipments, 11 sets of chemical plant equipments, and 5 sets of chemical fiber equipments, the total assets of the corporation amounts to 13.508 billion yuan. Tianjin Petrochemical's capacities include: 5 million tons/year of crude oil refining, 200,000 tons/year of ethane, 380,000 tons/year of toluene, 300,000 tons/year of PTA, 270,000 tons/year of polyester, 160,000 tons/year of terylene staple fiber, 90,000 tons/year of terylene thread, and 70,000 tons/year of polyaether. The corporation also has established oil storage area and corresponding facilities at Tianjin Port petrochemical dock and crude oil reserve capacity reaches 640,000 steres.

Under the guidance of the leadership of all levels, the whole staffs of Tianjin Petrochemical always hold the environment security and working healthiness with top-importance. Thanks to our unwavering adherence of “security the first, preventiveness the basic” guideline and positive execution of HSE management, no serious accidents have happened for four years in the corporation. At the same time, due to the efforts of company's scientific researchers, there are always new products being produced and patent being applied. With high-quality productions, advanced technology, strict management and favorable services, Tianjin Petrochemical will continually contribute to China's petrochemical industry and the prosperity of global economy.

炼油晨曦

乙烯厂全景

加氢裂化装置

地址: 天津市大港区北围堤路(西)160号
Add: No.160 North Weidi Road, Dagang District, Tianjin
邮编 Postal Coad: 300271
电话 Tel: +86 22 63804611
传真 Fax: +86 22 25990747

中国石油大港油田公司

PetroChina Dagang Oilfield Company

总经理 姚和清

大港油田公司是中国石油天然气股份公司下属的一个从事石油天然气勘探、开发的特大型石油企业，总部位于天津市东南60公里的渤海之滨，距天津国际机场70公里，距天津新港40公里，陆海空交通发达、便捷，地理环境优越。

大港油田公司东临渤海，西接冀中平原，东南与山东毗邻，北至津唐交界处，地跨津、冀、鲁25个区、市、县，勘探开发总面积18176平方千米。截止2005年底，大港油田已累积生产原油1.31亿吨，生产天然气157.5亿立方米。其中2005年生产原油510万吨、天然气3.3亿立方米。

目前，大港油田公司拥有资产总额130多亿元，有下属单位26个，在职员工12000余人。有专业技术人员4607人，硕士研究生以上学历86人，其中在职博士生35人。

进入新的世纪，大港油田公司将大力实施可持续发展战略、低成本战略、管理创新战略、科技领先战略、人才超前战略，立足陆上、推进滩海、加快合作、开拓新区，保持油气储量稳定增长。按照规划，大港油田从2004年开始，原油产量规模将保持450万吨并稳产10年，天然气产量保持3亿立方米以上。

PetroChina Dagang Oilfield Company is a large-sized enterprise, which is subordinated to PetroChina Company Limited, engaging in exploration, development and production of crude oil and natural gas, the head office lies on the seaside of Bohai 60 kilometers away from southeast Tianjin, 70 kilometers away from Tianjin International Airport, and 40 kilometers away from Tianjin Port. The transportation linked with railway, airway, highway and the waterway is very convenient.

Dagang Oilfield Company is situated at Dagang, with Bohai sea on the east, Jizhong plain on the west, Shandong province on the southeast, and border of Tianjin and Tangshan on the north, its extraction field covers 25 regions, cities and counties of Tianjin municipal, Hebei province and Shandong province with total areas of 18,176 square kilometers. By the end of 2005, it has produced crude oil of 0.131 billion tons and natural gas 15.75 billion tons. In 2005, the production of crude oil is 5.10 million tons, and natural gas is 0.33 billion tons.

At present, the total asset of Dagang Oilfield Company has reached more than 13 billion. There are 26 subcompanies, 12,000 working staff, 4,607 technical personnel, and 86 with master's degree, including 35 doctor's degree.

Entering into the new century, Dagang Oilfield Company continue to stick to the sustainable development strategy, low cost strategy, management innovation strategy, science leading strategy and talent advanced strategy, standing both on land and sea, cooperating with others and developing new areas, keeping the steady increase of the petroleum and natural gas reserves. According to the plan, since 2004, the output of the crude oil has kept to 4.5 million tons per year, and will last for 10 years, the output of the natural gas keeps to more than 0.3 billion tons.

地址: 天津市大港区三号院
Add: The Third Yard, Dagang District, Tianjin
邮政编码 Postal Code: 300280
电话 Tel: +86 22 25971708
传真 Fax: +86 22 25915115

中国石油大港石化公司

Petrochina Dagang Petrochemical Corporation

党委书记、总经理：庞晓东

中国石油大港石化公司位于天津市滨海新区，毗邻天津港、黄骅港、京唐港和曹妃甸港，地理环境优越，海、陆、空交通发达、便捷，具有得天独厚的区域、资源和市场优势，发展前景广阔。

公司现有员工2200余人，平均年龄37岁，具有高级职称85人，中级职称287人，大专以上学历871人。公司自1965年建厂，发展至今，目前原油年加工能力500万吨，拥有燃料油和润滑油两套生产线，固定资产原值达29.50亿元，净值17.68亿元。主要生产汽油、柴油、液化气、石油焦、丙烯、MTBE、燃料油、沥青、润滑油等产品，年销售收入超过百亿元。

面对党的十六届五中全会发展滨海新区给大港石化公司带来的发展机遇，大港石化公司认真落实科学发展观，大力实施可持续发展战略，坚持以人为本，内强素质，外塑形象，做精做细，做好做强，努力把大港石化公司建设成为渤海之滨的炼化明珠。

Petrochina Dagang Petrochemical Corporation is situated in Binhai New Area, among which there are Tianjin Port, Huanghua Port, Jingtang Port and Caofeidian Port. With an advantageous geographical position, convenient transportations and market predominance, we are definitely confident of future development.

Currently, there are 2,200 employees with an average age of 37 in our corporation, among which there are 85 persons with senior titles and 287 persons with middle titles. 871 of our employees have received high education. After 40 years of development since its formal establishment in 1965, the corporation has now two product-lines of fuel oil and lubricant oil, and can process 5 million tons of crude oil annually. The fixed capital of the enterprise amounts to 2.95 billion yuan and the net value is 1.768 billion yuan. Our products include gasoline, diesel oil, LPG, propylene, MTBE, fuel oil, asphalt and lubricant. Our annual sales revenue has now exceeded 10 billion yuan.

The resolution to develop Tianjin Binhai New Area passed in the fifth session of CPC National Congress as well brings great opportunities to the development of Dagang Petrochemical Corporation. Adhering to the strategy of sustainable development and the principle of people first, we will always earnestly carry out the concept of scientific development to enhance our quality and influence and assiduously, construct the corporation to be better and better.

地址: 天津市大港区三号院花园路东口
Add: The East Joint of Huayuan Road, The Third Yard, Dagang District, Tianjin
邮政编码 Postal Code: 300280
电话 Tel: +86 22 25921144

年产500万吨大港石化厂区现代化装置林立

大港油田集团石油化工公司煅烧焦厂

Dagang Oilfield Group Petrochemical Corporation Calcined Petroleum Factory

大港油田集团石油化工公司煅烧焦厂是中国石油大港油田集团有限责任公司所辖的专业生产和经营煅烧石油焦的国有生产企业。煅烧焦厂成立于2005年，位于天津市大港区，毗邻津京两大城市，交通便利。企业现主导产品为煅烧石油焦，采用回转窑煅烧方式，生产规模为20万吨/年。原料主要来自中国石油大港石化分公司100万吨/年延迟焦化装置的低硫、低灰份优质石油焦。

我厂生产设施配套，工艺先进、检测手段可靠、管理严谨。生产的产品质量稳定，各项指标均达到企业标准，属高品质低硫、低灰份煅烧焦，深受用户欢迎。产品主要用于生产铝厂用的预焙阳极和炭糊制品以及供钢铁厂使用的石墨电极、增碳剂等。

Dagang Oilfield Group Petrochemical Corporation Calcined Petroleum Factory is subordinated to Dagang Oilfield Group Co., Ltd. (DOGC), is a state-owned enterprise which produces and sells calcined petroleum. It established in 2005. It possesses convenient traffic, locates on Dagang District and near to Tianjin and Beijing, Its main product is calcined petroleum, it capacities reach 200,000 tons annually. Its raw materials come from Petrochina Dagang Petrochemical Corporation.

The factory is equipped with advanced technology, reliable test method and strict management. The products are welcomed because of stable quality and high-grade standard. Its products are mainly used by aluminium factories and steel factories.

低硫、低灰份石油焦

人工成型低硫煅后焦

煅后焦高纯粉末

地址: 天津市大港油田三号院
Add: The Third Yard, Dagang District, Tianjin
邮政编码 Postal Code: 300280
电话 Tel: +86 22 25969678
传真 Fax: +86 22 25969678

天津市建筑设计院

Tianjin Architecture Design Institute

天津市建筑设计院（简称 TADI）创立于 1952 年，是本市最大的综合建筑设计单位。现有员工近千人，其中全国工程设计大师 3 人，国务院批准享受政府特殊津贴专家 15 人，国家人事部批准有突出贡献的中青年专家 2 人，天津市中青年授衔专家 4 人，正高级建筑（工程）师 40 人，并有国家一级注册建筑师 63 人，国家一级注册结构工程师 74 人，国家级注册监理工程师 25 人，造价工程师 14 人。

TADI 具有多项国家建设部颁发的甲、乙级设计资质证书，主要承接民用建筑设计、工业建筑设计、城市规划及居住区、住宅小区规划设计、工程咨询、工程监理、工程项目总承包以及技术合作、技术成果转让等业务。

TADI 先后有 8 项设计获国家优秀设计奖，其中有三项获金质奖，近 200 项工程设计在市、部级评选中获奖。近几年完成了天津奥林匹克体育中心体育场、医科大学总医院、中华剧院、泰达国际会展中心、泰达体育场等一批大型重点公建项目，以其全新的设计理念和现代高新技术，展示了建院的技术实力和创新创优水平。

Established in 1952, Tianjin Architecture Design Institute (TADI), nowadays, has been one of the largest integrated architectural design institutes in China. At present, TADI possesses near 1000 employees, among which there are 3 State Engineering Masters, 15 experts who enjoy the government allowance approved by the State Council, 2 young experts who have outstanding contribution approved by the State Personnel Ministry, 4 young experts who are conferred titles by the municipality of Tianjin, 40 supreme architects (engineers), and 63 state 1st class registered architects, 74 state 1st class registered structural engineers, 25 state registered consultants, 14 cost engineers.

TADI has lots of qualifications and certificates issued by National Construction Ministry, and mainly works for civil architectural design, industrial architectural design, city plan and residential area design and plan; and it also takes charge in engineering consulting, project supervision, general contract to the engineering project and technical cooperation, technical fruits transfer etc..

Till now, 8 design works have awarded the Excellent Design Prizes of China, among which there are 3 won golden prizes. In addition, near 200 projects were awarded in the competitions of Municipality and Ministry. In recent years, TADI has completed a large group of public facility projects, such as Olympic Sports Center, General Hospital of Medical University, Zhong Hua Theater, TEDA International Conference and Exhibition Center, TEDA Stadium etc.. All of these projects express brand-new design concepts and modern high-tech technology, which reveal the technical power and creation capacity of TADI.

地址：天津市河西区气象台路 95 号
Add: No. 95 Qixiangtai Road, Hexi District, Tianjin
邮政编码 Postal Code: 300074
电话 Tel: +86 22 23543000
传真 Fax: +86 22 23345260
E-mail: tadi@tadi.net.cn
http://www.tadi.net.cn

人民日报新闻培训中心

中华剧院

医科大学总医院

天津大学建筑学院

Tianjin University School of Architecture

建筑教育家、教授：徐中

建筑大师、院士：彭一刚

建筑馆

建筑馆内景

天津大学建筑学院的前身为天津大学建筑系，成立于1952年9月，由原北方交通大学和津沽大学两校的建筑系合并而成。津沽大学的前身为天津工商学院，其建筑系创建于1935年；北方交通大学建筑系创建于1946年。

1997年6月天津大学进行学院制改革，在原建筑系的基础上，合并“王学仲艺术研究所”，成立了天津大学建筑学院。目前学院下辖建筑学系、城市规划系、环境艺术设计研究所、建筑设计及其理论研究所、建筑技术研究所、建筑历史与理论研究所、城市规划与设计研究所、城市规划设计研究院、计算机中心、211工程实验室、成人教育培训中心、天津大学建学科技开发公司等11个基层单位。

Tianjin University School of Architecture, growing out of Tianjin University Department of Architecture, established in September, 1952, which was merged by Department of Architecture of Original North Transportation University and Jingu University. Jingu University, growing out of Tianjin Industry & Commerce School, its Department of Architecture established in 1935, the Department of Architecture of North Transportation University established in 1946.

Tianjin University reformed its schools in June, 1997, founded School of Architecture, which merged Department of Architecture and Wangxuezhong Art Research Institute. In present, School of Architecture has 11 subordinated units, including Department of Architecture, Department of City Planning, Environment Art Design Research Institute, Architecture Design & Theory Research Institute, Architecture Technology Research Institute, Architecture History & Theory Research Institute, City Planning & Design Research Institute, City Planning & Design Research School, Computer Center, 211 Project Laboratory, Adult Education Training Center, Architecture Science & Technology Development Company.

地址：天津市南开区卫津路92号
Add: No. 92 Weijin Road, Nankai District, Tianjin
邮政编码 Postal Code: 300072
电话 Tel: +86 22 27404491
http://www2.tju.edu.cn/colleges/architecture/root.htm

天津大学建筑设计规划研究总院

Tianjin University Academy of Architecture Devise and Layout Research

电力通讯综合楼

本院创建于1958年，是国家甲级建筑设计、甲级城市规划设计、甲级工程咨询单位，依托于国家重点大学人才优势、学科优势和技术优势，凭借先进的技术装备和严谨的工作作风，近年来在全国范围完成各种类型、各种规模的建筑设计、城市规划设计屡获各类奖项。

本院现有一线设计人员150余人，其中45人为国家一级注册建筑师，35人为国家一级注册结构师，15人为国家注册城市规划师，拥有硕士学位的人员占全院总人数的40%以上。专业配套齐全，人员素质较高，使本院在教育和科研建筑、旅游和疗养建筑、办公和商贸建筑以及大型医院建筑、体育建筑设计和城市规划、古建筑保护规划等方面都有不同凡响的建树。此外，在工业建筑设计、古建筑复原设计、设计监理、深基坑支护以及建设项目策划和可行性研究等方面也具有较强的实力，并取得了较好的业绩。

“实事求是”作为天津大学的校训，已经深深的融入本院的企业文化与服务理念之中。特色鲜明、风格独具的天津大学建筑设计规划研究总院，愿为中国的城市建设精心勾绘最具地方特色、最具竞争力、最具时代精神的发展蓝图。

Established in 1958, Tianjin University Academy of Architecture Devise and Layout Research is one of national first-rank institute of architecture devise, urban layout and project counseling. Supported by the advantage of talent, knowledge and technology from national key university TJU and by its advanced technique and rigorous style in work, the academy has won several awards in architecture devise and urban layout nationwide.

At present, there are 150 designers working in the Academy, among which 45 are national first-class registered architects, 35 are national first-class registered construction designers, 15 are national registered civil planners; and 40% of them hold the Master's degree. Thanks to a complete range of specialities and a high-caliber team, the Academy specializes in a wide domain, including education and research architectures, tour and sanatorium architectures, office and business architecture, gymnasium devise and urban layout, protection of archaic architecture. Besides, we are also adept in devise of industrial architecture, renewal of archaic architecture, design supervision and feasibility research.

The motto of Tianjin University – “Seek Truth from Facts”, has also permeated into the academy’s enterprise culture and service notion. Tianjin University Academy of Architecture Devise and Layout Research, with its brilliant and inimitable characteristic, would like to draw for domestic city construction a blue print with the utmost competitiveness and time spirit.

地址: 天津市南开区卫津路92号
Add: No. 92 Weijin Road, Nankai District, Tianjin
邮政编码 Postal Code: 300072
电话 Tel: +86 22 27404753 27406626
传真 Fax: +86 22 27401845 27402460
E-mail: tdghy@126.com tdght@163.com

大学体育中心

校区总体规划

大学学生公寓

Welcome to MBA & MPA Education Center

天津大学公共管理学院

天津大学管理学院
MBA MPA 教育中心

MBA & MPA EDUCATION CENTER
SCHOOL OF MANAGEMENT

学院简介

天津大学的前身是北洋大学，成立于1895年10月2日，是中国近代史上第一所大学，是闻名世界的高等学府。天津大学管理学院成立于1984年，是全国高校中最早创立管理学院的四所院校之一。目前，天津大学管理学院与公共管理学院一体化运行，有1个博士后流动站、1个国家级重点学科、7个博士点、27个硕士点、7个本科专业，覆盖了管理科学与工程工商管理、公共管理三大一级学科，涉及应用经济学和控制科学与工程两个一级学科，成为全国高校中管理学科门类最齐全的管理学院之一。

管理学院现有教职工174人，其中教师132人。教师中有博士生导师34人，硕士生导师90人，教授38人，副教授62人，国家级有突出贡献专家2人，国家863专家1人，教育部“跨世纪优秀人才”2人，获杰出青年基金1人。学院每年都承接各级政府、各类组织机构、各类科学研究基金、国内外企业的大量科研课题和教育培训项目。

中心简介

天津大学管理学院MBA、MPA教育中心是专职负责天津大学MBA、MPA、EMBA等高等专业学位教育的机构。天津大学的MBA教育项目是1991年3月国务院学位委员会批准的全国首批可授予工商管理硕士(MBA)学位的九所院校之一；MPA教育项目是2000年国务院学位委员会批准的全国首批可授予公共管理硕士(MPA)学位的招生学校之一；EMBA项目是2002年国务院学位委员会首批批准的培养“高级管理人员工商管理硕士(EMBA)”专业学位试点单位。

天大MBA、MPA、EMBA等高等专业学位教育以“精术、明法、求道”为宗旨，开办至今，积累了丰富的经验，授课教师都是天津大学骨干教师和全国知名的专家学者。通过优秀的师资队伍，严谨的教学体系，现代化的教学方法，规范的教学管理，保证了这些专业学位教育项目的高水准。欢迎各界朋友选择优质教育资源，充实自己，缔造辉煌。

我们期待与您的合作！

天津大学管理学院MBA.MPA教育中心　地址：天津市南开区卫津路92号　邮编：300072
电话：+86 22 27401361　E-mail：mba_mpa@tju.edu.cn
传真：+86 22 27401360　http://mba-mpa.tju.edu.cn

天津科技大学

Tianjin University of Science and Technology (TUST)

天津科技大学泰达校区

天津科技大学是以工为主，工、理、文、经、管、法等学科协调发展的多科性大学，具有学士、硕士和博士学位授予权及接收外国留学生的资格，是为军队培养后备军官的签约高校。学校设有18个学院（部），现有学生18000余人，占地面积1600余亩，建筑面积50万平方米，教学科研仪器设备总值1.45亿元。学校师资力量雄厚，拥有一批富有教学经验和科研开发能力的专家教授。现有教职工近1500人，具有高级专业技术职务的教职工450余名。学校拥有“轻工技术与工程”一级学科博士学位授予权和博士后科研流动站，博士学位授权学科、专业10个；硕士学位授权学科、专业24个，工程硕士学位授权领域8个，高等学校在职培养研究生学科3个；本科专业和专业方向56个。省部级重点学科5个，省部级重点实验室3个，省部级工程研究中心及行业技术中心3个，研究所和研发中心26个。

我校泰达校区坐落于天津经济技术开发区高教园区内。目前，校区有博士、硕士、本科生和留学生共计8000余人。校区设置了海洋、生物、食品、化工等适合开发区高科技产业发展方向的专业和科研基地，包括市级重点实验室和工程中心等，为滨海新区和天津市经济发展服务。

Tianjin University of Science and Technology (TUST) is a scientific and technology university with a harmonious development of five major courses: engineering, science, liberal arts, economics and management. Besides the authority to confer degrees of bachelor, master and doctor, TUST also has qualification to enroll foreign students and to foster reserved officers for the Army. The campus where 18,000 students study occupies an area of 1,600 mu with a floor space up to 0.5 million square meters. The total value of education and research instruments amounts to 145 million yuan. TUST has a well-balanced faculty team in age and specialties, being equipped with excellent academic capability and creative spirit. Among the faculty of 1,500, 450 people are senior specialized technical personnel. TUST has a first-grade PhD program and Post-Doctoral research station of "technology and engineering in light industry". TUST offers 10 Doctoral programs, 24 Master's programs, 8 programs in engineering Master, 3 on-the-job Master's program, 56 undergraduate specialties. Besides, there are 5 provincial and municipal key specialties, 3 provincial and municipal key labs, 3 provincial and municipal engineering research centers and trade technology center and 26 research institutes.

The branch campus of TEDA is located in Tianjin Economic Development Area. At present, there are altogether 8,000 students on TEDA campus, including undergraduates, graduates for Master and Doctor's degree and foreign students. The campus has now established specialities and research centers in terms of oceanography, biology, food and chemical engineering, which are extraordinary adaptable to the development of Tianjin Economic Development Area and ultimately contributive to economic development of Binhai New Area and Tianjin.

地址：天津市河西区大沽南路1038号
Add: No. 1038 Dagu'nan Road, Hexi District, Tianjin
邮政编码 Postal Code: 300222
传真 Fax: +86 22 28340538
http://www.tust.edu.cn

天津科技大学教学主楼

天津科技大学泰达校区图书馆

天津市第四中心医院

天津市第四中心医院始建于1930年，是集医疗、教学、科研、预防保健于一体的大型综合性三级甲等医院，2001年被天津市政府确定为“北部区域医疗中心”。先后获得全国院内感染管理工作先进单位、天津市“十佳医院”、全国百姓放心示范医院等荣誉称号。是天津市耳鼻咽喉头颈外科医院、天津市交通事故急救定点医院、“120”急救中心河北分站、卫生部国际紧急救援中心网络医院。

设置病床880张，全院职工1200多人，各类专业技术人员900多人，其中副高以上医务人员120余人。设一级临床科室22个；医技科室8个。

现拥有菲利浦1.5T全新超导磁共振机、菲利浦V5000血管造影机、16排螺旋CT机、直线加速器、彩色多普勒诊断仪、ECT、大型遥控X光机、德国狼牌腔镜系列、全自动生化仪、人工肾、高压氧等先进设备。

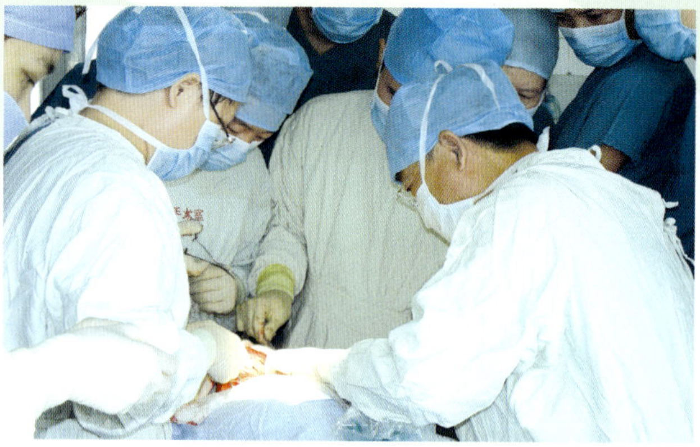

院长、耳鼻喉专家金国威教授(右一)为患者手术

领导为新楼剪彩

医院走科教兴院之路，耳鼻咽喉头颈外科在主任医师、硕士生导师、天津市授衔专家金国威教授的带领下，开展了新工作45项，11项科研成果通过鉴定，达国内领先、国际先进水平，经天津市卫生局批准建立了“天津市耳鼻咽喉头颈外科医院”。骨科开展的断肢再植、拇指再造、各类关节置换术、腰椎手术等多项技术达到国内先进水平。近几年，开展了体外循环心脏直视手术、心脏不停跳冠脉搭桥术、脑垂体瘤切除术、同种异体肾脏移植术、输尿管肾镜检查气压弹道碎石术、气囊飘浮导管进行血液动力学监测治疗急性心肌梗塞，各种心脏起搏器安装、冠脉造影支架安装、肾功能衰竭的透析治疗、运用腹腔镜、胸腔镜、关节镜实施微创手术、超声乳化治疗白内障等多项新技术。

建筑面积为37460平方米的急救中心综合大楼，从设计伊始，就注重流程上的先进性，在平面布局、科室设置、服务流程上，符合当代急救医学的发展要求，体现时间就是生命的理念，确保整个医疗环节的流畅，使急诊患者的检查、诊断、治疗过程在最短距离、最短时间完成，有效提高抢救的质量和效率。

急救中心集急诊科、放射检验等检查科室、综合ICU、手术室、住院病房于一体，急救中心由主管外系的副院长兼任主任，统一调度，同一管理。120急救中心河北分站安排在楼内，救护车时刻待命出发，保证院前的急救能力。影像中心的十六排螺旋CT、血管造影、放射、超声等大型设备以及检验中心设置在一楼和二楼，保证了急诊检查能在最短时间出报告，有效争取抢救时间。急诊科包括内、外、妇、儿、耳鼻喉、眼、口腔等诊室及设备一流的抢救室、观察室和急诊手术室。设置在三楼的手术室，拥有12个净化手术间，具备同时进行多台手术的能力。四楼是综合ICU，设床位22张，拥有国外最先进的呼吸机、监护设备和血液净化装置。内外科ICU合并管理，为救治各种危重症病人提供技术保证。多学科联合抢救是急救中心的一大特色，与急救密切相关的心内、心外、脑外、骨科、普外、妇产科、血液透析中心等均设置在楼内，遇紧急抢救、重大抢救，相关专业的主任、专家、医生能及时到位，给予专业性的抢救。

目前，医院已成为天津市北部区域规模最大、功能最全的现代化医院。

急救中心综合大楼

地址：天津市河北区中山路3号(天津北站旁)　Add: No. 3 Zhongshan Road, Hebei District, Tianjin　邮政编码 Postal Code: 300140
电话 Tel: +86 22 26181957(服务台)　26183657(门诊办公室)　26183637(医务科)

天津天士力制药股份有限公司简介

天士力制药股份有限公司（600535）位于天津北辰科技园区，建筑面积4万平方米，职工3100多人，拥有通过国家GMP、ISO9001、ISO14001和澳大利亚TGA认证的生产车间，是当前国内最大的滴丸剂型生产企业。

自主知识产权的全自动滴丸制剂生产线

几年来，天士力制药公司逐步建立了以现代中药生产经营为核心的产业化体系，主要产品有复方丹参滴丸、养血清脑颗粒、柴胡滴丸、藿香正气滴丸、荆花胃康胶丸、穿心莲内酯滴丸等。其中复方丹参滴丸已经成为我国心脑血管药品市场的主导产品之一，连续4年单品种销售额突破10亿，在百姓安全用药调查活动中，被评为“百姓放心药”，并第一个以药品身份通过美国食品与药品管理局临床用药申请（FDA IND），实现了中药进入世界医药主流市场的历史性突破。

Gep提取车间

天士力制药公司以“追求天人合一，提高生命质量”为理念，为推动中药走向世界，创造人类健康而不懈努力！

天津天士力制药股份有限公司
TIANJIN TASLY PHARMACEUTICAL CO.,LTD.

www.tasly.com

津港评估
Property Consulting & Appraisal

天津津港房地产咨询评估有限公司成立于1993年，是一家致力于房地产咨询、评估的专业化机构，凭借着优质的评估质量和完善的客户服务赢得了客户的认可和支持，目前已在天津市内多个区、县设立了分支机构。自1997年国家认定资格以来至今，连续被评为国家一级房地产评估机构，是您值得信赖的估价机构。

Tianjin Jin'gang Real Estate Consulting & Appraisal Co., Ltd. is incorporated in 1993. Jingang is specialized in real estate consultation and appraisal. Owing to our excellent appraisal quality and perfect customer services, we have won trusts and support from the customers. Up to now, we have already set up branches in several districts and counties of the city. Ever since 1997, when our qualification was accredited by the state, we have been chosen a national grade A real estate price appraisal agency. Our company is a trustworthy price appraisal agency.

- **房地产评估**
  包括各类房地产，为抵押、按揭、保险、买卖、租赁、补偿提供决策依据。
- **房地产经营咨询**
  房地产市场调查、预测、策划及推广。
- **房地产代理**
  代理房地产买卖、租赁、交换，商品房营销及策划。
- **项目可行性研究及评估**
  包括项目可行性论证、项目评估、项目策划及推广，项目市场前景研究及代办开发项目前期手续。
- **理论研究**
  包括房地产有关政策、法规咨询、市场分析、估价理论研究。
- **信息资料**
  提供本市及全国范围的房地产信息及其他与房地产业务相关的咨询代理。

资　信

- 建设部一级房地产价格评估机构
- 全国范围执业土地评估中介机构
- 天津市司法局司法鉴定资质机构
- 获得UKAS ISO9001 国际质量管理体系认证机构
- 中国房地产估价师学会常务理事单位
- 天津市建委、市消协、市房管局“放心中介”机构

地址: 天津市和平区重庆道6号
Add: No. 6 Chongqing Road, Heping District, Tianjin
邮政编码 Postal Code: 300050
电话 Tel: +86 22 23395218　23191964(总机)
传真 Fax: +86 22 23395298
E-mail: jg_appraisal@163.com

独立 INDEPENDENCE

MUTUALITY 客观

公正 IMPARTIALITY

ACCURACY 准确

CONVERGE ROOT
STYLE HOMETOWN
格调
故里

纯粹城粹

城市中央别墅社区

现房销售240万—600万

CONVERGE™ ROOT

City Central Villa Community

Interior
Front Yard Type Garden

在别墅的等级行列里，他就是「绅士」

如果说浓荫蔽日、自然幽谧的景观园林，与现代质感的建筑形式，形成了他后天的绅士面容；那么，几百年城市文化精髓所锻造的文化底蕴，无疑成就了他先天独有的绅士风度。**格调故里，作为城市中央唯一的别墅社区，以靓丽不失文雅的仪表、自然显露高贵气质、和庄重、谦恭的姿态迎纳品位相投的主人。**

现在**格调故里**已全景落成，欲深入了解其淳熟外表与深刻内涵，亲临现场，自会被其大气广博的城粹精神所震撼。

本资料为对不特定人的要约邀请，买卖双方的权利义务以合同为准。本公司保留对本资料的修改权，敬请留意最新资料。内容仅供参考，所有细节以政府批准图则与法规文件为准。(2005)津房售字第162号 NewGeniusAd 新基业 83525597

内环沿线：南开中学向西100米；**独体、双拼**、叠拼别墅和谐共生 150米樱花大道，300株原生成木再现中式私家园林的意境 2.2米层高夹层赠送，提供生活诸多可能性 木铝复合窗，中空LOW-E玻璃内充氩气；中央空调系统；中央吸尘系统；美国ISE（爱适易）食物垃圾处理器；安防系统等，将城市中央的别墅品质推至顶点。

售楼地址/位临南开中学、紧邻南开花园 TEL:27385500

投资商/天津泰达建设集团有限公司 **发展商**/泰达建设集团建设开发分公司 **景观设计**/贝尔高林(香港)有限公司 **建筑设计**/澳大利亚柏涛建筑设计公司

天津城投集团

Tianjin Infrastructure Investment Group

党委书记、董事长 王周喜

总经理 孟庆旺

2005年，城投集团围绕着“用好城市资源，服务天津发展”的经营宗旨，按照构建我市城市建设的投融资平台的企业发展定位，加大了项目管理、资金组织、企业管理工作力度，海河综合开发、快速路、路网改造、地铁建设、绿化环境等项目进展顺利，资金运营质量和效益进一步提高。企业融资思路不断创新，短期贷款、融资租赁、路桥冠名权拍卖等企业多元融资迈出可喜步伐，经营性项目开发取得突破。组建了城投建设公司等下属企业，组织架构和企业经营架构进一步完善，现代企业制度正在逐步健全。

2005年，城投集团融资到位额和固定资产投资额稳步增长，全年实现融资到位额192亿元，完成固定资产投资120亿元以上。海河开发项目实施进度加快，新建和改造了海河东路、海河西路等28条海河道路，以及大沽桥、北安桥、金汤桥等10座桥梁，大沽桥等4座桥梁竣工通车，建成解放公园、音乐公园等6处大型绿地，整修风貌建筑42栋。快速路项目通车里程达到120公里。地铁1号线于2005年12月28日实现试通车，进入综合调试阶段。城市路网改造和环境整治工程快速推进，到2005年底，累计新建、拓宽改造了156条道路，竣工通车136条，完成74公里铁路沿线环境综合整治和36.4公里市区二级河道治理。城市的交通功能和环境质量明显提高。

2006年，城投集团将按照我市“十一五”规划的要求，以科学发展观统领企业改革、发展和投融资工作全局，继续高标准、低成本的组织好500亿开行和106亿工商行贷款资金的“借、用、管、还”，加快海河综合开发等重点项目建设，地铁1号线实现试运营，开工建设地铁2、3号线，不断探索新的融资渠道，拓宽经营领域，加强资金监管，努力实现“十一五”时期的高起步。

地址：天津市和平区成都道60号
Add: No. 60 Chengdu Road, Heping District, Tianjin
邮政编码 Postal Code: 300050
电话 Tel: +86 22 23040792
传真 Fax: +86 22 23043431

In 2005, Tianjin Infrastructure Investment Group highlighted the business aim of "Using city source well, Providing service for Tianjin's development", following the development aim of forming investment platform of urban construction. The group strengthened project management, capital operation and enterprise management. Some projects ran smoothly, including comprehensive development of Haihe River, expressway construction, roads reconstruction, subway construction and green environment, etc.. The quality of capital operation and profit continued to improve. Breakthrough had been made in project development, short-term debt, rent, auction of road & bridge's name and other ways were used to absorb capital. It had some subsidiaries under its control, including Tianjin Infrastructure Investment Corporation and so on. The organization structure continued to improve and modern enterprise system was strengthened.

In 2005, the absorbed capital and fixed assets of the group increased steadily. The group absorbed capital of 19.2 billion yuan and the fixed assets was 12 billion in 2005. Comprehensive development of Haihe River quickened to construct. The newly constructed and reconstructed 28 roads and 10 bridges, including Haihe East Road, Haihe West Road, Dagu Bridge, Beian Bridge and Jintang Bridge. 4 bridges put in use. It constructed 6 green lands, including Jiefang Park and Music Park. It also reconstructed 42 scenic buildings. A total of 120 km expressway put in use. Subway Line 1 tested operation on Dec. 28, 2005. By the end of 2005, the grouped had newly constructed and widened 156 roads, 136 roads put in use, completed comprehensive treat along 74 km road line and river treat of 36.4 km. The urban traffic function and environment quality improved obviously.

In 2006, the group will encircle the demand of "11th five-year plan", implement the view of scientific development to carry out enterprise reform, development and absorbing capital. It will use 50 billion debt of Development Bank and 10.6 billion debt of Industrial and Commercial Bank of China, quicken to construct key projects. Subway Line1 will operation and Line2 and Line3 begin to construct. The group will continue to widen business field and strengthen capital management, hopes to have a good beginning of "11th five-year period".

地铁一号线

翔宇公园

梅江公交厂站

月牙河馨园

友谊路立交桥

海河夜景

天津住宅建设发展集团

Tianjin Residential Buildings Construction Development Group

天津市天鸿基业路桥建设工程有限公司

系国有企业天津市住宅建筑机械施工公司改制后建立的多元投资非国有控股的有限公司。注册资金5180万元。公司具有市政公用工程施工总承包二级资质，主要承接道路和桥梁建设、给排水管道及污水处理、基础施工、机电设备安装、拆除、钢结构、河道改造、住宅小区市政配套、建筑装修装饰、房屋建筑等工程。

公司拥有一支富有战斗力的施工队伍，曾经先后在华苑住宅小区、梅江生态居住小区以及卫津河、月牙河河道改造中，多次荣获天津市质量金奖和国家市政示范工程金杯奖。

公司全体员工精诚团结，戮力同心，践行诚信、精心施工，打造品牌，树立形象，为在最短时间内把企业打造成具有独立特色和相当竞争力的市政公用工程施工总承包一级企业而奋斗！

地址：天津市和平区鞍山道129号
Add: No. 129 Anshan Road, Heping District, Tianjin
邮政编码 Postal Code: 300070
电话 Tel: +86 22 23040936
传真 Fax: +86 22 23040936

恒华里经典大厦
获市级文明工地获年度部级QC成果奖

华苑久华里获住宅示范工程称号

梅江苏水园住宅小区
获住宅示范工程年度市级文明工地称号

天津市三房建建筑工程有限公司是原天津市建筑工程公司改制后重新组建的新型企业。公司严格按照现代企业制度的要求制作，依托原企业的基本格局，形成了除保留部分国有法人股外，其余以自然人和公司职工入股的多元投资为主体的有限责任公司。

公司具有房屋建筑工程施工一级资质及起重设备安装工程二级资质，主要经营范围包括：水暖、电梯安装及维修；建筑机械施工；建筑物拆除；周转材料；机械设备租赁；建筑装饰装修工程；钢结构工程；园林智能化工程；市政公用工程；机电设备安装工程；消防设施工程等，业已形成门类齐全、产品配套的产业链。

公司人才聚集、技术先进、设备精良、实力雄厚，并配有与企业资质相匹配的一级试验室。

公司以“服务社会、造福百姓”为己任，先后在和平路商业街改造、鼓楼商业步行街、华苑住宅小区、体北高层住宅、梅江生态小区、嘉华大厦、翠金园项目等大批工程中获得鲁班奖、市优质工程、金牌奖和市级文明工地等称号，公司历年承建的工程项目优良率达到75%以上，工程质量始终在全市名列前茅。

公司将传承在本市建筑领域的知名度，借助各方的鼎力支持，吸收先进的管理经验和吸纳各方面的精英为我所用，积极打造品牌、树立形象，尽快形成规模，不断发展壮大企业。公司董事长兼总经理钟金山率全体员工向社会郑重承诺：践行诚信，提供最佳服务，不向社会交付一平方米不合格产品。用我们的实力打造未来。

地址：天津市和平区汉阳道69号
Add: No. 69 Hanyang Road, Heping District, Tianjin
邮政编码 Postal Code: 300070
电话 Tel: +86 22 23041221
传真 Fax: +86 22 23040959

天津城建集团

TIANJIN URBAN CONSTRUCTION GROUP

天津城建集团有限公司是天津市政府批准的大型企业集团天津城建集团的核心企业，是具有公路工程施工总承包特级资质，市政公用工程施工总承包一级资质，公路路基、公路路面、桥梁工程专业承包一级资质、城市轨道交通工程专业承包资质，并通过了ISO9001:2000质量管理体系、ISO14001环境管理体系、OHSAS18001职业健康安全管理体系认证和获得对外经营权的大型企业。公司拥有20个全资、控股子公司，是以工程施工总承包为龙头，集市政、公路、桥梁、城市轨道、污水处理、建筑、环保、房地产开发的科研、设计、施工等为一体的规模化、多元化的大型企业集团。

党委书记、董事长：李凯建

公司及所属企业在天津和全国近20个省市承建了百余项有影响的大型市政、公路建设项目，所承建的京津塘高速公路、沪宁高速公路、山西太旧高速公路、京沈高速公路、广深珠高速公路、河北石安高速公路、苏嘉杭高速公路、安徽怀远蜗河三桥、江苏无锡芦村污水处理厂、天津“三环十四射”、城市道路网络工程、天津市区至滨海新区城市轨道工程、东南半环海河大桥、唐津高速公路津塘互通立交桥、天津市顺驰立交桥、大型污水处理厂等多项工程，以及刚刚竣工和目前正在建设中的天津滨海大桥、子牙河自锚式悬索桥、天津地铁一号线、天津快速路工程、天津市海河综合开发建设等一大批市政公路建设工程，赢得了“城建铁军”的称誉。获得国家优质工程金、银奖及中国建筑工程鲁班奖、中国市政工程金杯奖20余项和省市优工程50余项。并在城市立交、高等级公路路面摊铺和软基处理、污水处理厂等市政、公路工程的设计、施工领域达到了国内先进水平。

公司先后多次荣获了“全国施工优秀企业”、“全国工程建设管理先进单位”、“全国用户满意企业”、“全国市政工程优秀企业”、“天津市优秀企业”、“中国百家诚信示范企业”和“中国企业500强”等二十多项国家级奖项和荣誉称号，展现出一个国有大型建筑企业的雄厚竞争实力。

咸阳路污水处理厂

津滨轻轨

大沽桥

地址：天津市鞍山西道260号

Add: No. 260 Anshanxi Road, Tianjin

邮政编码 Postal Code: 300073

天津第一市政公路工程有限公司
Tianjin No. 1 Municipal Highway Engineering Co., Ltd.

董事长：殷增民

总经理：何大川

天津第一市政公路工程有限公司，始建于1950年，经建设部、交通部核准，是具有公路工程施工总承包一级、市政公用工程施工总承包一级施工资质的国家大型施工企业。主要承建各种结构桥梁、高等级公路、高速公路、地下铁路以及闸坝、给排水、供热与煤气管网、各类钢结构、水泥混凝土预制构件等。1997年经天津市建委、体改委批准，改制为国有独资公司。2002年公司改制为多元投资有限责任公司。

公司先后取得承建国际“菲迪克条款”工程资格和ISO9000质量体系认证，2004年，公司通过ISO9000、ISO14000、OHSAS18000三项管理体系综合认证。五十多年来，公司先后承建了巴基斯坦、赞比亚等十几个国家的援外工程，参与过天津、江苏、广东、四川等十几个省市的近百项重点工程建设。企业先后荣获国家优质工程金银奖7块，中国市政金杯奖7项，中国建筑工程鲁班奖7樽，中国土木詹天佑大奖2樽，天津市市优工程24项以及众多的社会荣誉，在天津市和全国施工企业中享有盛誉。近几年，公司还连续被评为全国用户满意施工企业、全国优秀施工企业、全国诚信经营示范单位、全国工程建设质量管理优秀企业。

地址: 天津市河东区东兴路111号
Add: No. 111 Dongxing Road, Hedong District, Tianjin
电话 Tel: + 86 22 24022401
传真 Fax: +86 22 24022870

Tianjin No. 1 Municipal Highway Engineering Co., Ltd. established in 1950. It is a large-sized state-owned construction enterprise, the first class enterprise in municipal engineering and highway construction contractor. The business fields are widely expanded to bridge, highway, subway, embankment, water supply, sewage treatment, heating, gas pipe, concrete processing and so on. It was re-registered as sole state-owned company approved by Tianjin Construction Committee and Tianjin System Reform Committee in 1997 and was re-registered as limited liability company in 2002.

The company has obtained the certificate of FIDIC and conformity of ISO9000. In 2004, it obtained the certificate of conformity of ISO9000, ISO14000 and OHSAS18000. During the past 50 years, it has constructed many projects in Pakistan, Zambia and other countries, about 100 domestic key projects in Tianjin, Jiangsu, Guangdong, Sichuan and other provinces. It was awarded 7 gold & silver prizes of national good quality engineering, 7 Gold Cup prize of China municipal engineering, 7 Luban prize, 2 Zhantianyou Prize, 24 Tianjin good quality engineering prize and other prizes. In recent years, It was awarded national customer satisfied construction enterprise, national good construction enterprise, national good credit model unit and national good engineering quality enterprise.

天津最大城市立交卫津南路立交桥

卫国道立交工程荣膺中国建筑工程鲁班奖

天津第二市政公路工程有限公司

Tianjin No. 2 Municipal Highway Engineering Co., Ltd.

董事长：韩占荣

天津城建集团第二市政公路工程有限公司为国有独资大型施工企业。公司历经40年的发展，逐渐成为能承揽各类市政工程、高等级公路工程、桥梁、隧道、城市地下轨道交通工程、污水处理、混凝土管材及沥青混凝土加工、销售等项目的综合建筑施工企业。公司于1996年通过ISO9000国家质量标准认证，2002年本市市政建设行业中率先通过国家职业安全健康管理体系认证，2003年通过国家环境体系认证。

公司现有职工1940人，有职称的工程技术人员和经济管理人员466人，其中高，中级职称有157人。有资质的项目经理共132人，公司技术力量雄厚，设备先进，拥有大中型机械设备1128台，其中美国沥青沥青砼拌合站和美国，德国沥青砼摊铺设备及其他进口机械设备57余部。

近年来公司承建的大型市政、公路工程项目有：天津东郊四十万吨污水处理厂、天津纪庄子污水处理厂扩建、天津北辰污水处理厂、轻轨快速轨道工程、天津地铁车站和盾构区间、京沈、京福、京深、津晋、津蓟、长余、丹拉、威乌、京沪等高速公路项目、广东珠海赛车场等。

公司曾荣获“中国五百家最大建筑施工企业”、“全国优秀施工企业”、“全国市政工程优秀施工单位”、“建设部工程质量优秀企业”、“全国工程建设管理先进单位”、“全国用户满意施工企业”、“天津市信用等级AAA企业称号”、“天津建筑业骨干企业”、并荣获“全国五一劳动奖状”。2005年获中华全国总工会“安康杯”五连贯的“连胜杯”。

企业永远坚持“质量第一，信誉至上，造价合理，服务为先”的经营宗旨，继续努力为国内，国外用户提供更多、更好、更全面的服务。

Tianjin No. 2 Municipal Highway Engineering Co., Ltd. is a large-sized state-owned construction enterprise. After the development of 40 years, the business fields are widely expanded to municipal engineering, highway, bridge, tunnel, subway, sewage treatment, tubes of concrete, concrete processing and sales, etc.. In 1996, the company obtained the certificate of conformity of ISO9000. In 2002, it obtained the certificate of conformity of safety. In 2003, it obtained the certificate of conformity of environment.

Now the corporation has 1,940 employees, including 466 technicians and managing persons, of which, 157 are medium & high-class qualified employees, 132 are project managers with intelligence. It has 1,128 sets of large and medium-sized mechanical equipment, including over 57 sets imported equipment. It has a abundant technique staff and advanced equipment.

In recent years, it has constructed many projects, such as Tianjin Sewage Disposal Factory of 400,000 tons, reconstruction of Jizhuangzi Sewage Disposal Factory, Beichen Sewage Disposal Factory, light-rail, subway underground station, Beijing-Shenyang expressway, Beijing-Fuzhou expressway, Beijing-Shenzhen expressway, Tianjin-Jixian expressway, Dandong-Lasa expressway, Beijing-Shanghai expressway, Zhuhai racing ground, etc..

The company has been granted many titles, such as “top 500 national construction enterprises”, “national advanced enterprise”, “national advanced municipal engineering enterprise”, “quality construction enterprise” of the Ministry of Construction, “national engineering management advanced unit”, “national customer satisfactory enterprise”, “Tianjin AAA credit enterprise”, “Tianjin key construction enterprise”, “Labor Day Prize”. In 2005, it was awarded “Ankang Cup” for the successive 5 years.

It respects contract and values one’s commitment. Following the principle of “credibility, efficiency, low cost and high quality”, we will cooperate with friends and provide better service for our clients.

办公大楼

地址：天津市南开区宜宾道13号　Add: No.13 Yibin Road, Nankai District, Tianjin
邮政编码 Postal Code: 300113　电话 Tel: +86 22 27615665　传真 Fax: +86 22 27616538

天津第三市政公路工程有限公司

Tianjin No. 3 Municipal Highway Engineering Co., Ltd.

我公司始建于1973年，原为天津市地下铁路工程公司，后于1979年更名为天津第三市政工程公司。1998年改制为国有独资有限责任公司，并更名为天津第三市政公路工程有限公司。具有市政公用工程施工总承包一级、桥梁工程专业承包一级，和公路工程施工总承包一级、路基、路面专业承包一级资质。

企业经过三十多年的发展壮大，现已成为以承担高等级公路、高速公路、各类型桥梁及市政工程为主，兼营建筑安装、大型土石方、给排水、水利水电、煤气和热力管网等施工项目的大型施工企业，形成了年产值8亿元以上的施工能力。

多年来，企业还多次获得政府和主管部门颁发的荣誉奖项，如："天津市质量管理奖"、"天津市先进企业"、"天津市重合同、守信誉单位"、"建设部先进单位"、"国家优秀施工企业"等。

公司于1998年通过ISO9002标准质量体系认证，又于2004年初通过ISO9001:2000、GB/T28001:2001兼容管理体系认证。

The company was initially found in 1973 with the registered name Tianjin Subway Engineering Company, and was renamed in 1979 as Tianjin No. 3 Municipal Highway Engineering Company. In 1998, as was transformed into totally state-owned company with limited liability, it's name was changed into Tianjin No. 3 Municipal Highway Engineering Co., Ltd.. The company was ratified with first-class qualification in general undertake of municipal public project construction and professional undertake of bridge engineering , first-class qualification in general undertakes of highway engineering construction and professional undertakes of roadbed and road-surface construction.

Through a development of more than thirty years, the company has now become a large-scale construction enterprise, which is mainly engaged in high-grade road and highway construction and all kinds of bridge and municipal engineering. The company also has businesses in construction installation, civil engineering, water supply and drainage system, water-and-electricity project, gas pipes and caliduct nets. The construction capability of the company has now reached 800 million Yuan per year.

The enterprise has been awarded many times by the government and departments in charge, such as "Tianjin municipal quality control medal", "Tianjin advanced enterprise", "Tianjin municipal credible unit", "advanced unit in construction industry", "national excellent construction enterprise".

The company successfully passed the authentication of ISO9002 Quality System Standards in 1998, and passed the authentication of ISO9001:2000, GB/T20041:1996 and GB/T28001:2001 Compatible Management System in early 2004.

子牙河大桥

地铁盾构

大沽桥

滨海大桥

地址：天津市河西区紫金山路3号
Add: No. 3 Zijinshan Road, Hexi District, Tianjin
邮政编码 Postal Code: 300074
电话 Tel: +86 22 23359888
传真 Fax: +86 22 23352313

天津第六市政公路工程有限公司

Tianjin No. 6 Municipal Highway Engineering Co., Ltd.

我公司成立于1987年3月1日，是“天津城建集团有限公司”下属的大型施工企业。

企业经营范围：市政工程建设、公路工程建设、沥青砼及水泥制品加工等。具有市政公用工程、公路施工总承包双一级资质。并已通过了ISO9000等三整合认证及国家计量检测认证。

近年来，我公司承建的工程：顺驰立交获鲁班奖；金纬路立交获全国市政金杯示范奖；津塘公路立交获国家优质工程银奖；津晋高速公路获市建设工程海河杯奖、市政（公路）工程质量金奖；唐津高速、津蓟高速、津滨高速获部优奖。

我公司作为“守合同、重信用”企业，坚持“诚信、务实、优质、高效”的经营宗旨，立足天津，服务全国。

董事长：赵惠川

Tianjin No. 6 Municipal Highway Engineering Co., Ltd. established on March 1, 1987, is a large-sized construction enterprise under the leadership of Tianjin Urban Construction Group Co., Ltd..

Its business field: municipal engineering construction, highway engineering construction and pitch & cement products processing. It is the first class enterprise in municipal engineering and highway construction contractor. It has passed ISO9000 certification and national metrology test certification.

In recent years, the company has constructed many projects, Shunchi flyway is awarded Luban prize, Jinwei Road Flyway is awarded gold cup prize, Jintang highway flyway is awarded silver prize of national good quality engineering, Jinjin expressway is awarded Haihe Cup prize and gold prize of engineering quality, Tangjin expressway, Jinji expressway and Jinbin expressway are awarded good quality prizes of ministry.

It respects contract and values one's commitment. Following the principal of "credibility, high quality, efficiency", it will develop in Tianjin and serve for the whole country.

东南半环快速路津塘立交工程

地址: 天津市南开区罗平道9号增2号
Add: Added No. 2 No. 9 Luoping Road, Nankai District, Tianjin
邮政编码 Postal Code: 300190
电话 Tel: +86 22 27616090

奉化桥

天津路桥建设工程有限公司

Tianjin Highway and Bridgc Construction Enginccring Company Ltd.

董事长、党委书记: 卢建国

总经理: 姚国强

天津路桥建设有限公司是由原天津市路桥总公司与天津通达路桥工程有限公司通过资产重组，2003年12月5日依章进行工商注册登记，具有国家交通部、建设部核准的公路工程施工总承包一级、市政公用工程施工总承包一级和桥梁工程专业承包一级资质的多元投资施工企业。公司核心管理层和基本施工队伍是由颇具实力的天津第一市政公路工程有限公司部分整建制桥梁、道路专业分公司和高素质管理骨干组成。企业经营范围主要为：高速公路、高等级公路、各类桥梁、给排水、地铁轻轨、机场码头建设施工等。

公司将在巩固现有主业的优势基础上，逐步向电力、港口、房地产等行业扩展延伸。在构成以高速公路、桥梁工程为主导的经营体系的基础上，利用嫁接重组、调控股比等方式延伸产业链条，提升产业层次，加速自身资本的积累，逐步建设成经营理念超前、核心技术领先、经营领域广泛、结构布局合理，施工技术先进，经济效益居优的现代企业。以“诚信经营、追求卓越”为立业宗旨，竭诚为广大客户提供满意服务。

Registered in Dec. 5, 2003, Tianjin Highway and Bridge Construction Engineering Company Ltd. established from the assets recombination of former Tianjin Highway and Bridge General Company and Tianjin Tongda Highway and Bridge Engineering Co., Ltd.. The Company is a multi-industry investment and construction enterprise, which is authorized by the national Ministries of Traffics and Construction with first-class qualification in highway engineering construction, in municipal public project construction, and in bridge engineering professional contracts. The central management and basic construction personnel are composed of some high-caliber managers coming form influential Tianjin No. 1 Municipal Highway Engineering Co., Ltd.. Businesses of the enterprise include: highway, high-level road, all kinds of bridges, water supply and drainage system, subway and lightweight railway, airport and dock construction, etc..

The company will consolidate its advantages in its current main businesses, and gradually extend to industries of electric power, port, and real estate. On the basic businesses system of highway and bridge engineering, the company will extend the industrial range, upgrade the industrial level, and accelerate the capital accumulation by ways of engraftation, recombination, and regulating stock config uration. We will endeavor to construct a modern enterprise with excellent manage conception, advanced kernel technology, comprehensive business domain, reasonable structure configuration, and high economic efficiency. Adhering to the business tenet of "performing with credit, pursuing the excellences", we are sincerely enthusiastic to serve our clients.

水上公园周边道路改造凌宾路工程

水上公园西路

福宁高速公路A2标段

地址: 天津市河东区卫国道36号
Add: No. 36 Weiguo Road, Hedong District, Tianjin
邮政编码 Postal Code: 300160
电话 Tel: +86 22 24332152　传真 Fax: +86 22 24332134
http://www.tjlqj.net

天津市津东房地产开发集团有限公司
Tianjin Jindong Real Estate Development Group Co., Ltd.

董事长：徐树山

天津市津东房地产开发集团有限公司成立于1992年10月。如今已拥有12家子公司，经营范围涉及房地产开发与经营、物业管理、酒店、大型商业零售业等，员工近千人，资产总值达12亿元人民币，已累计向国家上缴利税上亿元，是天津市的一级资质房地产企业，2004年率先通过了ISO9000质量管理体系认证。

公司成立13年，累计开发完成了近200万平方米的住宅及公建项目。连续四年被建委评为“天津市房地产开发二十强”企业，连续4年在天津市百强私企评选中名列前茅；并荣获了“危改先进企业”、“危改工程先进集体”、“开发危改项目立功集体”、“天津杰出房地产开发品牌企业”、“天津市房地产开发信誉度AAA企业等级企业”、“天津房地产十大公信力企业”等光荣称号，集团董事长徐树山本人也荣获了天津市优秀民营企业家、天津市优秀企业家、中国房地产企业卓越贡献者、2005全国年度管理人物等殊荣。

津东集团多年来秉承“以德立业、诚信为本”的经营理念、不断创新、超越自我的经营策略，精心策划、科学管理、产品创新、顾客满意的管理方针，打造了“津东米兰”这个享誉天津的房地产品牌。

Tianjin Jindong Real Estate Development Group Co., Ltd. established on Oct. 1992. It has 20 subsidiaries, the business fields include: real estate development, property management, restaurant, retail sales and so on. There are about 1,000 staff. The total assets reaches 1.2 billion yuan, the accumulative profit and taxes amount to over 100 million yuan. It is the first-class real estate enterprise in terms of capital and quality and passed ISO9000 Quality Standard Certification in 2004.

During the past 13 years since its foundation, a total of 2,000,000 square meters residential building and public buildings were constructed. It was awarded “top 20 Tianjin real estate enterprises” by Tianjin Construction Committee for successive four years. It listed leading position of “top 100 Tianjin private enterprises” for successive four years. It was also granted many titles, such as “Tianjin perfect real estate enterprise”, “credit AAA real estate enterprise”, “ten real estate enterprises who respect contract and value one’s commitment”. The chairman of the board, Mr. Xu Shushan was awarded “Tianjin perfect private entrepreneur”, “China real estate entrepreneur who made outstanding contribution”, “2005 national manager” and so on.

The group adheres to the business idea of “develop depending on prestige, honesty and credit”, the business tactics of “making innovation and overstepping itself”, the management principal of “elaborately planning, successfully management, product innovation and customer satisfaction”. It has created the famous brand “Jindong Milan” in Tianjin real estate market.

水西

家园

世纪

地址: 天津市河北区民主道米兰公寓17号3楼
Add: 3F, No. 17 Milan Condominium, Minzhu Road, Hebei District, Tianjin
邮政编码 Postal Code: 300010
电话 Tel: +86 22 24458775　传真 Fax: +86 22 24450762

天津市东达房地产开发有限公司
Tianjin Dongda Real Estate Development Co., Ltd.

总经理：牛世清

牛总经理视察供热

武备学堂

天津市东达房地产开发有限公司技术力量、经济实力雄厚。开发建设住宅、写字楼、商贸城等项目已达120多万平方米。

总经理牛世清以独到的眼光洞察了大直沽潜在的开发价值，带领东达公司率先开发改造危改难点大片大直沽地区，将危改与保护大直沽历史文化相结合，大幅度改善了大直沽的商业环境和文化教育氛围。目前重点规划建设的项目：集商贸、文化、体育、娱乐、旅游、住宅为一体的“直沽旅游商城”和生态型、科技型、智能型，规划总建筑面积为31.8万平方米的住宅小区“神州花园”，将成为天津市大规划中的一个独特景区。

近年来，公司企业规模不断扩大，先后获得了“明星企业”、“危改信得过开发企业”、“危陋平房改造先进集体”等荣誉称号，成为天津市房地产行业“百强企业”之一。

Tianjin Dongda Real Estate Development Co., Ltd. is equipped with strong technological and economic strength. It has developed and constructed over 1200,000 square meters of residential building, office building and trade city, etc..

General manager, Mr. Niu Shiqing has an insight into Dazhigu area and led the company be the first to develop Dazhigu area. During the development period, the company protected historic culture at the same time, improved its commercial environment and culture education surrounding. In present, the key projects, Zhigu Tour & Trade City and Shenzhou Garden will become the special district in Tianjin.

In recent years, the company continued to develop, had been awarded "star enterprise", "credit development enterprise for reforming old and dangerous houses" and "advanced unit for reforming old and dangerous houses". It is one of "top 100 real estate enterprise".

地址：天津市河东区大直沽五号路八纬路口
Add: The Joint of No. 5 Road and Bawei Road, Hedong District, Tianjin
邮政编码 Postal Code: 300170
电话 Tel: +86 22 24145678

天津市热力公司

Tianjin Heat Power Company

天津市热力公司是我市集中供热的骨干企业，中国城镇供热协会常务理事单位。公司成立于1985年，是天津市成立较早的供热企业，当年在体院北小区建设3万平方米的供热示范工程，拉开了我市集中供热的序幕。如今公司下设6个供热管理所，20个供热站，承担5万多户居民的供热任务，供热规模约500万平方米。二十多年来，公司始终坚持“服务人民、奉献社会”的服务理念，牢固树立“辛苦我一人、温暖千万家”的企业精神，按照“安全运行、均衡供热、诚信服务、用户满意”的质量方针，突出主题抓发展，严格规范抓管理，以人为本抓育才，立足用户抓创建，为天津市的供热事业做出了应有的贡献。

近两年来，公司领导班子以“三个代表”重要思想为指导，牢固树立科学发展观的思想，按照构建和谐社会、和谐企业的要求，带领广大干部职工奋力拼搏、锐意创新，开始了热力公司“二次创业”的历程，进入了一个新的上升期，形成了金谷园、华苑产业园区、水上国际村等区域30平方公里、2000万平方米以上的控规，2004、2005年共完成3台35吨锅炉房及锅炉的建设与安装，对两台20吨锅炉进行改造，敷设直径800—1000供热管网约77公里，投入资金2.36亿元。2006年热力公司将以更加崭新的精神风貌，确定发展工作目标，全力抓好科学发展，除继续完善3个热源基地的基本建设及设备安装配套外，还要再完成供热管网35公里，投入资金3.5亿元；重塑热力企业文化，提炼、形成具有热力特色的精神文化体系，重视、培养员工中庸儒雅、仁义诚信的行为道德规范，提高职工综合素质，增强企业凝聚力，叫响“天津热力”品牌，树立良好的企业形象；瞄准全国一流管理水平，明确方向，查找差距，夯实各项基础管理工作，制定3年赶超计划，在供热运行、服务、经营、能耗等方面跨入全国先进行列，为热力公司腾飞奠定坚实基础。

地址: 天津市河西区宾水道49号
Add: No. 49 Binshui Road, Hexi District, Tianjin
邮政编码 Postal Code: 300060
电话 Tel: +86 22 23010532
传真 Fax: +86 22 23010532

华苑工程北线2号换热站

李杰经理在金谷园供热站检查工作

天津送变电工程公司

Tianjin Power Transmission Engineering Corporation

领导班子成员

施工中的500KV输出线路

天津送变电工程公司成立于1953年，是具有国家一级资质的电力工程总承包施工企业（同时具有工民建、市政管网、电讯通讯等施工资质和能力）。其电缆对接及终端技术居全国领先地位，是瑞士布鲁克公司在东南亚的总代理。该公司隶属于天津市电力公司，注册资金9257万元，年施工能力为架设110千伏—500千伏输电线路200公里，敷设330千伏及以下电缆100公里，安装35千伏以上主变容器100万伏安，工民建200000平方米。2002年通过了ISO9001:2000国际标准体系认证，2001年获国家外经贸委批准的境外承包工程经营权。

公司历年来承建的数千项目工程合格率100%，优良品率在85%以上。先后被天津市人民政府授予“市级先进企业”、市“八五”、“九五”立功先进集体，连续十四年荣获“守合同，重信用”单位称号。并具备“AAA”信用等级。

Tianjin Power Transmission Engineering Corporation founded in 1953, is a first grade power engineering construction enterprise in terms of capital and quality(also including industry & civil construction, municipal pipe works, communication engineering). The cable joint and relative technology reaches national leading level. It is awarded general agent of Switzerland Cable Corporation in Southeast Asia. The corporation is subordinated to Tianjin Municipal Power Corporation with the registered capital of 92.57 million yuan. It can lay 200 kilometers of power transmission line from 110KV to 500KV, 100 kilometers cable of 330KV & under, construct 0.2 million square meters of industry & civil buildings per year. In 2002, it passed ISO9001:2000 International Standard System Certification. In 2001, it enjoyed autonomous right on undertaking foreign projects.

Thousands of projects constructed by the corporation are up to standard, of which, 85 percent of all the projects are high quality projects. The corporation was awarded “municipal-level advanced enterprise”, “eighth-five and ninth-five advanced unit”, “honor construction and abide by its words” unit for the successive 14 years. It also obtains “AAA” grade credit.

地址: 天津市河东区卫国道122号
Add: No. 122 Weiguo Road, Hedong District, Tianjin
邮政编码 Postal Code: 300161
电话 Tel: +86 22 24565026
传真 Fax: +86 22 24565026

中航油津京管道运输中心

China Aviation Oil Supply TSN-PEK Pipeline Transportation Center

中航油津京管道运输中心是经中国民航总局批准成立，隶属于中国航空油料总公司的具有独立法人资格的全民所有制企业。本企业主营航空油料、汽油、柴油、石脑油、清洗剂等有关的石油化工产品和各种机具、车辆所用油品及各种燃油的管道运输并兼营储备、调拨、零售、代购、代销、代运业务和相关的技术咨询和技术服务。

中航油津京管道运输中心总部位于天津滨海国际机场，注册资金2亿元人民币，拥有中转油库及185公里天津南疆码头至北京首都国际机场的可输送多种油品的管道，该管道不但具备多品种油顺序输送功能，还在沿线为开拓市场留出可发展的分输接口，管道沿线设三站三库，具备各种油品的储运和转输能力。

为促进管道沿线及周边地区的经济发展和建设，使津京输油管道充分发挥其在华北地区的重要作用，我们将以市场为导向，开发和利用现有的管输资源，为华北地区各客户输送多种油品，确保首都国际机场、天津滨海国际机场航油运输为经营思路，积极开拓市场，推动地区经济和民航事业的发展。

China Aviation Oil Supply TSN-PEK Pipeline Transportation Center is subordinated to China Aviation Oil General Company. It is a state-owned enterprise which is approved by China Civil Aviation Bureau. Its business mainly include pipeline transportation of aviation oil products, petrol, diesel oil, petroleum, cleaning products, also undertake to store, allocate, retail, buy & sell and transport on others' behalt, carry out technology consulting and services.

Its head quarter locates at Tianjin Binhai International Airport. The registered capital reaches 0.2 billion yuan. It is equipped with transfer oil storehouse and oil pipeline of 185 kilometers from Tianjin South Dock to Beijing International Airport. The oil pipelines not only transport kinds of oil, but also leave joints to transport oil along the pipelines. There are three stations and three storehouses which can store and transport oil.

In order to promote the development of regions along the oil pipeline, it will actively develop and utilize pipelines to meet the oil requirements of Beijing International Airport and Tianjin Coastal International Airport. It strives to develop market and contribute a lot for civil aviation and development of local economy.

塘沽站

北京站

自控中心

地址: 天津滨海国际机场
Add: Tianjin Binhai International Airport
邮政编码 Postal Code: 300300
电话 Tel: +86 22 24902221
传真 Fax: +86 22 24902249

天津一汽丰田发动机有限公司

Tianjin FAW TOYOTA ENGINE CO., LTD.

总经理：三重野英治

常务副总经理：陈培玉

天津一汽丰田发动机有限公司（TIANJIN FAW TOYOTA ENGINE CO., LTD. 简称TFTE），其前身是经国务院1996年5月批准，由天津汽车工业（集团）有限公司和日本丰田汽车公司共同出资兴建的天津丰田汽车发动机有限公司（简称TTME），注册资本2.48亿美元，中日双方各占50%的出资比率。经国家商务部批准，2003年12月天津汽车工业（集团）有限公司将所占合资公司的50%股份全部转让给中国第一汽车集团公司。

公司占地面积21万平方米，建筑面积8.6万平方米。主要产品是从日本丰田汽车公司引进的具有先进水平的A系列、K3/SZ系列、ZZ系列发动机及汽车铸件。为国内特锐、威姿、威乐、威驰、花冠等多种车型配套。

公司于2000年2月，通过ISO9002:1994标准的认证，并于2002年6月进行了换版认证（即ISO9001:2000）；同时公司为保护地球生态环境，注重并致力于环境管理，于2002年9月通过ISO14001:1996环境管理体系国内及UKAS国际认证。

公司以先进的丰田生产方式，不断地生产高品质、高性能、环保型的发动机来更好地服务于广大客户。

Tianjin FAW Toyota Engine Co., Ltd. (TFTE) is a joint-venture enterprise, has been developed by TTME which is invested by Tianjin Auto Industrial (Group) Co., Ltd. and Japan Toyota Auto Corporation. Approved by the State Council, it was founded in May, 1996. The registered capital is USD 0.248 billion at equal share of 50% each. Approved by the Ministry of Commerce, Tianjin Motor Industrial(Group) Co., Ltd. made over its 50% share to China No.1 Auto Group in December, 2003.

The corporation occupies an area of 210,000 square meters, the construction area reaches 86,000 square meters. Its major products include A series, K3/SZ series and ZZ series engine and auto casting parts which are equipped with international advanced technology imported from Japan Toyota Auto Corporation. The products are used for TERIOS, VIZI, VELA, VIOS, COROLLA and other domestic cars.

The corporation passed ISO9002:1994 Quality Standard System Certification in February, 2000 and ISO9001:2000 Quality Standard System Certification in June, 2002. Meanwhile, it pays attention to environmental management and passed ISO14001:1996 Environmental Management System Certification in September, 2002.

The corporation takes Toyota management pattern and produces engines with high quality, good performance and pollution-free for all customers.

地址: 天津市西青区杨柳青西青道266号　Add: No. 266 Xiqing Road Yangliuqing, Xiqing District, Tianjin

邮政编码 Postal Code: 300380　电话 Tel: +86 22 27911049　传真 Fax: +86 22 27390960

津英纺纱有限公司
Jinying Spinning Co., Ltd.

COATS

天津津英纺纱有限公司于1988年成立，1990年开业，尔后不断拓展运营规模，现公司投资总额累计已达4300余万美元，中外方各占50%。本公司原料以进口为主，主要生产高档纯涤短纤缝纫线、包芯线、长丝绣花装饰线及绳编类产品，产品70%以上出口。10余年来，公司一直在盈利中运营，在国际市场激烈竞争中不断地创新和发展，是具备一定规模，较强竞争力和世界一流技术和装备的合资经营企业。

李鹏等有关首脑要员，我市主要领导及国家有关部委领导人，均先后莅临公司参观视察。公司开业运营近十四年来，连年荣获国家及市政府授予的“最佳”、“双优”外商投资企业、“天津市工业百强企业”、“天津市优秀企业”、“全国纺织工业思想政治工作优秀企业”、“天津市模范职工之家”等荣誉称号，并于1991年跨入“中国规模最大500家外商投资工业企业”行列。2000年6月，天津市政府又对1990——1999年度连续10年荣获天津市先进外商投资企业称号的津英纺纱等8家企业，颁发奖牌，登报表彰。

十余年来，中外双方均能在友好协商、互惠互利的基础上，共谋企业发展。将来双方仍将致力于创新发展，不断调整产品结构、开发新品种、提高经济效益和社会效益，给投资者以合理回报。

英国Coats plc总裁Mr. Michael J Smithyman与公司董事局成员合影

天津市副市长杨栋梁亲切会见英国Coats plc总裁Mr. Michael J Smithyman

Jinying Spinning Co., Ltd. was established in 1988 and started from operation in 1990, then further developed. The total investment is USD 43 million, at equal share of 50% each the Sino-British. The company is export-oriented with major raw material is imported. The business scope of the company is to produce SSP synthetic yarn thread, PPC, filament and braid, and to maintain over 70% export. During the last ten years, the company has been running with profit and developing in the keen competitive market.

For the past years, the company received a lot of visitors from central and municipal government, including Premier Li Peng and many senior officials and guests from other countries. Jinying Spinning Co., Ltd. has received a lot of awards every year, such as “Double Excellent”, “Double Good” enterprises with foreign investment,“100 leading Industrial Enterprises in Tianjin” and “the excellent enterprise of Tianjin” , “the Ideological and Political excellent enterprise of Chinese Textile Industry” , “the Exemplary Family of employee in Tianjin” . In 1991, the company also listed in “the Largest 500 industrial Enterprises with Foreign Investment in China”. In June 2000, Jinying Spinning Co., Ltd. and other seven companies received special award of achievement for consecutive 10 years by Tianjin government.

During the last ten years, both sides were in friendly negotiation and on the mutual reciprocity & benefit to developed Jinying Spinning. In the future, we will be devoted to innovating and developing, pushing forward new product development, to create the best economic and social benefit and to give investor the good result.

地址: 天津市西青区李七庄津涞公路南
Add: South Jinlai Road, Liqizhuang, Xiqing District, Tianjin
邮政编码 Postal Code: 300381
电话 Tel: +86 22 83912847 83912940
传真 Fax: +86 22 83913935
E-mail: tjjysc@public1.tpt.tj.cn

理想成为世界顶级缝纫制造商

BS REGISTERED UKAS QUALITY MANAGEMENT 003
FM66227

WANHUA 天津万华股份有限公司

Tianjin Wanhua Co., Ltd.

天津万华股份有限公司成立于1992年，注册资本7425万元，总资产6.5亿元，作为一家高新技术企业，公司拥有一个市级技术中心，两大类支柱产品，三层梯队式人才队伍，超过百余人的各类高精尖、复合型研发技术人员，员工总数达500余人。

公司主营产品为“天华”牌BOPET双向拉伸塑料聚酯薄膜，主要生产设备是从德国布鲁克纳公司引进的具有国际领先水平、技术工艺先进的三层共挤BOPET薄膜生产线及从德国康普公司和英国阿特拉斯公司引进的分切设备。生产能力为年产BOPET薄膜25000吨，产品工艺先进、质量稳定，厚度规格为6~75 μm，幅宽达6.9米。主要用于食品医药和日用品的包装、真空镀铝、建筑装饰材料等的贴体保护膜、印刷基材、电子产品、电器绝缘、磁卡磁记录材料、感光胶片片基等，近年，我们又开发了电容器膜、转移膜、镭射膜、亚光膜、阳光膜等新型的高技术含量的产品，进一步丰富了薄膜产品的种类、扩大了应用领域。产品行销全国二十九个省市、自治区，并出口到韩国、日本、东南亚各国及美国、欧盟等国家和地区，在国内同行业中产销量、质量均名列前茅，并且由于产品质量稳定、技术含量高，在国内外享有一定的声誉和较高的知名度。

包装膜

地址: 天津市西青经济开发区兴华道7号
Add: No. 7 Xinghua Road, Xiqing Economic & Development Area, Tianjin
邮政编码 Postal Code: 300385
电话 Tel: +86 22 23979801　传真 Fax: +86 22 23970581
http://www.tj–wanhua.com

Tianjin Wanhua Co., Ltd. was established in 1992 with a registered capital of RMB 74,250,000 yuan, and the total assets have reached RMB 650,000,000 yuan. As a high-tech technology enterprise, the company holds one technical center at city level, two kinds of pillar products, three layers of echelon type talent's teams, more than one hundred high-level and advanced research and development technical staff, the total people number is more than 500.

The mainly product of the company is the biaxially oriented plastic polyester (BOPET) film with the brand "TianHua", and the 3-layers coextrusion BOPET film production line as the mainly equipment was imported from Bruckner Maschinenbau GmbH which held an international lead level and advanced technology and process, two slitters were respectively imported from Kampf GmbH, Germany and ATLAS corporation, England. The production capacity of BOPET film is 25,000 tons annually. The thickness specification of the product is 6-75 μm, with advanced process and steady quality, and web width is 6.9 meters. The product is professionally suitable for the packaging of food and medicine as well as daily commodities, and it is also applied for the vacuum metalizing, and as the adhesive protection film in architectural decoration materials, printing basic materials, electronic products, electric insulation, magnetic record materials for magcard, sensitization film and so on. In recently years, we have developed the new type products which have high-tech content, for the further enriching the sorts of the film products and enlarging its application fields, such as capacitor film, stamping film, hologram film, matte film, solar film etc.. The product has sales well more than 29 provinces and cities, as well as municipalities, and extended to Korea, Japan, Southeast Asia and America, EU etc.. The product and sale as well as quality are always ranking the industry at the very top among the country. A better reputation and highly popularity are enjoyed at home and abroad, due to the steady quality and high-tech content.

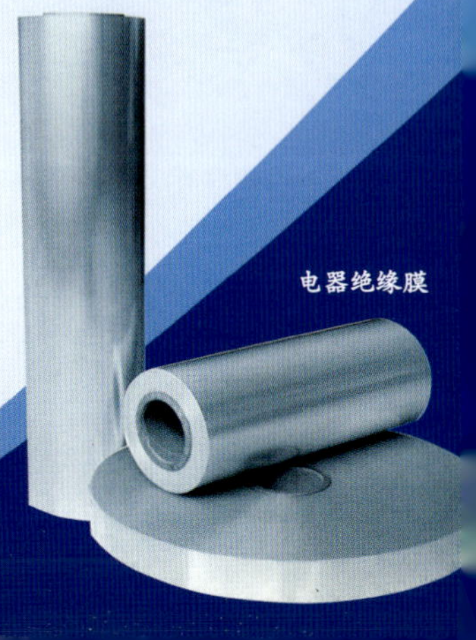

电器绝缘膜

天津市经纬电材有限公司

Tianjin Jingwei Electric Wire Co., Ltd.

天津市经纬电材有限公司是中外合资企业，公司技术力量雄厚、设备精良、工艺先进、检测手段完备，产品以优良的质量畅销全国，广受新老客户的欢迎。

公司主要生产漆包线、玻璃丝包线、纸包线、薄膜绕包线、铝绞合矩形线、组合线，铜、铝导线共五十余个品种。公司已通过GB/T19001–ISO9001质量体系认证，聚氨酯漆包线产品获得美国UL认证，公司具有自营进出口权。

“以质为本、满意客户”是我们的服务宗旨。本公司除供应国标系列产品外，还可按客户要求生产特殊用途的绕组线，热诚欢迎国内外客户洽谈订货，我们将为你提供优质服务。

Tianjin Jingwei Electric Wire Co., Ltd. is a joint venture manufacturing magnet wires. With strong technical power, Hi-tech equipments and process as well as advanced inspection instruments, high quality products have been produced. They are widely applied to wind coils of transformers, generators, welding machines, motors and so on.

More than fifty kinds of magnet wires could be manufactured in our company. The main products include most types of paper and Nomex paper covered wire, enameled copper wire, glass-fiber covered wire, film covered wire, combined wire and aluminum twist wire, etc.. The quality system has been set up and we have achieved ISO9001 status. Solderable polyurethane enameled round copper wire has earned UL approval. Also the company has the license for import and export.

“Quality first, Customer satisfied” is our aim. We will not only provide customers with the products according to international standard, but also can provide customers with products with specific requirement. Customers both at home and aboard are welcome warmly; we are ready to meet your request at any situation.

地址：天津市津南经济开发区(双港)旺港路12号

Add: No.12 (Shuanggang) Wanggang Road, Jinnan Economic Development Area, Tianjin

邮政编码 Postal Code: 300350

电话 Tel: +86 22 28571040

铝绞合矩形线▶

纸包线▶

120级缩醛漆包绕组线▶

天津兴业置业集团
Tianjin Xingye Property Group

兴业大厦

天津兴业置业集团组建于一九九三年十月，是以高科技、贸易、运输、三产业、房地产业、批发、零售、代购、代销，以及仓储、租赁、商品贸易为一体的大型综合性群体。

集团公司地处南开区中心，座落于鞍山西道、灵隐道、西湖道等处，占地面积22万多平方米，交通便利，地理位置优越，拥有资产5.3亿元，利税3000万元。

集团下属企业天津市业兴电子有限公司、必兴商贸有限公司、兴业劳务服务有限公司、兴运机械施工有限公司、兴科商贸有限公司，以及兴业鞋帽批发市场、兴业天宝旧物市场、农贸副食烟酒批发市场等。

为了加快发展步伐，集团正在进行产权制度改革，改革后的集团公司将以崭新的面貌展示于社会，诚信于社会，欢迎国内外商界朋友进行合作，共同发展。

董事长兼总经理刘长海向社会各界同仁致意。

Tianjin Xingye Property Group founded in October, 1993, is a large-sized comprehensive group, covering the fields of hi-tech, trade, transport, tertiary industry, real estate, wholesale, retail trade, agent for purchasing and sales, storage, rent and commodity trade.

The group locates at the center of Nankai District with convenient traffic and advantageous geographic location, occupying an area of 220,000 square meters. Its assets reaches 0.53 billion yuan and pre-tax profits total 30 million yuan.

Its subordinated enterprises include Tianjin Yexing Electronics Co., Ltd., Bixing Trade Co., Ltd., Xingye Labor Service Co., Ltd., Xingyun Machinery Construction Co., Ltd., Xingke Trade Co., Ltd., Xingye Shoes & Caps Wholesale Market, Xingye Tianbao Old Goods Market, Farm Products, Tobacco and Liquor Wholesale Market and so on.

In order to quicken the pace of development, the group is carrying out the reform of property rights. After the reform, the group will face to society with new feature. We hope to cooperate with friends at home and abroad and develop together.

The president, general manager, Mr. Liu Changhai gives his best wishes to social friends of all circles.

地址: 天津市南开区西湖道78号四楼

Add: 4F, No. 78 Xihu Road, Nankai District, Tianjin

电话 Tel: +86 22 27384817

天津市王顶堤集团公司

Tianjin Wangdingdi Group Co., Ltd.

集团公司党委书记、董事长：房贵英

天津市王顶堤集团公司是国家级乡镇企业集团公司，坐落在天津市南开区复康路西端城乡结合处，地理位置优越，交通便利。公司推行“以人为本，以德为先，以法为重心，以情为特质”的管理，发扬“团结拼搏，奋力开拓，勇于进取，敢于争先”的创业精神，秉承一个“诚”字，热情为用户服务。自1995年组建集团公司以来，经济迅速发展，2001年实现营业收入26516万元，增加值129.58万元，利润净额7792万元。

公司下属32个经济实体，其中第三产业企业有19个，覆盖多种行业，全部兴旺发达。尤以8大批发市场较为突出，形成总占地面积13万平方米，年交易额45亿元的王顶堤市场群，其中红旗路农贸批发市场已成为全国十大批发市场之一。公司的13个工业企业主要从事制药、化工、电子仪器、光学仪器、电线电缆、服装、食品等行业，其产品畅销国内31个省市，部分产品远销美国、西欧、日本、韩国、澳大利亚等国家。公司热诚欢迎国内外各界朋友进行广泛的合作与交流。

王顶堤红旗农贸批发市场进入全国农副产品批发市场百强行列。

Tianjin Wangdingdi Group Co., Ltd. is a state-rank township enterprise, locates at the western end of Fukang Road, Nankai District, at the junction of the city area and the county area, possessing the superiority of location and transportation. The company contiunes to pursuit in the management policy of "personnel as basis, morality as priority, law as axis, affection as speciality", and keeps up the pioneering spirit of "Unite and strive forward to gain the first place", always keeps in mind "Beijing honest" to serve the customers, Since 1995, it has gotten a considerable development. Its business revenue reached 265.16 million yuan, added-value totalled 1.2958 million yuan, net profits totalled 77.92 million yuan in 2001.

It covers 32 economic units, including 19 in the tertiary industry. These units are engaged in many sectors and all develop well. The eight wholesale markets with a total area of 130,000 square meters and an annual trade revenue of 4.5 billion yuan, have become a market group, of which, Hongqi Road Wholesale Market is one of the ten biggest markets. Its 13 industrial units are mainly engaged in pharmaceutical, chemical, electronic, devices, optical, devices, electronic cable, plastics, garments, foodstuff, etc.. All of the products sell well in 31 provinces, some products are sold abroad to the United States, Western Europe, Japan, Korea, Australia, etc.. We hope to cooperate and interchange with friends of all circles at home and abroad.

Hongqi Wholesale Market is listed among "Top 100 National Wholesale Markets of Form Sideline Products".

从意大利引进先进的挤奶设备

先进的检测设备

地址：天津市南开区复康路西头 Add: The west joint of Fukang Road, Nankai District, Tianjin
邮政编码 Postal Code: 300191 电话 Tel: +86 22 23364053 23689398 传真 Fax: +86 22 23691568

刘房子经济发展总公司

Liufangzi Economy Development General Company

公司承建的住宅小区

总经理：田东平

刘房子为我市西北部一颗璀璨的明珠，被市政府评为市级明星小康村。地理位置优越，与津霸公路、中环线、外环线、子牙河形成环围。远期规划前景宏大，在9平方公里的辖区内，780余户近2700人正以饱满的热情迎接二十一世纪的挑战。

改革开放十几年的发展，村经济已初具规模。现有村办集体企业十几家，三资企业数家；农业生产逐步走上科学、规模、效益型，现已形成的津霸公路刘房子村商业一条街，为第三产业的发展起到了促进作用。工业产值在村经济的比重日渐上升，已初步形成农、工、商合理发展，相互促进，比翼齐飞良性循环之势。

几年来教育事业得到长足发展。同时加大了社会福利、社会保障的投入。村容、村貌焕然一新，治安良好，民风纯朴，已实现精神文明与物质文明的共同发展。

刘房子领导正用战略眼光审视自己，以高度责任感率领全体人民共同努力、继往开来。

高级别墅

地址：天津市北辰区津霸公路

Add: Jinba Highway, Beichen District, Tianjin

邮政编码 Postal Code: 300400

电话 Tel: +86 22 26654384

教育从娃娃抓起

建设竣工后的高级别墅一角

Liufangzi, as a shining star in Northwest Tianjin, is a municipal level well-off star town with good geographic location, connected with Jinba Expressway, Middle-Ring Road, Extra-Ring Road and Ziya River, having a good developing potential. In its 9 square kilometers area, there are more than 780 families, nearly 2,700 people, who are heartedly welcoming the challenge of the 21st century.

与天津商学院联建的教学楼

After more than 10 years, development since the reform and opening to outside, the town's economy becomes scaled. There are over 10 township collective enterprises and several joint ventures in the town. Its agricultural production is becoming scientific efficient and on scale, a commercial street is setup in the town near Jinba Expressway, which plays an important role in the development of its tertiary industry. Its development of agriculture, industry and service industry become coordinated with each other.

Its education has also gotten improved rapidly. Its input in social welfare and social protection system is also enlarged. The town's environment and outlook are changed freshly which is socially securitied and civilized. The town is also realized co-development of spirital and material civilization.

天津海洋开关厂车间一角

The leaders of the town are inspecting themselves strategically, and leading its people to work hard together and success the past and looking forward the future. We are heartedly looking forward to actively cooperating with friends in different walks to achieve an excellent future.

我们将敞开胸怀，与各方有识之士积极合作，共创未来

天津市西青区大寺镇人民政府

大寺镇地处市区南部，位于城乡结合部，是全国环境优美乡镇。该镇地理位置得天独厚，交通便利，四通八达，外环线、津港公路、津淄公路、友谊路、梨双路四路一线贯穿南北、横跨东西。发展态势强劲的西青经济开发区、市微电子工业区坐落镇内。几年来，该镇党委政府坚持以人为本的思想，牢固树立和落实科学的发展观，坚持发展经济不放松、坚持为民办实事不放松、坚持保持安定团结不放松，统筹社会经济协调发展。2005年，该镇完成生产总值16.2亿元，财政收入9600万元，农民人均纯收入8881元，三个文明建设得到协调健康发展。

大寺镇人民政府

随着全球经济一体化的初步形成，该镇党委政府审时度势，狠抓对外开放，不断拓宽对外开放的深度与广度，在深层次、宽领域中进行招商引资。目前，有500余家国内外知名企业坐落境内，镇属企业48家通过ISO9000认证，国家、市级名牌产品9个，成为了天津市中外客商投资密度最大、最具活力的聚集区之一。大桥集团、太平洋科技集团等一批国内外知名企业给本镇的经济注入了时代的活力。

该镇历史文化底蕴丰厚，具有1300年历史的千年古刹峰山药王庙已成为本市民俗文化旅游胜地。小城镇建设日新月异，先后投入12亿，建成126万平米的高档次居民住宅楼，城市绿化率达到50%以上，绿地面积248万平米，绿化率达到35%以上。

一个富足、文明、和谐，具有时代气息的现代化小城镇正以崭新的姿态崛起。

Dasi Town, lying in the south of Tianjin downtown, at the conjunction of the urban and rural area, is a town with beautiful scenery. Thanks to the favorite geographic location, the transportation is very convenient. Outer Circulating Line, Jin'gang Road, Jinzi Road, Youyi Road, and Lishuang Road, connect the south to the north, and join the east to the west. Xiqing Economic Development Area and Microelectronic Industry Zone locate at here. In resent years, the government of the town has been sticking to the mind of people focuses, setting up and keeping the view of scientific development, keeping strictly to the economic development, keeping to the mind of doing good to the people, and keeping the society safe and steady, keeping the economic develop concordantly. In 2005, the town accomplished GDP of 1.62 billion yuan, finance income of 96 million yuan. Per capita annual net income of rural households was 8,881 yuan, the three civilization build-up has developed concordantly.

With the configuration of the integration of the world economy, the government of town is putting great effort into the opening up to the outside, making the opening up deepen and widen at the right time to attract the foreign company. Now, there are 500 famous enterprises have come to the town, 48 enterprises belonging to the town have passed the ISO9000 certification. There were 9 products approved "China or Tianjin Famous Brand". The town has become the most active district, having most foreign investment and national companies. Daqiao Group and Pacific Science & Technology Group and other famous enterprises have put new energy to the economy of the town.

The town has a long history and culture. Yaowang Temple, has become a folk custom scenic spot. The town is improving its construction, and has put into 1.2 billion yuan, building up 1.26 million square meters advanced residental buildings, the urbanize rate has reached 50%, the greening area is 2.48 million square meters, the greening rate is above 35%.

A rich, civilized, harmonic, and modern town is growing up.

地址: 天津市津港公路静水道　Add: Jingshui Road, Jin'gang Highway, Tianjin
邮政编码 Postal Code: 300385　电话 Tel: +86 22 23971295　传真 Fax: +86 22 23971295

河兴庄农工商联合公司

Hexingzhuang Agriculture, Industry & Commerce General Company

总经理：郭忠信

我公司地处河北区金钟河大街外环线交口处两侧。面对京津塘高速公路徐庄出入口，距天津机场、港口、天津站较近。海陆空方位畅通便利。我公司是多层次法人、代表机构，下设数十个经济实体企业，注册资金5千余万元。随着机构改革，人员调整，新的领导班子更是朝气蓬勃，秉承为民办实事，为百姓造福的理念。

我公司将继续以开拓进取、创新求实的精神热诚地与社会各界朋友真诚合作，共拓大业。

Hexingzhuang Agriculture, Industry & Commerce General Company locates at the two sides of the cross of Jinzhonghe Street with Outer Circle. It faces to the Xuzhuang Exit of Jing-Jin-Tang Highway. It near to airport, port, realway station and is equipped with convenient traffic. It possesses over 10 enterprises with a registered capital worth over 50 million yuan. Along with reform of company and adjustment of personnel, new leaders adhere to the idea of "Do things for people and earn benefits for pople".

The company will run along the road of renovation and development, sincerely hopes to cooperate with the friends coming from all fields and develops together.

地址: 天津市河北区北站外金钟河大街

Add: The Northern of the Cross of Jinzhonghe Street, Hebei District, Tianjin

邮政编码 Postal Code: 300240

电话 Tel: +86 22 26330640　26322586

天津市侯台商贸集团有限公司

Tianjin Houtai Trade Group Co., Ltd.

侯台科技园座落于天津市西青区中北镇，是天津市西青经济开发区的组成部分。占地4平方公里。位于天津市区西侧，紧邻天津市外环线500米绿化带。

- 园区位置优越，距首都北京120公里、天津机场30公里、天津新港40公里，交通便利。
- 园区各种基础配套设施完备，陕气入津减压调度总站位于园区北侧，天津市第四污水处理厂位于园区南侧。
- 园区以标准厂房出租方式招商。以电子信息、生物医药、精密机械、新型材料等高新技术产业项目为主。
- 园区引入现代工业物业管理模式，为企业生产经营活动提供高效、便捷、全程、优质的服务。

With an area of 4 square kilometers, Houtai Technological Park is located in Zhongbei Township, Xiqing District, Tianjin Municipality, which is a part of Xiqing Economic Development Area. It stands at the west of Tianjin Municipality, near to Tianjin section of Beijing-Shanghai expressway and 500-meter greenbelt of Tianjin outer ring road.

The park has superior regional location. It is 120 kilometers away from Beijing (the capital of China), 30 kilometers from Tianjin Airport and 40 kilometers from Tianjin New Harbor. It has convenient transportation.

The main control office of natural gas drawed from Shanxi Province in Tianjin situated in the north of the Park and The Fourth Sewage Treatment Plant of Tianjin lies in the west of the Park. The Park has basic conditions to set up all kinds of facilities.

The Park will attract investors according to the ways including, standard workshop rent, Many high and new technology industrial projects are encouraged, such as electronic information, biological medicine, precise machinery, etc..

The Park adopts modern industrial manage style to provide efficient, convenient, whole-course and high-quality services for enterprises.

地址: 天津市复康西路碧欣路
Add: Bixin Road, Fukangxi Road, Tianjin
邮政编码 Postal Code: 300384
电话 Tel: +86 22 23079566
传真 Fax: +86 22 23079566
http://www.tjhtjt.com

2006天津统计年鉴
TIANJIN STATISTICAL YEARBOOK

电子版
Electric Version

使用说明

《天津统计年鉴2006(电子版)》是新型的阅读工具，它使用简洁，界面美观，便于携带，全部文档均采用HTM格式。文字及图形资料装于一张光盘中，借助于计算机，可以方便快速地进行查询，并可将所需的资料打印出来。

[软件环境] 中文Windows 9x/2000/XP系统，Internet Explorer 5.0及以上，分辨率为800*600
[使用方法] 将光盘插入CD-ROM中，系统自动启动年鉴程序或者执行光驱中\2006nj\index.htm文件

本光盘中所有资料未经许可均不得用于营业性用途，否则必追究其法律责任。

User's Guide

Tianjin Statistical Yearbook 2006 (electric version) is a new type reading tool. It is equipped with beautiful interface and HTM files. You have the aid of computer to use the CD and it is convenient for you to search & read materials and print.

[Software Requirement]
Windows 9x/2000/XP, Internet Explorer 5.0 or higher, resolution 800*600
[Usage Method]
Insert CD into CD-ROM, then Yearbook program will start or to run\2006nj\index.htm

The date in this disk are not permitted for commercial purposes without written permission from the publisher. legal responsibilities are reserved to prosecute.